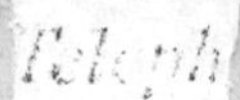

Renault Mégane & Scénic

Service and Repair Manual

Peter T Gill & A K Legg LAE MIMI

Models covered (3916-432)

Renault Mégane Hatchback, Saloon (Classic) & Coupé and Scénic MPV, including special/limited editions
Petrol engines: 1.4 litre (1390cc), 1.6 litre (1598cc) & 2.0 litre (1998cc)
Diesel engines: 1.9 litre (1870cc) including turbo

Does NOT cover Cabriolet or Scénic RX4 models
Does NOT cover 2.0 litre IDE or 1.8 litre petrol engines

ABCDE
FGHIJ
KLMNO
PQRS

A book in the **Haynes Service and Repair Manual Series**

ISBN **1 85960 916 3**

British Library Cataloguing in Publication Data
A catalogue record for this book is available from the British Library.

Printed in USA

Haynes Publishing
Sparkford, Nr Yeovil, Somerset BA22 7JJ, England

Haynes North America, Inc
861 Lawrence Drive, Newbury Park, California 91320, USA

Editions Haynes
4, Rue de l'Abreuvoir
92415 COURBEVOIE CEDEX, France

Haynes Publishing Nordiska AB
Box 1504, 751 45 UPPSALA, Sverige

Contents

LIVING WITH YOUR RENAULT MEGANE/SCENIC

Contents

REPAIRS & OVERHAUL

Advanced driving

Many people see the words 'advanced driving' and believe that it won't interest them or that it is a style of driving beyond their own abilities. Nothing could be further from the truth. Advanced driving is straightforward safe, sensible driving - the sort of driving we should all do every time we get behind the wheel.

An average of 10 people are killed every day on UK roads and 870 more are injured, some seriously. Lives are ruined daily, usually because somebody did something stupid. Something like 95% of all accidents are due to human error, mostly driver failure. Sometimes we make genuine mistakes - everyone does. Sometimes we have lapses of concentration. Sometimes we deliberately take risks.

For many people, the process of 'learning to drive' doesn't go much further than learning how to pass the driving test because of a common belief that good drivers are made by 'experience'.

Learning to drive by 'experience' teaches three driving skills:

- ☐ Quick reactions. (Whoops, that was close!)
- ☐ Good handling skills. (Horn, swerve, brake, horn).
- ☐ Reliance on vehicle technology. (Great stuff this ABS, stop in no distance even in the wet...)

Drivers whose skills are 'experience based' generally have a lot of near misses and the odd accident. The results can be seen every day in our courts and our hospital casualty departments.

Advanced drivers have learnt to control the risks by controlling the position and speed of their vehicle. They avoid accidents and near misses, even if the drivers around them make mistakes.

The key skills of advanced driving are **concentration,** effective all-round **observation, anticipation** and **planning.** When **good vehicle handling** is added to these skills, all driving situations can be approached and negotiated in a safe, methodical way, leaving nothing to chance.

Concentration means applying your mind to safe driving, completely excluding anything that's not relevant. Driving is usually the most dangerous activity that most of us undertake in our daily routines. It deserves our full attention.

Observation means not just looking, but seeing and seeking out the information found in the driving environment.

Anticipation means asking yourself what is happening, what you can reasonably expect to happen and what could happen unexpectedly. (One of the commonest words used in compiling accident reports is 'suddenly'.)

Planning is the link between seeing something and taking the appropriate action. For many drivers, planning is the missing link.

If you want to become a safer and more skilful driver and you want to enjoy your driving more, contact the Institute of Advanced Motorists on 0208 994 4403 or write to IAM House, Chiswick High Road, London W4 4HS for an information pack.

Working on your car can be dangerous. This page shows just some of the potential risks and hazards, with the aim of creating a safety-conscious attitude.

General hazards

Scalding

• Don't remove the radiator or expansion tank cap while the engine is hot.
• Engine oil, automatic transmission fluid or power steering fluid may also be dangerously hot if the engine has recently been running.

Burning

• Beware of burns from the exhaust system and from any part of the engine. Brake discs and drums can also be extremely hot immediately after use.

Crushing

• When working under or near a raised vehicle, always supplement the jack with axle stands, or use drive-on ramps. ***Never venture under a car which is only supported by a jack.***
• Take care if loosening or tightening high-torque nuts when the vehicle is on stands. Initial loosening and final tightening should be done with the wheels on the ground.

Fire

• Fuel is highly flammable; fuel vapour is explosive.
• Don't let fuel spill onto a hot engine.
• Do not smoke or allow naked lights (including pilot lights) anywhere near a vehicle being worked on. Also beware of creating sparks (electrically or by use of tools).
• Fuel vapour is heavier than air, so don't work on the fuel system with the vehicle over an inspection pit.
• Another cause of fire is an electrical overload or short-circuit. Take care when repairing or modifying the vehicle wiring.
• Keep a fire extinguisher handy, of a type suitable for use on fuel and electrical fires.

Electric shock

• Ignition HT voltage can be dangerous, especially to people with heart problems or a pacemaker. Don't work on or near the ignition system with the engine running or the ignition switched on.
• Mains voltage is also dangerous. Make sure that any mains-operated equipment is correctly earthed. Mains power points should be protected by a residual current device (RCD) circuit breaker.

Fume or gas intoxication

• Exhaust fumes are poisonous; they often contain carbon monoxide, which is rapidly fatal if inhaled. Never run the engine in a confined space such as a garage with the doors shut.

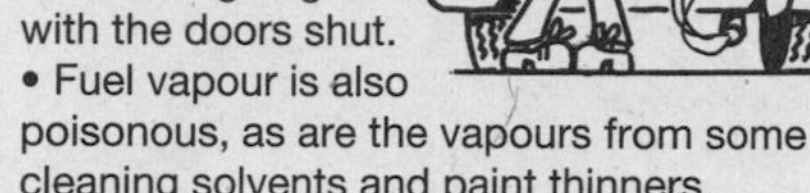

• Fuel vapour is also poisonous, as are the vapours from some cleaning solvents and paint thinners.

Poisonous or irritant substances

• Avoid skin contact with battery acid and with any fuel, fluid or lubricant, especially antifreeze, brake hydraulic fluid and Diesel fuel. Don't syphon them by mouth. If such a substance is swallowed or gets into the eyes, seek medical advice.
• Prolonged contact with used engine oil can cause skin cancer. Wear gloves or use a barrier cream if necessary. Change out of oil-soaked clothes and do not keep oily rags in your pocket.
• Air conditioning refrigerant forms a poisonous gas if exposed to a naked flame (including a cigarette). It can also cause skin burns on contact.

Asbestos

• Asbestos dust can cause cancer if inhaled or swallowed. Asbestos may be found in gaskets and in brake and clutch linings. When dealing with such components it is safest to assume that they contain asbestos.

Special hazards

Hydrofluoric acid

• This extremely corrosive acid is formed when certain types of synthetic rubber, found in some O-rings, oil seals, fuel hoses etc, are exposed to temperatures above 400°C. The rubber changes into a charred or sticky substance containing the acid. *Once formed, the acid remains dangerous for years. If it gets onto the skin, it may be necessary to amputate the limb concerned.*
• When dealing with a vehicle which has suffered a fire, or with components salvaged from such a vehicle, wear protective gloves and discard them after use.

The battery

• Batteries contain sulphuric acid, which attacks clothing, eyes and skin. Take care when topping-up or carrying the battery.
• The hydrogen gas given off by the battery is highly explosive. Never cause a spark or allow a naked light nearby. Be careful when connecting and disconnecting battery chargers or jump leads.

Air bags

• Air bags can cause injury if they go off accidentally. Take care when removing the steering wheel and/or facia. Special storage instructions may apply.

Diesel injection equipment

• Diesel injection pumps supply fuel at very high pressure. Take care when working on the fuel injectors and fuel pipes.

Warning: Never expose the hands, face or any other part of the body to injector spray; the fuel can penetrate the skin with potentially fatal results.

Remember...

DO

• Do use eye protection when using power tools, and when working under the vehicle.

• Do wear gloves or use barrier cream to protect your hands when necessary.

• Do get someone to check periodically that all is well when working alone on the vehicle.

• Do keep loose clothing and long hair well out of the way of moving mechanical parts.

• Do remove rings, wristwatch etc, before working on the vehicle – especially the electrical system.

• Do ensure that any lifting or jacking equipment has a safe working load rating adequate for the job.

DON'T

• Don't attempt to lift a heavy component which may be beyond your capability – get assistance.

• Don't rush to finish a job, or take unverified short cuts.

• Don't use ill-fitting tools which may slip and cause injury.

• Don't leave tools or parts lying around where someone can trip over them. Mop up oil and fuel spills at once.

• Don't allow children or pets to play in or near a vehicle being worked on.

The Phase 2 Renault Mégane was introduced in April 1999 and the Scénic in August 1999. There are four petrol engines available in the Mégane/Scénic range; 1.4 litre 8-valve, 1.4 litre 16-valve, 1.6 litre 16-valve and 2.0 litre 16-valve all using a fuel-injection system. (The 1.4 litre 8-valve petrol engine was phased out in October 2000.) The three diesel engines available are the 1.9 litre D, 1.9 litre Dti and the 1.9 litre dCi (Diesel Common rail engine) which was introduced in April 2000. The D diesel engine uses an indirect injection system, while the Dti and dCi engines use a direct injection system. (The 1.9 litre D Diesel engine was phased out in October 2000.) All the engines are of excellent design and, provided regular maintenance is carried out, are unlikely to give any trouble.

The Mégane is available in 2-door Coupé, 4-door Saloon and 5-door Hatchback body styles and the Scénic in a 5-door Hatchback body style, both having a wide range of fittings and interior trim depending on the model specification.

Models may be fitted with a five-speed manual, or a four-speed automatic transmission, mounted at the left-hand side of the engine. All models have a front-wheel-drive with fully-independent front and semi-independent rear suspension.

Renault Mégane

A wide range of standard and optional equipment is available within the Mégane/Scénic range to suit most tastes, including an anti-lock braking system.

The Mégane/Scénic is conventional in design, and the DIY mechanic should find most servicing work straightforward.

Your Renault Mégane/Scénic Manual

The aim of this manual is to help you get the best value from your vehicle. It can do so in several ways. It can help you decide what work must be done (even should you choose to get it done by a garage), provide information on routine maintenance and servicing, and give a logical course of action and diagnosis when random faults occur. However, it is hoped that you will use the manual by tackling the work yourself. On simpler jobs, it may even be quicker than booking the car into a garage and going there twice, to leave and collect it. Perhaps most important, a lot of money can be saved by avoiding the costs a garage must charge to cover its labour and overheads.

Renault Scénic

The manual has drawings and descriptions to show the function of the various components, so that their layout can be understood. Then the tasks are described and photographed in a clear step-by-step sequence.

References to the 'left' or 'right' are in the sense of a person in the driver's seat, facing forward.

Acknowledgements

Certain illustrations are the copyright of Renault (UK) Limited, and are used with their permission. Thanks are due to Draper Tools Limited, who provided some of the workshop tools, and to all those people at Sparkford who helped in the production of this manual.

Project vehicles

The main project vehicle used in the preparation of this manual, and appearing in many of the photographic sequences, was a Renault Scénic fitted with the 1.9 dCi (common rail) turbo diesel engine.

The following pages are intended to help in dealing with common roadside emergencies and breakdowns. You will find more detailed fault finding information at the back of the manual, and repair information in the main chapters.

If your car won't start and the starter motor doesn't turn

- ☐ If it's a model with automatic transmission, make sure the selector is in P or N.
- ☐ Open the bonnet and make sure that the battery terminals are clean and tight.
- ☐ Switch on the headlights and try to start the engine. If the headlights go very dim when you're trying to start, the battery is probably flat. Get out of trouble by jump starting (see next page) using a friend's car.

If your car won't start even though the starter motor turns as normal

- ☐ Is there fuel in the tank?
- ☐ Is there moisture on electrical components under the bonnet? Switch off the ignition, then wipe off any obvious dampness with a dry cloth. Spray a water-repellent aerosol product (WD-40 or equivalent) on ignition and fuel system electrical connectors like those shown in the photos. Pay special attention to the ignition coil wiring connector and HT leads.

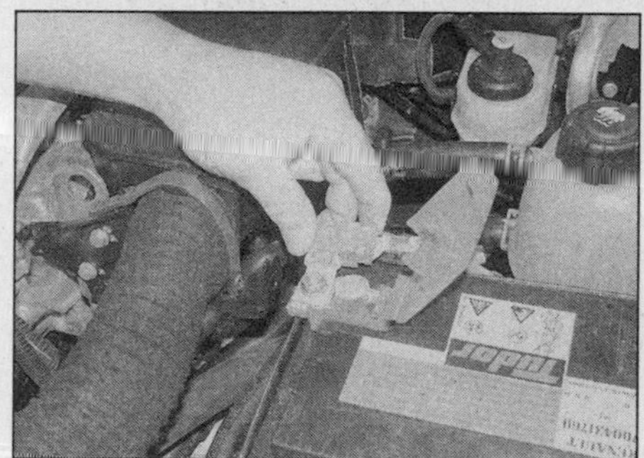

A Check the condition and security of the battery connections.

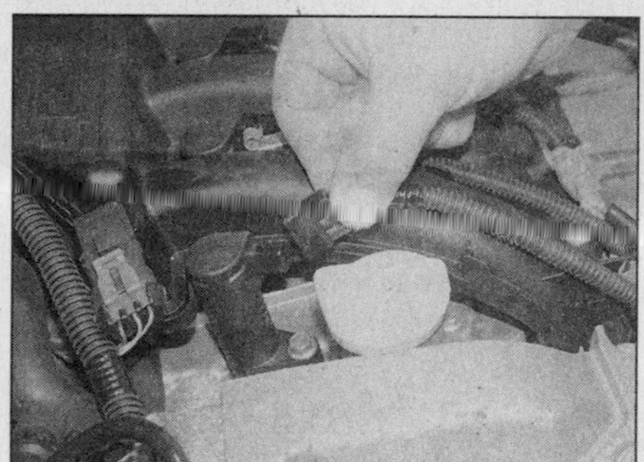

B Check that that wiring to the ignition coils/spark plugs is secure.

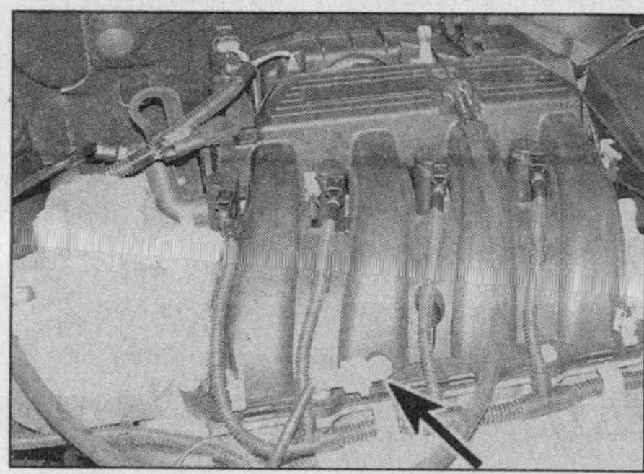

C Check that the wiring to the inlet air temperature sensor is secure.

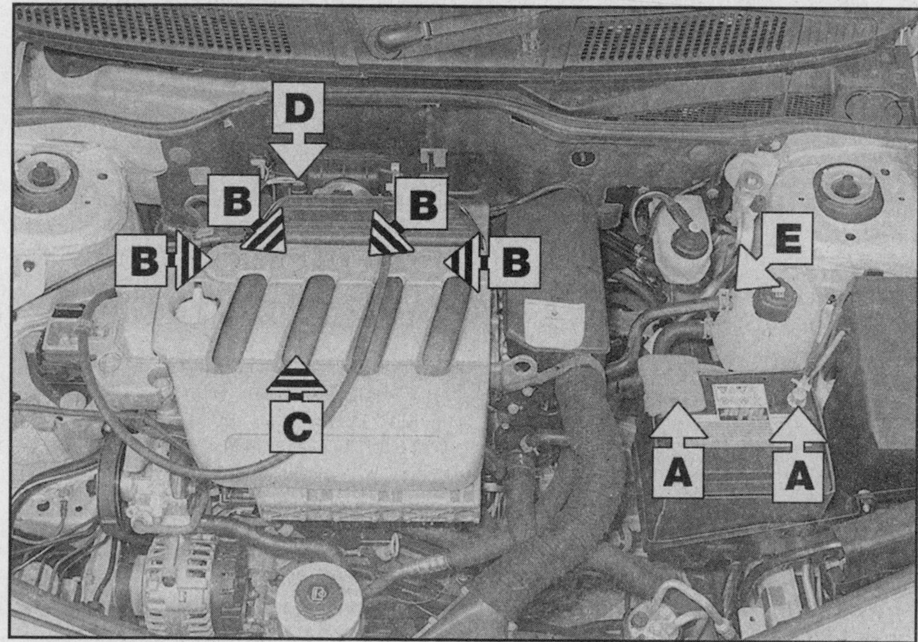

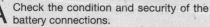

Check that electrical connections are secure (with the ignition switched off) and spray them with a water dispersant spray like WD-40 if you suspect a problem due to damp

D Check that the wiring to the throttle potentiometer is secure.

E Check that the fuel cut-off switch has not been activated.

Wheel changing

Warning: Do not change a wheel in a situation where you risk being hit by another vehicle. On busy roads, try to stop in a lay-by or a gateway. Be wary of passing traffic while changing the wheel – it is easy to become distracted by the job in hand.

Preparation

- ☐ When a puncture occurs, stop as soon as it is safe to do so.
- ☐ Park on firm level ground, if possible, and well out of the way of other traffic.
- ☐ Use hazard warning lights if necessary.
- ☐ If you have one, use a warning triangle to alert other drivers of your presence.
- ☐ Apply the handbrake and engage first or reverse gear.
- ☐ Chock the wheel diagonally opposite the one being removed – a couple of large stones will do for this.
- ☐ If the ground is soft, use a flat piece of wood to spread the load under the jack.

Changing the wheel

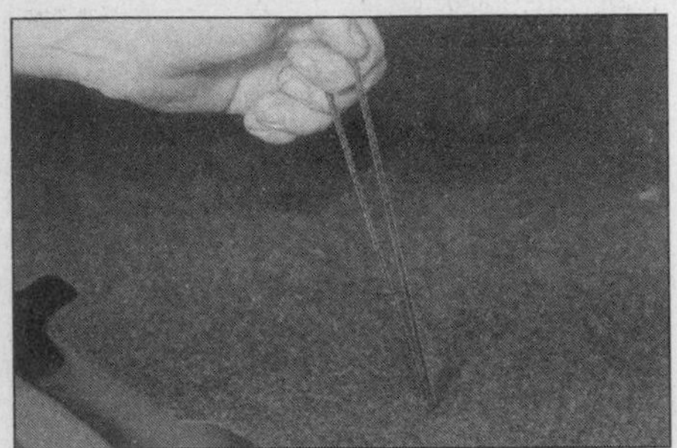

1 The spare wheel and tools are stored in the luggage compartment under the carpet.

2 Unscrew the retainer securing the spare wheel and tool holder.

3 Lift out the spare wheel.

4 Use the hook provided to remove the wheel trim.

5 Slacken each wheel bolt by half a turn.

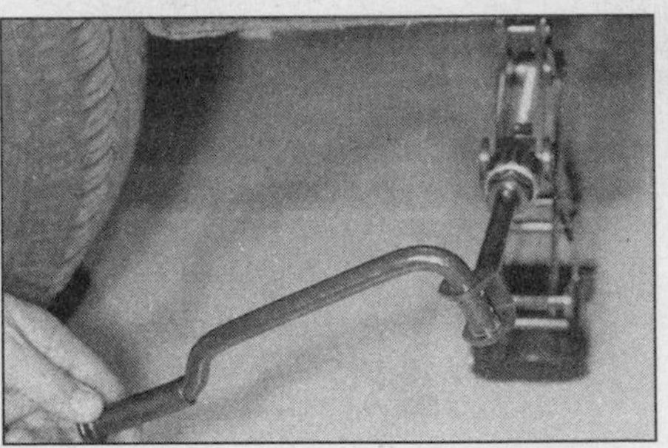

6 Locate the jack below the reinforced point on the sill (don't jack the vehicle at any other point of the sill) and on firm ground, then turn the jack handle clockwise until the wheel is raised clear of the ground.

7 Unscrew the wheel bolts using the brace provided, and remove the wheel. Fit the spare wheel, and screw in the bolts. Lightly tighten the bolts with the wheelbrace then lower the vehicle to the ground.

8 Securely tighten the wheel bolts in the sequence shown then (where applicable) refit the wheel trim. Stow the punctured wheel back in the spare wheel well. Note that the wheel bolts must be tightened to the specified torque at the earliest possible opportunity.

Finally...

- ☐ Remove the wheel chocks.
- ☐ Stow the jack and tools in the holder.
- ☐ Check the tyre pressure on the wheel just fitted. If it is low, or if you don't have a pressure gauge with you, drive slowly to the nearest garage and inflate the tyre to the right pressure.
- ☐ Have the damaged tyre or wheel repaired as soon as possible.

HAYNES HiNT *Jump starting will get you out of trouble, but you must correct whatever made the battery go flat in the first place. There are three possibilities:*

***1** The battery has been drained by repeated attempts to start, or by leaving the lights on.*

***2** The charging system is not working properly (alternator drivebelt slack or broken, alternator wiring fault or alternator itself faulty).*

***3** The battery itself is at fault (electrolyte low, or battery worn out).*

Jump starting

When jump-starting a car using a booster battery, observe the following precautions:

- ✔ Before connecting the booster battery, make sure that the ignition is switched off.
- ✔ Ensure that all electrical equipment (lights, heater, wipers, etc) is switched off.
- ✔ Take note of any special precautions printed on the battery case.
- ✔ Make sure that the booster battery is the same voltage as the discharged one in the vehicle.
- ✔ If the battery is being jump-started from the battery in another vehicle, the two vehicles MUST NOT TOUCH each other.
- ✔ Make sure that the transmission is in neutral (or PARK, in the case of automatic transmission).

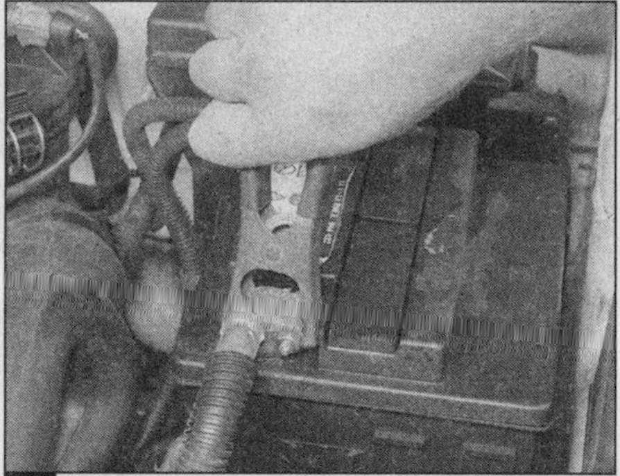

1 Connect one end of the red jump lead to the positive (+) terminal of the flat battery

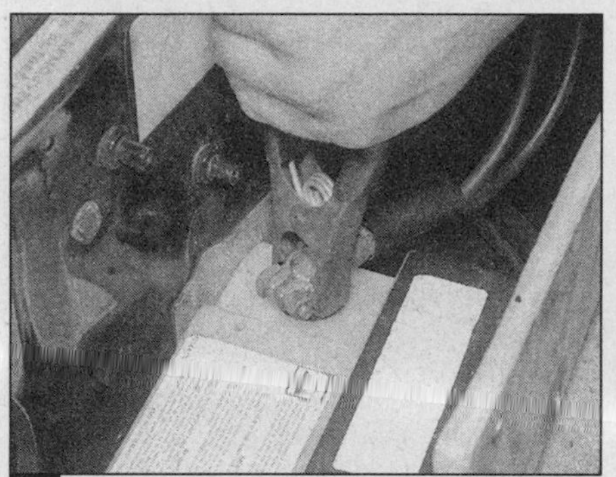

2 Connect the other end of the red lead to the positive (+) terminal of the booster battery.

3 Connect one end of the black jump lead to the negative (-) terminal of the booster battery

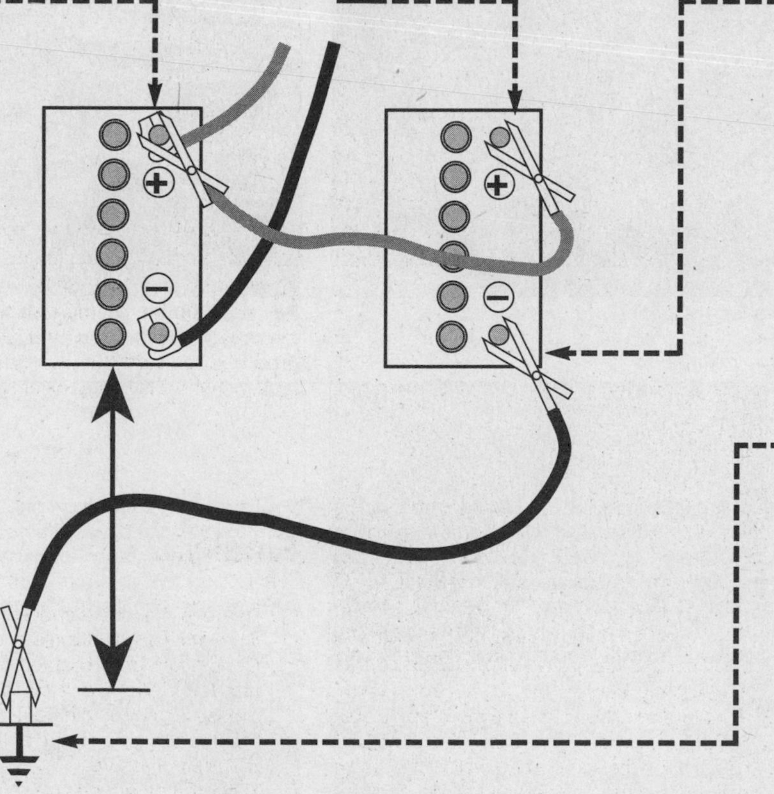

4 Connect the other end of the black jump lead to a bolt or bracket on the engine block, well away from the battery, on the vehicle to be started.

5 Make sure that the jump leads will not come into contact with the fan, drive-belts or other moving parts of the engine.

6 Start the engine using the booster battery and run it at idle speed. Switch on the lights, rear window demister and heater blower motor, then disconnect the jump leads in the reverse order of connection. Turn off the lights etc.

Identifying leaks

Puddles on the garage floor or drive, or obvious wetness under the bonnet or underneath the car, suggest a leak that needs investigating. It can sometimes be difficult to decide where the leak is coming from, especially if the engine bay is very dirty already. Leaking oil or fluid can also be blown rearwards by the passage of air under the car, giving a false impression of where the problem lies.

Warning: Most automotive oils and fluids are poisonous. Wash them off skin, and change out of contaminated clothing, without delay.

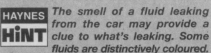

The smell of a fluid leaking from the car may provide a clue to what's leaking. Some fluids are distinctively coloured. It may help to clean the car carefully and to park it over some clean paper overnight as an aid to locating the source of the leak. Remember that some leaks may only occur while the engine is running.

Sump oil

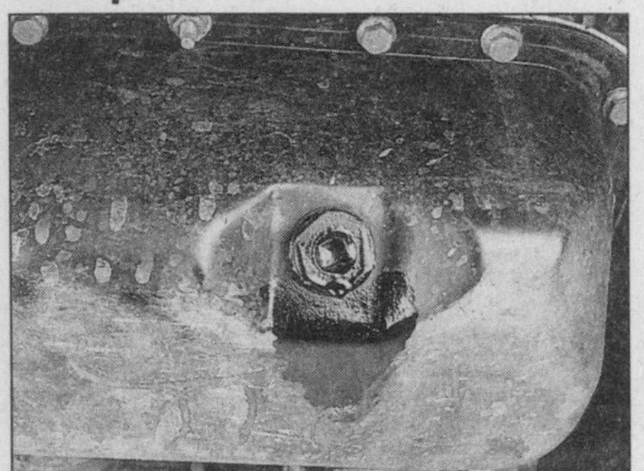

Engine oil may leak from the drain plug...

Oil from filter

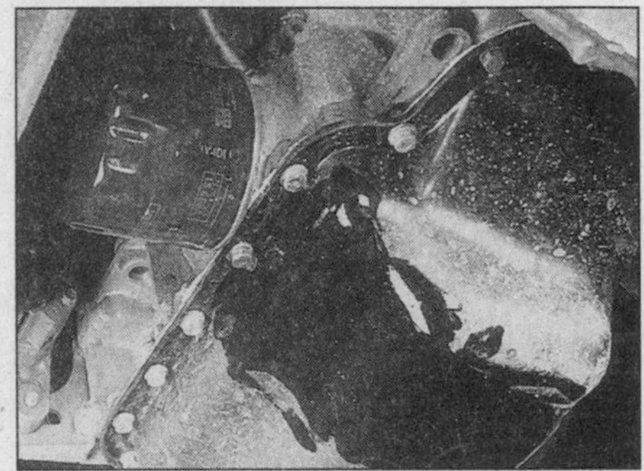

...or from the base of the oil filter.

Gearbox oil

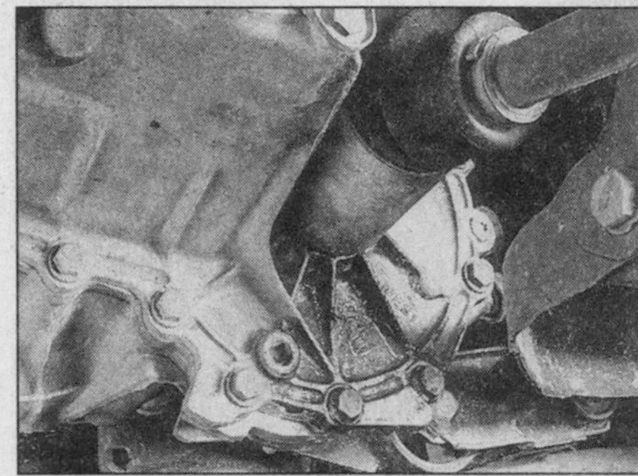

Gearbox oil can leak from the seals at the inboard ends of the driveshafts.

Antifreeze

Leaking antifreeze often leaves a crystalline deposit like this.

Brake fluid

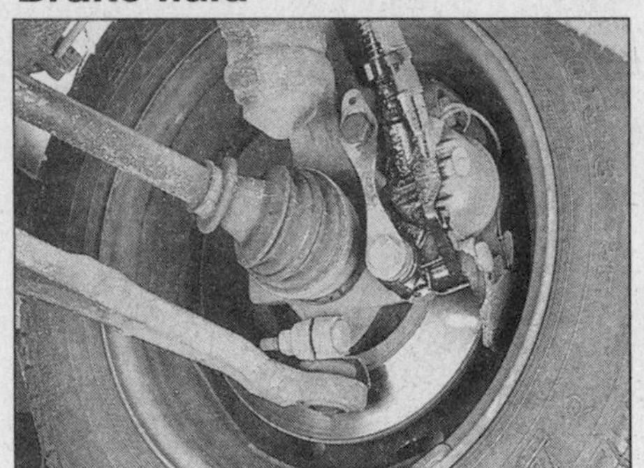

A leak occurring at a wheel is almost certainly brake fluid.

Power steering fluid

Power steering fluid may leak from the pipe connectors on the steering rack.

Towing

When all else fails, you may find yourself having to get a tow home – or of course you may be helping somebody else. Long-distance recovery should only be done by a garage or breakdown service. For shorter distances, DIY towing using another car is easy enough, but observe the following points:

☐ Use a proper tow-rope – they are not expensive. The vehicle being towed must display an ON TOW sign in its rear window.

☐ Always turn the ignition key to the 'on' position when the vehicle is being towed, so that the steering lock is released, and that the direction indicator and brake lights will work.

☐ Before being towed, release the handbrake and select neutral on the transmission.

☐ Note that greater-than-usual pedal pressure will be required to operate the brakes, since the vacuum servo unit is only operational with the engine running.

☐ The driver of the car being towed must keep the tow-rope taut at all times to avoid snatching.

☐ Make sure that both drivers know the route before setting off.

☐ Do not exceed 25 mph and do not tow for more than 30 miles. Drive smoothly and allow plenty of time for slowing down at junctions.

☐ A towing eye is provided in the tool kit in the luggage compartment under the spare wheel.

☐ To fit the towing eye at the front, screw it into the threaded hole located below the right-hand headlight. Tighten the eye using the brace.

☐ To fit the towing eye to the rear, screw the eye into the threaded hole below the right-hand side of the rear bumper. Tighten the eye using the brace.

Introduction

There are some very simple checks which need only take a few minutes to carry out, but which could save you a lot of inconvenience and expense.

These 'Weekly checks' require no great skill or special tools, and the small amount of time they take to perform could prove to be very well spent, for example;

☐ Keeping an eye on tyre condition and pressures, will not only help to stop them wearing out prematurely, but could also save your life.

☐ Many breakdowns are caused by electrical problems. Battery-related faults are particularly common, and a quick check on a regular basis will often prevent the majority of these.

☐ If your car develops a brake fluid leak, the first time you might know about it is when your brakes don't work properly. Checking the level regularly will give advance warning of this kind of problem.

☐ If the oil or coolant levels run low, the cost of repairing any engine damage will be far greater than fixing the leak, for example.

Underbonnet check points

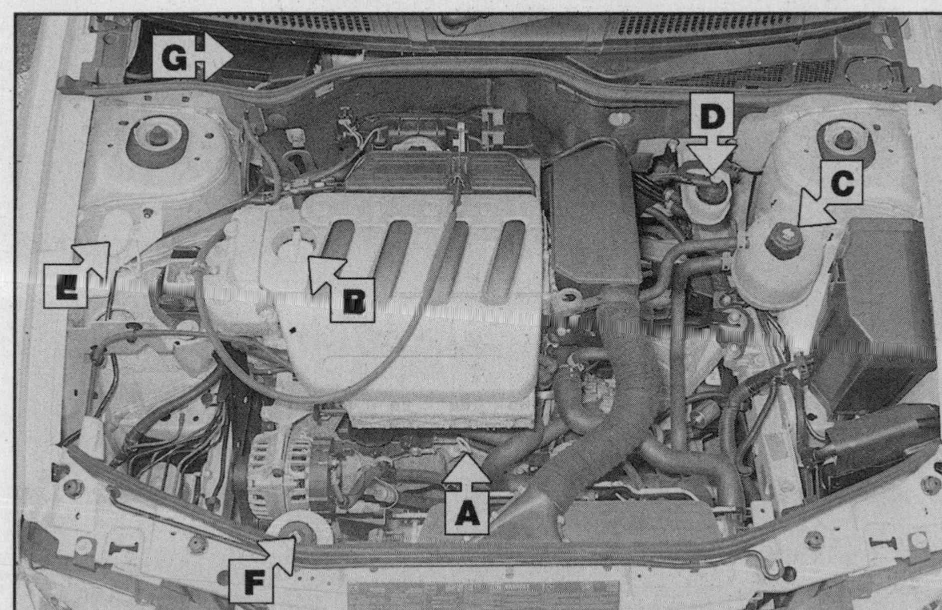

◀ **1.4 litre 16-valve (K4J) petrol engine**

A *Engine oil level dipstick*
B *Engine oil filler cap*
C *Coolant expansion tank*
D *Brake fluid reservoir*
E *Washer fluid reservoir*
F *Power steering fluid reservoir*
G *Battery*

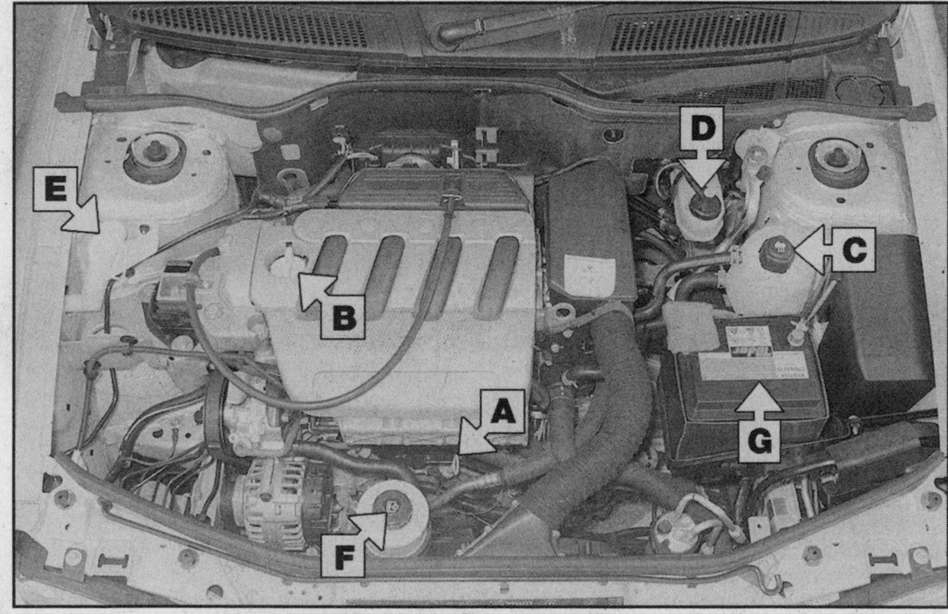

◀ **1.6 litre 16-valve (K4M) petrol engine**

A *Engine oil level dipstick*
B *Engine oil filler cap*
C *Coolant expansion tank*
D *Brake fluid reservoir*
E *Washer fluid reservoir*
F *Power steering fluid reservoir*
G *Battery*

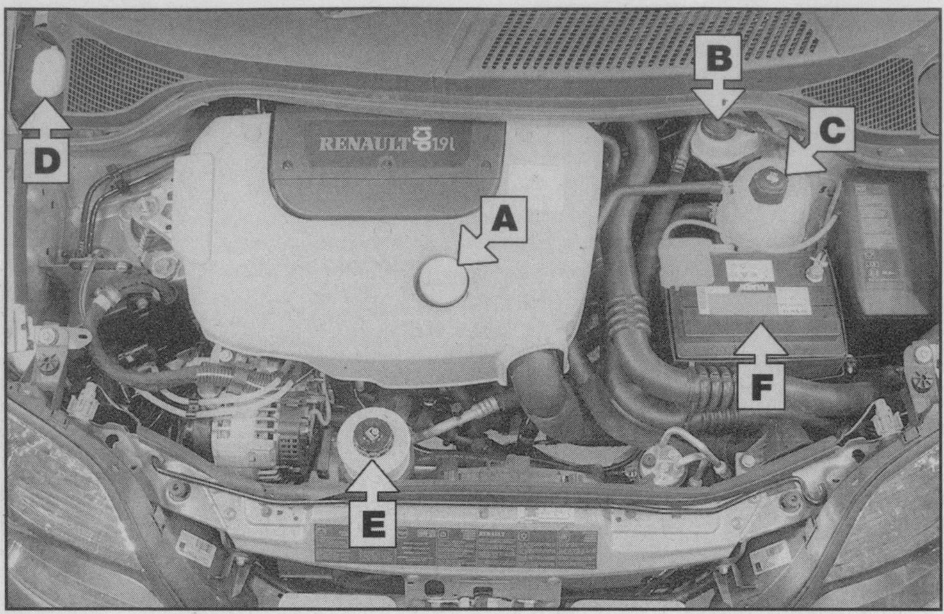

◀ 1.9 litre dCi (F9Q) diesel engine

A *Engine oil level dipstick and oil filler cap*
B *Brake fluid reservoir*
C *Coolant expansion tank*
D *Washer fluid reservoir*
E *Power steering fluid reservoir*
F *Battery*

Engine oil level

Before you start

✔ Make sure that your car is on level ground.
✔ Check the oil level before the car is driven, or at least 5 minutes after the engine has been switched off.

If the oil is checked immediately after driving the vehicle, some of the oil will remain in the upper engine components, resulting in an inaccurate reading on the dipstick.

The correct oil

Modern engines place great demands on their oil. It is very important that the correct oil for your car is used (see 'Lubricants and fluids').

Car Care

● If you have to add oil frequently, you should check whether you have any oil leaks. Place some clean paper under the car overnight, and check for stains in the morning. If there are no leaks, the engine may be burning oil.

● Always maintain the level between the upper and lower dipstick marks (see photo 3). If the level is too low, severe engine damage may occur. Oil seal failure may result if the engine is overfilled by adding too much oil.

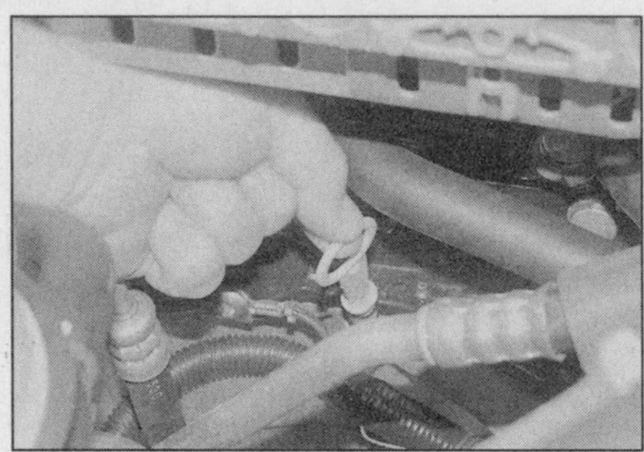

1 The dipstick is brightly coloured yellow and is located on the front of the engine or on F9Q diesels, part of the oil filler cap (see *Underbonnet Check Points* for exact location). Withdraw the dipstick.

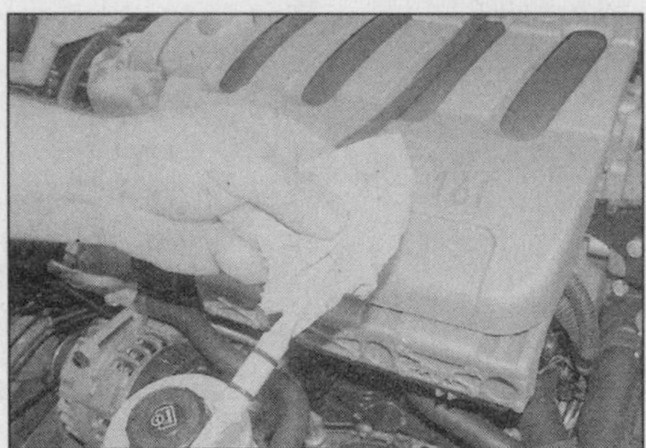

2 Using a clean rag or paper towel remove all oil from the dipstick. Insert the clean dipstick into the tube as far as it will go, then withdraw it again.

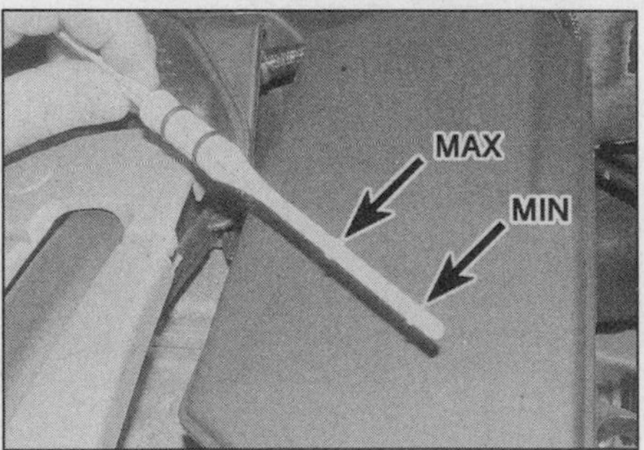

3 Note the oil level on the end of the dipstick, which should be between the upper (MAX) mark and lower (MIN) mark. Note that on some engines the MAX and MIN marks are indicated by notches. Approximately 1.5 litres (depending on engine) of oil will raise the level from the lower mark to the upper mark.

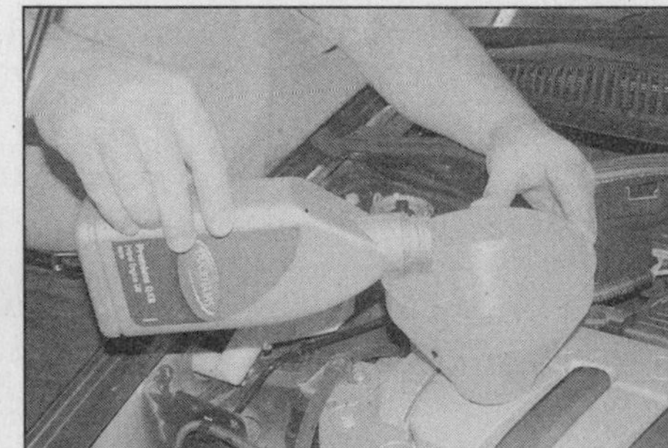

4 Oil is added through the filler cap. Twist the cap anti-clockwise and withdraw it. Top-up the level. A funnel may help to reduce spillage. Add the oil slowly, checking the level on the dipstick often. Do not overfill.

Coolant level

Warning: DO NOT attempt to remove the expansion tank pressure cap when the engine is hot, as there is a very great risk of scalding. Do not leave open containers of coolant about, as it is poisonous.

Car Care

● With a sealed-type cooling system, adding coolant should not be necessary on a regular basis. If frequent topping-up is required, it is likely there is a leak. Check the radiator, all hoses and joint faces for signs of staining or wetness, and rectify as necessary.

● It is important that antifreeze is used in the cooling system all year round, not just during the winter months. Don't top-up with water alone, as the antifreeze will become too diluted.

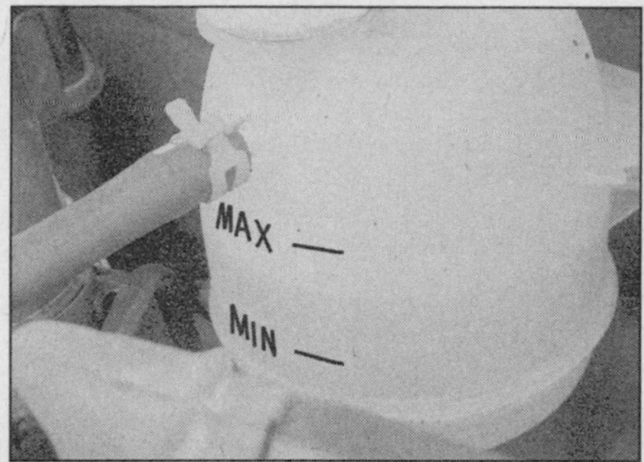

1 The coolant level varies with the temperature of the engine. When the engine is cold, the coolant level should be between the MIN and MAX marks (preferably near the MAX mark) on the side of the expansion tank. When the engine is hot, the level will rise.

2 If topping-up is necessary, **wait until the engine is cold**. Slowly unscrew the expansion tank cap, to release any pressure present in the cooling system, and remove it.

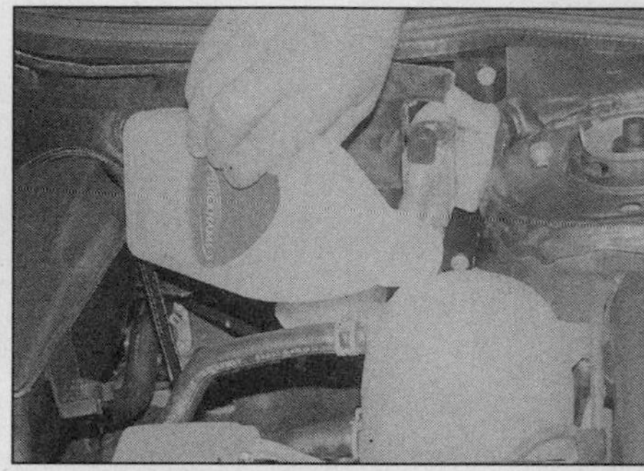

3 Add a mixture of water and antifreeze to the expansion tank until the coolant is up to the MAX level mark. Refit the cap and tighten it securely.

Brake fluid level

● Brake fluid can harm your eyes and damage painted surfaces, so use extreme caution when handling and pouring it.

● Do not use fluid that has been standing open for some time, as it absorbs moisture from the air, which can cause a dangerous loss of braking effectiveness.

HAYNES HiNT

• Make sure that your car is on level ground.

• The fluid level in the reservoir will drop slightly as the brake pads wear down, but the fluid level must never be allowed to drop below the MIN mark.

Safety First!

● If the reservoir requires repeated topping-up this is an indication of a fluid leak somewhere in the system, which should be investigated immediately.

● If a leak is suspected, the car should not be driven until the braking system has been checked. Never take any risks where brakes are concerned.

1 The MAX and MIN marks are indicated on the side of the reservoir. The fluid level must be kept between the marks at all times.

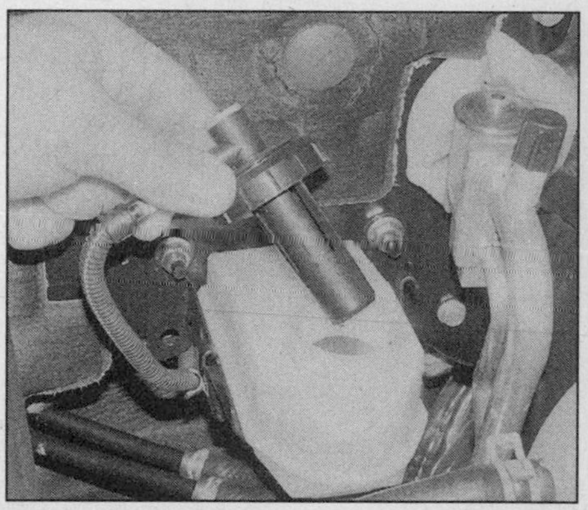

2 If topping-up is necessary, first wipe clean the area around the filler cap to prevent dirt entering the hydraulic system. Unscrew and remove the cap.

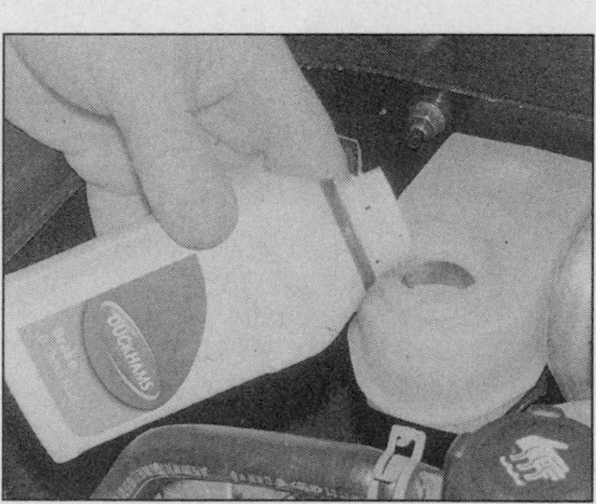

3 Carefully add fluid, taking care not to spill it onto the surrounding components. Use only the specified fluid; mixing different types can cause damage to the system. After topping-up to the correct level, securely refit the cap and wipe off any spilt fluid.

Power steering fluid level

Before you start

✔ Park the vehicle on level ground.
✔ Set the steering wheel straight-ahead.
✔ The engine should be turned off.

For the check to be accurate, the steering must not be turned once the engine has been stopped.

Safety First!

● The need for frequent topping-up indicates a leak, which should be investigated immediately.

1 The power steering fluid reservoir is located on the right-hand side of the radiator. The fluid level should be checked with the engine stopped. A translucent reservoir is fitted, with MAXI and MINI markings on the side of the reservoir.

2 The fluid level should be between the MAXI and MINI marks. If topping-up is necessary, and before removing the cap, wipe the surrounding area so that dirt does not enter the reservoir.

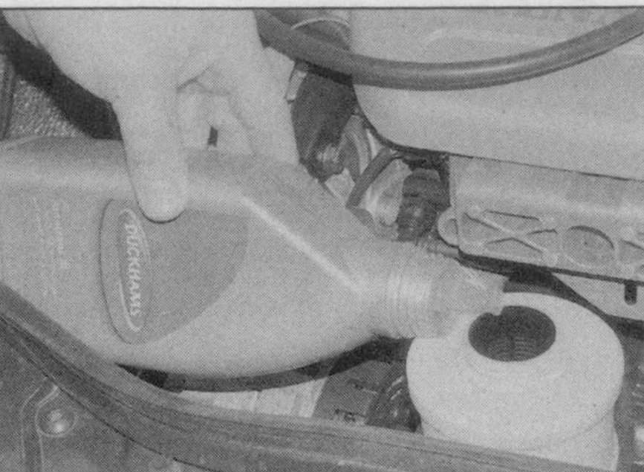

3 Unscrew the cap, allowing the fluid to drain from the bottom of the cap as it is removed. Top-up the fluid level to the MAXI mark, using the specified type of fluid (do not overfill the reservoir), then refit and tighten the filler cap.

Screen washer fluid level

Screenwash additives not only keep the windscreen clean, they also prevent the washer system freezing in cold weather – which is when you are likely to need it most. Don't top up using plain water as the screenwash will become too diluted, and will freeze during cold weather.

On no account use coolant antifreeze in the washer system – this could discolour or damage paintwork.

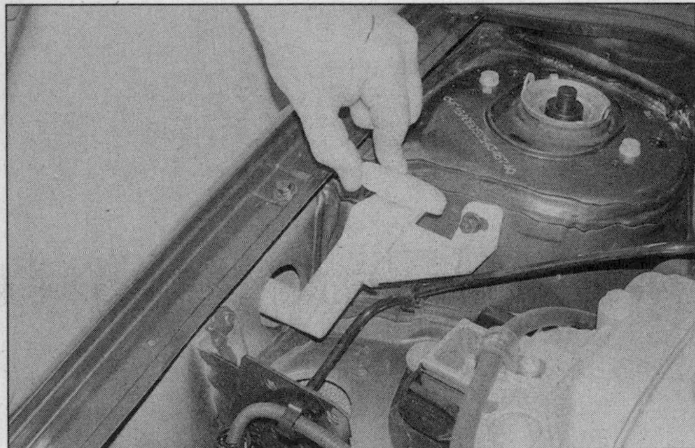

1 The reservoir for the windscreen and headlight washers (where fitted) is located at the right-hand side of the engine compartment. If topping-up is necessary, open the cap.

2 When topping-up the reservoir a screenwash additive should be added in the quantities recommended on the bottle.

Tyre condition and pressure

It is very important that tyres are in good condition, and at the correct pressure - having a tyre failure at any speed is highly dangerous. Tyre wear is influenced by driving style - harsh braking and acceleration, or fast cornering, will all produce more rapid tyre wear. As a general rule, the front tyres wear out faster than the rears. Interchanging the tyres from front to rear ("rotating" the tyres) may result in more even wear. However, if this is completely effective, you may have the expense of replacing all four tyres at once!

Remove any nails or stones embedded in the tread before they penetrate the tyre to cause deflation. If removal of a nail does reveal that the tyre has been punctured, refit the nail so that its point of penetration is marked. Then immediately change the wheel, and have the tyre repaired by a tyre dealer.

Regularly check the tyres for damage in the form of cuts or bulges, especially in the sidewalls. Periodically remove the wheels, and clean any dirt or mud from the inside and outside surfaces. Examine the wheel rims for signs of rusting, corrosion or other damage. Light alloy wheels are easily damaged by "kerbing" whilst parking; steel wheels may also become dented or buckled. A new wheel is very often the only way to overcome severe damage.

New tyres should be balanced when they are fitted, but it may become necessary to re-balance them as they wear, or if the balance weights fitted to the wheel rim should fall off. Unbalanced tyres will wear more quickly, as will the steering and suspension components. Wheel imbalance is normally signified by vibration, particularly at a certain speed (typically around 50 mph). If this vibration is felt only through the steering, then it is likely that just the front wheels need balancing. If, however, the vibration is felt through the whole car, the rear wheels could be out of balance. Wheel balancing should be carried out by a tyre dealer or garage.

1 ***Tread Depth - visual check***
The original tyres have tread wear safety bands (B), which will appear when the tread depth reaches approximately 1.6 mm. The band positions are indicated by a triangular mark on the tyre sidewall (A).

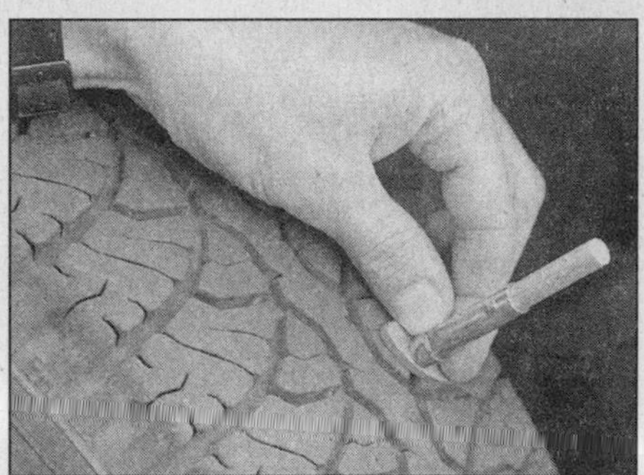

2 ***Tread Depth - manual check***
Alternatively, tread wear can be monitored with a simple, inexpensive device known as a tread depth indicator gauge.

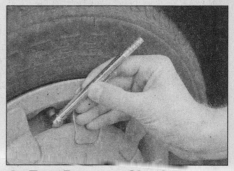

3 ***Tyre Pressure Check***
Check the tyre pressures regularly with the tyres cold. Do not adjust the tyre pressures immediately after the vehicle has been used, or an inaccurate setting will result.

Tyre tread wear patterns

Shoulder Wear

Underinflation (wear on both sides)
Under-inflation will cause overheating of the tyre, because the tyre will flex too much, and the tread will not sit correctly on the road surface. This will cause a loss of grip and excessive wear, not to mention the danger of sudden tyre failure due to heat build-up.
Check and adjust pressures
Incorrect wheel camber (wear on one side)
Repair or renew suspension parts
Hard cornering
Reduce speed!

Centre Wear

Overinflation
Over-inflation will cause rapid wear of the centre part of the tyre tread, coupled with reduced grip, harsher ride, and the danger of shock damage occurring in the tyre casing.
Check and adjust pressures

If you sometimes have to inflate your car's tyres to the higher pressures specified for maximum load or sustained high speed, don't forget to reduce the pressures to normal afterwards.

Uneven Wear

Front tyres may wear unevenly as a result of wheel misalignment. Most tyre dealers and garages can check and adjust the wheel alignment (or "tracking") for a modest charge.
Incorrect camber or castor
Repair or renew suspension parts
Malfunctioning suspension
Repair or renew suspension parts
Unbalanced wheel
Balance tyres
Incorrect toe setting
Adjust front wheel alignment
Note: *The feathered edge of the tread which typifies toe wear is best checked by feel.*

Battery

Caution: Before carrying out any work on the vehicle battery, read the precautions given in 'Safety first!' at the start of this manual.

✔ Make sure that the battery tray is in good condition, and that the clamp is tight. Corrosion on the tray, retaining clamp and the battery itself can be removed with a solution of water and baking soda. Thoroughly rinse all cleaned areas with water. Any metal parts damaged by corrosion should be covered with a zinc-based primer, then painted.

✔ Periodically (approximately every three months), check the charge condition of the battery as described in Chapter 5A.

✔ If the battery is flat, and you need to jump start your vehicle, see *Roadside Repairs*.

Battery corrosion can be kept to a minimum by applying a layer of petroleum jelly to the clamps and terminals after they are reconnected.

1 The battery is located on the left-hand side of the engine compartment (on some models the battery is located in the right-hand rear corner of the engine compartment, under the intake vent panel). Where necessary, prise open the plastic cover for access to the positive terminal. The exterior of the battery should be inspected periodically for damage such as a cracked case or cover.

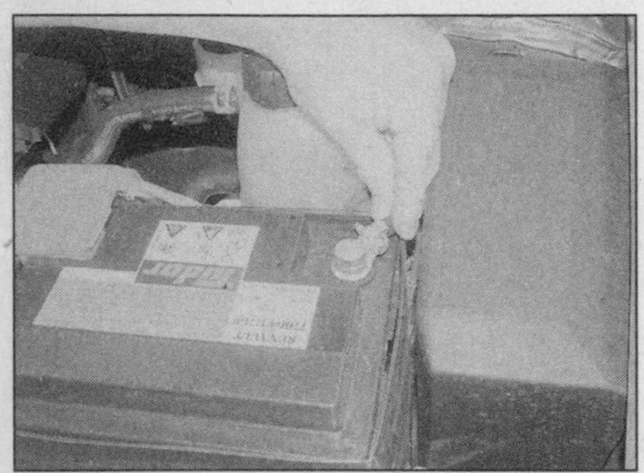

2 Check the tightness of battery clamps to ensure good electrical connections. You should not be able to move them. Also check each cable for cracks and frayed conductors.

3 If corrosion (white, fluffy deposits) is evident, remove the cables from the battery terminals, clean them with a small wire brush, then refit them. Automotive stores sell a tool for cleaning the battery post . . .

4 . . . as well as the battery cable clamps

Electrical systems

✔ Check all external lights and the horn. Refer to the appropriate Sections of Chapter 12 for details if any of the circuits are found to be inoperative.

✔ Visually check all accessible wiring connectors, harnesses and retaining clips for security, and for signs of chafing or damage.

If you need to check your brake lights and indicators unaided, back up to a wall or garage door and operate the lights. The reflected light should show if they are working properly.

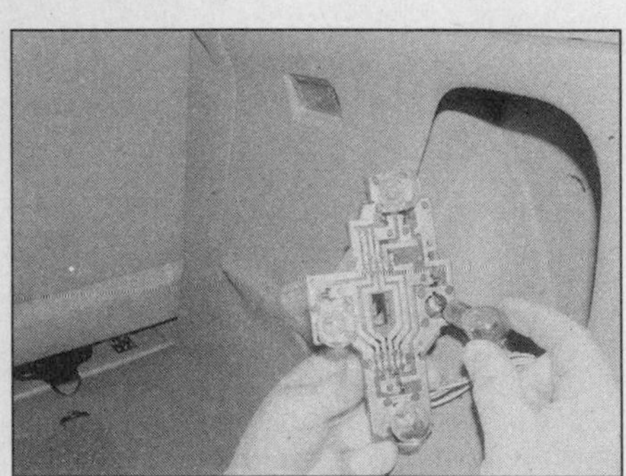

1 If a single indicator light, stop-light or headlight has failed, it is likely that a bulb has blown and will need to be replaced. Refer to *Electrical fault finding* in Chapter 12 for details. If both stop-lights have failed, it is possible that the switch has failed (see Chapter 9).

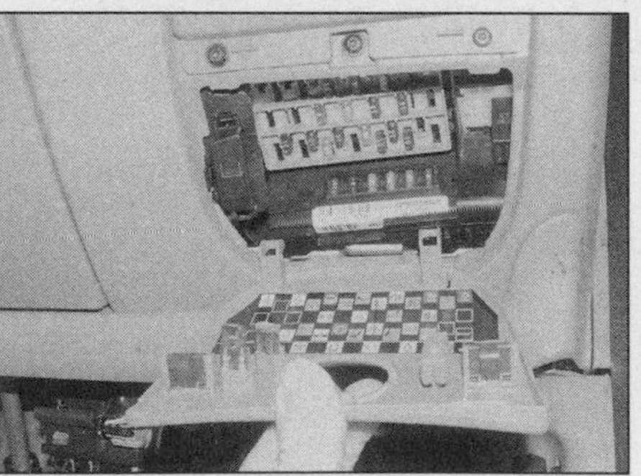

2 If more than one indicator light or headlight has failed, it is likely that either a fuse has blown or that there is a fault in the circuit (see Chapter 12). The fuses are located under a cover on the driver's side of the facia panel. Open the fusebox cover, and the fuse locations are indicated by symbols on the rear of the cover. Additional fuses and relays are located in the left-hand side of the engine compartment.

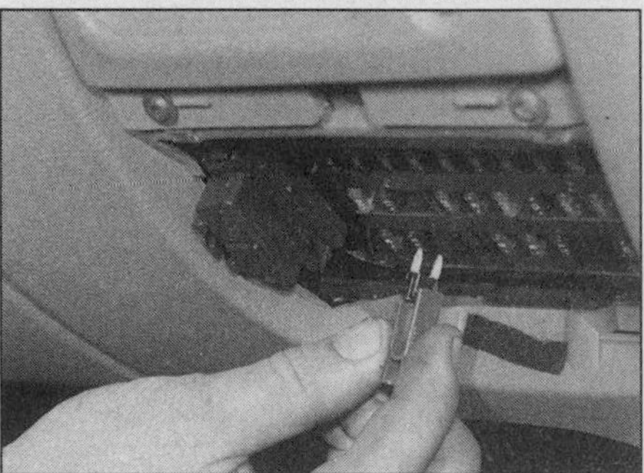

3 To replace a blown fuse, remove it using the plastic tool provided. Fit a new fuse of the same rating, available from car accessory shops. It is important that you find the reason that the fuse failed (see *Electrical fault finding* in Chapter 12).

Wiper blades

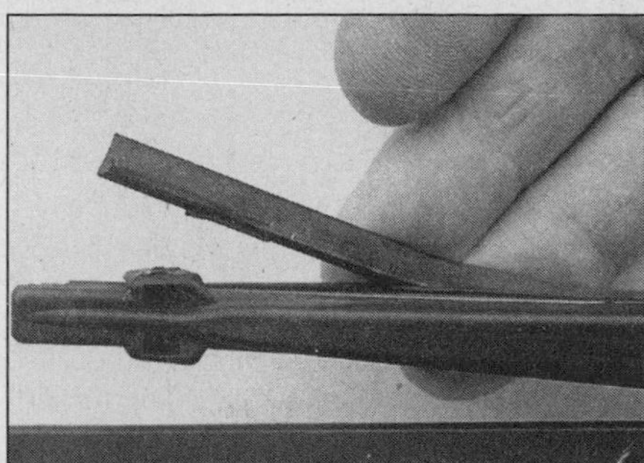

1 Check the condition of the wiper blades; if they are cracked or show any signs of deterioration, or if the glass swept area is smeared, renew them. For maximum clarity of vision, wiper blades should be renewed annually.

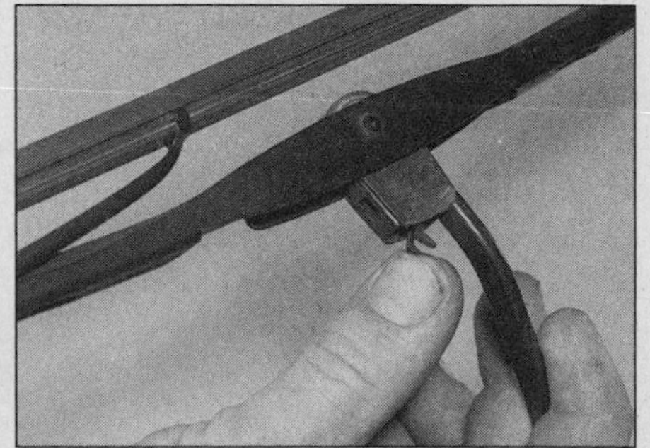

2 To remove a wiper blade, pull the arm fully away from the glass until it locks. Swivel the blade through 90°, then depress the locking clip at the base of the mounting block.

3 Slide the blade from the arm. When fitting the new blade, make sure that the blade locks securely into the arm, and that the blade is orientated correctly. Don't forget to check the tailgate wiper blade as well (where applicable)

Tyre pressures (cold)

Note: *Pressures apply to original-equipment tyres, and may vary if any other make or type of tyre is fitted; check with the tyre manufacturer or supplier for correct pressures if necessary. The pressures are given on the inside of the fuel filler flap.*

Mégane	**Front**	**Rear**
1.4 litre models		
Normal use	2.1 bar (30 psi)	2.0 bar (29 psi)
Full load	2.3 bar (33 psi)	2.2 bar (32 psi)
Emergency spare wheel	2.3 bar (33 psi)	
1.6 litre models		
Normal use	2.2 bar (32 psi)	2.0 bar (29 psi)
Full load	2.4 bar (35 psi)	2.2 bar (32 psi)
Emergency spare wheel	2.4 bar (35 psi)	
1.9 litre models		
Normal use	2.1 bar (30 psi)	2.0 bar (29 psi)
Full load	2.3 bar (33 psi)	2.2 bar (32 psi)
Emergency spare wheel	2.3 bar (33 psi)	
Scénic		
Normal use	2.2 bar (32 psi)	2.0 bar (29 psi)
Full load	2.3 bar (33 psi)	2.3 bar (33 psi)
Emergency spare wheel	2.3 bar (33 psi)	

Lubricants and fluids

Engine (petrol)	Multigrade engine oil, viscosity range SAE 15W/40 to 15W/50, to ACEA A1 and A3 *(Duckhams Fully Synthetic Engine Oil, QXR Premium Petrol Engine Oil, or Hypergrade Petrol Engine Oil)*
Engine (diesel)	Multigrade engine oil, viscosity range SAE 15W/40 to 15W/50, to ACEA B3 and B4 *(Duckhams Fully Synthetic Engine Oil, QXR Premium Diesel Engine Oil, or Hypergrade Diesel Engine Oil)*
Cooling system	Ethylene glycol-based antifreeze – RX Glaceol type D coolant *(Duckhams Antifreeze and Summer Coolant)*
Manual gearbox	Elf Tranself TRJ 75W/80W gear oil
Automatic transmission	Elf Renaultmatic D2, or MOBIL ATF 220 *(Duckhams ATF Autotrans III)*
Power steering reservoir	Elf Renaultmatic D2, Dexron II ATF *(Duckhams ATF Autotrans III)*
Brake fluid reservoir	Hydraulic fluid to SAE J1703F or DOT 4 *(Duckhams Universal Brake and Clutch Fluid)*

Choosing your engine oil

Engines need oil, not only to lubricate moving parts and minimise wear, but also to maximise power output and to improve fuel economy. By introducing a simplified and improved range of engine oils, Duckhams has taken away the confusion and made it easier for you to choose the right oil for your engine.

HOW ENGINE OIL WORKS

• *Beating friction*

Without oil, the moving surfaces inside your engine will rub together, heat up and melt, quickly causing the engine to seize. Engine oil creates a film which separates these moving parts, preventing wear and heat build-up.

• *Cooling hot-spots*

Temperatures inside the engine can exceed 1000° C. The engine oil circulates and acts as a coolant, transferring heat from the hot-spots to the sump.

• *Cleaning the engine internally*

Good quality engine oils clean the inside of your engine, collecting and dispersing combustion deposits and controlling them until they are trapped by the oil filter or flushed out at oil change.

OIL CARE - FOLLOW THE CODE

To handle and dispose of used engine oil safely, always:

- ***Avoid skin contact with used engine oil. Repeated or prolonged contact can be harmful.***
- ***Dispose of used oil and empty packs in a responsible manner in an authorised disposal site. Call 0800 663366 to find the one nearest to you. Never tip oil down drains or onto the ground.***

DUCKHAMS ENGINE OILS

For the driver who demands a premium quality oil for complete reassurance, we recommend synthetic formula **Duckhams QXR Premium Engine Oils**.

For the driver who requires a straightforward quality engine oil, we recommend **Duckhams Hypergrade Engine Oils.**

For further information and advice, call the Duckhams UK Helpline on 0800 212988.

Chapter 1 Part A:
Routine maintenance and servicing – petrol models

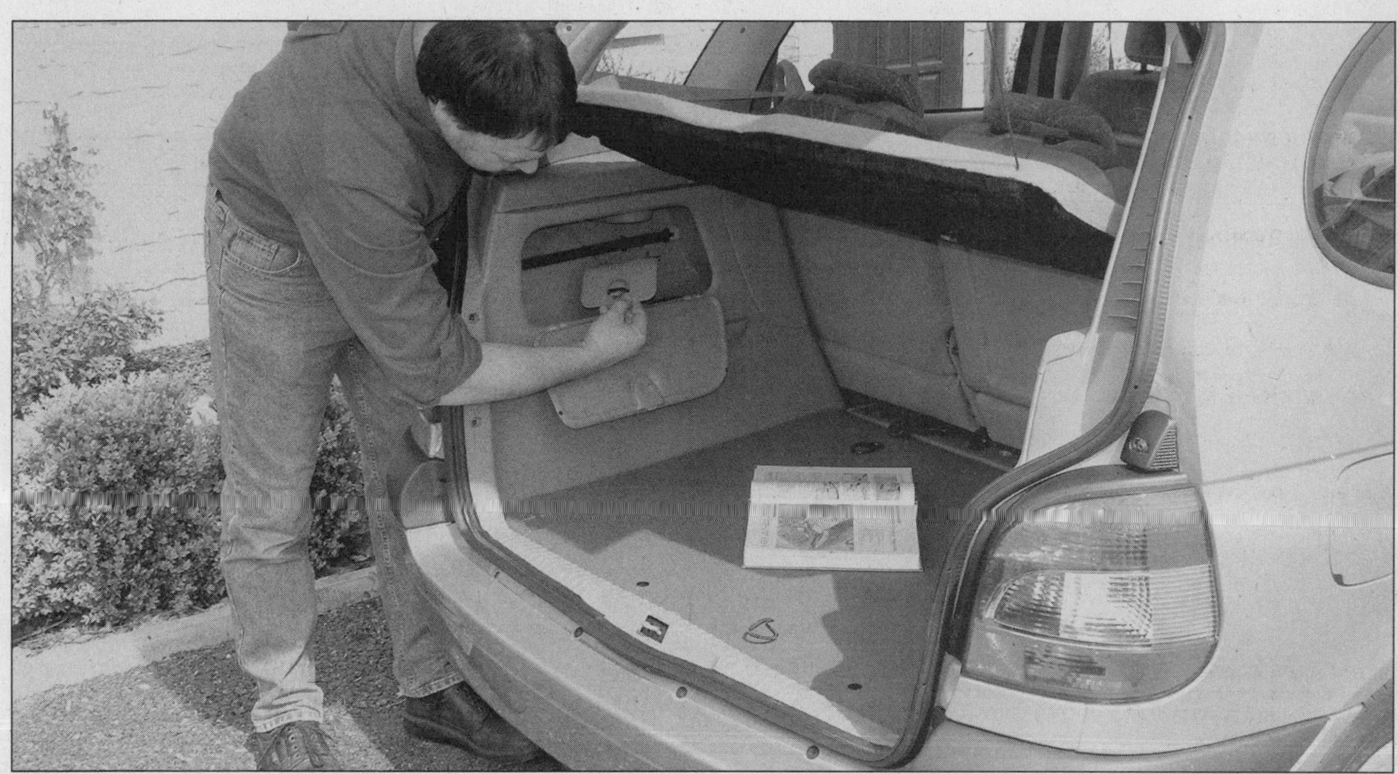

Contents

Degrees of difficulty

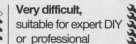

Easy, suitable for novice with little experience 	**Fairly easy,** suitable for beginner with some experience 	**Fairly difficult,** suitable for competent DIY mechanic 	**Difficult,** suitable for experienced DIY mechanic 	**Very difficult,** suitable for expert DIY or professional 

Specifications – petrol models

Lubricants and fluids

Refer to *Weekly checks*

Capacities

Engine oil

Including oil filter:	
1390cc and 1598cc engines	4.0 litres
1998cc engines	6.0 litres

Cooling system

1390cc and 1598cc engines	6.0 litres
1998cc engines	7.0 litres

Transmission

Manual transmission:	
JB1 and JB3	3.4 litres
JC5	3.1 litres
AD4 Automatic transmission:	
From dry:	
Main transmission	4.6 litres
Final drive	1.0 litre
Drain and refill:	
Main transmission	3.5 litres
Final drive	1.0 litre
DP0 Automatic transmission	6.0 litres

Power-assisted steering reservoir

Models with mechanical pump	1.1 litres

Fuel tank

All models	60 litres (13.2 gallons)

Engine codes

1.4 litre models:	
SOHC	E7J
DOHC	K4J
1.6 litre models	K4M
2.0 litre models	F4R

Cooling system

Antifreeze mixture:	**Antifreeze**	**Water**
Protection to –21°C	35%	65%
Protection to –37°C	50%	50%

Fuel system

Specified idle speed (non-adjustable)	750 ± 50 rpm
Idle mixture CO content (non-adjustable)	0.5% maximum (0.3% at 2500 rpm)

Ignition system

Firing order	1-3-4-2
Location of No 1 cylinder	Flywheel end
Ignition timing	Controlled by ECU – see Chapter 5B
Spark plugs:	
E7J	Eyquem FC52LS or NGK BCP5ES
K4J	Bosch RFC 50LZ2E
K4M	Bosch RFC 50LZ2E
F4R	Bosch FR7 LDC
Electrode gap	0.9 mm

Brakes

Front disc brakes:	**New**	**Minimum thickness**
Pad thickness (including backing):	18.2 mm	6.0 mm
Rear disc brakes:		
Pad thickness (including backing):	11.0 mm	5.0 mm
Rear drum brakes:		
Shoe thickness (including backing):		
Leading shoe	4.9 mm	2.0 mm
Trailing shoe	3.4 mm	2.0 mm

Torque wrench settings

	Nm	**lbf ft**
Engine oil drain plug	15 to 25	11 to 18
Roadwheel bolts	90	66
Spark plugs	25 to 30	19 to 22

The maintenance intervals in this manual are provided with the assumption that you, not the dealer, will be carrying out the work. These are the minimum maintenance intervals recommended by us for vehicles driven daily. If you wish to keep your vehicle in peak condition at all times, you may wish to perform some of these procedures more often. We encourage frequent maintenance, because it enhances the efficiency, performance and resale value of your vehicle.

If the vehicle is driven in dusty areas, used to tow a trailer, or driven frequently at slow speeds (idling in traffic) or on short journeys, more frequent maintenance intervals are recommended.

When the vehicle is new, it should be serviced by a factory-authorised dealer service department to preserve the factory warranty.

Every 250 miles (400 km) or weekly

- ☐ Refer to *Weekly checks*

Every 9000 miles (15 000 km) or 12 months

- ☐ Renew the engine oil and filter (Section 3)

Note: *Renault recommend that the engine oil and filter are changed every 18 000 miles, depending on the service programme. However, frequent oil and filter changes are good for the engine and we recommend that the oil and filter are renewed at the interval specified here, especially if the vehicle is used on a lot of short journeys or covers but a small annual mileage.*

Every 18 000 miles (30 000 km) or 2 years

In addition to all the items listed previously, carry out the following:

- ☐ Check the front brake pads and discs (Section 4)
- ☐ Check the condition of the exhaust system and mountings (Section 5)
- ☐ Check the suspension and steering components (Section 6)
- ☐ Check the driveshaft gaiters and CV joints (Section 7)
- ☐ Check all underbonnet components, hoses and brake lines for fluid leaks (Section 8)
- ☐ Check the tightness of the roadwheel bolts (Section 9)
- ☐ Renew the pollen filter (Section 10)
- ☐ Check the automatic transmission fluid level (Section 11)
- ☐ Check the operation of the clutch (Section 12)
- ☐ Check the exhaust emissions (Section 13)
- ☐ Check the operation of the air conditioning system (Section 14)
- ☐ Check the operation of all electrical systems (Section 15)
- ☐ Check the vehicle bodywork (Section 16)

Every 36 000 miles (60 000 km) or 4 years

In addition to all the items listed previously, carry out the following:

- ☐ Check the condition of the seat belts (Section 17)
- ☐ Check the condition of the auxiliary drivebelt (Section 18)
- ☐ Check the headlight beam adjustment (Chapter 12)
- ☐ Renew the spark plugs and check the ignition system (Section 19)
- ☐ Renew the air filter element (Section 20)
- ☐ Check the operation of the handbrake (Chapter 9)
- ☐ Check the heating system (Section 21)
- ☐ Lubricate all hinges and locks (Section 22)
- ☐ Check the spare fuses are in place (Section 23)
- ☐ Check the front wheel alignment (Chapter 10)
- ☐ Check the rear brakes (Section 24)
- ☐ Check the manual gearbox oil level (Section 25)
- ☐ Renew the automatic transmission fluid – AD4 transmission (Section 26)
- ☐ Renew the fuel filter (Section 27)
- ☐ Carry out a road test (Section 28)
- ☐ Renew the timing belt (Chapter 2A or 2B)

Note: *Renault recommend that the timing belt be renewed every 72 000 miles (120 000 km). However, if the vehicle is used mainly for short journeys or for a lot of stop-start driving or other severe use it is recommended that the belt be renewed earlier – consideration should be given to changing the belt at this interval. The actual belt renewal interval is very much up to the individual owner but, bearing in mind that severe engine damage will result if the belt breaks in use, we recommend you err on the side of caution.*

Every 72 000 miles (120 000 km) or 4 years

In addition to all the items listed previously, carry out the following:

- ☐ Renew the coolant (Section 29)
- ☐ Renew the brake fluid (Section 30)

Every 10 years

- ☐ Renew the batteries in the tyre pressure monitoring system
- ☐ Renew the air bag and seat belt pre-tensioners (Chapter 12)

Underbonnet view of a 1.6 litre Mégane

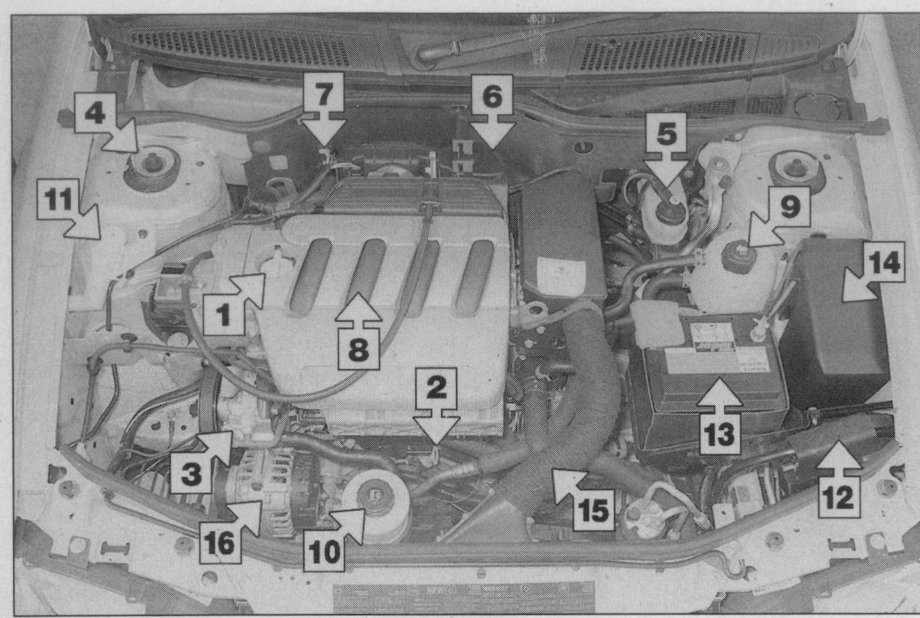

1 Engine oil filler cap
2 Engine oil level dipstick
3 Power steering pump
4 Front suspension strut upper mountings
5 Brake master cylinder fluid reservoir
6 Air cleaner
7 Absolute air pressure MAP sensor
8 Inlet manifold
9 Coolant expansion tank
10 Power steering fluid reservoir
11 Windscreen/headlight washer fluid reservoir
12 Engine management ECU
13 Battery
14 Engine related fusebox
15 Air inlet duct
16 Alternator

Front underbody view of a 1.6 litre Mégane

1 Engine oil sump drain plug
2 Manual transmission
3 Driveshafts
4 Front suspension subframe
5 Front suspension lower arms
6 Front anti-roll bar
7 Track rod ends
8 Front subframe rear links
9 Gearchange rod
10 Power steering gear
11 Exhaust catalytic converter

Rear underbody view of a 1.6 litre Mégane

1 Fuel tank
2 Handbrake cables
3 Fuel filter
4 Fuel feed and return lines
5 Rear axle assembly
6 Rear shock absorbers
7 Exhaust rear silencer and tailpipe
8 Torsion bars
9 Anti-roll bars

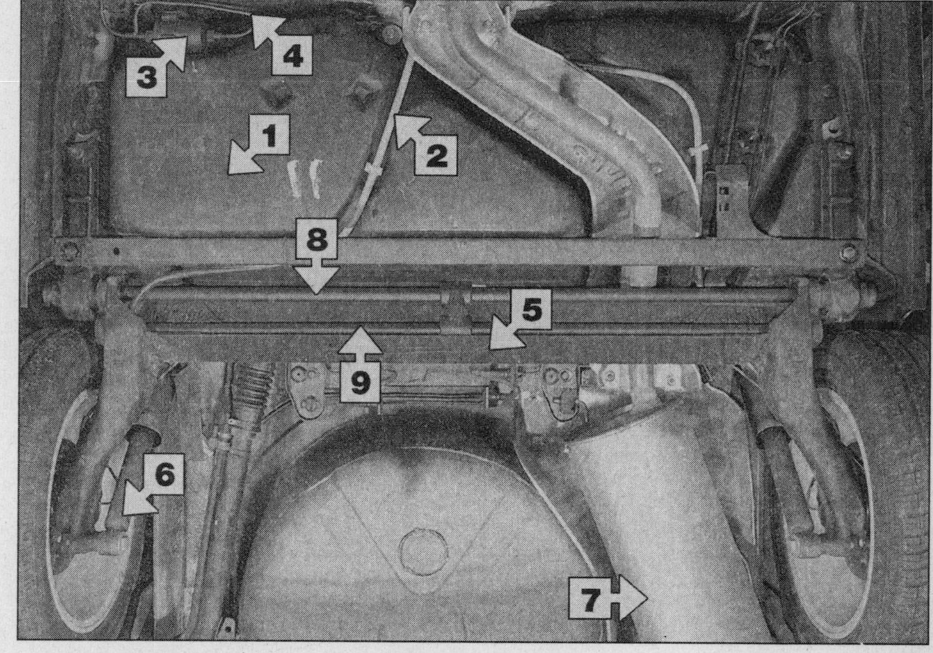

Underbonnet view of a petrol 1.4 litre (16-valve) Mégane

1 Engine oil filler cap
2 Engine oil level dipstick
3 Air inlet duct
4 Front suspension strut upper mountings
5 Brake master cylinder fluid reservoir
6 Air cleaner
7 Absolute air pressure MAP sensor
8 Inlet manifold
9 Coolant expansion tank
10 Power steering fluid reservoir
11 Windscreen/headlight washer fluid reservoir
12 Engine management ECU
13 Battery
14 Engine related fusebox
15 Alternator

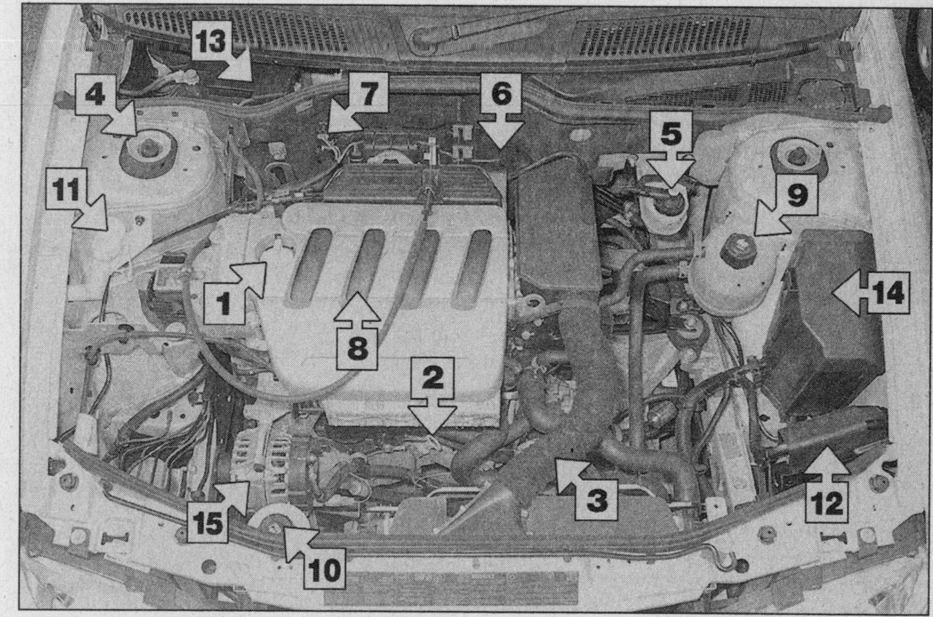

1 Introduction

This Chapter is designed to help the home mechanic maintain his/her vehicle for safety, economy, long life and peak performance.

The Chapter contains a master maintenance schedule, followed by Sections dealing specifically with each task in the schedule. Visual checks, adjustments, component renewal and other helpful items are included. Refer to the accompanying illustrations of the engine compartment and the underside of the vehicle for the locations of the various components.

Servicing your vehicle in accordance with the mileage/time maintenance schedule and the following Sections will provide a planned maintenance programme, which should result in a long and reliable service life. This is a comprehensive plan, so maintaining some items but not others at the specified service intervals, will not produce the same results.

As you service your vehicle, you will discover that many of the procedures can – and should – be grouped together, because of the particular procedure being performed, or because of the proximity of two otherwise-unrelated components to one another. For example, if the vehicle is raised for any reason, the exhaust can be inspected at the same time as the suspension and steering components.

The first step in this maintenance programme is to prepare yourself before the actual work begins. Read through all the Sections relevant to the work to be carried out, then make a list and gather all the parts and tools required. If a problem is encountered, seek advice from a parts specialist, or a dealer service department.

Caution: If the radio/cassette in your vehicle is equipped with an anti-theft system, make sure you have the correct activation code before disconnecting the battery.

2 Regular maintenance

If, from the time the vehicle is new, the routine maintenance schedule is followed closely, and frequent checks are made of fluid levels and high-wear items, as suggested throughout this manual, the engine will be kept in relatively good running condition, and the need for additional work will be minimised.

It is possible that there will be times when the engine is running poorly due to the lack of regular maintenance. This is even more likely if a used vehicle, which has not received regular and frequent maintenance checks, is purchased. In such cases, additional work may need to be carried out, outside of the regular maintenance intervals.

If engine wear is suspected, a compression test (refer to Chapter 2A or 2B as applicable) will provide valuable information regarding the overall performance of the main internal components. Such a test can be used as a basis to decide on the extent of the work to be carried out. If, for example, a compression test indicates serious internal engine wear, conventional maintenance as described in this Chapter will not greatly improve the performance of the engine, and may prove a waste of time and money, unless extensive overhaul work is carried out first.

The following series of operations are those most often required to improve the performance of a generally poor-running engine:

Primary operations

a) Clean, inspect and test the battery (refer to 'Weekly checks').
b) Check all the engine-related fluids (refer to 'Weekly checks').
c) Check the condition of the auxiliary drivebelt(s) (Section 18).
d) Check the condition of all hoses, and check for fluid leaks (Section 8).
e) Renew the spark plugs (Section 19).
f) Check the condition of the air filter, and renew if necessary (Section 20).
g) Check the fuel filter (Section 27).

If the above operations do not prove fully effective, carry out the following secondary operations:

Secondary operations

All items listed under *Primary operations*, plus the following:

a) Check the charging system (refer to Chapter 5A).
b) Check the ignition system (refer to Chapter 5B).
c) Check the fuel system (refer to Chapter 4A).

Every 9 000 miles (15 000 km) or 12 months

3 Engine oil and filter renewal

1 Frequent oil and filter changes are the most important preventative maintenance procedures which can be undertaken by the DIY owner. As engine oil ages, it becomes diluted and contaminated, which leads to premature engine wear.

2 Before starting this procedure, gather together all the necessary tools and materials **(see illustration)**. Also make sure that you have plenty of clean rags and newspapers handy, to mop up any spills. Ideally, the engine oil should be warm, as it will drain more easily and more built-up sludge will be removed with it. Take care not to touch the exhaust or any other hot parts of the engine when working under the vehicle. To avoid any possibility of scalding and to protect yourself from possible skin irritants and other harmful contaminants in used engine oils, it is advisable to wear gloves when carrying out this work.

3 Firmly apply the handbrake then jack up the front of the car and support it on axle stands (see *Jacking and vehicle support*). Where applicable, remove the engine undershield.

4 Remove the oil filler cap, then using an 8 mm square-section drain plug key, slacken the drain plug about half a turn. Position the draining container under the drain plug, then remove the plug completely – recover the sealing washer **(see illustration)**.

3.2 Tools and materials necessary for the engine oil change and filter renewal

5 Allow some time for the oil to drain, noting that it may be necessary to reposition the container as the oil flow slows to a trickle.

6 After all the oil has drained, wipe the drain plug and the sealing washer with a clean rag. Examine the condition of the sealing washer and renew it if it shows signs of scoring or other damage which may prevent an oil-tight seal. Clean the area around the drain plug opening and refit the plug complete with the

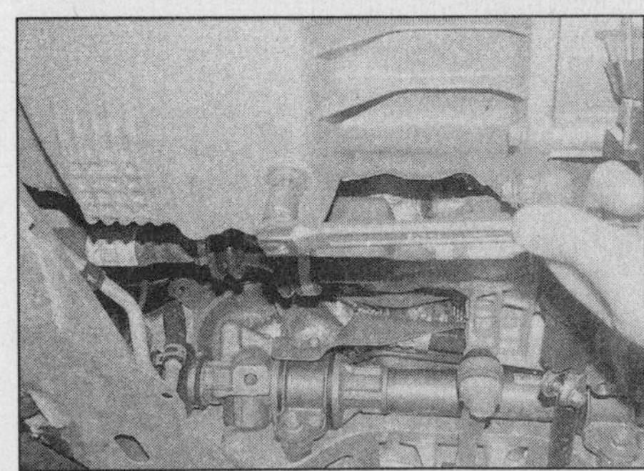

3.4 Engine oil drain plug (K4M engine)

As the drain plug threads release, move it sharply away so the stream of oil issuing from the sump runs into the container, not up your sleeve.

washer. Tighten it to the specified torque wrench setting.

7 Move the container into position under the oil filter which is located on the front of the cylinder block **(see illustration)**.

8 Use an oil filter removal tool to slacken the filter initially, then unscrew it by hand the rest of the way **(see illustration)**. Empty the oil from the old filter into the container.

9 Use a clean rag to remove all oil, dirt and sludge from the filter sealing area on the engine. Check the old filter to make sure that the rubber sealing ring has not stuck to the engine. If it has, carefully remove it.

10 Apply a light coating of clean engine oil to the sealing ring on the new filter, then screw the filter into position on the engine **(see illustration)**. Tighten the filter firmly by hand only – **do not** use any tools.

3.7 Oil filter location on the K4M engine

11 Remove the old oil and all tools from under the vehicle then lower the vehicle to the ground.

12 Fill the engine through the filler hole, using the correct grade and type of oil (refer to *Weekly checks* for details of topping-up). Pour in half the specified quantity of oil first, then wait a few minutes for the oil to drain into the sump. Continue to add oil, a small quantity at a time, until the level is up to the lower mark on the dipstick. Adding approximately a further 1.5 litres will bring the level up to the upper mark on the dipstick.

13 Start the engine and run it for a few minutes, while checking for leaks around the oil filter seal and the sump drain plug. Note that there may be a delay of a few seconds before the low oil pressure warning light goes out when the engine is first started, as the oil circulates through the new oil filter and the engine oil galleries before the pressure builds-up.

14 Stop the engine and wait a few minutes for the oil to settle in the sump once more. With the new oil circulated and the filter now completely full, recheck the level on the dipstick and add more oil as necessary.

15 Dispose safely of the used engine oil and the old filter with reference to *General repair procedures*.

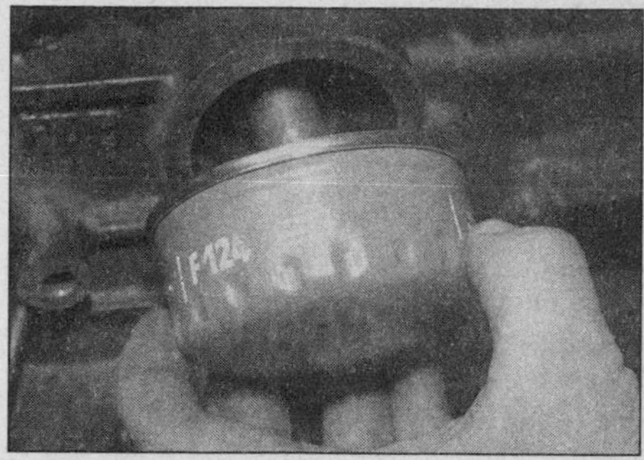

3.8 Removing the oil filter

3.10 Apply a light coating of clean engine oil to the sealing ring on the new filter

Every 18 000 miles (30 000 km) or 2 years

4 Front brake pad and disc check

1 Apply the handbrake, then jack up the front of the car and support it securely on axle stands. Remove the front roadwheels.

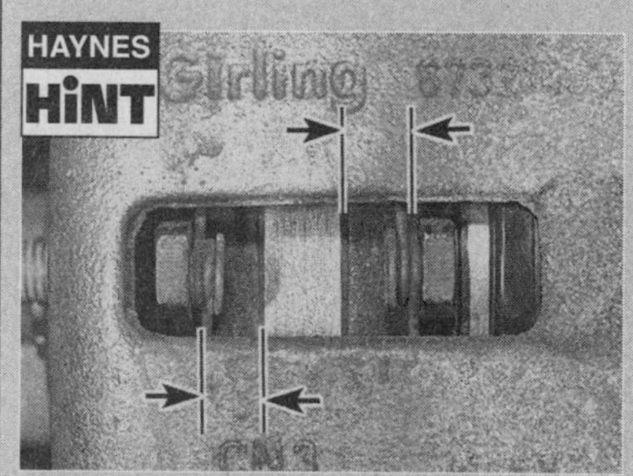

For a quick check, the thickness of friction material remaining on each brake pad can be measured through the aperture in the caliper body.

2 If any pads friction material is worn to the specified thickness or less, all four pads must be renewed as a set. Where pad wear warning contacts are fitted, it should not be used as an excuse for omitting a visual check.

3 For a comprehensive check, the brake pads should be removed and cleaned. The operation of the caliper can then also be checked and the condition of the brake disc itself can be fully examined on both sides. Refer to Chapter 9 for further information.

4 On completion refit the roadwheels and lower the car to the ground.

5 Exhaust system check

1 With the engine cold (at least an hour after the vehicle has been driven), check the complete exhaust system from the engine to the end of the tailpipe. The exhaust system is most easily checked with the vehicle raised on a hoist, or suitably supported on axle stands, so that the exhaust components are readily visible and accessible.

2 Check the exhaust pipes and connections for evidence of leaks, severe corrosion and damage. Make sure that all brackets and mountings are in good condition and that all relevant nuts and bolts are tight. Leakage at any of the joints or in other parts of the system will usually show up as a black sooty stain in the vicinity of the leak.

3 Rattles and other noises can often be traced to the exhaust system, especially the brackets and mountings. Try to move the pipes and silencers. If the components are able to come into contact with the body or suspension parts, secure the system with new mountings. Otherwise separate the joints (if possible) and twist the pipes as necessary to provide additional clearance.

6.4 Check for wear in the hub bearings by grasping the wheel and trying to rock it

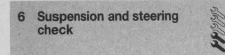

6 Suspension and steering check

Front suspension and steering check

1 Raise the front of the vehicle and securely support it on axle stands.

2 Visually inspect the balljoint dust covers and the steering gear gaiters for splits, chafing or deterioration. Any wear of these components will cause loss of lubricant, together with dirt and water entry, resulting in rapid deterioration of the balljoints or steering gear.

3 On vehicles with power steering, check the fluid hoses for chafing or deterioration and the pipe and hose unions for fluid leaks. Also check for signs of fluid leakage under pressure from the steering gear gaiters, which would indicate failed fluid seals within the steering gear.

4 Grasp the roadwheel at the 12 o'clock and 6 o'clock positions and try to rock it **(see illustration)**. Very slight free play may be felt, but if the movement is appreciable, further investigation is necessary to determine the source. Continue rocking the wheel while an assistant depresses the footbrake. If the movement is now eliminated or significantly reduced, it is likely that the hub bearings are at fault. If the free play is still evident with the footbrake depressed, then there is wear in the suspension joints or mountings.

5 Now grasp the wheel at the 9 o'clock and 3 o'clock positions and try to rock it as before. Any movement felt now may again be caused by wear in the hub bearings or the steering track rod balljoints. If the outer balljoint is worn, the visual movement will be obvious. If the inner joint is suspect, it can be felt by placing a hand over the steering gear gaiter and gripping the track rod. If the wheel is now rocked, movement will be felt at the inner joint if wear has taken place.

6 Using a large screwdriver or flat bar, check for wear in the suspension mounting bushes by levering between the relevant suspension component and its attachment point. Some movement is to be expected, as the mountings are made of rubber, but excessive wear should be obvious. Also check the condition of any visible rubber bushes, looking for splits, cracks or contamination of the rubber.

7 With the car standing on its wheels, have an assistant turn the steering wheel back-and-forth, about an eighth of a turn each way. There should be very little, if any, lost movement between the steering wheel and roadwheels. If this is not the case, closely observe the joints and mountings previously described. In addition, check the steering column universal joints for wear and also check the steering gear itself.

Rear suspension check

8 Chock the front wheels, engage reverse gear (or P on automatics) and release the handbrake. Jack up the rear of the vehicle and support securely on axle stands (see *Jacking and vehicle support*).

9 Working as described previously for the front suspension, check the rear hub bearings, the suspension bushes and the shock absorber mountings for wear.

Suspension strut/shock absorber check

10 Check for any signs of fluid leakage around the strut/shock absorber body, or from the rubber gaiter around the piston rod. Should any fluid be noticed, the strut/shock absorber is defective internally and should be renewed. **Note:** *Struts/shock absorbers should always be renewed in pairs on the same axle.*

11 The efficiency of the strut/shock absorber may be checked by bouncing the vehicle at each corner. Generally speaking, the body will return to its normal position and stop after being depressed. If it rises and returns on a rebound, the strut/shock absorber is probably suspect. Also examine the upper and lower mountings for any signs of wear.

7 Driveshaft rubber gaiter and CV joint check

1 With the car raised and securely supported on axle stands, turn the steering onto full lock, then slowly rotate the roadwheel. Inspect the condition of the outer constant velocity (CV) joint rubber gaiter while squeezing the gaiter to open out the folds **(see illustration)**. Check for signs of cracking, splits or deterioration of the rubber, which may allow the grease to escape and lead to the entry of water and grit into the joint. Also check the security and condition of the retaining clips/fasteners. Repeat these checks on the inner CV joint, then check the remaining driveshaft. If any damage or deterioration is found, the gaiter should be renewed as described in Chapter 8.

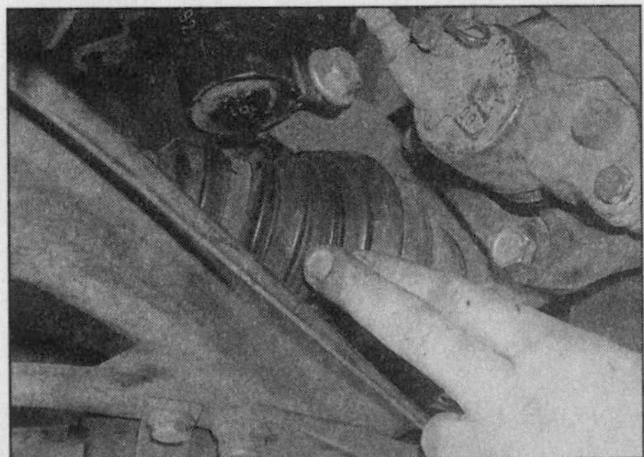

7.1 Checking a driveshaft outer gaiter for signs of damage

2 At the same time, check the general condition of the CV joints themselves by first holding the driveshaft and attempting to rotate the roadwheel. Repeat this check by holding the inner joint and attempting to rotate the driveshaft. Any appreciable movement indicates wear in the joints, in the driveshaft splines, or a loose driveshaft nut.

8 Hose, brake line and fluid leak check

1 Visually inspect the engine joint faces, gaskets and seals for any signs of water or oil leaks. Pay particular attention to the areas around the cylinder head cover, cylinder head, oil filter and sump joint faces. Bear in mind that, over a period of time, some very slight seepage from these areas is to be expected – what you are really looking for is any indication of a serious leak. Should a leak be found, renew the offending gasket or oil seal by referring to the appropriate Chapters in this manual.

2 Also check the security and condition of all the engine-related pipes and hoses and all braking system pipes and hoses. Ensure that all cable-ties or securing clips are in place and in good condition. Clips which are broken or missing can lead to chafing of the hoses, pipes or wiring, which could cause more serious problems in the future.

3 Carefully check the radiator hoses and heater hoses along their entire length. Renew any hose which is cracked, swollen or deteriorated. Cracks will show up better if the hose is squeezed. Pay close attention to the hose clips that secure the hoses to the cooling system components. Hose clips can pinch and puncture hoses, resulting in cooling

HAYNES HiNT

A leak in the cooling system will usually show up as white- or rust-coloured deposits on the area adjoining the leak.

10.1 Lift out the air intake vent panel . . .

10.2 . . . unclip the pollen filter cover . . .

10.3 . . . and withdraw the filter

system leaks. If the crimped-type hose clips are used, it may be a good idea to replace them with standard worm-drive clips.

4 Inspect all the cooling system components (hoses, joint faces, etc) for leaks.

5 Where any problems are found on system components, renew the component or gasket with reference to Chapter 3.

6 With the vehicle raised, inspect the fuel tank and filler neck for punctures, cracks and other damage. The connection between the filler neck and tank is especially critical. Sometimes a rubber filler neck or connecting hose will leak due to loose retaining clamps or deteriorated rubber.

7 Carefully check all rubber hoses and metal fuel lines leading away from the fuel tank. Check for loose connections, deteriorated hoses, crimped lines and other damage. Pay particular attention to the vent pipes and hoses, which often loop up around the filler neck and can become blocked or crimped. Follow the lines to the front of the vehicle, carefully inspecting them all the way. Renew damaged sections as necessary. Similarly, whilst the vehicle is raised, take the opportunity to inspect all underbody brake fluid pipes and hoses.

8 From within the engine compartment, check the security of all fuel, vacuum and brake hose attachments and pipe unions and inspect all hoses for kinks, chafing and deterioration.

9 Where applicable, check the condition of the power steering fluid pipes and hoses.

9 Roadwheel bolt check

1 Remove the wheel trims (where fitted) and slacken slightly (through one-quarter of a turn) each of the roadwheel bolts in turn. If any bolt is particularly difficult to unscrew, remove the roadwheel (see *Jacking and vehicle support*). Check that the threads and wheel-to-hub mating surfaces are clean and undamaged – the threads can be cleaned using a brass wire brush if rusty or corroded.

2 Clean each wheel thoroughly, inside and out, then examine the wheel rim for signs of rusting, corrosion or other damage. Light alloy wheels are easily damaged by 'kerbing' whilst parking and, similarly, steel wheels may become dented or buckled. Renewal of the wheel is very often the only course of remedial action possible. Check that any balance weights fitted are securely fastened.

3 Apply a thin smear of anti-seize compound to the threads and (if a wheel was found to be stuck in place with corrosion) to the wheel-to-hub mating surfaces. Refit the wheel, tightening the bolts only moderately at first.

4 Working in a diagonal sequence, tighten the bolts to the specified torque wrench setting. Refit the trim.

10 Pollen filter renewal

All models except Scénic

1 Open up the bonnet and unclip the small cover situated on the left-hand side of the intake vent panel **(see illustration)**.

2 Release the retaining clips and remove the pollen filter cover from the top of the blower motor housing **(see illustration)**.

3 Slide the pollen filter out of position and discard it **(see illustration)**.

4 Wipe clean the cover and housing and slide the new filter into position.

5 Securely clip the pollen filter cover onto the housing then clip the vent panel cover into position.

Scénic models

6 The filter is located inside the vehicle under the facia on the passenger's side.

7 Working in the passenger's footwell, undo the filter cover retaining screw and slide the cover forward (see arrow on cover) to release it from its location **(see illustrations)**.

8 Pull the pollen filter down out of position and discard it **(see illustration)**.

9 Wipe clean the cover and housing and slide the new filter into position.

10 Refit the cover and secure with the retaining bolt.

10.7a Undo the retaining screw (arrowed) . . .

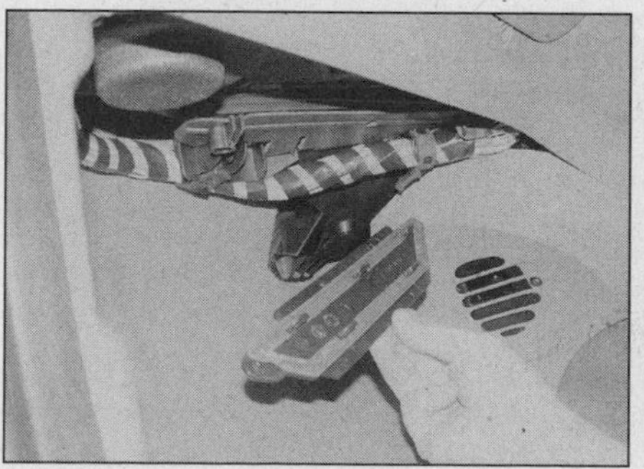
10.7b . . . remove the cover . . .

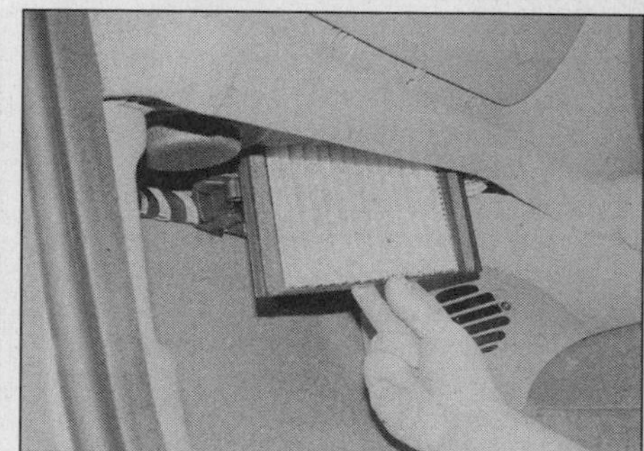
10.8 . . . and withdraw the pollen filter

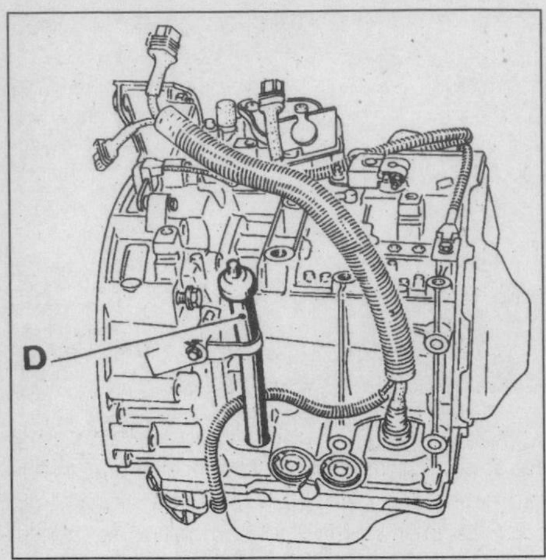

11.1a Automatic transmission fluid filler tube (D) on the AD4 type transmission

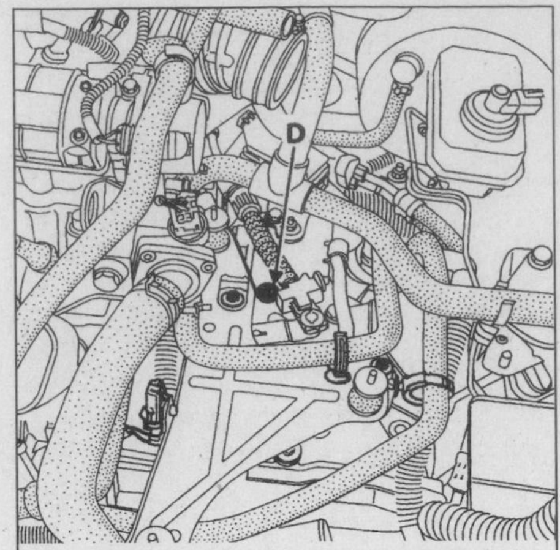

11.1b Automatic transmission fluid filler tube (D) on the DP0 type transmission

11 Automatic transmission fluid level check

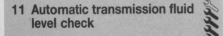

Transmission fluid

Note 1: *The transmission fluid level checking procedure is particularly complicated and the home mechanic would be well-advised to take the vehicle to a Renault dealer to have the work carried out, as special test equipment is necessary to carry out the check. However, the following procedure is given for those who have access to this equipment.*

Note 2: *The following procedure is mainly applicable to the AD4 type transmission. The DP0 type transmission is a 'sealed-for-life' unit and level checking will only be necessary if there has been a slight leak, or if it is suspected that the fluid level might be low.*

Note 3: *Refer to Chapter 7B for more information and transmission type identification.*

1 On AD4 type transmissions, remove the plug from the top of the filler tube D on the front of the transmission. On DP0 type transmissions, remove the air filter assembly as described in Chapter 4A, then unscrew the plug D from the top of the transmission **(see illustrations)**. Add 0.5 litre of the specified fluid to the transmission via the filler tube or opening, using a clean funnel with a fine-mesh filter, then refit the plug.

2 Position the vehicle over an inspection pit, on a ramp, or jack it up and support it on axle stands (see *Jacking and vehicle support*), ensuring that the vehicle remains level. If necessary, undo the retaining screws and remove the plastic undercover from beneath the engine/transmission.

3 Connect the Renault XR25 test meter to the diagnostic socket and enter DO4 (AD4 transmission) or D14 (DP0 transmission) then number 04. With the selector lever in Park, run the engine at idle speed until the fluid temperature, as shown on the test meter, reaches 60°C.

4 With the engine still running, unscrew the level plug from the transmission **(see illustrations)**. On the DP0 type transmission, the drain plug and level plug are incorporated into one unit – the level plug is the smaller of the two hexagonal headed plugs forming the draining/level checking unit. Allow the excess fluid to run out into a calibrated container drop-by-drop, then refit the plug. The amount of fluid should be more than 0.1 litre; if it is not, the fluid level in the transmission is incorrect.

5 If the level is incorrect, add an extra 0.5 litre of the specified fluid to the transmission, as described in paragraph 1. Allow the transmission to cool down to approx 50°C, then repeat the checking procedure again as described in the previous paragraphs. Repeat the procedure as required until more than the specified amount of fluid is drained as described in the previous paragraph, indicating that the transmission fluid level is correct, then securely tighten the level plug. Where necessary, refit the engine undercover and the air cleaner assembly.

Final drive oil – AD4 transmission

6 This is not a routine operation, but it may be considered necessary if there is reason to suspect that the oil level is incorrect – for instance if there has been an oil leak.

7 Either position the vehicle over an inspection pit, or jack up the front and rear of the vehicle and support it on axle stands (see *Jacking and vehicle support*). The vehicle must be level for the check to be accurate. Remove the engine undershield where fitted.

8 Unscrew the final drive filler/level plug located on the right-hand side of the transmission behind the driveshaft **(see illustration)**.

9 Check that the level of the oil is up to the bottom of the plug hole. If not, inject oil of the correct grade into the hole until if overflows.

10 Clean the plug, then refit and tighten it.

11 Lower the vehicle to the ground.

12 Clutch check

1 Check that the clutch pedal moves smoothly and easily through its full travel, and

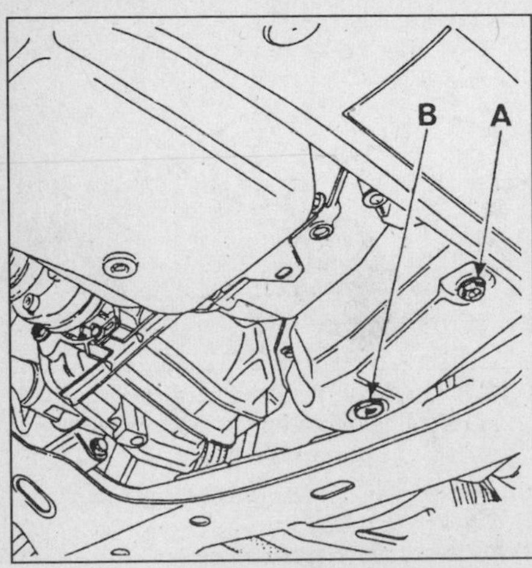

11.4a Automatic transmission level (A) and drain (B) plugs

11.4b Combined drain plug and level plug (A) on the DP0 type transmission

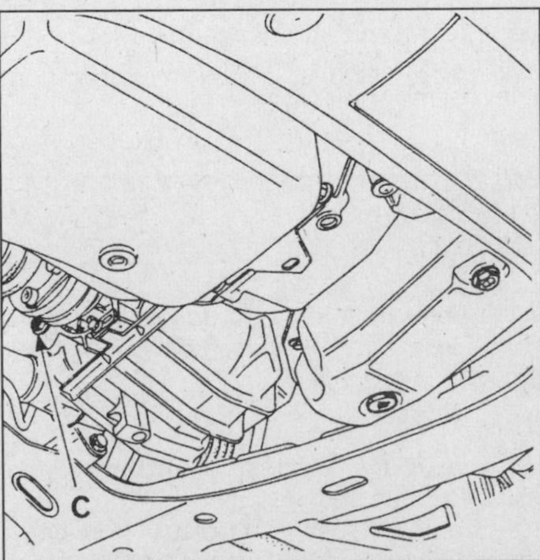

11.8 Automatic transmission final drive filler/level plug (C)

the clutch itself functions correctly, with no trace of slip or drag. If the movement is uneven or stiff in places, check that the cable is routed correctly, with no sharp turns.

2 Inspect the ends of the clutch inner cable, both at the gearbox end and inside the car, for signs of wear and fraying.

3 Lubricate its exposed inner cable section with multi-purpose grease.

4 Check and adjust the clutch cable as described in Chapter 6.

13 Exhaust emissions check

Both the idle speed and mixture (exhaust gas CO level) are automatically controlled by the ECU and cannot be adjusted. If either the idle speed or mixture settings are incorrect then a fault is present in the engine management system and the vehicle should be taken to a Renault dealer for testing.

14 Air conditioning system check

If the air conditioning system is functioning correctly, the only check needed is to ensure that the compressor drivebelt is correctly tensioned and in good condition (Section 18). If there is a problem with the air conditioning system the vehicle must be taken to a Renault dealer for testing.

15 Electrical systems check

1 Check the operation of all electrical equipment, ie, lights, direction indicators, horn, etc. Refer to the appropriate Sections of Chapter 12 for details if any of the circuits are found to be inoperative.

2 Note that the stop-light switch adjustment is described in Chapter 9.

3 Visually check all accessible wiring connectors, harnesses and retaining clips for security and for signs of chafing or damage. Rectify any faults found.

16 Vehicle bodywork check

Work slowly around the vehicle, paying particular attention to the bonnet, closely examining the paintwork for signs of damage such as stone chips. If damage is found, it should be repaired using a touch-in brush to prevent corrosion of the bodywork; colour-matched touch-in brushes are available from your Renault dealer. More serious damage can be repaired using the information given in Chapter 11.

Every 36 000 (60 000 km) or 4 years

17 Seat belt check

1 Carefully examine the seat belt webbing for cuts, or any signs of serious fraying or deterioration. If the belt is of the retractable type, pull the belt all the way out of the inertia reel and examine the full extent of the webbing.

2 Fasten and unfasten the belt, ensuring that the locking mechanism holds securely and releases properly when intended. If the belt is of the retractable type, check also that the retracting mechanism operates correctly when the belt is released.

3 Check the security of all seat belt mountings and attachments which are accessible without removing any trim or other components **(see illustration)**.

18 Auxiliary drivebelt(s) check and renewal

Note: *Renault state that a drivebelt must be renewed as a matter of course whenever it is removed.*

Checking

1 The auxiliary drivebelt is located at the right-hand side of the engine.

2 A number of different drivebelt configurations may be encountered, depending on engine type and whether the vehicle is equipped with air conditioning.

3 Due to their function and material makeup, drivebelts are prone to failure after a period of time and should therefore be inspected periodically.

4 Since the drivebelt is located very close to the right-hand side of the engine compartment, it is possible to gain better access by raising the front of the vehicle and removing the right-hand wheel, then removing the splash shield from inside the wheelarch.

5 With the engine stopped, inspect the full length of the drivebelt for cracks and separation of the belt plies. It will be necessary to turn the engine (using a spanner or socket and long extension bar on the crankshaft pulley bolt) to move the belt from the pulleys so that the belt can be inspected thoroughly. Twist the belt between the pulleys so that both sides can be viewed. Also check for fraying and glazing which gives the belt a shiny appearance. Check the pulleys for nicks, cracks, distortion and corrosion.

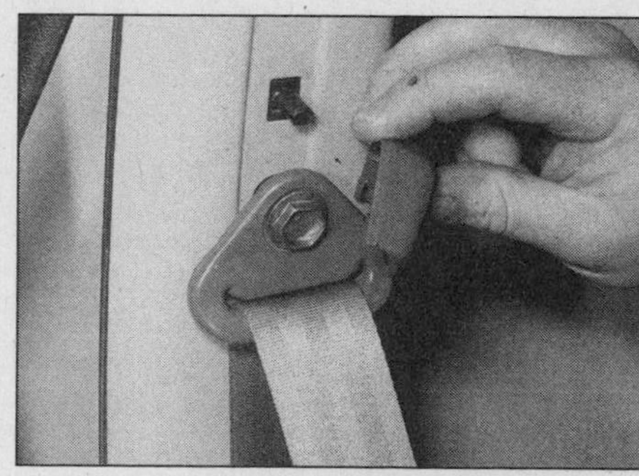

17.3 Check the security of the seat belt mountings

Tensioning

6 On models without air conditioning, a manual drivebelt adjuster is fitted. **Note:** *If the belt tension is checked using the special tool described below, the belt is fit for further use* ***only*** *if the value recorded is within the specified tolerance. If the value recorded is below the minimum specified, the belt must be renewed,* ***not*** *retensioned.*

7 The drivebelt tension is checked midway between the pulleys at the point indicated **(see illustration)**. A belt's tension can be set or checked accurately only by using the Renault tool Mot. 1273 (SEEM C. Tronic 105.6).

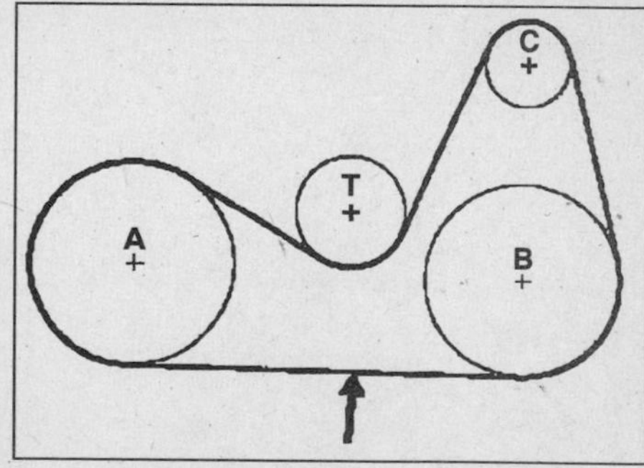

18.7 Auxiliary drivebelt configuration – 1.4 and 1.6 litre (16-valve) models without air conditioning

Arrow indicates tension checking point
A Crankshaft pulley
B Power-assisted steering pump
C Alternator
T Tensioner pulley

With experience, depressing the belt with moderate finger-pressure at the point indicated should give an adequate approximation of the correct tension. If the special tool is not available and there is any doubt about the tension of a drivebelt, the vehicle should be taken to a Renault dealer as soon as possible for the tension to be checked by qualified personnel using the special equipment.

8 On models with air conditioning, an automatic tensioner is used to maintain the correct drivebelt tension, and a value is not given by Renault.

9 If problems with belt squeal or slip are encountered, the belt should be renewed. If the problem continues, it will be necessary to renew the tensioner assembly.

Renewal

10 Disconnect the battery negative lead (refer to Chapter 5A).

11 On early E7J engines, when removing the PAS pump drivebelt, the alternator drivebelt must be removed first.

12 Apply the handbrake, then jack up the front of the car and support securely on axle stands (see *Jacking and vehicle support*). For improved access, remove the right-hand roadwheel, then remove the wheelarch liner, noting that it may be necessary to drill out the securing rivets on certain models.

1.4 & 1.6 litre engines without air conditioning

13 Loosen the bolt securing the tensioner bracket to the engine.

14 Loosen the locknut and back off the tensioner adjustment bolt until the drivebelt can be removed from the pulleys **(see illustration)**.

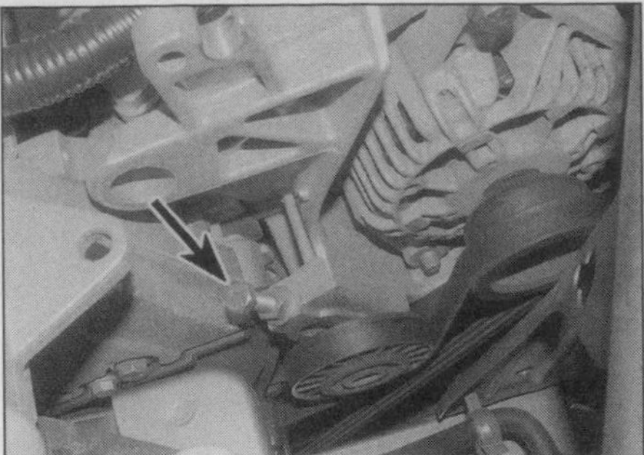

18.14 Alternator drivebelt tensioner adjustment bolt (arrowed)

15 Fit the new drivebelt around the pulleys making sure that it is routed correctly. Note that the drivebelt has five teeth and the alternator, PAS pump and crankshaft pulleys have six. When positioning the belt, ensure that the tooth on the end of the pulleys (furthest away from the engine) remains free **(see illustration)**.

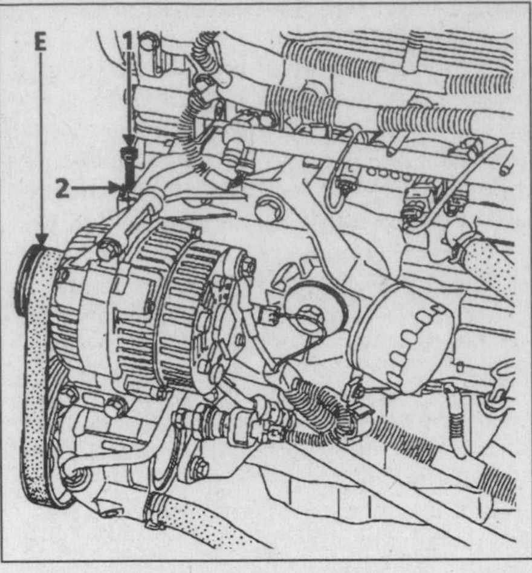

18.15 Ensure tooth (E) on the outer end of the pulley remains free

1 Adjusting bolt 2 Lock nut

16 To adjust the belt tension, slacken the tensioner mounting bolts and the adjuster bolt locknut (located next to the alternator). Turn the adjuster bolt to achieve the correct tension of 108 ± 6 SEEM units for the drivebelt.

17 Fully tighten the tensioner bracket bolt and the locknut for the adjustment bolt.

1.4 & 1.6 litre engines with air conditioning

18 Counterhold the automatic tensioner pulley using a spanner on the tensioner centre bolt, turn the tensioner clockwise to release the tension, then insert an Allen key in the hole in the tensioner bracket to lock the tensioner in the released position **(see illustration)**. Note the routing of the belt, then slip the drivebelt from the pulleys **(see illustration)**.

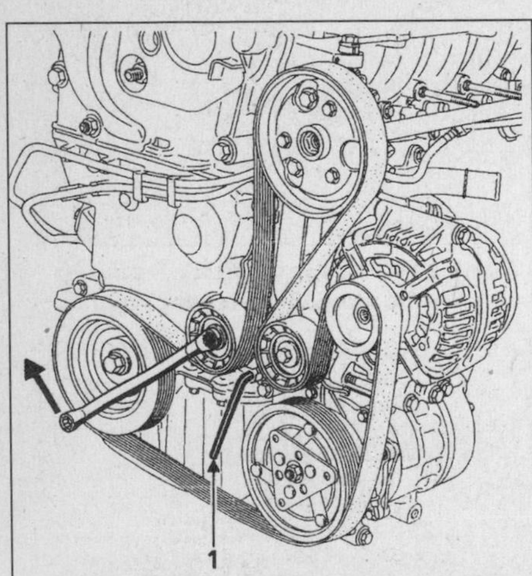

18.18a Releasing the drivebelt tensioner on 1.4 & 1.6 litre (16-valve) engines with air conditioning

Move the tensioner in the direction of the arrow then insert an Allen key (1) to lock the tensioner

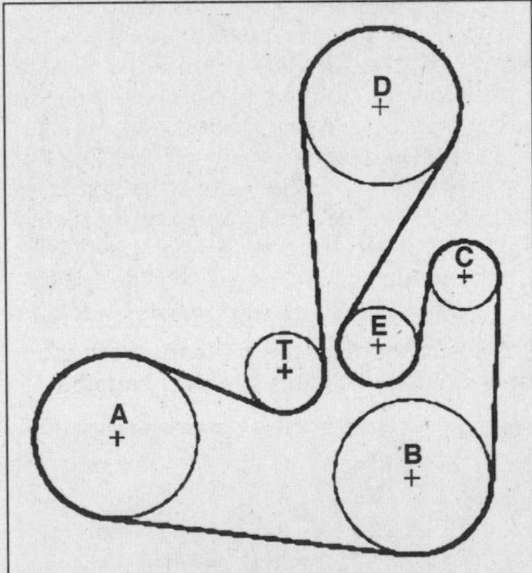

18.18b Auxiliary drivebelt configuration – 1.4 and 1.6 litre (16-valve) models with air conditioning

A Crankshaft pulley
B Air conditioning compressor
C Alternator
D Power-assisted steering pump
E Idler pulley
T Tensioner pulley

19 Fit the new belt around the pulleys making sure that it is correctly located in the grooves. Remove the Allen key and release the tensioner to automatically tension the belt.

2.0 litre engines

20 Counterhold the automatic tensioner pulley using a spanner on the tensioner centre bolt, turn the tensioner clockwise to release the tension, then insert an Allen key in the holes in the tensioner bracket to lock the tensioner in the released position **(see illustration)**. Note the routing of

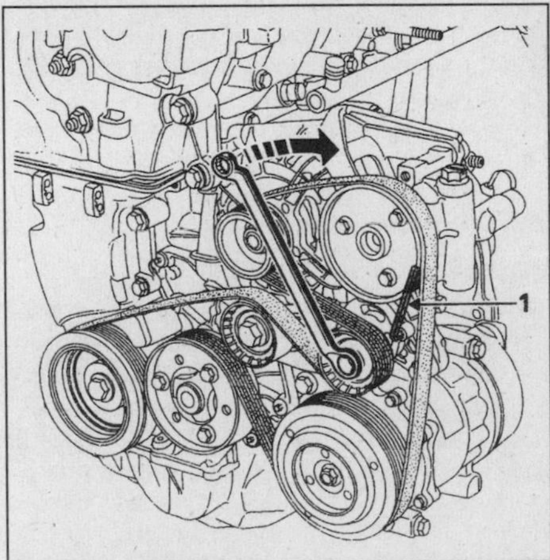

18.20a Releasing the drivebelt tensioner on 2.0 litre (16-valve) engines with air conditioning

Move the tensioner in the direction of the arrow then insert an Allen key (1) to lock the tensioner

the belt, then slip the drivebelt from the pulleys **(see illustration)**.

21 Fit the new drivebelt around the pulleys making sure that it is routed correctly. Note that the drivebelt has five teeth and the alternator, PAS pump and air conditioning pulleys have six. When positioning the belt, ensure that the tooth on the inner end of the pulleys (nearest the engine) remains free **(see illustration)**.

22 Remove the Allen key and release the tensioner to automatically tension the belt.

All engines

23 Run the engine for about 5 minutes, then recheck the tension. Refit the wheelarch liner and roadwheel.

24 Refit any components that were removed, then lower the car to the ground and reconnect the battery.

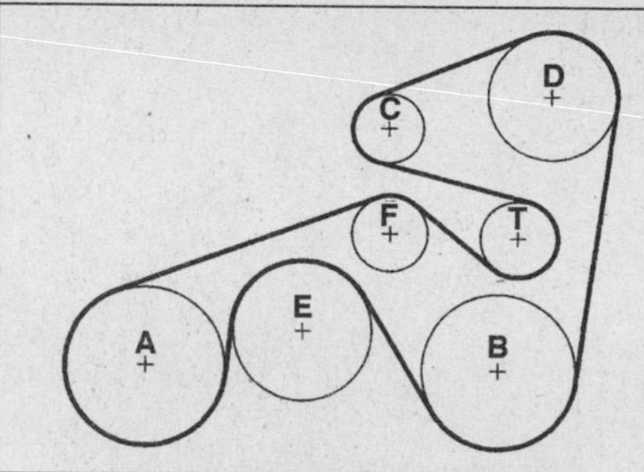

18.20b Auxiliary drivebelt configuration – 2.0 litre models with air conditioning

A Crankshaft pulley
B Air conditioning compressor
C Alternator
D Power-assisted steering pump
E Coolant pump
F Idler pulley
T Tensioner pulley

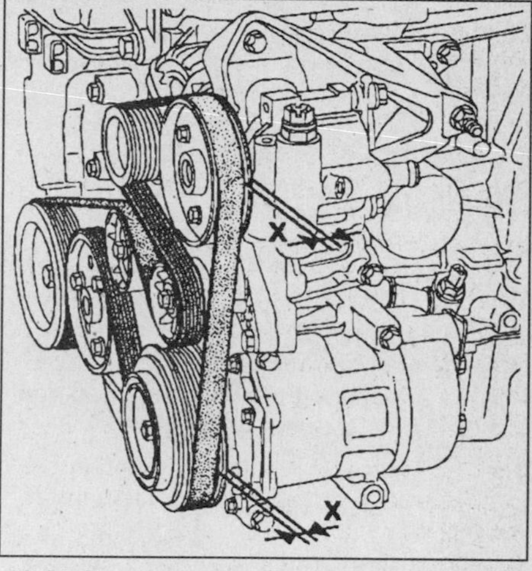

18.21 Ensure tooth (X) on the inner end of the pulley remains free

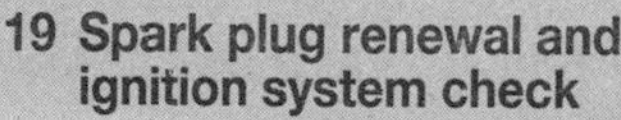

19 Spark plug renewal and ignition system check

Without suitable equipment, the DIY mechanic can only carry out a careful check of the entire ignition system in the conventional manner, checking each component in turn and cleaning, adjusting or renewing it as appropriate. Components such as the spark plugs must be renewed at each interval to ensure the continued reliability, economy and performance of the engine. The following procedures will allow the home mechanic to carry out a number of basic checks which will approximate as closely as possible the tests that would be made by a Renault dealer's mechanic. If there is the slightest doubt about the condition of any part of the system, the vehicle should be taken to a Renault dealer to be checked using the correct diagnostic equipment.

Spark plugs

Removal and examination

1 The correct functioning of the spark plugs is vital for the correct running and efficiency of the engine. It is essential that the plugs fitted are appropriate for the engine (a suitable type is specified at the beginning of this Chapter). If this type is used and the engine is in good condition, the spark plugs should not need attention between scheduled replacement intervals. Spark plug cleaning is rarely necessary and should not be attempted unless specialised equipment is available, as damage can easily be caused to the firing ends.

2 On E7J (1390cc) engines, carefully disconnect the HT leads from the spark plugs which are located on the front of the cylinder head **(see illustration)**.

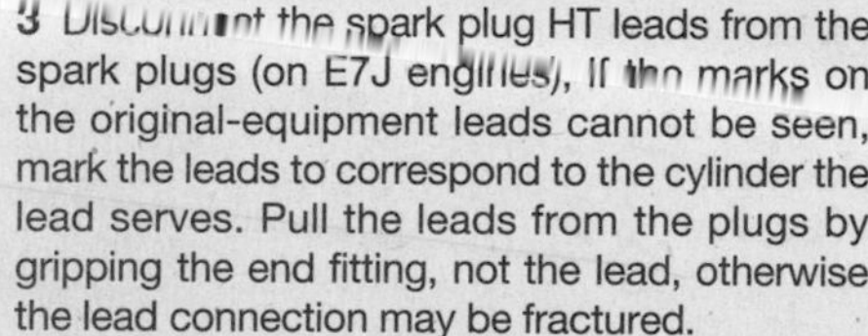

3 Disconnect the spark plug HT leads from the spark plugs (on E7J engines). If the marks on the original-equipment leads cannot be seen, mark the leads to correspond to the cylinder the lead serves. Pull the leads from the plugs by gripping the end fitting, not the lead, otherwise the lead connection may be fractured.

4 On K4J (1390cc), K4M (1598cc) and F4R (1998cc) engines, remove the ignition HT coils from the top of the spark plugs as described in Chapter 5B **(see illustration)**.

5 Undo the retaining bolt to disconnect the spark plug HT coil from the spark plugs (on K4J, K4M and F4R engines).

6 It is advisable to remove the dirt from the spark plug recesses using a clean brush, vacuum cleaner or compressed air before removing the plugs, to prevent dirt dropping into the cylinders.

7 Unscrew the plugs using a spark plug spanner, suitable box spanner or a deep socket and extension bar **(see illustrations)**. Keep the socket aligned with the spark plug – if it is forcibly moved to one side, the ceramic insulator may be broken off.

8 Examination of the spark plugs will give a

19.2 Disconnecting the HT leads from the spark plugs – 1.4 litre (8-valve) engines

19.4 Removing the ignition HT coils – 1.4 & 1.6 litre (16-valve) engines

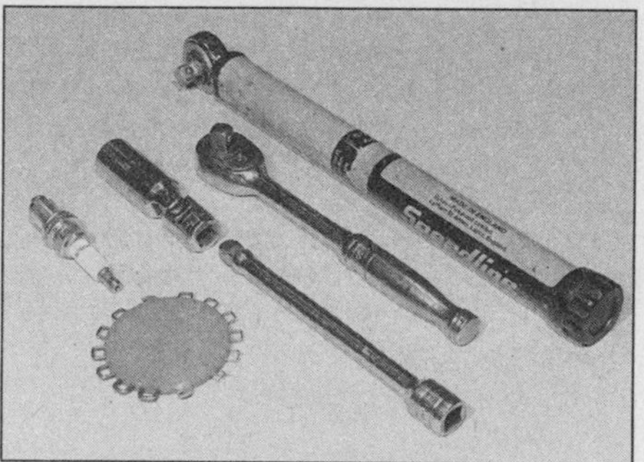

19.7a Tools required for spark plug removal, gap adjustment and refitting

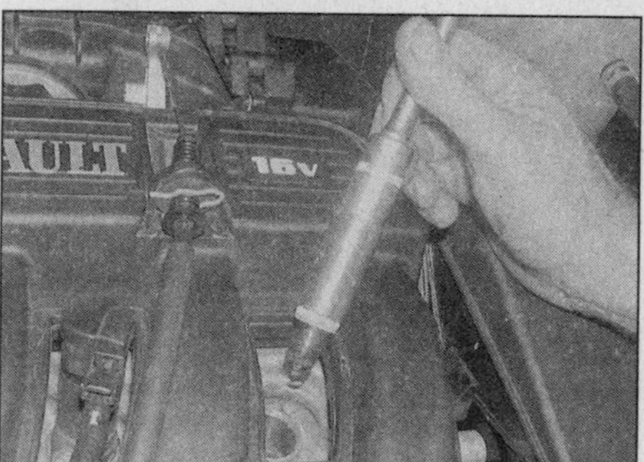

19.7b Using the special socket to remove the spark plugs

1

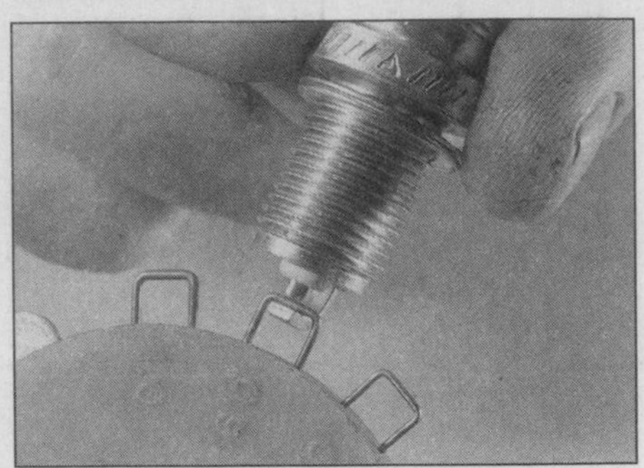

19.12a Measuring the electrode gap of a conventional spark plug – with a wire gauge . . .

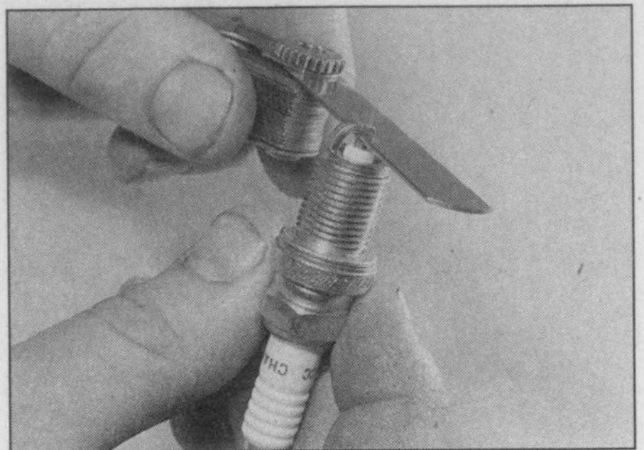

19.12b . . . and with a feeler gauge

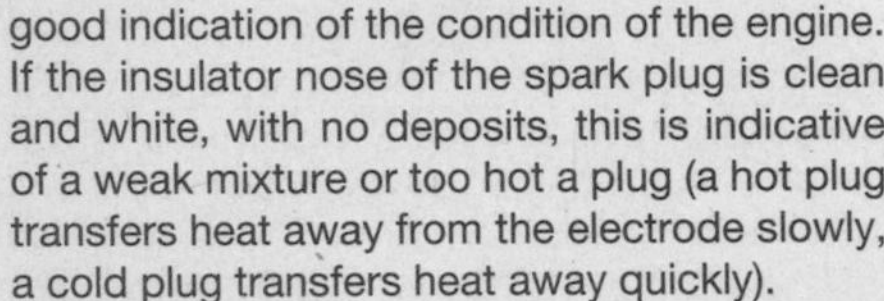

good indication of the condition of the engine. If the insulator nose of the spark plug is clean and white, with no deposits, this is indicative of a weak mixture or too hot a plug (a hot plug transfers heat away from the electrode slowly, a cold plug transfers heat away quickly).

9 If the tip and insulator nose are covered with hard black-looking deposits, then this is indicative that the mixture is too rich. Should the plug be black and oily, then it is likely that the engine is fairly worn, as well as the mixture being too rich.

10 If the insulator nose is covered with light tan to greyish-brown deposits, then the mixture is correct and it is likely that the engine is in good condition.

11 The spark plug electrode gap is of considerable importance as, if it is too large or too small, the size of the spark and its efficiency will be seriously impaired. The gap should be set to the value given in the Specifications at the beginning of this Chapter.

Adjustment

Note: *Some engines are fitted with multiple-earth (two or three) electrode spark plugs. The gaps on these are not adjustable (the value specified is a nominal one only) and, as noted above, cleaning is not recommended. If there is any doubt about their condition, all four spark plugs must be renewed as a set.*

12 To set the gap, measure it with a feeler gauge and then bend open, or closed, the outer plug electrode until the correct gap is achieved. The centre electrode should never be bent, as this may crack the insulator and cause plug failure, if nothing worse. If using feeler gauges, the gap is correct when the appropriate-size gauge is a firm sliding fit **(see illustrations)**.

13 Special spark plug electrode gap adjusting tools are available from most motor accessory shops, or from some spark plug manufacturers.

Refitting

14 Before fitting the spark plugs, check that the threaded connector sleeves are tight and that the plug exterior surfaces and threads are clean. Apply a thin smear of anti-seize compound to the threads of each spark plug.

15 Remove the rubber hose (if used) and tighten the plug to the specified torque using the spark plug socket and a torque wrench. Refit the remaining spark plugs in the same manner.

16 Connect the HT leads in their correct order, or where applicable, refit the ignition HT coils as described in Chapter 5B.

Ignition system check

Warning: Voltages produced by an electronic ignition system are considerably higher than those produced by conventional ignition systems. Extreme care must be taken when working on the system with the ignition switched on. Persons with surgically-implanted cardiac pacemaker devices should keep well clear of the ignition circuits, components and test equipment.

17 The spark plug HT leads (where fitted) should be checked whenever new spark plugs are fitted.

18 Ensure that the leads are numbered before removing them, to avoid confusion when refitting. Pull the leads from the plugs by gripping the end fitting, not the lead, otherwise the lead connection may be fractured.

19 Check inside the end fitting for signs of corrosion, which will look like a white crusty powder. Push the end fitting back onto the spark plug, ensuring that it is a tight fit on the plug. If not, remove the lead again and use pliers to carefully crimp the metal connector inside the end fitting until it fits securely on the end of the spark plug.

20 Using a clean rag, wipe the entire length of the lead to remove any built-up dirt and grease. Once the lead is clean, check for burns, cracks and other damage. Do not bend the lead excessively, nor pull the lead lengthways – the conductor inside might break.

21 Disconnect the other end of the lead from the distributor/ignition module – again, pull only on the end fitting. Check for corrosion and a tight fit in the same manner as the spark plug end. If an ohmmeter is available, check the resistance of the lead by connecting the meter between its two ends – no values are specified by the manufacturer but all leads should show a similar reading in the kilo ohms range – waggle the lead while testing it to check for intermittent faults caused by a partly-broken internal conductor. Renew any lead that shows infinite resistance (broken internal conductor) or a resistance reading significantly different from the others. Refit the lead securely on completion.

It's often difficult to insert spark plugs into their holes without cross-threading them. To avoid this possibility, fit a short piece of rubber hose over the end of the spark plug. The flexible hose acts as a universal joint, to help align the plug with the plug hole. Should the plug begin to cross-thread, the hose will slip on the spark plug, preventing thread damage to the aluminium cylinder head.

22 Check the remaining spark plug HT leads one at a time, in the same way. If any one lead shows any signs of a fault, renew all the leads as a matched set. Whenever new leads are required, purchase a set specifically for your car and engine.

23 Even with the ignition system in first-class condition, some engines may still occasionally experience poor starting attributable to damp ignition components. To disperse moisture, a water-dispersant aerosol can be very effective.

20 Air filter element renewal

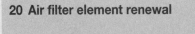

E7J engine

1 Unscrew the air cleaner mounting bolts from the top of the air cleaner. Where applicable, also unscrew the single cover retaining screw.

2 Release the retaining clips and remove the lid from the top of the air cleaner housing and lift out the air filter element.

3 Clean the inside of the air cleaner body and cover, being careful not to get dirt into the inlet duct.

4 Fit the new element using a reversal of the removal procedure.

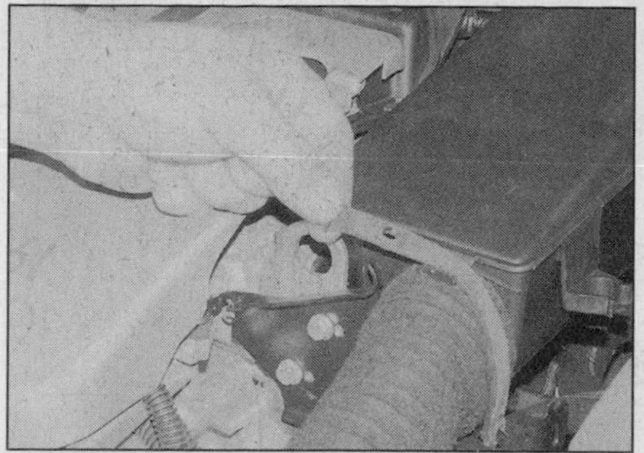
20.5a Unclip the rubber strap . . .

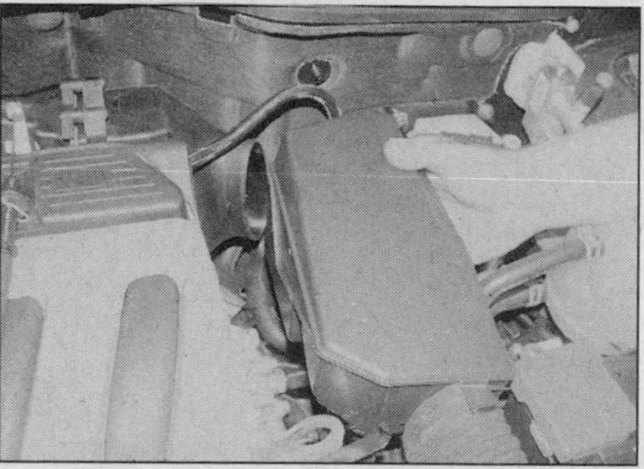
20.5b . . . and remove the air duct

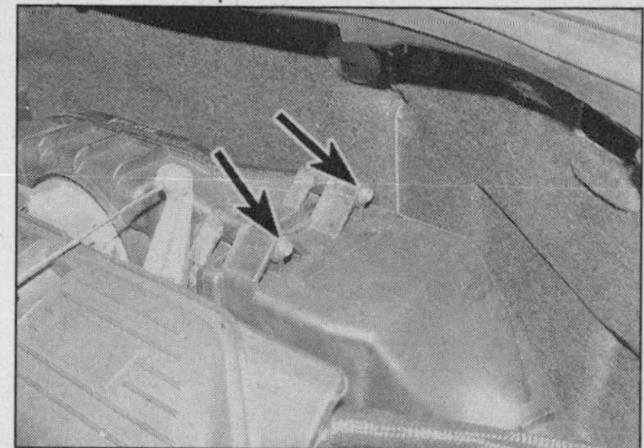
20.6a Undo the retaining screws (arrowed) . . .

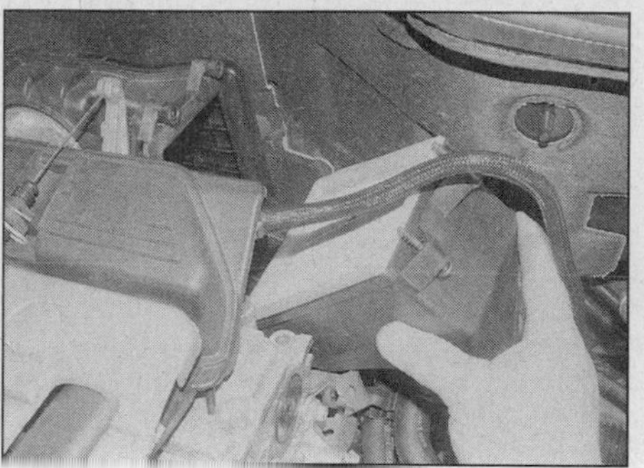
20.6b . . . and unclip the air filter housing

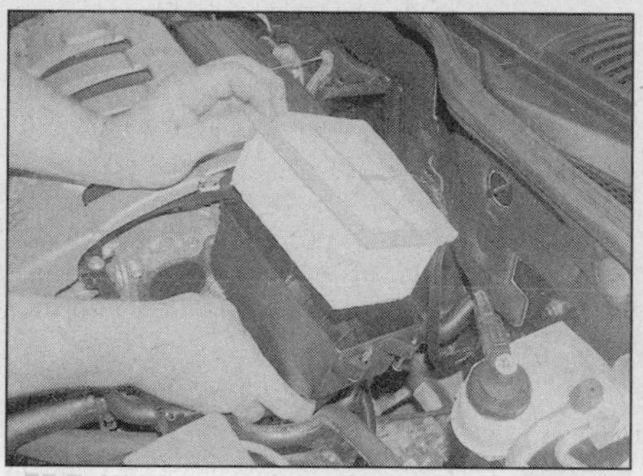
20.7 Withdraw the air filter element from the housing

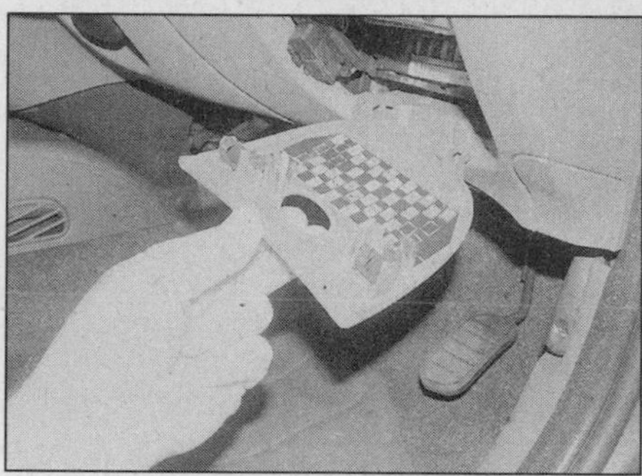
23.1 Spare fuses located in the fusebox cover

All other models

5 The air filter element is located at the left-hand rear of the engine. First unclip the rubber strap from the air inlet duct, and remove from the air cleaner housing **(see illustrations)**.

6 Undo the screws and unclip the element housing from the main body **(see illustrations)**.

7 Note how the element is fitted, then withdraw it from the housing **(see illustration)**.

8 Clean the inside of the air cleaner body and cover, being careful not to get dirt into the inlet duct.

9 Fit the new element using a reversal of the removal procedure.

21 Heating system check

Check that the heating controls move smoothly and easily with no sign of stiffness and check that the blower motor operates correctly. If there is a problem, check the heating ventilation system components as described in Chapter 3.

If the heating system seems to be giving out insufficient heat, check that the coolant level is correct and that there are no air locks in the cooling system (see Section 29).

22 Hinge and lock lubrication

Lubricate the hinges of the bonnet, doors and boot lid/tailgate with a light general purpose oil. Similarly, lubricate all latches, locks and lock strikers. At the same time, check the security and operation of all locks, adjusting them if necessary (see Chapter 11).

Lightly lubricate the bonnet release mechanism with a suitable grease.

23 Spare fuse check

Check that spare fuses are in place in the locations provided in the fusebox cover **(see illustration)**. It is advisable to carry at least one spare of each rating of fuse fitted (see Chapter 12). Spare fuses can be obtained from most car accessory shops, or from a Renault dealer.

24 Rear brake check

Drum brakes

1 Apply the handbrake, then jack up the rear of the car and support it securely on axle stands.

2 For a comprehensive check, remove the rear brake drums and check the brake shoes for signs of wear or contamination. At the same time, also inspect the wheel cylinders for signs of leakage and the brake drum for signs of wear. Refer to the relevant Sections of Chapter 9 for further information.

3 On completion lower the car to the ground.

Disc brakes

4 Apply the handbrake, then jack up the rear of the car and support it securely on axle stands then refer to Section 4.

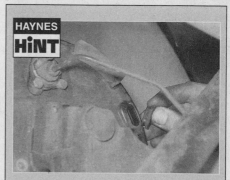

HAYNES HiNT

For a quick check, the thickness of the rear brake shoe can be checked through the aperture in the backplate once the rubber plug has been removed.

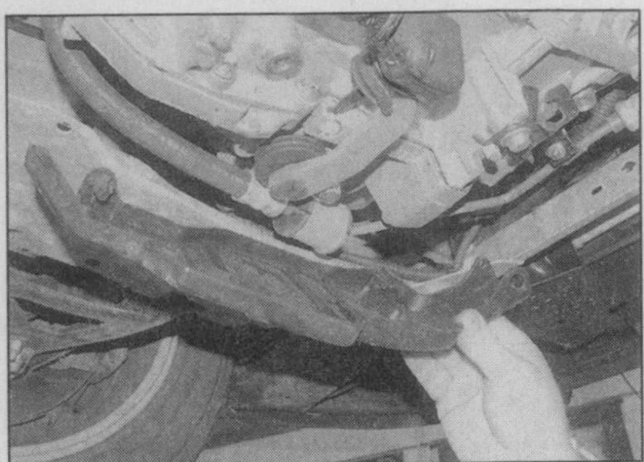
25.1 Unclipping the cover from under the transmission

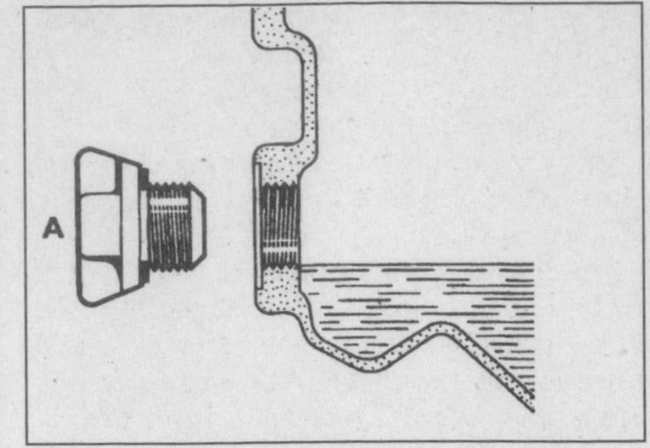

25.3 Manual gearbox filler/level plug (A) – correct oil level shown

25.4 Topping-up the manual gearbox oil level

25 Manual gearbox oil level check

1 Either position the vehicle over an inspection pit, or jack up the front and rear of the vehicle and support it on axle stands (see *Jacking and vehicle support*). The vehicle must be level for the check to be accurate. Remove the engine/transmission undershield where fitted **(see illustration)**.
2 Clean the area around the filler/level plug on the front of the gearbox, then unscrew the plug.
3 The gearbox oil level should be up to the lower edge of the filler/level plug aperture **(see illustration)**.
4 If necessary, top-up using the specified type of lubricant until the oil level is correct. Fill the gearbox until oil starts to flow out and allow excess oil to drain **(see illustration)**.
5 Once the gearbox oil level is correct, refit the filler/level plug and tighten it securely.
6 Refit the engine/transmission undercover then lower the vehicle to the ground. Note that frequent need for topping-up indicates a leakage, possibly through an oil seal. The cause should be investigated and rectified.

26 Automatic transmission fluid renewal – AD4 type transmission

Note 1: *Refer to Section 11 to find out what is involved in checking the transmission fluid level before draining the transmission. Note that the final drive oil does not need to be renewed.*
Note 2: *The following procedure is only applicable to the AD4 type transmission. The DP0 type transmission is a 'sealed-for-life' unit and fluid renewal is not a service operation.*
Note 3: *Refer to Chapter 7B for more information and transmission type identification.*
1 Take the vehicle on a short run, to warm the transmission up to operating temperature.
2 Park the car on level ground, then switch off the ignition and apply the handbrake firmly. Jack up the front of the car and support it securely on axle stands (see *Jacking and vehicle support*). Note that, when refilling and checking the fluid level, the car must be level to ensure accuracy. Remove the engine undershield where fitted.
3 Position a suitable container under the transmission. Unscrew the transmission drain plug **(see illustration 11.4a)** from the sump and allow the fluid to drain completely into the container.

Warning: If the fluid is hot, take precautions against scalding.

4 Clean the drain plug, being especially careful to wipe any metallic particles off the magnetic insert. Discard the original sealing washer; this should be renewed whenever it is disturbed.
5 When the fluid has finished draining, clean the drain plug threads and those of the transmission casing. Fit a new sealing washer to the drain plug and refit the plug to the transmission, tightening it securely.
6 Make sure the vehicle is level then refill the transmission with the specified type and amount of fluid via the filler tube (Section 11). Refilling the transmission is an awkward operation, use a funnel with a fine mesh gauze, to avoid spillage and to ensure that no foreign matter enters the transmission. Allow plenty of time for the fluid level to settle properly.
7 Check the transmission fluid level as described in Section 11.
8 Dispose safely of the used transmission fluid with reference to *General repair procedures*.

27 Fuel filter renewal

Warning: Before carrying out the following operation refer to the precautions given in 'Safety first!' at the beginning of this manual and follow them implicitly. Petrol is a highly dangerous and volatile liquid and the precautions necessary when handling it cannot be overstressed.

1 The fuel filter is located underneath the vehicle, just in front of the fuel tank **(see illustration)**. Wash down the filter and its surroundings before starting work, so that you can see what you are doing. Wipe carefully the fuel unions before disconnecting them to minimise the risk of dirt entering the fuel system.
2 Bearing in mind the information given on depressurising the fuel system in Section 7 of Chapter 4A, disconnect the hoses from the fuel filter. The hoses are equipped with quick-release fittings to ease removal. To disconnect each hose, slide out the locking tab (where fitted) from the collar then depress the collar and detach each hose. Disconnect both hoses, noting the correct fitted position of the sealing rings and plug the hose ends to minimise fuel loss.
3 Slacken the clamp screw then slide the filter out of position, noting its correct fitted orientation. The arrow on the filter should point in the direction of fuel flow (towards the throttle body/fuel rail).
4 Slide the new filter into position making sure its arrow is pointing in the direction of fuel flow. Make sure the rubber mounting is correctly positioned then securely tighten the clamp bolt.
5 Ensure that the sealing rings are in position and reconnect the hoses to the fuel filter. Check the end fittings are clipped securely in position and (where necessary) refit the locking tabs to the collars.
6 Lower the vehicle to the ground then start the engine and check the filter for signs of fuel leakage.
7 Dispose safely of the old filter with reference to *General repair procedures*.

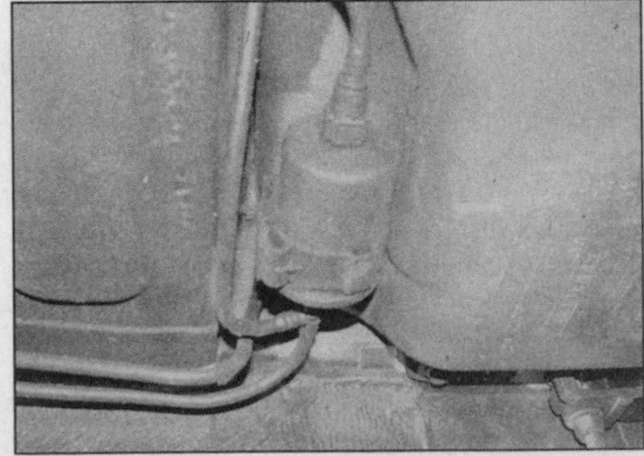
27.1 Fuel filter location just in front of the fuel tank

28 Road test

Instruments and electrical equipment

1 Check the operation of all instruments and electrical equipment.

2 Make sure that all instruments read correctly and switch on all electrical equipment in turn, to check that it functions properly.

Steering and suspension

3 Check for any abnormalities in the steering, suspension, handling or road 'feel'.

4 Drive the vehicle and check that there are no unusual vibrations or noises.

5 Check that the steering feels positive, with no excessive 'sloppiness', or roughness and check for any suspension noises when cornering and driving over bumps.

Drivetrain

6 Check the performance of the engine, clutch, transmission and drive-shafts.

7 Listen for any unusual noises from the engine, clutch and transmission.

8 Make sure that the engine runs smoothly when idling and that there is no hesitation when accelerating.

9 Check that, where applicable, the clutch action is smooth and progressive, that the drive is taken up smoothly and that the pedal travel is not excessive. Also listen for any noises when the clutch pedal is depressed.

10 Check that all gears can be engaged smoothly without noise and that the gearlever action is smooth and not vague or 'notchy'.

11 On automatic transmission models, make sure that all gearchanges occur smoothly, without snatching and without an increase in engine speed between changes. Check that all of the gear positions can be selected with the vehicle at rest. If any problems are found, they should be referred to a Renault dealer.

12 Listen for a metallic clicking sound from the front of the vehicle, as the vehicle is driven slowly in a circle with the steering on full-lock. Carry out this check in both directions. If a clicking noise is heard, this indicates wear in a driveshaft joint (see Chapter 8).

Braking system

13 Make sure that the vehicle does not pull to one side when braking and that the wheels do not lock prematurely when braking hard (or at all on ABS-equipped models).

14 Check that there is no vibration through the steering when braking.

15 Check that the handbrake operates correctly, without excessive movement of the lever and that it holds the vehicle stationary on a slope.

16 Test the operation of the brake servo unit as follows. Depress the footbrake four or five times to exhaust the vacuum, then start the engine. As the engine starts, there should be a noticeable 'give' in the brake pedal as vacuum builds-up. Allow the engine to run for at least two minutes and then switch it off. If the brake pedal is now depressed again, it should be possible to detect a hiss from the servo as the pedal is depressed. After about four or five applications, no further hissing should be heard and the pedal should feel considerably harder.

Every 72 000 (120 000 km) or 4 years

29 Coolant renewal

Warning: Wait until the engine is cold before starting this procedure. Do not allow antifreeze to come in contact with your skin, or with the painted surfaces of the vehicle. Rinse off spills immediately with plenty of water. Never leave antifreeze lying around in an open container, or in a puddle in the driveway or on the garage floor. Children and pets are attracted by its sweet smell, but antifreeze can be fatal if ingested.

Cooling system draining

1 With the engine completely cold, remove the expansion tank filler cap. Turn the cap anti-clockwise, wait until any pressure remaining in the system is released, then unscrew it and lift it off.

2 To assist draining, open the cooling system bleed screw(s). On E7J engines, the bleed screw is located in the hose leading from the thermostat housing to the heater matrix. On K4J, K4M and F4R engines, the bleed screw is located on the thermostat housing **(see illustrations)**.

3 Where applicable, remove the undershield, then position a suitable container beneath the radiator bottom hose connection. Slacken the hose clip, pull off the hose and allow the coolant to drain into the container.

4 To ensure the complete draining of the cooling system remove the cylinder block drain plug (where fitted). It is located either on the front left-hand side or rear right-hand side of the cylinder block. Remove the drain plug, and allow the coolant to drain into the container.

5 If the coolant has been drained for a reason other than renewal, then provided it is clean and less than two years old, it can be re-used, though this is not recommended.

6 Refit the radiator bottom hose on completion of draining. Where applicable, apply a few drops of a suitable sealant to the threads of the drain plug and refit it to the cylinder block; tighten it securely.

Cooling system flushing

7 If coolant renewal has been neglected, or if the antifreeze mixture has become diluted, then in time, the cooling system may gradually lose efficiency, as the coolant passages become restricted due to rust, scale deposits and other sediment. The cooling system efficiency can be restored by flushing the system clean.

8 The radiator should be flushed independently of the engine, to avoid unnecessary contamination.

Radiator flushing

9 Disconnect the top and bottom hoses and any other relevant hoses from the radiator, with reference to Chapter 3.

10 Insert a garden hose into the radiator top inlet. Direct a flow of clean water through the radiator and continue flushing until clean water emerges from the radiator bottom outlet.

11 If after a reasonable period, the water still

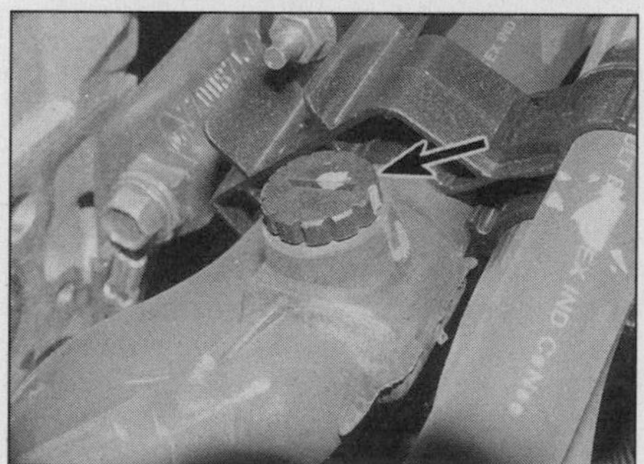

29.2a Cooling system bleed screw located in the heater hose – 1.4 litre (8-valve) engine

29.2b Coolant bleed screw (arrowed) in the thermostat housing

does not run clear, the radiator can be flushed with a good proprietary cleaning agent. It is important that their manufacturer's instructions are followed carefully. If the contamination is particularly bad, insert the hose in the radiator bottom outlet and reverse-flush the radiator.

Engine flushing

12 To flush the engine, remove the thermostat as described in Chapter 3, then temporarily refit the top hose at its engine connection.

13 With the top and bottom hoses disconnected from the radiator, insert a garden hose into the radiator top hose. Direct a clean flow of water through the engine and continue flushing until clean water emerges from the radiator bottom hose.

14 On completion of flushing, refit the thermostat and reconnect the hoses with reference to Chapter 3.

Cooling system filling

15 Before attempting to fill the cooling system, make sure that all hoses and clips are in good condition and that the clips are tight. Note that an antifreeze mixture must be used all year round, to prevent corrosion of the engine components.

16 Remove the expansion tank filler cap.

17 Open the cooling system bleed screw(s).

18 Place a wad of rags around the expansion tank.

19 Slowly fill the system until the coolant level reaches the top of the expansion tank filler neck.

20 Close the bleed screw(s) when coolant free from air bubbles emerges.

21 Start the engine and run it at a fast idle speed (do not exceed 2000 rpm) for approximately 4 minutes. Keep the level topped-up to the top of the expansion tank filler neck.

22 Refit and tighten the expansion tank filler cap.

23 Allow the engine to run for approximately 20 minutes at 2000 rpm until the cooling fan cuts in and out.

24 Stop the engine and check the coolant level, which should be up to the MAXI mark on the side of the tank. Check that the expansion tank filler cap is tight.

25 Allow the engine to cool, then recheck the coolant level with reference to *Weekly checks*. Top-up the level if necessary and refit the expansion tank filler cap. Where applicable, refit the undershield.

Antifreeze mixture

26 The antifreeze should always be renewed at the specified intervals. This is necessary not only to maintain the antifreeze properties, but also to prevent corrosion which would otherwise occur as the corrosion inhibitors become progressively less effective.

27 Always use an ethylene-glycol based antifreeze which is suitable for use in mixed-metal cooling systems. The quantity of antifreeze and levels of protection are given in the Specifications.

28 Before adding antifreeze, the cooling system should be completely drained, preferably flushed and all hoses checked for condition and security.

29 After filling with antifreeze, a label should be attached to the expansion tank, stating the type and concentration of antifreeze used and the date installed. Any subsequent topping-up should be made with the same type and concentration of antifreeze.

30 Do not use engine antifreeze in the windscreen/tailgate washer system, as it will damage the vehicle's paintwork. A screenwash additive should be added to the washer system in the quantities stated on the bottle.

31 Dispose safely of the used coolant with reference to *General repair procedures*.

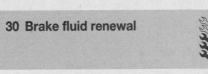

30 Brake fluid renewal

Warning: Brake hydraulic fluid can harm your eyes and damage painted surfaces, so use extreme caution when handling and pouring it. Do not use fluid that has been standing open for some time, as it absorbs moisture from the air. Excess moisture can cause a dangerous loss of braking effectiveness.

Caution: On models equipped with ABS, disconnect the battery before carrying out the following operation and do not reconnect the battery until after the operation is complete. Failure to do this could lead to air entering the hydraulic unit. If air enters the hydraulic unit pump, it will prove very difficult (in some cases impossible) to bleed the unit. Refer to Chapter 5A when disconnecting the battery.

1 The procedure is similar to that for the bleeding of the hydraulic system as described in Chapter 9, except that the brake fluid reservoir should be emptied by syphoning, using a clean poultry baster or similar before starting and allowance should be made for the old fluid to be expelled when bleeding a section of the circuit.

2 Working as described in Chapter 9, open the first bleed screw in the sequence and pump the brake pedal gently until nearly all the old fluid has been emptied from the master cylinder reservoir. Top-up to the MAXI level with new fluid and continue pumping until only the new fluid remains in the reservoir and new fluid can be seen emerging from the bleed screw. Tighten the screw and top the reservoir level up to the MAXI level.

Old brake fluid is invariably much darker in colour than the new, making it easy to distinguish between the two.

3 Work through all the remaining bleed screws in the sequence until new fluid can be seen at all of them. Be careful to keep the master cylinder reservoir topped-up to above the MINI level at all times, or air may enter the system and greatly increase the length of the task.

4 When the operation is complete, check that all bleed screws are securely tightened and that their dust caps are refitted. Wash off all traces of spilt fluid and recheck the master cylinder reservoir fluid level.

5 Check the operation of the brakes before taking the car on the road.

6 Dispose safely of the used brake fluid with reference to *General repair procedures*.

Chapter 1 Part B:
Routine maintenance and servicing – diesel models

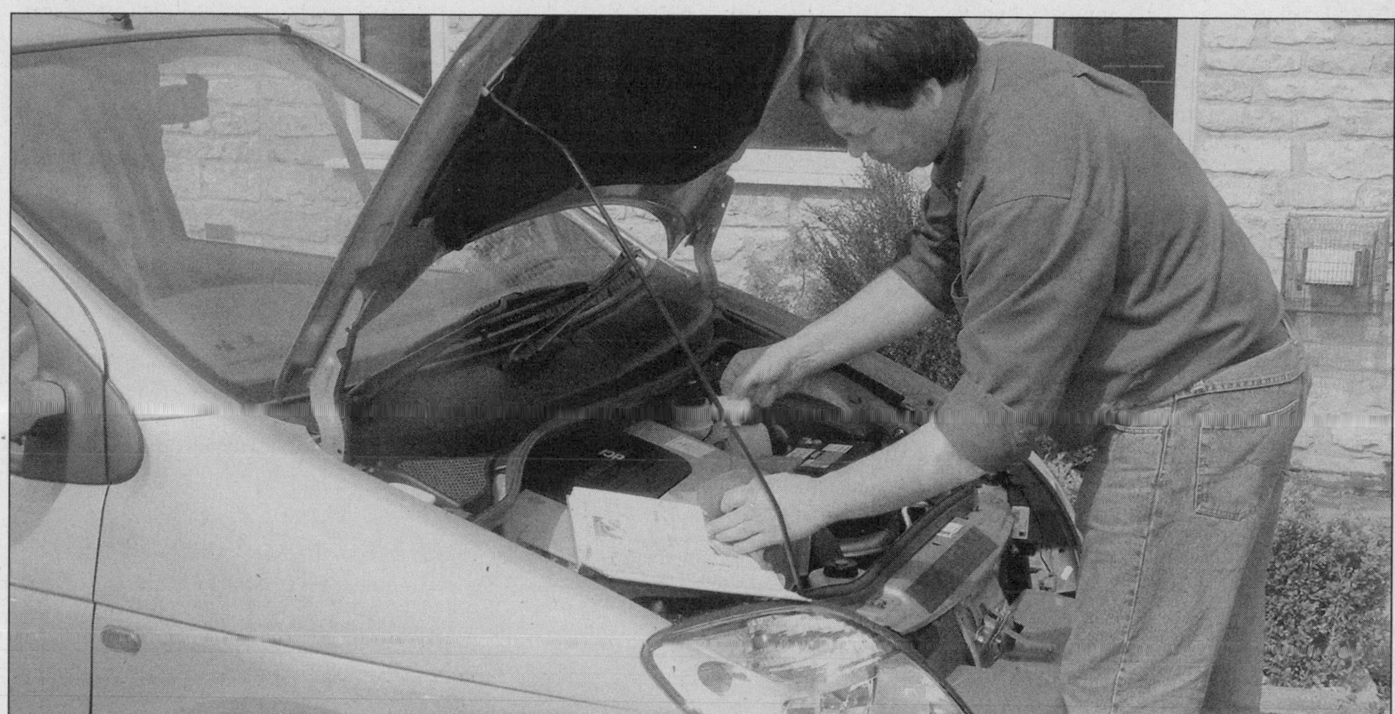

1B

Contents

Degrees of difficulty

Easy, suitable for novice with little experience		**Fairly easy,** suitable for beginner with some experience		**Fairly difficult,** suitable for competent DIY mechanic		**Difficult,** suitable for experienced DIY mechanic	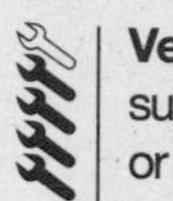	**Very difficult,** suitable for expert DIY or professional	

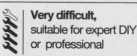

Specifications – diesel models

Lubricants and fluids	Refer to *Weekly checks*

Capacities

Engine oil	
Including filter	5.5 litres*
Oil filter capacity	0.5 litre
Difference between MAX and MIN dipstick marks	2.0 litres
Cooling system	7.5 litres
Fuel tank	60 litres (13.2 gallons)
Gearbox	
JB1 unit	3.4 litres
JC5 unit	3.1 litres
Power-assisted steering reservoir	1.1 litres

* **Note:** *4.8 litres on some F9Q engines*

Engine codes

Non-turbo engines – D models	F8Q 620, F8Q 622, F8Q 788
Turbo engines:	
Indirect injection – dT models	F8Q 784, F8Q 786
Direct injection – dTi models	F9Q 730, F9Q 734
Direct common-rail injection – dCi models	F9Q 732

Cooling system

Antifreeze mixtures:	**Antifreeze**	**Water**
Protection down to –21°C	35%	65%
Protection down to –37°C	50%	50%

Auxiliary drivebelt tension	
F9Q 732 models without air conditioning	188 ± 5 hertz
F8Q and F9Q 730/734 models without air conditioning:	
Fitting/checking	97 ± 3 SEEM units
Minimum value	67 SEEM units
F8Q models with air conditioning*	Automatic tensioner
F9Q models with air conditioning	Automatic tensioner

* **Note:** *For models with F8Q engine and air conditioning, a nominal fitting/checking value of 61 to 77 SEEM units is quoted.*

Braking system

	New	**Minimum thickness**
Front disc brakes:		
Pad thickness (including backing)	18.2 mm	6.0 mm
Rear drum brakes:		
Shoe thickness (including backing):		
Leading shoe	4.9 mm	2.0 mm
Trailing shoe	3.4 mm	2.0 mm
Rear disc brakes:		
Pad thickness (including backing)	11.0 mm	5.0 mm

Torque wrench settings

	Nm	**lbf ft**
Engine oil drain plug	15	11
Roadwheel bolts	90	66

The maintenance intervals in this manual are provided with the assumption that you, not the dealer, will be carrying out the work. These are the minimum maintenance intervals recommended by us for vehicles driven daily. If you wish to keep your vehicle in peak condition at all times, you may wish to perform some of these procedures more often. We encourage frequent maintenance, because it enhances the efficiency, performance and resale value of your vehicle.

If the vehicle is driven in dusty areas, used to tow a trailer, or driven frequently at slow speeds (idling in traffic) or on short journeys, more frequent maintenance intervals are recommended.

When the vehicle is new, it should be serviced by a factory-authorised dealer service department to preserve the factory warranty.

Every 250 miles (400 km) or weekly

- ☐ Refer to *Weekly checks*

Every 9000 miles (15 000 km) or 12 months

- ☐ Renew the engine oil and filter (Section 3)*
- ☐ Drain any water from the fuel filter (Section 4)

*** Note:** *Renault recommend that the engine oil and filter are changed every 18 000 miles (10 000 miles on 1.9D engines) or 2 years. However, frequent oil and filter changes are good for the engine and we recommend that the oil and filter are renewed more frequently, perhaps every 9000 miles or every 12 months, especially if the vehicle is used on a lot of short journeys or covers a small annual mileage.*

Every 18 000 miles (30 000 km) or 2 years

In addition to all the items listed previously, carry out the following:

- ☐ Check the front brake pads and discs (Section 5)
- ☐ Check the condition of the exhaust system and mountings (Section 6)
- ☐ Check the suspension and steering components (Section 7)
- ☐ Check the driveshaft gaiters and CV joints (Section 8)
- ☐ Check all underbonnet components, hoses and brake lines for fluid leaks (Section 9)
- ☐ Check the tightness of the roadwheel bolts (Section 10)
- ☐ Check the operation of the clutch (Section 11)
- ☐ Check the exhaust emissions (Section 12)
- ☐ Check the operation of the air conditioning system (Section 13)

Every 18 000 miles (30 000 km) or 2 years (continued)

- ☐ Check the operation of all electrical systems (Section 14)
- ☐ Check the vehicle bodywork (Section 15)
- ☐ Check the boost pressure – turbo models only (Section 16)
- ☐ Check the condition of the seat belts (Section 17)
- ☐ Check the condition of the auxiliary drivebelt (Section 18)
- ☐ Check the headlight beam adjustment (Chapter 12)
- ☐ Renew the air filter element (Section 19)*
- ☐ Renew the pollen filter (Section 20)

*** Note:** *On 1.9D engine models, this task is carried out every 36 000 miles (60 000 km).*

Every 36 000 miles (60 000 km) or 4 years

In addition to all the items listed previously, carry out the following:

- ☐ Check the operation of the handbrake (Chapter 9)
- ☐ Renew the fuel filter (Section 21)
- ☐ Check the heating system (Section 22)
- ☐ Lubricate the hinges and locks (Section 23)
- ☐ Check the spare fuses are in place (Section 24)
- ☐ Check the front wheel alignment (Chapter 10)
- ☐ Check the rear brakes (Section 25)
- ☐ Check the manual gearbox oil level (Section 26)
- ☐ Carry out a road test (Section 27)
- ☐ Renew the timing belt (Section 28)*

*** Note:** *Renault recommend that the timing belt be renewed every 72 000 miles/120 000 km (45 000 miles/75 000 km on 1.9dTi engine). However, if the vehicle is used mainly for short journeys or for a lot of stop-start driving or other severe use it is recommended that the belt be renewed earlier – consideration should be given to changing the belt at this interval. The actual belt renewal interval is very much up to the individual owner but, bearing in mind that severe engine damage will result if the belt breaks in use, we recommend you err on the side of caution.*

Every 72 000 miles (120 000 km) or 4 years

In addition to all the items listed previously, carry out the following:

- ☐ Renew the coolant (Section 29)
- ☐ Renew the brake fluid (Section 30)

Component locations – diesel models

Underbonnet view of a dTi turbo Mégane (with engine cover in place)

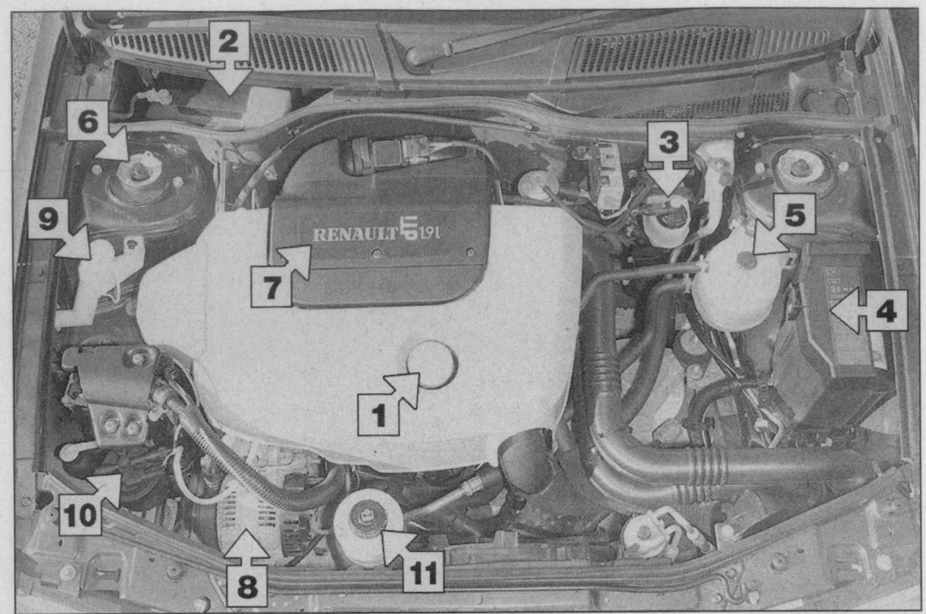

1 Engine oil filler cap and oil level dipstick
2 Battery
3 Brake fluid reservoir
4 Engine related fuse box
5 Coolant expansion tank
6 Suspension strut upper mounting
7 Air filter housing
8 Alternator
9 Washer fluid reservoir
10 Fuel filter
11 Power steering fluid reservoir

Underbonnet view of a dCi turbo Scénic (engine cover removed)

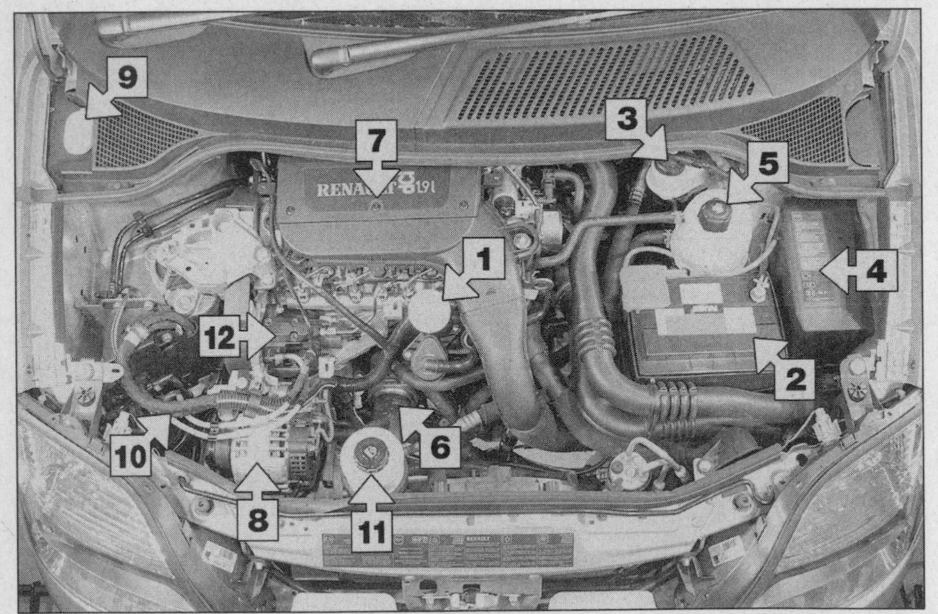

1 Engine oil filler cap and oil level dipstick
2 Battery
3 Brake fluid reservoir
4 Engine related fuse box
5 Coolant expansion tank
6 Engine oil filter
7 Air filter housing
8 Alternator
9 Washer fluid reservoir
10 Fuel filter
11 Power steering fluid reservoir
12 Injection pump

Front underbody view of a dCi turbo Scénic

1 Radiator
2 Engine oil drain plug
3 Gearbox
4 Front suspension lower arms
5 Front anti-roll bar
6 Driveshafts
7 Gearchange rod
8 Front brake calipers
9 Steering track rod ends
10 Steering gear
11 Engine rear mounting
12 Exhaust front downpipe

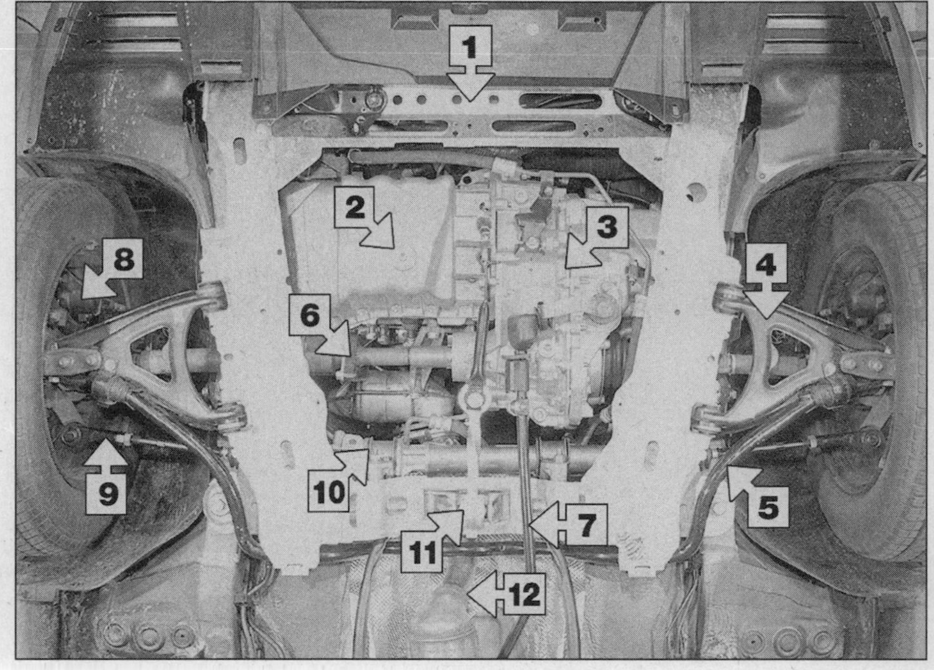

Rear underbody view a dCi turbo Scénic

1 Handbrake cables
2 Rear axle assembly
3 Torsion bars
4 Fuel tank
5 Rear suspension shock absorbers
6 Exhaust tailpipe and silencer
7 Spare wheel well
8 Fuel tank filler pipe and vent

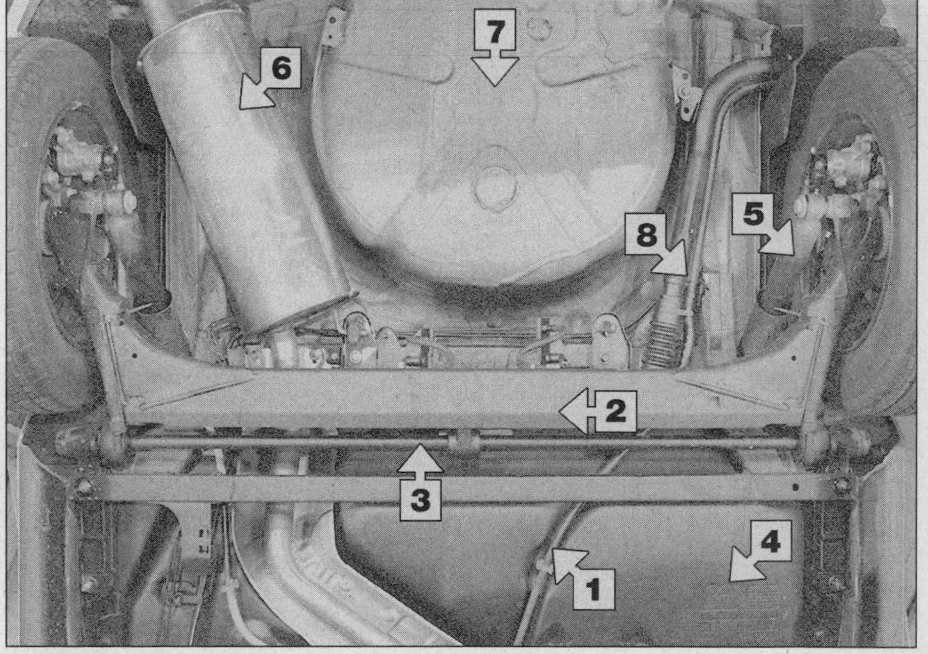

1 Introduction

This Chapter is designed to help the home mechanic maintain his/her vehicle for safety, economy, long life and peak performance.

The Chapter contains a master maintenance schedule, followed by Sections dealing specifically with each task in the schedule. Visual checks, adjustments, component renewal and other helpful items are included. Refer to the accompanying illustrations of the engine compartment and the underside of the vehicle for the locations of the various components.

Servicing your vehicle in accordance with the mileage/time maintenance schedule and the following Sections will provide a planned maintenance programme, which should result in a long and reliable service life. This is a comprehensive plan, so maintaining some items but not others at the specified service intervals will not produce the same results.

As you service your vehicle, you will discover that many of the procedures can – and should – be grouped together, because of the particular procedure being performed, or because of the close proximity of two otherwise-unrelated components to one another. For example, if the vehicle is raised for any reason, the exhaust can be inspected at the same time as the suspension and steering components.

The first step in this maintenance programme is to prepare yourself before the actual work begins. Read through all the Sections relevant to the work to be carried out, then make a list and gather together all the parts and tools required. If a problem is encountered, seek advice from a parts specialist, or a dealer service department.

2 Regular maintenance

If, from the time the vehicle is new, the routine maintenance schedule is followed closely and frequent checks are made of fluid levels and high-wear items, as suggested throughout this manual, the engine will be kept in relatively good running condition and the need for additional work will be minimised.

It is possible that there will be times when the engine is running poorly due to the lack of regular maintenance. This is even more likely if a used vehicle, which has not received regular and frequent maintenance checks, is purchased. In such cases, additional work may need to be carried out, outside of the regular maintenance intervals.

If engine wear is suspected, a compression test or leakdown test (refer to Chapter 2C) will provide valuable information regarding the overall performance of the main internal components. Such a test can be used as a basis to decide on the extent of the work to be carried out. If, for example, a compression test indicates serious internal engine wear, conventional maintenance as described in this Chapter will not greatly improve the performance of the engine and may prove a waste of time and money, unless extensive overhaul work is carried out first.

The following series of operations are those usually required to improve the performance of a generally poor-running engine:

Primary operations

a) Clean, inspect and test the battery (See 'Weekly checks')
b) Check all the engine-related fluids (See 'Weekly checks')
c) Check the condition and tension of the auxiliary drivebelt (Section 18)
d) Check the condition of the air filter element and renew if necessary (Section 19)
e) Check the fuel filter – drain off any water and renew the filter if necessary (Sections 4 and 21)
f) Check the condition of all hoses and check for fluid leaks (Section 9)
g) Check the idle speed and anti-stall speed (Chapter 4B)

If the primary operations do not prove fully effective, carry out the following secondary operations:

Secondary operations

All items listed under *Primary operations*, plus the following:

a) Check the charging system (Chapter 5A)
b) Check the pre-heating system (Chapter 5C)
c) Check the fuel system (Chapter 4B)

Every 9000 miles (15 000 km) or 12 months

3 Engine oil and filter renewal

1 Frequent oil and filter changes are the most important preventative maintenance procedures which can be undertaken by the DIY owner. As engine oil ages, it becomes diluted and contaminated, which leads to premature engine wear.

2 Before starting this procedure, gather together all the necessary tools and materials **(see illustration)**. Also make sure that you have plenty of clean rags and newspapers handy, to mop up any spills. Ideally, the engine oil should be warm, as it will drain more easily and more built-up sludge will be removed with it. Take care not to touch the exhaust or any other hot parts of the engine when working under the vehicle. To avoid any possibility of scalding and to protect yourself from possible skin irritants and other harmful contaminants in used engine oils, it is advisable to wear gloves when carrying out this work.

3 Firmly apply the handbrake then jack up the front of the vehicle and support it on axle stands (see *Jacking and vehicle support*). Where applicable, remove the engine undershield.

4 Remove the oil filler cap. Where applicable, remove the engine cover.

5 Using an 8 mm square-section drain plug key, slacken the drain plug about half a turn **(see illustration)**. Position the draining container under the drain plug, then remove the plug completely – recover the sealing washer.

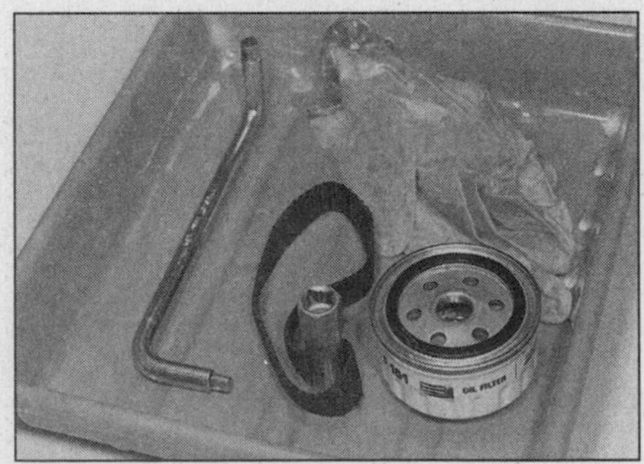

3.2 Tools and materials necessary for engine oil change and filter renewal

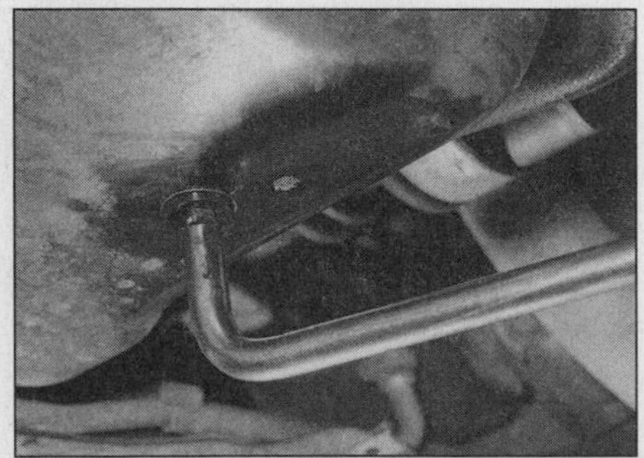

3.5 Using a drain plug key to unscrew the engine oil drain plug

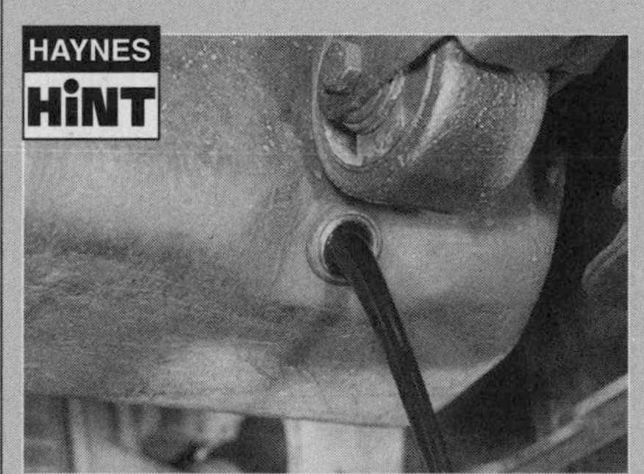

As the drain plug threads release, move it sharply away so the stream of oil issuing from the sump runs into the container, not up your sleeve.

6 Allow some time for the oil to drain, noting that it may be necessary to reposition the container as the oil flow slows to a trickle.

7 After all the oil has drained, wipe the drain plug and the sealing washer with a clean rag. Examine the condition of the sealing washer and renew it if it shows signs of scoring or other damage which may prevent an oil-tight seal. Clean the area around the drain plug opening and refit the plug complete with the washer. Tighten it to the specified torque wrench setting.

8 Move the container into position under the oil filter which is located on the front of the cylinder block.

9 Use an oil filter removal tool to slacken the filter initially, then unscrew it by hand the rest of the way **(see illustration)**. Empty the oil from the old filter into the container.

10 Use a clean rag to remove all oil, dirt and sludge from the filter sealing area on the engine. Check the old filter to make sure that the rubber sealing ring has not stuck to the engine. If it has, carefully remove it.

11 Apply a light coating of clean engine oil to the sealing ring on the new filter, then screw the filter into position on the engine. Tighten the filter firmly by hand only – **do not** use any tools **(see illustration)**.

12 Remove the old oil and all tools from under the vehicle then lower the vehicle to the ground.

3.9 Using an oil filter removal tool to slacken the oil filter

13 Fill the engine through the filler hole, using the correct grade and type of oil (refer to *Weekly Checks* for details of topping-up). Pour in half the specified quantity of oil first, then wait a few minutes for the oil to drain into the sump. Continue to add oil, a small quantity at a time, until the level is up to the lower mark on the dipstick. Adding approximately a further 2.0 litres will bring the level up to the upper mark on the dipstick. Refit and tighten the oil filler cap.

14 Note that when a non-turbo engine is first started, there will be a delay of a few seconds before the oil pressure warning light goes out while the new filter fills with oil (for turbo models the procedure described in the following paragraph **must** be followed). Do not race the engine while the warning light is on.

15 On turbo models, the following procedure must be observed before starting the engine:

a) *Disconnect the wiring from the stop solenoid on the injection pump and insulate the connector or remove the pump fuse/relay.*

b) *Crank the engine on the starter motor until the oil pressure warning light goes out (this may take several seconds).*

c) *Reconnect the wiring to the stop solenoid or refit the pump fuse/relay, then start the engine using the normal procedure.*

d) *Run the engine at idle speed and check the turbocharger oil and coolant unions for leakage. Rectify any problems without delay.*

16 Run the engine for a few minutes and check that there are no leaks around the oil filter seal and the sump drain plug.

17 Stop the engine and wait a few minutes for the oil to settle in the sump once more. With the new oil circulated and the filter now completely full, recheck the level on the dipstick and add more oil as necessary.

18 Dispose safely of the used engine oil and the old filter with reference to *General repair procedures*.

3.11 Tighten the new filter by hand only

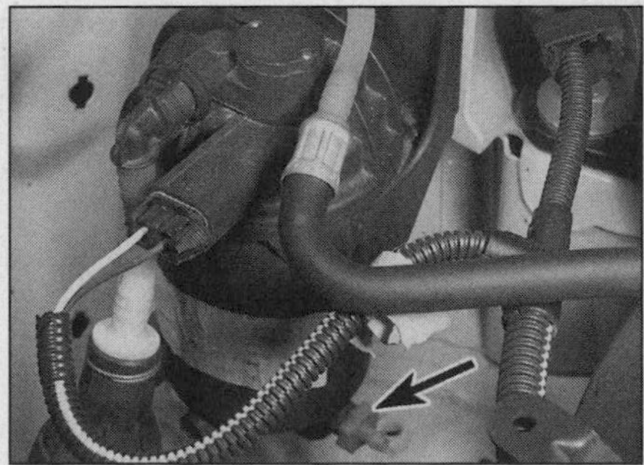

4.1 The water drain tap is at the base of the fuel filter

4 Fuel filter water draining

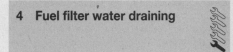

HAYNES HiNT

This is not a pleasant task, unless you like the smell of diesel fuel in your skin. Wear a pair of light plastic disposable gloves, like those available at the diesel pumps of most filling stations, to protect your hands and have plenty of newspaper or clean rag handy for mopping-up spills. Ensure that diesel fuel does not spill on to the coolant hoses, electrical wiring, alternator, engine mountings or the auxiliary drivebelt – protect them, if necessary, with a plastic sheet. Drain the fuel into a clean container so that you can be sure of seeing any water or other foreign bodies which might be present in the system.

1 A water drain cock is provided at the base of the fuel filter assembly **(see illustration)**.

2 Place a suitable container beneath the drain cock. To make draining easier, a suitable length of tubing can be attached to the cock outlet to direct the fuel flow into a clean glass jar – on some models a drain tube is provided as standard. **Note:** *If desired, access can be improved by unscrewing the nuts securing the filter head to the body and by raising the complete filter assembly to a more convenient position – if this is done, take care not to strain the fuel hoses and electrical wiring.*

3 Slacken the bleed screw on the injection pump's fuel inlet union (see Chapter 4B, Section 7), then open the drain cock by turning it anti-clockwise. It may be found that no fuel emerges at first (because the system is under negative pressure) – on models so equipped, fuel flow can be started by operating the hand priming pump.

4 Allow sufficient of the filter's contents – usually 100 ml is enough – to drain into the container to be sure that any traces of water or of other impurities have been flushed out of the system, then securely tighten the drain cock and the bleed screw.

5 Prime and bleed the fuel system as described in Chapter 4B.

6 Dispose safely of the drained fuel with reference to *General repair procedures*.

Every 18 000 miles (30 000 km) or 2 years

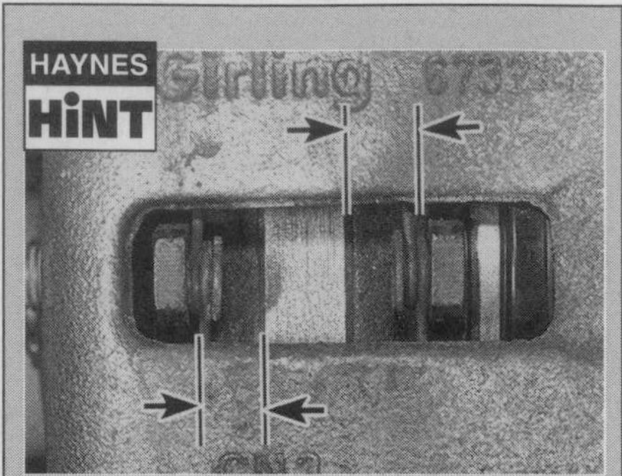

For a quick check, the thickness of each brake pad can be measured through the aperture in the caliper body.

5 Front brake pad and disc check

1 Apply the handbrake, then jack up the front of the car and support it securely on axle stands. Remove the front roadwheels.

2 For a comprehensive check, the brake pads should be removed and cleaned. The operation of the caliper can then also be checked and the condition of the brake disc itself can be fully examined on both sides. Refer to Chapter 9 for further information.

3 On completion refit the roadwheels and lower the car to the ground.

6 Exhaust system check

1 With the engine cold (at least an hour after the vehicle has been driven), check the complete exhaust system from the engine to the end of the tailpipe. The exhaust system is most easily checked with the vehicle raised on a hoist, or suitably supported on axle stands, so that the exhaust components are readily visible and accessible.

2 Check the exhaust pipes and connections for evidence of leaks, severe corrosion and damage. Make sure that all brackets and mountings are in good condition and that all relevant nuts and bolts are tight. Leakage at any of the joints or in other parts of the system will usually show up as a black sooty stain in the vicinity of the leak.

3 Rattles and other noises can often be traced to the exhaust system, especially the brackets and mountings. Try to move the pipes and silencers. If the components are able to come into contact with the body or suspension parts, secure the system with new mountings. Otherwise separate the joints (if possible) and twist the pipes as necessary to provide additional clearance.

7.4 Check for wear in the hub bearings by grasping the wheel and trying to rock it

7 Suspension and steering check

Front suspension and steering check

1 Raise the front of the vehicle and securely support it on axle stands.

2 Visually inspect the balljoint dust covers and the steering gear gaiters for splits, chafing or deterioration. Any wear of these components will cause loss of lubricant, together with dirt and water entry, resulting in rapid deterioration of the balljoints or steering gear.

3 On vehicles with power steering, check the fluid hoses for chafing or deterioration and the pipe and hose unions for fluid leaks. Also check for signs of fluid leakage under pressure from the steering gear gaiters, which would indicate failed fluid seals within the steering gear.

4 Grasp the roadwheel at the 12 o'clock and 6 o'clock positions and try to rock it **(see illustration)**. Very slight free play may be felt, but if the movement is appreciable, further investigation is necessary to determine the source. Continue rocking the wheel while an assistant depresses the footbrake. If the movement is now eliminated or significantly reduced, it is likely that the hub bearings are at fault. If the free play is still evident with the footbrake depressed, then there is wear in the suspension joints or mountings.

5 Now grasp the wheel at the 9 o'clock and 3 o'clock positions and try to rock it as before. Any movement felt now may again be caused by wear in the hub bearings or the steering track rod balljoints. If the outer balljoint is worn, the visual movement will be obvious. If the inner joint is suspect, it can be felt by placing a hand over the steering gear gaiter and gripping the track rod. If the wheel is now rocked, movement will be felt at the inner joint if wear has taken place.

6 Using a large screwdriver or flat bar, check for wear in the suspension mounting bushes by levering between the relevant suspension component and its attachment point. Some movement is to be expected, as the mountings are made of rubber, but excessive wear should be obvious. Also check the condition of any visible rubber bushes, looking for splits, cracks or contamination of the rubber.

7 With the car standing on its wheels, have an assistant turn the steering wheel back-and-forth, about an eighth of a turn each way. There should be very little, if any, lost movement between the steering wheel and roadwheels. If this is not the case, closely observe the joints and mountings previously described. In addition, check the steering column universal joints for wear and also check the steering gear itself.

Rear suspension check

8 Chock the front wheels, engage reverse gear and release the handbrake. Jack up the rear of the vehicle and support securely on axle stands (see *Jacking and vehicle support*).

9 Working as described previously for the front suspension, check the rear hub bearings, the suspension bushes and the shock absorber mountings for wear.

Suspension strut/shock absorber check

10 Check for any signs of fluid leakage around the strut/shock absorber body, or from the rubber gaiter around the piston rod. Should any fluid be noticed, the strut/shock absorber is defective internally and should be renewed. **Note:** *Struts/shock absorbers should always be renewed in pairs on the same axle.*

11 The efficiency of the strut/shock absorber may be checked by bouncing the vehicle at each corner. Generally speaking, the body will return to its normal position and stop after being depressed. If it rises and returns on a rebound, the strut/shock absorber is probably suspect. Also examine the upper and lower mountings for any signs of wear.

8 Driveshaft rubber gaiter and CV joint check

1 With the car raised and securely supported on axle stands, turn the steering onto full lock, then slowly rotate the roadwheel. Inspect the condition of the outer constant velocity (CV) joint rubber gaiter while squeezing the gaiter

8.1 Checking a driveshaft outer gaiter for signs of damage

to open out the folds **(see illustration)**. Check for signs of cracking, splits or deterioration of the rubber, which may allow the grease to escape and lead to the entry of water and grit into the joint. Also check the security and condition of the retaining clips/fasteners. Repeat these checks on the inner CV joint, then check the remaining driveshaft. If any damage or deterioration is found, the gaiter should be renewed as described in Chapter 8.

2 At the same time, check the general condition of the CV joints themselves by first holding the driveshaft and attempting to rotate the roadwheel. Repeat this check by holding the inner joint and attempting to rotate the driveshaft. Any appreciable movement indicates wear in the joints, in the driveshaft splines, or a loose driveshaft nut.

9 Hose, brake line and fluid leak check

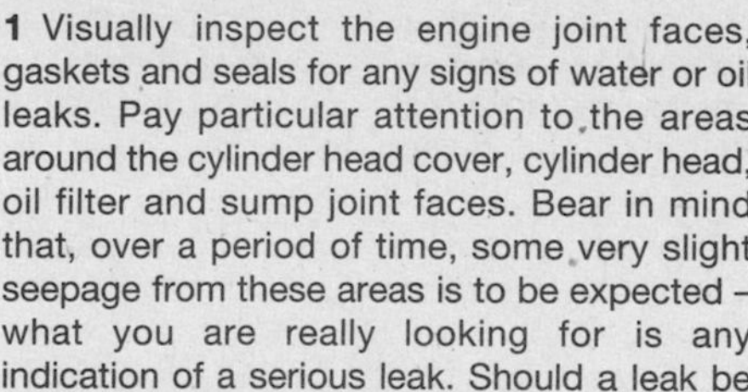

1 Visually inspect the engine joint faces, gaskets and seals for any signs of water or oil leaks. Pay particular attention to the areas around the cylinder head cover, cylinder head, oil filter and sump joint faces. Bear in mind that, over a period of time, some very slight seepage from these areas is to be expected – what you are really looking for is any indication of a serious leak. Should a leak be found, renew the offending gasket or oil seal by referring to the appropriate Chapters in this manual.

2 Also check the security and condition of all the engine-related pipes and hoses and all braking system pipes and hoses. Ensure that all cable-ties or securing clips are in place and in good condition. Clips which are broken or missing can lead to chafing of the hoses, pipes or wiring, which could cause more serious problems in the future.

3 Carefully check the radiator hoses and heater hoses along their entire length. Renew any hose which is cracked, swollen or deteriorated. Cracks will show up better if the hose is squeezed. Pay close attention to the hose clips that secure the hoses to the cooling system components. Hose clips can pinch and puncture hoses, resulting in cooling

A leak in the cooling system will usually show up as white- or rust-coloured deposits on the area adjoining the leak.

system leaks. If the crimped-type hose clips are used, it may be a good idea to replace them with standard worm-drive clips.

4 Inspect all the cooling system components (hoses, joint faces, etc) for leaks.

5 Where any problems are found on system components, renew the component or gasket with reference to Chapter 3.

6 With the vehicle raised, inspect the fuel tank and filler neck for punctures, cracks and other damage. The connection between the filler neck and tank is especially critical. Sometimes a rubber filler neck or connecting hose will leak due to loose retaining clamps or deteriorated rubber.

7 Carefully check all rubber hoses and metal fuel lines leading away from the fuel tank. Check for loose connections, deteriorated hoses, crimped lines and other damage. Pay particular attention to the vent pipes and hoses, which often loop up around the filler neck and can become blocked or crimped. Follow the lines to the front of the vehicle, carefully inspecting them all the way. Renew damaged sections as necessary. Similarly, whilst the vehicle is raised, take the opportunity to inspect all underbody brake fluid pipes and hoses.

8 From within the engine compartment, check the security of all fuel, vacuum and brake hose attachments and pipe unions and inspect all hoses for kinks, chafing and deterioration.

9 Where applicable, check the condition of the power steering fluid pipes and hoses.

10 Roadwheel bolt check

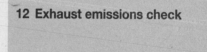

1 Remove the wheel trims (where fitted) and slacken slightly (through one-quarter of a turn) each of the roadwheel bolts in turn. If any bolt is particularly difficult to unscrew, remove the roadwheel (see *Jacking and vehicle support*). Check that the threads and wheel-to-hub mating surfaces are clean and undamaged – the threads can be cleaned using a brass wire brush if rusty or corroded.

2 Clean each wheel thoroughly, inside and out, then examine the wheel rim for signs of rusting, corrosion or other damage. Light alloy wheels are easily damaged by 'kerbing' whilst parking and, similarly, steel wheels may become dented or buckled. Renewal of the wheel is very often the only course of remedial action possible. Check that any balance weights fitted are securely fastened.

3 Apply a thin smear of anti-seize compound to the threads and (if a wheel was found to be stuck in place with corrosion) to the wheel-to-hub mating surfaces. Refit the wheel, tightening the bolts only moderately at first.

4 Working in a diagonal sequence, tighten the bolts to the specified torque wrench setting. Refit the trim.

11 Clutch check

1 Check that the clutch pedal moves smoothly and easily through its full travel, and the clutch itself functions correctly, with no trace of slip or drag. If the movement is uneven or stiff in places, check that the cable is routed correctly, with no sharp turns.

2 Inspect the ends of the clutch inner cable, both at the gearbox end and inside the car, for signs of wear and fraying.

3 Lubricate its exposed inner cable section with multi-purpose grease.

4 Check and adjust the clutch cable as described in Chapter 6.

1B

12 Exhaust emissions check

The exhaust emission control system can only be tested accurately using a suitable exhaust gas analyser (suitable for use with diesel engines). Have the test carried out by a Renault dealer or a diesel specialist, after the engine oil and filter have been changed (use only high-quality diesel-specific engine oil of the standard specified in *Lubricants and fluids*) and the air filter has been checked and renewed if necessary.

Check the engine idle and anti-stall speeds as described in Chapter 4B.

13 Air conditioning system check

If the air conditioning system is functioning correctly, the only check needed is to ensure that the compressor drivebelt is correctly tensioned and in good condition (Section 18). If there is a problem with the air conditioning system the vehicle must be taken to a Renault dealer for testing.

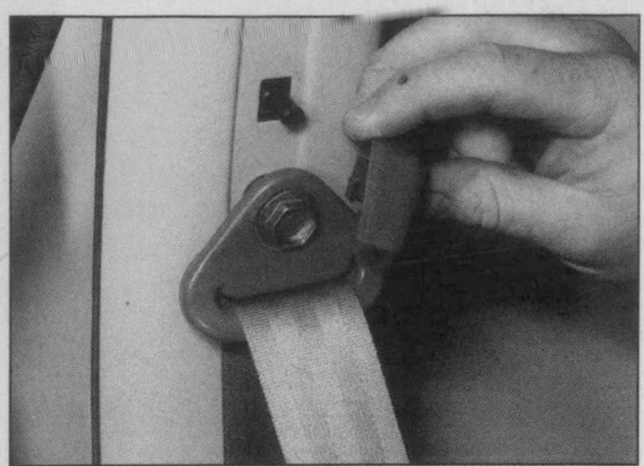

17.3 Check the security of the seat belt mountings

14 Electrical systems check

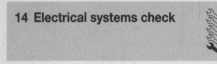

1 Check the operation of all electrical equipment, ie, lights, direction indicators, horn, etc. Refer to the appropriate Sections of Chapter 12 for details if any of the circuits are found to be inoperative.

2 Note that the stop-light switch adjustment is described in Chapter 9.

3 Visually check all accessible wiring connectors, harnesses and retaining clips for security and for signs of chafing or damage. Rectify any faults found.

15 Vehicle bodywork check

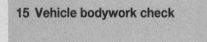

Work slowly around the vehicle, paying particular attention to the bonnet, closely examining the paintwork for signs of damage such as stone chips. If damage is found, it should be repaired using a touch-in brush to prevent corrosion of the bodywork; colour-matched touch-in brushes are available from your Renault dealer. More serious damage can be repaired with reference to Chapter 11.

16 Boost pressure check (turbo only)

This work must be carried out by a Renault dealer.

17 Seat belt check

1 Carefully examine the seat belt webbing for cuts, or any signs of serious fraying or deterioration. If the belt is of the retractable type, pull the belt all the way out of the inertia reel and examine the full extent of the webbing.

2 Fasten and unfasten the belt, ensuring that the locking mechanism holds securely and releases properly when intended. If the belt is of the retractable type, check also that the retracting mechanism operates correctly when the belt is released.

3 Check the security of all seat belt mountings and attachments which are accessible without removing any trim or other components **(see illustration)**.

18 Auxiliary drivebelt check and renewal

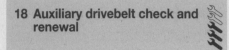

Note: *Renault state that a drivebelt must be renewed as a matter of course whenever it is removed.*

Checking

1 The auxiliary drivebelt is located at the right-hand side of the engine.

2 Two different drivebelt configurations may be encountered, depending on whether the vehicle is equipped with air conditioning or not **(see illustrations)**.

3 Due to their function and material makeup, drivebelts are prone to failure after a period of time and should therefore be inspected periodically.

4 Since the drivebelt is located very close to the right-hand side of the engine compartment, it is possible to gain better access by raising the front of the vehicle and removing the right-hand wheel, then removing the splash shield from inside the wheelarch. On certain models it will also be necessary to remove the lower timing belt cover. Where applicable, remove the engine cover if better access is required.

5 With the engine switched off, inspect the full length of the drivebelt for cracks and separation of the belt plies. It will be necessary to turn the crankshaft (using a spanner or socket and long extension bar on the crankshaft pulley bolt) to move the belt along the pulleys so that the full length of the belt can be inspected thoroughly. Twist the belt between the pulleys so that both sides can be viewed. Also check for fraying and glazing which gives the belt a shiny appearance. Check the pulleys for nicks, cracks, distortion and corrosion.

Tensioning

6 The tension of each drivebelt is checked midway between the pulleys at the point indicated in illustration 18.2a or 18.2b. For models without air conditioning, a belt's tension can be set or checked accurately only by using the appropriate Renault tool.

With experience, depressing the belt with moderate finger-pressure at the point indicated should give an adequate approximation of the correct tension. If the special tool is not available and there is any doubt about the tension of a drivebelt, the vehicle should be taken to a Renault dealer as soon as possible for the tension to be checked by qualified personnel using the special equipment.

7 For models without air conditioning, if the belt tension is checked using the special tool described below, the belt is fit for further use **only** if the value recorded is within the specified tolerance. If the value recorded is between the lower end of the fitting/checking value tolerance range and the minimum operating value, the belt should **not** be retightened – if the value recorded is below the minimum specified, the belt must be renewed.

8 On models with air conditioning, a spring-loaded tensioner is fitted to automatically maintain the correct tension on the belt. If there is any reason to suspect that the

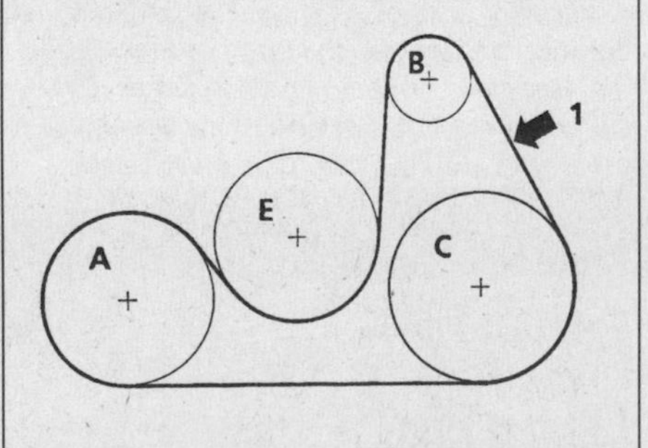

18.2a Auxiliary drivebelt tension checking – models without air conditioning

1 Tension checking point
A Crankshaft pulley
B Alternator
C Power-assisted steering pump
E Coolant pump

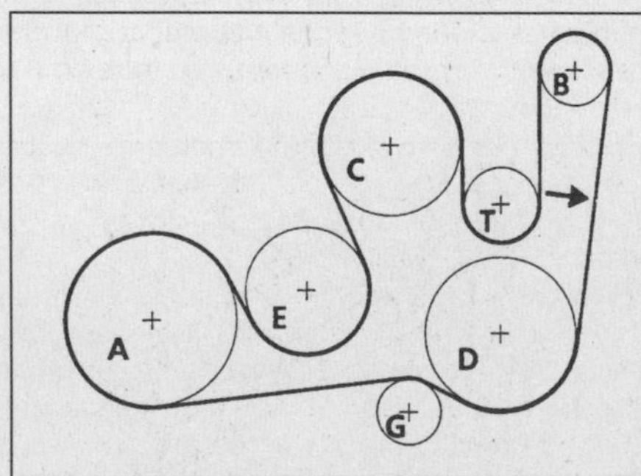

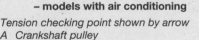

18.2b Auxiliary drivebelt tension checking – models with air conditioning

Tension checking point shown by arrow
A Crankshaft pulley
B Alternator
C Power-assisted steering pump
D Air conditioning compressor
E Coolant pump
G Roller
T Tensioner

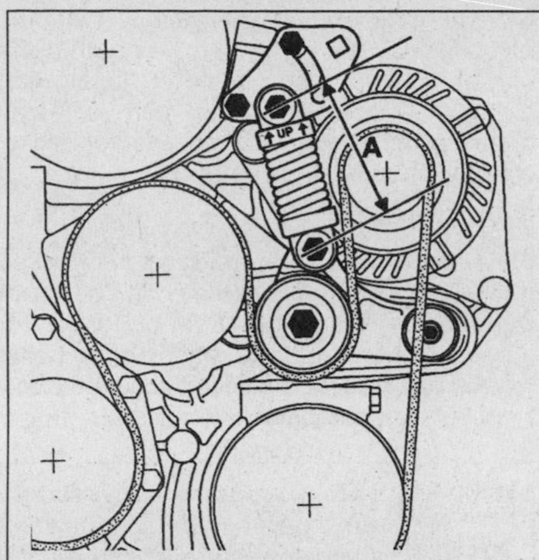

18.8 The operation of the auxiliary drivebelt automatic tensioner is checked by measuring the distance (A) – models with air conditioning

drivebelt tension is incorrect, it will be necessary to have this checked by a Renault dealer. A special gauge, tool Mot. 1387, is used to check the distance between centres of the tensioner mounting bolts, which then records on the gauge as correct or incorrect **(see illustration)**. As an actual distance between centres value is not specified by Renault, having this checked by use of the gauge is the only alternative. In practice, however, as long as the tensioner is initially set as described below when refitting the belt, no problems should be encountered.

9 If the gauge is available, proceed as follows: Slacken the gauge's knurled locking wheel, fit the gauge to the tensioner so that the ends of its arms engage on the heads of the tensioner mounting bolts, then tighten the knurled wheel to lock the gauge. Withdraw the gauge and check that the distance between centres is within the indicated tolerance range **(see illustrations)**. If the distance is below the minimum tolerance range check first that the tensioner mounting plate is positioned correctly (rotated clockwise to the limit of the elongated mounting bolt slot), that the belt is of the correct type (not too short) and that it is correctly routed, as shown in illustration 18.2b. If the distance is above the maximum tolerance range check first that the tensioner mounting plate is positioned correctly, that the belt is of the correct type (not too long) and that it is correctly routed – if the distance is still incorrect, the belt must be renewed.

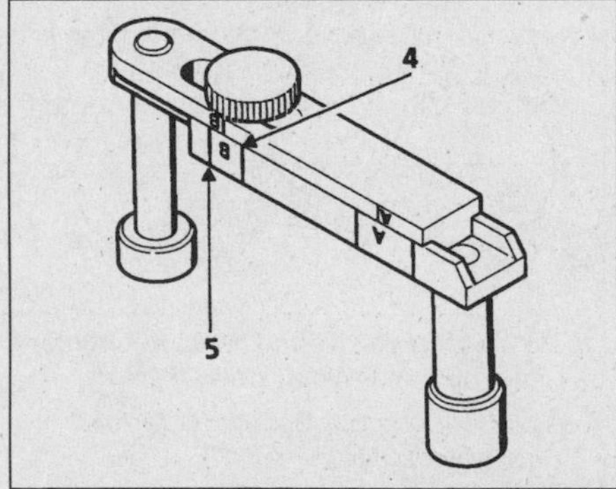

18.9b Checking the distance between centres of the auxiliary drivebelt automatic tensioner – models with air conditioning

4 Minimum tolerance range
5 Maximum tolerance range

Renewal

Models without air conditioning

10 To remove a belt, loosen the alternator mounting and pivot bolts, and slacken the belt tension fully. Slip the belt off the pulleys, then fit the new belt ensuring that it is routed correctly.

11 With the belt in position, loosen the adjustment locknut and turn the adjustment bolt as required until the tension is correct. Tighten the adjustment, mounting and pivot bolts on completion **(see illustration)**. Run the engine for about 5 minutes, then recheck the tension.

Models with air conditioning

Note: *Before the belt is removed, the distance between centres of the tensioner mounting bolts must be checked using the Renault tool Mot. 1387 (see paragraph 9 above).*

12 Unbolt the fuel filter-to-injection pump hose support bracket.

13 Engage a 9 mm square drive (ie, the end of a socket wrench) in the square hole in the tensioner mounting plate.

14 While holding the plate with the square drive, slacken the lower, then the upper, tensioner plate mounting bolts **(see illustration)**.

15 Move the tensioner plate anti-clockwise (as viewed from the side of the car) to the extent allowed by the elongated mounting bolt slot, to release the belt tension.

16 Slip the belt off the pulleys, then fit the new belt ensuring that it is routed correctly.

17 Set the automatic adjuster initial position by moving the tensioner mounting plate clockwise to the limit of the elongated mounting bolt slot. Hold the plate in this position and tighten the two mounting bolts.

18 Refit the hose support bracket and any other components disturbed for access.

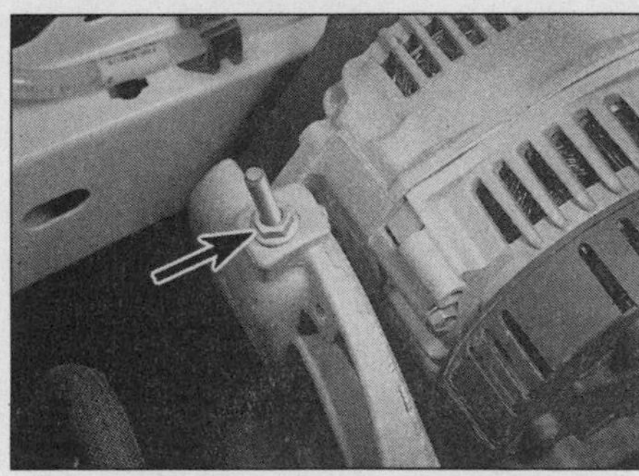

18.11 Auxiliary drivebelt adjustment bolt – models without air conditioning

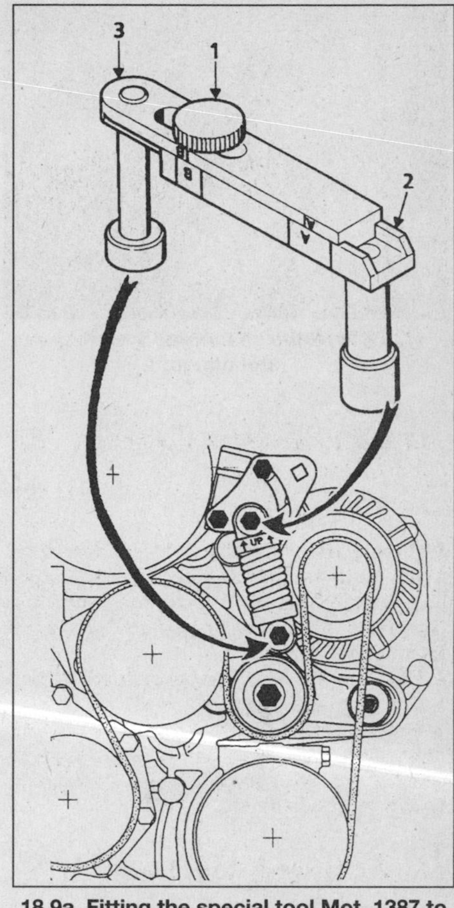

18.9a Fitting the special tool Mot. 1387 to check the operation of the auxiliary drivebelt automatic tensioner – models with air conditioning

1 Knurled locking wheel
2, 3 Tool arms

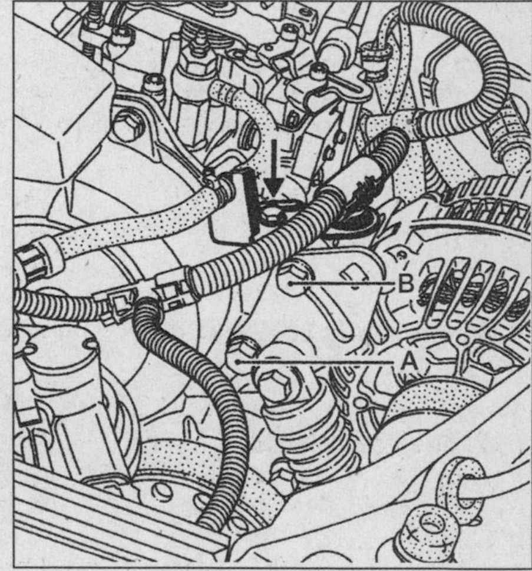

18.14 Auxiliary drivebelt automatic tensioner mounting plate – models with air conditioning

A Lower mounting bolt
B Upper mounting bolt
Arrow indicates fuel hose support bracket bolt.

19.1a Remove the side securing screws . . .

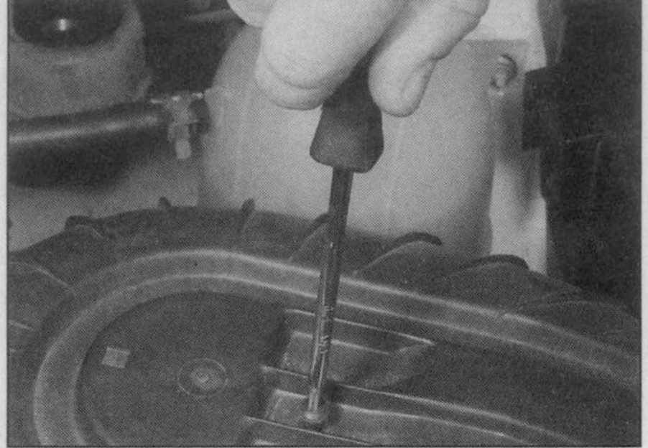

19.1b . . . and the centre securing screw . . .

19.1c . . . then withdraw the air cleaner cover

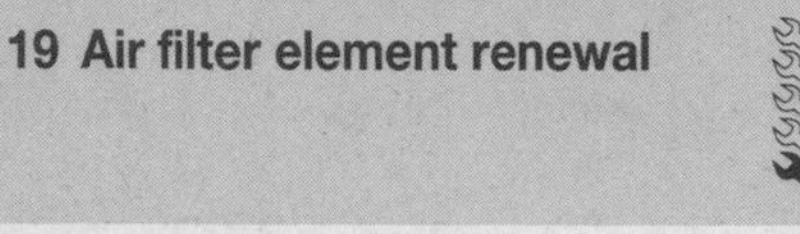

19 Air filter element renewal

Non-turbo models

1 Remove the securing screws (noting that one of the screws is located in the centre of the cover) and withdraw the air cleaner cover **(see illustrations)**.

2 Lift the filter element from the air cleaner casing **(see illustration)**.

3 Clean the inside of the air cleaner casing and the cover and fit a new filter element.

4 Refit the cover using a reversal of the removal procedure.

Turbo models

5 Loosen the captive securing bolts and lift off the air cleaner cover **(see illustration)**.

6 Lift the filter assembly from the air cleaner casing and withdraw the air filter element **(see illustrations)**.

7 Clean the inside of the air cleaner casing and the cover and fit a new filter element.

8 Refit the cover using a reversal of the removal procedure.

19.2 Removing the filter element – non-turbo model

19.5 Slacken and remove the retaining bolts

19.6a Lift out the air filter assembly . . .

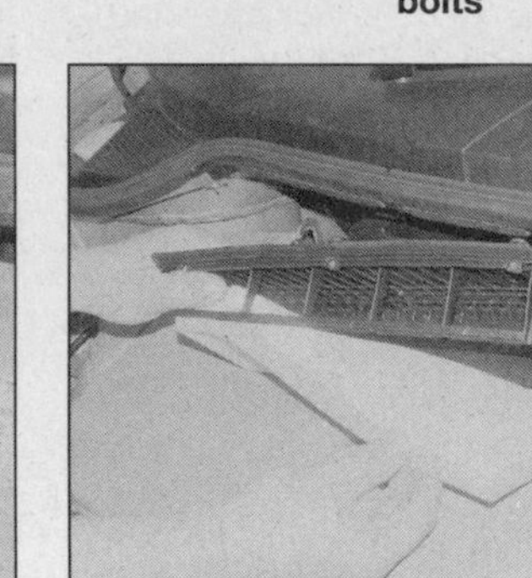

19.6b . . . and withdraw the air filter element

20 Pollen filter renewal

All models except Scénic

1 Open the bonnet and unclip the small cover situated on the left-hand side of the intake vent panel **(see illustration)**.

2 Release the retaining clips and remove the pollen filter cover from the top of the blower motor housing **(see illustration)**.

3 Slide the pollen filter out of position and discard it **(see illustration)**.

4 Wipe clean the cover and housing and slide the new filter into position.

5 Securely clip the pollen filter cover onto the

20.1 Lift out the air intake vent panel . . .

20.2 . . . unclip the pollen filter cover. . .

20.3 . . . and withdraw the filter

20.7a Undo the retaining screw (arrowed) . . .

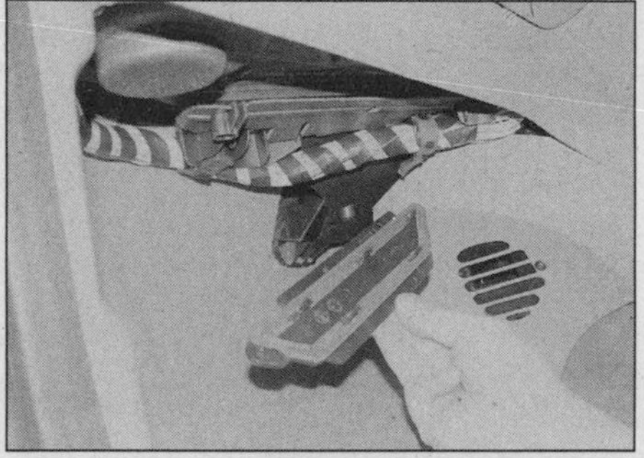

20.7b . . . remove the cover . . .

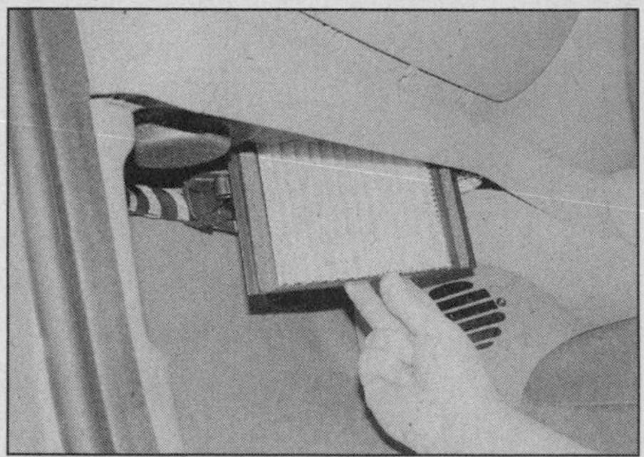

20.8 . . . and withdraw the pollen filter

housing then clip the vent panel cover into position.

Scénic models

6 The filter is located inside the vehicle under the facia on the passenger's side.

7 Working in the passenger's footwell, undo the filter cover retaining bolt and slide the cover forward (see arrow on cover) to release it from its location **(see illustrations)**.

8 Pull the pollen filter down out of position and discard it **(see illustration)**.

9 Wipe clean the cover and housing and slide the new filter into position.

10 Refit the cover and secure with the retaining bolt.

Every 36 000 miles (60 000 km)

21 Fuel filter renewal

Caution: Do not allow dirt to enter the fuel system during this procedure.

Note: *The disconnection of the fuel hose quick-release fittings requires the use of the Renault tool Mot. 1311-06.*

1 Drain the contents of the fuel filter as described in Section 4 – read carefully the related notes and Hint.

2 Unplug the fuel heater wiring from the filter head.

3 Disconnect the fuel hoses from the top of the filter assembly and plug or cover the open unions to keep dirt out and to minimise the spillage of fuel and the entry of air into the system. The unions are equipped with quick-release fittings which are intended to be uncoupled using the Renault tool – this is a small forked implement which is passed between the two outer 'spokes' of the fitting and pressed to disengage the retaining claws. The hose can then be pulled off the union. If the tool is not available, the very careful use of two small electrical screwdrivers should serve to release the union.

4 Whether of Lucas or of Bosch manufacture, the filter consists of a separate element held in a filter bowl (black plastic on models with Lucas filter assemblies) which is secured by a through-bolt to the filter head. **Note:** *If desired, access can be improved by unscrewing the nuts securing the filter head to the body and by changing the filter element on the bench.* Unscrew the through-bolt from the top of the filter head and carefully lower the filter bowl away from its underside. Note carefully the location and orientation of the various seals (check carefully the underside of the filter head to ensure that none are missed) – on Lucas filter assemblies the through-bolt has O-ring seals above and below the filter head, while on Bosch filters there is only one seal – recover all such seals.

5 Note which way round it is fitted and withdraw the element from the filter bowl and wipe out the bowl using a clean, lint-free rag. Recover the filter sealing ring. All seals, O-rings and sealing washers disturbed on dismantling must be renewed as a matter of course – new ones will be supplied with any good-quality replacement filter.

6 On reassembly, smear the new seals with clean diesel fuel and ensure that all of them are correctly installed, using the notes made on dismantling – if a drain cock seal is supplied with the new filter, replace this also. Ensure that the drain cock is securely tightened and insert the new filter element, ensuring that it is the right way up, fit the new filter sealing ring and fill the filter bowl with clean diesel fuel. Working very carefully to avoid spillage's of fuel, offer up the bowl to the filter head, refit the through-bolt (with its seals already in place) and tighten it securely. This procedure is awkward and potentially very messy, but will save a lot of time and battery effort on start-up, especially for those models without hand priming pumps.

7 Where applicable, refit the filter head to the body, tightening securely the retaining nuts. Connect the fuel hoses to the filter assembly, ensuring that each is connected to the correct union and that the quick-release fittings lock securely. Connect the fuel heater wiring.

8 Prime and bleed the fuel system as described in Chapter 4B.

9 Dispose safely of the drained-off fuel and the old filter with reference to *General repair procedures*.

22 Heating system check

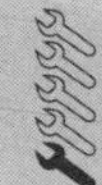

Check that the heating controls move smoothly and easily with no sign of stiffness and check that the blower motor operates correctly. If there is a problem check the heating ventilation system components as described in Chapter 3.

If the heating system seems to be giving out insufficient heat, check that the coolant level is correct and that there are no air locks in the cooling system (see Section 29).

23 Hinge and lock lubrication

Lubricate the hinges of the bonnet, doors and boot lid/tailgate with a light general purpose oil. similarly, lubricate all latches, locks and lock strikers. At the same time, check the security and operation of all locks, adjusting them if necessary (see Chapter 11).

Lightly lubricate the bonnet release mechanism with a suitable grease.

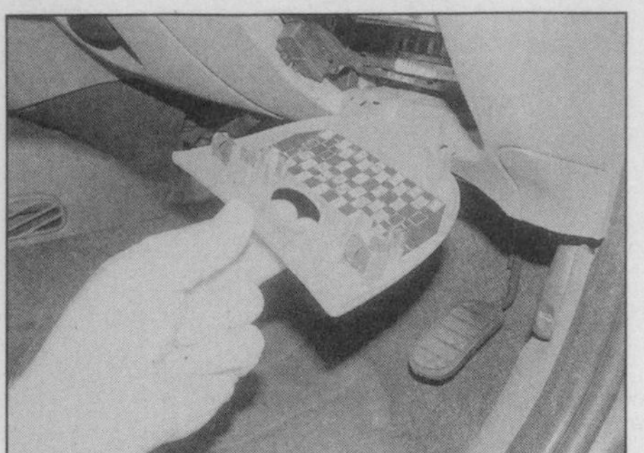

24.1 Spare fuses located in the fusebox cover

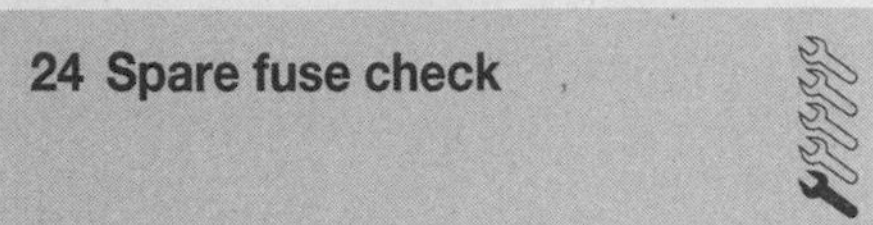

24 Spare fuse check

Check that spare fuses are in place in the locations provided in the fusebox cover **(see illustration)**. It is advisable to carry at least one spare of each rating of fuse fitted (see Chapter 12). Spare fuses can be obtained from most car accessory shops, or from a Renault dealer.

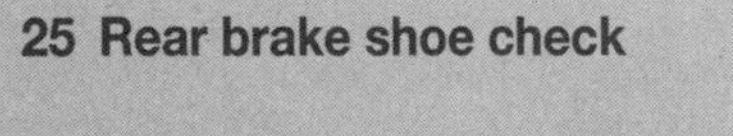

25 Rear brake shoe check

Drum brakes

1 Apply the handbrake, then jack up the rear of the car and support it securely on axle stands.

2 For a comprehensive check, remove the rear brake drums and check the brake shoes for signs of wear or contamination. At the same time, also inspect the wheel cylinders for signs of leakage and the brake drum for signs of wear. Refer to the relevant Sections of Chapter 9 for further information.

3 On completion lower the car to the ground.

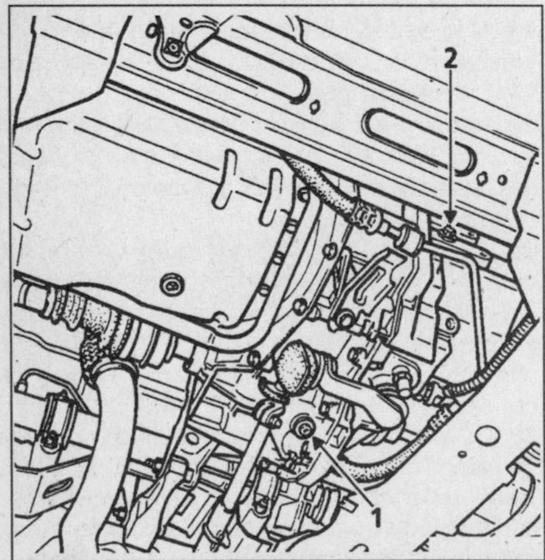

26.2 Gearbox drain (1) and filler/level (2) plugs

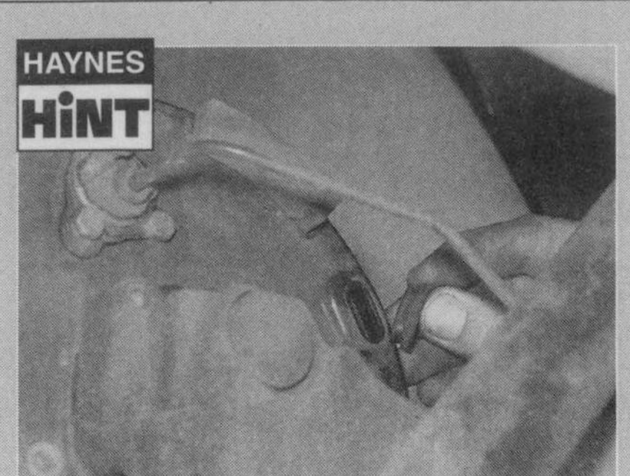

For a quick check, the thickness of the rear brake shoe can be checked through the aperture in the backplate once the rubber plug has been removed.

Disc brakes

1 Apply the handbrake, then jack up the rear of the car and support it securely on axle stands, then refer to Section 5.

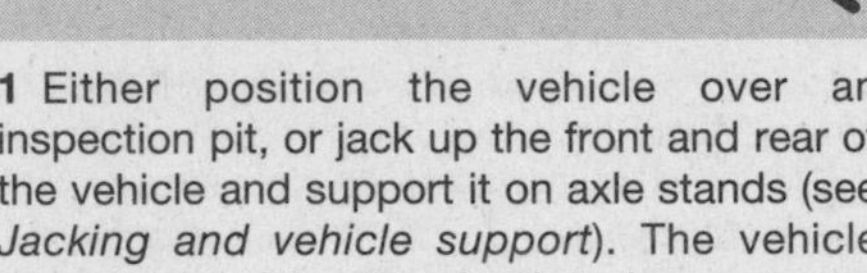

26 Manual gearbox oil level check

1 Either position the vehicle over an inspection pit, or jack up the front and rear of the vehicle and support it on axle stands (see *Jacking and vehicle support*). The vehicle must be level for the check to be accurate. Remove the engine undershield where fitted.

2 Clean the area around the filler/level plug on the front of the gearbox, then unscrew the plug **(see illustration)**.

3 The gearbox oil level should be up to the lower edge of the filler/level plug aperture **(see illustration)**.

4 If necessary, top-up using the specified type of lubricant until the oil level is correct. Fill the gearbox until oil starts to flow out, then allow excess oil to drain **(see illustration)**.

5 Once the gearbox oil level is correct, refit the filler/level plug and tighten it securely.

6 Lower the vehicle to the ground. Note that frequent need for topping-up indicates a leakage, possibly through an oil seal. The cause should be investigated and rectified.

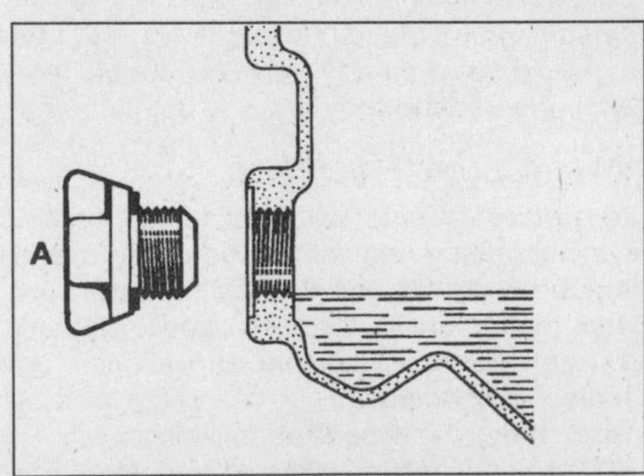

26.3 Gearbox filler/level plug (A) – correct oil level shown

27 Road test

Instruments and electrical equipment

1 Check the operation of all instruments and electrical equipment.

2 Make sure that all instruments read correctly and switch on all electrical equipment in turn, to check that it functions properly.

Steering and suspension

3 Check for any abnormalities in the steering, suspension, handling or road 'feel'.

4 Drive the vehicle and check that there are no unusual vibrations or noises.

5 Check that the steering feels positive, with no excessive 'sloppiness', or roughness and check for any suspension noises when cornering and driving over bumps.

Drivetrain

6 Check the performance of the engine, clutch, transmission and driveshafts.

7 Listen for any unusual noises from the engine, clutch and transmission.

8 Make sure that the engine runs smoothly when idling and that there is no hesitation when accelerating.

9 Check that, where applicable, the clutch action is smooth and progressive, that the drive is taken up smoothly and that the pedal travel is not excessive. Also listen for any noises when the clutch pedal is depressed.

10 Check that all gears can be engaged smoothly without noise and that the gearlever action is smooth and not vague or 'notchy'.

11 Listen for a metallic clicking sound from the front of the vehicle, as the vehicle is driven slowly in a circle with the steering on full-lock. Carry out this check in both directions. If a clicking noise is heard, this indicates wear in a driveshaft joint (see Chapter 8).

Braking system

12 Make sure that the vehicle does not pull to one side when braking and that the wheels do not lock prematurely when braking hard (or at all on ABS-equipped models).

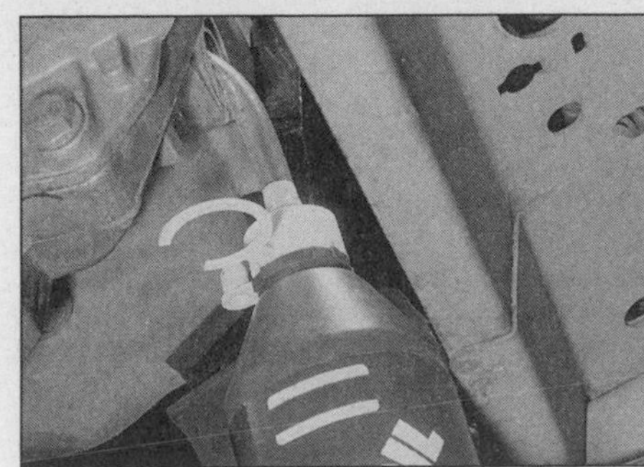

26.4 Topping-up the gearbox oil level

13 Check that there is no vibration through the steering when braking.
14 Check that the handbrake operates correctly, without excessive movement of the lever and that it holds the vehicle stationary on a slope.
15 Test the operation of the brake servo unit as follows. Depress the footbrake four or five times to exhaust the vacuum, then start the engine. As the engine starts, there should be a noticeable 'give' in the brake pedal as vacuum builds-up. Allow the engine to run for at least two minutes and then switch it off. If the brake pedal is now depressed again, it should be possible to detect a hiss from the servo as the pedal is depressed. After about four or five applications, no further hissing should be heard and the pedal should feel considerably harder.

28 Timing belt renewal

Refer to Chapter 2C for information on the removal and refitting of the timing belt.

Every 72 000 miles (120 000 km) or 4 years

29 Coolant renewal

Cooling system draining

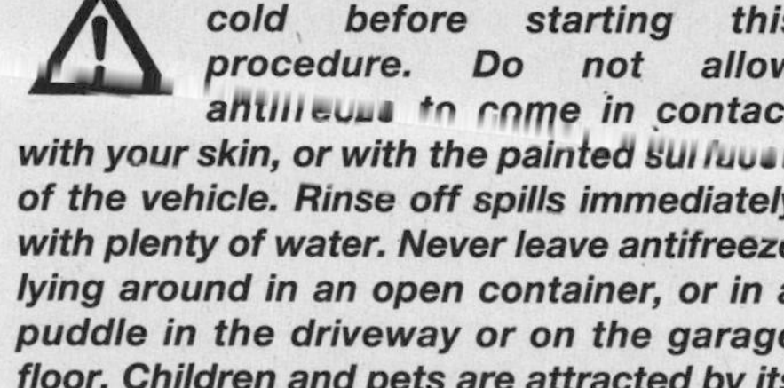
Warning: Wait until the engine is cold before starting this procedure. Do not allow antifreeze to come in contact with your skin, or with the painted surfaces of the vehicle. Rinse off spills immediately with plenty of water. Never leave antifreeze lying around in an open container, or in a puddle in the driveway or on the garage floor. Children and pets are attracted by its sweet smell, but antifreeze can be fatal if ingested.

1 With the engine completely cold, remove the expansion tank filler cap. Turn the cap anti-clockwise, wait until any pressure remaining in the system is released, then unscrew it and lift it off.
2 To assist draining, open the cooling system bleed screw(s). These are located in the heater hose at the bulkhead, in the thermostat housing or at the top right-hand side of the radiator. Where applicable, remove the engine cover if better access is required.
3 Where applicable, remove the undershield, then position a suitable container beneath the radiator bottom hose connection. Slacken the hose clip, pull off the hose and allow the coolant to drain into the container.
4 To ensure the complete draining of the cooling system, unscrew the cooling system drain plug on the engine. Where fitted, this is located at the rear of the cylinder block on the right-hand side, above the auxiliary shaft housing.
5 If the coolant has been drained for a reason other than renewal, then provided it is clean and less than two years old, it can be re-used, though this is not recommended.
6 Refit the radiator bottom hose on completion of draining. Where applicable, apply a few drops of a suitable sealant to the threads of the drain plug and refit it to the cylinder block; tighten it securely.

Cooling system flushing

7 If coolant renewal has been neglected, or if the antifreeze mixture has become diluted, then in time, the cooling system may gradually lose efficiency, as the coolant passages become restricted due to rust, scale deposits and other sediment. The cooling system efficiency can be restored by flushing the system clean.
8 The radiator should be flushed independently of the engine, to avoid unnecessary contamination.

Radiator flushing

9 Disconnect the top and bottom hoses and any other relevant hoses from the radiator, with reference to Chapter 3.
10 Insert a garden hose into the radiator top inlet. Direct a flow of clean water through the radiator and continue flushing until clean water emerges from the radiator bottom outlet.
11 If after a reasonable period, the water still does not run clear, the radiator can be flushed with a good proprietary cleaning agent. It is important that their manufacturer's instructions are followed carefully. If the contamination is particularly bad, insert the hose in the radiator bottom outlet and reverse-flush the radiator.

Engine flushing

12 To flush the engine, remove the thermostat as described in Chapter 3, then temporarily refit the top hose at its engine connection.
13 With the top and bottom hoses disconnected from the radiator, insert a garden hose into the radiator top hose. Direct a clean flow of water through the engine and continue flushing until clean water emerges from the radiator bottom hose.
14 On completion of flushing, refit the thermostat and reconnect the hoses with reference to Chapter 3.

Cooling system filling

15 Before attempting to fill the cooling system, make sure that all hoses and clips are in good condition and that the clips are tight. Note that an antifreeze mixture must be used all year round, to prevent corrosion of the engine components.
16 Remove the expansion tank filler cap.
17 Open the cooling system bleed screws.
18 Place a wad of rags around the expansion tank.
19 Slowly fill the system until the coolant level reaches the top of the expansion tank filler neck.
20 Close the bleed screws when coolant free from air bubbles emerges.
21 Start the engine and run it at a fast idle speed (do not exceed 2500 rpm) for approximately 4 minutes. Keep the level topped-up to the top of the expansion tank filler neck.
22 Refit and tighten the expansion tank filler cap.
23 Allow the engine to run for approximately 20 minutes at 2500 rpm until the cooling fan cuts in and out.
24 Stop the engine and check the coolant level, which should be up to the MAXI mark on the side of the tank. Check that the expansion tank filler cap is tight.
25 Allow the engine to cool, then recheck the coolant level with reference to *Weekly checks*. Top-up the level if necessary and refit the expansion tank filler cap. Where applicable, refit the undershield.

Antifreeze mixture

26 The antifreeze should always be renewed at the specified intervals. This is necessary not only to maintain the antifreeze properties, but also to prevent corrosion which would otherwise occur as the corrosion inhibitors become progressively less effective.
27 Always use an ethylene-glycol based antifreeze which is suitable for use in mixed-metal cooling systems. The quantity of antifreeze and levels of protection are given in the Specifications.
28 Before adding antifreeze, the cooling system should be completely drained, preferably flushed and all hoses checked for condition and security.
29 After filling with antifreeze, a label should be attached to the expansion tank, stating the type and concentration of antifreeze used and the date installed. Any subsequent topping-up should be made with the same type and concentration of antifreeze.
30 Do not use engine antifreeze in the windscreen/tailgate washer system, as it will damage the vehicle's paintwork. A screenwash additive should be added to the washer system in the quantities stated on the bottle.
31 Dispose safely of the used coolant with reference to *General repair procedures*.

30 Brake fluid renewal

Warning: Brake hydraulic fluid can harm your eyes and damage painted surfaces, so use extreme caution when handling and pouring it. Do not use fluid that has been standing open for some time, as it absorbs moisture from the air. Excess moisture can cause a dangerous loss of braking effectiveness.

Caution: On models equipped with ABS, disconnect the battery before carrying out the following operation and do not reconnect the battery until after the operation is complete. Failure to do this could lead to air entering the hydraulic unit. If air enters the hydraulic unit pump, it will prove very difficult (in some cases impossible) to bleed the unit. Refer to Chapter 5A, Section 1, when disconnecting the battery on Scénic models.

1 The procedure is similar to that for the bleeding of the hydraulic system as described in Chapter 9, except that the brake fluid reservoir should be emptied by syphoning, using a clean poultry baster or similar before starting and allowance should be made for the old fluid to be expelled when bleeding a section of the circuit.

2 Working as described in Chapter 9, open the first bleed screw in the sequence and pump the brake pedal gently until nearly all the old fluid has been emptied from the master cylinder reservoir. Top-up to the MAXI level with new fluid and continue pumping until only the new fluid remains in the reservoir and new fluid can be seen emerging from the bleed screw. Tighten the screw and top the reservoir level up to the MAXI level line.

Old brake fluid is invariably much darker in colour than the new, making it easy to distinguish the two.

3 Work through all the remaining bleed screws in the sequence until new fluid can be seen at all of them. Be careful to keep the master cylinder reservoir topped-up to above the MINI level at all times, or air may enter the system and greatly increase the length of the task.

4 When the operation is complete, check that all bleed screws are securely tightened and that their dust caps are refitted. Wash off all traces of spilt fluid and recheck the master cylinder reservoir fluid level.

5 Check the operation of the brakes before taking the car on the road.

6 Dispose safely of the used brake fluid with reference to *General repair procedures*.

Chapter 2 Part A:
1.4 and 1.6 litre petrol engine in-car repair procedures

Contents

Degrees of difficulty

Easy, suitable for novice with little experience 	**Fairly easy,** suitable for beginner with some experience 	**Fairly difficult,** suitable for competent DIY mechanic	**Difficult,** suitable for experienced DIY mechanic	**Very difficult,** suitable for expert DIY or professional

Specifications

General

Type	Four-cylinder, in-line, single-overhead camshaft (SOHC) on E7J engine, double-overhead camshaft (DOHC) on K4J and K4M engines
Designation:	
1.4 litre models	E7J 764, K4J 750
1.6 litre models	K4M 700, K4M 701
Bore:	
E7J engine	75.8 mm
K4J and K4M engines	79.5 mm
Stroke:	
E7J engine	77.0 mm
K4J engine	70.0 mm
K4M engine	80.5 mm
Capacity:	
E7J engine	1390 cc
K4J engine	1390 cc
K4M engine	1598 cc
Firing order	1-3-4-2 (No 1 cylinder at flywheel/driveplate end)
Direction of crankshaft rotation	Clockwise viewed from pulley end
Compression ratio:	
E7J engine	9.5 : 1
K4J and K4M engines	10 : 1

Valve clearances (cold) – E7J engine

Inlet	0.10 mm
Exhaust	0.25 mm

Timing belt tension value (see text):

Fitting/checking value	30 ± 10% SEEM units	
Minimum operating tension value	26 SEEM units	

Camshaft

Endfloat:		
E7J engine	0.06 to 0.15 mm	
K4J and K4M engines	0.08 to 0.178 mm	
Bearing journal diameters:		
No 1 to No 5 bearings	24.979 to 25.000 mm	
No 16 bearing	27.979 to 28.000 mm	

Lubrication system

System pressure:		
At idle	1.0 bar	
At 4000 rpm (E7J) or 3000 rpm (K4J and K4M)	3.0 bars	
Oil pump clearances:	**Minimum**	**Maximum**
Gear to body	0.110 mm	0.249 mm
Gear endfloat	0.020 mm	0.086 mm

Torque wrench settings

	Nm	**lbf ft**
Cylinder head cover bolts:		
E7J engine	10	7
K4M and K4J engines:		
Stage 1 – bolts 22, 23, 20 and 13	8	6
Stage 2 – bolts 1 to 12, 14 to 19, 21 to 24	12	9
Stage 3 – bolts 22, 23, 20 and 13	Slacken fully	
Stage 4 – bolts 22, 23, 20 and 13	12	9
Camshaft sprocket bolt:		
E7J engine	55	41
K4M and K4J engines:		
Stage 1	30	22
Stage 2	Angle-tighten through 84°	
Connecting rod (big-end) cap – oiled:		
E7J engine:		
Stage 1	10	7
Stage 2	45	33
K4J and K4M engines	43	32
Crankshaft pulley bolt:		
E7J engine:		
Stage 1	20	15
Stage 2	Angle-tighten through 68° ± 6°	
K4M and K4J engines:		
Stage 1	20	15
Stage 2	Angle-tighten through 135° ± 15°	
Cylinder head bolts – E7J engine*:		
Stage 1 – all bolts	20	15
Stage 2 – all bolts	Angle-tighten through 97° ± 2°	
Stage 3 – all bolts	Wait for at least 3 minutes for the gasket to settle	
Stage 4 – bolts 1 and 2	Slacken fully	
Stage 5 – bolts 1 and 2	20	15
Stage 6 – bolts 1 and 2	Angle-tighten through 97° ± 2°	
Stage 7 – bolts 3, 4, 5 and 6	Slacken fully	
Stage 8 – bolts 3, 4, 5 and 6	20	15
Stage 9 – bolts 3, 4, 5 and 6	Angle-tighten through 97° ± 2°	
Stage 10 – bolts 7, 8, 9 and 10	Slacken fully	
Stage 11 – bolts 7, 8, 9 and 10	20	15
Stage 12 – bolts 7, 8, 9 and 10	Angle-tighten through 97 ± 2°	
Cylinder head bolts – K4J and K4M engines*:		
Stage 1	20	15
Stage 2	Angle-tighten through 240° ± 6°	
Engine/automatic transmission mountings (see Section 14):		
Rear mounting	62	46
Right-hand engine mounting central nut	40	30
Right-hand engine mounting to body and engine	62	46
Left-hand engine mounting central nut	62	46
Left-hand engine mounting to transmission	62	46
Left-hand engine mounting to body	21	15

Torque wrench settings (continued)	Nm	lbf ft
Engine/manual gearbox mountings (see Section 14):		
Right-hand engine mounting nut:		
E7J engine	40	30
K4J and K4M engines	44	32
Left-hand engine mounting nut	45	33
Rear mounting link to transmission	65	48
Rear mounting link to subframe	75	55
Flywheel/driveplate bolts	53	39
Front suspension strut-to-hub carrier bolts	See Chapter 10	
Main bearing cap:		
E7J, K4J and K4M engines:		
Stage 1	25	18
Stage 2	Angle-tighten through 47° ± 5°	
Oil pump:		
Mounting bolts	25	18
Sprocket bolts	10	7
Oil separator to cylinder head cover	13	10
Roadwheel bolts	90	66
Rocker shaft bolts – oiled	23	17
Strengthening bracket/flywheel cover:		
On engine	50	37
On transmission	25	19
Subframe-to-underbody bolts:		
10 mm bolts	60	44
12 mm bolts	110	81
Sump:		
E7J engine	8	6
K4M and K4J engines:		
Stage 1	8	6
Stage 2	14	10
Timing belt idler pulley bolt	45	33
Timing belt tensioner pulley nut:		
E7J engine	50	37
K4M and K4J engines:		
Pre-tighten	7	5
Final	27	20
Valve adjustment screw locknut	15	11

*** Note:** *There is no requirement to retighten the cylinder head bolts after the engine has first been run.*

1 General information

How to use this Chapter

This Part of Chapter 2 is devoted to in-car repair procedures for the 1.4 and 1.6 litre petrol engines. Similar information covering the other engine types can be found in Parts B and C. All procedures concerning engine removal and refitting, and engine block/cylinder head overhaul can be found in Part D of this Chapter.

Refer to *Vehicle identification numbers* in the Reference Section at the end of this manual for details of engine code locations.

Most of the operations included in this Part are based on the assumption that the engine is still installed in the car. Therefore, if this information is being used during a complete engine overhaul, with the engine already removed, many of the steps included here will not apply.

Engine description

The engine is of four-cylinder, in-line, overhead camshaft type, mounted transversely in the front of the car. A single overhead camshaft is fitted to engine E7J, and double overhead camshafts are fitted to engines K4J and K4M.

The cylinder block is of cast iron. Renewable wet liners are fitted to the E7J engine, while the K4J and K4M engines have conventional dry liners bored directly into the cylinder block. The crankshaft is supported within the cylinder block on five shell-type main bearings. Thrustwashers are fitted at the upper centre main bearing to control crankshaft endfloat.

The connecting rods are attached to the crankshaft by horizontally-split shell-type big-end bearings and to the pistons by gudgeon pins which are an interference-fit in the connecting rods. The aluminium alloy pistons are fitted with three piston rings, comprising two compression rings and a scraper-type oil control ring.

On the E7J engine, the overhead camshaft rotates in five plain bearings machined directly in the aluminium alloy cylinder head and is driven by the crankshaft via a toothed rubber timing belt, which also drives the water pump. The camshaft operates the valves via rocker arms located on a rocker shaft bolted to the top of the cylinder head.

On K4J and K4M engines, the overhead camshafts are each mounted in the cylinder head by six plain bearings with matching caps, and are driven by the crankshaft by a toothed rubber timing belt, which also drives the water pump. The camshafts operate the valves by hydraulic tappets and roller-followers located below the camshafts in the cylinder head.

A fully-enclosed crankcase ventilation system is employed.

Lubrication is by pressure feed from a gear-type oil pump, which is chain-driven direct from the crankshaft.

Repair operations possible with the engine in the vehicle

The following operations can be carried out without having to remove the engine from the car:

a) Removal and refitting of the cylinder head.
b) Removal and refitting of the timing belt and sprockets.
c) Renewal of the camshaft oil seals.
d) Removal and refitting of the camshaft.
e) Removal and refitting of the pressed-steel sump.
f) Removal and refitting of the connecting rods and pistons.*
g) Removal and refitting of the oil pump.
h) Renewal of the crankshaft timing belt end oil seal.
i) Renewal of the engine mountings.

* **Note:** *Although the operation marked with an asterisk can be carried out with the engine in the car after removal of the sump, it is better for the engine to be removed, in the interests of cleanliness and improved access. For this reason, these procedures are described in Part D of this Chapter.*

Caution: If the radio/cassette in your vehicle is equipped with an anti-theft system, make sure you have the correct activation code before disconnecting the battery.

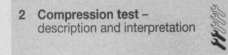

2 Compression test – description and interpretation

Note: *A compression gauge will be required for this test.*

1 A compression check will tell you what mechanical condition the top end (pistons, rings, valves, head gaskets) of the engine is in. Specifically, it can tell you if the compression is down due to leakage caused by worn piston rings, defective valves and seats or a blown head gasket. **Note:** *The engine must be at normal operating temperature and the battery must be fully charged, for this check.*

2 Begin by cleaning the area around the spark plugs before you remove them (compressed air should be used, if available, otherwise a small brush or even a bicycle tyre pump will work). The idea is to prevent dirt from getting into the cylinders as the compression check is being done.

3 Remove all the spark plugs from the engine (see Chapter 1A).

4 Disable the engine management system by removing the engine protection fuse from the engine compartment fusebox.

5 Fit the compression gauge into the No 1 spark plug hole – the type of tester which screws into the plug thread is to be preferred.

6 Have an assistant hold the accelerator pedal fully depressed, while at the same time cranking the engine over several times on the starter motor. Observe the compression gauge – the compression should build-up quickly in a healthy engine. Low compression on the first stroke, followed by gradually-increasing pressure on successive strokes, indicates worn piston rings. A low compression reading on the first stroke, which does not build-up during successive strokes, indicates leaking valves or a blown head gasket (a cracked head could also be the cause). Deposits on the undersides of the valve heads can also cause low compression. Record the highest gauge reading obtained, then repeat the procedure for the remaining cylinders.

7 Add some engine oil (about three squirts from a plunger-type oil can) to each cylinder, through the spark plug hole and repeat the test.

8 If the compression increases after the oil is added, the piston rings are worn. If the compression does not increase significantly, the leakage is occurring at the valves or head gasket. Leakage past the valves may be caused by burned valve seats and/or faces, or warped, cracked or bent valves.

9 If two adjacent cylinders have equally low compression, there is a strong possibility that the head gasket between them is blown. The appearance of coolant in the combustion chambers or the crankcase would verify this condition.

10 Actual compression pressures for the engines covered by this manual are not specified by the manufacturer. However, bearing in mind the information given in the preceding paragraphs, the results obtained should give a good indication of engine condition and what course of action, if any, to take.

3 Top Dead Centre (TDC) for No 1 piston – locating

1 Top Dead Centre (TDC) is the highest point in the cylinder that each piston reaches as the crankshaft turns. Each piston reaches TDC at the end of the compression stroke and again at the end of the exhaust stroke; however, for the purpose of timing the engine, TDC refers to the position of No 1 piston at the end of its compression stroke. No 1 piston is at the flywheel end of the engine.

2 Apply the handbrake, then jack up the front right-hand side of the car and support it on axle stands. Remove the right-hand roadwheel.

3 Remove the plastic liners from within the right-hand wheelarch to give access to the crankshaft pulley bolt.

4 Remove the spark plugs as described in Chapter 1A.

5 Place a finger over the No 1 spark plug hole in the cylinder head (nearest the flywheel) as the spark plugs are deeply recessed (especially the K4J and K4M engines), or alternatively use the handle of a screwdriver. Turn the engine in a clockwise direction, using a socket or spanner on the crankshaft pulley bolt, until pressure is felt in the No 1 cylinder. This indicates that No 1 piston is rising on its compression stroke.

E7J engine

6 Remove the plug from the aperture in the upper timing belt cover. Look through the aperture, and continue to turn the crankshaft until the TDC timing mark on the camshaft sprocket is aligned with the reference mark on the top of the bracket/timing belt cover. If the upper timing belt cover is removed, the reference mark on the camshaft sprocket should be aligned with the reference mark at the top of the cylinder head cover **(see illustrations)**. **Note:** *The camshaft sprocket has five reference marks. Only the rectangular reference mark on one of the teeth represents TDC. The other semi-circular marks are used to adjust the valve clearances. Due to parallax, it is tricky to see whether the reference marks are aligned when the timing belt cover is fitted. Provided that the crankshaft sprocket timing mark is aligned with the mark on the oil pump flange, and the camshaft sprocket reference mark is visible through the hole in the engine mounting bracket/timing belt cover, No 1 piston is at TDC.*

7 If the crankshaft pulley is now removed (see Sections 5), the timing mark on the crankshaft sprocket should be aligned with the TDC mark

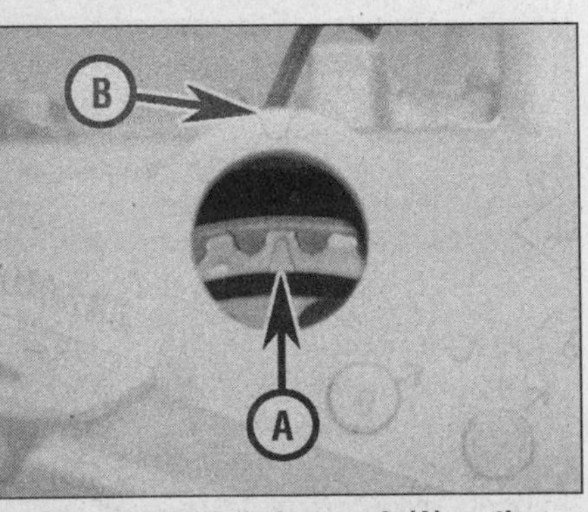

3.6a The TDC timing mark (A) on the camshaft sprocket should align with the reference mark (B) on the top of the lower engine mounting bracket/upper timing belt cover . . .

3.6b . . . or the reference mark (C) at the top of the valve cover

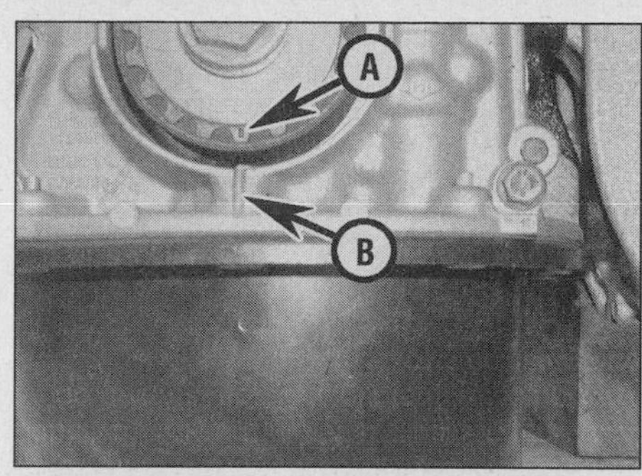

3.7 The timing mark (A) on the crankshaft sprocket should be aligned with the timing mark (B) on the oil pump flange

at the bottom of the oil pump flange **(see illustration)**.

K4M and K4J engines

Note: *A TDC pin from a Renault dealer is required for this operation.*

8 Remove the air cleaner and resonator from the left-hand side of the engine with reference to Chapter 4A.

9 Using a screwdriver, pierce the centres of the two plastic plugs at the left-hand end of the cylinder head, and pull out the plugs **(see illustration)**. With No 1 piston approaching TDC, the grooves in the ends of the camshafts should be positioned approximately at 30° angle from the horizontal, with the offset below the centreline **(see illustration 5.18)**.

10 Unscrew the TDC plug from the left-hand front of the cylinder block, then fully screw in the TDC pin. **Note:** *If the pin is not available, an alternative method of determining the TDC position is to use a dial gauge on the top of piston No 1 after removing the spark plug.*

11 Carefully turn the crankshaft clockwise until the crankshaft web is in contact with the TDC pin. At this point, the No 1 piston is at TDC on its compression stroke, and the grooves in the ends of the camshafts will now be positioned horizontally. Renault technicians use a special tool to lock the camshafts in their TDC position. The tool is attached to the left-hand end of the cylinder head to hold the camshafts with their grooves horizontal, and a similar tool may be fabricated from metal plate if necessary.

3.9 Using a screwdriver, prise the camshaft sealing plugs from the left-hand end of the cylinder head

12 Note that the crankshaft sprocket is not keyed to the crankshaft as is the normal arrangement, therefore if the crankshaft pulley is removed it is important to have an accurate method of determining the TDC position of No 1 piston.

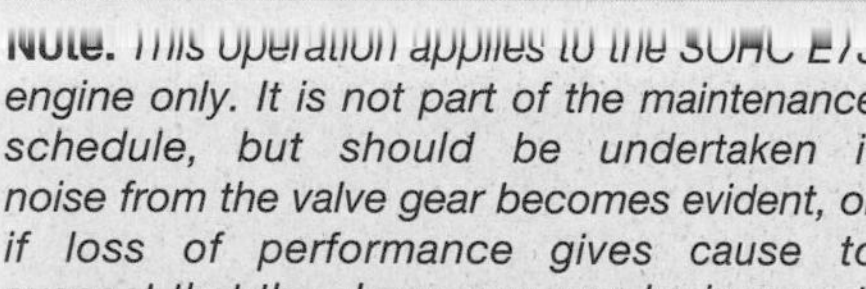

4 Valve clearances – checking and adjustment

Note: *This operation applies to the SOHC E7J engine only. It is not part of the maintenance schedule, but should be undertaken if noise from the valve gear becomes evident, or if loss of performance gives cause to suspect that the clearances may be incorrect. A new cylinder head cover gasket will be required.*

1 Remove the air cleaner assembly with reference to Chapter 4A, then, where applicable disconnect the accelerator cable from the throttle housing. If necessary, unbolt the accelerator cable support from the cylinder head cover.

2 Disconnect the crankcase ventilation hoses from the cylinder head cover **(see illustrations)**.

3 Unscrew the bolts and remove the cylinder head cover and gasket **(see illustrations)**.

4 Remove the spark plugs (Chapter 1A) to make turning the engine easier.

5 Draw the valve positions on a piece of paper, numbering them 1 to 4 inlet and exhaust according to their cylinders, from the flywheel/driveplate end of the engine (ie, 1E, 1I, 2E, 2I and so on). The inlet valves are on the inlet manifold side of the cylinder head and the exhaust valves are on the exhaust manifold side. As the valve clearances are adjusted, cross them off.

6 There are three methods of adjusting the valve clearances:

Method 1

7 Turn the crankshaft to bring No 1 piston to TDC on compression, as described in Section 3. Continue to turn the crankshaft until the first of the valve clearance adjustment marks (semi-circular marks) on the camshaft sprocket is aligned with the reference mark on the engine upper timing belt cover, or the

2A

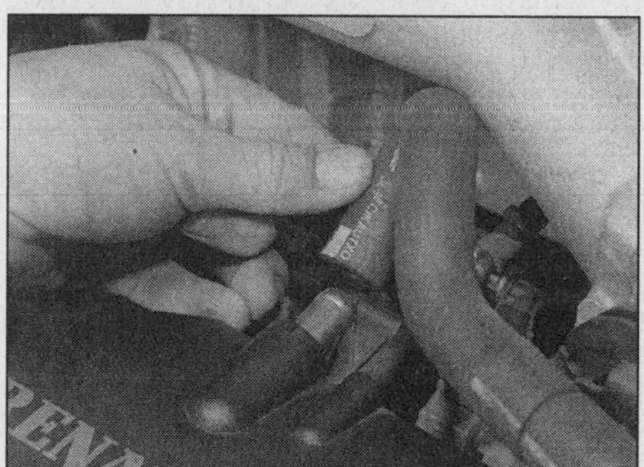

4.2a Disconnecting the large (to air cleaner) . . .

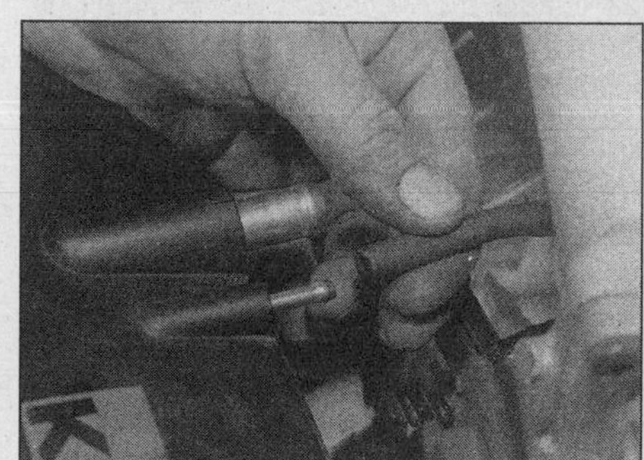

4.2b . . . and small (to inlet manifold) crankcase ventilation hoses from the cylinder head cover

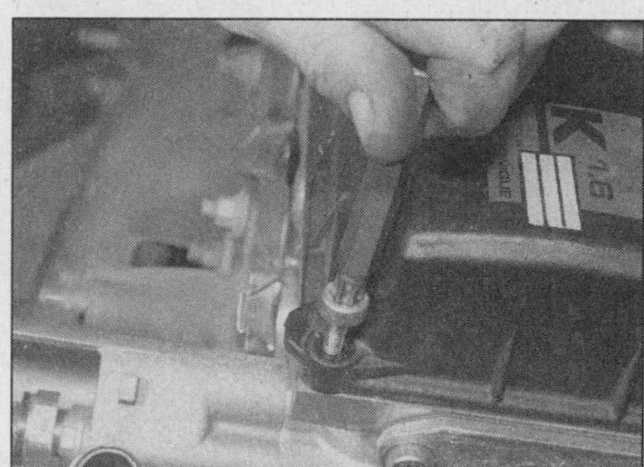

4.3a Removing the cylinder head cover bolts

4.3b Removing the cylinder head cover . . .

4.3c . . . and gasket

cylinder head cover, as applicable (if necessary, temporarily refit the cylinder head cover to check this) **(see illustration)**.

8 Insert a feeler blade of the correct thickness (see Specifications) between the No 1 cylinder exhaust valve stem and the end of the rocker arm. It should be a firm sliding fit. If adjustment is necessary, loosen the locknut on the rocker arm using a ring spanner, and turn the adjustment screw until the fit is correct **(see illustrations)**. Hold the adjustment screw, tighten the locknut and recheck the adjustment. Repeat the adjustment procedure on No 3 cylinder exhaust valve.

9 Turn the engine in a clockwise direction until the second valve clearance adjustment mark on the camshaft sprocket is aligned with the reference mark on the top of the timing belt cover or cylinder head cover (as applicable) **(see illustration 4.7)**. Adjust the valve clearances on No 1 inlet and No 3 inlet valves. Note that the valve clearances for the inlet and exhaust valves are different. Continue to adjust the valve clearances in the following sequence.

Valve clearance mark in alignment	Valves to adjust
First	No 1 exhaust and No 3 exhaust
Second	No 1 inlet and No 3 inlet
Third	No 2 exhaust and No 4 exhaust
Fourth	No 2 inlet and No 4 inlet

10 Remove the socket or spanner from the crankshaft pulley bolt.

11 Refit the spark plugs, with reference to Chapter 1A.

12 Refit the cylinder head cover using a new gasket, and tighten the securing bolts to the specified torque in a spiral sequence (working from the centre outwards).

13 Reconnect the crankcase ventilation hoses, HT leads and air cleaner assembly.

Method 2

14 Turn the crankshaft in a clockwise direction until No 1 exhaust valve is completely open (ie, the valve spring is completely compressed).

15 Insert a feeler blade of the correct thickness (see Specifications) between the No 3 cylinder inlet valve stem and the end of the rocker arm. It should be a firm sliding fit. If adjustment is necessary, loosen the locknut on the rocker arm

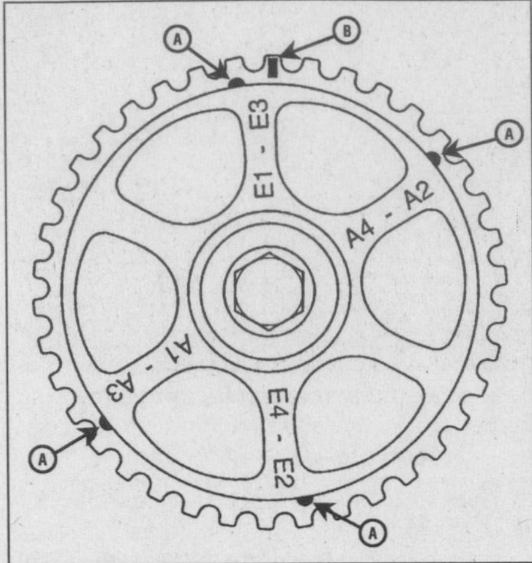

4.7 The first of the valve clearance adjustment marks (A), marked E1-E3 on the camshaft sprocket spoke, should be aligned with the reference mark (B) on the valve cover (temporarily refit the valve cover)

using a ring spanner, and turn the adjustment screw until the fit is correct. Tighten the locknut and recheck the adjustment, then repeat the adjustment procedure on No 4 cylinder exhaust valve. Note that the clearances for the inlet and exhaust valves are different.

16 Turn the engine in a clockwise direction until No 3 exhaust valve is completely open, then adjust the valve clearances on No 4 inlet and No 2 exhaust valves. Continue to adjust the valve clearances in the following sequence.

Exhaust valve fully open	Inlet valve to adjust	Exhaust valve to adjust
1	3	4
3	4	2
4	2	1
2	1	3

17 Remove the socket or spanner from the crankshaft pulley bolt.

18 Refit the spark plugs, with reference to Chapter 1A.

19 Refit the cylinder head cover using a new gasket, and tighten the securing bolts to the specified torque in a spiral sequence (working from the centre outwards).

20 Reconnect the crankcase ventilation hoses, HT leads and air cleaner assembly.

Method 3

21 Turn the crankshaft in a clockwise direction until the valves for cylinder No 1 are rocking. The exhaust valve must be just closing and the inlet valve must be just opening. If necessary, turn the crankshaft backwards and forwards to confirm the correct position.

22 Insert a feeler blade of the correct thickness (see Specifications) between the No 4 cylinder inlet valve stem and the end of the rocker arm. It should be a firm sliding fit. If adjustment is necessary, loosen the locknut on the rocker arm using a ring spanner, and turn the adjustment screw until the fit is correct. Tighten the locknut and recheck the adjustment, then repeat the adjustment procedure on No 4 exhaust valve. Note that the clearances for the inlet and exhaust valves are different.

23 Turn the engine in a clockwise direction until No 3 valves are rocking, then adjust the valve clearances on Nos 2 inlet and exhaust valves. Continue to adjust the valve clearances in the following sequence.

Exhaust valves rocking	Adjust valves
1	4
3	2
4	1
2	3

24 Remove the socket or spanner from the crankshaft pulley bolt.

25 Refit the spark plugs, with reference to Chapter 1A.

26 Refit the cylinder head cover using a new gasket, and tighten the securing bolts to the specified torque in a spiral sequence (working from the centre outwards).

27 Reconnect the crankcase ventilation hoses, HT leads and air cleaner assembly.

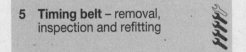

5 Timing belt – removal, inspection and refitting

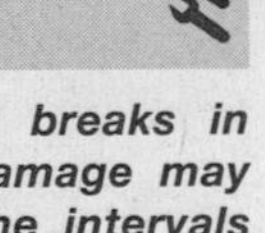

Caution: If the timing belt breaks in service, extensive engine damage may result. Renew the belt at the intervals specified in Chapter 1A, or earlier if its condition is at all doubtful.

4.8a Loosening the rocker arm adjustment locknut

4.8b Turning the adjustment screw to alter the valve clearance

4.8c Tightening the adjustment locknut with a torque wrench

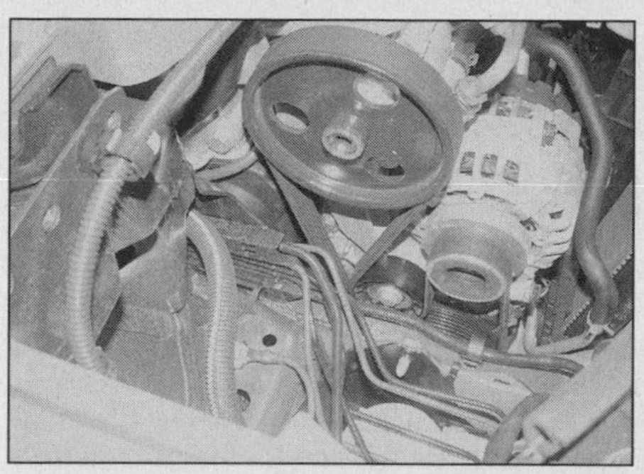
5.4 Alternator and power steering pump drivebelt

5.8a Loosening the crankshaft pulley bolt

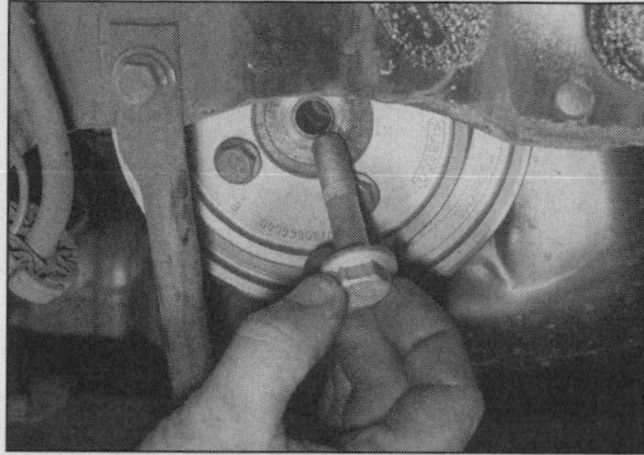
5.8b Removing the crankshaft pulley bolt

Removal

1 Disconnect the battery negative lead (refer to *Disconnecting the battery*).

2 Apply the handbrake, then jack up the front right-hand side of the vehicle and support on axle stands (see *Jacking and vehicle support*). Remove the right-hand roadwheel. Where fitted, remove the engine compartment undertray.

3 Remove the right-hand wheelarch liners, after pulling out the plastic retainers and removing the screws.

4 Remove the alternator and power steering pump drivebelt(s) as applicable as described in Chapter 1A **(see illustration)**.

5 Set the engine at TDC for No 1 piston as described in Section 3.

6 Carefully, position a trolley jack and a large block of wood under the sump to support the engine. Raise the jack to just take the weight of the engine.

E7J engine

7 On manual transmission models, to prevent the crankshaft from rotating while the pulley bolt is unscrewed, have an assistant engage 4th gear and depress firmly the brake pedal. Alternatively, and on automatic transmission models, the crankshaft may be held stationary by unbolting the crankshaft speed/position sensor from the top of the transmission and wedging a screwdriver in the starter ring gear teeth through the sensor's opening in the bellhousing.

5.8c Removing the crankshaft pulley

5.9a Timing cover lower mounting nut

8 Unscrew the crankshaft pulley bolt, then remove the pulley together with the hub, noting the key on the end of the crankshaft **(see illustrations)**. **Note:** *The bolt is very tight.* Alternatively, the pulley may be unbolted from the hub first, then the hub bolt unscrewed.

9 Unbolt and remove the timing belt covers **(see illustrations)**.

10 Check that the TDC mark on the camshaft sprocket is pointing upwards and in line with the mark on the cylinder head cover. On some models there is also an alignment mark on the crankshaft timing belt end oil seal housing which must line up with the timing mark in the 6 o'clock position, opposite to the keyway, on the crankshaft sprocket – on later models, mark the housing as an aid to refitting **(see illustration)**.

11 Loosen the nut on the timing belt tensioner, turn the tensioner pulley clockwise to release the tension, then temporarily tighten the nut to hold the pulley away from the timing belt.

12 Check if the belt is marked with arrows to indicate its running direction, and mark it if necessary. Release the belt from the camshaft, water pump and crankshaft sprockets and remove it from the engine. If the belt is to be re-used,

5.9b Removing the timing cover

5.10 Mark the oil seal housing in line with the crankshaft sprocket timing mark

5.12a The arrows on the timing belt show its running direction

5.12b Removing the timing belt from the camshaft sprocket

5.18 Turn the crankshaft until the slots in the camshafts are initially positioned at approximately a 30° angle from the horizontal, with the offsets below the centreline

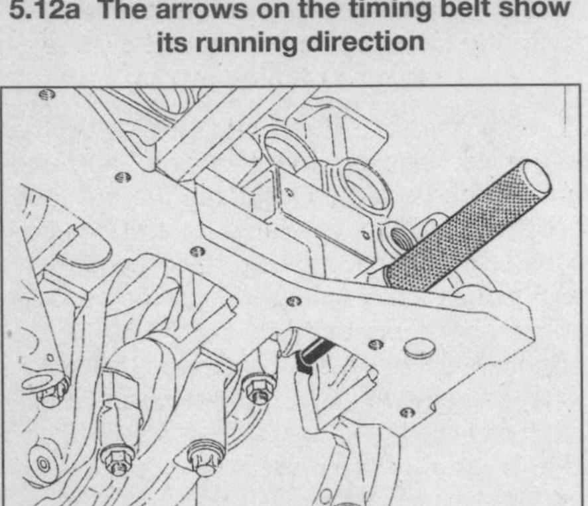

5.19 TDC pin on the left-hand front of the cylinder block

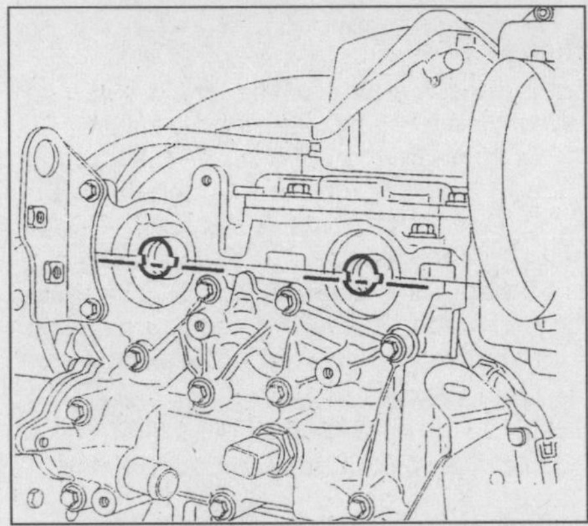

5.20a With the crankshaft at TDC the grooves in the end of the camshafts will be positioned horizontally

be careful not to kink or otherwise damage it **(see illustrations)**.

13 Clean the sprockets and tensioner and wipe them dry. Also clean the cylinder head and block behind the timing belt running area.

K4M and K4J engines

Note: *A Renault TDC pin is required for this operation.*

14 Remove the right-hand upper engine mounting bracket from the engine and body with reference to Section 14.

15 Remove the wiring loom from the right-hand end of the engine by disconnecting it over the inlet manifold and unbolting the support bracket at the right-hand front of the cylinder head. Also disconnect the vacuum pipe from the inlet manifold. Unclip the loom from the upper timing cover and position it to one side.

16 Unclip the fuel pipes from the lower timing cover.

17 Remove the air cleaner and resonator as described in Chapter 4A.

18 Using a screwdriver, pierce the centres of the two plastic plugs at the left-hand end of the camshafts, and pull the plugs from the cylinder head. With No 1 piston approaching TDC, the grooves in the ends of the camshafts should be as shown **(see illustration).**

19 Unscrew the TDC plug from the left-hand front of the cylinder block, then fully screw in the TDC pin **(see illustration)**. **Note:** *If the pin is not available, an alternative method of determining the TDC position is to use a dial gauge on the top of piston No 1 after removing the spark plug.*

20 Carefully turn the crankshaft clockwise until the crankshaft web is in contact with the TDC pin. At this point, the No 1 piston is at TDC on its compression stroke, and the grooves in the ends of the camshafts will now be positioned horizontally. Renault technicians use a special tool to lock the camshafts in their TDC position, however, a length of metal bar may be fabricated **(see illustrations and Tool Tip)**.

21 Before loosening the crankshaft pulley bolt, note that the crankshaft sprocket is **not** keyed to the crankshaft as is the normal arrangement, therefore if the crankshaft pulley is removed it is important to have an accurate method of

5.20b Engage the camshaft holding tool with the camshaft slots . . .

5.20c . . . and secure the tool using a suitable bolt screwed into the cylinder head

TOOL TIP

To make a camshaft holding tool, obtain a length of steel strip and cut it to length so that it will fit across the rear of the cylinder head. Obtain a second length of steel strip of suitable thickness to fit snugly in the slots in the camshafts. Cut the second strip into two lengths and drill accordingly so that they can be bolted to the first strip in the correct position to engage with the camshaft slots. Secure a suitably drilled small piece of steel angle to the first strip so that the tool can be bolted to the threaded hole in the cylinder head upper section.

5.29a Align the timing band on the inside of the belt with the crankshaft sprocket timing mark

5.29b The timing belt is also marked on its outside surface

5.29c Align the timing belt upper band with the camshaft sprocket and cylinder head cover timing marks

determining the TDC position of No 1 piston (refer to paragraph 19). Although the sprocket is not keyed to the crankshaft, there is still a groove in the crankshaft nose which is at the 12 o'clock position when piston No 1 is at TDC. To prevent the crankshaft from rotating while the pulley bolt is unscrewed, first remove the metal bar from the camshafts, then have an assistant engage top gear and depress firmly the brake pedal. Alternatively, and on automatic transmission models, the crankshaft may be held stationary by unbolting the crankshaft speed/position sensor from the top of the transmission and wedging a screwdriver in the starter ring gear teeth through the sensor's opening in the bellhousing. Unscrew the crankshaft pulley bolt, then remove the pulley/hub. **Note:** *The bolt is very tight*. The bolt may be re-used if its length from under the head to its end does not exceed 49.1 mm. If the length is greater than this, renew the bolt.

22 Unbolt the lower timing cover followed by the upper timing cover.

23 Loosen the nut on the timing belt tensioner, then turn the tensioner hub anti-clockwise to release the tension.

24 Check if the belt is marked with arrows to indicate its running direction, and if it is to be re-used, mark it to ensure correct refitting. Release the belt from the camshaft sprockets, water pump sprocket, crankshaft sprocket, tensioner pulley and idler pulley and remove it from the engine.

25 Clean the sprockets, tensioner and idler and wipe them dry. Also clean the cylinder head and block behind the timing belt running area.

Inspection

Note: *Renault state that the timing belt must be renewed whenever it is removed.*

26 Examine the timing belt carefully for any signs of cracking, fraying or general wear, particularly at the roots of the teeth. Renew the belt if there is any sign of deterioration of this nature, or if there is any oil or grease contamination. Renew any leaking oil seals. The belt **must** be renewed if it has completed the mileage given in Chapter 1A.

27 Renault state that the tensioner and idler pulley must also be renewed whenever the timing belt is renewed.

28 Thoroughly clean the nose of the crankshaft and the bore of the crankshaft sprocket, and also the contact surfaces of the sprocket and pulley. This is necessary to prevent the possibility of the sprocket slipping in use.

Refitting

E7J engine

29 Check the directional mark (arrows) and timing bands on the new timing belt. Fit the belt on the crankshaft sprocket so that one of the timing bands is aligned with the marks on the sprocket (in the 6 o'clock position, opposite to the keyway) and on the oil seal housing. The other timing band should be positioned so that it will locate on the camshaft sprocket in alignment with that sprocket's, and with the cylinder head cover's, timing marks. Having engaged the belt on the crankshaft sprocket, pull it taut over the water pump sprocket and onto the camshaft sprocket, then position it over the tensioner pulley **(see illustrations)**.

30 With the belt fully engaged with the sprockets, slacken the tensioner nut and tension the belt, then retighten the nut **(see illustration)**. The tensioner is not spring-loaded, so it will have to be rotated manually to tension the belt. A screwdriver can be used as a lever between bolts in the holes in the tensioner hub, or use a two-pronged tool which engages in the holes in the tensioner. Check that the timing marks are still aligned correctly.

31 The belt tension must now be checked – this can be set or checked accurately only by using the Renault tool Mot. 1273 (SEEM C. Tronic 105.6). If this equipment is not available, set the belt's tension as carefully as possible using the method outlined below, then take the vehicle to a Renault dealer as soon as possible for the tension to be checked by qualified personnel using the special equipment. Do not take the vehicle on any long journeys or rev the engine to high speeds until the timing belt's tension has been checked and is known to be correct.

Timing belt tension may be judged to be approximately correct when the belt can be twisted 90° with moderate pressure between the finger and thumb, checking midway between the pulleys on the belt's longest run.

32 If the adjustment is incorrect, the tensioner will have to be repositioned. The tensioner nut must be tightened to the specified torque wrench setting, since if it were to come loose, considerable engine damage would result.

33 Refit the crankshaft pulley and its bolt. Using a socket on the pulley bolt, turn the engine through two complete revolutions in its normal direction, then recheck the timing belt tension and make sure that the timing marks are still in alignment. Tighten the crankshaft pulley bolt to the specified torque (and angle) while the assistant holds the crankshaft stationary as described earlier in this Section **(see illustration)**.

34 Refit the timing belt covers, and tighten the retaining bolts securely.

5.30 It is important that the tensioner nut is tightened with a torque wrench

5.33 Angle-tightening the crankshaft pulley bolt

2A

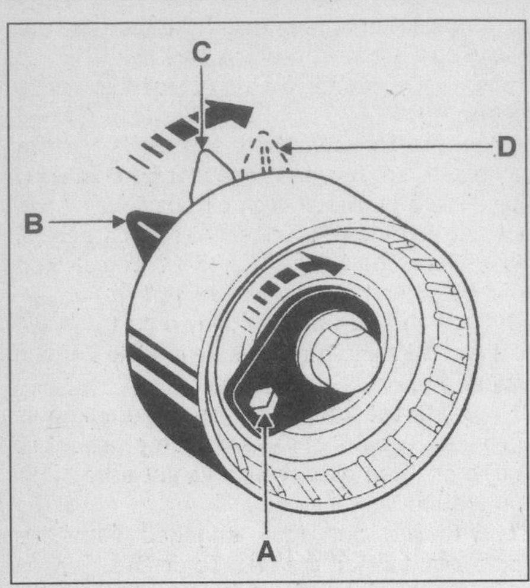

5.41 Timing belt tensioner pulley details

A Slot for Allen key in tensioner arm
B Position of moving index pointer in the 'at rest' position
C Fixed index pointer
D Moving index pointer positioned 7.0 to 8.0 mm to the right of the fixed index pointer

35 Refit the alternator drivebelt followed by the power-assisted steering drivebelt and tension them as described in Chapter 1A.
36 Refit the right-hand wheelarch liners, and engine compartment undertray, then refit the roadwheel and lower the vehicle to the ground.
37 Reconnect the battery negative lead.

K4M and K4J engines

38 Check that the lug on the rear of the tensioner is correctly located in the groove.
39 Check that the camshafts and No 1 piston are still at TDC. Fit the timing belt on the crankshaft sprocket, then locate it around the water pump sprocket and idler, over the camshafts and around the tensioner. Make sure that the belt is taut between the camshaft sprockets, and the correct way round if refitting the original.

5.48 Fitting new plastic plugs to the cylinder head using a large socket

40 Check that the idler retaining bolt is tightened to the specified torque.
41 With the belt fully engaged with the sprockets, slacken the tensioner nut and tension the belt. To do this, use an Allen key to turn the index finger on the tensioner 7.0 to 8.0 mm to the right of the static index, then retighten the nut to the specified torque **(see illustration)**. Check that the camshafts and crankshaft are still at TDC.
42 Refit the crankshaft pulley and tighten the bolt to the specified torque and angle.
43 Remove the locking tool from the camshafts and the TDC pin from the cylinder block. Turn the crankshaft clockwise two complete turns, then reset the piston to TDC as described earlier.
44 Remove the locking tool and TDC pin, then unscrew the tensioner bolt by one turn only. Using the Allen key, align the index finger with the static index. Tighten the tensioner bolt to the specified torque.
45 Turn the crankshaft two complete turns and recheck the TDC position and tensioner index setting.
46 Refit the upper timing cover and lower timing cover, and tighten the bolts.
47 Refit the TDC plug to the cylinder block and tighten securely.
48 Fit two new plastic plugs in the cylinder head on the left-hand end of the camshafts. Renault technicians use special tools to drive the plugs into position, however suitable sockets or blocks of wood may be used instead **(see illustration)**.
49 Refit the air cleaner and resonator with reference to Chapter 4A.
50 Clip the fuel pipes to the lower timing cover.
51 Reconnect the vacuum pipe to the inlet manifold and attach the wiring loom to the upper timing cover. Refit the support bracket and tighten the bolts, reconnect the wiring and attach it to the support.
52 Refit the right-hand upper engine mounting bracket to the engine and body with reference to Section 14. Lower the jack and block of wood from the sump.
53 Refit the alternator drivebelt followed by the power-assisted steering drivebelt and tension them as described in Chapter 1A.
54 Refit the right-hand wheelarch liners, and engine compartment undertray, then refit the roadwheel and lower the vehicle to the ground.
55 Reconnect the battery negative lead.

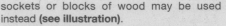

6 Timing belt sprockets and tensioner – removal, inspection and refitting

Removal

E7J engine

1 Remove the timing belt as described in Section 5.
2 To remove the camshaft sprocket, hold the sprocket stationary using a home-made tool fabricated from two metal bars with one bolt and nut as a pivot and with two bolts at its tips inserted into the holes in the pulley, then unscrew the bolt. The Renault tool is also shown **(see illustrations)**.
3 Remove the sprocket from the end of the camshaft. Note that it has a tab on its inner face which locates in a slot in the end of the camshaft.
4 A puller may be necessary to remove the crankshaft sprocket if it is tight **(see Tool tip)**. Note that the key is incorporated in the

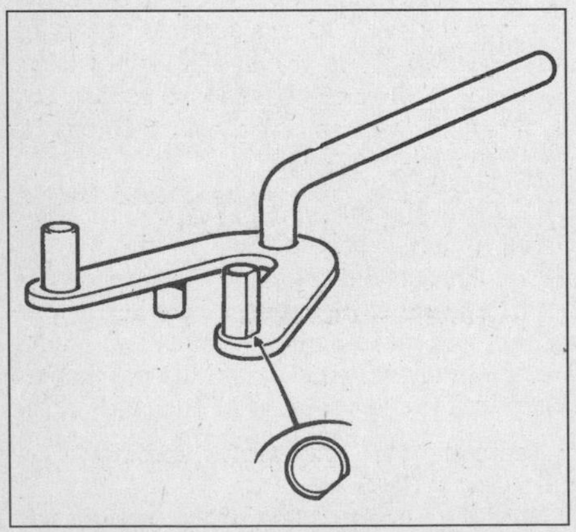

6.2a Tools for holding the camshaft sprocket – Renault tool Mot. 799-01 . . .

6.2b . . . and a home-made equivalent

6.2c Removing the camshaft sprocket bolt

It is easy to make up a puller for the crankshaft sprocket using two bolts, a metal bar and the existing crankshaft pulley bolt. By unscrewing the crankshaft pulley bolt against the bar, the sprocket is drawn off the crankshaft.

sprocket and is not separate **(see illustration)**.

5 Unscrew the nut and withdraw the washer and tensioner pulley from the stud on the crankshaft timing belt end oil seal housing **(see illustrations)**.

K4M and K4J engines

Caution: The timing belt sprockets are not keyed to the camshafts, neither is the crankshaft sprocket keyed to the crankshaft. Before starting work, make sure that you have the necessary tooling to accurately set the camshafts and crankshaft to TDC.

6 Remove the timing belt as described in Section 5.

7 Slide the crankshaft sprocket from the nose of the crankshaft, noting which way round it is fitted.

8 Use a suitable tool to hold each camshaft sprocket stationary while the retaining nuts are loosened, then unscrew and remove the nuts and withdraw the sprockets from the camshafts.

9 To remove the tensioner, unscrew the centre nut and withdraw the unit from the stud on the water pump. Note the groove in the water pump cover for the tensioner lug.

10 To remove the idler, unscrew the centre bolt and withdraw it from the cylinder head.

6.4 Removing the crankshaft sprocket

Inspection

11 Inspect the teeth of the sprockets for signs of nicks and damage. Also examine the water pump sprocket teeth. The teeth are not prone to wear and should normally last the life of the engine.

12 Spin the tensioner pulley by hand and check it for any roughness or tightness. Do not attempt to clean it with solvent, as this may enter the bearing. If wear is evident, renew the tensioner. **Note:** *Renault state that the tensioner and idler pulley must be renewed whenever the timing belt is renewed.*

Refitting

E7J engine

13 Locate the tensioner on the stud on the oil seal housing, then refit the nut and washer and tighten it finger-tight at this stage.

14 Slide the sprocket fully onto the crankshaft engaging the key with the groove in the crankshaft. Use a metal tube if necessary to tap it into position.

15 Locate the sprocket on the end of the camshaft, making sure that the tab locates in the special slot, then screw in the bolt. Tighten the bolt to the specified torque, holding the sprocket stationary using the method described in paragraph 2.

16 Fit a new timing belt as described in Section 5.

K4M and K4J engines

17 Locate the idler on the cylinder head, then insert the bolt and tighten to the specified torque.

18 Locate the tensioner on the stud on the water pump cover, making sure that the lug engages the groove. Fit the nut loosely at this stage.

19 Locate the camshaft sprockets on the camshafts so that the Renault logo engraved spokes are at the 12 o'clock position. Fit the pulley retaining nuts loosely at this stage. A clearance of between 0.5 and 1.0 mm should exist between the nuts and the pulleys.

20 Slide the crankshaft pulley onto the nose of the crankshaft, making sure it is the correct way round.

21 Locate the timing belt on the crankshaft sprocket, around the water pump sprocket and idler, then over the camshaft sprockets and around the tensioner.

22 With the belt fully engaged with the sprockets, tension the belt. To do this, use an Allen key to turn the index finger on the tensioner 7.0 to 8.0 mm to the right of the static index, then tighten the nut to the specified torque.

23 Refit the crankshaft pulley and tighten the bolt to the specified torque.

24 Check that the crankshaft is at TDC with the crank web touching the TDC pin. Check that the camshafts are both at TDC with the TDC tool in position on the left-hand end of the cylinder head.

25 The camshaft sprockets must now be held stationary while the retaining nuts are tightened in the specified stages. Renault technicians use a metal plate bolted to the cylinder head which clamps the two sprockets stationary, however, the tool used to hold the sprockets on removal can be used provided care is taken not to move the camshafts or crankshaft during the tightening procedure.

26 Remove the locking tool from the camshafts and the TDC pin from the cylinder block. Turn the crankshaft clockwise two complete turns, then reset the piston to TDC as described earlier.

27 Remove the locking tool and TDC pin, then unscrew the tensioner bolt by one turn only. Using the Allen key, align the index finger with the static index. Tighten the tensioner bolt to the specified torque.

28 Turn the crankshaft two complete turns and recheck the TDC position and tensioner index setting. If the camshafts do not align correctly, it will be necessary to loosen the camshaft sprocket retaining nuts, then repeat the tensioning procedure.

29 The remaining procedure is described in Section 5 for the timing belt refitting.

6.5a Unscrew the nut and withdraw the washer . . .

6.5b . . . then remove the tensioner pulley

7 Camshaft oil seals – renewal

1 Remove the camshaft sprocket as described in Section 6.

2 Note the fitted position of the old oil seal. Using a small screwdriver, prise out the oil seal from the cylinder head.

2A

3 Wipe clean the seating in the cylinder head.
4 Smear a little oil on the outer perimeter and sealing lip of the new oil seal. Locate the seal squarely in the cylinder head. Drive the seal into position using a metal tube or socket which has an external diameter slightly less than that of the bore in the cylinder head **(see illustrations)**. Make sure that the oil seal is the correct way round, with the lip facing inwards.
5 Refit the camshaft sprocket as described in Section 6.

7.4a Smear a little grease on the oil seal . . .

7.4b . . . before driving it into the cylinder head with a suitable socket

8 Camshaft(s) and rocker components – removal, inspection and refitting

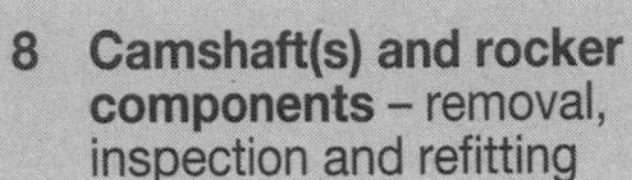

E7J engine

Removal

1 Remove the cylinder head as described in Section 9 and place it on the workbench.
2 Progressively unscrew the bolts holding the rocker shaft and retaining plate to the cylinder head and withdraw the shaft **(see illustrations)**.
3 Hold the camshaft stationary using a spanner on the special flats provided on the camshaft, or with a suitable tool inserted through the sprocket holes, then unscrew the bolt and withdraw the sprocket.
4 Using a Torx key, unscrew the two bolts and remove the distributor. There is no need to mark the distributor, as it is not possible to adjust its position; although there is an elongated slot for one of the bolts, the other bolt locates in a single hole.
5 Using a dial gauge, measure the endfloat of the camshaft and compare with that given in the Specifications. This will give an indication of the amount of wear in the thrustplate.
6 Unscrew the two bolts and lift the thrustplate out of the slot in the camshaft **(see illustrations)**.
7 Withdraw the camshaft from the sprocket end of the cylinder head, taking care not to damage the bearing surfaces **(see illustration)**.

Inspection

8 Examine the camshaft bearing surfaces and cam lobes for wear ridges and scoring. Also examine the rocker shaft for wear. If necessary, the rocker shaft may be dismantled for inspection **(see illustration)**. Renew worn components as necessary.
9 Examine the condition of the bearing surfaces both on the camshaft and in the cylinder head. If the head bearing surfaces are worn excessively, a new cylinder head will be required.

Refitting

10 Lubricate the bearing surfaces in the cylinder head and the camshaft journals, then insert the camshaft into the head.
11 Refit the thrustplate, then insert and tighten the bolts.
12 Measure the endfloat as described in paragraph 6 and make sure that it is within the limits given in the Specifications. Excessive endfloat can only be due to wear of the thrustplate or the camshaft.

8.2a Unscrew the bolts . . .

8.2b . . . then withdraw the rocker shaft

8.6a Unscrew the two bolts . . .

8.6b . . . and withdraw the thrustplate from the slot in the camshaft

8.7 Removing the camshaft

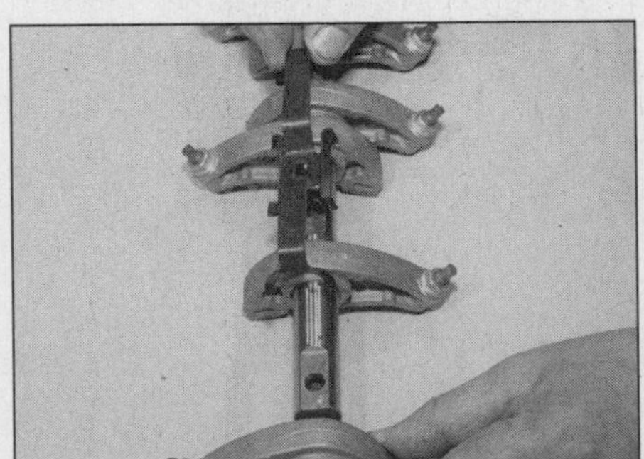
8.8 If necessary, the rockers may be removed from their shaft, but keep all the components in order

8.15 Tightening the rocker shaft mounting bolts

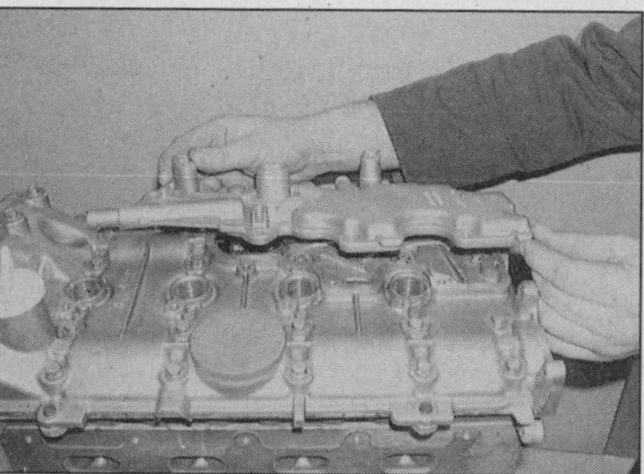

8.31 Undo the eight bolts and remove the oil separator housing

8.32 Removing the valve cover/bearing cap from the cylinder head

13 Refit the distributor and tighten the two bolts using a Torx key.

14 Renew the oil seal (Section 7) then refit the camshaft sprocket, making sure that the tab engages with the cut-out in the end of the camshaft. Hold the camshaft stationary with a spanner on the special flats, then insert the bolt and tighten it to the specified torque.

15 Refit the rocker shaft and retaining plate, then insert the bolts in their original positions and tighten them to the specified torque **(see illustration)**. Note that the bolt threads and head contact surfaces must be oiled before inserting them. The hollow bolts are located at each end and in the middle.

16 Refit the cylinder head (see Section 9).

K4M and K4J engines

Removal

17 Disconnect the battery negative (earth) lead and position it away from the terminal.

18 Remove the timing belt as described in Section 5.

19 Remove the camshaft sprockets as described in Section 6.

20 Disconnect the accelerator cable from the throttle housing with reference to Chapter 4A, Section 14.

21 Disconnect the fuel supply and return hoses from the fuel rail with reference to Chapter 4A.

22 Remove the injector gallery protector, then disconnect the wiring from the injectors and coils and position it to one side.

23 Unbolt the inlet air duct unit, then remove the cooling system expansion bottle and position it to one side.

24 Unbolt the catalytic converter mountings and remove it from the exhaust manifold.

25 Remove the throttle body as described in Chapter 4A.

26 Disconnect the wiring from the lambda (oxygen) sensor.

27 Unbolt and remove the exhaust manifold support strut and the engine lifting eye.

28 Disconnect the brake vacuum pipe from the inlet manifold.

29 Unbolt and remove the inlet manifold.

30 Remove the ignition coils as described in Chapter 5B.

31 Unbolt and remove the oil separator unit **(see illustration)**

32 Progressively unscrew the cylinder head cover/bearing cap retaining bolts, then release the cover by using a copper mallet to tap the lugs at each rear corner and using a screwdriver to lever up the lugs on the front of the cover. Once the cover is free, lift it squarely from the cylinder head **(see illustration)**. The camshafts will rise up slightly under the pressure of the valve springs – be careful they don't tilt and jam. Remove the cover/bearing cap.

33 Identify each camshaft for location and TDC position, then carefully lift them from the cylinder head. The inlet camshaft should have the marking AM on it and the exhaust should have the marking EM. If these are not visible, identify the camshafts with dabs of paint. Remove the oil seals from the camshafts, noting their fitted positions.

34 Obtain a box with 16 compartments and mark the valve positions clearly on it. Remove each rocker arm and place it in its compartment for safe keeping **(see illustration)**.

35 Obtain a metal box with 16 compartments identified with the valve positions, and fill it with fresh engine oil. Carefully remove the hydraulic tappets from the cylinder head and place them in their correct compartments, making sure that they are completely immersed in the oil **(see illustration)**.

Inspection

36 Inspect the cam lobes and the camshaft bearing journals for scoring or other visible evidence of wear.

37 If the camshafts appear satisfactory, measure the bearing journal diameters and compare the figures obtained with those given in the Specifications. If the diameters are not as specified, consult a Renault dealer or engine overhaul specialist. Wear of the camshaft bearings will almost certainly be accompanied by similar wear of the bearings in the cylinder head, which will entail renewal of the cylinder head upper and lower sections together with the camshafts.

38 Inspect the rocker arms and hydraulic tappets for scuffing, cracking or other damage and renew any components as necessary. Also check the condition of the tappet bores in the cylinder head. As with the camshafts, any wear in this area will necessitate cylinder head renewal.

Refitting

39 Clean the sealant from the mating surfaces of the cylinder head cover/bearing cap and cylinder head.

40 To prevent any possibility of the valves contacting the pistons when the camshafts are refitted, remove the TDC pin or dowel rod used to lock the crankshaft, and turn the crankshaft clockwise a quarter turn.

41 Lubricate the tappet bores in the cylinder head with clean engine oil.

42 If the hydraulic tappets have not been kept immersed in oil, the oil will drain from them and they will need to be re-primed before refitting. To check whether they require re-priming, depress the top of the tappet with a thumb – if the piston goes down, the tappet

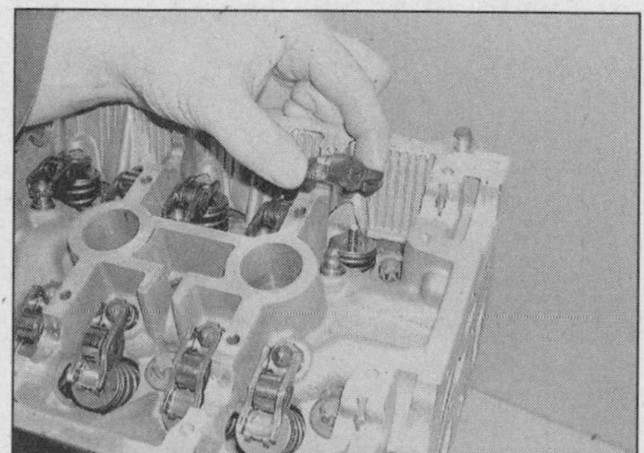

8.34 Lift out the rocker arms and place them in a marked box or containers

8.35 Similarly lift out the tappets and place them upright in a marked box or containers filled with oil

8.45a Refit the camshafts in the cylinder head

requires re-priming. Renault recommend that the tappets are immersed in diesel fuel and operated until they are primed.

43 Remove the hydraulic tappets from their compartments and insert them in their correct positions in the head.

44 One at a time, remove the rocker arms from their compartments and locate them on the hydraulic tappets and valve stems.

45 Lubricate the bearings and journals of the inlet and exhaust camshafts with fresh engine oil, then carefully locate them on the cylinder head in their correct positions and at TDC as previously noted. The grooves at the left-hand end of the camshafts must be horizontal **(see illustrations)**.

46 Check that the cylinder head cover/bearing cap mating surfaces are clean and dry, then apply Loctite 518 (or a suitable alternative) to the cover surface using a roller **(see illustration)**. Make several applications until the colour is **reddish.**

47 Locate the cylinder head cover/bearing cap on the cylinder head, insert the bolts, and progressively tighten them to the specified torque in the sequence and stages given in the Specifications **(see illustration)**. Make sure that the camshafts are located correctly on the rockers and in the cover.

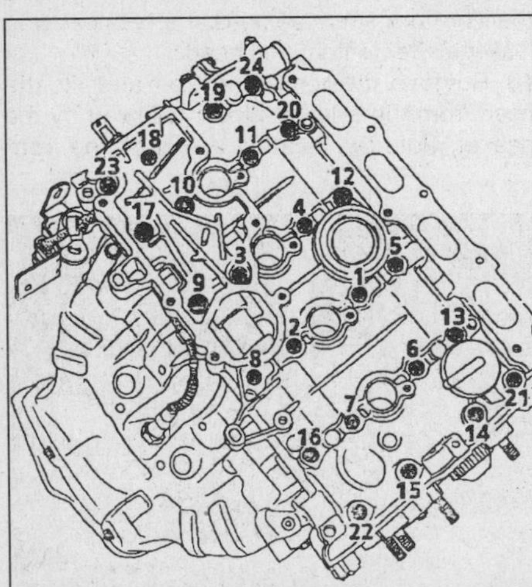

8.47 Cylinder head cover/bearing cap retaining bolt tightening sequence

8.45b Position the camshafts in their TDC position so that the grooves are horizontal and the offset is below the centreline

48 Check that the oil separator mating surfaces are clean and dry, then apply Loctite 518 (or a suitable alternative) to the separator surface using a roller **(see illustration)**. Make several applications until the colour is **reddish.**

49 Locate the oil separator on the cylinder head cover, insert the bolts, and tighten them to the specified torque in the sequence shown **(see illustration)**.

50 Refit the ignition coils with reference to Chapter 5B.

51 Refit the engine lifting eye to the cylinder head and tighten the bolts securely.

52 Refit the support bracket to the right-hand side of the exhaust manifold, and tighten the bolts securely.

53 Reconnect the wiring to the lambda (oxygen) sensor on the rear left-hand side of the engine.

54 Refit the throttle body with reference to Chapter 4A.

55 Refit the catalytic converter to the exhaust manifold with reference to Chapter 4A.

56 Refit the inlet manifold together with new seals with reference to Chapter 4A.

57 Reconnect the brake servo vacuum hose to the inlet manifold.

58 Refit the expansion bottle to the bulkhead.

59 Reconnect the wiring to the ignition coil and fuel injectors, and attach the wiring loom to the front of the engine.

60 Reconnect the fuel supply and return hoses to each end of the fuel rail, and tighten the clips.

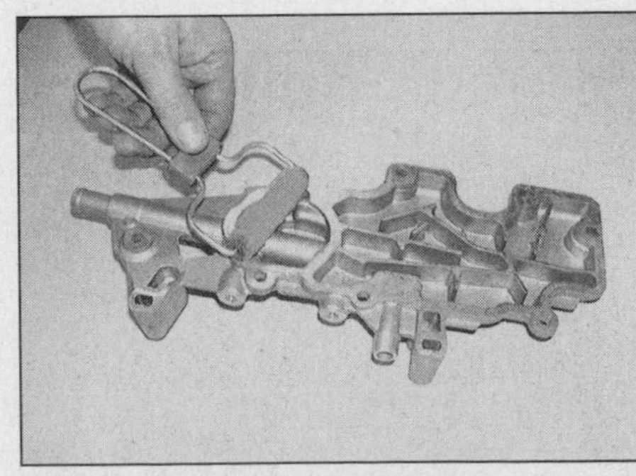
8.48 Apply an even coating of Loctite 518 gasket solution to the mating face of the oil separator housing

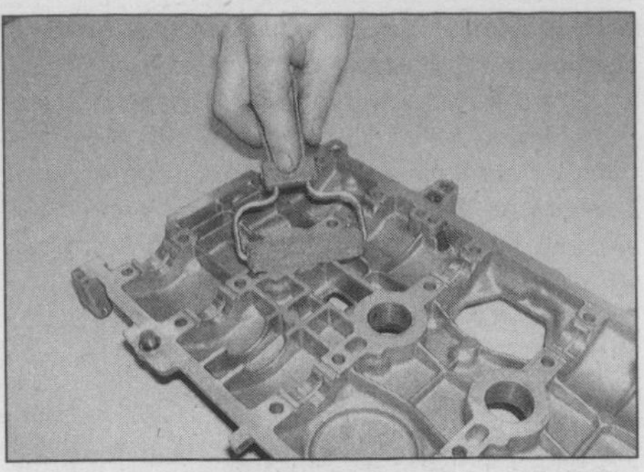
8.46 Apply an even coating of Loctite 518 gasket solution to the mating face of the valve cover/bearing cap

61 Refit the injector gallery protector.

62 Reconnect the accelerator cable to the throttle body with reference to Chapter 4A.

63 Refit the camshaft sprockets as described in Section 6.

64 Refit the timing belt with reference to Section 5 of this Chapter.

65 Remove the trolley jack and block of wood from under the sump.

66 Reconnect the battery negative lead.

67 Refill the engine with fresh oil, with reference to Chapter 1A.

68 Refit the engine undertray and lower the vehicle to the ground.

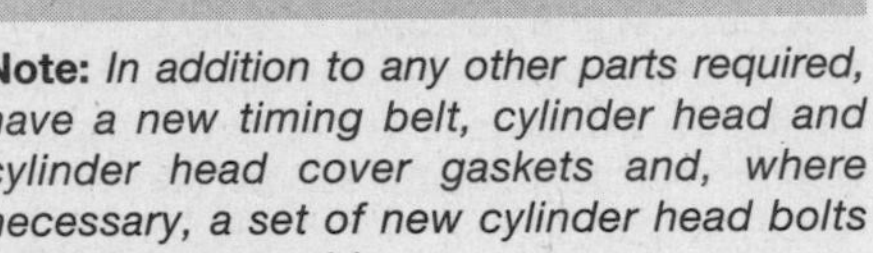

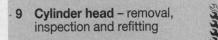

9 Cylinder head – removal, inspection and refitting

Note: *In addition to any other parts required, have a new timing belt, cylinder head and cylinder head cover gaskets and, where necessary, a set of new cylinder head bolts ready for reassembly.*

Note: *Renault state that the tensioner and idler pulley must be renewed whenever the timing belt is renewed.*

E7J engine

1 Disconnect the battery negative lead (refer to *Disconnecting the battery*).

2 For additional working room, remove the bonnet as described in Chapter 11.

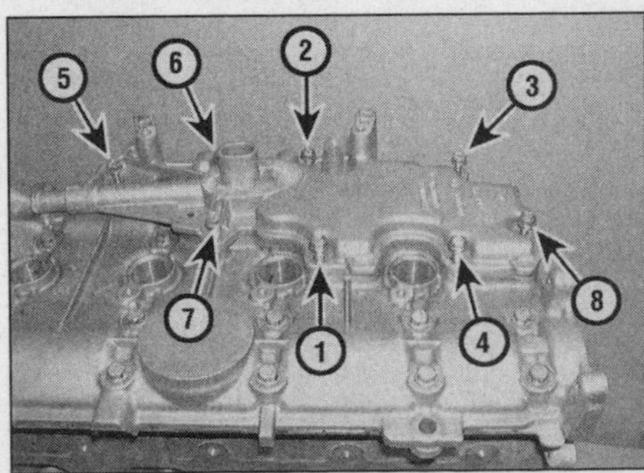

8.49 Oil separator housing retaining bolt tightening sequence

3 Remove the timing belt with reference to Section 5 of this Chapter.
4 Where fitted, remove the engine undertray, then drain the cooling system including the cylinder block with reference to Chapter 1A (it is important to drain the block, because if the wet cylinder liners are disturbed, the coolant will drain into the sump).
5 Drain the engine oil with reference to Chapter 1A.
6 Remove the complete air cleaner assembly as described in Chapter 4A.
7 Disconnect the accelerator cable from the throttle body with reference to Chapter 4A. Also unbolt the support from the cylinder head cover.
8 Disconnect the HT leads from the spark plugs, then unbolt the ignition coil assembly from the top of the cylinder head cover.
9 Disconnect the crankcase ventilation hose(s) from the rear of the cylinder head cover.
10 Unscrew the bolts and remove the cylinder head cover and gasket.
11 Where fitted, unbolt the earth strap from the right-hand side of the bulkhead.
12 Disconnect the fuel inlet and return hoses from the fuel rail.
13 Disconnect the evaporation emission control solenoid valve hose.
14 Disconnect the wiring from the throttle position potentiometer.
15 Disconnect the wiring from the absolute pressure sensor on the inlet manifold. Also disconnect the brake servo vacuum pipe.
16 Disconnect the wiring from the stepper motor on the throttle body.
17 On models with air conditioning, carefully position a trolley jack and a large block of wood under the sump to support the engine. Raise the jack to just take the weight of the engine, then unbolt and remove the right-hand engine mounting as described in Section 14.
18 Disconnect the wiring from the air temperature sensor, then remove the air inlet duct.
19 Disconnect the wiring from the ignition coils, and also disconnect the wiring at the connector near the coils.
20 Disconnect the wiring and the vacuum pipes from the right-hand rear of the cylinder head.

9.24 Disconnecting the heater hose from the thermostat housing

21 Unbolt the engine lifting eye from the left-hand end of the cylinder head.
22 Disconnect the wiring from the fuel injectors.
23 Disconnect the wiring from the temperature sensor on the thermostat housing at the left-hand end of the cylinder head.
24 Release the clips and disconnect the radiator top hose, heater hoses and expansion tank hose from the thermostat housing **(see illustration)**.
25 Unbolt the hot air shroud from the exhaust manifold, then unbolt the exhaust downpipe from the manifold with reference to Chapter 4A.

Models without air conditioning

26 Remove the alternator as described in Chapter 5A.
27 Remove the power steering pressostat mounting from the right hand front of the cylinder block. Also disconnect the power steering pump wiring at the connector.
28 Refer to Chapter 10 and unbolt the power-assisted steering pump from the right-hand front of the cylinder block. Tie the pump to one side out of the way.
29 Unscrew the multi-function support mounting bolts and move it to one side.

Models with air conditioning

30 Remove the radiator grille as described in Chapter 11, Section 8.
31 Remove the front bumper as described in Chapter 11. This procedure also includes removing the left-hand wheelarch liner.
32 Unscrew the centre lower and upper outer bolts and move the engine compartment front crossmember to one side.
33 Refer to Chapter 10 and unbolt the power-assisted steering pump from the right-hand front of the cylinder block. Tie to pump to one side out of the way.
34 Refer to Chapter 3 and unbolt the air conditioning compressor from the right-hand front of the cylinder block and tie it to one side. Do not disconnect the refrigerant pipes from the compressor.
35 Unscrew the multi-function support mounting bolts and move it to one side.
36 Unbolt the intermediate support from the right-hand end of the cylinder head.

All models

37 Remove the spark plugs as described in Chapter 1A.
38 Unbolt the support bracket securing the inlet manifold to the right-hand end of the cylinder head.
39 Unbolt the engine level dipstick tube from the right-hand end of the cylinder head.
40 Release the wiring loom from the clip on the right-hand end of the cylinder head.
41 Unbolt and remove the rocker shaft and retaining plate, then progressively slacken the cylinder head bolts in the **reverse** order to that shown in illustration 9.86a **(see illustrations)**. Remove all the bolts except the one positioned on the front right-hand corner, which should be unscrewed by only three or four turns.
42 The joint between the cylinder head, gasket and cylinder block must now be broken. It is important not to lift or disturb the 'wet' cylinder liners as the head is removed. To avoid this, pull the left-hand end of the cylinder head forward so as to swivel it around the single bolt still fitted, then move the head back to its original position. If this procedure is not followed, there is a possibility of the cylinder liners moving and their bottom seals being disturbed, causing leakage after refitting the head.
43 Remove the remaining bolt and lift the head from the cylinder block, followed by the gasket. Note the locating dowel on the front

9.41a Removing a rocker shaft end bolt – the bolt is hollow for oil supply to the rockers

9.41b Slackening a cylinder head bolt

9.41c Removing a cylinder head bolt

9.43a Removing the cylinder head assembly

9.43b Removing the cylinder head gasket

right-hand corner of the block **(see illustrations)**.

44 Remove the inlet and exhaust manifolds with reference to Chapter 4A.

45 Note that the crankshaft must not be rotated with the cylinder head removed, otherwise the cylinder liners may be displaced. If it is necessary to turn the crankshaft (e.g. to clean the piston crowns), clamp the liners using bolts and washers, or make up some retaining clamps out of flat metal bar, held in place with bolts screwed into the block **(see illustration)**.

K4M and K4J engines

46 Disconnect the battery negative lead (refer to *Disconnecting the battery*).

47 For additional working room, remove the bonnet as described in Chapter 11.

48 Remove the timing belt with reference to Section 5 of this Chapter. This procedure includes supporting the engine and removing the right-hand engine mounting from the engine and body. Carefully, position a trolley jack and a large block of wood under the sump to support the engine. Raise the jack to just take the weight of the engine.

49 Where fitted, remove the engine undertray, then drain the cooling system with reference to Chapter 1A.

50 Drain the engine oil with reference to Chapter 1A.

51 Release the power steering hydraulic hoses from the support on the right-hand side of the front subframe. Also unclip the power steering fluid reservoir from its mounting and tie it to one side.

52 Disconnect the accelerator cable from the throttle body with reference to Chapter 4A.

53 Unbolt and remove the injector gallery protector.

54 Refer to Section 6 and remove both camshaft sprockets.

55 Disconnect the fuel supply and return hoses from each end of the fuel rail. Take care not to allow spilt fuel to enter the alternator – if necessary cover the alternator with a plastic bag.

56 Disconnect the engine wiring loom at the front of the engine, and also disconnect the wiring from the ignition coils and fuel injectors.

57 Disconnect the brake servo vacuum pipe at the inlet manifold.

58 Disconnect the wiring from the power steering fluid pressure switch on the fluid pipe.

59 Remove the air cleaner assembly as described in Chapter 4A. On Scénic models it will be necessary to remove the soundproofing panel from the rear of the engine compartment.

60 Refer to Chapter 4A and remove the catalytic converter from the exhaust manifold. Also unbolt and remove the support strut from the manifold.

61 Remove the throttle body as described in Chapter 4A.

62 Disconnect the wiring plug from the lambda (oxygen) sensor on the left-hand rear of the engine.

63 Unbolt and remove the engine lifting eye from the right-hand rear of the cylinder head.

64 Unbolt the air distributor from the top of the cylinder head.

65 Remove the ignition coils with reference to Chapter 5B.

66 Unbolt and remove the oil separator.

67 Unbolt the engine lifting bracket from the left-hand end of the cylinder head.

68 Progressively, unscrew and remove the bolts from the cylinder head cover then release the cover and remove it. If necessary, carefully use a screwdriver to lever up the cover at the lugs provided at the rear corners and front edge. Take care not to damage the cover.

69 Remove the camshafts and followers with reference to Section 8.

70 Loosen the clips and disconnect the coolant hoses from the cylinder head.

71 Disconnect the wiring from the coolant temperature sensor on the thermostat housing **(see illustration)**. Also unbolt the wiring loom support brackets from the rear of the engine.

72 Check that all relevant attachments have been disconnected from the cylinder head.

73 Remove the spark plugs as described in Chapter 1A.

74 Progressively unscrew and remove the cylinder head bolts in the **reverse** order to that shown in illustration 9.134b.

75 Lift the head from the cylinder block, followed by the gasket.

Inspection – all engines

76 The mating faces of the cylinder head and block must be perfectly clean before refitting the head. Use a scraper to remove all traces of gasket and carbon and also clean the tops of the pistons. Take particular care with the aluminium cylinder head, as the soft metal is easily damaged. Also, make sure that debris is not allowed to enter the oil and water channels – this is particularly important for the oil circuit, as carbon could block the oil supply to the camshaft and rocker arms or crankshaft bearings. Using adhesive tape and paper, seal the water, oil and bolt holes in the cylinder block. Clean the piston crowns in the same way.

To prevent carbon entering the gap between the pistons and bores, smear a little grease in the gap. After cleaning the piston, rotate the crankshaft so that the piston moves down the bore, then wipe out the grease and carbon with a cloth rag.

77 Check the block and head for nicks, deep scratches and other damage. If slight, they may be removed carefully with a file. It may be possible to repair more serious damage by machining, but this is a specialist job.

78 If warpage of the cylinder head is suspected, use a straight-edge to check it for distortion. On the E7J engine, also check the protrusion of the cylinder liners. Either of these items can be associated with the head

9.45 Clamps holding the liners in place

9.71 Coolant temperature sensor on the thermostat housing (K4M engine)

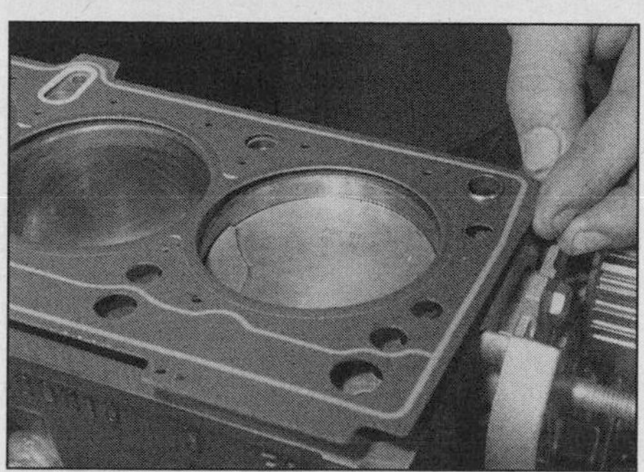
9.84 Place the new cylinder head gasket over the locating dowel on the block

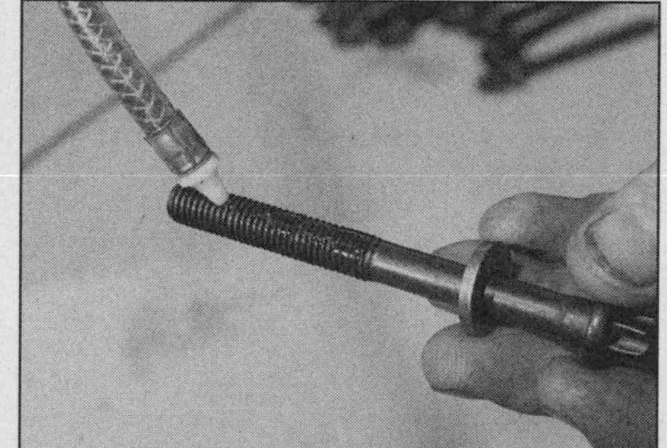
9.85a Oil the cylinder head bolts . . .

9.85b . . . before inserting them

gasket blowing. Refer to Part D of this Chapter for further information.

79 Clean out all the bolt holes in the block using a pipe cleaner, or a rag and screwdriver. Make sure that all oil is removed, otherwise there is a possibility of the block being cracked by hydraulic pressure when the bolts are tightened.

80 Examine the bolt threads and the threads in the cylinder block for damage. If necessary, use the correct-size tap to chase out the threads in the block and use a die to clean the threads on the bolts. In view of the severe stresses to which they are subjected, owners may wish to renew the bolts as a matter of course whenever they are disturbed. If any of the bolts shows the slightest sign of wear or of damage, all the bolts should be renewed as a set. On K4M and K4J engines, the bolts may be re-used if their length between the bolt head and end does not exceed 117.7 mm – if any one bolt is longer than this dimension, renew all the bolts as a set.

E7J engine

81 Refit the inlet and exhaust manifolds to the cylinder head, referring to Chapter 4A.

82 Check that No 1 piston is positioned at TDC, then wipe clean the faces of the head and block. Remove the cylinder liner clamps.

83 Check that the locating dowel is in place on the front right-hand corner of the block.

84 Position the new gasket on the block and over the dowel – it can only be fitted one way round **(see illustration)**.

85 Lower the cylinder head onto the block. Oil the threads and under the heads of the cylinder head bolts, fit their washers, then insert the bolts – note that the shorter bolts are located on the inlet side of the head – and initially screw them in finger-tight **(see illustrations)**.

86 Tighten the cylinder head bolts to the specified torques in the sequence shown **(see illustrations)** and in the stages given in the Specifications at the beginning of this Chapter. The initial Stages pre-compress the gasket and the subsequent Stages are the main tightening procedure. When angle-tightening the bolts, put paint marks on the bolt heads and cylinder head as a guide for the correct angle, or obtain a special angle-tightening tool. Note that, provided the bolts are tightened exactly as specified, there will be no need to retighten them once the engine has been started and run after reassembly.

87 Refit the rocker shaft and retaining plate with reference to Section 8. If the cylinder head has been overhauled, it is worthwhile checking the valve clearances at this stage, to prevent any possibility of the valves touching the pistons when the timing belt is being fitted. Turn the crankshaft so that there are no pistons at TDC. Use a socket on the camshaft pulley bolt to turn the camshaft and check the valve clearances. After carrying out the adjustment, reposition the camshaft and pistons at TDC.

88 Refit the wiring loom to the clip on the right-hand end of the cylinder head.

89 Refit the engine level dipstick tube and tighten the bolt securely.

90 Refit the inlet manifold support bracket and tighten the bolts securely.

91 Refit the spark plugs with reference to Chapter 1A.

Models without air conditioning

92 Refit the multi-function support mounting and tighten the bolts.

93 Refit the power-assisted steering pump with reference to Chapter 10.

94 Refit the pressostat mounting and reconnect the wiring.

95 Refit the alternator with reference to Chapter 5A.

Models with air conditioning

96 Refit the intermediate support to the right-hand end of the cylinder head.

97 Refit the multi-function support mounting and tighten the bolts.

98 Refit the air conditioning compressor with reference to Chapter 3.

99 Refit the power steering pump with reference to Chapter 10.

100 Refit the engine compartment front crossmember.

101 Refit the front bumper and left-hand wheelarch liner with reference to Chapter 11, Sections 6 and 24.

102 Refit the radiator grille with reference to Chapter 11, Section 8.

All models

103 Refit the exhaust downpipe to the manifold, and refit the hot air shroud with reference to Chapter 4A.

104 Reconnect the radiator top hose, heater hoses and expansion tank hose to the thermostat housing and tighten the clips.

2A

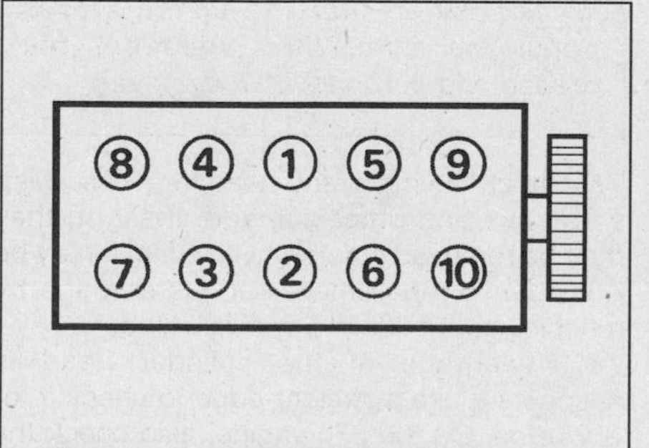

9.86a Cylinder head bolt tightening sequence

9.86b Torque-tightening a cylinder head bolt

9.86c Angle-tightening a cylinder head bolt

9.130 Locate a new cylinder head gasket on the cylinder block . . .

9.132 . . . and carefully lower the cylinder head into position

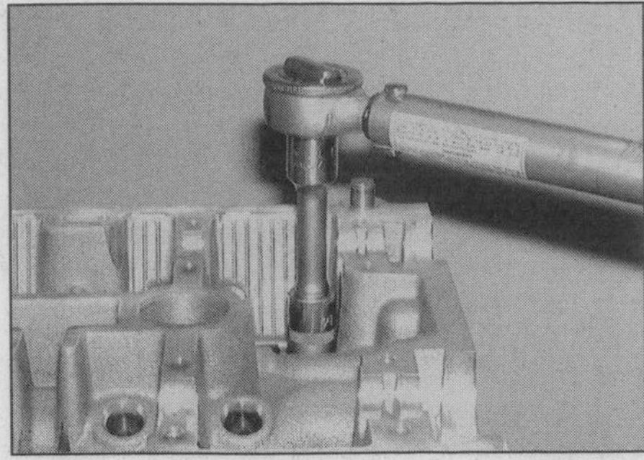
9.134a Tighten the cylinder head retaining bolts to the Stage 1 torque setting using a torque wrench

105 Reconnect the wiring to the temperature sensor on the thermostat housing.
106 Refit the cylinder head cover with a new gasket and tighten the bolts evenly to the specified torque wrench setting.
107 Reconnect the wiring to the fuel injectors.
108 Refit the engine lifting eye and tighten the bolts securely.
109 Reconnect the wiring and vacuum pipes to the right-hand rear of the cylinder head.
110 Reconnect the wiring to the ignition coils including the connector near the coils.
111 Refit the air inlet duct and reconnect the wiring to the air temperature sensor.
112 Refit the right-hand engine mounting with reference to Section 14, then remove the jack from under the sump.
113 Reconnect the wiring to the stepper motor on the throttle body.
114 Refit the brake vacuum pipe to the inlet manifold, then reconnect the wiring to the absolute pressure sensor.
115 Reconnect the wiring to the throttle position potentiometer.
116 Reconnect the evaporation emission control solenoid valve hose.
117 Reconnect the fuel supply and return hoses to the fuel rail.
118 Refit the earth strap (where fitted) and tighten the bolt.
119 Reconnect the crankcase ventilation hose(s) to the rear of the cylinder head cover.
120 Refit the ignition coil assembly to the cylinder head cover and reconnect the HT leads to the spark plugs.
121 Reconnect the accelerator cable to the throttle body with reference to Chapter 4A. Also refit the support to the cylinder head cover.
122 Refit the air cleaner complete with reference to Chapter 4A.
123 Fit a new timing belt with reference to Section 5 of this Chapter.
124 Where removed, refit the bonnet with reference to Chapter 11.
125 Refill the engine with fresh oil, with reference to Chapter 1A.
126 Reconnect the battery negative lead.
127 Refit the block drain plug, then refill and bleed the cooling system with reference to Chapter 1A.
128 Where necessary, refit the engine undertray, then lower the vehicle to the ground.

K4M and K4J engines

129 It is recommended that No 1 piston is positioned half-way up its cylinder before refitting the cylinder head as a safeguard against the valves touching the tops of the pistons. Turn the crankshaft clockwise until No 1 piston rises to the mid-cylinder position.
130 Position a new gasket on the block making sure it is the correct way up **(see illustration)**.
131 If the lower inlet manifold was removed, it can be refitted at this stage with reference to Chapter 4A making sure that the timing end is flush with the end of the cylinder head before tightening the bolts.
132 Carefully lower the cylinder head onto the block making sure that the gasket is not displaced **(see illustration)**.
133 If new bolts are being fitted, **do not** lubricate their threads, however if the old bolts are being refitted, lubricate their threads with fresh engine oil. Insert the bolts and initially screw them in finger-tight.
134 Tighten the cylinder head bolts to the specified torques in the sequence shown and in the Stages given in the Specifications **(see illustrations)**. The first Stage pre-compresses the gasket and the second Stage is the main

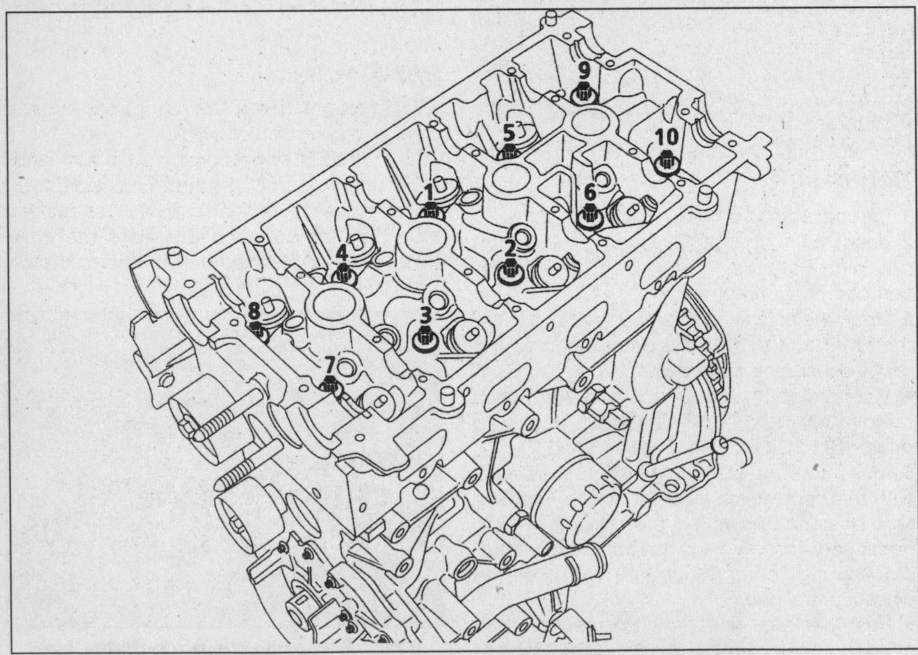

9.134b Cylinder head retaining bolt tightening sequence

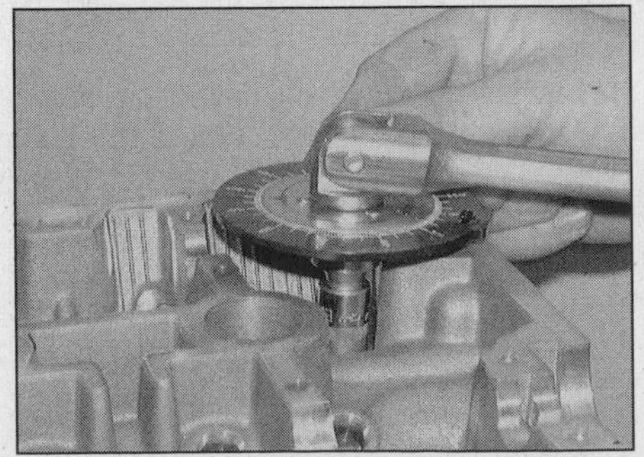
9.134c Using an angle tightening gauge to tighten the cylinder head retaining bolts through the Stage 2 angle

tightening procedure. When angle-tightening the bolts, put paint marks on the bolt heads and cylinder head as a guide for the correct angle, or obtain a special angle-tightening tool. Note that, provided the bolts are tightened exactly as specified, there will be no need to retighten them once the engine has been started and run after reassembly.

135 Refit the spark plugs with reference to Chapter 1A.

136 Refit the engine lifting eye to the left-hand end of the cylinder head.

137 Refit the wiring loom support bracket to the cylinder head and tighten the bolts.

138 Reconnect the radiator top hose, heater hoses and expansion tank to the thermostat housing and tighten the clips.

139 Reconnect the wiring to the temperature sensor on the thermostat housing.

140 If the hydraulic tappets have not been kept immersed in oil, the oil will drain from them and they will need to be re-primed before refitting. To check whether they require re-priming, depress the top of the tappet with a thumb – if the piston goes down, the tappet requires re-priming. Renault recommend that the tappets are immersed in diesel fuel and operated until they are primed.

141 Remove the hydraulic tappets from their compartments and insert them in their correct positions in the head.

142 One at a time, remove the cam followers from their compartments and locate them on the hydraulic tappets and valve stems.

143 Lubricate the bearings and journals of the inlet and exhaust camshafts with fresh engine oil, then carefully locate them on the cylinder head in their correct positions and at TDC as previously noted. The grooves at the left-hand end of the camshafts must be horizontal.

144 Turn the crankshaft clockwise to position No 1 piston at TDC. Refer to Section 3 if necessary.

145 Check that the cylinder head cover/bearing cap mating surfaces are clean and dry, then apply Loctite 518 (or a suitable alternative) to the cover surface using a roller. Make several applications until the colour is **reddish.**

146 Locate the cylinder head cover on the cylinder head, insert the bolts, and tighten them to the specified torque in the sequence and stages given in the Specifications **(see illustration 8.47)**.

147 Check that the oil separator mating surfaces are clean and dry, then apply Loctite 518 (or a suitable alternative) to the separator surface using a roller. Make several applications until the colour is **reddish.**

148 Locate the oil separator on the cylinder head cover, insert the bolts, and tighten them to the specified torque in the sequence shown **(see illustration 8.49)**.

149 Refit the ignition coils with reference to Chapter 5B.

150 Refit the engine lifting eye to the cylinder head and tighten the bolts securely.

151 Refit the support bracket to the right-hand side of the exhaust manifold, and tighten the bolts securely.

152 Reconnect the wiring to the lambda (oxygen) sensor on the rear left-hand side of the engine.

153 Refit the throttle body with reference to Chapter 4A.

154 Refit the catalytic converter to the exhaust manifold with reference to Chapter 4A.

155 Refit the inlet manifold together with new seals with reference to Chapter 4A.

156 Reconnect the brake servo vacuum hose to the inlet manifold.

157 Refit the expansion bottle to the bulkhead.

158 Reconnect the wiring to the ignition coil and fuel injectors, and attach the wiring loom to the front of the engine.

159 Reconnect the fuel supply and return hoses to each end of the fuel rail, and tighten the clips.

160 Refit the injector gallery protector.

161 Reconnect the accelerator cable to the throttle body with reference to Chapter 4A.

162 Refit the timing belt with reference to Section 5 of this Chapter.

163 Remove the trolley jack and block of wood from under the sump.

164 Where removed, refit the bonnet with reference to Chapter 11.

165 Reconnect the battery negative lead.

166 Refill the engine with fresh oil, with reference to Chapter 1A.

167 Refill and bleed the cooling system with reference to Chapter 1A.

168 Where necessary, refit the engine undertray, then lower the vehicle to the ground.

10 Sump – removal and refitting

Note: *An engine lifting hoist is required during this procedure.*

Removal

1 Disconnect the battery negative lead.

2 Jack up the front of the vehicle and support on axle stands. Remove the engine compartment undertray.

3 Drain the engine oil referring to Chapter 1A, then refit and tighten the drain plug using a new washer **(see illustration)**.

4 Remove both front roadwheels, then remove the right-hand wheelarch liner with reference to Chapter 11, Section 24.

5 Make sure the steering wheel is positioned with the front wheels straight-ahead, and use tape or string to hold it in this position. This is necessary to prevent damage to the airbag clockspring located beneath the steering wheel central pad.

6 Push back the gaiter and unscrew the bolt securing the steering column intermediate shaft to the steering gear pinion.

7 Refer to Chapter 10 and disconnect the front suspension lower arms from the hub carriers.

8 Unscrew the nuts and disconnect the track rod ends from the steering arms with reference to Chapter 10.

9 Detach the front suspension subframe tie-rods from the body. Also disconnect the gearchange rods from the transmission.

10 Loosen only the bolts securing the rear engine mounting link to the body.

11 Unscrew and remove the front bumper lower mounting fasteners.

12 Where necessary, unbolt and remove the exhaust manifold heat shield and remove the catalytic converter with reference to Chapter 4A.

13 Where necessary, unbolt the power-assisted steering pipe supports from the cylinder block. Also unbolt the multi-function support.

14 Unbolt the front suspension lower arms from the subframe with reference to Chapter 10.

15 Unscrew each subframe mounting bolt in turn and replace them with lengths of threaded rods and nuts. These are required to lower the subframe approximately 13.0 cm in order to remove the sump. With the rods in position, lower the subframe until the gap between the subframe and body is 9.0 cm at the rear mounting and 13.0 cm at the front mounting. As the subframe is being lowered, disconnect the steering gear pinion from the column intermediate shaft.

16 Unscrew the bolts securing the sump to the cylinder block. Tap the sump with a hide or plastic mallet to break the seal, then remove the sump. On the E7J engine, recover the half-moon gaskets from each end of the sump and discard them, as new ones must be used on refitting. On K4M and K4J engines, recover the gaskets.

Refitting

17 Thoroughly clean the mating surfaces of the sump and cylinder block.

18 On the E7J engine, apply a 3.0 mm bead of Rhodorseal 5661 sealant (available from Renault dealers) to the sump flanges making sure that the bead goes around the inner sides of the bolt holes and is approximately

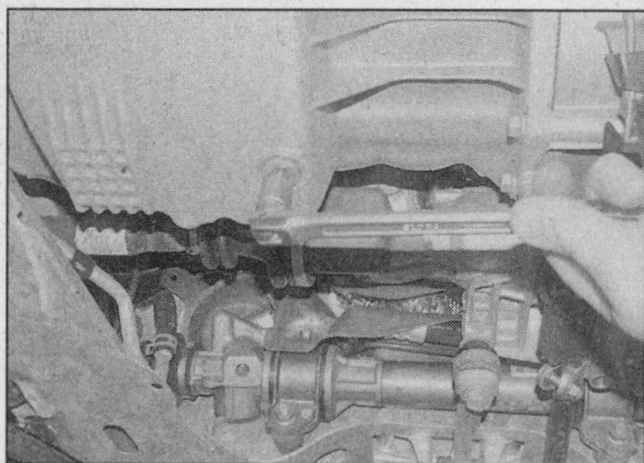

10.3 Removing the sump drain plug (K4M engine)

10.18a On K4M and K4J engines, apply sealant to the joint areas of the front oil seal housing . . .

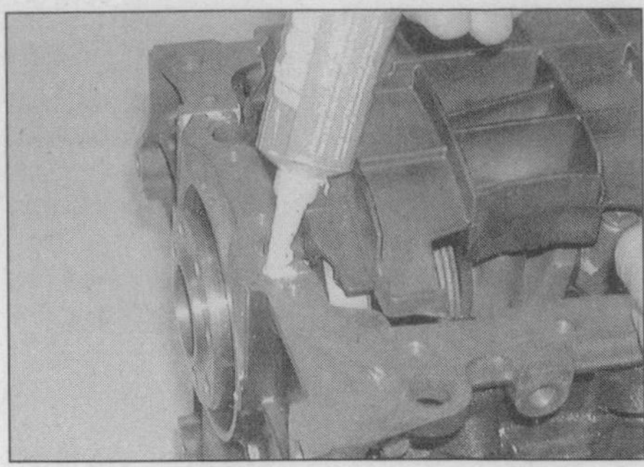
10.18b . . . and rear main bearing cap . . .

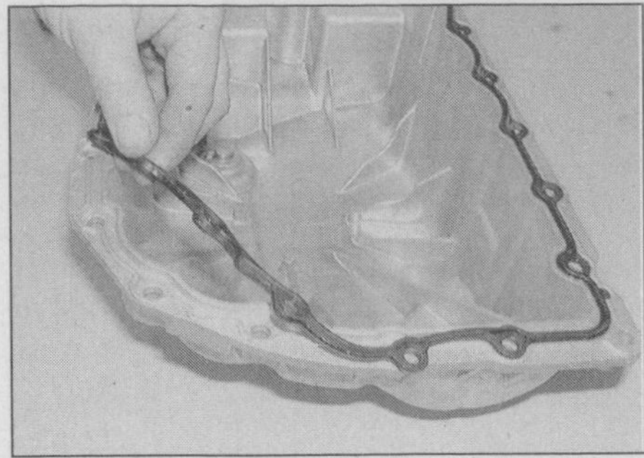
10.18c . . . then locate a new gasket on the sump

midway across the flange between the bolt holes. Do not apply any sealant to the half-moon areas of the sump. On K4M and K4J engines apply some Rhodorseal 5661 sealant to the joint areas where the front oil seal housing and rear main bearing cap meet the cylinder block, then locate a new gasket on the sump **(see illustrations)**.

19 Locate new half-moon gaskets in position, and lift the sump into position on the cylinder block. Insert the bolts and tighten them progressively to the specified torque. If the engine is removed from the car, use a straight-edge to maintain the alignment between the left-hand end of the sump and cylinder block **(see illustration)**.

20 Raise the subframe and replace the threaded rods with the mounting bolts. As the subframe is being raised, make sure that the steering gear pinion locates in the column intermediate shaft correctly (see Chapter 10). Tighten the bolts to the specified torque (see Chapter 10).

21 Refit the front suspension lower arms to the subframe with reference to Chapter 10.

22 Refit the multi-function and power steering pipe supports.

23 Refit the catalytic converter and exhaust manifold heat shield with reference to Chapter 4A.

24 Refit and tighten the front bumper lower mounting fasteners.

25 Tighten the rear engine mounting link bolts to the specified torque.

26 Reconnect the gearchange rods to the transmission, and refit the front suspension subframe tie-rods to the body.

27 Refit the track rod ends to the steering arms with reference to Chapter 10.

28 Reconnect the front suspension lower arms to the hub carriers with reference to Chapter 10.

29 With the front roadwheels straight-ahead, refit and tighten the bolt securing the intermediate shaft to the steering gear pinion. Locate the gaiter over the shaft, then remove the tape or string from the steering wheel.

30 Refit the wheelarch liner and right-hand front roadwheel. Also refit the engine compartment undertray, then lower the vehicle to the ground.

31 Reconnect the battery negative lead.

32 Fill the engine with fresh oil with reference to Chapter 1A.

11 Oil pump and sprockets – removal, inspection and refitting

E7J engine

Removal

1 Remove the timing belt and the crankshaft sprocket, with reference to Sections 5 and 6.

2 Remove the sump referring to Section 10.

3 Remove the Woodruff key (when fitted) from its slot in the crankshaft.

10.19 If the engine is removed, use a straight-edge to maintain the alignment between the left-hand end of the sump and cylinder block

4 Unbolt the crankshaft timing belt end oil seal housing from the cylinder block **(see illustration)**.

5 Unscrew the bolts securing the sprocket to the oil pump hub. Use a screwdriver through one of the holes in the sprocket to hold it stationary **(see illustrations)**.

6 Remove the sprocket from the oil pump.

7 Slide off the oil seal spacer **(see illustration)**.

8 Slide the drive sprocket from the crankshaft, then release both sprockets from the chain **(see illustration)**. **Note:** *The sprocket is not keyed to the crankshaft, but relies on the pulley bolt being tightened correctly to clamp the sprocket. It is most important that the pulley bolt is correctly*

11.4 Removing the oil seal housing from the cylinder block

11.5a Using a screwdriver to hold the oil pump sprocket when loosening the bolts

11.5b Removing the sprocket bolts from the oil pump

11.7 Slide off the oil seal spacer

11.8 Removing the oil pump sprockets and chain from the crankshaft

11.9a Unscrew the bolts . . .

tightened otherwise there is the possibility of the oil pump not functioning.

9 Unscrew the two mounting bolts and withdraw the oil pump. If the two locating dowels are displaced, refit them in the cylinder block **(see illustrations)**.

Inspection

10 Unscrew the retaining bolts and lift off the pump cover and pick-up tube **(see illustrations)**.

11 Using a feeler gauge, check the clearance between each of the gears and the oil pump body. Also check the endfloat of both gears by measuring the clearance between the gears and the cover joint face. If any clearance is outside the tolerances given in the Specifications, the oil pump must be renewed **(see illustrations)**.

12 Depress the relief valve end stop and extract the spring clip (with the piston at rest there is very little spring tension on the end stop, since the oil pressure release hole is located some way up the piston bore). Release the end stop and remove the spring and piston **(see illustrations)**.

13 Examine the relief valve piston and bore for signs of wear and damage. If evident, renew the oil pump complete.

14 If the components are serviceable, clean them and reassemble in the reverse order to dismantling. Before refitting the cover, fill the pump with fresh engine oil to assist circulation when the engine is first started. A new pump should also be primed with oil.

15 Examine the chain for excessive wear and renew it if necessary. Similarly check the sprockets.

Refitting

16 Wipe clean the oil pump and cylinder block mating surfaces.

17 Check that the two locating dowels are fitted in the cylinder block, then position the oil pump on them and insert the two mounting bolts. Tighten the bolts to the specified torque.

11.9b . . . and remove the oil pump

11.10a Unscrewing the bolts securing the cover and pick-up tube to the oil pump

2A

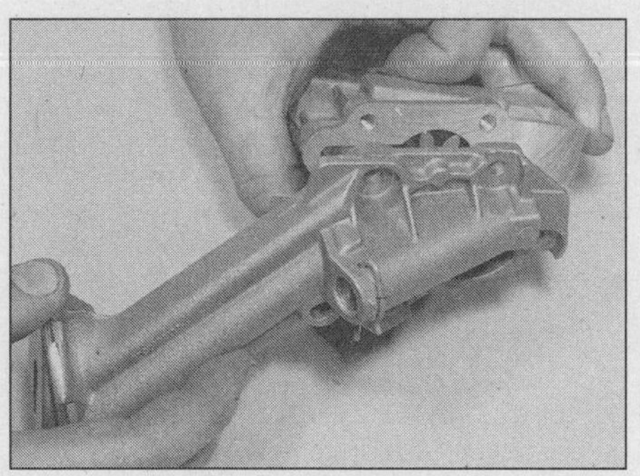
11.10b Removing the cover and pick-up tube

11.11a Measuring the oil pump gear-to-body clearance

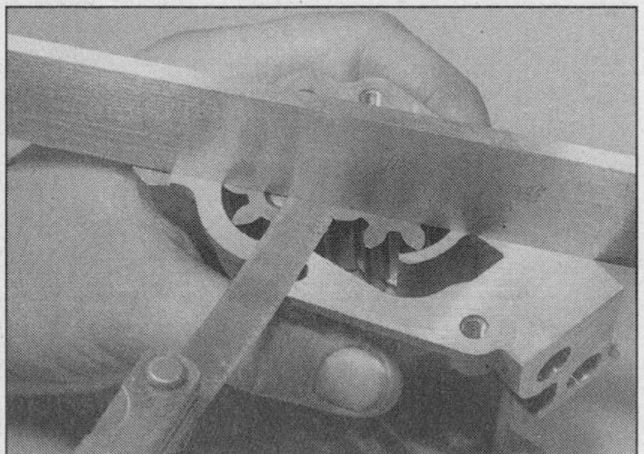
11.11b Measuring the oil pump gear endfloat

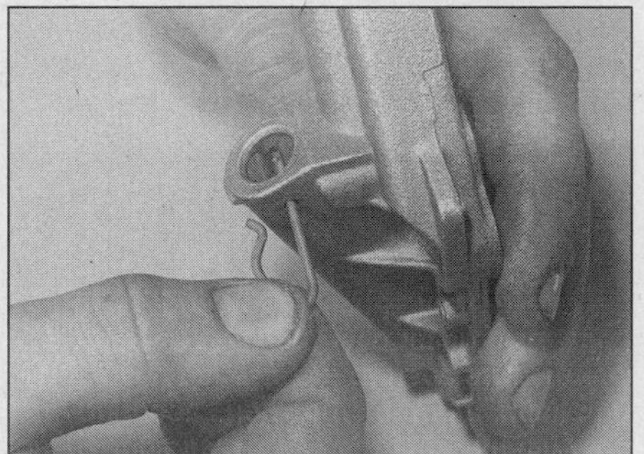
11.12a Extract the spring clip . . .

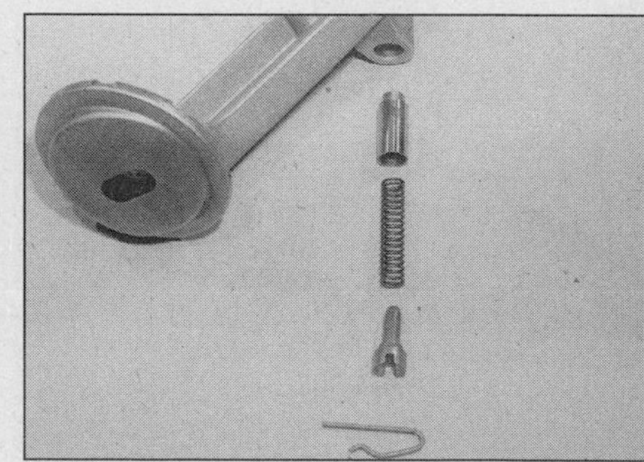
11.12b . . . and remove the end stop, spring and piston

18 Slide the drive sprocket onto the crankshaft.

19 Engage the oil pump sprocket with the chain, then engage the chain with the crankshaft drive sprocket and locate the sprocket on the oil pump hub.

20 Align the holes, then insert the sprocket bolts and tighten them to the specified torque while holding the sprocket stationary with a screwdriver.

21 The crankshaft timing belt end oil seal should be renewed whenever the housing is removed. Note the fitted position of the old seal, then prise it out with a screwdriver and wipe clean the seating. Smear the outer perimeter of the new seal with fresh engine oil and locate it squarely on the housing with its closed side facing outwards. Place the housing on a block of wood, then use a socket or metal tube to drive in the oil seal.

22 Clean all traces of sealant from the oil seal housing and block mating faces. Apply a 0.6 to 1.0 mm diameter bead of sealant to the housing, then refit it to the cylinder block and tighten the bolts securely. The sealant must be applied around the inner edges of the bolt holes **(see illustration)**.

23 Smear the oil seal with a little engine oil, then slide the spacer onto the crankshaft end. Turn the spacer slightly as it enters the oil seal, to prevent damage to the seal lip. If the spacer is worn where the old oil seal contacted it, it can be turned around so that the new oil seal contacts the unworn area.

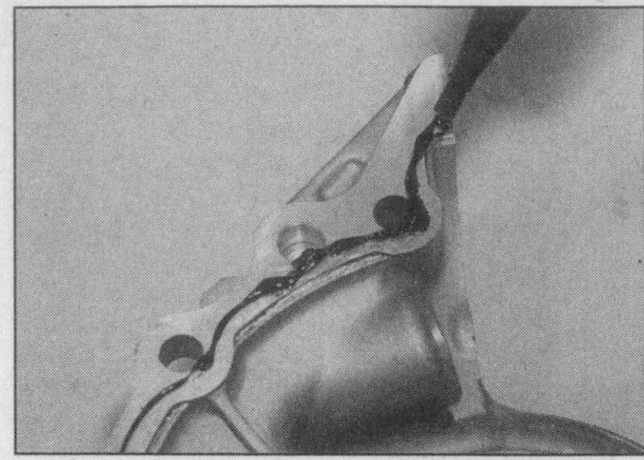

11.22 Apply sealant as directed to the oil seal housing

24 Refit the Woodruff key (when fitted) to its slot in the crankshaft.

25 Refit the sump (refer to Section 10).

26 Refit the crankshaft sprocket and fit the new timing belt with reference to Sections 6 and 5.

K4M and K4J engines

Removal

27 To remove the oil pump alone, first remove the sump as described in Section 10.

28 Unscrew the oil pump mounting bolts and the additional bolt(s) securing the anti-emulsion plate to the crankcase **(see illustration)**.

29 Withdraw the oil pump slightly and remove the anti-emulsion plate. Tilt the pump to disengage its sprocket from the drive chain and lift away the pump **(see illustrations)**. If the locating dowels are displaced, refit them in their locations.

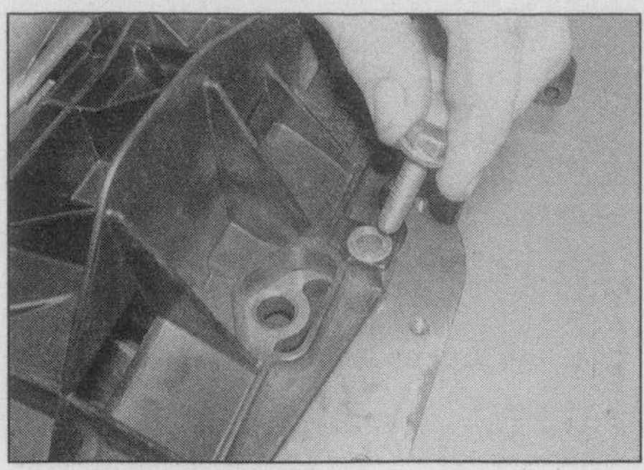

11.28 Unscrew the anti-emulsion plate retaining bolt(s)

30 To remove the pump complete with its drive chain and sprockets, first remove the sump as described in Section 10, then remove the crankshaft timing belt end oil seal housing as described in Section 12.

31 Remove the oil pump as described in paragraphs 27 and 28 above.

32 Slide the drive sprocket together with the chain from the crankshaft **(see illustration)**. Note that the drive sprocket is not keyed to the crankshaft, but relies on the pulley bolt being tightened correctly to clamp the sprocket.

Inspection

33 Extract the retaining clip, and remove the oil pressure relief valve spring retainer, spring and plunger **(see illustrations)**.

11.29a Remove the anti-emulsion plate . . .

11.29b . . . then tilt the pump to disengage its sprocket from the drive chain

11.32 Slide the drive sprocket together with the chain from the crankshaft

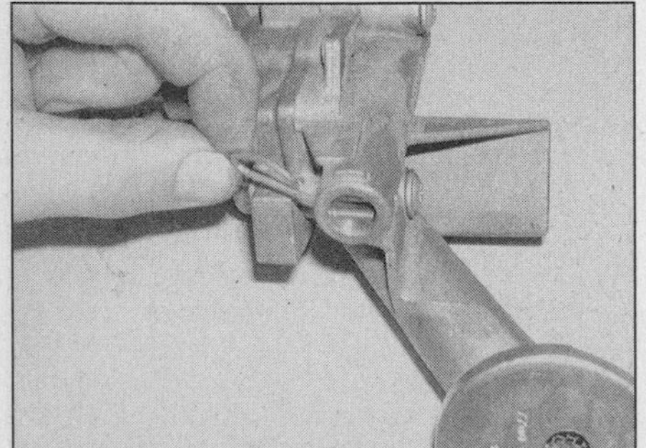

11.33a Extract the oil pressure relief valve retaining clip . . .

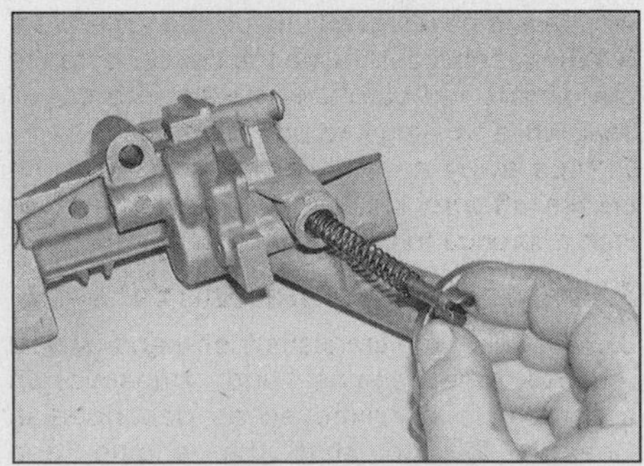

11.33b . . . remove the oil pressure relief valve spring retainer and spring . . .

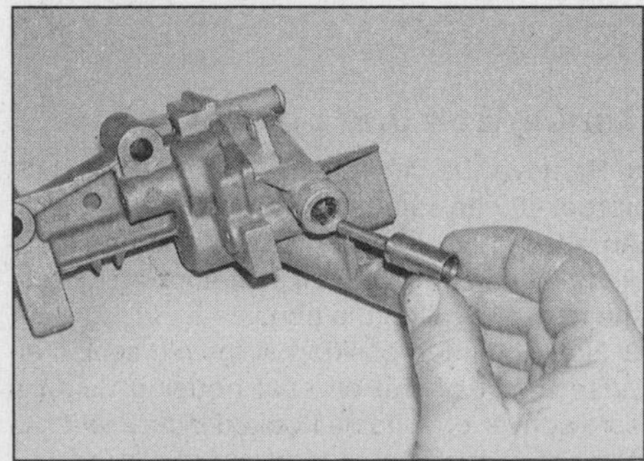

11.33c . . . followed by the plunger

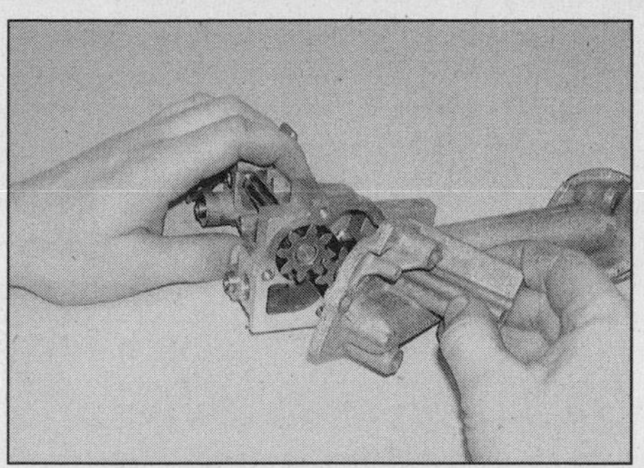

11.34 Unscrew the retaining bolts, and lift off the oil pump cover

11.36a Using feeler blades, measure the clearance between the pump body and the gears . . .

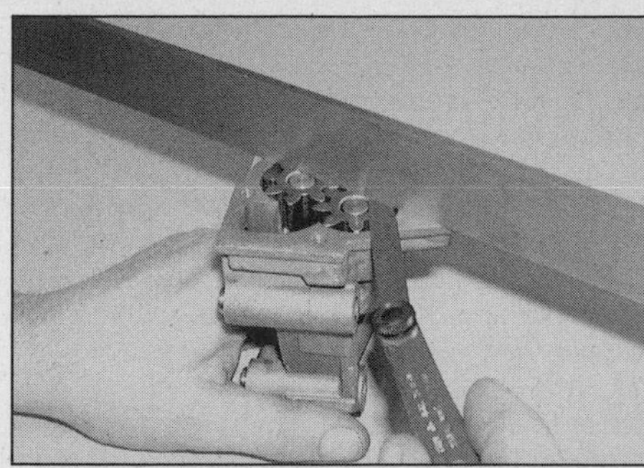

11.36b . . . and measure the gear endfloat

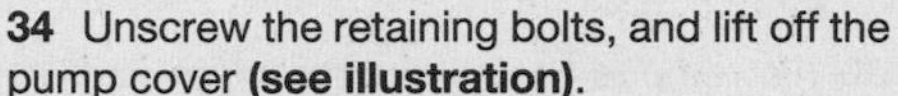

34 Unscrew the retaining bolts, and lift off the pump cover **(see illustration)**.

35 Carefully examine the gears, pump body and relief valve plunger for any signs of scoring or wear. Renew the pump complete if excessive wear is evident.

36 If the components appear serviceable, measure the clearance between the pump body and the gears using feeler blades. Also measure the gear endfloat, and check the flatness of the end cover **(see illustrations)**. If the clearances exceed the specified tolerances, the pump must be renewed.

37 If the pump is satisfactory, reassemble the components in the reverse order of removal. Fill the pump with oil, then refit the cover and tighten the bolts securely **(see illustration)**.

Refitting

38 Wipe clean the oil pump and cylinder block mating surfaces.

39 Locate the drive sprocket onto the end of the crankshaft, ensuring that it is fitted with the projecting boss facing away from the crankshaft **(see illustration)**. Engage the pump with the dowels, fit the two retaining bolts and tighten them to the specified torque.

40 Refit the anti-emulsion plate and secure with the retaining bolt(s).

41 Refit the oil seal housing as described in Section 12.

42 Refit the sump as described in Section 10.

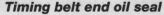

12 Crankshaft oil seals – renewal

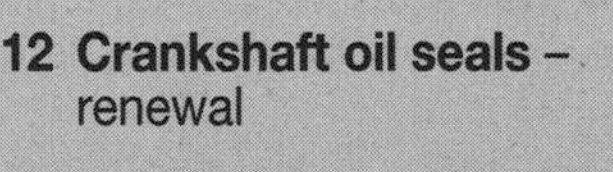

Timing belt end oil seal

1 Remove the timing belt and the crankshaft sprocket with reference to Sections 5 and 6. An alternative, though longer, method is to remove the sump and oil seal housing, and fit the new oil seal on the bench.

2 Note the fitted position of the old seal, then prise it out of the oil seal housing using a screwdriver or suitable hooked instrument. An alternative method of removing the oil seal is to drill carefully two small holes opposite each other in the oil seal and insert self-tapping screws, then pull on the screws with grips. Take care not to damage the surface of the spacer/crankshaft or the seal housing.

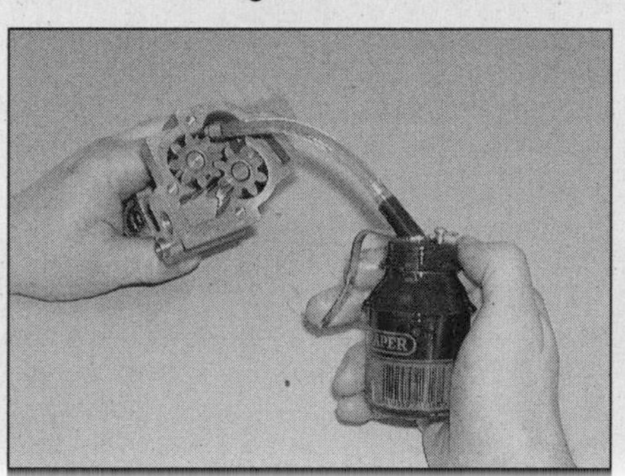

11.37 Fill the pump with oil, then refit the cover

11.39 Ensure that the oil pump drive sprocket is fitted with the projecting boss facing away from the crankshaft

3 With the oil seal removed, where applicable slide the spacer from the crankshaft, noting which way round it is fitted.

4 Examine the spacer for excessive oil seal wear and polish off any burrs or raised edges which may have caused the seal to fail in the first place. If necessary, the spacer can be refitted so that the new oil seal contacts an unworn area. Clean the oil seal seating in the housing.

5 Smear the lips and outer perimeter of the new seal with fresh engine oil and locate it over the crankshaft with its closed side facing outwards. Using hand pressure, press the oil seal squarely into the housing a little way, then use a socket or metal tube to drive the oil seal to the previously noted position – take great care not to damage the seal lips during fitting **(see illustration)**. Do not drive it in too far or it will have to be removed and possibly renewed.

6 Where applicable, slide the spacer onto the crankshaft and carefully press it into the oil seal, while twisting it to prevent damage.

7 Wipe away any excess oil, then refit the crankshaft sprocket and fit the new timing belt with reference to Sections 6 and 5.

Flywheel/driveplate end oil seal

8 Renewal of the crankshaft left-hand oil seal requires the engine and transmission assembly to be removed as described in Chapter 2D so that the engine and transmission can be separated on the bench (see Chapter 7A or 7B), the clutch (where fitted – see Chapter 6) and the flywheel/driveplate (see Section 13 of this Chapter) can be removed.

9 Prise out the old oil seal using a small screwdriver, taking care not to damage the surface on the crankshaft. Alternatively, the oil seal can be removed by drilling two small holes diagonally opposite each other and inserting self-tapping screws in them. A pair of grips can then be used to pull out the oil seal, by pulling on each side in turn.

10 Inspect the seal rubbing surface on the crankshaft. If it is grooved or rough in the area where the old seal was fitted, the new seal should be fitted slightly less deeply, so that it rubs on an unworn part of the surface.

11 Wipe clean the oil seal seating, then dip the new seal in fresh engine oil, and locate it over the crankshaft with its closed side facing

12.5 Using a socket to drive the new crankshaft oil seal into the housing

2A

12.11 Fitting a new crankshaft flywheel end oil seal

outwards **(see illustration)**. Make sure that the oil seal lip is not damaged as it is located on the crankshaft.

12 Using a metal tube, drive the oil seal squarely into the bore until flush. A block of wood cut to pass over the end of the crankshaft may be used instead.

13 Refit the flywheel/driveplate with reference to Section 13. Refit the clutch as described in Chapter 6, reconnect the transmission to the engine and refit the engine/transmission unit as described in the relevant Chapters of this Manual.

13 Flywheel/driveplate – removal, inspection and refitting

Note: *Removal of the flywheel or driveplate requires the engine and transmission assembly to be removed as described in Chapter 2D so that the engine and transmission can separated on the bench.*

Removal

1 Remove the manual gearbox or automatic transmission as described in Chapter 7A or 7B.

2 On manual gearbox models, remove the clutch as described in Chapter 6.

3 Mark the flywheel/driveplate in relation to the crankshaft to aid refitting. Note that the flywheel/driveplate can only be refitted in one position, as the bolts are unequally spaced.

4 The flywheel/driveplate must now be held stationary while the bolts are loosened. To do this, locate a long bolt in one of the transmission-to-engine mounting bolt holes, and either insert a wide-bladed screwdriver in the starter ring gear, or use a piece of bent metal bar engaged with the ring gear.

5 Unscrew the mounting bolts, and withdraw the flywheel/driveplate; be careful – it is heavy. Renault recommend that the bolts are renewed whenever removed. New bolts have locking compound already applied.

Inspection

6 Examine the flywheel/driveplate for wear or chipping of the ring gear teeth. If the ring gear is worn or damaged, it may be possible to renew it separately, but this job is best left to a Renault dealer or engineering works. The temperature to which the new ring gear must be heated for installation is critical and, if not done accurately, the hardness of the teeth will be destroyed.

7 Check the flywheel/driveplate carefully for signs of distortion, and for hairline cracks around the bolt holes, or radiating outwards from the centre. If damage of this sort is found, it must be renewed.

8 Examine the flywheel for scoring of the clutch face. If the clutch face is scored, the flywheel may be machined until flat, but renewal is preferable.

Refitting

9 Clean the flywheel/driveplate and crankshaft mating surfaces, then locate the flywheel/driveplate on the crankshaft, making sure that any previously-made marks are aligned.

10 Fit the new bolts and tighten them in a diagonal sequence to the specified torque wrench setting.

11 Refit the manual gearbox or automatic transmission as described in Chapter 7A or 7B, then refit the engine/transmission assembly with reference to Chapter 2D.

14 Engine/transmission mountings – inspection and renewal

Inspection

1 Apply the handbrake, then jack up the front of the car and support it on axle stands (see *Jacking and vehicle support*). Where fitted, remove the engine compartment undershield.

2 Visually inspect the rubber pads on the two front and one rear engine/transmission mountings for signs of cracking and deterioration **(see illustration)**. Careful use of a lever will help to determine the condition of the rubber pads. If there is excessive movement in the mounting, or if the rubber has deteriorated, the mounting should be renewed.

3 Lower the vehicle to the ground.

Renewal

Right-hand front mounting

4 Support the right-hand end of the engine with a trolley jack and block of wood beneath the sump.

5 Unbolt the mounting brackets from the engine and inner wing panel. **Note:** *On early E7J engines, the bracket is located on the right-hand front of the cylinder block, however on later versions of this engine and on all 16-valve engines, the bracket is located on the right-hand end of the cylinder head.*

6 Fit the new mounting using a reversal of the removal procedure, but tighten the nuts/bolts to the specified torque wrench settings.

Left-hand front mounting

7 Remove the air inlet ducts from the left-hand side of the engine as applicable, for access to the engine/transmission left-hand mounting. Remove the battery as described in Chapter 5A.

8 Support the left-hand end of the transmission with a trolley jack and block of wood beneath the sump.

9 Unbolt the mounting brackets from the transmission and inner wing panel.

10 Fit the new mounting using a reversal of the removal procedure, but tighten the nuts/bolts to the specified torque wrench setting.

Rear mounting

11 Apply the handbrake, then jack up the front of the vehicle and support it on axle stands (see *Jacking and vehicle support*).

12 Unbolt the link bar from the transmission or bracket, and from the subframe.

13 Where applicable, unbolt the bracket from the transmission.

14 Fit the new mounting using a reversal of the removal procedure, but tighten the nuts/bolts to the specified torque setting.

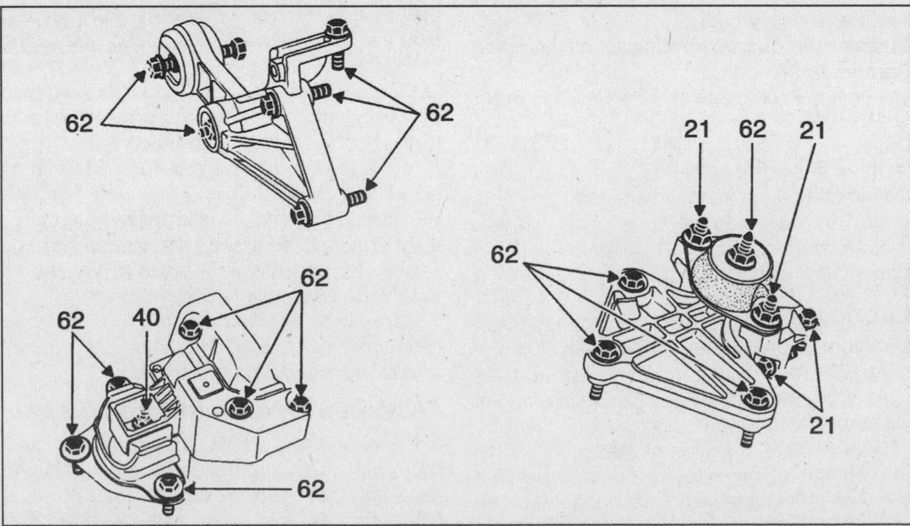

14.2 Torque wrench settings (in Nm) of the engine mountings on models fitted with automatic transmission

Chapter 2 Part B:
2.0 litre petrol engine in-car repair procedures

Contents

Degrees of difficulty

Easy, suitable for novice with little experience 	**Fairly easy,** suitable for beginner with some experience 	**Fairly difficult,** suitable for competent DIY mechanic 	**Difficult,** suitable for experienced DIY mechanic 	**Very difficult,** suitable for expert DIY or professional

Specifications

General

Type	Four-cylinder, 16-valve, in-line, double-overhead camshaft (DOHC)
Designation	F4R 740, F4R 741
Bore	82.7 mm
Stroke	93.0 mm
Capacity	1998 cc
Firing order	1-3-4-2 (No 1 cylinder at flywheel/driveplate end)
Direction of crankshaft rotation	Clockwise viewed from pulley end
Compression ratio	9.8 : 1

Camshafts

Drive	Toothed belt
Number of bearings	6
Camshaft bearing journal diameters:	
No 1 to No 5 bearings	24.979 to 25.000
No 6 bearing	27.979 to 28.000
Camshaft endfloat	0.08 to 0.178 mm

Lubrication system

Minimum oil pressure at 80°C:	
At 1000 rpm	1.0 bars
At 3000 rpm	3.0 bars
Oil pump clearances:	
Gear to body:	
Minimum	0.110 mm
Maximum	0.249 mm
Gear endfloat:	
Minimum	0.020 mm
Maximum	0.086 mm

Torque wrench settings

	Nm	lbf ft
Auxiliary components mounting bracket bolts	44	32
Connecting rod (big-end) caps*:		
Stage 1	20	15
Stage 2	Angle-tighten through 40°	
Crankshaft pulley bolt:		
Stage 1	20	15
Stage 2	Angle-tighten through 115°	
Cylinder head lower section to block:		
Stage 1	20	15
Stage 2	Angle-tighten through 165°	
Cylinder head upper section to lower section:		
Stage 1 – bolts 22, 23, 20 and 13	8	6
Stage 2 – bolts 1 to 12, 14 to 19, 21 and 24	12	9
Stage 3 – bolts 22, 23, 20 and 13	Slacken fully	
Stage 4 – bolts 22, 23, 20 and 13	12	9
Engine/transmission mountings:		
Right-hand mounting:		
Engine bracket-to-cylinder head bolts	62	46
Engine bracket-to-rubber mounting nut	40	30
Rubber mounting-to-body bolts	105	77
Left-hand mounting:		
Mounting bracket-to-transmission bolts	60	44
Mounting stud nut	67	49
Rubber mounting bolts	70	52
Rear mounting:		
Mounting bracket-to-transmission bolts	62	46
Mounting link bolts	105	77
Exhaust camshaft sprocket nut*:		
Stage 1	30	22
Stage 2	Angle-tighten through 84°	
Flywheel/driveplate bolts*	55	41
Inlet camshaft sprocket/phase-shifter bolt*	100	74
Inlet camshaft sprocket/phase-shifter plug	25	19
Main bearing cap bolts*	65	48
Oil pump-to-cylinder block bolts	22	16
Oil seal housing bolts (timing belt end)	15	11
Oil separator to cylinder head upper section	13	10
Roadwheel bolts	90	66
Sump bolts:		
Stage 1	8	6
Stage 2	14	10
Timing belt idler pulley bolts	45	33
Timing belt lower cover	20	15
Timing belt tensioner pulley nut	27	20
Timing belt upper cover:		
M10 nuts/bolts	38	28
M8 bolts	18	13

** New bolts must be used*

1 General information

How to use this Chapter

This Part of Chapter 2 is devoted to in-car repair procedures for the 2.0 litre petrol engine. Similar information covering the other engine types can be found in Parts A and C. All procedures concerning engine removal and refitting, and engine block/cylinder head overhaul can be found in Part D of this Chapter.

Refer to *Vehicle identification numbers* in the Reference Section at the end of this manual for details of engine code locations.

Most of the operations included in this Part are based on the assumption that the engine is still installed in the car. Therefore, if this information is being used during a complete engine overhaul, with the engine already removed, many of the steps included here will not apply.

Engine description

The 2.0 litre 16-valve engine covered in this part of Chapter 2 is of four-cylinder, in-line, double overhead camshaft type, incorporating two inlet valves and two exhaust valves per cylinder. The engine is mounted transversely at the front of the vehicle with the transmission bolted to the left-hand side.

The crankshaft is supported in five shell-type main bearings. Crankshaft endfloat is controlled by thrustwashers fitted to the No 2 main bearing.

The connecting rods are attached to the crankshaft by horizontally-split shell-type big-end bearings, and to the pistons by gudgeon pins. The gudgeon pins are a press fit in the connecting rods. The aluminium alloy pistons are of the slipper type, and are fitted with three piston rings – two compression rings and a scraper-type oil control ring.

The cylinder head comprises an upper and lower section, mated along the centre line of the camshafts. The upper section of the cylinder head functions as a combined valve cover and camshaft cover, the camshafts run in plain bearings integral to the two cylinder head sections. The camshafts operate the inlet and exhaust valves via roller rocker arms which are supported at their pivot ends by hydraulic self-adjusting tappets.

Drive to the camshafts is by a toothed timing belt and sprockets and incorporating an automatic tensioning mechanism. The inlet camshaft sprocket incorporates a phase-shifter which provides variable valve timing by advancing the inlet valve timing during certain operating conditions. The phase-shifter is activated by the engine management ECU via an electrically-controlled solenoid valve located on the top, right-hand side of the cylinder head.

The water pump is mounted on the front right-hand side of the engine, and is driven by the multi-ribbed auxiliary drivebelt from the crankshaft pulley. The same drivebelt drives the alternator, power steering pump and air conditioning compressor (where fitted).

A semi-closed crankcase ventilation system is employed; crankcase fumes are drawn from an oil separator on the cylinder head, and passed via a hose to the inlet manifold.

The lubrication system is of the full-flow, pressure-feed type. Oil is drawn from the sump by a chain-driven gear-type oil pump located beneath the crankshaft. Oil under pressure passes through a filter before being fed to the various shaft bearings and to the valve gear.

Repair operations possible with the engine in the vehicle

The following operations can be carried out without having to remove the engine from the car:

a) Compression pressure testing.
b) Timing belt and sprockets – removal and refitting.
c) Camshaft oil seals – renewal.
d) Camshafts, tappets and rocker arms – removal and refitting.
e) Cylinder head – removal and refitting.
f) Cylinder head and pistons – decarbonising.
g) Crankshaft oil seals – renewal.
h) Sump – removal and refitting.
i) Pistons and connecting rods – removal and refitting.*
j) Oil pump – removal and refitting.
k) Flywheel – removal and refitting.
l) Engine mountings – removal and refitting.

* **Note:** *Although the operation marked with an asterisk can be carried out with the engine in the car after removal of the sump, it is better for the engine to be removed, in the interests of cleanliness and improved access. For this reason, the procedure is described in Part D of this Chapter.*

Caution: If the radio/cassette in your vehicle is equipped with an anti-theft system, make sure you have the correct activation code before disconnecting the battery.

2 Compression test – description and interpretation

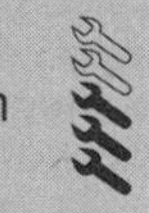

Note: *A compression gauge will be required for this test.*

1 When engine performance is down, or if misfiring occurs which cannot be attributed to the ignition or fuel systems, a compression test can provide diagnostic clues as to the engine's condition. If the test is performed regularly, it can give warning of trouble before any other symptoms become apparent.

2 The engine must be fully warmed-up to normal operating temperature, the battery must be fully charged, and all the spark plugs must be removed (see Chapter 1A). The aid of an assistant will also be required.

3 Disable the ignition system by disconnecting the crankshaft sensor wiring at the connector located on the left-hand side of the engine. Also disconnect the wiring connectors to each fuel injector to prevent unburned fuel from damaging the catalytic converter.

4 Fit a compression tester to the No 1 cylinder spark plug hole – the type of tester which screws into the plug thread is to be preferred.

5 Have the assistant hold the throttle wide open, and crank the engine on the starter motor; after one or two revolutions, the compression pressure should build-up to a maximum figure, and then stabilise. Record the highest reading obtained.

6 Repeat the test on the remaining cylinders, recording the pressure in each.

7 All cylinders should produce very similar pressures; a difference of more than 2 bars between any two cylinders indicates a fault. Note that the compression should build-up quickly in a healthy engine; low compression on the first stroke, followed by gradually-increasing pressure on successive strokes, indicates worn piston rings. A low compression reading on the first stroke, which does not build-up during successive strokes, indicates leaking valves or a blown head gasket (a cracked cylinder head could also be the cause). Deposits on the undersides of the valve heads can also cause low compression.

8 If the pressure in any cylinder is low, carry out the following test to isolate the cause. Introduce a teaspoonful of clean oil into that cylinder through its spark plug hole, and repeat the test.

9 If the addition of oil temporarily improves the compression pressure, this indicates that bore or piston wear is responsible for the pressure loss. No improvement suggests that leaking or burnt valves, or a blown head gasket, may be to blame.

10 A low reading from two adjacent cylinders is almost certainly due to the head gasket having blown between them; the presence of coolant in the engine oil will confirm this.

11 If one cylinder is about 20 percent lower than the others and the engine has a slightly rough idle, a worn camshaft lobe could be the cause.

12 If the compression reading is unusually high, the combustion chambers are probably coated with carbon deposits. If this is the case, the cylinder head should be removed and decarbonised.

13 On completion of the test, refit the spark plugs and reconnect the ignition system and fuel injectors.

3 Timing belt – removal and refitting

Note: *This is a complicated operation requiring the use of certain special tools. Read through the entire procedure to familiarise yourself with the work involved then either obtain the manufacturer's special tools or, where applicable, fabricate the home-made alternatives described, before proceeding.*

General information

1 The function of the timing belt is to drive the camshafts. Should the belt slip or break in service, the valve timing will be disturbed and piston to valve contact will occur, resulting in serious engine damage.

2 The timing belt should be renewed at the specified intervals (see Chapter 1A), earlier if it is contaminated with oil, or if it is at all noisy in operation (a 'scraping' noise due to uneven wear). Note that the manufacturer recommends that the timing belt should be renewed whenever it is removed, and that the timing belt tensioner and idler pulley should also be renewed at the same time. Additionally, new camshaft sealing caps will be required, and a new crankshaft pulley retaining bolt and camshaft sprocket retaining nuts may be needed, depending on the condition of the components and/or the tensioning method being used when refitting.

3 Before carrying out this procedure, it will be necessary to obtain or fabricate a crankshaft TDC positioning pin and a camshaft holding tool, as described later in this Section. Do not attempt to remove the timing belt unless the special tools or their alternatives are available.

4 The design of the camshaft and crankshaft timing belt sprockets are slightly unusual in that no method of positive location of the sprockets (such as that afforded by a Woodruff key) is employed. Instead, the sprockets are retained purely by the clamping action of the sprocket retaining bolts/nuts. Due to this arrangement, there are two different procedures for tensioning the timing belt when refitting. The first method is used for routine timing belt renewal when the camshaft sprockets have not been disturbed. The second method is used if either of the camshaft sprockets have been removed, or their retaining nuts slackened prior to refitting the timing belt.

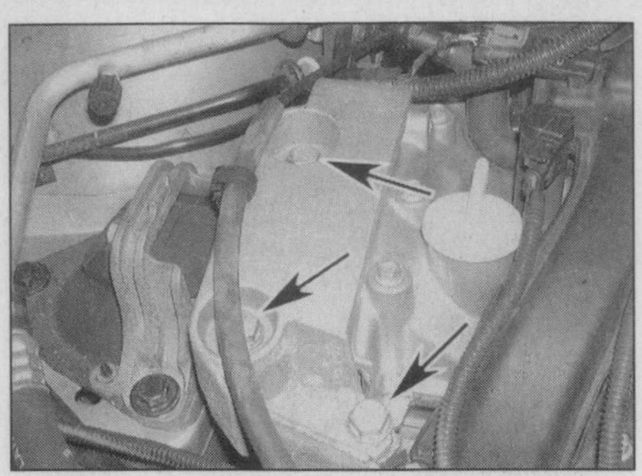
3.10a Undo the three bolts (arrowed) securing the right-hand engine mounting bracket to the cylinder head . . .

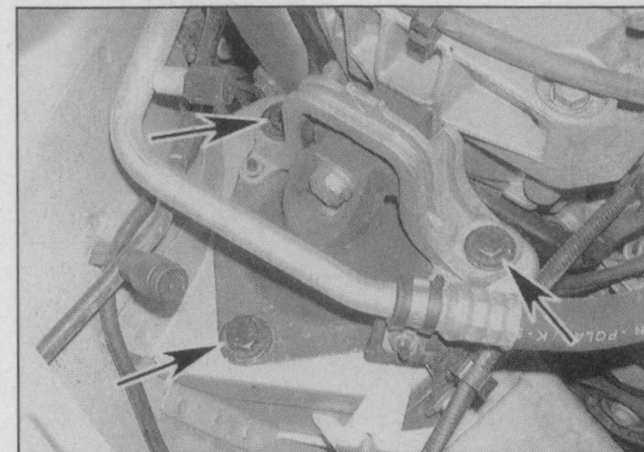
3.10b . . . and the three bolts (arrowed) securing the rubber mounting to the body

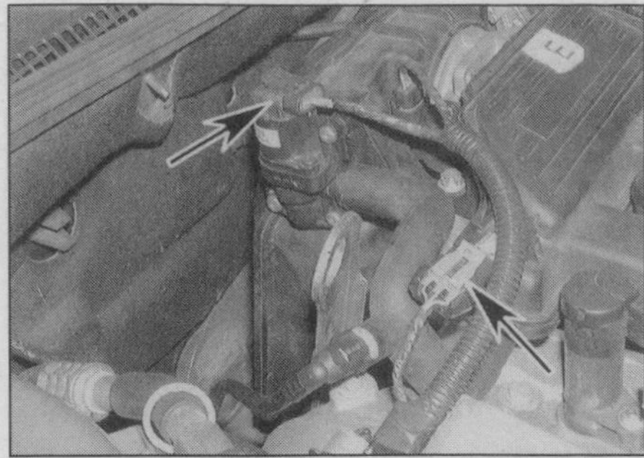
3.11 Disconnect the wiring connectors at the idle speed stepper motor, throttle position sensor and MAP sensor (arrowed)

Removal

5 Disconnect the battery negative terminal (refer to *Disconnecting the battery* in the Reference Section of this manual).

6 Apply the handbrake, then jack up the front of the car and support it on axle stands (see *Jacking and vehicle support*). Remove the right-hand front roadwheel, then undo the retaining screws and remove the engine undercover and the front and rear protective covers from the right-hand wheelarch.

3.13 Using a screwdriver, prise the camshaft sealing caps from the left-hand end of the cylinder head

7 Remove the auxiliary drivebelt as described in Chapter 1A.

8 Remove the complete air cleaner assembly and inlet ducts as described in Chapter 4A.

9 Position an engine hoist, or an engine lifting beam across the engine compartment and attach the jib to the right-hand engine lifting eyelet. Raise the lifting gear to take up the slack, so that it is just supporting the weight of the engine.

10 Undo the three bolts securing the right-hand engine mounting bracket to the cylinder head **(see illustration)**. Similarly, undo the three bolts securing the rubber mounting to the body **(see illustration)**. Release the relevant cable clips and remove the complete mounting assembly.

11 Disconnect the wiring connectors at the idle speed stepper motor, throttle position sensor and MAP sensor, then unclip the wiring harness from the upper timing belt cover and move the harness to one side **(see illustration)**.

12 Release the fuel pipes from the clips on the lower timing belt cover.

13 Prise the sealing caps from the left-hand end of the cylinder head, to expose the ends of both camshafts. The caps cannot be re-used, so the easiest way to remove them is to punch a small hole in the centre of each cap and lever them out with a stout screwdriver **(see illustration)**.

14 With the help of an assistant to slowly turn the crankshaft using a socket or spanner on the crankshaft pulley bolt, observe the position of the slots in the ends of the camshafts. Turn the crankshaft in a clockwise direction (as viewed from the timing belt end), until the camshaft slots are nearly horizontal, with the offset below the centreline **(see illustration)**.

15 Unscrew the plug from the TDC pin hole on the left-hand end of the front of the cylinder block, located just below the engine identification plate. Insert the crankshaft TDC pin (Renault special tool Mot. 1054) into the hole until it contacts the crankshaft. Alternatively, insert a dowel rod of suitable diameter to be a snug fit in the hole **(see illustrations)**.

16 While maintaining slight pressure on the

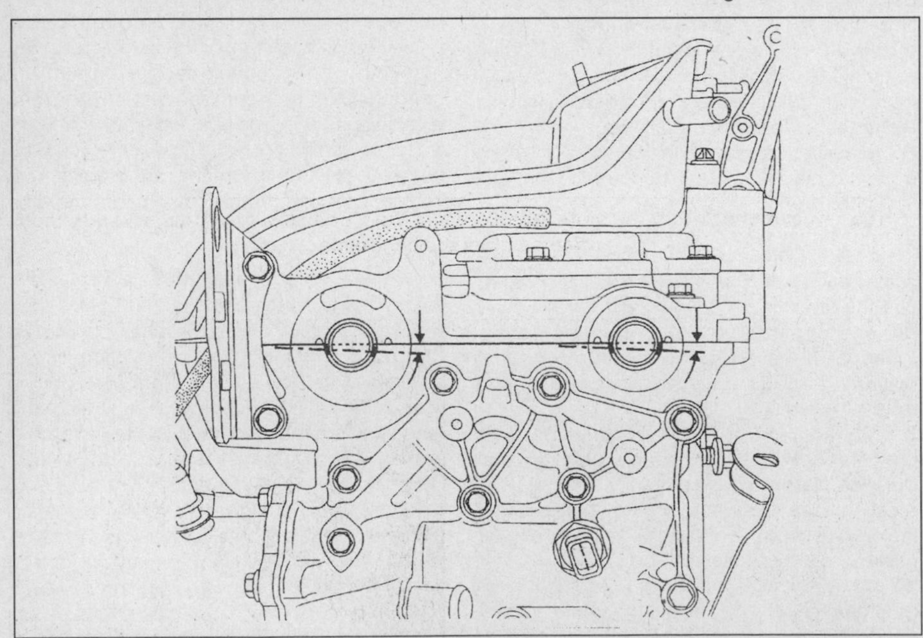
3.14 Turn the crankshaft until the camshaft slots are nearly horizontal, with the offset below the centreline

3.15a Unscrew the plug from TDC pin hole on the left-hand end of the front of the cylinder block . . .

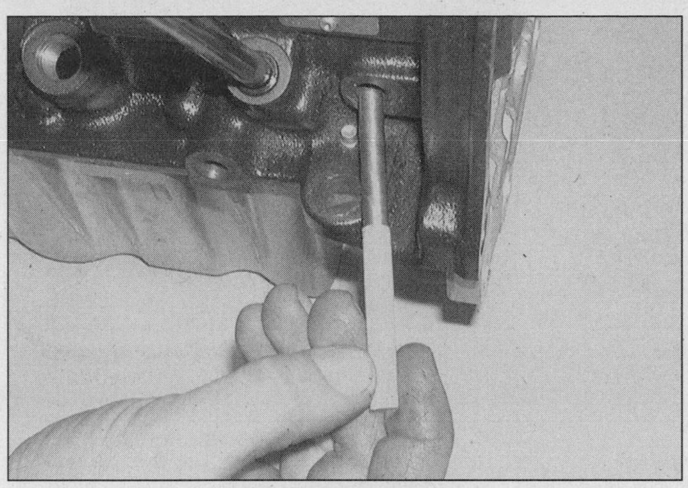

3.15b . . . and insert the special tool or a dowel rod of suitable diameter to be a snug fit in the hole

3.16a Turn the crankshaft until the special tool or dowel rod (A) enters the crankshaft setting slot (B)

TDC pin or dowel rod, continue to turn the crankshaft clockwise very slightly until the pin or rod enters the slot provided for this purpose in the crankshaft web. Note that there is a balance hole in the crankshaft web adjacent to the TDC setting slot. If care is not taken, it is very easy for the TDC pin or dowel rod to engage with the balance hole and not the setting slot. If the tool has entered the setting slot, the slots in the ends of the camshafts should now be horizontal (ie, parallel to the join between the upper and lower cylinder head sections) with their offsets below the centreline **(see illustrations)**.

17 Using a socket and extension bar, slacken the crankshaft pulley bolt. Hold the crankshaft stationary while the bolt is unscrewed by engaging a screwdriver with the flywheel ring gear teeth through the opening at the lower rear of the cylinder block. Unscrew the bolt and remove the washer and crankshaft pulley.

18 Unscrew the nuts and bolts and remove the lower timing belt cover followed by the upper cover, then collect the spacers from the mounting studs **(see illustrations)**.

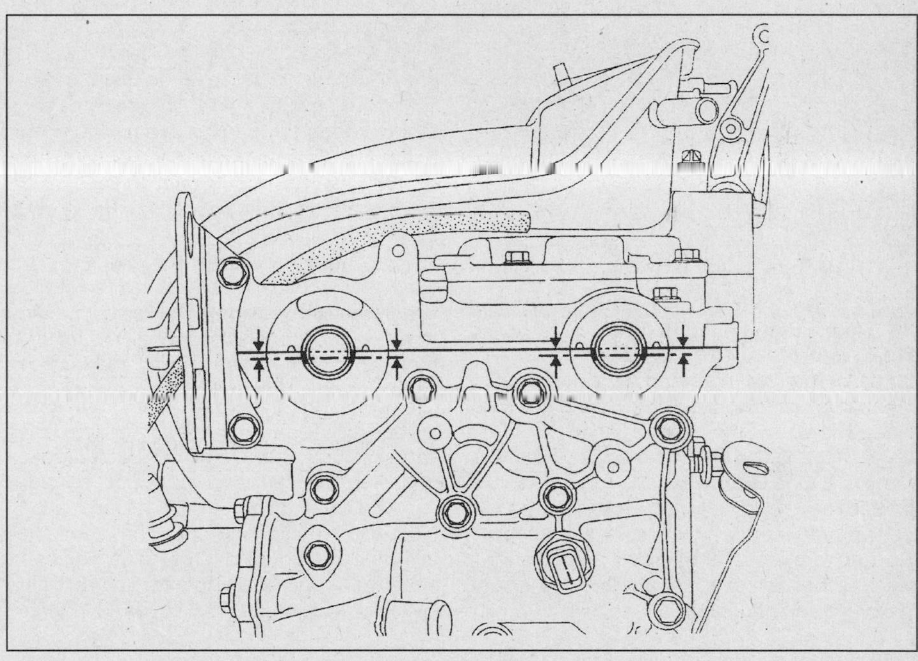

3.16b . . . and check that the slots in the ends of the camshafts are horizontal with their offsets below the centreline

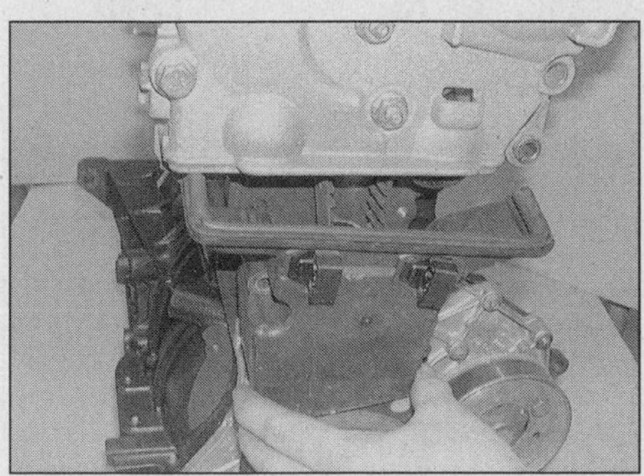

3.18a Unscrew the nuts and bolts and remove the lower timing belt cover . . .

3.18b . . . followed by the upper cover . . .

3.18c . . . then collect the spacers from the studs

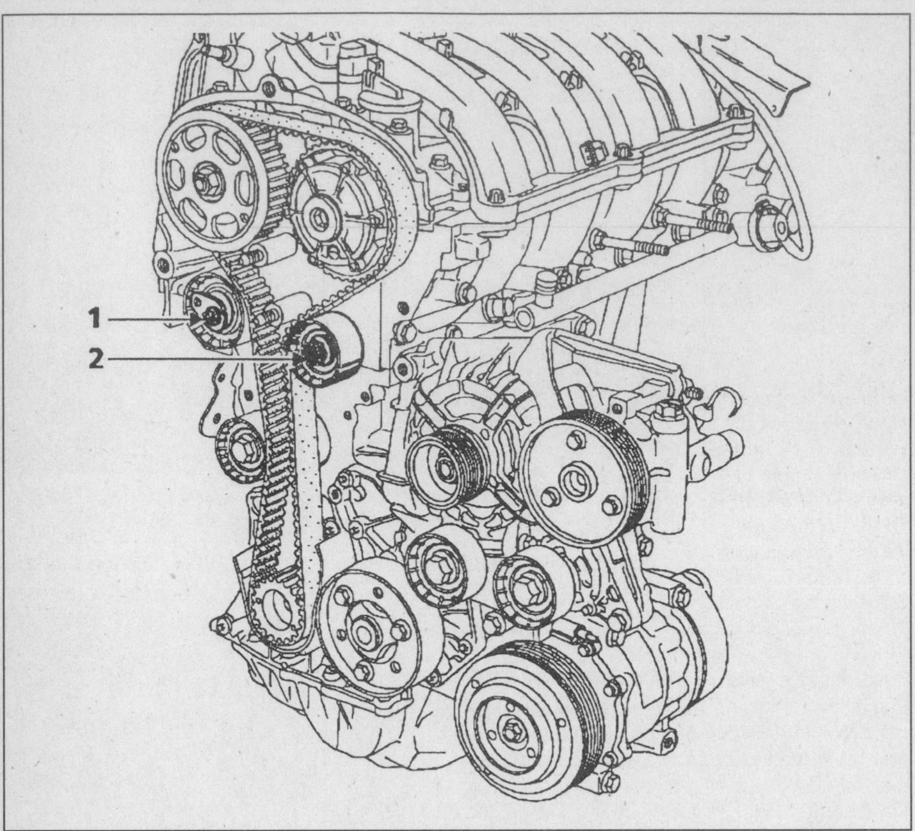

3.19 Timing belt tensioner pulley centre retaining nut (1) and idler pulley bolt (2)

3.20 Unscrew the bolt and remove the timing belt idler pulley and the spacer

19 Slacken the timing belt tensioner pulley centre retaining nut **(see illustration)**.

20 Unscrew the mounting bolt and remove the timing belt idler pulley and the spacer **(see illustration)**.

21 Slip the timing belt off the sprockets and remove it **(see illustration)**. Clearance is very limited at the crankshaft sprocket and a certain amount of manipulation is necessary. Do not rotate the crankshaft or camshafts with the belt removed, as there is the risk of piston-to-valve contact.

22 Obtain a new timing belt, new tensioner and idler pulleys and new camshaft sealing caps prior to refitting. If method two is being used for the refitting and tensioning procedure, remove the exhaust camshaft sprocket and the inlet camshaft sprocket/ phase-shifter; a new camshaft sprocket retaining nut and bolt will also be required.

23 Measure the length of the crankshaft pulley retaining bolt, from the underside of the head to the end of the thread. The bolt must be renewed if the length exceeds 49.1 mm.

Refitting and tensioning

Method one

Note: *Method one should be used for refitting and tensioning the timing belt when the camshaft sprockets have not been disturbed. If either of the camshaft sprockets have been removed, or their retaining nuts slackened prior to refitting the timing belt, method two described later in this Section should be used instead.*

24 Fit the new tensioner pulley to the mounting stud ensuring that the lug on the rear of the tensioner body engages in the slot in the cylinder head **(see illustration)**. Screw on the retaining nut, finger tight only at this stage.

25 Check that the crankshaft is still locked with the TDC pin or dowel rod. Slip the crankshaft sprocket off the end of the crankshaft and check that the keyway in the crankshaft is uppermost. Note that although there is a keyway in both the crankshaft and crankshaft sprocket, a Woodruff key is not used.

26 Using a suitable solvent, thoroughly clean the end of the crankshaft, crankshaft sprocket bore, and the crankshaft and sprocket mating faces. It is essential that all traces of oil and grease are removed from these areas to allow the sprocket to be securely clamped when the

3.21 Slip the timing belt off the sprockets and remove it

3.24 Fit the new tensioner pulley to the stud ensuring that the lug (arrowed) on the tensioner engages in the cylinder head slot

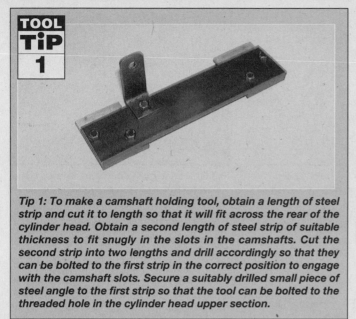

Tip 1: To make a camshaft holding tool, obtain a length of steel strip and cut it to length so that it will fit across the rear of the cylinder head. Obtain a second length of steel strip of suitable thickness to fit snugly in the slots in the camshafts. Cut the second strip into two lengths and drill accordingly so that they can be bolted to the first strip in the correct position to engage with the camshaft slots. Secure a suitably drilled small piece of steel angle to the first strip so that the tool can be bolted to the threaded hole in the cylinder head upper section.

3.29 Engage the camshaft holding tool with the camshaft slots and secure the tool using a suitable bolt screwed into the cylinder head

pulley and retaining bolt are refitted. If the sprocket slips in service, serious engine damage will result.

27 Check that the camshafts are still correctly positioned with the slots parallel to the join between the upper and lower cylinder head sections, with their offsets below the centreline. It may be necessary to turn the camshafts slightly using a spanner on the sprocket retaining nuts, to correctly align the slots.

28 The camshafts must now be retained in this position either by using Renault special tool Mot. 1496, or by fabricating a home-made alternative **(see Tool Tip 1)**.

29 Engage the Renault special tool or the home-made alternative with the slots in the camshafts and secure the tool to the cylinder head using a suitable bolt **(see illustration)**. With the crankshaft against the TDC pin and the camshafts secured with the holding tool, refit the crankshaft sprocket to the end of the crankshaft.

30 Check that the inlet camshaft sprocket/phase-shifter is neither advanced or retarded **(see illustration)**. Locate the new timing belt over the crankshaft and camshaft sprockets, and around the tensioner pulley **(see illustration)**.

31 Fit the new idler pulley and spacer and tighten the retaining bolt to the specified torque. Ensure that the spacer is fitted the correct way round **(see illustration)**.

32 Refit the crankshaft pulley and the retaining bolt and washer. If the original bolt is being re-used, lightly lubricate the threads with engine

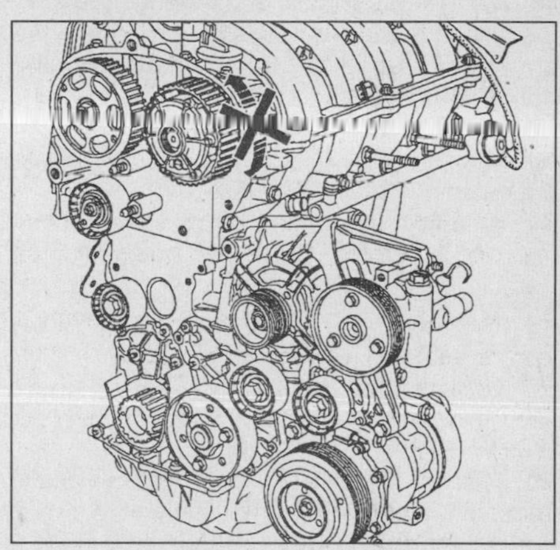

3.30a Check that the sprocket/phase-shifter is neither advanced or retarded before refitting the timing belt

2B

3.30b Locate the new timing belt over the sprockets and around the tensioner pulley

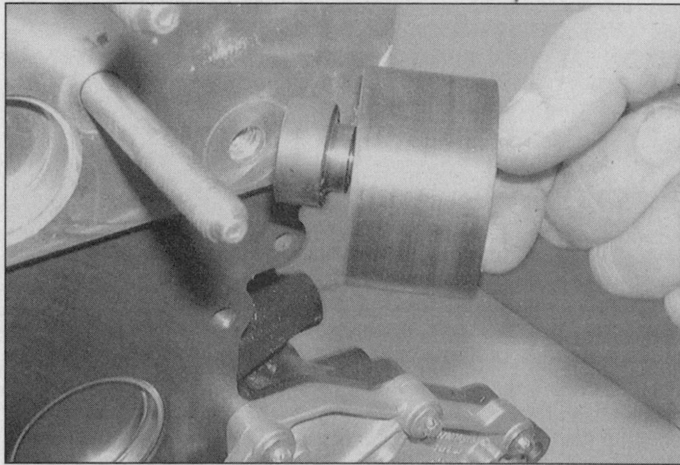

3.31 Fit the new idler pulley and spacer ensuring that the spacer is fitted the correct way round

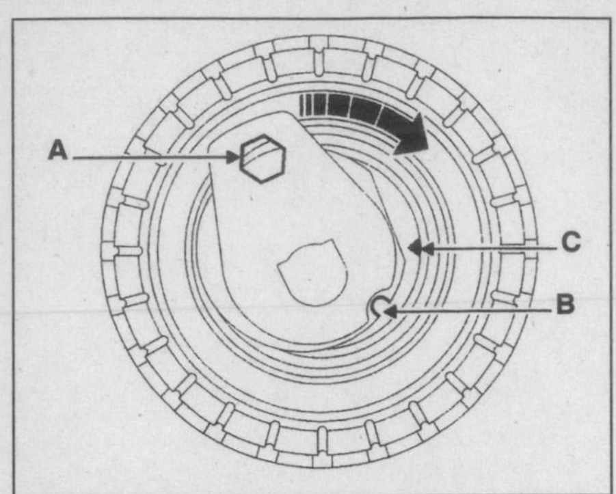

3.33a Using an Allen key in the tensioner arm slot (A) rotate the arm until the indentation (B) is aligned with the notch (C) in the pulley body

oil. If a new bolt is being used it should be fitted dry. Tighten the bolt so there is approximately 2.0 to 3.0 mm clearance between the bolt and the pulley. The crankshaft sprocket must be free to turn on the crankshaft for the timing belt to be tensioned correctly.

33 Using a 6.0 mm Allen key engaged with the hole in the tensioner pulley arm, rotate the arm clockwise until the indentation on the pulley arm is aligned with the notch on the pulley body **(see illustrations)**. Hold the tensioner in this position and initially tighten the retaining nut to 7 Nm (5 lbf ft).

34 Initially tighten the crankshaft pulley retaining bolt to the Stage 1 torque setting as given in the Specifications.

35 Using quick-drying paint, make alignment marks between the camshaft sprockets and cylinder head upper section to use as reference marks in the following procedure **(see illustration)**.

36 Remove the TDC pin or dowel rod and the camshaft holding tool, then finally tighten the crankshaft pulley bolt through the Stage 2 angle as given in the Specifications. Lock the crankshaft using a screwdriver engaged with the flywheel ring gear to prevent crankshaft rotation as the bolt is tightened.

37 Turn the crankshaft clockwise through two complete revolutions, but just before completing the second revolution, ie, half a tooth before the previously-made reference marks on the sprockets and cylinder head upper section align, refit the TDC pin or dowel rod. Continue turning the crankshaft until the pin or rod fully engage with the crankshaft setting slot.

38 Remove the TDC pin or dowel rod and check that the indentation on the tensioner pulley arm is still aligned with the notch on the pulley body. If not, slacken the tensioner nut and repeat the procedure in paragraphs 33 and 37. If the tensioner pulley is correctly positioned, finally tighten the retaining nut to the specified torque.

39 With the belt correctly tensioned, recheck the timing by once again turning the crankshaft clockwise through two complete revolutions, and stopping just before completing the second revolution (just before the previously made sprocket reference marks align). Refit the TDC pin or dowel rod, then continue turning the crankshaft until the pin or rod fully engage with the crankshaft setting slot.

3.33b Hold the tensioner and tighten the retaining nut

40 Check that with the crankshaft locked with the TDC pin or dowel rod, it is possible to fit the camshaft holding tool to the slots in the camshafts without force. If the slots are not correctly positioned and the tool will not fit, repeat the complete refitting and tensioning procedure.

41 If the timing is correct, remove the TDC pin and camshaft holding tool and continue with the refitting procedure as described in paragraphs 65 to 74.

Method two

Note: *Method two should be used for refitting and tensioning the timing belt if either of the camshaft sprockets have been removed, or their retaining nuts slackened for any reason prior to refitting the belt. If the camshaft sprockets have not been disturbed, method one described earlier in this Section should be used instead.*

42 Check that the crankshaft is still locked with the TDC pin or dowel rod. Slip the crankshaft sprocket off the end of the crankshaft and check that the keyway in the crankshaft is uppermost. Note that although there is a keyway in both the crankshaft and crankshaft sprocket, a Woodruff key is not used.

43 Using a suitable solvent, thoroughly clean the end of the crankshaft, crankshaft sprocket bore, and the crankshaft and sprocket mating faces. Similarly clean the camshaft ends, camshaft sprocket bores and mating faces. It is essential that all traces of oil and grease are removed from these areas to allow the sprockets to be securely clamped when the pulley and retaining bolt/nuts are refitted. If the sprockets slip in service, serious engine damage will result.

44 Check that the camshafts are still correctly positioned with the slots parallel to the join between the upper and lower cylinder head sections, with their offsets below the centreline. If necessary, temporarily refit the old camshaft sprocket retaining nut/bolt and turn the camshafts slightly using a spanner to correctly align the slots.

3.35 Make alignment marks between the camshaft sprockets and cylinder head upper section to use as reference marks

45 The camshafts must now be retained in this position either by using Renault special tool Mot. 1496, or by fabricating a home-made alternative **(see Tool Tip 1)**.

46 Engage the Renault special tool or the home-made alternative with the slots in the camshafts and secure the tool to the cylinder head using a suitable bolt. With the crankshaft against the TDC pin and the camshafts secured with the holding tool, refit the crankshaft sprocket to the end of the crankshaft.

47 Refit the camshaft sprockets, together with a new retaining nut or bolt (as applicable). Tighten the nut/bolt so there is approximately 0.5 to 1.0 mm clearance between the nuts and the sprockets, and the sprockets are free to turn. Where applicable, position the sprockets so that the Renault logo stamped on one of the spokes is vertically uppermost **(see illustration)**.

48 Fit the new tensioner pulley to the mounting stud ensuring that the lug on the rear of the tensioner body engages in the slot in the cylinder head **(see illustration 3.24)**. Screw on the retaining nut, finger tight only at this stage.

49 Check that the inlet camshaft sprocket/phase-shifter is neither advanced or retarded **(see illustration 3.30a)**. Locate the new timing belt over the crankshaft and camshaft sprockets, and around the tensioner pulley.

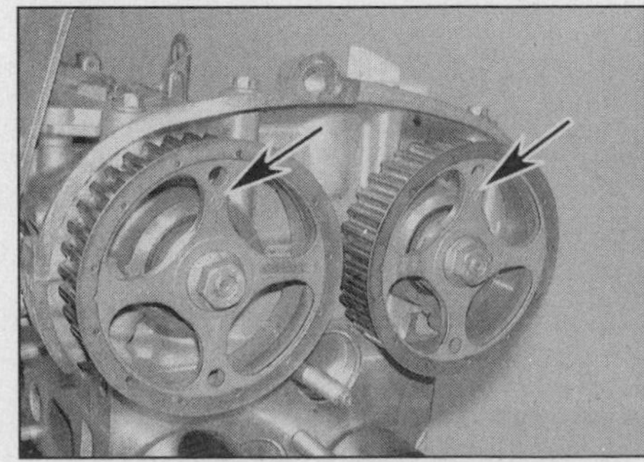

3.47 Position the sprockets so that the Renault logo (arrowed) is uppermost

Tip 2: To make a camshaft sprocket holding tool, obtain two lengths of steel strip 6 mm thick by 30 mm wide or similar, one 600 mm long, the other 200 mm long (all dimensions approximate). Bolt the two strips together to form a forked end, leaving the bolt slack so that the shorter strip can pivot freely. At the end of each 'prong' of the fork, drill a suitable hole and fit a nut and bolt to engage with the holes in the sprocket.

50 Fit the new idler pulley and spacer and tighten the retaining bolt to the specified torque. Ensure that the spacer is fitted the correct way round **(see illustration 3.31)**.

51 Refit the crankshaft pulley and the retaining bolt and washer. If the original bolt is being re-used, lightly lubricate the threads with engine oil. If a new bolt is being used it should be fitted dry. Tighten the bolt so there is approximately 2.0 to 3.0 mm clearance between the bolt and the pulley. The crankshaft and camshaft sprockets must all be free to turn for the timing belt to be tensioned correctly.

52 Using a 6.0 mm Allen key engaged with the hole in the tensioner pulley arm, rotate the arm clockwise until the indentation on the pulley arm is aligned with the notch on the pulley body **(see illustrations 3.33a and 3.33b)**. Hold the tensioner in this position and initially tighten the retaining nut to 7 Nm (5 lbf ft).

53 Turn the exhaust camshaft sprocket through six complete revolutions to initially settle and pre-tension the timing belt. The sprocket can be turned using a suitable forked tool engaged with the holes in the sprocket **(see Tool Tip 2)**. During this operation, ensure that the sprocket retaining nut/bolt remains slack to allow the sprockets to turn freely.

54 Check that the indentation on the tensioner pulley arm is still aligned with the notch on the pulley body. If not, slacken the tensioner nut and repeat the procedure in paragraphs 52 and 53. If the tensioner pulley is correctly positioned, finally tighten the retaining nut to the specified torque.

55 Initially tighten the crankshaft pulley retaining bolt to the Stage 1 torque setting as given in the Specifications **(see illustration)**.

56 Using quick-drying paint, make alignment marks between the camshaft sprockets and cylinder head upper section to use as reference marks in the following procedure **(see illustration 3.35)**.

57 Remove the TDC pin or dowel rod and finally tighten the crankshaft pulley bolt through the Stage 2 angle as given in the Specifications **(see illustration)**. Lock the crankshaft using a screwdriver engaged with the flywheel ring gear to prevent crankshaft rotation as the bolt is tightened.

58 Turn the crankshaft clockwise through two complete revolutions, but just before completing the second revolution, ie, half a tooth before the previously-made reference marks on the sprockets and cylinder head upper section align, refit the TDC pin or dowel rod. Continue turning the crankshaft until the pin or rod fully engage with the crankshaft setting slot.

3.55 Initially tighten the crankshaft pulley retaining bolt to the Stage 1 torque setting

3.57 Finally tighten the pulley bolt through the Stage 2 angle

59 Tighten the camshaft sprocket retaining nut and bolt to their specified torques. The forked tool described in Tool Tip 2 can be used to hold the sprockets as the nuts are tightened **(see illustrations)**.

60 Remove the TDC pin or dowel rod and the camshaft holding tool. Turn the crankshaft clockwise through two complete revolutions, but just before completing the second revolution, ie, half a tooth before the previously-made reference marks on the sprockets and cylinder head upper section align, refit the TDC pin or dowel rod. Continue turning the crankshaft until the pin or rod fully engage with the crankshaft setting slot.

61 Remove the TDC pin or dowel rod and check that the indentation on the tensioner pulley arm is still aligned with the notch on the pulley body. If not, slacken the tensioner nut and realign the indentation and notch as described in paragraph 52. Tighten the tensioner nut to the specified torque, then turn the crankshaft through a further two revolutions and recheck the setting **(see illustration)**.

62 With the belt correctly tensioned, recheck the timing by once again turning the crankshaft clockwise through two complete revolutions, and stopping just before completing the second revolution, (just before the previously-made sprocket reference marks align). Refit the TDC pin or dowel rod, then continue turning the crankshaft until the pin or rod fully engage with the crankshaft setting slot.

2B

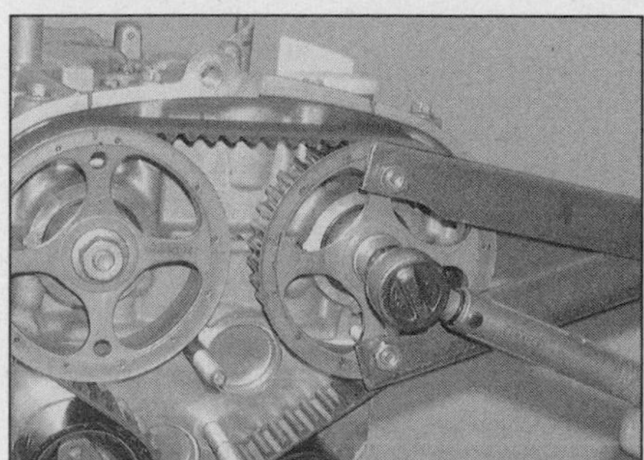

3.59a Tighten both camshaft sprocket retaining nuts to the Stage 1 torque setting . . .

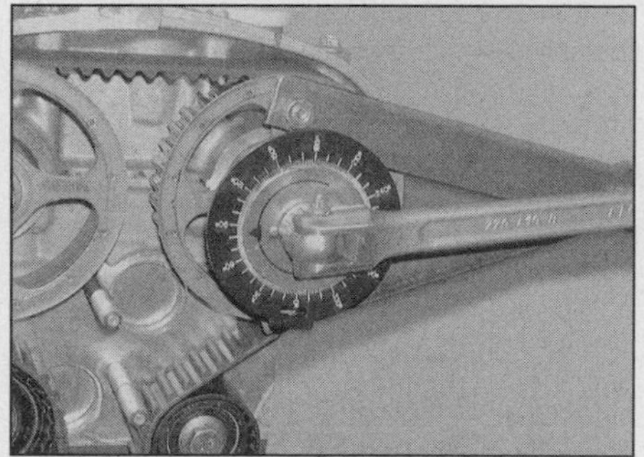

3.59b . . . then through the Stage 2 angle (where applicable)

3.61 Hold the tensioner arm and tighten the retaining nut to the specified torque

3.65 Fit the new sealing caps to the cylinder head and tap them into place using a large socket

63 Check that with the crankshaft locked with the TDC pin or dowel rod, it is possible to fit the camshaft holding tool to the slots in the camshafts without force. If the slots are not correctly positioned and the tool will not fit, repeat the complete refitting and tensioning procedure.

64 If the timing is correct, remove the TDC pin and camshaft holding tool, then proceed as follows.

65 Refit the new camshaft sealing caps to the left-hand end of the cylinder head and carefully tap them into place using a large socket or similar tool **(see illustration)**.

66 Apply sealing compound to the TDC pin plug then refit the plug to the cylinder block, tightening it securely.

67 Refit the timing belt upper cover followed by the lower cover and tighten the retaining nuts and bolts to the specified torque, where applicable.

68 Secure the fuel pipes with the clips on the lower timing belt cover.

69 Reconnect the wiring connectors at the idle speed stepper motor, throttle position sensor and MAP sensor, then clip the wiring harness to the upper timing belt cover.

70 Locate the right-hand engine mounting assembly into position and refit the bolts securing the mounting bracket to the cylinder head. Tighten the bolts to the specified torque. Refit the three bolts securing the rubber mounting to the body. Ensure that the movement limiter is positioned centrally over the mounting rubber then tighten the three bolts to the specified torque.

4.4 Withdraw the appropriate sprocket from the camshaft for access to the oil seal

71 Remove the engine hoist or lifting beam from the engine compartment.

72 Refit the auxiliary drivebelt as described in Chapter 1A, and the air cleaner components as described in Chapter 4A.

73 Refit the engine undercover and wheelarch covers then refit the right-hand roadwheel. Tighten the wheel bolts to the specified torque.

74 Lower the car to the ground and reconnect the battery.

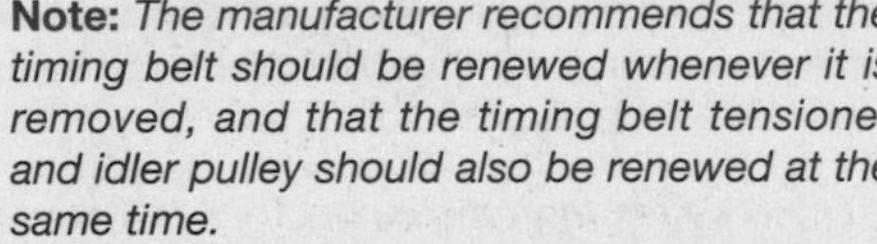

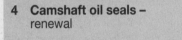

4 Camshaft oil seals – renewal

Note: *The manufacturer recommends that the timing belt should be renewed whenever it is removed, and that the timing belt tensioner and idler pulley should also be renewed at the same time.*

1 Remove the timing belt as described in Section 3.

2 If both camshaft sprockets are to be removed, suitably mark them inlet and exhaust for identification when refitting. On all engines, the inlet sprocket is nearest the front of the car.

3 Undo the retaining nut and remove the appropriate camshaft sprocket for access to the failed seal. Restrain the sprocket with a suitable forked tool as described in Section 3, which will engage with the sprocket holes. Note that new sprocket retaining nut and bplt will be required for refitting.

4 Withdraw the appropriate sprocket from the camshaft **(see illustration)**.

5 Carefully extract the seal by prising it out with a small screwdriver or hooked tool. Take great care to avoid damaging the shaft sealing face.

6 Clean the seal seat. Examine the shaft sealing face for wear or damage which could cause premature failure of the new seal.

7 Lubricate the new oil seal. Fit the seal over the shaft, lips inwards, and tap it home using a large socket or piece of tube until its outer face is flush with the housing **(see illustrations)**.

8 Refit the camshaft sprocket and timing belt using the 'method two' refitting and tensioning procedure described in Section 3.

5 Camshafts, tappets and rocker arms – removal, inspection and refitting

Note: *For this procedure, Renault special tool Mot.1367 will be required to support the engine from below while the engine mounting and lifting brackets are removed. Details for fabricating a home-made alternative are given in the text. A tube of the specified type of liquid gasket, and a short-haired application roller (available from Renault dealers) will be required when refitting the cylinder head upper section and the oil separator housing. New gaskets, seals and O-rings will also be*

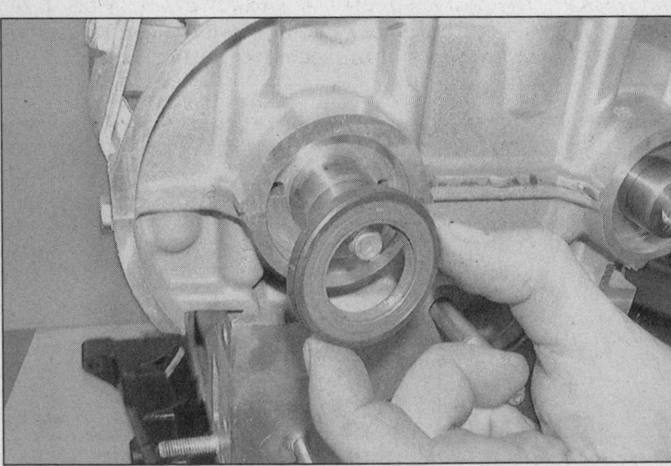

4.7a Fit the new oil seal over the camshaft . . .

4.7b . . . and tap it home using a large socket or piece of tube

required for refitting certain other components.

Note: *The manufacturer recommends that the timing belt should be renewed whenever it is removed, and that the timing belt tensioner and idler pulley should also be renewed at the same time.*

Removal

1 Disconnect the battery negative terminal (refer to *Disconnecting the battery* in the Reference Section of this manual).

2 Drain the cooling system as described in Chapter 1A.

3 Remove the timing belt as described in Section 3.

4 Suitably mark the inlet and exhaust camshaft sprockets for identification when refitting. On all engines, the inlet sprocket is nearest the front of the car.

5 Restrain the camshaft sprockets with a suitable forked tool as described in Section 3, or alternatively use the Renault special tool **(see illustration)**. Using a 14 mm hexagon key, unscrew and remove the plug from the inlet camshaft sprocket/phase-shifter **(see illustration)**. Undo the retaining nut from the exhaust camshaft sprocket and the bolt from the inlet camshaft sprocket/phase-shifter, then remove both sprockets from the camshafts. Note that a new sprocket retaining nut and bolt will be required for refitting.

6 The engine must now be supported from below so that the engine hoist or lifting beam used for timing belt removal can be removed for access to the top of the engine. If possible, obtain Renault special tool Mot.1367, or fabricate a home-made alternative out of square-section steel tube **(see Tool Tip)**.

7 Disconnect the accelerator cable from the throttle housing and inlet manifold as described in Chapter 4A.

8 Detach the power steering fluid reservoir from its mounting and move it to one side without disconnecting the fluid hoses.

9 Disconnect the wiring connector at the inlet air temperature sensor on the front of the inlet manifold, and the wiring connectors at each of the four ignition coils **(see illustration)**. Release the ignition coil wiring from the clips on the inlet manifold upper section and move the wiring clear.

10 Undo the nuts securing the fuel injector and fuel rail protective cover at the front of the inlet manifold. Release the wiring harness from the cable clips and remove the cover **(see illustration)**.

11 Undo the bolts and remove the engine lifting brackets from the right-hand and left-hand ends of the cylinder head.

12 Disconnect the brake servo vacuum hose from the inlet manifold upper section.

13 Undo the two bolts at the base of the throttle housing and remove the housing from

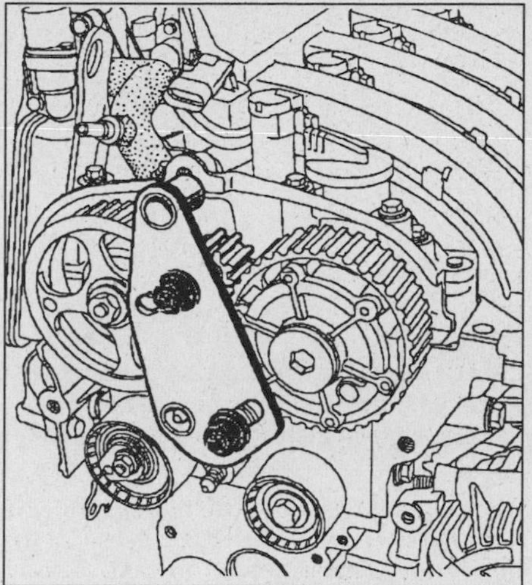

5.5a Renault tool for holding the camshaft sprockets

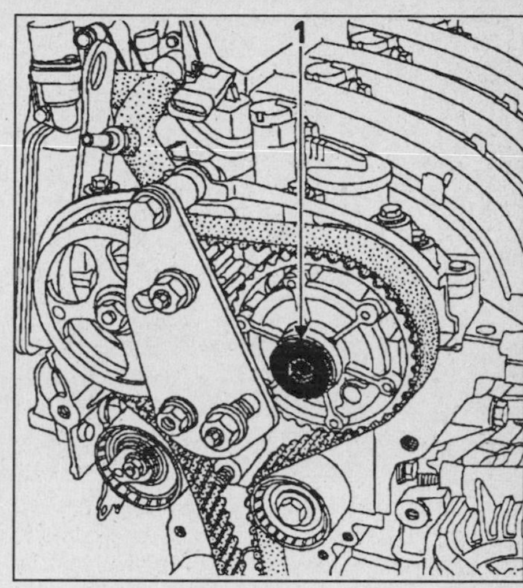

5.5b Plug (1) on the inlet camshaft sprocket/phase-shifter

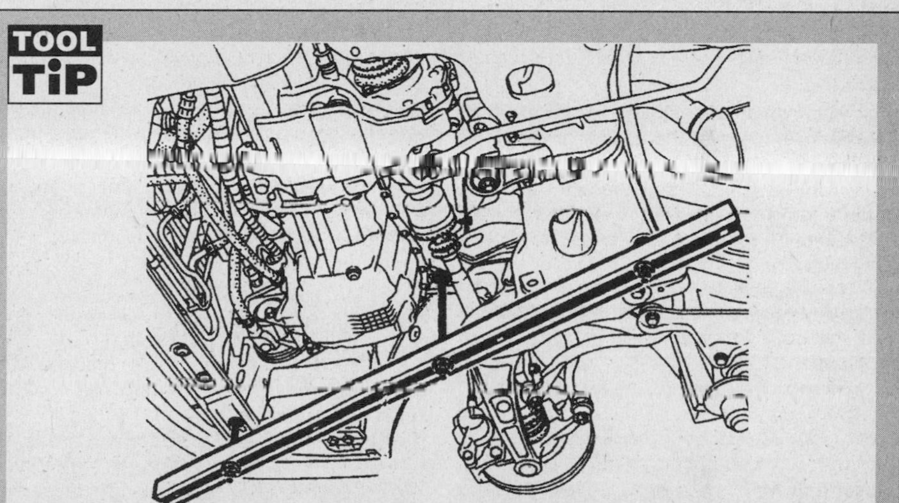

To make an engine support tool, obtain a suitable length of square-section steel tube. Drill the tube at both ends so that it can be bolted to the crossmember below the radiator at the front, and to the suspension crossmember at the rear, using suitable nuts, bolts and spacers. Drill a third hole to allow a length of threaded rod to be attached using nuts and washers. The position of the hole should be directly below a suitable location on the engine to allow the upper end of the threaded bar to be attached, either directly with nuts and washers, or by means of a small bracket.

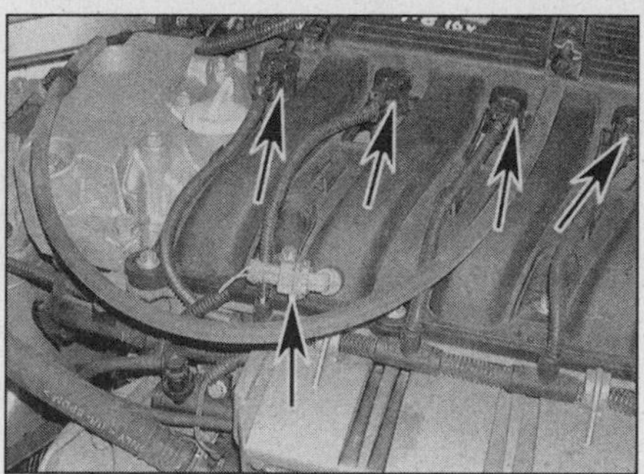

5.9 Disconnect the wiring connectors at the inlet air temperature sensor and at each of the four ignition coils (arrowed)

5.10 Undo the nuts and remove the fuel injector and fuel rail protective cover (arrowed) at the front of the inlet manifold

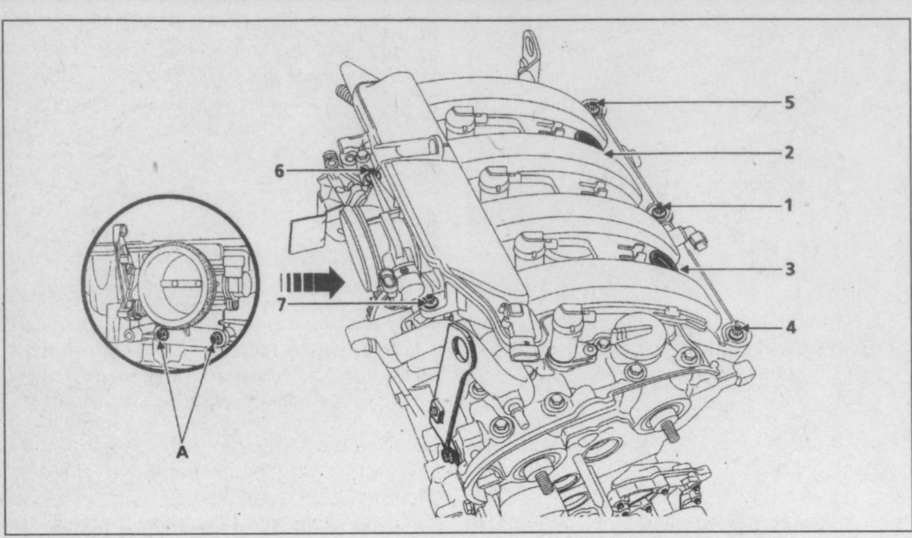

5.13 Inlet manifold upper section and throttle housing attachments

1 to 7 Inlet manifold upper section retaining bolts (numbers also indicate bolt tightening sequence when refitting)
A Throttle housing retaining bolts

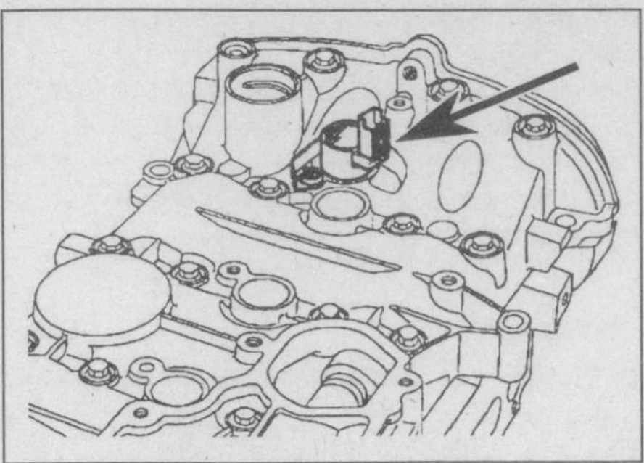

5.15 Variable valve timing control solenoid valve (arrowed)

the inlet manifold upper section **(see illustration)**. Recover the gasket or O-ring as applicable.

14 Undo the five bolts at the front and two bolts at the rear securing the inlet manifold upper section to the lower section, and to the oil separator housing. Lift off the manifold and recover the seals.

15 Undo the mounting bolts and remove the four ignition coils from the spark plugs and cylinder head upper section. Also disconnect the wiring from the variable valve timing control solenoid valve on the upper section. If necessary, the solenoid valve can be unbolted, and the oil seal removed **(see illustration)**.

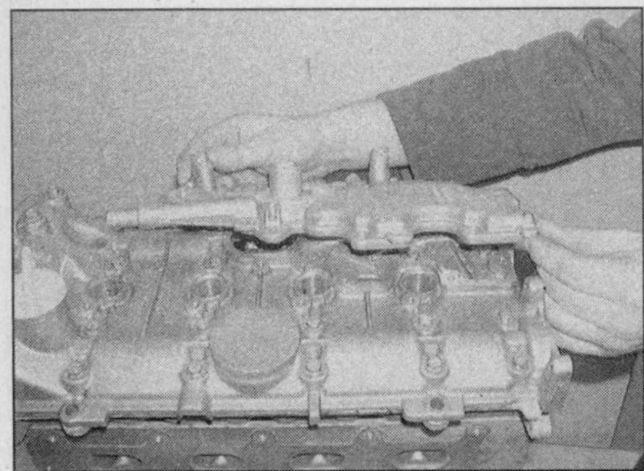

5.16 Undo the eight bolts and remove the oil separator housing

16 Undo the eight bolts and remove the oil separator housing from the cylinder head upper section **(see illustration)**.

17 In a progressive sequence, slacken then remove all the bolts securing the cylinder head upper section.

18 Using a soft-faced mallet and a protected screwdriver, gently tap and prise the cylinder head upper section upwards off the lower section **(see illustration)**. Note that lugs are provided to allow the upper section to be struck or prised against without damage. Do not insert the screwdriver or similar tool into the joint between the two sections as a means of separation. The upper section will be quite tight as it is located on several dowels.

19 Once the upper section is free, lift it squarely from the cylinder head. The camshafts will rise up slightly under the pressure of the valve springs – be careful they don't tilt and jam in either section.

20 Suitably mark the camshafts, inlet and exhaust and lift them out complete with the oil seals. Be careful of the lobes, which may have sharp edges.

21 Remove the oil seals from the camshafts, noting their fitted positions. Obtain new seals for reassembly.

22 Have ready two suitable boxes divided into sixteen segments each, or some containers or other means of storing and identifying the rocker arms and hydraulic tappets after removal. The box or containers for the hydraulic tappets must be oil tight and deep enough to allow the tappets to be almost totally submerged in oil. Mark the segments in the boxes or the containers with the number for each rocker arm and tappet (ie, 1 to 8 inlet and 1 to 8 exhaust).

23 Lift out the rocker arms and place them in their respective positions in the box or containers **(see illustration)**.

24 Similarly lift out the tappets and place them upright in their respective positions in the box or containers **(see illustration)**. Once all the tappets have been removed, add clean engine oil to the box or container so that the tappet is submerged.

Inspection

25 Inspect the cam lobes and the camshaft bearing journals for scoring or other visible evidence of wear. Once the surface hardening of the cam lobes has been eroded, wear will

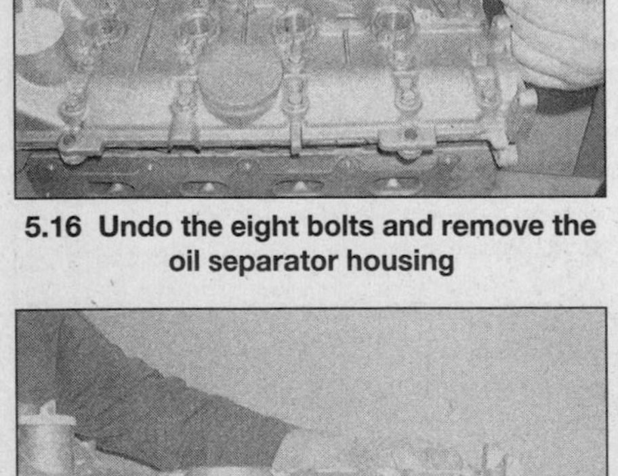

5.18 Gently tap and prise the cylinder head upper section upwards off the lower section

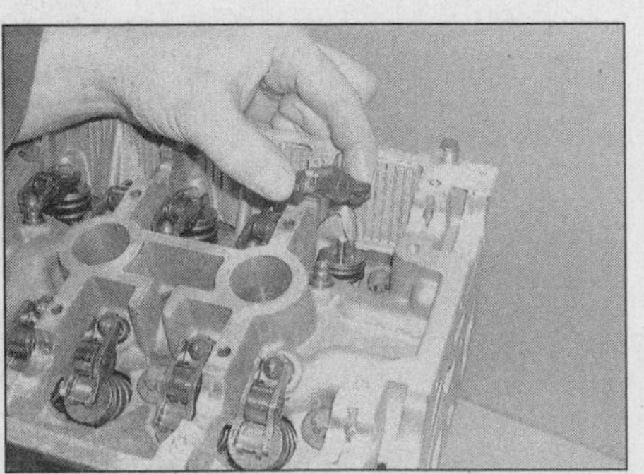

5.23 Lift out the rocker arms and place the in a marked box or containers

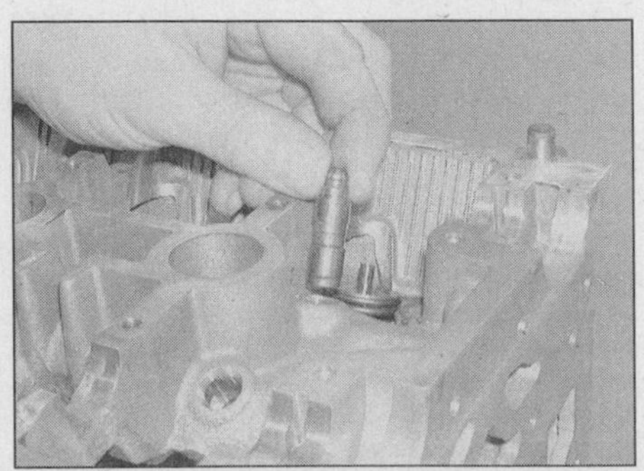

5.24 Similarly lift out the tappets and place them upright in a marked box or containers filled with oil

5.36a Refit the camshafts in the cylinder head lower section, with the inlet camshaft at the front of the engine

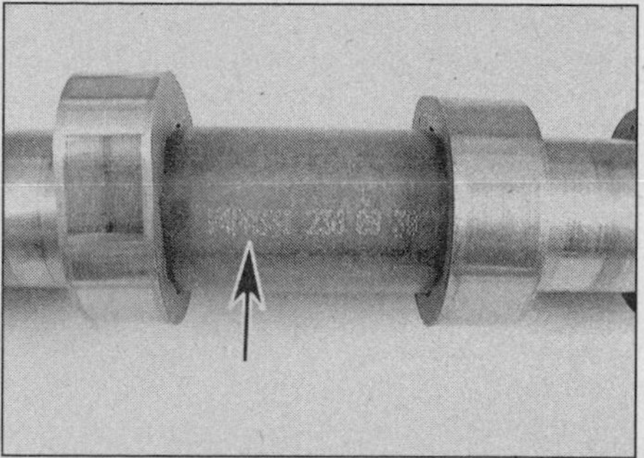
5.36b Camshaft identification code marking A (arrowed)

5.37 Position the camshafts so that the slots are horizontal with the offset below the centreline

occur at an accelerated rate. **Note:** *If these symptoms are visible on the tips of the camshaft lobes, check the corresponding rocker arm, as it will probably be worn as well.*

26 If the camshafts appear satisfactory, measure the bearing journal diameters and compare the figures obtained with those given in the Specifications. If the diameters are not as specified, consult a Renault dealer or engine overhaul specialist. Wear of the camshaft bearings will almost certainly be accompanied by similar wear of the bearings in the cylinder head, which will entail renewal of the cylinder head upper and lower sections together with the camshafts.

27 Inspect the rocker arms and tappets for scuffing, cracking or other damage and renew any components as necessary. Also check the condition of the tappet bores in the cylinder head. As with the camshafts, any wear in this area will necessitate cylinder head renewal.

Refitting

28 Thoroughly clean the sealant from the mating surfaces of the upper and lower cylinder head sections. Use a suitable liquid gasket dissolving agent (available from Renault dealers) together with a soft putty knife; do not use a metal scraper or the faces will be damaged. As there is no conventional gasket used, the cleanliness of the mating faces is of the utmost importance.

29 Clean off any oil, dirt or grease from both components and dry with a clean lint-free cloth. Ensure that all the oilways are completely clean.

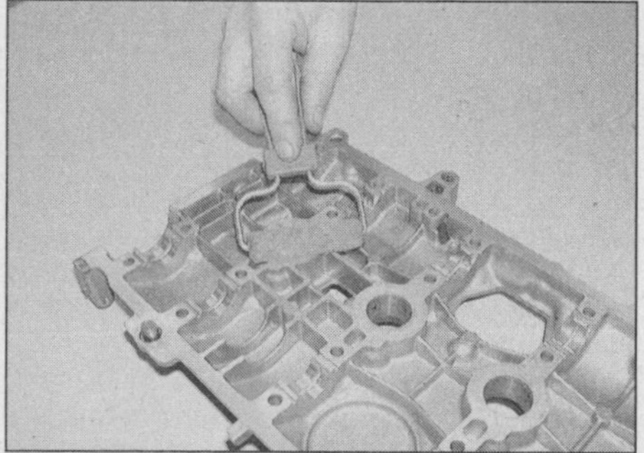
5.39 Apply an even coating of Loctite 518 gasket solution to the mating face of the cylinder head upper section

30 To prevent any possibility of the valves contacting the pistons when the camshafts are refitted, remove the TDC pin or dowel rod used to lock the crankshaft, and turn the crankshaft clockwise a quarter turn.

31 Liberally lubricate the tappet bores in the cylinder head lower section with clean engine oil.

32 Prior to refitting each tappet, remove it from its container, place it on the bench the correct way up and press down on the top of the tappet (the stop piston) with your thumb. If it is possible to depress the stop piston then the tappet must be primed by operating it in a container of diesel fuel before refitting.

33 Insert the tappets into their original bores in the cylinder head lower section unless they have been renewed.

34 Lubricate the rocker arms and place them over their respective tappets and valve stems.

35 Lubricate the camshaft journals in the cylinder head lower section sparingly with oil, taking care not to allow the oil to spill over onto the upper and lower section contact areas.

36 Lay the camshafts in their correct locations in the lower section, remembering that the inlet camshaft must be at the front of the engine. If new camshafts are being fitted, or if the identification marks made during removal have been lost, the camshafts can be identified by referring to the markings located between two of the cam lobes. The markings consist of a series of manufacturer's numbers and letters, together with a code to identify the camshaft. The fourth digit in the series denotes the camshaft code – A for inlet camshaft and E for exhaust camshaft **(see illustrations).**

37 Turn the camshafts so that the slot in the end of each camshaft is horizontal (ie, parallel to the join between the upper and lower cylinder head sections) with the offset below the centreline **(see illustration).**

38 Ensure that the mating faces of both cylinder head sections are clean and free of any oil or grease.

39 Using the short-haired roller, apply an even coating of Loctite 518 liquid gasket solution to the mating face of the cylinder head upper section only **(see illustration).** Ensure that the whole surface is coated to a **reddish** colour, but take care to keep the solution out of the oilways.

40 With the camshafts correctly positioned, lay the upper section in place on the lower section.

41 Insert all the upper section retaining bolts and progressively tighten them just sufficiently to pull the upper section down into contact with the lower section.

42 The upper section retaining bolts must now be tightened in four stages in the order given in the Specifications **(see illustration).**

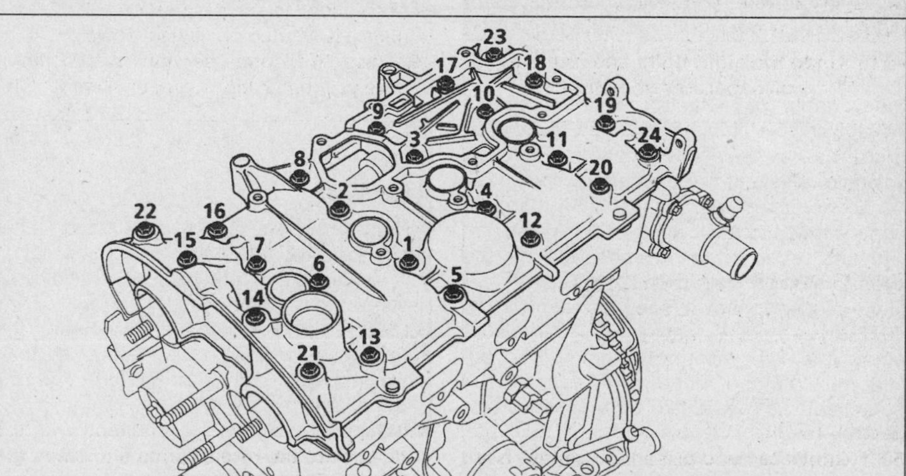

5.42 Cylinder head upper section retaining bolt identification

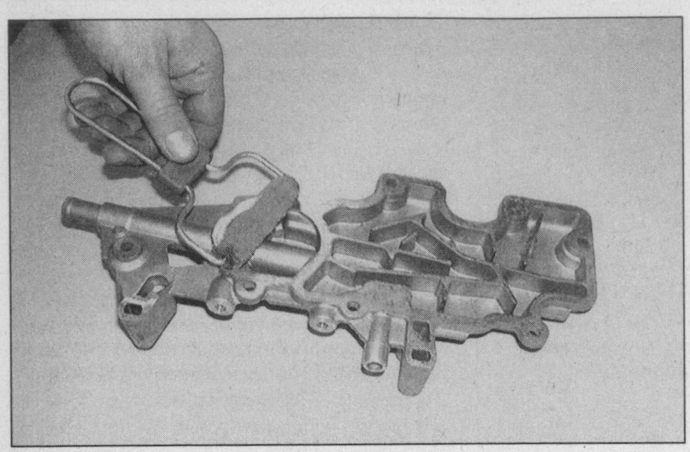

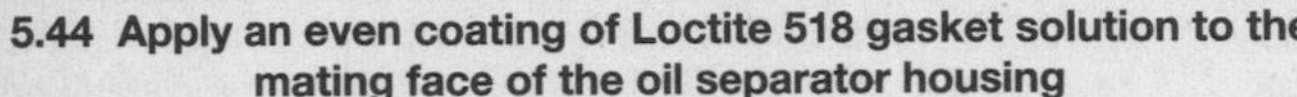

5.44 Apply an even coating of Loctite 518 gasket solution to the mating face of the oil separator housing

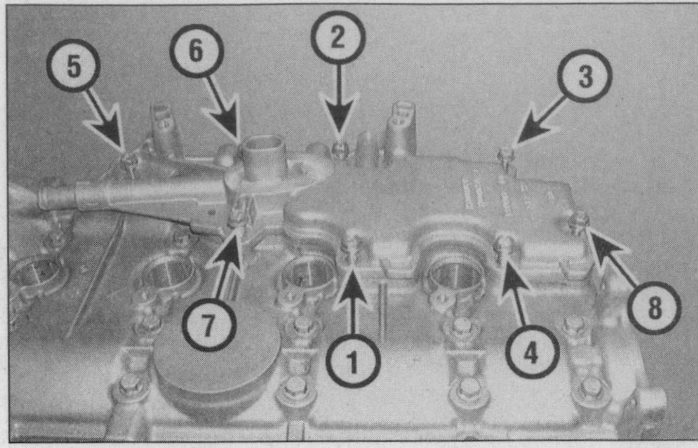

5.45 Oil separator housing retaining bolt tightening sequence

First tighten the four bolts indicated in the Specifications in the correct sequence to the setting given (Stage 1). Tighten the remaining bolts in the correct sequence to the setting given (Stage 2). Slacken the original four bolts completely (Stage 3), then finally tighten the original four bolts in the correct sequence to the setting given (Stage 4).

43 Ensure that the mating faces of the oil separator housing and cylinder head upper section are clean and free of any oil or grease.

44 Using the short-haired roller, apply an even coating of Loctite 518 liquid gasket solution to the mating face of the oil separator housing until it is **reddish** in colour **(see illustration)**.

45 Refit the oil separator housing to the cylinder head upper section. Insert the retaining bolts and tighten them to the specified torque in the sequence shown **(see illustration)**.

46 Lubricate the lips of the two new camshaft oil seals. Fit each seal the correct way round over the camshaft, and tap it home with a large socket or piece of tube until its outer face is flush with the housing; refer to the information in Section 4 for guidance.

47 Refit the four ignition coils to the spark plugs and cylinder head upper section and secure with the retaining bolts tightened securely. Where removed, fit a new oil seal for the variable valve timing control solenoid valve, using a suitable socket and hammer to drive the new seal into position. Refit the solenoid valve and tighten the retaining bolt.

48 Using new seals, refit the inlet manifold upper section to the lower section and secure with the seven retaining bolts. Tighten the bolts to the specified torque (see Chapter 4A) in the sequence shown **(see illustration 5.13)**.

49 Using a new gasket or O-ring as applicable, refit the throttle housing to the inlet manifold and secure with the two bolts tightened to the specified torque (see Chapter 4A).

50 Reconnect the brake servo vacuum hose to the inlet manifold.

51 Refit the engine lifting brackets to the right-hand and left-hand ends of the cylinder head. The engine can now be re-attached to the engine hoist or lifting beam allowing the support tool to be removed from below. Alternatively, the tool can be left in position until after the timing belt is refitted.

52 Reconnect the wiring to the four ignition coils and the inlet air temperature sensor on the front of the inlet manifold. Secure the wiring harness with the clips provided on the manifold.

53 Refit the fuel injector and fuel rail protective cover to the front of the inlet manifold, and secure the wiring harness with the cable clips.

54 Refit the power steering fluid reservoir to its mounting.

55 Refer to Chapter 4A and reconnect the accelerator cable.

56 Turn the crankshaft back a quarter of a turn to the TDC position then, referring to the information given in Section 3, lock the crankshaft with the TDC pin.

57 Refit the timing belt using the 'method two' refitting and tensioning procedure described in Section 3.

58 On completion, refill the cooling system as described in Chapter 1A.

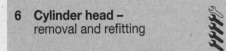

6 Cylinder head – removal and refitting

Removal

1 Remove the camshafts tappets and rocker arms as described in Section 5.

2 Remove the inlet and exhaust manifolds as described in Chapter 4A.

3 Disconnect the radiator top hose, the heater hoses and expansion tank hose from the thermostat housing on the left-hand end of the cylinder head.

4 Disconnect the wiring connector at the coolant temperature sensor on the side of the thermostat housing.

5 Undo the retaining bolts and release the wiring harness support bracket from the left-hand end of the cylinder head.

6 Working in the reverse of the sequence shown in illustration 6.21b, progressively slacken the cylinder head bolts by half a turn at a time until all the bolts can be unscrewed by hand and removed.

7 Lift the cylinder head upwards and off the cylinder block. If it is stuck, tap it upwards using a hammer and block of wood. Do not try to turn it (it is located by two dowels), nor attempt to prise it free using a screwdriver inserted between the block and head faces. If the locating dowels are a loose fit, remove them and store them with the head for safe-keeping

8 Remove the cylinder head gasket from the cylinder block.

9 If the cylinder head is to be dismantled for overhaul, refer to Part D of this Chapter.

Preparation for refitting

10 The mating faces of the cylinder head and cylinder block must be perfectly clean before refitting the head. Use a soft putty knife to remove all traces of gasket and carbon; also clean the piston crowns. Take particular care during the cleaning operations, as aluminium alloy is easily damaged. Also, make sure that the carbon is not allowed to enter the oil and water passages – this is particularly important for the lubrication system, as carbon could block the oil supply to the engine's components. Using adhesive tape and paper, seal the water, oil and bolt holes in the cylinder block. To prevent carbon entering the gap between the pistons and bores, smear a little grease in the gap. After cleaning each piston, use a small brush to remove all traces of grease and carbon from the gap, then wipe away the remainder with a clean rag. Clean all the pistons in the same way.

11 Check the mating surfaces of the cylinder block and the cylinder head for nicks, deep scratches and other damage. If slight, they may be removed carefully with a file, but if excessive, machining may be the only alternative to renewal.

6.17 **Locate a new cylinder head gasket on the cylinder block . . .**

6.18 **. . . and carefully lower the cylinder head into position**

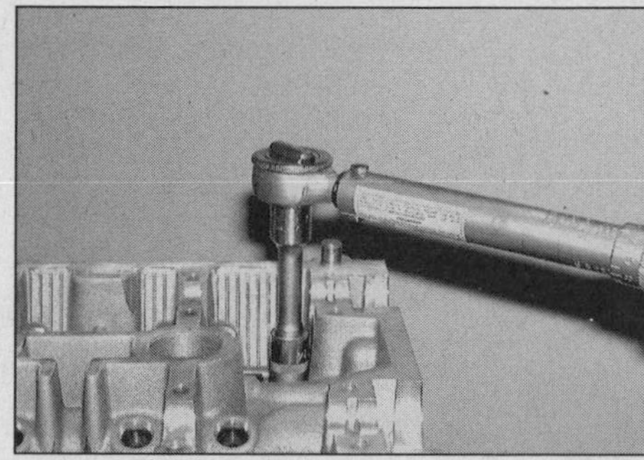

6.21a **Tighten the cylinder head retaining bolts to the Stage 1 torque setting using a torque wrench**

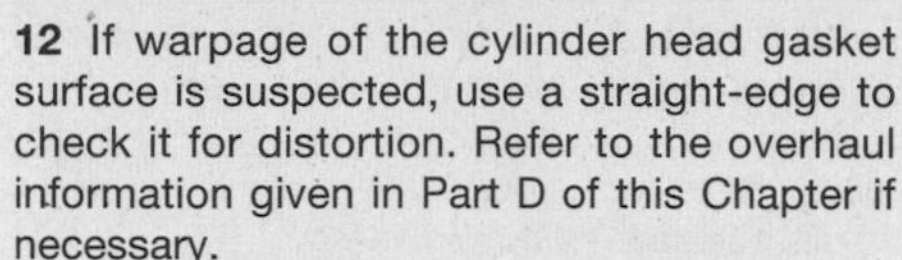

12 If warpage of the cylinder head gasket surface is suspected, use a straight-edge to check it for distortion. Refer to the overhaul information given in Part D of this Chapter if necessary.

13 Examine the cylinder head bolt threads in the cylinder block for damage. If necessary, use the correct-size tap to chase out the threads in the block. Ensure that the bolt holes are clean and free of oil. Syringe or soak up any oil left in the bolt holes. This is most important in order that the correct bolt tightening torque can be applied and to prevent the possibility of the block being cracked by hydraulic pressure when the bolts are tightened.

14 Check the condition of the cylinder head bolts, and particularly their threads, whenever they are removed. Wash the bolts in a suitable solvent, and wipe them dry. Check each bolt for any sign of visible wear or damage, renewing them if necessary.

15 If the bolt condition is satisfactory, measure the length of each bolt, from the underside of the head to the end of the thread. If the length of any bolt exceeds 118.5 mm, all the bolts must be renewed.

Refitting

16 Ensure that the mating faces of the cylinder block and head are spotlessly clean, that the retaining bolt threads are also clean and dry, and that they screw easily in and out of their locations.

17 Ensure that the locating dowels are correctly fitted to the block and fit a new cylinder head gasket, making sure it is the right way up **(see illustration)**.

18 Carefully lower the cylinder head onto the block, engaging it over the dowels **(see illustration)**.

19 If new cylinder head bolts are being used, they should be fitted dry. If the original bolts are being re-used, lightly oil them, both on their threads and under their heads and allow any excess oil to drain off.

20 Fit the bolts and screw them in until they just contact the cylinder head.

21 Working progressively and in the sequence shown, tighten the cylinder head bolts to their Stage 1 torque setting, using a torque wrench and suitable socket **(see illustrations)**.

22 Once all the bolts have been tightened to their Stage 1 setting, working again in the given sequence, angle-tighten the bolts through the specified Stage 2 angle, using a socket and extension bar. It is recommended that an angle-measuring gauge is used during this stage of the tightening, to ensure accuracy **(see illustration)**.

23 Reconnect the coolant hoses to the thermostat housing and securely tighten their retaining clips.

24 Refit the wiring harness support bracket to the left-hand end of the cylinder head and reconnect the coolant temperature sensor wiring connector.

25 Refit the inlet and exhaust manifolds as described in Chapter 4A.

26 Refit the camshafts tappets and rocker arms as described in Section 5.

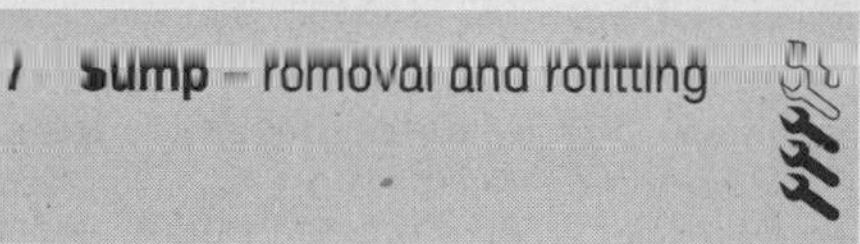

7 Sump – removal and refitting

Removal

1 Apply the handbrake, then jack up the front of the car and support it on axle stands (see *Jacking and vehicle support*). Where fitted, remove the engine undertray.

2 Drain the engine oil as described in Chapter 1A, then refit and tighten the drain plug.

3 Remove both front roadwheels and the liners from the wheelarches.

4 Unbolt the subframe-to-body support rods from each side of the vehicle.

5 With the steering gear in the straight-ahead position, working in the engine compartment, pull back the rubber grommet then unscrew and remove the eccentric bolt securing the bottom of the steering inner column to the steering gear, and separate the column (refer

6.21b **Cylinder head retaining bolt tightening sequence**

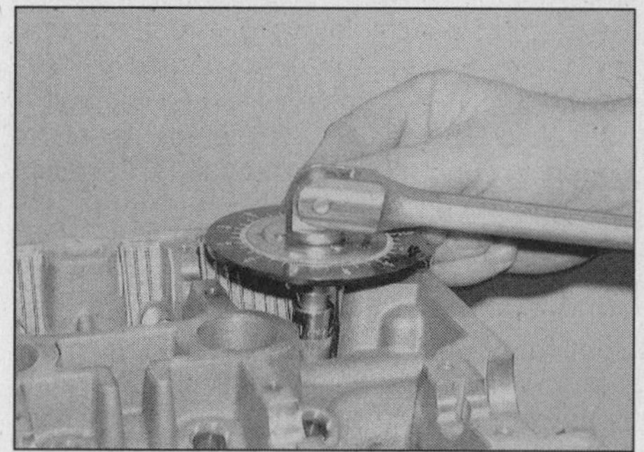

6.22 **Using an angle tightening gauge to tighten the cylinder head retaining bolts through the Stage 2 angle**

2B

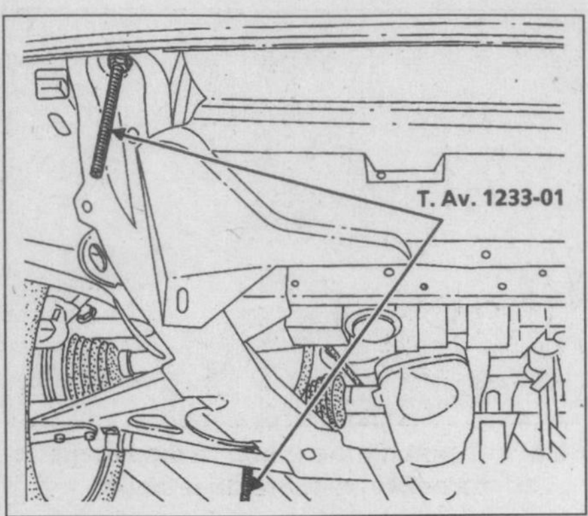

7.9 Renault tools, replacing the four subframe-to-underbody bolts at the corners of the subframe, to maintain location of the subframe while lowering it

to Chapter 10 for more information) from the steering gear.

Caution: It is important that the airbag rotary switch beneath the steering wheel is not damaged. Before removing the column the steering wheel must be immobilised with the wheels straight using a steering wheel locking tool.

6 Remove the horns (see Chapter 12).

7 Unscrew the bolts securing the exhaust downpipe to the exhaust manifold. Release the downpipe and support it.

8 Unbolt the supports securing the power-assisted steering fluid pipe to the subframe.

9 Unscrew one of the subframe-to-underbody bolts from the corners of the subframe, noting the location of spacers and washers, then fit one of the Renault special tools No. T. Av. 1233-01 in its place, tightening securely the tool's threaded rod into the underbody and tightening the nut and washer against the subframe's underside **(see illustration)**. Repeat for the remaining three subframe-to-underbody bolts. If the Renault tools are not available, four threaded rods can be used instead, each of the same thread size (10 mm at the front, 12 mm at the rear) and pitch as the subframe-to-underbody bolts, and with an appropriate nut and washer.

10 Carefully and evenly unscrew the nuts at the subframe corners so that the subframe is lowered in a safe and controllable fashion by

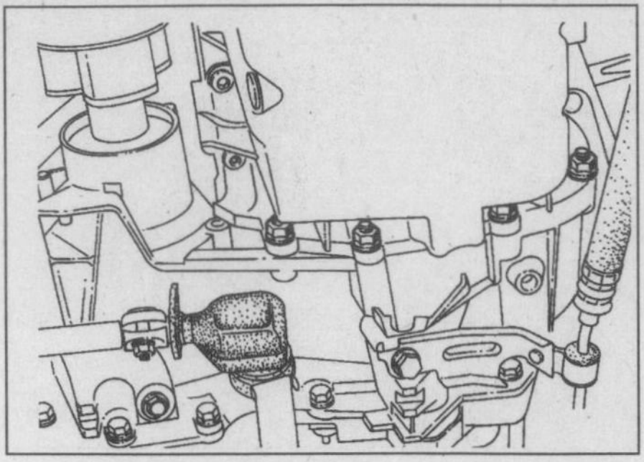

7.11 Engine-to-transmission nuts on sump

55 to 60 mm from the underbody mounting points.

11 Unscrew the four engine-to-transmission nuts on the sump, then unscrew the studs as well, using two nuts locked together on each stud to do so **(see illustration)**.

12 Unscrew the bolts securing the sump to the cylinder block, but leave two diagonally-opposite bolts entered on a few threads until the sump joint has been released.

13 Using a palette knife or similar tool, release the sump from the bottom of the cylinder block. Do not use a screwdriver as this may damage the mating surfaces.

14 Unscrew the two remaining bolts and lower the sump from the engine. Recover the gasket, where fitted.

15 Clean all traces of gasket/sealant from the cylinder block and sump and wipe them dry.

Refitting

16 Where a gasket is fitted, apply a bead of Rhodorseal 5661 sealant (available from Renault dealers) to the join between the crankshaft oil seal housing and cylinder block, and to the join between the main bearing cap and cylinder block, then locate the gasket in position on the sump **(see illustrations)**.

17 Where sealant is used, apply a 1 mm wide bead of suitable sealant – Renault recommend Rhodorseal 5661 – to the mating face of the sump, making sure that the bead is to the outside of the sump groove.

18 It is important that the sump is positioned correctly the first time and not moved around after the sealant (where applicable) has

7.16a Apply a bead of sealant to the join between the crankshaft oil seal housing and cylinder block . . .

touched the cylinder block. Temporary long bolts or dowel rods may be used to help achieve this. To prevent oil dripping from the oil pump and cylinder block, wipe these areas clean before refitting the sump.

19 Offer up the sump to the cylinder block and insert two diagonally-opposite bolts. Gently tighten these bolts, then refit the four engine-to-transmission studs to the gearbox bellhousing, using two nuts locked together on each stud to do so. Tighten the studs securely and refit the nut and washer to each. If the engine is in the car, ensure that the left-hand end of the sump is in contact with the transmission bellhousing flange. If the engine is removed from the car, use a straight-edge to maintain the alignment between the left-hand end of the sump and cylinder block **(see illustration)**.

20 Refit the remaining sump bolts. Progressively tighten all the bolts in diagonal sequence to the specified torque wrench setting.

21 Raise the subframe against the underbody by tightening evenly the nut on each of the threaded rods. When the subframe is back in place, remove each tool in turn and refit the subframe-to-underbody bolt. Tighten all four subframe-to-underbody bolts to the torque wrench settings specified in Chapter 10.

22 Refit the power-assisted steering fluid pipe to the supports on the subframe and tighten the bolts securely.

23 Refit the exhaust downpipe and tighten the bolts.

7.16b . . . and to the join between the main bearing cap and cylinder block

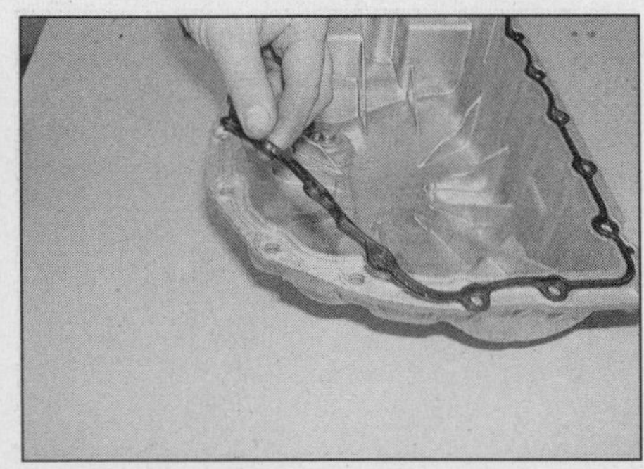

7.16c Locate the new gasket on the top of the sump

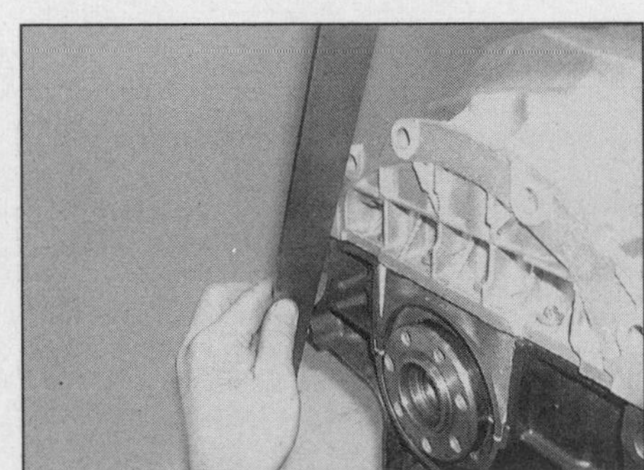

7.19 If the engine is removed, use a straight-edge to maintain the alignment between the left-hand end of the sump and cylinder block

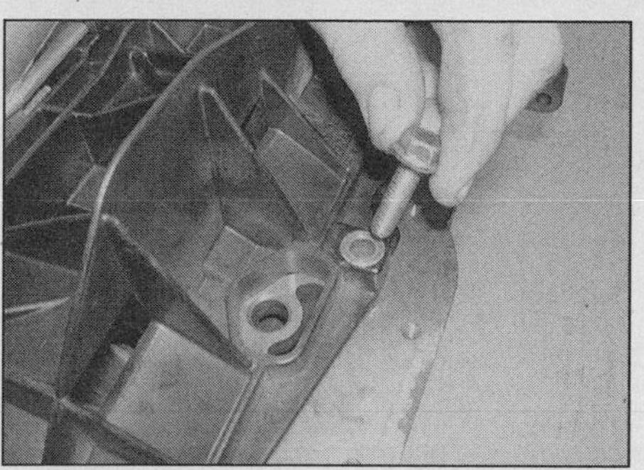

8.2 Unscrew the baffle plate retaining bolt(s)

8.3a Remove the anti-emulsion plate . . .

8.3b . . . then tilt the pump to disengage its sprocket from the drive chain

24 Refit the horns (see Chapter 12).

25 Refer to Chapter 10 when connecting the steering column to the steering gear. Refit the eccentric bolt and tighten it to the specified torque wrench setting.

26 Refit the subframe-to-body support rods and tighten the bolts securely.

27 Refit the liners beneath the wheelarches and the engine compartment undershield, if fitted.

28 Refit the front roadwheels and lower the vehicle to the ground. Tighten the roadwheel bolts to the specified torque wrench setting.

29 Reconnect the battery negative lead.

30 Refill the engine with oil (see Chapter 1A).

8 Oil pump – removal, inspection and refitting

Note: *The manufacturer recommends that the timing belt should be renewed whenever it is removed, and that the timing belt tensioner and idler pulley should also be renewed at the same time.*

Removal

1 To remove the oil pump alone, first remove the sump as described in Section 7.

2 Unscrew the oil pump mounting bolts and the additional bolt(s) securing the baffle plate to the crankcase **(see illustration)**.

3 Withdraw the oil pump slightly and remove the baffle plate. Tilt the pump to disengage its sprocket from the drive chain and lift away the pump **(see illustrations)**. If the locating dowels are displaced, refit them in their locations.

4 To remove the pump complete with its drive chain and sprockets, first remove the sump as described in Section 7, then remove the crankshaft timing belt end oil seal housing as described in Section 9.

5 Remove the oil pump as described in paragraphs 1 and 2 above.

6 Slide the drive sprocket together with the chain from the crankshaft **(see illustration)**. Note that the drive sprocket is not keyed to the crankshaft, but relies on the pulley bolt being tightened correctly to clamp the sprocket.

Inspection

7 Extract the retaining clip, and remove the oil pressure relief valve spring retainer, spring and plunger **(see illustrations)**.

8 Unscrew the retaining bolts, and lift off the pump cover **(see illustration)**.

9 Carefully examine the gears, pump body and relief valve plunger for any signs of scoring or wear. Renew the pump complete if excessive wear is evident.

10 If the components appear serviceable, measure the clearance between the pump body and the gears using feeler blades. Also measure the gear endfloat, and check the

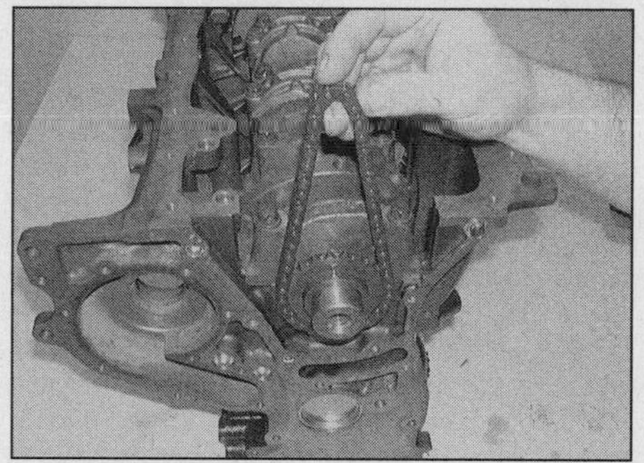

8.6 Slide the drive sprocket together with the chain from the crankshaft

8.7a Extract the oil pressure relief valve retaining clip . . .

2B

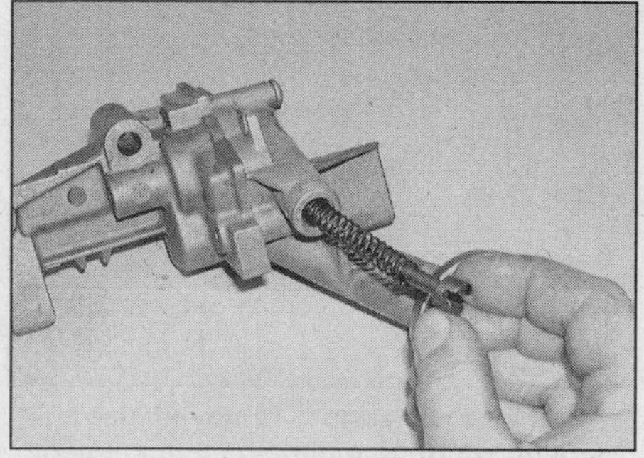

8.7b . . . remove the oil pressure relief valve spring retainer and spring . . .

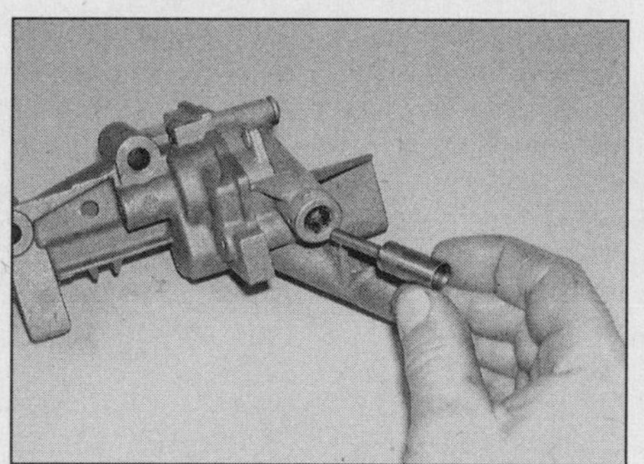

8.7c . . . followed by the plunger

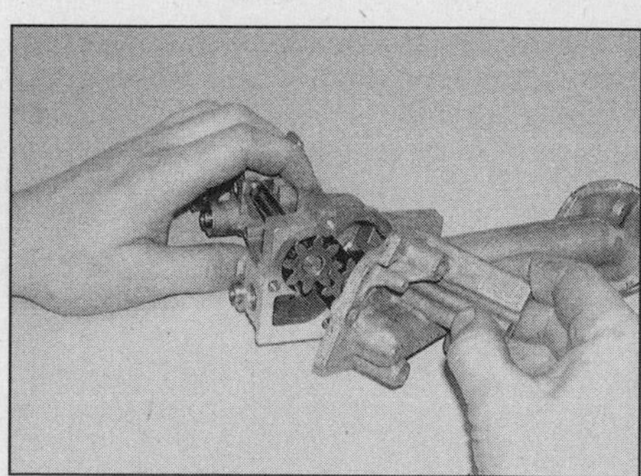

8.8 Unscrew the retaining bolts, and lift off the oil pump cover

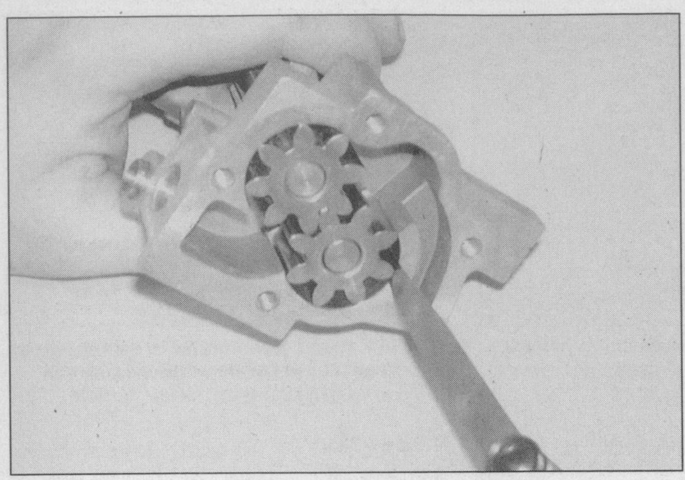

8.10a Using feeler blades, measure the clearance between the pump body and the gears . . .

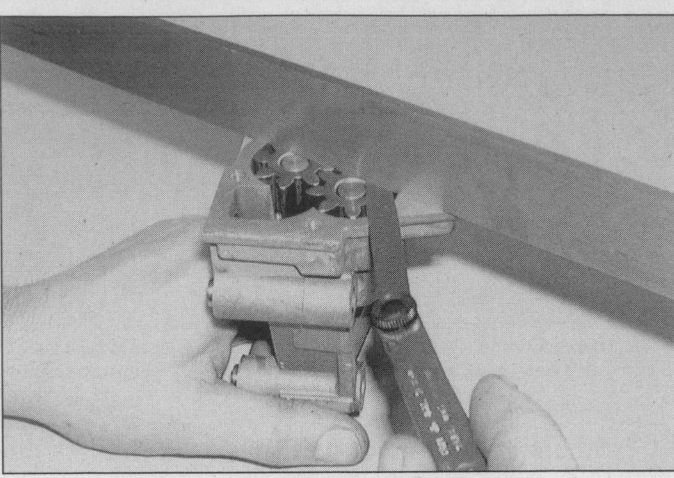

8.10b . . . and measure the gear endfloat

flatness of the end cover **(see illustrations)**. If the clearances exceed the specified tolerances, the pump must be renewed.

11 If the pump is satisfactory, reassemble the components in the reverse order of removal. Fill the pump with oil, then refit the cover and tighten the bolts securely **(see illustration)**.

Refitting

12 Wipe clean the oil pump and cylinder block mating surfaces.

13 Locate the drive sprocket onto the end of the crankshaft, ensuring that it is fitted with the projecting boss facing away from the crankshaft **(see illustration)**. Engage the chain with the sprocket and push the sprocket fully home.

14 Check that the locating dowels are in place either on the pump or on the cylinder block, then engage the oil pump sprocket with the drive chain. Engage the pump with the dowels, fit the two retaining bolts and tighten them to the specified torque.

15 Refit the baffle plate and secure with the retaining bolt(s).

16 Refit the oil seal housing as described in Section 9.

17 Refit the sump as described in Section 7.

9 Crankshaft oil seals – renewal

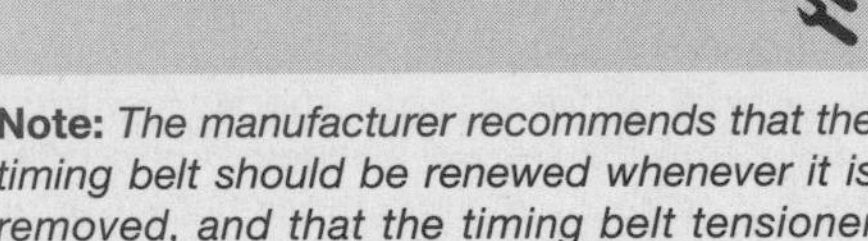

Note: *The manufacturer recommends that the timing belt should be renewed whenever it is removed, and that the timing belt tensioner and idler pulley should also be renewed at the same time.*

Timing belt end oil seal

1 Remove the timing belt as described in Section 3, the withdraw the sprocket from the end of the crankshaft.

2 Make a note of the correct fitted depth of the seal then punch or drill two small holes opposite each other in the oil seal. Screw a self-tapping screw into each and pull on the screws with pliers to extract the seal.

3 Clean the seal housing and polish off any burrs or raised edges which may have caused the seal to fail in the first place.

4 Lubricate the lips of the new seal with clean engine oil and ease it into position on the end of the shaft. Press the seal into its housing until it is positioned at the same depth as the original was prior to removal.

5 If necessary, a suitable tubular drift, such as a socket, which bears only on the hard outer edge of the seal can be used to tap the seal into position. Take great care not to damage the seal lips during fitting and ensure that the seal lips face inwards. Note that if the surface of the shaft was noted to be badly scored, press the new seal slightly further into its housing so that its lip is running on an unmarked area of the shaft.

6 Refit and tension the new timing belt using the 'method one' procedure described in Section 3.

Timing belt end oil seal housing

7 Remove the timing belt as described in Section 3, the withdraw the sprocket from the end of the crankshaft.

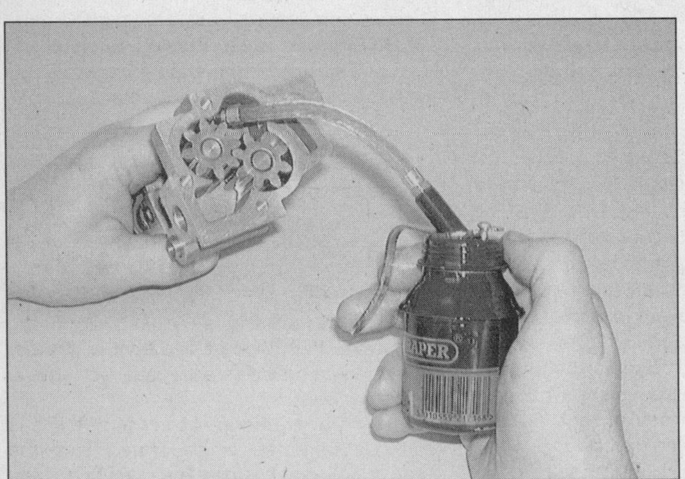

8.11 Fill the pump with oil, then refit the cover

8.13 Ensure that the oil pump drive sprocket is fitted with the projecting boss facing away from the crankshaft

9.12 Use a suitable socket or metal tube to drive the new crankshaft oil seal into the housing

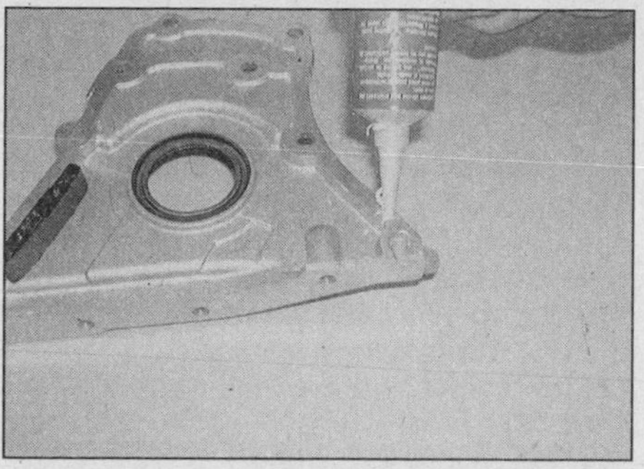

9.14a Lightly coat the oil seal housing mating surface with sealant . . .

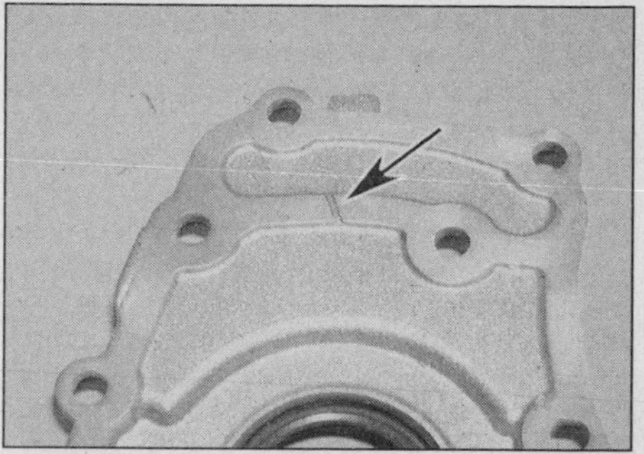

9.14b . . . taking care not to allow the sealant to block the small oil channel (arrowed) at the top of the housing

8 Remove the sump as described in Section 7.

9 Unscrew the retaining bolts and withdraw the oil seal housing, noting the locating dowels around its two lower bolt holes. If it is stuck in place, a leverage point is provided on the upper edge (near the timing belt idler pulley) to allow a screwdriver to be used to gently prise the housing free.

10 Note the presence of the oil pump drive chain guide block and of its two locating dowels, Check that the guide block is fit for further use and renew it if there is any doubt about its condition.

11 The oil seal should be renewed whenever the housing is removed. Note the fitted position of the old seal then prise it out with a screwdriver and wipe clean the seating.

12 Lubricate the outer surface of the new seal then locate it squarely on the housing with its closed side facing outwards. Place the housing on blocks of wood, then use a suitable socket or metal tube to drive in the oil seal **(see illustration)**.

13 Clean all traces of sealant from the housing and cylinder block mating faces. Check that the chain guide block is correctly fitted and that the housing locating dowels are in place.

14 Lightly coat the housing mating surface with Rhodorseal 5661 sealant (available from Renault dealers). Do not allow the sealant to block the small oil channel at the top of the housing **(see illustrations)**.

15 Lubricate the lips of the oil seal then locate the housing on the cylinder block. Refit the retaining bolts and tighten them progressively to the specified torque.

16 Refit the sump as described in Section 7.

17 Refit and tension the new timing belt using the 'method one' procedure described in Section 3.

Flywheel/driveplate end oil seal

18 Remove the flywheel/driveplate as described in Section 10.

19 Prise out the old oil seal using a small screwdriver, taking care not to damage the surface of the crankshaft. Alternatively, the oil seal can be removed as described in paragraph 2.

20 Inspect the seal rubbing surface on the crankshaft. If it is grooved or rough in the area where the old seal was fitted, the new seal should be fitted slightly less deeply, so that it rubs on an unworn part of the surface.

21 Wipe clean the oil seal seating, then dip the new seal in fresh engine oil. Locate it over the crankshaft, making sure its sealing lip is facing inwards. Make sure that the oil seal lip is not damaged as it is located on the crankshaft.

22 Using a metal tube, drive the oil seal squarely into the bore until flush. A block of wood cut to pass over the end of the crankshaft may be used instead.

23 Refit the flywheel/driveplate with reference to Section 10.

10 Flywheel/driveplate – removal, inspection and refitting

Note: *Removal of the flywheel or driveplate requires the engine and transmission assembly to be removed as described in Chapter 2D so that the engine and transmission can separated on the bench.*

Removal

1 Remove the manual gearbox or automatic transmission as described in Chapter 7A or 7B.

2 On manual gearbox models, remove the clutch as described in Chapter 6.

3 Mark the flywheel/driveplate in relation to the crankshaft to aid refitting. Note that the flywheel/driveplate can only be refitted in one position, as the bolts are unequally spaced.

4 The flywheel/driveplate must now be held stationary while the bolts are loosened. To do this, locate a long bolt in one of the transmission-to-engine mounting bolt holes, and either insert a wide-bladed screwdriver in the starter ring gear, or use a piece of bent metal bar engaged with the ring gear.

5 Unscrew the mounting bolts, and withdraw the flywheel/driveplate; be careful – it is heavy.

Inspection

6 Examine the flywheel/driveplate for wear or chipping of the ring gear teeth. If the ring gear is worn or damaged, it may be possible to renew it separately, but this job is best left to a Renault dealer or engineering works. The temperature to which the new ring gear must be heated for installation is critical and, if not done accurately, the hardness of the teeth will be destroyed.

7 Check the flywheel/driveplate carefully for signs of distortion, and for hairline cracks around the bolt holes, or radiating outwards from the centre. If damage of this sort is found, it must be renewed.

8 Examine the flywheel for scoring of the clutch face. If the clutch face is scored, the flywheel may be machined until flat, but renewal is preferable.

Refitting

9 Clean the flywheel/driveplate and crankshaft mating surfaces, then locate the flywheel/driveplate on the crankshaft, making sure that any previously-made marks are aligned.

10 Apply a few drops of locking fluid to the mounting bolt threads, fit the bolts and tighten them in a diagonal sequence to the specified torque wrench setting.

11 Refit the manual gearbox or automatic transmission as described in Chapter 7A or 7B, then refit the engine/transmission assembly with reference to Chapter 2D.

11 Engine mountings – inspection and renewal

Inspection

1 If improved access is required, apply the handbrake, then jack up the front of the car and support it on axle stands (see *Jacking and vehicle support*).

2 Check the mounting rubber to see if it is cracked, hardened or separated from the metal at any point; renew the mounting if any such damage or deterioration is evident.

3 Check that all the mounting's fasteners are

securely tightened; use a torque wrench to check if possible.

4 Using a large screwdriver or a crowbar, check for wear in the mounting by carefully levering against it to check for free play. Where this is not possible, enlist the aid of an assistant to move the engine/transmission back-and-forth, or from side-to-side, while you watch the mounting. While some free play is to be expected even from new components, excessive wear should be obvious. If excessive free play is found, check first that the fasteners are correctly secured, then renew any worn components as described below.

Renewal

Right-hand mounting

5 Disconnect the battery negative terminal (refer to *Disconnecting the battery* in the Reference Section of this manual).

6 Place a jack beneath the engine, with a block of wood on the jack head (remove the undercover to improve access to the sump). Raise the jack until it is supporting the weight of the engine. Alternately, attach an engine support bar to the lifting brackets and support the weight of the engine with the bar.

7 Undo the bolt securing the rubber mounting to the engine mounting bracket. Slacken and remove the three bolts securing the engine mounting bracket to the cylinder head/timing cover. Release the accelerator cable from the cable clip and lift off the bracket.

8 Unscrew the three retaining bolts and remove the rubber mounting and movement limiter from the body.

9 Check carefully for signs of wear or damage on all components, and renew them where necessary.

10 On reassembly, refit the bracket to the cylinder head/timing cover and tighten the retaining bolts to the specified torque.

11 Fit the rubber mounting and movement limiter to the body, insert the retaining bolts but tighten them finger tight only at this stage.

12 Refit the bolt securing the rubber mounting to the engine mounting bracket and tighten it to the specified torque.

13 Centralise the movement limiter around the rubber mounting then tighten the three bolts to the specified torque.

14 Remove the jack from underneath the engine or the engine support bar (as applicable), and reconnect the battery negative terminal.

Left-hand mounting

15 Disconnect the battery negative terminal (refer to *Disconnecting the battery* in the Reference Section of this manual).

16 Refer to Chapter 4A and remove the air cleaner and inlet components as necessary for access to the mounting.

17 Place a jack beneath the transmission, with a block of wood on the jack head. Raise the jack until it is supporting the weight of the transmission.

18 Slacken and remove the mounting rubber's centre nut, and two retaining bolts and remove the mounting from the engine compartment.

19 If necessary, undo the retaining bolts and remove the mounting bracket from the top of the transmission housing. The mounting stud can be separated from the bracket once its lower retaining nut has been undone.

20 Check carefully for signs of wear or damage on all components, and renew them where necessary.

21 Refit the stud to the mounting bracket and tighten its to the specified torque.

22 Refit the bracket to the transmission, tightening its mounting bolts to the specified torque.

23 Fit the mounting rubber to the bracket and tighten its retaining bolts and centre nut to the specified torque.

24 Refit the air cleaner and inlet components removed for access.

25 Remove the jack from underneath the transmission and reconnect the battery negative terminal.

Rear mounting

26 Disconnect the battery negative terminal (refer to *Disconnecting the battery* in the Reference Section of this manual).

27 If not already done, apply the handbrake, then jack up the front of the car and support it on axle stands (see *Jacking and vehicle support*).

28 Position a jack with a block of wood on its head underneath the sump. Raise the jack until it is supporting the weight of the engine.

29 Slacken and remove the nut and bolt from each end of the mounting link and remove the link from underneath the vehicle. If necessary, undo the retaining nuts and bolts and remove the mounting bracket from the engine/transmission.

30 Check carefully for signs of wear or damage on all components, and renew them where necessary.

31 On reassembly, fit the mounting bracket (where removed) to the rear of the transmission and tighten its retaining bolts to the specified torque.

32 Fit the mounting link, and tighten both its bolts to their specified torque settings.

33 Lower the vehicle to the ground and reconnect the battery negative terminal.

Chapter 2 Part C:
Diesel in-car engine repair procedures

Contents

2C

Degrees of difficulty

Easy, suitable for novice with little experience 

Fairly easy, suitable for beginner with some experience 

Fairly difficult, suitable for competent DIY mechanic 

Difficult, suitable for experienced DIY mechanic

Very difficult, suitable for expert DIY or professional

Specifications

General

Type	Four-cylinder, in-line, single overhead camshaft
Designation:	
Non-turbo engines – D models	F8Q 620*, F8Q 622*, F8Q 788
Turbo engines:	
dT models – indirect injection	F8Q 784*, F8Q 786
dTi models – direct injection	F9Q 730*, F9Q 734
dCi models – direct common-rail injection	F9Q 732
Bore	80.0 mm
Stroke	93.0 mm
Capacity	1870 cc
Compression ratio:	
F8Q non-turbo engines	21.5:1
F8Q turbo engines	20.5:1
F9Q engines	19.0:1
Firing order	1-3-4-2 (No 1 cylinder at flywheel end)
Direction of crankshaft rotation	Clockwise viewed from timing belt end

* **Note:** *Engines with auxiliary shaft.*

Compression pressures (engine warm – approximately 80°C)

Normal pressure:	
F8Q engines	27 bars
F9Q engines	22 bars
Minimum pressure	20 bars
Maximum difference between cylinders	4 bars

Camshaft

Endfloat	0.05 to 0.13 mm

Valve clearances (engine cold)

Inlet	0.20 mm
Exhaust	0.40 mm

Timing belt tension value (see text)

F8Q engines:	
HTD timing belt	38 ± 10% SEEM units
HTD2 timing belt	47 ± 10% SEEM units
F9Q engines	38 ± 10% SEEM units

Lubrication system

Minimum oil pressure at 80°C:		
At 1000 rpm	1.2 bars	
At 3500 rpm	3.5 bars	
Oil pump clearances:	**Minimum**	**Maximum**
Gear to body	0.100 mm	0.240 mm
Gear endfloat	0.020 mm	0.085 mm

Torque wrench settings

	Nm	lbf ft
Air conditioning compressor	25	18
Auxiliary shaft sprocket bolt	50	37
Camshaft bearing caps:		
8 mm diameter fasteners	20	15
6 mm diameter fasteners	10	7
Camshaft sprocket bolt:		
F8Q engines	50	37
F9Q engines	60	44
Connecting rod (big-end) cap bolts:		
Except F9Q engines	45 to 50	33 to 37
F9Q engines:		
Stage 1	20	15
Stage 2	Angle-tighten through 40° ± 6°	
Crankshaft pulley bolt:		
Early engines	90 to 100	66 to 74
Later engines with HTD2 timing belt – locking fluid on threads:		
Stage 1	20	15
Stage 2	Angle-tighten through 115°	
Cylinder head bolts – F8Q 620, F8Q 622, F8Q 788 and all F9Q engines*:		
Stage 1 – all bolts	30	22
Stage 2 – all bolts:		
Except F9Q 732	Angle-tighten through 50° ± 4°	
F9Q 732	Angle-tighten through 100° ± 4°	
Stage 3	Wait for at least 3 minutes for the gasket to settle	
Stage 4 – bolts 1 and 2	Slacken fully	
Stage 5 – bolts 1 and 2	25	18
Stage 6 – bolts 1 and 2	Angle-tighten through 213° ± 7°	
Stage 7 – bolts 3 and 4	Slacken fully	
Stage 8 – bolts 3 and 4	25	18
Stage 9 – bolts 3 and 4	Angle-tighten through 213° ± 7°	
Stage 10 – bolts 5 and 6	Slacken fully	
Stage 11 – bolts 5 and 6	25	18
Stage 12 – bolts 5 and 6	Angle-tighten through 213° ± 7°	
Stage 13 – bolts 7 and 8	Slacken fully	
Stage 14 – bolts 7 and 8	25	18
Stage 15 – bolts 7 and 8	Angle-tighten through 213° ± 7°	
Stage 16 – bolts 9 and 10	Slacken fully	
Stage 17 – bolts 9 and 10	25	18
Stage 18 – bolts 9 and 10	Angle-tighten through 213° ± 7°	

Torque wrench settings

	Nm	lbf ft
Cylinder head bolts – F8Q 784 and F8Q 786 engines*:		
Stage 1 – all bolts	30	22
Stage 2 – all bolts	Angle-tighten through 50° ± 4°	
Stage 3	Wait for at least 3 minutes for the gasket to settle	
Stage 4 – bolts 1 and 2	Slacken fully	
Stage 5 – bolts 1 and 2	25	18
Stage 6 – bolts 1 and 2	Angle-tighten through 213° ± 7°	
Stage 7 – bolts 3 and 4	Slacken fully	
Stage 8 – bolts 3 and 4	25	18
Stage 9 – bolts 3 and 4	Angle-tighten through 213° ± 7°	
Stage 10 – bolts 5 and 6	Slacken fully	
Stage 11 – bolts 5 and 6	25	18
Stage 12 – bolts 5 and 6	Angle-tighten through 213° ± 7°	
Stage 13 – bolts 7 and 8	Slacken fully	
Stage 14 – bolts 7 and 8	25	18
Stage 15 – bolts 7 and 8	Angle-tighten through 213° ± 7°	
Stage 16 – bolts 9 and 10	Slacken fully	
Stage 17 – bolts 9 and 10	25	18
Stage 18 – bolts 9 and 10	Angle-tighten through 213° ± 7°	
Stage 19	Run engine to normal operating temperature (when the cooling fan has cut in), then switch off	
Stage 20	Allow engine to cool completely	
Stage 21 – bolts 1 and 2	Angle-tighten through a **further** 120° ± 7°	
Stage 22 – bolts 3 and 4	Angle-tighten through a **further** 120° ± 7°	
Stage 23 – bolts 5 and 6	Angle-tighten through a **further** 120° ± 7°	
Stage 24 – bolts 7 and 8	Angle-tighten through a **further** 120° ± 7°	
Stage 25 – bolts 9 and 10	Angle-tighten through a **further** 120° ± 7°	
Cylinder head cover nuts/bolts	12	9
Engine/gearbox mountings	See Section 13	
Engine oil drain plug	15	11
Flywheel bolts*	50 to 55	37 to 41
Injection pump or high pressure pump sprocket nut	See Chapter 4B	
Main bearing caps	60 to 65	44 to 48
Oil pump bolts:		
Engines with auxiliary shaft:		
6 mm diameter bolts	10	7
8 mm diameter bolts	22	10
All other engines:		
Mounting bolts	Not available	
Sprocket bolts	Not available	
Piston oil spray jet securing bolts	20 ± 2	15 ± 1
Roadwheel bolts	90	66
Strengthening bracket/flywheel cover:		
On engine	50	37
On gearbox	25	18
Sump bolts:		
Except F9Q 732 engine	12 to 15	9 to 11
F9Q 732 engine:		
Stage 1	8	6
Stage 2	15	11
Timing belt tensioner nut	50	37

*** Note:** *Use new bolts.*

1 General information

How to use this Chapter

This Part of Chapter 2 is devoted to in-car repair procedures on diesel engines. Details on engine removal and refitting and engine block/cylinder head overhaul, can be found in Chapter 2D.

Refer to *Vehicle identification numbers* in the Reference Section of this manual for details of engine code locations.

Most of the operations in Chapter 2C assume that the engine is still installed in the car. Therefore, if this information is being used during a complete engine overhaul, with the engine already removed, many of the steps included here will not apply.

Engine description

The engine is of four-cylinder, in-line, single overhead camshaft type, mounted transversely at the front of the vehicle.

The crankshaft is supported in five shell-type main bearings. Thrustwashers are fitted to No 2 main bearing to control crankshaft endfloat.

The connecting rods are attached to the crankshaft by horizontally-split shell-type big-end bearings and to the pistons by gudgeon pins. The gudgeon pins are fully floating and are retained by circlips. The aluminium alloy pistons are of the slipper type and are fitted with three piston rings; two compression rings and a scraper-type oil control ring.

The single overhead camshaft is mounted in five plain bearings machined directly in the aluminium alloy cylinder head and is driven by the crankshaft via a toothed timing belt.

The camshaft operates the valves via inverted bucket-type followers, which operate in bores machined directly in the cylinder head. Valve clearance adjustment is by shims located externally between the followers and the cam lobes on early models, or by different thickness followers. The inlet and exhaust valves are mounted vertically in the cylinder head and are each closed by a single valve spring.

On early engines (F8Q 620, F8Q 622, F8Q 784 and F9Q 730) an auxiliary shaft located alongside the crankshaft is also driven by the timing belt and actuates the oil pump via a skew gear. On later engines the oil pump is driven by chain from the crankshaft: no auxiliary shaft is fitted, but its sprocket is retained as an idler.

The fuel injection pump (except F9Q 732 engine) or high pressure pump (F9Q 732 engine) is driven by the timing belt and is described in detail in Chapter 4B.

A semi-closed crankcase ventilation system is employed and crankcase fumes are drawn from an oil separator on the cast iron cylinder block and passed via a hose (and in certain cases, a second oil separator) to the inlet tract (see Chapter 4C for further details).

Engine lubrication is by pressure feed from a gear-type oil pump located beneath the crankshaft. Engine oil is fed through an externally-mounted oil filter to the main oil gallery feeding the crankshaft, auxiliary shaft (where fitted) and camshaft. Oil spray jets are fitted to the cylinder block to supply oil to the underside of the pistons. Certain models are fitted with an oil cooler mounted on the cylinder block.

Repair operations possible with the engine in the vehicle

The following operations can be carried out without having to remove the engine from the vehicle:

a) Removal and refitting of the cylinder head.
b) Removal and refitting of the timing belt and sprockets.
c) Renewal of the camshaft oil seals.
d) Removal and refitting of the camshaft.
e) Removal and refitting of the sump.
f) Removal and refitting of the connecting rods and pistons.*
g) Removal and refitting of the oil pump.
h) Renewal of the crankshaft oil seals.
i) Renewal of the engine mountings.

* **Note:** *Although the operation marked with an asterisk can be carried out with the engine in the car after removal of the sump, it is better for the engine to be removed in the interests of cleanliness and improved access. For this reason, the procedure is described in Chapter 2D.*

Caution: If the radio/cassette in your vehicle is equipped with an anti-theft system, make sure you have the correct activation code before disconnecting the battery

2.2 Carrying out a compression test

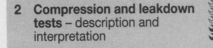

2 Compression and leakdown tests – description and interpretation

Compression test

Note: *A compression tester specifically designed for diesel engines must be used for this test.*

1 When engine performance is down, or if misfiring occurs which cannot be attributed to a fault in the fuel system, a compression test can provide diagnostic clues as to the engine's condition. If the test is performed regularly it can give warning of trouble before any other symptoms become apparent.

2 A compression tester specifically intended for diesel engines must be used, because of the higher pressures involved. The tester is connected to an adapter which screws into the glow plug or injector hole **(see illustration)**. It is unlikely to be worthwhile buying such a tester for occasional use, but it may be possible to borrow or hire one – if not, have the test performed by a garage.

3 Unless specific instructions to the contrary are supplied with the tester, observe the following points:

a) The battery must be in a good state of charge, the air filter must be clean and the engine should be at normal operating temperature.
b) All the injectors or glow plugs should be removed before starting the test. If removing the injectors, also remove the fire seal washers (which must be renewed when the injectors are refitted – see Chapter 4B), otherwise they may be blown out.
c) Where applicable, it is advisable to disconnect the stop solenoid on the pump to reduce the amount of fuel discharged as the engine is cranked.

4 There is no need to hold the accelerator pedal down during the test because the diesel engine air inlet is not throttled.

5 The actual compression pressures measured are not as important as the balance between cylinders. Values are given in the Specifications.

6 The cause of poor compression is less easy to establish on a diesel engine than on a petrol one. The effect of introducing oil into the cylinders ('wet' testing) is not conclusive, because there is a risk that the oil will sit in the swirl chamber or in the recess on the piston crown instead of passing to the rings. However, the following can be used as a rough guide to diagnosis.

7 All cylinders should produce very similar pressures; any difference greater than that specified indicates the existence of a fault. Note that the compression should build-up quickly in a healthy engine; low compression on the first stroke, followed by gradually increasing pressure on successive strokes, indicates worn piston rings. A low compression reading on the first stroke, which does not build-up during successive strokes, indicates leaking valves or a blown head gasket (a cracked head could also be the cause).

8 A low reading from two adjacent cylinders is almost certainly due to the head gasket having blown between them.

Leakdown test

9 A leakdown test measures the rate at which compressed air fed into the cylinder is lost. It is an alternative to a compression test and in many ways it is better, since the escaping air provides easy identification of where pressure loss is occurring (piston rings, valves or head gasket).

10 The equipment needed for leakdown testing is unlikely to be available to the home mechanic. If poor compression is suspected, have the test performed by a suitably-equipped garage.

3 Top Dead Centre (TDC) for No 1 piston – locating

1 Top Dead Centre (TDC) is the highest point in the cylinder that each piston reaches as the crankshaft turns. Each piston reaches TDC at the end of the compression stroke and again at the end of the exhaust stroke; however, for the purpose of timing the engine, TDC refers to the position of No 1 piston at the end of its compression stroke. No 1 piston is at the flywheel end of the engine.

2 When No 1 piston is at TDC, the timing mark on the camshaft sprocket should be aligned with the pointer on the timing belt outer cover (the sprocket mark can be viewed through the cut-out in the cover, below the pointer). Additionally, the timing mark on the flywheel should be aligned with the TDC mark on the gearbox bellhousing.

3 To align the timing marks, the crankshaft must be turned. This should be done by using a spanner on the crankshaft pulley bolt. Improved access to the pulley bolt can be obtained by jacking up the front right-hand corner of the vehicle and removing the

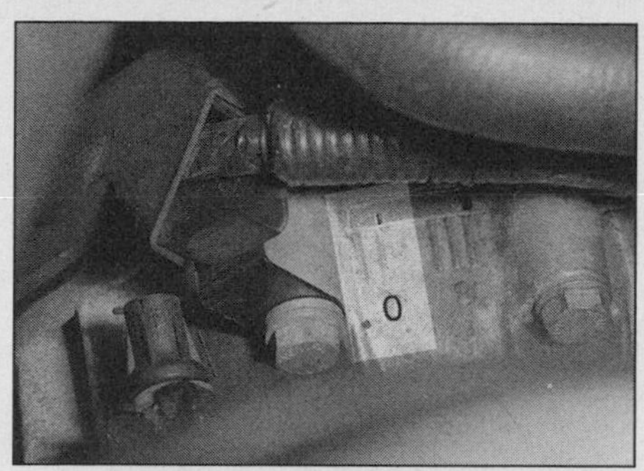

3.4 Flywheel timing mark aligned with TDC (0°) mark on bellhousing

3.6 Camshaft sprocket timing mark aligned with pointer on timing belt outer cover

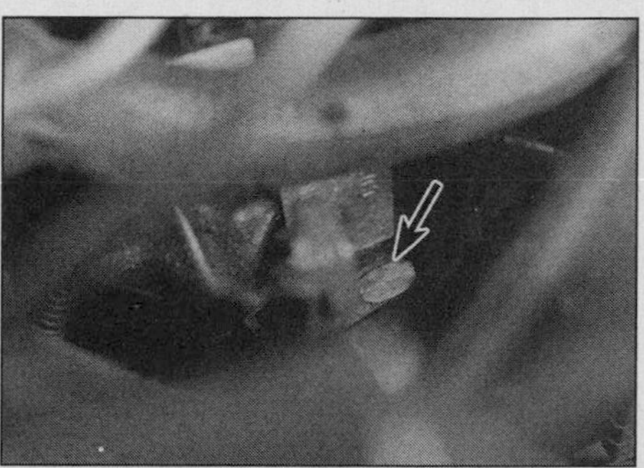
3.8a Remove the blanking plug from the cylinder block . . .

roadwheel and the wheelarch lower liner (secured by plastic clips). If desired, to enable the engine to be turned more easily, remove the glow plugs (Chapter 5C) or the fuel injectors (Chapter 4B).

4 Look through the timing aperture in the gearbox bellhousing and turn the crankshaft until the timing mark on the flywheel is aligned with the TDC (0°) mark on the bellhousing **(see illustration)**.

5 On F8Q-engined models, unscrew the three securing bolts and remove the timing belt upper/engine right-hand mounting plastic cover from the mounting upper bracket, noting the locations of any brackets secured by the bolts. On F9Q-engined models, unscrew the retaining nuts and withdraw the engine sound-insulating cover.

6 Check that the timing mark on the camshaft sprocket is aligned with the pointer on the timing belt outer cover **(see illustration)**. The engine is now positioned with No 1 piston at TDC on its compression stroke.

7 It is possible to check the crankshaft position as follows. If necessary, remove the air cleaner housing assembly (Chapter 4B).

If the special Renault tool mentioned in this Section is not available, an 8 mm diameter rod or drill bit can be used instead. On some engines, however, an 8 mm diameter rod may be too slack a fit in the cylinder block plug aperture for the crankshaft position to be determined accurately – it will therefore be necessary in such cases to have a stepped pin made up, with an 8 mm diameter at its tip to engage in the crankshaft slot and a larger diameter as necessary to fit precisely in the cylinder block aperture.

8 For absolute accuracy, the crankshaft position can be checked by inserting a timing pin – Renault tool Mot. 861 (early version) or Mot. 1054 (latest version) **(see Tool tip)**. To do this, unscrew the blanking plug from the front left-hand end of the cylinder block, next to the base of the oil level dipstick tube, and insert the timing pin so that it engages in the

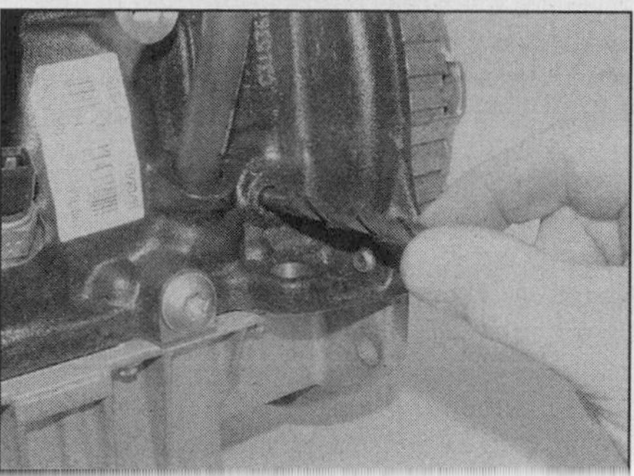
3.8b . . . and insert a suitable drill to check the crankshaft position

3.8c Using the purpose-made TDC timing pin

timing slot provided for this purpose in the crankshaft, noting that it may be necessary to rock the crankshaft very slightly backwards or forwards to do this **(see illustrations)**. Once in place it should be impossible to turn the crankshaft – if the crankshaft will still move to-and-fro slightly, then the timing pin has entered a balance hole in the crankshaft instead of the timing slot. **Note:** *Do not attempt to rotate the engine whilst the timing pin is in place. If the engine is to be left in this state for a long period of time, it is a good idea to place warning notices inside the vehicle and in the engine compartment. This will reduce the possibility of the engine being accidentally cranked on the starter motor, which will cause severe damage if done with the timing pin in place.*

Caution: These timing pins are intended SOLELY for the purpose of checking the position of the crankshaft during various engine overhaul procedures. DO NOT use them as locking tools to prevent crankshaft rotation while the pulley or flywheel bolts are unscrewed or tightened.

9 On completion, remove the timing pin and refit all removed components.

4 Valve clearances – checking and adjustment

Note: *This operation is not part of the maintenance schedule. It should be undertaken if noise from the valvegear*

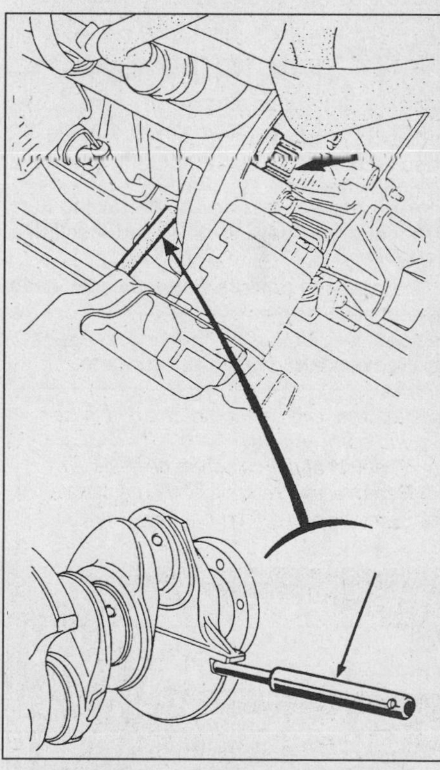
3.8d With No 1 cylinder at TDC – TDC mark on flywheel can be viewed through bellhousing aperture – the crankshaft position can be checked using a timing pin – early version (Mot. 861) of Renault tool shown

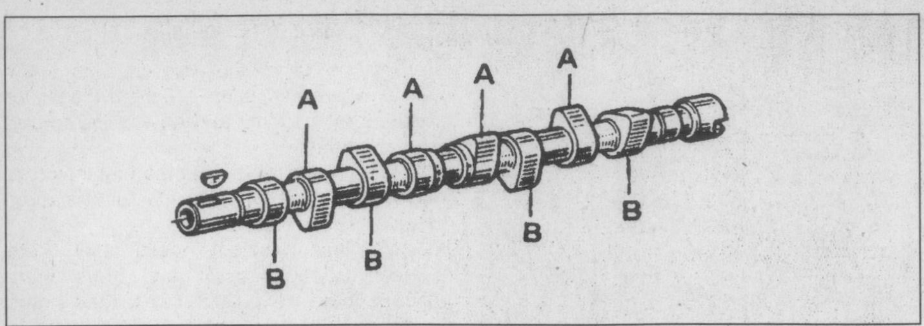

4.6 Valve location details
A Inlet B Exhaust

4.8 Measuring a valve clearance (early model)

becomes evident, or if loss of performance gives cause to suspect that the clearances may be incorrect. A new cylinder head cover gasket may be required on refitting.

Note: *It is permissible to move adjustment shims to different followers to correct valve clearances, but new followers will have to be used if adjustment is not by shims, as the old followers will have worn into their bores.*

Checking

1 Where necessary for improved access, unclip any hoses which are routed across the top of the cylinder head cover and move them to one side out of the way. If fuel lines are disconnected, cover open unions to prevent dirt ingress.

2 On F8Q-engined models, unscrew the securing bolts and remove the timing belt upper/engine right-hand mounting plastic cover, noting the locations of any brackets secured by the bolts. On F9Q-engined models, unscrew the retaining nuts and withdraw the engine sound-insulating cover.

3 Unscrew the nuts from the cylinder head cover retaining nuts (F8Q engines) or bolts (F9Q engines) and withdraw the cover from the engine. Recover the gasket.

VALVES ROCKING ON CYLINDER	CHECK CLEARANCE ON CYLINDER
1	4
3	2
4	1
2	3

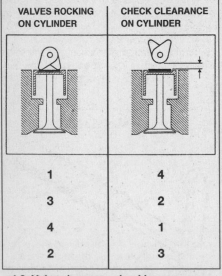

4.9 Valve clearance checking sequence

4 During the following procedure, the crankshaft must be turned, using a spanner on the crankshaft pulley bolt. Improved access to the pulley bolt can be obtained by jacking up the front right-hand corner of the vehicle and removing the roadwheel and the wheelarch lower liner (secured by plastic clips).

5 If desired, to enable the crankshaft to be turned more easily, remove the glow plugs (Chapter 5C) or the fuel injectors (Chapter 4B).

6 Draw the valve positions on a piece of paper, numbering them 1 to 8 from the flywheel end of the engine. Identify them as inlet or exhaust (ie, 1E, 2I, 3E, 4I, 5I, 6E, 7I, 8E) **(see illustration)**.

7 Turn the crankshaft until the valves of No 1 cylinder (flywheel end) are rocking – the exhaust valve will be closing and the inlet valve will be opening. The piston of No 4 cylinder will be at the top of its compression stroke, with both valves fully closed – the clearances for both valves of No 4 cylinder may now be checked.

8 Insert a feeler gauge of the correct thickness (see Specifications) between the cam lobe and the top of the follower or shim (early models) and check that it is a firm sliding fit **(see illustration)**. If it is not, use the feeler gauges to ascertain the exact clearance and record this for use when calculating the new follower/shim thickness required. Note that the inlet and exhaust valve clearances are different (see Specifications).

9 With No 4 cylinder valve clearances checked, turn the engine through half a turn so that No 3 valves are rocking, then check the valve clearances of No 2 cylinder in the same way. Similarly check the remaining valve clearances in the sequence shown **(see illustration)**.

Adjustment

F8Q engines

Note: *A micrometer will be required for this operation. Note that on most later models, a shim is not fitted, and the followers are available in different thicknesses for adjustment. Removal of the followers for adjustment requires removal of the camshafts first as described in Section 8.*

10 Where a valve clearance differs from the specified value, then the follower (or shim if applicable) for that valve must be substituted with a thinner or thicker one accordingly. Where shims are fitted, each shim's thickness is etched on the bottom face of the shim, but it is prudent to use a micrometer to measure the true thickness of any shim removed, as it may have been reduced by wear **(see illustrations)**. Where no shims are fitted, the thickness of the followers must be measured after their removal.

11 The thickness of follower/shim required is calculated as follows. If the measured clearance is less than specified, subtract the measured clearance from the specified clearance and deduct the result from the

4.10a Thickness is etched on the underside of each shim

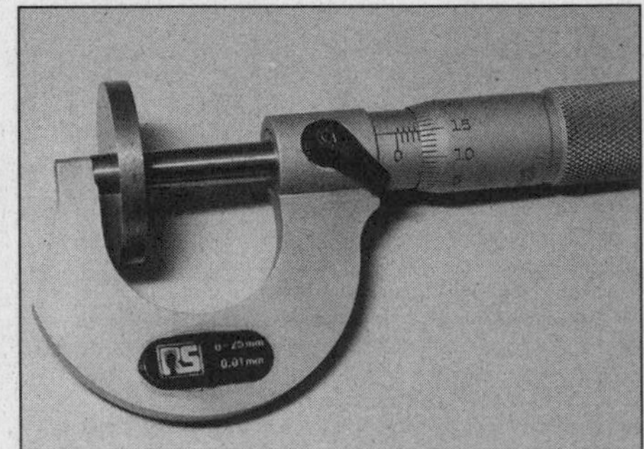

4.10b Checking a shim's thickness with a micrometer

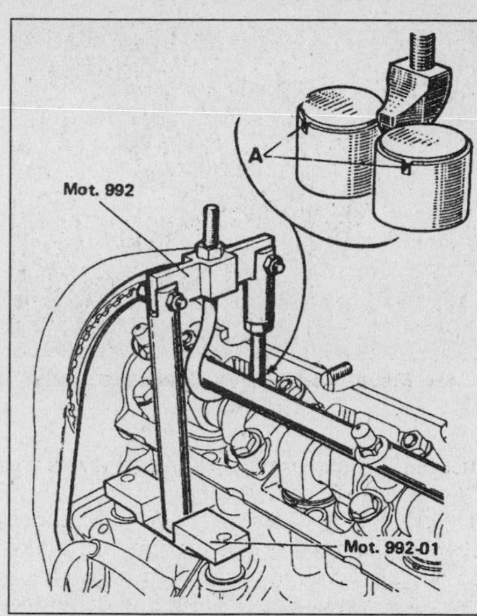

4.13 Renault tools for depressing and holding cam followers (F8Q engine)

Position follower notches (A) at right-angles to the camshaft before depressing them

thickness of the existing follower/shim. For example:

Sample calculation – clearance too small

Clearance measured (A) = 0.15 mm
Desired clearance (B) = 0.20 mm
Difference (B – A) = 0.05 mm
Follower/shim thickness fitted = 3.70 mm
Follower/shim
required = 3.70 – 0.05 = 3.65 mm

12 If the measured clearance is greater than specified, subtract the specified clearance from the measured clearance and add the result to the thickness of the existing follower/shim. For example:

Sample calculation – clearance too big

Clearance measured (A) = 0.50 mm
Desired clearance (B) = 0.40 mm
Difference (A – B) = 0.10 mm
Follower/shim thickness fitted = 3.45 mm
Follower/shim
required = 3.45 + 0.10 = 3.55 mm

13 Where shims are not fitted, the camshaft and followers must be removed as described in Section 8. Where shims are fitted, they can

4.14 Removing a shim from a cam follower using screwdrivers (F8Q engine)

be removed from their locations on top of the followers without removing the camshaft if the Renault tools shown can be borrowed, or a suitable alternative fabricated **(see illustration)**.

14 To remove a shim, the follower has to be pressed down against valve spring pressure just far enough to allow the shim to be slid out. Theoretically, this could be done by levering against the camshaft between the cam lobes with a suitable screwdriver or similar tool to push the follower down, but this is not recommended by the manufacturers. If this method is to be used, take great care not to damage the camshaft, cylinder head, or follower **(see illustration)**.

15 An arrangement similar to the Renault tools can be made by bolting a bar to the camshaft bearing studs and levering down against this with a stout screwdriver. The contact pad should be a triangular-shaped metal block with a lip filed along each side to contact the edge of the followers. Levering down against this will open the valve and allow the shim to be withdrawn.

16 Make sure that the cam lobe peaks are uppermost when depressing a follower and rotate the followers so that their notches are at right-angles to the camshaft centre-line. When refitting the shims, ensure that the thickness markings face the followers (ie, face downwards).

17 If the Renault tools cannot be borrowed or a suitable alternative improvised, then it will be necessary to remove the camshaft to reach the shims, as described in Section 8.

18 Remove the spanner from the crankshaft pulley bolt.

19 Refit the cylinder head cover, using a new gasket where necessary – tighten the cover retaining nuts evenly to the specified torque wrench setting.

20 Where applicable, refit the fuel injectors (as described in Chapter 4B), or the glow plugs (Chapter 5C).

21 Refit/reconnect any hoses which were moved for access. If fuel lines were disconnected, reconnect them, then prime and bleed the fuel system as described in Chapter 4B.

22 Refit the timing belt upper/engine right-hand mounting plastic cover.

F9Q engines

Note: *A micrometer will be required for this operation. Note that on most later models, a shim is not fitted, and the followers are available in different thicknesses for adjustment. Removal of the followers for adjustment requires removal of the camshafts first as described in Section 8.*

23 Where a valve clearance differs from the specified value, then the follower (or shim if applicable) for that valve must be substituted with a thinner or thicker one accordingly. The follower/shim thickness can be measured using a micrometer and then the thickness of new one required can be calculated as described for the F8Q engines in paragraphs 11 and 12 above **(see illustrations)**.

24 Where shims are not fitted, the camshaft and followers must be removed as described in Section 8. Where shims are fitted, they have a round projection on their lower face which locates in a recess in the follower. This arrangement makes it very difficult to remove the shims with the camshaft installed. The procedure requires the use of the Renault special tool shown **(see illustration)**, or a suitable home-made alternative, but it is first necessary to remove the inlet and exhaust manifolds and the turbocharger (see Chapter 4B).

25 To remove a shim, turn the crankshaft in the normal direction of rotation until the valve to be adjusted is fully open. Insert the tool through the cylinder head port so that the

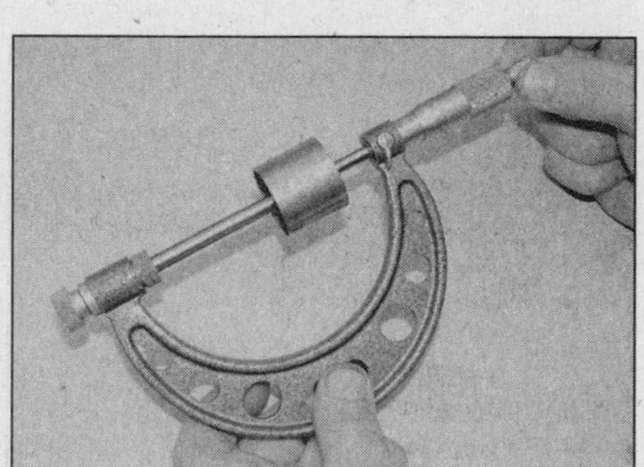

4.23a Measuring the thickness of a follower (F9Q 732 engine)

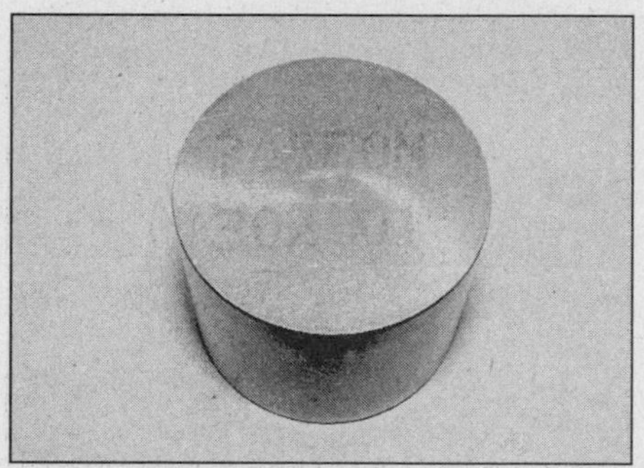

4.23b The follower thickness may still be visible (F9Q 732 engine)

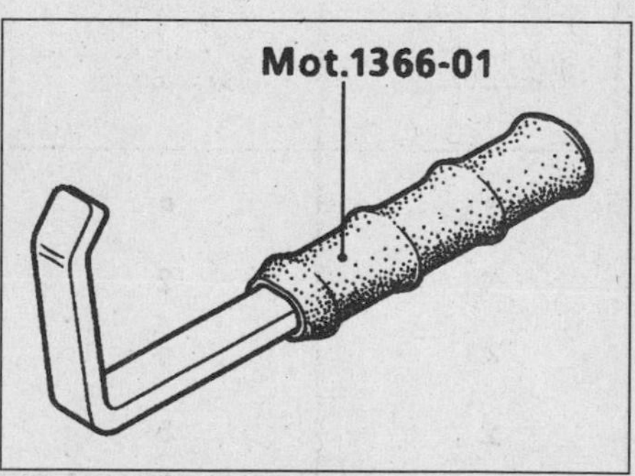

4.24 Renault tool for holding valves open (F9Q engine)

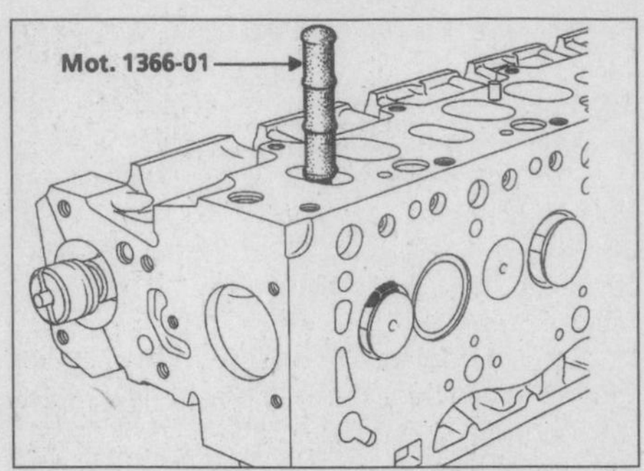

4.25 Method of inserting and using Renault tool to hold valves open (F9Q engine)

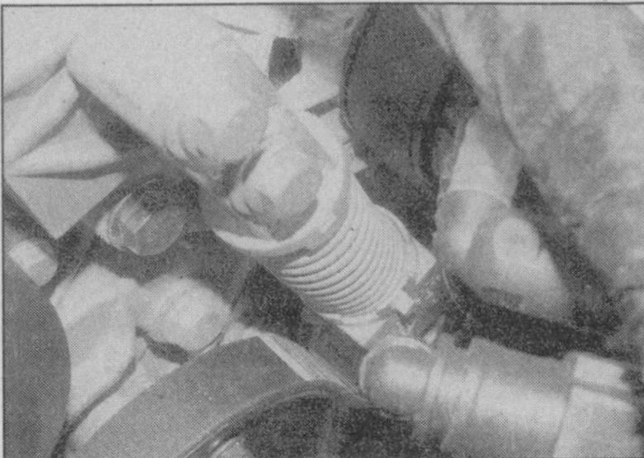
5.4a The auxiliary drivebelt tensioner on F9Q 732 engines

5.4b Removing the auxiliary drivebelt

shaped end of the tool locates on the valve seat **(see illustration)**.

26 If removing an inlet valve shim, turn the crankshaft a further 180°, in the normal direction of rotation, to allow the valve to close and contact the tool. The tool will trap the valve, preventing it from closing fully, which will allow sufficient clearance for the shim to be removed with a screwdriver. The same procedure is used for the exhaust valves except that the crankshaft must be turned 180° in the **opposite** direction to normal rotation.

27 Before refitting a shims, wipe the top of the follower and ensure that all the oil is removed from the shim locating recess in the follower's upper face. Fit the shim to the follower with the projection on the shim engaged with the follower's recess.

28 If the Renault tool cannot be borrowed or a suitable alternative improvised, then it will be necessary to remove the camshaft to gain access to the shims, as described in Section 8.

29 Remove the spanner from the crankshaft pulley bolt.

30 Refit the cylinder head cover, using a new gasket where necessary – tighten the cover retaining bolts evenly to the specified torque wrench setting.

31 Where applicable, refit the fuel injectors (as described in Chapter 4B), or the glow plugs (Chapter 5C).

32 Refit the inlet and exhaust manifolds and the turbocharger as described in Chapter 4B.

33 Refit/reconnect any hoses which were moved for access. If fuel lines were disconnected, reconnect them, then prime and bleed the fuel system as described in Chapter 4B.

34 Refit the engine sound-insulating cover.

5 Timing belt – removal, inspection and refitting

Caution: If the timing belt breaks or slips in service, extensive engine damage may result. Renew the belt at the intervals specified in Chapter 1B, or earlier if its condition is at all doubtful.

Note: *F8Q 620 and early F8Q 784 engines are fitted with timing belts marked HTD, while later F8Q units and all F9Q engines are fitted with timing belts of a different tooth profile that are marked HTD2. The change in tooth profile necessitates different sprockets which are usually marked to match their respective timing belts – if not, physical differences (the early camshaft sprockets have six spokes while the later ones have three) will serve for identification purposes. Whenever the timing belt is renewed, ALWAYS ensure that the correct replacement type is obtained to match the sprockets – if any of the sprockets are ever to be renewed, the converse applies.*

Note: *A suitable tool will be required to check the timing belt tension on completion of refitting – see text. A suitable puller may be required to remove the crankshaft pulley.*

Removal

1 Disconnect the battery negative lead. On early Scénic models, refer to Chapter 5A and disconnect the battery positive lead at the secondary terminal unit in the engine compartment and also the negative lead at the battery itself. With the battery disconnected, undo the mounting bolt and move the secondary terminal unit to one side.

2 Jack up the front right-hand corner of the vehicle (see *Jacking and vehicle support*) and remove the roadwheel and the wheelarch lower liner (secured by plastic clips). Where fitted, remove the engine top cover and the engine compartment undershield. On Scénic models, the following procedure may be necessary in order to locate an engine support bar across the engine compartment – remove the windscreen wiper arms, then remove the grilles and the plenum chamber closure panel located beneath the front of the windscreen. If an ordinary hoist is being used, this work is not required.

3 On F8Q-engined models, unscrew the securing bolts and remove the timing belt upper/engine right-hand mounting plastic cover, noting the locations of any brackets secured by the bolts. On F9Q-engined models, unscrew the retaining nuts and withdraw the engine top cover, then on early models disconnect the wiring plug from the injection control unit, undo the two mounting bolts and move the control unit to one side.

4 Remove the auxiliary drivebelt as described in Chapter 1B. On air conditioning models, note the position of the drivebelt tensioner as a guide to refitting. On F9Q 732 engines, press down on the tensioner before loosening the upper mounting bolts, then release the tension slowly **(see illustrations)**. If desired, to improve access, unbolt the strengthening bar (where fitted) from between the front suspension strut turrets.

5 Unscrew the crankshaft pulley bolt while holding the crankshaft stationary. To hold the crankshaft, have an assistant firmly depress the foot brake pedal with 4th gear engaged while the bolt is loosened (note that at least two of the front wheel retaining bolts should be fitted on each side). Alternatively, remove the engine-to-gearbox strengthening bracket/flywheel cover, then refit one of the cover plate-to-gearbox bolts to act as a fulcrum and have an assistant insert a screwdriver or similar tool in the starter ring gear teeth.

6 Remove the bolt and the pulley from the crankshaft end **(see illustrations)**. Use a suitable puller if the pulley is tight.

7 To improve access, unscrew the two bolts

5.6a Remove the crankshaft pulley bolt . . .

5.6b . . . and the pulley

5.9a On Scénic models, remove the plastic covers . . .

5.9b . . . and locate the lifting bar on the front suspension strut towers

5.14a Removing the timing belt cover from the injection pump sprocket (early models)

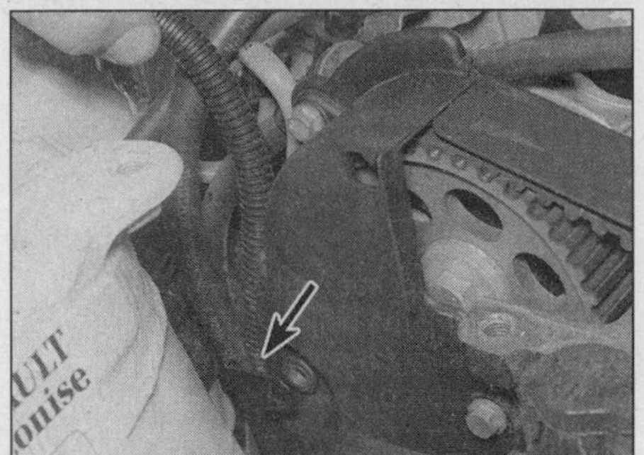

5.14b Note the location of any brackets secured by the bolts . . .

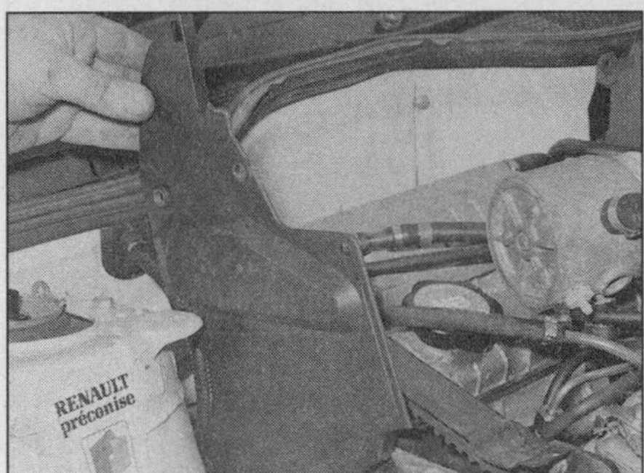

5.14c . . . and remove the timing belt cover from the camshaft sprocket (early models)

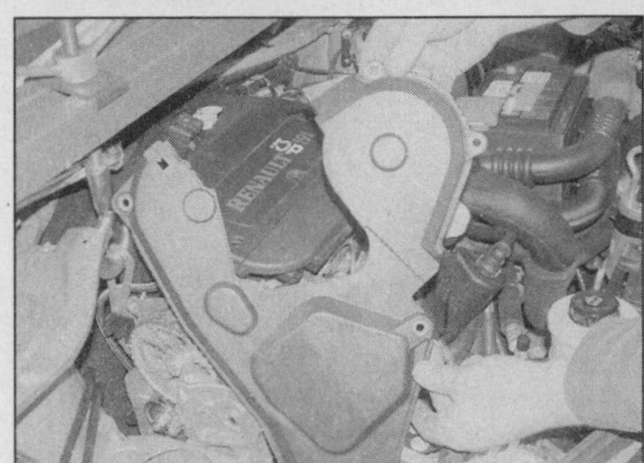

5.14d Removing the upper outer timing cover (later models)

securing the fuel filter assembly to the body panel, then unclip the filter hoses from the brackets on the engine. The assembly can be moved to one side (on top of the engine) until completion of refitting.

8 Temporarily refit the crankshaft pulley bolt. Turn the crankshaft to position No 1 piston at TDC on the compression stroke and insert a timing pin to check the crankshaft position as described in Section 3.

9 The engine right-hand front mounting must be dismantled to enable the timing belt to be removed; therefore the engine must be supported. The assembly can be supported using a jack and a suitable block of wood to spread the load under the sump. Alternatively, connect a hoist or lifting bar and suitable lifting tackle to the right-hand engine lifting bracket (in this case, where applicable, the fuel return hose will have to be disconnected from the injection pump and withdrawn from the hole in the engine rear lifting bracket). On Scénic models, remove the plastic covers from the strut towers and locate the lifting bar on the inner body **(see illustrations)**.

10 Ensure that the engine/gearbox assembly is adequately supported, then unscrew the nut securing the mounting upper bracket to the mounting rubber/movement limiter assembly – refer to Section 13 for details if required.

11 Unscrew the three bolts securing the mounting upper bracket to the main bracket on the engine, then withdraw the bracket.

12 Unbolt the engine mounting rubber/ movement limiter assembly from the body. On F8Q and F9Q engines, also unbolt the rear mounting link (Section 13).

13 Where necessary, unscrew the bolts securing the exhaust downpipe to the exhaust manifold (see Chapter 4B). Release the downpipe and support it.

14 Unscrew the securing bolts and withdraw the timing belt outer cover, noting the location of any brackets secured by the bolts. On early models this is in two sections, however on later models it is in one piece, and must be tilted to remove **(see illustrations)**.

15 With No 1 piston at TDC on the compression stroke (see paragraph 8), where applicable, note the position of the timing mark on the fuel injection pump sprocket. **Note:** *On engines fitted with an MAA-type injection pump sprocket, the sprocket timing mark may differ from those shown for the one-piece sprocket. If this is the case, take note of the type of mark found and its location, for use when refitting.* Note that on models with a one-piece sprocket, there are two timing marks on the sprocket. The mark used depends on whether a Bosch or Lucas injection pump is fitted **(see illustrations)**. **Note:** *On the F9Q 732, there are no timing marks on the high pressure fuel pump.*

16 If the original belt is to be re-used (contrary to Renault's recommendation), check that the belt is marked with arrows to indicate its running direction and if necessary mark it. Similarly, note that the belt should be marked with bands across its width to act as timing marks corresponding to the timing marks on the camshaft, fuel injection pump

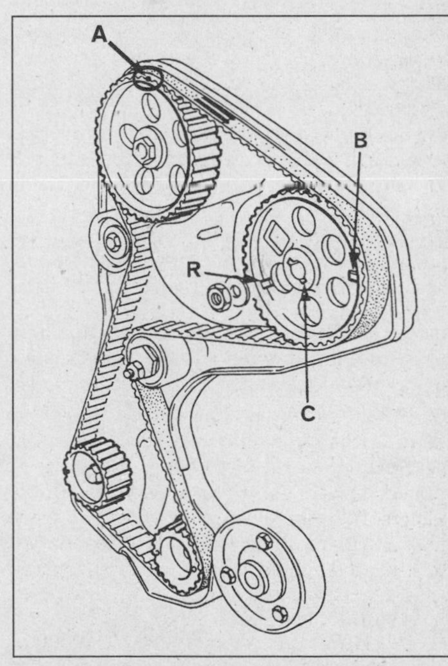

5.15a Camshaft and injection pump sprocket timing mark positions with No 1 piston at TDC (F8Q 620 engine)

A Camshaft sprocket mark (aligned with pointer on timing belt outer cover – removed in this view)
B Injection pump sprocket mark for use with Bosch pump
C Woodruff keyway
R Injection pump sprocket mark for use with Lucas pump

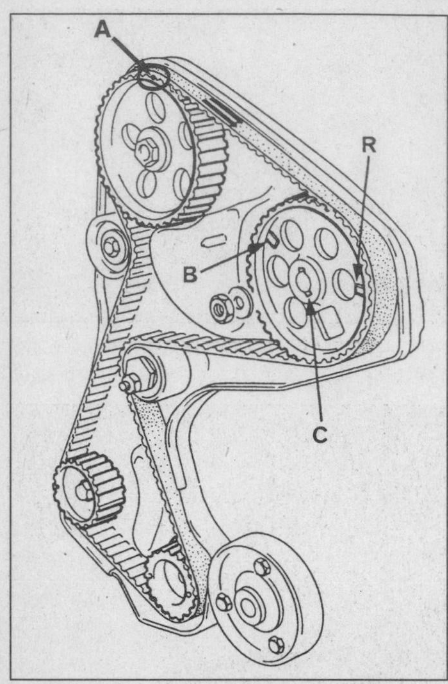

5.15b Camshaft and injection pump sprocket timing mark positions with No 1 piston at TDC (F8Q 784, F8Q 786 and F8Q 788 engines)

A Camshaft sprocket mark (aligned with pointer on timing belt outer cover – removed in this view)
B Injection pump sprocket mark for use with Bosch pump
C Woodruff keyway
R Injection pump sprocket mark for use with Lucas pump

Note: *On engines fitted with an MAA-type injection pump sprocket, the actual sprocket timing mark may differ from those shown – see text*

(except F9Q 732 engine) and crankshaft sprockets. If the original timing bands have deteriorated, make accurate alignment marks on the belt.

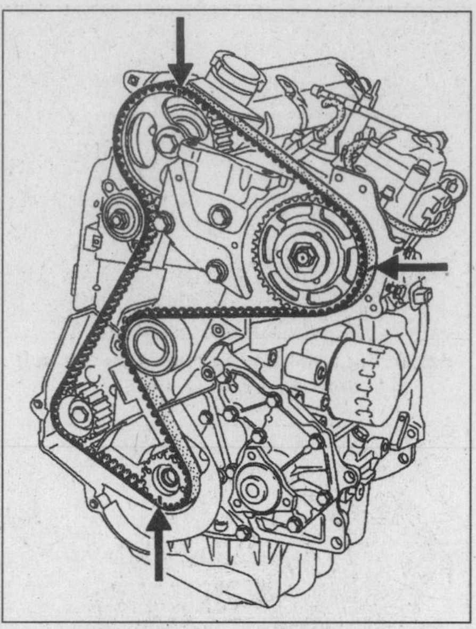

5.15c Sprocket timing mark positions with No 1 piston at TDC (F9Q engine)

17 Loosen the retaining nut and bolt, then push back the tensioner to relieve the tension on the timing belt **(see illustration)**. Retighten the nut.

18 Release the belt first from the camshaft sprocket, then from the fuel injection/high pressure pump, idler, crankshaft and auxiliary shaft/idler, and remove it from the engine **(see illustration)**.

19 Do not turn the camshaft or the crankshaft whilst the timing belt is removed, as there is a risk of piston-to-valve contact. If it is necessary to turn the camshaft for any reason, before doing so, remove the timing pin and turn the crankshaft anti-clockwise (viewed from the timing belt end of the engine) by a quarter-turn to position all four pistons halfway down their bores.

Inspection

Note: *Renault state that the timing belt must be renewed as a matter of course whenever it is removed.*

20 Clean the sprockets, idler pulley and tensioner and wipe them dry – **do not** apply excessive amounts of solvent to the idler pulley and tensioner otherwise the bearing lubricant may be removed. Also clean the timing belt inner cover and the related surfaces of the cylinder head and block.

21 Examine the timing belt carefully for any signs of cracking, fraying or general wear, particularly at the roots of the teeth. Renew the belt if there is any sign of deterioration of this nature, or if there is any oil or grease contamination. Renew any leaking oil seals. The belt **must**, of course, be renewed if it has completed the mileage given in the maintenance schedule in Chapter 1B.

Refitting

22 Ensure that the crankshaft is at the TDC position for No 1 cylinder, with the timing pin in place to ensure complete accuracy, as described previously. If the pistons have been positioned halfway down their bores, temporarily refit the timing belt outer cover which covers the camshaft sprocket and check that the timing mark on the sprocket is aligned with the pointer on the timing belt outer cover, then turn the crankshaft clockwise (viewed from the timing belt end of the engine) until the timing pin can be refitted. To enable the tensioner to be adjusted, screw a 6 mm bolt into the threaded hole provided in the timing belt inner cover (temporarily remove the bolt already in position, where necessary). The bolt will bear against the rear of the tensioner pulley and enable adjustments of the belt tension to be made **(see illustration 5.26)**.

23 Align the timing bands on the belt with the marks on the crankshaft, camshaft and fuel injection pump (except F9Q 732 engine) sprockets, ensuring that the running direction arrows on the belt are pointing clockwise (viewed from the timing belt end of the engine). Fit the timing belt over the crankshaft

5.17 Loosen the timing belt tensioner nut

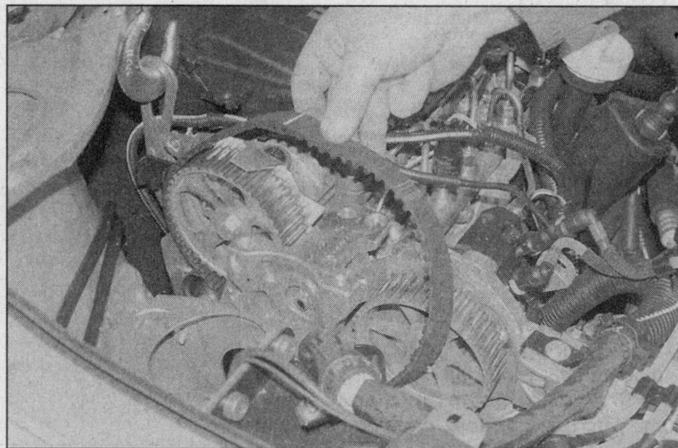

5.18 Removing the timing belt

5.23a The running direction arrows on the belt must point clockwise

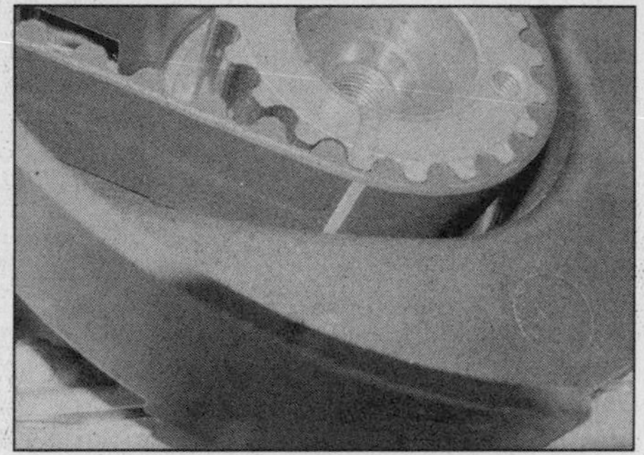
5.23b Align the timing bands on the belt with the crankshaft . . .

5.23c . . . camshaft . . .

5.23d . . . and injection pump sprocket timing marks (engine with Lucas pump)

sprocket first, followed by the idler pulley, fuel injection/high pressure pump sprocket, camshaft sprocket, tensioner and auxiliary shaft/idler sprocket **(see illustrations)**.

24 Check that all the timing marks are still aligned and remove all slack from the timing belt by tightening the bolt fitted to the timing belt inner cover. **Note:** *As a further check (except on the F9Q 732 engine), count the number of timing belt teeth between the camshaft sprocket's timing mark and the injection pump sprocket's timing mark – if the valve timing is correct, there will be 29 teeth on F8Q engines, 30 teeth on F9Q engines.*

25 The belt tension must now be checked –

With experience, timing belt tension may be judged to be approximately correct when the belt can be twisted 45 to 90° with moderate pressure between the finger and thumb, checking midway between the sprockets on the belt's longest run.

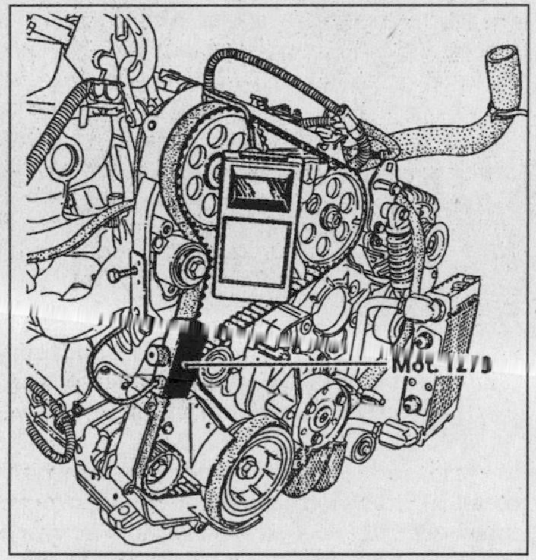

5.25a Using Renault tool Mot. 1273 to check the timing belt tension

this can be set or checked accurately **only** by using the Renault tool Mot. 1273 (SEEM C. Tronic 105.6), Mot. 1505 or Mot. 1543. When using Mot. 1543, apply a torque of 11 Nm (8 lbf ft) to the tool in order to pre-tension the front run of the timing belt, before carrying out the main tensioning procedure **(see illustrations)**. If this equipment is not available, set the belt's tension as carefully as possible **(see Haynes Hint)**, then take the vehicle to a Renault dealer as soon as possible for the tension to be checked by qualified personnel using the special equipment. Do not take the vehicle on any long journeys or rev the engine to high

5.25b Using Mot. 1543 to pre-tension the timing belt before checking the tension with a gauge

speeds until the timing belt's tension has been checked and is known to be correct.

26 If the adjustment is incorrect, the tensioner will have to be repositioned by loosening the tensioner nut and by screwing in or out the bolt fitted to the timing belt inner cover **(see illustration)**.

27 With the correct tension applied, retighten the tensioner nut to the specified torque. This torque is critical, since if the nut were to come loose, considerable engine damage would result. Unscrew the bolt fitted to the timing belt inner cover, and where necessary, refit the original.

28 Remove the crankshaft timing pin, then refit the crankshaft pulley and securing bolt. Prevent the crankshaft turning using the method described previously and tighten the bolt to the specified torque (and angle on later models) **(see illustration)**. Refit the engine-to-

5.26 M6 bolt fitted to timing belt inner cover to adjust timing belt tension

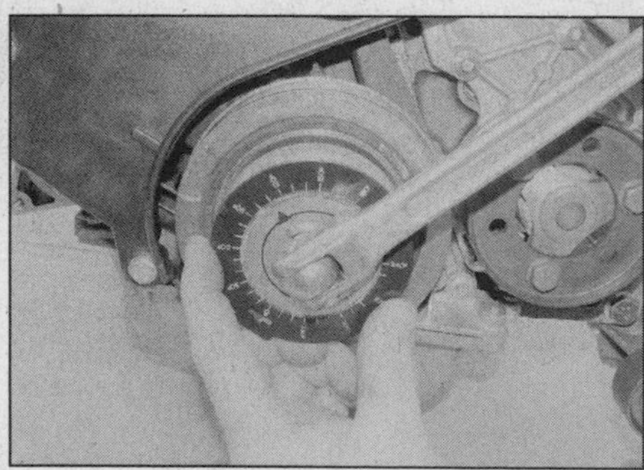
5.28 Angle-tightening the crankshaft pulley bolt (F9Q 732 engine)

gearbox strengthening bracket/flywheel cover.

29 Check that the crankshaft is still positioned with No 1 piston at TDC (by temporarily refitting the crankshaft timing pin), then remove the timing pin and turn the crankshaft two complete turns in the normal direction of rotation, returning it to the TDC position again. Re-insert the timing pin in the cylinder block.

30 Temporarily refit the timing belt outer cover which covers the camshaft sprocket and check that the sprocket timing mark still aligns with the pointer on the cover, as noted before removal (see Section 3).

31 Recheck the belt tension as described previously. If the tension is incorrect, the setting and checking procedure must be repeated until the correct tension is achieved.

32 With the belt tensioned correctly, remove the M6 bolt from the timing belt inner cover and remove the timing pin from the cylinder block, if not already done. Refit the blanking plug to the cylinder block and tighten it securely, also the tensioner retaining bolt.

33 Except on models with the F9Q 732 engine, check the fuel injection pump timing as described in Chapter 4B.

34 Refit the timing belt upper outer covers, ensuring that any brackets secured by the bolts are in position as noted before removal.

35 Refit the engine mounting rubber/movement limiter assembly to the body and the mounting upper bracket to the engine, as described in Section 13. Withdraw the jack or the lifting tackle, as applicable, used to support the engine.

36 Refit the fuel filter assembly to the body and clip the hoses into position. On F8Q turbo engines, refit the rear mounting tie-bar (Section 13) and the exhaust downpipe (see Chapter 4B). On F9Q engines, refit the rear mounting tie-bar.

37 Refit the auxiliary drivebelt as described in Chapter 1B.

38 Where applicable, refit the strengthening bar to the front suspension turrets.

39 On F8Q-engined models, refit the timing belt upper/engine right-hand mounting plastic cover, ensuring that any brackets secured by the bolts are in position as noted before removal. On F9Q-engined models, refit the injection control unit and the wiring plug, then refit the engine sound-insulating cover.

40 Where applicable, refit the engine top cover and engine compartment undershield, then refit the wheelarch liner and the roadwheel and lower the vehicle to the ground. Where necessary on Scénic models, refit the plenum chamber closure panel beneath the windscreen, followed by the grilles and windscreen wiper arms.

41 Reconnect the battery negative lead and, on early Scénic models, the secondary terminal unit.

6.2a Removing the crankshaft sprocket

6 Timing belt sprockets and tensioner – removal and refitting

Note: *F8Q 620 and early F8Q 784 engines are fitted with timing belts marked HTD, while later F8Q units and all F9Q engines are fitted with timing belts of a different tooth profile that are marked HTD2. The change in tooth profile necessitates different sprockets which are usually marked to match their respective timing belts – if not, physical differences (the early camshaft sprockets have six spokes while the later ones have three) will serve for identification purposes. Whenever the timing belt is renewed, ALWAYS ensure that the correct replacement type is obtained to match the sprockets – if any of the sprockets are ever to be renewed, the converse applies.*

Note: *A new timing belt must be used on refitting.*

Crankshaft sprocket

Note: *A suitable puller may be required for this operation.*

Removal

1 Remove the timing belt as described in Section 5.

2 It should be possible simply to pull the sprocket off the crankshaft. However in some cases a puller may be required to draw off the sprocket – one can be made up as shown in the **Tool Tip** in Chapter 2A, Section 6. On the F9Q 732 engine, although not essential, the inner timing covers may be unbolted to provide improved access, however, the auxiliary/idle shaft sprocket must be removed first **(see illustrations)**.

3 Recover the Woodruff key if it is loose. Examine the oil seal for signs of oil leakage and, if necessary renew as described in Section 12.

Refitting

4 Refitting is a reversal of removal. Refit the Woodruff key to the crankshaft keyway and slide on the sprocket, making sure it is correctly engaged with the key and with its flange against the cylinder block/timing belt inner cover.

5 Fit the new timing belt as described in Section 5.

Auxiliary shaft/idler sprocket

Removal

6 Remove the timing belt and inner covers as described in Section 5.

7 On engines with an auxiliary shaft (see Specifications), hold the sprocket stationary using a suitable gear-holding tool. Alternatively, the old timing belt can be wrapped around the sprocket and held firmly with a pair of grips.

8 Unscrew the securing bolt, then draw the sprocket off the end of the shaft. If necessary, use two levers or screwdrivers to free the sprocket (if necessary, a puller can be used as described previously for the crankshaft sprocket). Note that on some engines the Woodruff key is an integral part of the sprocket. On engines without an auxiliary shaft, undo the idler sprocket bolt and withdraw the sprocket; if necessary, the idler mounting can be unbolted from the block flange **(see illustrations)**.

Refitting

9 On engines with an auxiliary shaft, refit the Woodruff key (where fitted) to the shaft and slide on the sprocket making sure it is correctly engaged with the key. Refit the

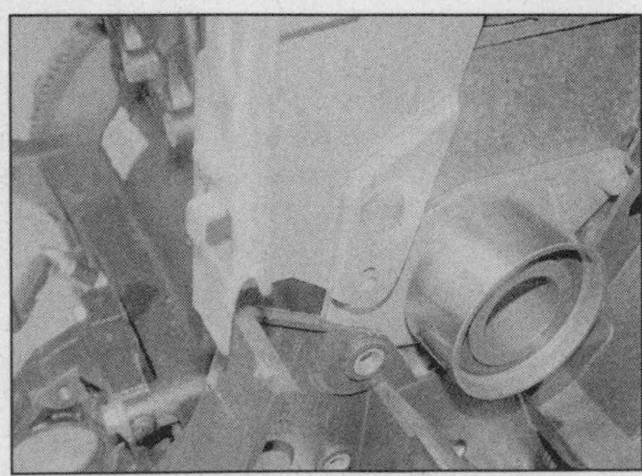

6.2b Unbolting the upper timing inner cover . . .

6.2c . . . and lower timing inner cover

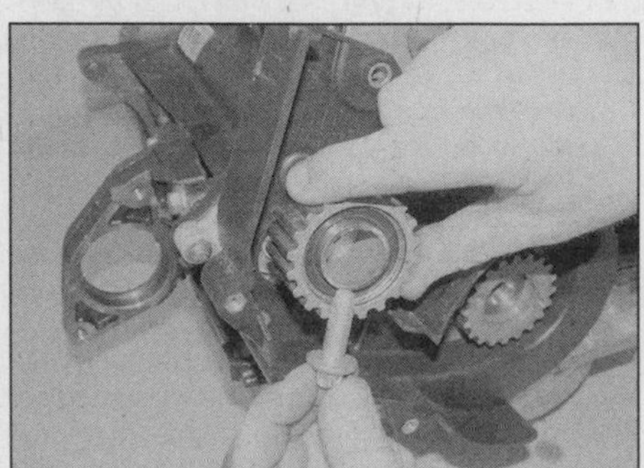

6.8a Removing the auxiliary shaft sprocket on the F9Q 732 engine

6.8b The idler mounting on the cylinder block

6.12a Unscrewing the fuel injection pump sprocket nut . . .

6.12b . . . and removing the sprocket (F8Q 620 engine)

sprocket retaining bolt and tighten it to the specified torque using the method employed on removal to prevent rotation. On engines without an auxiliary shaft, refit the idler sprocket and tighten its retaining bolt securely.

10 Fit the new timing belt as described in Section 5.

Fuel injection pump sprocket (except F9Q 732 engine)

Note: *On F8Q 620 engines, a suitable puller will be required for this operation. On early versions of F8Q turbo engines (principally F8Q 784 types), the MAA-type injection pump sprocket must be removed using the Renault tools Mot. 1359 and Mot. 1357, and a torque wrench suitable for left-hand threaded fasteners will be required on refitting. On later versions of these engines – especially the F8Q 786 and F8Q 788 types – and on all F9Q engines, the MAA-type injection pump sprocket is secured by a gold-coloured nut with an integral washer, which acts as an extractor. For all engines, refer to Section 22 of Chapter 4B for further information.*

Removal

11 On all engines, remove the timing belt (see Section 5).

12 On F8Q 620 engines, with a single-piece sprocket, proceed as follows **(see illustrations)**:

a) *Hold the sprocket stationary using either the Renault holding tool Mot. 1200 (see Chapter 4B, Section 22) or a suitable gear-holding tool. Alternatively, the old timing belt can be wrapped around the sprocket and held firmly with a pair of grips.*
b) *Unscrew the sprocket nut, as far as the end of the pump shaft. Do not remove the nut at this stage.*
c) *Note the location of the Woodruff key in the end of the injection pump shaft. There are two keyways in the sprocket (for use with Bosch and Lucas injection pumps – see illustrations 5.15a and 5.15b). Mark the keyway used to ensure correct refitting.*
d) *Using a suitable puller acting on the sprocket nut (not on the end of the pump shaft), release the sprocket from the taper on the pump shaft.*
e) *Remove the puller, then remove the sprocket nut and recover the washer.*
f) *Remove the sprocket and recover the Woodruff key from the end of the pump shaft if it is loose.*

Caution: On early versions of F8Q turbo engines (principally F8Q 784 types), the MAA-type injection pump sprocket is secured by a conventional nut with separate washer and must be removed using the Renault tools Mot. 1359 and Mot. 1357. On later versions of these engines – especially the F8Q 786 type and including the non-turbo F8Q 788 type – and on all F9Q engines, the MAA-type injection pump sprocket is secured by a gold-coloured nut with an integral washer, which acts as an extractor. For all engines, check carefully the pulley fastening before starting work and proceed according to the relevant instructions below – refer to Section 22 of Chapter 4B for further information.

13 On early versions of F8Q turbo engines (MAA-type injection pump sprocket secured by a conventional nut with separate washer), proceed as follows:

a) *Fit Renault holding tool Mot. 1131 (early version) or Mot. 1200 (latest version) to prevent the sprocket from rotating. It may be necessary to rotate the crankshaft slightly clockwise to allow the tool to engage on the sprocket teeth – ensure that the timing pin has been removed from the cylinder block before attempting to turn the crankshaft.*
b) *Unscrew the sprocket nut and recover the washer.*
c) *Using the Renault tool Mot. 1359, unscrew* ***clockwise*** *the sprocket centre bolt – the bolt has a* ***left-hand thread****.*
d) *In place of the centre bolt, screw in* ***anti-clockwise*** *and tighten securely Renault tool Mot. 1357, then into the centre of this tool screw an M12 x 1.25 bolt, 40 mm long. Tighten the bolt into the tool to draw off the sprocket.*
e) *Remove the sprocket and recover the Woodruff key from the end of the pump shaft if it is loose.*

14 On later versions of F8Q turbo engines and all F9Q engines, (MAA-type injection pump sprocket secured by a gold-coloured nut with an integral washer), proceed as follows:

a) *Fit Renault holding tool Mot. 1131 (early version) or Mot. 1200 (latest version) to prevent the sprocket from rotating. It may be necessary to rotate the crankshaft slightly clockwise to allow the tool to engage on the sprocket teeth – ensure that the timing pin has been removed from the cylinder block before attempting to turn the crankshaft.*
b) *Unscrew the sprocket nut to draw off the sprocket – the nut will slacken at first and then tighten as its extracting action is brought to bear against the sprocket centre bolt. Continue 'unscrewing' the nut until the pulley is free of the pump shaft's taper.*
c) *Remove the sprocket and recover the Woodruff key from the end of the pump shaft if it is loose.*

Refitting

15 Refitting is a reversal of removal, bearing in mind the following points:

a) *On F8Q 620 engines with a single-piece sprocket, ensure that the Woodruff key is engaged with the correct sprocket keyway.*
b) *Tighten the sprocket nut to the specified torque wrench setting (see Chapter 4B).*
c) *Fit and tension the new timing belt as described in Section 5.*
d) *Before refitting the timing belt outer cover over the injection pump sprocket, check the injection timing as described in Chapter 4B.*

High pressure pump sprocket (F9Q 732 engine)

Note: *A suitable puller may be required for this operation.*

Removal

16 Remove the timing belt (see Chapter 5).

17 Hold the sprocket stationary using a suitable gear-holding tool. Alternatively, the old timing belt can be wrapped around the sprocket and held firmly with a pair of grips.

18 Unscrew and remove the sprocket nut. Alternatively, depending on the type of puller to be used, leave it engaged with a few threads so that the puller will bear on the nut to prevent damage to the end of the shaft.

19 Using the puller, release the sprocket from the taper on the pump shaft. Note there is no location key.

6.20 Angle-tightening the high pressure pump retaining nut

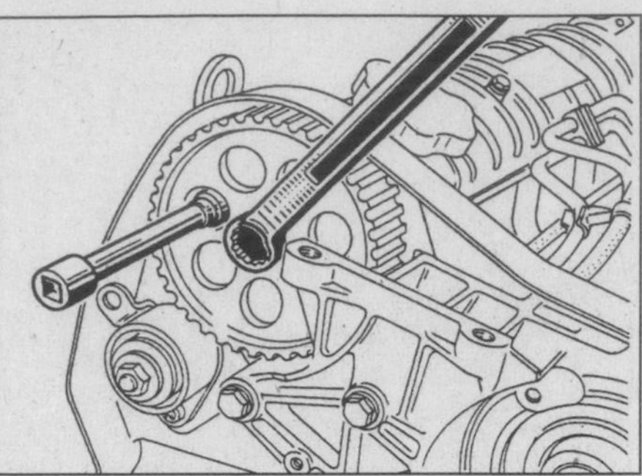

6.24a Using a socket and extension bar to counterhold the camshaft sprocket whilst unscrewing the sprocket bolt

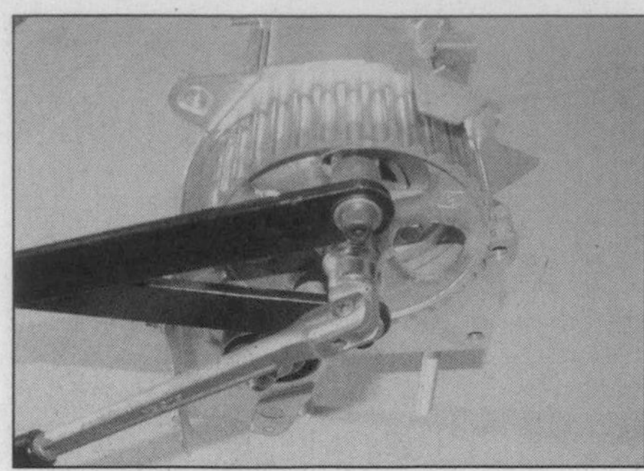

6.24b Using a home-made tool to hold the camshaft sprocket stationary while the bolt is loosened

Refitting

20 Refitting is a reversal of removal, but tighten the retaining nut to the specified torque (and angle if applicable) **(see illustration)**, then refit the timing belt with reference to Section 5.

Camshaft sprocket

Note: *A suitable puller will be required for this operation.*

Removal

21 Remove the timing belt as described in Section 5. If it is necessary to turn the camshaft for any reason, before doing so, remove the timing pin and turn the crankshaft anti-clockwise (viewed from the timing belt end of the engine) by a quarter-turn to position all four pistons halfway down their bores.

22 On models with F9Q engines and air conditioning, unbolt the auxiliary drivebelt tensioner mounting plate (see Chapter 1B), then remove the high pressure pump and alternator.

6.25 Removing the sprocket from the camshaft

23 Unscrew the bolts securing the engine right-hand mounting main bracket to the engine and withdraw the bracket.

24 Unscrew the camshaft sprocket bolt. The sprocket can be held using a suitable socket and extension bar engaged with one of the timing belt inner cover securing bolts **(see illustrations)**. Alternatively, use the old timing belt wrapped around the pulley, held with a pair of grips. Recover the washer.

25 Remove the bolt, washer and sprocket from the camshaft **(see illustration)**. A suitable puller may be required, in which case ensure that the legs of the puller act on the holes in the sprocket, **not** on the sprocket teeth.

26 Recover the Woodruff key from the end of the camshaft if it is loose – note that on later engines the key is an integral part of the sprocket **(see illustration)**.

Refitting

27 Refit the Woodruff key (where separate) to the camshaft keyway. Refit the sprocket with its projecting hub towards the cylinder head and ensuring that the key engages correctly with the keyway.

28 Ensure that the washer is in place, then refit the sprocket bolt and tighten it to the specified torque, holding the sprocket as during removal.

29 Refit the engine right-hand mounting main bracket to the engine and tighten the securing bolts. Where applicable, refit the upper two bolts to the holes in the bracket before the bracket is refitted.

30 Refit the bolts securing the auxiliary drivebelt tensioner mounting plate and the alternator/fuel injection/high pressure pump mounting bolt disturbed on removal.

31 Fit the new timing belt as described in Section 5.

Idler pulley

Removal

32 Remove the timing belt and inner covers as described in Section 5.

33 Unscrew the two securing bolts and withdraw the idler pulley assembly **(see illustration)**.

Refitting

34 Refitting is a reversal of removal, but check that the pulley turns freely without binding or excessive play.

35 Fit the new timing belt as described in Section 5.

Tensioner

Removal

36 Remove the timing belt as described in Section 5.

37 Remove the securing nut and its washer, unscrew the retaining bolt, then withdraw the tensioner assembly **(see illustration)**.

Refitting

38 Refitting is a reversal of removal, but

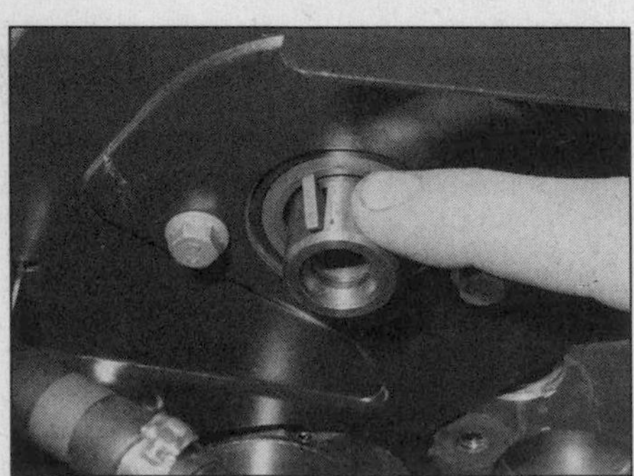

6.26 Recover the Woodruff key from the end of the camshaft if it is loose

6.33 Idler pulley

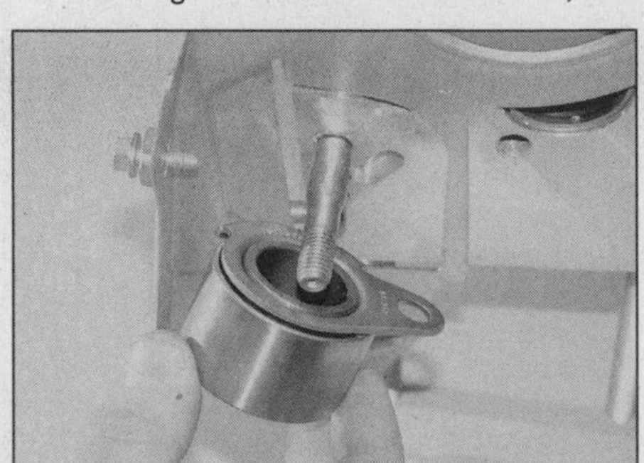

6.37 Removing the tensioner

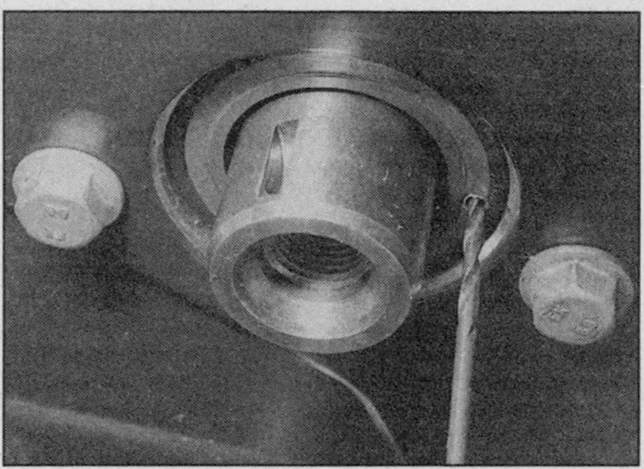

7.3a Drill a small hole . . .

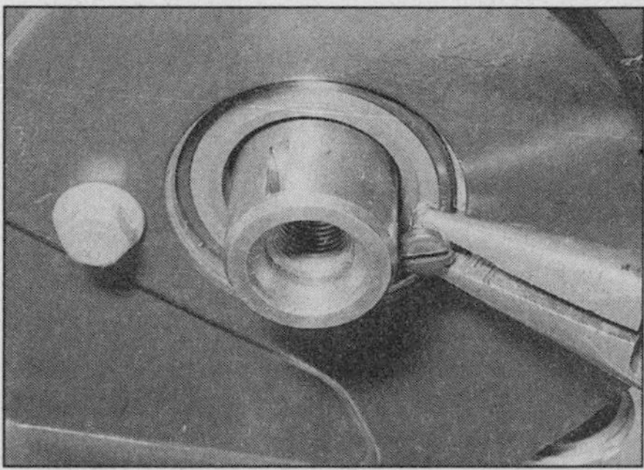

7.3b . . . and use a screw and pliers to pull out the seal

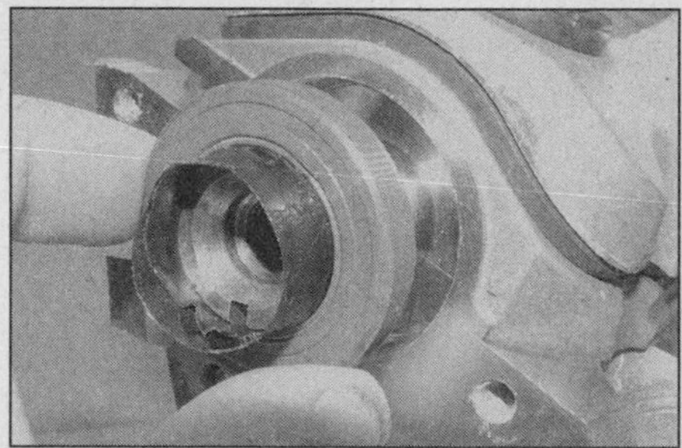

7.4 Wrap some adhesive tape over the end of the camshaft to prevent damage to the oil seal

check that the roller turns freely without binding or excessive play. Ensure that the peg on the cylinder block engages with the hole in the tensioner bracket.

39 Fit the new timing belt as described in Section 5.

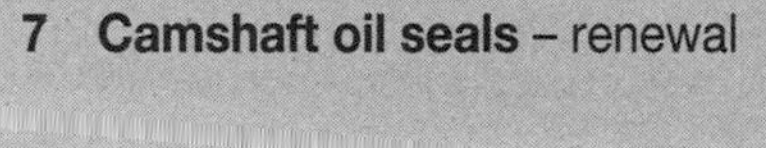

7 Camshaft oil seals – renewal

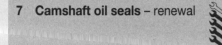

Timing belt end oil seal

1 Remove the camshaft sprocket as described in Section 6. For improved access, also remove the inner timing cover.

2 Remove the Woodruff key (where separate) from the end of the camshaft, if not already done.

3 Make a note of the fitted depth of the old seal then, using a small screwdriver, prise it out of the cylinder head, taking care not to damage the surface of the camshaft. Alternatively, the oil seal can be removed by drilling a small hole and inserting a self-tapping screw. A pair of grips can then be used to pull out the oil seal, by pulling on the screw **(see illustrations)**. If difficulty is experienced, insert two screws diagonally opposite each other.

4 Wipe clean the oil seal seating in the cylinder head, then dip the new seal in fresh engine oil and locate it over the camshaft with its closed side facing outwards. Make sure that the oil seal lip is not damaged as it is located on the camshaft – to prevent this, wrap some adhesive tape over the end of the camshaft **(see illustration)**.

5 Using a tube of suitable diameter, drive the oil seal squarely into the housing to the previously noted depth **(see illustration)**. A block of wood cut to pass over the end of the camshaft may be used instead.

6 Refit the inner timing cover and camshaft sprocket as described in Section 6 **(see illustrations)**.

Flywheel end oil seal

7 No oil seal is fitted to the flywheel end of the camshaft. The sealing is provided by a gasket between the cylinder head and the brake vacuum pump housing and on certain models by an O-ring fitted between the pump and the housing. The gasket and the O-ring, where applicable, can be renewed after unbolting the pump from the cylinder head (see Chapter 9).

8 Camshaft and followers – removal, inspection and refitting

2C

Note: *A new camshaft timing belt end oil seal should be fitted and a new cylinder head cover gasket may be required on refitting. Suitable sealant will be required for the camshaft bearing caps and thread-locking compound for the bearing cap bolts.*

Removal

1 Remove the camshaft sprocket as described in Section 6.

2 Remove the timing belt tensioner as described in Section 6 **(see illustration)**.

3 Unscrew the two bolts securing the timing belt upper inner cover to the cylinder head **(see illustration)**.

7.5 Use a suitable socket to drive the new oil seal into the cylinder head

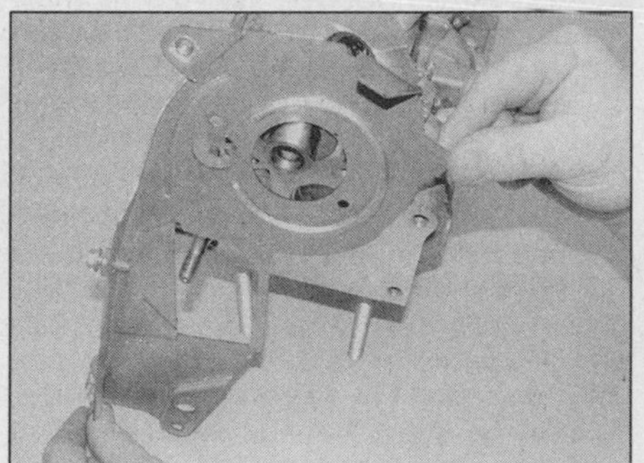

7.6a Refitting the inner timing cover . . .

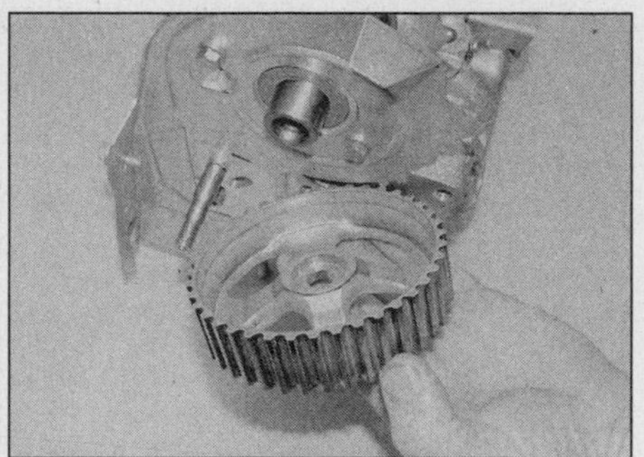

7.6b . . . and camshaft sprocket

8.2 Withdraw the timing belt tensioner

8.3 Remove the bolts securing the timing belt upper inner cover to the cylinder head

8.7a Removing the brake vacuum pump . . .

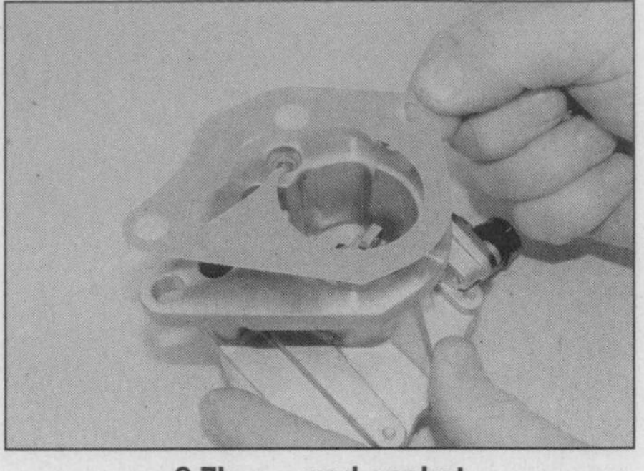

8.7b . . . and gasket

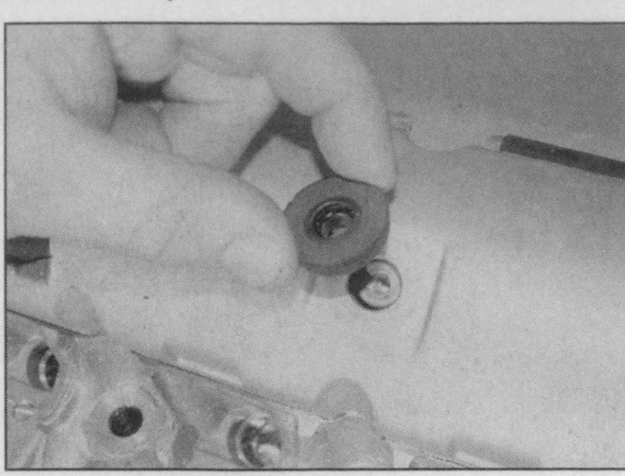

8.9a Unscrew the nuts . . .

4 Unscrew the lower bolt(s) securing the timing belt upper inner cover to the cylinder block.

5 Remove the timing belt idler pulley securing bolt which also passes through the timing belt inner cover.

6 Manipulate the timing belt inner cover from the camshaft end and, where possible, withdraw the cover from the engine.

7 Remove the brake vacuum pump as described in Chapter 9 **(see illustrations)**.

8 Where necessary for improved access, unclip any hoses which are routed across the top of the cylinder head cover and move them to one side out of the way. If any fuel lines are disconnected, cover the open unions to prevent dirt ingress.

9 Unscrew the cylinder head cover nuts or bolts and withdraw the cover. Recover the gasket **(see illustrations)**.

10 Using a dial gauge, measure the camshaft endfloat and compare with the value given in the Specifications **(see illustration)**. This will give an indication of the amount of wear present on the thrust surfaces. **Note:** *If preferred, the camshaft endfloat can be checked with the followers removed; this will make the checking procedure easier as the cam lobes will not be in contact with the followers.*

11 If the original camshaft is to be refitted, it is advisable to measure the valve clearances at this stage, as described in Section 4, so that the followers/shims required can be obtained before the camshaft is refitted.

12 Where applicable, check the camshaft bearing caps for identification marks and if none are present, make identifying marks so that they can be refitted in their original positions and the same way round. Number the caps from the flywheel end of the engine. **Note:** *On the F9Q 732 engine, the caps are integral in a ladder-type retainer.*

13 Progressively slacken the bearing cap bolts (and studs where applicable) until the valve spring pressure is relieved. Remove the bolts and studs (noting their locations to ensure correct refitting) and the bearing caps themselves. Note that No 1 bearing cap is secured by two studs and two additional bolts **(see illustrations)**.

14 Lift out the camshaft with the oil seal **(see illustration)**.

15 Remove the followers, keeping each with

8.9b . . . remove the cylinder head cover . . .

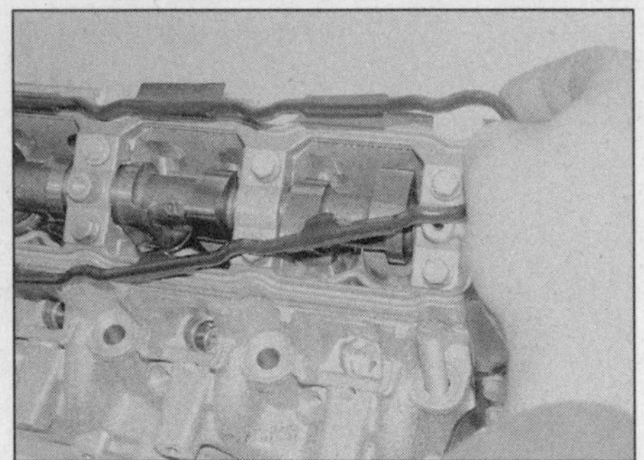

8.9c . . . and recover the gasket

8.10 Measuring camshaft endfloat

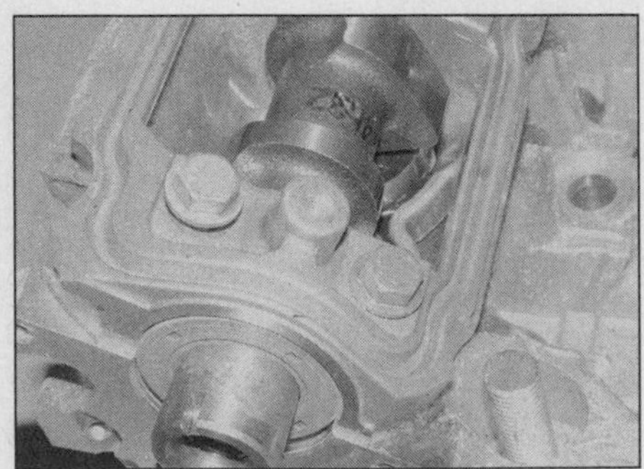

8.13a Unscrew the bolts . . .

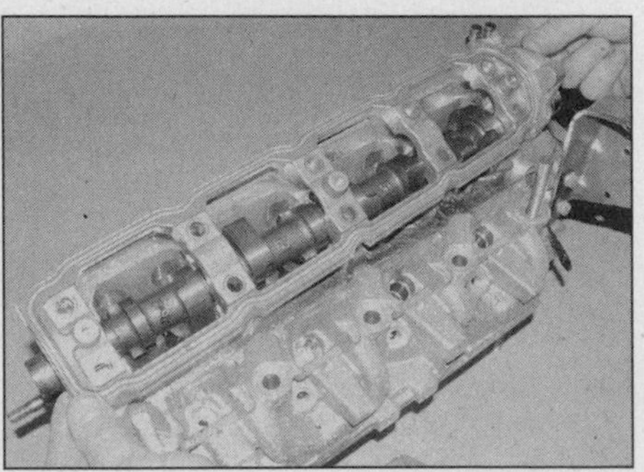

8.13b . . . and lift the camshaft bearing cap retainer from the cylinder head

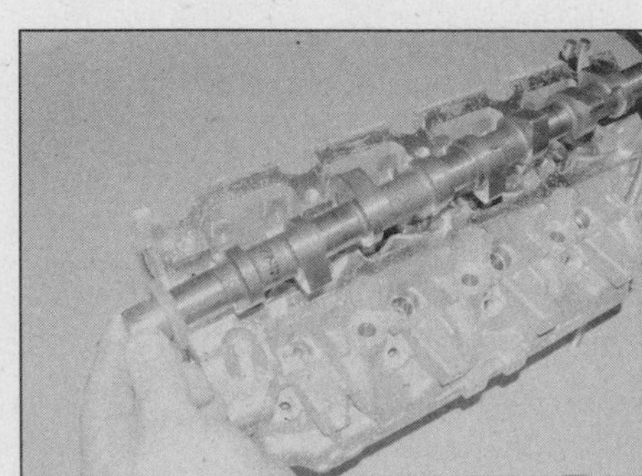

8.14 Lifting out the camshaft with oil seal

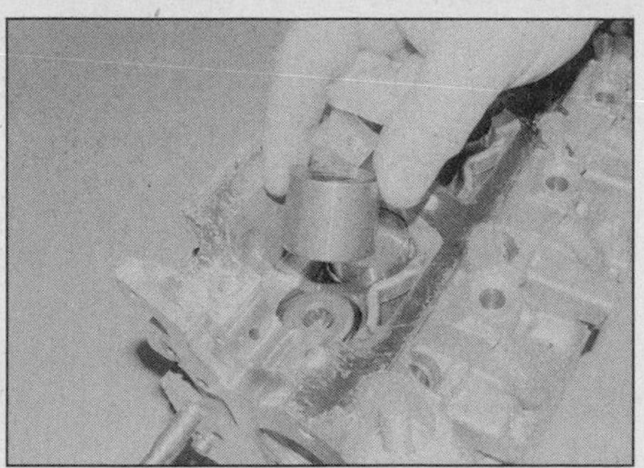
8.15 Lifting out a cam follower

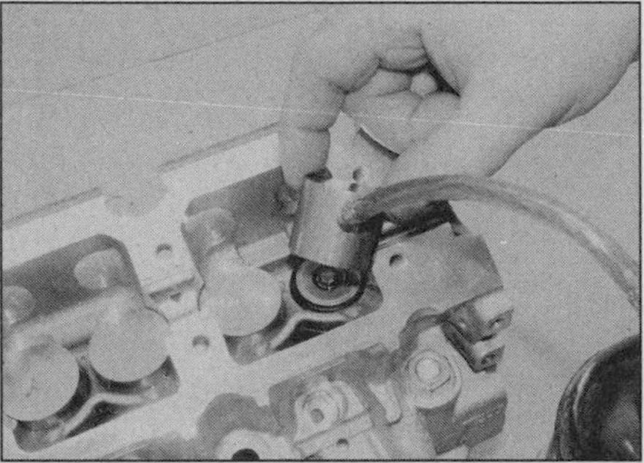
8.21 Oil the followers before refitting them in their correct bores

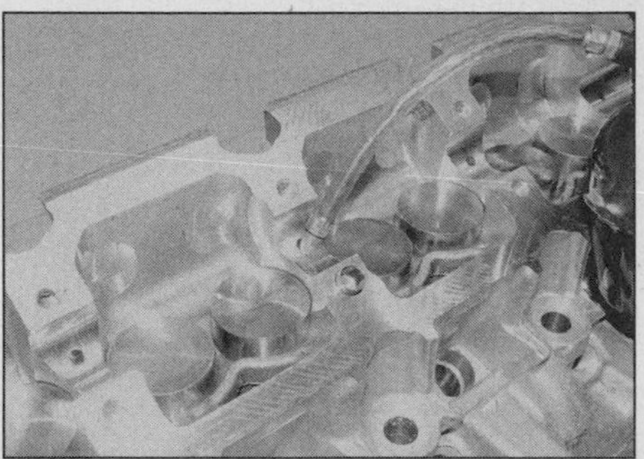
8.22a Oiling the camshaft bearing surfaces

its shim, where applicable **(see illustration)**. Place them in a compartmented box, or on a sheet of card marked into eight sections, so that they may be refitted to their original locations. Write down the follower/shim thicknesses – they will be needed later if any of the valve clearances are incorrect. The thickness is etched on the follower/shim, but it is prudent to use a micrometer to measure the true thickness of any component removed, as it may have been reduced by wear.

Inspection

16 Examine the camshaft bearing surfaces and cam lobes for wear ridges, pitting or scoring. Renew the camshaft if evident.

17 Renew as a matter of course the oil seal at the timing belt end of the camshaft. Lubricate the lips of the new seal before fitting and store the camshaft so that its weight is not resting on the seal.

18 Examine the camshaft bearing surfaces in the cylinder head and bearing caps. Deep scoring or other damage means that the cylinder head must be renewed.

19 Inspect the followers (and shims where applicable) for scoring, pitting and wear ridges. Renew as necessary.

Refitting

20 Ensure that the pistons are positioned halfway down their bores, as described for sprocket removal in Section 6.

21 Oil the followers and fit them to the bores from which they were removed **(see illustration)**. Where applicable, fit the correct shim, numbered side downwards, to each follower. **Note:** *If valve clearance adjustment is achieved by fitting different thickness followers (see Section 4) this will have to be done before refitting the camshaft.*

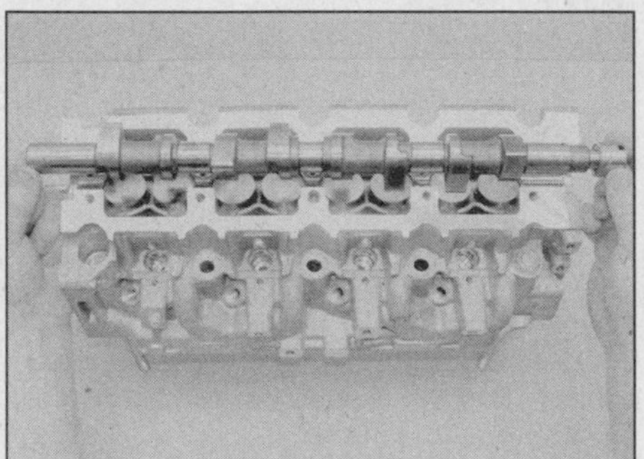
8.22b Refitting the camshaft (F9Q 732 engine)

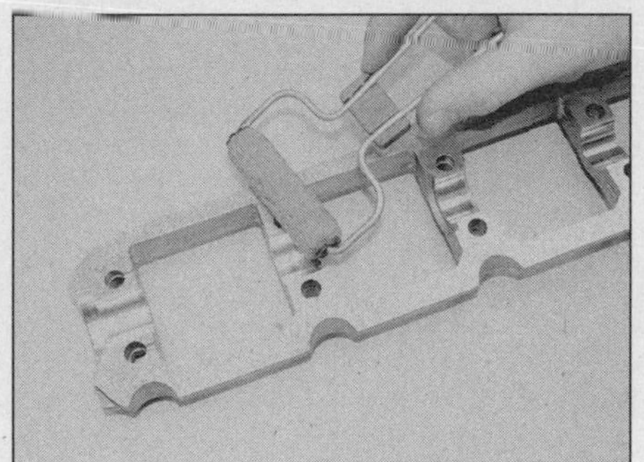
8.23 Applying Locktite 518 liquid gasket to the camshaft bearing ladder on the F9Q 732 engine

22 Oil the camshaft bearings. Place the camshaft onto the cylinder head. If necessary, the oil seal can be fitted at this stage, but make sure that it is positioned so that it is flush with the cylinder head face **(see illustrations)**.

23 On all engines except the F9Q 732, apply sealant (CAF 4/60 THIXO, Rhodorseal 5661, or a suitable equivalent) to the cylinder head mating faces of the camshaft right- and left-hand bearing caps (Nos 1 and 5). On the F9Q 732 engine, use a short haired roller to apply an even coating of Loctite 518 liquid gasket solution to the mating face of the camshaft bearing ladder until it is **reddish** in colour **(see illustration)**.

24 Refit the camshaft bearing cap(s) to their original locations, ensuring that the right-hand oil seal is correctly located in the bearing cap **(see illustration)**.

25 Apply a few drops of thread-locking compound to the threads of the bearing cap bolts (and studs). Fit the bolts (and studs) and tighten them progressively to the specified torque **(see illustrations)**.

26 If a new camshaft has been fitted, measure the endfloat using a dial gauge and check that it is within the specified limits.

27 Refit the brake vacuum pump with reference to Chapter 9.

28 Refit the timing belt upper inner cover, then refit and tighten the bolts securing it to the cylinder block and to the head.

29 Refit and tighten the bolt securing the timing belt idler pulley assembly.

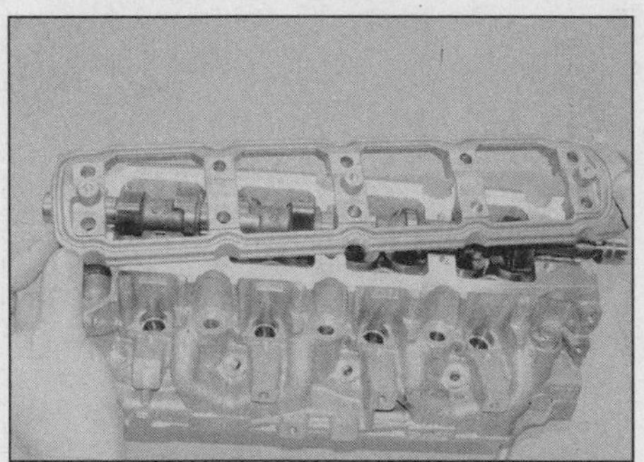
8.24 Refit the camshaft bearing ladder

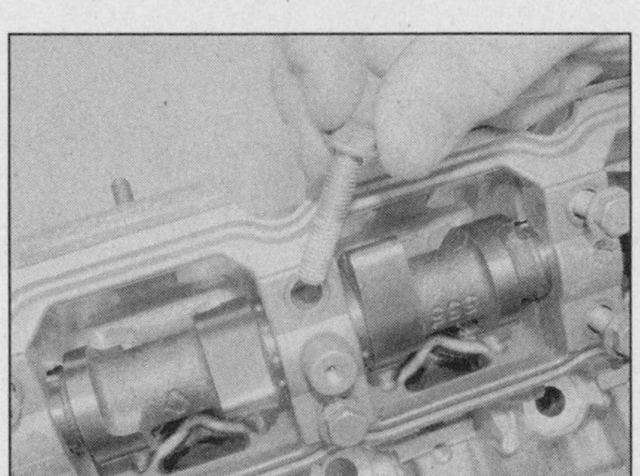
8.25a Insert the bolts . . .

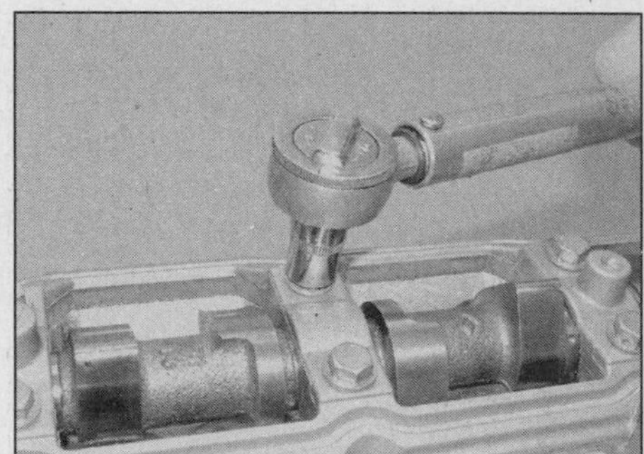
8.25b . . . and tighten them progressively to the specified torque

30 Refit the timing belt tensioner, ensuring that the peg on the cylinder block engages with the hole in the tensioner bracket.
31 Refit the camshaft sprocket as described in Section 6.
32 Check the valve clearances as described in Section 4 and take any corrective action necessary.
33 Refit the cylinder head cover, using a new gasket where necessary – tighten the cover retaining nuts or bolts evenly to the specified torque wrench setting.
34 Refit/reconnect any hoses which were moved for access. If fuel lines were disconnected, reconnect them, then prime and bleed the fuel system as described in Chapter 4B.
35 Reconnect the battery negative lead.

9 Cylinder head – removal, inspection and refitting

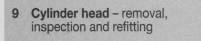

Note: *A new cylinder head gasket and cylinder head bolts must be fitted, and a new cylinder head cover gasket may be required on refitting – see text.*

All engines except F9Q 732

Removal

1 The following procedure describes removal and refitting of the cylinder head complete with manifolds and the fuel injection pump.
2 Disconnect the battery negative lead (refer to Chapter 5A). On F9Q-engined models, unscrew the retaining nuts and withdraw the engine sound-insulating cover.
3 Drain the cooling system, including the cylinder block (where a drain plug is provided), with reference to Chapter 1B.
4 To improve access, unbolt the strengthening bar (where fitted) from between the front suspension strut turrets.
5 Remove the auxiliary drivebelt (Chapter 1B). On models with F9Q engines and air conditioning, unbolt the auxiliary drivebelt tensioner mounting plate (see Chapter 1B), then unscrew the associated alternator/fuel injection pump mounting bolt.
6 Unbolt the earth strap from the rear of the engine.
7 On F8Q-engined models, disconnect the accelerator cable from the fuel injection pump and move the cable clear of the engine, noting its routing (refer to Chapter 4B if necessary).
8 Undo the banjo union and disconnect the fuel supply pipe from the injection pump **(see illustration)**. Recover the sealing washers from the banjo union. Plug the open end of the pipe and the opening in the pump to keep dirt out (the banjo bolt can be refitted to the pump and covered).
9 Remove the securing clip and disconnect the main fuel return hose from the pipe on the fuel injection pump. Feed the hose through the engine rear lifting bracket, located at the rear of the cylinder head and move the hose clear of the engine. Plug the open ends of the pipe and the hose to prevent dirt ingress.
10 Disconnect the air trunking running from the air cleaner to the inlet manifold or turbocharger, as applicable, and remove the trunking (note that, where applicable, the breather hoses which connect to the trunking will also have to be disconnected).
11 On turbo engines, disconnect the air trunking running from the intercooler to the turbocharger and remove the trunking.
12 Remove the timing belt as described in Section 5 and its tensioner as described in Section 6. Since the cylinder head will be removed, it is not possible to support the engine/gearbox with a hoist. Renault technicians use special support tools located beneath the right-hand front of the cylinder block and the subframe and an additional support bracket bolted beneath the water pump. If care is exercised, blocks of wood may be used instead. Note that the engine **must** be supported adequately as the cylinder head bolts are tightened to a high torque.
13 Unbolt the hose bracket from the front of the fuel injection pump mounting bracket and move the hoses and bracket clear of the pump.
14 Disconnect the breather hose(s) from the crankcase oil separator(s) and, on turbo engines, disconnect the hose from the boost pressure corrector on the injection pump. Similarly, disconnect the corresponding ends of the hoses from the manifold.
15 Unclip the hose bracket from the engine front lifting bracket, unbolt the remaining hose bracket from the brake vacuum pump and remove the hose assembly from the engine.
16 On non-turbo engines, disconnect the coolant hose from the thermostat housing.
17 On turbo engines, unbolt the thermostat housing from the cylinder head and move it to one side, leaving the hoses and sensor wiring connected **(see illustration)**.
18 Disconnect the coolant hose from the left-hand rear corner of the cylinder head and move the hose clear.
19 Disconnect the vacuum hose from the brake vacuum pump **(see illustration)**.
20 Disconnect all relevant wiring from the fuel injection pump. Note that on certain pumps, this can be achieved by simply disconnecting the wiring connectors at the brackets on the pump. On some pumps it will be necessary to disconnect the wiring from the individual components (some connections may be protected by rubber covers). Label all connections to aid correct refitting.
21 Disconnect the electrical feed wires from the relevant glow plugs.
22 On non-turbo engines, disconnect the wiring plug from the temperature gauge/warning light sender unit, located in the thermostat housing underneath the brake vacuum pump.
23 Disconnect all relevant pipes and hoses from the manifolds and the turbocharger where applicable, with reference to the relevant Section(s) of Chapter 4B. Label all pipes and hoses to aid correct refitting.
24 Where applicable, unbolt any hose brackets from the manifolds and surrounding area and move the hoses to one side.
25 On turbo engines, remove the two bolts securing the turbocharger inlet elbow to the bracket on the gearbox. Remove the nut and bolt securing the bracing bracket to the turbocharger and the inlet elbow and remove the elbow.
26 Remove the bolt(s) securing the timing belt upper inner cover to the cylinder block.
27 Remove the timing belt idler pulley securing bolt which also passes through the timing belt inner cover.
28 Remove the exhaust front section as described in Chapter 4B.
29 On turbo engines, unscrew the union nut securing the turbocharger oil feed pipe to the

9.8 Unscrewing the fuel supply pipe banjo union

9.17 Unbolt the thermostat housing and move it to one side (turbo engine)

9.19 Disconnecting the brake vacuum pump hose

9.32 Slackening a cylinder head bolt

9.34 Lifting the cylinder head assembly from the engine (turbo engine)

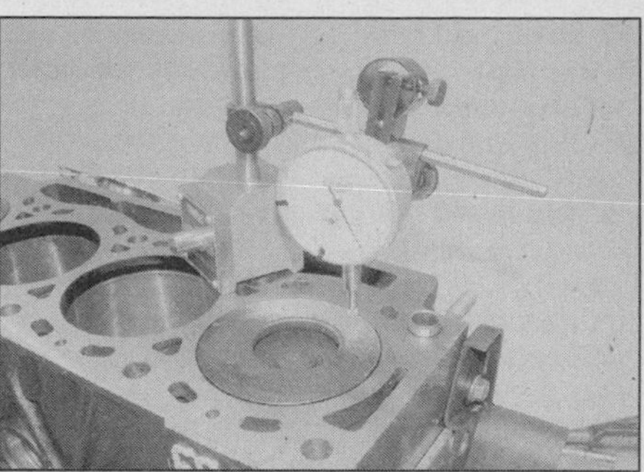

9.42 Measuring piston protrusion

union on the cylinder block and remove the pipe/hose assembly.

30 On turbo engines, remove the bolts securing the turbocharger support bracket to the turbocharger and the engine and remove the support bracket.

31 If not already done, remove the timing pin from the cylinder block and turn the crankshaft anti-clockwise (viewed from the timing belt end of the engine) by a quarter-turn to position all four pistons halfway down their bores.

32 Working in the **reverse** of the sequence shown in illustration 9.51, progressively slacken the cylinder head bolts by half a turn at a time until all bolts can be unscrewed by hand and removed **(see illustration)**. Discard the bolts.

33 The cylinder head assembly complete with ancillaries is heavy and it is advisable to attach a hoist and suitable lifting tackle to the lifting brackets on the cylinder head to lift it from the engine.

34 Lift the cylinder head (complete with manifolds, injection pump and timing belt upper inner cover) upwards and off the cylinder block **(see illustration)**. If it is stuck, tap it upwards using a hammer and block of wood (taking care not to damage the fuel injection pump). **Do not** try to turn the cylinder head (it is located by two dowels), nor attempt to prise it free using a screwdriver inserted between the block and head faces. If the locating dowels are a loose fit, remove them and store them with the head for safe-keeping.

35 If desired, the manifolds, turbocharger (where applicable) and fuel injection pump can be removed from the cylinder head with reference to the relevant Sections of Chapter 4B.

Inspection

36 The mating faces of the cylinder head and block must be perfectly clean before refitting the head. Use a scraper to remove all traces of gasket and carbon and also clean the tops of the pistons. Take particular care with the aluminium cylinder head, as the soft metal is damaged easily. Also, make sure that debris is not allowed to enter the oil and water channels – this is particularly important for the oil circuit, as carbon could block the oil supply to the camshaft or crankshaft bearings. Using adhesive tape and paper, seal the water, oil and bolt holes in the cylinder block. Clean the piston crowns in the same way.

To prevent carbon entering the gap between the pistons and bores, smear a little grease in the gap. After cleaning the piston, rotate the crankshaft so that the piston moves down the bore, then wipe out the grease and carbon with a cloth rag.

37 Check the block and head for nicks, deep scratches and other damage. If slight, they may be removed carefully with a file. More serious damage may be repaired by machining, but this is a specialist job.

38 If warpage of the cylinder head is suspected, use a straight-edge to check it for distortion. Refer to Chapter 2D if necessary.

39 Clean out the cylinder head bolt holes in the block using a pipe cleaner, or a rag and screwdriver. Make sure that all oil is removed, otherwise there is a possibility of the block being cracked by hydraulic pressure when the bolts are tightened.

40 Examine the cylinder head bolt threads in the cylinder block for damage – if necessary, use the correct-size tap to chase out the threads in the block. The cylinder head bolts must be discarded and renewed, regardless of their apparent condition.

Gasket selection

41 Turn the crankshaft to bring piston Nos 1 and 4 to just below the TDC position (just below the top face of the cylinder block). Position a dial test indicator (DTI) on the cylinder block and zero it on the block face. Transfer the probe to the centre of No 1 piston, then slowly turn the crankshaft back and forth past TDC, noting the highest reading produced on the indicator. Record this reading.

42 Repeat this measurement procedure on No 4 piston, then turn the crankshaft half a turn (180°) and repeat the procedure on Nos 2 and 3 pistons **(see illustration)**. Ensure that all measurements are taken along the longitudinal centreline of the crankshaft (this will eliminate errors due to piston slant).

43 If a dial test indicator is not available, piston protrusion may be measured using a straight-edge and feeler gauges or vernier calipers. However, these methods are inevitably less accurate and cannot therefore be recommended.

44 Ascertain the greatest piston protrusion measurement and use this to determine the appropriate thickness cylinder head gasket from the following table. The identification holes are located at the front corner of the gasket, at the flywheel end **(see illustrations)**. **Note:** *The gasket thickness identification holes are located in an area 25 mm from the flywheel end of the gasket. Do not take into account any other holes outside this area.*

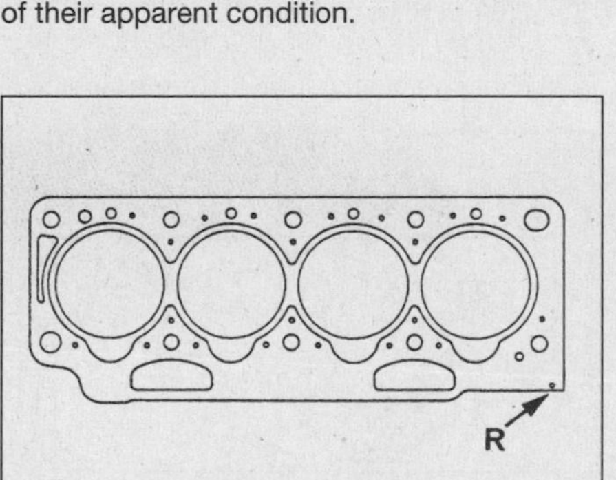

9.44a Cylinder head gasket thickness marking location (R)

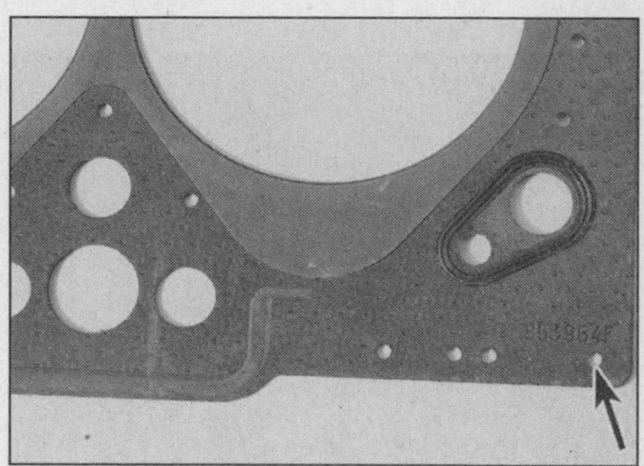

9.44b Cylinder head gasket thickness marking – 1 hole type shown (ignore remaining holes – see text)

2C

Piston protrusion	Gasket identification
F8Q non-turbo engines	
Up to 0.868 mm	*2 holes*
0.868 to 1.000 mm	*1 hole*
More than 1.000 mm	*3 holes*
F8Q turbo engines	
Up to 0.073 mm	*2 holes*
0.073 to 0.206 mm	*1 hole*
More than 0.206 mm	*3 holes*
F9Q engines except F9Q 732	
Up to 0.653 mm	*2 holes*
0.653 to 0.786 mm	*1 hole*
More than 0.786 mm	*3 holes*
F9Q 732 engine	
Up to 0.72 ± 0.077 mm	*2 holes*

Cylinder head bolts

45 The manufacturer recommends that the cylinder head bolts are renewed as a matter of course whenever they are disturbed.

Refitting

46 Where applicable, refit the manifolds, turbocharger (where applicable) and fuel injection pump to the cylinder head, with reference to the relevant Sections of Chapter 4B.

47 Remove the timing pin from the cylinder block and turn the crankshaft clockwise (viewed from the timing belt end) until Nos 1 and 4 pistons pass bottom dead centre (BDC) and begin to rise, then position them halfway up their bores (this is to prevent the possibility of piston-to-valve contact). Nos 2 and 3 pistons will also be at their midway positions, but descending their bores. Do not turn the crankshaft again until the timing belt is to be refitted.

48 Ensure that the cylinder head locating dowels are fitted to the cylinder block, then fit the correct gasket the right way round on the cylinder block with the identification mark(s) at the front corner of the engine at the flywheel end **(see illustration)**.

49 Lower the cylinder head onto the block. Ensure that the timing belt upper inner cover engages correctly with the lower inner cover on the cylinder block. Where applicable, disconnect the lifting tackle and hoist. On F8Q engines, ensure that the swirl chambers do not drop out of their locations in the cylinder head as it is lowered into position.

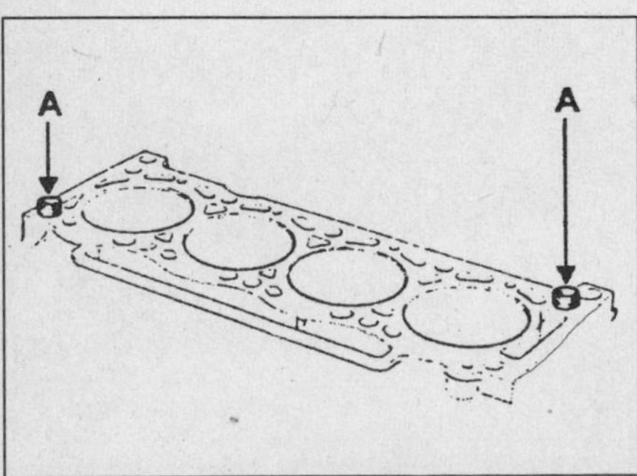

9.48 Cylinder head locating dowel positions (A)

50 Lightly oil the new cylinder head bolts, both on their threads and under their heads. Allow excess oil to drain off then insert the bolts, with their washers, and tighten them finger-tight.

51 Tighten the cylinder head bolts to the specified torques in the sequence shown and in the stages given in the Specifications at the beginning of this Chapter **(see illustration)**. The initial stages pre-compress the gasket and the remaining stages are the main tightening procedure. When angle-tightening the bolts, put paint marks on the bolt heads and cylinder head as a guide for the correct angle, or obtain a special angle-tightening tool. Note that, provided the bolts are tightened exactly as specified on F8Q non-turbo or F9Q engines, there will be no need to retighten them once the engine has been started and run after reassembly. On F8Q turbo engines however, additional tightening will be necessary on completion of reassembly after the engine has been run to normal operating temperature then allowed to cool.

Warning: The final tightening stages involve very high forces. Ensure that the tools used are in good condition. If the engine has been removed from the vehicle, it is recommended that the final tightening stages are carried out with the engine refitted to the vehicle (it may be necessary to remove the engine right-hand mounting upper bracket for access to one of the bolts with the engine in the vehicle).

52 On turbo engines, refit the turbocharger support bracket and tighten the securing bolts.

53 On turbo engines, refit the turbocharger oil feed pipe/hose assembly and tighten the union to the cylinder block.

54 Refit the exhaust front section with reference to Chapter 4B.

55 Refit the timing belt idler pulley securing bolt.

56 Refit the bolts securing the timing belt upper inner cover to the cylinder block, then refit the timing belt tensioner as described in Section 6.

57 Fit the new timing belt as described in Section 5.

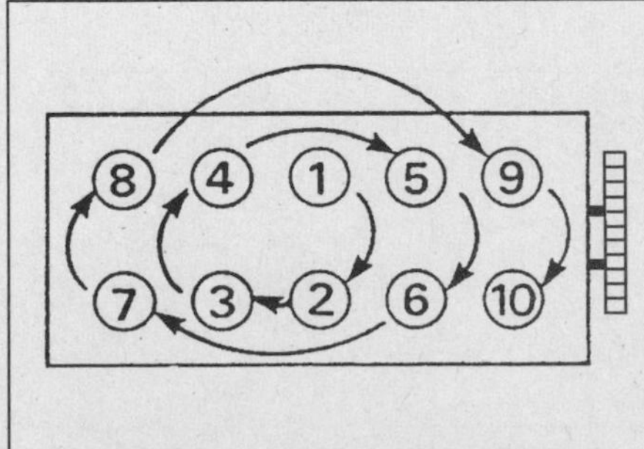

9.51 Cylinder head bolt tightening sequence

58 On turbo engines, examine the sealing ring in the turbocharger inlet elbow and renew it if necessary. Refit the elbow and the bracing bracket.

59 Refit any hose brackets to the manifolds, as noted before removal.

60 Reconnect all relevant pipes and hoses to the manifolds and the turbocharger where applicable, as noted before removal.

61 On non-turbo engines, reconnect the wiring plug to the temperature gauge/warning light sender unit.

62 Reconnect the feed wires to the glow plugs.

63 Reconnect all wiring to the fuel injection pump.

64 Reconnect the engine earth lead to the engine rear lifting bracket.

65 Reconnect the coolant hose to the cylinder head and the brake vacuum hose to the vacuum pump.

66 Reconnect the air trunking between the air cleaner, inlet manifold, turbocharger and intercooler, as applicable. Ensure that any breather hoses are correctly reconnected.

67 On turbo engines, examine the sealing ring between the thermostat housing and the cylinder head and renew it if necessary. Refit the thermostat housing to the cylinder head.

68 On non-turbo engines, reconnect the coolant hose to the thermostat housing.

69 Reconnect the crankcase breather hose(s) and on turbo engines, the boost pressure corrector hose, ensuring that the connections are securely made. Refit the brackets to the engine lifting bracket and the brake vacuum pump.

70 Refit the hose bracket to the fuel injection pump mounting bracket.

71 Feed the main fuel return hose through the engine lifting bracket and reconnect it to the fuel injection pump pipe.

72 Reconnect the fuel supply hose to the injection pump.

73 Reconnect the accelerator cable with reference to Chapter 4B.

74 Where applicable, refit the strengthening bar to the front suspension strut turrets.

75 Check that the cylinder block drain plug (where fitted) is securely fastened, then refill and bleed the cooling system as described in Chapter 1B.

76 Refit the auxiliary drivebelt tensioner and bracket, followed by the drivebelt (refer to Chapter 1B if necessary).

77 Reconnect the battery negative lead.

78 Prime and bleed the fuel system as described in Chapter 4B.

79 On turbo engines, follow the procedure described in Chapter 4B, Section 30 (priming the turbocharger oil circuit) before starting the engine. On F9Q-engined models, refit the engine sound-insulating cover.

80 On F8Q turbo engines, tighten the cylinder head bolts to the final stage (refer to the Specifications) after running the engine up to normal operating temperature and allowing it to cool. It may be necessary to remove the

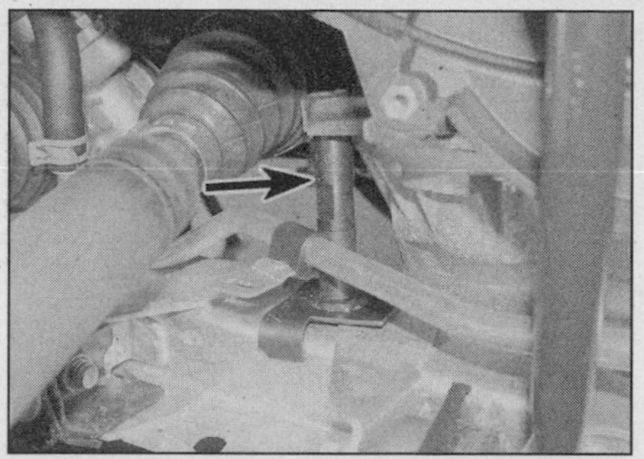

9.83 Home-made engine support positioned beneath the rear of the cylinder block

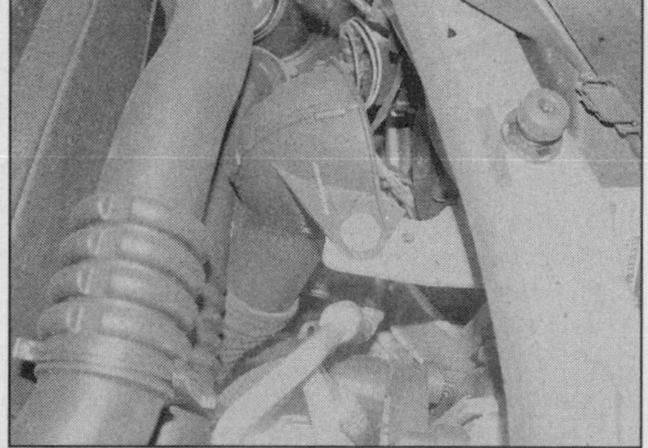

9.84a Front mounting of the inlet air duct

9.84b Removing the air cleaner assembly

engine right-hand mounting upper bracket, with reference to Section 13, for access to one of the bolts.

F9Q 732 engine

Removal

81 Disconnect the battery negative lead (refer to Chapter 5A). Also remove the engine top cover.

82 Drain the cooling system, including the cylinder block (where a drain plug is provided), with reference to Chapter 1B.

83 Remove the timing belt and tensioner as described in Sections 5 and 6 but note the following. Since the cylinder head will be removed, it is not possible to support the engine/gearbox with a hoist. Renault technicians use special support tools located beneath the right-hand front of the cylinder block and the subframe and an additional support bracket bolted beneath the water pump. A home-made support can be made out of metal tube, alternatively, if care is exercised, blocks of wood may be used instead **(see illustration)**. Note that the engine **must** be supported adequately as the cylinder head bolts are tightened to a high torque. The timing belt removal procedure includes disconnecting the rear engine mounting link, however, it is recommended that the link is refitted before removing the cylinder head in order to support the engine adequately. Where necessary, detach the two power steering pipe mountings from the right-hand side of the subframe.

84 Remove the air cleaner assembly and inlet duct with reference to Chapter 4B **(see illustrations)**.

85 Disconnect the wiring from the injectors and heater plugs, and from the EGR valve **(see illustrations)**.

86 Disconnect the wiring from the high pressure pump and the fuel pressure sensor on the fuel rail. Unbolt the wiring support from the left-hand end of the cylinder head, and disconnect the plug. Also disconnect the wiring from the temperature sensor on the thermostat housing and from the electric coolant heater unit on the left-hand side of the cylinder head **(see illustrations)**.

87 Disconnect the crankcase ventilation hose from the oil separator.

88 Disconnect the vacuum hose from the brake servo pump on the left-hand end of the cylinder head **(see illustration)**.

89 Loosen the clips and disconnect the coolant hoses from the thermostat housing **(see illustration)**.

2C

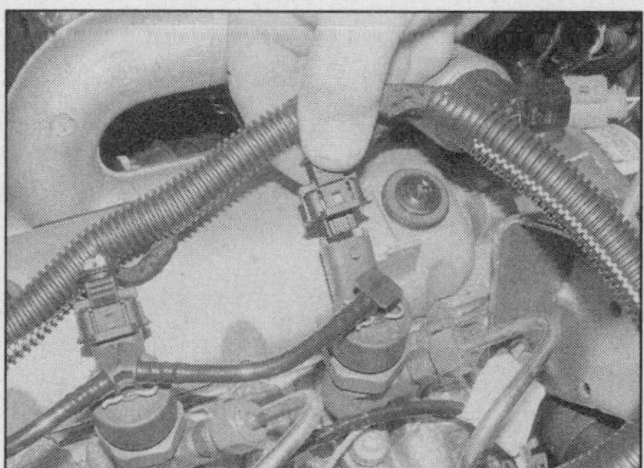

9.85a Disconnect the wiring from the injectors . . .

9.85b . . . and EGR valve

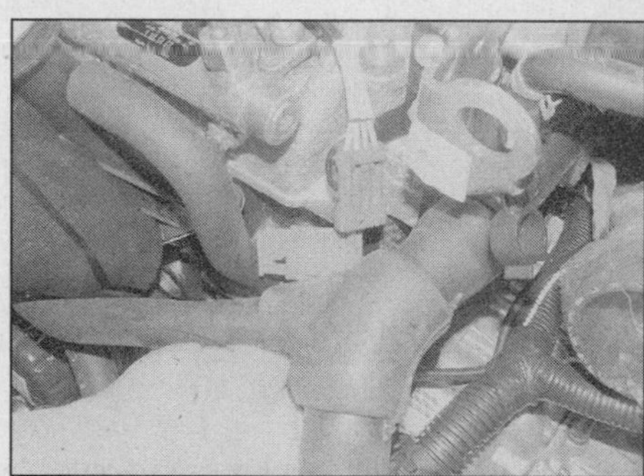

9.86a Disconnecting the wiring plug on the left-hand end of the cylinder head

9.86b Wiring on the electric coolant heater unit

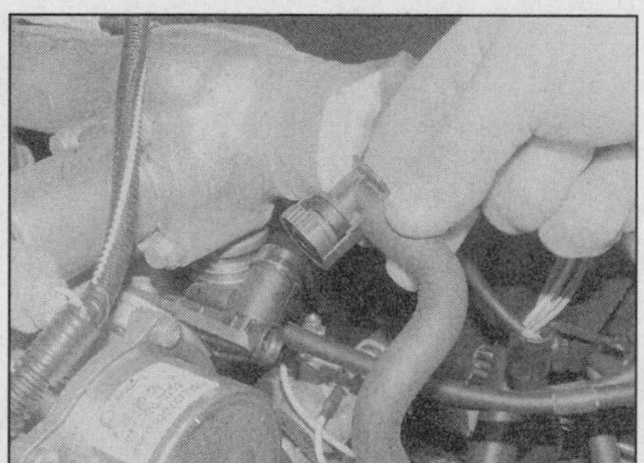

9.88 Disconnecting the vacuum hose from the brake servo pump

9.89 Coolant hoses on the thermostat housing

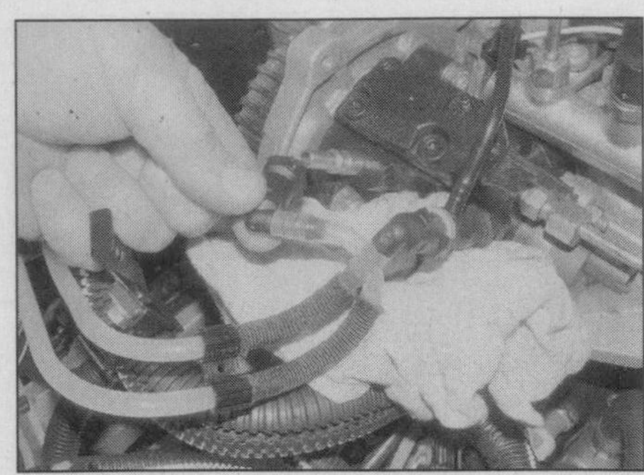
9.91a Disconnecting the fuel pipes from the high pressure pump

9.91b Seal the ends of the pipes and apertures to prevent entry of dust and dirt

9.92a Unbolt the wiring mounting . . .

9.92b . . . then unbolt and remove the alternator mounting bracket

9.93a Disconnecting the wiring from the camshaft position sensor

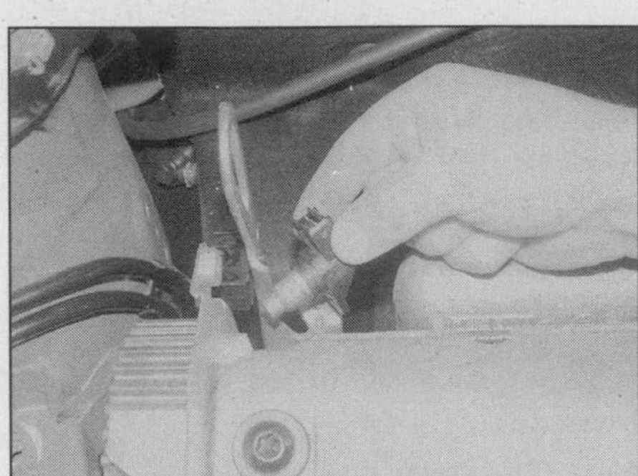
9.93b Removing the camshaft position sensor

90 Note the location of the vacuum pipes on the bulkhead, then disconnect them.

91 Disconnect the fuel pipes from the filter and high pressure pump. Plug the apertures and ends of the pipes **(see illustrations)**.

92 Unbolt the wiring mounting from the alternator mounting bracket, then unbolt and remove the bracket **(see illustrations)**.

93 Disconnect the wiring from the camshaft position sensor on the right-hand rear of the cylinder head. To provide access to the right-hand rear cylinder head bolt, remove the sensor completely **(see illustrations)**.

94 Disconnect the wiring from the low pressure electric pump, located on the lower, right-hand side of the engine compartment, just above the subframe.

95 Remove the alternator as described in Chapter 5A. Also unbolt and remove the alternator mounting bracket and auxiliary drivebelt tensioner complete with spring.

96 Unscrew the bolts and disconnect the exhaust downpipe from the flange on the catalytic converter. Recover the gasket.

97 Unscrew and remove the catalytic converter mountings.

98 Unscrew the stay bolt from the bottom of the catalytic converter.

99 Unscrew the bolt from the turbocharger oil pipe support on the inlet manifold.

100 Unscrew the union nut and disconnect the oil supply pipe from the top of the turbocharger. Tie the pipe to one side on the bulkhead.

101 Unscrew the nuts and remove the catalytic converter from the turbocharger. Recover the gasket. If necessary, move the engine towards the radiator to provide additional working room.

102 Remove the oil return pipe from the turbocharger and cylinder block **(see illustration)**.

103 Unscrew and remove the upper bolt securing the lower timing cover to the cylinder block **(see illustration)**, then loosen the remaining cover mounting bolts so that they are just on their last threads.

104 Working in the **reverse** of the sequence shown in illustration 9.51, progressively slacken the cylinder head bolts by half a turn at a time until all bolts can be unscrewed by

9.102 Turbocharger oil return pipe connection to the cylinder block

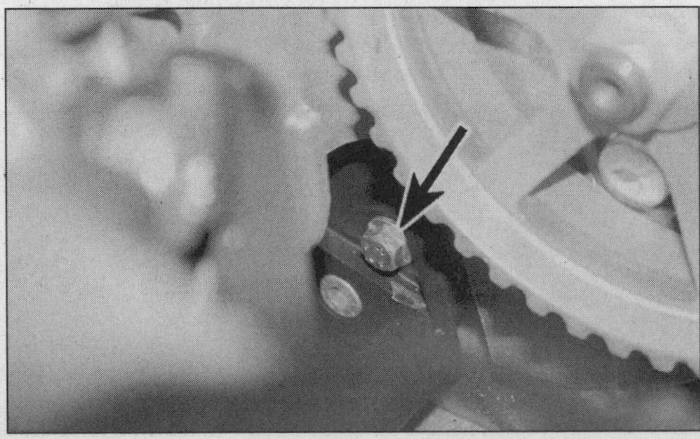
9.103 Upper bolt securing the lower timing cover to the cylinder block

hand and removed. Discard the bolts as the manufacturer states they must be renewed after removal.

105 The cylinder head assembly complete with ancillaries is heavy and it is advisable to attach a hoist and suitable lifting tackle to the lifting brackets on the cylinder head to lift it from the engine.

106 Lift the cylinder head (complete with manifolds, high pressure pump and timing belt upper inner cover) upwards and off the cylinder block and remove the gasket **(see illustrations)**. If it is stuck, tap it upwards using a hammer and block of wood. **Do not** try to turn the cylinder head (it is located by two dowels), nor attempt to prise it free using a screwdriver inserted between the block and head faces. If the locating dowels are a loose fit, remove them and store them with the head for safe-keeping. Make sure that the upper section of the inner timing cover clears the lower cover and bolt as the head is lifted.

107 If desired, the manifolds, turbocharger and high pressure pump can be removed from the cylinder head with reference to the relevant Sections of Chapter 4B.

Inspection

108 Refer to paragraphs [illegible] to [illegible].

Gasket selection

109 Refer to paragraphs 41 to 44, however note that the maximum protrusion is 0.72 ± 0.077 mm.

Piston protrusion	Gasket identification
Up to 0.72 ± 0.077 mm	*2 holes*

Cylinder head bolts

110 Refer to paragraph 45.

Refitting

111 Where applicable, refit the manifolds, turbocharger and high pressure pump to the cylinder head, with reference to the relevant Sections of Chapter 4B.

112 Remove the timing pin from the cylinder block and turn the crankshaft clockwise (viewed from the timing belt end) until Nos 1 and 4 pistons pass bottom dead centre (BDC) and begin to rise, then position them halfway up their bores (this is to prevent the possibility of piston-to-valve contact). Nos 2 and 3 pistons will also be at their midway positions,

9.106a Lifting the cylinder head from the cylinder block

but descending their bores. Do not turn the crankshaft again until the timing belt is to be refitted.

113 Ensure that the cylinder head locating dowels are fitted to the cylinder block **(see illustration)**, then fit the correct gasket the right way round on the cylinder block with the identification mark(s) at the front corner of the engine at the flywheel end.

114 Lower the cylinder head onto the block. Ensure that the timing belt upper inner cover engages correctly with the lower inner cover on the cylinder block. Where applicable, disconnect the lifting tackle and hoist.

115 Lightly oil the new cylinder head bolts, both on their threads and under their heads. Allow excess oil to drain off then insert the bolts, with their washers, and tighten them finger-tight **(see illustration)**.

116 Tighten the cylinder head bolts to the specified torques in the sequence shown in illustration 9.51 and in the stages given in the Specifications at the beginning of this Chapter. The initial stages pre-compress the gasket and the remaining stages are the main tightening procedure. When angle-tightening the bolts, put paint marks on the bolt heads and cylinder head as a guide for the correct angle, or obtain a special angle-tightening tool **(see illustration)**. Note that, provided the bolts are tightened exactly as specified, there will be no need to retighten them once the engine has been started and run after reassembly.

Warning: The final tightening stages involve very high forces. Ensure that the tools used are in

9.106b Removing the cylinder head gasket

good condition. If the engine has been removed from the vehicle, it is recommended that the final tightening stages are carried out with the engine refitted to the vehicle (it may be necessary to remove the engine right-hand mounting upper bracket for access to one of the bolts with the engine in the vehicle).

117 Insert and tighten the timing cover mounting bolts.

118 Refit the oil return pipe to the turbocharger and cylinder block and tighten the union nuts.

119 Refit the exhaust front section to the turbocharger together with a new gasket, and tighten the nuts to the specified torque (see Chapter 4B).

120 Refit the oil supply pipe to the top of the turbocharger and tighten the union nut. Also insert and tighten the pipe support bolt on the inlet manifold.

121 Refit the stay bolt to the bottom of the catalytic converter.

122 Refit the catalytic converter mountings.

123 Refit the exhaust downpipe to the flange on the catalytic converter together with a new gasket, and tighten the bolts securely.

124 Refit the auxiliary drivebelt tensioner and spring, and also the alternator mounting bracket, then refit the alternator with reference to Chapter 5A.

125 Reconnect the wiring to the low pressure electric pump, and the camshaft position sensor.

126 Refit the wiring mounting to the high pressure pump.

127 Reconnect the fuel pipes to the filter and high pressure pump.

2C

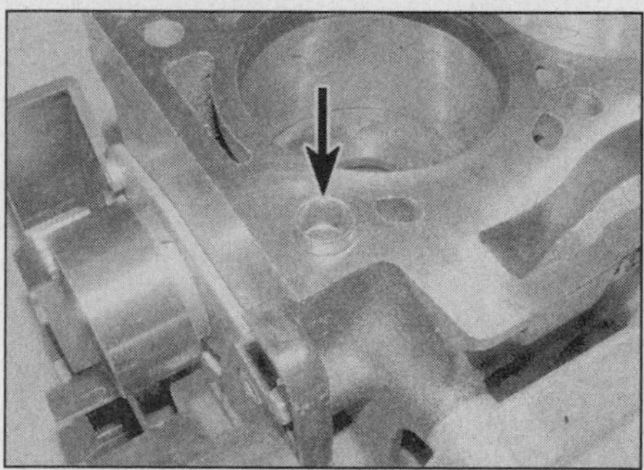

9.113 Cylinder head locating dowel on the block

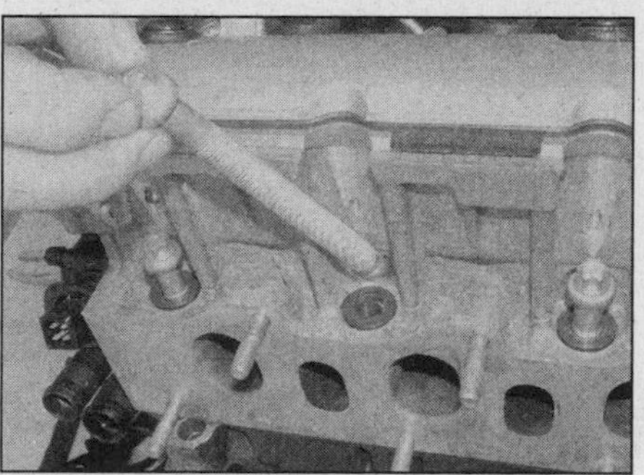

9.115 Inserting the cylinder head bolts

9.116 Angle-tightening the cylinder head bolts

128 Reconnect the vacuum pipes on the bulkhead.
129 Reconnect the coolant hoses to the thermostat housing and tighten the clips.
130 Reconnect the vacuum hose to the brake servo pump.
131 Reconnect the crankcase ventilation hose to the oil separator.
132 Reconnect the wiring to the temperature sensor on the thermostat housing, to the fuel pressure sensor on the fuel rail, and to the high pressure pump.
133 Reconnect the wiring to the injectors and heater plugs.
134 Refit the air cleaner assembly and inlet duct with reference to Chapter 4B.
135 Refit the timing belt with reference to Section 5, and remove the engine support blocks.
136 Refill the cooling system with reference to Chapter 1B.
137 Prime and bleed the fuel system as described in Chapter 4B.
138 Refit the engine top cover and reconnect the battery negative lead (refer to Chapter 5A).

10 Sump – removal and refitting

Note: *A new sump gasket or suitable sealant (as applicable) must be used on refitting.*

All engines except F9Q 732

Removal

1 Disconnect the battery negative lead (refer to Chapter 5A).
2 Drain the engine oil (see Chapter 1B), then refit and tighten the drain plug to its specified torque wrench setting using a new washer.
3 Jack up the front of the vehicle and support on axle stands (see *Jacking and vehicle support*). Where fitted, remove the engine compartment undershield.
4 Unbolt the strengthening bar (where fitted) from between the front suspension turrets.
5 On F8Q-engined models, unscrew the securing bolts and remove the timing belt upper/engine right-hand mounting plastic cover, noting the locations of any brackets secured by the bolts. On F9Q-engined models, unscrew the retaining nuts and withdraw the engine sound-insulating cover.
6 Using a hoist, support the weight of the engine/gearbox.
7 Unscrew the bolts securing the exhaust downpipe to the exhaust manifold. Release the downpipe and support it.
8 Unbolt the engine-to-gearbox strengthening bracket/flywheel cover. Note that one of the bolts secures the engine rear mounting bracket to the gearbox and that the bolts securing the bracket to the engine require a Torx key to unscrew them.
9 Unbolt the supports securing the power-assisted steering fluid pipe to the right-hand side of the subframe.
10 Unscrew the nut securing the engine right-hand mounting upper bracket to the engine mounting rubber/movement limiter assembly on the body.
11 Lift the engine only sufficient to provide room to remove the sump. Remember that the driveshafts and remaining engine mountings are still connected.

Caution: Make sure the engine/gearbox assembly is supported adequately before removing the sump.

12 Unscrew the bolts securing the sump to the cylinder block, but leave two diagonally-opposite bolts entered on a few threads until the sump joint has been released.
13 Using a palette knife or similar tool, release the sump from the bottom of the cylinder block. Do not use a screwdriver as this may damage the mating surfaces.
14 Unscrew the two remaining bolts and lower the sump from the engine. Recover the gasket where fitted.
15 Clean all traces of gasket or sealant from the cylinder block and sump and wipe them dry.

Refitting

16 Clean all traces of gasket or sealing compound from the mating faces of the sump and cylinder block.
17 Where fitted, locate a new gasket on the sump, otherwise apply a 1 mm wide bead of suitable sealant – Renault recommend Rhodorseal 5661 – to the mating face of the sump, making sure that the bead is to the outside of the sump groove.
18 If a gasket is not fitted, it is important that the sump is positioned correctly the first time and not moved around after the sealant has touched the cylinder block. Temporary long bolts or dowel rods may be used to help achieve this.
19 To prevent oil dripping from the oil pump and cylinder block, wipe these areas clean before refitting the sump.
20 Lift the sump into position, then insert the bolts and tighten them progressively to the specified torque.
21 Lower the engine, then refit and tighten the engine right-hand mounting nut.
22 Refit the supports for the power-assisted steering fluid pipe.
23 Refit the engine-to-gearbox strengthening bracket/flywheel cover and tighten the securing bolts.
24 Refit the exhaust downpipe and tighten the bolts.
25 Remove the hoist and refit the timing belt upper/engine right-hand mounting plastic cover or engine sound-insulating cover, as applicable.
26 Where applicable, refit the strengthening bar between the front suspension turrets and tighten the bolts.
27 Reconnect the battery, then lower the vehicle to the ground.
28 Fill the engine with fresh oil with reference to Chapter 1B.

F9Q 732 engine

Removal

29 Disconnect the battery negative lead (refer to Chapter 5A).
30 Drain the engine oil (see Chapter 1B), then refit and tighten the drain plug to its specified torque wrench setting using a new washer.
31 Jack up the front of the vehicle and support on axle stands (see *Jacking and vehicle support*). Where fitted, remove the engine compartment undershield. Remove both front roadwheels.
32 Remove the wheelarch liner from under the front right-hand wing. Release the lower clip from the left-hand wheelarch liner.
33 Make sure that the front roadwheels are in their straight-ahead position. To prevent damage to the airbag clockspring in the steering wheel in the following procedure, tape or tie the steering wheel in its straight-ahead position. Refer to Chapter 10 if necessary.
34 Pull back the gaiter, and unscrew the nut and bolt securing the bottom of the steering column to the steering gear pinion.
35 Referring to Chapter 10, disconnect the steering track rod ends from the hub carriers, then unscrew and remove the bolts securing the front suspension lower arm balljoints to the hub carriers. Press the lower arms down from the hub carriers, and tie the hub carriers to one side.
36 Unbolt the support stays from the subframe and underbody.
37 Disconnect the gearchange control rod from the gearbox with reference to Chapter 7A.
38 Remove the horn as described in Chapter 12.
39 Unscrew and remove the bolt securing the rear engine mounting link to the gearbox, and loosen only the bolt securing the link to the subframe.
40 Unscrew the lower mountings of the front bumper.
41 Release the wiring from the left-hand side of the subframe.
42 The subframe must now be lowered. To do this, unscrew each subframe mounting bolt in turn, and insert a length of threaded rod of sufficient length to allow the subframe to be lowered 9.0 cm **(see illustration)**. Fit

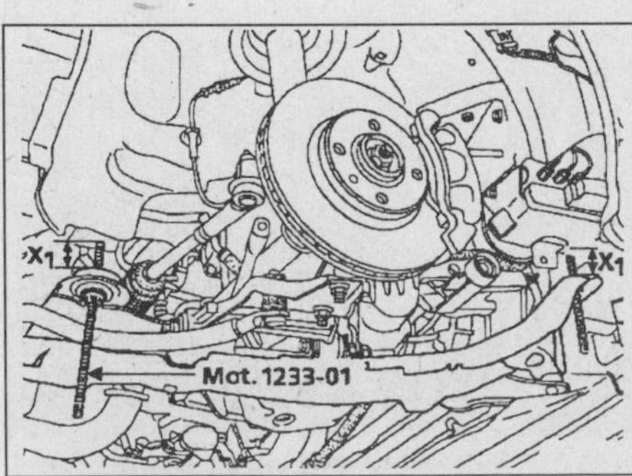

10.42 Lower the subframe by 9.0 cm (X1)

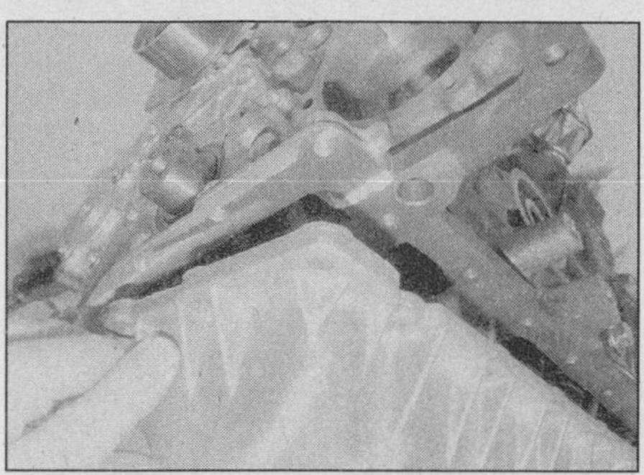
10.45a Removing the sump . . .

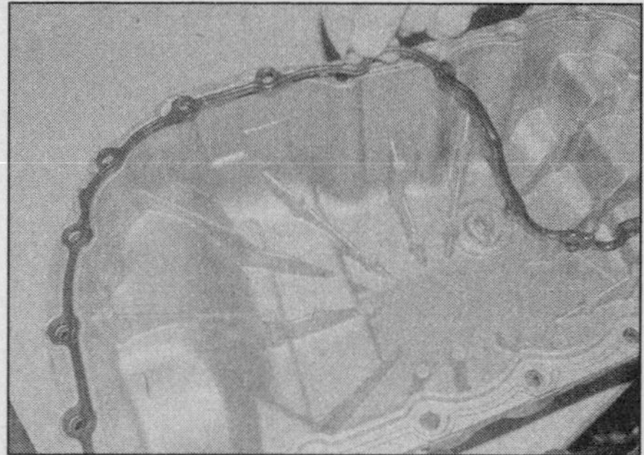
10.45b . . . and gasket

10.47 Applying sealant to the joint between the oil seal housing and block

nuts to the rod and lower the subframe. As the subframe is being lowered, release the column from the steering gear pinion.

43 Unscrew the bolts securing the sump to the cylinder block, but leave two diagonally-opposite bolts entered on a few threads until the sump joint has been released.

44 Using a palette knife or similar tool, release the sump from the bottom of the cylinder block. Do not use a screwdriver as this may damage the mating surfaces.

45 Unscrew the two remaining bolts and lower the sump from the engine. Recover the gasket **(see illustrations)**.

46 Clean all traces of gasket or sealant from the cylinder block and sump and wipe them dry.

Refitting

47 Apply a little Rhodorseal 5661 sealant, or similar, to the joint areas between the No 1 (flywheel end) main bearing cap and cylinder block, and to the areas between the oil seal housing and block **(see illustration)**.

48 Locate a new gasket on the sump.

49 To prevent oil dripping from the oil pump and cylinder block, wipe these areas clean before refitting the sump.

50 Lift the sump into position and align it with the flywheel end of the cylinder block **(see illustration)**, then insert the bolts and tighten them progressively to the specified torque. It is recommended that the bolts are tightened in the two stages given in the Specifications.

51 Raise the subframe and at the same time reconnect the steering column to the steering gear pinion, and tighten the clamp bolt. Refit the subframe mounting bolts and tighten to the specified torque. Remove the tape from the steering wheel.

52 Refit the wiring to the support on the subframe.

53 Refit and tighten the front bumper lower mountings.

54 Refit the rear engine mounting link and tighten the bolts to the specified torque.

55 Refit the horn (see Chapter 12).

56 Reconnect the gearchange control rod to the gearbox with reference to Chapter 7A.

57 Refit the support stays between the underbody and subframe.

58 Refit the front suspension lower arm balljoints and steering track rod ends with reference to Chapter 10.

59 Refit the right-hand wheelarch liner, and re-secure the left-hand liner.

60 Refit the front roadwheels and undershield (where fitted), then lower the vehicle to the ground.

61 Refill the engine with oil and reconnect the battery negative lead.

11 Oil pump – removal, inspection and refitting

Engines with auxiliary shaft

Removal

1 Remove the sump (see Section 10).

2 Unscrew the four retaining bolts and withdraw the pump from the cylinder block and drivegear **(see illustration)**. Note the locating dowel which is fitted over the pump driveshaft.

10.50 Using a straight-edge to align the sump with the end of the cylinder block

3 If necessary, unscrew the two retaining bolts and remove the oil pump drivegear cover and sealing ring from the rear of the cylinder block. Withdraw the drivegear from the block; the drivegear can be removed by screwing a 12 mm bolt into its threads and using the bolt to pull out the gear. Discard the sealing ring; a new one should be used on refitting.

Inspection

4 Unscrew the retaining bolts and lift off the pump cover. Withdraw the idler gear and the drivegear/shaft. Mark the idler gear before removal, so that it can be refitted in its original position.

5 Extract the retaining clip and remove the oil pressure relief valve spring retainer, spring, spring seat and plunger **(see illustrations)**.

11.2 Removing the oil pump

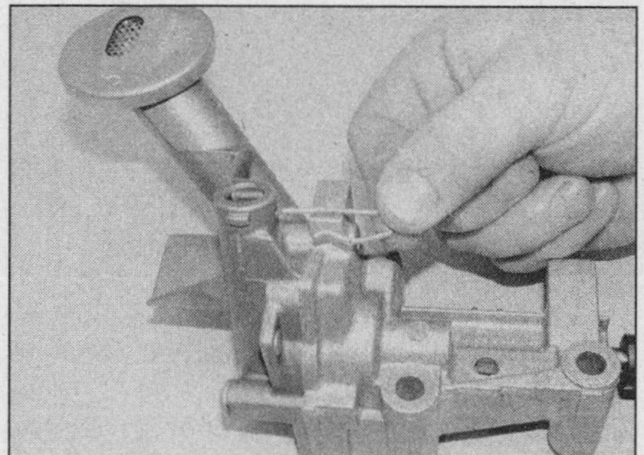
11.5a Extract the retaining clip . . .

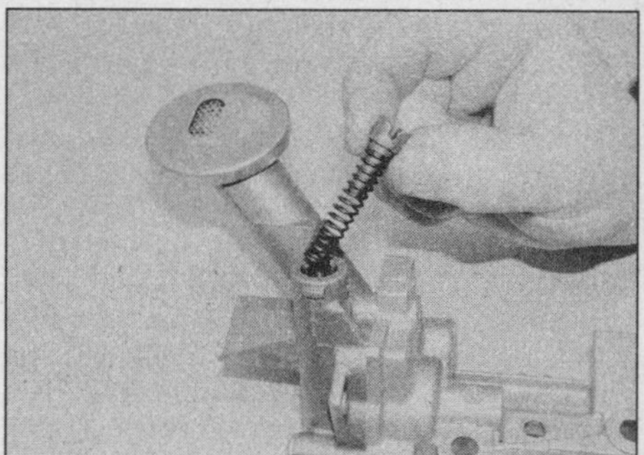
11.5b . . . and remove the oil pressure relief valve components

11.7a Measuring the oil pump gear-to-body clearance

11.7b Measuring the oil pump gear endfloat

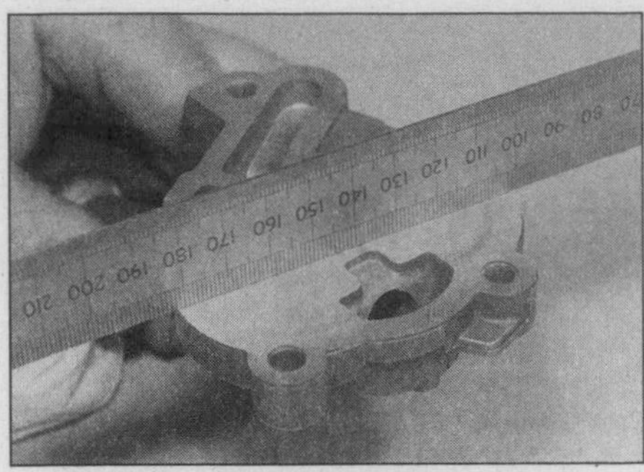
11.7c Checking the flatness of the oil pump cover

6 Clean the components and carefully examine the gears, pump body and relief valve plunger for any signs of scoring or wear. Renew the complete pump assembly if excessive wear is evident (no spare parts are available).

7 If the components appear serviceable, measure the clearance between the pump body and the gears using feeler gauges. Also measure the gear endfloat and check the flatness of the end cover **(see illustrations)**. If the clearances exceed the specified tolerances, the pump must be renewed. There should be no discernible wear or distortion of the end cover.

8 If the pump is satisfactory, reassemble the components in the reverse order of removal, but bend the end of the retaining clip to ensure it remains in position **(see illustration)**. Fill the pump with oil, then refit the cover and tighten the bolts securely. Prime the oil pump by filling it with clean engine oil whilst rotating the driveshaft.

Refitting

9 Where necessary, refit the pump drivegear to the cylinder block making sure it is correctly engaged with the auxiliary shaft. Refit the drivegear cover using a new sealing ring and securely tighten its retaining bolts.

10 Wipe clean the mating faces of the oil pump and cylinder block.

11 Ensure that the locating dowel is correctly fitted to the oil pump then lift the pump into position, engaging the driveshaft with the drivegear splines and seat the pump fully in position. Refit the pump retaining bolts and tighten them to the specified torque.

12 Refit the sump as described in Section 10.

Engines without auxiliary shaft

Removal

13 To remove the oil pump alone, first remove the sump, referring to Section 10. On F9Q 732 engines, also unbolt and unclip the anti-emulsion panel **(see illustrations)**.

14 Unscrew the two mounting bolts and withdraw the oil pump, tilting it to disengage its sprocket from the drive chain **(see illustrations)**. If the two locating dowels are displaced, refit them in their locations.

15 To remove the oil pump complete with its drive chain and sprockets, first remove the sump (Section 10), then unbolt the crankshaft timing belt end oil seal housing, as described in Section 12 **(see illustration)**. Where fitted, note the presence of the chain guide block and of its two locating dowels.

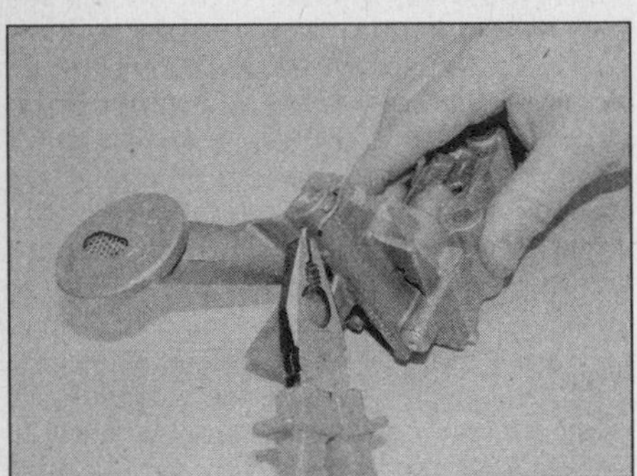
11.8 Bend the end of the retaining clip to ensure it remains in position

11.13a Unscrew the bolts . . .

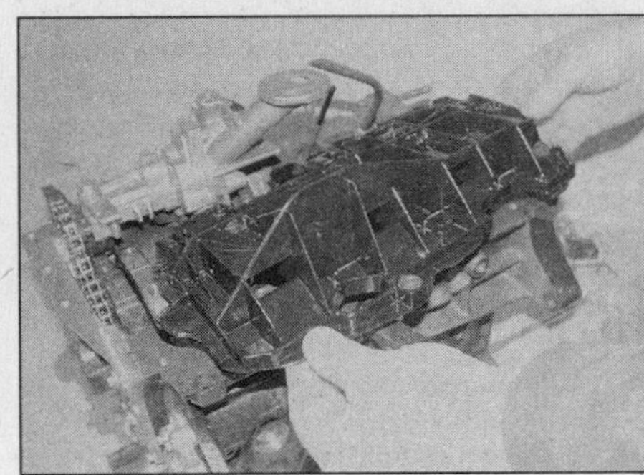
11.13b . . . then unclip and remove the anti-emulsion panel

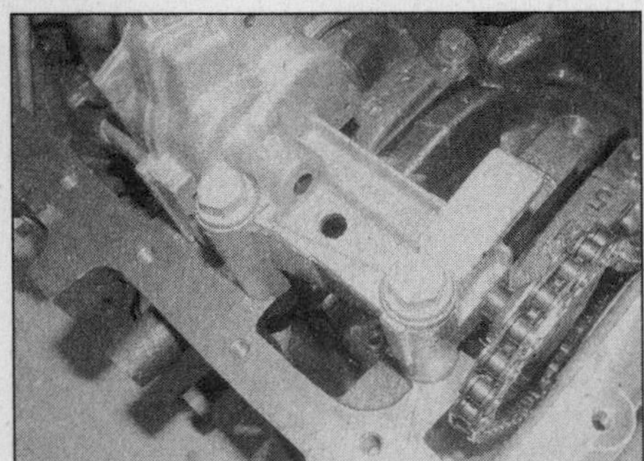
11.14a Oil pump mounting bolts

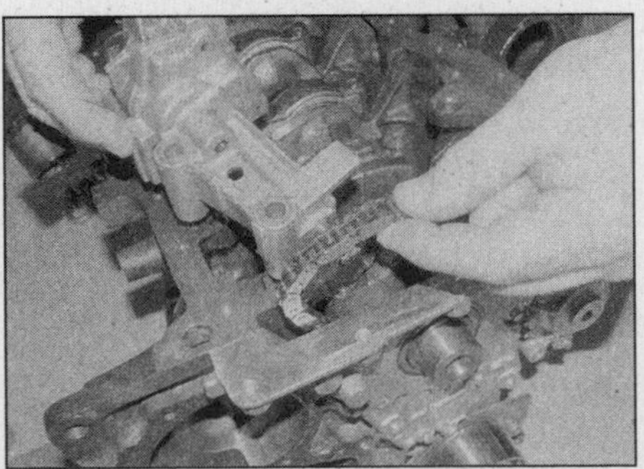
11.14b Disengaging the oil pump sprocket from the drive chain

11.15 Removing the timing belt end oil seal housing

16 Where applicable, unscrew the bolts securing the sprocket to the oil pump hub. Use a screwdriver through one of the holes in the sprocket to hold it stationary.
17 Slide the drive sprocket from the crankshaft together with the chain **(see illustration)**. Note that the drive sprocket is not keyed to the crankshaft, but relies on the pulley bolt being tightened correctly to clamp the sprocket. It is most important that the pulley bolt is correctly tightened otherwise there is the possibility of the oil pump not functioning.
18 Unbolt the oil pump as described in paragraph 14 above.

Inspection

19 Proceed as described in paragraphs 4 to 8 above.

Refitting

20 Wipe clean the oil pump and cylinder block mating surfaces.
21 Check that the two locating dowels are fitted in the cylinder block, then position the oil pump on them and insert the two mounting bolts. Tighten the bolts securely.
22 Engage the sprockets on the chain (if removed), then refit both sprockets and the chain as an assembly. Slide the drive sprocket fully onto the crankshaft and locate the driven sprocket on the oil pump hub.
23 Align the holes, then insert the sprocket bolts and tighten them securely while holding the sprocket stationary with a screwdriver.
24 Refit the oil seal housing as described in Section 12 – do not forget the chain guide block and its two locating dowels – and the sump (refer to Section 10).

12 Crankshaft oil seals – renewal

Timing belt end oil seal

1 Remove the crankshaft sprocket, as described in Section 6.
2 Note the fitted position of the old seal, then prise it out of the oil seal housing using a screwdriver or suitable hooked instrument. An alternative method of removing the oil seal is to drill carefully two small holes opposite each other in the oil seal and insert self-tapping screws, then pull on the screws with grips **(see illustration)**. Take care not to damage the surface of the crankshaft or spacer, or the seal housing. **Note:** *On some models it may be necessary to remove the timing belt lower inner cover to allow the seal to be withdrawn. If this is the case, remove the auxiliary shaft/idler sprocket and idler pulley (see Section 6) then unbolt the cover.*
3 Clean the seal housing and polish off any burrs or raised edges which may have caused the seal to fail in the first place. Inspect the seal rubbing surface on the crankshaft. If it is grooved or rough in the area where the old seal was fitted, the new seal should be fitted slightly less deeply, so that it rubs on an unworn part of the crankshaft surface. On early F8Q 784 engines which have a separate spacer fitted over the crankshaft end, withdraw the spacer – if it is worn where the old oil seal contacted it, it may be possible to turn the spacer around so that the new oil seal contacts its unworn area. If the spacer is excessively worn at this point, it must be renewed.

11.17 Removing the oil pump drive sprocket and chain

4 Wipe clean the oil seal seating, then dip the new seal in fresh engine oil and locate it over the crankshaft with its closed side facing outwards. Make sure that the oil seal lip is not damaged as it is located on the crankshaft.
5 Using a tube of suitable diameter, drive the oil seal squarely into the housing to the previously noted position **(see illustration)** – take great care not to damage the seal lips during fitting. Note that if the surface of the shaft was noted to be badly scored, press the new seal slightly further into its housing so that its lip is running on an unmarked area of the shaft. Where a separate spacer is fitted, lubricate it with clean engine oil, then slide it onto the crankshaft and carefully press it into the oil seal, while twisting it to prevent damage.
6 Where necessary, refit the timing belt lower inner cover/seal housing **(see illustration)** and install the idler pulley and auxiliary shaft/idler sprocket as described in Section 6. Refit the crankshaft sprocket as described in Section 6 and fit the new timing belt as described in Section 5.

12.5 Using a socket to drive in the new oil seal

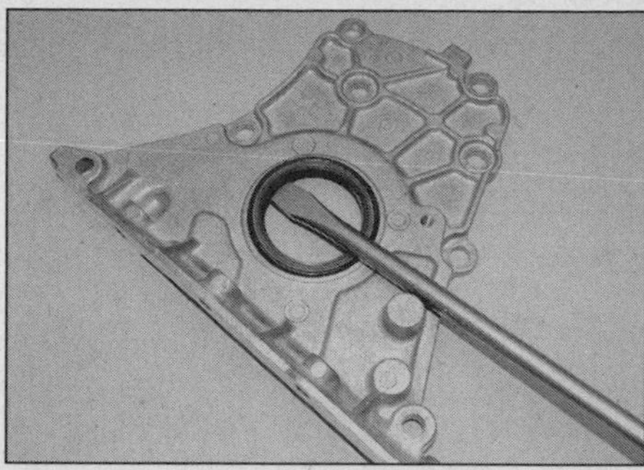

12.2 Removing the timing belt end oil seal (timing cover removed)

Timing belt end oil seal housing

7 Remove the timing belt as described in Section 5, and the crankshaft and auxiliary shaft/idler sprockets and the idler pulley with reference to Section 6. Remove the Woodruff key from the crankshaft keyway, then unbolt the timing belt lower inner cover from the cylinder block.
8 Unscrew the bolts (approximately four in number, depending on engine version) securing the sump to the oil seal housing.
9 Unscrew the retaining bolts and carefully withdraw the oil seal housing, noting the locating dowels around its two lower bolt holes. If it is stuck in place a leverage point is provided on its upper edge (near the timing belt idler pulley) to allow a screwdriver or similar to be used gently to prise the housing away from the cylinder block without risking damage to the delicate mating surfaces of either. If the sump gasket is damaged, the sump will have to be removed to renew it. On engines without an auxiliary shaft, note the presence of the oil pump drive chain guide block and of its two locating dowels – check that the guide block is fit for further use and renew it if there is any doubt about its condition. On early F8Q 784 engines, note also the presence of the separate spacer fitted over the crankshaft end.
10 The oil seal should be renewed whenever the housing is removed. Note the fitted position of the old seal, then prise it out with a screwdriver and wipe clean the seating. Smear the outer perimeter of the new seal with fresh engine oil and locate it squarely on

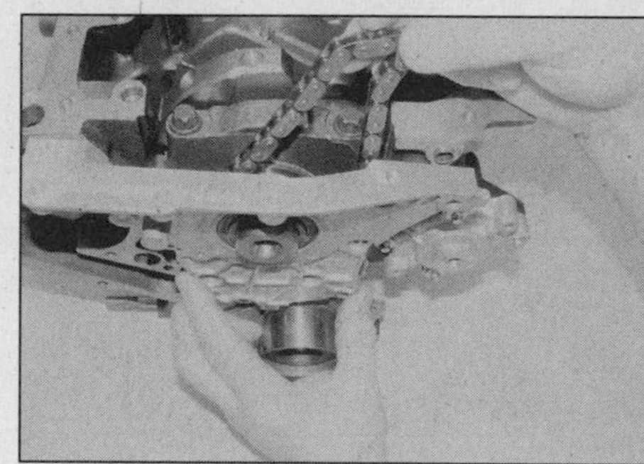

12.6 Refitting the oil seal housing

the housing with its closed side facing outwards. Place the housing on a block of wood, then use a socket or metal tube to drive in the oil seal.

11 On refitting, clean all traces of sealant from the housing, sump and block mating faces. Check that the chain guide block (where applicable) is correctly fitted and that the housing's locating dowels are in place.

12 Apply a 0.6 to 1.0 mm diameter bead of sealant (Renault recommend CAF 4/60 THIXO or Rhodorseal 5661) to the housing's gasket surfaces, around the inner edges of the bolt holes and apply a smear of sealant to the threads of the two bolts (nearest the oil seal) which project inside the cylinder block. Do **NOT** allow sealant to foul the oil gallery at the upper end of the housing. Refit the housing to the cylinder block and sump, tightening the bolts securely and evenly.

13 Refit the separate spacer (where applicable) as described in paragraph 5 above. On all engines, refit the Woodruff key to the crankshaft keyway, then refit the timing belt lower inner cover to the cylinder block, tightening securely its retaining bolts.

14 Refit the crankshaft and auxiliary shaft/idler sprockets and the idler pulley, and fit the new timing belt with reference to Sections 6 and 5.

Flywheel end oil seal

15 Renewal of the crankshaft left-hand oil seal requires the gearbox to be removed from the engine compartment so that the clutch and the flywheel can be withdrawn – refer to Chapter 7A and to Chapter 6. Remove the flywheel as described in Section 16.

16 Prise out the old oil seal using a small screwdriver, taking care not to damage the surface on the crankshaft **(see illustration)**. Alternatively, the oil seal can be removed by drilling two small holes diagonally opposite each other and inserting self-tapping screws in them. A pair of grips can then be used to pull out the oil seal, by pulling on each side in turn.

17 Inspect the seal rubbing surface on the crankshaft. If it is grooved or rough in the area where the old seal was fitted, the new seal should be fitted slightly less deeply, so that it rubs on an unworn part of the surface.

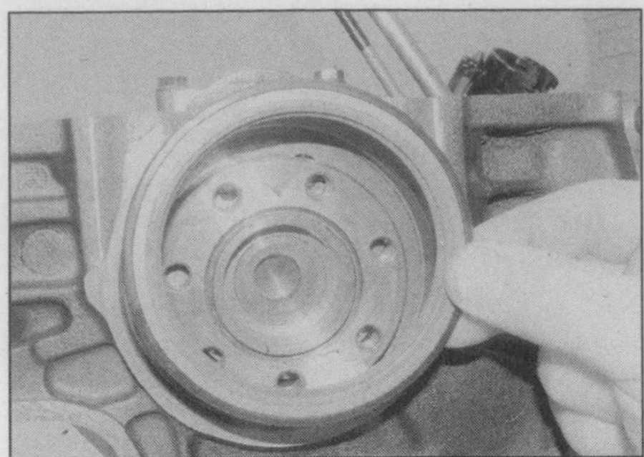

12.16 Removing the flywheel end crankshaft oil seal

18 Wipe clean the oil seal seating, then dip the new seal in fresh engine oil, and locate it over the crankshaft with its closed side facing outwards. Make sure that the oil seal lip is not damaged as it is located on the crankshaft.

19 Using a metal tube, drive the oil seal squarely into the bore until flush. A block of wood cut to pass over the end of the crankshaft may be used instead.

20 Refit the flywheel with reference to Section 16. Refit the clutch as described in Chapter 6, then refit the gearbox and reconnect it to the engine as described in Chapter 7A.

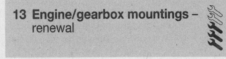

13 Engine/gearbox mountings – renewal

Inspection

1 Apply the handbrake, then jack up the front of the car and support it on axle stands (see *Jacking and vehicle support*). Where fitted, remove the engine compartment undershield.

2 Visually inspect the rubber pads on the two front and one rear engine/gearbox mountings for signs of cracking and deterioration. Careful use of a lever will help to determine the condition of the rubber pads. Check that all the mounting's fasteners are securely tightened; use a torque wrench to check if possible. If there is excessive movement in the mounting, or if the rubber has deteriorated, the mounting should be renewed.

13.5 Right-hand engine mounting on a late Scénic with F9Q 732 engine

Renewal

Right-hand mounting

3 Connect a hoist and suitable lifting tackle to the engine lifting brackets to support the engine/gearbox assembly while the mounting is removed. Alternatively, the assembly can be supported using a jack and a suitable block of wood to spread the load under the sump.

4 On F8Q-engined models, unscrew the securing bolts and remove the timing belt upper/engine right-hand mounting plastic cover, noting the locations of any brackets secured by the bolts. On F9Q-engined models, unscrew the retaining nuts and withdraw the engine top cover.

5 Ensure that the engine/gearbox assembly is adequately supported, then unscrew the nut securing the mounting upper bracket to the mounting rubber/movement limiter assembly on the body **(see illustration)**. On certain models it is necessary to counterhold the mounting threaded rod using a suitable Allen key or hexagon bit, whilst loosening the nut with an open-ended spanner.

6 Unscrew the three bolts securing the mounting upper bracket to the main bracket on the engine **(see illustrations)**, then withdraw the bracket. Note that on some models it is necessary to detach the accelerator cable support from the mounting.

7 Unscrew the bolts securing the engine mounting rubber/movement limiter assembly to the body and withdraw the assembly **(see illustration)**.

8 With the mounting cover and upper bracket

13.6a Removing the right-hand engine mounting upper bracket on the F9Q 732 engine

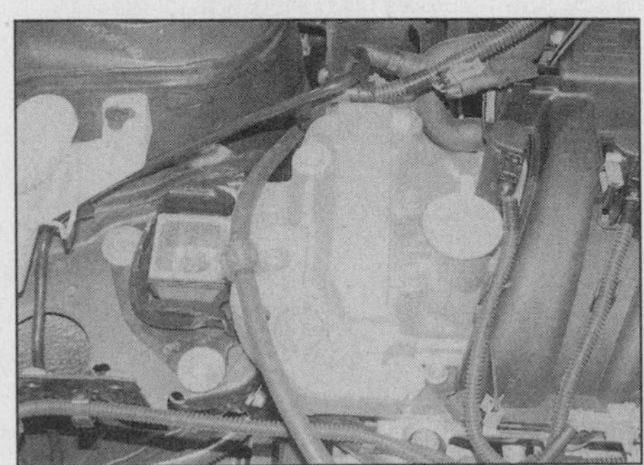

13.6b Right-hand engine mounting

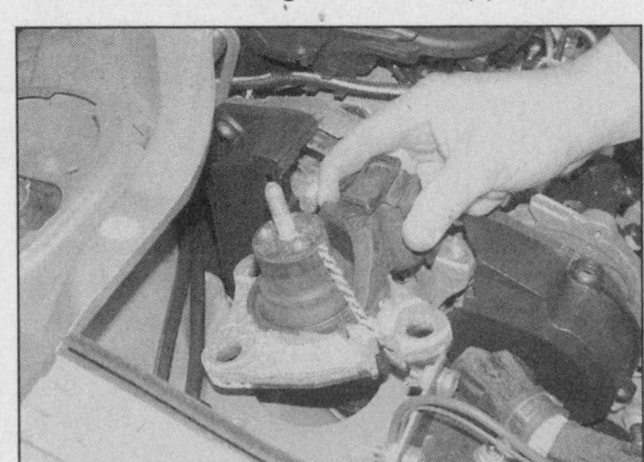

13.7 Removing the engine mounting rubber/movement limiter from the body

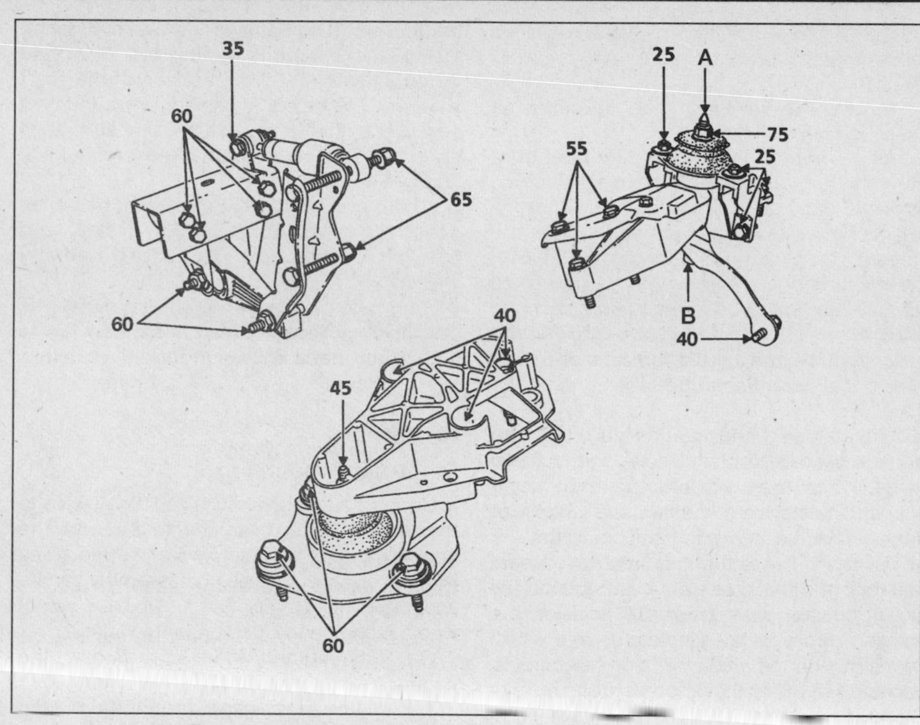

13.13 Torque wrench settings (in Nm) of engine/gearbox mountings

A Tighten the stud to 60 Nm *B Tighten the nut to 40 Nm*

removed, remove the timing belt outer covers to reach the main bracket's mounting bolts on the engine. Unscrew the bolts and withdraw the main bracket; tighten the bolts securely on refitting.

9 Refit the mounting rubber/movement limiter assembly. On F8Q-engined models, do not fully tighten the securing bolts at this stage.

10 Refit the upper mounting bracket and tighten to the specified torque wrench setting the bolts securing it to the main bracket. At this stage, on F8Q-engined models, do not fully tighten the nut securing the bracket to the mounting rubber/movement limiter assembly.

11 Remove the hoist or jack from the engine/gearbox assembly.

12 On F8Q-engined models, the mounting rubber/movement limiter assembly must now be centred before tightening the body mounting bolts – on F9Q-engined models, the assembly is self-centring. Renault technicians use a special forked tool, Mot. 1289-03, which is inserted through the slots in the bracket. If this tool is not available it may be possible to make up a similar tool out of strips of metal.

13 With the mounting centred, tighten to the specified torque wrench settings the body mounting bolts and the upper bracket-to-mounting rubber/movement limiter assembly nut **(see illustration)**. Remove the tool after making the adjustment and also refit the plastic cover or engine cover, as applicable.

Left-hand mounting

14 Remove the left-hand roadwheel.

15 Using a jack and block of wood, support the weight of the gearbox.

16 Unscrew the nut securing the lower mounting stud to the upper bracket. Using a soft-faced mallet, tap the stud to release it from the upper bracket.

17 Unbolt the upper mounting rubber and bracket.

18 Unbolt the lower mounting bracket.

19 Fit the new mounting components using a reversal of the removal procedure, but tighten the stud, the nuts and the bolts to the specified torque wrench settings shown in illustration 13.13.

Rear mounting and link

20 If removing the link only, apply the handbrake, then jack up the front of the vehicle and support it on axle stands (see *Jacking and Vehicle Support*). Support the engine/gearbox, then remove the engine compartment undertray and unbolt the link from the gearbox bracket and subframe **(see illustrations)**.

21 To remove the bracket, first remove the air cleaner assembly as described in Chapter 4B. From within the engine compartment, reach down behind the left-hand side of the engine and unscrew the nuts from the bolts securing the rear mounting bracket to the gearbox. At the same time, where applicable, unbolt the shock absorber from the top of the mounting.

22 Using a hoist or trolley jack and block of wood, take the weight of the engine/gearbox off the rear mounting.

23 Unscrew the bolts from the bracket and manoeuvre the bracket from the gearbox and subframe. The bracket is a tight fit and it may be necessary to raise the engine/gearbox further to provide room to remove it.

24 Fit the new mounting using a reversal of the removal procedure, but tighten the bolts to the specified torque wrench settings shown in illustration 13.13.

14 Engine oil cooler – removal and refitting

Removal

1 Drain the cooling system as described in Chapter 1B.

2 Remove the oil filter (refer to Chapter 1B).

3 Loosen the clips and disconnect the coolant hoses from the oil cooler.

4 Unscrew the oil filter mounting stud, which also secures the oil cooler and withdraw the oil cooler from the engine. Recover the sealing ring **(see illustrations)**.

13.20a Rear engine mounting link on a late Scénic

13.20b Removing the rear engine mounting link bolt from the gearbox bracket

14.4a Remove the oil filter mounting stud . . .

2C

14.4b . . . then withdraw the oil cooler and recover the sealing ring

Refitting

5 Refitting is a reversal of removal, but use a new sealing ring.

15 Auxiliary shaft oil seal – renewal

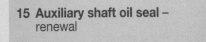

Note: *This procedure applies only to those engines fitted with auxiliary shafts. There is no oil seal or gasket behind the idler sprocket of those engines which do not have auxiliary shafts.*

1 Remove the auxiliary shaft sprocket as described in Section 6.

2 Make a note of the correct fitted depth of the seal then punch or drill two small holes opposite each other in the oil seal. Screw a self-tapping screw into each and pull on the screws with pliers to extract the seal. **Note:** *On some models it may be necessary to remove the timing belt lower inner cover to allow the seal to be withdrawn. If this is the case, remove the crankshaft sprocket and idler pulley (see Section 6) then unbolt the cover.*

3 Clean the seal housing and polish off any burrs or raised edges which may have caused the seal to fail in the first place.

4 Lubricate the lips of the new seal with clean engine oil and ease it into position on the end of the shaft. Press the seal into its housing until it is positioned at the same depth as the original was prior to removal. If necessary, a suitable tubular drift, such as a socket, which bears only on the hard outer edge of the seal can be used to tap the seal into position. Take great care not to damage the seal lips during fitting and ensure that the seal lips face inwards. Note that if the surface of the shaft was noted to be badly scored, press the new seal slightly further into its housing so that its lip is running on an unmarked area of the shaft.

5 Where necessary, refit the timing belt inner cover and install the idler pulley and crankshaft sprocket as described in Section 6.

6 Refit the auxiliary shaft sprocket as described in Section 6 and fit the new timing belt as described in Section 5.

16 Flywheel – removal, inspection and refitting

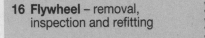

1 Proceed as described in Chapter 2A, noting that on diesel models the gearbox can be removed separately as described in Chapter 7A – there is no need to remove the complete engine/gearbox assembly to reach the flywheel **(see illustrations)**.

16.1a Removing the flywheel

16.1b Fit the bolts . . .

16.1c . . . and tighten them to the specified torque

Chapter 2 Part D:
Engine removal and overhaul procedures

Contents

Degrees of difficulty

Easy, suitable for novice with little experience 	**Fairly easy,** suitable for beginner with some experience 	**Fairly difficult,** suitable for competent DIY mechanic 	**Difficult,** suitable for experienced DIY mechanic 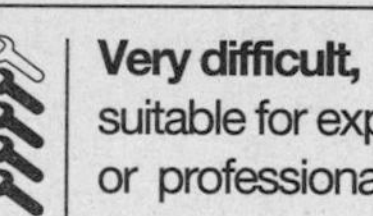	**Very difficult,** suitable for expert DIY or professional

Specifications

General

Engine designation:	
Petrol models:	
1.4 litre engine	E7J 764, K4J 750
1.6 litre engine	K4M 700, K4M 701
2.0 litre engine	F4R 740, F4R 741
Diesel models:	
Non-turbo engines – D models	F8Q 620*, F8Q 622*, F8Q 788
Turbo engines:	
dT models – indirect injection	F8Q 784*, F8Q 786
dTi models – direct injection	F9Q 730*, F9Q 734
dCi models – direct common-rail injection	F9Q 732

** Engines with an auxiliary shaft*

Cylinder head

Height:		
E7J engine	113.0 mm ± 0.05 mm	
K4J and K4M engines	137.0 mm	
F4R engine	138.15 mm	
F8Q engine	159.50 ± 0.20 mm	
F9Q engine	162.00 ± 0.10 mm	
Maximum acceptable gasket face distortion	0.05 mm	
Refinishing limit	No refinishing permitted	
Swirl chamber protrusion (F8Q engine)	0.01 to 0.04 mm	
Valve depth below cylinder head gasket face:		
F8Q engines:	**Inlet**	**Exhaust**
Non-turbo engines	0.85 ± 0.09 mm	0.97 ± 0.09 mm
Turbo engines	0.65 ± 0.09 mm	0.57 ± 0.09 mm
F9Q engines (excluding F9Q 732)	0.65 ± 0.09 mm	0.57 ± 0.09 mm
Valve protrusion above cylinder head gasket face:		
F9Q 732 engines:		
Inlet and exhaust	0.09 ± 0.12 mm	
Valve seat angle:		
E7J and F8Q engines:		
Inlet	120°	
Exhaust	90°	
F9Q engines:		
Inlet	90°	
Exhaust	90°	
K4J, K4M and F4R engines:		
Inlet and exhaust	89°	
Valve seat width:		
E7J engine	1.7 mm ± 0.1 mm	
K4J, K4M and F4R engines:		
Inlet	1.3 +1.4 –0 mm	
Exhaust	1.4 +1.3 –0 mm	
F8Q and F9Q engines	1.8 mm	
Valve guide bore (diesel engines):		
F8Q engines	8.0 mm	
F9Q engines – nominal	7.0 mm +0.02 mm	
Valve guide outer diameter (diesel engines):		
F8Q engines:		
Standard	13.00 mm	
Oversize	13.30 mm	
F9Q engines:		
Standard	12.00 mm +0.03 mm to +0.05 mm	
Oversize	Not available	

Pistons and piston rings

Piston ring end gaps	Rings supplied pre-set
Piston ring thickness:	
Top compression ring:	
E7J engine	1.75 mm
K4J, K4M and F4R engines	1.2 mm
F8Q engines	2.0 mm
F9Q engines	2.5 mm
Second compression ring:	
E7J engine	1.75 mm
K4J and K4M engines	1.5 mm
F4R engine	1.47 to 1.495 mm
F8Q and F9Q engines	2.0 mm
Oil control ring:	
E7J engine	3.0 mm
K4J and K4M engines	2.5 mm
F4R engine	1.94 mm
F8Q and F9Q engines	3.0 mm
Piston clearance in liner/bore (suggested values):	
Petrol engines	0.045 to 0.065 mm
Diesel engines	0.015 to 0.030 mm

Valves

Head diameter:	Inlet	Exhaust
E7J engine	37.5 ± 0.1 mm	33.5 ± 0.1 mm
K4J and K4M engines	32.7 ± 0.12 mm	27.96 ± 0.12 mm
F4R engine	33.5 ± 0.12 mm	29.0 ± 0.12 mm
F8Q 620, F8Q 622 and F8Q 788 engines:		
Conventional inlet valve seat	36.100 mm	31.500 mm
Stellite inlet valve seat*	36.350 mm	31.500 mm
F8Q 784 and F8Q 786 engines	36.225 ± 0.125 mm	31.620 ± 0.120 mm
F9Q engines	35.200 mm	32.500 mm

Stem diameter:	
E7J engine:	
Inlet and exhaust	7.0 mm
K4J and K4M engines:	
Inlet	5.484 ± 0.01 mm
Exhaust	5.473 ± 0.01 mm
F4R engine:	
Inlet	5.471 ± 0.009 mm
Exhaust	5.447 ± 0.009 mm
F8Q 620, F8Q 622 and F8Q 788 engines	8.000 mm
F8Q 784 and F8Q 786 engines	7.985 ± 0.040 mm
F9Q engines	7.000 –0.010 mm to –0.020 mm
Valve spring free length:	
E7J engine:	
Black marking	46.64 mm
Orange marking	44.93 mm
K4J, K4M and F4R engines	41.30 mm
F8Q 620, F8Q 622 and F8Q 788 engines	43.41 mm
F8Q 784 and F8Q 786 engines	47.57 mm
F9Q engines	45.80 mm

** Cylinder heads with steel inlet valve seats and Stellited valves can be identified by the ribs on them.*

Cylinder block

Wet liner dimensions – E7J engine:	
Liner height:	
Total	130.0 mm
From shoulder to top	91.5 mm +0.035 +0.005 mm
Cylinder block depth – from top to liner locating shoulder	91.5 mm –0.015 –0.055 mm
Liner protrusion – without O-ring	0.02 to 0.09 mm
Maximum difference in protrusion between adjacent liners	0.05 mm
Bore diameter:	
E7J engine (wet liners)	75.8 mm +0.03 –0.00 mm
K4J and K4M engines	79.5 mm +0.03 –0.00 mm
F4R engine:	
Class A or 1	82.710 to 82.720 mm
Class B or 2	82.720 to 82.730 mm
F8Q engines*:	
Class A or 1	80.000 to 81.015 mm
Class B or 2	80.015 to 80.030 mm
F9Q engines – nominal	80.000 mm

*** Note:** *The bore size classes are shown by drillings on the side of the block, just below the cylinder head gasket surface.*

Connecting rods

Big-end bearing running clearance:	
Except F4R engine	0.014 to 0.053 mm
F4R engine	0.02 to 0.071 mm
Big-end cap side play:	
E7J engines	0.310 to 0.572 mm
K4J and K4M engines	0.310 to 0.604 mm
F4R engine	0.220 to 0.402 mm
F8Q and F9Q engines	0.220 to 0.400 mm

Auxiliary shaft

Endfloat	0.07 to 0.15 mm

2D

Crankshaft

Number of main bearings	5
Main bearing journal diameter:	
E7J engine:	
Standard	54.795 mm ± 0.01 mm
1st undersize	54.545 mm ± 0.01 mm
K4J and K4M engines:	
Standard	47.990 to 47.997 mm
1st undersize	47.997 to 48.003 mm
2nd undersize	48.003 to 48.010 mm
F4R engine:	
Standard	54.795 mm ± 0.01 mm
F8Q engine:	
Standard	54.795 ± 0.01 mm
1st undersize	54.545 ± 0.01 mm
F9Q engines:	
Standard	54.790 ± 0.01 mm
Undersize	Not available
Main bearing running clearance:	
Except F4R engine	0.020 to 0.058 mm
F4R engine	0.04 to 0.075 mm
Crankpin (big-end) journal diameter:	
E7J engine:	
Standard	43.980 mm +0 –0.02 mm
1st undersize	43.730 mm +0 –0.02 mm
K4J and K4M engines:	
Standard	43.97 ± 0.01 mm
F4R engine:	
Standard	48.00 +0 –0.02 mm
F8Q engine:	
Standard	48.00 mm
Undersize	47.75 mm +0.02 mm –0.00 mm
F9Q engines:	
Standard	48.00 mm +0.02 mm
Undersize	Not available
Crankshaft endfloat:	
E7J engine:	
New	0.045 to 0.252 mm
Maximum	0.852 mm
K4J and K4M engines:	
New	0.045 to 0.252 mm
Maximum	0.852 mm
F8Q, F9Q and F4R engines	0.070 to 0.230 mm
Thrustwasher thicknesses (diesel engines)	2.30, 2.35, 2.40 and 2.45 mm

Torque wrench settings

Refer to Parts A, B, and C of this Chapter.

1 General information

Included in this part of Chapter 2 are the general overhaul procedures for the cylinder head, cylinder block/crankcase and internal engine components.

The information ranges from advice concerning preparation for an overhaul and the purchase of replacement parts, to detailed step-by-step procedures covering removal, inspection, renovation and refitting of internal engine parts.

The following Sections have been compiled based on the assumption that the engine has been removed from the car. For information concerning in-car engine repair, as well as the removal and refitting of the external components necessary for the overhaul, refer to Part A or B (petrol engines) or Part C (diesel engine) of this Chapter and to Section 7 of this Part.

Caution: If the radio/cassette in your vehicle is equipped with an anti-theft system, make sure you have the correct activation code before disconnecting the battery.

2 Engine overhaul – general information

It is not always easy to determine when, or if, an engine should be completely overhauled, as a number of factors must be considered.

High mileage is not necessarily an indication that an overhaul is needed, while low mileage does not preclude the need for an overhaul. Frequency of servicing is probably the most important consideration. An engine which has had regular and frequent oil and filter changes, as well as other required maintenance, will most likely give many thousands of miles of reliable service. Conversely, a neglected engine may require an overhaul very early in its life.

Excessive oil consumption is an indication that piston rings, valve stem oil seals and/or valves and valve guides are in need of attention. Make sure that oil leaks are not responsible before deciding that the rings and/or guides are bad. Perform a cylinder compression check to determine the extent of the work required.

Check the oil pressure with a gauge fitted in place of the oil pressure warning light switch and compare it with the value given in the Specifications. If it is extremely low, the main and big-end bearings and/or the oil pump are probably worn out.

Loss of power, rough running, knocking or metallic engine noises, excessive valve gear noise and high fuel consumption may also point to the need for an overhaul, especially if they are all present at the same time. If a complete tune-up does not remedy the situation, major mechanical work is the only solution.

An engine overhaul involves restoring the internal parts to the specifications of a new engine. During an overhaul, the pistons and rings are renewed and the cylinder bores are reconditioned. New main bearings, connecting rod bearings and camshaft bearings are generally fitted and, if necessary, the crankshaft may be reground to restore the journals. The valves are also serviced as well, since they are usually in less-than-perfect condition at this point. While the engine is being overhauled, other components, such as the distributor, starter and alternator, can be overhauled as well. The end result should be a like-new engine that will give many trouble-free miles. **Note:** *Critical cooling system components such as the hoses, drivebelts, thermostat and water pump MUST be renewed when an engine is overhauled. The radiator should be checked carefully, to ensure that it is not clogged or leaking. Also, it is a good idea to renew the oil pump whenever the engine is overhauled.*

Before beginning the engine overhaul, read through the entire procedure to familiarise yourself with the scope and requirements of the job. Overhauling an engine is not difficult if you follow all of the instructions carefully, have the necessary tools and equipment and pay close attention to all specifications; however, it can be time-consuming. Plan on the vehicle being tied up for a minimum of two weeks, especially if parts must be taken to an engineering works for repair or reconditioning. Check on the availability of parts and make sure that any necessary special tools and equipment are obtained in advance. Most work can be done with typical hand tools, although a number of precision measuring tools are required for inspecting parts to determine if they must be renewed. Often the engineering works will handle the inspection of parts and offer advice concerning reconditioning and renewal. **Note:** *Always wait until the engine has been completely disassembled and all components, especially the engine block, have been inspected before deciding what service and repair operations must be performed by an engineering works. Since the condition of the block will be the major factor to consider when determining whether to overhaul the original engine or buy a reconditioned unit, do not purchase parts or have overhaul work done on other components until the block has been thoroughly inspected.* As a general rule, time is the primary cost of an overhaul, so it does not pay to fit worn or substandard parts.

As a final note, to ensure maximum life and minimum trouble from a reconditioned engine, everything must be assembled with care and in a spotlessly-clean environment.

3 Engine removal – methods and precautions

If you have decided that an engine must be removed for overhaul or major repair work, several preliminary steps should be taken.

Locating a suitable place to work is extremely important. Adequate work space, with storage space for the vehicle, will be needed. If a garage is not available, at the very least a flat, level, clean work surface is required.

Cleaning the engine compartment and engine before beginning the removal procedure will help keep tools clean and organised.

An engine hoist or A-frame will also be necessary. Make sure the equipment is rated in excess of the combined weight of the engine and transmission. Safety is of primary importance, considering the potential hazards involved in lifting the engine out of the vehicle.

If the engine is being removed by a novice, an assistant should be available. Advice and aid from someone more experienced would also be helpful. There are many instances when one person cannot simultaneously perform all of the operations required when lifting the engine out of the vehicle.

Plan the operation ahead of time. Arrange for, or obtain, all of the tools and equipment you will need prior to beginning the job. Some of the equipment necessary to perform engine removal and installation safely and with relative ease are (in addition to an engine hoist) a heavy-duty floor jack, complete sets of spanners and sockets as described in the *Tools and working facilities* section of this manual, wooden blocks and plenty of rags and cleaning solvent for mopping up spilled oil, coolant and fuel. If the hoist must be hired, make sure that you arrange for it in advance and perform all of the operations possible without it beforehand. This will save you money and time.

Plan for the vehicle to be out of use for quite a while. An engineering works will be required to perform some of the work which the do-it-yourselfer cannot accomplish without special equipment. These places often have a busy schedule, so it would be a good idea to consult them before removing the engine, in order to accurately estimate the amount of time required to rebuild or repair components that may need work.

Always be extremely careful when removing and refitting the engine. Serious injury can result from careless actions. Plan ahead, take your time and you will find that a job of this nature, although major, can be accomplished successfully.

4 Petrol engine and manual gearbox – removal and refitting

Removal

1.4 and 1.6 litre models

Note: *The engine is removed upwards from the engine compartment together with the gearbox, then separated on the bench.*

1 Disconnect the battery negative lead (refer to Chapter 5A).

2 Remove the radiator with reference to Chapter 3. Also disconnect the top hose from the thermostat housing and the bottom hose from the coolant pipe **(see illustration)**.

3 Drain the gearbox oil with reference to Chapter 7A **(see illustration)**.

4 If necessary, drain the engine oil with reference to Chapter 1A.

5 Remove the bonnet with reference to Chapter 11.

6 Where applicable, unbolt the strengthening bar from between the front suspension strut turrets.

7 Remove the air cleaner assembly with reference to Chapter 4A.

8 Apply the handbrake, then jack up the front of the car and support it on axle stands (see *Jacking and vehicle support*). Remove both

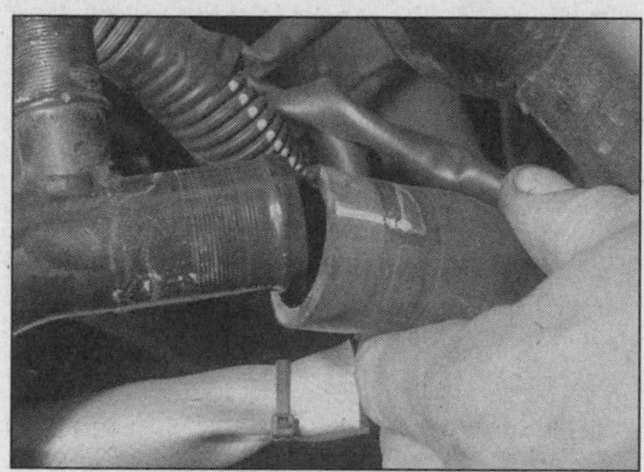

4.2 Disconnecting the bottom hose from the coolant pipe

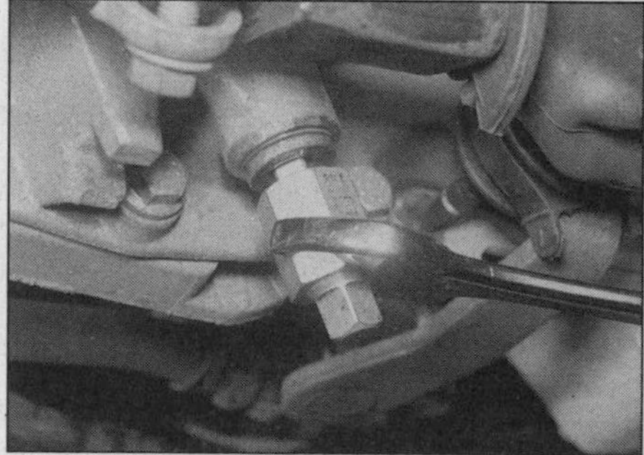

4.3 Unscrewing the drain plug from the manual transmission

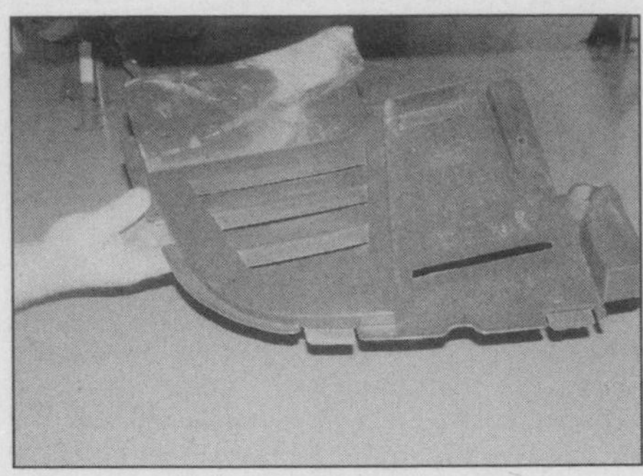
4.8a Removing the side covers . . .

4.8b . . . and the wheelarch liners

4.9 Disconnecting the track rod end from the steering arm on the stub axle carrier

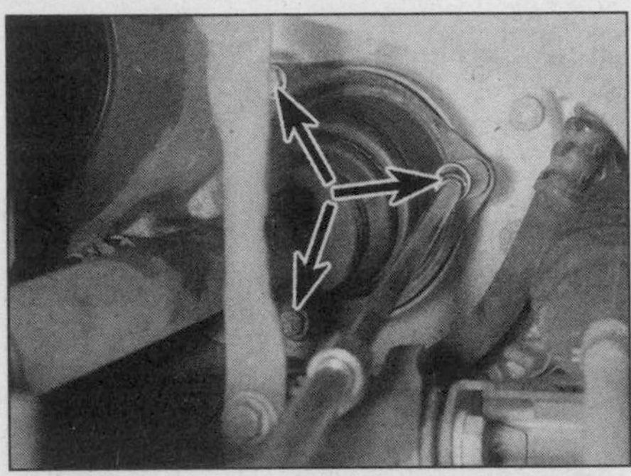
4.10 Remove the three bolts (arrowed) securing the left-hand driveshaft inner rubber boot and metal ring to the transmission

4.11a Unscrew the guide pin bolts . . .

4.11b . . . remove the left-hand brake caliper . . .

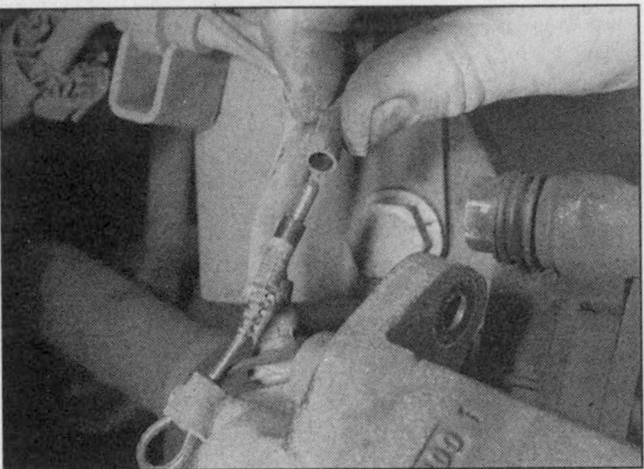
4.11c . . . and disconnect the pad wear warning wiring

front roadwheels and the left- and right-hand front wheelarch liners and side covers **(see illustrations)**. Where fitted, remove the engine compartment undershield.

9 Unscrew the nut from the left-hand track rod end and disconnect it from the swivel hub steering arm using a balljoint separator tool **(see illustration)**.

10 Unscrew the bolts securing the left-hand driveshaft inner rubber boot and metal ring to the transmission **(see illustration)**.

11 Unscrew the two guide pin bolts securing the left-hand brake caliper to the mounting bracket and disconnect the pad wear warning wiring. Tie the caliper to the coil spring, taking care not to strain the hose **(see illustrations)**.

12 Unscrew and remove fully the pinch-bolt securing the left-hand front lower arm balljoint to the swivel hub **(see illustration)**.

13 Unscrew and remove fully both bolts securing the front suspension left-hand strut to the swivel hub (note that the nuts are on the rear of the carrier) **(see illustrations)**.

14 Lever the suspension lower arm downwards, then pull the driveshaft from the sun-gear and withdraw it with the swivel hub. Make sure the tripod components remain in position on the inner end of the driveshaft, otherwise they may fall into the transmission. There may be some oil loss from the gearbox,

4.12 Removing the pinch-bolt securing the left-hand front lower balljoint to the bottom of the stub axle carrier

4.13a Unscrew the nuts . . .

4.13b . . . and tap out the bolts securing the stub axle carrier to the bottom of the suspension strut

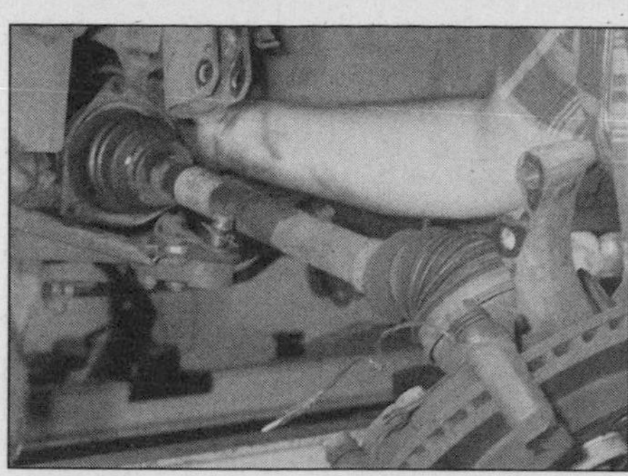
4.14 Withdrawing the left-hand driveshaft from the transmission

so place a small container on the floor to catch it **(see illustration)**.

15 Working beneath the car, drive out the roll pin (early models) securing the right-hand driveshaft to the differential sun-gear shaft. Note that if the original double roll pin is renewed, the new one will be of single coiled type **(see illustrations)**.

16 Unscrew the nut from the right-hand track rod end and disconnect it from the swivel hub steering arm using a balljoint separator tool.

17 Unscrew and remove fully the upper bolt securing the front suspension right-hand strut to the swivel hub (note that the nut is on the rear of the carrier). Loosen only (do not remove) the lower bolt.

18 Pull out the driveshaft and disconnect the inner end from the splines on the transmission sun-gear shaft. Tie the driveshaft to the steering gear. **Note:** *Where the driveshaft has an intermediate section, remove the driveshaft completely.*

19 Remove the exhaust front downpipe and catalytic converter as described in Chapter 4A.

20 Undo the screws and remove the plastic cover from the bottom of the transmission, then mark the position of the gearchange main rod on the clevis at the rod's transmission end, loosen the clamp bolt and disconnect the two sections of the rod **(see illustrations)**.

21 Where applicable, detach the power-assisted steering hydraulic fluid pipes from the transmission.

22 Pull out the spring clip and remove the vehicle speed sensor from the rear of the transmission **(see illustrations)**.

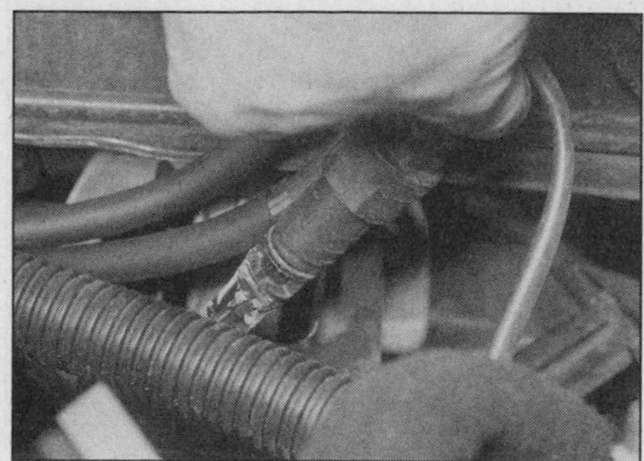
4.22b ... and remove the vehicle speed sensor from the transmission

4.15a Roll pin (arrowed) securing the driveshaft to the transmission sun gear

23 Disconnect the wiring from the reversing light switch on the transmission **(see illustration)**.

24 On models without air conditioning, remove the power-assisted steering pump and fluid reservoir from the engine with reference to Chapter 10, but do not disconnect the fluid pipes. Position the pump to one side **(see illustration)**.

25 On models fitted with air conditioning,

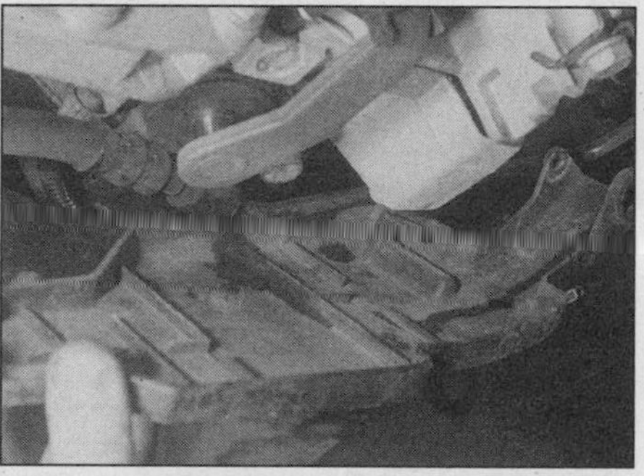
4.20a Remove the plastic cover from the bottom of the transmission ...

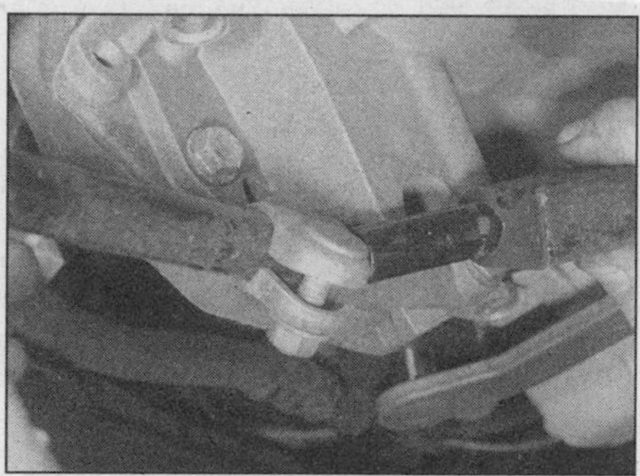
4.20c ... loosen the clamp, and disconnect the gearchange rod

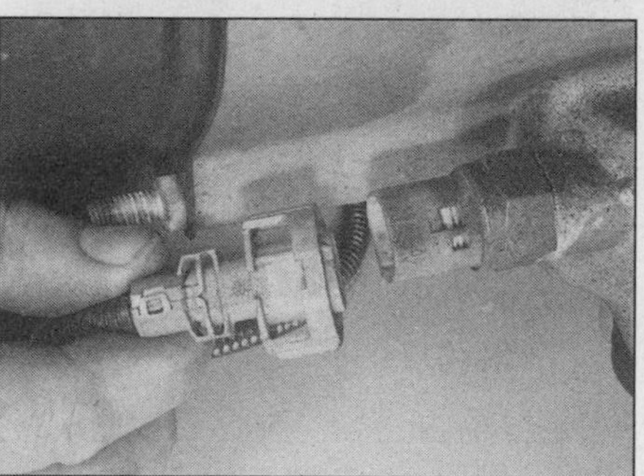
4.23 Disconnecting the wiring from the reversing light switch

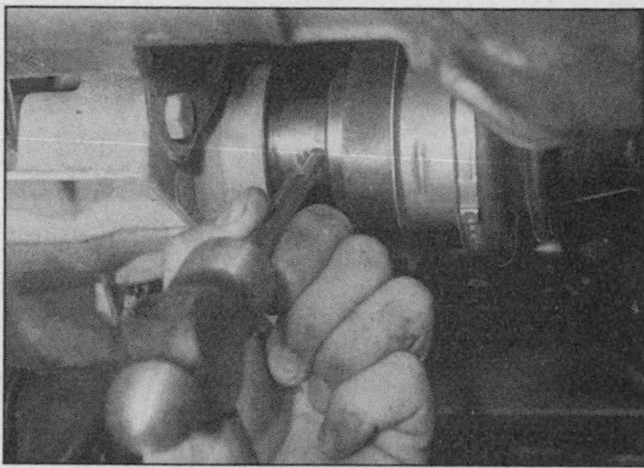
4.15b Using a punch to drive out the driveshaft roll pin

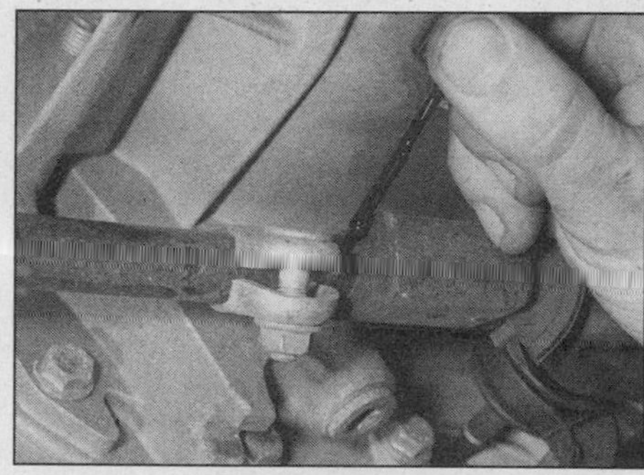
4.20b ... then mark the position of the gearchange rod clamp with paint ...

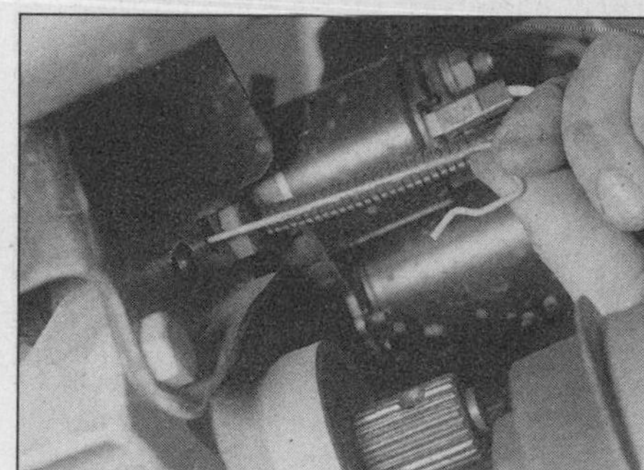
4.22a Pull out the spring clip ...

4.24 Removing the power-assisted steering pump and fluid reservoir from the bracket on the engine

4.25 Power steering pump location

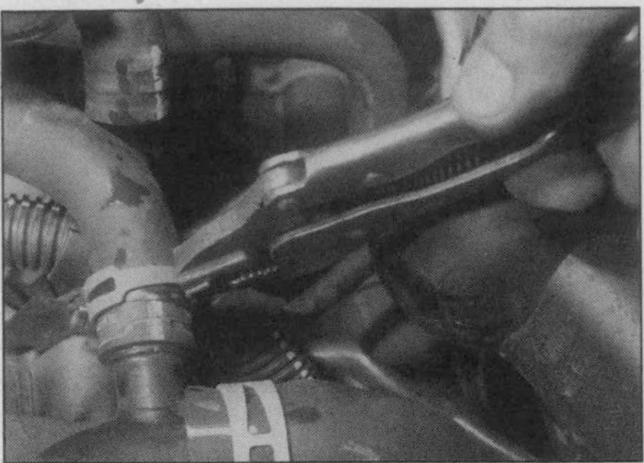
4.28 Disconnecting the heater hose from the coolant pipe – note the use of pliers to compress the hose retaining clip

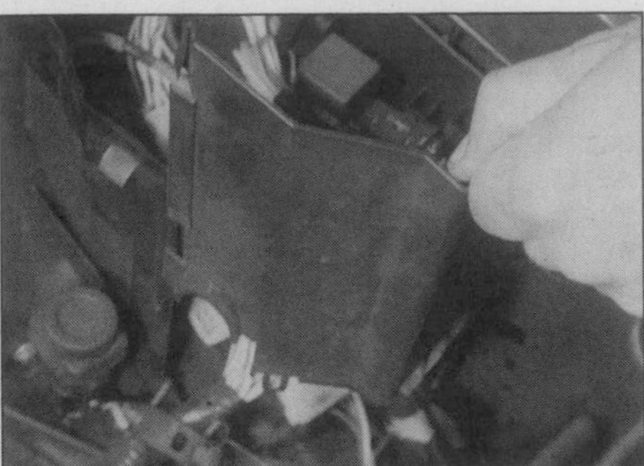
4.30a Remove the covers . . .

remove the power-assisted steering pump pulley and position the pump and air conditioning compressor to one side **(see illustration)**, but leave the hoses attached. **Do not** open any refrigerant lines. Alternatively, if preferred, disconnect the power-assisted steering pump hoses and drain the fluid into a suitable container – if this method is used the power steering pump can remain on the engine.

26 Disconnect the accelerator cable from the throttle body with reference to Chapter 4A.

27 Disconnect the clutch cable from the transmission with reference to Chapter 6.

28 Disconnect the remaining hoses from the thermostat housing and/or the coolant pipe (as applicable) on the left-hand side of the engine. These include the coolant expansion tank hose and the heater hoses **(see illustration)**.

29 Unbolt the coolant expansion tank and tie it to the left-hand side of the engine compartment.

4.30b . . . and disconnect the wiring from the relay box

30 Remove the top and side covers from the relay box on the left-hand side of the engine compartment, then release the relay plate and wiring cable-ties and position the wiring on the engine **(see illustrations)**.

31 Disconnect the wiring from the radiator fan and thermostatic switch.

32 Disconnect the brake vacuum servo unit hose from the inlet manifold.

33 Disconnect the manifold absolute pressure sensor hose from the inlet manifold and disconnect the sensor wiring.

34 Unscrew the mounting nuts and remove the engine management system control unit from the right-hand side of the engine compartment. Tie the control unit on top of the engine to prevent it being damaged when the assembly is lifted out.

35 Loosen the clips and disconnect the fuel supply and return hoses from the throttle body housing or fuel rail.

36 Unbolt the earth cable from the bulkhead.

37 Disconnect the evaporative carbon canister hose from the solenoid valve on the inlet manifold.

38 Disconnect the wiring from the ignition amplifier module on the bulkhead, or the ignition HT coils on the cylinder head.

39 Disconnect the starter main supply cable from the battery. To do this, remove the battery (Chapter 5A) and disconnect the wiring at the connector box, then release the cable from the cover/grommet in the engine compartment bulkhead panel. Also disconnect the fuel injection feed wire. On Scénic models, unbolt the battery secondary terminal unit in the engine compartment and move it to one side.

40 Unscrew the engine/transmission front lower mounting nuts and recover the spacer plate from the right-hand mounting.

41 Connect a hoist to the engine lifting eyes and take the weight of the engine/transmission assembly.

42 Unscrew the bracket bolts and through-bolt from the engine/transmission rear mounting. Lift the assembly slightly and remove the rear mounting bracket.

43 With the help of an assistant, slowly lift the engine/transmission assembly from the engine compartment, taking care not to damage any components on the surrounding panels. When high enough, lift the assembly over the body front panel and lower to the ground.

44 If the engine is to be overhauled, remove the wiring loom from the engine, noting the location and routing of each part **(see illustrations)**.

2.0 litre models

Note: *The engine is lowered downwards from the engine compartment together with the gearbox, then separated on the bench. Some assistance will be required.*

45 Carry out the preliminary dismantling operations described in paragraphs 1 to 23 above. Remove the left- and right-hand front wheelarch liners.

46 On models fitted with air conditioning,

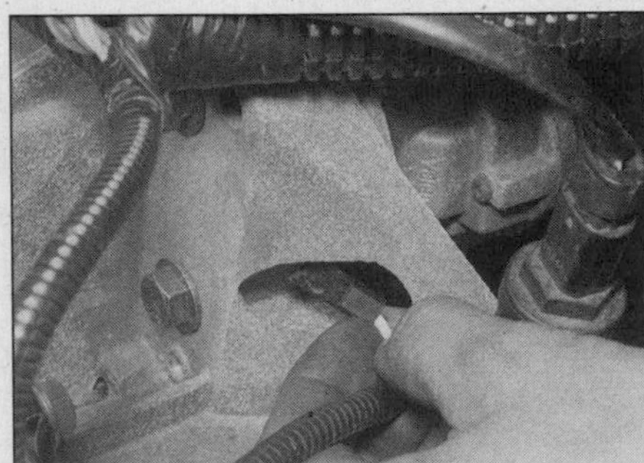
4.44a Disconnecting the wiring from the starter motor . . .

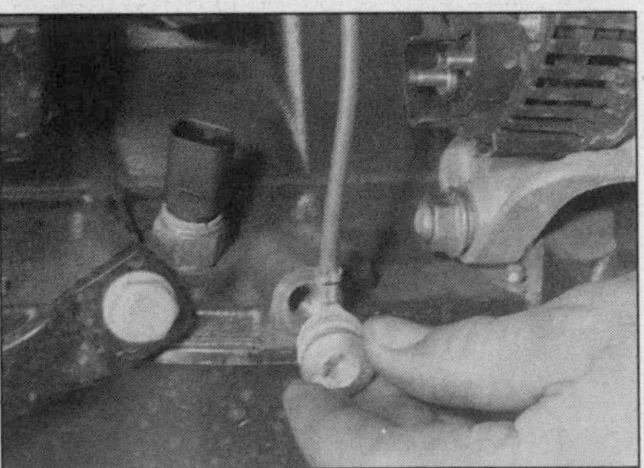
4.44b . . . the earth wire from the cylinder block . . .

4.44c . . . and the loom support from the transmission

disconnect the wiring from the pressure switch and from the compressor.

47 Where applicable, disconnect the power-assisted steering pressure switch.

48 Disconnect the accelerator cable from the throttle housing with reference to Chapter 4A.

49 Disconnect the clutch cable from the transmission with reference to Chapter 6.

50 Disconnect the heater hoses from the heater matrix unions on the bulkhead.

51 Disconnect the remaining coolant hoses from the thermostat housing.

52 Disconnect its coolant hoses and unbolt the coolant expansion tank, then tie it to the left-hand side of the engine compartment.

53 Remove the top and side covers from the relay box on the left-hand side of the engine compartment, then release the relay plate and wiring cable-ties and position the wiring on the engine.

54 Disconnect the wiring from the radiator fan and thermostatic switch.

55 Disconnect the brake vacuum servo unit hose from the inlet manifold.

56 Disconnect the manifold absolute pressure sensor hose from the inlet manifold and disconnect the sensor wiring.

57 Unscrew the mounting nuts and remove the engine management system control unit from the right-hand side of the engine compartment. Tie the control unit on top of the engine to prevent it being damaged when the assembly is lifted out.

58 Loosen the clips and disconnect the fuel supply and return hoses from the fuel rail. Where applicable, release the pipes from the clips on the timing belt intermediate outer cover.

59 Unbolt the earth cable from the bulkhead.

60 Disconnect the evaporative carbon canister hose from the solenoid valve on the inlet manifold.

61 Disconnect the wiring from the ignition HT coils on the cylinder head.

62 Disconnect the starter main supply cable from the battery. To do this, remove the battery (Chapter 5A) and disconnect the wiring at the connector box, then release the cable from the cover/grommet in the engine compartment bulkhead panel. Also disconnect the fuel injection feed wire. On early Scénic models, unbolt the battery secondary terminal unit in the engine compartment and move it to one side.

63 Remove the auxiliary drivebelt as described in Chapter 1A.

64 Remove the pulley from the power-assisted steering pump with reference to Chapter 10.

65 Unscrew the three power-assisted steering pump mounting bolts and where applicable, the four air conditioning compressor mounting bolts. Position to one side the pump and compressor, but do not disconnect the fluid pipes or refrigerant lines. However, if preferred, the power steering pump can remain on the engine if the fluid hoses are disconnected and the fluid drained into a suitable container.

66 Unclip the air conditioning system low-pressure refrigerant line from the engine/transmission lower mounting.

67 Slacken the engine/transmission right- and left-hand front mounting nuts to remove them (see Chapter 2B).

68 Connect a hoist to the engine lifting eyes and take the weight of the engine/transmission assembly.

69 Unscrew (but do not remove) the nut from the rear bolt of the engine/transmission rear mounting link, then unscrew and remove the link front bolt. Also unbolt the rear mounting bracket from the transmission.

70 With the steering gear in the straight-ahead position, unscrew and remove the eccentric bolt securing the bottom of the steering inner column to the steering gear, and separate the column (refer to Chapter 10 for more information) from the steering gear.

Caution: It is important that the airbag rotary switch beneath the steering wheel is not damaged. Before removing the column the steering wheel must be immobilised with the wheels straight using a steering wheel locking tool.

71 Unscrew the four subframe-to-underbody bolts at the subframe corners so that the subframe is lowered in a safe and controllable fashion by 10 mm from the underbody mounting points.

72 Slacken the bolts securing the two strengthening brackets to the underbody.

73 Unscrew as far as possible the steering gear mounting bolts. The two strengthening brackets must be left in place.

74 Unbolt the supports securing the power-assisted steering fluid pipe to the subframe.

75 Remove its mounting bolts and tie the steering gear as high as possible, clear of the subframe.

76 Unbolt and remove the heat shields from underneath the gearlever, then unhook the return spring from the gearchange rod.

77 Swing the rod around to the rear and secure it.

78 Remove the horn.

79 Remove the crankshaft speed/position sensor, disconnect its wiring and release the wiring from the subframe.

80 Prepare a wheeled engine removal dolly with wooden blocks to take the subframe and ensure that the engine/transmission assembly is securely supported on the subframe – wedge wooden blocks in place as necessary. Renault mechanics will have access to the special wheeled cradle (Renault tool Mot. 1040-01) and support tools Mot. 1159 and Mot. 1159-02 – if these can be borrowed or hired, they will obviously make the operation easier and safer.

81 Unscrew the subframe-to-underbody bolts, noting the location of spacers and washers. Don't forget to remove the power-assisted steering pipe bolts to the subframe.

82 With the help of several assistants, lift the vehicle body to clear the assembly, then release the handbrake and move the vehicle away. Two of the assistants must support the struts and care must be taken not to damage any components on the surrounding panels. With the vehicle clear of the assembly, carefully lower it to the ground and apply the handbrake.

83 Make a final check that all components have been removed or disconnected which might prevent or hinder the removal of the engine/transmission assembly. Remove the assembly from the subframe.

Refitting

84 Refitting is a reversal of removal, with reference to the Chapters needed for removal, but tighten all nuts and bolts to the specified torque. On 2.0 litre models, when attaching the subframe to the underbody, the use of 100 mm long rods temporarily screwed into the nuts will help alignment of the bolt holes. With the front of the subframe aligned, the rear bolts can be inserted, then the temporary rods can be removed and the front bolts inserted. Refer to Chapter 10 when connecting the steering column to the steering gear. Top-up the power steering fluid level as described in *Weekly checks.* Fill the engine with fresh oil and fill the cooling system with coolant with reference to Chapter 1A. Before taking the vehicle on the road, depress the brake pedal several times to bring the brake pads to their normal position.

5 Petrol engine and automatic transmission – removal and refitting

Removal

Note: *Renault recommend that the engine is removed downwards from the engine compartment together with the automatic transmission. The help of several assistants will be required to lift the body upwards over the assembly.*

1 Disconnect the battery negative lead (refer to Chapter 5A).

2 Remove the radiator with reference to Chapter 3.

3 Drain the automatic transmission fluid with reference to Chapter 1A.

4 If necessary, drain the engine oil with reference to Chapter 1A.

5 Remove the bonnet with reference to Chapter 11.

6 Apply the handbrake, then jack up the front of the car and support it on axle stands (see *Jacking and vehicle support*). Remove both front roadwheels. Where fitted, remove the engine compartment undershield.

7 Remove the left- and right-hand front wheelarch liners.

8 Unbolt the subframe-to-body support rods from each side of the vehicle.

9 Unbolt the front brake calipers from the swivel hubs with reference to Chapter 9 and support them on axle stands or tie them to the body.

10 On models fitted with ABS, unbolt the wheel sensors and remove them from the swivel hubs.

11 Remove the front bumper as described in Chapter 11.

12 Remove the exhaust front downpipe and catalytic converter, referring to Chapter 4A.

13 Remove the horn with reference to Chapter 12.

14 Remove the air cleaner assembly with reference to Chapter 4A.

15 Unbolt the earth cable from the bulkhead.

16 Disconnect the manifold absolute pressure sensor hose from the inlet manifold and disconnect the wiring from the sensor.

17 Remove the coolant expansion tank and attach it to the engine/transmission assembly.

18 Disconnect the accelerator cable from the throttle housing.

19 Disconnect the wiring from the kickdown switch.

20 Disconnect the brake vacuum servo unit hose from the inlet manifold.

21 Remove the top and side covers from the relay box on the left-hand side of the engine compartment, then release the relay plate and wiring cable-ties and position the wiring on the engine.

22 Disconnect the wiring from the automatic transmission control unit on the left-hand side of the engine compartment.

23 Disconnect the evaporative carbon canister hose from the solenoid valve on the inlet manifold.

24 Disconnect the starter main supply cable from the battery. To do this, remove the battery (Chapter 5A) and disconnect the wiring at the connector box, then release the cable from the cover/grommet in the engine compartment bulkhead panel. Also disconnect the fuel injection feed wire.

25 Loosen the clips and disconnect the fuel supply and return hoses from the fuel rail.

26 Disconnect the heater hoses from the thermostat housing.

27 Disconnect the selector control from the transmission (see Chapter 7B).

28 Remove the auxiliary drivebelt (see Chapter 1A).

29 Remove the pulley from the power-assisted steering pump with reference to Chapter 10.

30 Unscrew the three power-assisted steering pump mounting bolts and where applicable, the four air conditioning compressor mounting bolts. Position to one side the pump and compressor, but do not disconnect the fluid pipes or refrigerant lines.

31 Unclip the air conditioning system low-pressure refrigerant line from the engine/transmission lower mounting.

32 Remove the left-hand engine/ transmission mounting. First wedge a block of wood between the transmission and the left-hand side of the subframe to support the weight of the transmission. Where applicable, unscrew the nut from the top of the mounting then using a soft-faced mallet tap the mounting stud to release it.

33 Remove the right-hand engine/transmission mounting.

34 Connect a hoist to the engine lifting eyes and take the weight of the engine/ transmission assembly.

35 Unscrew (but do not remove) the nut from the rear bolt of the engine/transmission rear mounting link, then unscrew and remove the link front bolt. Also unbolt the rear mounting bracket from the transmission.

36 With the front wheels in the straight-ahead position, working in the engine compartment pull back the rubber grommet then unscrew the eccentric bolt securing the bottom of the steering inner column to the steering gear and separate the column (refer to Chapter 10 for more information) **(see illustration)**.

Caution: It is important that the airbag rotary switch beneath the steering wheel is not damaged. Before removing the column the steering wheel must be immobilised with the wheels straight using a steering wheel locking tool.

37 Unscrew the four subframe-to-underbody bolts at the subframe corners so that the subframe is lowered in a safe and controllable fashion by 10 mm from the underbody mounting points.

38 Slacken the bolts securing the two strengthening brackets to the underbody.

39 Unscrew as far as possible the steering gear mounting bolts. The two strengthening brackets must be left in place.

40 Unbolt the supports securing the power-assisted steering fluid pipe to the subframe.

41 Remove its mounting bolts and tie the steering gear as high as possible, clear of the subframe.

42 Refer to Chapter 7B, Section 5, and disconnect the selector cable from the transmission.

43 Remove the crankshaft speed/position sensor, disconnect its wiring and release the wiring from the subframe.

44 Prepare a wheeled engine removal dolly with wooden blocks to take the subframe and ensure that the engine/transmission assembly is securely supported on the subframe – wedge wooden blocks in place as necessary. Renault mechanics will have access to the special wheeled cradle (Renault tool Mot. 1040-01) and support tools Mot. 1159 and Mot. 1159-02 – if these can be borrowed or hired, they will obviously make the operation easier and safer.

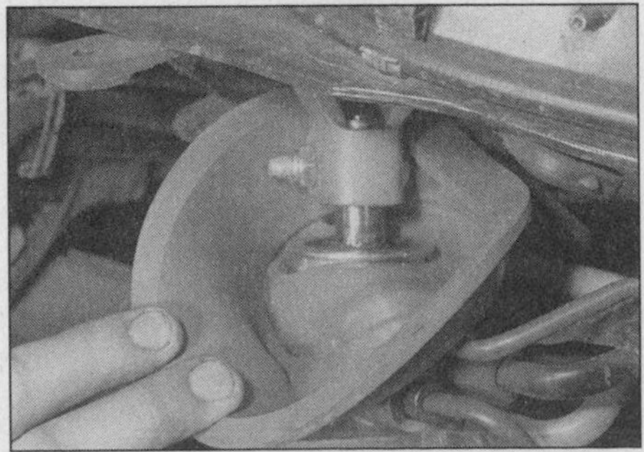

5.36 Pull back the rubber grommet, then remove the bolt securing the bottom of the steering inner column to the steering gear

45 Unscrew the subframe-to-underbody bolts, noting the location of spacers and washers. Don't forget to remove the power-assisted steering pipe bolts to the subframe.

46 Unscrew the front suspension strut upper mounting bolts from the turrets.

47 With the help of several assistants, lift the vehicle body to clear the assembly, then release the handbrake and move the vehicle away. Two of the assistants must support the struts and care must be taken not to damage any components on the surrounding panels.

48 With the vehicle clear of the assembly, carefully lower it to the ground and apply the handbrake.

49 Have an assistant move the tops of the suspension struts outwards while the driveshafts are released from the transmission. Support the driveshafts making sure that the CV joints are not angled excessively.

50 Make a final check that all components have been removed or disconnected which might prevent or hinder the removal of the engine/transmission assembly. Remove the assembly from the subframe.

Refitting

51 Refitting is a reversal of removal, with reference to the Chapters needed for removal, but tighten all nuts and bolts to the specified torque. When attaching the subframe to the underbody, the use of 100 mm long rods temporarily screwed into the nuts will help alignment of the bolt holes. With the front of the subframe aligned, the rear bolts can be inserted, then the temporary rods can be removed and the front bolts inserted. Refer to Chapter 10 when connecting the steering column to the steering gear. Top-up the power steering fluid level as described in *Weekly checks*. Fill the engine with fresh oil and fill the cooling system with coolant with reference to Chapter 1A. Fill the automatic transmission with fresh fluid with reference to Chapter 7B. Before taking the vehicle on the road, depress the brake pedal several times to bring the brake pads to their normal position.

6 Diesel engine and gearbox – removal and refitting

Note: *Renault recommend that the engine is removed downwards from the engine compartment together with the transmission and subframe. The engine/transmission can then be removed from the subframe and the transmission separated from the engine. The first sub-Section (except F9Q 732 engines) describes lowering the engine together with the subframe, however, the sub-Section for the F9Q 732 engine describes removal of the subframe before lowering the engine and transmission to the floor.*

Except F9Q 732 engine

Removal

1 Disconnect the battery negative lead (refer to Chapter 5A).

2 Remove the radiator with reference to Chapter 3. Also disconnect the top hose from the thermostat housing and the bottom hose from the coolant pipe.

3 Drain the manual gearbox oil with reference to Chapter 7A.

4 If necessary, drain the engine oil with reference to Chapter 1B.

5 Remove the bonnet with reference to Chapter 11.

6 Remove the air cleaner assembly and air duct with reference to Chapter 4B. On turbo models, remove the air ducting connecting the intercooler to the turbocharger and inlet manifold. Disconnect the coolant hoses on the turbocharger.

7 Apply the handbrake, then jack up the front of the car and support it on axle stands (see *Jacking and vehicle support*). Remove both front roadwheels. Where fitted, remove the engine compartment undershield.

8 Remove the front wheelarch liners from both sides.

9 Remove the auxiliary drivebelt as described in Chapter 1B.

10 On models fitted with air conditioning, remove the compressor with reference to Chapter 3, but leave the hoses attached and position the pump to one side. **Do not** open any refrigerant lines.

11 Remove the oil filter as described in Chapter 1B.

12 Remove the power-assisted steering pump and fluid reservoir from the engine with reference to Chapter 10, but do not disconnect the fluid pipes. Position the pump to one side.

13 Identify then disconnect the heater hoses from the thermostat housing on the left-hand side of the cylinder head.

14 Disconnect the brake vacuum servo unit hose from the inlet manifold on the left-hand side of the cylinder head.

15 Disconnect the pipes and wiring from the fast idle and EGR solenoid valves. On F9Q engines, disconnect the injection pump wiring harness at the injection control unit and all relevant sensor wiring connectors attached to the engine wiring harness.

16 On F8Q engines, remove the pre/post-heating control unit and tie it to the engine (refer to Chapter 5C).

17 Disconnect the accelerator cable (where fitted) and clutch cable from the engine with reference to Chapters 4B and 6.

18 On non-turbo models, disconnect the wiring from the altitude sensor corrector.

19 Remove the top and side covers from the relay box on the left-hand side of the engine compartment; release the relay plate and wiring cable-ties and place the wiring on the engine.

20 Squeeze the connector and disconnect the fuel supply pipe from the fuel filter. Disconnect the wiring from the fuel filter.

21 Detach the fuel return union from the injection pump.

22 Unbolt the earth strap from the bulkhead.

23 Where applicable, unbolt the strengthening bar from between the front suspension strut turrets.

24 Remove the battery as described in Chapter 5A. On Scénic models, unbolt the battery secondary terminal unit in the engine compartment and move it to one side.

25 Disconnect the starter main cable and the pre/post-heating cable from the wiring connector on the right-hand side of the battery compartment.

26 Unscrew the nut from the left-hand track rod end and disconnect it from the swivel hub steering arm using a balljoint separator tool.

27 Unscrew the bolts securing the left-hand driveshaft inner rubber boot and metal ring to the transmission.

28 Unscrew the two mounting bolts securing the left-hand brake caliper to the swivel hub and disconnect the pad wear warning wiring. Tie the caliper to the coil spring, taking care not to strain the hose.

29 Unscrew and remove fully the pinch-bolt securing the left-hand front lower arm balljoint to the swivel hub.

30 Unscrew and remove fully both bolts securing the front suspension left-hand strut to the swivel hub (note that the nuts are on the rear of the carrier).

31 Lever the suspension lower arm downwards, then pull the driveshaft from the sun-gear and withdraw it with the swivel hub.

32 Make sure that the tripod components remain in position on the inner end of the driveshaft, otherwise they may fall into the transmission. There may be some loss of oil from the gearbox, so position a small container on the floor to catch it.

33 Working beneath the car, drive out the roll pin (where fitted) securing the right-hand driveshaft to the differential sun-gear shaft **(see illustration)**. Note that if the original double roll pin is renewed, the new one will be of single coiled type.

34 Unscrew the nut from the right-hand track rod end and disconnect it from the swivel hub steering arm using a balljoint separator tool.

35 Unscrew and remove fully the upper bolt securing the front suspension right-hand strut to the swivel hub (note that the nut is on the rear of the carrier). Loosen only (do not remove) the lower bolt.

36 Pull out the driveshaft and disconnect the inner end from the splines on the transmission sun-gear shaft. Tie the driveshaft to the steering gear. **Note:** *Where an intermediate bearing is fitted, remove the driveshaft completely.*

37 Remove the exhaust front downpipe as described in Chapter 4B.

38 Undo the screws and remove the plastic cover from the bottom of the transmission, then mark the position of the gearchange main rod on the clevis at the rod's transmission end, loosen the clamp bolt and disconnect the two sections of the rod.

39 Where applicable, detach the power-assisted steering hydraulic fluid pipes from the transmission.

40 Pull out the spring clip and remove the vehicle speed sensor from the rear of the transmission.

41 Disconnect the wiring from the reversing light switch on the transmission.

42 Disconnect the oil cooler pipes located beneath the oil filter.

43 Connect a hoist to the engine lifting eyes and take the weight of the engine/transmission assembly.

44 Unscrew (but do not remove) the nut from the rear bolt of the engine/transmission rear mounting link, then unscrew and remove the link front bolt. Note which way round the shock absorber is, then unbolt it from the top of the rear mounting. Also unbolt the rear mounting bracket from the transmission.

45 Remove the engine right-hand mounting plastic cover. Unscrew the nuts securing the engine mounting/right-hand mounting rubber to the engine and body. Remove the rubber from the mounting.

46 Unscrew the nuts securing the engine mounting/left-hand mounting rubber to the transmission and body, as well as the strengthening bracket nut. Remove the rubber from the mounting.

47 With the steering gear in the straight-ahead position, unscrew and remove the eccentric bolt securing the bottom of the steering inner column to the steering gear, and separate the column (refer to Chapter 10 for more information) from the steering gear.

Caution: It is important that the airbag rotary spring beneath the steering wheel is not damaged. Before removing the column the steering wheel must be immobilised with the wheels straight using a steering wheel locking tool.

48 Unscrew the four subframe-to-underbody bolts at the subframe corners so that the subframe is lowered in a safe and controllable

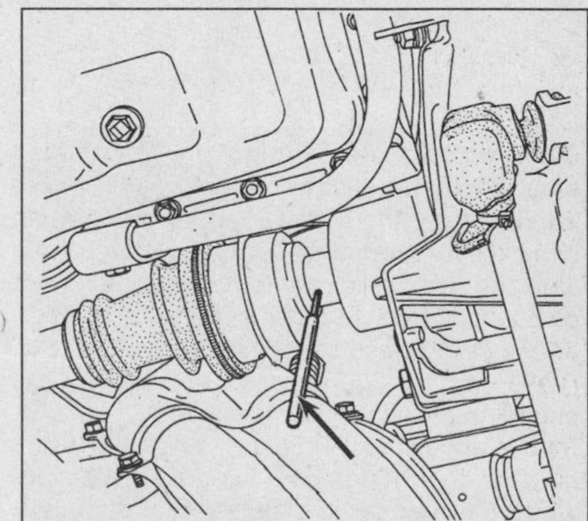

6.33 Using a pin punch (arrowed) to drive out the driveshaft roll pin

6.60 Separating the gearbox from the engine

6.62 Battery tray

fashion by 10 mm from the underbody mounting points.

49 Slacken the bolts securing the two strengthening brackets to the underbody.

50 Unscrew as far as possible the steering gear mounting bolts. The two strengthening brackets must be left in place.

51 Unbolt the supports securing the power-assisted steering fluid pipe to the subframe.

52 Remove its mounting bolts and tie the steering gear as high as possible, clear of the subframe.

53 Unbolt and remove the heat shields from underneath the gearlever, then unhook the return spring from the gearchange rod.

54 Swing the rod around to the rear and secure it.

55 Remove the crankshaft speed/position sensor, disconnect its wiring and release the wiring from the subframe.

56 Remove the horn.

57 Prepare a wheeled engine removal dolly with wooden blocks to take the subframe and ensure that the engine/transmission assembly is securely supported on the subframe – wedge wooden blocks in place as necessary. Renault mechanics will have access to the special wheeled cradle (Renault tool Mot. 1040-01) and support tools Mot. 1159 and Mot. 1159-02 – if these can be borrowed or hired, they will obviously make the operation easier and safer.

58 Unscrew the subframe-to-underbody bolts, noting the location of spacers and washers. Don't forget to remove the power-assisted steering pipe bolts to the subframe.

59 With the help of several assistants, lift the vehicle body to clear the assembly, then release the handbrake and move the vehicle away. Two of the assistants must support the struts and care must be taken not to damage any components on the surrounding panels. With the vehicle clear of the assembly, carefully lower it to the ground and apply the handbrake.

60 Make a final check that all components have been removed or disconnected which might prevent or hinder the removal of the engine/transmission assembly. Remove the assembly from the subframe, and separate the gearbox from the engine with reference to Chapter 7A **(see illustration)**.

Refitting

61 Refitting is a reversal of removal, with reference to the Chapters needed for removal, but tighten all nuts and bolts to the specified torque. When attaching the subframe to the underbody, the use of 100 mm long rods temporarily screwed into the nuts will help alignment of the bolt holes. With the front of the subframe aligned, the rear bolts can be inserted, then the temporary rods can be removed and the front bolts inserted. Refer to Chapter 10 when connecting the steering column to the steering gear. Top-up the power steering fluid level as described in *Weekly checks.* Fill the engine with fresh oil, the cooling system with coolant and the transmission with fresh fluid with reference to Chapter 1A. Prime and bleed the fuel system as described in Chapter 4B. On turbo models, before starting the engine ensure that the lubrication system has been primed as described in Chapter 4B, Section 30. Before taking the vehicle on the road, depress the brake pedal several times to bring the brake pads to their normal position.

F9Q 732 engine

Removal

62 Disconnect the battery negative lead then remove the battery and tray (refer to Chapter 5A) **(see illustration)**.

63 Apply the handbrake, then jack up the front of the vehicle and support it on axle stands (see *Jacking and vehicle support*). Remove the front roadwheels and the engine undertray. Also remove the engine top cover **(see illustrations)**.

64 Drain the cooling system by disconnecting the radiator bottom hose from the water pump inlet tube on the front of the cylinder block (refer to Chapter 1B if necessary). The hose clips are of the spring type and are difficult to remove. It is possible to release them with large pliers, however, a simple removal tool can be made out of a worm-drive clip **(see illustrations)**.

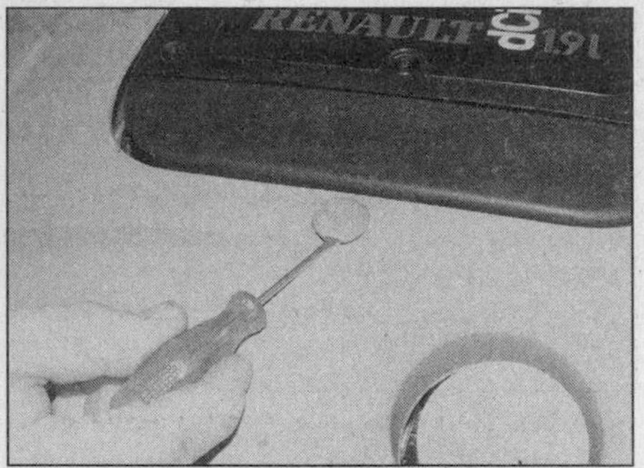

6.63a Prise out the covers . . .

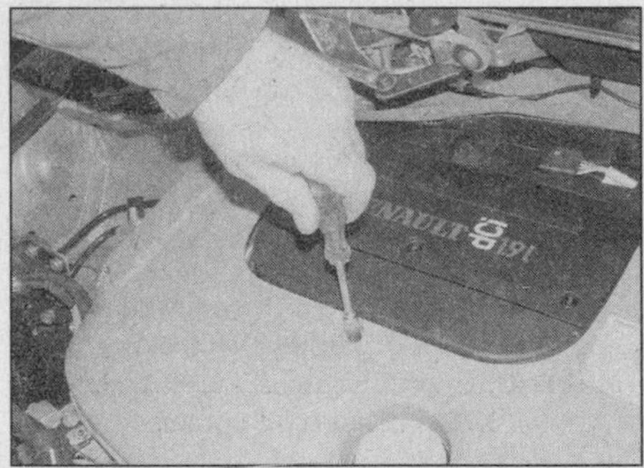
6.63b . . . undo the screws . . .

6.63c . . . and remove the engine top cover

6.64a Using a home-made tool to release the hose clips

6.64b Disconnecting the radiator bottom hose from the water pump inlet tube

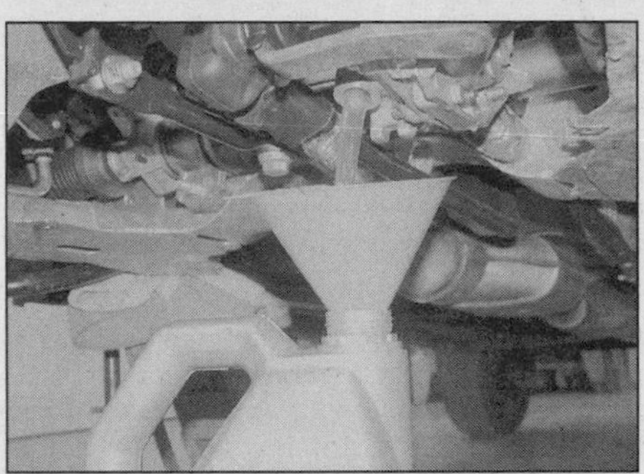
6.66 Draining the transmission oil

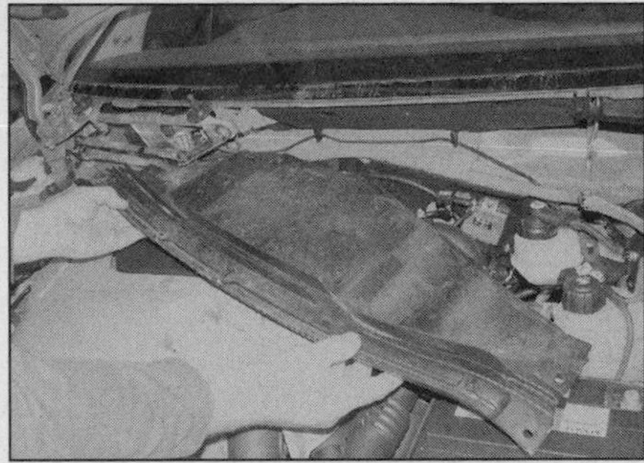
6.67 Removing the plenum cover on Scénic models

6.68 Disconnecting the crankcase ventilation hose from the oil separator

65 If necessary, drain the engine and transmission oil with reference to Chapter 1B **(see illustration)**.

66 On Scénic models, remove the windscreen wiper arms and the grilles from the heater air intake, then remove the plenum cover from just in front of the windscreen **(see illustration)**.

67 Remove the air cleaner assembly and inlet ducting with reference to Chapter 4B.

68 Disconnect the crankcase ventilation hose from the oil separator **(see illustration)**.

69 Remove the ducting from between the turbocharger and intercooler.

70 Disconnect the hoses from the expansion tank, thermostat housing and oil cooler **(see illustrations)**.

71 Remove the electric cooling fan and radiator as described in Chapter 3. Note that the air conditioning drier unit is attached to the electric cooling fan and must be tied to one side away from the engine **(see illustrations)**. Also the power steering fluid reservoir must be tied to one side.

72 Remove the front sections of the wheelarch liners on both sides.

73 Remove the front bumper as described in Chapter 11.

74 Remove the horn with reference to Chapter 12.

75 Release the power-assisted steering hydraulic fluid hoses from the subframe. Also unbolt the support **(see illustration)**.

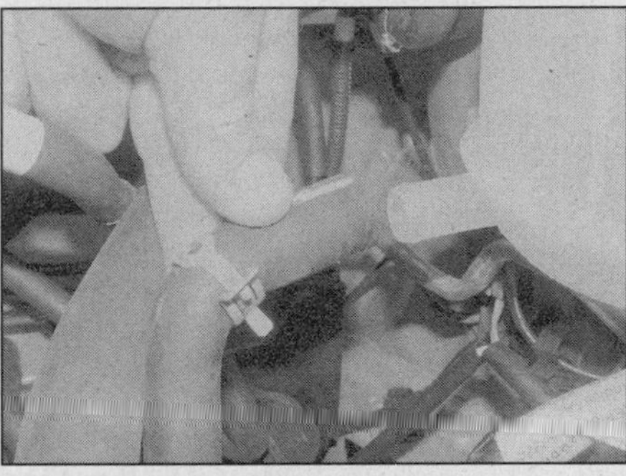
6.70a Disconnecting the hoses from the expansion tank . . .

6.70b . . . thermostat housing . . .

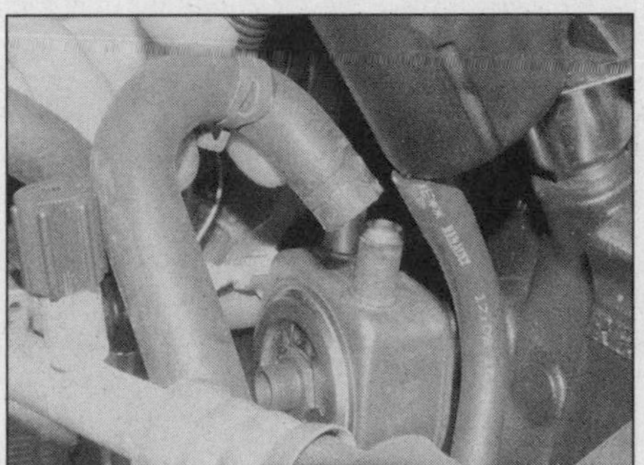
6.70c . . . and oil cooler

6.71a Removing the electric cooling fan . . .

2D

6.71b . . . and radiator

6.71c Air conditioning drier unit mounting on the electric cooling fan unit

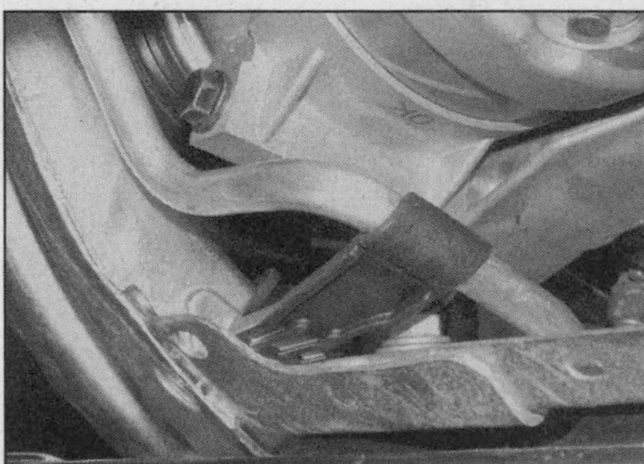
6.75 Power steering hydraulic fluid line support on the subframe

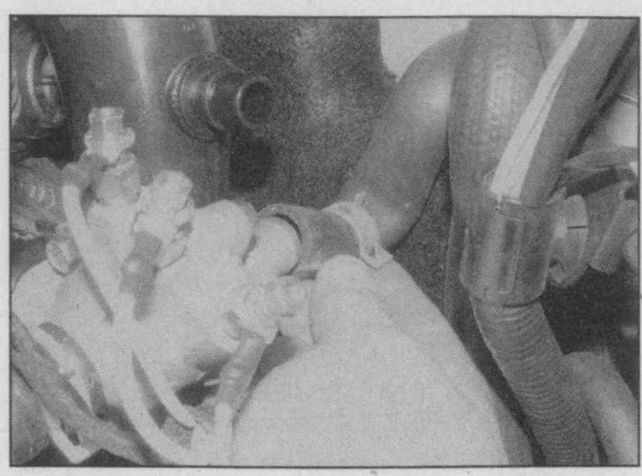

6.76a Disconnecting the wiring from the electric coolant heater on the left-hand side of the cylinder head

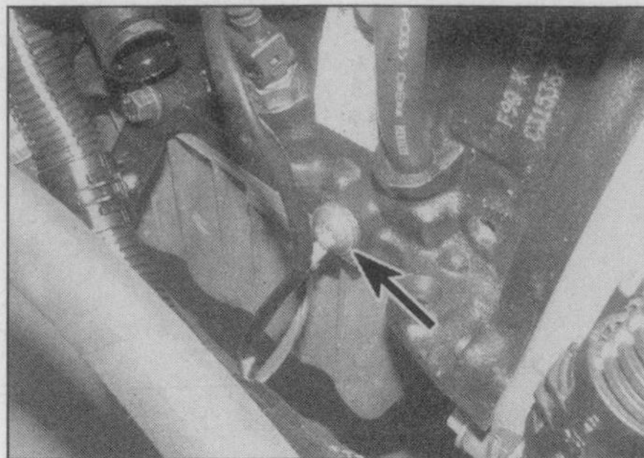

6.76b Earth cable on the front of the cylinder block

6.76c Fuel cut-off inertia switch

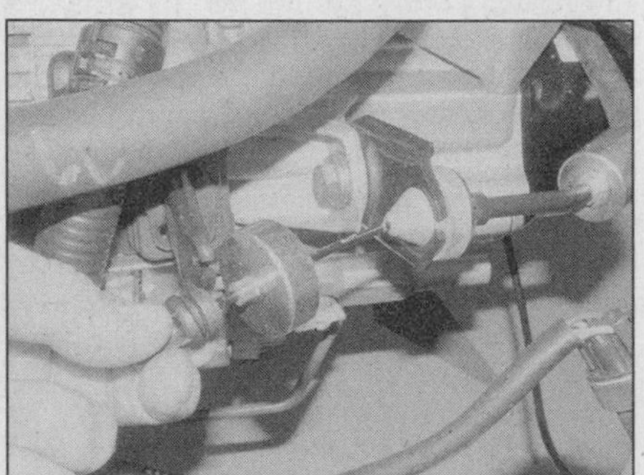

6.77 Disconnecting the clutch cable from the release lever on the transmission

6.78a Disconnecting the outlet line from the power steering pump

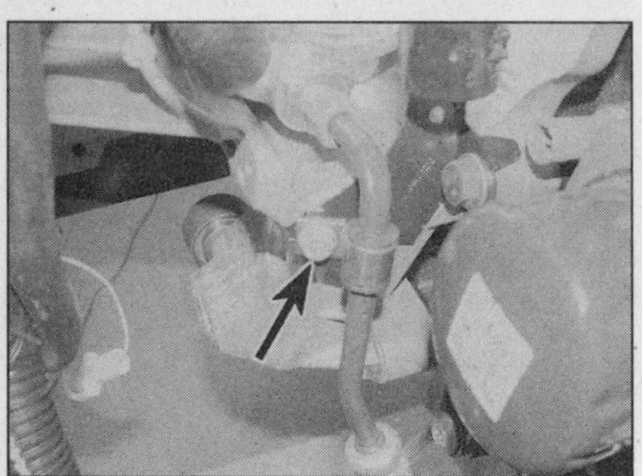

6.78b Power steering fluid line support

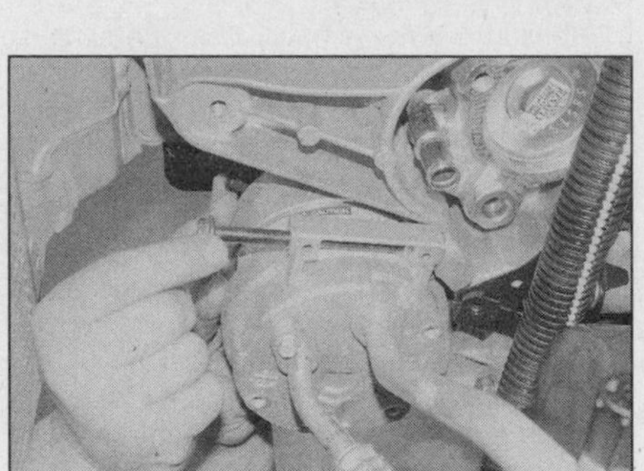

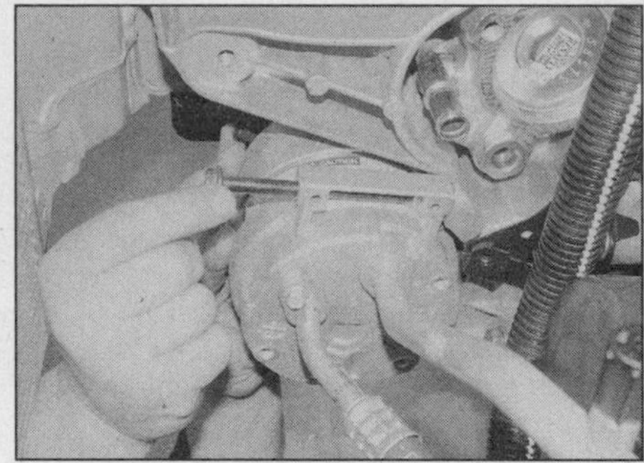

6.79a Unscrew the air conditioning compressor mounting bolts . . .

76 Disconnect the wiring from the post/pre-heating control unit, inertia switch and map sensor on the bulkhead. Also disconnect the wiring from the electric coolant heater unit on the left-hand side of the cylinder head, and unbolt the earth cable from the front of the cylinder block **(see illustrations)**.

77 Disconnect the clutch cable from the gearbox with reference to Chapter 6 **(see illustration)**.

78 Position a container beneath the power steering pump location on the front of the engine, then disconnect the hydraulic fluid lines from the pump and allow the fluid to completely drain. The outlet line is attached with a union nut **(see illustration)** but the inlet line is attached with a hose clamp. Also unbolt the line support **(see illustration)**, and move the line to one side.

79 On models equipped with air conditioning, the manufacturer recommends that the refrigerant is discharged from the system, however, an alternative method is to unbolt the compressor from the engine and tie it to one side **(see illustrations)**.

80 Unbolt the tie rods from the subframe and underbody.

81 Detach the left-hand steering track rod end from the hub carrier with reference to Chapter 10 **(see illustrations)**.

82 Refer to Chapter 9 and unbolt the left-hand brake caliper and mounting bracket from

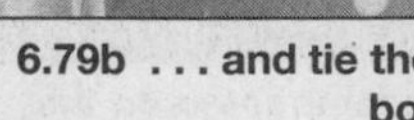

6.79b . . . and tie the compressor to the body

6.81a Unscrew the nuts . . .

6.81b . . . then use a balljoint separator tool to disconnect the steering track rod ends from the hub carriers

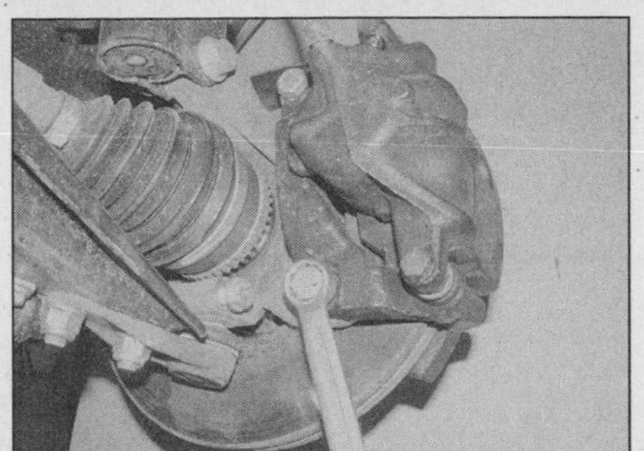

6.82a Unbolting the brake calipers and mounting brackets from the hub carriers

6.82b Removing the ABS sensors from the hub carriers

their hub carrier. **Note:** *If only the caliper is removed, there is insufficient room to remove the balljoint clamp bolt.* Where applicable, remove the ABS sensor as well. Tie the caliper and bracket to the front suspension coil spring making sure that the flexible hose is not damaged or strained **(see illustrations)**.

83 Unscrew and remove the bolts securing the left-hand driveshaft gaiter to the transmission.

84 Unscrew and remove the clamp bolt securing the left-hand lower balljoint to the bottom of the hub carrier, then lever down the lower arm and disconnect the balljoint from the carrier. If possible, retain the lower arm down to prevent damage to the driveshaft gaiter.

85 Unscrew and remove the bolts securing the left-hand hub carrier to the bottom of the front suspension strut **(see illustration)**. Release the carrier from the strut, then withdraw it together with the left-hand driveshaft and place it away from the vehicle. Check that the driveshaft inner joint roller bearings are all in position – if the joint is worn excessively, the rollers may become detached.

86 Refer to Chapter 9 and unbolt the right-hand front brake caliper together with the bracket from the hub carrier without disconnecting the hydraulic brake line. Suspend the caliper from the suspension coil spring using wire. **Note:** *If only the caliper is removed, there is insufficient room to remove the balljoint clamp bolt.*

87 Remove the right-hand ABS sensor from the hub carrier with reference to Chapter 9.

88 Disconnect the right-hand track rod end from the steering arm on the hub carrier with reference to Chapter 10.

89 Unscrew and remove the clamp bolt securing the right-hand lower ball joint to the bottom of the hub carrier, then lever down the lower arm and disconnect the balljoint from the carrier. If possible, retain the lower arm down to prevent damage to the driveshaft gaiter.

90 Where applicable (early models), remove the roll pin securing the inner end of the driveshaft to the differential sun-gear.

91 Where applicable (models with an intermediate bearing), unbolt the intermediate bearing retainer from the rear of the cylinder block. Unscrew and remove the bolts securing the right-hand hub carrier to the bottom of the front suspension strut. Release the carrier from the strut, then withdraw it together with the right-hand driveshaft and place it away from the vehicle. Refer to Chapter 8 if necessary.

92 Disconnect the exhaust from the exhaust manifold/catalytic converter with reference to Chapter 4B.

93 Unbolt the subframe support tie rods on each side, and either remove them completely or leave the lower bolts loose and swivel down the rods.

94 Release the wiring loom from the clips on the left-hand side of the subframe. Also unbolt the earth cable from the transmission.

95 Unbolt the power steering pipe mountings from the right-hand side of the subframe and from behind the steering gear.

96 Unbolt the heat shield from under the gearlever.

97 Disconnect the return spring (where fitted) then undo the screws and remove the plastic cover from the bottom of the transmission. Mark the position of the gearchange main rod on the clevis at the rod's transmission end, loosen the clamp bolt and disconnect the two sections of the rod **(see illustrations 4.20a, 4.20b and 4.20c)**. In order to move the gearchange rod to one side, unbolt the exhaust heatshields from the underbody.

98 Unscrew and remove the bolt securing the rear engine mounting link to the transmission, then loosen the link bolt on the subframe and swivel the link to the rear.

99 Where applicable, unscrew the nuts and remove the heat shield from the steering gear.

100 Make sure that the steering wheel is in its central position with the front wheels facing straight-ahead.

Caution: To prevent possible damage to the airbag rotary spring, tie the steering wheel in its central position.

101 Unscrew the bolts/nuts securing the steering gear to the rear of the subframe. Remove the mounting clamps and carefully prise the steering gear away from the subframe.

102 Tie the track rod ends to the front suspension coils on each side in order to support the steering gear while the subframe is being lowered.

103 Use trolley jacks or axle stands to support the weight of the front subframe, then unscrew and remove the subframe mounting bolts and lower the unit to the floor.

104 Withdraw the subframe from under the vehicle **(see illustration)**.

105 Disconnect the wiring from the reversing light switch and speedometer sender (if fitted) on the transmission. Where applicable on early models, disconnect the speedometer cable.

106 Disconnect the wiring from the injectors, high pressure pump, oil pressure sender, coolant temperature sender and oil level sender. Also unbolt the crankshaft speed/position (TDC) sensor from the top of the gearbox bellhousing. Position the wiring to one side **(see illustrations)**.

107 Where applicable, unbolt the power steering hydraulic fluid pipe supports from the transmission. Tie the pipe to one side so that it will not interfere with the removal of the engine/transmission.

108 Disconnect the brake vacuum hose from the inlet manifold.

6.85 Removing the bolts securing the struts to the hub carriers

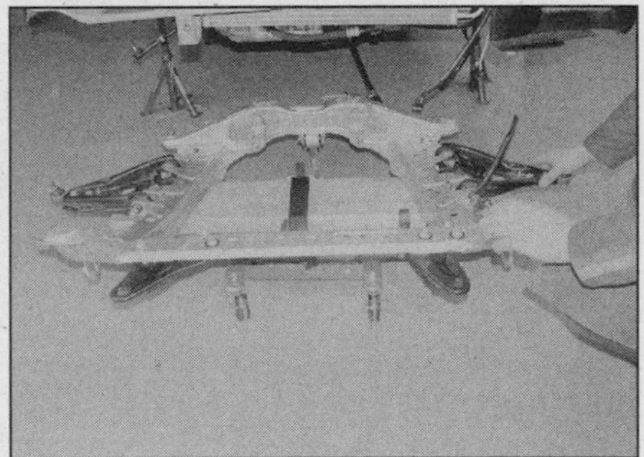

6.104 Removing the subframe from under the vehicle

6.106a Oil level sender located on the front of the cylinder block (F9Q 732 engine)

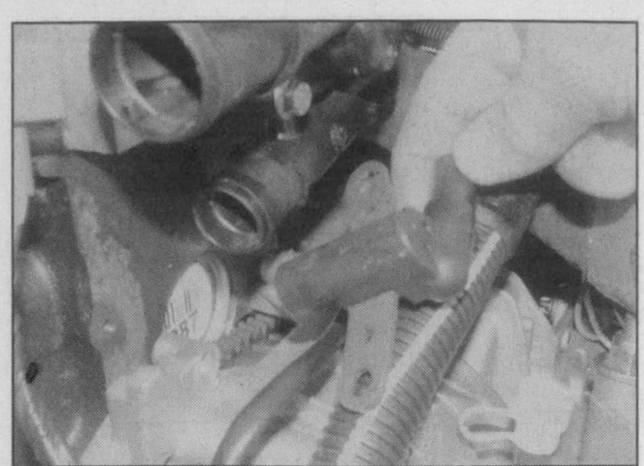
6.106b Removing the TDC sensor from the top of the gearbox bellhousing

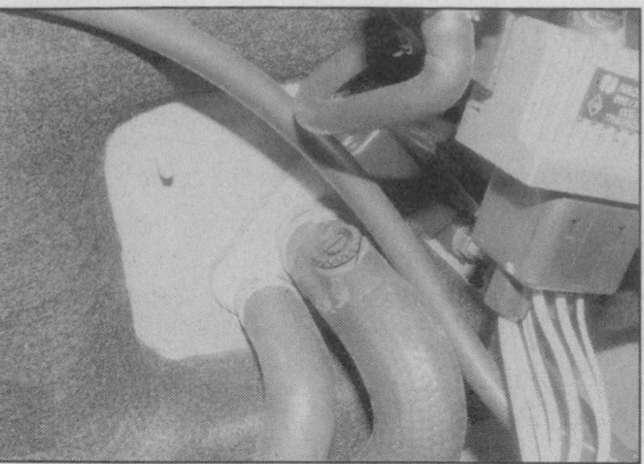
6.109 Disconnect the heater hose on the bulkhead

6.113a Left-hand engine mounting

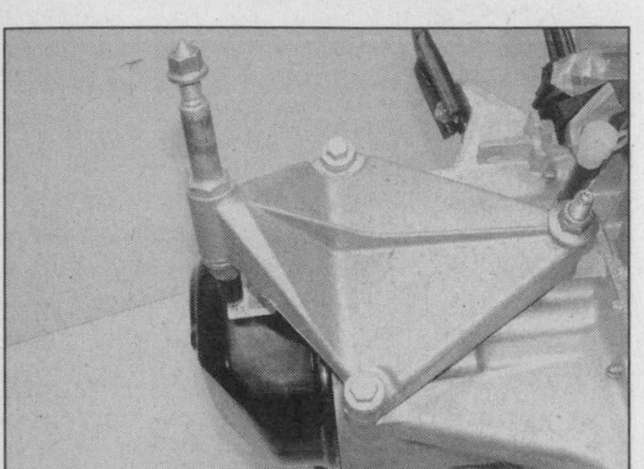
6.113b Engine mounting bracket on the transmission

109 Loosen the clips and disconnect the hoses on the bulkhead from the heater matrix pipes **(see illustration)**.

110 Disconnect the vacuum hoses from the fuel cut-off inertia switch and map sensor on the bulkhead.

111 Disconnect the fuel pipes from the fuel filter and high pressure pump.

112 Attach a suitable hoist to the engine/transmission assembly and just take its weight. The lifting chain should be arranged on the lifting eyes so that the engine/transmission is level.

113 Unbolt and remove the right-hand engine mounting cover, and similarly unscrew the centre nut from the left-hand engine/transmission mounting. Also unbolt the left-hand mounting from the body, but leave the lower section of the mounting on the transmission **(see illustrations)**.

114 Make a final check that all components have been removed or disconnected which might prevent or hinder the removal of the engine/transmission assembly. Make sure that all relevant wiring has also been disconnected.

115 With the help of an assistant, lower the engine/transmission from the vehicle body to the floor, making sure that it clears the surrounding components in the engine bay. Protect the air conditioning condenser by placing a piece of card over it.

116 Separate the gearbox from the engine with reference to Chapter 7A.

Refitting

117 Refitting is a reversal of removal, with reference to the Chapters needed for removal, but tighten all nuts and bolts to the specified torque. When attaching the subframe to the underbody, the use of 100 mm long rods temporarily screwed into the nuts will help alignment of the bolt holes. With the front of the subframe aligned, the rear bolts can be inserted, then the temporary rods can be removed and the front bolts inserted. Top-up the power steering fluid level as described in *Weekly checks*. Fill the engine with fresh oil, the cooling system with coolant and the transmission with fresh fluid with reference to Chapter 1B. Prime and bleed the fuel system as described in Chapter 4B. On turbo models, before starting the engine ensure that the lubrication system has been primed as described in Chapter 4B, Section 30. Before taking the vehicle on the road, depress the brake pedal several times to bring the brake pads to their normal position.

7 Engine overhaul – dismantling sequence

1 It is much easier to disassemble and work on the engine if it is mounted on a portable engine stand. These stands can often be hired from a tool hire shop. Before the engine is mounted on a stand, the flywheel/driveplate should be removed from the engine, so that the engine stand bolts can be tightened into the end of the cylinder block.

2 If a stand is not available, it is possible to disassemble the engine with it blocked up on a sturdy workbench or on the floor. Be extra careful not to tip or drop the engine when working without a stand.

3 If you are going to obtain a reconditioned engine, all the external components must be removed first, and be transferred to the replacement engine (just as they will if you are doing a complete engine overhaul yourself). Check with the engine supplier for details. Normally these components include:

Petrol engine models

a) Alternator and brackets ***(see illustration).***
b) HT leads and spark plugs (see Chapters 1A and 5B).
c) Thermostat and cover (see Chapter 3).
d) Fuel injection equipment.
e) Inlet and exhaust manifolds.
f) Oil filter ***(see illustration).***
g) Engine mountings, lifting brackets and hose brackets **(see illustration)**.

7.3a Alternator on the K4M engine

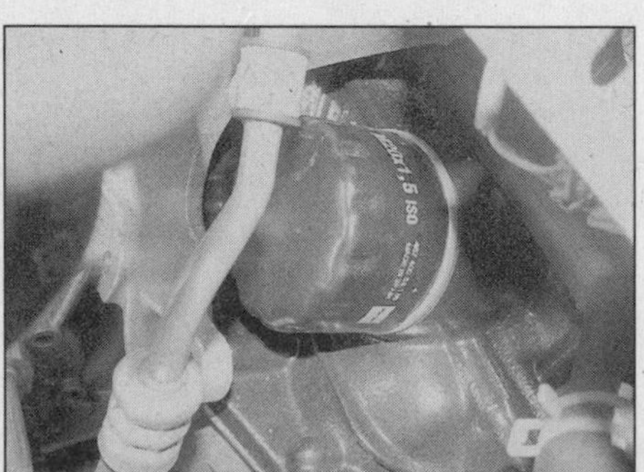
7.3b Oil filter location on the K4M engine

7.3c Removing the front engine lifting bracket

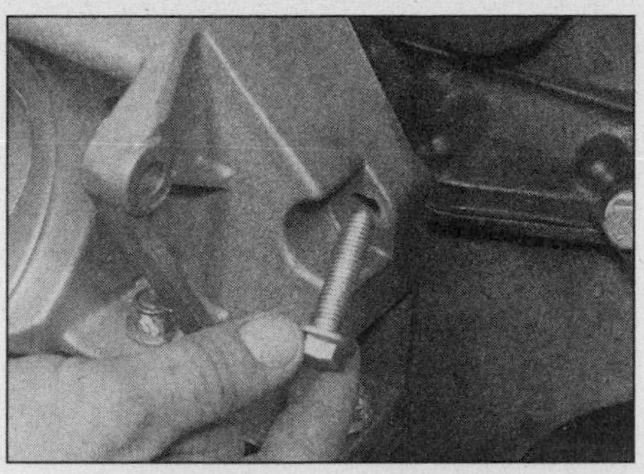

7.3d Removing the power-assisted steering pump bracket from the engine

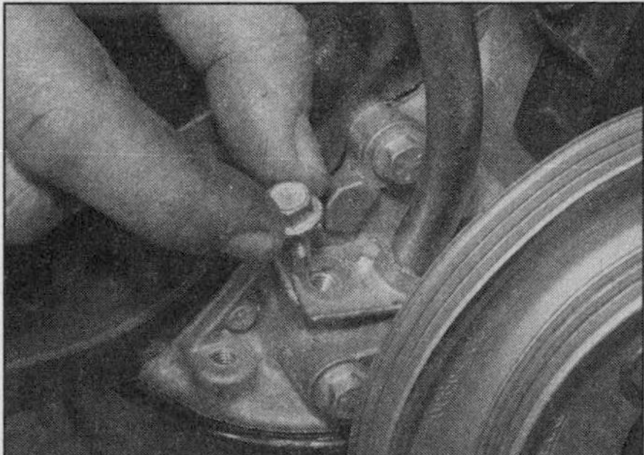

7.3e Unscrew the bolt . . .

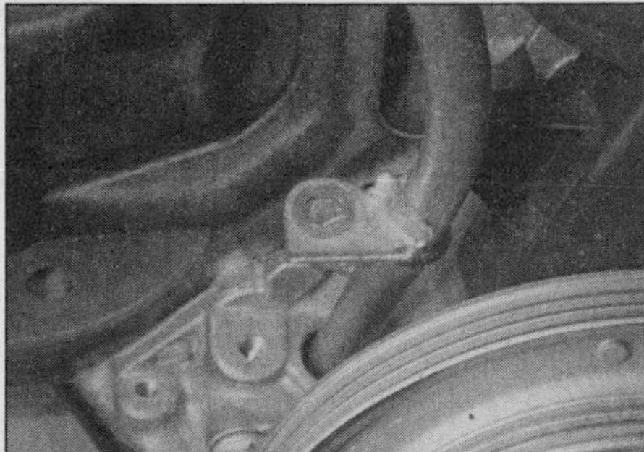

7.3f . . . lift the oil filler tube and dipstick from the front cover . . .

h) Ancillary (power steering pump, air conditioning compressor) brackets **(see illustration)**.
i) Oil filler tube and dipstick **(see illustrations)**.
j) Coolant pipes and hoses **(see illustration)**.
k) Flywheel (or driveplate where applicable) (see Chapter 2A or 2B).

Diesel engine models

a) Alternator mounting bracket.
b) Fuel injection pump and mounting bracket/high pressure pump, fuel injectors and glow plugs (see Chapters 4B and 5C).
c) Thermostat and cover (see Chapter 3).
d) Turbocharger, where applicable (see Chapter 4B).
e) Inlet and exhaust manifolds (see Chapter 4B).
f) Oil filter and cooler (see Chapter 2C) ***(see illustration)****.*
g) Engine mountings, lifting brackets and hose brackets.
h) Ancillary (power steering pump, air conditioning compressor) brackets ***(see illustrations)****.*
i) Oil pressure warning light switch and oil level sensor (where applicable) (see Chapter 5A).
j) Coolant temperature sensors (see Chapter 3).
k) Wiring harnesses and brackets.
l) Oil filler tube and dipstick.
m) Coolant pipes and hoses (see Chapter 3).
n) Flywheel (see Chapter 2C).

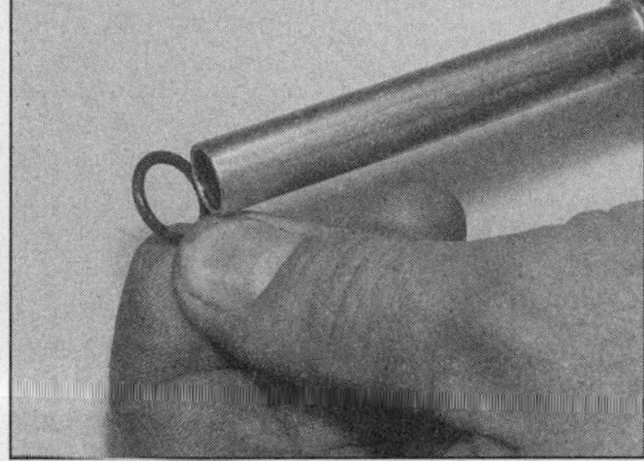

7.3g . . . and remove the sealing O-ring

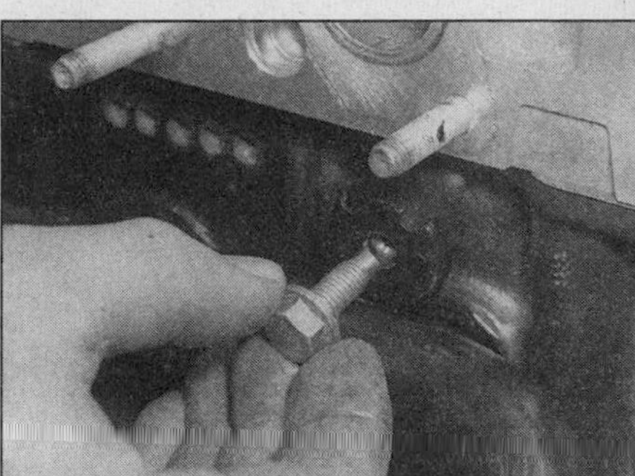

7.3h Unbolting the coolant pipe from the cylinder block

7.3i Oil filter and cooler on the F9Q 732 engine

7.3j Remove the power steering pump pulley . . .

7.3k . . . then unbolt the wiring loom bracket . . .

7.3l . . . unbolt the power steering pump . . .

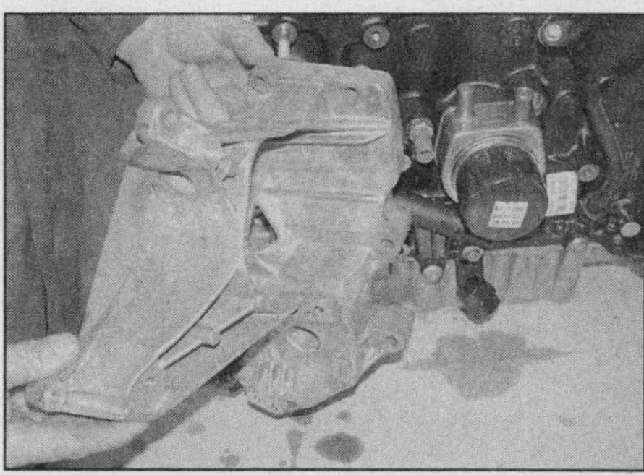

7.3m . . . and unbolt the mounting bracket

7.5a Unbolting the water pump from the cylinder block (petrol engine)

7.5b Removing the water pump (diesel engine)

7.5c Removing the cylinder head

All engine models

Note: *When removing the external components from the engine, pay close attention to details that may be helpful or important during refitting. Note the fitted position of gaskets, seals, spacers, pins, washers, bolts and other small items.*

4 If you are obtaining a 'short' motor (which, when available, consists of the engine cylinder block, crankshaft, pistons and connecting rods all assembled), then the cylinder head, sump, oil pump and timing belt will have to be removed also.

5 If you are planning a complete overhaul, the engine can be disassembled and the internal components removed in the following order:

a) Inlet and exhaust manifolds.
*b) Timing belt and pulleys and water pump **(see illustrations)**.*
*c) Cylinder head **(see illustration)**.*
d) Flywheel/driveplate.
e) Pistons.
f) Crankshaft.

6 Before beginning the disassembly and overhaul procedures, make sure that you have all of the correct tools necessary. Refer to the *Tool and working facilities* at the end of this manual for further information.

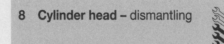

8 Cylinder head – dismantling

Note: *New and reconditioned cylinder heads are available from the manufacturers and from engine overhaul specialists. Due to the fact that some specialist tools are required for the dismantling and inspection procedures and new components may not be readily available, it may be more practical and economical for the home mechanic to purchase a reconditioned head rather than dismantle, inspect and recondition the original head.*

Petrol engines

1 Referring to Chapter 2A or 2B, as applicable, remove the camshaft(s).

Diesel engines

2 Remove the right-hand engine mounting bracket, brake vacuum pump (see Chapter 9), the fuel injectors, the thermostat housing, the injection pump or high pressure pump (as applicable), if removed with the cylinder head (Chapter 4B), and the camshaft and followers (Chapter 2C). Also where necessary, unbolt the upper inner timing cover and engine lifting eye bracket **(see illustrations)**.

8.2a Right-hand engine mounting bracket on the cylinder head

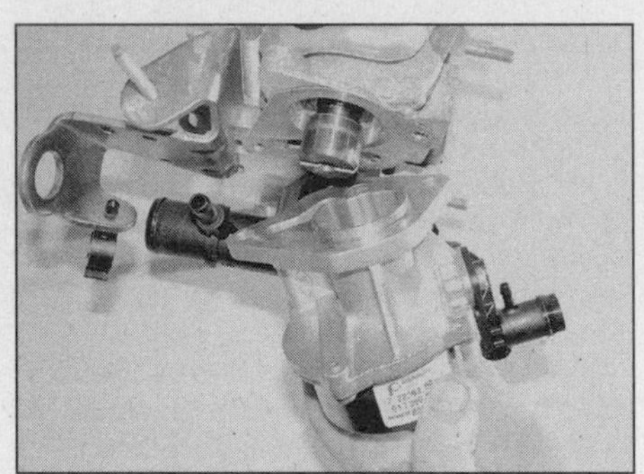
8.2b Removing the brake vacuum pump . . .

8.2c . . . and gasket

8.2d Thermostat housing on the left-hand end of the cylinder head

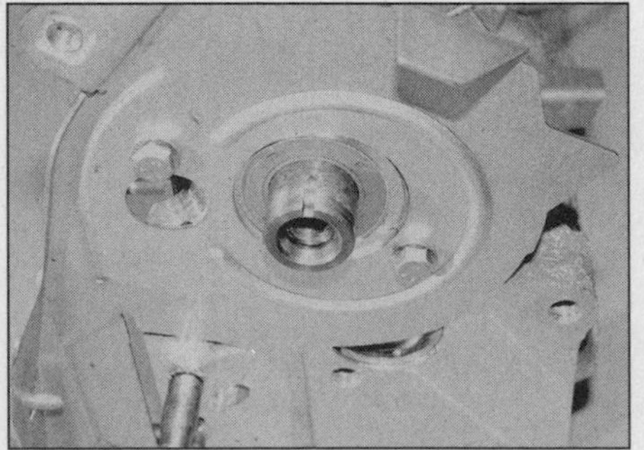
8.2e Bolts securing the upper inner timing cover to the cylinder head

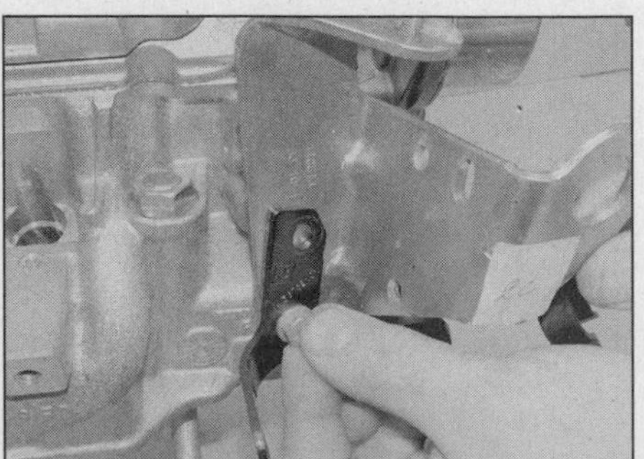
8.2f Unbolting the engine lifting eye bracket

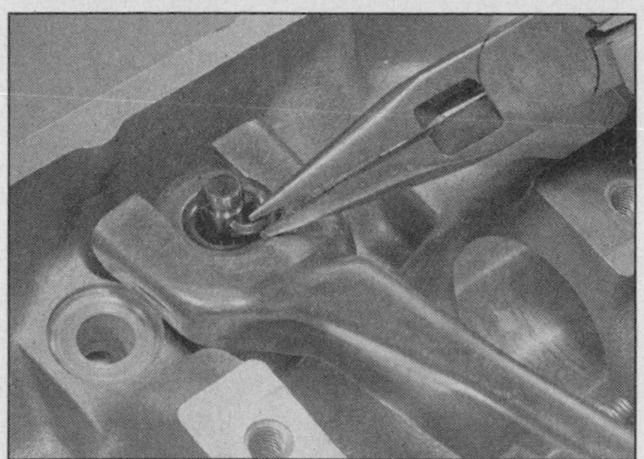
8.3a Removing the split collets . . .

8.3b . . . and lift off the cap and valve spring . . .

8.3c . . . followed by the spring seat

All engines

3 Using a valve spring compressor, compress each valve spring in turn until the split collets can be removed. Release the compressor and lift off the cap, spring and spring seat. If, when the valve spring compressor is screwed down, the valve spring cap refuses to free and expose the split collets, gently tap the top of the tool, directly over the cap, with a light hammer. This will free the cap **(see illustrations)**.

4 Withdraw the oil seal from the top of the valve guide, then remove the valve through the combustion chamber **(see illustrations)**.

5 It is essential that the valves and associated components are kept in their correct sequence, unless they are so badly worn that they are to be renewed. If they are going to be kept and used again, place them in labelled polythene bags, or in a compartmented box **(see illustrations)**.

8.4a Removing the oil seal from the top of the valve guide

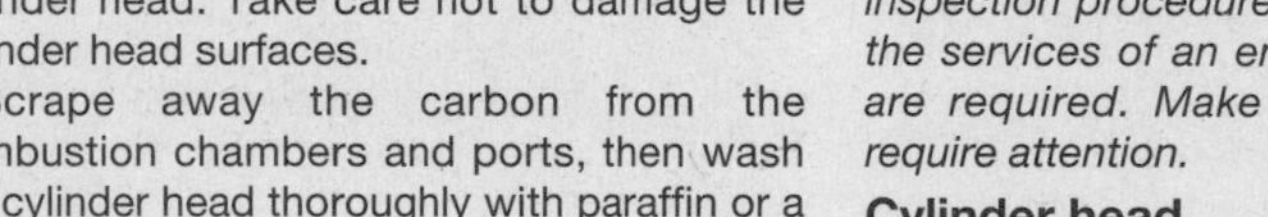
8.4b Withdrawing a valve from the combustion chamber

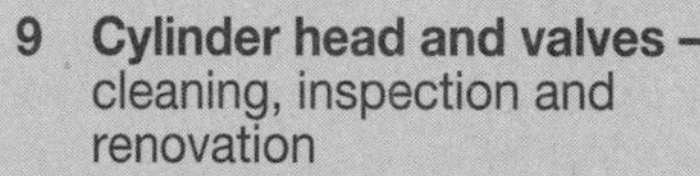

9 Cylinder head and valves – cleaning, inspection and renovation

1 Thorough cleaning of the cylinder head and valve components, followed by a detailed inspection, will enable you to decide how much valve service work must be carried out during the engine overhaul.

Cleaning

2 Scrape away all traces of old gasket material and sealing compound from the cylinder head. Take care not to damage the cylinder head surfaces.

3 Scrape away the carbon from the combustion chambers and ports, then wash the cylinder head thoroughly with paraffin or a suitable solvent.

4 Scrape off any heavy carbon deposits that may have formed on the valves, then use a power-operated wire brush to remove deposits from the valve heads and stems.

5 On F8Q engines, the swirl chambers should be removed from their locations if they are loose (if this is done, mark the swirl chambers so that they can be refitted in their original locations) **(see illustration)**.

6 If the head is extremely dirty, it should be steam-cleaned. On completion, make sure that all oil holes and oil galleries are cleaned.

Inspection and renovation

Note: *Be sure to perform all the following inspection procedures before concluding that the services of an engine overhaul specialist are required. Make a list of all items that require attention.*

Cylinder head

7 Inspect the head very carefully for cracks, evidence of coolant leakage and other damage. If cracks are found, a new cylinder head should be obtained.

8 Use a straight-edge and feeler gauge to check that the cylinder head surface is not distorted. On F8Q engines, do not position the straight-edge over the swirl chambers, as these may be proud of the cylinder head face. If the specified distortion limit is exceeded, machining of the gasket face is not recommended by the manufacturers, so the only course of action is to renew the cylinder head. Check that the overall height of the cylinder head is as specified, which will

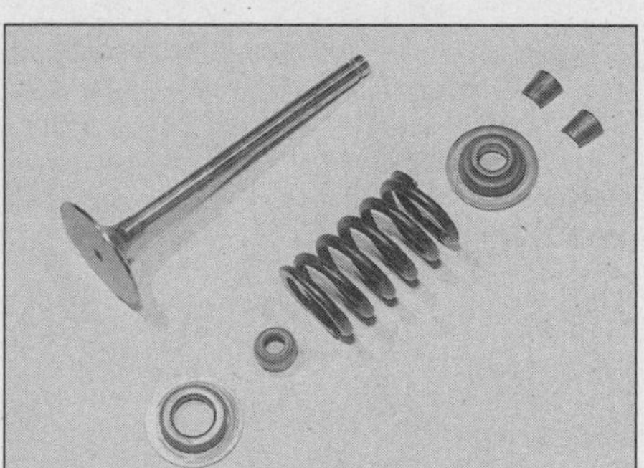
8.5a Valve components

8.5b Store the valve components in a labelled polythene bag

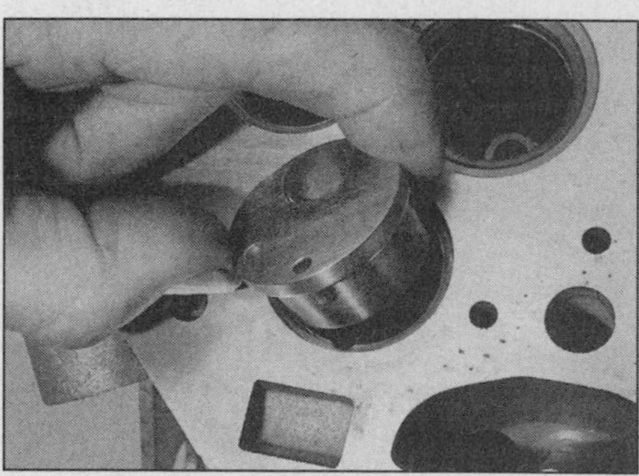
9.5 Removing a swirl chamber (F8Q engine)

2D

9.8a Checking the cylinder head surface for distortion with feeler blades

9.8b Checking the overall height of the cylinder head (F8Q engine)

9.9a Measuring the valve depth with a dial gauge . . .

indicate if the head has been machined in a mistaken attempt to compensate for surface distortion **(see illustrations)**.

9 Examine the valve seats in each of the combustion chambers. If they are severely pitted, cracked or burned, then they will need to be renewed or recut by an engine overhaul specialist. If they are only slightly pitted, this can be removed by grinding the valve heads and seats together with coarse, then fine, grinding paste as described below. Note that on diesel engines the valve seats can only be recut to a limited depth, to avoid decreasing the compression ratio. Using a dial test indicator, check that valve depth below (or above) the cylinder head gasket surface is within the limits given in the Specifications **(see illustration)**.

10 If the valve guides are worn, indicated by a side-to-side motion of the valve in the guide, new guides must be fitted. A dial gauge may be used to determine the amount of side play of the valve. Recheck the fit using a new valve if in doubt, to decide whether it is the valve or the guide which is worn. If new guides are to be fitted, the valves must be renewed in any case. Valve guides may be renewed using a press and a suitable mandrel, making sure that they are at the correct height. The work is best carried out by an engine overhaul specialist, since if it is not done skillfully, there is a risk of damaging the cylinder head.

11 On F8Q engines, inspect the swirl chambers for burning or cracks. If required, the chambers can be renewed by an engine overhaul specialist. Using a dial test indicator check that the swirl chamber protrusion is within the limits given in the Specifications. Zero the dial test indicator on the gasket surface of the cylinder head, then measure the protrusion of the swirl chamber **(see illustrations)**.

12 Where applicable, check the follower bores in the cylinder head for wear. If excessive wear is evident, the cylinder head must be renewed.

13 Examine the camshaft bearing surfaces in the cylinder head (and bearing caps/carriers where applicable). Wear here can only be corrected by renewing the head. Also examine the camshaft as described in Chapter 2A, 2B or 2C.

Valves

14 Examine the head of each valve for pitting, burning, cracks and general wear, and check the valve stem for scoring and wear ridges. Rotate the valve and check for any obvious indication that it is bent. Look for pits and excessive wear on the end of each valve stem. If the valve appears satisfactory at this stage, measure the valve stem diameter at several points using a micrometer **(see illustration)**. Any significant difference in the readings obtained indicates wear of the valve stem. Should any of these conditions be apparent, the valve(s) must be renewed. If the valves are in satisfactory condition, or if new valves are being fitted, they should be ground (lapped) into their respective seats to ensure a smooth gas-tight seal.

15 Valve grinding is carried out as follows. Place the cylinder head upside-down on a bench, with a block of wood at each end to give clearance for the valve stems.

16 Smear a trace of coarse carborundum paste on the seat face and press a suction grinding tool onto the valve head. With a semi-rotary action, grind the valve head to its seat, lifting the valve occasionally to redistribute the grinding paste **(see illustration)**. When a dull-

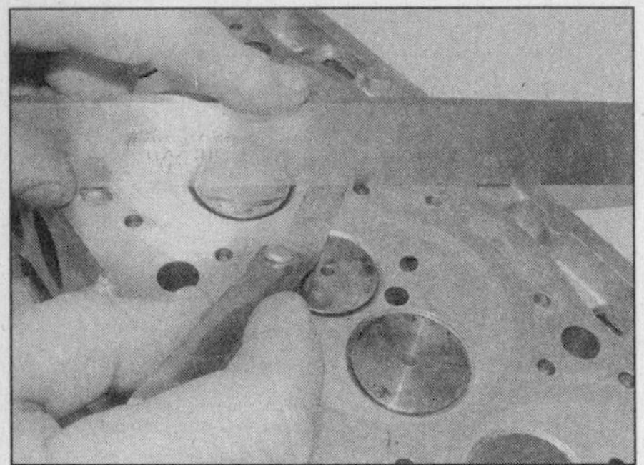
9.9b . . . or valve protrusion with a feeler blade and straight-edge (F9Q 732 engine)

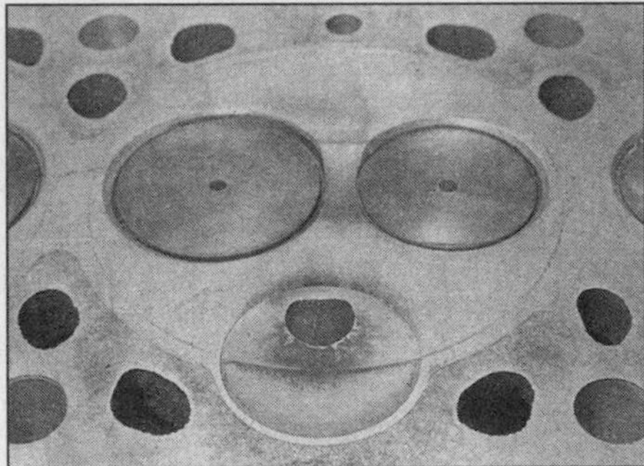
9.11a This swirl chamber shows the initial stages of cracking and burning (F8Q engine)

9.11b Measuring the swirl chamber protrusion using a dial gauge (F8Q engine)

9.14 Measuring a valve stem using a micrometer

9.16 Grinding a valve to its seat – lift the valve to redistribute the paste

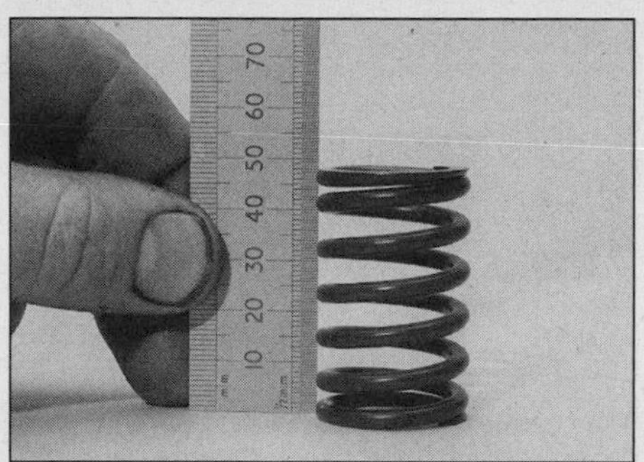

9.17 Checking a valve spring free length

10.2a Fitting the valve stem oil seals to the valve guides

10.2b Using a special tool to fit the valve stem oil seals

matt even surface is produced on both the valve seat and the valve, wipe off the paste and repeat the process with fine carborundum paste. A light spring placed under the valve head will greatly ease this operation. When a smooth unbroken ring of light grey matt finish is produced on both the valve and seat, the grinding operation is complete. Be sure to remove all traces of grinding paste, using paraffin or a suitable solvent, before reassembly of the cylinder head.

Valve components

17 Examine the valve springs for signs of damage and discoloration and also measure their free length using vernier calipers or a steel rule **(see illustration)** or by comparing the existing spring with a new component.

18 Stand each spring on a flat surface and check it for squareness. If any of the springs are damaged, distorted or have lost their tension, obtain a complete new set of springs. It is normal to renew the springs as a matter of course during a major overhaul.

19 Where applicable, check the followers and the shims for scoring, pitting (especially on the shims) and wear ridges. Renew any components as necessary. Some scuffing is to be expected and is acceptable provided that the followers are not scored.

Rocker arm components – E7J engine

20 Check the rocker arm contact surfaces for pits, wear, score marks or any indication that the surface-hardening has worn through. Dismantle the rocker shaft and check the rocker arm and rocker shaft pivot and contact areas in the same way. Measure the internal diameter of each rocker and check their fit on the shaft. Clean out the oil spill holes in each rocker using a length of wire. Renew the rocker arm or the rocker shaft itself if any are suspect.

Valve stem oil seals

21 The valve stem oil seals should be renewed as a matter of course.

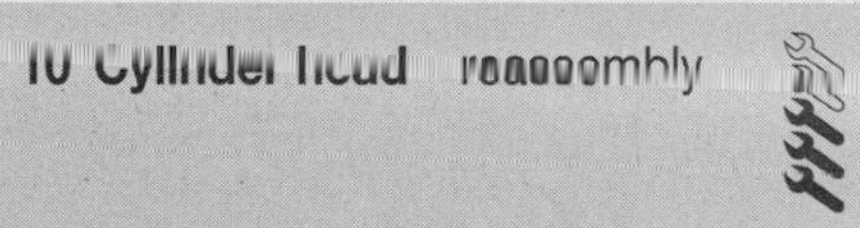

10 Cylinder head reassembly

1 On F8Q engines, if the swirl chambers have been removed, refit them to their original locations.

2 Lubricate the valve stem oil seals with clean engine oil, then fit them by pushing into position in the cylinder head using a suitable socket or special tool **(see illustrations)**. Ensure that the seals are fully engaged with the valve guide.

3 Insert the valves into their original locations. If new valves are being fitted, insert them into the locations to which they have been ground. Take care not to damage the valve stem oil seal as each valve is fitted **(see illustration)**.

4 Locate the spring seat on the guide, followed by the spring and cap **(see illustrations)**.

5 Compress the valve spring and locate the split collets in the recess in the valve stem. Release the compressor, then repeat the procedure on the remaining valves. Use a little grease to hold the collets in place **(see illustrations)**.

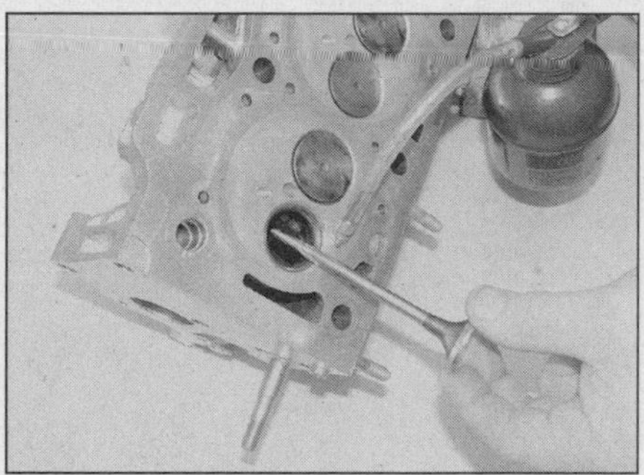

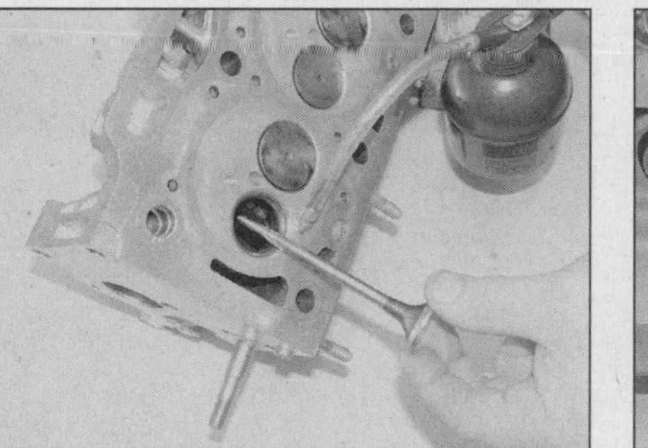

10.3 Lubricate the valve stems before inserting the valves

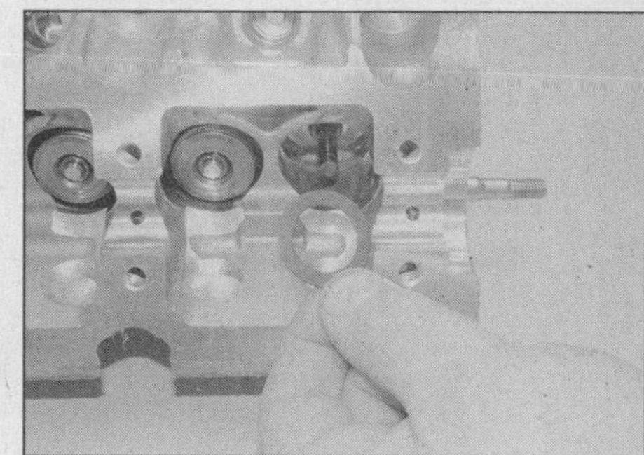

10.4a Fit the spring seat . . .

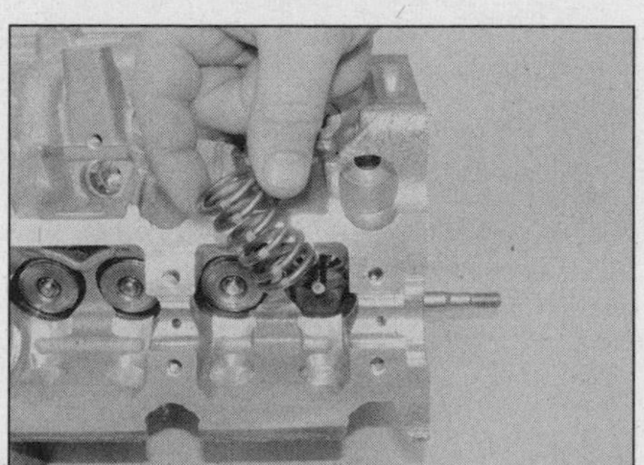

10.4b . . . spring . . .

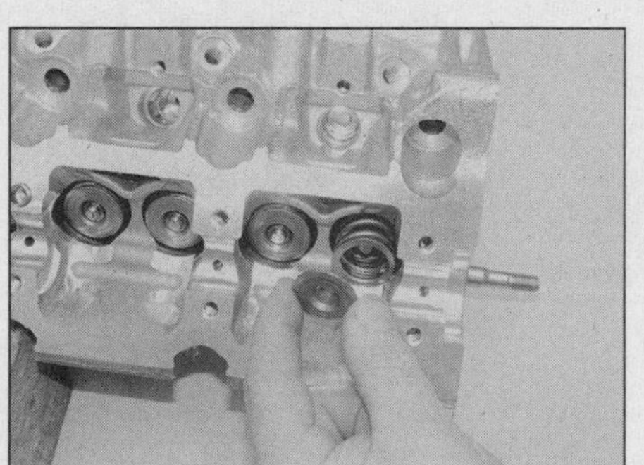

10.4c . . . and cap over the valve stem

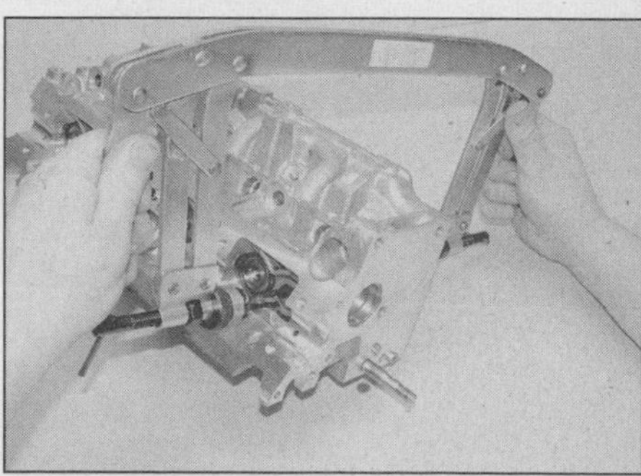

10.5a Compress the valve spring with the compressor tool . . .

10.5b . . . then fit the collets, using a little grease to hold them in place

10.7 Fit a new sealing ring when refitting the thermostat housing

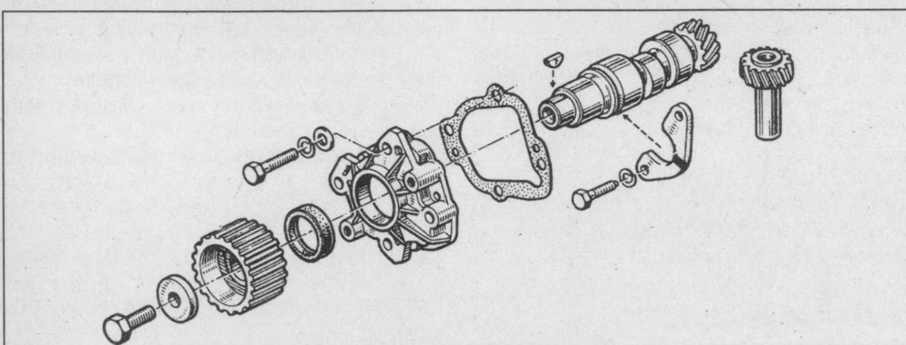
11.5a Auxiliary shaft components

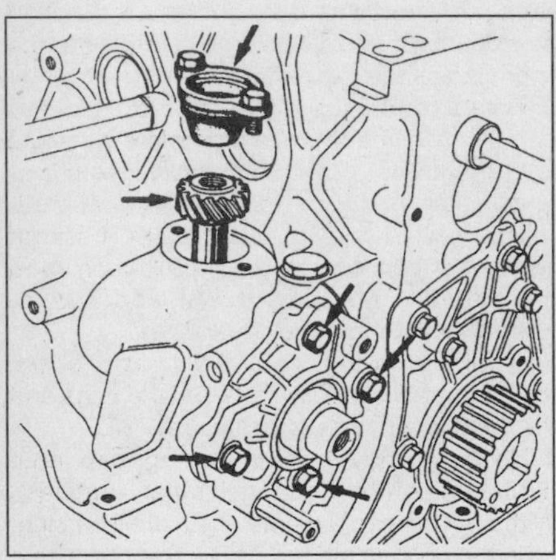
11.5b Auxiliary shaft housing retaining bolt locations, oil pump driveshaft and cover plate

6 With all the valves installed, place the cylinder head flat on the bench and, using a hammer and interposed block of wood, tap the end of each valve stem to settle the components.

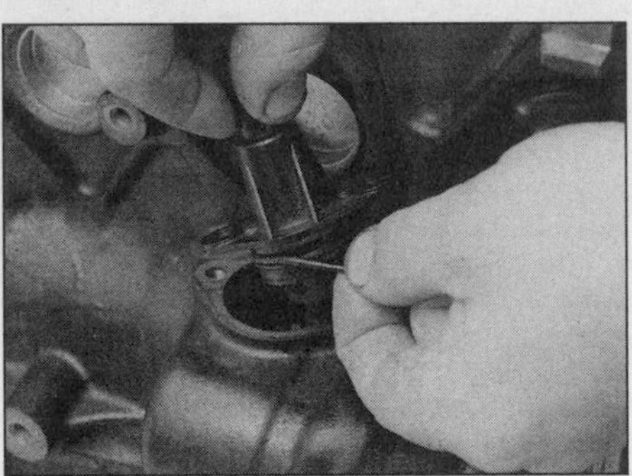
11.6a Removing the oil pump drivegear cover plate/breather and O-ring

7 The previously-removed components can now be refitted with reference to paragraphs 1 or 2 (as applicable) of Section 8 – fit new gaskets and sealing rings where necessary **(see illustration)**.

11 Auxiliary shaft – removal and refitting

Note: *The following procedure is applicable only to early diesel engines. A new timing belt, auxiliary shaft oil seal, housing gasket (or suitable sealant, as applicable) and oil pump drivegear cover plate O-ring will be required on refitting.*

Removal

1 With the engine removed from the vehicle, proceed as follows.
2 Remove the timing belt (see Chapter 2C).
3 Remove the auxiliary shaft sprocket with reference to Chapter 2C.
4 Unbolt the timing belt lower inner cover and remove it.
5 Unscrew the four bolts and withdraw the auxiliary shaft housing **(see illustrations)**, then remove the gasket (if fitted). Note that the housing locates on two dowels.
6 Unscrew the two bolts and withdraw the oil pump drivegear cover plate/breather noting the location of the O-ring. Withdraw the drivegear from its location. Use a screwdriver or similar tool to hook the drivegear out if necessary **(see illustrations)**.
7 Unscrew the two bolts and washers and lift out the auxiliary shaft thrustplate and the auxiliary shaft **(see illustrations)**.

Inspection

8 Examine the auxiliary shaft and oil pump driveshaft for pitting, scoring or wear ridges on the bearing journals and for chipping or wear of the gear teeth. Renew as necessary. Check the auxiliary shaft bearings in the cylinder block for wear and, if worn, have these renewed by your Renault dealer or suitably-equipped engineering works. Wipe them clean if they are still serviceable.
9 Temporarily fit the thrustplate to its position on the auxiliary shaft and use a feeler gauge

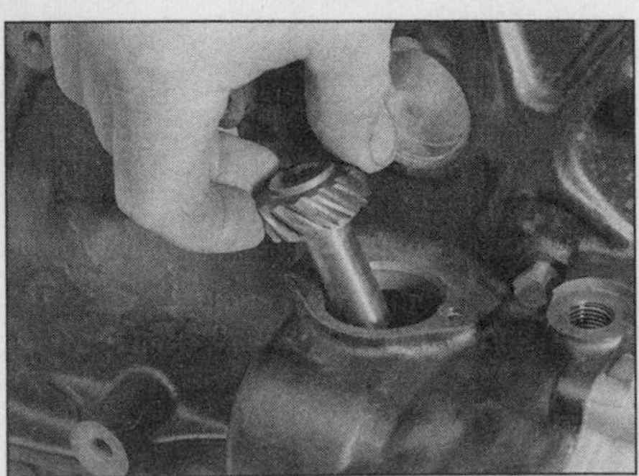
11.6b Removing the oil pump drivegear

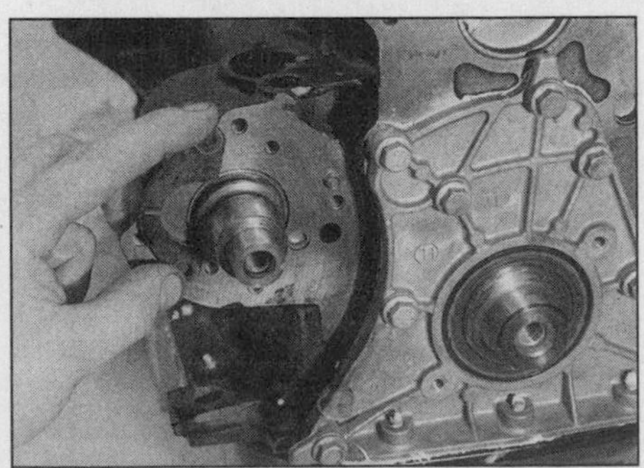
11.7a Removing the auxiliary shaft thrustplate . . .

11.7b . . . and the auxiliary shaft

11.9 Measuring the auxiliary shaft endfloat with a feeler blade

11.10a Prising the auxiliary shaft oil seal from the housing

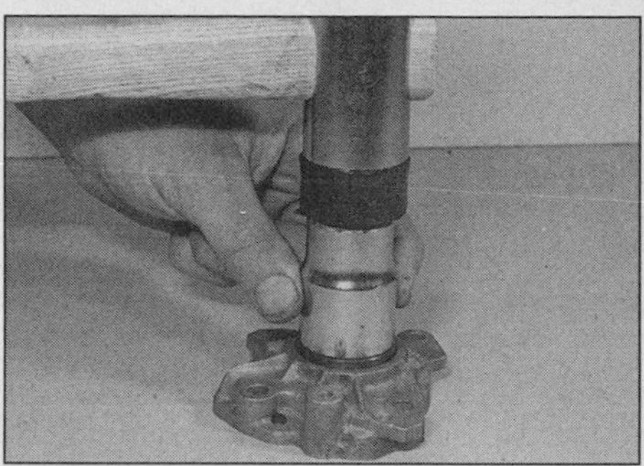

11.10b Fitting a new auxiliary shaft oil seal

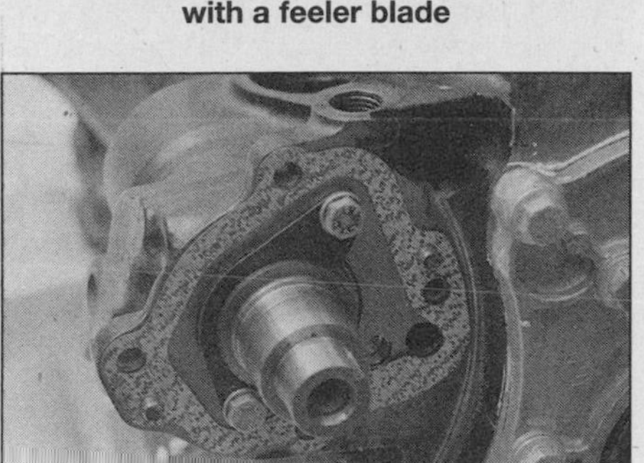

11.13 Auxiliary shaft gasket positioned over the dowels

11.14 Refitting the auxiliary shaft housing. Note tape around front of shaft

to check that the endfloat is as given in the Specifications **(see illustration)**. If it is greater than the upper tolerance, a new thrustplate should be obtained, but first check the thrust surfaces on the shaft to ascertain if wear has occurred here.

Refitting

10 Clean off all traces of the old gasket or sealant from the auxiliary shaft housing and prise out the oil seal with a screwdriver. Install the new oil seal using a block of wood, or a suitable socket and tap it in until it is flush with the outer face of the housing. The open side of the seal must be towards the engine **(see illustrations)**.

11 Liberally lubricate the auxiliary shaft and slide it into its bearings.

12 Place the thrustplate in position with its curved edge away from the crankshaft and refit the two retaining bolts, tightening them securely.

13 Place a new housing gasket in position over the dowels of the cylinder block **(see illustration)**. If a gasket was not used previously, apply a bead of CAF 4/60 THIXO sealant (or an alternative) to the housing mating face.

14 Wind a length of tape around the end of the auxiliary shaft, to prevent damage to the oil seal as the housing is refitted. Liberally lubricate the oil seal lips and then locate the housing in place, engaging it with the dowels **(see illustration)**. Refit and tighten the housing retaining bolts progressively in a diagonal sequence. Remove the tape from the end of the shaft.

15 Lubricate the oil pump drivegear and lower the gear into its location. Ensure that the splines on the drivegear engage with the oil pump.

16 Inspect the O-ring seal on the oil pump drivegear cover plate/breather and renew it if necessary. Fit the cover plate/breather and secure with the two retaining bolts.

17 Refit the timing belt lower inner cover to the cylinder block and tighten the bolts.

18 Refit the auxiliary shaft sprocket with reference to Chapter 2C.

19 Fit the new timing belt as described in Chapter 2C.

12 Piston/connecting rod assemblies – removal

1 With the cylinder head, sump and oil pump removed (see Chapter 2A, 2B or 2C), proceed as follows. On the E7J engine, make sure the liner clamps are in position.

2 Rotate the crankshaft so that No 1 big-end cap (nearest the flywheel/driveplate position) is at the lowest point of its travel. If the big-end cap and rod are not already numbered, mark them with a marker pen – it is not recommended to use a centre-punch **(see illustration)**. Mark both cap and rod to identify the cylinder they operate in.

3 Before removing the big-end caps, check the amount of side play between the caps and the crankshaft webs **(see illustration)**.

4 Unscrew the big-end bearing cap nuts (E7J engine) or bolts (all other engines). Withdraw the cap, complete with shell bearing, from the connecting rod. Strike the cap with a wooden or copper mallet if it is stuck **(see illustration)**. Note that on the F9Q 732 engine the big-end caps and connecting

12.2 Marking the big-end caps

12.3 Checking the side play between a big-end cap and the crankshaft web with a feeler blade

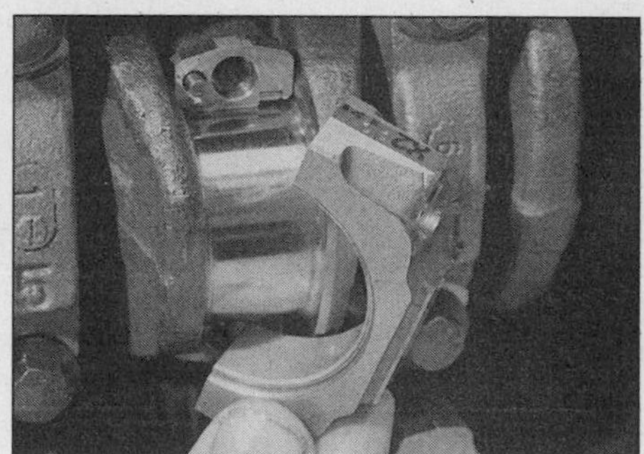

12.4a Removing a big-end bearing cap (E7J engine)

12.4b Removing a big-end bearing cap (F9Q 732 engine)

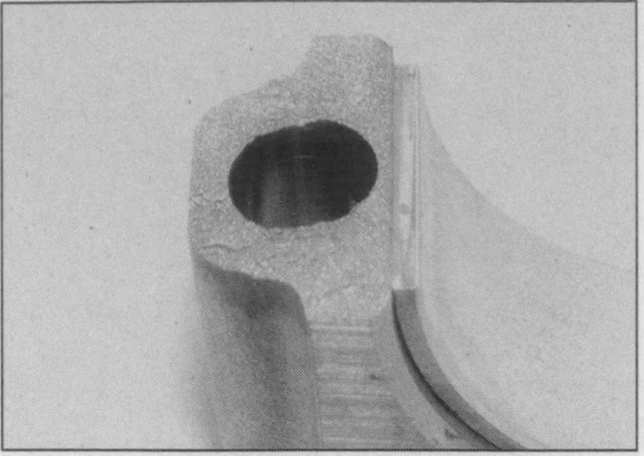
12.4c Cracked interface on the big-end bearing cap (F9Q 732 engine)

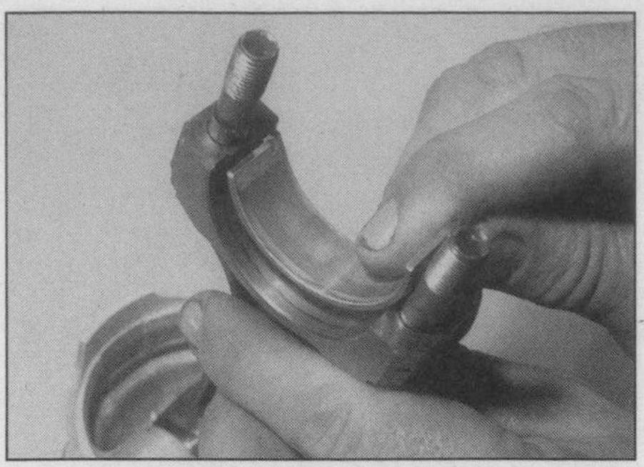
12.5 Removing a big-end bearing upper shell

rods are not machined but have a 'cracked' interface, and also the shell bearings are not located with tabs but are held in position by the clamping effect of the cap **(see illustrations)**. Make sure that the positions of the shells and caps are accurately noted to ensure correct reassembly.

5 If only the bearing shells are being attended to, push the connecting rod up and off the crankpin and remove the upper bearing shell **(see illustration)**. Keep the bearing shells and cap together in their correct sequence if they are to be refitted.

E7J engine

6 Remove the liner clamps and withdraw each liner, together with piston and connecting rod, from the top of the cylinder block. Mark the liners using masking tape, so that they may be refitted in their original locations.

7 Withdraw the piston from the bottom of the liner. Keep each piston with its respective liner if they are to be re-used.

8 Repeat the procedure for the remaining piston/connecting rod assemblies. Ensure that the caps and rods are marked before removal, as described previously and keep all components in order.

All other engines

9 Push the connecting rod up and remove the piston and rod from the bore. Note that if there is a pronounced wear ridge at the top of the bore, there is a risk of damaging the piston as the rings foul the ridge. However, it is reasonable to assume that a rebore and new pistons will be required in any case if the ridge is so pronounced.

10 Repeat the procedure for the remaining piston/connecting rod assemblies. Ensure that the caps and rods are marked before removal, as described previously and keep all components in order.

13.2 Unscrewing the nuts/bolts securing the crankshaft timing belt end oil seal housing

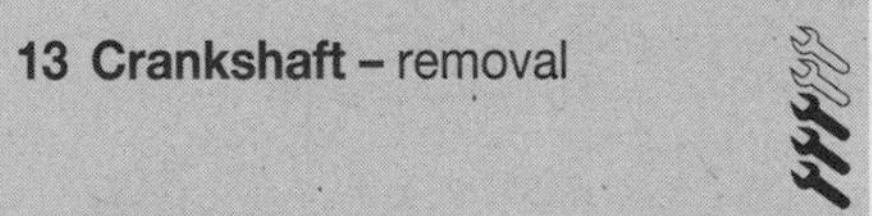

13 Crankshaft – removal

1 Remove the timing belt, crankshaft sprocket, oil pump and flywheel/driveplate. The pistons/connecting rods must be free of the crankshaft journals, however it is not essential to remove them completely from the cylinder block.

2 Unbolt the timing belt lower inner cover (where fitted), then unscrew the securing bolts/nuts and remove the crankshaft timing belt end oil seal housing and oil seal – refer if necessary to the relevant Sections of Parts A, B and C of this Chapter **(see illustration)**.

3 Before the crankshaft is removed, check the endfloat using a dial gauge in contact with the end of the crankshaft **(see illustration)**. Push the crankshaft fully one way and then zero the gauge. Push the crankshaft fully the other way and check the endfloat. The result can be compared with the specified amount and will give an indication as to whether new thrustwashers are required.

4 If a dial gauge is not available, feeler gauges can be used. First push the crankshaft fully towards the flywheel/driveplate end of the engine, then slip the feeler gauge between the web of No 2 crankpin and the thrustwasher of the centre main bearing (E7J, K4J and K4M engines), or between the web of No 1 crankpin and the thrustwasher of No 2 main bearing (all other engines).

5 Identification numbers should already be cast onto the base of each main bearing cap. If not, number the cap and crankcase using a marker pen, as was done for the connecting rods and caps **(see illustration)**.

6 Unscrew the main bearing cap retaining bolts and withdraw the caps, complete with bearing shells **(see illustrations)**. Tap the caps with a wooden or copper mallet if they

13.3 Checking the crankshaft endfloat with a dial gauge

13.5 The main bearing caps are numbered for position

13.6a Removing a main bearing cap bolt

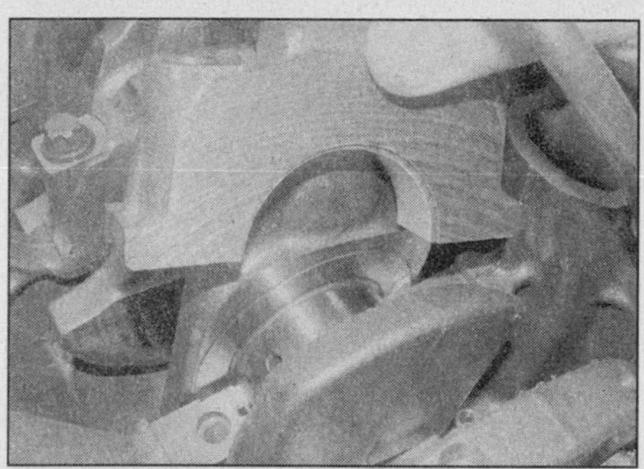

13.6b Removing a main bearing cap

are stuck. Note on the diesel engines, No 1 main bearing cap (flywheel end) is secured by Allen bolts and sealed to the cylinder block using silicone sealant or butyl seals. It is recommended that a tool is fabricated to remove the main bearing cap **(see Tool Tip)**.

7 Carefully lift the crankshaft from the crankcase **(see illustration)**.

8 Remove the thrustwashers at each side of the centre main bearing or No 2 main bearing (as applicable), then remove the bearing shell upper halves from the crankcase **(see illustration)**. Place each shell with its respective bearing cap. Note that on the F9Q 732 engine, there are no tabs to locate the bearing shells in either the block or main bearing cap, so each shell must be positively identified for position to ensure correct refitting.

9 Remove the oil seal from the flywheel/ driveplate end of the crankshaft.

14 Cylinder block/crankcase and bores – cleaning and inspection

Cleaning

1 For complete cleaning, the core plugs should be removed. Drill a small hole in them, then insert a self-tapping screw and pull out the plugs using a pair of grips or a slide-hammer. Also remove all external components and sensors (if not already done), noting their locations. As applicable unbolt the drivebelt tensioner bracket, coolant pipe and oil cooler from the cylinder block. On F8Q engines, remove the piston oil spray jets from the bottom of each bore by unscrewing the securing bolts. On F9Q engines the jets are pressed into the cylinder block **(see illustration)** and special tools are required to remove them, therefore this task should be performed by an engine reconditioning specialist. If necessary, unbolt the right-hand driveshaft bearing bracket, the alternator bracket and the oil separator **(see illustrations)**.

TOOL TIP

To make a main bearing cap removal tool, obtain a length of steel strip about 6 mm thick by 30 mm wide, and long enough to straddle the main bearing cap. Drill three holes in the strip as shown. Attach two suitable lengths of threaded rod, using two nuts each, to the outer two holes in the strip, or alternatively two old cylinder head bolts can be used instead. Make a lifting plate by cutting a second length of steel strip, long enough to fit over the bearing cap. Drill a hole in the centre, then mark and drill a hole each side so that the plate can be bolted to the holes in the cap. Attach a threaded rod to the lifting plate using two nuts and screw on another nut at the top.

13.7 Lifting the crankshaft from the crankcase

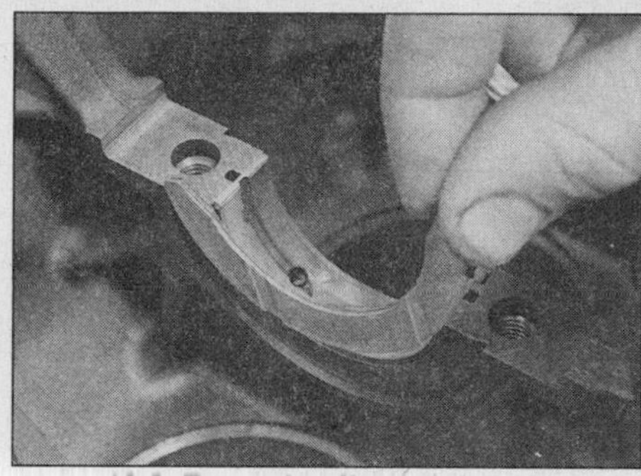

13.8 Removing the crankshaft thrustwashers

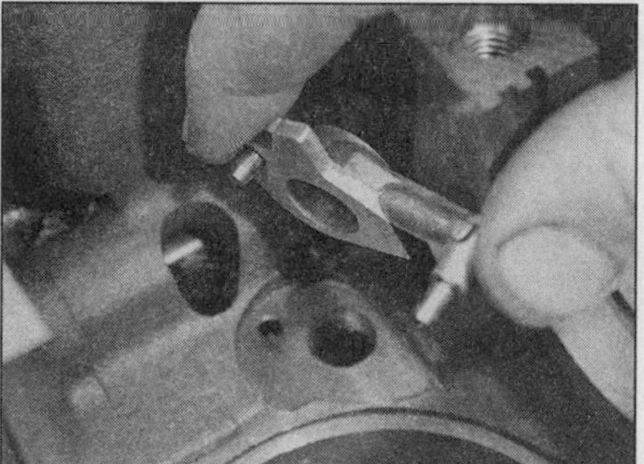

14.1a Removing a piston oil spray jet (F8Q engine)

14.1b On F9Q engines, the oil spray jets are pressed into position (F9Q 732 engine)

14.1c Right-hand driveshaft bearing bracket (F9Q 732 engine)

14.1d Removing the PAS pump/alternator/ air conditioning compressor mounting

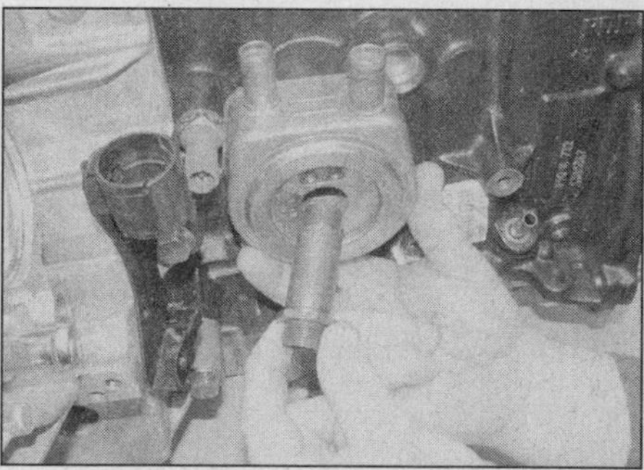

14.1e Removing the oil cooler

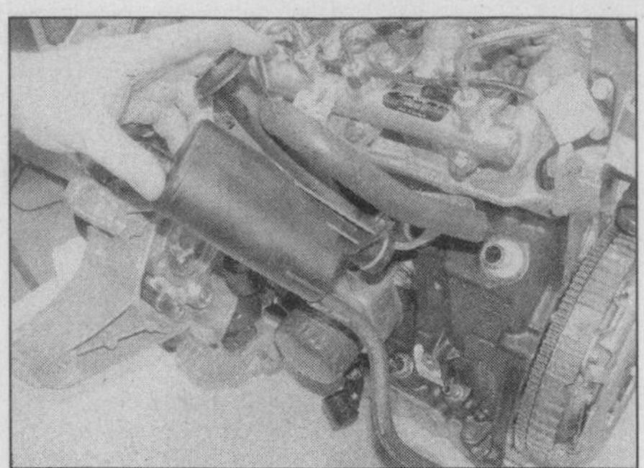

14.1f Removing the oil separator

2 Scrape all traces of gasket or sealant from the cylinder block, taking care not to damage the head and sump mating faces.

3 If the block is extremely dirty, it should be steam-cleaned.

4 If the block is not very dirty, you can do an adequate cleaning job with hot soapy water and a stiff brush. Take plenty of time and do a thorough job.

5 After the block has been cleaned, clean all oil holes and oil galleries one more time. Flush all internal passages with warm water until the water runs clear, dry the block thoroughly and wipe all machined surfaces with a light rust-preventative oil. If you have access to compressed air, use it to speed up the drying process and to blow out all the oil holes and galleries.

Warning: Wear eye protection when using compressed air.

6 The threaded holes in the block must be clean to ensure accurate torque wrench readings during reassembly. Run the proper-size tap into each of the holes to remove rust, corrosion, thread sealant or sludge and to restore damaged threads. If possible, use compressed air to clear the holes of debris produced by this operation. Now is a good time to clean the threads on the head bolts and the main bearing cap bolts as well.

7 Refit the main bearing caps and tighten the bolts finger-tight.

8 After coating the mating surfaces of the new core plugs with suitable sealant, refit them in the cylinder block. Make sure that they are driven in straight and seated properly, or leakage could result. Special tools are available for this purpose, but a large socket, with an outside diameter that will just slip into the core plug, will work just as well.

9 On diesel engines with piston oil spray jets secured with bolts, check the gauze filters and the oil holes in the piston oil spray jet securing bolts and the oil holes in the jets themselves for blockage **(see illustrations)**. Clean if necessary, then refit the jets and tighten the securing bolts to the specified torque wrench setting. Ensure the locating pegs on the jets engage with the corresponding holes in the cylinder block.

10 If the engine is not going to be reassembled right away, cover it with a large plastic bag to keep it clean and prevent it rusting.

Inspection

11 Visually check the block for cracks, rust and corrosion. Look for stripped threads in the threaded holes. If there has been any history of internal water leakage, it may be worthwhile having an engine overhaul specialist check the block with special equipment. If defects are found, have the block repaired, if possible, or renewed.

12 Check the cylinder bores/liners for scuffing and scoring. Normally, bore wear will show up in the form of a wear ridge at the top of the bore. This ridge marks the limit of piston travel.

13 Measure the diameter of each cylinder at the top (just under the ridge area), centre and bottom of the cylinder bore, parallel to the crankshaft axis.

14 Next measure each cylinder's diameter at the same three locations across the crankshaft axis. If the difference between any of the measurements is greater than 0.20 mm, indicating that the cylinder is excessively out-of-round or tapered, then remedial action must be considered.

15 Repeat this procedure for the remaining cylinders.

16 If the cylinder walls are badly scuffed or scored, or if they are excessively out-of-round or tapered, obtain new cylinder liners (E7J engine) or have the cylinder block rebored (all other engines). New pistons (oversize in the case of a rebore) will also be required.

17 If the cylinders are in reasonably good condition, then it may only be necessary to renew the piston rings.

18 If this is the case, the bores should be honed in order to allow the new rings to bed in correctly and provide the best possible seal. The conventional type of hone has spring-loaded stones and is used with a power drill. You will also need some paraffin or honing oil and rags. The hone should be moved up and down the cylinder to produce a crosshatch pattern and plenty of honing oil should be used. Ideally, the crosshatch lines should intersect at approximately a 60° angle. Do not take off more material than is necessary to produce the required finish. If new pistons are being fitted, the piston manufacturers may specify a finish with a different angle, so their instructions should be followed. Do not withdraw the hone from the cylinder while it is still being turned, but stop it first. After honing a cylinder, wipe out all traces of the honing oil. If equipment of this type is not available, or if you are not sure whether you are competent to undertake the task yourself, an engine overhaul specialist will carry out the work at a moderate cost.

19 Before refitting the cylinder liners to the E7J engine, their protrusions must be checked as follows and new base O-rings fitted. Place the liner without a base O-ring in the cylinder block and press down to make sure that it is seated correctly. Using a dial gauge or straight-edge and feeler blade, check that the protrusion of the liner above the upper surface of the cylinder block is within the specified limits **(see illustrations)**.

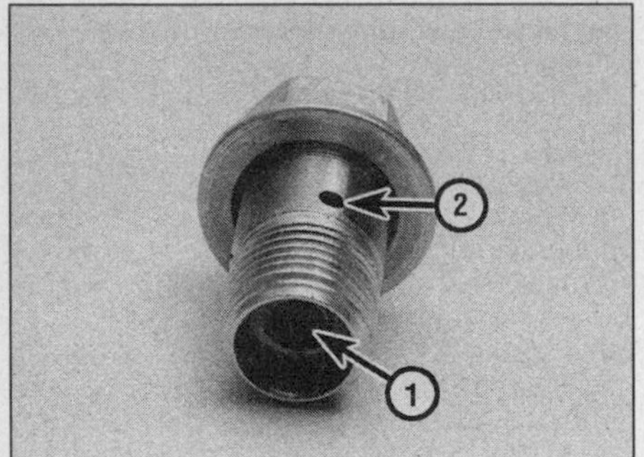

14.9a Check the gauze filters (1) and the oil holes (2) in the oil spray jet bolts . . .

14.9b . . . and the oil holes (arrowed) in the jets for blockage

14.19a Checking the liner protrusion with a dial gauge . . .

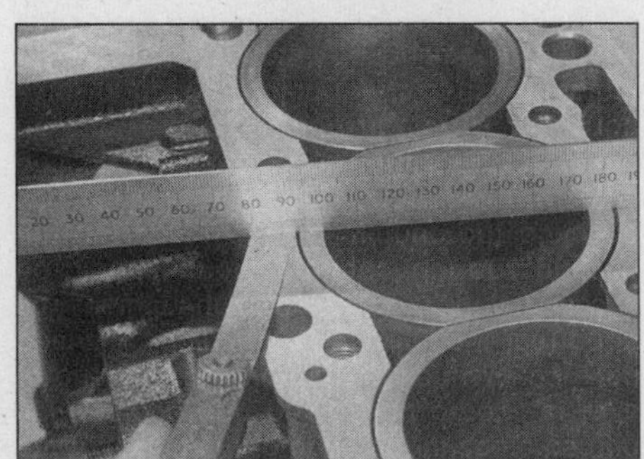

14.19b . . . and with feeler blades (E7J engine)

Check all of the liners in the same manner and record the protrusions. Note that there is also a limit specified for the difference of protrusion between two adjacent liners. If new liners are being fitted, it is permitted to interchange them to bring this difference within limits. The protrusions may be stepped upwards or downwards from the flywheel end of the engine.

20 Refit all external components and sensors in their correct locations, as noted before removal.

15 Piston/connecting rod assemblies – inspection and reassembly

Inspection

1 Before the inspection process can begin, the piston/connecting rod assemblies must be cleaned and the original piston rings removed from the pistons.

2 Carefully expand the old rings over the top of the pistons. The use of two or three old feeler blades will be helpful in preventing the rings dropping into empty grooves **(see illustration)**. Note that the oil control ring is in two sections.

3 Scrape away all traces of carbon from the top of the piston **(see illustration)**. A hand-held wire brush or a piece of fine emery cloth can be used once the majority of the deposits have been scraped away.

4 Remove the carbon from the ring grooves in the piston by cleaning them using an old ring. Break the ring in half to do this. Be very careful to remove only the carbon deposits; do not remove any metal, nor nick or scratch the sides of the ring grooves. Protect your fingers – piston rings are sharp.

5 Once the deposits have been removed, clean the piston/connecting rod assembly with paraffin or a suitable solvent and dry thoroughly. Make sure the oil return holes in the ring grooves are clear.

6 If the pistons and cylinder bores are not damaged or worn excessively and if the cylinder block does not need to be rebored or the liners renewed, the original pistons can be re-used. Normal piston wear appears as even vertical wear on the piston thrust surfaces and slight looseness of the top ring in its groove. New piston rings, however, should always be used when the engine is reassembled.

15.2 Removing a piston ring with the aid of a feeler blade

7 Carefully inspect each piston for cracks around the skirt, at the gudgeon pin bosses and at the piston ring lands (between the piston ring grooves).

8 Look for scoring and scuffing on the sides of the skirt, holes in the piston crown and burned areas at the edge of the crown. If the skirt is scored or scuffed, the engine may have been suffering from overheating and/or abnormal combustion, which caused excessively-high operating temperatures. The cooling and lubricating systems should be checked thoroughly. Scorch marks on the sides of the pistons show that blow-by has occurred and the rings are not sealing correctly. A hole in the piston crown is an indication that abnormal combustion (pre-ignition, knocking or detonation) has been occurring. If any of the above problems exist, the causes must be corrected, or the damage will occur again. On petrol engines, the causes may include inlet air leaks, incorrect fuel/air mixture or incorrect ignition timing. On diesel engines incorrect injection pump timing or a faulty injector may be the cause.

9 Corrosion of the piston, in the form of small pits, indicates that coolant is leaking into the combustion chamber and/or the crankcase. Again, the cause must be corrected, or the problem may persist in the rebuilt engine.

10 If new rings are being fitted to old pistons, measure the piston ring-to-groove clearance by placing a new piston ring in each ring groove and measuring the clearance with a feeler gauge. Check the clearance at three or four places around each groove. No values are specified, but if the measured clearance is excessive – say greater than 0.10 mm – new pistons will be required. If the new ring is excessively tight, the most likely cause is dirt remaining in the groove.

15.3 Top of the piston on the F9Q 732 engine

11 Check the piston-to-bore/liner clearance by measuring the cylinder bore/liner diameter (see Section 14) and the piston diameter. Measure the piston across the skirt, at 90° to the gudgeon pin, approximately half way down the skirt **(see illustration)**. Subtract the piston diameter from the bore/liner diameter to obtain the clearance. If this is greater than the figures given in the Specifications, the block will have to be rebored and new pistons and rings fitted – note the markings on the old pistons to ensure the correct replacements are obtained **(see illustrations)**. On the E7J engine, new pistons and liners are supplied in matched pairs.

12 Check the fit of the gudgeon pin by twisting the piston and connecting rod in opposite directions. Any noticeable play indicates excessive wear, which must be corrected by separating the pistons and connecting rods. This operation must be entrusted to a Renault garage or engine overhaul specialist for petrol engines. Note in the case of the diesel engines, the gudgeon pins are secured by circlips, so the pistons and connecting rods can be separated without difficulty. Note the position of the piston relative to the rod before dismantling and use new circlips on reassembly. If new

2D

15.11a Measuring a piston diameter using a micrometer

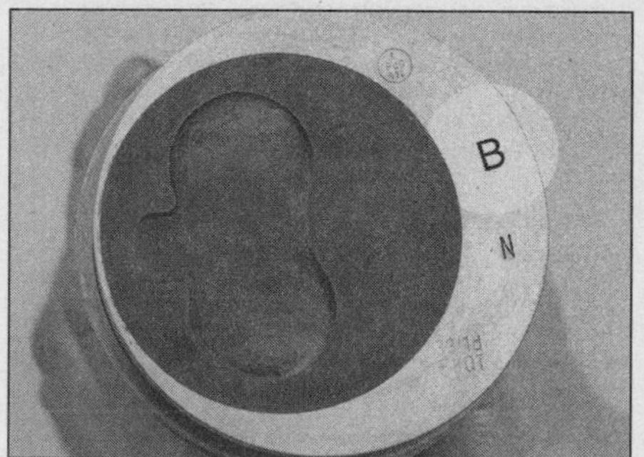

15.11b Piston diameter grade marked on piston crown

15.11c Markings on the piston crown on the F9Q 732 engine

15.12a Gudgeon pin retaining circlip (arrowed)

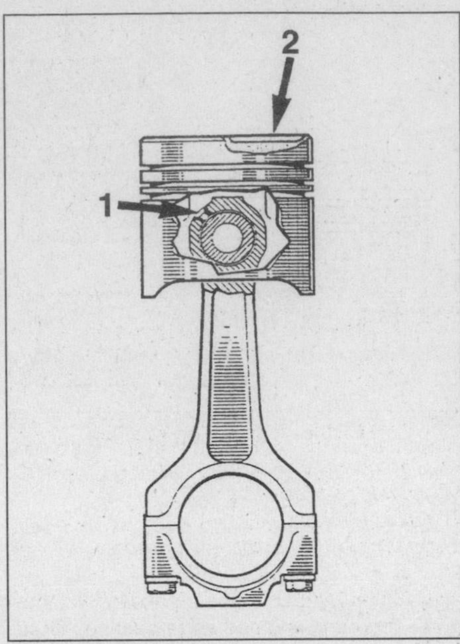

15.12b Oil hole (1) in connecting rod small-end should face away from combustion chamber (2) in piston crown (diesel engine)

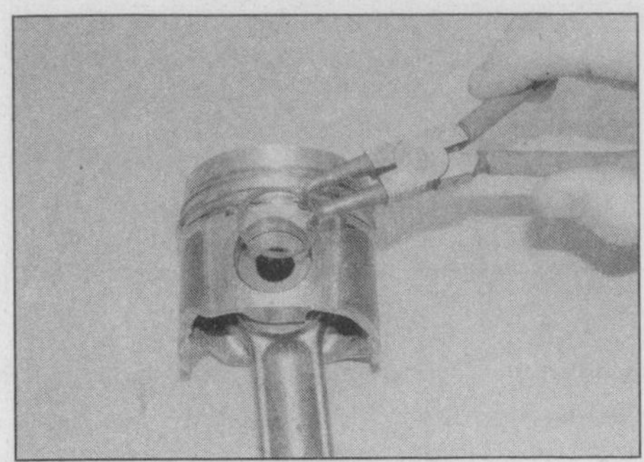

15.12c Removing the circlip . . .

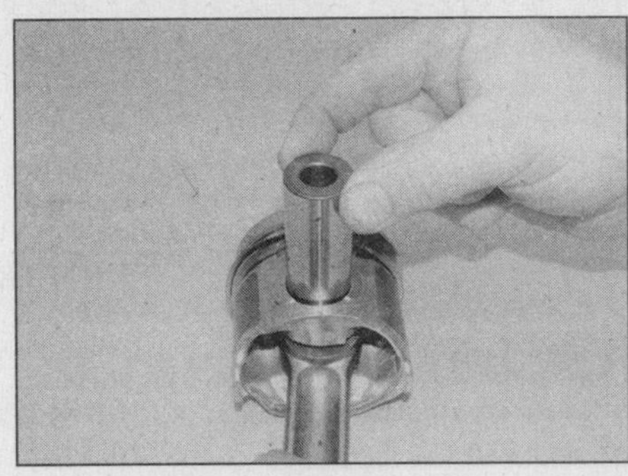

15.12d . . . gudgeon pin . . .

bearing shells are being fitted using the special Renault tool on the F9Q 732 engine, they should be fitted at this stage, before reassembling the piston to the connecting rod **(see illustrations)**.

13 Before refitting the rings to the pistons, check their end gaps by inserting each of them in their cylinder bores. Use the piston to make sure that they are square **(see illustrations)**. No values are specified, but typical gaps would be of the order of 0.50 mm for compression rings, perhaps somewhat greater for the oil control rings. Renault rings are supplied pre-gapped; no attempt should be made to adjust the gaps by filing.

Reassembly

14 Install the new rings by fitting them over the top of the piston, starting with the oil control scraper ring **(see illustrations)**. Use feeler blades in the same way as when removing the old rings. Note that the second compression ring is tapered and additionally stepped in the case of the K4J and K4M engines. Both compression rings must be fitted with the word TOP uppermost. Be careful when handling the compression rings; they will break if they are handled roughly or

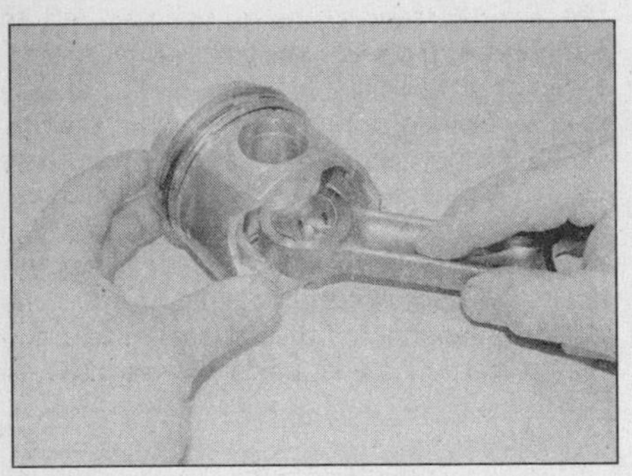

15.12e . . . and connecting rod (F9Q 732 engine)

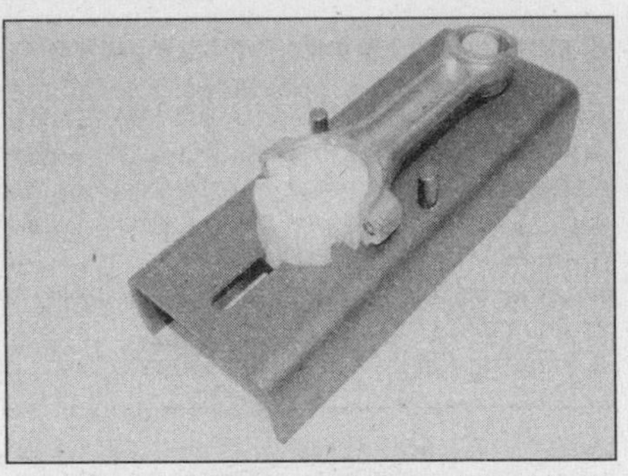

15.12f Using the special Renault tool to fit new bearing shells to the connecting rods (F9Q 732 engine)

15.13a Use the piston to push the rings into the cylinder bores . . .

15.13b . . . then measure the ring end gaps

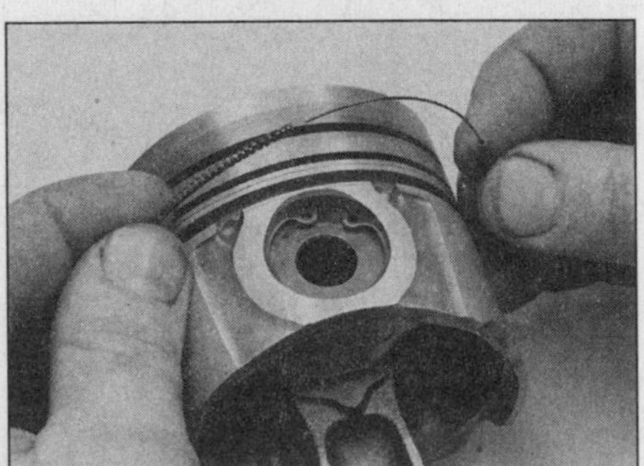

15.14a Fit the oil control ring expander . . .

15.14b . . . followed by the ring

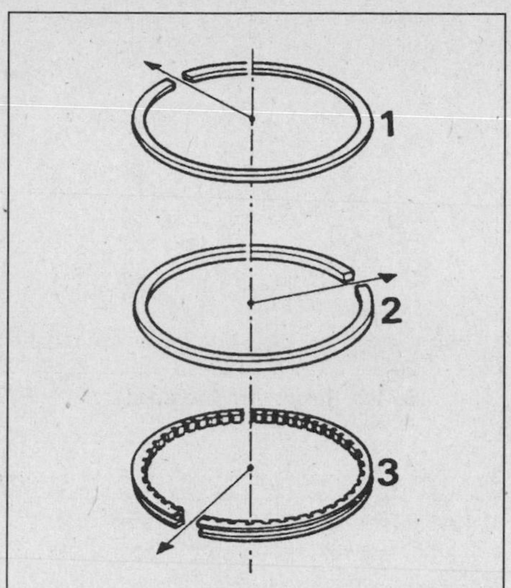

15.14c Position the piston ring end gaps 120° apart

1 Top compression ring
2 Lower compression ring
3 Oil control ring

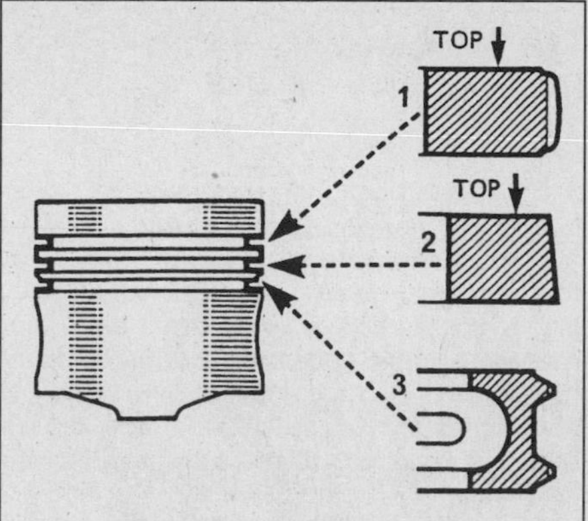

15.14d Piston ring profiles

1 Top compression ring
2 Lower compression ring
3 Oil control ring
Position the TOP markings as shown

16.4 Measuring a main bearing journal diameter using a micrometer

expanded too far. With all the rings in position, space the ring gaps at 120° to each other.

15 Note that on the E7J engine, if new piston and liner assemblies have been obtained, each piston is matched to its respective liner and they must not be interchanged.

16 Crankshaft – inspection

1 Clean the crankshaft and dry it with compressed air if available. Be sure to clean the oil holes with a pipe cleaner or similar probe.

Warning: Wear eye protection when using compressed air.

2 Check the main and big-end bearing journals for uneven wear, scoring, pitting and cracking.

3 If the crankshaft has been reground, check for burrs around the crankshaft oil holes (the holes are usually chamfered, so burrs should not be a problem unless regrinding has been carried out carelessly). Remove any burrs with a fine file or scraper and thoroughly clean the oil holes as described previously.

4 Using a micrometer, measure the diameter of the main bearing and connecting rod journals and compare the results with that given in the Specifications **(see illustration)**. By measuring the diameter at a number of points around each journal's circumference, you will be able to determine whether or not the journal is out-of-round. Take the measurement at each end of the journal, near the webs, to determine if the journal is tapered. If any of the measurements vary by more than 0.025 mm, the crankshaft will have to be reground and undersize bearings fitted.

5 Check the oil seal contact surfaces at each end of the crankshaft for wear and damage. If the seal has worn an excessive groove in the surface of the crankshaft, consult an engine overhaul specialist who will be able to advise whether a repair is possible or if a new crankshaft is necessary.

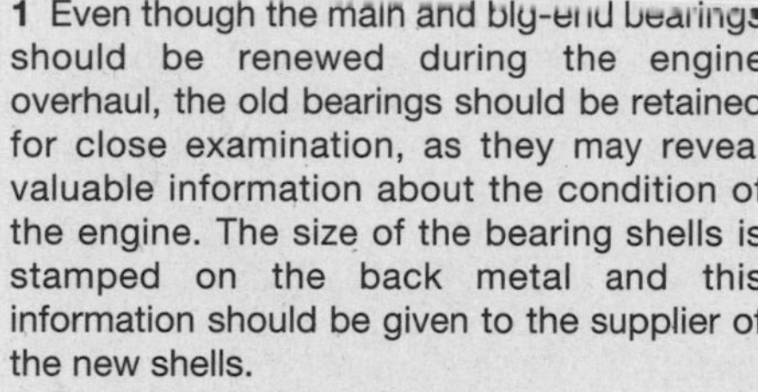

17 Main and big-end bearings – inspection

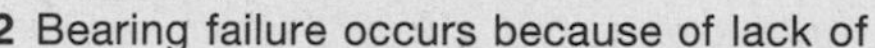

1 Even though the main and big-end bearings should be renewed during the engine overhaul, the old bearings should be retained for close examination, as they may reveal valuable information about the condition of the engine. The size of the bearing shells is stamped on the back metal and this information should be given to the supplier of the new shells.

2 Bearing failure occurs because of lack of lubrication, the presence of dirt or other foreign particles, overloading the engine and corrosion. Regardless of the cause of bearing failure, it must be corrected before the engine is reassembled, to prevent it from happening again **(see illustration)**.

3 When examining the bearings, remove them from the engine block, the main bearing caps, the connecting rods and the rod caps and lay them out on a clean surface in the same general position as their location in the engine. This will enable you to match any bearing problems with the corresponding crankshaft journal.

4 Dirt and other foreign particles get into the engine in a variety of ways. Dirt may be left in the engine during assembly, or it may pass through filters or the crankcase ventilation system. It may get into the oil and from there into the bearings. Metal chips from machining operations and normal engine wear are often present. Abrasives are sometimes left in engine components after reconditioning, especially when parts are not thoroughly cleaned using the proper cleaning methods. Whatever the source, these foreign objects often end up embedded in the soft bearing material and are easily recognised. Large particles will not embed in the bearing and will score or gouge the bearing and journal. The best prevention for this cause of bearing failure is to clean all parts thoroughly and

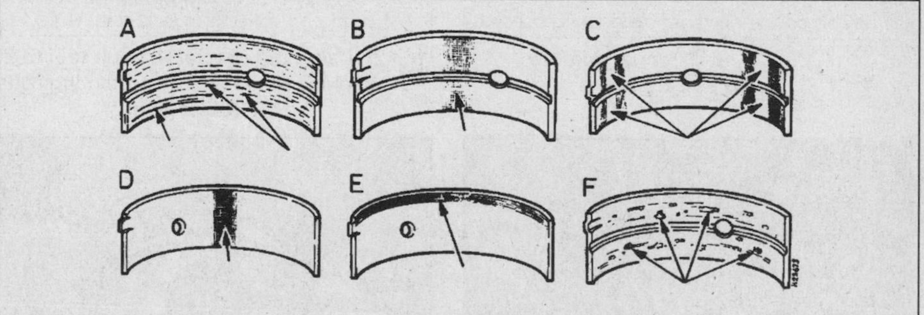

17.2 Typical bearing shell failures

A **Scratches** – *due to foreign bodies embedded in bearing material*
B **Overlay wiped out** *(copper underlay showing through) – due to lack of oil*
C **Bright (polished) sections** – *due to an improperly-seated shell*
D **Overlay gone from entire surface** – *due to excessive wear*
E **Wear on one edge** – *due to a tapered journal*
F **Cracks, craters or pockets** – *due to fatigue failure*

2D

keep everything spotlessly-clean during engine assembly. Frequent and regular engine oil and filter changes are also recommended.

5 Lack of lubrication (or oil breakdown) has a number of interrelated causes. Excessive heat (which thins the oil), overloading (which squeezes the oil from the bearing face) and oil leakage (from excessive bearing clearances, worn oil pump or high engine speeds) all contribute to lubrication breakdown. Blocked oil passages, which usually are the result of misaligned oil holes in a bearing shell, will also oil-starve a bearing and destroy it. When lack of lubrication is the cause of bearing failure, the bearing material is wiped or extruded from the steel backing of the bearing. Temperatures may increase to the point where the steel backing turns blue from overheating.

6 Driving habits can have a definite effect on bearing life. Full-throttle, low-speed operation (labouring the engine) puts very high loads on bearings, which tends to squeeze out the oil film. These loads cause the bearings to flex, which produces fine cracks in the bearing face (fatigue failure). Eventually, the bearing material will loosen in pieces and tear away from the steel backing. Short-trip driving leads to corrosion of bearings, because insufficient engine heat is produced to drive off the condensed water and corrosive gases. These products collect in the engine oil, forming acid and sludge. As the oil is carried to the engine bearings, the acid attacks and corrodes the bearing material.

7 Incorrect bearing installation during engine assembly will lead to bearing failure as well. Tight-fitting bearings leave insufficient bearing oil clearance and will result in oil starvation. Dirt or foreign particles trapped behind a bearing shell result in high spots on the bearing which lead to failure.

8 If new bearings are to be fitted, the bearing running clearances should be measured before the engine is finally reassembled, to ensure that the correct bearing shells have been obtained (see Sections 19 and 20). If the crankshaft has been reground, the engineering works which carried out the work will advise on the correct size bearing shells to suit the work carried out. If there is any doubt as to which bearing shells should be used, seek advice from a Renault dealer.

18 Engine overhaul – reassembly sequence

Before starting, ensure all new parts have been obtained and all necessary tools are available. Read through the entire procedure to familiarise yourself with the work involved and to ensure all items necessary for engine reassembly are at hand. In addition to all normal tools and materials, a thread-locking compound will be needed. A tube of RTV sealing compound will also be required for the joint faces that are fitted without gaskets; it is recommended that Rhodorseal 5661 paste is used for the crankshaft main bearing cap and sump and Loctite 518 for the water pump (E7J engine) and cylinder head end cover (K4J and K4M engines). Both sealants are available from Renault dealers.

To save time and avoid problems, assembly can be carried out in the following order:

a) Crankshaft.
b) Pistons/connecting rod assemblies.
c) Oil pump and sump.
d) Flywheel/driveplate.
e) Cylinder head.
f) Timing belt and sprockets.
g) Engine external components.

19 Crankshaft – main bearing clearance check and refitting

1 Before fitting the crankshaft and main bearings on the E7J petrol engine and diesel engines, decide whether the No 1 main bearing cap is to be sealed using butyl seals or silicone sealant. If butyl seals are to be used, it is necessary to determine the correct thickness of the seals to obtain from Renault. To do this, place the bearing cap in position without any seals and secure it with the two retaining bolts. Locate a twist drill, dowel rod or any other suitable implement which will just fit in the side seal groove **(see illustration)**. Now measure the implement – this dimension is the side seal groove size. If the dimension is less than or equal to 5 mm, a 5.10 mm thick side seal is needed. If the dimension is more than 5 mm, a 5.4 mm thick side seal is required. Having determined the side seal size and obtained the necessary seals, proceed as follows for the other types of engine as well. Note that silicone sealant is used instead of side seals when the engine is originally assembled at the factory.

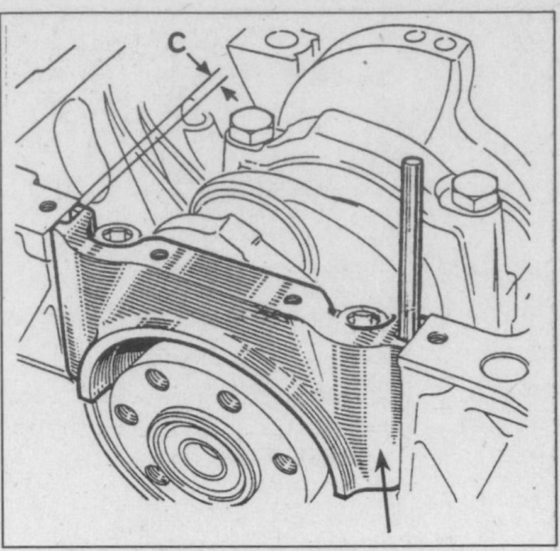

19.1 Measuring No 1 main bearing cap side seal grooves using a dowel rod

Bearing cap (arrowed)
C Seal groove measurement

Main bearing clearance check

2 Clean the backs of the bearing shells and the bearing recesses in both the cylinder block and main bearing caps.

3 Press the bearing shells into the caps and cylinder block, ensuring that the tag on the shell engages in the notch in the cap. Note that on K4J and K4M engines from July 1999-on, all F4R engines, and the F9Q 732 engine, tags are **not** incorporated in the shells. To ensure correct fitting, it is recommended that the Renault tool Mot. 1493 for F4R and F9Q engines, or Renault tool Mot. 1493-01 is obtained for K4J and K4M engines. Note, however, that with care it is possible to position the shells in their locations equally accurately without the tool. Press them into position so that they are exactly centred in their locations and their ends are flush with the surface of the block or cap **(see illustrations)**. Also note the following points.

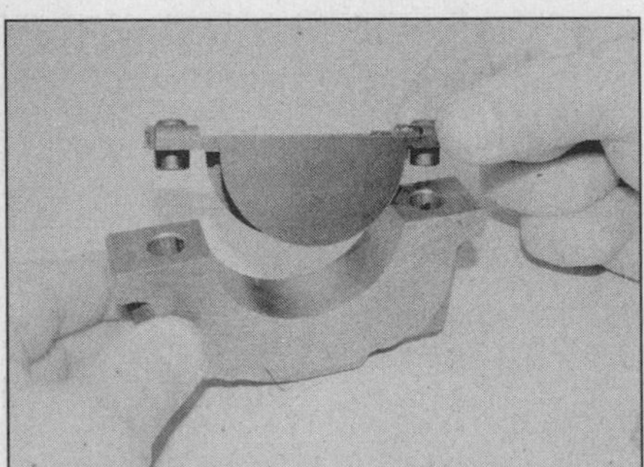

19.3a Tool for fitting main bearing shells

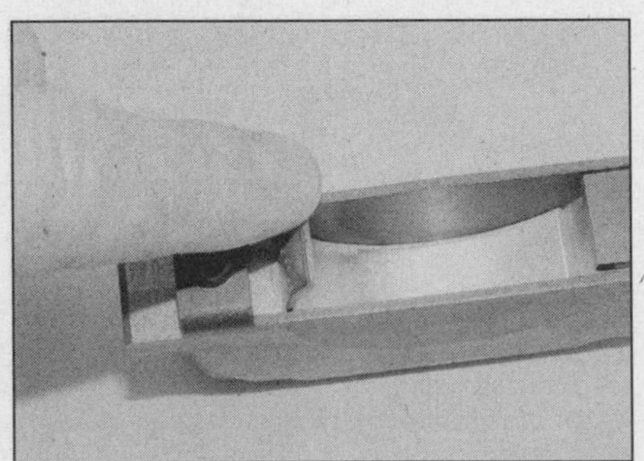

19.3b Press the bearing shell until it contacts the tool

19.3c If the Renault special tool is being used to fit the main bearing shells on the F4R engine, place the tool over the bearing location . . .

19.3d . . . insert the bearing shell into the tool . . .

19.3e . . . and press one end of the shell until the other end contacts the tool

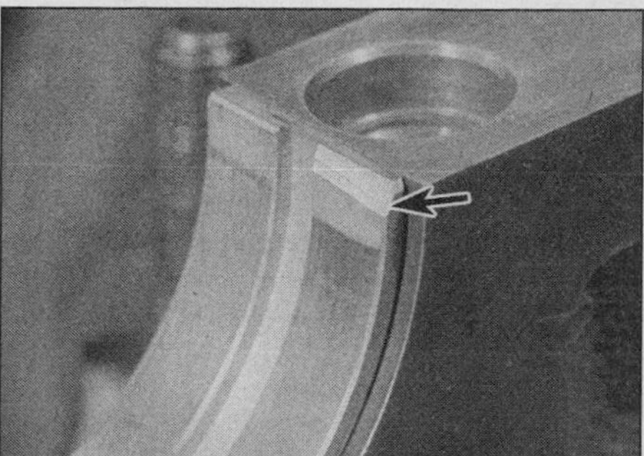

19.3f On the E7J engine, No 5 upper main bearing shell has an oil pump lubricating chamfer

a) On the E7J engine, the shells without grooves are located in the caps, but note that No 5 upper shell incorporates a chamfer to lubricate the oil pump drive gear.

b) On the K4J and K4M engines, the shells with grooves are located on the cylinder block. Bearing caps 2 and 4 have grooved shells, and bearing caps 1, 3 and 5 have non-grooved shells.

c) On the F4R engine, the shells with oil grooves are fitted to the cylinder block and the plain shells are fitted to the caps.

d) On the diesel engines, the shells with the oil holes are fitted to the cylinder block.

4 Note that if the original shells are being re-used, it is important that they are only refitted to their original locations in the block and caps.

5 Before the crankshaft can be permanently installed, the main bearing running clearance should be checked; this can be done in either of two ways. One method is to fit the main bearing caps to the cylinder block, with the bearing shells in place. With the cap retaining bolts tightened to the specified torque, measure the internal diameter of each assembled pair of bearing shells using a vernier dial indicator or internal micrometer. If the diameter of each corresponding crankshaft journal is measured and then subtracted from the bearing internal diameter, the result will be the main bearing running clearance. The second (and more accurate) method is to use a product known as Plastigauge. This consists of a fine thread of perfectly-round plastic which is compressed between the bearing cap and the journal. When the cap is removed, the deformation of the plastic thread is measured with a special card gauge supplied with the kit. The running clearance is determined from this gauge. The procedure for using Plastigauge is as follows.

6 With the upper main bearing shells in place, carefully lay the crankshaft in position **(see illustration)**. Do not use any lubricant; the crankshaft journals and bearing shells must be perfectly clean and dry.

7 Cut several pieces of the appropriate-size Plastigauge (they should be slightly shorter than the width of the main bearings) and place one piece on each crankshaft journal axis **(see illustration)**.

8 With the bearing shells in position in the caps, fit the caps to their numbered or previously-noted locations. Take care not to disturb the Plastigauge.

9 Starting with the centre main bearing and working outward, tighten the main bearing cap bolts progressively to their specified torque setting and where applicable to the specified angle. Don't rotate the crankshaft at any time during this operation.

10 Remove the bolts and carefully lift off the main bearing caps, keeping them in order. Don't disturb the Plastigauge or rotate the crankshaft. If any of the bearing caps are difficult to remove, tap them from side-to-side with a soft-faced mallet.

11 Compare the width of the crushed Plastigauge on each journal to the scale

19.3g Fitting a shell to No 1 main bearing cap (E7J engine)

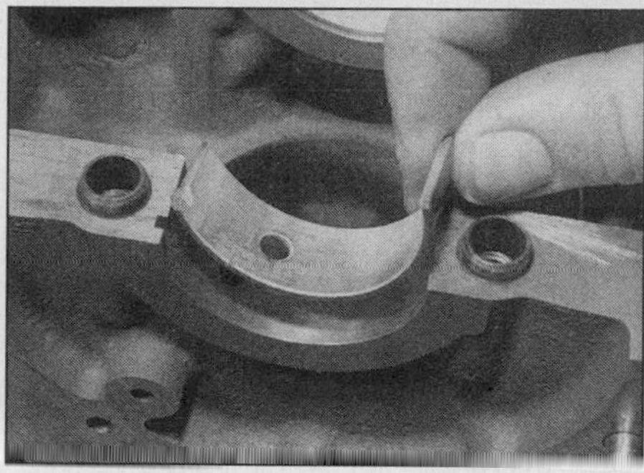

19.3h Fitting a main bearing shell to No 5 position (E7J engine)

2D

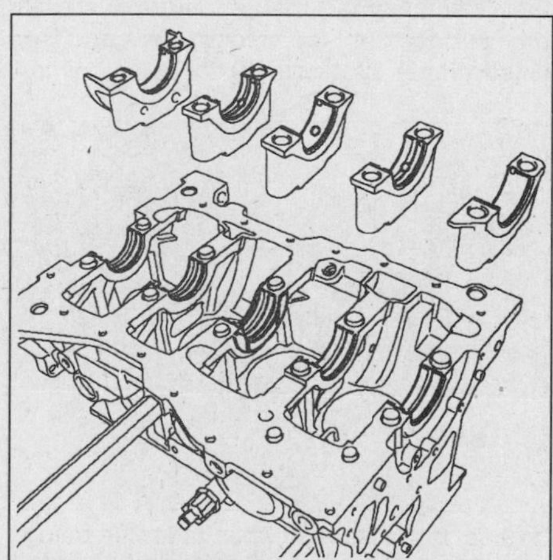

19.3i Bearing shell positions (K4J and K4M engines)

19.6 Lay the crankshaft in position in the crankcase

19.7 Strip of Plastigauge placed on No 5 main bearing journal

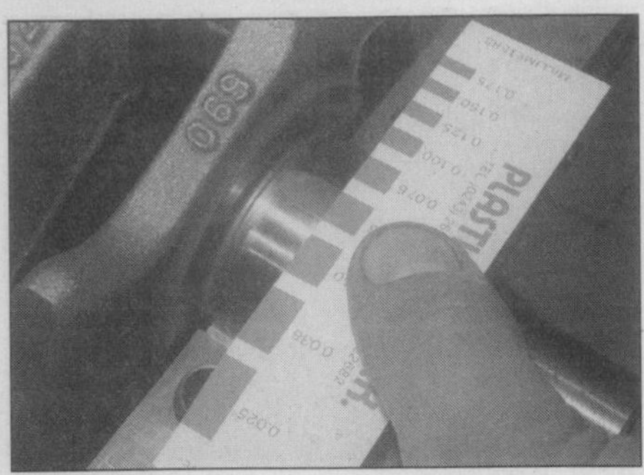
19.11 Using the gauge to check the main bearing running clearance

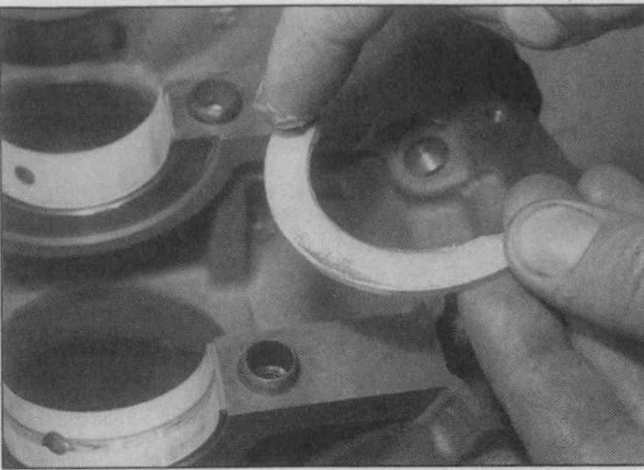
19.15a Smear a little grease on the crankshaft thrustwashers . . .

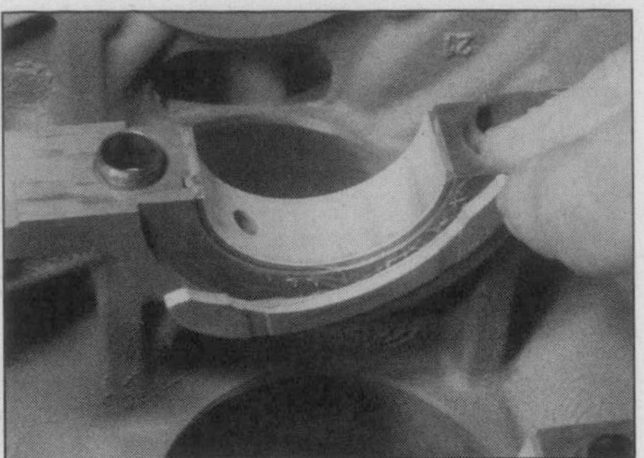
19.15b . . . and stick them to the appropriate main bearing

19.16 Lubricate the main bearing shells before fitting the crankshaft

19.17a Fitting No 5 main bearing cap

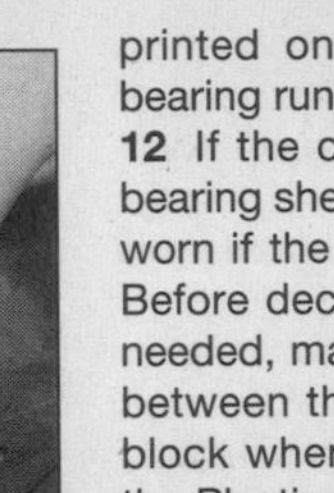

printed on the gauge to obtain the main bearing running clearance **(see illustration)**.

12 If the clearance is not as specified, the bearing shells may be the wrong size (or badly worn if the original shells are being re-used). Before deciding that different size shells are needed, make sure no dirt or oil was trapped between the bearing shells and the caps or block when the clearance was measured. If the Plastigauge was wider at one end than at the other, the journal may be tapered.

13 Carefully scrape away all traces of the Plastigauge material from the crankshaft and bearing shells, using a fingernail or something similar which is unlikely to score the shells.

Final refitting

14 Carefully lift the crankshaft out of the cylinder block once more.

15 Using a little grease, stick the thrustwashers to each side of the centre main bearing (E7J, K4J and K4M engines) or No 2 main bearing (all other engines). Ensure that the oilway grooves on each thrustwasher face outwards from the bearing location, towards the crankshaft webs **(see illustrations)**.

16 Liberally lubricate each bearing shell in the cylinder block and lower the crankshaft into position **(see illustration)**.

17 Lubricate the bearing shells, then fit the bearing caps in their numbered or previously-noted locations **(see illustrations)**. Note the following points.

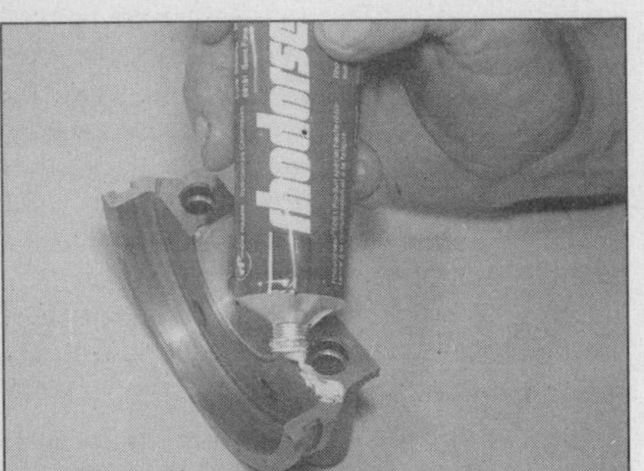
19.17b Apply a thin coating of sealant to the contact faces of No 1 main bearing cap . . .

19.17c . . . before refitting the cap

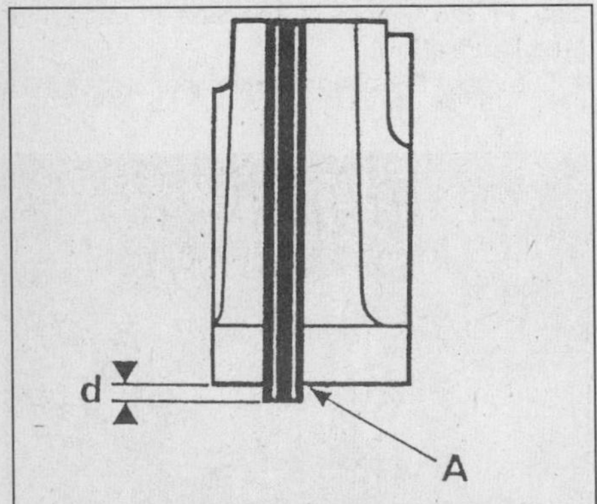

19.17d The butyl seals should protrude beyond the lower face (A) of No 1 main bearing cap

d = 0.2 mm

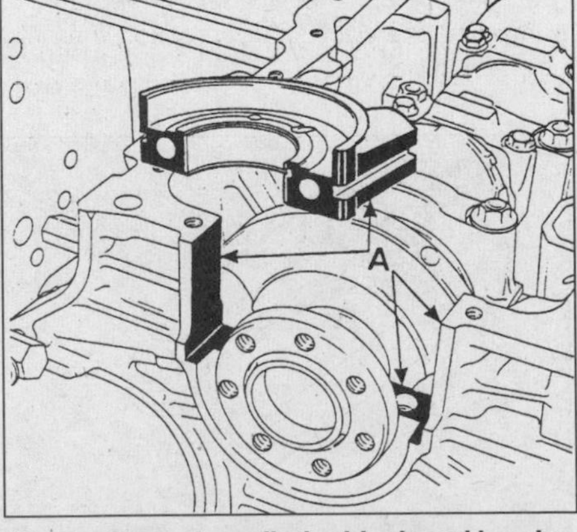

19.17e Clean the cylinder block and bearing cap mating faces (A) when using silicone sealant to seal No 1 main bearing cap . . .

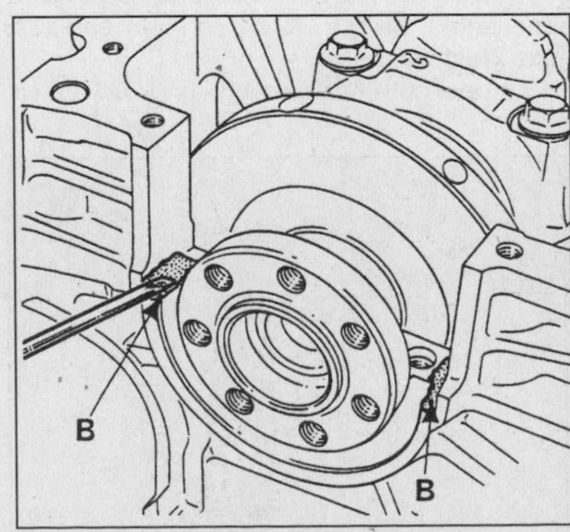

19.17f . . . and coat the lower faces of the cylinder block (B) with sealant

19.17g Injecting sealant into the side grooves of No 1 main bearing cap

19.18a Tighten the main bearing cap bolts to the specified torque . . .

19.18b . . . and angle

a) *On the E7J engine, apply a thin coating of sealant to the outer corners of No 1 main bearing cap*
b) *On the K4J and K4M engines, apply a thin coating of sealant to the complete contact faces of the No 1 main bearing cap.*
c) *If fitting butyl seals to No 1 main bearing cap, fit the seals with their grooves facing outwards. Position the seals so that approximately 0.2 mm of seal protrudes at the bottom-facing side (the side towards the crankcase). Lubricate the seals with a little oil and apply a little sealant to the bottom corners of the cap prior to fitting it. When the cap is being fitted, use the bolts as a guide by just starting them in their threads, then pressing the cap firmly into position. When the cap is almost fully home, check that the seals still protrude slightly at the cylinder block mating face.*
d) *If silicone sealant is to be used on the No 1 main bearing, do not press the cap right down onto the crankshaft, but leave it raised so that the first few threads of the main bearing bolts can just be entered. Now inject the sealant into each of the cap side grooves until it enters the space below the cap and completely fills the grooves.*

18 Fit the main bearing cap bolts and tighten them progressively to the specified torque (and angle on E7J, K4J and K4M engines) **(see illustrations)**.

19 Where butyl seals have been fitted to seal No 1 bearing cap, trim the protruding ends flush with the surface of the cylinder block sump mating face.

20 Where silicone sealant is to be used to seal No 1 main bearing cap, mix the sealant and the hardener as described in the instructions supplied with the kit **(see illustration)**. Inject the mixture into the bearing cap grooves, allowing the mixture to flow out slightly either side of the grooves and at the cylinder block sump mating face, to ensure that the grooves are completely filled. Allow the sealant to dry for a few minutes, then cut away surplus sealant from the joint face, both inside and outside the cylinder block and at the sump mating face.

21 Check that the crankshaft is free to turn. Some stiffness is normal if new components have been fitted, but there must be no jamming or tight spots.

22 Check the crankshaft endfloat with reference to Section 13.

23 Fit a new seal to the crankshaft timing belt end oil seal housing and refit the housing with reference to Chapter 2A, 2B or 2C.

24 Fit a new crankshaft flywheel/driveplate end oil seal, with reference to Chapter 2A, 2B or 2C.

25 Where applicable, refit the timing belt lower inner cover.

26 On completion, refit the piston/connecting rod assemblies, the flywheel/driveplate, oil pump and the crankshaft sprocket, then fit a new timing belt.

20 Piston/connecting rods – big-end bearing clearance check and refitting

1 Clean the backs of the big-end bearing shells and the recesses in the connecting rods and big-end caps. If new shells are being fitted, ensure that all traces of the protective grease are cleaned off using paraffin. Wipe the shells and connecting rods dry with a lint-free cloth.

2 Press the big-end bearing shells into the connecting rods and caps in their correct positions. Make sure that the location tabs are engaged with the cut-outs in the connecting rods. Note that on K4J and K4M engines from July 1999-on, all F4R engines, and the F9Q 732 engine, tags are not incorporated in the shells and, to ensure correct fitting, it is recommended that the Renault tool Mot. 1492 is obtained **(see illustration)**.

2D

Big-end bearing clearance check

E7J petrol engine

3 Place the four liners face down in a row on the bench, in their correct order. Turn them as necessary so that the flats on the edges of liners 1 and 2 are towards each other and the flats on liners 3 and 4 are towards each other also. Fit the O-rings to the base of each liner **(see illustration)**.

4 Lubricate the pistons and piston rings, then

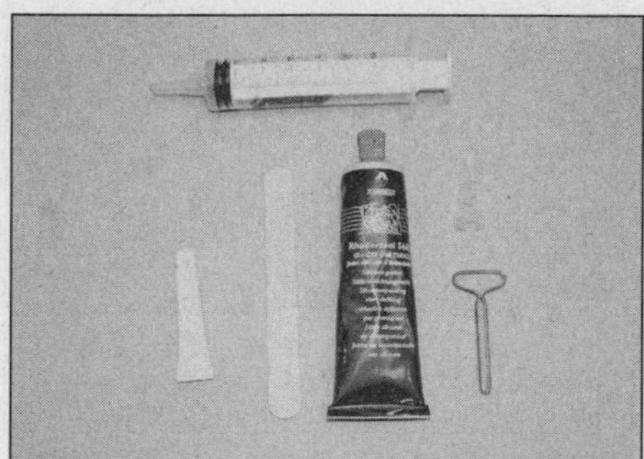

19.20 Main bearing silicone sealant injection kit

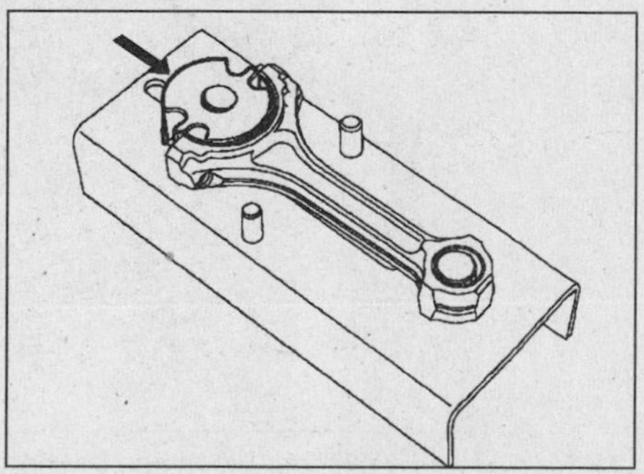

20.2 Using tool Mot. 1492 to fit the big-end shells

20.3 Fitting a liner base O-ring (E7J engines)

20.11 Clamp to hold the liners in place (E7J engines)

20.13 Lubricating the piston rings

place each piston and connecting rod assembly with its respective liner.

5 Starting with assembly No 1, make sure that the piston ring gaps are still spaced at 120° to each other. Clamp the piston rings using a piston ring compressor.

6 Insert the piston and connecting rod assembly into the bottom of the liner, ensuring that the arrow on the piston crown will be facing the flywheel/driveplate end of the engine. Using a block of wood or a hammer handle against the end of the connecting rod, tap the piston into the liner until the top of the piston is approximately 25 mm away from the top of the liner.

7 Repeat the procedure for the remaining three piston-and-liner assemblies.

8 Turn the crankshaft so that No 1 crankpin is at the bottom of its travel.

9 With the liner seal/O-ring in position, place No 1 liner, piston and connecting rod assembly into its location in the cylinder block. Ensure that the arrow on the piston crown faces the flywheel/driveplate end of the engine and that the flat on the liner is positioned as described previously.

10 To measure the big-end bearing running clearance, refer to the information contained in Section 19; the same general procedures apply. If the Plastigauge method is being used, ensure that the crankpin journal and the big-end bearing shells are clean and dry, then pull the connecting rod down and engage it with the crankpin. Place the Plastigauge strip on the crankpin, check that the marks made on the cap and rod during removal are next to each other, then refit the cap and retaining nuts. Tighten the nuts to the specified torque in two stages. Do not rotate the crankshaft during this operation. Remove the cap and check the running clearance by measuring the Plastigauge as previously described.

11 With the liner/piston assembly installed, retain the liner using a bolt and washer screwed into the cylinder head bolt holes, or using liner clamps **(see illustration)**.

12 Repeat the above procedures for the remaining piston-and-liner assemblies.

All other engines

13 Lubricate No 1 piston and piston rings and check that the ring gaps are spaced at 120° intervals to each other **(see illustration)**.

14 Fit a ring compressor to No 1 piston, then insert the piston and connecting rod into No 1 cylinder. On petrol engines, the V arrow must point to the flywheel end of the engine. On F8Q engines, the combustion chamber recess in the piston crown should be on the oil filter side of the engine. With No 1 crankpin at its lowest point, drive the piston carefully into the cylinder with the wooden handle of a hammer, at the same time guiding the connecting rod onto the crankpin **(see illustrations)**.

15 To measure the big-end bearing running clearance, refer to the information contained in Section 19; the same general procedures apply. If the Plastigauge method is being used, ensure that the crankpin journal and the big-end bearing shells are clean and dry, then engage the connecting rod with the crankpin. Place the Plastigauge strip on the crankpin, fit the bearing cap in its previously-noted

20.14a Markings on the top of the piston

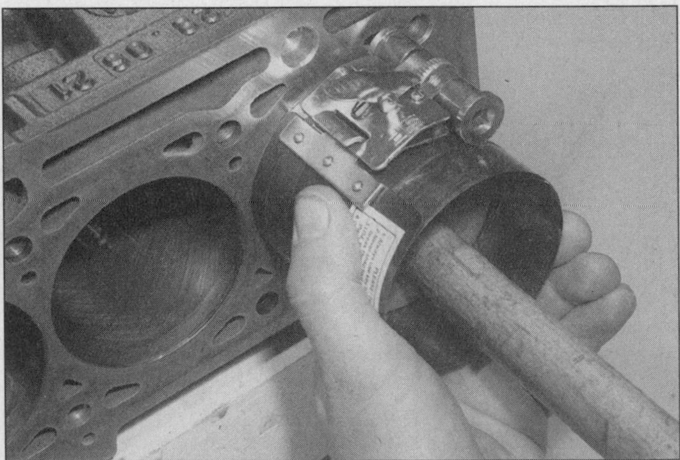
20.14b Using the wooden handle of a hammer to drive the piston into the bore

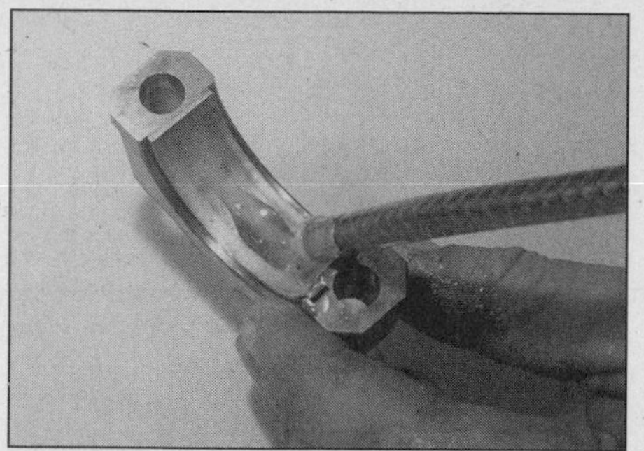

20.18a Lubricate both the cap . . .

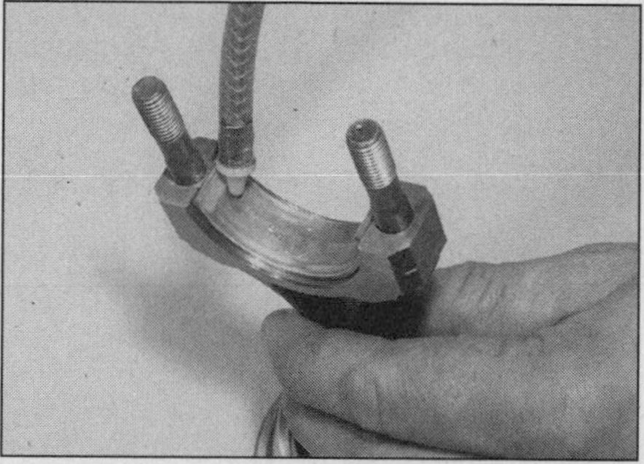

20.18b . . . and connecting rod shells before . . .

20.18c . . . refitting the cap . . .

position, then tighten the nuts/bolts to the specified torque. Do not rotate the crankshaft during this operation. Remove the cap and check the running clearance by measuring the Plastigauge as previously described.

16 Repeat the above procedures on the remaining piston/connecting rod assemblies.

Final refitting

17 Having checked the running clearance of all the crankpin journals and taken any corrective action necessary, clean off all traces of Plastigauge from the bearing shells and crankpin.

18 Liberally lubricate the crankpin journals and big-end bearing shells. Refit the bearing caps once more, ensuring correct positioning as previously described. Tighten the bearing cap nuts/bolts to the specified torque (and angle where applicable) and turn the crankshaft each time to make sure that it is free before moving on to the next assembly. On the E7J engine, check that all the liners are positioned relative to each other, so that a 0.1 mm feeler gauge can pass freely through the gaps between the liners. If this is not the case, it may be necessary to interchange one or more of the complete piston/liner assemblies to achieve this clearance **(see illustrations)**.

19 On completion, refit the oil pump, sump and cylinder head as described in Chapter 2A, 2B or 2C.

20.18d . . . screwing on the nuts . . .

20.18e . . . and tightening the nuts

20.18f Angle-tightening the big-end cap bolts (F9Q 732 engine)

20.18g Checking the gap between the liners (E7J engines)

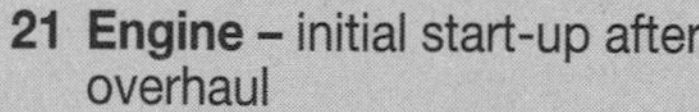

21 Engine – initial start-up after overhaul

1 With the engine refitted in the vehicle, double-check the engine oil and coolant levels. Make a final check that everything has been reconnected and that there are no tools or rags left in the engine compartment.

Petrol-engined models

2 With the spark plugs removed and the engine management system disabled by removing the engine protection fuse from the engine compartment fusebox, crank the engine on the starter motor until the oil pressure light goes out.

3 Refit the spark plugs and the fuse.

4 Start the engine, noting that this may take a little longer than usual, due to the fuel system being empty.

5 While the engine is idling, check for fuel, water and oil leaks. Where applicable, check the power steering pipe/hose unions for leakage. Do not be alarmed if there are some odd smells and smoke from parts getting hot and burning off oil deposits.

6 Keep the engine idling until hot water is felt circulating through the top hose, then switch it off.

7 After a few minutes, recheck the oil and water levels and top-up as necessary (see *Weekly checks*).

8 There is no requirement to retighten the cylinder head bolts.

9 If new pistons, rings or crankshaft bearings have been fitted, the engine must be run-in for the first 500 miles (800 km). Do not operate the engine at full-throttle, nor allow it to labour in any gear during this period. It is recommended that the oil and filter be changed at the end of this period.

Diesel-engined models

10 Prime the fuel system as described in Chapter 4B.

11 Prime the lubrication system by disconnecting the stop solenoid from the injection pump and by cranking the engine on the starter motor in 10 second bursts with pauses of 30 seconds in between. On completion, reconnect the stop solenoid (check that the oil pressure light goes out when the starter motor is being activated).

12 Fully depress the accelerator pedal, turn the ignition key to position M and wait for the pre-heating warning light to go out.

13 Start the engine. Additional cranking may be necessary to bleed the fuel system before the engine starts.

14 Once started, keep the engine running at fast tickover. Check that the oil pressure light goes out, then check that there are no leaks of oil, fuel and coolant. Where applicable, check the power steering pipe/hose unions for leakage. Do not be alarmed if there are some odd smells and smoke from parts getting hot and burning off oil deposits.

15 Keep the engine idling until hot coolant is felt circulating through the radiator top hose, indicating that the engine is at normal operating temperature, then stop the engine and allow it to cool.

16 On F8Q 784 and F8Q 786 engines, retighten the cylinder head bolts (refer to Chapter 2C).

17 Recheck the oil and coolant levels and top-up if necessary (see *Weekly checks*).

18 Check the fuel injection pump timing and the idle speed as described in Chapter 4B.

19 If new pistons, rings or bearings have been fitted, the engine must be run-in at reduced speeds and loads for the first 500 miles (800 km) or so. Do not operate the engine at full throttle, or allow it to labour in any gear during this period. It is beneficial to change the engine oil and filter at the end of this period.

Chapter 3
Cooling, heating and ventilation systems

Contents

Degrees of difficulty

Easy, suitable for novice with little experience 

Fairly easy, suitable for beginner with some experience 

Fairly difficult, suitable for competent DIY mechanic 

Difficult, suitable for experienced DIY mechanic 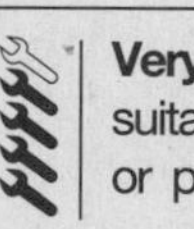

Very difficult, suitable for expert DIY or professional

Specifications

3

General

Air conditioning system:	
Refrigerant type	R134a
Compressor make	Delphi Harrison
Compressor oil	Planetelf PAG 488
Cooling system type	Pressurised, with belt-driven pump, front-mounted radiator and electric cooling fan
Coolant capacity	See Chapter 1A or 1B
System pressure	1.2 bar
Engine designation:	
Petrol models:	
1.4 litre engine	E7J 764, K4J 750
1.6 litre engine	K4M 700, K4M 701
2.0 litre engine	F4R 740, F4R 741
Diesel models:	
Non-turbo engines – D models	F8Q 620, F8Q 622, F8Q 788
Turbo engines:	
dT models – indirect injection	F8Q 784, F8Q 786
dTi models – direct injection	F9Q 730, F9Q 734
dCi models – direct common-rail injection	F9Q 732

Thermostat

Type	Wax
Opening temperatures:	
Starts to open	89°C
Fully open	101°C
Valve lift	7.5 mm

Torque wrench settings

	Nm	lbf ft
Air conditioning compressor bolts:		
Mégane	21	15
Scénic	30	22
Coolant pump:		
E7J (1390cc):		
Bolts	22	16
Nuts	10	7
K4J (1390cc) and K4M (1598cc):		
Stage 1	8	6
Stage 2 (M6 bolts)	11	8
Stage 3 (M8 bolts)	22	16
F4R (1998cc)	17	12
F9Q (1870cc)	17	12

1 General information and precautions

General information

The cooling system is of pressurised type, comprising a coolant pump (which is belt driven), an aluminium crossflow radiator, electric cooling fan(s), a thermostat, heater matrix, and all associated hoses and switches **(see illustrations)**.

The system functions as follows. Cold coolant in the bottom of the radiator passes through the bottom hose to the coolant pump, where it is pumped around the cylinder block and head passages, and through the oil cooler(s) (where fitted). After cooling the cylinder bores, combustion surfaces and valve seats, the coolant reaches the underside of the thermostat, which is initially closed. The coolant passes through the heater, and is returned via the cylinder block to the coolant pump.

When the engine is cold, the coolant circulates only through the cylinder block, cylinder head, and heater. When the coolant reaches a predetermined temperature, the thermostat opens, and the coolant passes through the top hose to the radiator. As the coolant circulates through the radiator, it is cooled by the inrush of air when the car is in forward motion. The airflow is supplemented by the action of the electric cooling fan(s) when necessary. Upon reaching the bottom of the radiator, the coolant has now cooled, and the cycle is repeated.

On diesel engine models, the coolant is also circulated through the engine oil cooler or water-to-oil intercooler and around the turbocharger (where fitted). On models with

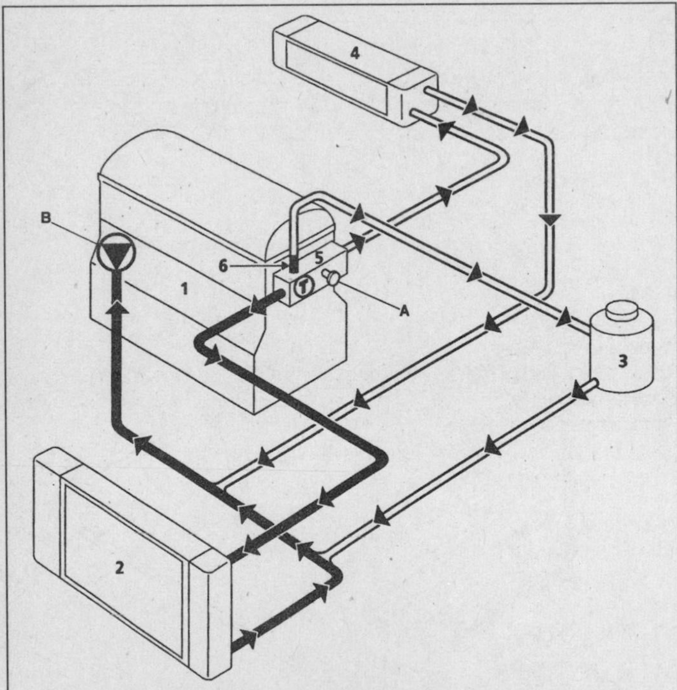

1.1a Cooling system schematic – K4J and K4M engines

1 Cylinder block
2 Radiator
3 Hot expansion bottle with permanent degassing
4 Heater matrix/radiator
5 Thermostat mounting
6 3mm diameter restriction
7 Oil heat exchanger
8 8mm diameter restriction
9 6mm diameter restriction
10 Thermoplunger mounting (where equipped)
A Bleed screws
B Water pump
C Fan thermostatic switch
T Thermostat

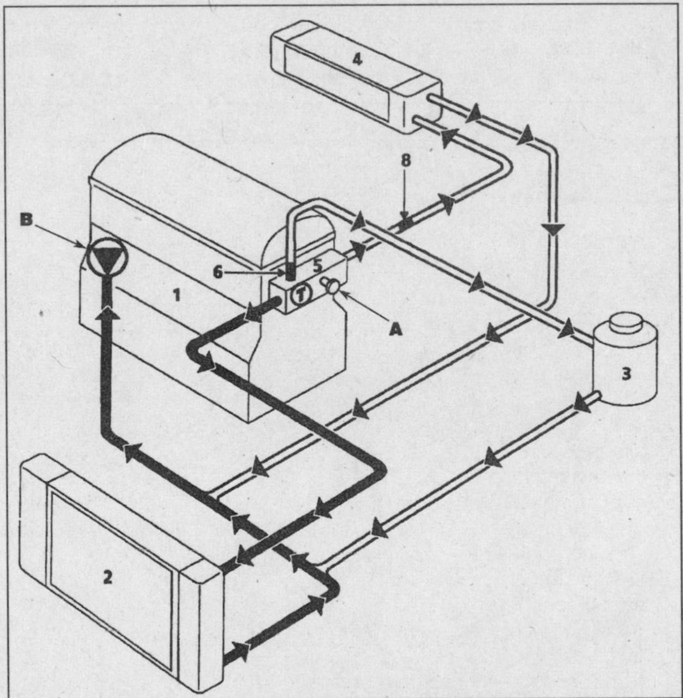

1.1b Cooling system schematic – F4R engines (manual transmission)

See illustration 1.1a for key

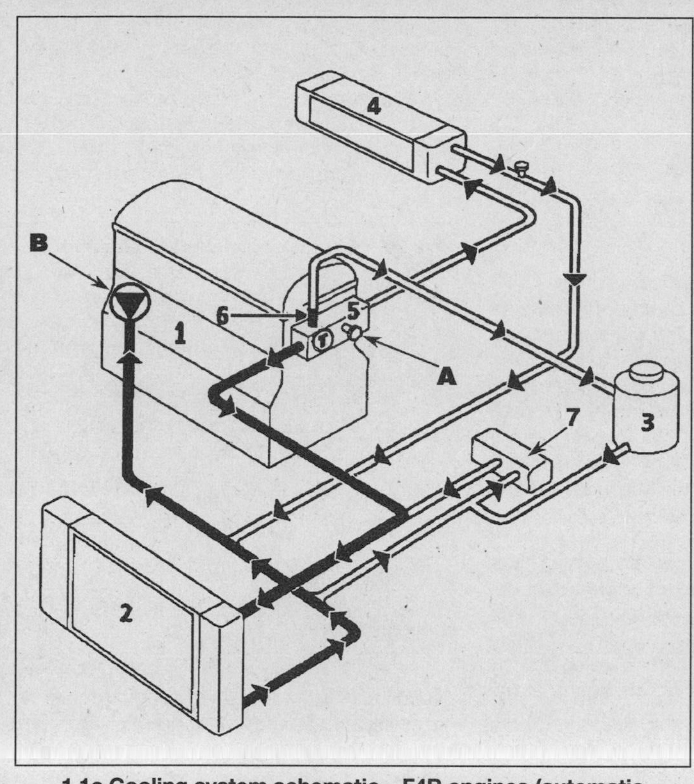

1.1c Cooling system schematic – F4R engines (automatic transmission)

See illustration 1.1a for key

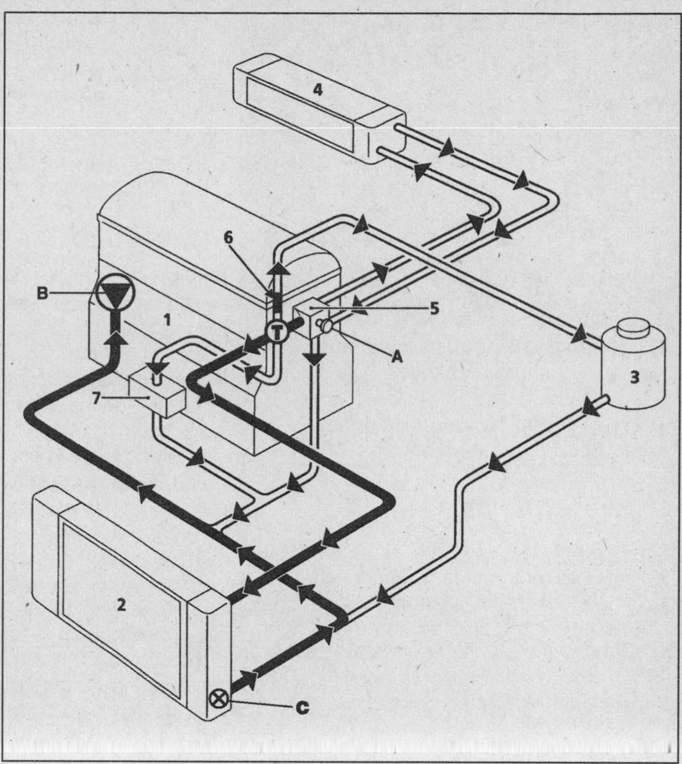

1.1d Cooling system schematic – F8Q engines

See illustration 1.1a for key

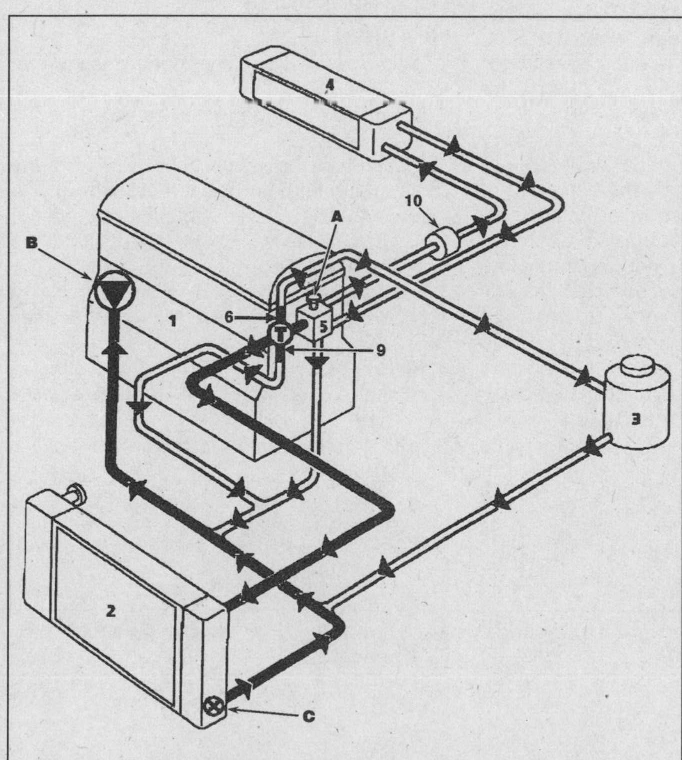

1.1e Cooling system schematic – F9Q (dTi) engines

See illustration 1.1a for key

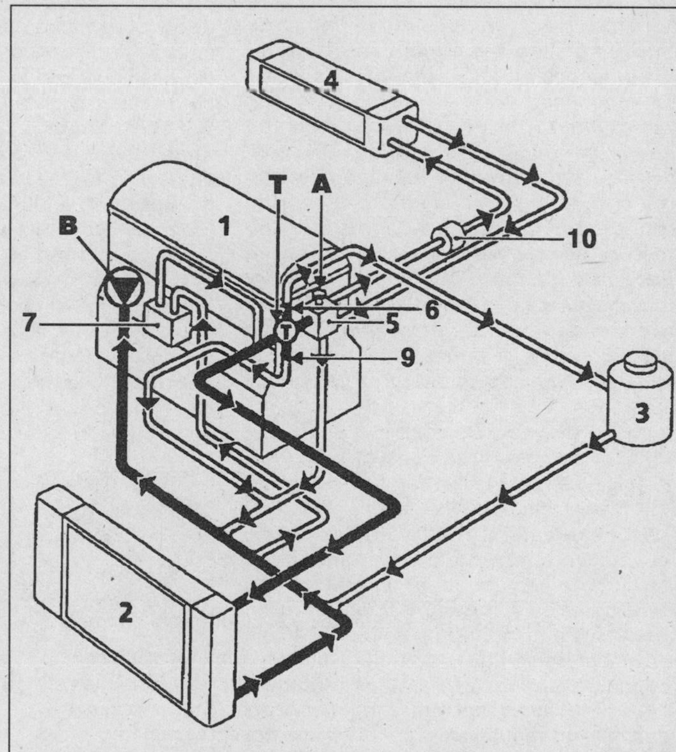

1.1f Cooling system schematic – F9Q (dCi) engines

See illustration 1.1a for key

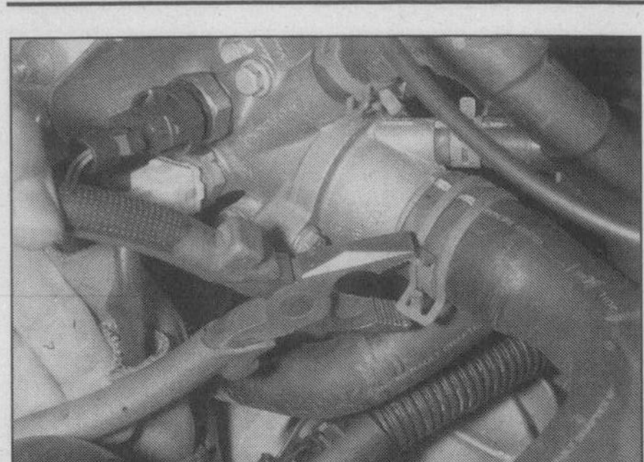
2.3 Removing a coolant hose spring clip using pliers

automatic transmission, the coolant is also passed through the fluid cooler on the top of the transmission.

When the engine is at normal operating temperature, the coolant expands, and some of it is displaced into the expansion tank. Coolant collects in the tank, and is returned to the radiator when the system cools.

The electric cooling fan mounted behind the radiator is controlled by a thermostatic switch. At a predetermined coolant temperature, the switch actuates the fan.

Precautions

Warning: Do not attempt to remove the expansion tank filler cap, or to disturb any part of the cooling system, while the engine is hot, as there is a high risk of scalding. If the expansion tank filler cap must be removed before the engine and radiator have fully cooled (even though this is not recommended), the pressure in the cooling system must first be relieved. Cover the cap with a thick layer of cloth to avoid scalding, and slowly unscrew the filler cap until a hissing sound is heard. When the hissing has stopped, indicating that the pressure has reduced, slowly unscrew the filler cap until it can be removed; if more hissing sounds are heard, wait until they have stopped before unscrewing the cap completely. At all times, keep well away from the filler cap opening, and protect your hands.

Warning: Do not allow antifreeze to come into contact with your skin, or with the painted surfaces of the vehicle. Rinse off spills immediately, with plenty of water. Never leave antifreeze lying around in an open container, or in a puddle in the driveway or on the garage floor. Children and pets are attracted by its sweet smell, but antifreeze can be fatal if ingested.

Warning: If the engine is hot, the electric cooling fan may start rotating even if the engine is not running. Be careful to keep your hands, hair, and any loose clothing well clear when working in the engine compartment.

Warning: Refer to Section 11 for precautions to be observed when working on models equipped with air conditioning.

2 Cooling system hoses – disconnection and renewal

Note: *Refer to the warnings given in Section 1 of this Chapter before proceeding. Hoses should only be disconnected once the engine has cooled sufficiently to avoid scalding.*

1 If the checks described in Chapter 1A or 1B reveal a faulty hose, it must be renewed as follows.

2 First drain the cooling system (Chapter 1A or 1B). If the coolant is not due for renewal, it may be re-used, providing it is collected in a clean container.

3 Release the hose clips from the hose concerned. Three types of clip are used: worm-drive, spring and crimped-type. The worm-drive clip is released by simply turning its screw. The spring clip is released by squeezing its tags together with pliers, at the same time working the clip away from the hose stub **(see illustration)**. The crimped-type clip is not re-usable, and is best cut off with snips or side-cutters and a standard worm-drive clip used instead. Release the clips at both ends, move them along the hose, and position them clear of the union.

4 Carefully work the hose free. The hoses can be removed with relative ease when new – on an older car, however, where the hoses have not been changed for some time, the rubber can become stuck to the hose stubs.

5 If a hose proves to be difficult to remove, try to release it by rotating its ends before attempting to free it. Gently prise the end of the hose with a blunt instrument (such as a flat-bladed screwdriver), but do not apply too much force, and take care not to damage the pipe stubs or hoses. Note in particular that the radiator inlet stub is fragile; do not use excessive force when attempting to remove the hose. If all else fails, cut the hose with a sharp knife, then slit it so that it can be peeled off in two pieces. Although this may prove expensive if the hose is otherwise undamaged, it is preferable to buying a new radiator. Check first, however, that a new hose is readily available.

6 When fitting a hose, first slide the clips onto the hose, then work the hose into position. If crimped-type clips were originally fitted, use standard worm-drive clips when refitting the hose.

If the hose is stiff, use a little soapy water as a lubricant, or soften the hose by soaking it in hot water. Do not use oil or grease, which may attack the rubber.

7 Work the hose into position, checking that it is correctly routed, then position the clips at the ends making sure they are properly adjusted before tightening them.

8 Refill the cooling system with reference to Chapter 1A or 1B.

9 Check thoroughly for leaks as soon as possible after disturbing any part of the cooling system.

3 Radiator – removal, inspection and refitting

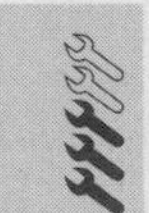

Note: *If leakage is the reason for removing the radiator, bear in mind that minor leaks can often be cured using a radiator sealant with the radiator in situ.*

Removal

1 Disconnect the battery negative lead (refer to Chapter 5A).

2 Drain the cooling system as described in Chapter 1A or 1B.

3 Disconnect the wiring connector from the radiator cooling fan **(see illustration)**. On some diesel engines, disconnect the radiator fan switch, which is screwed into the left-hand side of the radiator.

4 Release the retaining clips and disconnect the coolant hoses from the radiator (see Section 2).

5 Slacken and remove the nuts/bolts (as applicable) securing the radiator upper mounting brackets to the bonnet crossmember **(see illustration)**. If access

3.3 Disconnect the wiring connector from the cooling fan

3.5 Undo the upper radiator securing bolts (Scénic model shown)

3.7 Unclip the PAS reservoir from the radiator assembly

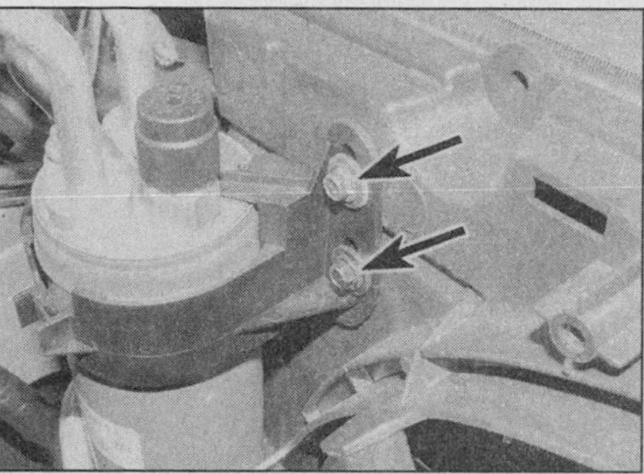

3.8 Undo the two drier rreservoir retaining screws (arrowed)

3.9 Withdraw the cooling fan assembly from the vehicle

cannot easily be gained to the mounting nut/bolt, it may prove sufficient to simply unclip the radiator from the bracket.

6 Where necessary, slacken and remove the bonnet crossmember mounting bolts, then remove the crossmember from the vehicle. Remove the upper mounting brackets and rubbers from the top of the radiator.

7 Unclip the power steering fluid reservoir and position it clear of the radiator **(see illustration)**.

8 On models with air conditioning, slacken and remove the retaining bolts and nuts, and free the drier reservoir from the rear of the radiator **(see illustration)**. Slacken and remove the bolts securing the condenser to the front of the radiator, and separate the two.

Warning: Do not attempt to open the refrigerant circuit. Refer to the precautions in Section 11.

9 Remove the cooling fan assembly from the radiator and withdraw from the engine compartment **(see illustration)**.

10 Check that all pipes/wiring is released, then lift the radiator out from the engine compartment, taking care not to lose the radiator lower mounting rubbers.

Inspection

11 If the radiator has been removed due to suspected blockage, reverse-flush it as described in Chapter 1A or 1B. Clean dirt and debris from the radiator fins, using an air line (in which case, wear eye protection) or a soft brush. Be careful, as the fins are sharp, and easily damaged.

12 If necessary, a radiator specialist can perform a 'flow test' on the radiator, to establish whether an internal blockage exists.

13 A leaking radiator must be referred to a specialist for permanent repair. Do not attempt to weld or solder a leaking radiator, as damage to the plastic components may result.

14 If the radiator is to be sent for repair or renewed, remove all hoses and the cooling fan switch (where fitted).

15 Inspect the condition of the radiator mounting rubbers, and renew them if necessary.

Refitting

16 Refitting is a reversal of removal, ensuring that all the mounting rubbers are correctly positioned, and that the upper mounting brackets are correctly engaged with the radiator. On completion, refill the cooling system as described in Chapter 1A or 1B.

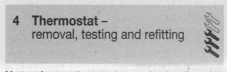

4 Thermostat – removal, testing and refitting

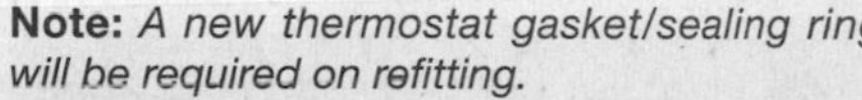

Note: *A new thermostat gasket/sealing ring will be required on refitting.*

Removal

1 Disconnect the battery negative lead (refer to Chapter 5A).

2 Where necessary, remove the engine cover and air cleaner assembly (Chapter 4A or 4B), then release any relevant wiring and hoses from the retaining clips, and position clear of the thermostat housing to improve access.

3 Drain the cooling system as described in Chapter 1A or 1B. The thermostat housing is mounted on the left-hand end of the cylinder head.

4 Disconnect the coolant hose(s) from the thermostat housing cover (see Section 2).

5 Unscrew the nuts/bolts (as applicable), and carefully withdraw the thermostat housing/cover to expose the thermostat **(see illustrations)**. Where necessary, remove the housing gasket/seal and discard it; a new one should be used on refitting.

6 Lift the thermostat from the housing, and recover the sealing ring **(see illustration)**.

4.5a Thermostat housing on the K4J engine . . .

4.5b . . . and on the K4M engine . . .

4.5c . . . and removing the housing on the F9Q engine

4.6 Remove the thermostat housing cover sealing ring

3

Testing

7 A rough test of the thermostat may be made by suspending it with a piece of string in a container full of water so that it is immersed in the water but not touching the sides or bottom of the container. Heat the water to bring it to the boil – the thermostat must open by the time the water boils. If not, renew it.
8 If a thermometer is available, the precise opening temperature of the thermostat may be determined; compare with the figures given in the Specifications. The opening temperature is also marked on the thermostat.
9 A thermostat which fails to close as the water cools must also be renewed.

Refitting

10 Refitting is a reversal of removal, bearing in mind the following points:

a) *Always fit a new sealing ring and ensure that the thermostat is fitted the correct way round, with the spring(s) facing into the housing. The housing gasket (where fitted) should also be renewed.*
b) *On completion, refill the cooling system as described in Chapter 1A or 1B.*

5 Electric cooling fan – testing, removal and refitting

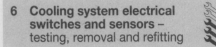

Testing

1 Current supply to the cooling fan is via the ignition switch and a fuse (see Chapter 12). On E7J petrol, F8Q diesel and F9Q dTi diesel engines the circuit is completed by the cooling fan thermostatic switch, which is mounted in the left-hand side of the radiator. On all the other petrol and F9Q dCi diesel engine models, the fan is controlled by the fuel injection ECU.
2 If a fan does not appear to work, first check the fuse. Run the engine until normal operating temperature is reached, then allow it to idle. The fan should cut in within a few minutes (before the temperature gauge needle enters the red section, or before the coolant temperature warning light comes on).
3 On models with a cooling fan switch, if the fan does not operate, switch off the ignition and disconnect the wiring plug from the cooling fan switch. Bridge the two contacts in the wiring plug using a length of spare wire, and switch on the ignition. If the fan now operates, the switch is probably faulty, and should be renewed.
4 If the fan still fails to operate, check that battery voltage is available at the feed wire to the switch; if not, then there is a fault in the feed wire. If there is no problem with the feed, check that there is continuity between the switch earth terminal and a good earth point on the body; if not, then the earth connection is faulty, and must be re-made.
5 If the switch and the wiring are in good condition, the fault must lie in the motor itself. The motor can be checked by disconnecting it from the wiring loom and connecting a 12 volt supply directly to it.

Removal

6 Disconnect the battery negative lead (refer to Chapter 5A).
7 Where necessary, unclip/unbolt the power steering fluid reservoir and position it clear of the cooling fan.
8 On models with air conditioning, slacken and remove the retaining bolts and nuts, and free the drier reservoir from the rear of the radiator.

Warning: Do not attempt to open the refrigerant circuit. Refer to the precautions in Section 11.

9 Disconnect the wiring connector from the cooling fan motor, and free the wiring from the fan shroud **(see illustration)**.
10 Slacken and remove the bolts securing the fan shroud to the rear of the radiator then manoeuvre the assembly out from the engine compartment.
11 If necessary, slide off retaining clip/undo the retaining screw (as applicable) and remove the fan from the motor spindle. The motor can then be unbolted and removed from the shroud **(see illustration)**. If the motor is faulty, the complete unit must be renewed, as no spares are available.

Refitting

12 Refitting is a reversal of removal, noting the following points.

a) *Prior to refitting, inspect the fan shroud mountings, renewing them if they show signs of wear or damage.*
b) *Ensure that the wiring is correctly routed and secured in position with all the relevant clips and ties, so that it is no danger of contacting the fan.*

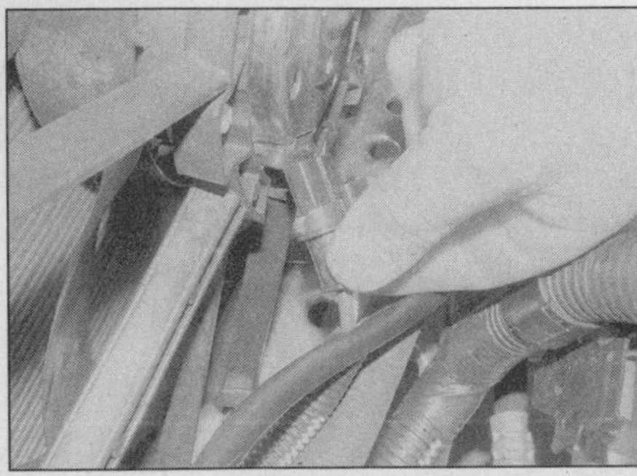
5.9 Disconnecting the cooling fan motor wiring connector

5.11 Undo the three retaining bolts (arrowed)

6 Cooling system electrical switches and sensors – testing, removal and refitting

Cooling fan thermostatic switch

Testing

1 Testing of the switch is described in Section 5, as part of the electric cooling fan test procedure.

Removal

2 On E7J petrol, F8Q diesel and F9Q dTi diesel engines, there is a switch located in the left-hand side of the radiator. The engine and radiator should be cold before removing the switch.
3 Disconnect the battery negative lead (refer to Chapter 5A).
4 Partially drain the cooling system to just below the level of the switch (as described in Chapter 1A or 1B). Alternatively, have ready a suitable bung to plug the switch aperture in the radiator when the switch is removed. If this method is used, take great care not to damage the radiator, and do not use anything which will allow foreign matter to enter the radiator.
5 Disconnect the wiring plug from the switch.
6 Carefully unscrew the switch from the radiator, and recover the sealing ring (where fitted). If the system has not been drained, plug the switch aperture to prevent further coolant loss.

Refitting

7 If the switch was originally fitted using a sealing ring, use a new sealing ring on refitting. Where no sealing ring was fitted, clean the switch threads thoroughly, and coat them with fresh sealing compound.
8 Refitting is a reversal of removal. Tighten the switch securely and refill (or top-up) the cooling system as described in Chapter 1A or 1B.
9 On completion, start the engine and run it until it reaches normal operating temperature. Continue to run the engine, and check that the cooling fan cuts in and out correctly.

Temperature gauge/warning light sender

Testing

10 The coolant temperature gauge/warning light sender is fitted to the thermostat housing on the left-hand end of the cylinder head. On petrol engine models, where two sender units are visible, the upper one is the temperature

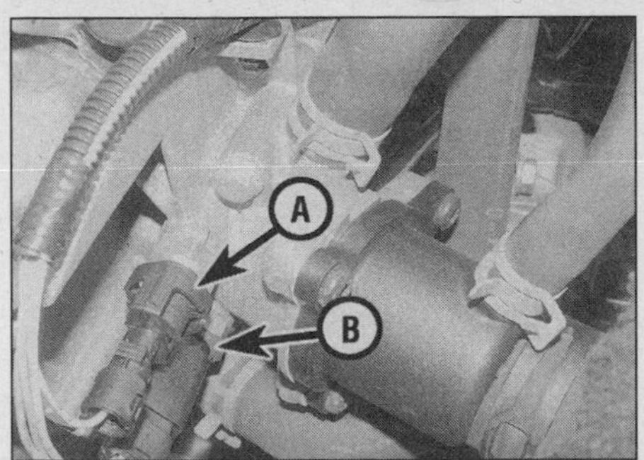

6.17a Temperature gauge sender (A) – K4J engine

Fuel injection system temperature sender (B) is also visible

gauge sender. On diesel engine models, the sender is fitted to the end of the housing.

11 The temperature gauge is fed with a stabilised voltage from the instrument panel feed (via the ignition switch and a fuse). The gauge earth is controlled by the sender. The sender contains a thermistor – an electronic component whose electrical resistance decreases as its temperature rises. When the coolant is cold, the sender resistance is high, current flow through the gauge is reduced and the gauge needle points towards the cold end of the scale. As the coolant temperature rises and the sender resistance falls, current flow increases, and the gauge needle moves towards the upper end of the scale. If the sender is faulty, it must be renewed.

12 The temperature warning light is fed with a voltage from the instrument panel. The light's earth is controlled by the sender. The sender is effectively a switch, which operates at a predetermined temperature to earth the light and complete the circuit.

13 If the gauge develops a fault, first check the other instruments; if they do not work at all, check the instrument panel electrical feed. If the readings are erratic, there may be a fault in the voltage stabiliser, which will necessitate renewal of the stabiliser (the stabiliser is integral with the instrument panel printed circuit board – see Chapter 12). If the fault lies in the temperature gauge alone, check it as follows.

14 If the gauge needle remains at the cold end of the scale when the engine is hot, disconnect the sender wiring plug, and earth the relevant wire to the cylinder head. If the needle then deflects when the ignition is switched on, the sender unit is proved faulty, and should be renewed. If the needle still does not move, remove the instrument panel (Chapter 12) and check the continuity of the wire between the sender unit and the gauge, and the feed to the gauge unit. If continuity is shown, and the fault still exists, then the gauge is faulty, and the gauge unit should be renewed.

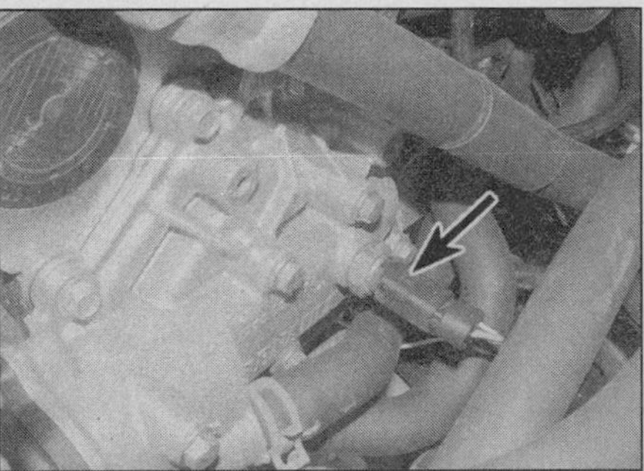

6.17b Temperature gauge sender (arrowed) in the thermostat housing – K4M engine

15 If the gauge needle remains at the hot end of the scale when the engine is cold, disconnect the sender wire. If the needle then returns to the cold end of the scale when the ignition is switched on, the sender unit is proved faulty, and should be renewed. If the needle still does not move, check the remainder of the circuit as described previously.

16 The same basic principles apply to testing the warning light. The light should illuminate when the relevant sender wire is earthed.

Removal and refitting

17 On petrol engine models, remove and refit the sender using the information given for the cooling fan switch (paragraphs 2 to 9) **(see illustrations)**.

18 On diesel engine models, refer to the information given in paragraphs 2 to 9 for the cooling fan switch, noting that the sender is clipped into the housing. Press the sender into the housing then, using a small flat-bladed screwdriver, lever out the retaining clip and remove the sender and sealing ring. On refitting, fit a new sealing ring to the sender, then press the sender into the thermostat housing and secure it in position with the retaining clip **(see illustrations)**.

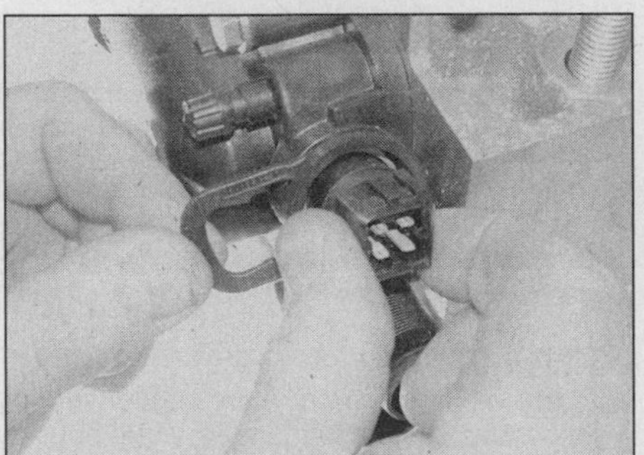

6.18a Unclip the temperature sender . . .

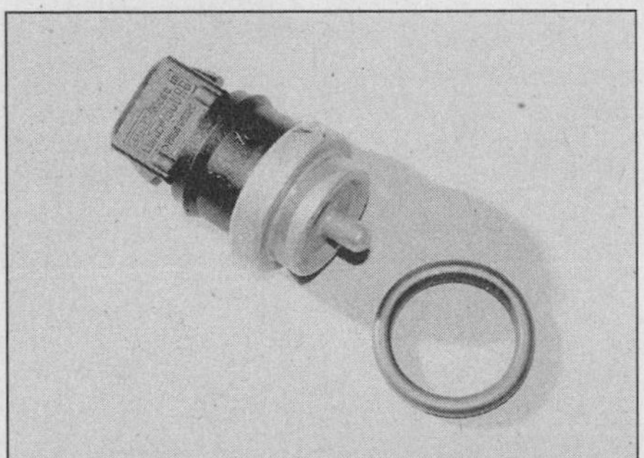

6.18b . . . and fit new sealing ring – F9Q diesel

Fuel injection system temperature sensor

Testing

19 The fuel injection system coolant temperature sensor on some petrol-engined models, is located in the thermostat housing on the left-hand end of the cylinder head. The sensor is the lower of the two sensors which are screwed into the front of the housing **(see illustration 6.17a)**.

20 The sensor is a thermistor (refer to paragraph 11). The fuel injection/engine management electronic control unit (ECU) supplies the sensor with a set voltage and then, by measuring the current flowing in the sensor circuit, it determines the engine's temperature. This information is then used, in conjunction with other inputs, to control the injector opening time (pulse width). On some models, the idle speed and/or ignition timing settings are also temperature-dependent.

21 If the sensor circuit should fail to provide adequate information, the ECU's back-up facility will override the sensor signal. In this event, the ECU assumes a predetermined setting which will allow the fuel injection/engine management system to run, albeit at reduced efficiency. When this occurs, the warning light on the instrument panel will come on, and the advice of a Renault dealer should be sought. The sensor itself can only be tested using special Renault diagnostic equipment. *Do not* attempt to test the circuit using any other equipment, as there is a high risk of damaging the ECU.

Removal and refitting

22 Remove and refit the sensor using the information given for the cooling fan switch (paragraphs 2 to 9).

7 Coolant pump – removal and refitting

1 If the coolant pump is leaking, or is noisy in operation, it must be renewed.

K4J and K4M engines

Note: *A tube of loctite 518 sealant will be required on refitting.*

Removal

2 Disconnect the battery negative lead, then drain the cooling system as described in Chapter 1A.

3 Remove the timing belt and timing belt tensioner as described in Chapter 2A.

4 Slacken and remove the coolant pump retaining bolts, noting the locations of the different size bolts.

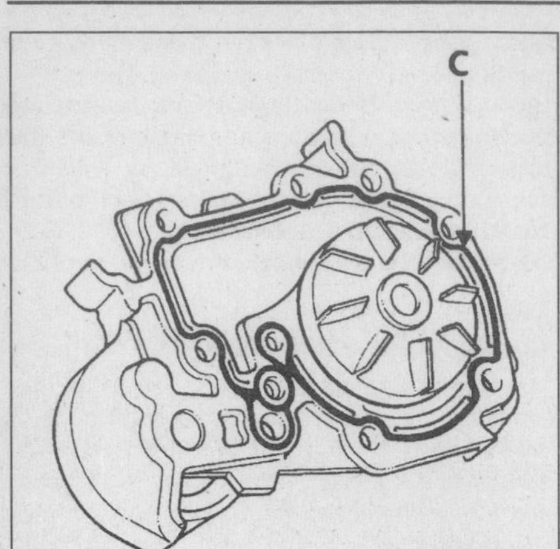

7.7 Apply a bead of sealant (C) – K4M and K4J engines

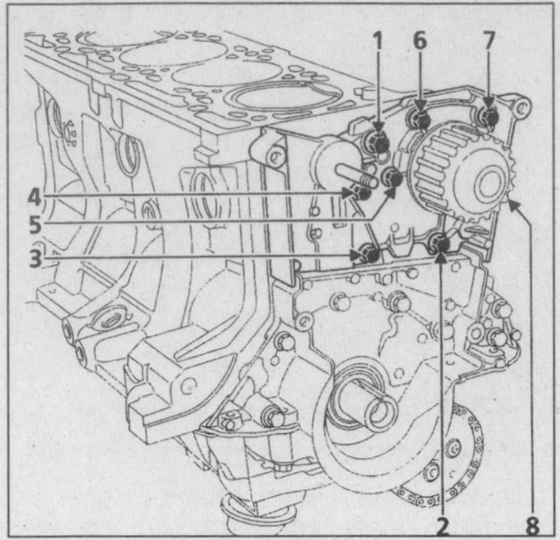

7.9 Coolant pump retaining bolts tightening sequence – K4M and K4J engine

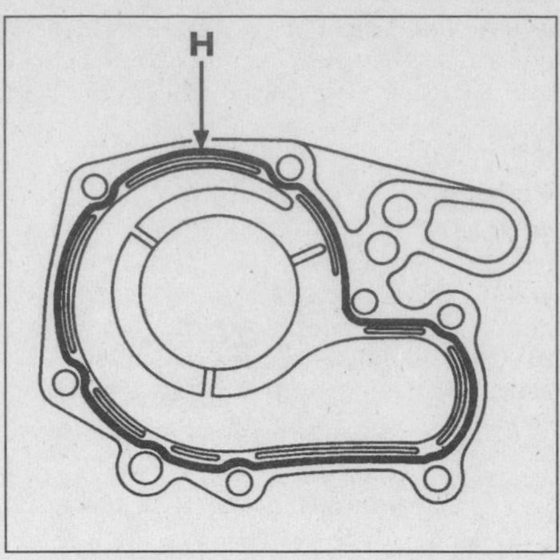

7.15 On E7J engines, apply a bead of sealant (H) to the coolant mating surface

5 Withdraw the pump from the block, tapping it with a soft-faced mallet if it is stuck.

Refitting

6 Commence refitting by thoroughly cleaning the mating surfaces of the pump and cylinder block, ensuring that all traces of sealant are removed.

7 Apply a 0.6 to 1.0mm wide band of Loctite 518 sealant to the pump mating face **(see illustration)**.

8 Locate the pump in position and refit the retaining bolts to their correct locations, tightening them to their specified torque. Note that a suitable thread sealant should be applied to the threads of bolts 1 and 4 **(see illustration 7.9)**.

9 Work in the sequence shown **(see illustration)**, to tighten all the bolts to the specified Stage 1 torque setting. Again working in sequence tighten the M6 bolts to the torque setting given for Stage 2, then tighten the M8 bolts to the setting given for Stage 3 (see specifications at the start of this Chapter).

10 Refit the timing belt tensioner and timing belt as described in Chapter 2A.

11 On completion, refill the cooling system as described in Chapter 1A.

E7J engine

Removal

12 Drain the cooling system (see Chapter 1A).

13 Remove the timing belt as described in Chapter 2A.

14 Slacken and remove the retaining bolts, and withdraw the pump assembly from the engine. Note the correct fitted location of the pump locating dowels, and remove them for safe-keeping if they are loose.

Refitting

15 Ensure that the mating surfaces of the pump and cylinder block are clean and dry, then apply a bead of sealant 0.6 to 1.0 mm thick (Renault recommend the use of Loctite 518 – available from your Renault dealer) to the pump sealing face **(see illustration)**.

16 Ensure that the locating dowels are correctly positioned then manoeuvre the pump into position. Refit the pump bolts and tighten them securely.

17 Refit the timing belt (see Chapter 2A).

18 Refill the cooling system as described in Chapter 1A.

F4R engine

Removal

19 Drain the cooling system (see Chapter 1A).

20 Jack up the front of the car and support on axle stands (see *Jacking and vehicle support*). Remove the right-hand front roadwheel and wheelarch liner.

21 Loosen the three coolant pump pulley retaining bolts, then remove the auxiliary drivebelt as described in Chapter 1A.

22 Remove the bolts from the lower timing cover and separate from the upper cover to withdraw.

23 Unscrew the securing bolts and remove the pump pulley.

24 Unscrew the bolts securing the pump to the cylinder block, and withdraw the pump from the block. If the pump is stuck, tap it free using a soft-faced mallet. Recover the gasket/seal.

7.28 Loosen the three coolant pump pulley bolts (arrowed) – diesel engine

Refitting

25 Refitting is a reversal of removal, bearing in mind the following points.

a) Thoroughly clean the mating faces of the pump and cylinder block.
b) Use a new pump gasket/seal.
c) Fit and tension the auxiliary drivebelt as described in Chapter 1A.
d) On completion, refill the cooling system as described in Chapter 1A.

Diesel models

Note: *A new thermostat gasket/sealing ring may be required on some models when refitting.*

Removal

26 Remove the auxiliary drivebelt as described in Chapter 1B, noting that the coolant pump (and PAS pump on F9Q dCi engines) pulley retaining bolts should be slackened before the belt is removed.

27 Drain the cooling system (see Chapter 1B). On F9Q dCi engines unclip the fuel filter and move it to one side.

28 Unscrew the retaining bolts, and remove the drivebelt pulley(s) from the coolant pump and PAS pump (where applicable) **(see illustration)**.

29 Unscrew the retaining bolts, then manoeuvre the coolant pump out of position **(see illustration)**. Where fitted, note the

7.29 Withdrawing the coolant pump – diesel engines

correct fitted location of the pump locating dowels, and remove them for safe-keeping if they are loose. Recover the pump gasket and discard it; a new one must be used on refitting.

Refitting

30 Ensure that pump and cylinder block/housing mating faces are clean and dry, and that the (where applicable) locating dowels are correctly positioned.

31 Offer up the new gasket and fit the pump assembly, tightening its retaining bolts securely.

32 Refit the coolant pump pulley, fit the drivebelt and tension as described in Chapter 1B, then securely tighten the pulley retaining bolts.

33 Refill the cooling system as described in Chapter 1B.

8 Heating and ventilation system – general information

The heating/ventilation system consists of a fully-adjustable blower motor, face level vents in the centre and at each end of the facia, and air ducts to the windows on the front doors, to the windscreen and to the footwells of both front and rear passengers.

The control unit is located in the facia, and the controls operate flap valves to deflect and mix the air flowing through the various parts of the heating/ventilation system. The flap valves are contained in the air distribution housing, which acts as a central distribution unit, passing air to the various ducts and vents.

Cold air enters the system through the grille at the rear of the engine compartment. If required, the airflow is boosted by the blower, and then flows through the various ducts, according to the settings of the controls. Stale air is expelled through ducts at the rear of the vehicle. If warm air is required, the cold air is passed over the heater matrix, which is heated by the engine coolant.

On some models, a recirculation switch enables the outside air supply to be closed off, while the air inside the vehicle is recirculated. This can be useful to prevent unpleasant odours entering from outside the vehicle – for instance, when driving in heavy traffic – but should only be used briefly, as the recirculated air inside the vehicle will soon become stale and may cause light misting.

9 Heater/ventilation components (all models except Scénic) – removal and refitting

Models without air conditioning

Heater/ventilation control unit

1 Disconnect the battery negative lead.

2 Remove the cigarette lighter as described in Chapter 12.

3 Unclip the control unit and withdraw it from the facia **(see illustration)**.

4 Disconnect the wiring connectors, then release the outer cable clips from the unit and detach the inner cables from their levers; note that the control cables are colour-coded for identification **(see illustrations)**. If necessary, unclip the control unit from the facia panel.

5 Refitting is a reversal of removal, but ensure that the control cables are securely reconnected to their original locations; the air temperature (hot/cold) cable is red, and the air distribution cable is blue. Check the operation of the controls prior to refitting the cigarette lighter.

Heater/ventilation control cables

6 Remove the control unit as described in paragraphs 1 to 4. Access to the cable fixings on the right-hand side of the air distribution housing can be gained both from beneath the facia and through the control unit aperture.

7 Make alignment marks between the control cables and their retaining clips on the side of the air distribution housing. The marks can then be used on refitting to ensure that the cables are correctly positioned.

8 Unhook the retaining clip(s) then detach the cable(s) from the housing and lever and withdraw from the facia; note that the control cables are colour-coded for identification.

9 On refitting, manoeuvre the cable(s) into position, noting that they are colour-coded; the air temperature (hot/cold) cable is red, and the air distribution cable is blue.

10 Engage the inner cable(s) with the housing levers, and seat the outer cable(s) on the housing. Align the retaining clips with the marks made prior to removal, and secure both cables in position with the retaining clips. Refit the control unit and check the operation of the cables.

Blower motor (standard system)

11 Disconnect the battery negative lead. Referring to Chapter 12, on right-hand-drive models remove the passenger side wiper arm, and on left-hand-drive models remove both windscreen wiper arms.

12 Remove the sealing strip from the top of the engine compartment bulkhead.

13 Undo the retaining screws and remove the inlet vent panel from beneath the left-hand side of the windscreen.

14 Undo the two retaining screws and remove the plastic cover from the left-hand side of the blower motor.

15 Disconnect the wiring connectors from the right-hand side of the blower motor assembly and remove the right-hand securing bolt which is underneath the wiring connectors.

16 Unbolt and remove the water deflector, then slacken and remove the left-hand mounting bolt of the blower motor assembly, manoeuvring the motor out from the left-hand side.

17 Refitting is the reverse of removal,

9.3 Unclip the heater control unit from the facia . . .

9.4a . . . and disconnect the wiring connectors

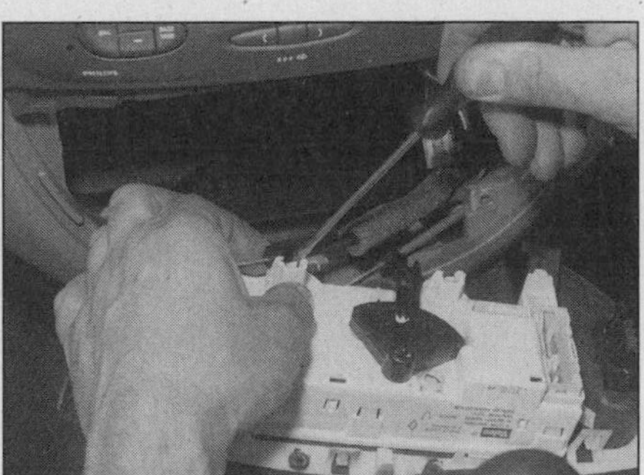

9.4b Release the outer cable retaining clips . . .

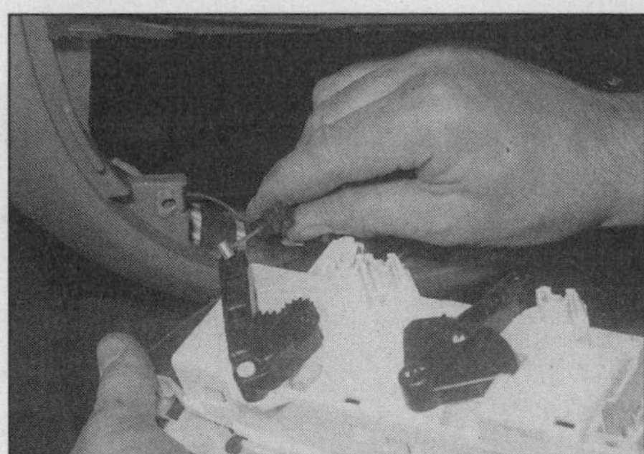

9.4c . . . then detach the inner cables from the levers, and remove the control unit from the vehicle

9.21 Where applicable, remove the manifold pressure sensor from the bulkhead panel

9.23 Unscrew the retaining nuts, and free the braking system master cylinder reservoir from the bulkhead

9.24 Undo the retaining bolts and remove the bulkhead panel to gain access to the blower motor housing

ensuring that the blower motor seal is in good condition.

Blower motor (system with an air recirculation switch)

18 Carry out the operations described in paragraphs 11 to 13.

19 Disconnect the wiring connectors from the right-hand end of the blower motor housing, then unscrew the end mounting bolt.

20 Unscrew the mounting bolts and remove the strengthening bar which is fitted between the front suspension strut turrets.

21 On petrol engine models, in order to allow the left-hand section of the engine compartment bulkhead to be removed, carry out the following operations.

a) *On 1.4 litre (8-valve) models, remove the air cleaner housing and free the MAP (manifold absolute pressure) sensor and the ignition control unit from the bulkhead (see Chapters 4A, Sections 2 and 13 or 14).*

b) *On 1.4 and 1.6 litre (16-valve) models, remove the air cleaner inlet duct and free the MAP (manifold absolute pressure) sensor from the bulkhead (see Chapter 4A, Sections 2 and 14)* **(see illustration).**

c) *On 2.0 litre models, remove the accelerator cable mounting and adjacent switches.*

22 On diesel engine models, in order to allow the left-hand section of the engine compartment bulkhead to be removed, carry out the following operations.

a) *Free the pre-heating unit from the bulkhead (see Chapter 5C).*

b) *Free the solenoid valves (where fitted) from the bulkhead.*

c) *Release all pipes/hoses and their mounting brackets from the bulkhead panel.*

23 On models fitted with a remotely-mounted brake-fluid reservoir slacken the retaining nuts, and free the braking system master cylinder fluid reservoir bracket from the bulkhead panel **(see illustration).** Position the reservoir clear, ensuring it stays upright to avoid fluid spillage.

24 On all models, slacken and remove the retaining bolts and remove the heat shield (where fitted). Slacken and remove the five retaining bolts and manoeuvre the bulkhead panel out from the engine compartment **(see illustration).**

25 On models with a two-piece blower motor housing, undo the retaining screws and remove the top cover. Unscrew the bolts securing the two halves of the housing together, then separate the two halves and remove the right-hand end section from the vehicle. Disconnect the wiring connector from the blower motor, then undo the two mounting bolts and remove the left-hand section of the blower motor housing. Undo the retaining screws and remove the blower motor assembly from its housing.

26 On models with a one-piece blower motor housing, undo the retaining screws and remove the top cover from the housing. Slacken and remove the retaining bolts, and manoeuvre the assembly out of position **(see illustrations).** At the time of writing, it was unclear whether the blower motor was available separately from the housing; refer to your Renault dealer for the latest parts information.

27 Refitting is the reverse of removal, ensuring all the housing seals are in good condition. Check the operation of the blower motor before refitting the bulkhead.

Blower motor control module

28 Disconnect the battery negative lead.

29 Referring to Chapter 12, on right-hand drive-models remove the passenger side wiper arm, and on left-hand-drive models remove both windscreen wiper arms.

30 Remove the sealing strip from the top of the engine compartment bulkhead.

31 Undo the retaining screws and remove the inlet vent panel from beneath the left-hand side of the windscreen.

32 On models where an air recirculation switch is incorporated into the system, disconnect the wiring connectors from the control module which is mounted on the right-hand end of the blower motor housing; on

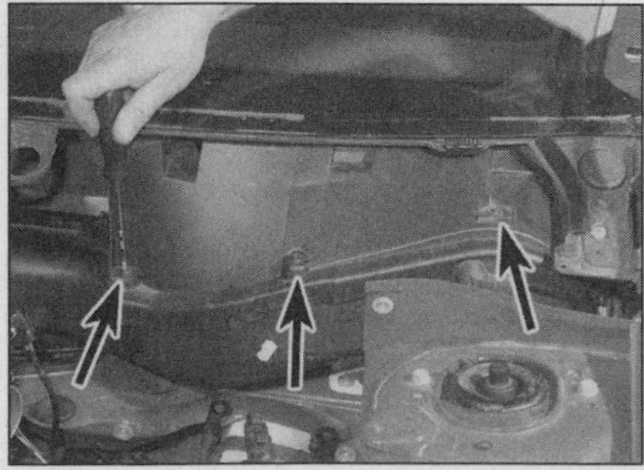
9.26a On models with a one-piece blower motor housing, undo the retaining screws (arrowed) . . .

9.26b . . . and remove the top cover from the housing

9.26c Unscrew the retaining bolts and remove the blower motor housing assembly from the vehicle

9.32 On some models, it will be necessary to disconnect the control module wiring from the motor (arrow) and release it from its clips to allow the module to be removed

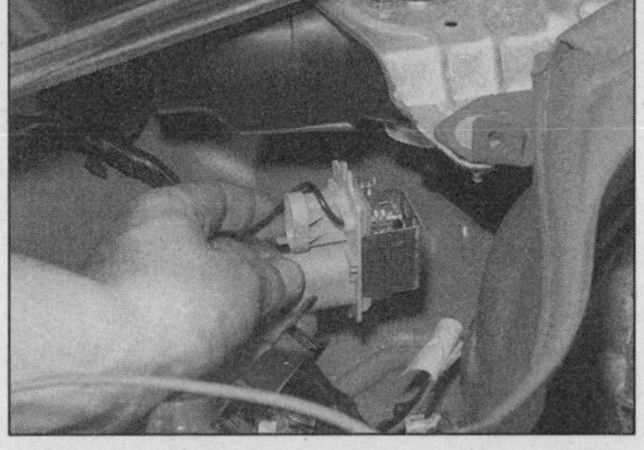

9.33 Removing the blower motor control module from the housing

9.37 Release the retaining clips and disconnect the coolant hoses (arrowed) from the heater matrix unions

some models it will also be necessary to disconnect the wiring connector from the blower motor and free it from its retaining clips so that it can be removed with the module housing **(see illustration)**. Undo the retaining screws then release the retaining clips and remove the control module.

33 On models without an air recirculation switch, the control module is mounted onto the right-hand side of the blower motor. Disconnect the wiring, then undo the retaining screws (where fitted) and unclip the unit from the blower motor housing **(see illustration)**.

34 Refitting is the reverse of removal.

Air distribution housing

35 Drain the cooling system as described in Chapter 1A or 1B. Alternatively, clamp the heater matrix hoses as close as possible to the engine compartment bulkhead.

36 Remove the facia assembly as described in Chapter 11.

37 Release the retaining clips, and disconnect the coolant hoses from the heater matrix unions **(see illustration)**.

38 Remove the blower motor/housing as described earlier in this Section to gain access to the air distribution housing retaining bolt. **Note:** *On models with a two-piece housing, it will only be necessary to remove the right-hand housing section.*

39 Slacken and remove the air distribution housing bolt **(see illustration)**.

40 From inside the vehicle, slacken and remove the housing mounting screws at centre console level, then unscrew the bolt securing the lower mounting bracket to the floor and remove the bracket **(see illustration)**.

41 Carefully ease housing and lower duct assembly clear of the bulkhead, and remove it from the vehicle **(see illustration)**. As the housing is removed, try and keep the heater matrix unions uppermost, to prevent coolant spillage on the interior. Place absorbent rags around the housing as a precaution, and mop up any spilt coolant immediately with a damp cloth to prevent staining.

42 Refitting is the reverse of removal, noting that the mounting bracket lower bolt should be tightened by hand only, and should only be fully tightened once the blower motor housing has been refitted. On completion, top-up/refill the cooling system as described in Chapter 1A or 1B.

Heater matrix

Note: *If leakage is the reason for removing the matrix, bear in mind that minor leaks can often be cured using a radiator sealant with the matrix in situ.*

43 Remove the air distribution housing as described earlier in this Section.

44 Slacken and remove the retaining screws (where fitted), then release the retaining clips and slide the matrix out from the housing, taking great care not to damage the matrix fins **(see illustrations)**.

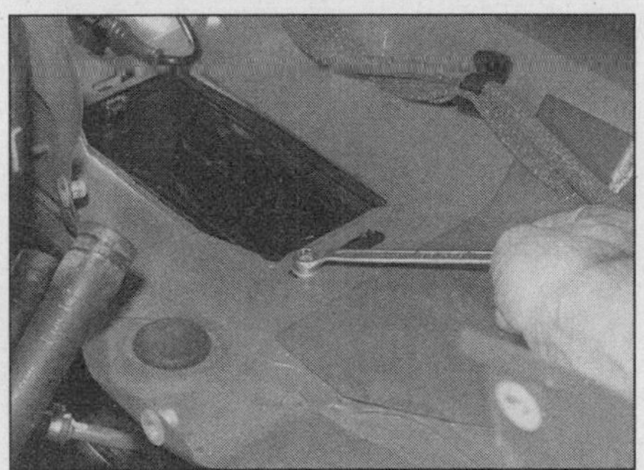

9.39 With the blower motor housing removed, slacken and remove the air distribution housing bolt

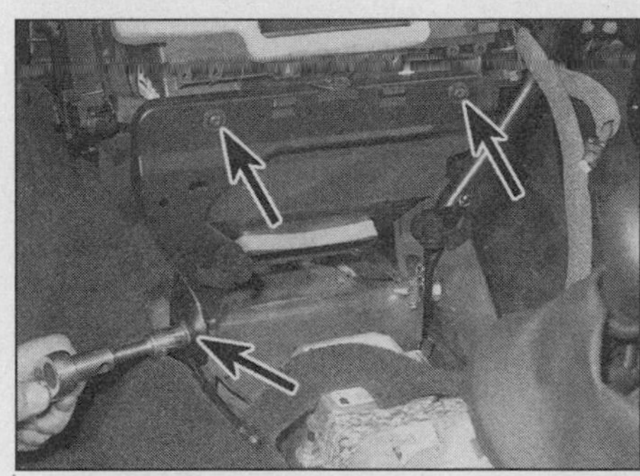

9.40 Slacken and remove the retaining screws and lower bolt (arrowed) and remove the mounting bracket . . .

3

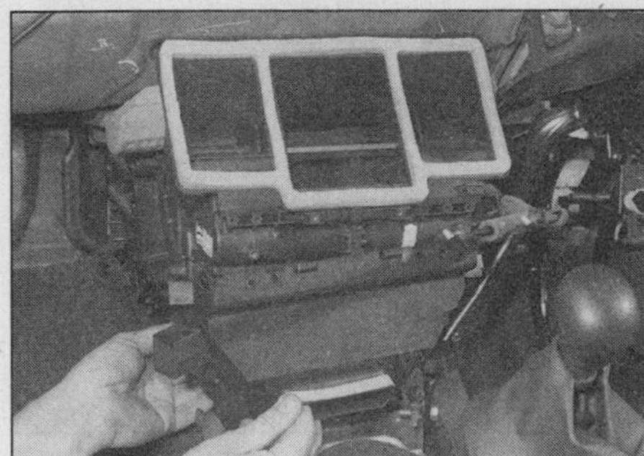

9.41 . . . then manoeuvre the lower duct and housing assembly out from the vehicle

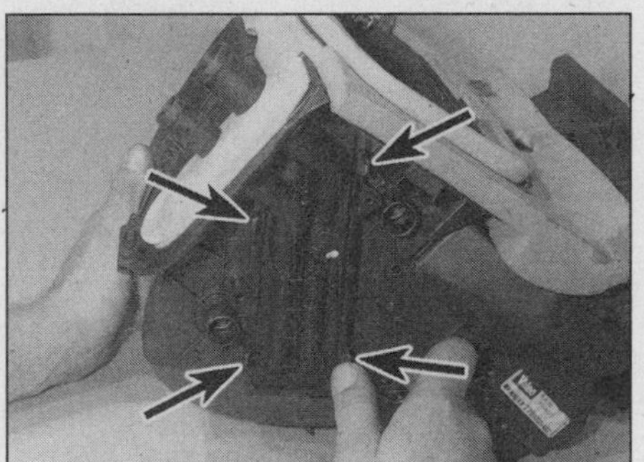

9.44a Release the retaining clips . . .

9.44b . . . and carefully slide the heater matrix out from the housing

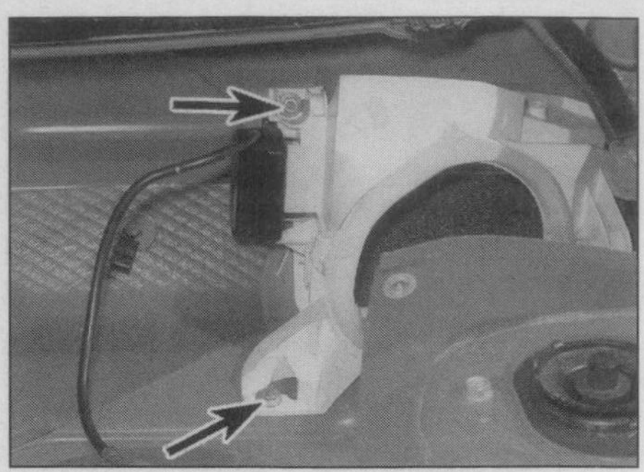

9.48 Slacken and remove the nuts (arrowed), and remove the recirculation flap valve assembly from the vehicle

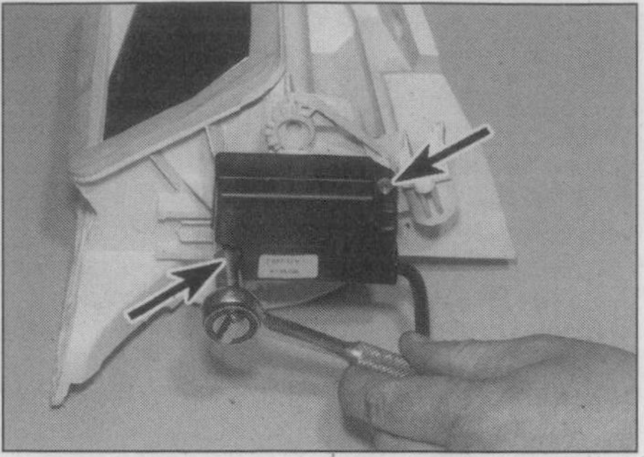

9.49a Undo the retaining screws . . .

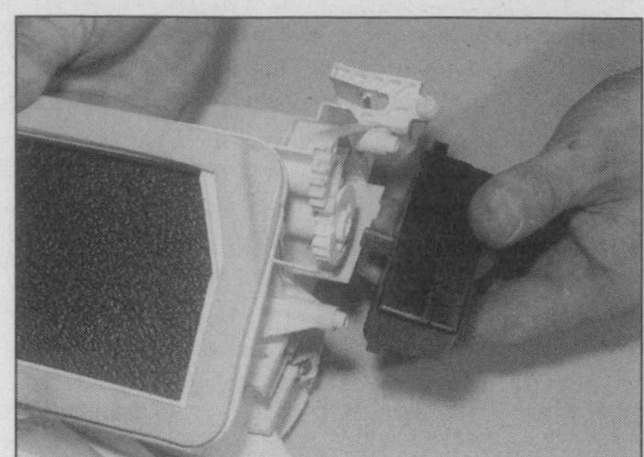

9.49b . . . and remove the motor and drive gears from the housing

45 Refitting is the reverse of removal. If the retaining clips were damaged on removal, secure the matrix in position with screws using the holes provided.

Recirculation valve flap motor

46 Remove the blower motor housing as described earlier in this Section.

47 Trace the wiring back from the flap motor, freeing it from the retaining clips, and disconnect its wiring connector.

48 Undo the retaining nuts and remove the flap housing assembly from the vehicle **(see illustration)**.

49 With the assembly on the bench, slacken and remove the retaining screws, and remove the motor and the flap drivegear from the housing **(see illustrations)**.

50 Refitting is the reverse of removal, ensuring that the drivegears are correctly engaged so that the slot on the motor gear aligns with the lug on the flap gear as they rotate **(see illustration)**. Engage the motor with the gear, and securely tighten its retaining screws.

Models with air conditioning

51 On models equipped with air conditioning, the only operations which can be easily performed by the home mechanic are removal/refitting of the heater/ventilation control panel and cables, and of the blower motor control module. These operations can be carried out using the information given earlier.

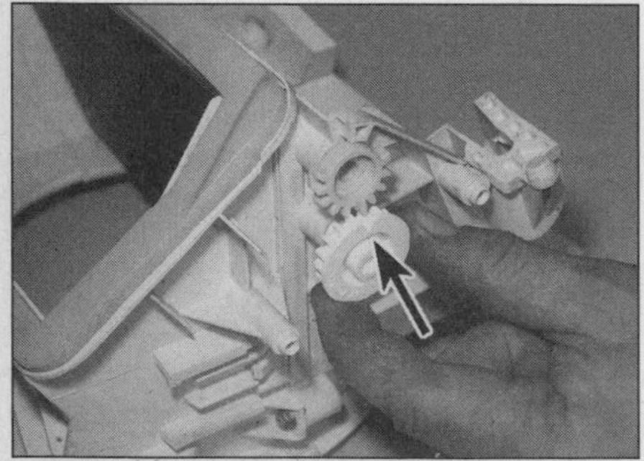

9.50 On refitting, ensure that the slot on the motor gear (arrowed) is correctly aligned with the lug on the flap gear

52 Removal of the blower motor, air distribution housing, heater matrix and recirculation valve flap motor will have to be entrusted to a Renault dealer with access to the necessary equipment required to discharge/recharge the system safely (see Section 11).

Warning: Do not attempt to open the refrigerant circuit. Refer to the precautions in Section 11.

10 Heater/ventilation components (Scénic models) – removal and refitting

Models without air conditioning

Heater/ventilation control unit

1 Disconnect the battery negative lead (refer to Chapter 5A).

2 Remove the cigarette lighter as described in Chapter 12.

3 Unclip the control unit and withdraw it from the facia.

4 Disconnect the wiring connectors, then release the outer cable clips from the unit and detach the inner cables from their levers; note that the control cables are colour-coded for identification. If necessary, unclip the control unit from the facia panel.

5 Refitting is a reversal of removal, but ensure that the control cables are securely reconnected to their original locations; the air temperature (hot/cold) cable is red, and the air distribution cable is blue. Check the operation of the controls prior to refitting the cigarette lighter.

Heater/ventilation control cables

6 Remove the control unit as described in paragraphs 1 to 4. Access to the cable fixings on the right-hand side of the air distribution housing can be gained both from beneath the facia and through the control unit aperture. Undo the bolt and remove the cover panel beneath the facia on the right-hand side for access **(see illustration)**.

7 Make alignment marks between the control cables and their retaining clips on the side of the air distribution housing. The marks can then be used on refitting to ensure that the cables are correctly positioned.

8 Unhook the retaining clip(s) then detach the cable(s) from the housing and lever and withdraw from the facia; note that the control cables are colour-coded for identification **(see illustration)**.

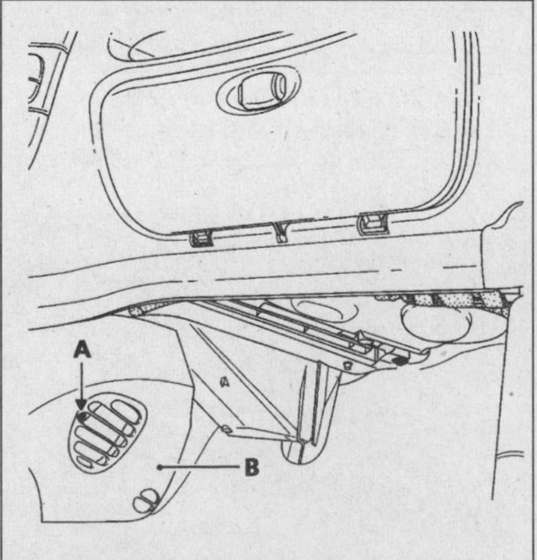

10.6 Remove the bolt (A) and cover panel (B) for access to the heater/ventilation control cables

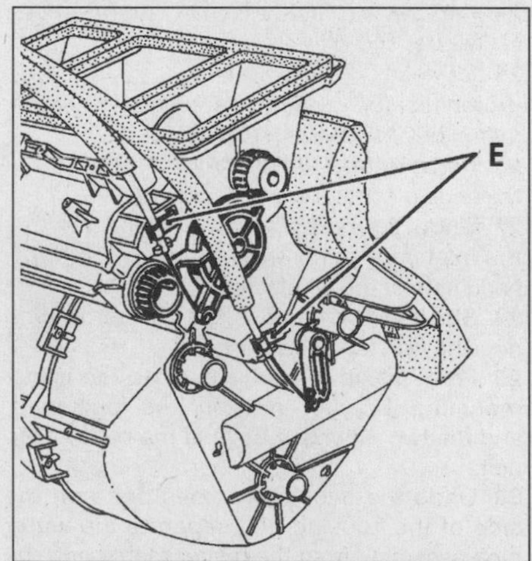

10.8 Heater/ventilation control cable retaining clips (E)

9 On refitting, manoeuvre the cable(s) into position, noting that they are colour-coded; the air temperature (hot/cold) cable is red, and the air distribution cable is blue.
10 Engage the inner cable(s) with the housing levers, and seat the outer cable(s) on the housing. Align the retaining clips with the marks made prior to removal, and secure both cables in position with the retaining clips. Refit the control unit and check the operation of the cables.

Heater blower motor

11 Disconnect the battery negative lead (refer to Chapter 5A).
12 Locally remove the door seal weather-strip on the right-hand side sufficiently to allow the plastic inner sill trim to be removed, then remove the sill trim.
13 Release the blower motor wiring harness under the facia at glovebox level, working towards the outside of the vehicle.
14 Remove the insulating foam under the blower, then disconnect the wiring connector.
15 Undo the three mounting bolts and withdraw the blower motor assembly from its location.
16 Turn the unit 90° anticlockwise and remove it from the car.
17 Refitting is the reversal of removal.

Heater blower motor control module

18 The control module is located behind the facia on the left-hand side.
19 Disconnect the battery negative lead (refer to Chapter 5A).
20 Disconnect the wiring then undo the control unit lower mounting bolt.
21 Slacken the upper mounting bolt, tilt the unit backwards and remove from its location.
22 Refitting is the reversal of removal.

Air distribution housing

23 Drain the cooling system as described in Chapter 1A or 1B. Alternatively, clamp the heater matrix hoses as close as possible to the engine compartment bulkhead.
24 Remove the facia assembly as described in Chapter 11.
25 Release the retaining clips, and disconnect the coolant hoses from the heater matrix unions **(see illustration 9.37)**.
26 Remove the sealing strip from the top of the engine compartment bulkhead.
27 Undo the retaining screws and remove the inlet vent panel from beneath the right-hand side of the windscreen.
28 Slacken and remove the air distribution housing bolt **(see illustration)**.
29 From inside the vehicle, undo the upper mounting bracket nut on the bulkhead, and the two mounting bolts at the base of the unit.
30 Undo the two water pipes bolts on the side of the housing and separate the water pipe assembly from the heater matrix and the housing body. As the pipe assembly is separated from the matrix, plug the pipe ends and matrix unions to prevent coolant spillage on the interior. Place absorbent rags around the housing as a precaution, and mop up any spilt coolant immediately with a damp cloth to prevent staining.
31 Check that all wiring and cables are moved clear and all attachments to the housing are released.
32 Carefully ease housing and lower duct assembly clear of the bulkhead, and remove it from the vehicle. Take precautions against coolant spillage as described previously.
33 Refitting is the reversal of removal, but use new seals when reconnecting the water pipes to the matrix. On completion, top-up/refill the cooling system as described in Chapter 1A or 1B.

Heater matrix

Note: *If leakage is the reason for removing the matrix, bear in mind that minor leaks can often be cured using a radiator sealant with the matrix in situ.*
34 Disconnect the battery negative lead (refer to Chapter 5A).
35 Drain the cooling system as described in Chapter 1A or 1B. Alternatively, clamp the heater matrix hoses as close as possible to the engine compartment bulkhead.
36 Release the retaining clips, and disconnect the coolant hoses from the heater matrix unions.
37 Drain as much water as possible from the matrix by blowing through the upper matrix pipe union using a short length of hose. Be prepared for water to flow quickly from the lower union and if possible, direct the flow away from the engine.
38 Undo the bolt and remove the cover panel beneath the facia on the left-hand side.
39 Undo the bolt securing the water pipes to the side of the matrix, and the remaining three bolts securing the matrix to the air distribution housing.
40 Release the water pipes from the matrix, taking care to prevent coolant spillage on the interior. Place absorbent rags around the housing as a precaution, and mop up any spilt coolant immediately with a damp cloth to prevent staining.

10.28 Remove the air distribution housing bolt (arrowed)

41 Slide the matrix out from the housing, taking great care not to damage the matrix fins.
42 Refitting is the reversal of removal, but use new seals when reconnecting the water pipes to the matrix.

Models with air conditioning

43 On models equipped with air conditioning, the only operations which can be easily performed by the home mechanic are removal/refitting of the heater/ventilation control panel and cables, and of the blower motor control module. These operations can be carried out using the information given earlier.
44 Removal of the blower motor, air distribution housing, heater matrix and recirculation valve flap motor will have to be entrusted to a Renault dealer with access to the necessary equipment required to discharge/recharge the system safely (see Section 11).

Warning: Do not attempt to open the refrigerant circuit. Refer to the precautions in Section 11.

11 Air conditioning system – general information and precautions

General information

An air conditioning system is available on certain models. It enables the temperature of incoming air to be lowered, and also dehumidifies the air, which makes for rapid demisting and increased comfort.

The cooling side of the system works in the same way as a domestic refrigerator. Refrigerant gas at low pressure is drawn into a belt-driven compressor and passes into a condenser mounted on the front of the radiator, where it loses heat and becomes liquid. The liquid passes through an expansion valve to an evaporator, where it changes from liquid under high pressure to gas under low pressure. This change is accompanied by a drop in temperature, which cools the evaporator. The refrigerant returns to the compressor, and the cycle begins again.

Air blown through the evaporator passes to the air distribution unit, where it is mixed with hot air blown through the heater matrix to achieve the desired temperature in the passenger compartment.

The heating side of the system works in the same way as on models without air conditioning (see Section 8).

The operation of the system is controlled

electronically by the control unit, which controls the electric cooling fan(s), the compressor and the facia-mounted warning light. Any problems with the system should be referred to a Renault dealer.

Precautions

When an air conditioning system is fitted, it is necessary to observe special precautions whenever dealing with any part of the system, or its associated components. If for any reason the system must be disconnected, entrust this task to your Renault dealer or a refrigeration engineer.

Warning: The refrigeration circuit may contain a liquid refrigerant (Freon), and it is therefore dangerous to disconnect any part of the system without specialised knowledge and equipment.

The refrigerant is potentially dangerous, and should only be handled by qualified persons. If it is splashed onto the skin, it can cause frostbite. It is not itself poisonous, but in the presence of a naked flame (including a cigarette) it forms a poisonous gas. Uncontrolled discharging of the refrigerant is dangerous, and potentially damaging to the environment.

Do not operate the air conditioning system if it is known to be short of refrigerant, as this may damage the compressor.

12 Air conditioning system components – removal and refitting

Warning: Do not attempt to open the refrigerant circuit. Refer to the precautions in Section 11.

The only operation which can be carried out easily without discharging the refrigerant is the renewal of the compressor drivebelt. This is described in Chapter 1A or 1B. All other operations must be referred to a Renault dealer or an air conditioning specialist.

If necessary, the compressor can be unbolted and moved aside, without disconnecting its flexible hoses, after removing the drivebelt.

Chapter 4 Part A: Petrol engine fuel and exhaust systems

Contents

Degrees of difficulty

Easy, suitable for novice with little experience 

Fairly easy, suitable for beginner with some experience 

Fairly difficult, suitable for competent DIY mechanic 

Difficult, suitable for experienced DIY mechanic 

Very difficult, suitable for expert DIY or professional

4A

Specifications

Engine codes

1.4 litre models:	
SOHC	E7J
DOHC	K4J
1.6 litre models	K4M
2.0 litre models	F4R

System type

E7J engine	Siemens-Fenix 3 single-point injection with Bosch throttle body
K4J engine	Siemens-Sirius 32 sequential multi-point injection
K4M engine	Siemens-Sirius 32 sequential multi-point injection
F4R engine	Siemens-Sirius 32 sequential multi-point injection

Fuel system data

Fuel pressure regulator control pressure:	
E7J engine:	
Zero vacuum	3.0 ± 0.2 bars
500 mbars vacuum	2.5 ± 0.2 bars
K4J and K4M engines:	
With return circuit	3.0 ± 0.2 bars
Without return circuit	3.5 ± 0.2 bars
F4R engine	3.5 ± 0.2 bars

Fuel system data (continued)

Fuel pump flow output (minimum):	
E7J engine	80 litres/hour at 3.0 bars fuel pressure
K4J and K4M engines	60 to 80 litres/hour at 3.0 bars fuel pressure
F4R engine	130 litres/hour at 3.5 bars fuel pressure
Air temperature sensor resistance:	
E7J engine:	
At 0°C	7470 to 11 970 ohms
At 20°C	3060 to 4045 ohms
At 40°C	1315 to 1600 ohms
K4J and K4M engines:	
At 0°C	5290 to 6490 ohms
At 20°C	2400 to 2600 ohms
At 40°C	1070 to 1270 ohms
F4R engine:	
At -10°C	8525 to 10 450 ohms
At 25°C	1880 to 2120 ohms
At 50°C	760 to 860 ohms
Coolant temperature sensor resistance:	
E7J engine:	
At 20°C	2600 to 3000 ohms
At 40°C	1100 to 1300 ohms
At 80°C	270 to 300 ohms
At 90°C	200 to 215 ohms
K4J and K4M engines:	
At 20°C	3060 to 4045 ohms
At 40°C	1315 to 1600 ohms
At 80°C	300 to 370 ohms
At 90°C	210 to 270 ohms
F4R engine:	
At 25°C	2140 to 2360 ohms
At 50°C	770 to 850 ohms
At 80°C	275 to 290 ohms
At 110°C	112 to 117 ohms
Throttle potentiometer:	
E7J engine:	
Voltage	5.0 volts
Track resistance	4100 ± 800 ohms
Cursor resistance	1500 ± 150 ohms
K4J, K4M and F4R engines:	
Voltage	5.0 volts
Resistance:	
Track A-B	1250 ohms (no load), 1250 ohms (full load)
Track A-C	1245 ohms (no load), 2230 ohms (full load)
Track B-C	2230 ohms (no load), 1245 ohms (full load)
Stepper motor resistance:	
E7J engine	50.0 ohms
K4J, K4M and F4R engines	53.0 ± 5 ohms
Injector resistance:	
Single-point injection	2.0 ohms
Multi-point injection	14.5 ± 1.0 ohms
Crankshaft speed/position sensor resistance:	
E7J engine	220 ohms
K4J and K4M engines	200 to 270 ohms
F4R engine	200 to 270 ohms
Fuel tank level sender unit resistance at height of float pin (approx):	
At 47 mm	310 ± 10 ohms
At 52 mm	280 ± 20 ohms
At 81 mm	190 ± 16 ohms
At 110 mm	110 ± 10 ohms
At 143 mm	61 ± 7 ohms
At 164 mm	3.5 ± 3.5 ohms
Specified idle speed (non-adjustable)	750 ± 50 rpm
Idle mixture CO content (non-adjustable)	0.5% maximum (0.3% at 2500 rpm)

Recommended fuel

Minimum octane rating	95 RON unleaded. Leaded fuel and LRP must **not** be used

Torque wrench settings

	Nm	lbf ft
Air cleaner unit	9	7
Exhaust downpipe to manifold	20	15
Exhaust manifold:		
E7J engine	25	18
K4J, K4M and F4R engines	18	13
Fuel pump locking ring	35	26
Fuel rail mounting bolts	9	7
Fuel tank	21	15
Inlet manifold:		
E7J engine	25	18
K4J, K4M and F4R engines	10	7
Injector mounting shim	21	15
Lambda (oxygen) sensor:		
K4J and K4M engines	45	33
F4R engine:		
Upstream	45	33
Throttle body:		
E7J, K4J and K4M engines	13	10
F4R engine	15	11

1 General information and precautions

The fuel system consists of a fuel tank which is mounted under the rear of the vehicle with an electric fuel pump immersed in it, a fuel filter **(see illustration)** and the fuel feed and return lines. On single-point injection models, the fuel is supplied by a throttle body assembly which incorporates the single fuel injector and the fuel pressure regulator. On multi-point injection models, the fuel pump supplies fuel to the fuel rail, which acts as a reservoir for the four fuel injectors which inject fuel into the inlet tracts. In addition, there is an Electronic Control Unit (ECU) and various sensors, electrical components and related wiring.

1.1 Fuel filter location on a Mégane

Refer to Section 6 for further information on the operation of each fuel injection system, and to Section 16 for information on the exhaust system.

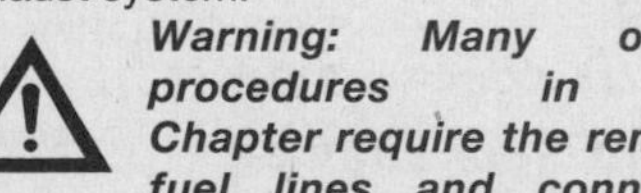

Warning: Many of the procedures in this Chapter require the removal of fuel lines and connections, which may result in some fuel spillage. Before carrying out any operation on the fuel system, refer to the precautions given in 'Safety first!' at the beginning of this manual, and follow them implicitly. Petrol is a highly-dangerous and volatile liquid, and the precautions necessary when handling it cannot be overstressed.

Note: *Residual pressure will remain in the fuel lines long after the vehicle was last used. When disconnecting any fuel line, first depressurise the fuel system as described in Section 7.*

Caution: If the radio/cassette in your vehicle is equipped with an anti-theft system, make sure you have the correct activation code before disconnecting the battery.

2 Air cleaner assembly and inlet ducts – removal and refitting

E7J engines

Note: *Some models may be fitted with a heat-sensitive wax capsule in the inlet ducting, to control the inlet air temperature. If the system does not function correctly, the air cleaner body must be renewed; it is not possible to renew the flap valve separately.*

Removal

1 Unscrew and remove the bolts and cover screw from the top of the air cleaner, then release the clips and remove the cover from the body. Remove the element from the body **(see illustrations)**.

2 Disconnect the warm air hose from the exhaust manifold shroud, then disconnect the ambient air hose from the inlet elbow on the air cleaner body **(see illustrations)**.

3 Release the rubber strap, then lift the body

4A

2.1a Removing the bolts . . .

2.1b . . . and cover screw (E7J engine)

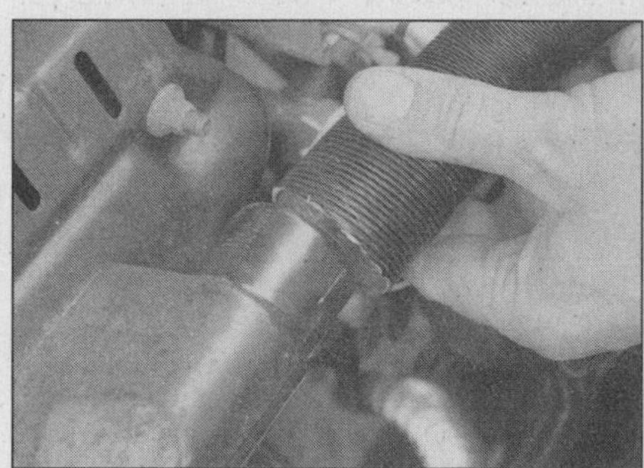

2.2a Disconnecting the warm air hose from the exhaust manifold shroud (E7J engine)

2.2b Loosen the clip . . .

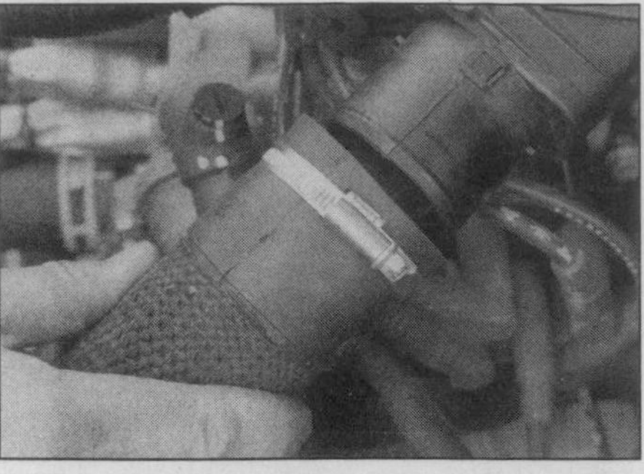
2.2c . . . and disconnect the ambient air hose (E7J engine)

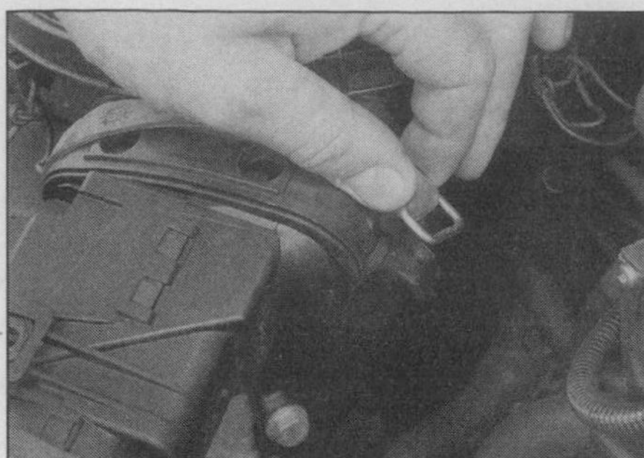
2.3a Release the rubber strap . . .

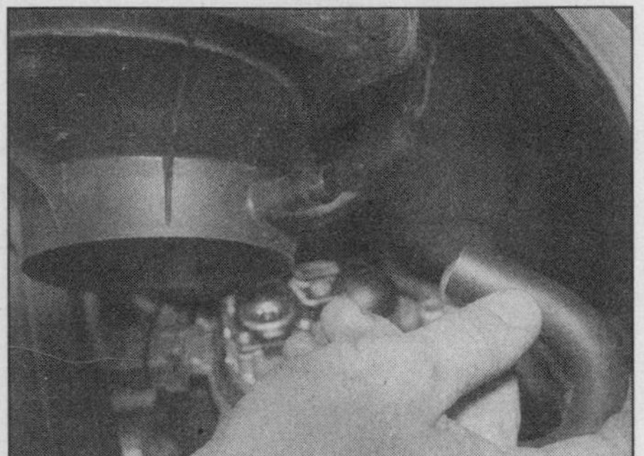
2.3b . . . and disconnect the crankcase ventilation hose (E7J engine)

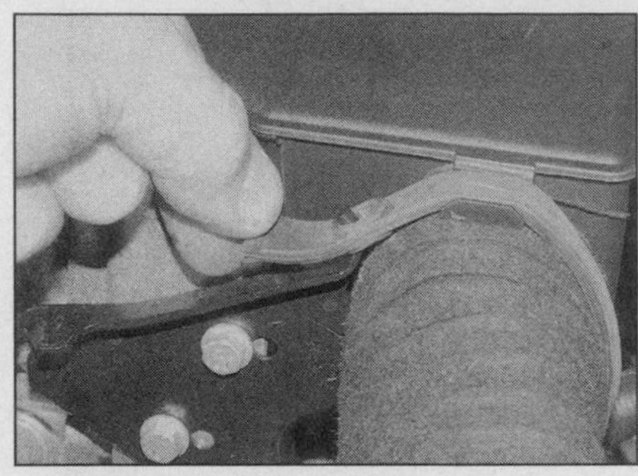
2.7a Unhook the retaining strap . . .

2.7b . . . remove the resonator . . .

from the throttle body and disconnect the crankcase ventilation hose **(see illustrations)**. If necessary, unbolt and remove the support bracket. Remove the hose and unbolt the air inlet duct from the front of the engine compartment.

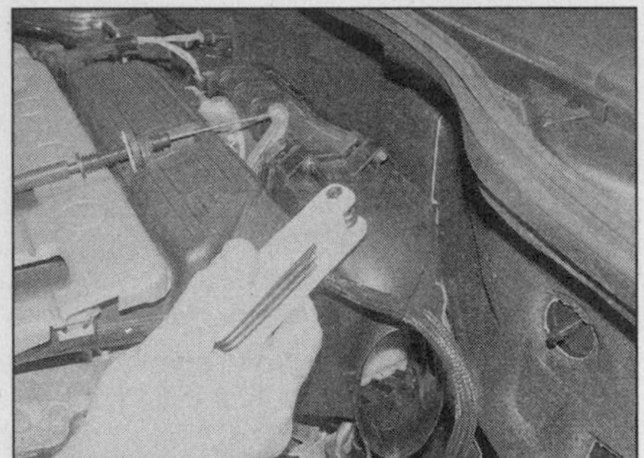
2.7c . . . then undo the screws . . .

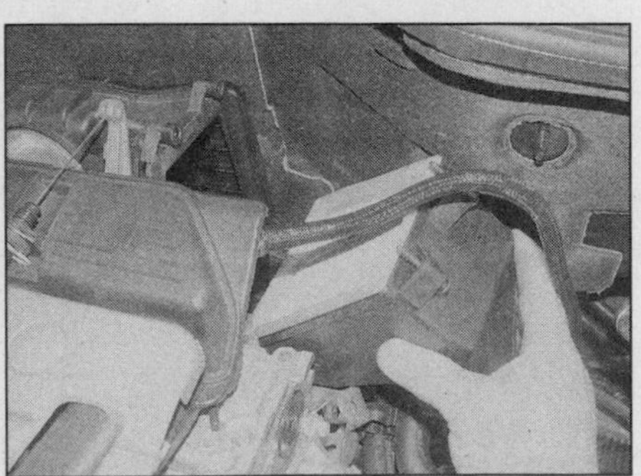
2.7d . . . and remove the air filter (K4M engine)

Refitting

4 Refitting is a reversal of removal.

K4J and K4M engines (Mégane models)

Removal

5 Disconnect the battery negative terminal (see Chapter 5A), then disconnect the brake vacuum hose from the inlet manifold.

6 Disconnect the wiring from the crankcase ventilation purge valve then disconnect the hose.

7 Remove the heat shield from the bulkhead and remove the air filter **(see illustrations)**.

8 Remove the plate from the bulkhead.

9 Remove the air resonator **(see illustration)**.

10 Unscrew the mounting bolts and withdraw the air cleaner assembly from the inlet manifold. It will be necessary to move the assembly to the right and manoeuvre it between the engine and bulkhead.

Refitting

11 Refitting is a reversal of removal, but check that the vacuum outlet from the exhaust manifold to the brake vacuum servo unit is not broken. If it is, the inlet manifold must be renewed.

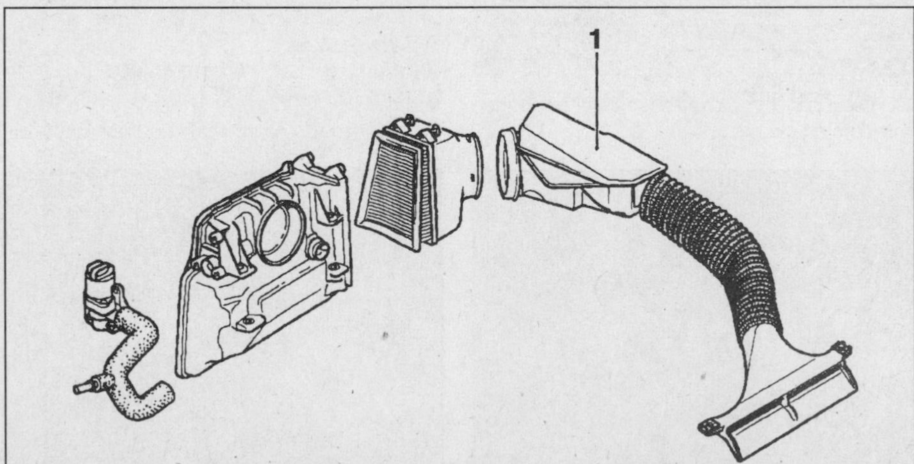

2.9 Air cleaner components, showing the resonator (1)

K4J and K4M engines (Scénic models)

Removal

12 Disconnect the battery negative (earth) lead and position it away from the terminal.
13 Remove the windscreen wiper arms and blades as described in Chapter 12.
14 Remove the plenum chamber cover from just in front of the windscreen.
15 Remove the bulkhead plate from the rear of the engine compartment.
16 Remove the inlet air resonator.
17 Disconnect the brake vacuum servo hose from the inlet manifold.
18 Unscrew the mounting bolts securing the air cleaner body to the inlet manifold.
19 Disconnect the wiring from the actuator on the right-hand side of the air cleaner.
20 Disconnect the crankcase ventilation hose from the air cleaner.
21 Manoeuvre the air cleaner to the right, then withdraw it from between the windscreen plenum area, the engine and the brake vacuum servo.

Refitting

22 Refitting is a reversal of removal, but check that the vacuum outlet from the exhaust manifold to the brake vacuum servo unit is not broken. If it is, the inlet manifold must be renewed.

F4R engines

Removal

23 Disconnect the battery negative (earth) lead and position it away from the terminal.
24 Remove the windscreen wiper arms and blades as described in Chapter 12.
25 Remove the plenum chamber cover from just in front of the windscreen.
26 Remove the bulkhead plate from the rear of the engine compartment.
27 Remove the inlet air resonator.
28 Disconnect the brake vacuum servo hose from the inlet manifold.
29 Unscrew the mounting bolts securing the air cleaner body to the inlet manifold.
30 Disconnect the wiring from the actuator on the right-hand side of the air cleaner.
31 Disconnect the crankcase ventilation hose from the air cleaner.
32 Manoeuvre the air cleaner to the right, then withdraw it from between the windscreen plenum area, the engine and the brake vacuum servo.

Refitting

33 Refitting is a reversal of removal, but check that the vacuum outlet from the exhaust manifold to the brake vacuum servo unit is not broken. If it is, the inlet manifold must be renewed.

3 Accelerator cable – removal, refitting and adjustment

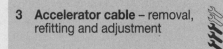

Removal

1 Remove the air cleaner assembly as described in Section 2. Where applicable, unbolt the strengthening bar from between the front suspension strut turrets.
2 On the throttle body/housing, turn the throttle quadrant by hand to release the cable tension. Disconnect the inner cable from the quadrant.
3 Remove the outer cable and grommet from the support bracket. On automatic transmission models, disconnect the kickdown sensor wiring from the end of the outer cable. If necessary, remove the spring clip from the end of the cable noting its position in the groove.
4 Working inside the car, remove the lower trim panel from under the steering column. Disconnect the cable from the accelerator pedal by squeezing the lugs of the cable end fitting **(see illustration)**.
5 Return to the engine compartment, release the outer cable from the bulkhead and withdraw the cable.

Refitting

6 Refitting is a reversal of removal, but adjust the cable if necessary. Make the adjustment before refitting the strengthening bar or the air cleaner assembly, as applicable.

Adjustment

7 With the spring clip removed from the accelerator outer cable, ensure that the throttle quadrant is fully against its stop. Gently pull the cable out of its grommet until all free play is removed from the inner cable.
8 With the cable held in this position, refit the spring clip to the last exposed outer cable groove in front of the rubber grommet and washer **(see illustration)**. When the clip is refitted and the outer cable is released, there should be only a small amount of free play in the inner cable. **Note:** *The idle speed control motor opens the throttle slightly when the ignition is switched off. There must be enough slack in the cable to allow the throttle to close past this position, otherwise a stable idle speed will not be obtained.*
9 Have an assistant depress the accelerator pedal, and check that the throttle quadrant opens fully and returns smoothly to its stop.

4 Accelerator pedal – removal and refitting

Removal

1 Remove the lower trim panel from under the steering column.
2 Disconnect the cable from the top of the accelerator pedal by squeezing the lugs of the cable end fitting.
3 Remove the nut which secures the accelerator pedal pivot and bush to the bulkhead **(see illustration)**.
4 Withdraw the accelerator pedal.
5 Examine the pedal and pivot for signs of wear and renew as necessary.

Refitting

6 Refitting is a reversal of removal. Check the adjustment of the accelerator cable as described in Section 4.

5 Unleaded petrol – general information and usage

The fuel recommended by Renault is given in the Specifications Section of this Chapter.

All petrol models are designed to run on fuel with a minimum octane rating of 95 RON. All models have a catalytic converter, and so

4A

3.4 Accelerator cable end fitting on the top of the pedal

3.8 Accelerator cable adjustment ferrule and support

4.3 Accelerator pedal pivot and bush mounting nut

must be run on unleaded fuel **only**. Under no circumstances should leaded fuel or LRP be used, as this may damage the converter.

Super unleaded petrol (98 octane) can also be used in all models if wished, though there is no advantage in doing so.

6 Fuel injection systems – general information

Single-point injection system

1.4 litre models with the E7J engine are equipped with a Siemens-Fenix 3 single-point fuel injection/ignition system with a Bosch throttle body. The system incorporates a closed-loop catalytic converter and an evaporative emission control system, and complies with the latest emission control standards. The fuel injection side of the system operates as follows; refer to Chapter 5B for information on the ignition system.

The fuel pump, immersed in the fuel tank, pumps fuel from the fuel tank to the fuel injector, via a filter mounted underneath the rear of the vehicle. Fuel supply pressure is controlled by the pressure regulator in the throttle body assembly. The regulator operates by allowing excess fuel to return to the tank.

The electrical control system consists of the ECU, along with the following sensors:

a) *Throttle potentiometer – informs the ECU of the throttle position, and the rate of throttle opening or closing.*
b) *Coolant temperature sensor – informs the ECU of engine temperature.*
c) *Inlet air temperature sensor – informs the ECU of the temperature of the air passing through the throttle body.*
d) *Lambda (oxygen) sensor – informs the ECU of the oxygen content of the exhaust gases (explained in greater detail in Part C of this Chapter).*
e) *Microswitch (built into idle speed stepper motor) – informs the ECU when the throttle is closed (ie, when the accelerator pedal is released).*
f) *Crankshaft speed/position (TDC) sensor – informs the ECU of engine speed and crankshaft position.*
g) *Power steering pressure switch – informs the ECU when the power steering pump is working so the engine idle speed can be increased to prevent stalling.*
h) *Knock sensor (where fitted) – informs the ECU when pre-ignition ('pinking') is occurring (explained in greater detail in Chapter 5B).*
i) *Manifold absolute pressure (MAP) sensor – informs the ECU of the engine load by monitoring the pressure in the inlet manifold.*
j) *Fuel vapour recirculation valve – operates the fuel evaporative control system (explained in greater detail in Part C of this Chapter).*

All the above information is analysed by the ECU and, based on this, the ECU determines the appropriate ignition and fuelling requirements for the engine. The ECU controls the fuel injector by varying its pulse width – the length of time the injector is held open – to provide a richer or weaker mixture, as appropriate. The mixture is constantly varied by the ECU, to provide the best setting for cranking, starting (with either a hot or cold engine), warm-up, idle, cruising, and acceleration.

The ECU also has full control over the engine idle speed, via a stepper motor which is fitted to the throttle body. The motor pushrod rests against a cam on the throttle spindle. When the throttle is closed (accelerator pedal released), the ECU uses the motor to vary the opening of the throttle valve and so control the idle speed.

The ECU also controls the exhaust and evaporative emission control systems, which are described in detail in Part C of this Chapter.

If there is an abnormality in any of the readings obtained from either the coolant temperature sensor, the inlet air temperature sensor or the lambda (oxygen) sensor, the ECU enters its back-up mode. In this event, the ECU ignores the abnormal sensor signal, and assumes a pre-programmed value which will allow the engine to continue running (albeit at reduced efficiency). If the ECU enters this back-up mode, the warning light on the instrument panel will come on, and the relevant fault code will be stored in the ECU memory.

If the warning light comes on, the vehicle should be taken to a Renault dealer at the earliest opportunity. A complete test of the engine management system can then be carried out, using a special electronic diagnostic test unit (Renault XR25 or the Haynes Fault Code Reader) which is simply plugged into the system's diagnostic connector (located on the fusebox on the facia panel) **(see illustrations)**.

A fuel cut-off inertia switch is incorporated into the fuel injection system. In the event of an impact the switch cuts off the electrical supply to the fuel pump and so prevents fuel being expelled should the fuel pipes/hoses be damaged in an accident.

Multi-point injection system

1.4 litre models with the K4J engine, and all 1.6 litre and 2.0 litre engines are equipped with a Siemens-Sirius sequential multi-point fuel injection/ignition system. The system is of closed-loop type incorporating two lambda (oxygen) sensors, one located upstream and the other downstream of the catalytic converter. An evaporative emission control system is fitted.

The multi-point injection system uses one injector and one ignition coil for each cylinder, and the injectors are operated individually and sequentially at the beginning of the inlet stroke. The electronic control unit (ECU) is able to determine which cylinder is on its inlet stroke without the use of a camshaft position sensor, however if the unit is renewed, the car must be taken for a road test lasting at least 25 minutes to enable the ECU to reprogram itself; the stepper motor must also be reset.

The system incorporates a closed-loop catalytic converter and an evaporative emission control system, and complies with the latest emission control standards. The fuel injection side of the system operates as follows; refer to Chapter 5B for information on the ignition system.

The fuel pump, immersed in the fuel tank, pumps fuel from the fuel tank to the fuel rail, via a filter mounted beneath the rear of the vehicle. Fuel supply pressure is controlled by the pressure regulator in the fuel rail (except F4R engine) or fuel pump (F4R engine). The regulator operates by allowing excess fuel to return to the tank. There are four injectors (one per cylinder) located in the inlet manifold downstream of the throttle valve. All the injectors are fed from the fuel rail.

The electrical control system consists of the ECU, along with the following sensors:

a) *Throttle potentiometer – informs the ECU of the throttle position, and the rate of throttle opening or closing.*
b) *Coolant temperature sensor – informs the ECU of engine temperature.*

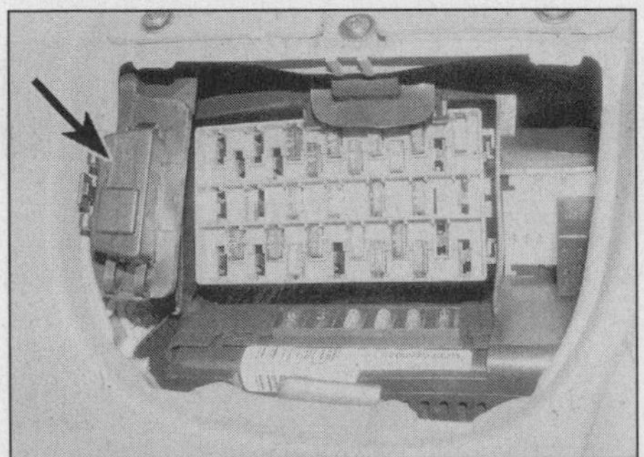

6.8a Diagnostic socket location on the fusebox

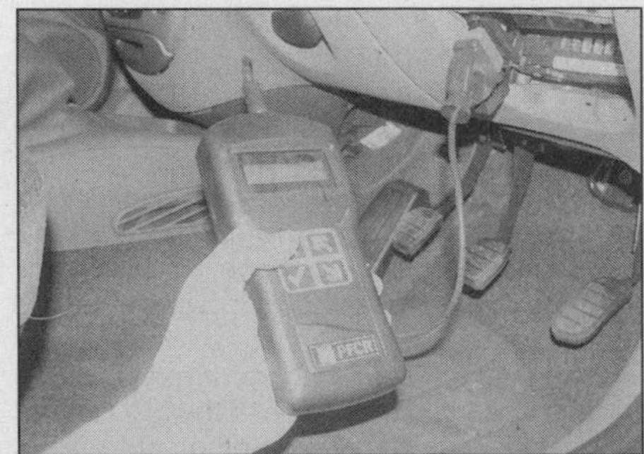

6.8b Using the Haynes Fault Code Reader connected to the diagnostic socket on the fusebox

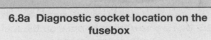

c) Inlet air temperature sensor – informs the ECU of the temperature of the air passing through the throttle body.

d) Lambda (oxygen) sensor – informs the ECU of the oxygen content of the exhaust gases (explained in greater detail in Part C of this Chapter).

e) Idle speed regulation stepper motor – controls the idle speed.

f) Crankshaft speed/position (TDC) sensor – informs the ECU of engine speed and crankshaft position.

g) Power steering pressure switch – informs the ECU when the power steering pump is working so the engine idle speed can be increased to prevent stalling.

h) Knock sensor (where fitted) – informs the ECU when pre-ignition ('pinking') is occurring (explained in greater detail in Chapter 5B).

i) Manifold absolute pressure (MAP) sensor – informs the ECU of the engine load by monitoring the pressure in the inlet manifold.

j) Fuel vapour recirculation valve – operates the fuel evaporative control system (explained in greater detail in Part C of this Chapter).

All the above information is analysed by the ECU and, based on this, the ECU determines the appropriate ignition and fuelling requirements for the engine. The ECU controls the fuel injector by varying its pulse width – the length of time the injector is held open – to provide a richer or weaker mixture, as appropriate. The mixture is constantly varied by the ECU, to provide the best setting for cranking, starting (with either a hot or cold engine), warm-up, idle, cruising, and acceleration. On automatic transmission models, information from sensors on the transmission is sent to the ECU for processing to determine the most efficient settings for the engine.

The ECU also has full control over the engine idle speed, via a stepper motor which is fitted to the throttle body. The motor pushrod rests against a cam on the throttle spindle. When the throttle is closed (accelerator pedal released), the ECU uses the motor to vary the opening of the throttle valve and so control the idle speed.

The ECU also controls the exhaust and evaporative emission control systems, which are described in detail in Part C of this Chapter.

If there is an abnormality in any of the readings obtained from either the coolant temperature sensor, the inlet air temperature sensor or the lambda (oxygen) sensor, the ECU enters its back-up mode. In this event, the ECU ignores the abnormal sensor signal, and assumes a pre-programmed value which will allow the engine to continue running (albeit at reduced efficiency). If the ECU enters this back-up mode, the warning light on the instrument panel will come on, and the relevant fault code will be stored in the ECU memory.

If the warning light comes on, the vehicle should be taken to a Renault dealer at the earliest opportunity. A complete test of the engine management system can then be carried out, using a special electronic diagnostic test unit (Renault XR25 or the Haynes Fault Code Reader) which is simply plugged into the system's diagnostic connector (located beneath the ashtray on the centre console).

A fuel cut-off inertia switch is incorporated into the fuel injection system. In the event of an impact the switch cuts off the electrical supply to the fuel pump and so prevents fuel being expelled should the fuel pipes/hoses be damaged in an accident. The switch is located in the left-hand rear corner of the engine compartment.

7 Fuel injection system – depressurisation

Warning: Refer to the warning note in Section 1 before proceeding. The following procedure will merely relieve the pressure in the fuel system – remember that fuel will still be present in the system components, and take precautions accordingly before disconnecting any of them.

Note: *The fuel system referred to in this Section includes the tank-mounted fuel pump, the fuel filter, the fuel injector(s) and the pressure regulator in the throttle body/fuel rail, and the metal pipes and flexible hoses of the fuel lines between these components. All these contain fuel which will be under pressure while the engine is running, and/or while the ignition is switched on. The pressure will remain for some time after the ignition has been switched off, and it must be relieved when any of these components are disturbed for servicing work.*

Method 1

1 Disconnect the battery negative lead (refer to Chapter 5A).

2 Place a suitable container beneath the connection or union to be disconnected, and have a large rag ready to soak up any escaping fuel not being caught by the container.

3 Slowly loosen the connection or union nut to avoid a sudden release of pressure, and position the rag around the connection, to catch any fuel spray which may be expelled. Once the pressure is released, disconnect the fuel line. Plug the pipe ends, to minimise fuel loss and prevent the entry of dirt into the fuel system.

Method 2

4 Remove the fuel pump relay located in the engine compartment fuse/relay box (see Chapter 12).

5 Start the engine and allow it to idle until it stops due to lack of fuel. Operate the starter motor a couple more times, to ensure that all fuel pressure has been relieved.

6 Switch off the ignition and refit the fuel pump relay.

8 Fuel pump – removal and refitting

Warning: Refer to the warning note in Section 1 before proceeding

Removal

1 Depressurise the fuel system with reference to Section 7, then disconnect the battery negative lead (refer to Chapter 5A) if not already done.

2 Remove the rear seat, or rear seat cushion as described in Chapter 11, for access to the fuel pump cover.

3 Using a screwdriver, carefully prise the plastic access cover from the floor to expose the fuel pump **(see illustration)**.

4 Disconnect the wiring connector from the fuel pump, and tape the connector to the vehicle body, to prevent it disappearing behind the tank **(see illustration)**.

5 Identify the fuel hoses for position; the green hose on the left-hand side is the supply to the engine compartment, and the red hose next to the wiring connector is the return (arrows on the top of the pump indicate the direction of fuel flow). The hoses are equipped

8.3 Use a screwdriver to prise up the fuel pump access cover

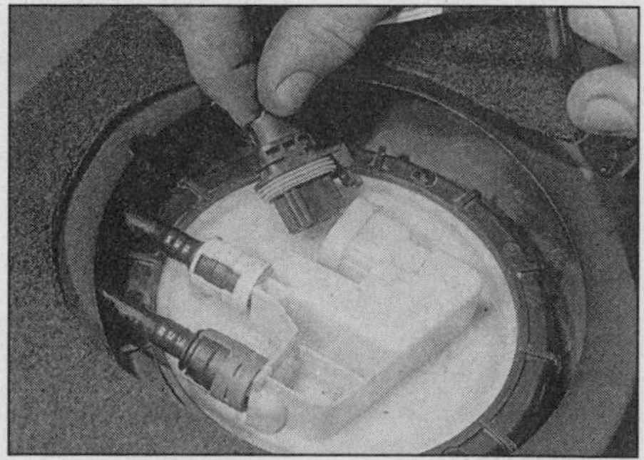

8.4 Disconnecting the fuel pump wiring

4A

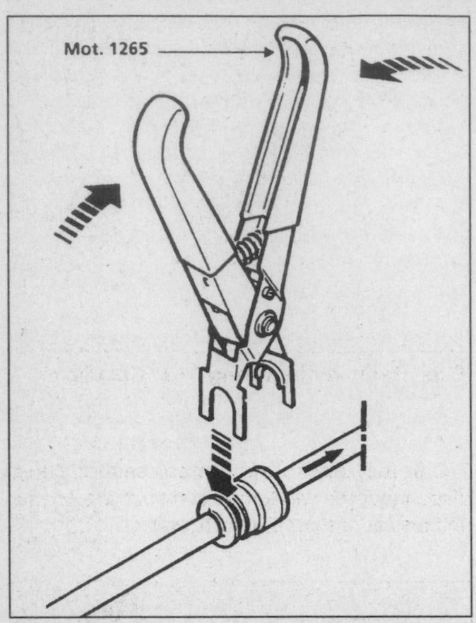

8.5a Renault service tool for releasing the fuel hose quick-release fittings

with quick-release fittings to ease removal. To disconnect each hose, slide out the locking tab from the collar then compress the collar and detach the hose from the pump. Renault technicians use a special tool to compress the collar – without this tool, it is possible to use a small screwdriver **carefully** to press back the locking collar inside the end of the special end fitting. Disconnect both hoses from the top of the pump, then plug the hose ends to minimise fuel loss **(see illustrations)**.

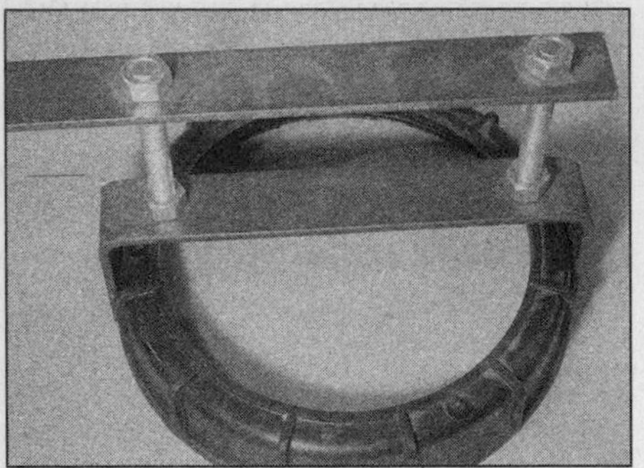

8.6a Home-made fuel pump locking ring removal tool

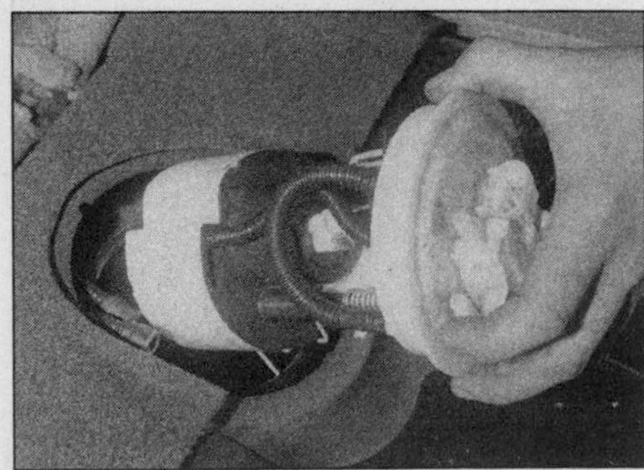

8.7a Lifting the fuel pump assembly from the fuel tank

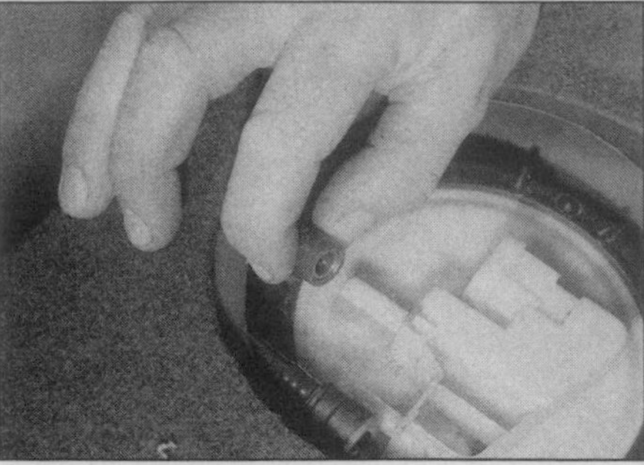

8.5b Disconnecting the fuel return hose from the fuel pump

6 Noting the alignment arrows on the pump cover and fuel tank, unscrew the locking ring and remove it from the tank. This can be accomplished by using a screwdriver on the raised ribs of the locking ring – carefully tap the screwdriver to turn the ring anti-clockwise until it can be unscrewed by hand. Alternatively a removal tool can be fabricated out of metal bar and two bolts **(see illustrations)**.

7 Carefully lift the fuel pump assembly out of the fuel tank, taking great care not to damage the fuel level gauge sender arm, or to spill fuel in the interior of the vehicle. Remove the rubber sealing ring and check it for deterioration; if it is in good condition, it may be re-used, however if the pump is to remain out of the fuel tank for several hours, the locking ring should be refitted temporarily to prevent the sealing ring from distorting. If the sealing ring is unserviceable, obtain a new one **(see illustrations)**.

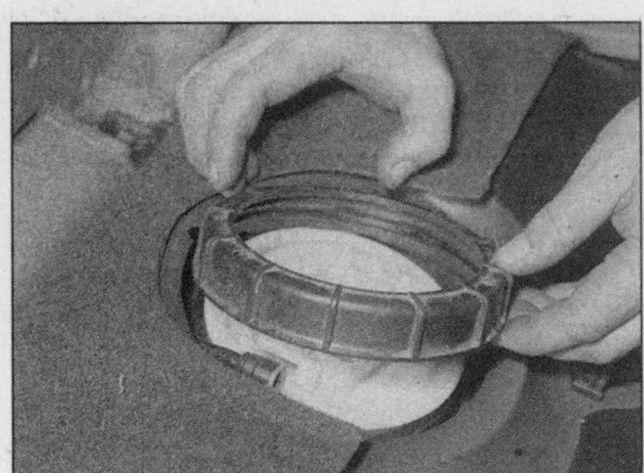

8.6b Removing the locking ring

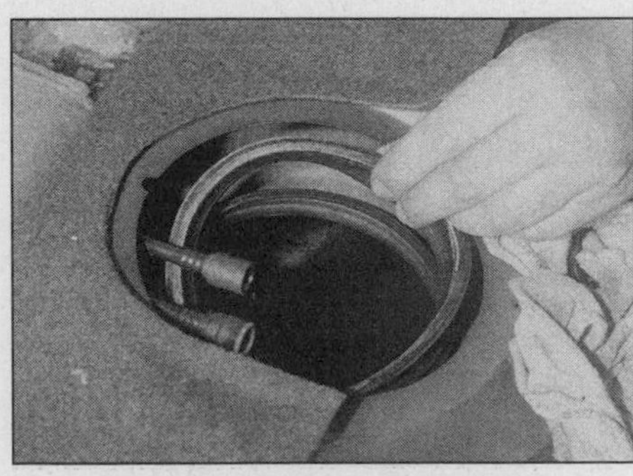

8.7b Removing the sealing ring

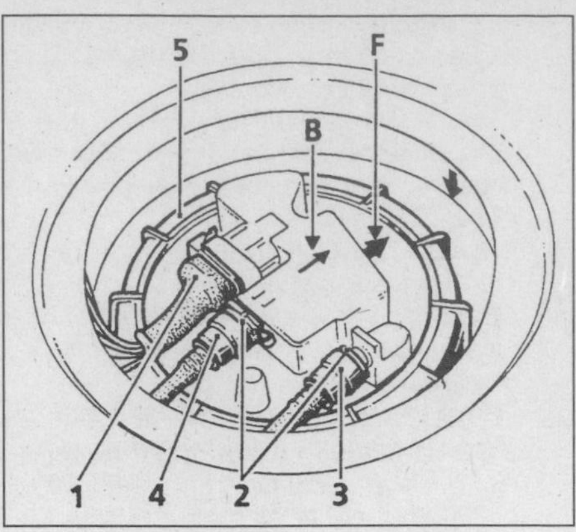

8.5c Fuel pump connections

1 Wiring connector
2 Quick-release clips
3 Fuel supply hose
4 Fuel return hose
5 Locking ring
B Arrow indicating flow of return fuel
F The arrow must be pointing to the rear and aligned with the longitudinal axis of the car

8 Note that the fuel pump/fuel gauge sender unit is only available as a complete assembly – no components are available separately.

Refitting

9 Ensure that the fuel pump pick-up filter is clean and free of debris. Fit the sealing ring to the top of the fuel tank.

10 Carefully manoeuvre the pump assembly into the fuel tank.

11 Align the arrow on the fuel pump cover with the arrow on the fuel tank (the arrow must point to the rear of the vehicle), then refit the locking ring. Securely tighten the locking ring, then recheck that the pump cover and tank marks are all correctly aligned. **Note:** *If a suitable adapter is available tighten the locking ring to the specified torque.*

12 Reconnect the feed and return hoses to the top of the fuel pump; it is not necessary to depress the collars when refitting the hoses. Check the hoses are securely in position.

13 Reconnect the wiring connector.

14 Reconnect the battery and start the engine. Check the fuel pump feed and return hoses for signs of leakage.

15 Refit the plastic access cover and the rear seat cushion.

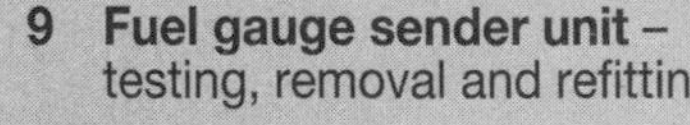
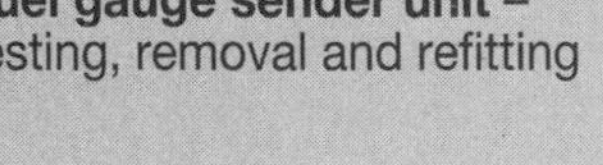

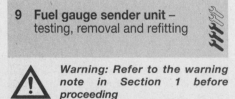

9 Fuel gauge sender unit – testing, removal and refitting

Warning: Refer to the warning note in Section 1 before proceeding

Testing

1 The fuel gauge sender unit is supplied as part of the fuel pump assembly, however it is possible to test its operation and remove it.

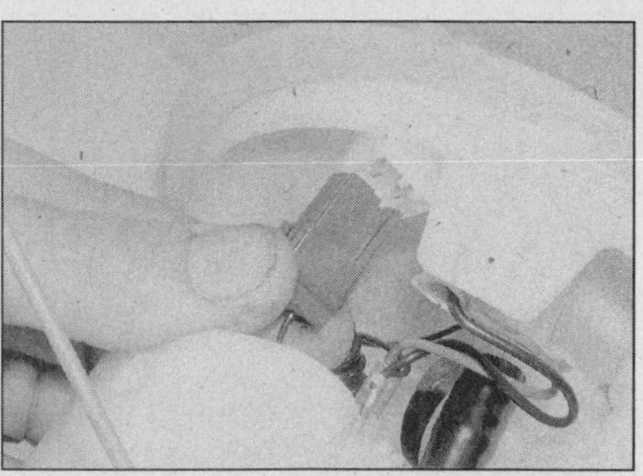
9.3 Disconnecting the wiring from the cover

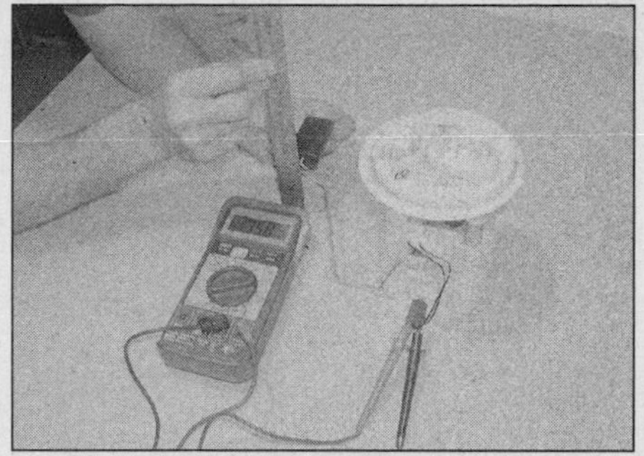
9.4 Testing the sender unit with an ohmmeter

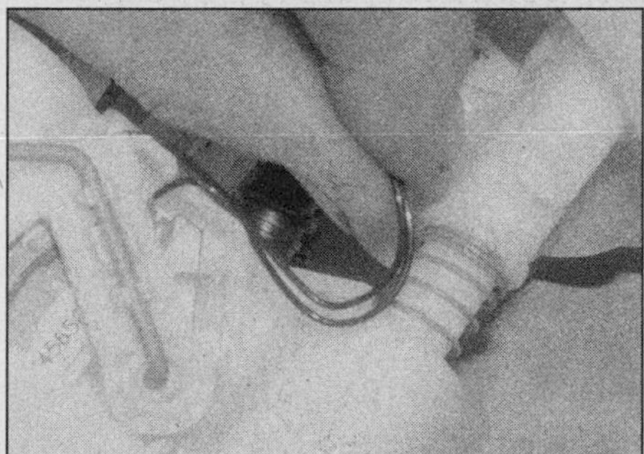
9.5a Remove the wiring from the clips . . .

2 To test the sender unit, first remove the pump as described in Section 8.

3 Disconnect the wiring plug from the cover and connect an ohmmeter to the two terminals **(see illustration)**.

4 With the pump assembly upright on the bench, measure the resistance of the sender unit at the different heights given in the Specifications **(see illustration)**. The resistances are approximate but is should be clear if the sender unit is not operating correctly.

Removal

5 To remove the sender unit, first release the wiring from the clips, then unclip and remove the cover from the main body **(see illustrations)**.

6 Using a screwdriver, prise off the gauze filter from the bottom of the unit. Also recover the O-ring seal from the spring location column **(see illustrations)**.

7 Carefully unclip the bottom section, then disconnect the wiring and slide out the sender unit and float **(see illustrations)**.

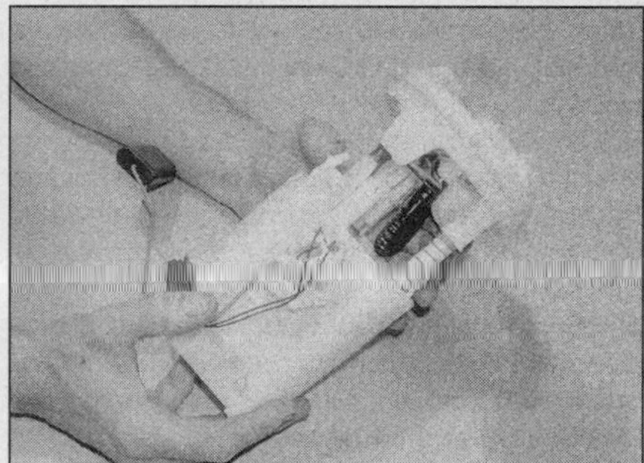
9.5b . . . then unclip the cover

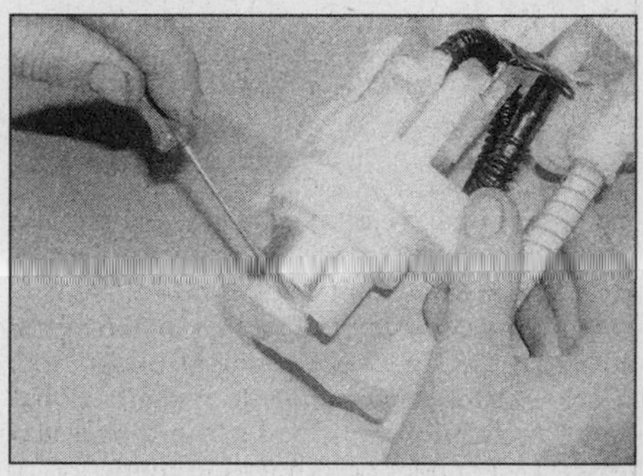
9.6a Insert a screwdriver . . .

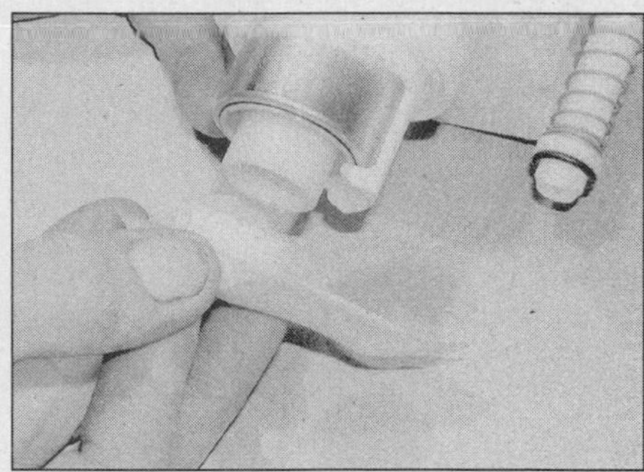
9.6b . . . prise off the gauze filter . . .

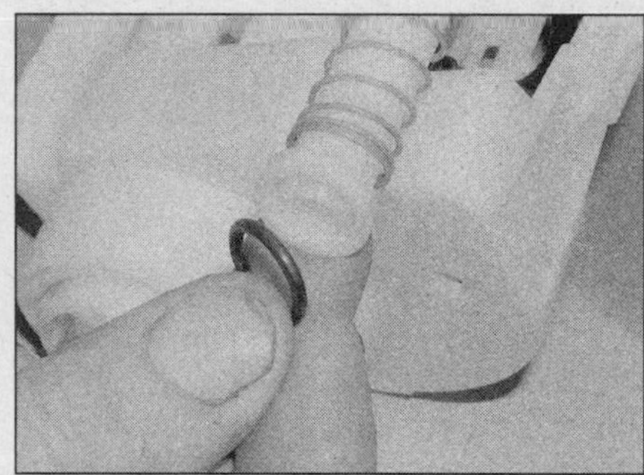
9.6c . . . and recover the O-ring seal

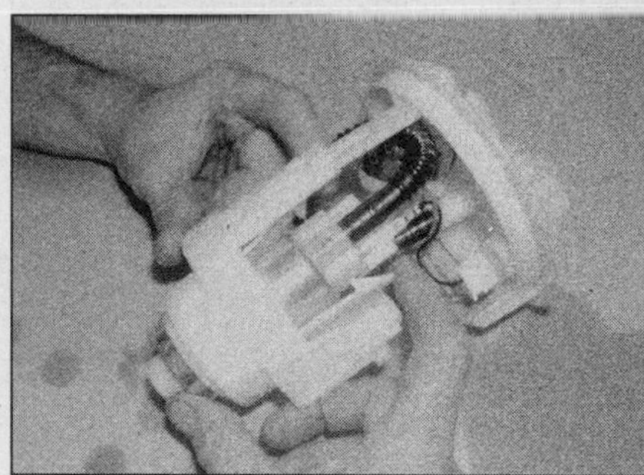
9.7a Unclip the bottom section . . .

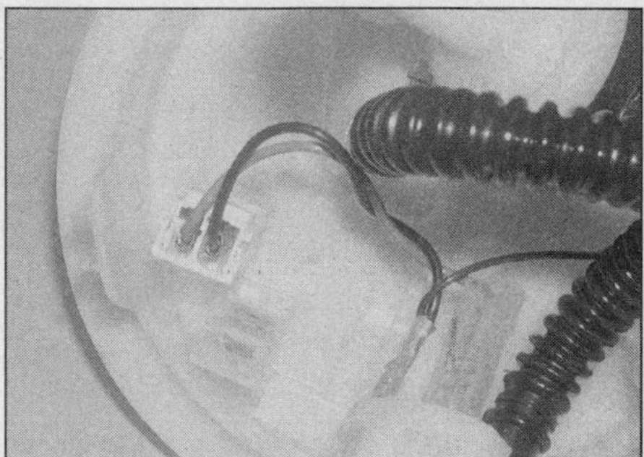
9.7b . . . then disconnect the wiring . . .

9.7c . . . and slide out the sender unit and float

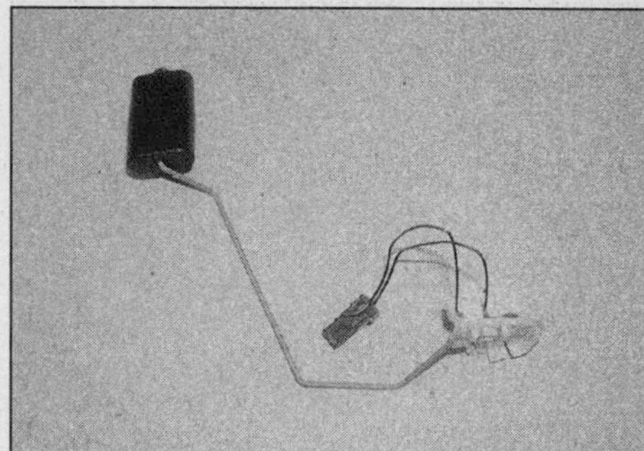
9.7d Sender unit and float removed

Refitting

8 Refitting is a reversal of removal, but test the unit before refitting the pump assembly to the tank.

10 Fuel tank – removal and refitting

Warning: Refer to the warning note in Section 1 before proceeding

Removal

1 Before removing the fuel tank, all fuel must be drained from it. Since a drain plug is not provided, it is preferable to carry out the removal operation when the tank is nearly empty.

2 Remove the rear seat, or rear seat cushion (Chapter 11), for access to the fuel pump cover.

3 Using a screwdriver, carefully prise the plastic access cover from the floor to expose the fuel pump.

4 If there is any fuel remaining in the fuel tank, it can be removed by disconnecting the fuel delivery hose and connecting a suitable hose leading to a container outside the vehicle (refer to Section 8 for disconnecting the hose). Remove the fuel pump relay located in the engine compartment fuse/relay box, and connect a bridging wire between terminals 3 and 5 (the terminals with the thick wires). Allow the fuel pump to operate until the fuel flow is intermittent, then disconnect the bridging wire and refit the relay.

5 Disconnect the wiring connector from the fuel pump, and tape the connector to the vehicle body, to prevent it disappearing behind the tank.

6 Disconnect the battery negative lead (refer to Chapter 5A).

7 Disconnect the return hose from the fuel pump with reference to Section 8.

8 Chock the front wheels then jack up the rear of the vehicle and support on axle stands (see *Jacking and vehicle support*). Remove the right-hand rear wheel.

9 Remove the exhaust system and relevant heat shield(s) with reference to Section 16.

10 Note the position of the adjustment nut on the rear of the handbrake lever equaliser rod, then unscrew and remove it and detach the handbrake cables from the supports on the underbody. Position the cables to one side away from the fuel tank.

11 Disconnect the hoses from the fuel filler neck (see Section 8 when disconnecting the special collar).

12 Place a trolley jack with an interposed block of wood beneath the tank, then raise the jack until it is supporting the weight of the tank.

13 Unscrew and remove the mounting bolts, then slowly lower the fuel tank out of position, disconnecting any other relevant vent pipes as they become accessible (where necessary), and remove the tank from underneath the vehicle. Note that it may be necessary to carefully bend the brake pipes to provide sufficient clearance when lowering the tank.

14 If the tank is contaminated with sediment or water, remove the fuel pump/sender unit (Section 8), and swill the tank out with clean fuel. The tank is injection-moulded from a synthetic material – if seriously damaged, it should be renewed. However, in certain cases, it may be possible to have small leaks or minor damage repaired. Seek the advice of a specialist before attempting to repair the fuel tank.

Refitting

15 Refitting is the reverse of the removal procedure, noting the following points:

a) *When lifting the tank back into position, take care to ensure that the hoses are not trapped between the tank and vehicle body.*

b) *Ensure that all pipes and hoses are correctly routed. Make sure the sealing rings are in position in the quick-release fittings prior to fitting and make sure they are securely clipped in position.*

c) *On completion, refill the tank with a small amount of fuel, and check for signs of leakage prior to taking the vehicle out on the road.*

11 Throttle body/housing – removal and refitting

Warning: Refer to the warning note in Section 1 before proceeding.

Removal

1 Depressurise the fuel system with reference to Section 7.

2 Disconnect the battery negative lead (refer to Chapter 5A) and proceed as described under the relevant heading.

E7J engine

3 Remove the air cleaner assembly as described in Section 2. Also remove the air inlet duct.

4 Disconnect the accelerator cable from the throttle quadrant.

5 Depress the retaining clips and disconnect the wiring connectors from the throttle potentiometer and idle control stepper motor **(see illustrations)**.

6 Unscrew and remove the bolts securing the throttle body assembly to the inlet manifold, then remove the assembly and gasket. Discard the gasket; a new one should be used on refitting.

All other engines

7 Remove the air cleaner assembly as described in Section 2. Also remove the airbox from the throttle housing.

8 Disconnect the accelerator cable from the throttle quadrant **(see illustration)**.

9 Disconnect the wiring from the throttle potentiometer.

10 Unscrew the bolts securing the throttle body assembly to the inlet manifold, then remove the assembly and gasket/seal. Discard the gasket/seal; a new one should be used on refitting.

Refitting

11 Clean the mating faces of the throttle body/housing and inlet manifold.

12 Refitting is a reversal of removal, but fit a new gasket/seal and check the adjustment of the accelerator cable with reference to Section 3.

11.5a Wiring connector for the air temperature sensor/injector (E7J engine)

11.5b Disconnecting the wiring for the throttle potentiometer (E7J engine)

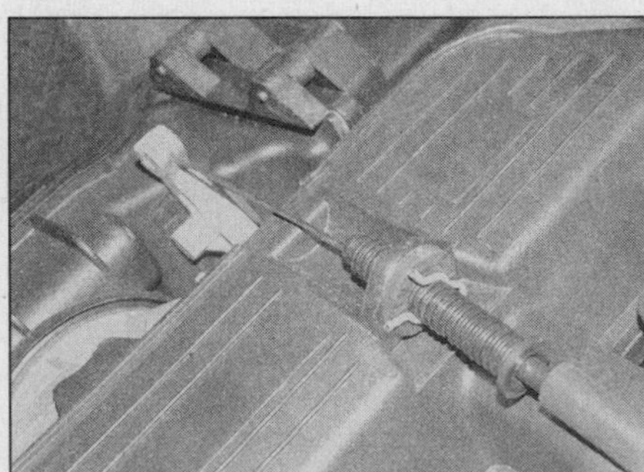

11.8 Accelerator cable adjustment and connection to throttle quadrant

12 Fuel injection system – testing and adjustment

Warning: Refer to the warning note in Section 1 before proceeding

Testing

1 If a fault appears in the fuel injection system, first ensure that all the system wiring connectors are securely connected and free of corrosion. Ensure that the fault is not due to poor maintenance; ie, check that the air cleaner filter element is clean, the spark plugs are in good condition and correctly gapped, the cylinder compression pressures are correct, the ignition timing is correct, and that the engine breather hoses are clear and undamaged, referring to the relevant parts of Chapters 1, 2 and 5 for further information.

2 If these checks fail to reveal the cause of the problem, the vehicle should be taken to a suitably-equipped Renault dealer for testing. A diagnostic connector is incorporated in the engine management circuit, into which a special electronic diagnostic tester can be plugged; the connector is located on the main fusebox. The tester will locate the fault quickly and simply, alleviating the need to test all the system components individually, which is a time-consuming operation that carries a risk of damaging the ECU. The Renault XR25 diagnostic tester is specific for Renault dealerships; at the time of writing there was no equivalent tester available. The tester uses a barchart configuration on a LCD screen; a fiche for the particular model is placed on the screen and each circuit can be checked instantly. There is no code output as such, so it is not possible for the home mechanic to determine a faulty area of the fuel injection system.

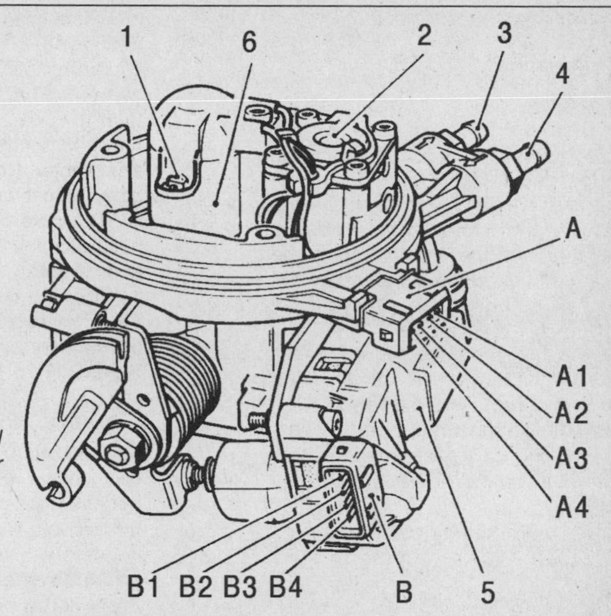

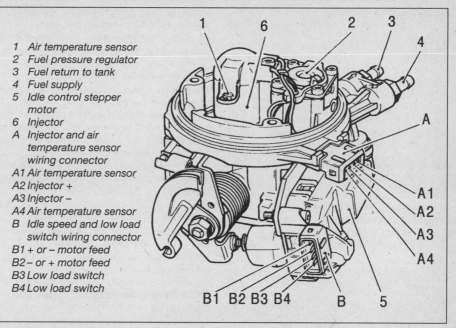

1 Air temperature sensor
2 Fuel pressure regulator
3 Fuel return to tank
4 Fuel supply
5 Idle control stepper motor
6 Injector
A Injector and air temperature sensor wiring connector
A1 Air temperature sensor
A2 Injector +
A3 Injector –
A4 Air temperature sensor
B Idle speed and low load switch wiring connector
B1 + or – motor feed
B2 – or + motor feed
B3 Low load switch
B4 Low load switch

12.4a Throttle body components and terminals (right-hand side) (E7J engine)

3 If the 'electronic incident' warning light illuminates on the instrument panel whilst driving, or remains illuminated longer than 3 seconds after switching on the ignition, a fault is indicated in one or more of the following components:

a) Manifold absolute pressure sensor.
b) Throttle potentiometer.
c) Injectors.
d) Idle speed stepper motor (certain engines only).
e) Vehicle speed sensor (when the vehicle is moving).
f) EGR solenoid valve (where fitted).
g) Automatic transmission computer.

4 Some individual components may be tested for resistance after removal using the information given in the Specifications, however other items (such as the idle speed stepper motor) cannot be checked and are not adjustable **(see illustrations)**.

Adjustment

5 Experienced home mechanics with a considerable amount of skill and equipment (including a tachometer and an accurately calibrated exhaust gas analyser) may be able to check the exhaust CO level and the idle speed. However, if these are found to be in need of adjustment, the car *must* be taken to a suitably-equipped Renault dealer for further testing. Neither the mixture adjustment (exhaust gas CO level) nor the idle speed are adjustable, and should either be incorrect, a fault must be present in the fuel injection system.

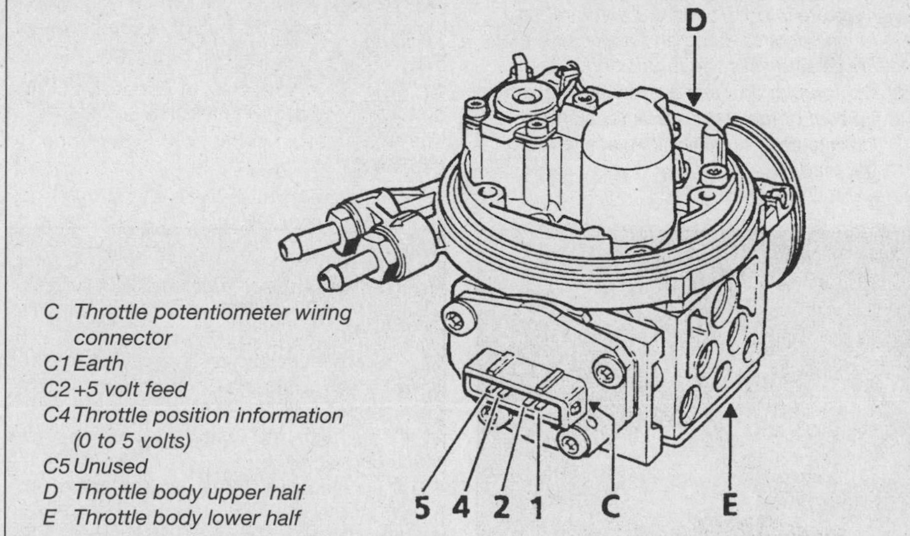

C Throttle potentiometer wiring connector
C1 Earth
C2 +5 volt feed
C4 Throttle position information (0 to 5 volts)
C5 Unused
D Throttle body upper half
E Throttle body lower half

12.4b Throttle body components and terminals (left-hand side) (E7J engine)

4A

13 Single-point injection system components – removal and refitting

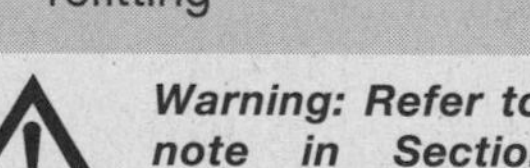

Warning: Refer to the warning note in Section 1 before proceeding

Fuel injector

Note: *If a faulty injector is suspected, before condemning the injector, it is worth trying the effect of one of the proprietary injector-cleaning treatments.*

Removal

1 Remove the inlet air temperature sensor as described later in this Section.

2 Note its fitted position, then lift out the injector and recover its sealing rings **(see illustration)**.

Refitting

3 Refitting is a reversal of the removal procedure ensuring that the injector sealing rings and injector cap O-ring are in good condition. When refitting the injector cap ensure that the injector pins are correctly aligned with the cap terminals; the terminals are marked + and – for identification.

Fuel pressure regulator

4 The fuel pressure regulator is an integral part of the upper half of the throttle body. If it is defective, the complete throttle body assembly must be renewed.

Inlet air temperature sensor

Removal

5 Remove the air cleaner assembly as described in Section 2.
6 Disconnect the sensor multi-plug.
7 Remove the single securing screw, and free the sensor cover **(see illustration)**.
8 Free the connector lugs, and withdraw the sensor together with the cover, wiring and connector.

Refitting

9 Refit by reversing the removal operations.

Idle speed control stepper motor

Removal

10 Remove the air cleaner assembly as described in Section 2.
11 Remove the throttle body securing screws. Carefully lift the throttle body to improve access to the motor.
12 Disconnect the motor multi-plug.
13 Remove the three mounting screws and withdraw the motor.

Refitting

14 Refit by reversing the removal operations, then perform an initial setting operation as follows.
15 Place a shim or feeler gauges of approximately 5 mm thickness between the throttle quadrant and the motor plunger. Switch the ignition on for a few seconds, then switch it off again. Remove the shim or gauges, then switch on and off again.
16 Run the engine and check that the idle speed and quality are satisfactory.

Throttle potentiometer

17 The throttle potentiometer is an integral part of the lower half of the throttle body. If it is defective, the complete throttle body assembly must be renewed. The idle speed control motor can be transferred from the old half-body to the new one.
18 After renewal, the initial setting of the potentiometer must be verified using the Renault XR25 diagnostic tester.

Coolant temperature sensor

19 The coolant temperature sensor is located on the front of the thermostat housing. Refer to Chapter 3, Section 6, for removal and refitting details.

Electronic control unit (ECU)

Removal

20 The ECU is located in the front right-hand corner of the engine compartment.
21 To remove the ECU first disconnect the battery negative lead.
22 Unbolt the bracket from the top of the ECU and release the strap. Alternatively the bracket can remain on the ECU until the assembly is removed.
23 Undo the mounting screws and remove the ECU and mounting bracket.
24 Disconnect the wiring connector and remove the ECU from the engine compartment.

Refitting

25 Refitting is a reverse of the removal procedure ensuring that the wiring connector is securely reconnected.

Manifold absolute pressure sensor

Removal

26 The sensor is mounted on the left-hand side of the engine compartment bulkhead.
27 Disconnect the wiring from the sensor.
28 Unscrew the mounting nuts and remove the sensor.

Refitting

29 Refitting is a reversal of removal.

Relays

Removal

30 The fuel injection system and fuel pump relays are located in the engine compartment fuse/relay box.
31 Remove the cover from the box.
32 Remove the relevant relay from the fuse/relay box.

Refitting

33 Refitting is the reverse of removal.

Crankshaft speed/position (TDC) sensor

Removal

34 The sensor is mounted on the top of the transmission housing at the left-hand end of the cylinder block.
35 To remove the sensor, disconnect the battery negative terminal (refer to Chapter 5A) then remove the air cleaner housing as described in Section 2.
36 Trace the wiring back from the sensor to the wiring connector, and disconnect it from the main harness.
37 Unscrew the retaining bolts and remove the sensor.

Refitting

38 Refitting is a reverse of the removal procedure. Ensure that the sensor retaining bolts are securely tightened – note that only the special shouldered bolts originally fitted must be used to secure the sensor; these bolts locate the sensor precisely to give the correct air gap between the sensor tip and the flywheel/driveplate.

Fuel cut-off inertia switch

Removal

39 The fuel cut-off inertia switch is located in the left-hand side of the engine compartment.
40 Unscrew and remove the switch retaining screws then disconnect its wiring connector and remove the switch from the engine compartment.

Refitting

41 Refitting is the reverse of removal. On completion, reset the switch by depressing its button.

Power steering pressure switch

Removal

42 The pressure switch is screwed into the power steering feed pipe from the pump to the steering gear.
43 To remove the switch, disconnect the wiring connector.
44 Wipe clean the area around the switch then unscrew the switch and remove it from the pipe. Plug the pipe aperture to prevent excess fluid leakage and prevent dirt entry into the hydraulic system.

13.2 Removing the fuel injector (E7J engine)

13.7 Inlet air temperature sensor cover retaining screw (E7J engine)

Refitting

45 Refitting is the reverse of removal. On completion check the power steering fluid level as described in *Weekly checks*.

Knock sensor (where fitted)

46 Refer to Chapter 5B.

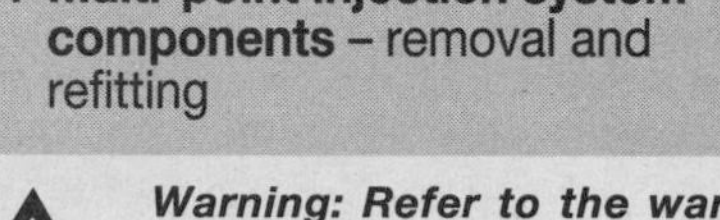

14 Multi-point injection system components – removal and refitting

Warning: Refer to the warning note in Section 1 before proceeding

Fuel rail and injectors

Note: *If a faulty injector is suspected, before condemning the injector, it is worth trying the effect of one of the proprietary injector-cleaning treatments.*

K4J and K4M engines

1 Depressurise the fuel system as described in Section 7, then disconnect the battery negative lead.
2 Remove the cover for access to the fuel rail.
3 Disconnect the fuel feed and return hoses from the fuel rail.
4 Disconnect the vacuum hose connecting the pressure regulator (on the fuel rail) to the inlet manifold.
5 Disconnect the wiring from the injectors and move the loom to one side.
6 Unscrew and remove the mounting bolts and carefully ease the fuel rail together with the injectors from the inlet manifold.
7 Note the fitted positions of the injectors, then remove the clips and ease the injectors from the fuel rail.
8 Remove the sealing rings from the grooves at each end of the injectors and obtain new ones.
9 Refitting is a reversal of the removal procedure, noting the following points:

a) Renew all sealing rings, using a smear of engine oil to aid installation.
b) Refit the fuel rail assembly to the manifold, making sure the sealing rings remain correctly positioned, and tighten the retaining bolts to the specified torque.
c) On completion start the engine and check for fuel leaks.

F4R engine

10 Depressurise the fuel system as described in Section 7, then disconnect the battery negative lead.
11 Remove the cover for access to the fuel rail. Disconnect the fuel feed hose and, where applicable, the return hose from the fuel rail. Also disconnect the vacuum hose connecting the pressure regulator (on the fuel rail) to the inlet manifold.
12 Remove the auxiliary drivebelt, then unbolt the power steering pump pulley, unscrew the pump mounting bolts and move the pump to one side without disconnecting the hydraulic fluid hoses.
13 Disconnect the wiring from the injectors and move the loom to one side.
14 Unscrew and remove the mounting bolts and carefully ease the fuel rail together with the injectors from the inlet manifold.
15 Note the fitted positions of the injectors, then remove the clips and ease the injectors from the fuel rail.
16 Remove the sealing rings from the grooves at each end of the injectors and obtain new ones.
17 To remove the lower inlet manifold, first remove the upper inlet manifold as described in Section 15, then unbolt the lower manifold from the cylinder head and recover the gasket.
18 Refitting is a reversal of the removal procedure, noting the following points:

a) Fit a new gasket when refitting the lower inlet manifold, but use a straight-edge to align the right-hand end of the manifold with the cylinder head.
b) Renew all sealing rings, using a smear of engine oil to aid installation.
c) Refit the fuel rail assembly to the manifold, making sure the sealing rings remain correctly positioned, and tighten the retaining bolts to the specified torque.
d) On completion start the engine and check for fuel leaks.

Fuel pressure regulator

Removal

19 Disconnect the vacuum pipe from the regulator.
20 Place a wad of rag over the regulator to catch any spilled fuel, then extract the retaining spring and ease the regulator from the fuel rail.
21 Remove the sealing rings from the grooves in the pressure regulator and obtain new ones.

Refitting

22 On refitting, fit new sealing rings to the regulator grooves and apply a smear of engine oil to them to ease installation. Ease the regulator back into the end of the fuel rail and refit the retaining spring and vacuum pipe.

Throttle potentiometer

Removal

23 Remove the throttle housing as described in Section 11.
24 Undo the retaining screws and remove the potentiometer from the throttle housing.

Refitting

25 Refitting is a reverse of the removal procedure ensuring that the potentiometer is correctly engaged with the throttle spindle. **Note:** *Renault recommend that the potentiometer operation should be checked, whenever it is disturbed, using the XR25 diagnostic tester.*

Inlet air temperature sensor

Removal

26 Unscrew and remove the inlet air temperature sensor from the air inlet duct or air cleaner body as applicable.

Refitting

27 Refitting is a reversal of removal.

Coolant temperature sensor

28 The sensor is located on the thermostat housing at the left-hand end of the cylinder head. Refer to Chapter 3, Section 6, for removal and refitting details.

Power steering pressure switch

Removal

29 The switch is screwed into the feed pipe from the power steering pump to the steering gear.
30 To remove the switch, disconnect the wiring connector.
31 Wipe clean the area around the switch then unscrew the switch and remove it from the pipe. Plug the pipe aperture to prevent excess fluid leakage and prevent dirt entry into the hydraulic system.

Refitting

32 Refitting is the reverse of removal. On completion check the power steering fluid level as described in *Weekly checks*.

Knock sensor (where fitted)

33 Refer to Chapter 5B.

Idle speed control stepper motor

Removal

34 The idle speed control stepper motor is mounted on the top of the throttle housing. To remove it first remove the throttle housing as described in Section 11.
35 Undo the retaining screws and remove the stepper motor from the throttle housing. Recover the gasket and discard it; a new one should be used on refitting.

Refitting

36 Refitting is a reversal of the removal procedure using a new gasket.

Manifold absolute pressure sensor

Removal

37 The pressure sensor is located on the left-hand end of the inlet manifold. Where necessary, remove the air cleaner assembly for access to the sensor.
38 Disconnect the wiring from the sensor.
39 Unscrew and remove the sensor.

Refitting

40 Refitting is a reversal of removal.

Relays

Removal

41 The fuel injection system and fuel pump relays are located in the engine compartment fuse/relay box (see Chapter 12).
42 Remove the cover from the box.

14.45 The crankshaft speed/position sensor is mounted on top of the transmission

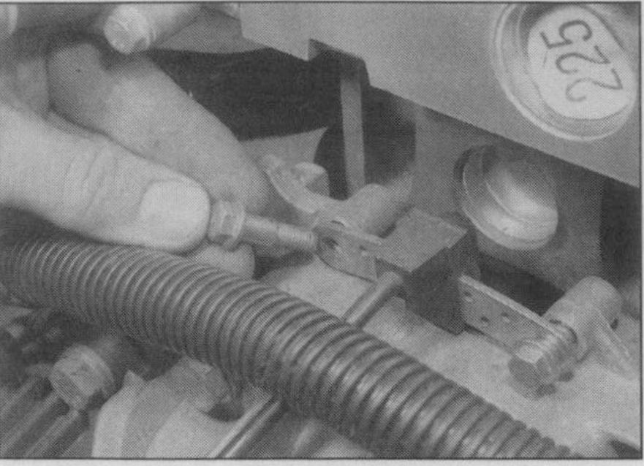
14.48 Note the special bolts used to locate and secure the crankshaft speed/position sensor

14.50 Fuel cut-off inertia switch

43 Remove the relevant relay from the fuse/relay box.

Refitting

44 Refitting is the reverse of removal.

Crankshaft speed/position (TDC) sensor

Removal

45 The sensor is mounted on the top of the transmission bellhousing at the left-hand end of the cylinder block **(see illustration)**.
46 To remove the sensor, disconnect the battery negative terminal (refer to Chapter 5A) then, where applicable, remove the air cleaner housing as described in Section 2.
47 Trace the wiring back from the sensor to the wiring connector, and disconnect it from the main harness.
48 Unscrew the retaining bolts and remove the sensor **(see illustration)**.

Refitting

49 Refitting is a reverse of the removal procedure. Ensure that the sensor retaining bolts are securely tightened – note that only the special shouldered bolts originally fitted must be used to secure the sensor; these bolts locate the sensor precisely to give the correct air gap between the sensor tip and the flywheel/driveplate.

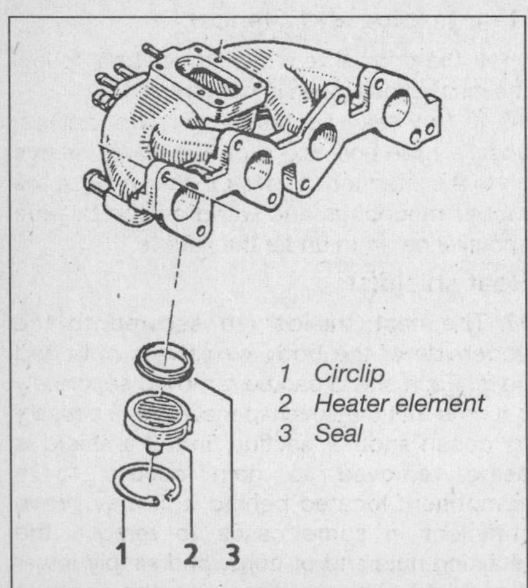

15.5 Inlet manifold heater components (E7J engine)

Fuel cut-off inertia switch

Removal

50 The switch is located in the left-hand side of the engine compartment **(see illustration)**.
51 Unscrew and remove the switch retaining screws then disconnect its wiring connector and remove the switch from the engine compartment.

Refitting

52 Refitting is the reverse of removal. On completion, reset the switch by depressing its button.

Electronic control unit (ECU)

Removal

Note: *The ECU is electronically-coded to match the engine immobiliser. If the ECU is being removed to enable a new unit to be fitted, the new unit must be programmed with the vehicle code as described.*
53 The ECU is located in the left-hand side of the engine compartment. First disconnect the battery negative lead (refer to Chapter 5A).
54 Where applicable, unbolt the bracket from the top of the ECU and release the strap. Alternatively the bracket can remain on the ECU until the assembly is removed.
55 Undo the mounting screws and remove the ECU and mounting bracket.
56 Disconnect the wiring connector and remove the ECU from the engine compartment.

15.9 Wiring to the throttle potentiometer and air temperature sensor

Refitting

57 Refitting is a reverse of the removal procedure ensuring that the wiring connector is securely reconnected. If a new ECU has been fitted, reprogramme it as follows. Turn the ignition on for a few seconds, then turn it off. Now remove the key to operate the immobiliser. After 10 seconds, the red immobiliser warning light should start to flash.

15 Manifolds – removal and refitting

Inlet manifold

E7J engine

1 Remove the throttle body as described in Section 11.
2 Drain the cooling system as described in Chapter 1A, then disconnect the coolant hoses from the inlet manifold.
3 Disconnect the brake servo vacuum hose and the wiring connector from the heater on the bottom of the inlet manifold.
4 Progressively unscrew the nuts, then withdraw the inlet manifold from the studs on the cylinder head. Remove the gasket.
5 If necessary, the heater may be removed from the bottom of the inlet manifold, by first extracting the circlip. Note the location of the seal **(see illustration)**.
6 Refitting is a reversal of removal but use a new gasket and tighten the mounting nuts to the specified torque. Ensure that the cylinder head and manifold mating surfaces are clean, and use a new gasket. Refill the cooling system with reference to Chapter 1A.

K4J, K4M and F4R engines

7 Disconnect the battery negative (see Chapter 5A).
8 Remove the air cleaner assembly as described in Section 2.
9 Disconnect the wiring from the throttle potentiometer, absolute pressure sensor, ignition coils and air temperature sensor **(see illustration)**.
10 Disconnect the accelerator cable from the throttle body with reference to Section 3.

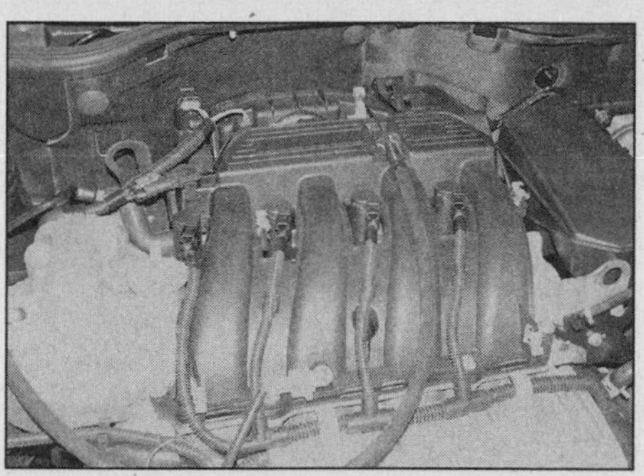

15.12 Inlet manifold on the K4M engine

11 Unscrew and remove the throttle body mounting bolts and position the throttle body to one side.

12 Progressively unscrew and remove the bolts securing the inlet manifold to the cylinder head **(see illustration)**.

13 Withdraw the inlet manifold and recover the gasket. On the F4R engine, unbolt the lower inlet manifold.

14 Refitting is a reversal of removal but use new gaskets and tighten the mounting bolts to the specified torque. Ensure that the cylinder head and manifold mating surfaces are clean.

Exhaust manifold

Removal

15 Disconnect the battery negative lead (see Chapter 5A).

16 Apply the handbrake, then jack up the front of the vehicle and support it on axle stands (see *Jacking and vehicle support*).

17 Remove the air cleaner assembly as described in Section 2.

18 Disconnect the wiring and remove the lambda (oxygen) sensor from the exhaust manifold with reference to Chapter 4C, Section 2.

19 Unbolt and remove the heatshield from the exhaust manifold.

20 Disconnect the exhaust downpipe from the manifold with reference to Section 16, and support it to one side on an axle stand or block of wood. Recover the gasket. **Note:** *Take care not to damage the flexible section of the catalytic converter.*

21 Unbolt the support strut between the exhaust manifold and cylinder block.

16.6 Downstream lambda (oxygen) sensor on the K4M engine

22 Unscrew the mounting nuts, then tilt the exhaust manifold through 45° and withdraw it from the cylinder head.

Refitting

23 Refitting is a reversal of removal, but tighten the nuts progressively to the specified torque. Ensure that the cylinder head and manifold mating surfaces are clean, and use new gaskets. Also make sure that the heat shield is correctly refitted between the lambda (oxygen) sensor and manifold and that the wiring is routed away from the manifold.

16 Exhaust system – general information, removal and refitting

General information

1 On new vehicles the exhaust system consists of just two sections; the front downpipe (and catalytic converter) and the remaining system consisting of a resonator, tailpipe and silencer. The downpipe is attached to the rear section by a flanged joint with gasket or a cone-and-socket joint.

2 The rear section of the exhaust is located above the rear suspension. The system is suspended throughout its entire length by rubber mountings.

Removal

3 To remove a part of the system, first jack up the front or rear of the car, and support it on axle stands (see *Jacking and vehicle support*). Alternatively, position the car over an inspection pit, or on car ramps. Where fitted, remove the engine compartment undershield.

Front pipe and catalytic converter

4 Remove the air cleaner assembly as described in Section 2.

5 To provide additional clearance between the front subframe and exhaust downpipe, the subframe must be lowered by 20 mm at the front and 40 mm at the rear. To do this, unscrew the subframe tie rod bolts, disconnect the bottom of the steering column from the steering gear (see Chapter 10), then unscrew and remove the subframe mounting bolts one at a time, replacing them with threaded rod which will allow the subframe to be lowered. As each rod is fitted, initially fit a nut to keep the subframe in position, then unscrew them when all of the rods are fitted in order to lower the subframe.

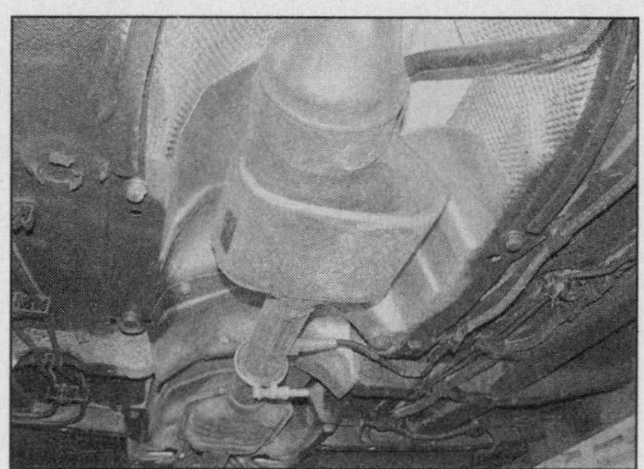

16.7 Front pipe and catalytic converter on the K4M engine

6 Where fitted, disconnect the wiring from the lambda (oxygen) sensor located downstream of the catalytic converter **(see illustration)**.

7 Working beneath the vehicle, loosen the clamp bolt securing the catalytic converter to the intermediate exhaust section **(see illustration)**. Separate the sections and support them.

8 Unbolt the relevant heat shields from the underbody.

9 Unscrew the bolts/nuts and release the downpipe from the exhaust manifold.

10 Withdraw the front pipe and catalytic converter from under the vehicle, taking care not to damage the heat shields.

Intermediate pipe and resonator

11 Unscrew and remove the clamp or flange bolts (as applicable) attaching the front pipe and catalytic converter to the rear section. Recover the gasket where applicable.

12 If the original rear section is fitted, it must be cut in half using either a hacksaw or pipe cutter. Locate the cutting area which is situated approximately midway between the resonator and rear silencer. The cutting point is marked with two circular punch marks on the side of the pipe. The punch marks are 90 mm apart and the exhaust section should be cut at the mid-point between the two punch marks. **Note:** *Ensure that the exhaust pipe is cut squarely, or else it will be difficult to obtain a gas-tight seal when the exhaust is refitted.*

13 With the intermediate pipe cut, withdraw the intermediate exhaust section from under the vehicle.

14 If the rear section is in two halves, unscrew the bolt and slide the clamp sleeve on to the rear section then release the rubber mountings and withdraw the intermediate section from under the vehicle.

Rear tailpipe and silencer

15 If the original rear section is fitted, follow the instructions given in paragraph 12.

16 If the rear section is in two halves, unscrew the bolt and slide the clamp sleeve on to the intermediate section then release the rubber mountings and withdraw the tailpipe and silencer from under the vehicle.

Heat shield(s)

17 The heat shields are secured to the underside of the body by various nuts and bolts. Each shield can be removed separately but note that they overlap making it necessary to loosen another section first. If a shield is being removed to gain access to a component located behind it, it may prove sufficient in some cases to remove the retaining nuts and/or bolts, and simply lower the shield, without disturbing the exhaust system. Otherwise remove the exhaust section as described earlier.

Refitting

18 Each section is refitted by reversing the removal sequence, noting the following points:

a) *Ensure that all traces of corrosion have been removed from the flanges, and renew all necessary gaskets.*
b) *Inspect the rubber mountings for signs of damage or deterioration, and renew as necessary.*
c) *When reconnecting the intermediate pipe to the tailpipe, apply a smear of exhaust system jointing paste (Renault recommend the use of Sodicam) to the sleeve inner surface, to ensure a gas-tight seal. Make sure both inner ends of the cut pipe are positioned squarely against the stop of the clamp sleeve. Position the sleeve bolt vertically on the left-hand side of the pipe and securely tighten the nut until it is heard to click; the clamp bolt has a groove in it to ensure that the nut is correctly tightened (equivalent to a tightening torque of approximately 25 Nm/18 lbf ft).*
d) *Prior to tightening the exhaust system fasteners, ensure that all rubber mountings are correctly located, and that there is adequate clearance between the exhaust system and vehicle underbody.*

Chapter 4 Part B:
Diesel engine fuel and exhaust systems

Contents

Degrees of difficulty

Easy, suitable for novice with little experience

Fairly easy, suitable for beginner with some experience

Fairly difficult, suitable for competent DIY mechanic

Difficult, suitable for experienced DIY mechanic

Very difficult, suitable for expert DIY or professional

Specifications

Engine codes

Non-turbo engines – D models	F8Q 620, F8Q 622, F8Q 788
Turbo engines:	
Indirect injection – dT models	F8Q 784, F8Q 786
Direct injection – dTi models	F9Q 730, F9Q 734
Direct common-rail injection – dCi models	F9Q 732

Note: *The engine code is on a plate attached to the engine. Refer to 'Vehicle identification numbers' for further details.*

General

System type	Rear-mounted fuel tank, fuel injection pump with integral transfer pump (except F9Q 732) or high-pressure pump with common-rail (F9Q 732), indirect injection
Firing order	1-3-4-2 (No 1 at flywheel end)

Maximum no-load speed

F8Q 620/788 engines	5200 ± 100 rpm
F8Q 622 engine	5175 ± 50 rpm
F8Q 784/786 engines	5000 ± 100 rpm
F9Q 730/734 engines	4800 ± 100 rpm*
F9Q 732 engine	4700 ± 150 rpm*

**On F9Q engines the maximum speed is controlled by the injection ECU and is not adjustable*

Idle speed

F8Q 620/788 engines	825 ± 25 rpm
F8Q 622 engine	825 ± 50 rpm*
F8Q 784/786 engines	825 ± 25 rpm*
F9Q 730/734 engines	850 ± 25 rpm*
F9Q 732 engine	835 ± 50 rpm*

** The idle speed is controlled by the injection ECU and is not adjustable*

Fast idle speed

F8Q 620 engine	950 ± 25 rpm
Other F8Q and F9Q engines	Not adjustable*

** The fast idle speed is controlled by the injection ECU*

Anti-stall speed

F8Q 620 engine (with 4 mm shim – see text)	1150 ± 25 rpm
F8Q 622 engine	Controlled by the injection ECU and not adjustable
Other F8Q engines (with 4 mm shim – see text)	1250 ± 25 rpm
F9Q engines	Controlled by the injection ECU and not adjustable

Smoke opacity

	Approval value*	Legal maximum
F8Q 620 engine	1.24 m^{-1} (40%)	2 m^{-1} (55%)
F8Q 622 engine	1.0 m^{-1} (33%)	2.5 m^{-1} (64%)
F8Q 784/786/788 engines	1.4 m^{-1} (44%) or 1.8 m^{-1} (52%)	3 m^{-1} (71%)
F9Q 730/734 engines	1.24 m^{-1} (40%)	2.5 m^{-1} (64%)
F9Q 732 engine	1.5 m^{-1} (46%)	3 m^{-1} (70%)

*** Note:** *The values given are for reference only – for further details refer to the label located in the engine compartment.*

Injection pump (Bosch)

Type:
- F8Q 620 engine: VE 4/8F 2300R 598,
  - VE 4/8F 2300R 598-1 (with air conditioning and fast idle vacuum actuator),
  - VE 4/8F 2300R 598-2 (with coded fuel cut-off solenoid valve),
  - VE 4/8F 2300R 598-3 (with air conditioning, fast idle vacuum actuator and coded fuel cut-off solenoid valve) or
  - VE 4/8F 2300R 598-4

F9Q 730 engine	VE 4/11 E2000R 672
F9Q 734 engine	VE 4/11 E2000R V1763
Direction of rotation	Clockwise viewed from pulley end
Static timing:	
Engine position	No 1 cylinder at TDC
Pump position:	
F8Q 620 engine	0.82 ± 0.04 mm
F9Q 730/734 engines	0.45 ± 0.02 mm
Dynamic timing	No information available at time of writing

Injection pump (Lucas)

Type:	
F8Q 622 engine	EPIC R8640 A111A H111.027
F8Q 784/786 engines	DPCN R8448B020A or R8448B021A (with coded fuel cut-off solenoid valve)
F8Q 788 engines	DPCN R8448B130A
Direction of rotation	Clockwise viewed from pulley end
Static timing:	
Engine position	No 1 cylinder at TDC
Pump position	Value shown on pump
Dynamic timing	No information available at time of writing

High-pressure pump (Bosch)

Type:	
F9Q 732 engine	Bosch CR/CP153/R65/10-15
Pressure	250 to 1350 bars
Pressure regulator resistance	5.0 ohms at 20°C

Injectors

Type:	
Except F9Q 732 engine	Standard Pintle
F9Q 732 engine	Solenoid injector
Opening pressure:	
F8Q engine	130 + 8 – 5 bars (max. tolerance 8 bars)
F9Q engine (except F9Q 732)	200 + 12 – 0 bars (1st level)*
Maximum pressure (F9Q 732 engine)	1525 bars
Solenoid injector resistance (F9Q 732 engine)	2.0 ohms
Injector needle lift resistance (sensor type)	105 ohms

** Not adjustable (factory set)*

Sensor resistances (F8Q 622 engine)

Advance cam position sensor	52 ± 4 ohms
Advance solenoid valve	31 ± 2 ohms
Air temperature sensor:	
0°C	5290 to 6490 ohms
20°C	2400 to 2600 ohms
40°C	1070 to 1270 ohms
Coolant temperature sensor:	
0°C	5290 to 6490 ohms
20°C	2400 to 2600 ohms
40°C	1070 to 1270 ohms
80°C	300 to 450 ohms
Flow valve position sensor	41 ± 4 ohms
Electrical solenoid valve	1.39 ± 0.1 ohms
Negative flow solenoid valve	31 ± 2 ohms
Positive flow solenoid valve	31 ± 2 ohms
Pump temperature thermistor	2716 ± 60 ohms at 20°C

Turbocharger

Type	Garrett T2
Boost pressure (full load at 2500 to 3000 rpm)	900 + 50 – 100 mbar

Fuel tank

Fuel tank level sender unit resistance at height of float pin (approx):	
At 47 mm	310 ± 10 ohms
At 52 mm	280 ± 20 ohms
At 81 mm	190 ± 16 ohms
At 110 mm	110 ± 10 ohms
At 143 mm	61 ± 7 ohms
At 164 mm	3.5 ± 3.5 ohms

Torque wrench settings

	Nm	lbf ft
Advance solenoid valve	30	22
Altimetric solenoid valve	30	22
Cold start timing advance solenoid valve bolt (F9Q engines)	10	7
Coolant pipe-to-turbocharger union nuts	25	18
Exhaust front section-to-turbocharger nuts:		
F8Q engine	45	33
F9Q engine	26	19
Fuel injector clamp bolts to cylinder head (F9Q engines)	27	20
Fuel injectors to cylinder head (F8Q engines)	70	52
Fast idle thermostatic actuator to cylinder head	35	26
Fuel gauge sender unit locking ring	35	26
Fuel pipe union nuts and bolts	25	18
Fuel supply and return hose banjo union bolt (Bosch pump)	25	18
Fuel tank	21	15
High-pressure pipe unions (F9Q 732 engine)	25	18
High-pressure pump mounting (F9Q 732 engine)	32	24
High-pressure pump sprocket nut (F9Q 732 engine):		
Alternative 1	50	37
Alternative 2:		
Stage 1	15	11
Stage 2	Angle-tighten through 60° ± 10°	
Injection pump cover bolts (F9Q engines)	7	5
Injection pump hydraulic head bolt (F9Q engine models)	12	9
Injection pump left-hand mounting nuts and bolts:		
F8Q 620 engine	25	18
Other F8Q engines	20	15
F9Q engines	Not available	
Injection pump right-hand mounting bolts:		
F8Q 620 engine	25	18
Other F8Q engines	30	22
F9Q engines	22	16
Injection pump sprocket centre bolt (LH thread) with micrometric adjustment:		
Stage 1	20	15
Stage 2	90	66

Torque wrench settings (continued)	Nm	lbf ft
Injection pump sprocket securing nut:		
One-piece sprocket (F8Q 620 engine)	65	48
MAA-type sprocket:		
Conventional nut with separate washer	65	48
Gold-coloured extractor nut with integral washer:		
Stage 1	20	15
Stage 2	45	33
Injection pump timing hole blanking plug:		
F8Q 620 engines	25	18
Other F8Q engines	6	4
F9Q engines	Not available	
Inlet/exhaust manifold mounting nuts:		
F8Q engines	25	18
F9Q engines	28	21
Inlet/exhaust manifold studs (F9Q engines)	8	6
Oil feed pipe-to-turbocharger union nut:		
F8Q engine	20	15
F9Q engine	20	15
Oil return pipe-to-turbocharger union nut:		
F8Q engines	40	30
F9Q engines	9	7
Stop solenoid	20	15
Turbocharger-to-exhaust manifold nuts:		
F8Q engines	45	33
F9Q engines	26	19
Wastegate actuator rod locknut	7	5
Wastegate bracket-to-turbocharger bolts*	15	11

**Coat the bolt threads with thread-locking compound*

1 General information and precautions

General information

The fuel system consists of a rear-mounted fuel tank, a fuel filter with integral water separator, either a fuel injection pump or high-pressure pump (common-rail system), injectors and associated components **(see illustrations)**. Before passing through the filter, the fuel is heated by an electric heating element which is fitted to the filter housing.

On engines with a fuel injection pump (ie, except F9Q 732), fuel is drawn from the fuel tank to the fuel injection pump by a vane-type transfer pump incorporated in the fuel injection pump. Before reaching the pump, the fuel passes through a fuel filter, where foreign matter and water are removed. Excess fuel lubricates the moving components of the pump, and is then returned to the tank. The fuel injection pump is driven at half crankshaft speed by the timing belt. The high-pressure required to inject the fuel into the compressed air in the swirl chambers is achieved by two opposed pistons forced together by rollers running in a cam ring. The fuel passes through a central rotor with a single outlet drilling which aligns with ports leading to the injector pipes. The four fuel injectors inject a homogeneous spray of fuel into the swirl chambers located in the cylinder head. The injectors are calibrated to open and close at critical pressures to provide efficient and even

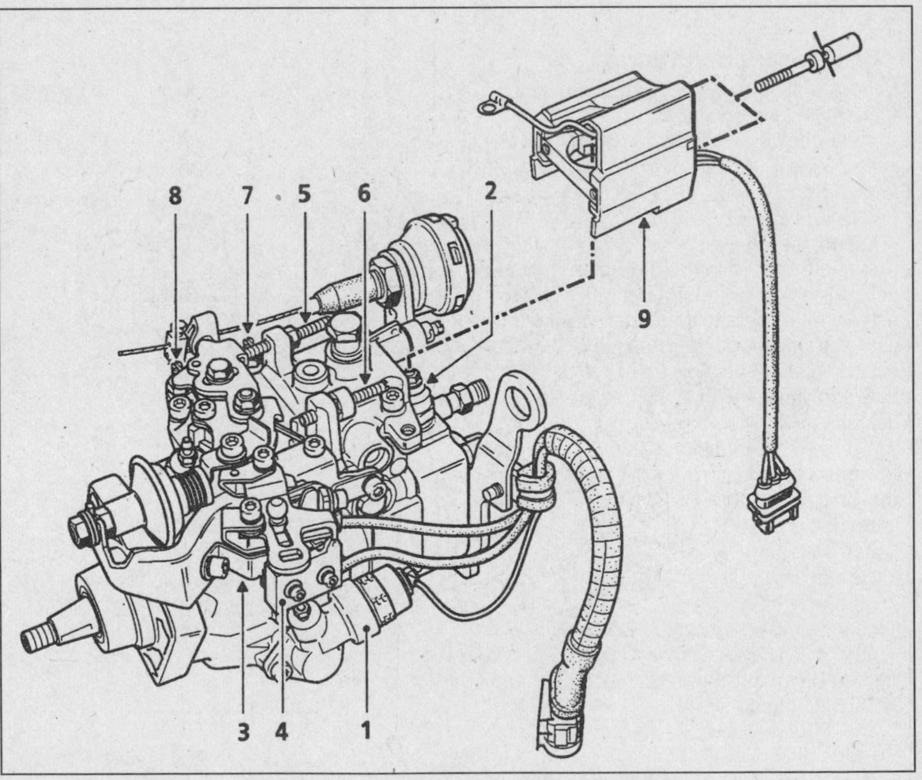

1.1a Bosch fuel injection pump components

1 *Load dependence control solenoid valve (ALFB)*
2 *Fuel cut-off solenoid*
3 *Post-heating/EGR valve cutting microswitch*
4 *Air conditioning microswitch*
5 *Anti-stall adjustment screw*
6 *Maximum speed adjustment screw*
7 *Idle adjustment screw*
8 *Fast idle adjustment screw*
9 *Coded solenoid valve electronic unit*

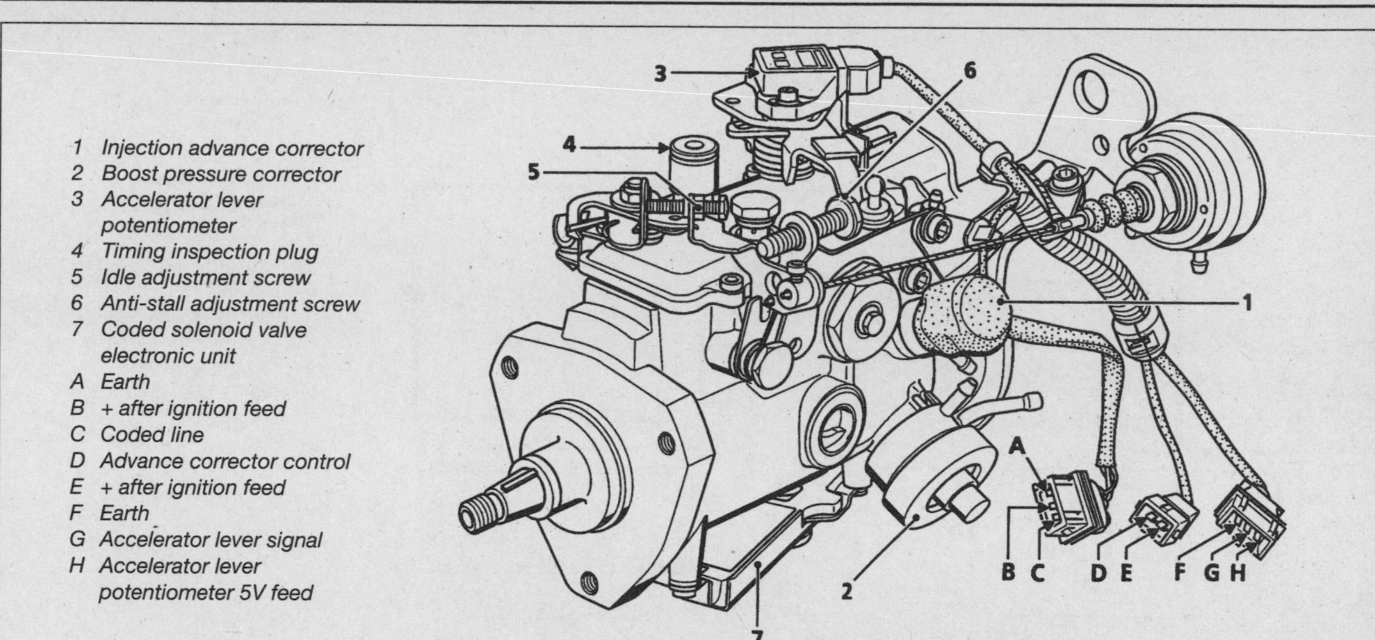

1.1b Early Lucas fuel injection pump components

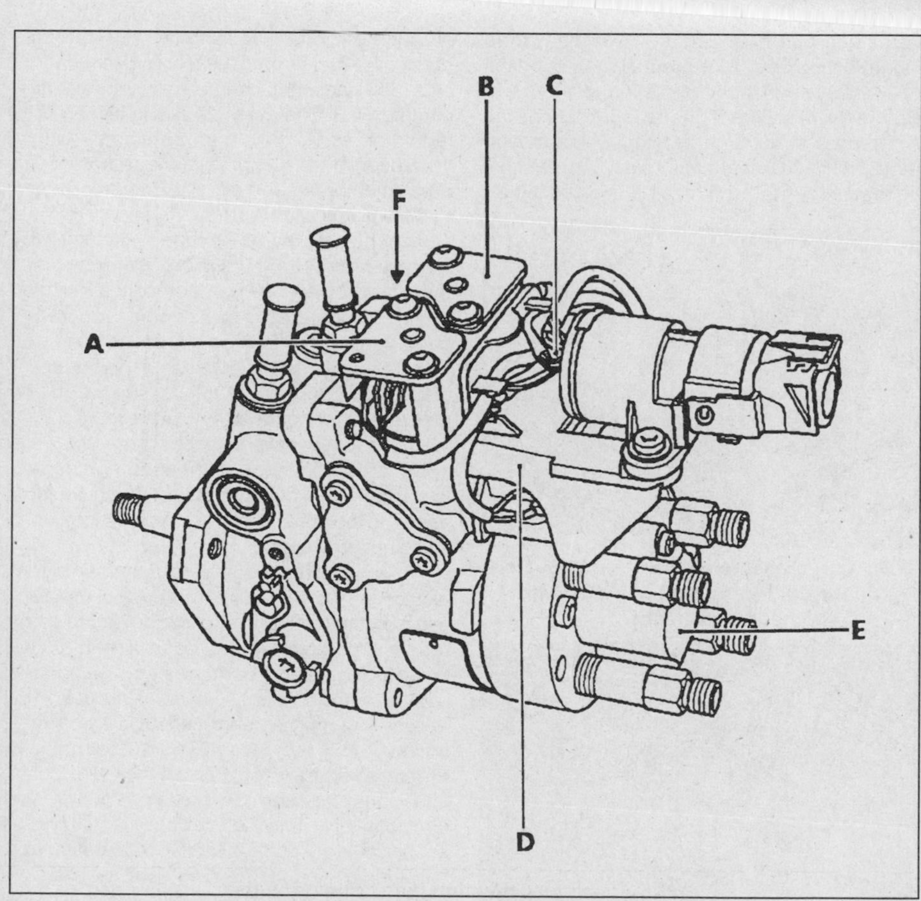

1.1c Lucas EPIC fuel injection pump components

A Advance solenoid valve
B Positive flow solenoid valve
C Negative flow solenoid valve
D Electrical solenoid valve
E Flow valve position sensor (cannot be removed)
F Advance valve position sensor (cannot be removed)

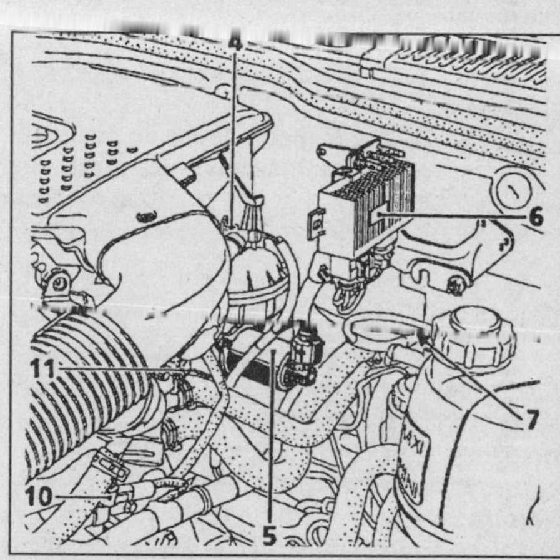

1.1d Lucas EPIC system components

4 Inlet air temperature sensor
5 EGR valve
6 Pre/post-heating unit
7 Accelerator pedal position potentiometer
10 TDC sensor
11 Coolant temperature sensor

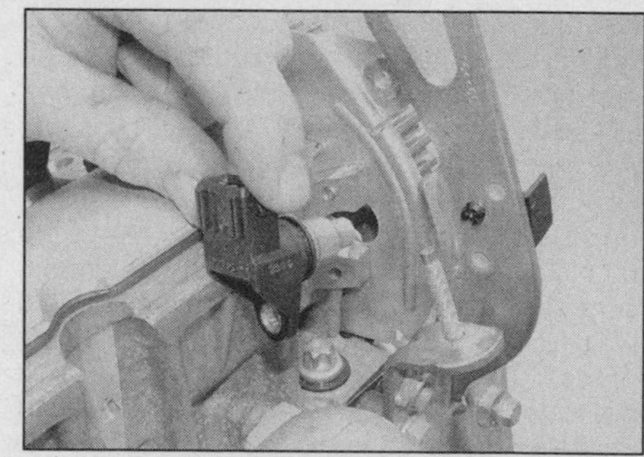

1.1e Camshaft position sensor (F9Q 732 engine)

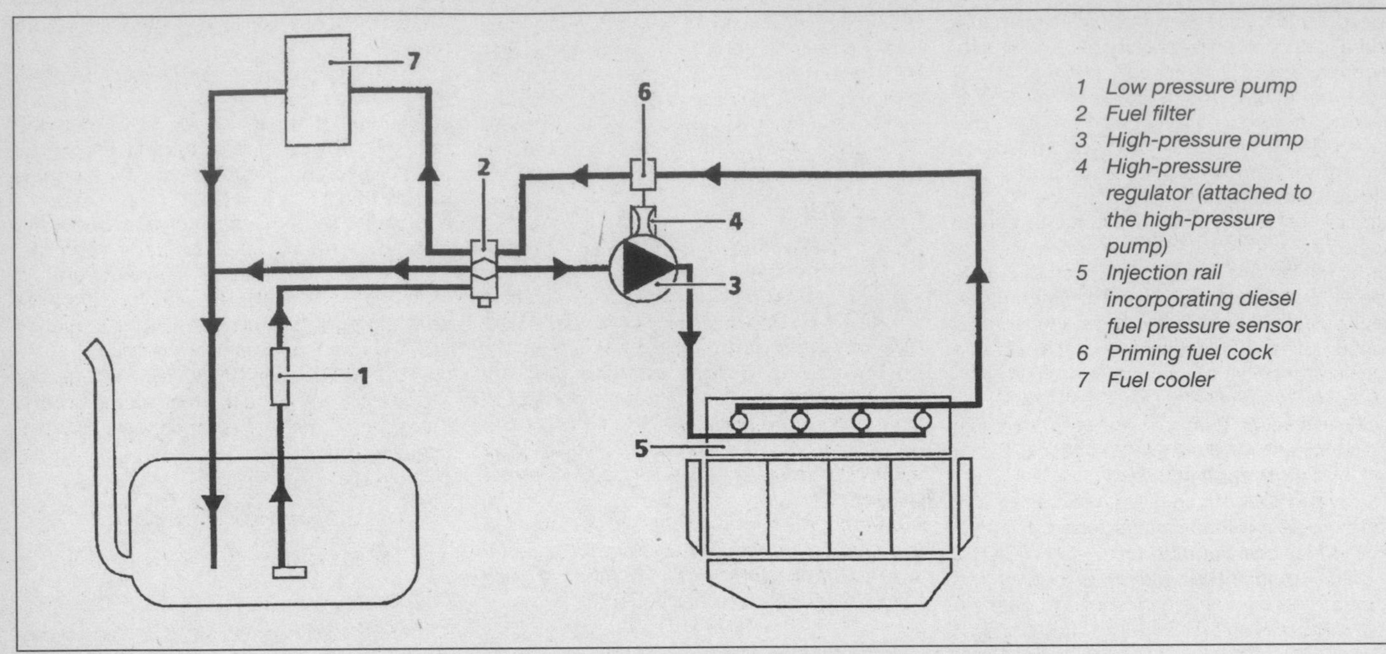

1.3a Common rail direct high-pressure injection system components

combustion. Each injector needle is lubricated by fuel, which accumulates in the spring chamber.

On the F9Q 732 engine with the common-rail injection system, fuel is drawn from the fuel tank to the high-pressure pump by a low pressure electric pump located on the right-hand side of the engine compartment **(see illustrations)**. The low pressure pump operates at a pressure of between 2.5 and 4.0 bars. Before reaching the high-pressure pump, the fuel passes through a fuel filter, where foreign matter and water are removed. As the fuel passes through the filter, it is heated by an electric heater. On reaching the high-pressure pump, the fuel is pressurised to between 250 and 1350 bars and accumulates in the injection common-rail. The pressure is modulated by a regulator on the high-pressure pump, controlled by the engine management ECU. Each injector is supplied with the pressurised fuel from the common-rail via separate steel pipes. Each injector is operated electrically by a signal from the ECU, which also determines the exact timing and duration of the injection period according to engine operating conditions. The ECU also determines the correct fuel pressure necessary for efficient engine operation, and sends signals to the pressure regulator on the high-pressure pump. The four fuel injectors inject a homogeneous spray of fuel into the combustion chambers located in the cylinder head. Each injector needle is lubricated by fuel, which accumulates in the spring chamber.

1.3b Fuel common rail (F9Q 732 engine)

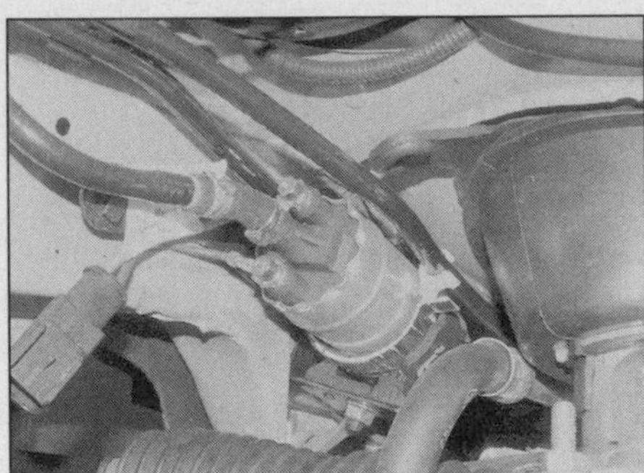

1.3c Low pressure electric pump located on the right-hand side of the engine compartment

1.4a Airflow meter (F9Q 732 engine)

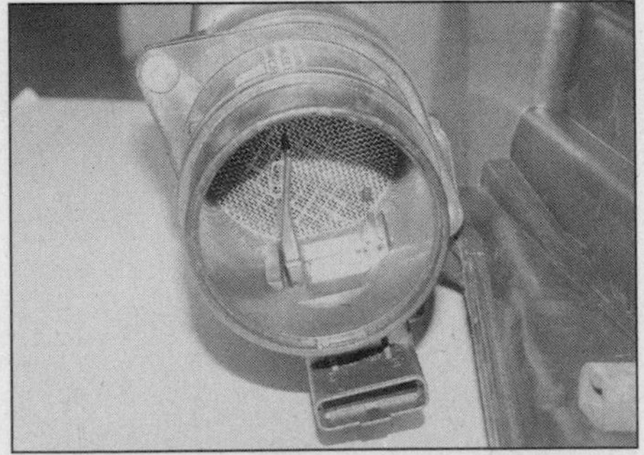

1.4b The air temperature sensor is incorporated in the airflow meter on the F9Q 732 engine

To enable the engine to meet stringent exhaust emission regulations, the fuel metering and injection timing is accurately controlled by the injection electronic control unit (ECU) located in the left-hand rear corner of the engine compartment. On early models, the injection pump has semi-electronic controls, however on the later EPIC (**E**lectronically **P**rogrammed **I**njection **C**ontrol) injection pump and common-rail high-pressure pump, the controls are fully electronic. This highly sophisticated system is similar in operation to a full engine management system as used on petrol engine vehicles and uses similar sensors to provide data to the ECU on engine operating conditions. The sensors typically monitor coolant temperature, air temperature (included in the airflow meter on F9Q 732 engine) **(see illustrations)**, fuel flow, engine speed, vehicle speed, atmospheric pressure, fuel temperature and accelerator pedal position. From the data received, the ECU controls injection pump fuel metering and injection advance, pre/post-heating system, idle speed, exhaust gas recirculation, the anti-theft system engine immobiliser, and the electric stop control. This allows precise control of all engine fuelling requirements providing optimum engine operation and minimal exhaust emissions under all engine operating conditions. Idle speed is dependent on coolant temperature, gear selected, battery voltage and electrical consumption. If one of the tracks in the accelerator pedal potentiometer is faulty, the idle speed is set at 1000 rpm, if both tracks are faulty, it is set to 1300 rpm. In 1st gear the idle speed is set to 850 rpm, in 2nd gear 875 rpm and in all other gears 900 rpm.

Provided that the specified maintenance is carried out, the fuel injection equipment will give long and trouble-free service. The injection pump itself may well outlast the engine. The main potential cause of damage to the injection pump and injectors is dirt or water in the fuel.

Servicing of the injection pump or high-pressure pump, injectors, and electronic equipment and sensors is very limited for the home mechanic, and any dismantling or adjustment other than that described in this Chapter must be entrusted to a Renault dealer or fuel injection specialist.

If a fault appears in the injection system, first ensure that all the system wiring connectors are securely connected and free of corrosion. Ensure that the fault is not due to poor maintenance; ie, check that the air cleaner filter element is clean, the cylinder compression pressures are correct, and that the engine breather hoses are clear and undamaged.

Should the fault persist, the vehicle should be taken to a Renault dealer or specialist who can test the system on a diagnostic tester. The tester will locate the fault quickly and simply, alleviating the need to test all the system components individually, which is a time-consuming operation that carries a risk of damaging the ECU. The specific Renault XR25 tester uses a bar chart configuration on a LCD screen; a fiche for the particular model is placed on the screen and each circuit can be checked instantly. It is also advisable to have any faulty components renewed by the dealer as in most instances the XR25 tester is required to re-program the ECU in the event of component or sensor renewal.

Precautions

Warning: It is necessary to take certain precautions when working on the fuel system components, particularly the fuel injectors and high-pressure pump (where fitted). Before carrying out any operations on the fuel system, refer to the precautions given in 'Safety first' at the beginning of this manual, and to any additional warning notes at the start of the relevant Sections.

Caution: If the radio/cassette in your vehicle is equipped with an anti-theft system, make sure you have the correct activation code before disconnecting the battery.

2 Air cleaner housing assembly – removal and refitting

Non-turbo models

Removal

1 Remove the securing screws (noting that one of the screws is located in the centre of the cover), and withdraw the air cleaner cover.

2 Lift the filter element from the air cleaner body.

3 Disconnect the inlet manifold air hose from the air cleaner body.

4 Disconnect the fresh air hose from the bottom of the air cleaner body and from the front left-hand corner of the engine compartment.

5 Unscrew the mounting nuts from below and withdraw the air cleaner body from the bracket in the engine compartment. If necessary, unbolt the air inlet from the front crossmember, and also unbolt the mounting bracket from the engine compartment.

6 Check the condition of the rubber mountings and renew them as necessary. Also check the hoses and hose clips for condition.

Refitting

7 Refitting is a reversal of removal.

Turbo models

Removal

8 Undo the screws and lift off the air cleaner cover **(see illustration)**.

9 Remove the filter cassette from the air cleaner body then remove the element from the cassette **(see illustrations)**.

10 Where fitted, release the strap securing the air cleaner body to the support bracket.

11 Disconnect the air trunking connecting the air cleaner body or airflow meter to the turbocharger. Where applicable, also disconnect the wiring from the airflow meter **(see illustrations)**.

2.8 Removing the air cleaner cover

2.9a Remove the filter cassette . . .

4B

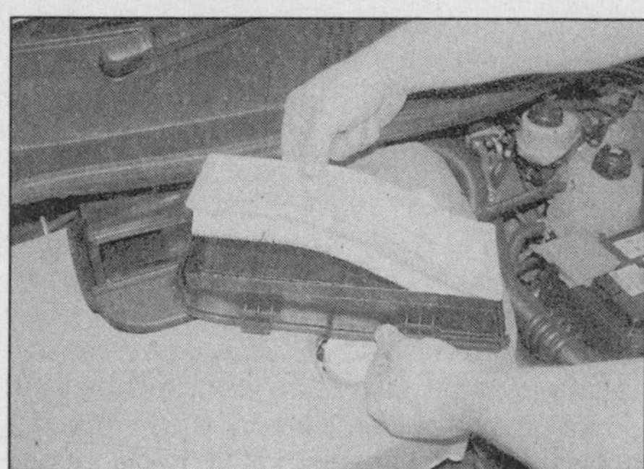

2.9b . . . then remove the element from the cassette

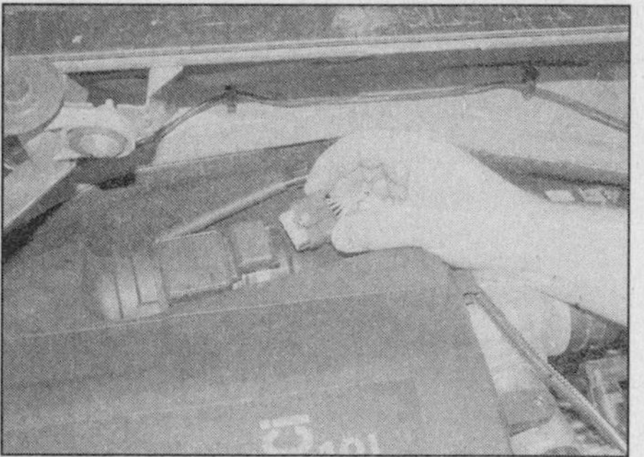

2.11a Disconnecting the wiring from the airflow meter

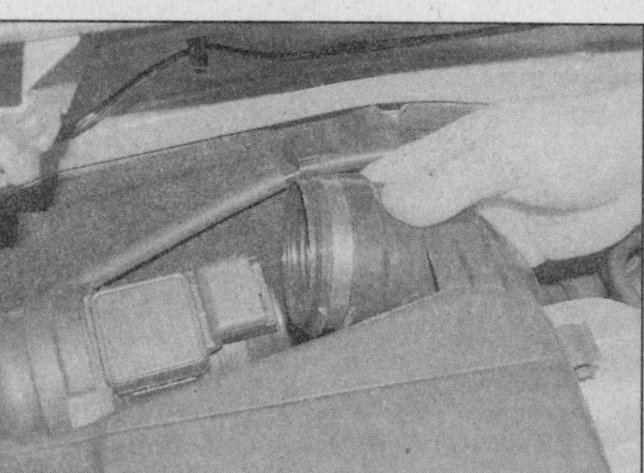

2.11b Disconnecting the turbocharger air duct from the airflow meter

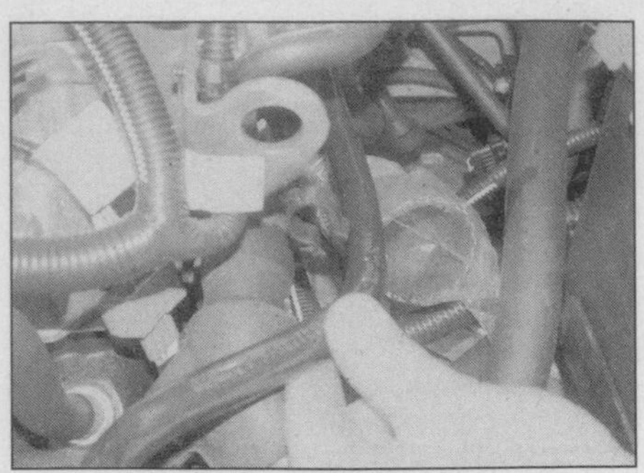
2.12a Disconnect the crankcase ventilation hose . . .

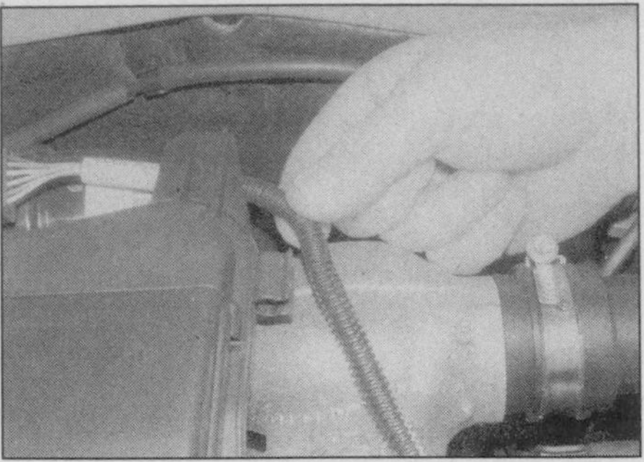
2.12b . . . unclip the wiring . . .

2.12c . . . unscrew the mounting nuts . . .

2.12d . . . withdraw the air cleaner body . . .

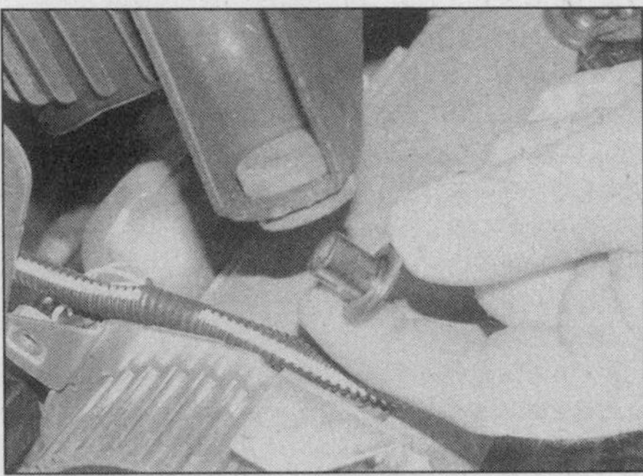
2.12e . . . and recover the mounting bushes

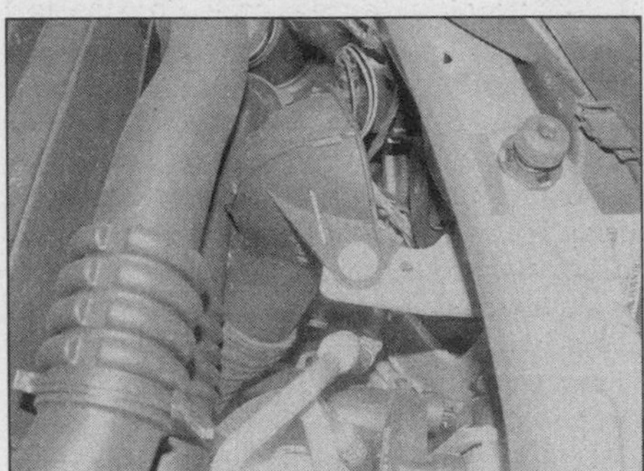
2.13 Air inlet mounting on the front crossmember

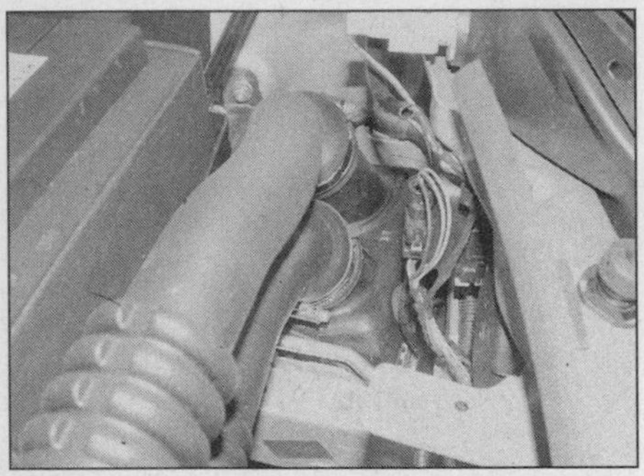
2.14a Air ducts connection to the intercooler

2.14b Removing the intercooler air ducts

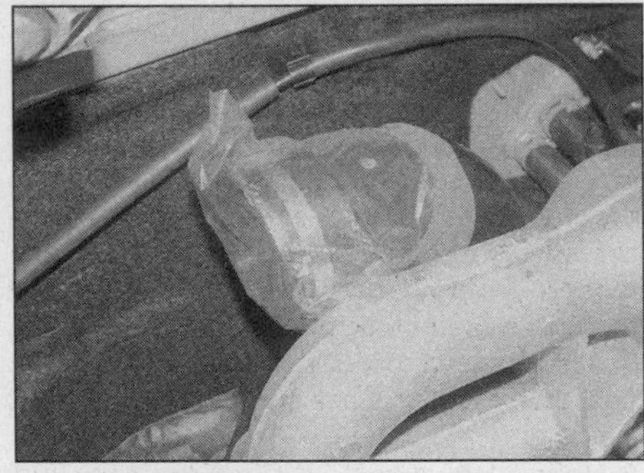
2.14c Seal the turbocharger air ducts to prevent entry of foreign matter

12 Where applicable, disconnect the crankcase ventilation hose from the bottom of the air cleaner and lift the air cleaner body from its mounting bracket. On F9Q 732 engines, unclip the wiring from the air cleaner body then unbolt the body from the engine – recover the mounting bushes **(see illustrations)**.
13 If necessary, unbolt the air inlet from the front crossmember **(see illustration)**, and also unbolt the mounting bracket from the engine compartment.
14 To remove the intercooler air ducts, release them from the intercooler, inlet manifold and turbocharger. Seal the turbocharger ducts to prevent entry of any foreign matter which may damage the turbines **(see illustrations)**.
15 Check the condition of the securing strap and the hoses and hose clips.

Refitting

16 Refitting is a reversal of removal.

3 Fuel gauge sender unit – removal, testing and refitting

Warning: Refer to the precautions in Section 1 before proceeding.

Removal

1 Disconnect the battery negative lead (refer to Chapter 5A).
2 Remove the rear seat or rear seat cushion as described in Chapter 11, for access to the fuel gauge sender unit cover. On Scénic models, remove the remove the seat mounting covers and remove the floor covering **(see illustrations)**.

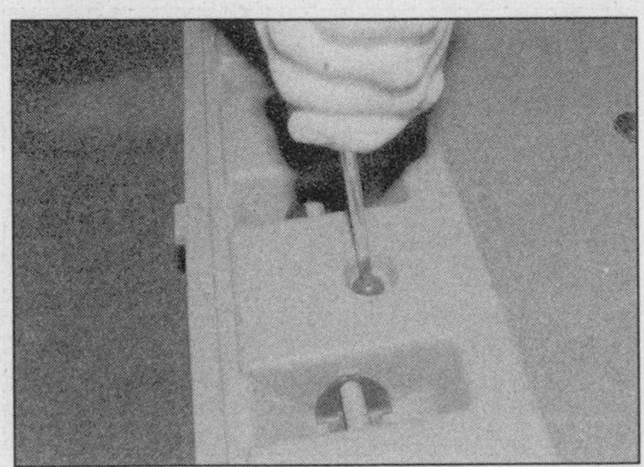
3.2a Undo the screws . . .

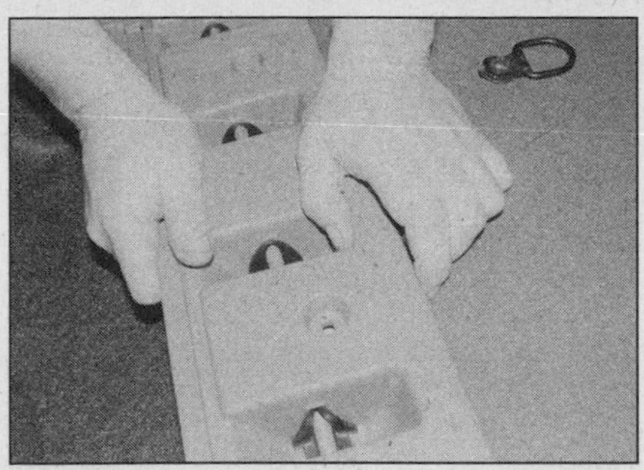

3.2b . . . remove the seat mounting covers . . .

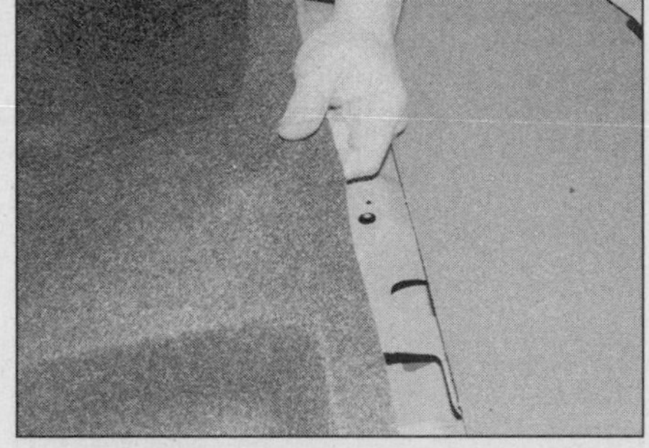

3.2c . . . and remove the floor covering

3.3 Remove the plastic cover . . .

3 Prise the plastic access cover from the floor to expose the fuel gauge sender unit **(see illustration)**.

4 Disconnect the wiring connector from the fuel gauge sender unit, and tape the connector to the vehicle body to prevent it disappearing behind the tank **(see illustration)**.

5 Identify the fuel hoses for position; the green hose on the left-hand side is the supply to the engine compartment, and the red hose next to the wiring connector is the return (arrows on the top of the fuel gauge sender unit indicate the direction of fuel flow). The hoses are equipped with quick-release fittings to ease removal. To disconnect each hose, slide out the locking tab from the collar then compress the collar and detach the hose from the fuel gauge sender unit. Renault technicians use a special tool to compress the collar (see Chapter 4A, Section 8), however it is possible to use a small screwdriver to **carefully** press back the locking collar inside the end of the special end fitting. On later models, simply release the clip to disconnect the hoses **(see illustration)**. Disconnect both hoses from the top of the fuel gauge sender unit, then plug the hose ends to minimise fuel loss.

6 Noting the alignment arrows on the fuel gauge sender unit cover and fuel tank, unscrew the locking ring and remove it from the tank. This can be accomplished by using a screwdriver on the raised ribs of the locking ring – carefully tap the screwdriver to turn the ring anti-clockwise until it can be unscrewed by hand. Alternatively a removal tool can be fabricated out of metal bar as shown in Chapter 4A, Section 8.

7 Carefully lift the fuel gauge sender unit out of the fuel tank, taking care not to damage the gauge sender arm, or to spill fuel in the interior of the vehicle **(see illustration)**. Remove the rubber sealing ring and check it for deterioration; if it is in good condition, it may be re-used, however if the pump is to remain out of the fuel tank for several hours, the locking ring should be refitted temporarily to prevent the sealing ring from distorting. If the sealing ring is unserviceable, obtain a new one.

Testing

8 Note that the fuel gauge sender unit is only available as a complete assembly, however it is possible to test its operation and to remove it. To test the unit, disconnect the wiring plug from the cover and connect an ohmmeter to the two terminals.

9 With the pump assembly upright on the bench, measure the resistance of the sender unit at the different heights given in the Specifications. The resistances are approximate but is should be clear if the sender unit is not operating correctly.

10 To remove the sender unit, first release the wiring from the clips, then unclip and remove the cover from the main body.

11 Using a screwdriver, prise off the gauze filter from the bottom of the unit. Also recover the O-ring seal from the spring location column.

12 Carefully unclip the bottom section, then disconnect the wiring and slide out the sender unit and float.

Refitting

13 Ensure that the fuel gauge sender unit pick-up filter is clean and free of debris. Fit the sealing ring to the top of the fuel tank.

14 Carefully manoeuvre the fuel gauge sender unit assembly into the fuel tank.

15 Align the arrow on the fuel gauge sender unit cover with the arrow on the fuel tank (the arrow must point to the rear of the vehicle), then refit the locking ring. Tighten the locking ring until the alignment marks on the unit and securing ring are aligned, then recheck that the fuel gauge sender unit cover and tank marks are all correctly aligned **(see illustration)**. **Note:** *If a suitable adapter is available tighten the locking ring to the specified torque.*

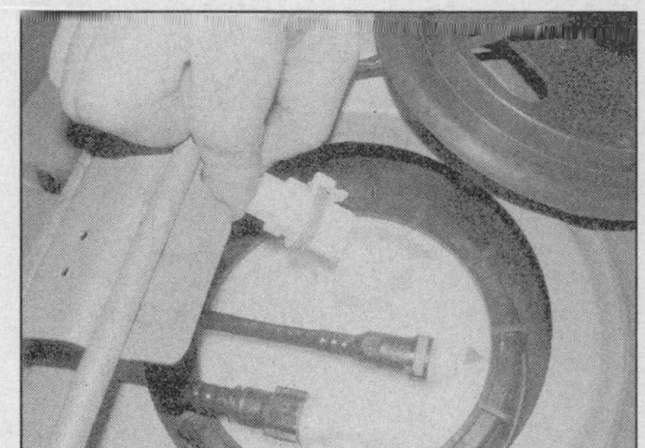

3.4 . . . and disconnect the wiring plug

4B

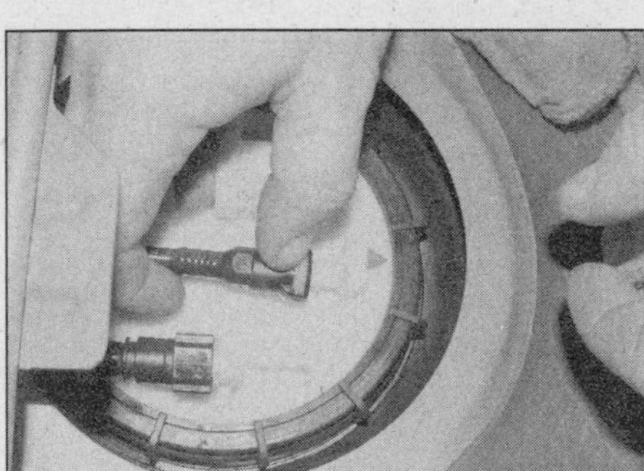

3.5 Disconnecting the fuel hoses

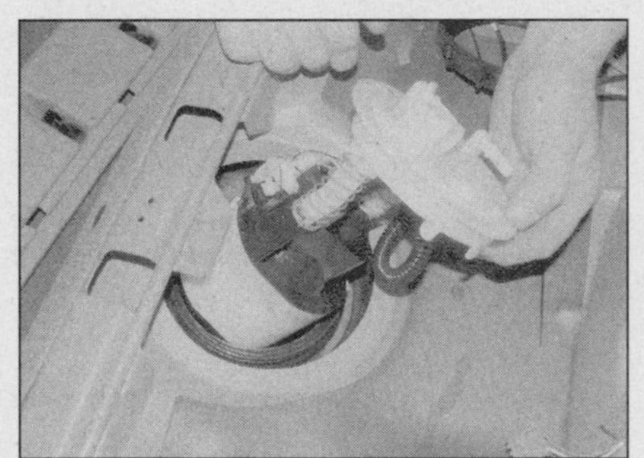

3.7 Lifting the fuel gauge sender unit from the fuel tank

3.15 Alignment marks on the sender unit and securing ring

16 Reconnect the feed and return hoses to the top of the fuel gauge sender unit; it is not necessary to depress the collars when refitting the hoses. Check the hoses are securely in position.

17 Reconnect the wiring connector.

18 Reconnect the battery negative lead, and start the engine. Check the fuel gauge sender unit feed and return hoses for signs of leakage.

19 Refit the plastic access cover and the rear seat cushion.

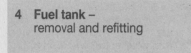

4 Fuel tank – removal and refitting

Warning: Refer to the precautions in Section 1 before proceeding.

Removal

1 Before removing the fuel tank, all fuel must be drained from it. Since a drain plug is not provided, it is preferable to carry out the removal operation when the tank is nearly empty.

2 Disconnect the battery negative lead (refer to Chapter 5A).

3 Remove the rear seat or rear seat cushion as described in Chapter 11, for access to the fuel gauge sender unit cover.

4 Using a screwdriver, carefully prise the plastic access cover from the floor to expose the sender unit.

5 If there is any fuel remaining in the fuel tank, it can be removed by disconnecting the fuel delivery hose and connecting an external syphoning pump to the tank outlet union.

6 Disconnect the wiring connector from the fuel gauge sender unit, and tape the connector to the vehicle body to prevent it disappearing behind the tank.

7 Disconnect the feed and, where applicable, the return hoses.

8 Chock the front wheels then jack up the rear of the vehicle and support on axle stands (see *Jacking and vehicle support*). Remove the right-hand rear wheel.

9 Remove the exhaust system and relevant heat shield(s) with reference to Section 34.

10 Note the position of the adjustment nut on the rear of the handbrake lever equaliser rod, then unscrew and remove it and detach the handbrake cables from the supports on the underbody. Position the cables to one side away from the fuel tank.

11 Disconnect the hoses from the fuel filler neck (see Chapter 4A, Section 8).

12 Place a trolley jack with an interposed block of wood beneath the tank, then raise the jack until it is supporting the weight of the tank.

13 Unscrew and remove the mounting bolts, then slowly lower the fuel tank out of position, disconnecting any other relevant vent pipes as they become accessible (where necessary), and remove the tank from underneath the vehicle. Note that it may be necessary to carefully bend the brake pipes to provide sufficient clearance when lowering the tank. **Do not** bend the pipes excessively.

14 If the tank is contaminated with sediment or water, remove the fuel gauge sender unit and swill the tank out with clean fuel. The tank is injection-moulded from a synthetic material – if seriously damaged, it should be renewed. However, in certain cases, it may be possible to have small leaks or minor damage repaired. Seek the advice of a specialist before attempting to repair the fuel tank.

Refitting

15 Refitting is the reverse of the removal procedure, noting the following points:

a) *When lifting the tank back into position, take care to ensure that the hoses are not trapped between the tank and vehicle body.*
b) *Ensure that all pipes and hoses are correctly routed. Make sure the sealing rings are in position in the quick-release fittings prior to fitting and make sure they are securely clipped in position.*
c) *On completion, refill the tank with a small amount of fuel, and check for signs of leakage prior to taking the vehicle out on the road.*

5 Accelerator cable – removal, refitting and adjustment

Note: *The following procedures are only applicable to certain engine models. On F8Q 622 and F9Q engine models accelerator pedal position is determined electronically by a sensor which sends the appropriate information to the system ECU (the sensor is located on the left-hand side of the bulkhead).*

Removal

1 Working in the engine compartment, operate the accelerator lever on the fuel injection pump, and release the inner cable from the lever. Alternatively, on models with a press-fit balljoint cable end fitting, pull the cable end from the lever **(see illustration)**.

2 Pull the outer cable ferrule from the grommet in the fuel injection pump bracket. Note that on models with a balljoint end fitting, it will be necessary to prise the balljoint from the rubber cable end fitting to enable the cable to pass through the pump bracket **(see illustrations)**.

3 Working inside the vehicle, remove the lower trim panel from under the steering column. Disconnect the cable from the accelerator pedal by squeezing the lugs of the cable end fitting.

4 Return to the engine compartment, release the outer cable from the bulkhead and withdraw the cable.

Refitting and adjustment

5 Refitting is a reversal of removal, ensuring that the cable is routed as noted before

5.1 Disconnecting the accelerator cable from the injection pump lever

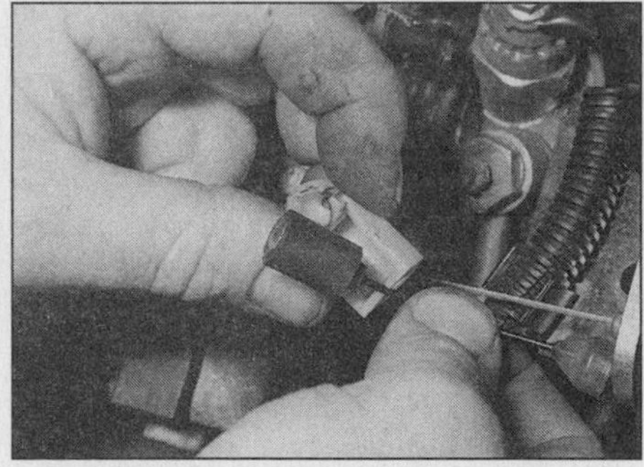

5.2a Remove the balljoint . . .

5.2b . . . to enable the cable to pass through the bracket (early Lucas pump)

5.2c Accelerator cable end fitting (Bosch pump)

removal, and on completion, check the cable adjustment as follows.

6 Have an assistant fully depress the accelerator pedal, then check that the accelerator lever on the injection pump is touching the maximum speed adjustment screw. If adjustment is required, remove the spring clip from the adjustment ferrule, reposition the ferrule as necessary, then insert the clip in the next free groove on the ferrule.

7 With the accelerator pedal fully released, check that the accelerator lever is touching the anti-stall adjustment screw.

6 Accelerator pedal – removal and refitting

Removal

1 Remove the lower trim panel from under the steering column.

2 On F8Q engine models, disconnect the cable from the top of the accelerator pedal by squeezing the lugs of the cable end fitting. On F9Q engine models, disconnect the accelerator pedal position sensor link from the pedal.

3 Remove the nut which secures the accelerator pedal pivot and bush to the bulkhead.

4 Withdraw the accelerator pedal.

5 Examine the pedal and pivot for signs of wear and renew as necessary.

Refitting

6 Refitting is a reversal of removal. On F8Q engine models, check the adjustment of the accelerator cable as described in Section 5.

7 Fuel system – priming and bleeding

Warning: Refer to the precautions in Section 1 before proceeding.

1 After disconnecting part of the fuel supply system or running out of fuel, it is necessary to prime the system and bleed off any air which may have entered the system components.

2 Some early engines fitted with a standard injection pump may be fitted with a hand-operated priming bulb located in the right-hand corner of the engine compartment, in the feed line to the fuel filter. Later models are not fitted with the priming bulb and an alternative procedure must be used.

Where a hand-operated priming bulb is not fitted, priming of the fuel system after filter renewal will be greatly improved if the filter element is filled with clean diesel fuel before securing it to the filter head. To avoid spillages of fuel, keep the filter upright during refitting.

3 On models fitted with a hand-operated priming bulb, to prime the system, loosen the bleed screw located on the top of the injection pump near the fuel inlet union, then squeeze the priming bulb several times until fuel free from air bubbles emerges from the bleed screw **(see illustrations)**. Retighten the bleed screw and continue pumping until firm resistance is felt. Attempt to start the engine at this stage. If it refuses to start, repeat the priming procedure and try again.

4 On standard injection engine models (ie, not F9Q 732) not fitted with a hand-operated priming bulb, the engine may be difficult to start. In order not to drain the battery, crank the engine on the starter motor in 4 to 5 second bursts followed by pauses of 8 to 10 seconds. As soon as the engine starts, let it run at fast idle speed until a regular idle speed is reached. Stop the engine and start it again in order to purge the system of air bubbles.

5 On models with the common-rail injection F8Q 732 engine, prime the fuel system as follows. First, close the fuel cock located on the fuel filter by turning the valve until the two coloured lines are **not** aligned with each other. **Note:** *If a fuel cock is not fitted, follow the procedure given in paragraph 4.* Switch on the ignition so that the electric low pressure pump is started, then switch it off. Switch the ignition on and off several times in order to prime the system. Start the engine, then open the fuel cock by turning the valve until the coloured lines are aligned with each other.

Warning: On the F8Q 732 engine, do not attempt to bleed the system by loosening the unions on the fuel rail.

6 On standard injection engine models, if air has entered the injector pipes, place wads of rag around the injector pipe unions at the injectors (to absorb spilt fuel), then slacken the unions. Crank the engine on the starter motor until fuel emerges from the unions, then stop cranking the engine and retighten the unions. Mop up spilt fuel.

Warning: Be prepared to stop the engine if it should fire, to avoid fuel spray and spillage.

7.3a Loosen the fuel system bleed screw located on the fuel pump inlet union . . .

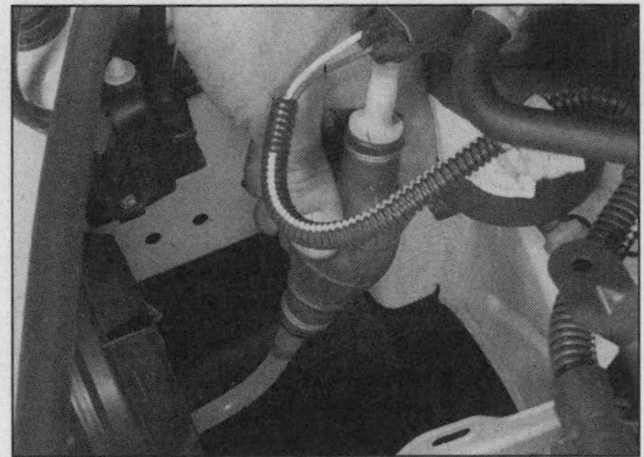

7.3b . . . and squeeze the priming bulb (where fitted)

8 Idle speed and anti-stall speed – check and adjustment

Note: *The following procedure is only applicable to F8Q 620 and F8Q 788 engine models. On F8Q 622, F8Q 784, F8Q 786 and all F9Q engines the idle speed and anti-stall speed is controlled by the injection ECU.*

1 The usual type of tachometer (rev counter), which works from ignition system pulses, cannot be used on diesel engines. A diagnostic socket is provided for the use of Renault test equipment, but this will not normally be available to the home mechanic. If it is not felt that adjusting the idle speed 'by ear' is satisfactory, one of the following alternatives may be used.

a) Purchase or hire of an appropriate tachometer.
b) Delegation of the job to a Renault dealer or other specialist.
c) Timing light (strobe) operated by a petrol engine running at the desired speed. If the timing light is pointed at a mark on the diesel engine's camshaft or injection pump sprockets, the mark will appear stationary when the two engines are running at the same speed (or multiples of that speed). The sprocket will be rotating at half the crankshaft speed but this will not affect the adjustment. (In practice it was found impossible to use this method on the crankshaft pulley due to the acute viewing angle.)

2 Before making adjustments warm-up the engine to normal operating temperature (the cooling fan must have operated at least twice). Make sure that the accelerator cable is correctly adjusted (see Section 5).

Idle speed

3 With the accelerator lever resting against the idle stop, check that the engine idles at the specified speed (see Specifications). If necessary adjust as follows.

Lucas injection pump

4 Loosen the locknut on the idle speed adjustment screw. Turn the screw as

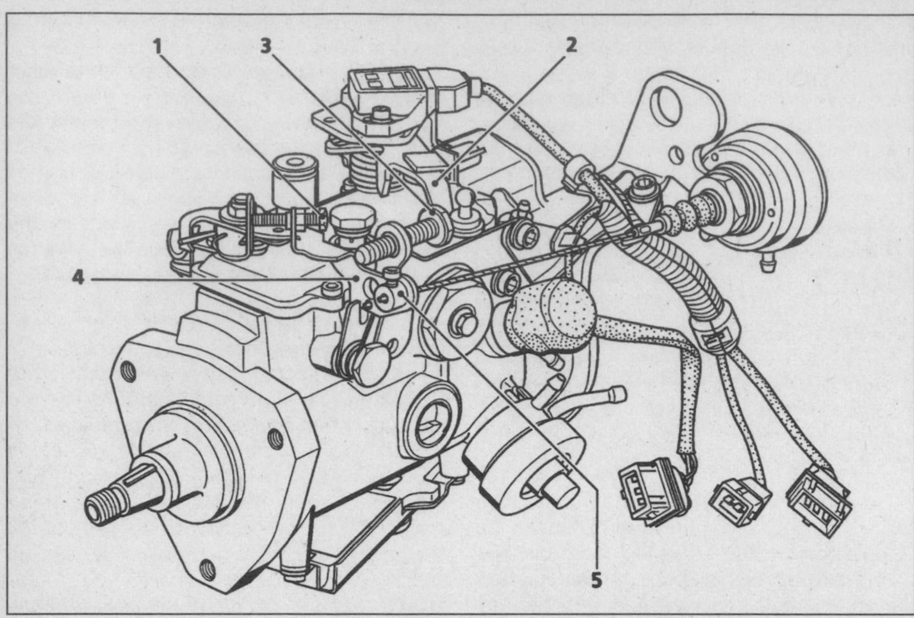

8.4 Idle speed and anti-stall speed adjustment points (Lucas pump)

1 Idle speed adjustment screw
2 Accelerator lever
3 Anti-stall speed adjustment screw
4 Fast idle lever
5 Fast idle cable end fitting

required and retighten the locknut **(see illustration)**.

5 Check the anti-stall adjustment as described later in this Section.

6 Stop the engine and disconnect the tachometer.

Bosch injection pump

7 Loosen the locknut and unscrew the anti-stall speed adjustment screw until it is touching the pump accelerator lever **(see illustration)**.

8 Loosen the locknut and turn the idle speed adjustment screw as required, then retighten the locknut.

9 Check the anti-stall adjustment as described later in this Section.

10 Stop the engine and disconnect the tachometer.

Anti-stall speed

11 Make sure that the engine is at normal operating temperature (the cooling fan must have operated at least twice) and idling at the specified speed.

Lucas injection pump

12 Insert a 4.0 mm thick shim or feeler blade between the pump accelerator lever and the anti-stall adjustment screw.

13 The engine speed should increase to the specified anti-stall speed (see Specifications).

14 If adjustment is necessary, loosen the locknut, turn the anti-stall adjustment screw as required, then retighten the locknut.

15 Remove the shim or feeler blade and check the idle speed as described previously.

16 Move the pump accelerator lever to increase the engine speed to approximately 3000 rpm, then quickly release the lever. The deceleration period should be approximately 2.5 to 3.5 seconds, and the engine speed should drop to approximately 50 rpm below idle.

17 If the deceleration is too fast and the engine stalls, unscrew the anti-stall adjustment screw 1/4 turn towards the accelerator lever. If the deceleration is too slow, resulting in poor engine braking, turn the screw 1/4 turn away from the lever.

18 Retighten the locknut after making an adjustment, then recheck the idle speed and adjust if necessary as described previously.

19 On completion, disconnect the tachometer.

Bosch injection pump

20 Insert a 4.0 mm thick shim or feeler blade between the pump accelerator lever and the anti-stall speed adjustment screw **(see illustration)**.

21 The engine speed should increase to the specified anti-stall speed (see Specifications).

22 If adjustment is necessary, loosen the locknut and turn the anti-stall speed adjustment screw as required. Retighten the locknut.

23 Remove the shim or feeler blade and allow the engine to idle.

24 Move the fast idle lever fully towards the flywheel end of the engine and check that the engine speed increases to the specified fast idle speed. If necessary, loosen the locknut and turn the fast idle adjusting screw as required, then retighten the locknut.

25 Disconnect the tachometer on completion and stop the engine.

26 After making the adjustment, the deceleration damper must be adjusted as follows.

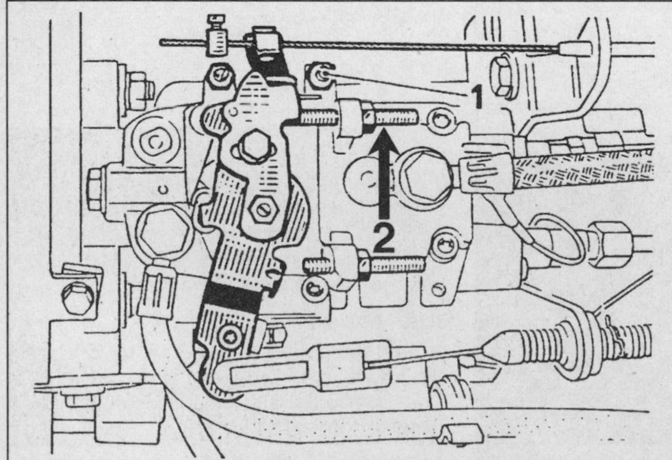

8.7 Idle speed adjustment screw (1) and anti-stall speed adjustment screw (2) (Bosch pump)

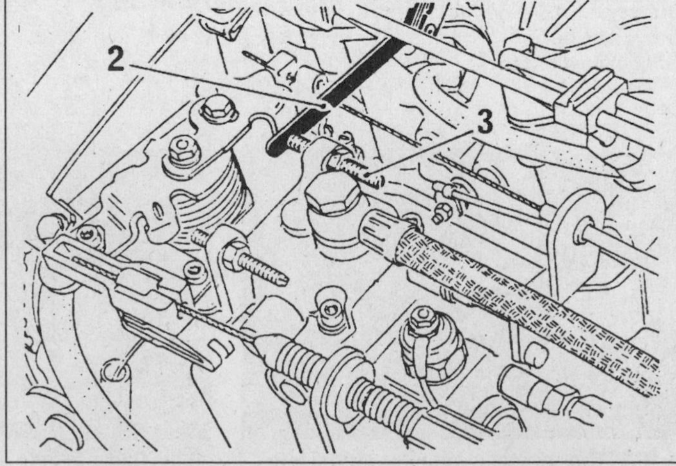

8.20 Checking the anti-stall speed adjustment (Bosch pump)
2 Feeler blade 3 Anti-stall speed adjustment screw

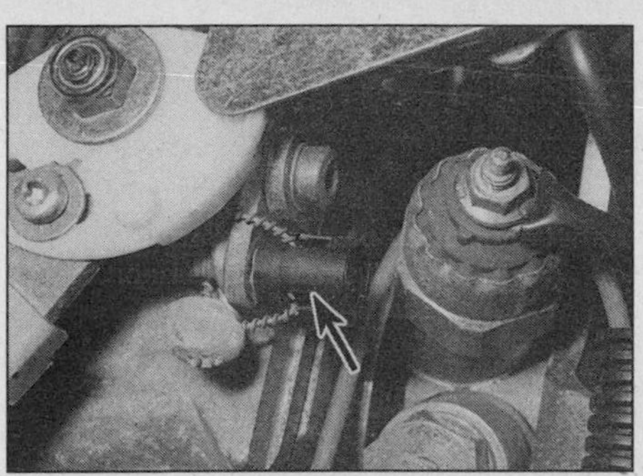

9.3 Maximum speed adjustment screw on a Lucas pump

27 Loosen the two screws securing the damper operating lever to the accelerator lever.

28 Insert a 1.0 mm thick shim or feeler blade between the operating lever and the end of the damper, then push the lever onto the stop. Make sure that the accelerator lever is in contact with the anti-stall speed adjustment screw, then tighten the two securing screws.

29 Remove the shim and check that the accelerator lever is still in contact with the anti-stall speed adjustment screw.

9 Maximum speed – checking and adjustment

Note: *The following procedure is only applicable to F8Q 620 engine models (Bosch injection pump). On engines equipped with a Lucas injection pump, the adjustment can only be carried out on a test bench. On F9Q engines the maximum speed setting is controlled by the injection ECU.*

Caution: The maximum speed adjustment screw is sealed by the manufacturers at the factory using paint or locking wire and a lead seal. There is no reason why it should require adjustment. Do not disturb the screw if the vehicle is still within the warranty period otherwise the warranty will be invalidated.

1 This adjustment requires the use of a tachometer, see Section 8. Run the engine to normal operating temperature.

2 Have an assistant fully depress the accelerator pedal and check that the maximum engine speed is as given in the Specifications. Do not keep the engine at maximum speed for more than two or three seconds.

3 If adjustment is necessary, stop the engine then loosen the locknut, turn the maximum speed adjustment screw as necessary, and retighten the locknut **(see illustrations 9.3 and 10.12)**.

4 Repeat the procedure in paragraph 2 to check the adjustment.

5 Stop the engine and disconnect the tachometer.

10 Fast idle thermostatic actuator and cable – removal, refitting, testing and adjustment

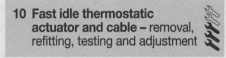

Note: *The following procedure is only applicable to early F8Q 620 engine models. A new sealing ring will be required on refitting.*

Removal

1 The thermostatic actuator is located at the left-hand end of the cylinder head **(see illustration)**.

2 Partially drain the cooling system as described in Chapter 1B.

3 Loosen the clamp screw or nut (as applicable) and slide the fast idle cable end fitting from the inner cable at the fast idle lever on the injection pump **(see illustration)**.

4 Slide the outer cable from the bracket on the fuel injection pump.

5 Unscrew the thermostatic actuator from the cylinder head, and withdraw the actuator complete with the cable. Recover the sealing ring **(see illustration)**.

Refitting

6 Fit the actuator, using a new sealing ring, and tighten it.

7 Refill the cooling system as described in Chapter 1B.

8 Insert the outer cable through the bracket on the injection pump.

9 Insert the inner cable through the fast idle lever, and position the end fitting on the cable, but do not tighten the clamp screw or nut (as applicable).

10 Adjust the cable as described in the following paragraphs.

Testing and adjustment

Note: *During this procedure, it is necessary to measure the engine speed. The usual type of tachometer (rev counter), which works from ignition system pulses, cannot be used on diesel engines. A diagnostic socket is provided for the use of Renault test equipment, but this will not normally be available to the home mechanic. If it is not felt that adjusting the idle speed 'by ear' is satisfactory, or that (where fitted) the instrument panel tachometer is not sufficiently reliable, one of the following alternatives may be used.*

a) *Purchase or hire of an appropriate tachometer.*
b) *Delegation of the job to a Renault dealer or other specialist.*
c) *Timing light (strobe) operated by a petrol engine running at the desired speed. If the timing light is pointed at a mark on the diesel engine's camshaft or injection pump sprockets, the mark will appear stationary when the two engines are running at the same speed (or multiples of that speed). The sprocket will be rotating at half the crankshaft speed but this will not affect the adjustment. (In practice it was found impossible to use this method on the crankshaft pulley due to the acute viewing angle.)*

11 With the engine warm (the cooling fan should have cut in and out once) and running at the correct idle speed (see Section 8), proceed as follows.

12 Move the fast idle lever on the injection pump towards the flywheel end of the engine

10.1 Thermostatic actuator on the left-hand end of the cylinder head

10.3 Thermostatic actuator fast idle cable end fitting

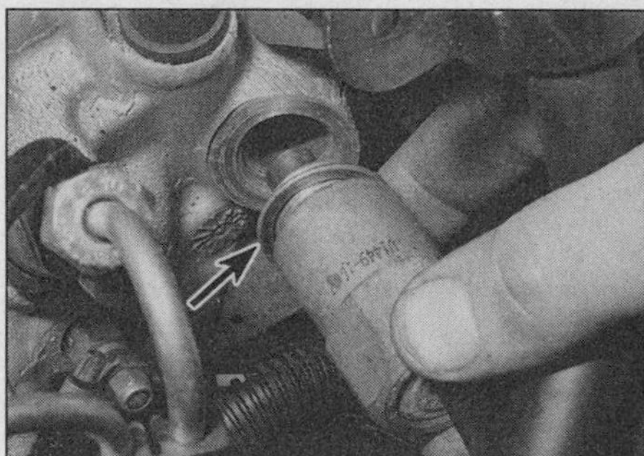

10.5 Unscrew the thermostatic actuator from the cylinder head. Note the sealing ring (arrowed)

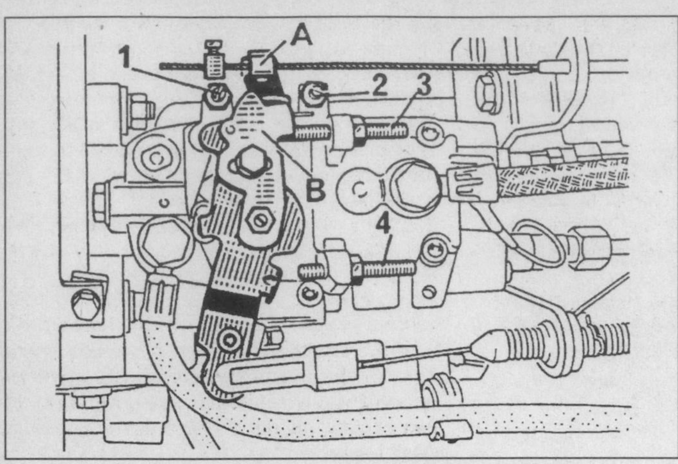

10.12 Bosch injection pump adjustment screws

A Fast idle lever
B Accelerator lever
1 Fast idle adjustment screw
2 Idle adjustment screw
3 Anti-stall adjustment screw
4 Maximum speed adjustment screw

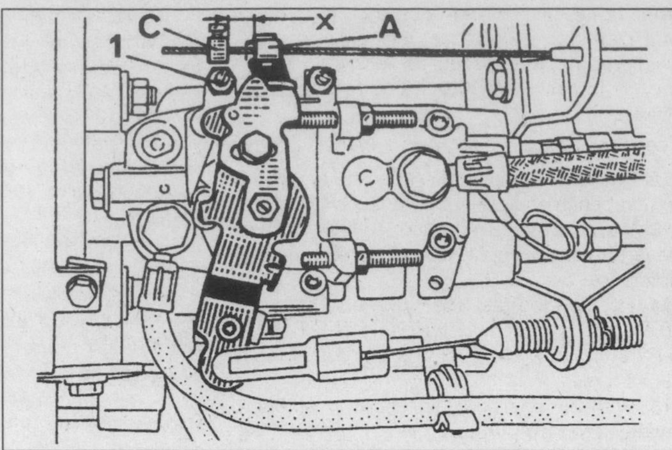

10.17 Bosch injection pump fast idle cable adjustment (thermostatic actuator)

A Fast idle lever
C Cable end fitting
1 Fast idle adjustment screw
x = 6.0 ± 1 mm

so that it contacts the fast idle adjustment screw **(see illustration)**.

13 Check that the fast idle speed is as specified in the Specifications. If necessary, loosen the locknut and turn the adjustment screw to give the specified fast idle speed. Retighten the locknut on completion.

14 Stop the engine, and disconnect the tachometer where applicable.

15 The fast idle cable should now be adjusted as follows.

16 With the engine still at normal operating temperature, and the fast idle lever in its rest position (resting against the idle speed adjustment screw, **not** the fast idle adjustment screw), gently pull the fast idle cable taut.

17 Position the end fitting on the cable so that the dimension between the end of the fast idle lever and the end fitting is correct **(see illustration)**.

18 With the end fitting correctly positioned, tighten the clamp screw.

19 When the engine has cooled, check that the cable has pulled the fast idle lever so that it rests against the fast idle adjustment screw. Recheck that with the engine at normal operating temperature the dimension x between the end of the fast idle lever and the cable end fitting is as specified **(see illustration 9.17)**. If not, it is likely that the thermostatic actuator is faulty.

11 Fast idle system components – removal, refitting, testing and adjustment

Note: *The following procedure is only applicable to late F8Q 620 and F8Q 788 engine models. On other F8Q and all F9Q engines the fast idle is controlled by the injection ECU and no additional mechanical components are used.*

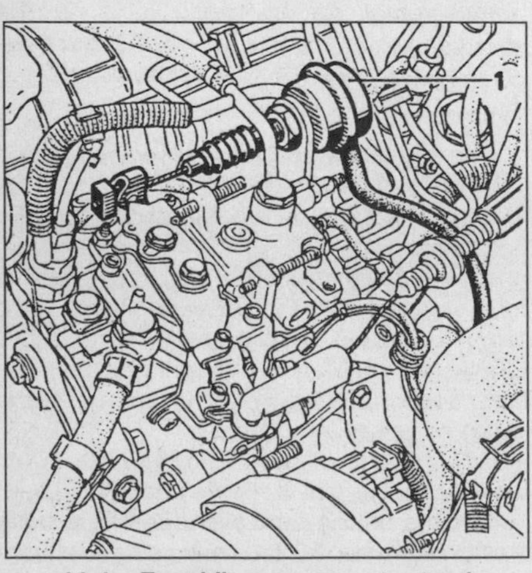

11.4a Fast idle vacuum actuator 1 (Bosch pump)

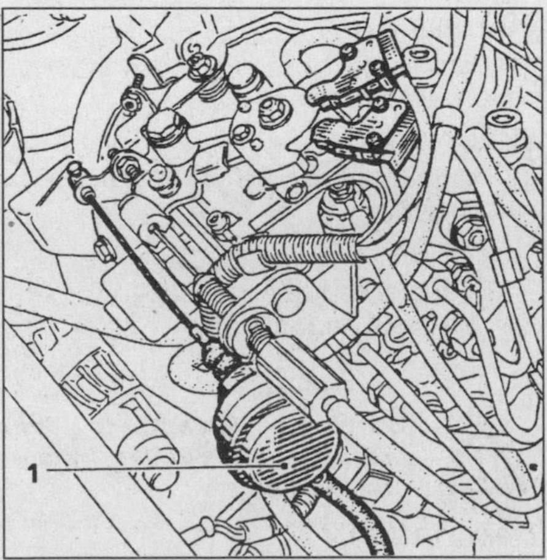

11.4b Fast idle vacuum actuator 1 (Lucas pump)

Vacuum actuator and cable

Removal

1 The vacuum actuator is attached to a bracket located on the end of the injection pump.

2 Loosen the clamp screw or nut (as applicable) and slide the fast idle cable end fitting from the inner cable at the fast idle lever on the injection pump.

3 Disconnect the vacuum hose from the actuator.

4 Unscrew the nut securing the actuator to the bracket, and withdraw the actuator, passing the cable through the bracket as it is withdrawn **(see illustrations)**.

Refitting

5 Refit the actuator to the bracket, and tighten the securing nut.

6 Reconnect the vacuum hose.

7 Insert the inner cable through the fast idle lever, and position the end fitting on the cable, but do not tighten the clamp screw or nut (as applicable).

8 Adjust the cable as described in the following paragraphs.

Testing and adjustment – Bosch pump

9 Proceed as described in Section 10, paragraphs 11 to 18 inclusive, with reference to the note at the beginning of paragraph 11, except that the dimension between the end of the fast idle lever and the end fitting must be 2 ± 1 mm.

10 If a faulty vacuum actuator is suspected, first test the solenoid valve as described later in this Section.

11 The actuator can be tested using a vacuum pump. With the engine stopped, disconnect the vacuum hose from the actuator, and connect the vacuum pump in its place. With a vacuum of 500 mbars applied, the actuator should operate the cable sufficiently to pull the fast idle lever so that it rests against the fast idle adjustment screw. If not, it is likely that the vacuum actuator is faulty.

Testing and adjustment – Lucas pump

12 The fast idle speed is set at the factory on a test bench and cannot be adjusted.
13 With the engine stopped, and the fast idle lever in the rest position, gently pull the fast idle cable taut.
14 Position the fast idle cable end fitting on the cable so that the dimension between the end of the fast idle lever and the end fitting is 2 ± 1 mm.
15 With the end fitting correctly positioned, tighten the clamp nut.
16 The actuator can be tested with reference to paragraphs 10 and 11, but note that the fast idle lever should rest against the lever stop rather than the fast idle adjustment screw.

Solenoid valve

Removal

17 The solenoid valve is located on the bulkhead in the engine compartment, next to the preheating control unit.
18 Disconnect the wiring and vacuum hoses from the solenoid valve.
19 Slacken the two securing screws and withdraw the valve.

Refitting

20 Refitting is a reversal of removal ensuring that the vacuum hoses and the wiring are securely reconnected. Tighten the screws securely.

Testing

21 Remove the solenoid valve as described previously.
22 Attempt to blow gently through one of the vacuum hose connections. No air should pass through the valve.
23 With a 12 volt supply connected across the solenoid terminals, again attempt to blow through the valve. Air should now pass through.
24 If the valve proves to be faulty, it should be renewed.

12 Cold start timing advance solenoid – testing, removal and refitting

Warning: Refer to the precautions in Section 1 before proceeding.

Testing

Note: *The following procedure is only applicable to F8Q 620 engine models. On other F8Q and all F9Q engines, cold start operation is controlled by the injection ECU.*

1 To check the operation of the system, start the engine from cold, and listen for a knocking or harshness, disappearing after between 30 seconds and 2 minutes 45 seconds. This shows that the system is working correctly – if dynamic timing equipment is available, this can be used to check the advance.
2 If the system does not seem to be working, check for voltage at the solenoid feed wire with the starter motor cranking, and for 5 to 6 seconds after start-up (the feed to the solenoid is controlled by the preheating system control unit).
3 If voltage is present, but the system is still not working, the solenoid valve is probably faulty, and should be renewed.

Removal

F8Q engines

Note: *Be careful not to allow dirt into the injection pump during this procedure. A new sealing washer must be used on refitting.*

4 Disconnect the battery negative lead (refer to Chapter 5A) then disconnect the solenoid wiring connector.
5 Unscrew the solenoid valve from the pump and recover the sealing washer. Take great care not to allow dirt to enter the pump.

F9Q engines

6 Slacken the high-pressure pipes bolts on the injection pump and fuel injectors. Secure the pump connectors while slackening the bolts. Remove the pipes. To prevent the entry of dirt cover the end of the connectors with small plastic bags or fingers cut from discarded (but clean) rubber gloves.
7 Disconnect the two wiring connectors from the pump.
8 Remove the right-hand plate which secures the pump to the engine.
9 Remove the steel plate. This plate is secured by a bolt which secures the hydraulic head.
10 Clean the area where the advance solenoid valve is secured to the pump, then remove the valve. Check that the O-ring is not still attached inside the pump body.

Refitting

F8Q engines

11 Refitting is a reversal of removal, using a new sealing washer.

F9Q engines

12 Refitting is a reversal of removal, using a new O-ring.

13 Stop solenoid – description, removal and refitting

Warning: Refer to the precautions in Section 1 before proceeding.

Description

1 The stop solenoid is located on the end of the fuel injection pump. Its purpose is to cut the fuel supply when the ignition is switched off. If an open circuit occurs in the solenoid or supply wiring it will be impossible to start the engine, as the fuel will not reach the injectors. The same applies if the solenoid plunger jams in the 'stop' position. If the solenoid jams in the 'run' position, the engine will not stop when the ignition is switched off.
2 If the solenoid has failed and the engine will not run, a temporary repair may be made by removing the solenoid as described in the following paragraphs. Refit the solenoid body without the plunger and spring. Tape up the wire so that it cannot touch earth. The engine can now be started as usual, but it will be necessary to use the manual stop lever on the fuel injection pump (or to stall the engine in gear) to stop it.

Without coded electronic unit

Removal

Caution: Be careful not to allow dirt into the injection pump during this procedure. A new sealing washer or O-ring must be used on refitting.

3 Disconnect the battery negative lead (refer to Chapter 5A).
4 Withdraw the rubber boot (where applicable), then unscrew the terminal nut and disconnect the wire from the top of the solenoid.
5 Carefully clean around the solenoid, then unscrew and withdraw the solenoid, and recover the sealing washer or O-ring (as applicable). Recover the solenoid plunger and spring if they remain in the pump. Operate the hand priming pump (where applicable) as the solenoid is removed to flush away any dirt.

Refitting

6 Refitting is a reversal of removal, using a new sealing washer or O-ring. Tighten the solenoid to the specified torque setting.

With coded electronic unit

Note: *A special kit is available from Renault dealers to drill out the shear-head screws which retain the electronic unit on the injection pump. New shear-head screws will be required for refitting the electronic unit.*

Removal

7 The coded solenoid valve is secured on the left-hand side of the injection pump.
8 Disconnect the battery negative lead (refer to Chapter 5A).
9 On models fitted with a Bosch injection pump, disconnect the accelerator end cable from the pump control lever. Remove the crankcase ventilation oil separator from the left-hand front of the engine for access to the solenoid valve mounting bolts.
10 The heads of the mounting bolts must now be drilled out. If the Renault kit is used, locate the drilling tube over one of the bolts and drill to a depth of 4.0 mm using a 4.0 mm drill (lightly oil the drill to facilitate drilling). Using the extractor and its handle, remove the

mounting bolt. If not available, cut the head of the bolt with a small chisel or a punch and remove it with a stud extractor tool. Repeat the procedure on the remaining bolts.

11 Disconnect the wiring to remove the coded electronic unit from the pump. Remove the plastic cover and unscrew the valve.

12 On models fitted with a Lucas injection pump, the replacement of the solenoid valve requires the injection pump to be removed from the engine (see Section 22).

13 With the pump on the bench, remove the valve protective fittings.

14 The protective fittings are mounted using sealed bolts. The heads of these bolts must now be drilled out in order to remove them as described above in paragraph 10.

15 Disconnect the wiring to remove the coded electronic unit and its spacers (where fitted). Remove the cover and unscrew the valve.

Refitting

16 On models fitted with a Bosch injection pump, tighten the valve securing nut securely and refit the plastic cover. Tighten the electronic control unit new mounting bolts until the heads break off.

17 On models fitted with a Lucas injection pump, tighten the valve to the specified torque setting. Fit a heat shrink cover to the valve, ensuring that the wiring is correctly routed. Refit the protective fittings using new sealed bolts, ensuring that the spacers (where fitted) are correctly fitted. Tighten the bolts securely then remove the heads of the bolts by twisting, using a tube fitted to the head of the bolt. Refit the injection pump to the engine (see Section 22).

14 Diesel fuel temperature sensor – removal and refitting

Note: *Only F9Q 730 and F9Q 734 engines are equipped with a diesel fuel temperature sensor linked to the fuel injection system control unit. The sensor must be removed in extremely clean conditions.*

Warning: Refer to the precautions in Section 1 before proceeding.

Removal

1 The sensor is located on top of the injection pump. Before removing it, clean the upper section very carefully.

2 Place a cloth under the pump and on the alternator to soak up the diesel which might flow out of the pump.

3 Remove the three bolts which secure the pump cover. In order to remove the 4th bolt securing the cover, use the Bosch tool 0986 612 605. Remove the cover. Ensure that no impurities enter the pump.

4 Slacken the two Torx bolts and remove the sensor. Clean the surfaces of the sensor electrical connections.

Refitting

5 Fit the sensor and tighten the bolts securely.

6 Clean the sealing surface of the upper section of the pump and the cover. Fit the cover and the bolts, then tighten them to the specified torque setting in a cross formation.

15 Advance solenoid valve – removal and refitting

Note: *After removal and refitting of the valve, it is recommended that the ECU memory is checked and if necessary erased.*

Warning: Refer to the precautions in Section 1 before proceeding.

F8Q 788 engine

Removal

1 The advance solenoid valve is located on the front-facing side of the injection pump.

2 The two wires for the valve must be removed from the multi-plug connector for the pump. To do this, first separate the connectors, then press the two tabs and remove the yellow guide. The wires can now be removed using a small screwdriver to prise the retaining tabs to one side. Release the wiring from the main loom.

3 Remove the cover from the valve, then unscrew and remove the valve from the pump.

4 Recover the return connection, seals and filter **(see illustration)**. Note that the filter must be renewed whenever the valve is removed.

15.4 Advance solenoid valve

1 *Solenoid valve*
2 *Protective cover*
3 *Small filter*
4 *Seal*
5 *Return connection*
6 *Seal*
7 *Seal*

Refitting

5 Refitting is a reversal of removal, but tighten the valve to the specified torque and bleed the fuel system as described in Section 7.

F9Q 730 and F9Q 734 engines

Removal

6 The advance solenoid valve is located on the rear of the injection pump **(see illustration)**.

7 Unscrew the union nuts and disconnect the injector pipes as a complete assembly.

8 Disconnect the wiring at the connectors located between the injection pump and power steering fluid reservoir.

9 Unbolt the mounting bracket from the rear of the injection pump.

10 Unscrew the single hydraulic head bolt and remove the steel bracket from the injection pump.

11 Clean the area around the advance solenoid valve, then unbolt and remove the valve.

Refitting

12 Refitting is a reversal of removal, but make sure that the O-ring seals are correctly located in the grooves of the valve, and tighten all bolts and nuts to the specified torque.

16 Altimetric solenoid valve – removal and refitting

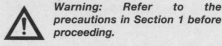

Note: *The altimetric solenoid valve is fitted to F8Q 788 engines.*

Warning: Refer to the precautions in Section 1 before proceeding.

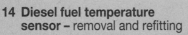

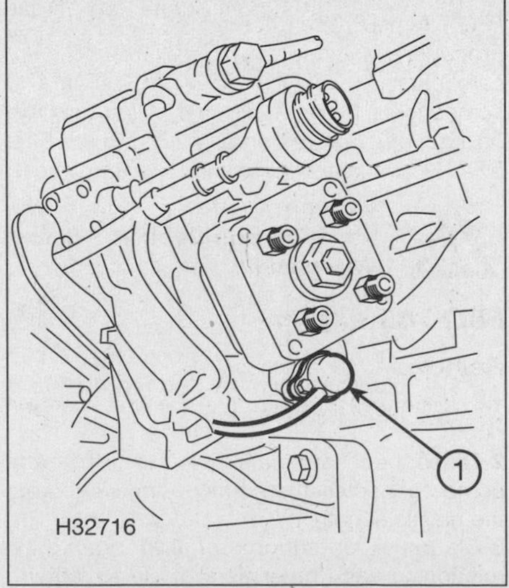

15.6 Advance solenoid valve (1) with bracket removed (F9Q 730/734 engine)

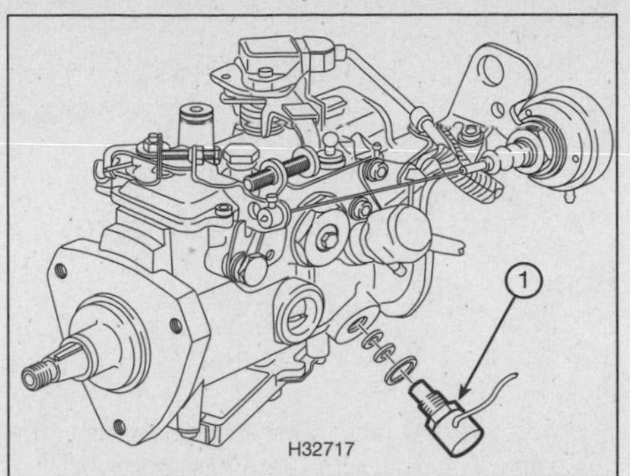

16.1 Altimetric solenoid valve (1)

Removal

1 The altimetric corrector valve is located on the front of the injection pump **(see illustration)**, and its purpose is to reduce the fuel flow at altitudes above 1000 metres.
2 Disconnect terminals 1 and 6 from the pump wiring connector as follows. To do this, first separate the connectors, then press the two tabs and remove the yellow guide. The wires can now be removed using a small screwdriver to prise the retaining tabs to one side. Release the wiring from the main loom.
3 Remove the cover from the valve, then unscrew and remove the valve from the pump.
4 Recover the small filter. Note that the filter must be renewed whenever the valve is removed.

Refitting

5 Refitting is a reversal of removal, but tighten the valve to the specified torque and bleed the fuel system as described in Section 7.

17 Load potentiometer – removal and refitting

Note: *The load potentiometer is fitted to F8Q 788 and F9Q 732 engines. The following procedure is a delicate operation, and extra care must be taken to prevent damage to components. If a new unit is fitted, the 'full load' position must be reprogrammed into the ECU by a Renault dealer using specialist equipment.*

Warning: Refer to the precautions in Section 1 before proceeding.

F8Q 788 engine

Removal

1 Disconnect the wiring from the injection pump.
2 Disconnect terminals 3, 4 and 5 from the pump connector, then remove the wires from the plastic sheath.
3 Mark the potentiometer and bracket in relation to each other as a guide to refitting the unit.
4 Undo the mounting screws, then use a small screwdriver to release the slide contact from the lever. Turn the insert 90° to remove it.
5 With the load lever in the 'full load' position, turn the potentiometer 90° anti-clockwise and remove it **(see illustration)**.

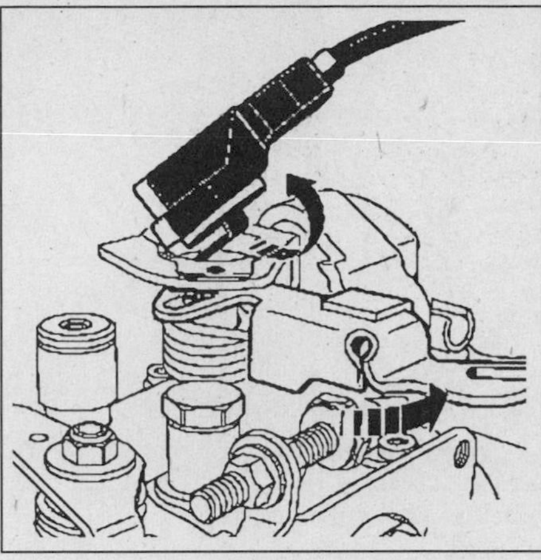

17.5 Removing the load potentiometer (F8Q 788 engine)

Refitting

6 Refitting is a reversal of removal, but if a new unit has been fitted, have the 'full load' position reprogrammed into the ECU by a Renault dealer.

F9Q 732 engine

Removal

7 Remove the engine top cover and the air inlet ducts from the left-hand side of the engine compartment.
8 The load potentiometer is located over the steering gear in the left-hand rear of the engine compartment **(see illustration)**. First disconnect the wiring plug.
9 Unbolt the potentiometer and detach the cable.

17.8 Load potentiometer (F9Q 732 engine)

Refitting

10 Refitting is a reversal of removal.

18 Advance and positive flow solenoid valves – removal and refitting

Note: *The advance and positive flow solenoid valves are fitted to the F8Q 622.*
Warning: Refer to the precautions in Section 1 before proceeding.

Removal

1 The advance and positive flow solenoid valves are located on the top of the injection pump and are in one unit. To remove them, first disconnect the battery negative (earth) lead and position it away from the terminal.
2 Disconnect the main wiring plug from the connector.
3 Unbolt the connector body from its mounting, then pull out the plug by depressing the tabs.
4 Remove the pin plate, then carefully pull out the plastic clip and remove the pin holder.
5 Note the location of the four wires for the solenoid valve, then remove them together with the terminals **(see illustration)**. Renault

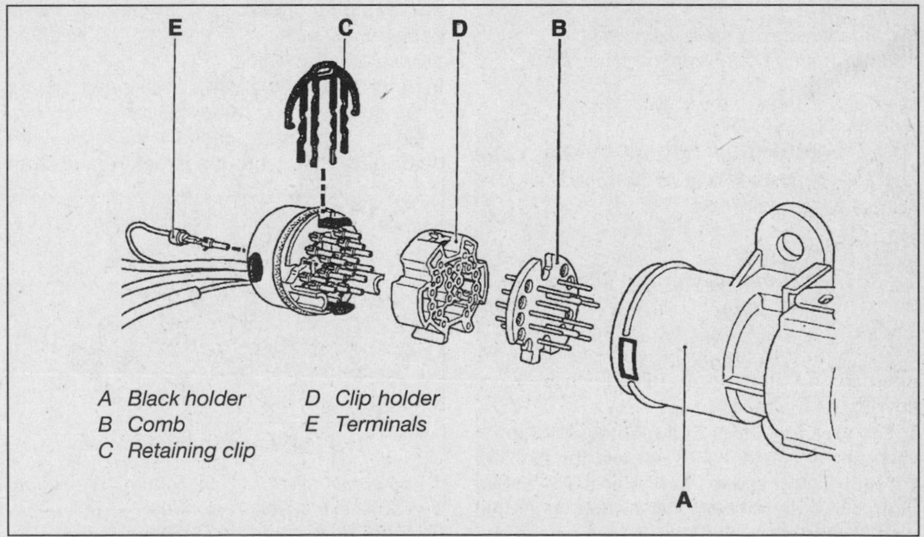

18.5 Injection pump wiring connector

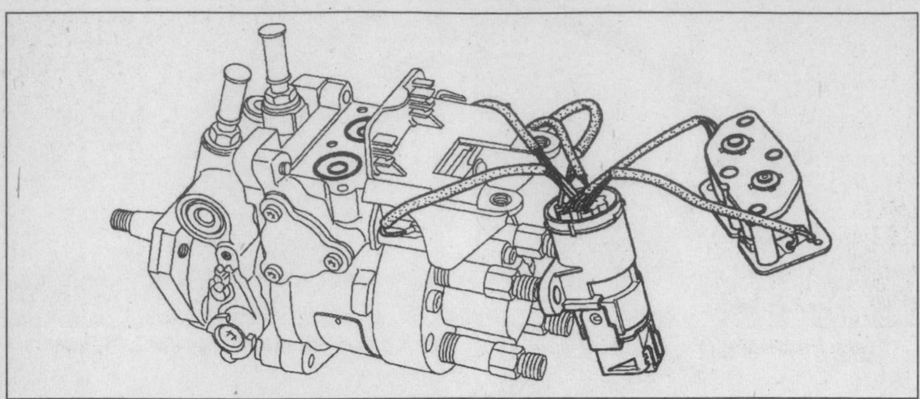

18.6 Removing the advance and positive flow solenoid valves

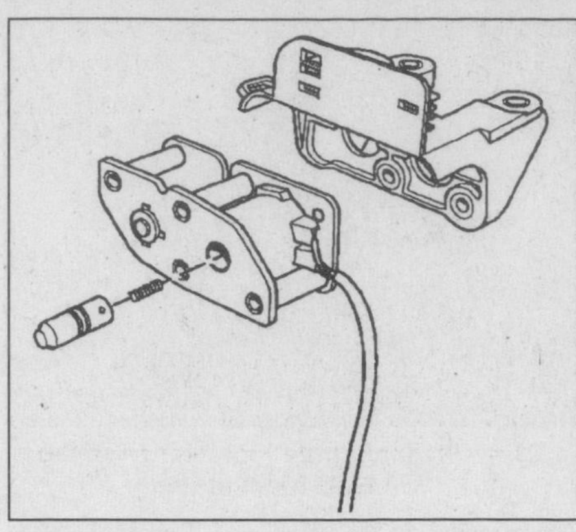

19.6 Negative flow and electrical solenoid valves

technicians use a special tool for this, however a paper clip or similar tool may be used instead.

6 Unbolt the solenoid valve assembly from the injection pump and recover the four O-ring seals **(see illustration)**. Discard the seals as new ones must be fitted.

Refitting

7 Wipe clean the mating surfaces of the valve assembly and injection pump using lint-free cloth. Do not use any solvent.

8 Locate the new O-ring seals on the injection pump. Do not locate them on the solenoid valve assembly.

9 Locate the solenoid valve assembly on the pump, insert the bolts and hand-tighten them.

10 Tighten the bolts securely, tightening the inner bolts first then the outer bolts.

11 Refit the wires and terminals in their correct locations. Each terminal must be carefully pushed in then pulled back to lock the tabs.

12 Refit the pin holder and retain with the plastic clip, then refit the pin plate.

13 Reconnect the plug then refit the connector body and tighten the mounting bolts.

14 Reconnect the main wiring plug.

15 Reconnect the battery negative lead.

19 Negative flow and electrical solenoid valves – removal and refitting

Note: *The negative flow and electrical solenoid valves are fitted to the F8Q 622 engine.*

Warning: Refer to the precautions in Section 1 before proceeding.

Removal

1 The negative flow and electrical solenoid valves are located on the lower part of the injection pump and are in one unit. To remove them, first disconnect the battery negative (earth) lead and position it away from the terminal.

2 Disconnect the main wiring plug from the connector.

3 Unbolt the connector body from its mounting, then pull out the plug by depressing the tabs.

4 Remove the pin plate, then carefully pull out the plastic clip and remove the pin holder.

5 Note the location of the wires for the solenoid valve, then remove them together with the terminals. Renault technicians use a special tool for this, however a paper clip or similar tool may be used instead.

6 Unbolt the solenoid valve assembly and plastic mounting from the injection pump loosening the outer bolts first. As it is being removed note the position of the core and spring **(see illustration)**. Recover the 3 O-ring seals. Discard the seals as new ones must be fitted. **Note:** *The valves are matched to the body, and it is important to obtain a new component with identical references.*

Refitting

7 Wipe clean the mating surfaces of the valve assembly and injection pump using lint-free cloth. Do not use any solvent.

8 Locate the new O-ring seals on the injection pump, using diesel fuel to hold them in position. Do not locate them on the solenoid valve assembly.

9 Refit the solenoid valve assembly together with core, spring and plastic mounting, making sure that the O-rings are not disturbed. Insert the inner bolts hand-tight while pressing the assembly onto the pump, then insert the outer bolts hand-tight. Tighten the bolts securely.

10 Refit the wires and terminals in their correct locations. Each terminal must be carefully pushed in then pulled back to lock the tabs.

11 Refit the pin holder and retain with the plastic clip, then refit the pin plate.

12 Reconnect the plug then refit the connector body and tighten the mounting bolts.

13 Reconnect the main wiring plug.

14 Reconnect the battery negative lead.

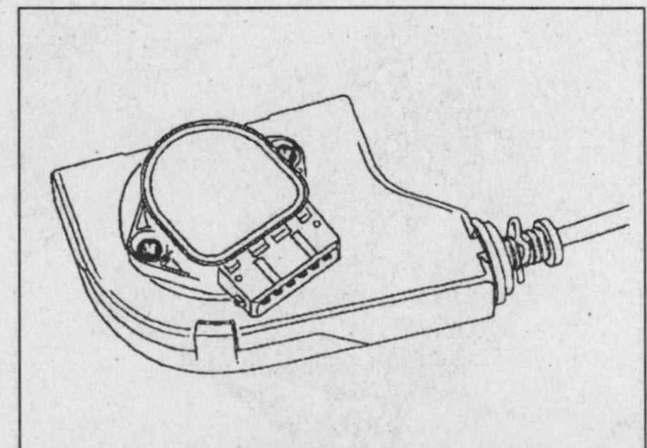

20.1a Accelerator potentiometer (F8Q 622 engine)

20 Accelerator potentiometer – removal and refitting

Note: *The accelerator potentiometer is fitted to the F8Q 622 and F9Q 732 engines.*

Removal

1 The accelerator potentiometer is located beneath the brake master cylinder. It is connected to the accelerator pedal by cable **(see illustrations)**.

2 Remove the unit from under the master cylinder, then prise open the plastic cover.

3 Turn the potentiometer segment slightly and unhook the cable end fitting.

4 Release the cable ferrule from the potentiometer.

20.1b Accelerator potentiometer (F9Q 732 engine)

21.4 Unclipping the fuel filter from the ECU bracket

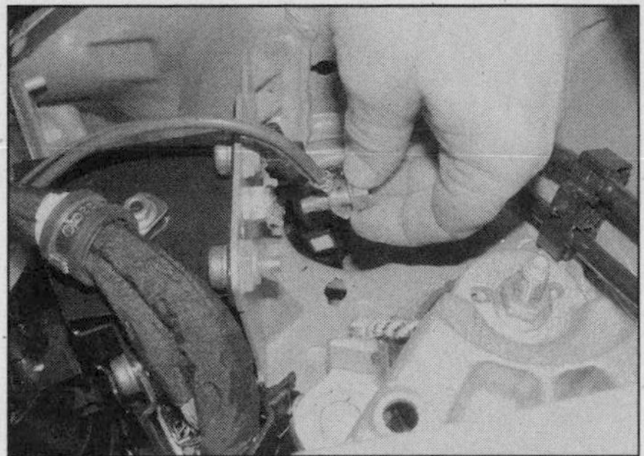

21.6a Removing the mounting screws

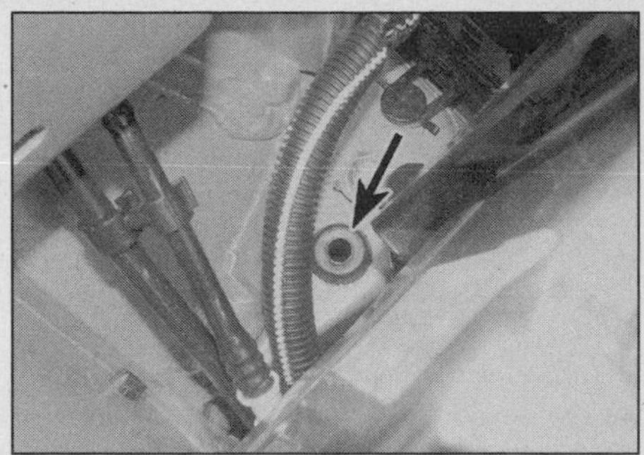

21.6b Rubber mounting grommet

Refitting

5 Refitting is a reversal of removal, but note that the engine management ECU should be checked by a Renault dealer for faults residing in its memory.

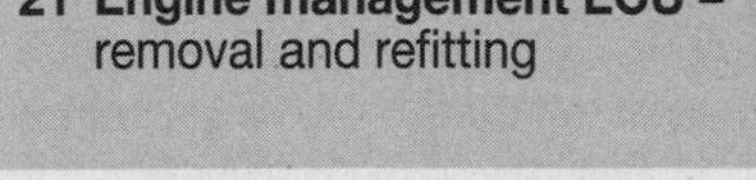

21 Engine management ECU – removal and refitting

Note: *The ECU is electronically-coded to match the engine immobiliser. If the ECU is being removed to enable a new unit to be fitted, the new unit must be programmed with the vehicle code as described.*

Removal

1 The ECU (also referred to as a DCU – Diesel Control Unit) is located in the left-hand side of the engine compartment, in front of the fuse/relay box or on the right-hand side of the compartment behind the fuel filter. It is fitted to engine codes F8Q 622 and all F9Q engines.

2 Disconnect the battery negative lead (refer to Chapter 5A).

3 On Scénic models where the battery is located in the engine compartment, and where the ECU is located on the left-hand side, remove the battery completely with reference to Chapter 5A.

4 Where the ECU is located on the right-hand side of the engine compartment, first unclip the fuel filter from the ECU bracket **(see illustration)**.

5 Where applicable, unbolt the bracket from the top of the ECU and release the strap. On some later models, this is not possible as an internal clip prevents the bracket from being removed, and in this case, the bracket must be unbolted before removing the ECU.

6 Undo the mounting screws and remove the ECU and mounting bracket. Note the rubber mounting grommets and check their condition **(see illustrations)**.

7 Undo the bolts, and slide the ECU from the mounting bracket **(see illustrations)**.

8 Disconnect the wiring connector and remove the ECU from the engine compartment **(see illustration)**.

Refitting

9 Refitting is a reversal of the removal procedure ensuring that the wiring connector is securely reconnected. If a new ECU has been fitted, reprogramme it as follows. Turn the ignition on for a few seconds, then turn it off. Now remove the key to operate the immobiliser. After 10 seconds, the red immobiliser warning light should start to flash.

22 Fuel injection pump – removal and refitting

Warning: Refer to the precautions in Section 1 before proceeding.

Note: *Be careful not to allow dirt into the pump or injector pipes during this procedure. New sealing rings should be used on the fuel pipe banjo unions when refitting.*

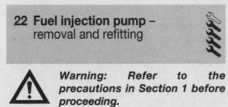

Removal

F8Q engines

Note: *On engines with air conditioning, in order to gain access to the injection pump securing bolts, the alternator and its mounting bracket must be removed. If air conditioning is not fitted, start at paragraph 10.*

1 Disconnect the battery negative lead (refer to Chapter 5A).

2 Where necessary, remove the alternator as described in Chapter 5A, and the injection ECU where it is located on the right-hand side of the engine compartment.

3 Where necessary, unscrew the securing bolts, and remove the power steering pump pulley from the pump drive flange. Note that it will be necessary to counterhold the pulley (eg, using an old drivebelt) in order to loosen the bolts.

4 Remove the securing bolts, and withdraw the auxiliary drivebelt guide roller/bracket assembly.

5 Remove the two upper bolts securing the air conditioning compressor to the alternator mounting bracket.

6 Apply the handbrake, then jack up the front of the vehicle and support securely on axle stands (see *Jacking and vehicle support*). Where fitted, remove the engine compartment undershield.

7 Remove the right-hand front roadwheel and the wheelarch liner.

8 Loosen the lower air conditioning compressor mounting nuts and bolts, then pivot the compressor downwards to enable the alternator mounting bracket to be removed from above.

21.7a Undo the bolts . . .

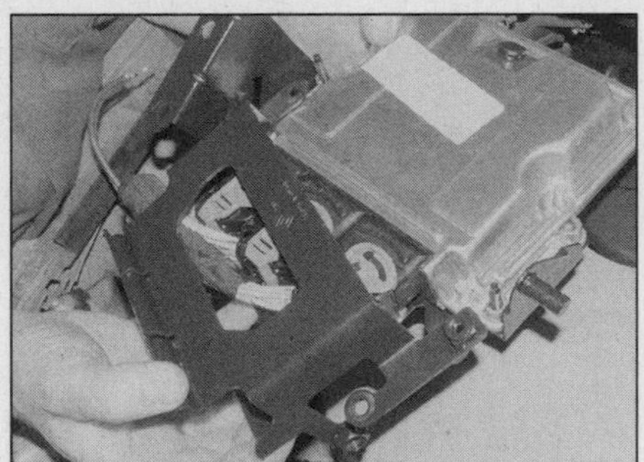

21.7b . . . and slide the ECU from the bracket

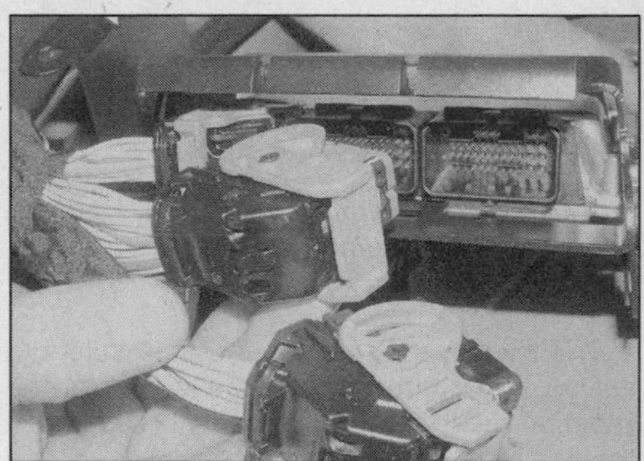

21.8 Pull up the levers and disconnect the wiring plugs

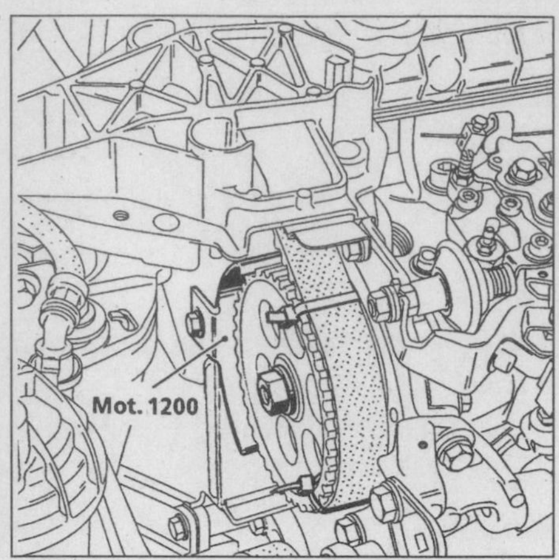

22.14 Renault sprocket holding tool in position

9 Proceed as described in the following paragraphs for all models.

10 If not already done, disconnect the battery negative lead (refer to Chapter 5A).

11 Unbolt and remove the engine right-hand upper mounting cover.

12 Turn the crankshaft to bring No 1 piston to TDC on the compression stroke, and fit the timing pin to check the crankshaft's position, as described in Chapter 2C.

13 Unscrew the securing bolts and remove the timing belt cover which covers the fuel injection pump sprocket.

14 If an injection pump sprocket holding tool (Renault Mot. 1200) is available, remove the timing pin, turn the engine back from TDC by one camshaft sprocket tooth, and fit the injection pump sprocket holding tool (turning the engine back by one sprocket tooth will ensure that sufficient adjustment is available to set the pump timing on refitting) **(see illustration)**.

22.18 Disconnect the hose connecting the boost pressure fuel delivery corrector to the inlet manifold (turbo models)

15 If a holding tool is not available, remove the timing belt as described in Chapter 2C.

16 Disconnect the accelerator cable from the injection pump, with reference to Section 5 if necessary.

17 On engines with a fast idle thermostatic actuator, disconnect the fast idle cable from the injection pump, with reference to Section 10 if necessary. On models with a fast idle vacuum actuator, disconnect the cable from the pump lever and the vacuum hose from the actuator (see Section 11).

18 On turbo models, disconnect the hose connecting the boost pressure fuel delivery corrector to the inlet manifold **(see illustration)**.

22.19a Fuel supply hose (1) and main return hose (2) (Bosch pump)

19 Undo the banjo union bolt where necessary, then disconnect the fuel supply hose from the injection pump. Cover the open end of the hose or pipe, and plug the opening in the injection pump to keep dirt out. Proceed in the same way for the main return hose **(see illustrations)**.

20 Disconnect the main fuel leak-off return hose from the relevant fuel injector **(see illustration)**.

21 Where applicable, disconnect the auxiliary fuel return hose from the pump. On turbo models, the auxiliary hose is connected to the boost pressure fuel delivery corrector on the pump (also unclip it from the accelerator cable bracket) **(see illustration)**.

22 Disconnect all relevant wiring from the pump. Note that on certain pumps, this can be achieved by simply disconnecting the wiring connectors at the brackets on the pump. On some pumps it will be necessary to disconnect the wiring from the individual components (some connections may be protected by rubber covers) **(see illustration)**. On engines with Lucas pumps, disconnect the following wiring: the coded solenoid valve electronic unit, the injection advance corrector and the accelerator lever potentiometer.

23 Unscrew the union nuts securing the injector pipes to the injection pump and injectors. Counterhold the unions on the pump, when unscrewing the pipe-to-pump union nuts. Remove the pipes as a set. Cover open unions to keep dirt out, using small plastic bags or fingers cut from discarded (but clean) rubber gloves. Note that the leak-off hoses will have to be removed from the fuel injectors to enable the injectors to be covered **(see illustration)**.

22.19b Disconnecting the main fuel return pipe union (Lucas pump)

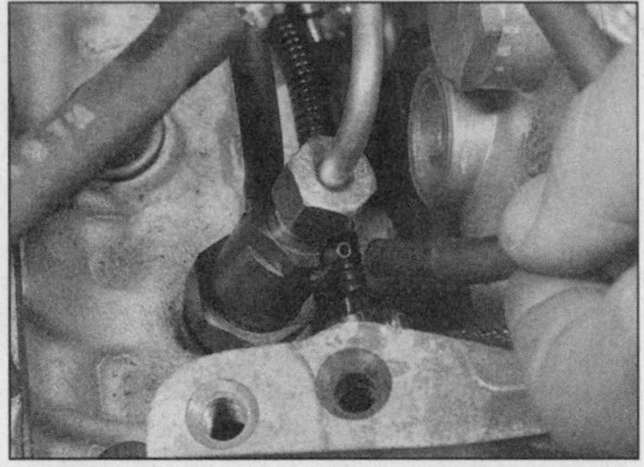

22.20 Disconnect the main fuel leak-off return hose from the relevant fuel injector

22.21 Disconnecting the auxiliary fuel return hose (turbo models)

22.22 Wiring terminal on the ALFB solenoid valve (Bosch pump)

22.23 Unscrewing an injector pipe union on the pump

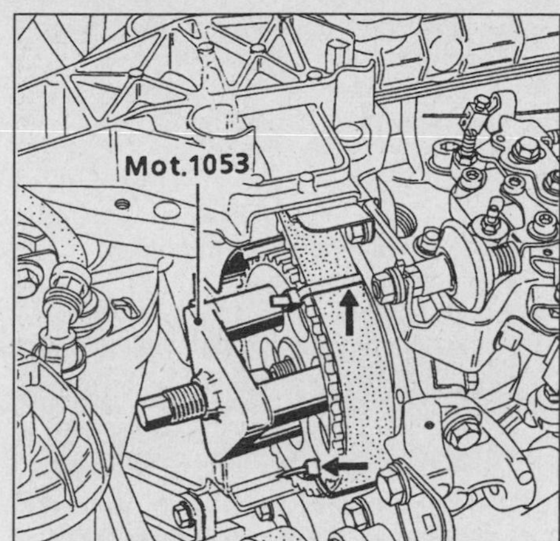

22.28 Removal of a Bosch pump's sprocket using the special Renault tool – note the two plastic ties (arrows) retaining the timing belt

24 Where applicable, remove the alternator plastic shield from below the injection pump. Note the locations of any brackets secured by the shield securing nut and bolt.

25 Where applicable, disconnect the vacuum hose from the LDA anti-stall device on the front of the injection pump.

26 Unscrew the injection pump sprocket securing nut, and remove the washer. If a Renault sprocket holding tool is not available, counterhold the sprocket using an improvised tool engaged with the holes in the sprocket (**not** the sprocket teeth).

27 Mark the sprocket in relation to the end of the pump shaft to ensure correct refitting. This is necessary regardless of whether the timing belt has been removed, because there are two keyways in the sprocket (for use with different injection pump types), and it is possible to refit the sprocket to the pump shaft incorrectly.

28 Fit the special Renault tool (Mot. 1053) to the pump sprocket, and free the sprocket from the pump shaft **(see illustration)**. It is advised to retain the timing belt using two plastic ties before sprocket removal. **Note:** *The puller must locate in the sprocket holes,* **not** *on the teeth. On the MAA-type sprocket a special puller will be required which locates on the hub of the sprocket.* **Do not** hammer on the end of the pump shaft to free it, as this will damage the internal components of the pump.

29 Remove the puller. Unless an injection pump sprocket holding tool has been fitted and the timing belt is still in position, remove the sprocket.

30 On early engines, proceed as follows:

Caution: On early engines, the MAA-type sprocket is secured to the injection pump shaft by a conventional nut with separate washer. A special Renault puller (Mot. 1357) will be required which locates on the hub of the sprocket. On later engines, the MAA-type sprocket is secured to the injection pump shaft by a gold-coloured nut with an integral washer which acts as an extractor. The sprocket can be freed from the pump shaft by slackening the nut. Before starting work, check carefully the sprocket fastening.

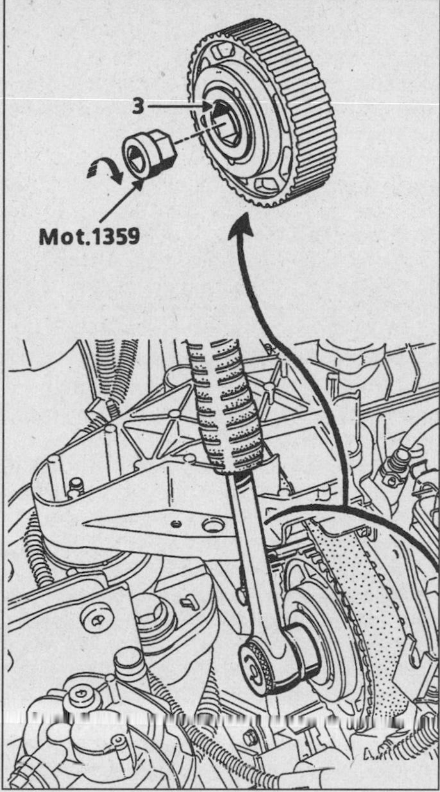

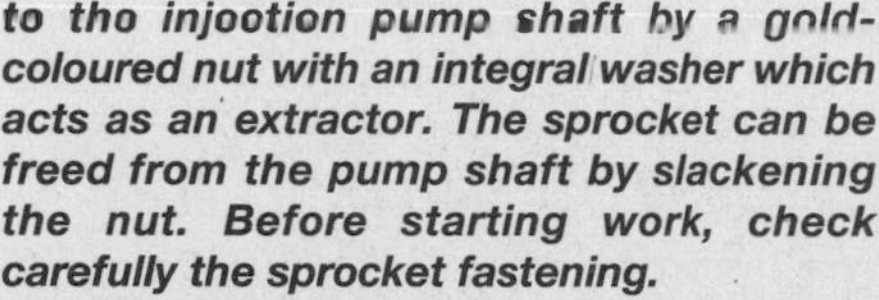

22.31 Unscrewing an MAA-type sprocket's centre bolt (3) using the special Renault tool – the bolt has a left-hand thread (Lucas pump)

31 Using the special Renault tool (Mot. 1359), remove the sprocket centre bolt with its plate: the bolt has a left-hand thread **(see illustration)**.

32 In place of the centre bolt, screw in the special Renault tool (Mot. 1357). Then screw a M12x125, 40 mm long bolt into the tool in order to release the sprocket **(see illustration)**.

33 On all models, unscrew the bolts and nuts securing the injection pump left-hand mounting bracket to the cylinder head **(see illustration)**.

34 Make a final check to ensure that all relevant pipes, hoses and wires have been disconnected to facilitate pump removal.

35 Make alignment marks between the pump and the mounting bracket. This will aid pump timing on refitting.

36 Unscrew the three pump mounting bolts, and withdraw the pump from its mounting bracket, leaving the sprocket engaged with the timing belt, where applicable **(see illustrations)**. On F8Q 620 engines, access to the lower pump mounting bolt is most easily

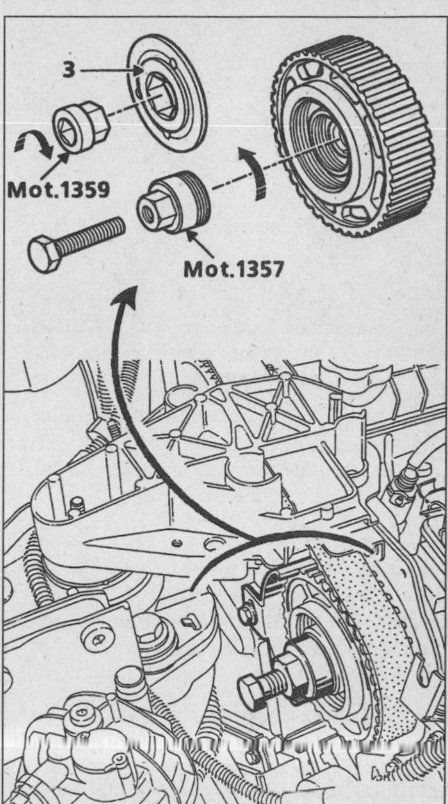

22.32 Removal of a Lucas pump's MAA-type sprocket using the special Renault tool and a 12 mm bolt (early F8Q engine)

22.33 Unscrew the bolts and nuts securing the pump left-hand mounting bracket (Lucas pump)

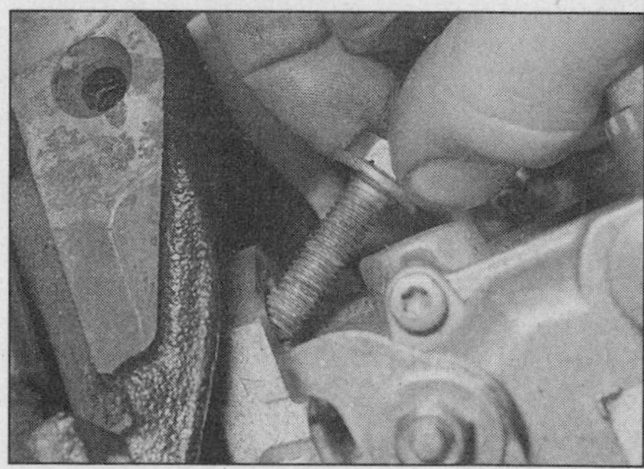

22.36a Remove the pump right-hand mounting bolts . . .

22.36b . . . and withdraw the pump (Lucas pump)

obtained from the pump's left-hand end. A special Renault tool (Mot. 902-02) will be required for this procedure. If not available, use a deep socket and extension. On engines with a Lucas pump and MAA-type sprocket, unscrew the bolts with a Torx key T40, minimum length 60 mm – move the pump back as the bolts are slackened.

37 Recover the Woodruff key from the end of the pump shaft if it is loose.

38 If desired, the pump's left-hand mounting bracket and the accelerator cable bracket can be unbolted from the pump.

F9Q engines

39 Disconnect the battery negative lead (refer to Chapter 5A).

40 Disconnect the ECU wiring connector then unbolt and remove the ECU from its bracket.

41 Disconnect the two fuel hoses from the top of the fuel filter assembly. The unions are equipped with quick-release fittings which are intended to be uncoupled using the Renault tool Mot. 1311-06 – this is a small forked implement which is passed between the two outer 'spokes' of the fitting and pressed to disengage the retaining claws. The hose can then be pulled off the union. If the tool is not available, the very careful use of two small electrical screwdrivers should serve to release the union. To stop diesel fuel from spilling cover the open ends of the hoses.

42 Disconnect the pump wiring harness at the main socket connector attached to the ECU mounting bracket. Release the wiring from the retaining clips and move it clear.

43 Disconnect the wiring connector at the fuel heater connection on the filter.

44 Unbolt and remove the fuel filter assembly and the ECU mounting bracket.

45 Unbolt and remove the engine right-hand upper mounting cover and the injection pump sprocket cover.

46 Turn the crankshaft to bring No 1 piston to TDC on the compression stroke, and fit a timing pin to check the crankshaft's position, as described in Chapter 2C.

47 Fit the injection pump sprocket holding tool (Renault Mot. 1200) to secure the pump sprocket **(see illustration 22.14)**.

48 Disconnect the injection pump fuel return hose quick-release union. Cover the open ends of the hose to keep dirt out.

49 Disconnect the main fuel leak-off return hose from the relevant fuel injector.

50 Disconnect the two wiring connectors at the base of the injection pump.

51 Unscrew the union nuts securing the injector pipes to the injection pump and injectors. Counterhold the unions on the pump, when unscrewing the pipe-to-pump union nuts. Remove the pipes as a set. Cover open unions to keep dirt out, using small plastic bags or fingers cut from discarded (but clean) rubber gloves.

52 Unscrew the bolts securing the injection pump left-hand mounting bracket to the cylinder block.

53 Make alignment marks between the pump and the right-hand mounting. This will aid pump timing on refitting.

54 Using a suitable socket inserted through the slots in the pump sprocket, slacken the three pump right-hand mounting bolts.

55 Mark the sprocket in relation to the end of the pump shaft to ensure correct refitting, then slacken the centre nut securing the sprocket to the pump shaft.

56 Alternately, continue slackening the three pump mounting bolts then the sprocket retaining nut until they are completely released. Withdraw the pump from the sprocket and right-hand mounting and remove it from the engine, leaving the sprocket still in place and engaged with the timing belt. Recover the Woodruff key from the end of the pump shaft if it is loose.

Refitting

F8Q engines

57 Where applicable, refit the pump's left-hand mounting bracket and the accelerator cable bracket to the pump.

58 Commence refitting by fitting the Woodruff key to the end of the pump shaft. On F8Q 784, 786 and 788 engines, this key should be positioned in line with the axis of the high-pressure outlet of No 1 cylinder injector **(see illustration)**. On all engines, make sure that the pump shaft is perfectly dry – otherwise degrease it.

59 Offer the pump to the right-hand mounting bracket. If the sprocket is still engaged with the timing belt, engage the pump shaft with the sprocket. Align the marks made on the sprocket and the pump shaft

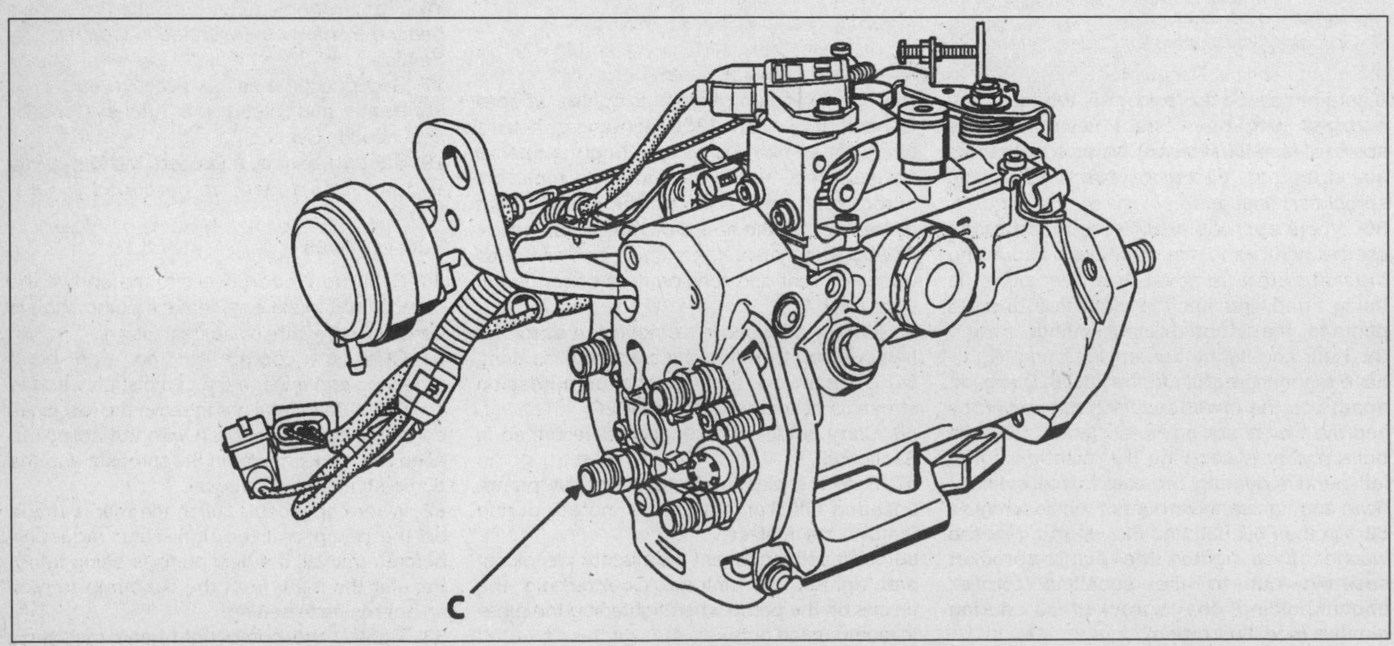

22.58 Sprocket shaft Woodruff key must align with the axis of the outlet (C) for injector No 1 (Lucas pump)

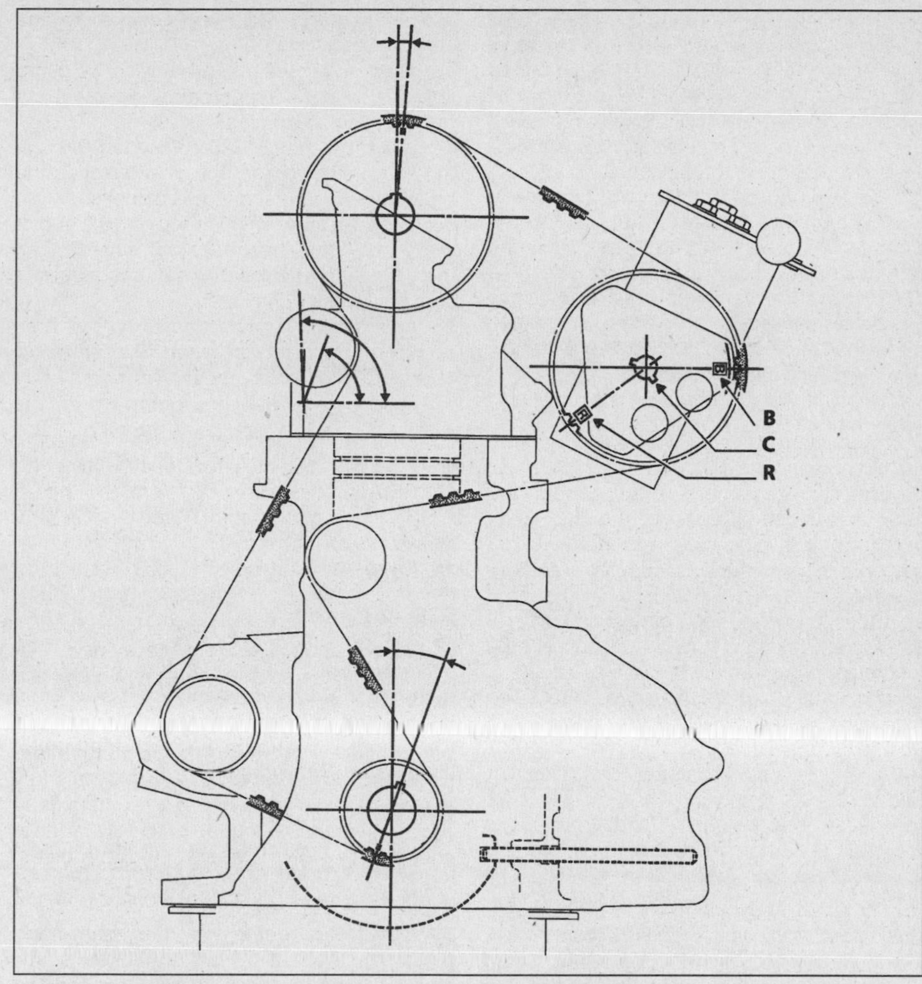

22.59 Alignment of timing marks on camshaft and injection pump sprockets (engine shown with No 1 cylinder at TDC) (F8Q 620 engine)

B Sprocket timing mark for Bosch injection pump
C Keyway to be used
R Sprocket timing mark for Lucas injection pump

before removal. Ensure that the Woodruff key engages with the correct keyway in the sprocket **(see illustration)**. Make sure that the key does not fall out of the shaft as the sprocket is engaged.

60 Where applicable, align the marks made on the pump and the right-hand mounting bracket before removal. If a new pump is being fitted, transfer the mark from the old pump to give an approximate setting.

61 Refit and lightly tighten the pump right-hand mounting bolts. On the F8Q 620 engine, access to the lower securing nut is greatly improved by removing No 4 injector. Refit the bolts and nuts securing the injection pump left-hand mounting bracket to the cylinder head and tighten them but not too securely.

62 On the F8Q 620 and 622 engine, refit the washer, then tighten the pump sprocket securing nut to the specified torque, counterholding the sprocket as during removal **(see illustration)**.

63 On F8Q 784, 786 and 788 engines, refit the sprocket centre bolt using the special Renault tool Mot. 1359 tightening it to a torque of 90 Nm (66 lbf ft). Using the special Renault tool used on removal, lock the sprocket in place and refit the securing nut tightening it to the specified torque setting.

64 On all engines, if the timing belt has been removed, refit and tension it as described in Chapter 2C.

65 Where applicable, remove the sprocket holding tool, then turn the crankshaft to bring No 1 piston to TDC on the compression stroke as described in Chapter 2C.

66 Carry out injection timing as described in Section 25.

67 Refit the plastic shield under the pump, ensuring that any brackets noted during removal are in place.

68 Refit and reconnect the injector fuel pipes, and tighten the unions. Counterhold the unions on the pump when tightening the pipe-to-pump union nuts.

69 Reconnect all relevant wiring to the pump.

22.62 Using a home-made tool to hold the pump sprocket while tightening its retaining nut

70 Reconnect the fuel supply and return pipes and hoses, and where necessary tighten the banjo union bolt to the specified torque. Use new sealing washers on the banjo unions. Also reconnect the leak-off hoses.

71 Reconnect the accelerator cable and adjust as described in Section 5.

72 On F8Q 620 engines with air conditioning, reverse the removal operations. Refit and tighten the auxiliary drivebelt, referring to Chapter 1B.

73 Where applicable, on models with a fast idle thermostatic actuator, reconnect and adjust the fast idle cable, noting that final adjustment must be carried out after the engine has been started and reached normal operating temperature.

74 On models with a fast idle vacuum actuator, reconnect the hose to the actuator, and check the fast idle cable adjustment as described in Section 11.

75 Refit the timing belt cover over the injection pump sprocket and the engine upper right-hand mounting cover and tighten the bolts securely.

76 Where applicable, check the post-heating system as described in Chapter 5C, Section 1.

77 Reconnect the battery negative lead.

78 Prime and bleed the fuel system as described in Section 7.

79 Start the engine, and check the idle speed and anti-stall speed, as described in Section 8.

F9Q engines

80 Refit the Woodruff key to the end of the pump shaft. Make sure that the pump shaft is perfectly dry – otherwise degrease it.

81 Offer the pump to the right-hand mounting and engage the pump shaft with the sprocket. Be careful not to move the key while engaging the pump shaft with the sprocket. Align the marks made on the sprocket and the pump shaft before removal.

82 Where applicable, align the marks made on the pump and the right-hand mounting before removal. If a new pump is being fitted, transfer the mark from the old pump to give an approximate setting.

83 Tighten the pump right-hand mounting bolts lightly then refit the sprocket centre bolt

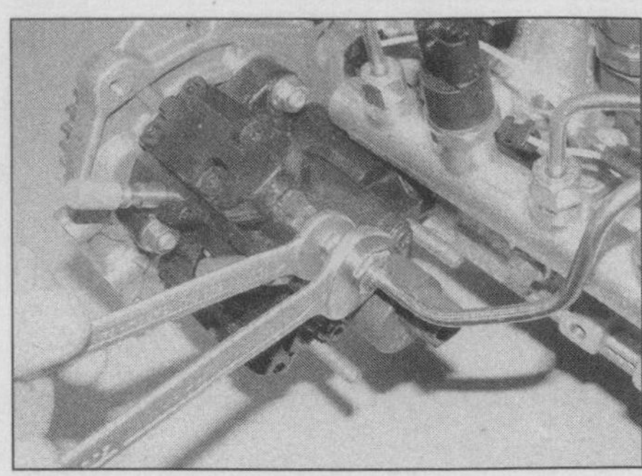
23.6 Loosening the fuel pipe union nuts

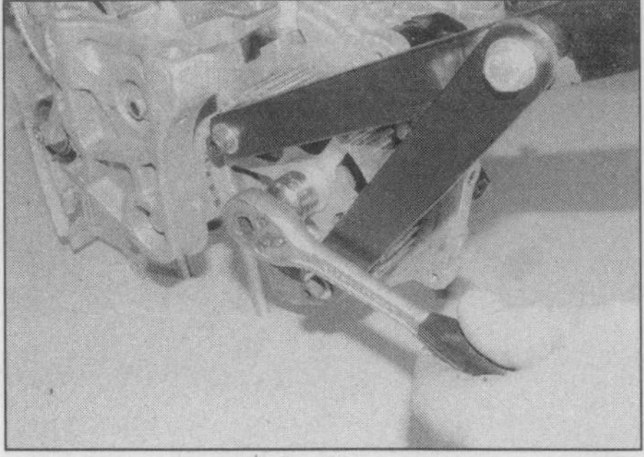
23.9 Loosening the high-pressure pump sprocket bolt

23.10a Using a puller to release the sprocket from the high-pressure pump shaft

using the Renault special tool Mot. 1359. Tighten it to a torque of 90 Nm (66 lbf ft). Using the special Renault tool used on removal, lock the sprocket in place and refit the securing nut tightening it to the specified torque setting.

84 Refit and tighten the bolts securing the pump's left-hand mounting bracket to the cylinder head.

85 Refit and reconnect the injector fuel pipes, and tighten the unions. Counterhold the unions on the pump when tightening the pipe-to-pump union nuts.

86 Refit the timing belt cover over the injection pump sprocket and the engine upper right-hand mounting cover and tighten the bolts securely.

87 Refit the fuel filter assembly and ECU mounting bracket.

88 Reconnect the fuel supply and return pipes and hoses.

89 Refit the ECU and bracket and reconnect all relevant wiring to the pump.

90 Lower the vehicle to the ground and reconnect the battery negative lead.

91 Prime and bleed the fuel system as described in Section 7.

92 On completion check and adjust the injection timing (see Section 25).

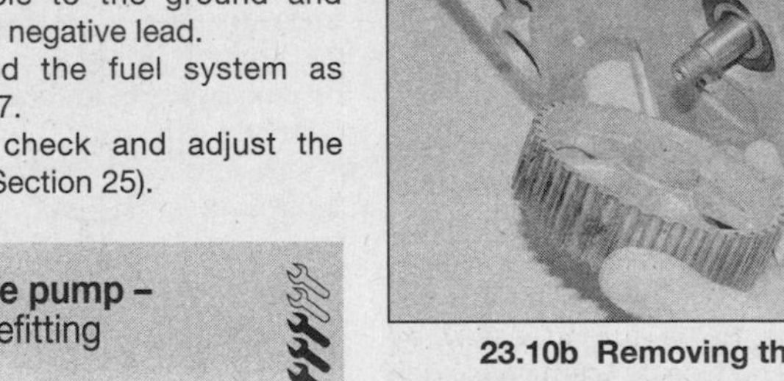

23 High-pressure pump – removal and refitting

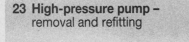

Note: *The high-pressure pump is only fitted to the F9Q 732 engine.*

Warning: Refer to the precautions in Section 1 before proceeding.

Removal

1 Disconnect the battery negative (earth) lead and position it away from the terminal (see Chapter 5A).

2 Set the engine to TDC as described in Chapter 2C. **Note:** *If a sprocket holder tool is being used, this is unnecessary.*

3 Release the fuel filter from its support bracket.

4 Remove the injection computer mounting.

5 Unbolt and remove the sprocket cover from the high-pressure pump.

6 Using two spanners (one to hold the adapter stationary), unscrew the union nuts and remove the fuel pipe from between the high-pressure pump and common-rail **(see illustration)**. Plug or tape over the pipe apertures to prevent entry of dust and dirt.

7 Unscrew the union nuts and disconnect the fuel return pipe from the high-pressure pump. Plug or tape over the aperture. **Note:** *The manufacturers stipulate that the return pipe is renewed whenever it is removed.*

8 Fit the sprocket holding tool (Renault Mot. 1200-01) to secure the pump sprocket **(see illustration 22.14)**. If a holding tool is not available, it will be necessary to remove the timing belt as described in Chapter 2C.

9 Slacken the centre nut securing the sprocket to the pump shaft, while holding the sprocket with a suitable tool **(see illustration)**.

10 Release the sprocket from the pump shaft, if necessary using a suitable puller **(see illustrations)**.

11 Disconnect the wiring from the sensor on the rear of the high-pressure pump **(see illustration)**.

12 Unbolt the rear support bracket from the cylinder head. Support the high-pressure pump, then unscrew the mounting nuts while holding the bolts with another spanner. Lift the pump and withdraw it from the engine flange **(see illustrations)**.

Refitting

13 Refitting is a reversal of removal, but take care not to place the high-pressure pipe under any stress. If using the angle-tightening

23.10b Removing the sprocket

23.11 Disconnect the wiring from the sensor on the rear of the high-pressure pump

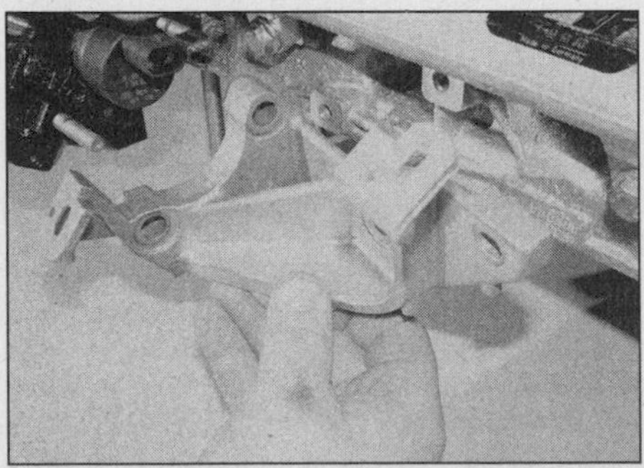
23.12a Removing the high-pressure pump rear mounting bracket

23.12b Removing the high-pressure pump

23.13 Angle-tightening the high-pressure pump sprocket bolt

method, use an angle protractor **(see illustration)**. Connect the pipe to the fuel rail and pump and hand-tighten the union nuts before finally fully tightening them to the specified torque. Prime and bleed the fuel system as described in Section 7.

24 Injection timing – checking methods and adjustment

Note: *Injection timing does not apply to engine F9Q 732.*

1 Checking the injection timing is not a routine operation. It is only necessary after the injection pump has been disturbed.

2 Dynamic timing equipment does exist, but it is unlikely to be available to the home mechanic. The equipment works by converting pressure pulses in an injector pipe into electrical signals. If such equipment is available, use it in accordance with its maker's instructions.

3 Static timing as described in this Chapter is possible if carried out carefully. A dial test indicator/DTI (usually known as a dial gauge) will be needed, with probes and adapters appropriate to the type of injection pump, and the necessary timing pins for ensuring that the crankshaft is accurately positioned **(see illustration)**. Read through the procedures before starting work to find out what is involved.

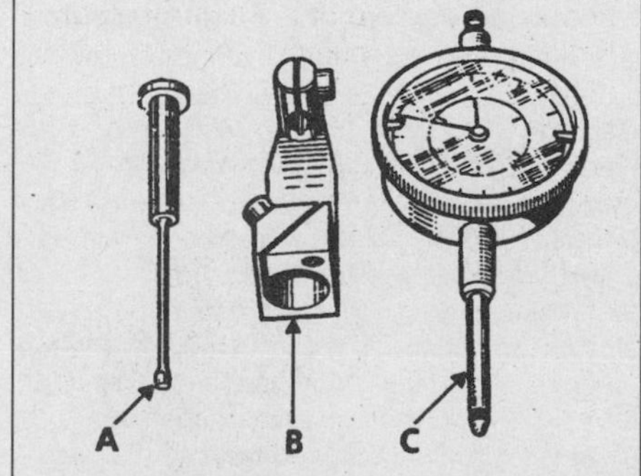

25.5 Components of Lucas injection pump timing tool set (Renault Mot. 1079)

A Probe B Adapter
C Dial test indicator (dial gauge)

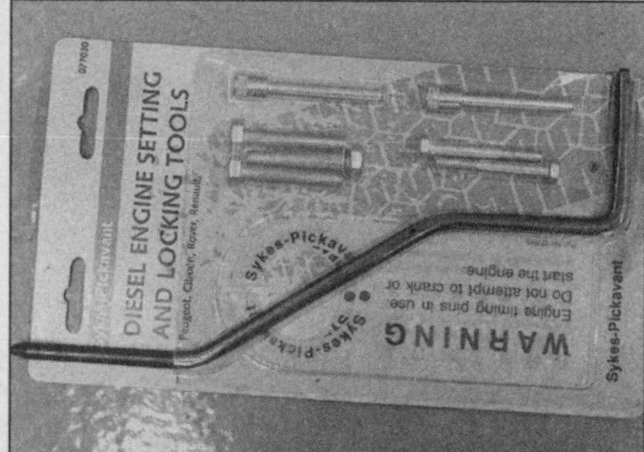

24.3 Tools for checking crankshaft position when setting injection timing on diesel engines

25 Injection timing – checking and adjustment

Note: *Injection timing only applies to engines with an injection pump; it does not apply to engine F9Q 732 with common-rail injection and high-pressure pump.*

Caution: Some of the injection pump settings and access plugs may be sealed by the manufacturers at the factory using paint or locking wire and lead seals. Do not disturb the seals if the vehicle is still within the warranty period, otherwise the warranty will be invalidated. Also do not attempt the timing procedure unless accurate instrumentation is available. Suitable special tools for carrying out pump timing are available from motor factors, and a dial test indicator will be required regardless of the method used.

Warning: Refer to the precautions given in Section 1 of this Chapter before proceeding.

1 Disconnect the battery negative lead (refer to Chapter 5A).

2 Apply the handbrake, then jack up the front right-hand corner of the vehicle until the wheel is just clear of the ground. Support the vehicle on an axle stand (see *Jacking and vehicle support*) and engage 4th or 5th gear. This will enable the engine to be turned easily by turning the right-hand wheel. Alternatively, the engine can be turned using an open-ended spanner on the crankshaft pulley bolt.

25.6a Unscrewing the timing inspection plug from the top of a Lucas pump

3 Turn the crankshaft to bring No 1 piston to TDC on the compression stroke and fit a timing pin to check the crankshaft's position, as described in Chapter 2C.

4 Cover the alternator with a plastic bag or rags as a precaution against spillage of fuel.

F8Q 784, 786 and 788 engines

5 A dial test indicator will now be required, along with a suitable special probe (Renault tool Mot. 1079, or an alternative available from motor factors) **(see illustration)**. Note that the probe of the Renault tool is 'waisted' to allow it to clear the pump rotor and rest on the timing shoulder.

6 Remove the inspection plug from the top of the pump and recover the sealing washer. Position the timing probe in the aperture so that the tip of the probe rests on the rotor timing piece shoulder **(see illustrations)**.

7 Position the dial test indicator securely on the injection pump body, so that it can read the movement of the timing probe. Ensure that the gauge is positioned directly in line with the probe, with the gauge plunger at the mid-point of its travel.

8 Remove the timing pin, then turn the crankshaft approximately a quarter-turn anti-clockwise (viewed from the timing belt end of the engine), and zero the dial test indicator. Check that the timing probe is seated on the timing shoulder.

9 Turn the crankshaft clockwise slowly until the crankshaft locking tool can be re-inserted (bringing the engine back to TDC). Only turn the engine clockwise – if it is turned anti-clockwise, repeat the setup procedure. To determine the exact timing position, maintain pressure on the crankshaft locking tool until it enters the TDC timing hole.

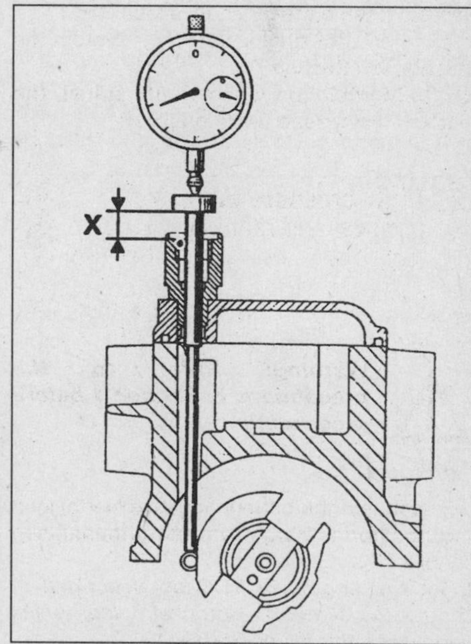

25.6b Timing probe details (Renault tool Mot. 1079) (Lucas pump)

X = Timing value marked on pump

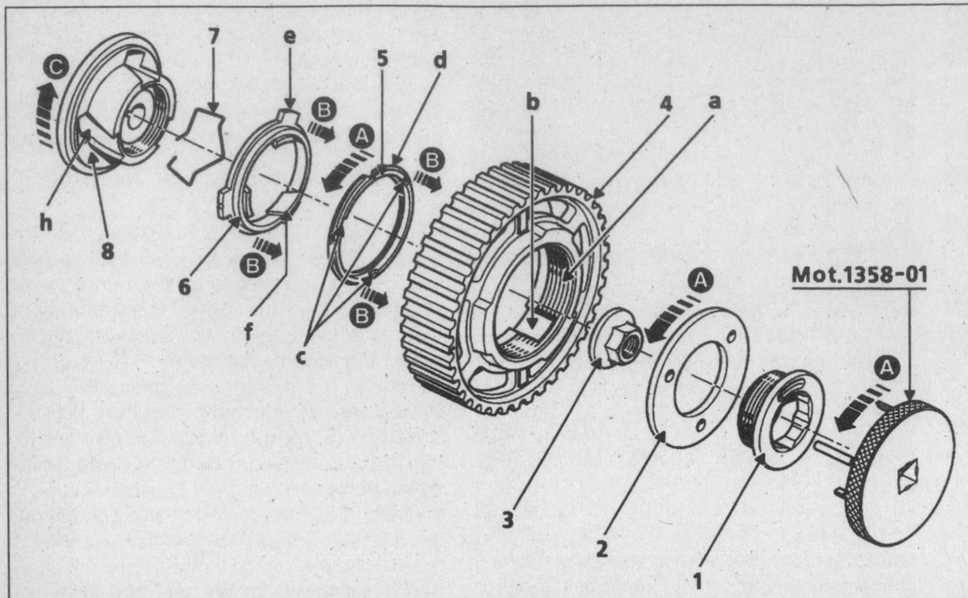

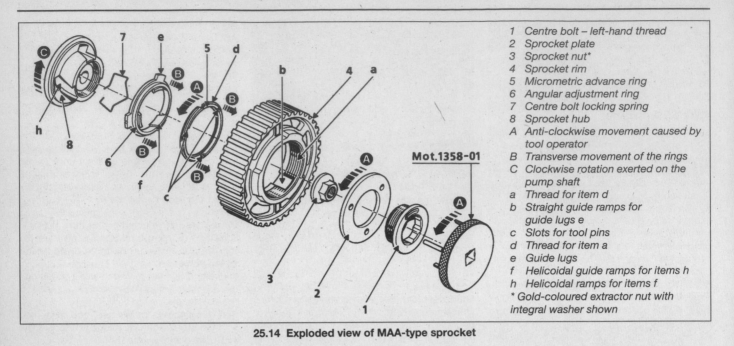

1 Centre bolt – left-hand thread
2 Sprocket plate
*3 Sprocket nut**
4 Sprocket rim
5 Micrometric advance ring
6 Angular adjustment ring
7 Centre bolt locking spring
8 Sprocket hub
A Anti-clockwise movement caused by tool operator
B Transverse movement of the rings
C Clockwise rotation exerted on the pump shaft
a Thread for item d
b Straight guide ramps for guide lugs e
c Slots for tool pins
d Thread for item a
e Guide lugs
f Helicoidal guide ramps for items h
h Helicoidal ramps for items f
** Gold-coloured extractor nut with integral washer shown*

25.14 Exploded view of MAA-type sprocket

10 Read the dial test indicator; the reading should correspond to the value marked on a tag on the pump cover. If the reading is not as specified, proceed as follows.
11 Unbolt the cover from over the injection pump sprocket.
12 Remove the crankshaft locking tool.
13 Withdraw the timing probe and lock the pump sprocket with the Renault special tool Mot. 1200-01 or an alternative tool.
14 The injection pump MAA-type sprocket (**M**icrometric **A**angular **A**djustment) consists of a hub and toothed rim which are locked together by a centre ring (left-hand thread) **(see illustration)**. The plate incorporates three holes into which a special tool (Renault Mot. 1358-01) is inserted to turn the pump shaft. First, the centre ring must be loosened (turn clockwise) using Renault tool Mot. 1359 or a suitable equivalent. The ring must be loosened sufficiently so that the adjacent flange can rotate freely.

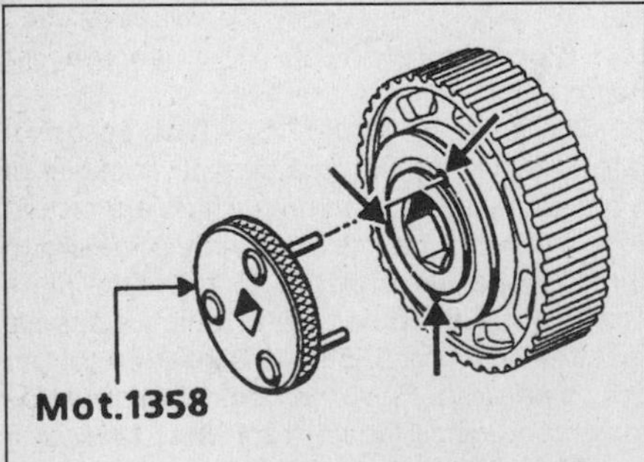

25.15 Renault tool for turning the MAA-type sprocket's plate

Note: *Tool Mot. 1358 is designed for MAA-type sprockets and HTD-type timing belts. If an HTD2-type timing belt is fitted, either tool Mot. 1358 must be modified to suit (see illustration 25.68) or tool Mot. 1358-01 must be used*

15 Fit the special tool in the three holes and turn the plate assembly so that the three pins of the tool engage in the three slots in the advance ring **(see illustration)**.
16 Now rotate the plate assembly clockwise until the tool locks. This allows the sprocket to be set to the position for starting adjustment.
17 Remove the sprocket locking tool and turn the engine 2 turns clockwise (bringing No 1 piston back to TDC).
18 Refit the timing probe and dial test indicator and zero as previously described. Reset the engine to TDC and insert the crankshaft locking tool.
19 Now turn the tool Mot. 1358-01 anti-clockwise until the correct timing value is obtained on the dial gauge. If the timing value is exceeded, turn it fully back before making the adjustment again.
20 Remove the special tool, then tighten the centre ring (left-hand thread) to a torque of 20 Nm (15 lbf ft). The dial gauge should not move.
21 Remove the crankshaft locking tool.
22 Fit the tool Mot. 1200-01 (or alternative tool) to immobilise the sprocket, then tighten the centre ring to a torque of 90 Nm (66 lbf ft).
23 Remove the sprocket locking tool, turn the engine 2 complete turns and check the pump timing once more.
Caution: If the correct injection timing cannot be obtained, check the alignment of the camshaft and injection pump sprockets (see illustration 22.59). This alignment is correct if all timing marks are lined up and if there are 30 teeth between the camshaft sprocket mark and that of the injection pump.
24 When the timing is correct, remove the dial test indicator. Remove the probe from the inspection hole, and refit the inspection plug securely, ensuring that the sealing washer is in place.
25 Lower the vehicle to the ground and reconnect the battery negative lead. Remove the plastic bag or rags from the alternator.
26 Prime and bleed the fuel system (see Section 7).
27 Check and if necessary adjust the idle speed and anti-stall speed as described in Section 8.

F8Q 622 engine

Note: *Renault tools Mot. 1200-01, 1525, 1520 and 1522 are required for this procedure.*
28 Unbolt the diesel fuel filter and position it to one side, then remove the cover from the injection pump.
29 Fit Renault tool Mot. 1200-01 to the injection pump sprocket then loosen the sprocket retaining nut. Using tool Mot. 1525, release the sprocket from the pump shaft.
30 Fit the adjusting wheel tool Mot. 1522 to the end of the injection pump shaft.
31 Position a suitable container beneath the injection pump, then unscrew and remove the setting plug. Allow the diesel fuel to drain.
Caution: Do not loosen the two bolts securing the setting plug housing to the pump. If these are loosened, the injection pump will have to be returned to a diesel injection specialist for calibration.
32 While looking through the timing hole, slowly turn the pump shaft using the wheel tool until the timing groove appears. Using tool Mot. 1520, find the point where the setting pin engages with the groove in the pump shaft.
33 Carefully tighten the pump sprocket centre nut to lock the sprocket to the pump shaft.
34 Remove all of the tools and refit the setting plug.

35 Refit the cover to the injection pump, and refit the fuel filter.
36 Remove the crankshaft locking tool.
37 Lower the vehicle to the ground and reconnect the battery negative lead.
38 Prime and bleed the fuel system (see Section 7).

F8Q 620 engine

39 A dial test indicator will be required, along with a special probe and adaptor to screw into the hole in the end of the pump on the left-hand side (Renault tool Mot. 856 or an alternative available from motor factors) **(see illustration)**.
40 Unscrew the union nuts securing the injector pipes to the fuel injection pump. Counterhold the unions on the pump, when unscrewing the nuts. Cover the open unions to keep dirt out, using small plastic bags or fingers cut from discarded (but clean) rubber gloves.
41 Unscrew the blanking plug from the left-hand side of the injection pump between the injector pipe connections. Be prepared for the loss of some fuel.
42 Insert the probe and connect it to the dial test indicator positioned directly over the inspection hole.
43 Remove the timing pin and turn the engine approximately a quarter-turn anti-clockwise (viewed from the timing belt end of the engine), then zero the dial test indicator. For this operation, apply the handbrake, then jack up the front right-hand corner of the vehicle until the wheel is just clear of the ground. Support the vehicle on an axle stand (see *Jacking and vehicle support*) and engage 4th gear. This will enable the engine to be turned easily by turning the right-hand wheel. Alternatively, the engine can be turned using an open ended-spanner on the crankshaft pulley bolt.
44 Turn the crankshaft clockwise slowly (bringing the engine back to TDC) until the timing pin can be re-inserted.

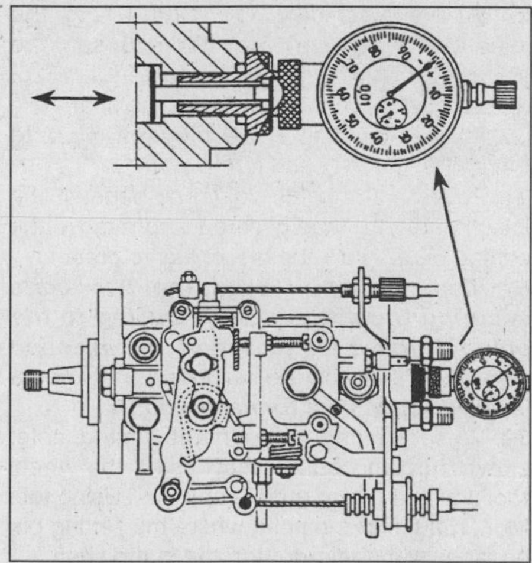

25.39 Dial test indicator and timing probe for use with Bosch pump

Note: *Pump cable linkages may differ from that shown*

45 Read the dial test indicator; the reading should correspond to the value given in the Specifications. Note that the timing value is also marked on the pump accelerator lever.
46 If the reading is not as specified, proceed as follows:
47 Slacken the three pump right-hand mounting bolts and the pump left-hand mounting nuts, then slowly rotate the pump body until the point is found where the specified reading is obtained on the dial gauge. When the pump is correctly positioned, tighten the mounting nuts and bolts, ensuring that the reading on the dial gauge does not change as the fixings are tightened.
48 Remove the timing pin and rotate the crankshaft through one and three quarter turns clockwise. Check that the dial test indicator is reading zero.
49 Rotate the crankshaft slowly clockwise (bringing No 1 piston back to TDC) until the timing pin can be reinserted. Recheck the timing measurement.
50 If adjustment is necessary, slacken the pump mounting nuts and bolts, and repeat the operations described in paragraphs 47 to 49.
51 When the timing is correct, remove the dial test indicator, remove the probe from the inspection hole, and refit the blanking plug tightening it to the specified torque setting. Tighten the three pump right-hand mounting bolts and the pump left-hand mounting nuts to the specified torque setting.
52 Reconnect the fuel injector pipes to the pump and tighten the union nuts securely.
53 Remove the plastic bag or rags from the alternator.
54 Remove the timing pin.
55 Lower the vehicle to the ground and reconnect the battery negative lead.
56 Prime and bleed the fuel system as described in Section 7.
57 Check and if necessary adjust the idle speed and anti-stall speed as described in Section 8.

F9Q engines (Bosch pump)

Note: *Special tools are required for timing adjustment, otherwise it will be necessary to take the vehicle to a Renault dealer. A dial test indicator will be required, along with a special probe and adaptor to screw into the hole in the end of the pump on the left-hand side (Renault tool Mot. 856-02 or an alternative available from motor factors).*

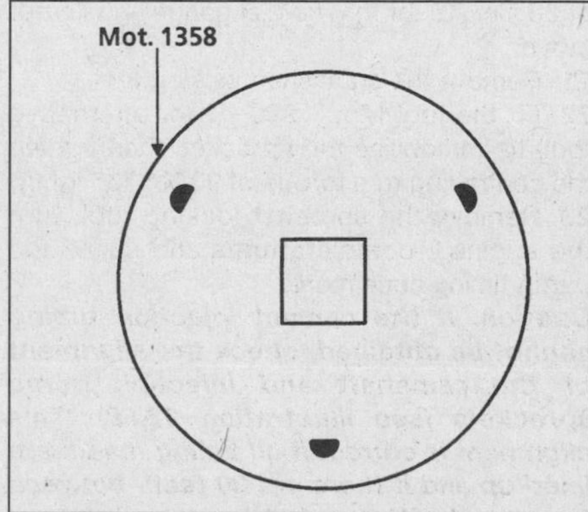

25.68 Renault tool Mot. 1358 – note that 1.5 mm must be filed or ground off the tool pins to allow it to fit an HTD2-type sprocket

58 Remove the crankcase ventilation oil separator.
59 Unscrew the union nuts securing the injector pipes to the fuel injection pump. Counterhold the unions on the pump, when unscrewing the nuts. Cover the open unions to keep dirt out, using small plastic bags or fingers cut from discarded (but clean) rubber gloves.
60 Unscrew the blanking plug from the left-hand side of the injection pump between the injector pipe connections. Be prepared for the loss of some fuel.
61 Insert the probe and connect it to the dial test indicator positioned directly over the inspection hole.
62 Remove the timing pin and turn the engine approximately a quarter-turn anti-clockwise (viewed from the timing belt end of the engine), then zero the dial test indicator. For this operation, apply the handbrake, then jack up the front right-hand corner of the vehicle until the wheel is just clear of the ground. Support the vehicle on an axle stand (see *Jacking and vehicle support*) and engage 4th or 5th gear. This will enable the engine to be turned easily by turning the right-hand wheel. Alternatively, the engine can be turned using an open-ended spanner on the crankshaft pulley bolt.
63 Turn the crankshaft clockwise slowly (bringing the engine back to TDC) until the timing pin can be re-inserted.
64 Read the dial test indicator; the reading should correspond to the value given in the Specifications. Note that the timing value is also marked on the pump accelerator lever.
65 If the reading is not as specified, first unbolt and remove the injection pump sprocket cover.
66 Fit the injection pump sprocket holding tool (Renault Mot. 1200-01) to secure the pump sprocket.
67 The injection pump MAA-type sprocket (Micrometric Angular Adjustment) consists of a hub/plate and toothed rim which are locked together by a centre bolt with a left-hand thread **(see illustration 25.14)**. The plate incorporates three holes into which a special tool (Renault Mot. 1358-01) is inserted to turn the pump shaft. First, the centre bolt must be loosened using Renault tool Mot. 1359 or a suitable equivalent.
68 Fit the special tool in the three holes and turn the tool/plate assembly so that the three claws of the tool engage in the three slots in the advance ring. Note that if tool Mot. 1358-01 is not available, tool Mot. 1358 must be modified by filing the interior surface of the three pins on the tool by 1.5 mm **(see illustration)**.

69 Now rotate the tool/plate assembly clockwise until the tool locks. This allows the sprocket to be set to the position for starting adjustment.
70 Remove the sprocket locking tool and turn the engine 2 turns (bringing No 1 piston back to TDC) until the timing probe can be reinserted.
71 Now turn the tool Mot. 1358-01 anti-clockwise until the correct timing value is obtained on the dial gauge. If the timing value is exceeded when the timing is carried out, turn it back 0.7 mm below the value before making the adjustment again.
72 Remove the special tool, then tighten the centre bolt (left-hand thread) to a torque of 20 Nm (15 lbf ft) with another tool Mot. 1359.
73 Remove the timing pin.
74 Fit the tool Mot. 1200-01/02 to immobilise the sprocket. Turn the engine by hand in an anti-clockwise direction to bring the locking tool into contact with the sprocket.
75 Tighten the centre bolt to a torque of 90 Nm (66 lbf ft) with tool Mot. 1359.
76 Remove the sprocket locking tool, turn the engine 2 turns and check the pump timing once more.
Caution: If correct injection timing cannot be obtained, check the alignment of the camshaft and injection pump sprockets. This alignment is correct if all timing marks are well lined up and if there are 30 teeth between the camshaft sprocket mark and that of the injection pump.
77 When the timing is correct, remove the dial test indicator. Remove the probe from the inspection hole, and refit the inspection plug securely.
78 Refit and reconnect the injector fuel pipes, and tighten the unions. Counterhold the unions on the pump when tightening the pipe-to-pump union nuts.
79 Refit the crankcase ventilation oil separator.
80 Refit the timing belt cover over the injection pump sprocket.
81 Remove the plastic bag or rags from the alternator.
82 Lower the vehicle to the ground and reconnect the battery negative lead.
83 Prime and bleed the fuel system as described in Section 7.

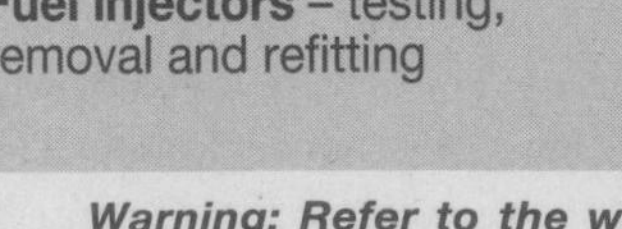

26 Fuel injectors – testing, removal and refitting

Warning: Refer to the warning note in Section 1 before proceeding. Exercise extreme caution when working on the fuel injectors. Never expose the hands or any part of the body to injector spray, as the high working pressure can cause the fuel to penetrate the skin, with possibly fatal results. You are strongly advised to have any work which involves testing the injectors under pressure carried out by a dealer or fuel injection specialist.

Testing

1 Injectors do deteriorate with prolonged use and it is reasonable to expect them to need reconditioning or renewal after 60 000 miles (100 000 km) or so. Accurate testing, overhaul and calibration of the injectors must be left to a specialist. On standard injection models (ie, not F9Q 732), a defective injector which is causing knocking or smoking can be located without dismantling as follows. **Do not** use this method on the common-rail injection engine (F9Q 732).
2 Run the engine at a fast idle. Slacken each injector union in turn, placing rag around the union to catch spilt fuel and being careful not to expose the skin to any spray. When the union on the defective injector is slackened, the knocking or smoking will stop.

Removal

Note: *Take care not to allow dirt into the injectors or fuel pipes during this procedure.*
3 Carefully clean around the injectors and injector pipe union nuts. Note on Scénic models it is necessary to remove the bulkhead and scuttle panels together with the air inlet ducts.
4 Where applicable, pull out the retaining clips, then pull the leak-off pipes from the injectors. Also disconnect the pipe assembly from the high-pressure pump. Seal the fuel system with suitable plastic covers **(see illustrations)**.
5 On the F9Q 732 engine, disconnect the wiring from each injector, and also depressurise the common-rail by wrapping cloth around the inlet union, then carefully loosening the union nut.
6 Unscrew the union nuts securing the injector pipes to the fuel injection pump or high-pressure pump (as applicable). Counterhold the unions on the pump, when unscrewing the nuts. Cover open unions to keep dirt out, using small plastic bags or fingers cut from discarded (but clean) rubber gloves.
7 Unscrew the union nuts and disconnect the pipes from the injectors **(see illustration)**. If necessary, the injector pipes may be completely removed. Note the locations of any clips attached to the pipes. Cover the ends of the injectors to prevent dirt ingress.

F8Q engines

8 Unscrew the injectors using a deep socket

26.4a Pull out the retaining clips . . .

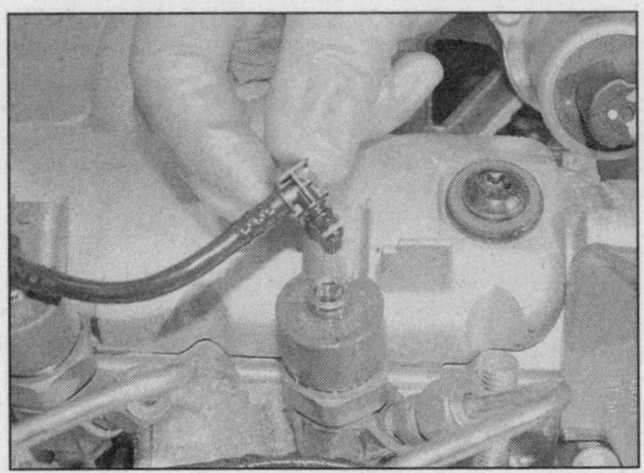

26.4b . . . and disconnect the leak-off pipes from the fuel injectors . . .

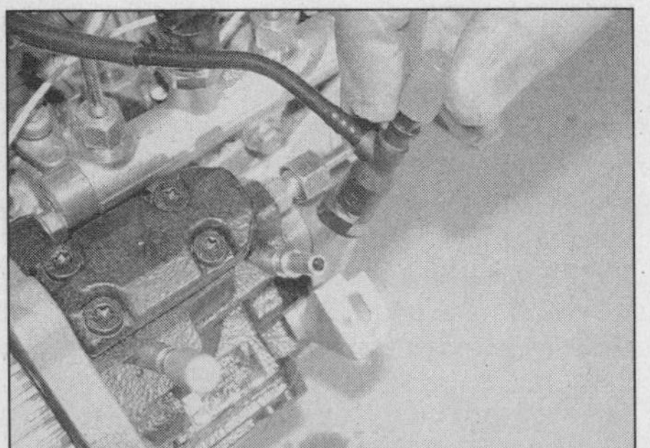

26.4c . . . and high-pressure pump

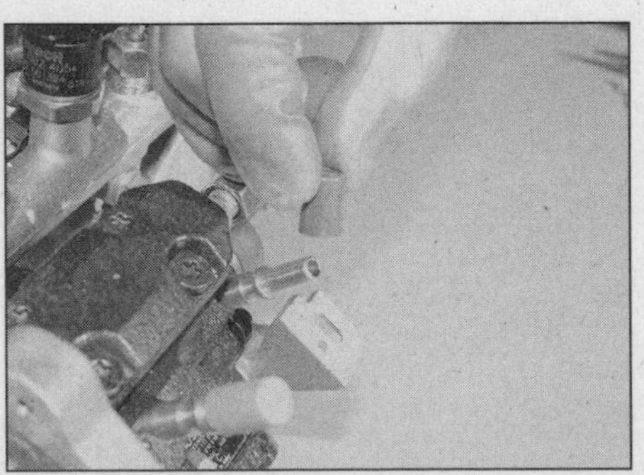

26.4d Using plastic covers to seal the fuel system

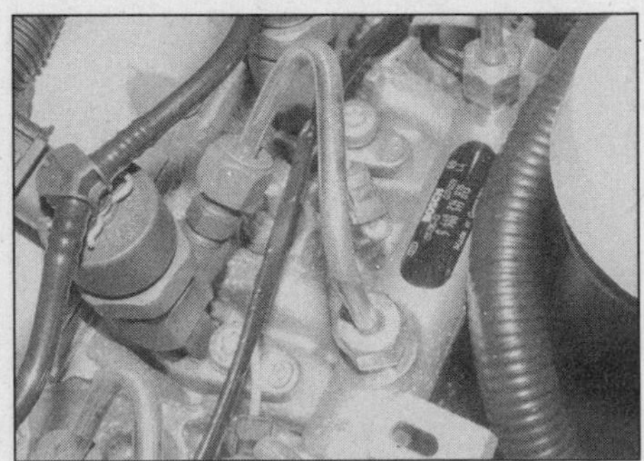

26.7 Disconnect the fuel pipes from the injectors

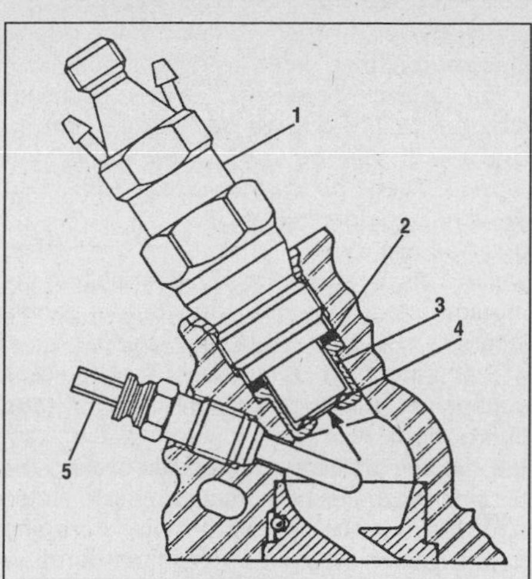

26.8a Cross-section of a fuel injector (F8Q engine)

1 Fuel injector
2 Copper washer
3 Sleeve
4 Fire seal washer
5 Glow plug

or box spanner (27 mm across flats) and remove them from the cylinder head. On turbo engines, a needle lift sensor is integral in the injector holder (cylinder No 1) and removal of the injector will require the use of a special tool. If not available, make a cut-out in a deep socket for the sensor wiring **(see illustrations)**. Note that where No 3 injector incorporates a needle lift sensor, it will be necessary to disconnect the wiring prior to removing it. Ideally, a deep socket with a slot for the wiring should be used.

26.8b Unscrew the injectors . . .

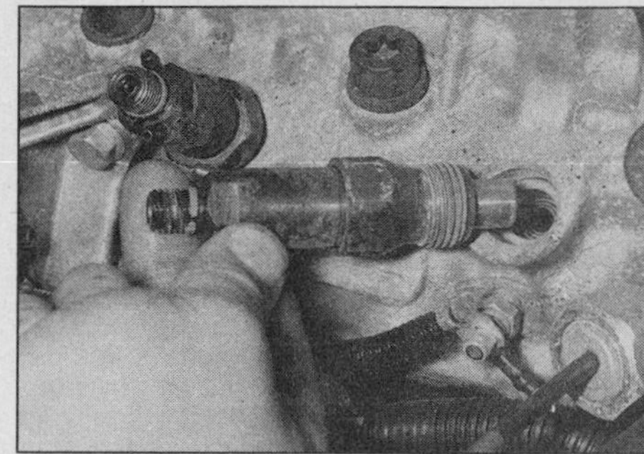

26.8c . . . and withdraw them from the cylinder head

9 Recover the copper washers and fire seal washers from the cylinder head. Also recover the sleeves if they are loose **(see illustrations)**.

F9Q engines

10 On F9Q engines, unscrew the bolt securing each injector clamp plate to the cylinder head. Lift off the clamp plates and remove the injectors then recover the sealing shims between the injectors and the cylinder head **(see illustrations)**.

Refitting

11 Take care not to drop the injectors or allow the needles at their tips to become damaged. The injectors are precision-made to fine limits and must not be handled roughly. In particular, do not mount them in a bench vice.

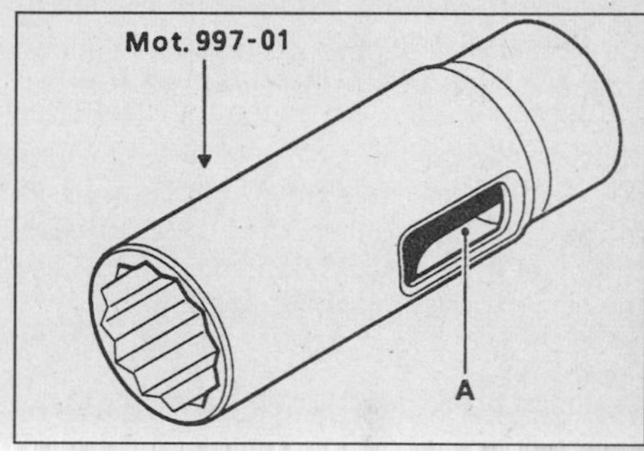

26.8d Renault tool for removing No 1 injector (with needle lift sensor)

A Cut-out for sensor wiring

26.9a Recover the copper washers . . .

26.9b . . . and the fire seal washers

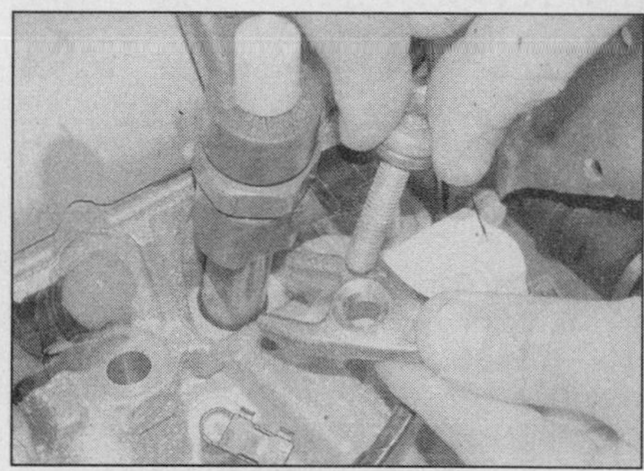

26.10a Unscrew the bolt and remove the retaining clamp plate . . .

26.10b . . . then remove the injector . . .

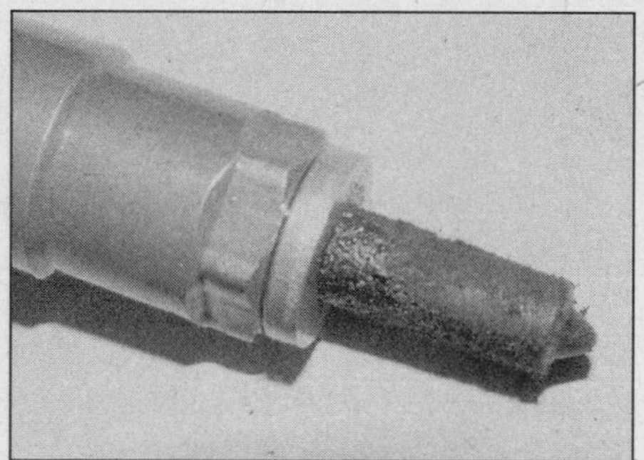

26.10c . . . and recover the sealing shim

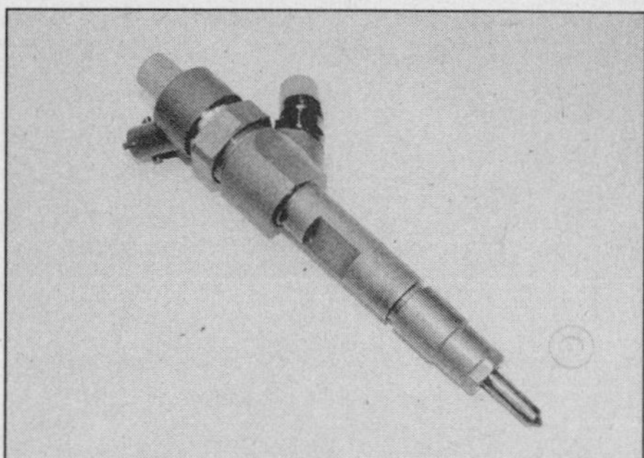

26.10d Fuel injector removed from the cylinder head

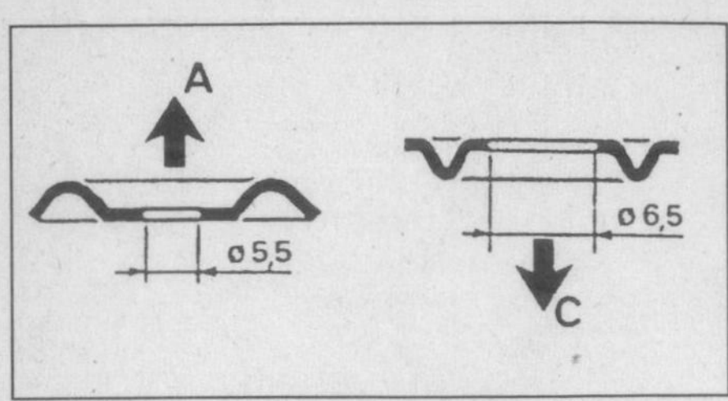

26.13 Fire seal washer fitting details (F8Q engine)

A Early type washer – convex side upwards
C Later type washer – convex side downwards

F8Q engines

12 Obtain new copper washers and fire seal washers. Also renew the sleeves if they are damaged.

13 Commence refitting by inserting the sleeves (if removed) into the cylinder head. Fit the new fire seal washers to the cylinder head. Note that the fire seal washers must be fitted the correct way up **(see illustration)**.

14 Fit the new copper washers to the cylinder head.

15 Insert the injectors and tighten them to the specified torque. On turbo engines, use the special tool to tighten injector No 1 with needle lift sensor.

F9Q engines

16 Fit new sealing shims between the injectors and the cylinder head. Insert the injectors then fit the clamp plates. Tighten the clamp plate bolts to the specified torque.

All engines

17 Refit the injector pipes and tighten the union nuts securely. Position any clips attached to the pipes as noted before removal.

18 On the F9Q 732 engine, reconnect the wiring to each injector.

19 Reconnect the leak-off pipes.

20 On Scénic models, refit the air inlet ducts, scuttle panel and bulkhead panel.

21 Start the engine. If difficulty is experienced, bleed and prime the fuel system, referring to Section 7.

27 Injector rail (common-rail) – removal and refitting

Warning: Refer to the precautions in Section 1 before proceeding.

Removal

Note: *Refer to the precautions given in Section 1 of this Chapter before proceeding. Be careful not to allow dirt into the pump or injector pipes during this procedure.*

1 Remove the engine top cover, then remove the air cleaner and inlet duct as described in Section 2.

2 Depressurise the common-rail by wrapping cloth around the outlet union **(see illustration)**, then carefully loosening the inlet union nut until all pressure has been released. ***Caution: If the engine has been running, there will still be high-pressure in the pipes. Take adequate precautions to prevent personal injury.***

3 On Scénic models, remove the windscreen wiper arms (see Chapter 12), then pull up the moulding and remove the scuttle panels located just in front of the windscreen.

4 Disconnect the wiring from the pressure sensor on the high-pressure pump **(see illustration)**. Also disconnect the wiring from the injectors and camshaft position sensor.

5 Unscrew the union nuts and remove all the high-pressure pipes from the injectors and pump. Cover all outlets to prevent entry of foreign matter into the fuel system, and put the pipes in a polythene bag for protection **(see illustrations)**.

6 Unscrew the mounting bolts and withdraw the injection rail from the cylinder head **(see illustration)**.

Refitting

7 Refitting is a reversal of removal, but before fully tightening any of the mounting bolts/nuts, assemble the rail and all of the pipes finger-tight. Tighten the pipe union nuts on the injectors, then the union nuts on the rail, followed by the rail mounting bolts and finally the pipe union nuts from the high-pressure pump **(see illustration)**.

27.2 Outlet union on the high-pressure pump

27.4 Pressure sensor on the common rail

27.5a The high-pressure pipes to the injectors are identical

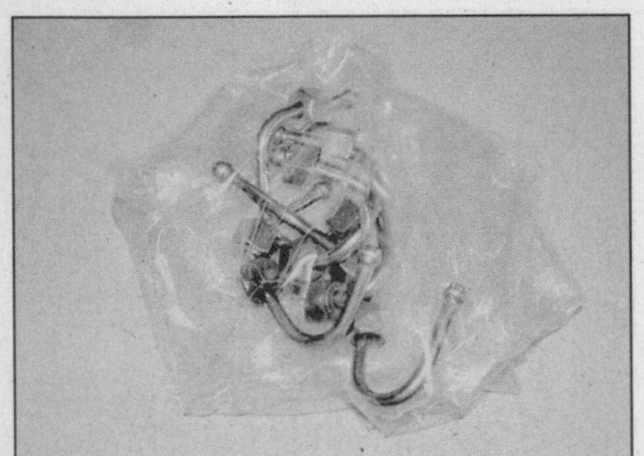

27.5b Put all of the pipes in a polythene bag for protection

27.6 Removing the injection rail

27.7 Tightening the fuel pipe union nuts with a torque wrench

28 Manifolds – removal and refitting

Note: *A new gasket must be used on refitting.*

Non-turbo models

Removal

1 Although the manifolds are separate, they are retained by the same nuts, since the stud holes are split between the manifold flanges.

2 To improve access, unscrew the securing bolts, and remove the strengthening bar, where fitted, from between the front suspension strut turrets. Also jack up the front of the vehicle and support on axle stands (see *Jacking and vehicle support*). Where fitted, remove the engine compartment undershield. On Scénic models, remove the windscreen wiper arms, scuttle panel, bulkhead panel, and air cleaner assembly.

3 Note the location of any wiring or hose brackets/clips attached to the manifolds, and remove them.

4 Loosen the securing clip, and disconnect the air inlet hose from the inlet manifold.

5 Where applicable, disconnect the hoses from the oil separator mounted on the inlet manifold. If desired, the oil separator can be unbolted from its bracket.

6 Where applicable, disconnect the breather hose(s) from the inlet manifold.

7 On models fitted with an EGR system, remove the recirculation valve and pipe as described in Chapter 4C, Section 3.

8 Detach the exhaust front downpipe from the exhaust manifold with reference to Section 34.

9 Progressively unscrew the nuts securing the inlet and exhaust manifolds and withdraw them from the cylinder head. Recover the manifold gasket.

Refitting

10 Refitting is a reversal of removal, bearing in mind the following points.

a) *Ensure that the cylinder head and manifold mating surfaces are clean and use a new gasket. Tighten all fixings to the specified torque.*
b) *Reconnect the exhaust front section to the manifold with reference to Section 34.*
c) *Where applicable, refit the EGR recirculation valve and pipe with reference to Chapter 4C.*
d) *Ensure that any wiring or hose brackets/clips are positioned as noted before removal.*

Turbo models

Removal

11 Although the manifolds are separate, they are retained by the same nuts, since the stud holes are split between the manifold flanges.

12 To improve access, where fitted, unbolt the strengthening bar from between the front suspension strut turrets. Also jack up the front of the vehicle and support on axle stands (see *Jacking and vehicle support*). Where fitted, remove the engine compartment undertray. On Scénic models, remove the windscreen wiper arms, scuttle panel, bulkhead panel, and air cleaner assembly.

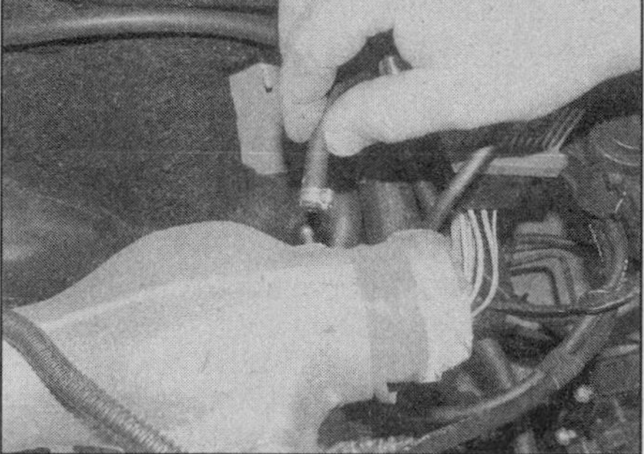

28.14 Disconnecting the pipe leading to the pressure sensor

13 Note the location of any wiring or hose brackets/clips attached to the manifolds, and remove them.

14 Disconnect the breather and inlet hoses from the inlet manifold, noting their locations to aid refitting. On the F9Q 732 engine, disconnect the pipe leading to the pressure sensor on the inlet manifold **(see illustration)**.

15 Remove the turbocharger as described in Section 30.

16 On models fitted with an EGR system, remove the recirculation valve (and pipe where fitted) as described in Chapter 4C, Section 3.

17 Unbolt the engine earth strap from the engine lifting bracket at the right-hand end of the inlet manifold, then unbolt the coolant heater bracket from the left-hand end of the manifold – also disconnect the coolant pipe **(see illustration)**.

18 Progressively unscrew the nuts securing the inlet and exhaust manifolds and withdraw them from the cylinder head. Recover the manifold gasket **(see illustrations)**.

Refitting

19 Refitting is a reversal of removal, bearing in mind the following points.

28.17 Unbolting the coolant heater bracket from the left-hand end of the manifold

a) *Ensure that the cylinder head and manifold mating surfaces are clean and use a new gasket. Note that the central lower four mounting nuts and washers may be started on their studs before refitting the exhaust manifold as the manifold is slotted. Tighten all fixings to the specified torque.*
b) *Ensure that the breather hoses are correctly reconnected as noted before removal.*
c) *Ensure that any wiring or hose brackets/clips are positioned as noted before removal.*

29 Turbocharger – description

A turbocharger increases engine efficiency by raising the pressure in the inlet manifold above atmospheric pressure. Instead of the air simply being sucked into the cylinders, it is forced in. Additional fuel is supplied in proportion to the increased air intake.

Energy for the operation of the turbocharger comes from the exhaust gas. The gas flows through a specially-shaped housing (the turbine housing) and in so doing, spins the turbine wheel. The turbine wheel is attached to a shaft, at the end of which is another vaned wheel known as the compressor wheel. The compressor wheel spins in its own housing and compresses the inducted air on the way to the inlet manifold.

Between the turbocharger and the inlet manifold, the compressed air passes through an intercooler. This is an air-to-air heat

28.18a Remove the manifolds . . .

28.18b . . . and recover the gasket

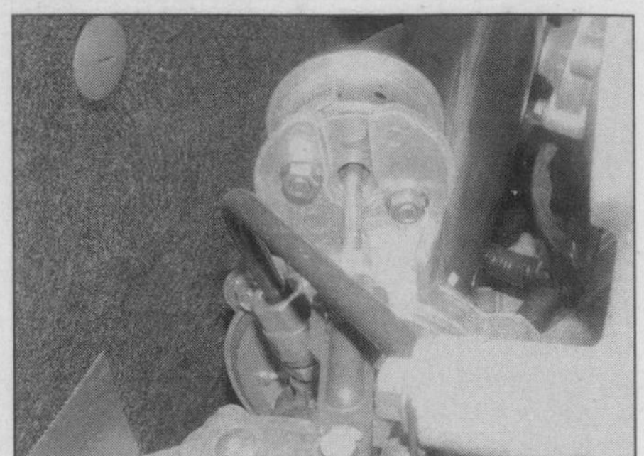
29.4a Wastegate located on the turbocharger

29.4b Turbocharging pressure regulator solenoid

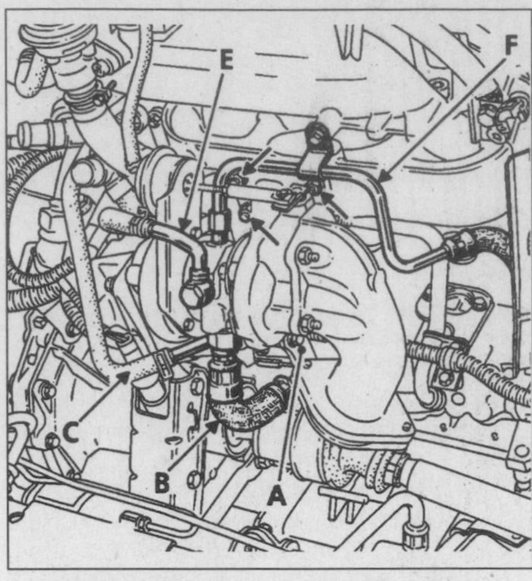

30.6a Turbocharger mountings and hose/pipe connections (early models)

Arrows indicate wastegate bracket bolts and turbocharger-to-manifold nuts
A Lower support bracket
B Oil return pipe union
C Lower turbocharger coolant hose
E Upper turbocharger coolant hose
F Oil feed pipe union

exchanger, mounted on the left-hand side of the car behind the front bumper, and supplied with cooling air ducted through the front spoiler. The purpose of the intercooler is to remove, from the inducted air, some of the heat gained in being compressed. Because cooler air is denser, removal of this heat further increases engine efficiency.

Boost pressure (the pressure in the inlet manifold) is limited by a wastegate **(see illustration)**, which diverts the exhaust gas away from the turbine wheel in response to a pressure-sensitive actuator. Turbocharging pressure is controlled by a pressure sensor located on the bulkhead **(see illustration)**.

The turbo shaft is pressure-lubricated by an oil feed pipe from the main oil gallery. The shaft 'floats' on a cushion of oil. A drain pipe returns the oil to the sump.

The turbocharger bearings are cooled by circulating engine coolant. After switching off the ignition, an electric pump continues to circulate coolant for several minutes to prevent overheating of the bearings and to prolong their life.

Precautions

The turbocharger operates at extremely high speeds and temperatures. Certain precautions must be observed to avoid premature failure of the turbo or injury to the operator.

Do not race the engine immediately after start-up, especially if it is cold. Give the oil a few seconds to circulate.

Always allow the engine to return to idle speed before switching it off – do not blip the throttle and switch off, as this will leave the turbo spinning without lubrication.

Allow the engine to idle for several minutes before switching off after a high-speed run.

Observe the recommended intervals for oil and filter changing, and use a reputable oil of the specified quality. Neglect of oil changing, or use of inferior oil, can cause carbon formation on the turbo shaft and subsequent failure.

Warning: Do not operate the turbo with any parts exposed. Foreign objects falling onto the rotating vanes could cause excessive damage and (if ejected) personal injury.

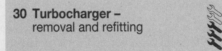

30 Turbocharger – removal and refitting

Note: *New turbocharger-to-exhaust manifold nuts must be used on refitting. If a new turbocharger is to be fitted, new exhaust elbow-to-turbocharger nuts and new coolant pipe seals will be required.*

Removal

1 Whilst the engine is still warm, spray the turbocharger mounting bolts with a penetrating oil to ease removal.

2 Apply the handbrake, then jack up the front of the vehicle, and support securely on axle stands (see *Jacking and vehicle support*).

3 Ensure that the engine has cooled sufficiently to avoid scalding, then, on F8Q engines, drain the cooling system as described in Chapter 1B.

4 Where applicable, remove the engine undershield and top cover.

5 Remove the exhaust front section/downpipe/catalytic converter with reference to Section 34.

6 Working under the vehicle, unscrew the upper securing nut and bolt, and the lower bolt, and remove the turbocharger lower support bracket **(see illustrations)**.

7 Remove the air cleaner assembly as described in Section 2. On Scénic models with the F9Q 732 engine, remove the windscreen wiper arms, scuttle panel, and bulkhead panel, then disconnect the airflow meter and remove the air unit.

8 On early models, unscrew the turbocharger oil return pipe union from the outlet on the underside of the turbocharger. On later models, remove the return pipe completely **(see illustrations)**. Be prepared for oil spillage.

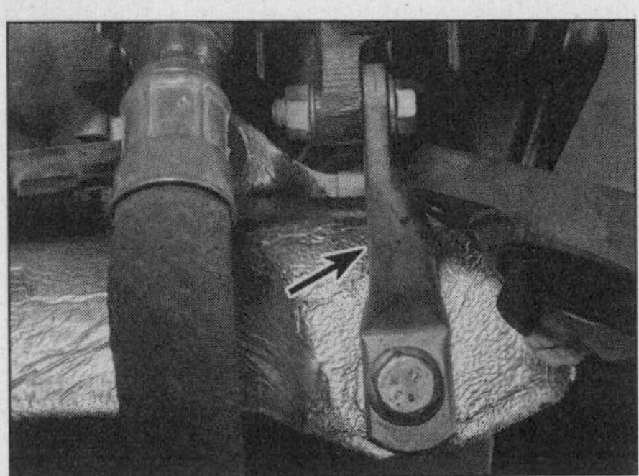
30.6b Turbocharger lower support bracket (arrowed) viewed with engine removed (early models)

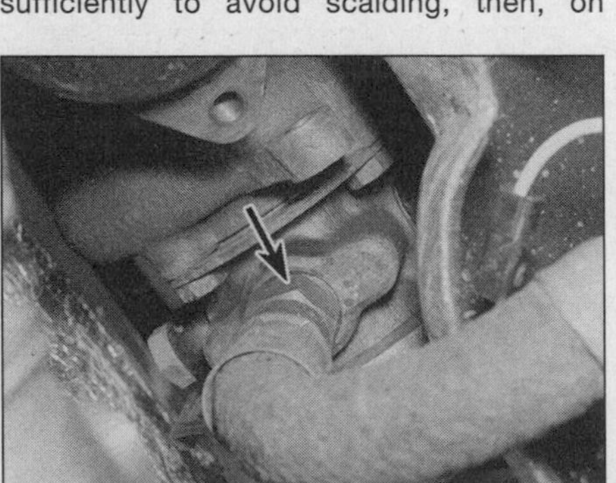
30.8a Turbocharger oil return pipe union (arrowed) viewed from underneath vehicle (early models)

30.8b Detach the oil return pipe from the turbocharger . . .

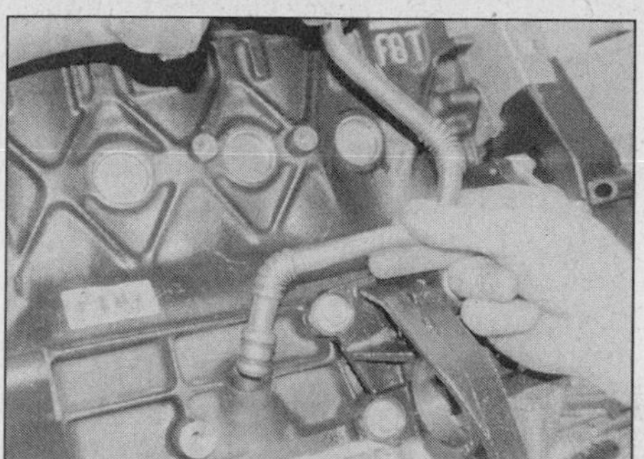
30.8c . . . and block

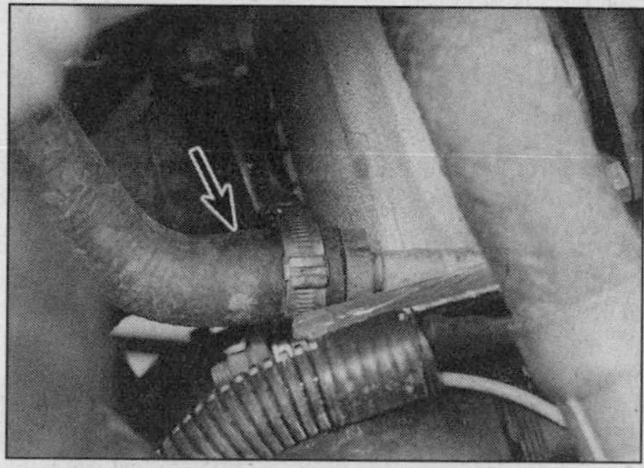
30.9 Disconnect the lower coolant hose (arrowed) from the turbocharger pipe, viewed from underneath vehicle

30.15 Unscrew the brake vacuum pump pipe union

9 On F8Q engine models, cut the hose clamp, and disconnect the lower coolant hose from the turbocharger pipe **(see illustration)**. Be prepared for coolant spillage.

10 Where applicable, unbolt the strengthening bar from between the front suspension strut turrets.

11 Loosen the clamps, and remove the air trunking connecting the inlet manifold to the intercooler tube.

12 Loosen the clamps, and remove the air trunking connecting the air cleaner to the turbocharger. Also disconnect the breather hose connecting the air trunking to the inlet manifold. Note the locations of any clips attached to the air trunking.

13 Loosen the clamp and disconnect the air outlet trunking (running to the intercooler) from the turbocharger.

14 Remove the nut securing the pre/post-heating system control unit to the bulkhead, and move the unit to one side, leaving the wiring connected.

15 Unscrew the union nut, and disconnect the vacuum pipe from the brake vacuum pump **(see illustration)**.

16 On F8Q engine models, disconnect the coolant hose from the rear of the cylinder head, and move the hose to one side, clear of the working area **(see illustration)**. Be prepared for coolant spillage.

17 Similarly, disconnect the upper turbocharger coolant hose **(see illustration)**.

18 Unscrew the union nut, and disconnect the oil feed pipe from the top of the turbocharger. If preferred, the pipe can be removed completely **(see illustrations)**. It may be necessary to remove the wastegate bracket bolts to enable access to the union nut.

19 Remove the bolt and the nut securing the turbocharger-to-air elbow bracket, and withdraw the bracket **(see illustration)**.

20 Disconnect the boost pressure pipe **(see illustration)**.

21 Unscrew the four turbocharger-to-manifold nuts, and slide the turbocharger

30.16 Disconnect coolant hose (arrowed) from the rear of the cylinder head

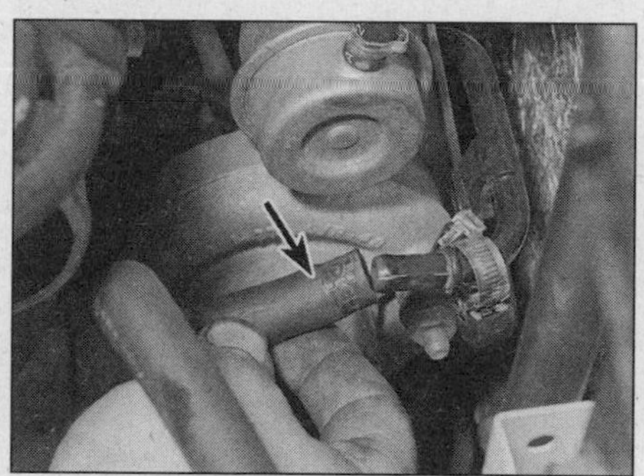
30.17 Disconnecting the upper turbocharger coolant hose (arrowed)

30.18a Unscrewing the turbocharger oil feed pipe union nut (arrowed)

30.18b Removing the oil feed pipe

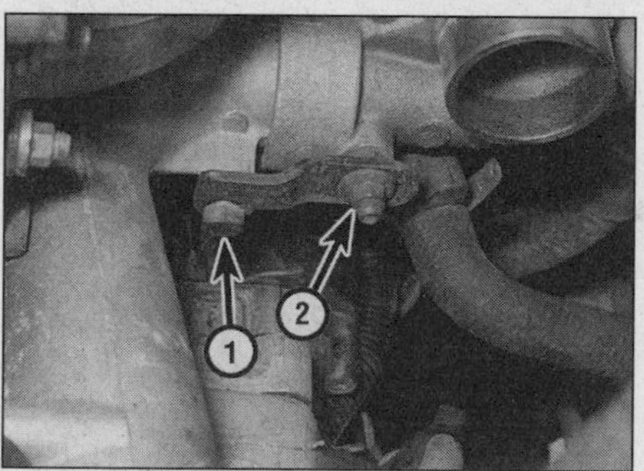

30.19 Turbocharger-to-air elbow bracket bolt (1) and nut (2)

30.20 Disconnecting the boost pressure pipe (arrowed) from the inlet manifold

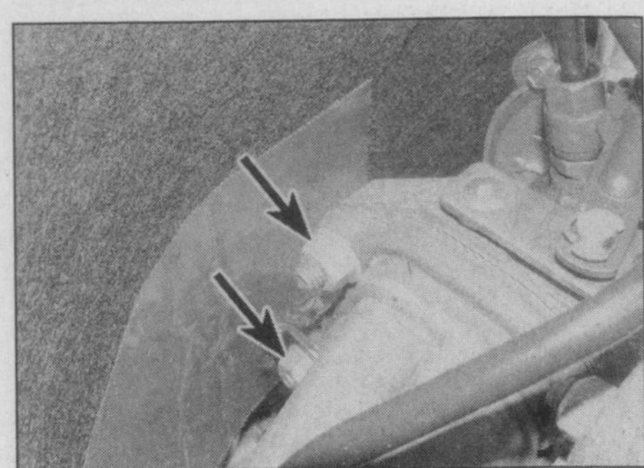

30.21 Two of the turbocharger-to-manifold nuts

from the manifold studs **(see illustration)**. Access to the lower right-hand nut is easiest from underneath the vehicle. For improved access to the nuts, unbolt the exhaust elbow from the turbocharger.

22 Withdraw the turbocharger from above the engine compartment, by passing it below the brake vacuum pump, and then manipulating it between the vacuum pump and the coolant reservoir **(see illustration)**.

23 If a new turbocharger is to be fitted, where applicable remove the coolant pipes and the exhaust elbow from the old unit, and transfer them to the new unit. Use new nuts when fitting the exhaust elbow, and new seals when fitting the coolant pipes.

Refitting

24 Refitting is a reversal of removal, but renew any damaged hose clamps, and use new turbocharger-to-exhaust manifold nuts which should be tightened to the specified torque. Tighten the oil feed and return pipe-to-turbocharger union nuts to the specified torque. Where applicable, the exhaust elbow should be refitted to the turbocharger using new nuts. Note that if the wastegate bracket bolts were removed, they must be refitted using a suitable thread-locking compound before tightening to the specified torque. Refill the cooling system as described in Chapter 1B.

25 On completion, the following procedure must be observed before starting the engine.

a) Disconnect the wiring from the stop solenoid or fuel pressure rail (as applicable).

b) Crank the engine on the starter motor until the instrument panel oil pressure warning light goes out (this may take several seconds).

c) Reconnect the wiring to the stop solenoid, then start the engine using the normal procedure.

d) Run the engine at idle speed, and check the turbocharger oil unions for leakage. Rectify any problems without delay.

26 After the engine has been run, check the engine oil level, and top up if necessary.

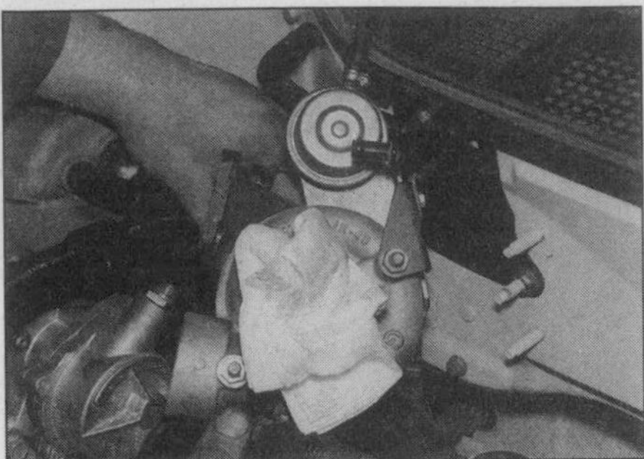

30.22 Withdrawing the turbocharger

31 Turbocharger – examination and renovation

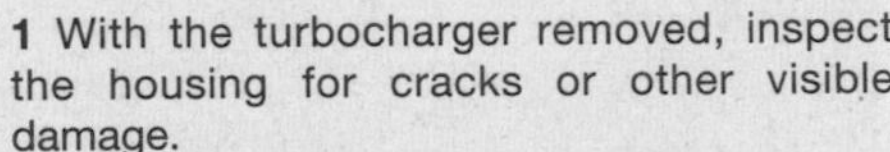

1 With the turbocharger removed, inspect the housing for cracks or other visible damage.

2 Spin the turbine or the compressor wheel to verify that the shaft is intact and to feel for excessive shake or roughness. Some play is normal since in use the shaft is 'floating' on a film of oil. Check that the wheel vanes are undamaged.

3 The wastegate actuator is a separate unit, and can be renewed independently of the turbocharger. Consult a Renault dealer or other specialist if it is thought that testing or renewal is necessary.

4 If the exhaust or inlet passages are oil-contaminated, the turbo shaft oil seals have probably failed. On the inlet side, this will also have contaminated the intercooler, which if necessary should be flushed with a suitable solvent.

5 Check the oil feed and return pipes for contamination or blockage and clean if necessary.

6 No DIY repair of the turbocharger is possible. A new unit may be available on an exchange basis.

32 Boost pressure fuel delivery corrector (turbo models) – general information

Note: *The following information is only applicable to F8Q engine models. On F9Q engines fuel metering and turbo boost pressure are controlled by the injection ECU.*

This device is mounted on the side of the injection pump, and its purpose is to adjust the injection pump fuel metering in relation to the turbocharger boost pressure. Effectively, the quantity of fuel injected is increased as the boost pressure increases.

An adjustment screw is provided, but this is sealed at the factory, and no attempt should be made to carry out adjustments without the use of specialist test equipment.

If a fault with the device is suspected, consult a Renault dealer or a suitably-qualified specialist.

33 Intercooler (turbo models) – removal and refitting

Removal

1 The intercooler is located at the front left-hand side of the engine compartment, behind the front bumper.

2 Remove the front bumper as described in Chapter 11.

3 Loosen the securing clamps, and disconnect the intake duct connecting the turbocharger to the inlet manifold from the intercooler **(see illustration)**.

4 Working from outside the wing panel, unscrew the two bolts securing the intercooler mounting bracket to the body panel. Where applicable, also remove the bracket mounting nut **(see illustration)**.

5 Working at the inner edge of the intercooler, remove the bolt securing the clamp plate to the body panel, and withdraw the clamp plate.

6 Push the intercooler up to release the upper securing clip from the lip of the body panel (the clip is visible from the engine compartment), then withdraw the intercooler

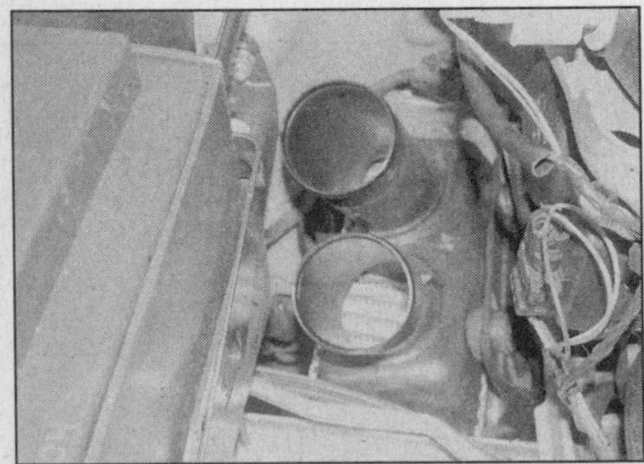

33.3 Intercooler inlet and outlet stubs (left-hand front corner of the engine compartment)

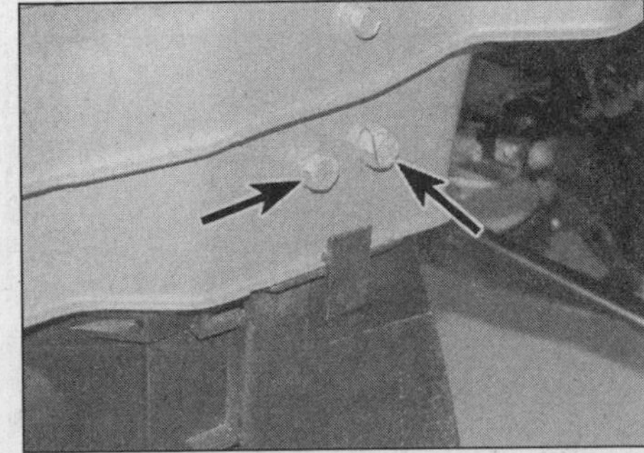

33.4 Intercooler mounting bolts (arrowed)

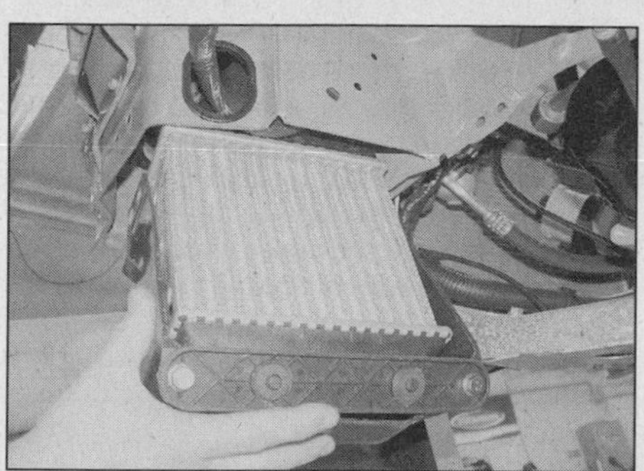

33.6 Lowering the intercooler and bracket from the body

and bracket assembly from under the vehicle **(see illustration)**.

7 The intercooler can be removed from its bracket after unscrewing the two securing bolts on early models, or releasing it from the mounting rubbers **(see illustration)**.

Refitting

8 Refitting is a reversal of removal, bearing in mind the following points.

a) When positioning the assembly, take care not to damage the wiring harness located beneath the wheelarch.

b) Ensure that the upper securing clip is correctly located on the body panel (push the intercooler upwards until the clip engages over the lip of the body panel).

c) Ensure that the intake duct securing clamps are securely tightened.

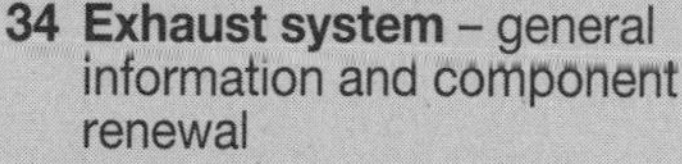

34 Exhaust system – general information and component renewal

General information

1 On new vehicles, the exhaust system consists of just two sections; the front downpipe and the remaining system consisting of a catalytic converter or resonator (according to model), and the tailpipe and silencer. The downpipe is attached to the rear section by a flanged joint with gasket.

2 The rear section of the exhaust is located above the rear suspension. The system is suspended throughout its entire length by rubber mountings.

Removal

3 To remove a part of the system, first jack up the front or rear of the car, and support it on axle stands (see *Jacking and vehicle support*). Alternatively, position the car over an inspection pit, or on car ramps. Where fitted, remove the engine compartment undertray.

Front pipe

4 Where applicable, unbolt the front pipe from the mounting bracket.

5 Unscrew and remove the nuts/bolts securing the front pipe flange joint to the manifold or turbocharger (as applicable), and recover the gasket.

33.7 Removing the intercooler from its bracket

6 Unscrew and remove the flange bolts, and disconnect the front pipe from the catalytic converter or intermediate section. Withdraw the pipe from under the vehicle.

Catalytic converter (except F9Q 732)

7 Unscrew and remove the flange bolts attaching the front pipe to the catalytic converter and recover the gasket.

8 If the original rear section is fitted, it must be cut just behind the catalytic converter using either a hacksaw or pipe cutter. The cutting point is marked with two circular punch marks on the side of the pipe. The punch marks are 90 mm apart and the exhaust section should be cut at the mid-point between the two punch marks. **Note:** *Ensure that the exhaust pipe is cut squarely else it will be difficult to obtain a gas-tight seal when the exhaust is refitted.*

9 With the intermediate pipe cut, withdraw the catalytic converter from under the vehicle.

Catalytic converter (F9Q 732)

10 The front subframe must be lowered in order to remove the catalytic converter on F9Q 732 engines. First apply the handbrake, then jack up the front of the vehicle and support it on axle stands (see *Jacking and vehicle support*). For improved access, remove both front roadwheels.

11 Each subframe mounting bolt must be replaced by a threaded rod so that the subframe may be lowered 40 mm at the front and 60 mm at the rear. Unscrew the first bolt and screw in the threaded rod, then fit a nut and washer and tighten. Replace all of the bolts in the same way.

12 Unbolt the subframe tie-rods on each side.

13 Unscrew and remove the clamp bolt securing the steering intermediate column to the steering gear (refer to Chapter 10 if necessary).

14 Unbolt the rear engine mounting link with reference to Chapter 2C.

15 Progressively unscrew the nuts and lower the subframe to the amounts given in paragraph 11. At the same time release the intermediate column from the steering gear.

16 Unbolt the exhaust mounting bracket, then unscrew and remove the catalytic converter mounting bolts and withdraw it from under the vehicle taking care not to damage the underbody heat shields. Recover the gasket **(see illustrations)**.

34.16a Catalytic converter and turbocharger on the rear of the F9Q 732 engine

34.16b Unbolt the lower bracket . . .

4B

34.16c . . . and stay . . .

34.16d . . . then unbolt the catalytic converter from the turbocharger . . .

34.16e . . . and recover the gasket

Intermediate pipe (and resonator)

17 On models without a catalytic converter, unscrew and remove the flange bolts attaching the front pipe to the intermediate pipe and recover the gasket.

18 On models with a catalytic converter, remove the catalytic converter as described in paragraphs 7 to 9.

19 If the original rear section is fitted, it must be cut in half using either a hacksaw or pipe cutter. The cutting point is marked with two circular punch marks on the side of the pipe. The punch marks are 90 mm apart and the exhaust section should be cut at the mid-point between the two punch marks. **Note:** *Ensure that the exhaust pipe is cut squarely else it will be difficult to obtain a gas-tight seal when the exhaust is refitted.*

20 With the intermediate pipe cut, withdraw the intermediate exhaust section from under the vehicle.

21 If the rear section is already in two halves, unscrew the bolt and slide the clamp sleeve onto the rear section then release the rubber mountings and withdraw the intermediate section from under the vehicle.

Rear tailpipe and silencer

22 If the original rear section is fitted, follow the instructions given in paragraph 8.

23 If the rear section is in two halves, unscrew the bolt and slide the clamp sleeve onto the intermediate section then release the rubber mountings and withdraw the tailpipe and silencer from under the vehicle.

Heat shield(s)

24 The heat shields are secured to the underside of the body by various nuts and bolts. Each shield can be removed separately but note that they overlap making it necessary to loosen another section first. If a shield is being removed to gain access to a component located behind it, it may prove sufficient in some cases to remove the retaining nuts and/or bolts, and simply lower the shield, without disturbing the exhaust system.

Refitting

25 Each section is refitted by reversing the removal sequence, noting the following points:

a) *Ensure that all traces of corrosion have been removed from the flanges, and renew all necessary gaskets.*
b) *Inspect the rubber mountings for signs of damage or deterioration, and renew as necessary.*
c) *When reconnecting sections which have been cut, apply a smear of exhaust system jointing paste (Renault recommend the use of Sodicam) to the sleeve inner surface, to ensure a gas-tight seal. Make sure both inner ends of the cut pipe are positioned squarely against the stop of the clamp sleeve. Position the sleeve bolt vertically on the left-hand side of the pipe and securely tighten the nut until it is heard to click; the clamp bolt has a groove in it to ensure that the nut is correctly tightened (equivalent to a tightening torque of approximately 25 Nm/18 lbf ft).*
d) *Prior to tightening the exhaust system fasteners, ensure that all rubber mountings are correctly located, and that there is adequate clearance between the exhaust system and vehicle underbody.*

Chapter 4 Part C:
Emissions control systems

Contents

Degrees of difficulty

Easy, suitable for novice with little experience 	**Fairly easy,** suitable for beginner with some experience 	**Fairly difficult,** suitable for competent DIY mechanic 	**Difficult,** suitable for experienced DIY mechanic 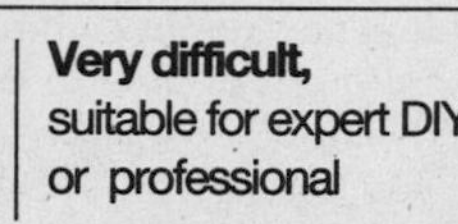	**Very difficult,** suitable for expert DIY or professional

Specifications

Engine designation

Petrol models:	
1.4 litre engine	E7J 764, K4J 750
1.6 litre engine	K4M 700, K4M 701
2.0 litre engine	F4R 740, F4R 741
Diesel models:	
Non-turbo engines – D models	F8Q 620, F8Q 622, F8Q 788
Turbo engines:	
dT models – indirect injection	F8Q 784, F8Q 786
dTi models – direct injection	F9Q 730, F9Q 734
dCi models – direct common-rail injection	F9Q 732

General

EGR solenoid valve resistance:	
F8Q 620 and F8Q 784 engines	10.0 ± 5.0 ohms
F8Q 622, F9Q 730, F9Q 732 and F9Q 734 engines	8.0 ± 0.5 ohms at 20°C
F8Q 788 engine	5.5 ± 1.0 ohms
EGR sensor resistance:	
F8Q 622 and F9Q 732 engines	4000 ohms at 20°C
EVAP solenoid valve resistance:	
K4J 750 and K4M 700 engines	26.0 ± 4.0 ohms at 23°C
F4R 740 and F4R 741 engines	26.0 ± 4.0 ohms at 23°C
E7J 764 engine	26.0 ± 4.0 ohms at 23°C
Engines from January 1998 (valve integrated in canister)	40.0 ± 4.0 ohms
Lambda (oxygen) sensor (petrol engines):	
Heating resistance:	
F4R 740 and F4R 741 engines	9.0 ohms at ambient temperature
K4J 750 and K4M 700 engines:	
Upstream	9.0 ohms at ambient temperature
Downstream	3.4 ohms at ambient temperature
Sensor voltage at 850°C:	
Rich mixture:	
F4R 740 and F4R 741 engines	840 ± 70 mvolts
K4J 750 and K4M 700 engines (upstream sensor)	840 ± 70 mvolts
Lean mixture:	
F4R 740 and F4R 741 engines	20 ± 50 mvolts
K4J 750 and K4M 700 engines (upstream sensor)	20 ± 50 mvolts

Torque wrench settings

	Nm	lbf ft
EGR solenoid valve bolt	21	16
Lambda (oxygen) sensor – petrol engines	45	33
Steel pipe for EGR solenoid valve	21	16

4C

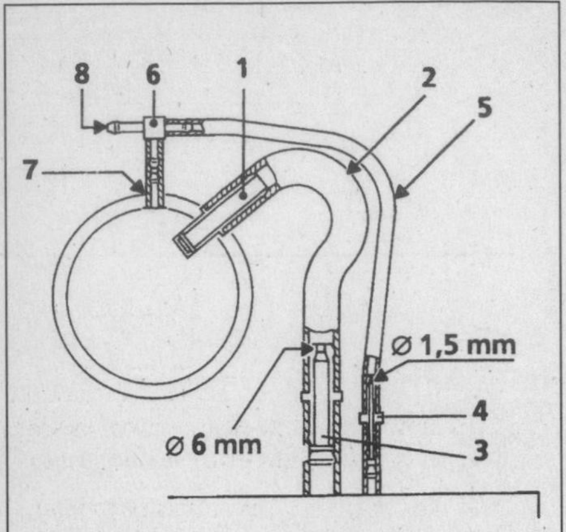

1.4a Crankcase emission control system (E7J engine)

1 Air cleaner inlet
2 Valve cover-to-air cleaner hose
3 Large restrictor
4 Small restrictor
5 Valve cover-to-inlet manifold hose
6 Tee-piece
7 Inlet manifold inlet
8 To EVAP canister

1.4b Crankcase emission control system (K4J and K4M engine)

A Oil vapour outlet

1 General information and precautions

Petrol models

1 All petrol engine models are designed to use unleaded petrol and also have various other features built into the fuel system to help minimise harmful emissions. In addition, all models are equipped with the crankcase emissions control system described below.

2 All models are also equipped with a catalytic converter and an evaporative emissions control system.

3 The emissions control systems function as follows.

Crankcase emissions control

4 To reduce the emission of unburned hydrocarbons from the crankcase into the atmosphere, the engine is sealed and the blow-by gases and oil vapour are drawn from inside the crankcase, and into the inlet manifold or throttle body to be burned by the engine during normal combustion **(see illustrations)**.

5 Under conditions of high manifold depression (idling, deceleration) the gases will be sucked positively out of the crankcase. Under conditions of low manifold depression (acceleration, full-throttle running), the gases are forced out of the crankcase by the (relatively) higher crankcase pressure; if the engine is worn, the raised crankcase pressure (due to increased blow-by) will cause some of the flow to return under all manifold conditions.

6 The crankcase ventilation hoses and restrictors should be periodically cleaned to ensure correct operation of the system.

Exhaust emissions control

7 To minimise the amount of pollutants which escape into the atmosphere, all models are fitted with a catalytic converter in the exhaust system. The system is of the closed-loop type, in which a lambda (oxygen) sensor in the exhaust system downpipe provides the fuel injection/ignition system ECU with constant feedback, enabling the ECU to adjust the mixture to provide the best possible conditions for the converter to operate. Except on K4M engines the oxygen sensor is located in the exhaust downpipe, however on the K4M engine there are two sensors, one located on the top of the exhaust manifold and the other located downstream of the catalytic converter **(see illustration)**.

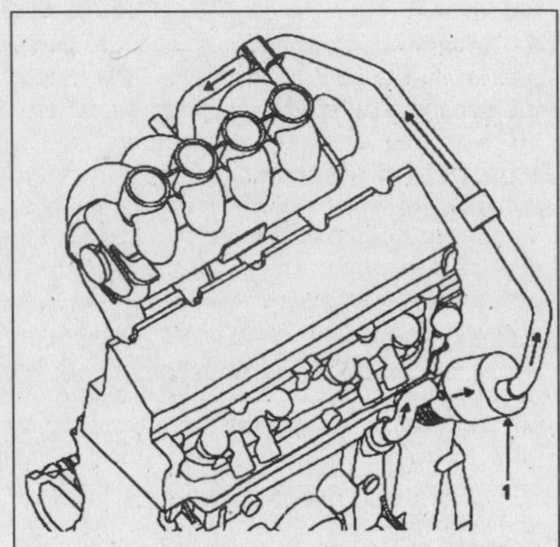

1.4c Crankcase emission control system (F8Q 788 engine)

1 Oil separator

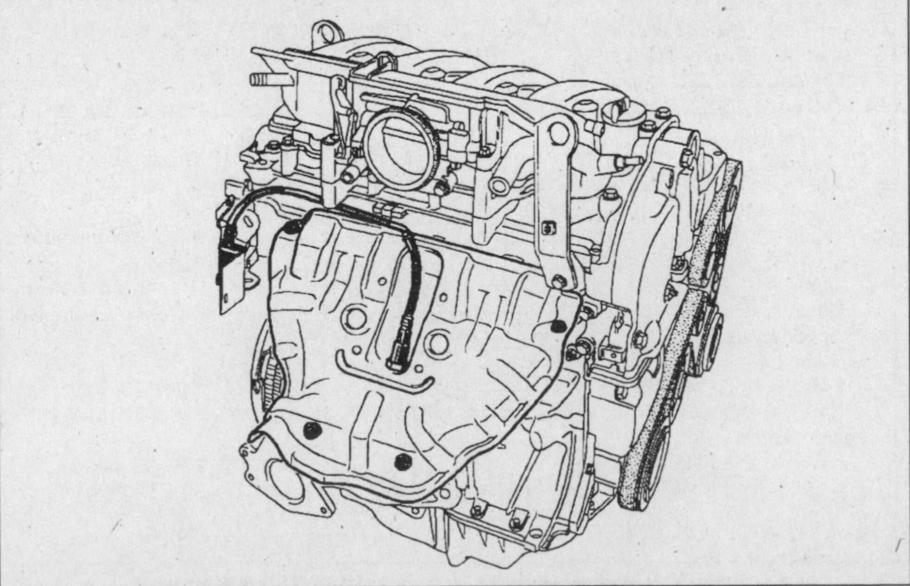

1.7 On the K4M engine, the upstream oxygen sensor is located on the exhaust manifold

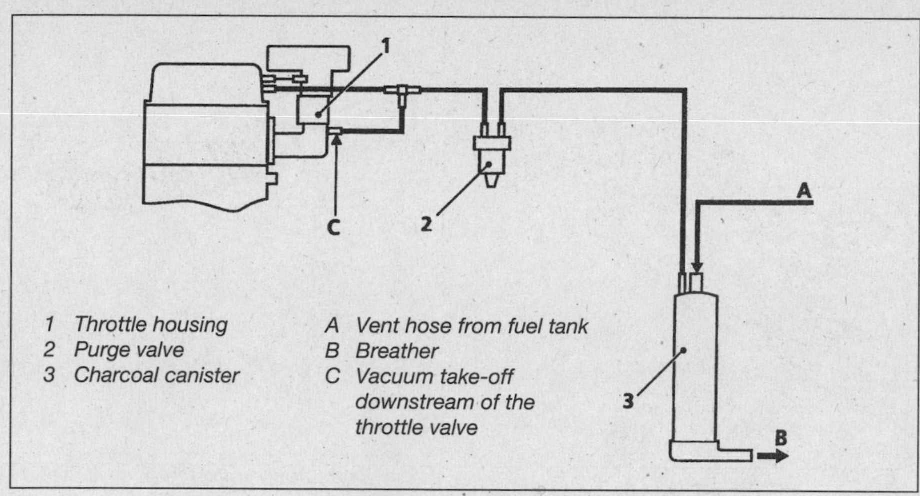

1.9a Evaporative emission control system (early E7J engine)

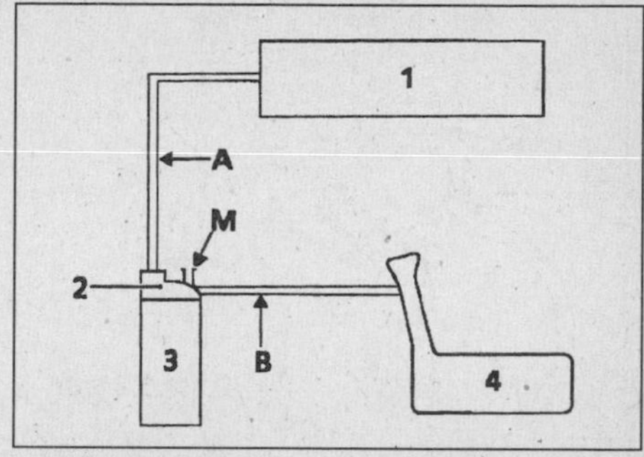

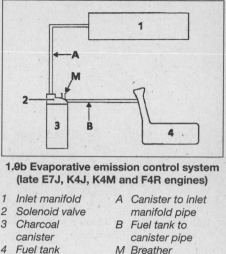

1.9b Evaporative emission control system (late E7J, K4J, K4M and F4R engines)

1 Inlet manifold
2 Solenoid valve
3 Charcoal canister
4 Fuel tank
A Canister to inlet manifold pipe
B Fuel tank to canister pipe
M Breather

8 The lambda sensor has a heating element built-in that is controlled by the ECU through the sensor relay quickly to bring the sensor's tip to an efficient operating temperature. The sensor's tip is sensitive to oxygen and sends the ECU a varying voltage depending on the amount of oxygen in the exhaust gases; if the inlet air/fuel mixture is too rich, the exhaust gases are low in oxygen so the sensor sends a low-voltage signal, the voltage rising as the mixture weakens and the amount of oxygen rises in the exhaust gases. Peak conversion efficiency of all major pollutants occurs if the inlet air/fuel mixture is maintained at the chemically-correct ratio for the complete combustion of petrol of 14.7 parts (by weight) of air to 1 part of fuel (the 'stoichiometric' ratio). The sensor output voltage alters in a large step at this point, the ECU using the signal change as a reference point and correcting the inlet air/fuel mixture accordingly by altering the fuel injector pulse width.

Evaporative emissions control

9 To minimise the escape into the atmosphere of unburned hydrocarbons, an evaporative emissions control system is also fitted to all models **(see illustrations)**. The fuel tank filler cap is sealed and a charcoal canister is mounted on the front right-hand side of the engine compartment behind the bumper mounting. The canister collects the petrol vapours generated in the tank when the car is parked and stores them until they can be cleared from the canister (under the control of the fuel injection/ignition system ECU) via the purge valve into the inlet manifold to be burned by the engine during normal combustion.

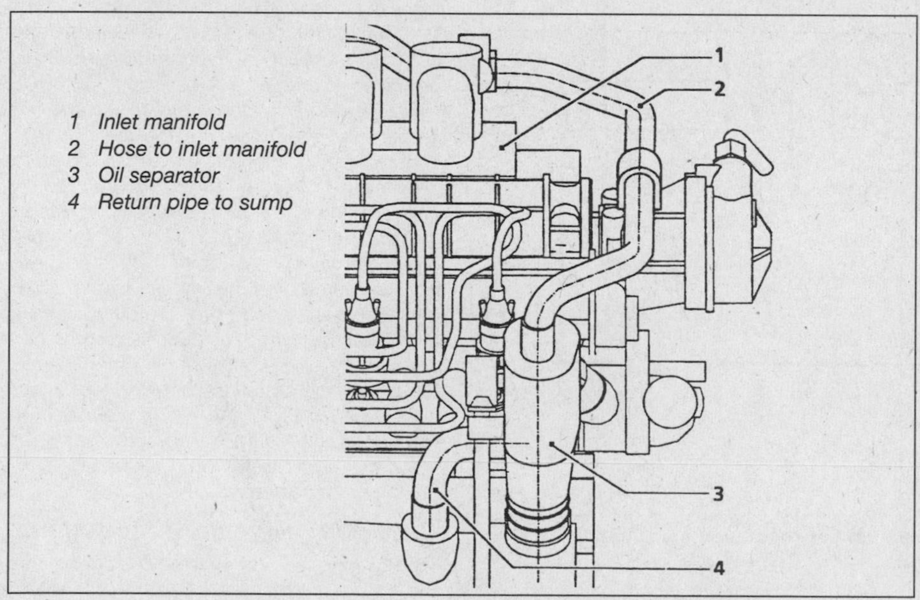

1.13a Crankcase emission control system (F8Q 620 engine)

10 To ensure that the engine runs correctly when it is cold and/or idling and to protect the catalytic converter from the effects of an over-rich mixture, the purge control valve is not opened by the ECU until the engine has warmed-up, and the engine is under load; the valve solenoid is then modulated on and off to allow the stored vapour to pass into the inlet manifold.

Diesel models

11 All diesel engine models are designed to meet strict emission requirements and are also equipped with a crankcase emissions control system. In addition to this, all models are fitted with an unregulated catalytic converter to reduce harmful exhaust emissions. To further reduce emissions, an exhaust gas recirculation (EGR) system is also fitted.

12 The emissions control systems function as follows.

Crankcase emissions control

13 To reduce the emission of unburned hydrocarbons from the crankcase into the atmosphere, the engine is sealed and the blow-by gases and oil vapour are drawn from inside the crankcase, through an oil separator located on the front left-hand side of the cylinder block, and into the inlet manifold to be burned by the engine during normal combustion **(see illustrations)**.

14 There are no restrictors in the system hoses, since the minimal depression in the inlet manifold remains constant during all engine operating conditions.

Exhaust emissions control

15 To minimise the amount of pollutants which escape into the atmosphere, an unregulated catalytic converter is fitted in the exhaust system. The catalytic converter operates remotely in the exhaust system, and there is no lambda sensor as fitted to the petrol engines.

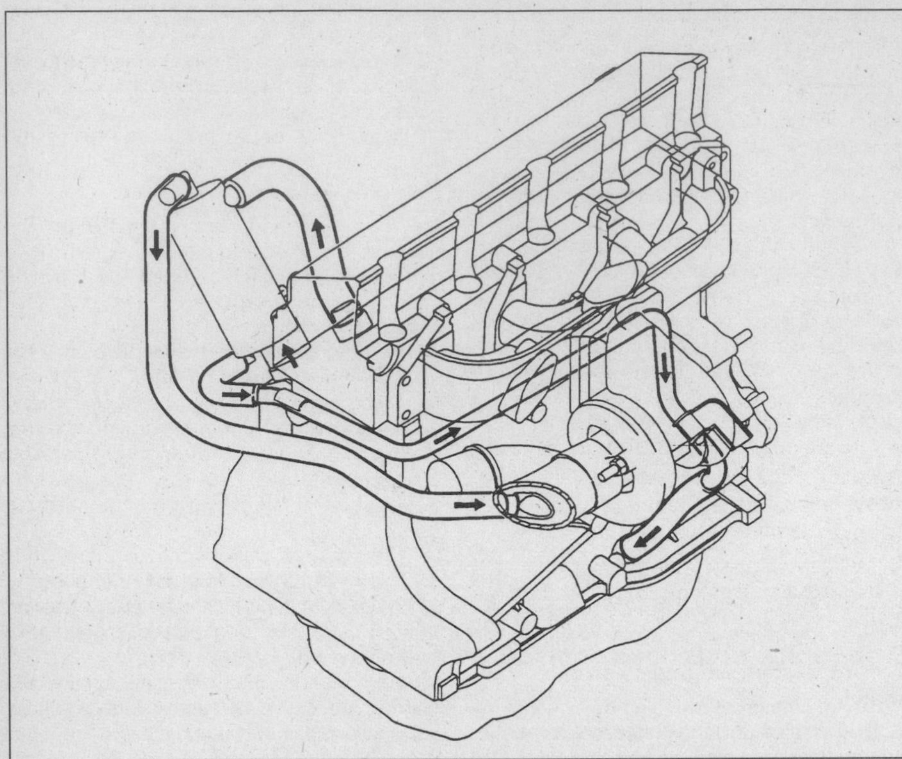

1.13b Crankcase emission control system (F8Q turbo engine)

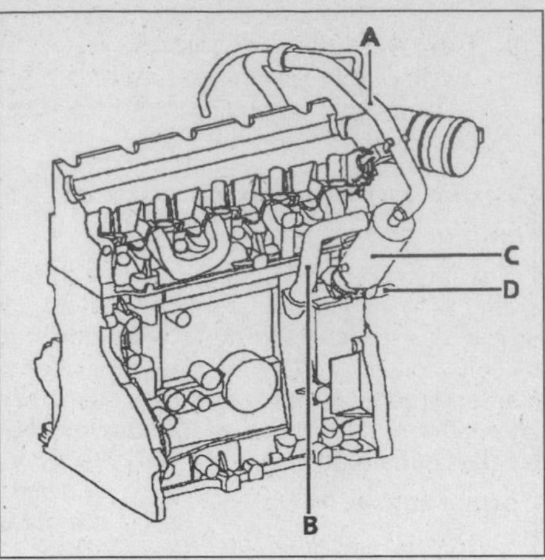

1.13c Crankcase emission control system components (F9Q 732 engine)

A Pipe to inlet manifold
B Pipe from cylinder block
C Oil separator
D Pipe linked to inlet pipes

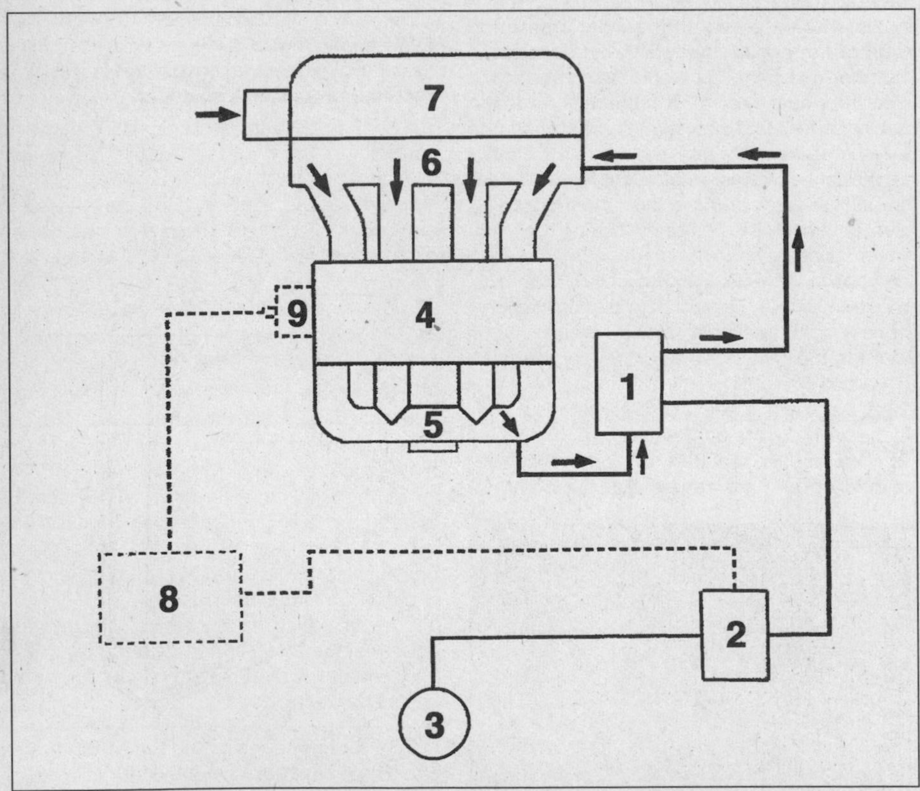

1.16 Typical schematic view of exhaust gas recirculation system

1 EGR valve
2 EGR solenoid
3 Vacuum pump
4 Engine
5 Exhaust manifold
6 Inlet manifold
7 Air filter
8 Injection computer
9 Coolant temperature sensor

Exhaust gas recirculation (EGR) system

16 The system is designed to recirculate small quantities of exhaust gas into the inlet manifold, and into the combustion chambers **(see illustration)**, reducing the level of oxides of nitrogen present in the final exhaust gas which is released into the atmosphere. The system is controlled by the engine management ECU (sometimes referred as the **D**iesel **C**ontrol **U**nit (DCU) which uses several sensors to determine when to switch the system on and off. The system is switched off at idle speed, if the air temperature is less than 16°C, if the coolant temperature is less than 45°C, or if the engine speed/load is greater than a specific threshold. The system is switched on when the vehicle reaches a speed of 6 mph.

17 The volume of exhaust gas recirculated is controlled either by a vacuum- or electrically-operated exhaust gas recirculation (EGR) valve located between the exhaust and inlet manifolds. The vacuum-operated type is controlled by a solenoid valve mounted on the bulkhead, whereas on the electrically-operated type, the solenoid valve is integral with the EGR valve. On the vacuum-operated type, vacuum is supplied by the brake vacuum pump, and the system is operated by a micro-switch on the injection pump which is also used to shut off the post-heating function and is controlled by the engine management ECU. A temperature valve fitted in the vacuum supply line cuts off the vacuum supply until the engine has warmed-up sufficiently. The electrically-operated type is regulated by the engine management ECU.

Catalytic converter precautions

18 For long life and satisfactory operation of the catalytic converter, certain precautions must be observed. These are listed in Section 4 of this Chapter.

2 Petrol engine emissions control systems – testing and component renewal

Crankcase emissions control

Testing

1 There is no specific test procedure for the crankcase emissions control system. If problems are suspected (sometimes indicated by oil contamination of the air cleaner element), check that the hoses are clean internally, and that the restrictors are not blocked or missing.

Component renewal

2 This is self-evident. Mark the various hoses before disconnecting them, if there is any possibility of confusion on reassembly.

Exhaust emissions control

Testing

3 An exhaust gas analyser (CO meter) will be needed. The ignition system must be in good condition, the air cleaner element must be clean, and the engine must be in good mechanical condition.

4 Bring the engine to normal operating temperature, then connect the exhaust gas analyser in accordance with the equipment maker's instructions.

5 Run the engine at 2500 rpm for about 30 seconds, then allow it to idle and check the CO level (Chapter 1A Specifications). If the CO level is within the specified limits, the system is operating correctly.

6 If the CO level is higher than specified, try the effect of disconnecting the lambda sensor wiring. If the CO level rises when the sensor is disconnected, this suggests that the lambda sensor is OK and that the catalytic converter is faulty. If disconnecting the sensor has no effect, this suggests a fault in the sensor.

7 If a digital voltmeter is available, the lambda sensor output voltage can be measured. Voltage should alternate between 625 to 1100 mV (rich mixture) and 0 to 80 mV (lean mixture).

8 Renew the lambda sensor if it is proved faulty.

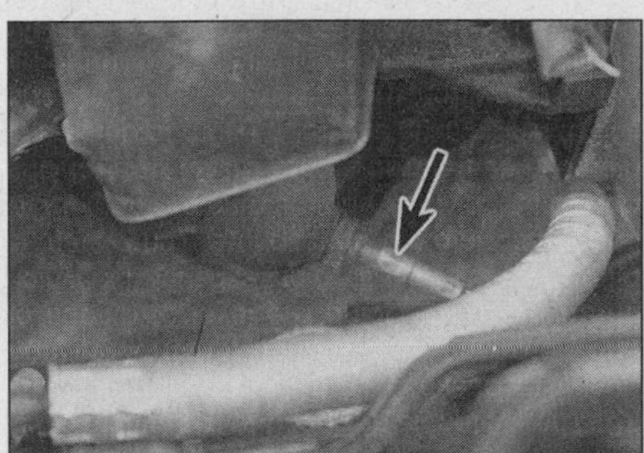

2.10 Lambda sensor viewed from inside the engine compartment (E7J engine)

Lambda sensor renewal

9 Raise the front of the vehicle and support it on axle stands (see *Jacking and vehicle support*). Where necessary, remove the engine compartment undershield. Disconnect the sensor wiring.

10 Unscrew the sensor from the exhaust manifold, downpipe or catalytic converter as applicable, and remove it **(see illustration)**.

11 Clean the threads in the exhaust pipe, and the threads of the sensor (if it is to be refitted).

12 Note that if the sensor wires are broken, the sensor must be renewed. No attempt should be made to repair them.

13 Apply high-temperature anti-seize compound to the sensor threads. Screw the sensor in by hand, then tighten it fully.

14 Reconnect the sensor wiring, refit the undershield where applicable, and lower the vehicle to the ground.

Catalytic converter renewal

15 The catalytic converter is renewed as part of the exhaust system. Refer to Part A, Section 16, of this Chapter.

Evaporative emissions control

Testing

16 The operating principle of the system is that the solenoid valve is open only when the engine is warm with the throttle at least at the part-throttle position.

17 Bring the engine to normal operating temperature, then switch it off. Connect a vacuum gauge (range 0 to 1000 mbars) into the hose between the canister and the solenoid valve. Connect a voltmeter to the solenoid valve terminals.

18 Start the engine and allow it to idle. There should be no vacuum shown on the gauge, and no voltage present at the solenoid.

19 If manifold vacuum is indicated although no voltage is present, the solenoid valve may be stuck open. Temporarily disconnect the hoses from the solenoid valve and blow through the outlets to dislodge any particles of carbon.

20 If voltage is present at idle, there is a fault in the wiring or the computer.

21 Depress the accelerator slightly. Voltage should appear momentarily at the solenoid terminals, and manifold vacuum be indicated on the gauge.

2.26 Evaporative emission canister located in the right-hand front corner of the engine compartment

22 If vacuum is not indicated even though voltage is present, either there is a leak in the hoses, or the valve is not opening.

23 If no voltage appears, there is a fault in the wiring or the computer.

Canister renewal

24 The canister is located at the front of the right-hand wheelarch. First, apply the handbrake, then jack up the front of the vehicle and support it on axle stands (see *Jacking and vehicle support*).

25 Remove the engine undertray and the right-hand front wheelarch liner.

26 Disconnect and plug the hose coming from the purge solenoid valve, and the fuel tank vent hose from the top of the canister **(see illustration)**.

27 Disconnect the wiring from the solenoid valve.

28 Unscrew and remove the mounting bolts and lower the canister from the inner body.

29 Dispose of the old canister safely, bearing in mind that it may contain liquid fuel and/or fuel vapour.

30 Fit the new canister using a reversal of the removal procedure. Make sure that the hoses are connected correctly.

Solenoid valve renewal

31 The solenoid valve is located on top of the canister, and may be accessed from the front right-hand corner of the engine compartment. First disconnect the hoses and multi-plug from the valve **(see illustration)**.

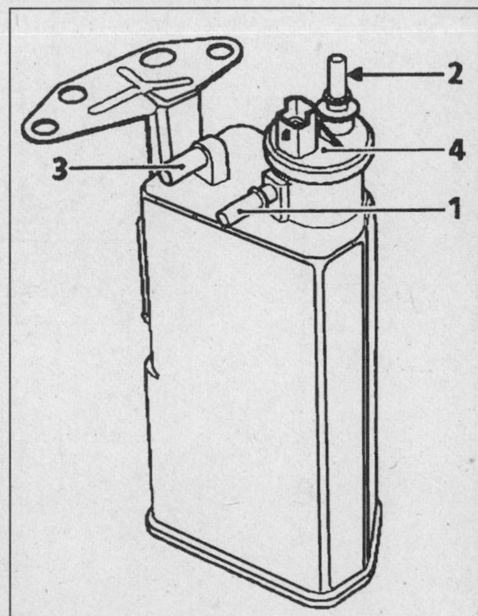

2.31 Connections to the top of the fuel evaporative canister (K4J and K4M engines)

1 *From fuel tank (quick-release connection)*
2 *To engine*
3 *Canister breather*
4 *Solenoid valve*

2.32 Evaporative emission solenoid valve (E7J engine)

32 Release the valve from its mountings and remove it **(see illustrations)**.

33 Fit the new valve using a reversal of the removal procedure. Make sure that the hoses are connected correctly.

3 Diesel engine emissions control systems – testing and component renewal

Crankcase emissions control

Testing

1 If the system is thought to be faulty, first check that the hoses are unobstructed. On high mileage vehicles, particularly when regularly used for short journeys, a jelly-like deposit may be evident inside the system

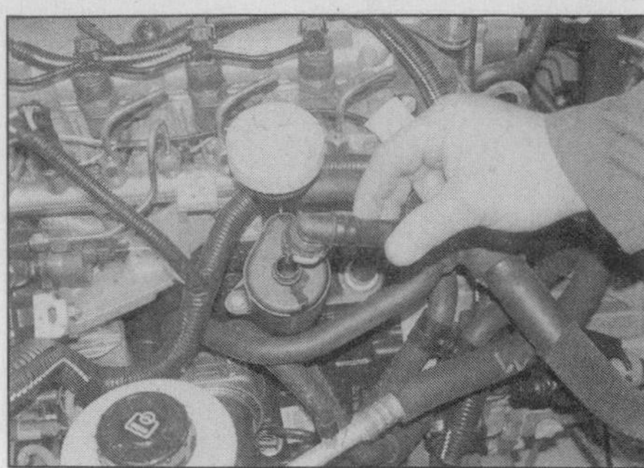

3.3 Removing the crankcase emission hose from the oil separator (F9Q 732 engine)

hoses and oil separators. If excessive deposits are present, the relevant component(s) should be removed and cleaned.

2 Periodically inspect the system components for security and damage, and renew them as necessary.

Component renewal

3 This is self-evident. Mark the various hoses before disconnecting them, if there is any possibility of confusion on reassembly **(see illustration)**.

Exhaust emissions control

Testing

4 The system can only be tested accurately using a suitable exhaust gas analyser (suitable for use with diesel engines).

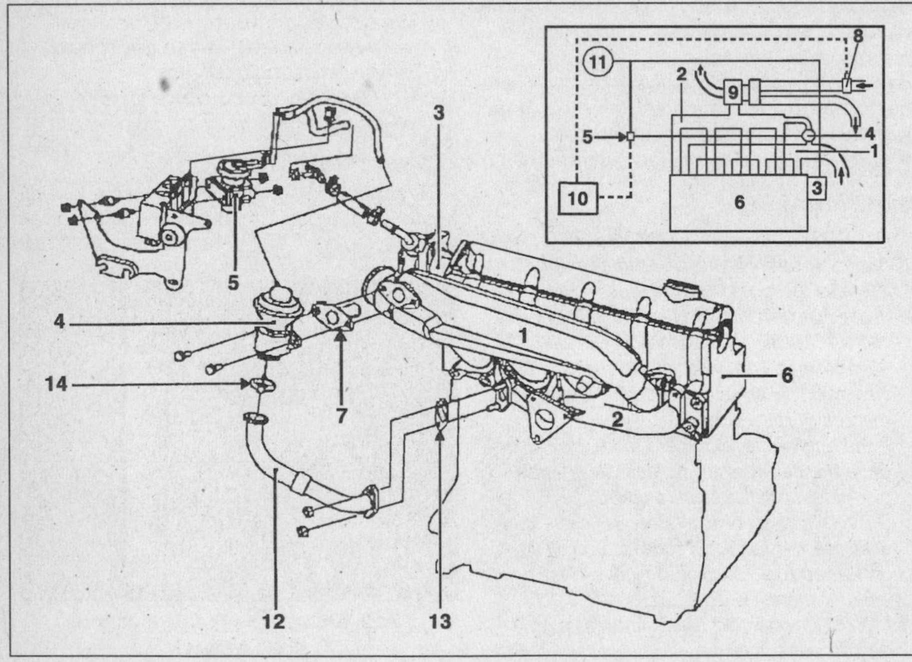

3.13 Exhaust gas recirculation components (F9Q engine)

1 Inlet manifold	*6 Cylinder head*	*11 Brake servo*
2 Exhaust manifold	*7 Venturi*	*12 Steel pipe*
3 Vacuum pump	*8 Flow meter*	*13 Seal*
4 EGR valve	*9 Turbocharger*	*14 Clamp*
5 EGR solenoid valve	*10 Computer*	

Catalytic converter renewal

5 The catalytic converter is renewed as part of the exhaust system. Refer to Part B of this Chapter.

Exhaust gas recirculation

Testing

Note: *The following procedure applies to the vacuum-operated type EGR valve only. Due to the need for Renault dedicated test equipment to test the electrically-operated type, this work should be entrusted to a Renault dealer.*

6 Start the engine, and run it until it reaches normal operating temperature (the cooling fan should have cut in and out at least once).

7 With the engine idling, disconnect the vacuum hose from the recirculation valve. As the hose is disconnected, it should be possible to hear the valve click shut. If no click is heard, proceed as follows.

8 Check that vacuum is present at the recirculation valve end of the vacuum hose. If a vacuum gauge is available, check that the vacuum is at least 500 mbars. If vacuum is present, it is likely that the recirculation valve is faulty (jammed or pierced diaphragm). If no vacuum is present, carry out the following checks.

9 Check the security of all vacuum hose connections.

10 Check the electrical feed to the solenoid valve.

11 Check the operation of the temperature valve. This can be done by checking that vacuum will pass through the valve with the engine at normal operating temperature. Stop the engine and disconnect the temperature valve vacuum hoses at the recirculation valve and the solenoid valve, and check that it is possible to blow through the hoses. If not, it is likely that the temperature valve is faulty, or the hoses are obstructed.

12 Check the operation of the post-heating systems as described in Chapter 5C, Section 1.

Vacuum-operated EGR valve renewal

Note: *Where applicable, new gaskets should be used on refitting.*

13 The valve is located at the rear of the engine, and is either bolted or pressed into the exhaust manifold or inlet manifold. The valve is connected to the remaining manifold via a metal pipe bolted between the valve and the manifold **(see illustration)**.

14 Disconnect the vacuum hose from the valve.

15 Where the valve is secured with bolts, remove the bolts and disconnect the valve pipe from the inlet or exhaust manifold, as applicable. Recover the gasket. Unbolt the valve body from the relevant manifold, and recover the gasket. Remove the valve complete with the pipe.

16 Where the valve is pressed into the manifold, it is recommended that the manifold

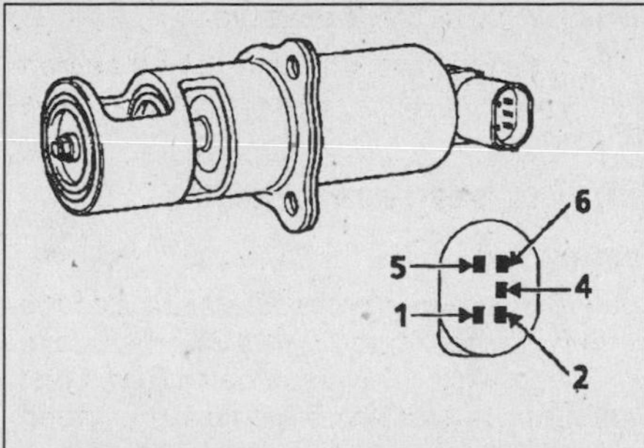

3.19 Electrically-operated EGR valve

1 *Solenoid supply*
2 *Sensor supply*
4 *Sensor earth*
5 *Solenoid earth*
6 *Sensor output*

is removed from the engine and a suitable press used to remove the valve. Refer to Chapter 4B for the manifold removal and refitting information.

17 Where necessary, unscrew the securing bolts or release the clamp, and transfer the pipe to the new valve, using a new gasket.

18 Refitting is a reversal of removal, using new gaskets where applicable.

Electrically-operated EGR valve renewal

19 Disconnect the wiring from the valve located on the left-hand end of the inlet manifold **(see illustration)**.

20 Mark the valve and manifold in relation to each other to ensure correct refitting, then unscrew the bolts and withdraw the valve from the manifold **(see illustration)**. Recover the gasket.

21 Refitting is a reversal of removal, but clean the mounting surfaces and use a new gasket.

Solenoid valve (vacuum-operated EGR valve) renewal

22 The valve is located on a bracket attached to the engine compartment bulkhead **(see illustration)**.

23 Disconnect the wiring plug and the vacuum hoses from the valve.

24 Unscrew the securing nut(s), and withdraw the valve complete with its bracket.

25 Refitting is a reversal of removal, ensuring that the vacuum hoses are securely reconnected.

Temperature valve renewal (F8Q engines)

26 The temperature valve is located in the coolant hose at the left-hand front corner of the cylinder block.

27 To remove the valve, simply disconnect the wiring plug and unscrew the valve from the hose. Be prepared for coolant spillage.

3.20 Electrically-operated EGR valve (F9Q 732 engine)

28 Refitting is reversal of removal, but check for coolant leaks on completion, and if necessary, top-up the coolant level.

Altimetric capsule renewal

Note: *on F8Q turbo engines and on F9Q engines the altimetric capsule is incorporated in the ECU and cannot be separated from it.*

29 The capsule is located on the front left-hand wheelarch behind the headlight in the engine compartment **(see illustration)**.

30 Disconnect the wiring plug from the capsule, then unscrew the securing nut(s) and withdraw the capsule.

31 Refitting is a reversal of removal.

4 Catalytic converter – general information and precautions

The catalytic converter is a reliable and simple device which needs no maintenance in itself, but there are some facts of which an owner should be aware if the converter is to function properly for its full service life.

Petrol models

a) DO NOT use leaded petrol (or LRP) in a car equipped with a catalytic converter – the lead will coat the precious metals, reducing their converting efficiency and will eventually destroy the converter.

b) Always keep the ignition and fuel systems well-maintained in accordance with the manufacturer's schedule.

c) If the engine develops a misfire, do not drive the car at all (or at least as little as possible) until the fault is cured.

d) DO NOT push- or tow-start the car – this will soak the catalytic converter in unburned fuel, causing it to overheat when the engine does start.

e) DO NOT switch off the ignition at high engine speeds.

3.22 Vacuum-operated EGR solenoid valve location

f) DO NOT use fuel or engine oil additives – these may contain substances harmful to the catalytic converter.

g) DO NOT continue to use the car if the engine burns oil to the extent of leaving a visible trail of blue smoke.

h) Remember that the catalytic converter operates at very high temperatures. DO NOT, therefore, park the car on dry undergrowth, over long grass or piles of dead leaves after a long run.

i) Remember that the catalytic converter is FRAGILE – do not strike it with tools during servicing work or drop it.

j) In some cases a sulphurous smell (like that of rotten eggs) may be noticed from the exhaust. This is common to many catalytic converter-equipped cars and once the car has covered a few thousand miles the problem should disappear.

k) The catalytic converter, used on a well-maintained and well-driven car, should last for between 50 000 and 100 000 miles – if the converter is no longer effective it must be renewed.

Diesel models

Refer to the information given in parts f, g, h, and i of the petrol models information given above.

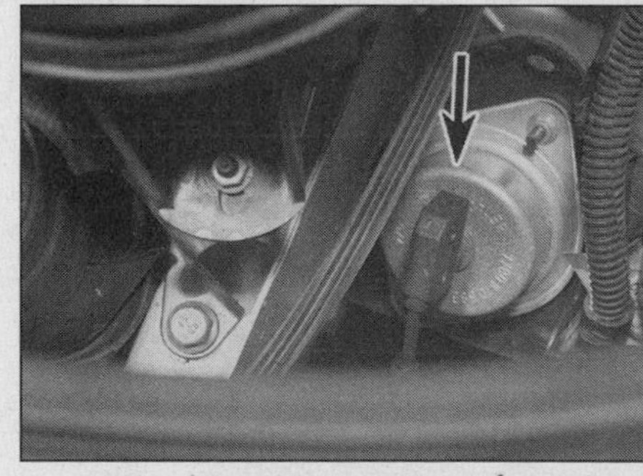

3.29 Altimetric capsule location (F8Q engine)

Notes

Chapter 5 Part A:
Starting and charging systems

Contents

Degrees of difficulty

Easy, suitable for novice with little experience 

Fairly easy, suitable for beginner with some experience 

Fairly difficult, suitable for competent DIY mechanic 

Difficult, suitable for experienced DIY mechanic 

Very difficult, suitable for expert DIY or professional

Specifications

Engine designation

Petrol models:	
1.4 litre engine	E7J 764, K4J 750
1.6 litre engine	K4M 700, K4M 701
2.0 litre engine	F4R 740, F4R 741
Diesel models:	
Non-turbo engines – D models	F8Q 620, F8Q 622, F8Q 788
Turbo engines:	
dT models – indirect injection	F8Q 784, F8Q 786
dTi models – direct injection	F9Q 730, F9Q 734
dCi models – direct common-rail injection	F9Q 732

Battery

Type:	
All models except Scénic	Lead-acid, low-maintenance or 'maintenance-free'
Scénic models	'Maintenance-free' only
Charge condition:	
Poor	12.5 volts
Normal	12.6 volts
Good	12.7 volts

Alternator

Type	Valeo or Bosch
Output:	
K4J and K4M engines	75, 98 or 110 amps (according to model)
F4R engine	98 amps
F9Q engine	75, 80 or 120 amps (according to model)
All other engines	75 or 110 amps (depending on model)
Regulated voltage	13.5 to 14.8 volts

Starter motor

Type	Valeo, Bosch or Mitsubishi (depending on model)

Torque wrench setting

Torque wrench setting	Nm	lbf ft
Alternator	25	18

1 General information and precautions

General information

The engine electrical system consists mainly of the charging and starting systems. Because of their engine-related functions, these components are covered separately from the body electrical devices such as the lights, instruments, etc (which are covered in Chapter 12). On petrol engine models, refer to Part B for information on the ignition system, and on diesel models, refer to Part C for information on the pre-heating system.

The electrical system is of the 12 volt negative earth type.

The battery is of the low maintenance or 'maintenance-free' (sealed for life) type, and is charged by the alternator, which is belt-driven from the crankshaft pulley.

The starter motor is of the pre-engaged type, incorporating an integral solenoid. On starting, the solenoid moves the drive pinion into engagement with the flywheel ring gear before the starter motor is energised. Once the engine has started, a one-way clutch prevents the motor armature being driven by the engine until the pinion disengages from the flywheel.

Battery disconnection and information – general

On Mégane models, the battery is located in the right-hand rear bulkhead area of the engine compartment.

On early Scénic models, the battery is located in a special compartment beneath the right-hand front seat and the positive lead is extended to a secondary terminal unit in the engine compartment, however on later models it is located in the engine compartment. For all operations requiring battery disconnection on early models, the battery positive lead should be disconnected at the secondary terminal unit which is accessible after removing the terminal unit cover **(see illustration)**. On later Scénic and all Mégane models, disconnect the negative terminal from the battery located in the engine compartment.

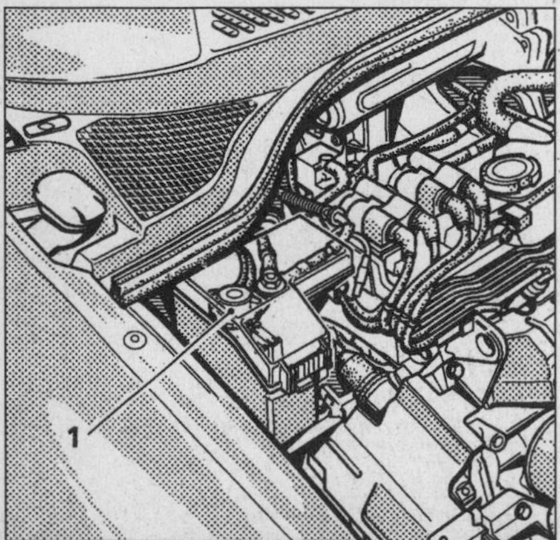

1.6 Battery positive terminal (1) in the secondary terminal unit on Scénic models

Note: *On early models, if the engine is being started using jump leads and a slave battery, use the secondary terminal for the positive, red-coloured, lead connection, not the battery post itself. This also applies when connecting a battery charger.*

Precautions

Warning: It is necessary to take extra care when working on the electrical system, to avoid damage to semi-conductor devices (diodes and transistors), and to avoid the risk of personal injury. In addition to the precautions given in 'Safety first!' at the beginning of this manual, observe the following when working on the system:

Always remove rings, watches, etc, before working on the electrical system. Even with the battery disconnected, capacitive discharge could occur if a component's live terminal is earthed through a metal object. This could cause a shock or nasty burn.

Do not reverse the battery connections. Components such as the alternator, electronic control units, or any other components having semi-conductor circuitry could be irreparably damaged

Never disconnect the battery terminals, the alternator, any electrical wiring or any test instruments with the engine running.

Do not allow the engine to turn the alternator when the alternator is not connected.

Never 'test' for alternator output by 'flashing' the output lead to earth.

Never use an ohmmeter of the type incorporating a hand-cranked generator for circuit or continuity testing.

Always ensure that the battery negative lead is disconnected when working on the electrical system.

If the engine is being started using jump leads and a slave battery, connect the batteries ***positive-to-positive*** and ***negative-to-negative*** (see *Jump starting* at the beginning of the manual). This also applies when connecting a battery charger.

Before using electric-arc welding equipment on the car, ***disconnect the battery, alternator and components such as the electronic control units*** to protect them from the risk of damage.

The radio/cassette unit fitted as standard equipment by Renault is equipped with a built-in security code, to deter thieves. If the power source to the unit is cut, the anti-theft system will activate. Refer to 'Disconnecting the battery' in the Reference Section.

Caution: If the radio/cassette in your vehicle is equipped with an anti-theft system, make sure you have the correct activation code before disconnecting the battery

2 Electrical fault finding – general information

Refer to Chapter 12.

3 Battery – testing and charging

Note: *The following information does not apply to gel-type batteries fitted to early Scénic models.*

Standard and low maintenance battery – testing

1 If the vehicle covers a small annual mileage, it is worthwhile checking the specific gravity of the electrolyte every three months to determine the state of charge of the battery. Use a hydrometer to make the check and compare the results with the following table (the temperatures quoted are ambient temperatures). Note that the specific gravity readings assume an electrolyte temperature of 15°C (60°F); for every 10°C (18°F) below 15°C (60°F) subtract 0.007. For every 10°C (18°F) above 15°C (60°F) add 0.007.

	Above 25°C	Below 25°C
Fully-charged	*1.210 to 1.230*	*1.270 to 1.290*
70% charged	*1.170 to 1.190*	*1.230 to 1.250*
Discharged	*1.050 to 1.070*	*1.110 to 1.130*

2 If the battery condition is suspect, first check the specific gravity of electrolyte in each cell. A variation of 0.040 or more between any cells indicates loss of electrolyte or deterioration of the internal plates.

3 If the specific gravity variation is 0.040 or more, the battery should be renewed. If the cell variation is satisfactory but the battery is discharged, it should be charged as described later in this Section.

Maintenance-free battery – testing

4 In cases where a 'sealed for life' maintenance-free battery is fitted, topping-up and testing of the electrolyte in each cell is not possible. The condition of the battery can therefore only be tested using a battery condition indicator or a voltmeter.

5 Certain models may be fitted with a 'Delco' type maintenance-free battery, with a built-in charge condition indicator. The indicator is located in the top of the battery casing, and indicates the condition of the battery from its colour. If the indicator shows green, then the battery is in a good state of charge. If the indicator turns darker, eventually to black, then the battery requires charging, as described later in this Section. If the indicator shows clear/yellow, then the electrolyte level in the battery is too low to allow further use, and the battery should be renewed. **Do not** attempt to charge, load or jump start a battery when the indicator shows clear/yellow.

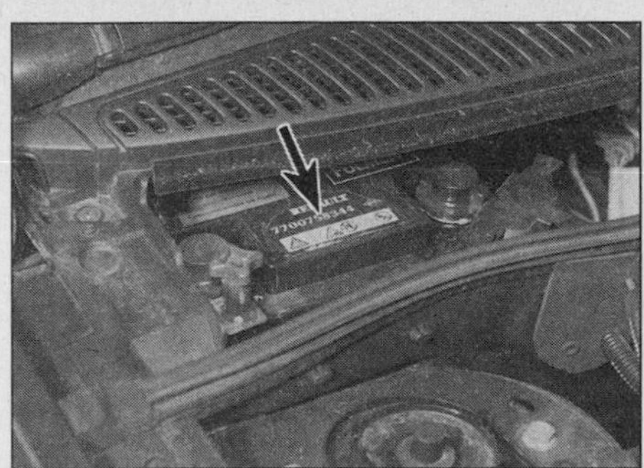

4.1 On Mégane models, the battery is located at the right-hand rear of the engine compartment

4.2a Unscrew the mounting screws . . .

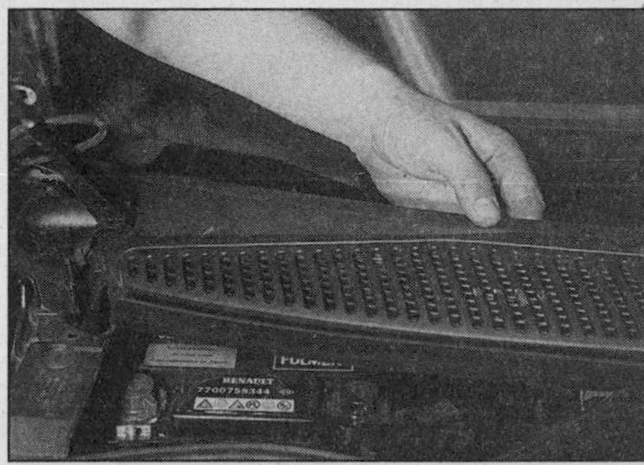

4.2b . . . and remove the scuttle grille from the right-hand side of the bulkhead

6 If testing the battery using a voltmeter, connect it to the terminals and compare the result with that given in the Specifications. The test is only accurate if the battery has not been subjected to any kind of charge for the previous six hours. If this is not the case, switch on the headlights for 30 seconds, then wait four to five minutes before testing the battery after switching off the headlights. All other electrical circuits must be switched off, so check that the doors and tailgate/bootlid are fully shut when making the test.

7 If the voltage reading is less than 12.2 volts, then the battery is discharged, whilst a reading of 12.2 to 12.4 volts indicates a partially-discharged condition.

8 If the battery is to be charged, remove it from the vehicle (Section 4) and charge it as described later in this Section.

Standard and low-maintenance battery – charging

Note: *The following is intended as a guide only. Always follow the maker's recommendations (often printed on a label attached to the battery) before charging a battery.*

9 Charge the battery at a rate of 3.5 to 4 amps, and continue to charge the battery at this rate until no further rise in specific gravity is noted over a four-hour period.

10 Alternatively, a trickle charger charging at the rate of 1.5 amps can safely be used overnight.

11 Specially-rapid 'boost' charges which are claimed to restore the power of the battery in 1 to 2 hours are not recommended, as they can cause serious damage to the battery plates through overheating.

12 While charging the battery, note that the temperature of the electrolyte should never exceed 37.8°C (100°F).

Maintenance-free battery – charging

Note: *The following is intended as a guide only. Always follow the maker's recommendations (often printed on a label attached to the battery) before charging a battery.*

13 This battery type takes considerably longer to fully recharge than the standard type, the time taken being dependent on the extent of discharge, but it can take anything up to three days.

14 A constant voltage type charger is required, to be set, when connected, to 13.9 to 14.9 volts with a charger current below 25 amps. Using this method, the battery should be usable within three hours, giving a voltage reading of 12.5 volts, but this is for a partially discharged battery and, as mentioned, full charging can take considerably longer.

15 If the battery is to be charged from a fully discharged state (condition reading less than 12.2 volts), have it recharged by your Renault dealer or local automotive electrician, as the charge rate is higher and constant supervision during charging is necessary.

4 Battery – removal and refitting

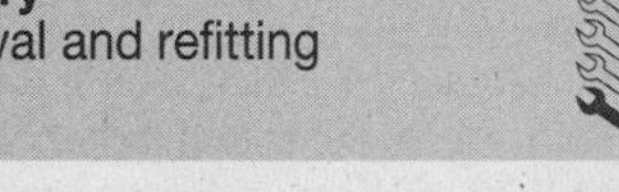

Removal

Early Mégane models

1 The battery is located in the right-hand rear bulkhead area of the engine compartment **(see illustration)**.

2 Unscrew the mounting screws, and remove the scuttle grille from the right-hand side of the bulkhead compartment in front of the windscreen. The inner end of the grille must be unclipped from the left-hand grille **(see illustrations)**.

3 Loosen the plastic terminal nut and disconnect the clamp from the battery negative (earth) terminal.

4 Loosen the plastic terminal nut and disconnect the positive terminal lead in the same way **(see illustration)**.

5 Unscrew the special bolt and remove the battery retaining clamp **(see illustrations)**.

6 Lift the battery out of the bulkhead compartment.

7 If necessary, remove the battery tray.

Early Scénic models

8 The battery is located in a special compartment beneath the right-hand front seat.

9 Slide the seat fully rearward, then release

5A

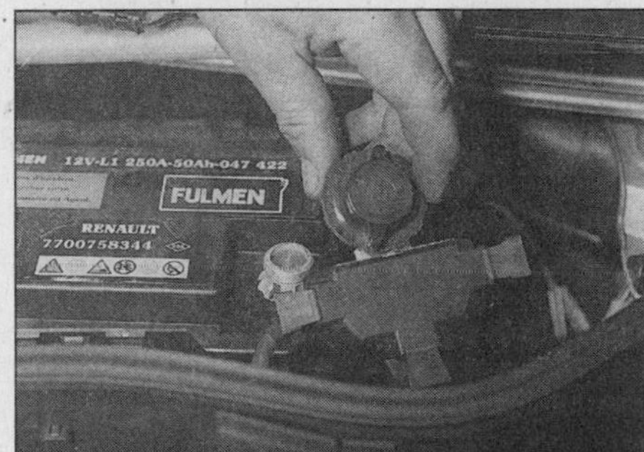

4.4 Removing the positive terminal lead from the battery

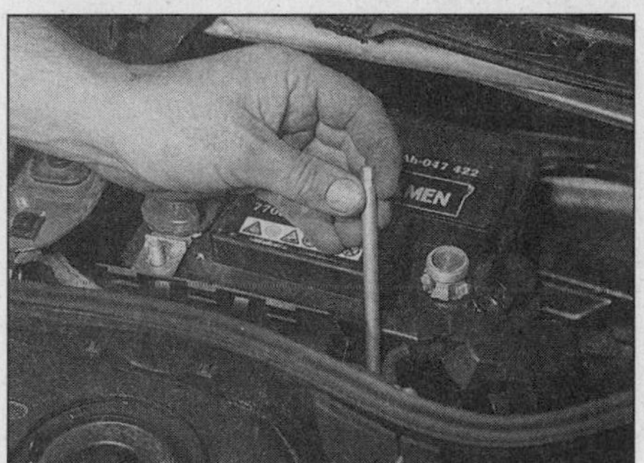
4.5a Unscrew the special bolt . . .

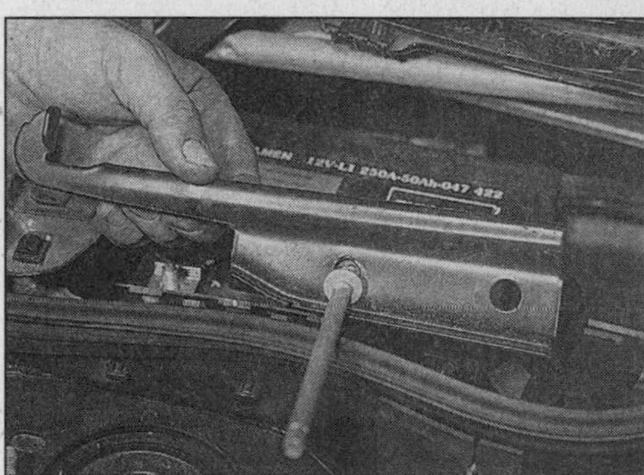

4.5b . . . and remove the battery retaining clamp

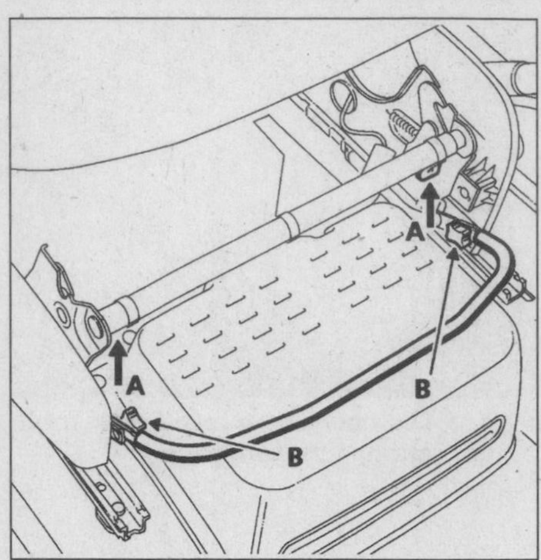

4.9 On early Scénic models, release the two levers (A) on the tilt locking bar, then slacken the two nuts (B) on the longitudinal adjustment bar

the two levers on the tilt locking bar **(see illustration)**.

10 Slacken the two nuts on the longitudinal adjustment bar and lift the bar upwards. Tilt the seat backwards for access to the battery cover.

11 Turn the two cover fasteners a quarter turn anti-clockwise and lift off the cover.

12 Slacken the terminal nut and disconnect the clamp from the battery negative (earth) terminal.

13 Slacken the terminal nut and disconnect the positive terminal lead in the same way.

14 Unscrew the two bolts and remove the battery retaining clamp.

15 Lift the battery out of the tray and remove it from the vehicle.

Later Mégane and Scénic models

16 The battery is located on the left-hand side of the engine compartment.

17 Unscrew the clamp bolt and disconnect the negative lead from the battery **(see illustration)**.

18 Lift the protective cover then unscrew the clamp bolt and disconnect the positive lead from the battery **(see illustration)**.

19 Unscrew the bolt and remove the battery mounting clamp **(see illustration)**.

4.17 Disconnecting the negative battery terminal

20 Where fitted, slide the insulator from the battery, then lift and remove the battery from the engine compartment. If necessary, the tray may be unbolted from the inner body panel **(see illustrations)**.

Refitting

21 Refitting is a reversal of removal, but smear petroleum jelly on the terminals when reconnecting the leads, and always reconnect the positive lead first, and the negative lead last. When refitting the battery cover on early Scénic models, turn the two fasteners a quarter turn clockwise until the reference marks align.

5 Charging system – testing

Note: *Refer to the warnings given in 'Safety first!' and in Section 1 of this Chapter before starting work.*

1 If the ignition warning light fails to illuminate when the ignition is switched on, first check the alternator wiring connections for security. If satisfactory, check that the warning light bulb has not blown, and that the bulbholder is secure in its location in the instrument panel (see Chapter 12). If the light still fails to illuminate, check the continuity of the warning light feed wire from the alternator to the bulbholder. If all is satisfactory, the alternator

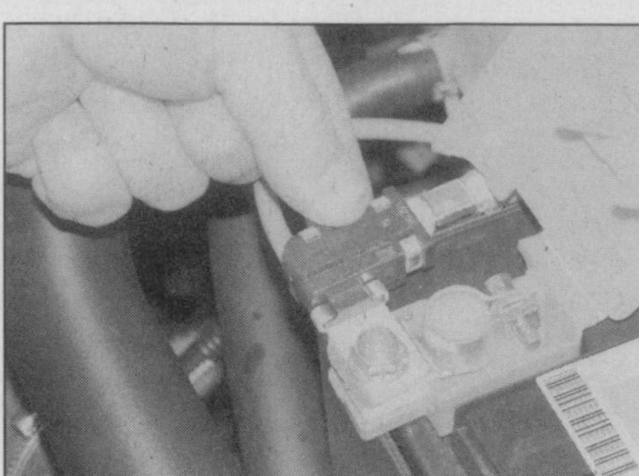
4.18 Disconnecting the positive battery terminal

is at fault, and should be renewed or taken to an auto-electrician for testing and repair.

2 If the ignition warning light illuminates when the engine is running, stop the engine and check that the drivebelt is correctly tensioned (see Chapter 1A or 1B) and that the alternator connections are secure. If all is so far satisfactory, have the alternator checked by an auto-electrician for testing and repair.

3 If the alternator output is suspect even though the warning light functions correctly, the regulated voltage may be checked as follows.

4 Connect a voltmeter across the battery terminals and start the engine. On early Scénic models, connect the voltmeter positive lead to the secondary terminal unit in the engine compartment and the negative lead to a good earth point.

5 Increase the engine speed until the voltmeter reading remains steady; the reading should be approximately 12 to 13 volts, and no more than 14 volts.

6 Switch on as many electrical accessories (eg, the headlights, heated rear window and heater blower) as possible, and check that the alternator maintains the regulated voltage at around 13 to 14 volts.

7 If the regulated voltage is not as stated, the fault may be due to worn brushes, weak brush springs, a faulty voltage regulator, a faulty diode, a severed phase winding, or worn or damaged slip rings. The alternator should be renewed or taken to an auto-electrician for testing and repair.

4.19 Battery mounting clamp bolt

4.20a Removing the insulator from the battery

4.20b Removing the battery tray

6 Alternator drivebelt – removal, refitting and tensioning

Refer to the procedure given for the auxiliary drivebelt(s) in the appropriate part of Chapter 1.

7 Alternator – removal and refitting

Removal

1 Disconnect the battery negative lead (refer to Section 1). Release the auxiliary drivebelt tension as described in Chapter 1A or 1B and disengage the drivebelt from the alternator pulley. **Note:** *Renault recommend that the drivebelt be renewed whenever it is disturbed.*

E7J engine

2 If not already done for drivebelt removal, apply the handbrake, then jack up the front of the vehicle and support on axle stands (see *Jacking and vehicle support*). Remove the right-hand roadwheel, the engine undershield and the wheelarch liner. Access to the alternator is best achieved from underneath the vehicle.

3 If the drivebelt is to be renewed on models without air conditioning, remove the power steering drivebelt first as described in Chapter 1A. If it is not being renewed, there is no need to remove the power steering drivebelt.

4 Remove the rubber covers (where fitted) from the alternator terminals, then unscrew the retaining nuts and disconnect the wiring from the rear of the alternator **(see illustrations)**.

5 Loosen the pivot and adjusting bolt and swivel the alternator towards the engine. Slip the drivebelt from the pulley.

6 Unscrew and remove the alternator upper adjusting bolt.

7 Unscrew and remove the alternator lower pivot bolt, and temporarily support the alternator.

8 Disconnect the steering track rod end from the right-hand swivel hub with reference to Chapter 10.

9 On all models except Scénic, unscrew and remove the right-hand suspension strut upper mounting bolts from the top of the suspension turret with reference to Chapter 10.

10 On Scénic models, remove the bolt securing the subframe front support bar to the wing valance, and the nut securing it to the lower arm front pivot and remove the support bar. Remove the subframe rear support bar in the same way. With reference to Chapter 10, remove the two nuts and washers from the bolts securing the swivel hub to the suspension strut, noting that the nuts are positioned on the rear side of the strut. Withdraw the bolts and support the swivel hub assembly.

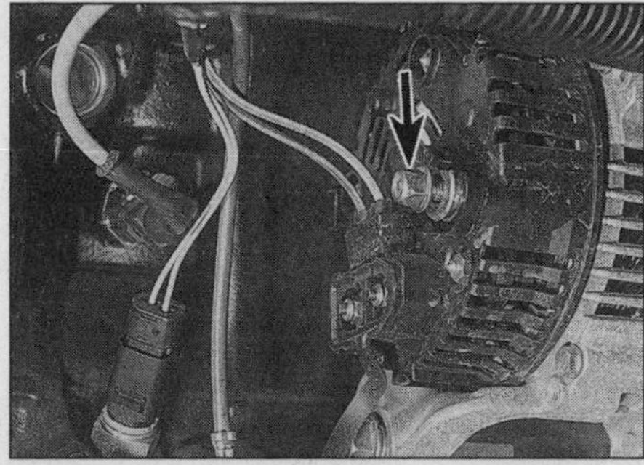

7.4a Main battery cable retaining nut on the alternator B+ terminal

11 Under the vehicle, have an assistant pull or lever the right-hand suspension downwards as far as possible, while the alternator is being removed through the wheelarch inner panel.

F4R engine

12 If not already done for drivebelt removal, apply the handbrake, then jack up the front of the vehicle and support on axle stands (see *Jacking and vehicle support*). Remove the right-hand roadwheel, the engine undershield and the wheelarch liner. Access to the alternator is best achieved from underneath the vehicle.

13 Remove the power steering fluid reservoir from its mounting and position it to one side.

14 Remove the power steering fluid pipe from the multifunction unit support.

15 Refer to Chapter 10 and remove the power steering pump pulley, pump and mounting bracket **(see illustration)**. Position the pump to one side.

16 Remove the rubber covers (where fitted) from the alternator terminals, then unscrew the retaining nuts and disconnect the wiring from the rear of the alternator.

17 Unscrew the alternator mounting bolts and nuts and remove the unit from the engine.

K4J and K4M engines

18 If not already done for drivebelt removal,

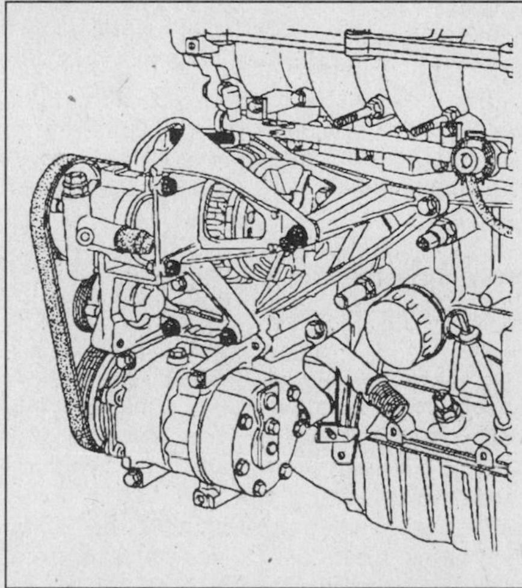

7.15 On the F4R engine, the power steering pump mounting bracket must be removed for access to the alternator

7.4b Disconnecting the wiring from the rear of the alternator

apply the handbrake, then jack up the front of the vehicle and support on axle stands (see *Jacking and vehicle support*). Remove the right-hand roadwheel, the engine undershield and the wheelarch liner. Access to the alternator is best achieved from underneath the vehicle.

19 Unclip the power steering fluid reservoir from the cooling fan assembly and position it to one side.

20 Remove the rubber covers (where fitted) from the alternator terminals, then unscrew the retaining nuts and disconnect the wiring from the rear of the alternator.

21 Unscrew the alternator mounting bolts and nuts and remove the unit from the engine.

F9Q engine

22 Remove the rubber covers (where fitted) from the alternator terminals, then unscrew the retaining nuts and disconnect the wiring from the rear of the alternator **(see illustration)**.

23 Release the fuel filter from its mounting then unclip the power steering fluid reservoir and position it to one side.

24 On the F9Q 732 engine, release the air conditioning pipe from its support on the right-hand side of the engine compartment. Also, unbolt the wiring loom support near the alternator.

25 On the F9Q 730 and F9Q 734 engine models, disconnect the wiring from the injection computer, then unbolt it and move it to one side.

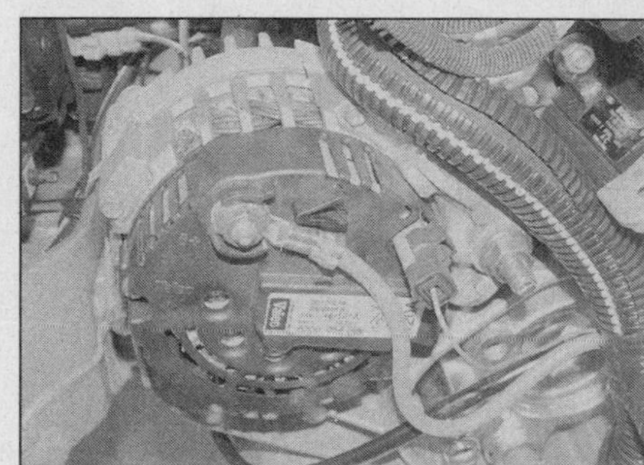

7.22 Wiring on the rear of the alternator (F9Q 732 engine)

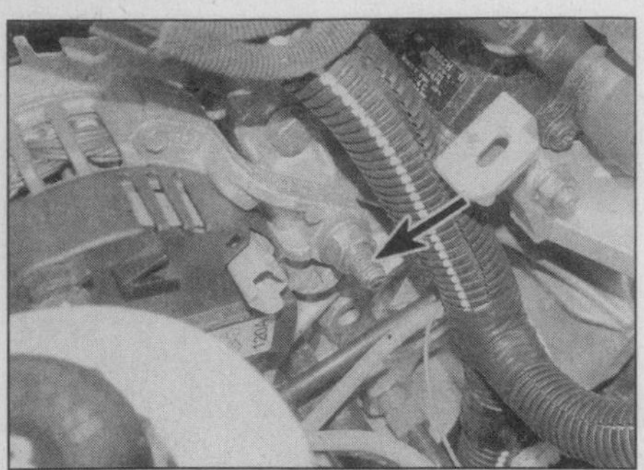

7.28a Alternator mounting bolt (engine side)

7.28b Removing the alternator from the engine (F9Q engine)

7.28c Alternator removed from the engine

26 Remove the auxiliary drivebelt as described in Chapter 1B. Note that the drivebelt tensioner bracket must be marked for position before removal. Rotate the bracket anti-clockwise to release the tension, using a suitable tool engaged with the 9.35 mm square.

27 Unbolt and remove the drivebelt tensioner.

28 Unscrew the alternator mounting bolts and remove the unit from the engine **(see illustrations)**.

F8Q engine

29 Just behind the alternator, unscrew the bolt from the fuel pipe support bracket, and position the bracket to one side.

30 If the drivebelt is to be renewed, raise the front of the vehicle and support on axle stands (see *Jacking and vehicle support*), then unbolt and remove the lower timing cover.

31 Remove the rubber covers (where fitted) from the alternator terminals, then unscrew the retaining nuts and disconnect the wiring from the rear of the alternator.

32 Unscrew and remove the mounting bolts, slip the drivebelt from the pulley, then withdraw the alternator from the engine.

Refitting

33 Refitting is a reversal of removal. Refer to Chapter 10 for torque wrench settings applicable to the suspension and steering components, and to Chapter 1A or 1B for details of fitting and tensioning the drivebelt(s).

8 Alternator – testing and overhaul

If the alternator is thought to be suspect, it should be removed from the vehicle and taken to an automotive electrician for testing. Most auto-electricians will be able to supply and fit brushes at a reasonable cost. However, check on the cost of repairs before proceeding, as it may prove more economical to obtain a new or exchange alternator.

9 Starting system – testing

Note: *Refer to the precautions given in 'Safety first!' and in Section 1 of this Chapter before starting work.*

1 If the starter motor fails to operate when the ignition key is turned to the appropriate position, the following may be the possible causes:

a) The battery is faulty.
b) The electrical connections between the switch, solenoid, battery and starter motor are somewhere failing to pass the necessary current from the battery through the starter to earth.
c) The solenoid is faulty.
d) The starter motor is mechanically or electrically defective.

2 To check the battery, switch on the headlights. If they dim after a few seconds, this indicates that the battery is discharged. If this is the case, recharge (see Section 3) or renew the battery. If the headlights glow brightly, operate the ignition switch and observe the lights. If they dim, then this indicates that current is reaching the starter motor, therefore the fault must lie in the starter motor. If the lights continue to glow brightly (and no clicking sound can be heard from the starter motor solenoid), this indicates that there is a fault in the circuit or solenoid (see following paragraphs). If the starter motor turns slowly when operated, but the battery is in good condition, then this indicates that either the starter motor is faulty, or there is considerable resistance somewhere in the circuit.

3 If a fault in the circuit is suspected, disconnect the battery leads (including the earth connection to the body), the starter/solenoid wiring and the engine/transmission earth strap. Thoroughly clean the connections, and reconnect the leads and wiring, then use a voltmeter or test lamp to check that full battery voltage is available at the battery positive lead connection to the solenoid, and that the earth is sound.

HAYNES HiNT ***Smear petroleum jelly around the battery terminals to prevent corrosion – corroded connections are amongst the most frequent causes of electrical system faults.***

4 If the battery and all connections are in good condition, check the circuit by disconnecting the wire from the solenoid terminal. Connect a voltmeter or test lamp between the wire end and a good earth (such as the battery negative terminal), and check that the wire is live when the ignition switch is turned to the 'start' position. If it is, then the circuit is sound. If it is not, then the circuit wiring can be checked as described in Chapter 12.

5 If the circuit is sound, the fault must lie in the starter motor. In this event, it may be possible to have the starter motor overhauled by a specialist, but check on the cost of spares before proceeding, as it may prove more economical to obtain a new or exchange motor.

10 Starter motor – removal and refitting

Removal

1 Disconnect the battery negative lead (refer to Section 1).

E7J engine

2 Remove the air cleaner housing as described in Chapter 4A.

3 Firmly apply the handbrake, then jack up the front of the vehicle and support it on axle stands (see *Jacking and vehicle support*). Remove the engine undershield where fitted.

4 Where fitted, unbolt and remove the support bracket from the rear of the starter motor.

5 Unscrew the nut and disconnect the main cable from the starter motor solenoid. Recover the washers under the nuts.

10.6 Disconnecting the starter motor solenoid trigger wire

10.7a Unscrew the starter motor mounting bolts . . .

10.7b . . . noting the location of the support bracket . . .

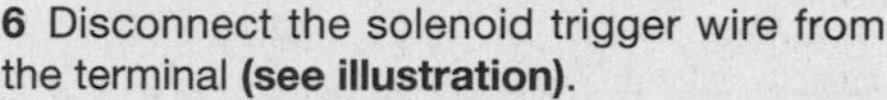

6 Disconnect the solenoid trigger wire from the terminal **(see illustration)**.

7 Unscrew and remove the three bolts securing the starter motor to the transmission housing, noting the location of the support bracket, then remove the motor downwards and out of position, noting the locating dowel which is fitted to the rear mounting bolt hole **(see illustrations)**.

K4J and K4M engines

8 Apply the handbrake, then jack up the front of the vehicle and support it on axle stands (see *Jacking and vehicle support*). Remove the front right-hand roadwheel and the engine compartment undertray.

9 Refer to Chapter 10 and disconnect the right-hand steering track rod end from the hub carrier. Also remove the upper bolt securing the hub carrier to the suspension strut, then loosen the lower bolt. Tilt the hub carrier outwards and disconnect the inner end of the driveshaft from the transmission using a lever (refer to Chapter 8).

10 In the engine compartment, remove the air resonator (refer to Chapter 4A, Section 16).

11 At the left-hand front of the engine, unscrew the nut for the starter motor supply wire and disconnect the solenoid connector.

12 Unbolt the heat shield and loosen the lower mounting for the strut on the transmission.

13 Remove the oil level sensor.

14 Unscrew the mounting bolts and withdraw the starter motor from below the engine.

F4R petrol engine

15 Apply the handbrake, then jack up the front of the vehicle and support it on axle stands (see *Jacking and vehicle support*). Remove the front right-hand roadwheel and the engine compartment undertray.

16 Refer to Chapter 10 and disconnect the right-hand steering track rod end from the hub carrier. Also remove the upper bolt securing the hub carrier to the suspension strut, then loosen the lower bolt. Tilt the hub carrier outwards and disconnect the inner end of the driveshaft from the transmission (refer to Chapter 8).

17 Unbolt the heat shield from the bottom of the starter motor, then loosen the

10.7c . . . then withdraw the starter motor from the transmission

lower mounting of the flange and remove the shield.

18 Unscrew the nut and disconnect the main wiring cable from the starter terminal, then disconnect the small wire from the solenoid.

19 In the engine compartment, remove the air inlet ducting, then unscrew and remove the starter motor mounting bolts and lower the unit to remove it.

Non-turbo diesel engined-models

20 Remove the air cleaner housing as described in Chapter 4B.

21 Firmly apply the handbrake, then jack up the front of the vehicle and support it on axle stands (see *Jacking and vehicle support*). Remove the engine undershield where fitted.

22 Undo the retaining screws and nut, and remove the protective cover from the starter motor.

23 Disconnect the wiring connector from the starter solenoid, then undo the retaining nut and disconnect the main feed cable from the solenoid. Recover the washer under the nut.

24 Undo the retaining nuts and bolts, and remove the rear mounting bracket from the starter motor.

25 Slacken and remove the three bolts securing the starter motor to the transmission housing, and remove the motor from the engine compartment. Recover the locating dowel which is fitted to the rear mounting bolt hole.

Turbo diesel engined-models

26 Firmly apply the handbrake, then jack up the front of the vehicle and support it on axle stands (see *Jacking and vehicle support*).

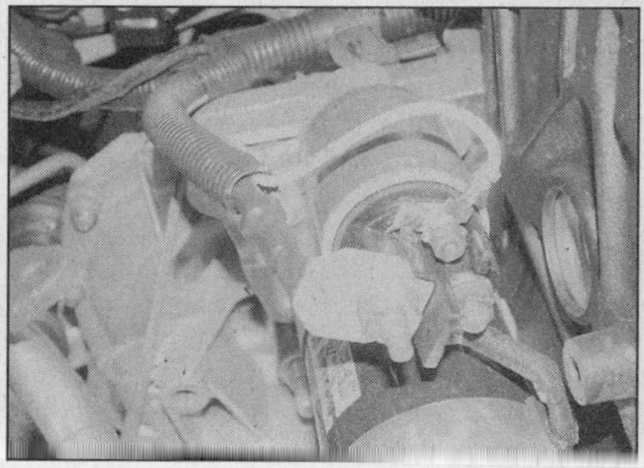

10.31 Starter motor wiring

Remove the right-hand front roadwheel and the engine undershield.

27 On Scénic models remove the scuttle panel and closure panel in front of the windscreen.

28 Loosen the securing clips, and remove the air ducting connecting the inlet manifold to the intercooler.

29 Similarly, remove the air ducting connecting the turbocharger to the intercooler.

30 As applicable, remove or disconnect the exhaust front downpipe, and remove the catalytic converter as described in Chapter 4B. On some models, it may be necessary to move the engine slightly forwards towards the front of the engine compartment. Also, where necessary, detach the oil return pipe.

31 Disconnect the wiring connector from the starter solenoid, then undo the retaining nut and disconnect the main feed cable from the solenoid **(see illustration)**. Recover the washer under the nut.

32 If fitted, remove the two support struts at the rear of the starter, using a Torx key where necessary.

33 Unscrew the three bolts securing the starter motor to the gearbox bellhousing. Where applicable, note the location of any wiring brackets secured by the bolts.

34 Depending on engine and equipment fitted, it may be possible to manipulate the starter from its location without further dismantling. However, on some models it will be necessary to proceed as described in the following paragraphs.

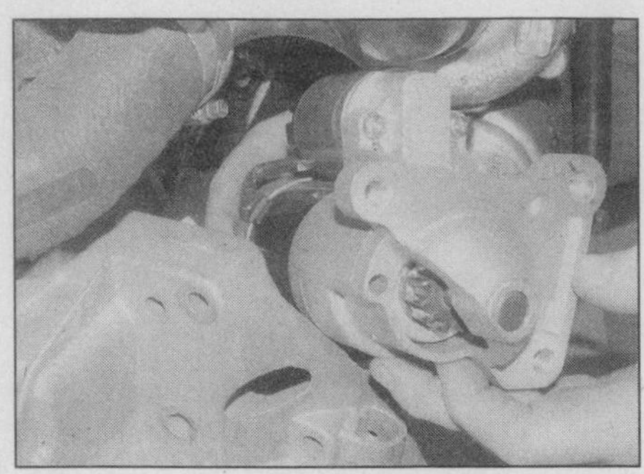

10.44a Removing the starter motor from the engine

10.44b Starter motor removed from the engine

35 Working beneath the right-hand side of the vehicle, use a pin punch to drive out the roll pin (where fitted) securing the right-hand driveshaft to the gearbox differential sun wheel stub shaft. Note that if the original double roll pin is renewed, the new one will be of single coiled type.

36 Loosen the two nuts and bolts securing the right-hand stub axle carrier to the suspension strut. Remove the upper nut and bolt, but leave the lower nut and bolt in position. Note that the nuts are on the rear side of the strut. **Note:** *Where an intermediate driveshaft if fitted to a bearing on the rear of the cylinder block, remove the driveshaft completely.*

37 Pull the top of the stub axle carrier outwards until the inner end of the driveshaft is released from the stub shaft. Support the driveshaft using string or wire – do not allow it to hang under its own weight.

38 Move the driveshaft as necessary to allow access to the two nuts securing the turbocharger oil return pipe to the cylinder block.

39 Remove the two securing nuts, and disconnect the turbocharger oil return pipe from the cylinder block. Recover the gasket. Plug the hole in the cylinder block to prevent dirt ingress.

40 Remove the nut securing the wiring bracket to the bottom of the rear starter motor mounting bracket, then disconnect the wiring from the starter motor.

41 Remove the bolt securing the turbocharger support bracket to the rear starter motor support bracket (note that the bolt also secures the heat shield). Loosen the nut and bolt securing the support bracket to the turbocharger, and pivot the support bracket clear of the starter motor.

42 Remove the nuts and bolts securing the rear starter motor mounting bracket to the engine and the starter motor.

43 Remove the remaining bolt securing the heat shield.

44 Withdraw the starter motor, rear mounting bracket and heat shield from underneath the vehicle **(see illustrations)**.

Refitting

45 Refitting is a reversal of removal, and tighten the mounting bolts securely. Where fitted, make sure that the location dowel is fitted between the starter motor and transmission housing.

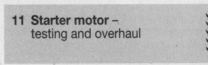

11 Starter motor – testing and overhaul

If the starter motor is thought to be suspect, it should be removed from the vehicle and taken to an auto-electrician for testing. Most auto-electricians will be able to supply and fit brushes at a reasonable cost. However, check on the cost of repairs before proceeding, as it may prove more economical to obtain a new or exchange motor.

12 Ignition switch – removal and refitting

Removal

1 Disconnect the battery negative lead (refer to Section 1).

2 Remove the steering wheel and steering column shrouds as described in Chapter 10.

3 Release the ignition switch wiring connector from its location beneath the steering column by pivoting it, then disconnect it. Note the routing of the wiring for correct refitting.

4 Unscrew and remove the mounting bolt from the ignition switch.

5 Insert the ignition key and turn it to position 3.

6 Depress the side peg and withdraw the ignition switch together with the wiring.

Refitting

7 Refitting is a reversal of removal, but make sure the wiring is correctly routed.

13 Oil pressure warning light switch – removal and refitting

Removal

1 The switch is located at the lower front right-hand side of the cylinder block, next to the oil filter **(see illustration)**.

2 Apply the handbrake, then jack up the front of the vehicle and support on axle stands (see *Jacking and vehicle support*).

3 Disconnect the wiring from the switch.

4 Unscrew the switch from the cylinder block **(see illustration)**, and recover the sealing washer. Be prepared for oil spillage, and if the switch is to be left removed from the engine, plug the hole in the cylinder block.

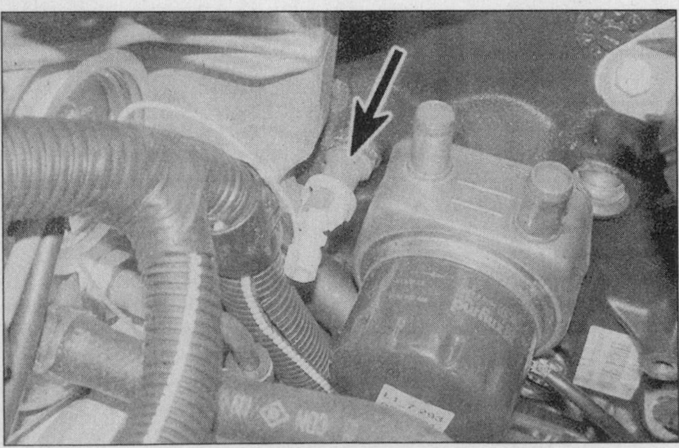

13.1 The oil pressure switch is located next to the oil filter

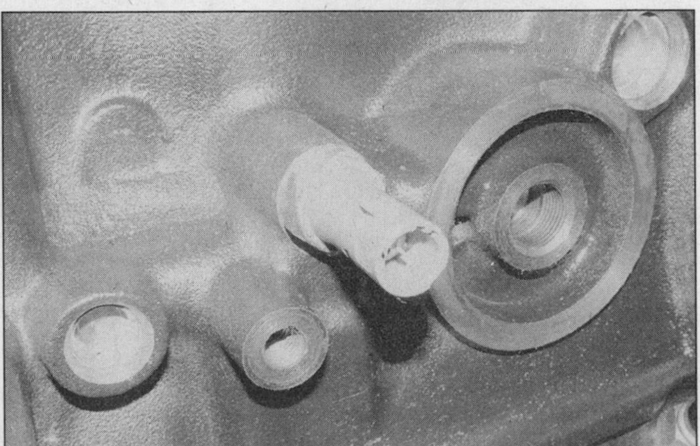

13.4 Oil pressure switch (oil filter removed)

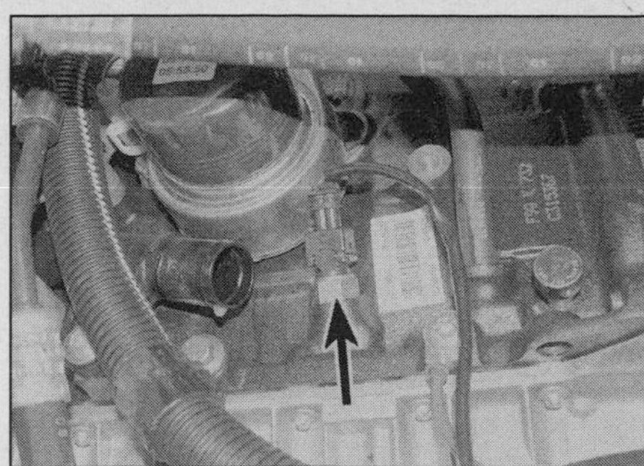

14.1 The oil level sensor is located below the oil filter

Refitting

5 Examine the sealing washer for signs of damage or deterioration, and if necessary renew it.

6 Refit the switch, complete with washer, and tighten it securely. Reconnect the wiring connector.

7 If necessary, top-up the engine oil as described in *Weekly checks*.

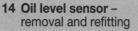

14 Oil level sensor – removal and refitting

Removal

1 The oil level sensor is located on the front of the cylinder block, below the oil filter **(see illustration)**.

2 Apply the handbrake, then jack up the front of the vehicle and support on axle stands (see *Jacking and vehicle support*).

3 Disconnect the wiring from the sensor.

4 Unscrew the sensor from the cylinder block, and recover the sealing washer. If the sensor is to be left removed from the engine, plug the hole in the cylinder block.

Refitting

5 Examine the sealing washer for signs of damage or deterioration, and if necessary renew it.

6 Refit the sensor, complete with washer, and tighten it securely. Reconnect the wiring connector.

Chapter 5 Part B:
Ignition system – petrol engines

Contents

Degrees of difficulty

Easy, suitable for novice with little experience 

Fairly easy, suitable for beginner with some experience 

Fairly difficult, suitable for competent DIY mechanic 

Difficult, suitable for experienced DIY mechanic 

Very difficult, suitable for expert DIY or professional

Specifications

General

Engine designation	
1.4 litre engine	E7J 764, K4J 750
1.6 litre engine	K4M 700, K4M 701
2.0 litre engine	F4R 740, F4R 741
Ignition system type:	
E7J engine	Fully-electronic, computer-controlled, with two dual output ignition coils serving cylinders 1 and 4, and 2 and 3
K4J, K4M and F4R engines	Fully-electronic, computer-controlled, with four individual ignition coils, one on each spark plug
Firing order	1 – 3 – 4 – 2
Location of No 1 cylinder	Flywheel end

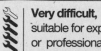

Ignition timing

Ignition timing	Controlled by the ECU

Ignition HT coil resistances

E7J engine:	
Primary resistance	0.5 ohms
Secondary resistance	11 000 ± 1000 ohms
K4J and K4M engines:	
Primary resistance	0.5 ± 0.02 ohms
Secondary resistance	7500 ± 1100 ohms
F4R engine:	
Primary resistance	0.5 ± 0.02 ohms
Secondary resistance	6800 ± 1000 ohms

Torque wrench settings

Torque wrench settings	Nm	lbf ft
Ignition coil	15	11
Knock sensor	20	15

1 Ignition system – general information and precautions

General information

The ignition system is integrated with the fuel injection system to form a combined engine management system under the control of one ECU (see Chapter 4A for further information). All engines are fitted with a distributorless ignition system.

On the E7J engine, the ignition system consists simply of two ignition HT coils formed into one unit, the crankshaft speed/position/TDC sensor and a knock sensor. Each coil supplies two cylinders (one coil supplies cylinders 1 and 4 and the other coil supplies cylinders 2 and 3). The ignition coils operate on the 'wasted spark' principle, ie, each spark plug sparks twice for every cycle of the engine, once on the compression stroke and once on the exhaust stroke.

On K4J, K4M and F4R engines, the ignition system uses one coil for each cylinder, with each coil mounted on the relevant spark plug. The coils are fed in series, two at a time, and the system operates on the 'wasted spark' principle as for the E7J engine.

The crankshaft speed/position (TDC) sensor (see Chapter 4A, Section 13 or 14) is used to determine piston position as well as engine speed.

The power module for the ignition is integrated in the engine management ECU. The ECU uses the inputs from the sensors to calculate the required ignition advance setting and coil charging time – an integral amplifier circuit within the ECU switches the ignition coil primary (LT) circuit.

The knock sensor is mounted on the cylinder block to inform the ECU when the engine is 'pinking'. Its sensitivity to a particular frequency of vibration allows it to detect the impulses which are caused by the shock waves set up when the engine starts to 'pink' (pre-ignite). The knock sensor sends an electrical signal to the ECU which retards the ignition advance setting until the 'pinking' ceases – the ignition timing is then gradually returned to the 'normal' setting. This maintains the ignition timing as close to the knock threshold as possible – the most efficient setting for the engine under normal running conditions.

Precautions

The following precautions must be observed, to prevent damage to the ignition system components and to reduce risk of personal injury.

a) *Ensure the ignition is switched off before disconnecting any of the ignition wiring.*

b) *Ensure that the ignition is switched off before connecting or disconnecting any ignition test equipment, such as a timing light.*

c) *Do not earth the coil primary or secondary circuits.*

Warning: Voltages produced by an electronic ignition system are considerably higher than those produced by conventional ignition systems. Extreme care must be taken when working on the system with the ignition switched on. Persons with surgically-implanted cardiac pacemaker devices should keep well clear of the ignition circuits, components and test equipment

Caution: If the radio/cassette in your vehicle is equipped with an anti-theft system, make sure you have the correct activation code before disconnecting the battery

2 Ignition system – testing

1 The components of ignition systems are normally very reliable; most faults are far more likely to be due to loose or dirty connections, or to 'tracking' of HT voltage due to dirt, dampness or damaged insulation than to the failure of any of the system's components. Always check all wiring thoroughly before condemning an electrical component and work methodically to eliminate all other possibilities before deciding that a particular component is faulty.

2 The old practice of checking for a spark by holding the live end of a spark plug HT lead a short distance away from the engine is not recommended; not only is there a high risk of a powerful electric shock, but the HT coil or ECU may be damaged. However, if necessary each plug can be checked individually by removing it, then reconnecting the HT lead or coil (as applicable) and connecting the body of the spark plug to a suitable earthing point on the engine using a battery 'jump' lead. It is important to make a good earth connection if using this method. Never try to 'diagnose' misfires by pulling off one HT lead at a time.

Engine will not start

3 If the engine either will not turn over at all, or only turns very slowly, first check the battery and starter motor as described in Chapter 5A.

4 If the engine turns over at normal speed but will not start, the HT circuit of the E7J engine can be checked by connecting a timing light to an HT lead (following the manufacturer's instructions) and turning the engine over on the starter motor. If the light flashes, voltage is reaching the spark plugs, so these should be removed and checked. If the light does not flash, check the spark plug HT leads themselves with reference to Chapter 1A. **Note:** *On K4J, K4M and F4R engines, the coils are mounted on each individual spark plug, so it is not possible to use a conventional timing light to check the system.*

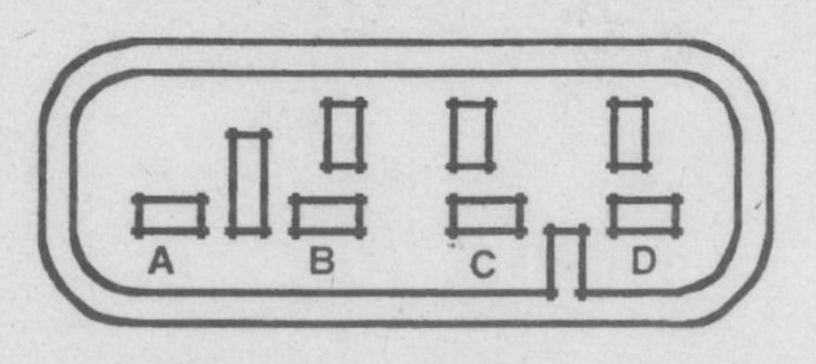

2.5 Ignition coil connector terminals (E7J engine)

A Control for cylinders 1 and 4
B Control for cylinders 2 and 3
C Supply
D Supply (internal connection)

5 If there is still no spark, use an ohmmeter to check the resistances of the coils and compare with the information given in the Specifications. On the E7J engine, the connector terminals are as shown **(see illustration)**; on other engines, the connectors can be disconnected from the coils for access to the terminals.

6 If these checks fail to reveal the cause of the problem, the vehicle should be taken to a Renault dealer for testing. A wiring block connector is incorporated in the engine management circuit, into which a special electronic diagnostic tester can be plugged. The tester will locate the fault quickly and simply, alleviating the need to test all the system components individually, which is a time-consuming operation that carries a high risk of damaging the ECU. If necessary, the system wiring and wiring connectors can be checked as described in Chapter 12, ensuring that the ECU wiring connector is first disconnected with the ignition switched off.

Engine misfires

7 An irregular misfire suggests either a loose connection or intermittent fault in the primary circuit, or an HT fault on the circuit between the coil and spark plugs.

8 With the ignition switched off, check carefully through the system ensuring that all connections are clean and securely fastened.

9 Check that the HT coil and the spark plug HT leads (where applicable) are clean and dry.

10 Regular misfiring of one spark plug may be due to a faulty spark plug, faulty injector, a faulty HT lead or loss of compression in the relevant cylinder. On E7J engines, regular misfiring of cylinders 1 and 4 only, or 2 and 3 only suggests a fault on the relevant coil. Regular misfiring of all the cylinders suggests a fuel supply fault, such as a clogged fuel filter or faulty fuel pump.

3 Ignition HT coils – removal, testing and refitting

Removal

1 Disconnect the battery negative lead (refer to Chapter 5A).

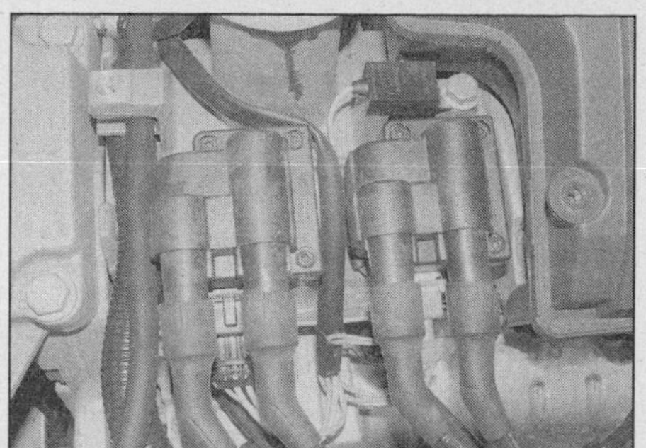

3.2 Ignition HT coils

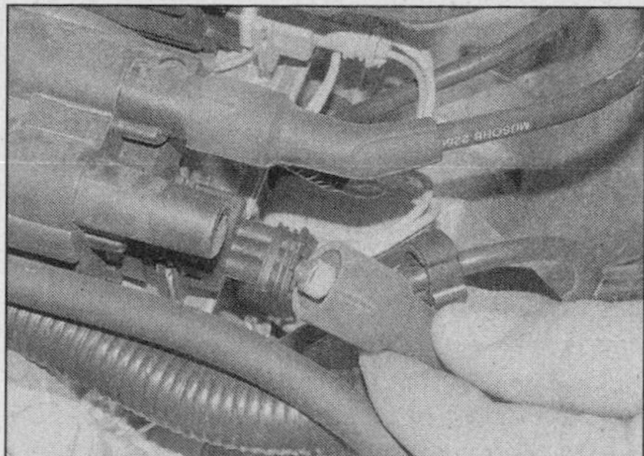

3.3a Disconnecting the HT leads from the coils . . .

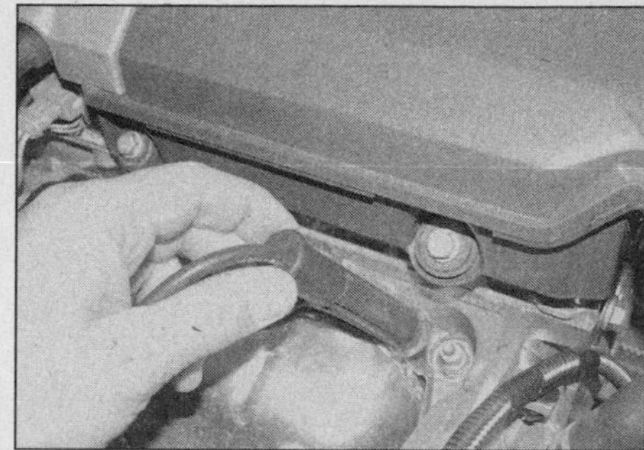

3.3b . . . and from the spark plugs

E7J engine

2 The ignition HT coils are located on the right-hand end of the camshaft cover **(see illustration)**.

3 Note their location, then disconnect the spark plug HT leads from the spark plugs and from the coils **(see illustrations)**. If necessary, identify each lead to ensure correct refitting.

4 Disconnect the wiring multiplug from each coil **(see illustration)**.

5 Undo the mounting screws and remove the coils from the mounting plate – note the location of the suppressor **(see illustration)**. **Note:** *The base of each coil is different to ensure that they only locate in one position.*

K4J, K4M and F4R engines

6 The ignition coils are accessible through the holes in the inlet manifold. First, carefully disconnect the wiring from each coil. Take care not to damage the connectors **(see illustration)**.

7 Unscrew the mounting screws and withdraw each coil off of its spark plug **(see illustrations)**.

8 Check the condition of the O-rings where the coils enter the camshaft cover, and if necessary renew them.

Testing

9 Each coil can be tested as described in the previous Section, using an ohmmeter to check for the resistances given in the Specifications **(see illustrations)**.

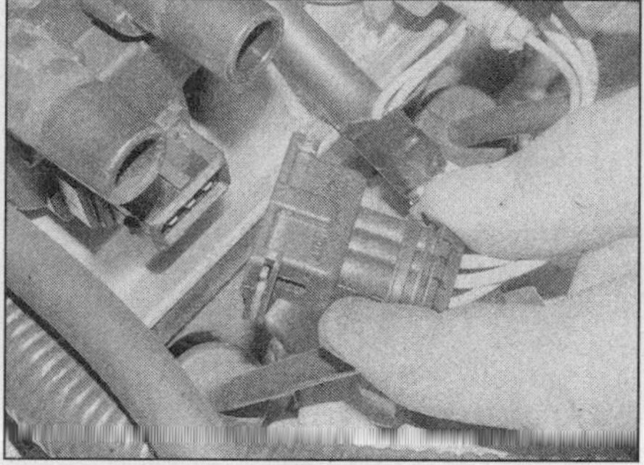

3.4 Disconnecting the wiring multi-plugs from the ignition coils

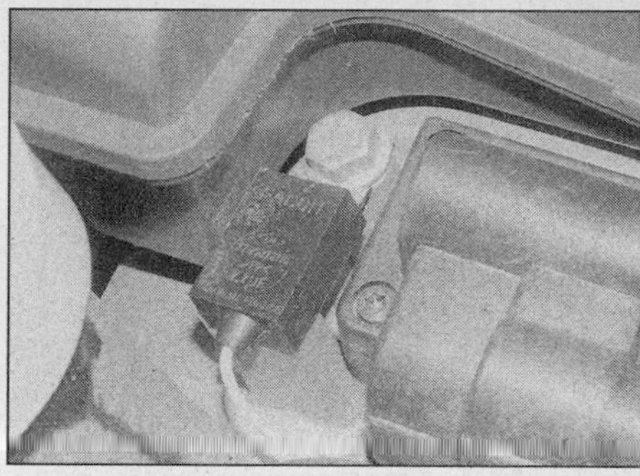

3.5 Note the location of the suppressor on one of the mounting screws

3.6 Disconnect the wiring from the ignition coil . . .

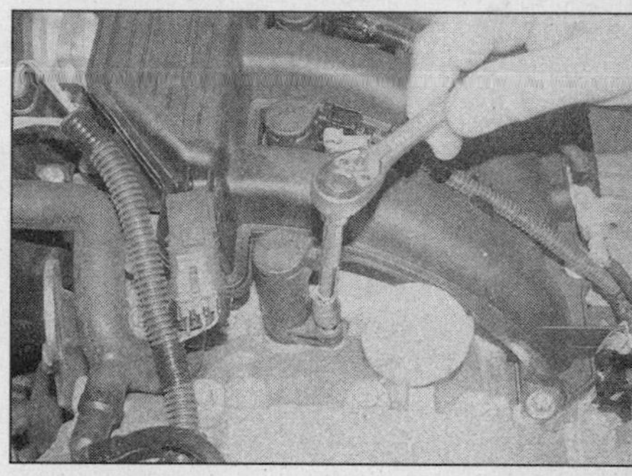

3.7a . . . then undo the mounting screw . . .

5B

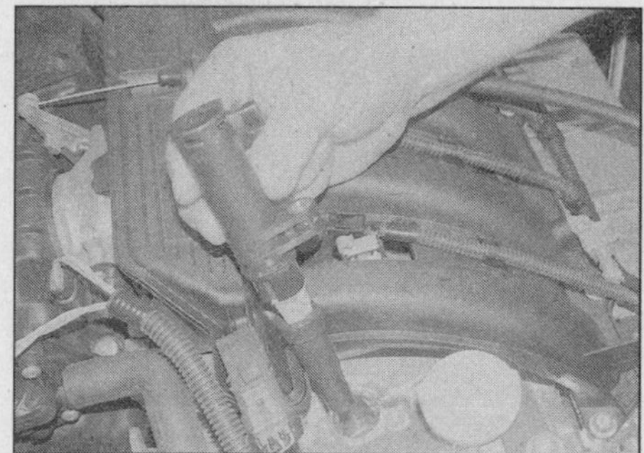

3.7b . . . and withdraw the coil off of its spark plug

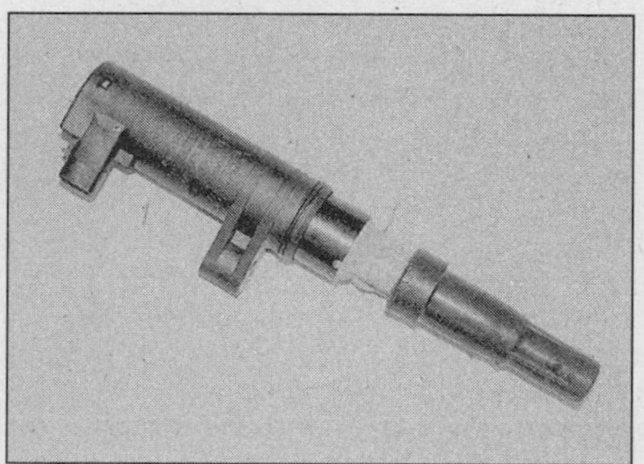

3.7c Ignition coil removed from the cylinder head

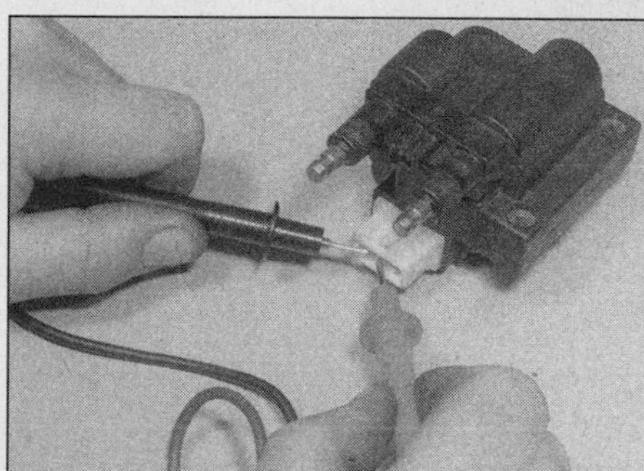

3.9a Testing an ignition coil's low tension circuits

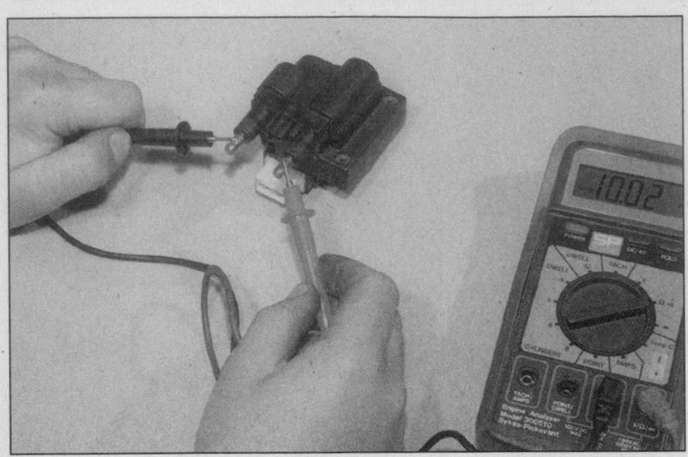

3.9b Testing an ignition coil's HT circuit

4.1 Knock sensor location (K4J engine)

10 Testing of the complete ignition system should be carried out by a Renault dealer using specialised equipment connected to the engine management diagnostic socket.

Refitting

11 Refitting is a reversal of removal, but tighten the mounting bolts to the specified torque, and ensure that the wiring connectors and spark plug HT leads are correctly and securely refitted.

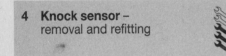

4 Knock sensor – removal and refitting

Removal

1 On the E7J engine, the knock sensor is located on the right-hand rear of the cylinder block. On K4J, K4M and F4R engines, it is located on the front of the cylinder block **(see illustration)**.

2 To remove the sensor, first disconnect the wiring, then unscrew it from the cylinder block.

Refitting

3 Refitting is a reversal of removal. Ensure that the sensor and its seating on the cylinder block or head are completely clean and tighten the sensor to the specified torque wrench setting. It is essential that these measures are scrupulously observed as if the sensor is not correctly secured to a clean mating surface it may not be able to detect the impulses caused by pre-ignition. If this were to happen the correction of ignition timing would not take place, with the consequent risk of severe engine damage.

5 Ignition timing – checking and adjustment

With this type of ignition system the ignition timing is constantly being monitored and adjusted by the engine management ECU and nominal checking values cannot be given. Therefore, it is not possible for the home mechanic to check the ignition timing. The only way in which the ignition timing can be checked is using special electronic test equipment, connected to the engine management system diagnostic connector. No adjustment of the ignition timing is possible. Should the ignition timing be incorrect, then a fault must be present in the engine management system.

Chapter 5 Part C: Pre/post-heating system – diesel engines

Contents

Degrees of difficulty

Easy, suitable for novice with little experience 	**Fairly easy,** suitable for beginner with some experience 	**Fairly difficult,** suitable for competent DIY mechanic 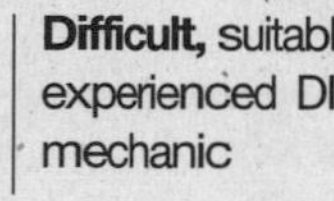	**Difficult,** suitable for experienced DIY mechanic 	**Very difficult,** suitable for expert DIY or professional

Specifications

Engine designation

Non-turbo engines – D models	F8Q 620, F8Q 622, F8Q 788
Turbo engines:	
dT models – indirect injection	F8Q 784, F8Q 786
dTi models – direct injection	F9Q 730, F9Q 734
dCi models – direct common-rail injection	F9Q 732

Glow plugs

Resistance	0.8 ohms

Thermal plungers (F9Q engines)

Resistance	0.45 ± 0.05 ohms

Coolant temperature sensor resistance

F8Q 620, F8Q 784, F8Q 786 and F8Q 788 engines:	
20°C	3060 to 4045 ohms
40°C	1315 to 1600 ohms
80°C	300 to 370 ohms
90°C	210 to 270 ohms
F8Q 622, F9Q 730, F9Q 734 and F9Q 732 engines:	
0°C	5290 to 6490 ohms
20°C	2400 to 2600 ohms
40°C	1070 to 1270 ohms
80°C	300 to 450 ohms

Torque wrench settings

	Nm	lbf ft
Glow plugs	20	15
Glow plug terminal nut	4	3

5C

1 Pre/post-heating system – description and testing

Description

1 The pre-heating/post-heating system consists of glow plugs screwed into the swirl chambers (indirect injection) or combustion chambers (direct injection), a control unit mounted on the left-hand side of the bulkhead, and a coolant temperature sensor located on the thermostat housing. The control unit is itself activated by the engine management ECU.

2 The glow plugs are supplied with current from the control unit in five phases, namely variable pre-heating, fixed pre-heating, starting heating, fixed post-heating and variable post-heating.

3 The variable pre-heating phase occurs when the ignition is switched on, and during this phase the pre-heating warning light is illuminated on the instrument panel. The period of pre-heating depends on the temperature of the coolant, battery voltage, and altitude. The maximum period of 15.5 seconds occurs if the coolant temperature is low, the battery voltage is less than 9.3 volts, and the altitude is higher than 2000 metres. The period varies from 15.5 seconds to zero seconds according to the temperature of the coolant, and when the temperature reaches 80°C, no pre-heating occurs.

4 The fixed pre-heating phase occurs immediately after the variable phase finishes, after the warning light has extinguished, and lasts for 8 seconds on F8Q 730/734 and F8Q 788 engines, 10 seconds on the F9Q 732 engine, and 30 seconds on the F8Q 622 engine. Normally, the driver will start the engine at some point during this phase.

5 During the period when the starter motor is in operation, the glow plugs are continuously supplied with current.

6 Fixed post-heating lasts for a period of 10 seconds after the engine has been started.

7 The variable post-heating phase occurs immediately after the fixed post-heating phase ends, and the period of post-heating depends on the temperature of the coolant, engine speed, and engine load which is determined by the load potentiometer on the injection pump lever. The maximum period of variable post-heating is 3 minutes, at which point the system is switched off. Variable post-heating will cease if the coolant temperature exceeds 60°C, if engine full load occurs for more than 3 seconds, or if battery voltage is greater than 16 volts. It is reintroduced within the time limit of 3 minutes, if the engine returns to idle speed or low load, or if the battery voltage is less than 15 volts.

8 If the coolant temperature sensor becomes faulty, the ECU uses the air temperature sensor to calculate the period of pre/post-heating. Note that a coolant heating system is fitted to certain F9Q engines supplied to very cold climates – three electric thermoplungers located in a unit beneath the inlet manifold, heat the coolant to assist engine warm-up.

Testing

9 If the system malfunctions, testing is best carried out by a Renault dealer using dedicated test equipment, however, some preliminary checks may be made as follows.

10 Connect a voltmeter or 12 volt test lamp between the glow plug supply cable and earth (engine or vehicle metal). Make sure that the live connection is kept clear of the engine and bodywork. Have an assistant switch on the ignition and check that voltage is applied to the glow plugs. Note the time for which the warning light is lit and the total time for which voltage is applied before the system cuts out, and compare to the times given in the description in paragraphs 1 to 7.

11 If there is no supply at all, the relay, control unit or associated wiring is at fault.

12 To locate a defective glow plug, disconnect the main supply cable and the interconnecting wire or strap from the top of the glow plugs. Be careful not to drop the nuts and washers. Using an ohmmeter, check for continuity between each glow plug terminal and earth. The resistance of a glow plug in good condition is very low (less than 1 ohm), so if the test lamp does not light or the continuity tester shows a high resistance the glow plug is defective.

13 If an ammeter is available, the current draw of each glow plug can be checked. After an initial surge of around 15 to 20 amps, each plug should draw around 10 amps. Any plug which draws much more or less than 10 amps is probably defective.

14 As a final check, the glow plugs can be removed and inspected as described in Section 2.

15 If the pre/post-heating system is faulty, first check the wiring to each individual component. If this does not locate the fault, ideally each component should be replaced with known good units until the fault is located. If this is not possible, take the vehicle to a Renault dealer or diesel specialist who will have the diagnostic equipment necessary to pin-point the fault quickly.

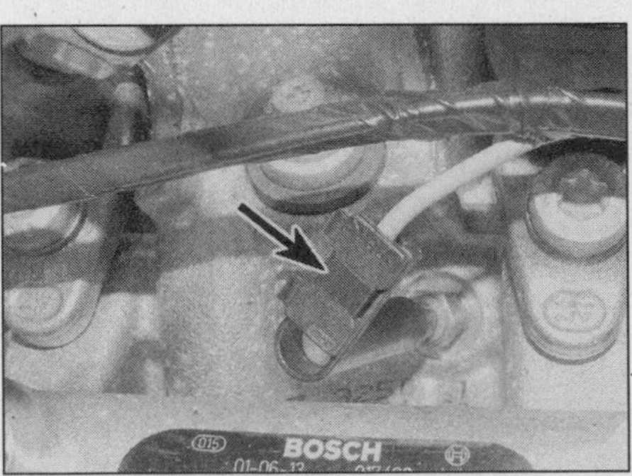

2.2 Disconnect the wiring (arrowed) from the glow plug terminal

2 Glow plugs – removal, inspection and refitting

Removal

Caution: If the pre-heating system has just been energised, or if the engine has been running, the glow plugs may be very hot.

1 Disconnect the battery negative (earth) lead and position it away from the terminal (see Chapter 5A).

Caution: If the radio/cassette in your vehicle is equipped with an anti-theft system, make sure you have the correct activation code before disconnecting the battery.

2 Where applicable, unscrew the nuts from the glow plug terminals, and recover the washers. Disconnect the wiring **(see illustration)**. Note that the main electrical feed wiring is connected to two of the plugs.

3 Unscrew the glow plugs and remove them from the cylinder head **(see illustration)**.

Inspection

4 Inspect the glow plugs for physical damage. Burnt or eroded glow plug tips can be caused by a bad injector spray pattern. Have the injectors checked if this sort of damage is found.

5 If the glow plugs are in good physical condition, check them electrically using a 12 volt test lamp or continuity tester with reference to the previous Section.

6 The glow plugs can be energised by applying 12 volts to them to verify that they heat up evenly and in the required time. Observe the following precautions:

a) Support the glow plug by clamping it carefully in a vice or self-locking pliers. Remember it will become red-hot.

b) Make sure that the power supply or test lead incorporates a fuse or overload trip to protect against damage from a short-circuit.

c) After testing, allow the glow plug to cool for several minutes before attempting to handle it.

7 A glow plug in good condition will start to glow red at the tip after drawing current for

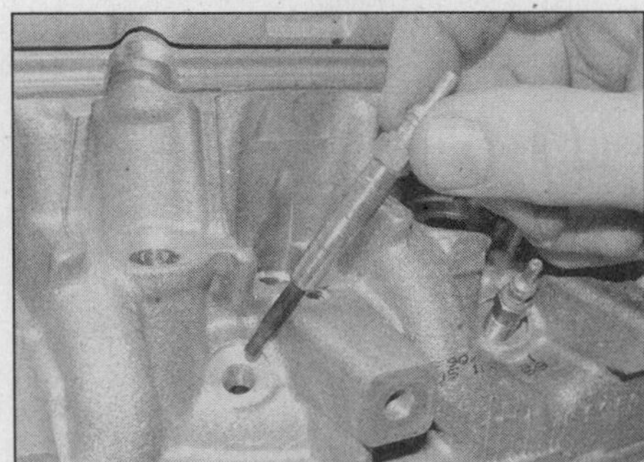
2.3 Removing a glow plug

5 seconds or so. Any plug which takes much longer to start glowing, or which starts glowing in the middle instead of at the tip, is defective.

Refitting

8 Refit by reversing the removal operations. Apply a smear of copper-based anti-seize compound to the plug threads and tighten the glow plugs to the specified torque. Do not overtighten, as this can damage the glow plug element.

3 Pre/post-heating system control unit – removal and refitting

Removal

1 The pre/post-heating control unit is located on a bracket on the bulkhead **(see illustration)**. Before proceeding, make sure that the ignition is switched off.

2 Disconnect the wiring from the control unit.

3 Unscrew the mounting nuts/bolts and remove the control unit from the mounting bracket.

Refitting

4 Refitting is a reversal of removal.

4 Coolant temperature sensor – removal, testing, and refitting

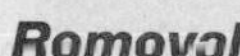

Removal

1 The coolant temperature sensor is located on the rear of the thermostat housing on the left-hand end of the cylinder head, below the brake vacuum pump.

2 Drain the cooling system as described in Chapter 1B. Alternatively, have the new sensor or a suitable bung to hand to quickly plug the hole and prevent liquid from being spilt while the sensor is being removed.

3 Disconnect the electrical connector, then unscrew the sensor. Recover the sealing ring.

Testing

Note: *A continuity tester or an ohmmeter will be required for testing.*

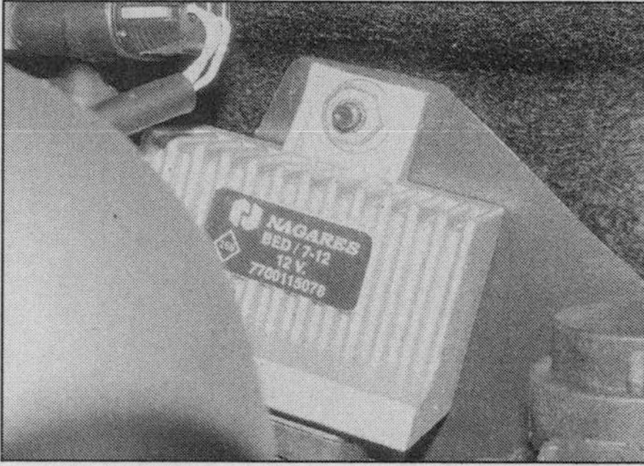

3.1 The pre/post-heating control unit is located on a bracket on the bulkhead

4 The sensor has two functions – the NTC (negative temperature coefficient) resistor informs the pre/post-heating control unit of the engine coolant temperature, and its switch interrupts the electrical supply to the EGR solenoid.

5 Connect a continuity tester or an ohmmeter to pins 1 and 4 of the sensor connector. There should be infinite resistance at room temperature, showing that the contacts of the thermoswitch are open.

6 Next suspend the sensor in a container of water (using string) so that it is immersed but not touching the sides or the base of the container. Dip a thermometer into the water, apply heat and then check that the contacts of the thermoswitch remain open up to 20°C but close at temperatures above 30°C. With the contacts closed, the ohmmeter must show zero resistance.

7 On all engines, connect an ohmmeter across the switch terminals 2 and 3. Heat the water and check that the resistance of the thermistor (coolant temperature sensor) is in accordance with the figures given in the Specifications.

8 If the results obtained are not as specified, the switch is proved faulty and should be renewed.

Refitting

9 Refitting is the reverse of removal, but fit a new sealing ring.

10 On completion, top-up or refill and bleed the cooling system, as necessary, as described in Chapter 1B.

5 Fuel filter heating system – general information and component renewal

General information

1 The fuel filter is located in the right-hand front of the engine compartment. An electrically-operated heating element is fitted in the fuel filter housing, to prevent the fuel 'waxing' at low temperatures. The heater is controlled by an internal thermostat. When the fuel temperature is below 0°C, current to the heater warms the fuel in the filter housing and filter. When the fuel temperature reaches 8°C, current supply to the heater ceases.

Component renewal

Caution: Be careful not to allow dirt into the fuel system during the following procedures.

Fuel filter heating element

2 Remove the fuel filter as described in Chapter 1B.

3 Disconnect the wiring connector then unscrew the centre bolt and remove the heating element from the base of the fuel filter housing. Recover the sealing ring which is fitted between the element and filter housing and discard; a new one should be used on refitting.

4 On refitting, fit the new sealing ring to the groove in the heating element and refit the element to the filter housing, tightening the centre bolt securely.

5 Reconnect the wiring connector and fit the fuel filter as described in Chapter 1B.

Temperature switch

6 Disconnect the wiring connector from the temperature switch.

7 Wipe clean the area around the temperature switch and fuel filter housing. Position a container to catch any spilt fuel then slacken and remove the switch from the fuel filter housing. Recover the sealing washers which are fitted on each side of the fuel hose union and discard them; new ones must be used on refitting.

8 Refitting is the reverse of removal, positioning a new sealing washer on each side of the fuel hose union.

Chapter 6
Clutch

Contents

Degrees of difficulty

Easy, suitable for novice with little experience 	**Fairly easy,** suitable for beginner with some experience 	**Fairly difficult,** suitable for competent DIY mechanic 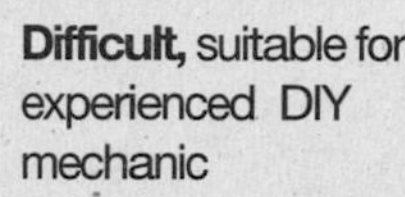	**Difficult,** suitable for experienced DIY mechanic 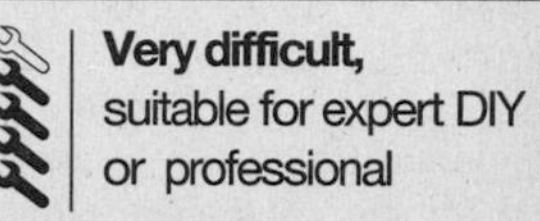	**Very difficult,** suitable for expert DIY or professional

Specifications

Engine designation

Petrol models:	
1.4 litre engine	E7J 764, K4J 750
1.6 litre engine	K4M 700, K4M 701
2.0 litre engine	F4R 740, F4R 741
Diesel models:	
Non-turbo engines – D models	F8Q 620, F8Q 622, F8Q 788
Turbo engines:	
dT models – indirect injection	F8Q 784, F8Q 786
dTi models – direct injection	F9Q 730, F9Q 734
dCi models – direct common rail injection	F9Q 732

General

Clutch type	Single dry plate, diaphragm spring, cable-operated
Adjustment	Automatic

Clutch friction disc

Diameter:	
E7J engine	180 mm
K4J engine	200 mm
K4M engine	215 mm
F4R engine	215 mm
F8Q engine	200 mm
F9Q engine	200 mm
Number of springs:	
E7J engine	6
K4J engine	6
K4M engine	6
F4R engine	4
F8Q engine	4
F9Q engine	4
Lining thickness (new, and in compressed position):	
E7J engine	8.3 mm
K4J engine	6.8 mm
K4M engine	6.8 mm
F4R engine	6.8 mm
F8Q engine	8.4 mm
F9Q engine	8.4 mm

Torque wrench setting	**Nm**	**lbf ft**
Clutch pressure plate bolts	20	15

1 General information

All manual gearbox models are equipped with a cable-operated clutch. The unit consists of a steel pressure plate which is dowelled and bolted to the rear face of the flywheel, and contains the diaphragm spring.

The clutch friction disc is free to slide along the gearbox splined input shaft. The disc is held in position between the flywheel and the pressure plate by the pressure of the diaphragm spring. Friction lining material is riveted to the disc, which has a spring-cushioned hub to absorb transmission shocks and help ensure a smooth take-up of the drive.

The clutch is actuated by a cable, controlled by the clutch pedal. The clutch release mechanism consists of a release arm and bearing which are in permanent contact with the fingers of the diaphragm spring.

Depressing the clutch pedal actuates the release arm by means of the cable. The arm pushes the release bearing against the diaphragm fingers, so moving the centre of the diaphragm spring inwards. As the centre of the spring is pushed in, the outside of the spring pivots out, so moving the pressure plate backwards and disengaging its grip on the friction disc.

When the pedal is released, the diaphragm spring forces the pressure plate into contact with the friction linings on the friction disc. The disc is now firmly sandwiched between the pressure plate and the flywheel, thus transmitting engine power to the gearbox.

Wear of the friction material on the disc is automatically compensated for by a self-adjusting mechanism. The mechanism consists of a serrated quadrant, a notched cam and a tension spring integrated into the top of the clutch pedal. The mechanism functions as follows. One end of the clutch cable is attached to the quadrant, which is free to pivot, but is kept in tension by a spring. When the pedal is depressed, the notched cam contacts the quadrant, thus locking it and allowing the pedal to pull the cable and operate the clutch. When the pedal is released, the tension spring causes the notched cam to move free of the quadrant, and at the same time tension is maintained on the cable, keeping the release bearing in contact with the diaphragm spring. As the friction material on the disc wears, the self-adjusting quadrant will rotate when the pedal is released, and the pedal free play will be maintained between the notched cam and the quadrant.

Caution: If the radio/cassette in your vehicle is equipped with an anti-theft system, make sure you have the correct activation code before disconnecting the battery.

2 Clutch cable – removal and refitting

Removal

1 In order to gain access to the clutch cable on the gearbox bellhousing, remove the air cleaner or air inlet ducting, according to model as described in Chapter 4A or 4B.

2 Disengage the inner cable from the release fork, then withdraw the outer cable from the bracket on the bellhousing.

Caution: Do not lift the release fork as it may become detached from the release bearing inside the bellhousing.

3 Working inside the car, remove the clutch pedal as described in Section 3 and tie a length of string to the end of the clutch cable.

4 With the inner cable already disconnected, release the outer cable from its bracket on the transmission, then work along its length, freeing it from the retaining clips and ties whilst noting its correct routing.

5 Release the clutch cable end fitting from the bulkhead and remove the cable from the vehicle. When the end of the cable appears, untie the string and leave it in position; it can then be used to draw the cable back through into position on refitting.

6 Examine the cable, looking for worn end fittings or a damaged outer casing, and for signs of fraying of the inner wire. Check the cable's operation; the inner wire should move smoothly and easily through the outer casing. Remember that a cable that appears serviceable when tested off the car may well be much heavier in operation when in its working position. Renew the cable if it shows signs of excessive wear or any damage.

Refitting

7 Manoeuvre the cable into position, making sure it is correctly routed, and use the string to draw the cable end through into the passenger compartment. Untie the string, and seat the cable end fitting securely in the bulkhead.

8 Secure the cable in position with all the relevant clips and ties, and locate the transmission end of the outer cable in its mounting bracket. Slip the outer end of the cable through the bellhousing bracket, and connect the inner cable to the release fork. Refit the cable to the support clips.

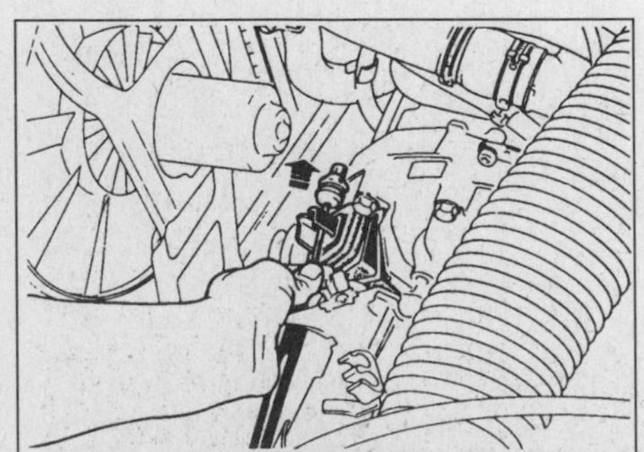

2.11 Checking the clutch inner cable freeplay at the release fork end

9 Refit the clutch pedal as described in Section 3. Place the inner cable over the self-adjusting cam, and onto the quadrant. Refit the inner cable guide where applicable. Check the operation of the automatic adjustment mechanism as described in Section 3. When the pedal is depressed, the outer cable will be drawn into its locating hole in the bulkhead. At the same time, the inner cable guide (where fitted) will be automatically pulled onto the top of the pedal to hold the inner cable in position.

10 Depress the clutch pedal several times in order to allow the self-adjusting mechanism to set the correct free play.

11 When the self-adjusting mechanism on the clutch pedal is functioning correctly, there should be a minimum of 20 mm slack in the cable. To check this dimension, pull out the inner cable near the release fork on the gearbox **(see illustration)**. If there is less than the minimum slack in the cable, the self-adjusting quadrant should be checked for seizure or possible restricted movement.

12 Depress the clutch pedal fully, and check that the total movement at the end of the release fork is as follows **(see illustration)**.

E7J, F8Q and F9Q engines	*7.4 to 30.7 mm*
F4R engine	*25.4 to 25.9 mm*
K4J and K4M engines	*27.0 to 30.5 mm*

This movement ensures that the clutch pedal stroke is correct. If not, make sure that the quadrant is free to turn, and that the spring has not lost its tension. If necessary, check the free length of the spring against a new one. Also check that the inner cable is not seizing in the outer cable.

13 Refit the air cleaner assembly and air inlet ducting.

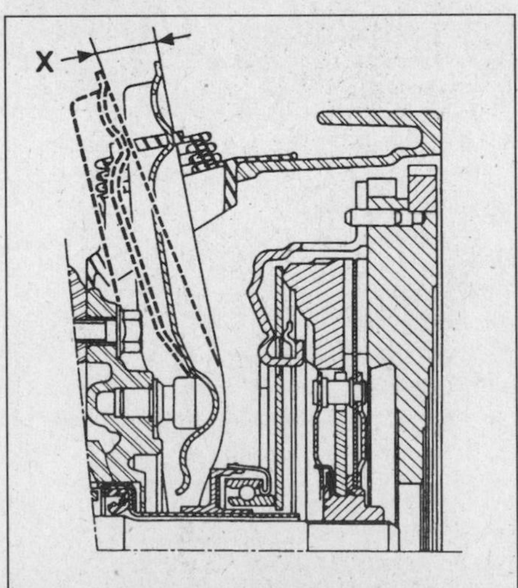

2.12 Checking the clutch release fork movement (X)

For dimension X, see text

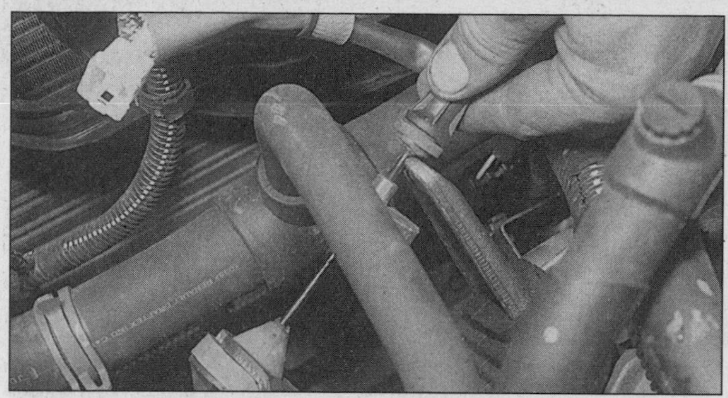

3.6 Releasing the end of the clutch cable from the release fork

3.8 Nut on the clutch/brake pedal pivot bolt

3 Clutch pedal – removal and refitting

Checking

1 The clutch pedal assembly incorporates the automatic adjustment mechanism, and the operation of the mechanism can be checked as follows.

2 First measure the clutch cable freeplay. To check this, with the clutch pedal in the at-rest position, pull out the transmission end of the clutch inner cable and measure the length of exposed cable. If the mechanism is operating correctly, there should be at least 20 mm freeplay in the cable. If there is less than this, the automatic adjustment quadrant should be checked for seizure or possible restricted movement.

3 Have an assistant depress and release the clutch pedal fully whilst you measure the total movement of the release fork end; if the mechanism is operating correctly, this should be as given in Section 2. This movement ensures that the clutch pedal stroke is correct. If not, make sure that the automatic adjustment mechanism teeth are undamaged, and that the spring has not lost its tension. Also check that the inner cable is not seizing in the outer cable.

Removal

4 Disconnect the battery negative lead (refer to Chapter 5A).

5 Remove the air cleaner assembly and air ducting as described in Chapter 4A or 4B.

6 Working in the engine compartment, unhook the end of the clutch cable from the release fork on the transmission **(see illustration)**.

7 Undo the securing screws and remove the steering column lower shroud to gain access to the clutch pedal assembly.

8 Unscrew and remove the nut and washer from the pedal pivot bolt **(see illustration)**. Where applicable, undo the retaining nut/bolt and remove the support bracket from the end of the pivot bolt.

9 Partially withdraw the clutch/brake pedal pivot shaft until it is possible to remove the clutch pedal along with its pivot bushes and spacer. Note the positions of the pivot bushes to ensure correct refitting.

10 Detach the clutch inner cable from the top of the pedal, then free it from the quadrant and remove the pedal assembly from the vehicle. With the clutch pedal removed, slide the pivot bolt back into position to securely retain the brake pedal.

11 Examine the pedal assembly for signs of wear or damage, paying particular attention to the automatic adjustment mechanism. Do not attempt to dismantle the assembly as no components are available separately; the pedal assembly must be renewed as a unit if damaged. Renew the pivot bushes if they show signs of wear or damage.

Refitting

12 Apply some multi-purpose grease to the bearing surfaces of the pedal spacer and bushes, and also to the surface of the adjustment mechanism teeth.

13 Fit the bushes to the pedal, making sure they are located in the previously noted positions. Ensure that the locating lug of each bush is correctly engaged with the pedal cut-out, then slide the spacer into position.

14 Manoeuvre the pedal assembly into position under the facia. Engage the clutch cable end fitting with the self-adjust mechanism, then seat the pedal in position.

15 Ensure the clutch cable is correctly seated in the adjustment mechanism quadrant, then refit the support bracket (where fitted), tightening its nut/bolt lightly only at this stage.

16 Slide the pivot bolt fully into position, then refit the washer and nut. Tighten both the pivot bolt and support bracket nut/bolt securely.

17 Hook the transmission end of the cable back onto the release fork in the engine compartment.

18 Depress the clutch pedal several times, whilst ensuring that the cable remains correctly seated in the quadrant. This will allow the automatic adjustment mechanism to set the correct free play/pedal stroke.

19 Check the operation of the adjustment mechanism as described in paragraphs 1 to 3.

20 Refit the steering column lower shroud, the air cleaner assembly and air ducting (as applicable), and reconnect the battery negative lead.

4 Clutch assembly – removal, inspection and refitting

Warning: Dust created by clutch wear and deposited on the clutch components may contain asbestos which is a health hazard. DO NOT blow it out with compressed air or inhale any of it. DO NOT use petrol or petroleum-based solvents to clean off the dust. Brake system cleaner or methylated spirit should be used to flush the dust into a suitable receptacle. After the clutch components are wiped clean with rags, dispose of the contaminated rags and cleaner in a sealed, marked container.

Removal

1 Access to the clutch may be gained in one of two ways. Either the gearbox may be removed independently, as described in Chapter 7A, or the engine/gearbox unit may be removed as described in Chapter 2D, and the gearbox separated from the engine on the bench.

2 Having separated the gearbox from the engine, first use paint or a marker pen to mark the relationship of the pressure plate assembly to the flywheel **(see illustration)**.

4.2 Mark the relationship of the clutch pressure plate and flywheel before removing the pressure plate

4.3a Slacken the pressure plate bolts progressively . . .

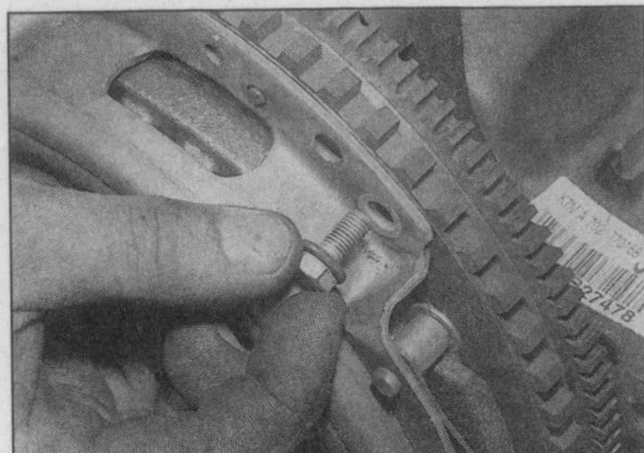
4.3b . . . before removing them

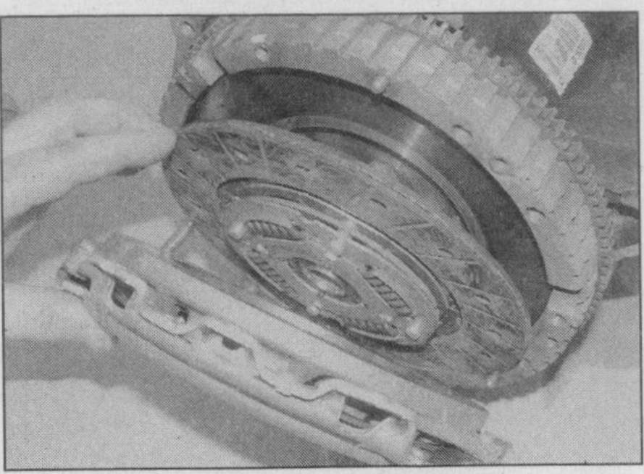
4.4 Removing the clutch pressure plate and disc

3 Unscrew and remove the pressure plate assembly retaining bolts. Work in a diagonal sequence and slacken the bolts only a few turns at a time. Hold the flywheel stationary by positioning a screwdriver over the dowel on the cylinder block and engaging it with the starter ring gear **(see illustrations)**.

4 Ease the pressure plate assembly off its locating dowels. Be prepared to catch the friction disc, which will drop out as the assembly is removed **(see illustration)**. Note which way round the disc is fitted.

Inspection

5 With the clutch assembly removed, clean off all traces of asbestos dust using a dry cloth. This is best done outside or in a well-ventilated area (refer to the warning at the beginning of this Section).

6 Examine the linings of the disc for wear or loose rivets, and the disc rim for distortion, cracks, broken torsion springs and worn splines. The surface of the friction linings may be highly glazed, but as long as the friction material pattern can be clearly seen, this is satisfactory. If there is any sign of oil contamination, indicated by shiny black discoloration, the disc must be renewed and the source of the contamination traced and rectified. This will be a leaking crankshaft oil seal, gearbox input shaft oil seal, or both. The renewal procedure for the crankshaft oil seal is given in the appropriate part of Chapter 2. Renewal of the gearbox input shaft oil seal should be entrusted to a Renault garage, as it involves dismantling the gearbox and the renewal of the clutch release bearing guide tube using a press. The disc must also be renewed if the linings have worn down to, or just above, the level of the rivet heads.

7 Check the machined faces of the flywheel and pressure plate. If either is grooved, or heavily scored, renewal is necessary. The pressure plate must also be renewed if any cracks are apparent, or if the diaphragm spring is damaged or its pressure suspect.

8 Take the opportunity to check the condition of the release bearing, as described in Section 6.

9 It is good practice to renew the friction disc, pressure plate and release bearing at the same time.

Refitting

10 Before commencing the refitting procedure, apply a little high-melting-point grease to the splines of the gearbox input shaft. Distribute the grease by sliding the friction disc on and off the splines a few times. Remove the disc and wipe away any excess grease. Also smear a little grease to the guide tube on the gearbox.

11 It is important that no oil or grease is allowed to come into contact with the friction material of the disc or the pressure plate and flywheel faces. It is advisable to refit the clutch assembly with clean hands, and to wipe the pressure plate and flywheel faces with a clean dry rag before assembly begins.

12 There are several different types of clutch alignment tool available to the home mechanic; the conventional type uses a spigot which centralises the disc with the hole in the end of the crankshaft, however, an alternative clamp-type tool centralises the disc onto the pressure plate before refitting them both to the flywheel.

Using a conventional alignment tool

13 Place the friction disc against the flywheel, with the side having the larger offset facing away from the flywheel, and hold the disc in position using the alignment tool **(see illustration)**.

14 Place the pressure plate assembly over the dowels, and where applicable, align it with the previously made mark **(see illustration)**. Refit the retaining bolts and tighten them

4.13 Using the clutch aligning tool to hold the friction disc in position

4.14 Refitting the pressure plate assembly

4.20a Centralise the pressure plate on the disc . . .

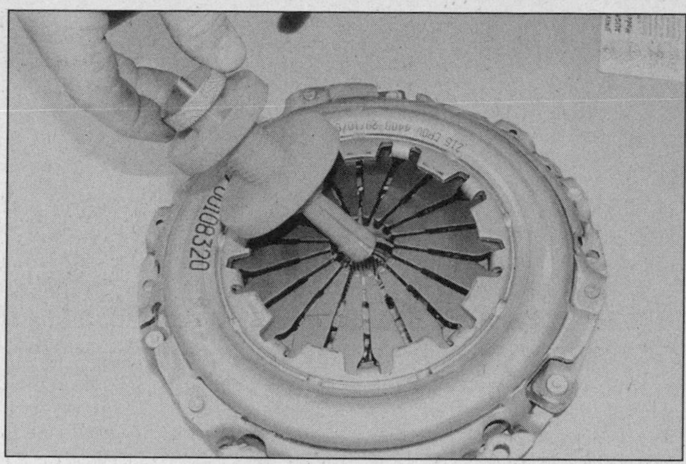

4.20b . . . fit the tool and tighten to clamp the disc to the pressure plate . . .

finger-tight so that the disc is gripped, but can still be moved.

15 The disc must now be centralised so that, when the engine and gearbox are reconnected, the splines of the gearbox input shaft will pass through the splines in the centre of the disc hub. If this is not done accurately, it will be impossible to refit the gearbox.

16 Centralisation can be carried out quite easily by inserting a round bar through the hole in the centre of the disc, so that the end of the bar rests in the hole in the end of the crankshaft. Note that a plastic centralising tube is supplied with Renault clutch kits, making the use of a bar unnecessary.

17 If a bar is being used, move it sideways or up-and-down until the disc is centralised. Centralisation can be judged by removing the bar and viewing the disc hub in relation to the bore in the end of the crankshaft. When the bore appears exactly in the centre of the disc hub, all is correct.

18 Once the clutch is centralised, progressively tighten the pressure plate bolts in a diagonal sequence to the correct torque setting. Remove the centralising tool.

19 The gearbox can now be refitted with reference to Chapter 7A or 2D as applicable.

Using a clamp-type alignment tool

20 Position the pressure plate centrally on the friction disc, then insert the alignment tool and clamp the two items together with the tool **(see illustrations)**. Check that the disc is correctly aligned with the pressure plate by viewing it from the flywheel side.

21 Position the plate and disc on the flywheel and insert the retaining bolts finger-tight **(see illustration)**. Where applicable, align the previously made marks on the plate and flywhool.

22 Progressively tighten the pressure plate bolts to the specified torque, then remove the tool **(see illustration)**.

23 The gearbox can now be refitted to the engine with reference to Chapter 7A or 2D as applicable.

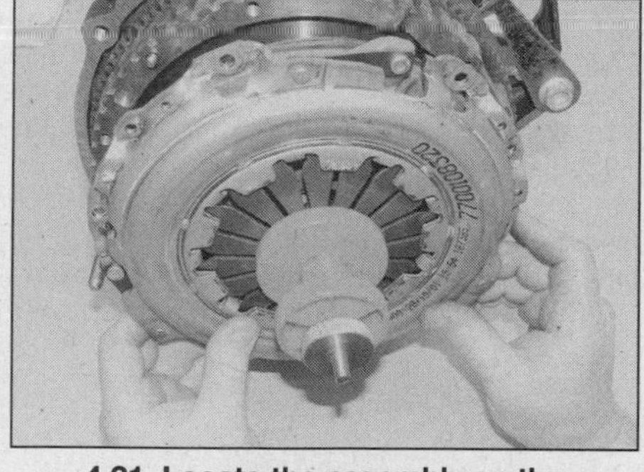

4.21 Locate the assembly on the flywheel . . .

4.22 . . . then progressively tighten the bolts to the specified torque

6 Clutch release bearing – removal, inspection and refitting

Removal

1 Access to the clutch release bearing may be gained in one of two ways. Either the gearbox may be removed independently, as described in Chapter 7A, or the engine/gearbox unit may be removed as described in Chapter 2D, and the gearbox separated from the engine on the bench.

2 Having separated the gearbox from the engine, tilt the release fork and slide the bearing assembly off the gearbox input shaft guide tube **(see illustration)**. Note how the fork locates in the release bearing.

3 To remove the release fork, disengage the rubber cover and then pull the fork off its pivot ball stud **(see illustrations)**.

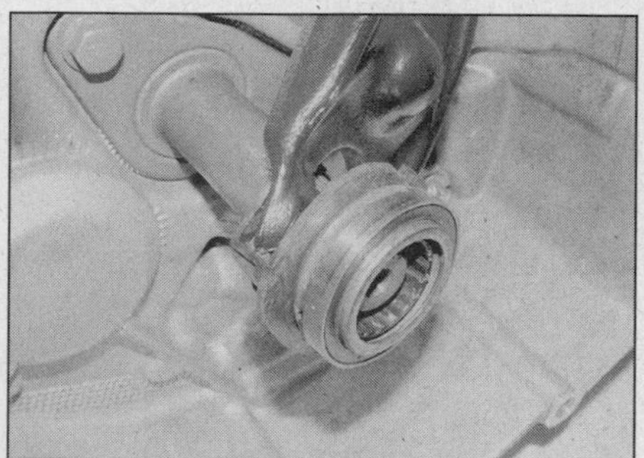

6.2 Removing the release bearing from the guide tube and fork

6.3a Showing the rubber cover on the release lever

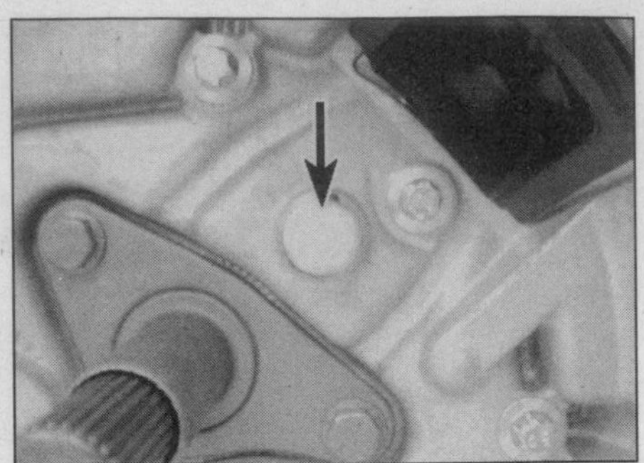

6.3b Release lever pivot ball stud

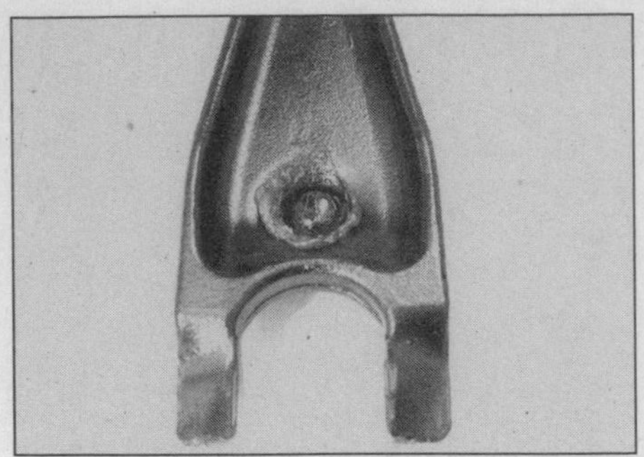

6.3c The release lever has an indentation to locate on the pivot ball stud

6.5 Smear molybdenum disulphide grease on the pivot stud before refitting the release fork

Inspection

4 Check the bearing for smoothness of operation. Renew it if there is any roughness or harshness as the bearing is spun. It is good practice to renew the bearing as a matter of course during clutch overhaul, regardless of its apparent condition.

Refitting

5 Refitting the release fork and release bearing is a reversal of the removal procedure, but note the following points.

a) Lubricate the release fork pivot ball stud, the release bearing-to-diaphragm spring contact areas and the guide tube sparingly with molybdenum disulphide grease ***(see illustration)****.*

b) Ensure that the release fork engages correctly with the lugs on the bearing.

Chapter 7 Part A: Manual gearbox

Contents

Degrees of difficulty

Easy, suitable for novice with little experience

Fairly easy, suitable for beginner with some experience

Fairly difficult, suitable for competent DIY mechanic

Difficult, suitable for experienced DIY mechanic

Very difficult, suitable for expert DIY or professional

Specifications

Engine designation

Petrol models:	
1.4 litre engine	E7J 764, K4J 750
1.6 litre engine	K4M 700, K4M 701
2.0 litre engine	F4R 740, F4R 741
Diesel models:	
Non-turbo engines – D models	F8Q 620, F8Q 622, F8Q 788
Turbo engines:	
dT models – indirect injection	F8Q 784, F8Q 786
dTi models – direct injection	F9Q 730, F9Q 734
dCi models – direct common-rail injection	F9Q 732

General

Type	Five forward speeds (all synchromesh) and reverse. Final drive differential integral with main gearbox
Designation:	
E7J and F8Q engines	JB1
K4J and K4M engines	JB3
F4R and F9Q engines	JC5

Gear ratios

JB1 gearbox:	
1st	3.4 : 1
2nd	1.9 : 1
3rd	1.3 : 1
4th	1.0 : 1
5th	0.8 : 1
Reverse	3.6 : 1
Final drive	4.1 : 1
JB3 gearbox:	
1st	3.7 : 1 or 3.4 : 1
2nd	2.1 : 1 or 1.9 : 1
3rd	1.4 : 1 or 1.3 : 1
4th	1.0 : 1
5th	0.8 : 1
Reverse	3.6 : 1
Final drive	4.2 : 1 or 4.1 : 1 or 4.5 : 1
JC5 gearbox:	
1st	3.4 : 1
2nd	1.9 : 1
3rd	1.3 : 1
4th	1.0 : 1
5th	0.8 : 1
Reverse	3.6 : 1
Final drive	3.9 : 1

Torque wrench settings

	Nm	lbf ft
Clutch release bearing guide tube bolts – JC5 unit	24	18
Engine to transmission:		
Mounting nuts	35	26
Mounting bolts	30	22
Gearchange lever assembly to floor	15	11
Gearchange rod:		
Clamp bolt	30	22
Clevis-to-transmission bolt	30	22

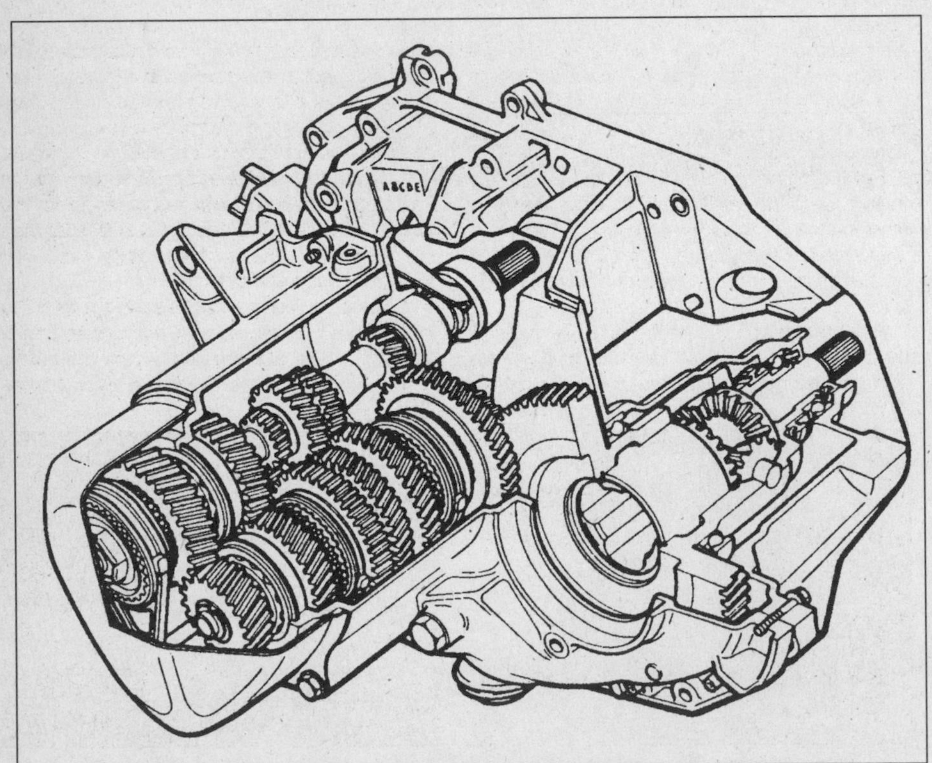

1.1a Cutaway view of the gearbox

1 General information

The transmission is equipped with five forward gears, one reverse gear and a final drive differential, incorporated in one casing bolted to the left-hand end of the engine. The transmission type code is either on an identification plate attached to the top of the gearbox or stamped into the bottom of the gearbox casing **(see illustrations)**.

Drive is transmitted from the crankshaft via the clutch to the input shaft which rotates in

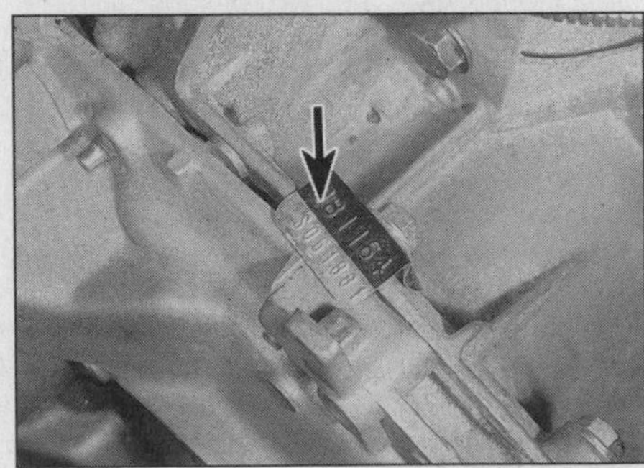

1.1b The identification number starts with the gearbox type code

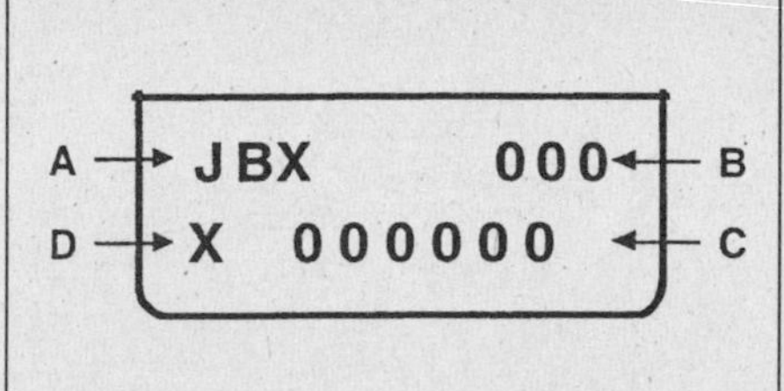

1.1c Gearbox identification number stamped on the bottom of the casing

A Type
B Gearbox suffix
C Fabrication number
D Factory of manufacture

sealed ball bearings, and has a splined extension to accept the clutch friction disc. From the input shaft, drive is transmitted to the output shaft, which rotates in a roller bearing at its right-hand end, and a sealed ball-bearing at its left-hand end. From the output shaft, drive is transmitted to the differential crownwheel, which rotates with the differential gears and planetary gears, thus driving the sun gears and driveshafts. The rotation of the planetary gears on their shaft allows the inner roadwheel to rotate at a slower speed than the outer roadwheel when the car is cornering.

The input and output shafts are arranged side-by-side, parallel to the crankshaft and driveshafts, so that their gear pinion teeth are in constant mesh. In the neutral position, the output shaft gear pinions rotate freely, so that drive cannot be transmitted to the crownwheel. Synchromesh is provided on all forward speeds. Gear selection is via a floor-mounted lever and rod mechanism.

The gearbox selector rod causes the appropriate selector fork to move its respective synchro-sleeve along the shaft, in order to lock the gear pinion to the synchro-hub. Since the synchro-hubs are splined to the output shaft, this locks the pinion to the shaft, so that drive can be transmitted. To ensure that gearchanging can be made quickly and quietly, a synchro-mesh system is fitted to all forward gears, consisting of baulk rings and spring-loaded fingers, as well as the gear pinions and synchro-hubs. The synchro-mesh cones are formed on the mating faces of the baulk rings and gear pinions.

2 Gearbox – draining and refilling

Note: *The filler plug is also used as the level plug.*

1 This operation is much quicker and more efficient if the car is first taken on a journey of sufficient length to warm the engine/transmission up to operating temperature.

2 Park the car on level ground, switch off the ignition and apply the handbrake firmly. For improved access, jack up the front of the car and support it securely on axle stands (see *Jacking and vehicle support*), or alternatively position the vehicle over an inspection pit or on car ramps. Remove the engine compartment undertray or the small cover from the bottom of the transmission (as applicable) **(see illustration)**. Note that to ensure accuracy, the car must be level when checking the oil level.

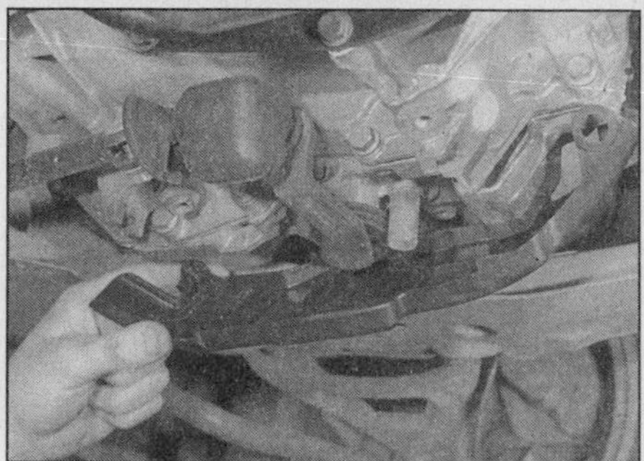

2.2 Removing the plastic cover from the bottom of the gearbox

3 Remove all traces of dirt from around the drain and filler plugs, then unscrew the filler/level plug from the front face of the gearbox **(see illustration)**.

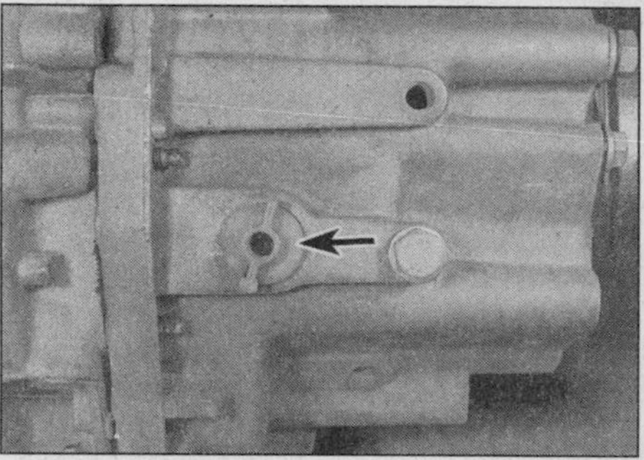

2.3 Oil filler plug on the front of the gearbox

4 Position a suitable container under the gearbox, then unscrew the drain plug and allow the oil to drain completely into the container **(see illustrations)**. If the oil is hot, take precautions against scalding. Clean both the filler/level and the drain plugs, being especially careful to wipe any metallic particles off the magnetic inserts. The sealing washers should be renewed whenever they are disturbed.

2.4a Unscrew the drain plug . . .

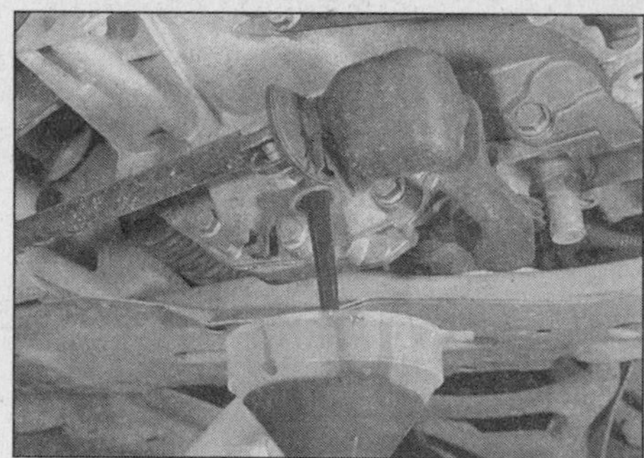

2.4b . . . and drain the oil

5 When the oil has finished draining, clean the drain plug threads and those of the gearbox casing, and refit the drain plug, tightening it securely.

6 Refilling the gearbox is an extremely awkward operation. Above all, allow plenty of time for the oil level to settle properly before checking it. Note that the car must be parked on flat level ground when checking the oil level.

7 Refill the gearbox with the exact amount of the specified type of oil (see the appropriate part of Chapter 1 and *Weekly checks*), then check the oil level as described in Chapter 1A or 1B. When the level is correct, refit the filler level plug with a new sealing washer and tighten securely.

8 Refit the plastic cover to the gearbox or the engine undertray (as applicable), then lower the vehicle to the ground.

3 Gearchange mechanism – adjustment

Note: *A special Renault service tool (B.Vi. 1133 or 1133-01) will be required to accurately adjust the gearchange linkage.*

1 Firmly apply the handbrake, then jack up the front of the vehicle and support it securely on axle stands (see *Jacking and vehicle support*). As applicable, remove the engine compartment undertray or unclip the small cover from the bottom of the gearbox.

2 Unbolt the heat shields from the underbody to gain access to the bottom of the gearlever.

3 Scoop out the old grease from the gearchange linkage balljoint on the gearbox, and refill the socket with suitable new grease. Also check that the gearchange rod mounting bolt at the gearbox lever is tightened to the correct torque. If it is too tight, stiff operation will result. If it is too loose, difficult gearchanging will result.

4 On models where a return spring is fitted to the bottom of the gearlever, make sure that it is in place. On later models where the return spring is incorporated into the lever on the

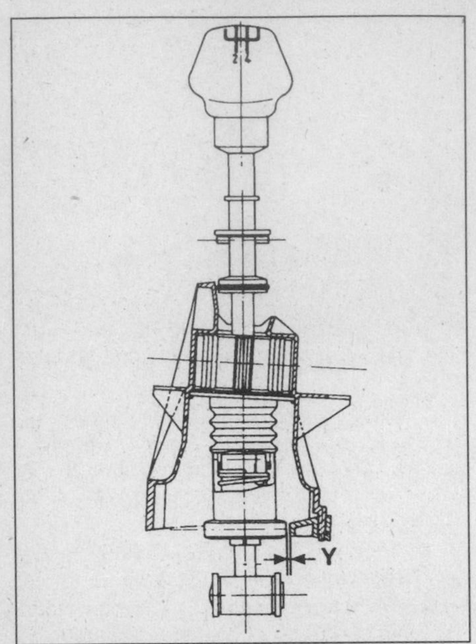

3.5a The adjustment clearance between the gearlever and inclined plane

Y Measuring point

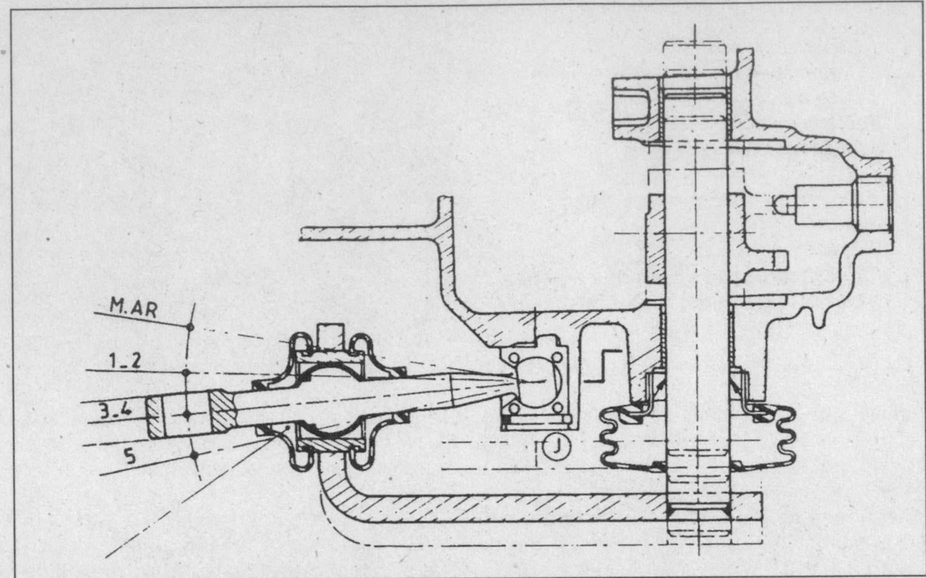

3.6a Gear positions for the gearbox lever

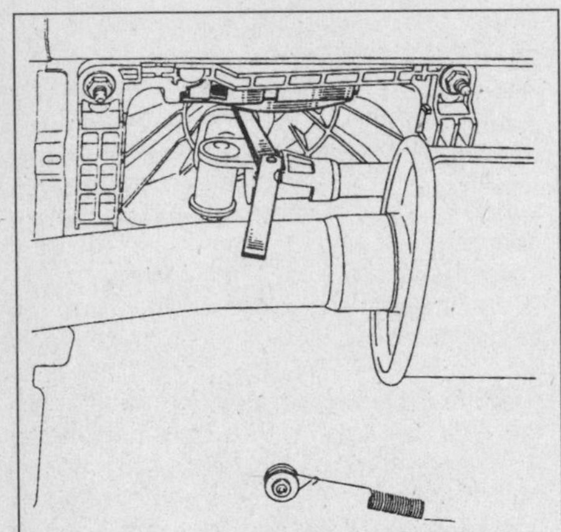

3.5b Using a feeler blade to make the adjustment

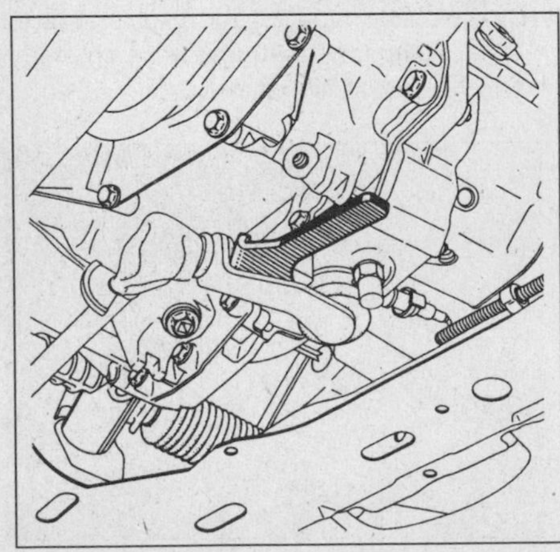

3.6b Using the Renault tool B.Vi.1133 to hold the gearchange lever in position

gearbox, it is still necessary to apply a force of 15 Nm (11 lbf ft) to the bottom of the gearlever when making the adjustment; this can be done either by fitting an old spring, or by using a spring balance attached to the bottom of the gearlever. Make sure that the force is applied to the left-hand side of the lever.

5 Note that two readings must be made; one with the gearlever in the 1st gear position and the other with the lever in the 2nd gear position. Both readings should be added together, then divided by 2 to give an average reading. First select 1st gear, then use a feeler blade to measure the clearance (a) between the reverse stop-ring on the gearlever and the inclined plane on the right-hand side of the gearlever **(see illustrations)**. Now select 2nd gear and measure the clearance (b) at the same point. Add the two clearances (a + b) together and divide by 2; the result should be between 4.0 mm and 7.0 mm (early models with return spring on bottom of lever) or between 7.0 mm and 10.0 mm (later models with return spring on gearbox lever). If not, adjust the clearance as follows.

6 Select 1st gear and make sure that the lever on the gearbox is also in the 1st gear position. To hold the lever securely in the 1st gear position, fit the Renault tool B.Vi.1133 or B.Vi.1133-01 **(see illustrations).** In the absence of the special tool, a suitable alternative can be made from a flat metal bar or a piece of wood.

7 Loosen the clamp bolt at the transmission end of the gearchange rod so that the rod can be moved.

8 Make sure that the gearlever is positioned so that the reverse stop-ring is against the inclined plane on the housing, then insert a 4.0 mm (early models with return spring on bottom of lever) or 7.0 mm (later models with return spring on gearbox lever) feeler blade between the ring and plane. Hold the lever in this position, then tighten the clamp bolt to the specified torque setting.

9 Remove the holding tool, then recheck the clearance as described in paragraph 5.

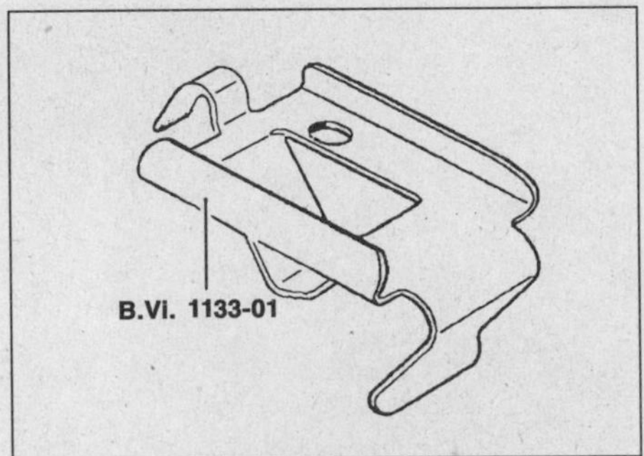

3.6c Renault tool B.Vi.1133-01

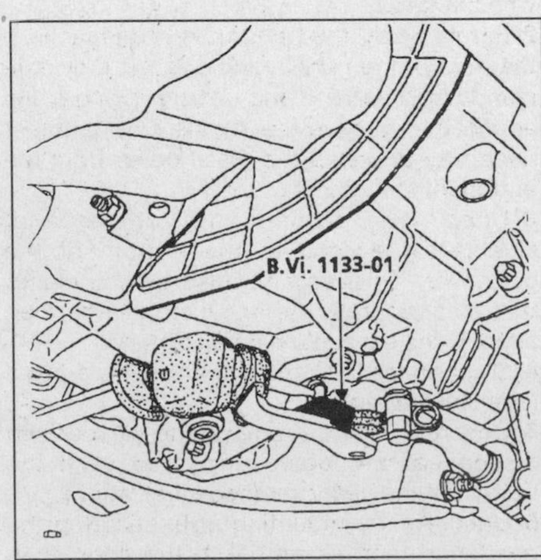

3.6d Using the Renault tool B.Vi.1133-01 to hold the gearchange lever in position

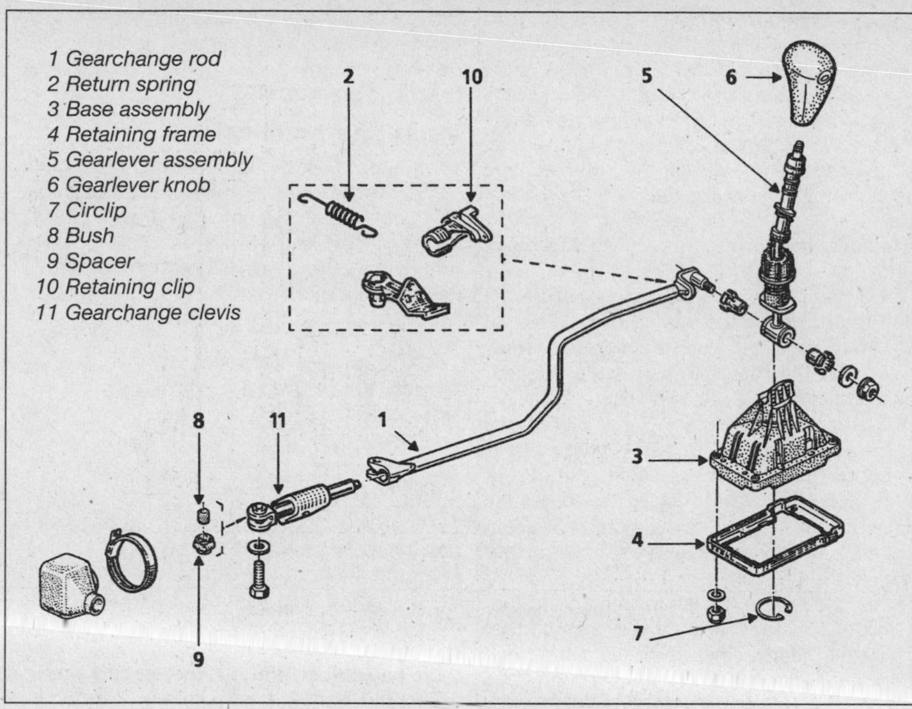

4.1 Gearchange linkage components

10 Check that all gears can be selected, then refit the heat shields, plastic cover or undertray before lowering the vehicle to the ground.

4 Gearchange mechanism – removal and refitting

Removal

1 Working inside the vehicle, carefully prise the gearchange lever gaiter out of the centre console **(see illustration)**. Pull the knob off the top of the gearchange lever and remove it with the gaiter.
2 Firmly apply the handbrake, then jack up the front of the vehicle and support it on axle stands (see *Jacking and vehicle support*). As applicable, remove the engine compartment undertray or unclip the small cover from the bottom of the gearbox.
3 Unbolt and remove the exhaust heat shields for access to the bottom of the gearlever. If necessary, unscrew the clamp bolt and separate the exhaust system, then support the exhaust on an axle stand.
4 Disconnect the return spring where fitted **(see illustration)**.
5 Unscrew the nut, remove the washer and disconnect the gearchange rod from the bottom of the gearlever **(see illustration)**.
6 Unscrew the mounting nuts securing the gearlever base assembly to the floor, then lower the assembly and remove it from under the car. If the exhaust is still in position, it will be necessary to push it to one side while removing the gearlever assembly.
7 Remove the frame from the base.
8 Mount the gearlever in a soft-jawed vice, then extract the circlip and separate the base and gaiter.

4.5 Nut securing the gearchange rod to the bottom of the gearlever

4.9b . . . unscrew and remove the bolt . . .

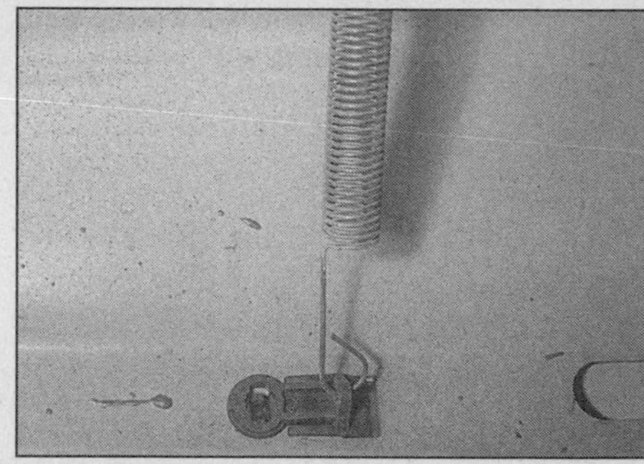
4.4 Return spring attachment to the floor tunnel

9 To remove the gearchange rod, release the rubber gaiter and unscrew the bolt at the front of the rod. Note the location of the bush and spacer **(see illustrations)**. Remove the rod from the transmission.
10 To separate the gearchange clevis, first mark it in relation to the main rod, then loosen the clamp bolt and separate the two sections.
11 Examine all components for signs of wear or damage, and renew as necessary.

Refitting

12 Lubricate all the pivot points with multi-purpose grease.
13 Where the gearchange rod has been dismantled, locate the clevis on the rod in its previously-noted position, and tighten the clamp bolt to the specified torque. Where new components are being fitted, locate the clevis on the rod so that approximately 7.0 to 8.0 mm of the knurled section is visible. Make

4.9a Pull back the rubber boot on the gearchange rod . . .

4.9c . . . and recover the bush from inside the lever

sure that the clevis is offset towards the transmission.

14 Attach the clevis to the gearbox lever and refit the bolt making sure that the bush and spacer are in their correct positions. Tighten the bolt to the specified torque.

15 Reassemble the gearlever components using a reversal of the removal procedure. Make sure the circlip is secure.

16 Lift the gearlever assembly into position in the floor aperture, then locate the frame and refit the mounting nuts. Tighten the nuts to the specified torque.

17 Connect the gearchange rod to the bottom of the gearlever, making sure that the bushes are correctly located and that the nut is positioned on the left-hand side. Refit the washer, then tighten the nut securely.

18 Check and adjust the gearchange with reference to Section 3.

19 Refit the heat shields, plastic cover and undertray, and exhaust system components as applicable, then lower the car to the ground.

20 Refit the gaiter and gearlever knob to the centre console. The knob should be bonded to the lever using suitable adhesive.

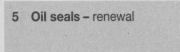

5 Oil seals – renewal

Right-hand driveshaft oil seal

Note: *On early models, a new driveshaft-to-differential side-gear roll pin will be required on refitting (see Chapter 8). Note that if the original double roll pin is renewed, the new one will be of single coiled type. Later models are not fitted with roll pins.*

1 Apply the handbrake, then jack up the front of the car and support it on axle stands (see *Jacking and vehicle support*). Remove the right-hand wheel.

2 Drain the gearbox oil as described in Section 2.

3 Referring to Chapter 8, disconnect the driveshaft from the transmission. Note that where a single driveshaft is fitted, it is not necessary to remove the driveshaft completely, the shaft can be left attached to the hub assembly and slid off from the differential gear splines as the hub assembly is pulled outwards. **Note:** *Do not allow it to hang down under its own weight, as this could damage the constant velocity joints/gaiters.* Where an intermediate driveshaft is fitted, it will be necessary to unbolt the intermediate bearing retainer from the rear of the cylinder block.

4 Remove the O-ring from the side-gear shaft.

5 Wipe clean the old oil seal, and measure its fitted depth below the casing edge. This is necessary to determine the correct fitted position of the new oil seal, if the special Renault fitting tool is not being used.

6 Free the old oil seal, using a small drift to tap the outer edge of the seal inwards so that the opposite edge of the seal tilts out of the casing **(see illustration)**. A pair of pliers or grips can then be used to pull out the oil seal. Take care not to damage the splines of the differential side-gear.

7 Wipe clean the oil seal seating in the casing. Wrap tape around the end of the differential gear splines to prevent the new seal being damaged.

8 Apply a smear of grease to the sealing lip of the new oil seal and, making sure its sealing lip is facing inwards, carefully slide it onto the differential gear shaft. Press the seal squarely into the gearbox until it is positioned at the same depth as the original was prior to removal. If necessary, the seal can be tapped into position using a piece of metal tube or a socket which bears only on the hard outer edge of the seal **(see illustrations)**.

9 Remove the tape from the end of the differential shaft, and slide a new O-ring into position.

10 Reconnect the driveshaft (and intermediate bearing where applicable) to the transmission as described in Chapter 8.

11 Refill the gearbox with oil as described in Section 2.

12 Refit the roadwheel and lower the car to the ground. Tighten the wheel bolts to the specified torque.

Left-hand driveshaft oil seal

13 On the left-hand side of the gearbox, there is no oil seal as the seal is formed by the driveshaft gaiter. If oil is leaking from the left-hand driveshaft-to-gearbox joint and/or bearing, renew the gaiter/bearing as described in Chapter 8.

Input shaft oil seal

14 It is not possible to renew the input shaft oil seal without first dismantling the gearbox. The guide tube assembly is a press fit in the housing, and is removed inwards. Oil seal renewal should therefore be entrusted to a Renault dealer or gearbox overhaul specialist.

6 Reversing light switch – testing, removal and refitting

Testing

1 The reversing light circuit is controlled by a plunger-type switch that is screwed into the left-hand side of the gearbox casing, next to the driveshaft inner joint. If a fault develops in the circuit, first ensure that the circuit fuse has not blown.

2 To test the switch, disconnect the wiring connector, and use a multimeter (set to the resistance function) or a battery-and-bulb test circuit to check that there is continuity between the switch terminals only when reverse gear is selected. If this is not the case, and there are no obvious breaks or other damage to the wires, the switch is faulty, and must be renewed.

Removal

3 Firmly apply the handbrake, then jack up the front of the vehicle and support it on axle stands (see *Jacking and vehicle support*).

4 Where fitted, remove the engine compartment undertray.

5 Disconnect the wiring, then unscrew the switch from the gearbox. Recover the sealing washer.

Refitting

6 Fit a new sealing washer to the switch, then screw it back into the gearbox casing and tighten it securely. Reconnect the wiring, and test the operation of the circuit. Where fitted, refit the engine compartment undertray, then

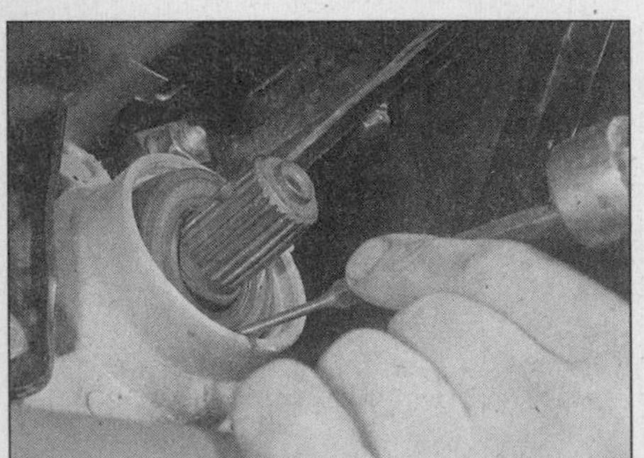

5.6 Tap the bottom of the driveshaft oil seal with a small drift to remove it

5.8a Locate the new oil seal carefully over the output shaft splines . . .

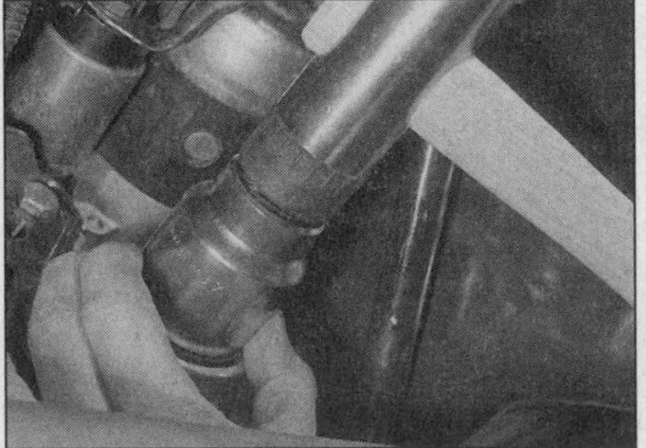

5.8b . . . and press into position with a socket or metal tube

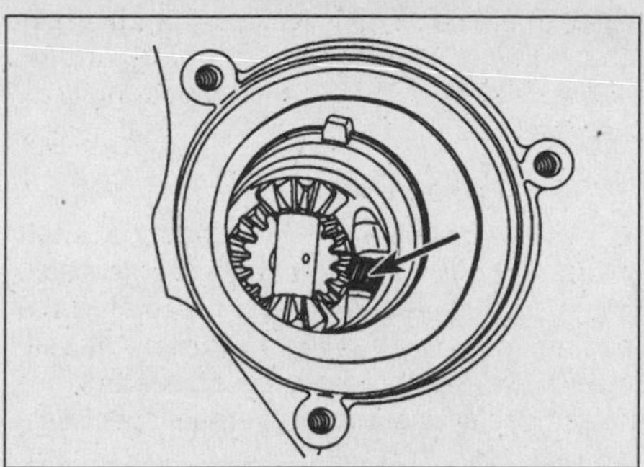

7.3 View of the speedometer drivegear (arrowed) with the differential sun wheel removed

7.4a Removing the vehicle speed sensor from the gearbox

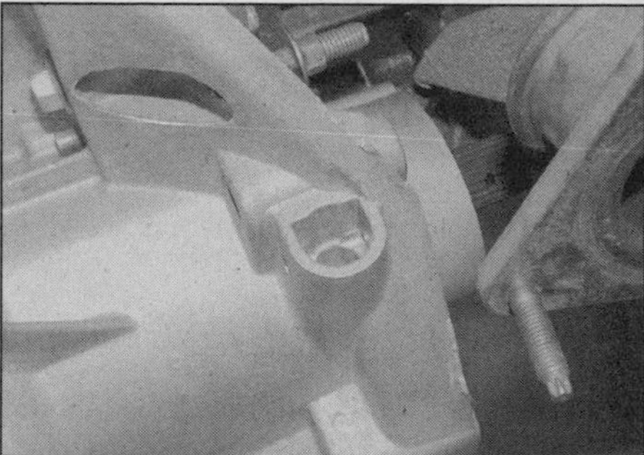

7.4b There is no speedometer drive on later models

lower the vehicle to the ground. If any oil was lost when the switch was removed, check the oil level as described in Chapter 1A or 1B.

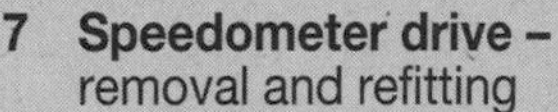

7 Speedometer drive – removal and refitting

Note: *The speedometer drive is taken from the right-hand side of the transmission, just above the driveshaft. On some later models, it is not possible to remove the drive – this later type can be identified by the plastic cable connection to the transmission instead of the clip-type connection on earlier models.*

Removal

1 Disconnect the left-hand driveshaft at the transmission end – refer to Chapter 8. Note that it is not necessary to remove the driveshaft completely; the shaft can be left attached to the hub assembly and slid from the differential sun gear as the hub assembly is pulled outwards. **Note:** *Support the driveshaft on an axle stand; do not allow it to hang down under its own weight, as this could damage the constant velocity joints/gaiters.*

2 Extract the circlip and thrustwasher, then withdraw the left-hand sun wheel from the differential. The sun wheel also acts as the driveshaft spider housing.

3 Turn the differential until the planetary gears are in a vertical plane so that the speedometer drivegear is visible **(see illustration)**.

4 Pull out the clip and disconnect the vehicle speed sensor from the outside of the gearbox **(see illustrations)**.

5 Using long-nosed pliers from the outside of the gearbox, extract the speedometer drivegear shaft vertically.

6 Using the same pliers, extract the speedometer drivegear from inside the differential housing, being very careful not to drop it.

7 Examine the drivegear teeth for wear and damage. Renew it if necessary. Note that if the drivegear teeth on the differential are worn or damaged, it will be necessary to dismantle the transmission – this work should be entrusted to a Renault dealer.

Refitting

8 Using long-nosed pliers, insert the speedometer drivegear into its location.

9 From outside the gearbox, refit the drivegear shaft. Make sure that it engages correctly with the gear location notches **(see illustration)**.

10 Refit the vehicle speed sensor and secure with its clip.

11 Insert the differential sun wheel, then refit the thrustwasher and circlip.

12 Reconnect the left-hand driveshaft with reference to Chapter 8.

8 Manual gearbox – removal and refitting

Note: *This Section describes the removal of the gearbox, leaving the engine in position in the car. Alternatively, the engine and gearbox can be removed together, as described in Chapter 2D, then separated on the bench. Where applicable on early models, a new right-hand driveshaft-to-differential sun wheel roll pin will be required on refitting, and suitable sealant will be required to seal the ends of the roll pin.*

Removal

1 Apply the handbrake, then jack up the front of the vehicle and support it on axle stands (see *Jacking and vehicle support*). As applicable, remove the engine compartment undertray or unclip the small cover from the bottom of the gearbox **(see illustration)**. Remove both front roadwheels.

2 Remove the battery and tray as described in Chapter 5A on all models except early Scénic models, in which case disconnect the battery negative lead.

3 Unscrew the drain plug and drain the gearbox oil into a suitable container **(see illustration)**. Clean the drain plug, refit it and tighten securely.

4 Remove the front section of the left-hand front wheelarch liner with reference to Chapter 11.

5 Refer to Chapter 9 and unbolt the left-hand front brake caliper from the hub carrier without disconnecting the hydraulic brake line. Suspend the caliper from the suspension coil spring using wire. For improved access to the lower balljoint clamp bolt, unbolt and remove the caliper bracket from the hub carrier.

7A

7.9 Notches in the speedometer drivegear engage with the shaft

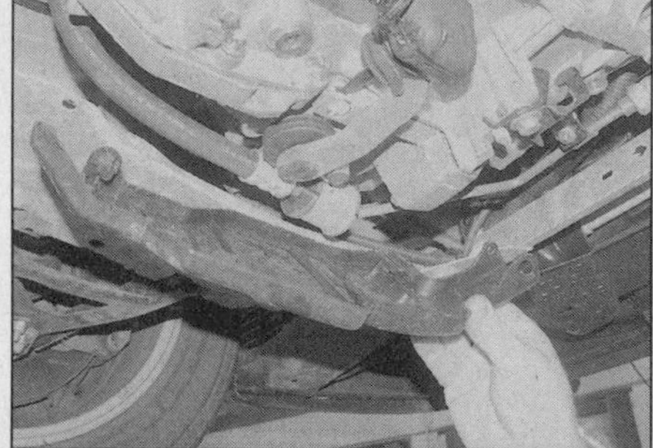

8.1 Unclip the small cover from the bottom of the gearbox

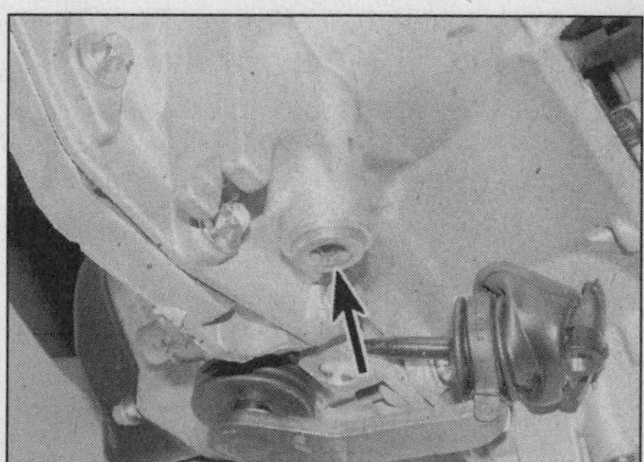

8.3 Gearbox drain plug

8.8 Bolts securing the left-hand driveshaft gaiter to the transmission

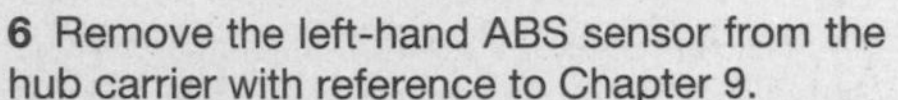

8.9 Unscrewing the clamp bolt securing the left-hand lower balljoint to the bottom of the hub carrier

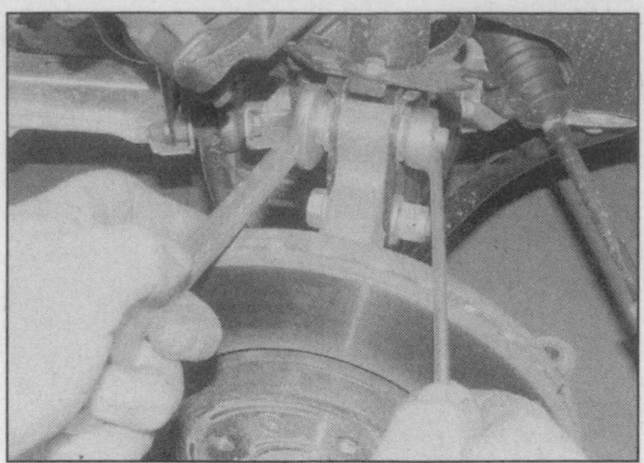

8.10a Unbolt the left-hand hub carrier from the bottom of the strut . . .

6 Remove the left-hand ABS sensor from the hub carrier with reference to Chapter 9.

7 Disconnect the left-hand track rod end from the steering arm on the hub carrier with reference to Chapter 10.

8 Unscrew and remove the bolts securing the left-hand driveshaft gaiter to the transmission **(see illustration)**.

9 Unscrew and remove the clamp bolt securing the left-hand lower balljoint to the bottom of the hub carrier **(see illustration)**, then lever down the lower arm and disconnect the balljoint from the carrier. If possible, keep the lower arm down to prevent damage to the driveshaft gaiter.

10 Unscrew and remove the bolts securing the left-hand hub carrier to the bottom of the front suspension strut. Release the carrier from the strut, then withdraw it together with the left-hand driveshaft and place it away from the vehicle **(see illustrations)**. Check that the driveshaft inner joint roller bearings are all in position – if the joint is worn excessively, the rollers may become detached.

11 Remove the right-hand front wheelarch liner.

12 Refer to Chapter 9 and unbolt the right-hand front brake caliper together with the bracket from the hub carrier without disconnecting the hydraulic brake line. Suspend the caliper from the suspension coil spring using wire. **Note:** *If only the caliper is removed, there is insufficient room to remove the balljoint clamp bolt.*

13 Remove the right-hand ABS sensor from the hub carrier with reference to Chapter 9.

14 Disconnect the right-hand track rod end from the steering arm on the hub carrier with reference to Chapter 10.

15 Unscrew and remove the clamp bolt securing the right-hand lower balljoint to the bottom of the hub carrier, then lever down the lower arm and disconnect the balljoint from the carrier. If possible, keep the lower arm down to prevent damage to the driveshaft gaiter.

16 Where applicable (early models), remove the roll pin securing the inner end of the driveshaft to the differential sun gear.

17 Where applicable (models with an intermediate bearing), unbolt the intermediate bearing retainer from the rear of the cylinder block. Unscrew and remove the bolts securing the right-hand hub carrier to the bottom of the front suspension strut. Release the carrier from the strut, then withdraw it together with the left-hand driveshaft and place it away from the vehicle **(see illustrations)**. Refer to Chapter 8 if necessary.

18 Disconnect the exhaust from the exhaust manifold/catalytic converter with reference to Chapter 4A or 4B.

19 Unbolt the subframe support tie rods on each side **(see illustration)**, and either remove them completely or leave the lower bolts loose and swivel down the rods.

20 Release the wiring loom from the clips on the left-hand side of the subframe. Also unbolt the earth cable from the transmission **(see illustration)**.

21 Unbolt the power steering pipe mountings from the right-hand side of the subframe and from behind the steering gear.

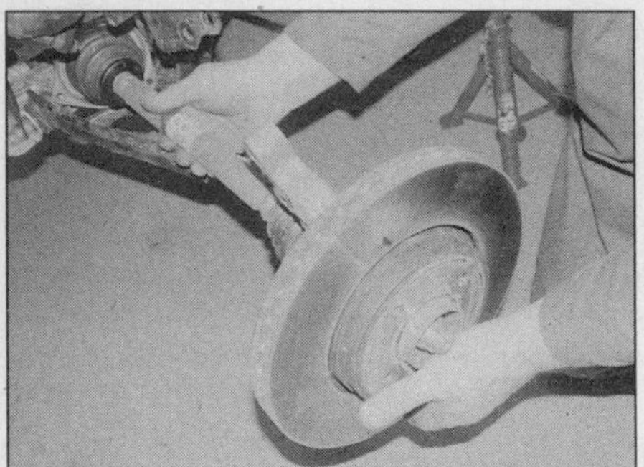

8.10b . . . then withdraw the driveshaft together with the hub carrier from the transmission

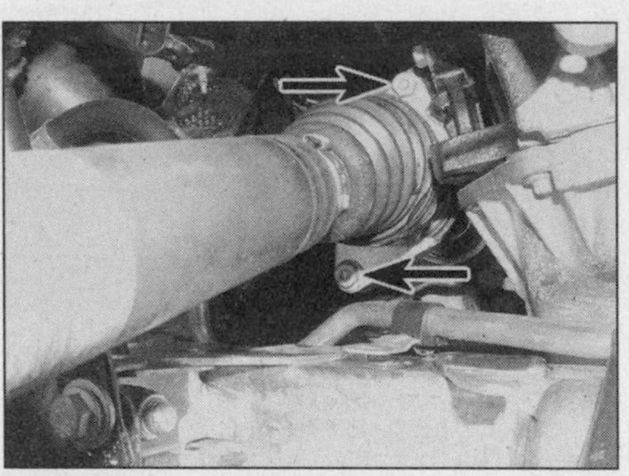

8.17a Right-hand driveshaft intermediate bearing and clamp

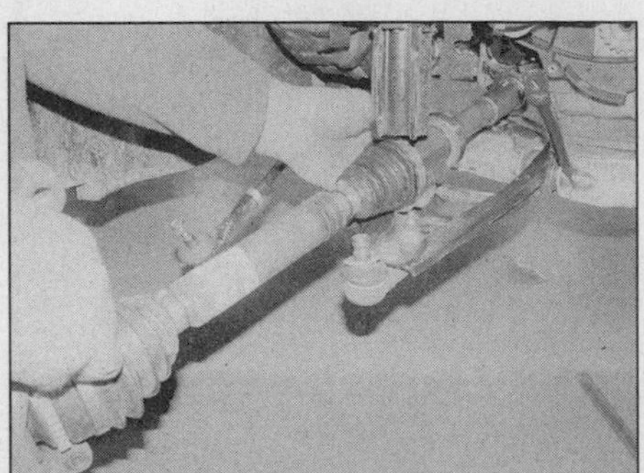

8.17b Removing the right-hand driveshaft together with the hub carrier

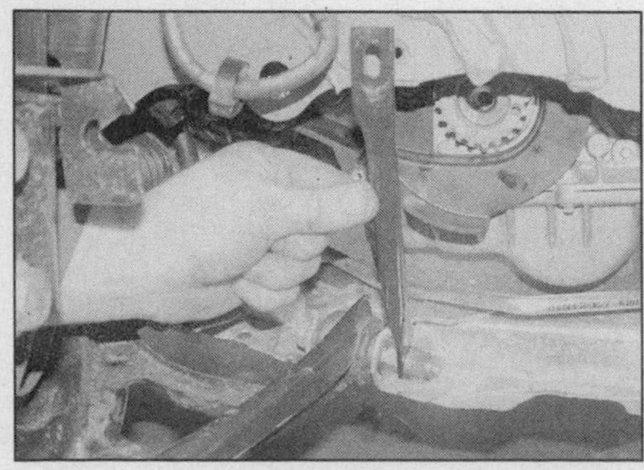

8.19 Removing the subframe support tie rods

8.20 Earth cable attached to the top of the transmission

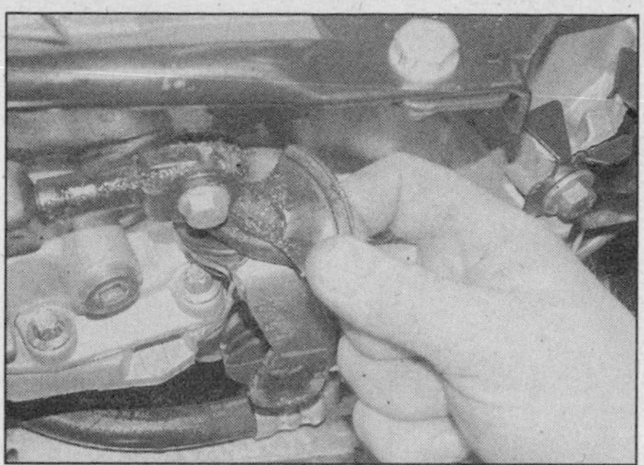
8.23a Pull back the rubber boot . . .

8.23b . . . then remove the pivot bolt, and disconnect the gearchange rod

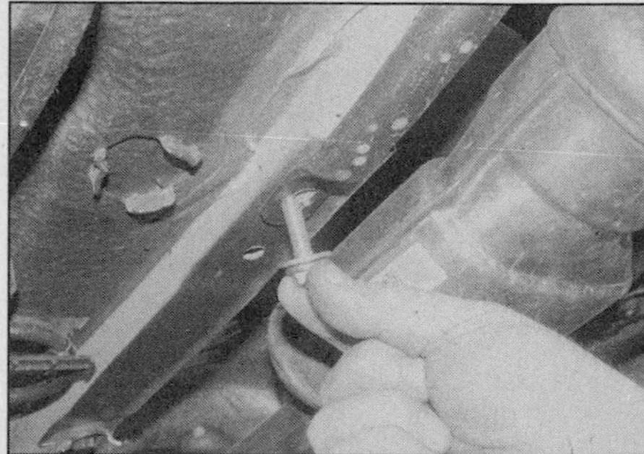
8.23c Unbolting the heat shields from the underbody

8.24a Rear engine mounting link

8.24b Removing the front mounting link bolt

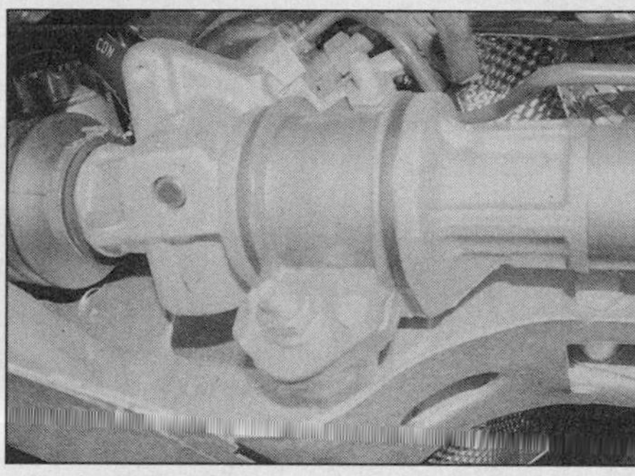
8.27a Steering gear mounting

22 Unbolt the heat shield from under the gearlever.

23 Disconnect the return spring (where fitted) then disconnect the gearchange rod from the transmission with reference to Section 4. In order to move the gearchange rod to one side, unbolt the exhaust heatshields from the underbody **(see illustrations)**.

24 Unscrew and remove the bolt securing the rear engine mounting link to the transmission, then loosen the link bolt on the subframe and swivel the link to the rear **(see illustration)**.

25 Where applicable, unscrew the nuts and remove the heat shield from the steering gear.

26 Make sure that the steering wheel is in its central position with the front wheels facing straight-ahead. To prevent possible damage to the airbag rotary spring, tie the steering wheel in its central position.

27 Unscrew the bolts/nuts securing the steering gear to the rear of the subframe. Remove the mounting clamps and carefully prise the steering gear away from the subframe. Tie the track rod ends to the front suspension coils on each side in order to support the steering gear while the subframe is being lowered **(see illustrations)**.

28 For additional working room, remove the front bumper as described in Chapter 11.

29 Unbolt and remove the horn with reference to Chapter 12.

30 Use trolley jacks or axle stands to support the weight of the front subframe, then unscrew and remove the subframe mounting bolts and lower the unit to the floor. Withdraw

8.27b Removing a steering gear mounting clamp

8.27c Support the steering gear by tying the track rod ends to the coil springs

8.30a Support the subframe with a trolley jack . . .

8.30b . . . then unscrew the mounting bolts . . .

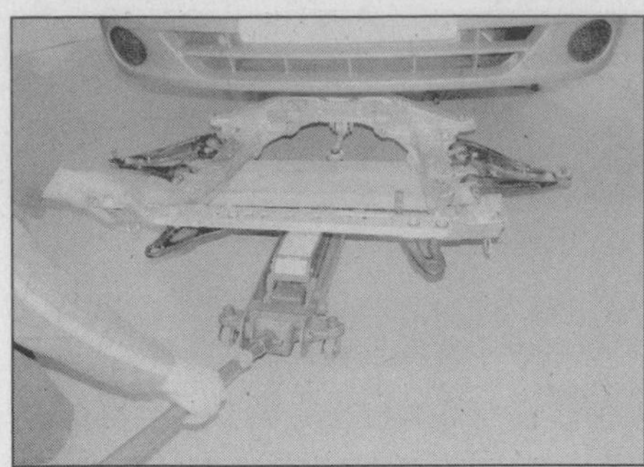
8.30c . . . and lower the subframe to the floor

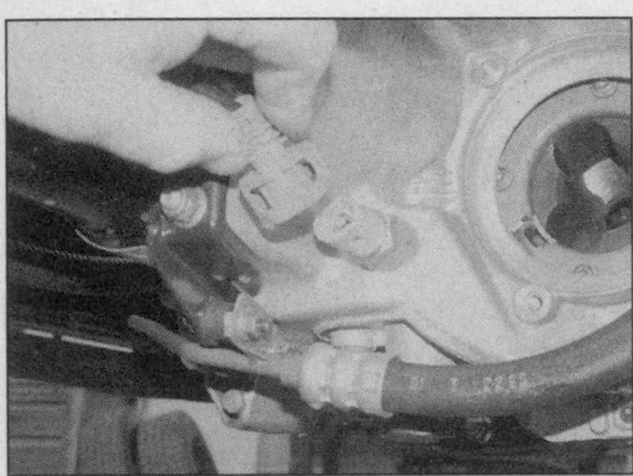
8.31 Disconnecting the wiring from the reversing light switch on the transmission

8.33 Using a support bar to support the left-hand end of the engine. Note the additional metal bar bolted to the chassis member

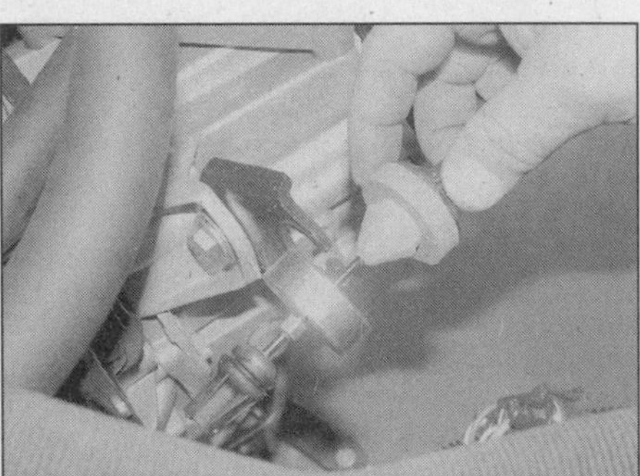
8.35 Disconnecting the outer clutch cable from the mounting bracket

the subframe from under the vehicle **(see illustrations)**.

31 Disconnect the wiring from the reversing light switch **(see illustration)** and speedometer sender (if fitted) on the transmission. Where applicable on early models, disconnect the speedometer cable.

32 Remove the air cleaner and inlet ducts with reference to Chapter 4A or 4B. On turbo-diesel models, remove the inlet and outlet ducts from the intercooler.

33 Attach a suitable hoist to the left-hand end of the engine and support its weight. A support bar across the engine compartment may be used if required. It may be necessary to make up an additional support for the bar since the front wings are of plastic and their channels are not strong enough to support the engine **(see illustration)**.

34 On Scénic models, if necessary remove the windscreen wiper arms, the scuttle panel seal, and the two scuttle panel grilles.

35 Disconnect the clutch cable from the gearbox by releasing the inner cable from the end of the release fork then removing the outer cable from the bracket **(see illustration)**. Position the cable to one side.

36 Unscrew the mounting bolts and remove the crankshaft speed/position (TDC) sensor from the top of the gearbox bellhousing **(see illustration)**. Position the sensor to one side.

37 Unscrew the three starter motor mounting bolts, noting the location of the wiring support on one of them **(see illustration)**.

8.36 Removing the crankshaft speed/position (TDC) sensor from the top of the gearbox

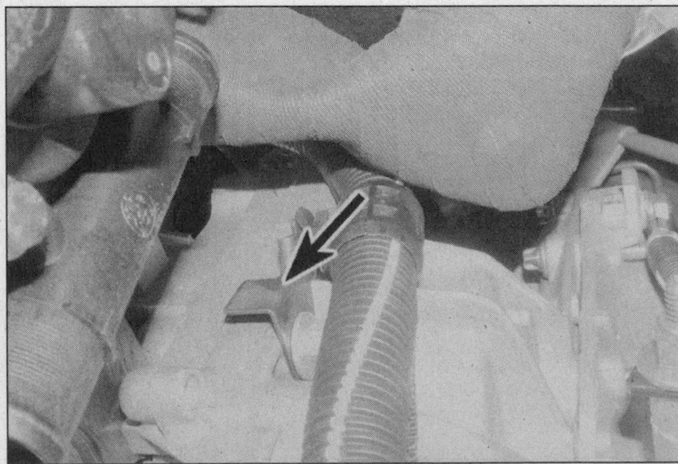
8.37 One of the starter motor mounting bolts has a wiring support bracket on it

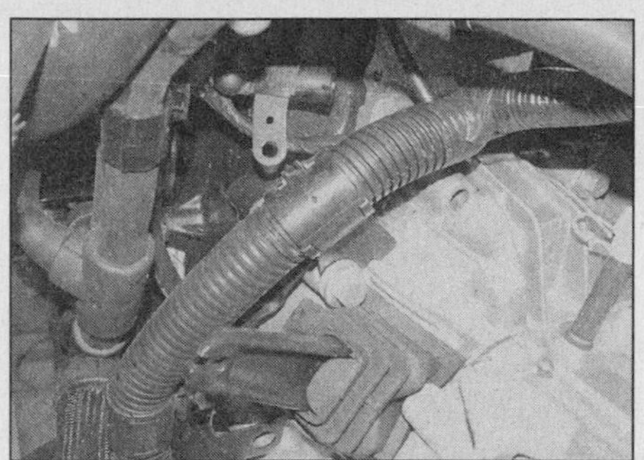
8.38 A bracket is also located on one of the upper transmission bolts

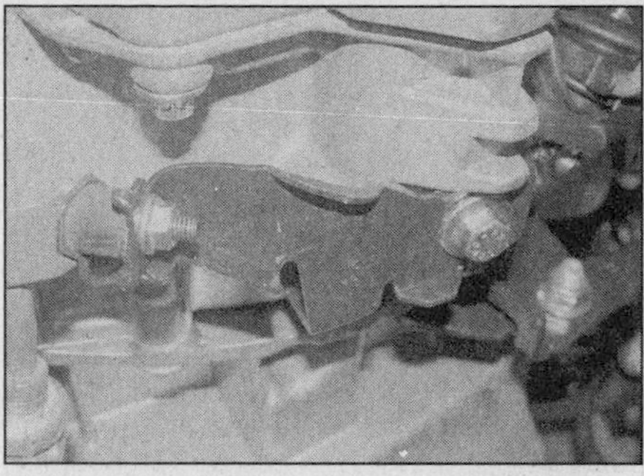
8.39a Power steering hydraulic fluid pipe support located on the bottom . . .

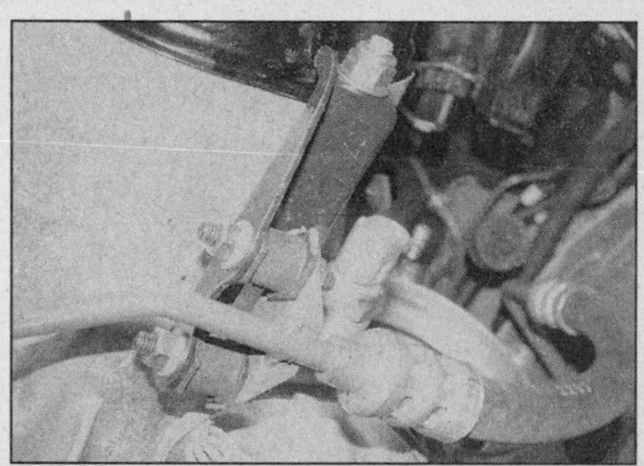
8.39b . . . and side of the transmission

38 Unscrew the two upper bolts securing the transmission to the engine, noting the location of the wiring harness bracket **(see illustration)**.

39 Where applicable, unbolt the power steering hydraulic fluid pipe supports from the transmission **(see illustrations)**. Tie the pipe to one side so that it will not interfere with the removal of the transmission.

40 Where applicable, unbolt the exhaust support bracket from the rear of the transmission.

41 Position a trolley jack beneath the transmission, and take its weight **(see illustration)**.

42 Remove the starter motor and position it to one side without disconnecting the wiring. Make sure that all other relevant wiring is disconnected from any additional components near the transmission.

43 Make sure that the engine is adequately supported with the hoist, then unscrew and remove the four bolts/nut securing the left-hand engine mounting to the transmission **(see illustrations)**.

44 Carefully lower the engine and transmission until there is sufficient clearance between the transmission and body. Make sure that the engine does not bear against the right-hand side of the engine compartment.

45 Unscrew and remove the remaining bolts and two nuts securing the transmission to the engine, then, with the help of an assistant, lift the transmission directly from the engine **(see illustrations)**. Do not allow the gearbox to

8.41 Supporting the transmission on a transmission cradle

8.43a Unscrew the bolts and nut . . .

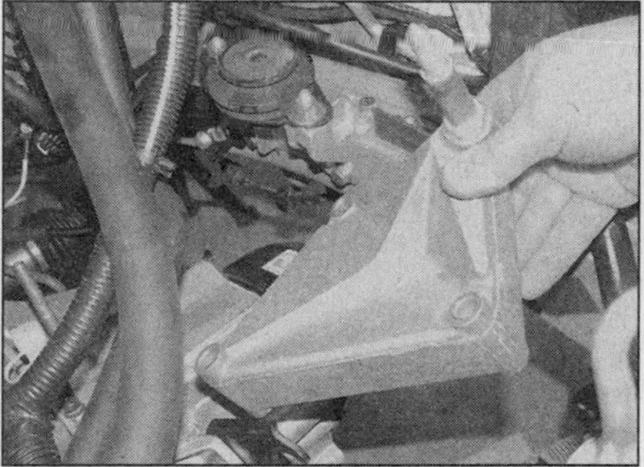
8.43b . . . and remove the left-hand mounting from the transmission

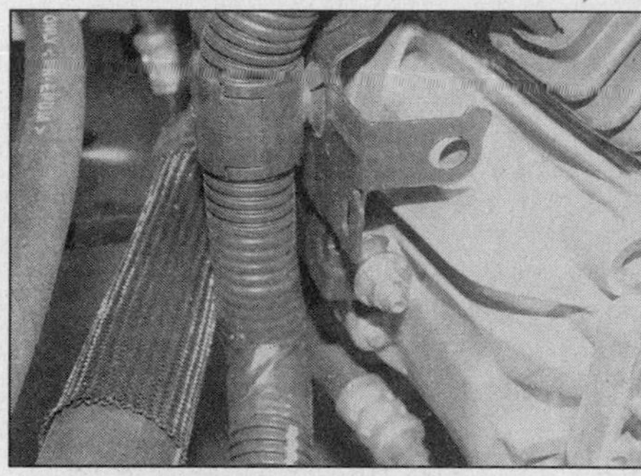
8.45a Front mounting nut securing the transmission to the engine

7A

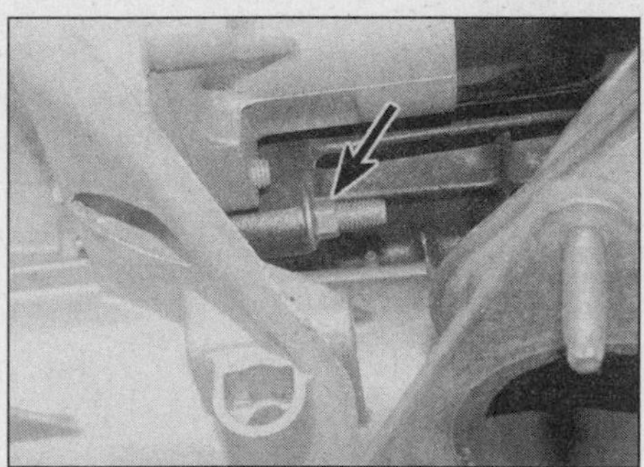
8.45b Rear mounting nut securing the transmission to the engine

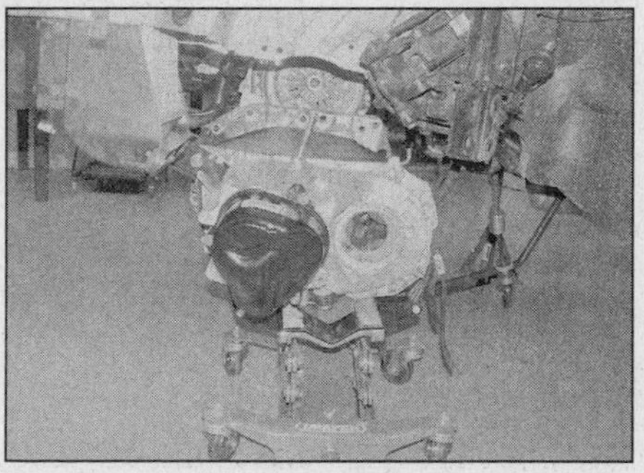
8.45c Removing the transmission from the engine

8.45d Transmission removed from the engine

hang on the input shaft and keep the gearbox in line with the engine until the input shaft has cleared the clutch. Lower the transmission to the ground and withdraw from under the vehicle.

Refitting

46 Refitting is a reversal of removal, noting the following additional points.

a) *Before assembling the gearbox to the engine, make sure that the release fork is correctly engaged with the release bearing. To ensure the fork remains engaged, tie it to the gearbox bellhousing.*
b) *Make sure that the location dowels are correctly positioned in the gearbox.*
c) *Apply a little high-melting-point grease to the splines of the gearbox input shaft. Do not apply too much, otherwise there is the possibility of the grease contaminating the clutch friction disc.*
d) *Make sure that the locating dowel for the starter motor is correctly fitted.*
e) *Before refitting the driveshafts, make sure that the rollers are in position (see paragraph 10).*
f) *Where applicable, use new roll pins when reconnecting the right-hand driveshaft, and seal the ends using a suitable sealant.*
g) *Check the gearbox oil level with reference to Chapter 1A or 1B.*
h) *Tighten all nuts and bolts to the specified torque.*

9 Manual gearbox overhaul – general information

Overhauling a manual gearbox is a difficult and involved job for the DIY home mechanic. In addition to dismantling and reassembling many small parts, clearances must be precisely measured and, if necessary, changed by selecting shims and spacers. Gearbox internal components are also often difficult to obtain, and in many instances, extremely expensive. Because of this, if the gearbox develops a fault or becomes noisy, the best course of action is to have the unit overhauled by a specialist repairer, or to obtain an exchange reconditioned unit.

Nevertheless, it is not impossible for the more experienced mechanic to overhaul a gearbox, provided the special tools are available and the job is done in a deliberate step-by-step manner so that nothing is overlooked.

The tools necessary for an overhaul include internal and external circlip pliers, bearing pullers, a slide-hammer, a set of pin punches, a dial test indicator, and possibly a hydraulic press. In addition, a large, sturdy workbench and a vice will be required.

During dismantling of the gearbox, make careful notes of how each component is fitted, to make reassembly easier and more accurate.

Before dismantling the gearbox, it will help if you have some idea what area is malfunctioning. Certain problems can be closely related to specific areas in the gearbox, which can make component examination and replacement easier. Refer to the *Fault finding* Section at the end of this manual for more information.

Chapter 7 Part B: Automatic transmission

Contents

Degrees of difficulty

Easy, suitable for novice with little experience 	**Fairly easy,** suitable for beginner with some experience 	**Fairly difficult,** suitable for competent DIY mechanic 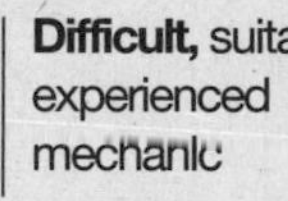	**Difficult,** suitable for experienced DIY mechanic	**Very difficult,** suitable for expert DIY or professional

Specifications

General

Type ... Electronically controlled with four forward speeds and reverse. Final drive differential integral with transmission

Designation:
- Models manufactured up to August 1999 (approx) ... AD4
- Models manufactured from September 1999-on (approx) ... DP0

Torque wrench settings	Nm	lbf ft
AD4 transmission		
Driveplate cover plate bolts	24	18
Engine to transmission	50	37
Fluid cooler bolts	25	18
Fluid filter mounting bolts	5	4
Torque converter-to-driveplate nuts:		
Original nut – yellow	25	18
Modified nut – black*	21	15
Transmission sump bolts	10	7
DP0 transmission		
Drain plug	25	18
Engine to transmission	45	33
Fluid cooler bolt	50	37
Modular connector mounting plate bolts	20	15
Multi-function switch mounting bolts	10	7
Topping-up overflow	35	26
Torque converter-to-driveplate nuts*	30	22

***Note:** *Use new nuts.*

1 General information

Automatic transmission models are fitted with a fully automatic four-speed, electronically-controlled transmission.

The transmission consists of a torque converter, an epicyclic geartrain, hydraulically-operated clutches and brakes, and an electronic control unit. Sensors fitted to the transmission include an input speed sensor, output speed sensor, fluid cooler flow control solenoid valve and a line pressure sensor **(see illustrations)**.

The AD4 type transmission was fitted to models manufactured up to approximately August 1999, and thereafter the type DP0 transmission was fitted. The main difference between the two types of transmission are that the DP0 type incorporates a 'shift-lock' and 'lock-up' facility. The shift-lock system prevents the gear selector lever from being moved without simultaneously depressing the brake pedal. The lock-up system consists of a mini clutch unit located inside the torque converter which locks the transmission directly to the engine during certain conditions in order to eliminate the slight slippage of the converter turbine which would otherwise occur. The lock-up function is controlled by the ECU.

The epicyclic geartrain provides the forward gears or reverse gear, depending on which of its component parts are held stationary or allowed to turn. The components of the geartrain are held or released by brakes and clutches which are activated by a hydraulic control unit. A fluid pump within the transmission provides the necessary hydraulic pressure to operate the brakes and clutches.

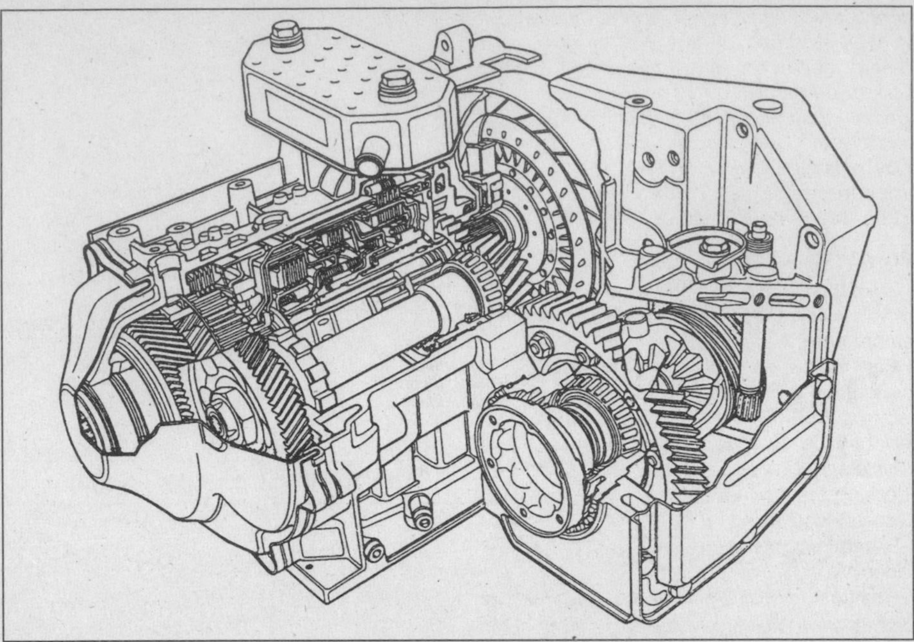

1.2a Cutaway view of the AD4 transmission unit

Impulses from switches and sensors connected to the transmission throttle and selector linkages are directed to the ECU computer module, which determines the ratio to be selected from the information received. The computer activates solenoid valves, which in turn open or close ducts within the hydraulic control unit. This causes the clutches and brakes to hold or release the various components of the geartrain, and provide the correct ratio for the particular engine speed or load. The information from the computer module can be overridden by use of the selector lever, and a particular gear can be held if required, regardless of engine speed.

The automatic transmission fluid is cooled by passing it through a cooler located on the top of the transmission. Coolant from the cooling system passes through the cooler.

Due to the complexity of the automatic transmission, any repair or overhaul work must be left to a Renault dealer with the necessary special equipment for fault diagnosis and repair. The contents of the following Sections are therefore confined to supplying general information, and any service information and instructions that can be used by the owner.

Caution: If the radio/cassette in your vehicle is equipped with an anti-theft system, make sure you have the correct activation code before disconnecting the battery.

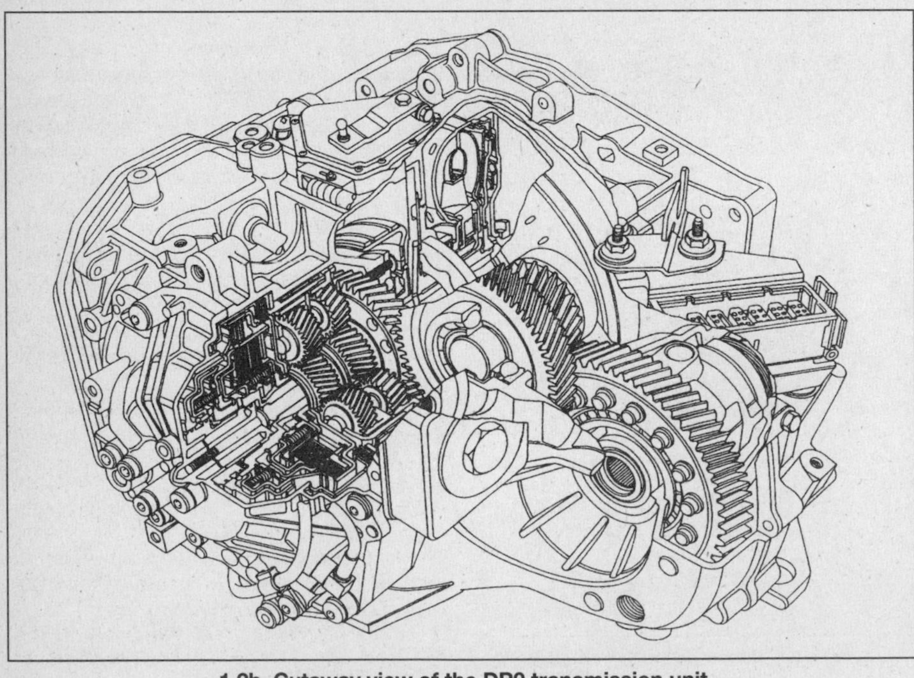

1.2b Cutaway view of the DP0 transmission unit

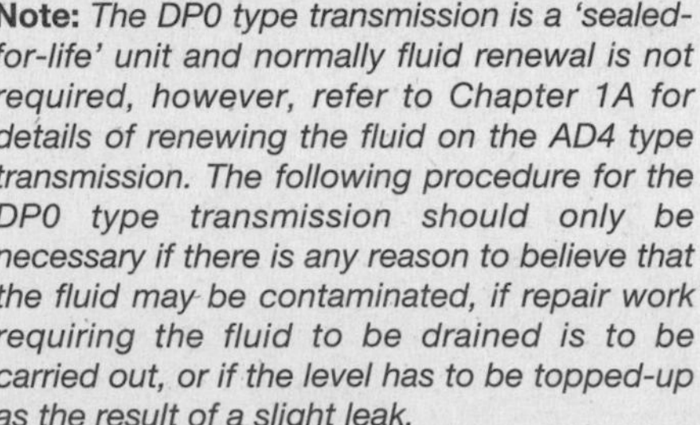

2 Automatic transmission fluid renewal – DP0 type transmission

Note: *The DP0 type transmission is a 'sealed-for-life' unit and normally fluid renewal is not required, however, refer to Chapter 1A for details of renewing the fluid on the AD4 type transmission. The following procedure for the DP0 type transmission should only be necessary if there is any reason to believe that the fluid may be contaminated, if repair work requiring the fluid to be drained is to be carried out, or if the level has to be topped-up as the result of a slight leak.*

Note: *The transmission fluid filling and level checking procedure is particularly* *complicated, and the home mechanic would be well-advised to take the vehicle to a Renault dealer for the draining and refilling work to be carried out. To ensure accuracy, special test equipment is necessary to measure the fluid temperature when carrying out the level check. However, the following procedure is given for those who may have access to this equipment.*

Draining

1 Take the vehicle on a short run, to warm the transmission up to normal operating temperature.

2 Park the car on level ground, then switch off the ignition and apply the handbrake firmly. Jack up the front of the car and support it securely on axle stands (see *Jacking and vehicle support*). Note that, when refilling and checking the fluid level, the car must be level to ensure accuracy.

3 Remove the engine compartment undertray.

4 Position a suitable container under the transmission. Unscrew the transmission drain plug and allow the fluid to drain completely into the container. Note that the drain plug and level checking plug are incorporated into one unit – the drain plug is the larger of the two hexagonal headed plugs forming the draining/level checking unit **(see illustrations)**.

Warning: If the fluid is hot, take precautions against scalding.

5 When the fluid has finished draining, clean the drain plug threads and those of the transmission casing. Fit a new sealing washer to the drain plug, and refit the plug to the transmission, tightening it securely.

Refilling

6 Refer to Chapter 4A and remove the air inlet duct from the engine compartment for access to the transmission filler plug. Unscrew the filler plug from the top of the transmission

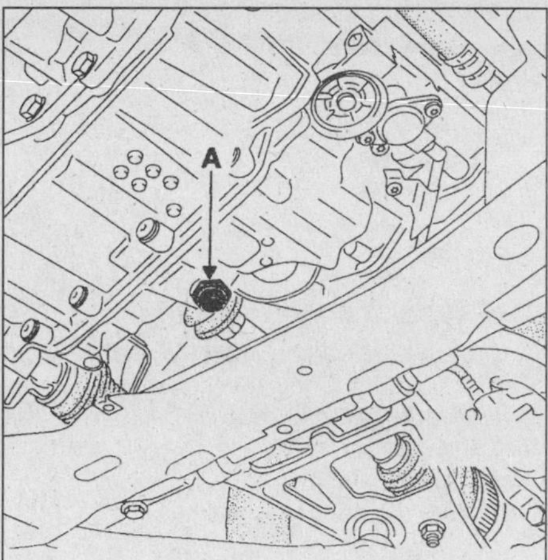

2.4a Combined drain plug and level checking plug unit (A)

(see illustration). Add 3.5 litres of the specified fluid to the transmission via the filler plug opening, using a clean funnel with a fine-mesh filter, then refit the plug.

7 Connect the Renault XR25 test meter to the diagnostic socket, and enter D14 then #04. With the selector lever in Park, run the engine at idle speed until the fluid temperature, as shown on the test meter, reaches 60 ± 1.0°C.

8 With the engine still running, unscrew the level plug from the centre of the draining/level checking unit. Allow the excess fluid to run out into a calibrated container drop-by-drop, then refit the plug. The amount of fluid should be more than 0.1 litre; if it is not, the fluid level in the transmission is incorrect.

9 If the level is incorrect, add an extra 0.5 litre of the specified fluid to the transmission, as described in paragraph 6. Allow the transmission to cool down to 50°C, then repeat the checking procedure again as described in the previous paragraphs. Repeat the procedure as required until more than the specified amount of fluid is drained as described in the previous paragraphs,

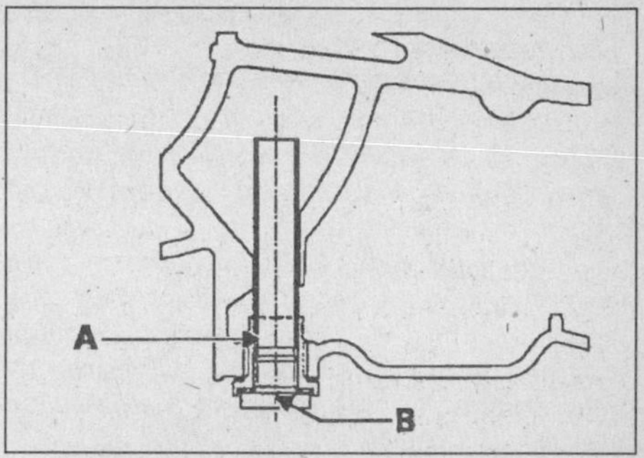

2.4b Cross-section of the combined drain/level plug unit

A Drain plug B Level (overflow) plug

indicating that the transmission fluid level is correct, then securely tighten the level plug. Refit the engine undertray and the air cleaner duct.

10 With the XR25 test meter still connected, enter the command G74* then the date to reset the oil ageing counter in the electronic control unit. Disconnect the test meter on completion.

3 Transmission fluid filter – renewal

Note: *This procedure applies to the AD4 type transmission only.*

1 The fluid filter should be changed whenever the transmission fluid has become contaminated.

2 Drain the transmission fluid as described in Chapter 1A.

3 Unbolt the coolant expansion tank from the left-hand side of the engine compartment, and position it to one side.

4 Remove the air cleaner assembly as described in Chapter 4A.

5 Apply the handbrake, then jack up the left-hand front of the car and support on axle stands (see *Jacking and vehicle support*). Remove the roadwheel.

6 Remove the left-hand front wheelarch liner which is retained by plastic clips and screws.

7 Using a trolley jack and block of wood, support the weight of the transmission.

8 Unscrew and remove the bolts securing the left-hand engine/transmission mounting to the body.

9 On models with ABS, unscrew and ABS pump mounting nut on the left-hand engine mounting.

10 Raise the transmission on the trolley jack to provide room to remove the transmission sump.

11 Slacken and remove the sump retaining bolts, and lower the sump away from the transmission. Recover the sump seal.

12 Unbolt the filter from the base of the transmission, and recover the filter gasket **(see illustration)**.

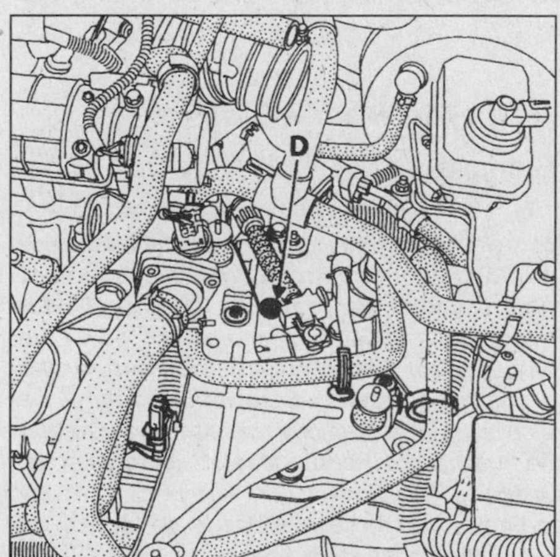

2.6 Transmission fluid filler plug (D)

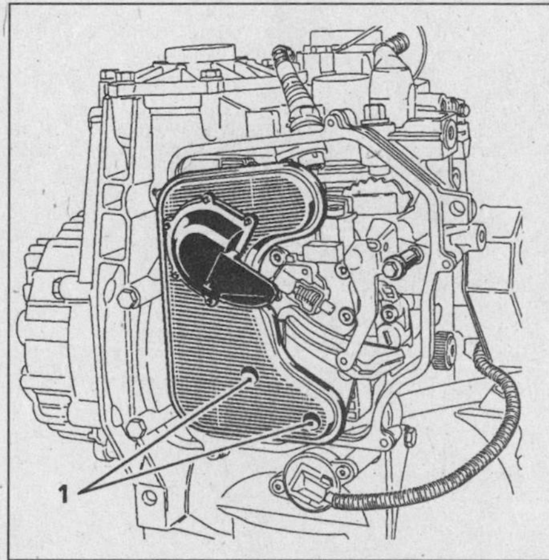

3.12 Fluid filter retaining bolts (1)

13 Remove the magnet from inside the sump, noting its correct fitted position, and clean away all traces of metal filings. The filings (if any) should be very fine; any sizeable chips of metal indicate a worn component in the transmission. Refit the magnet in the correct position.

14 Fit a new gasket on top of the filter element, and offer the filter to the transmission. Refit the retaining bolts, ensuring that the gasket is still correctly positioned, and tighten them to the specified torque.

15 Ensure that the seal is correctly located on the sump and refit the sump to the transmission, tightening its retaining bolts to the specified torque.

16 Lower the transmission, then refit the left-hand engine/transmission mounting bolts and tighten to the specified torque (see Chapter 2A or 2B).

17 On models with ABS, refit and tighten the pump mounting nut on the left-hand engine mounting.

18 Refit the wheelarch liner and roadwheel, and lower the vehicle to the ground. Tighten the roadwheel bolt to the specified torque setting.

19 Refit the air cleaner and coolant expansion tank.

20 Fill the transmission with the specified type and amount of fluid as described in Chapter 1A.

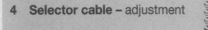

4 Selector cable – adjustment

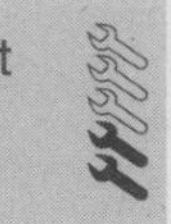

AD4 type transmission

1 Apply the handbrake, then jack up the front of the car and support it on axle stands (see *Jacking and vehicle support*). Remove the heat shield(s) for access to the underside of the selector assembly.

2 Remove the centre console as described in Chapter 11.

3 Remove the air cleaner assembly as described in Chapter 4A.

4 Disconnect the selector cable from the transmission lever by removing the clip(s) and pulling the end fitting from the balljoint.

5 Make sure the cable is attached to the lever assembly correctly, then turn the cable lock ring to ensure that the adjustment sleeve is free.

6 Position both the lever on the transmission and the selector lever inside the vehicle in 1st gear hold.

7 Offer the cable end fitting over the balljoint (but do not refit it at this stage) on the transmission, and check that it is aligned correctly. If not, adjust the cable by turning the sleeve. When correctly aligned, push the end fitting onto the balljoint, and lock the adjustment by turning the ring on the sleeve.

8 Refit the cable retaining clip(s).

9 Refit the centre console as described in Chapter 11.

10 Check that the selector lever moves freely, and that the starter motor will only operate with P or N selected. Also check that the Park function operates correctly.

11 Refit the air cleaner assembly as described in Chapter 4A.

12 Refit the heat shield(s) then lower the vehicle to the ground.

DP0 type transmission

13 Move the selector lever inside the car to the N position.

14 Disconnect the selector cable end fitting from the multi-function switch on top of the transmission. To improve access to the cable, remove the air cleaner inlet duct as described in Chapter 4A.

15 Check that the multi-function switch is in the N position, and if necessary set it accordingly.

16 Depress the tab on the side of the cable end fitting and suitably retain it in the released position.

17 Reconnect the selector cable to the multi-function switch then release the tab on the end fitting to lock the cable. Refit the air cleaner inlet duct as described in Chapter 4A.

18 Check that the selector lever moves freely, and that the starter motor will only operate with P or N selected. Also check that the Park function operates correctly.

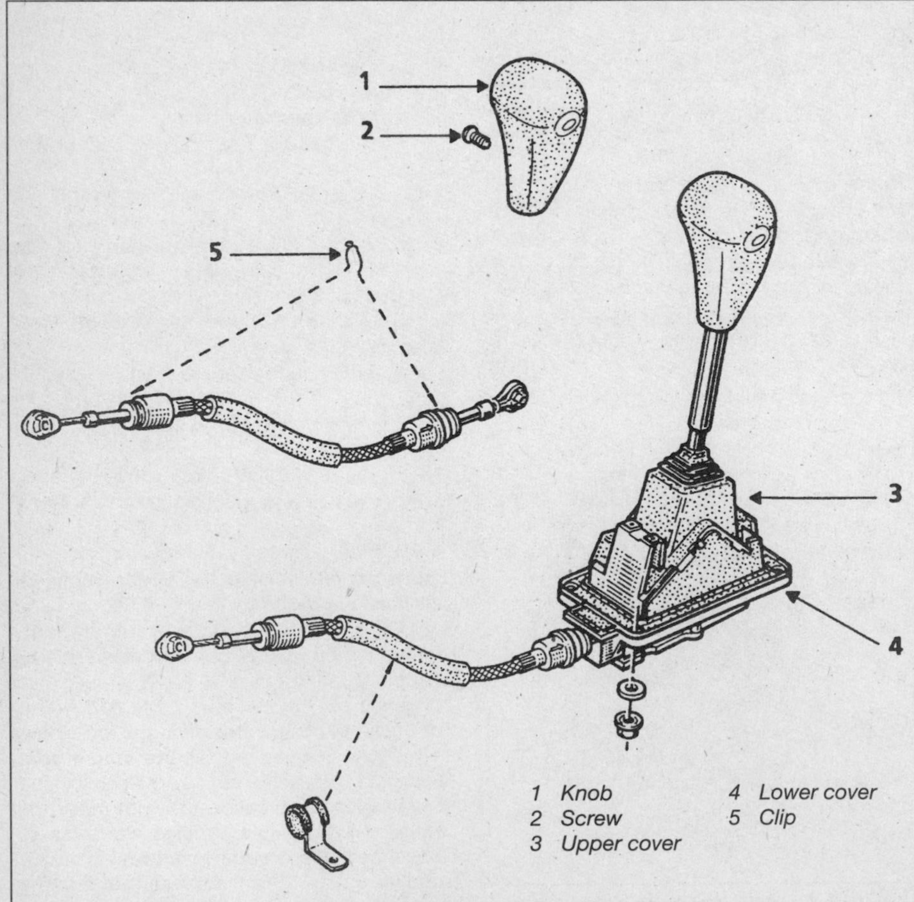

5.2 Selector cable and lever components

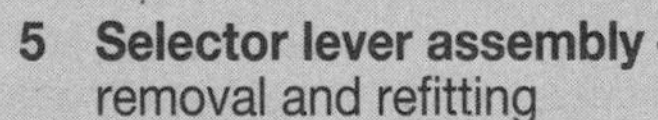

5 Selector lever assembly – removal and refitting

AD4 type transmission

Removal

1 Apply the handbrake, then jack up the front of the car and support it on axle stands (see *Jacking and vehicle support*). Remove the heat shield(s) for access to the underside of the selector assembly.

2 Inside the vehicle, unscrew the small screw and remove the knob from the top of the gearlever, then remove the centre console as described in Chapter 11 and disconnect the wiring **(see illustration)**.

3 Remove the air cleaner assembly as described in Chapter 4A.

4 Disconnect the selector cable from the transmission lever by removing the clip(s) and

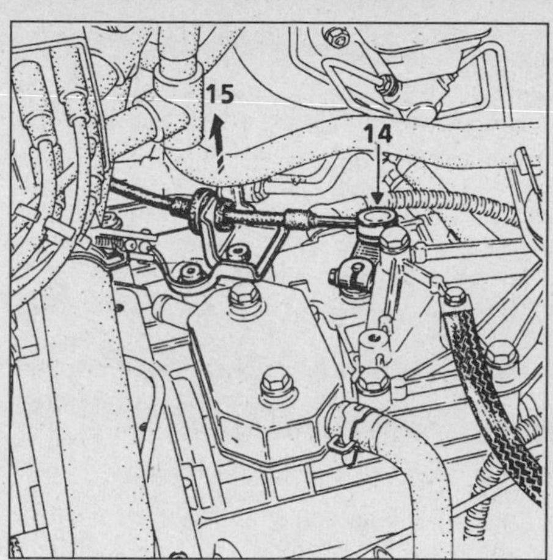

5.4 Disconnect the selector cable from the transmission lever by removing the clip(s) (15) and pulling the end fitting (14) from the balljoint

pulling the end fitting from the balljoint **(see illustration)**.

5 Unscrew the two bolts, and lift off the upper cover from the lever assembly **(see illustration)**.

6 Under the vehicle, unscrew the nuts securing the lever assembly to the floor.

7 Unscrew the bolt securing the selector cable to the underbody, and remove the assembly from under the vehicle.

8 Remove the cable from the lever assembly with reference to Section 6.

Refitting

9 Refitting is the reverse of removal, noting the following points:

a) *Prior to refitting, apply a smear of multi-purpose grease to the sliding surfaces of the selector lever mechanism.*

b) *On completion, check and adjust the selector cable as described in Section 4.*

DP0 type transmission

Removal

10 Apply the handbrake, then jack up the front of the vehicle and support it on axle stands (see *Jacking and vehicle support*). Remove the heat shield(s) for access to the underside of the selector assembly.

11 Inside the vehicle, remove the centre console as described in Chapter 11.

12 Disconnect the wiring from the selector lever assembly. There are two connectors under the right-hand side of the assembly, and one connector located just in front of the assembly.

13 Working under the vehicle, unclip the exhaust from its mounting, then unbolt the heat shields from the underbody for access beneath the selector assembly.

14 Remove the protector plate, then unscrew and remove the four mounting nuts securing the assembly to the floor. Recover the spacers.

15 Release the cable end fitting from its

5.5 Upper cover retaining bolts

balljoint on the bottom of the lever, then prise out the clip and remove the outer cable from the assembly. Withdraw the assembly from under the vehicle.

16 If necessary, the knob may be removed from the lever. To do this, undo the screw securing the knob to the lever and lift the knob to access the two wires. Identify the location of each wire, then disconnect them from the connector so that the knob may be removed separate. The wire locations are as follows.

Track	Colour
A1	Black
A2	Black
B1	White
B2	Light brown

17 Examine the selector lever assembly for signs of wear or damage and renew if necessary.

Refitting

18 Refitting is the reverse of removal, noting the following points.

a) *Prior to refitting, apply a smear of multi-purpose grease to the surfaces of the selector lever mechanism.*

b) *If the knob was removed, carefully feed the sport mode switch wires down the guides in the selector lever making sure the wires are not crossed **(see illustration)**. Seat the control knob in position and tighten its retaining screw. Crimp new wiring connectors onto the*

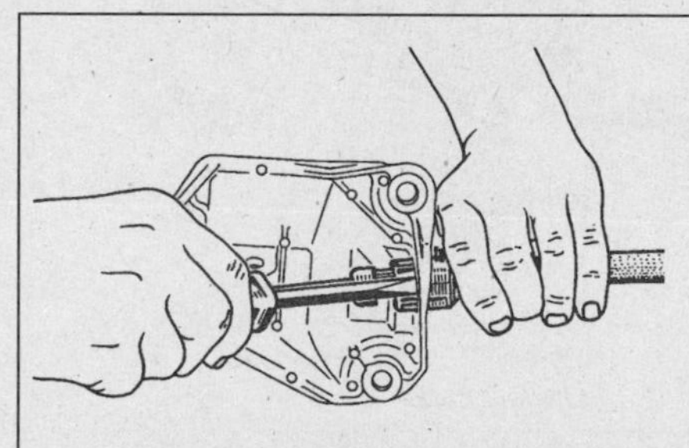

6.3 Using a screwdriver to release the cable from the lever assembly

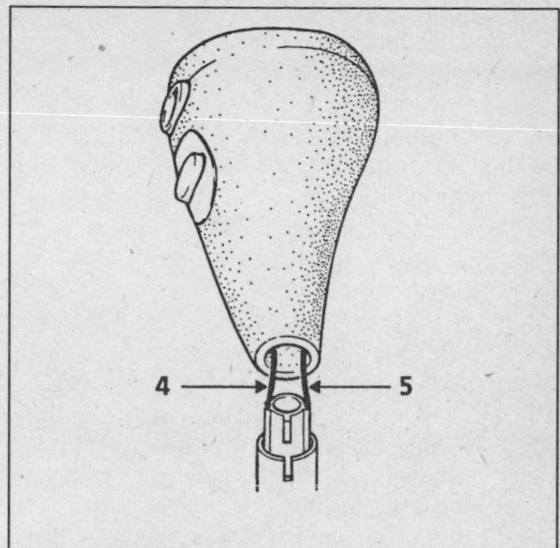

5.18 When refitting the selector lever knob, take great care to ensure the switch wires (4 and 5) are not crossed and are correctly routed down the lever guides

ends of the switch wires and locate the connectors in the connector.

c) *On completion check the operation of the selector lever and, if necessary, adjust the cable as described in Section 4.*

6 Selector cable – removal and refitting

AD4 type transmission

Removal

1 Remove the selector lever assembly as described in Section 5.

2 Unclip the cable from the bottom of the gearlever.

3 Using a screwdriver, release the clip and pull the cable from the lever assembly **(see illustration)**.

Refitting

4 Refitting is the reverse of removal. Refit the selector lever as described in Section 5, and adjust the cable as described in Section 4.

DP0 type transmission

Removal

5 Remove the selector lever assembly as described in Section 5.

6 Working in the engine compartment, remove the air inlet ducts with reference to Chapter 4A.

7 Disconnect the selector cable end fitting from the multi-function switch on top of the transmission. Release the outer cable from the support bracket by turning the two locking rings in opposite directions. **Do not** move the orange ring as the locking rings are released. Note that if the orange ring breaks during removal, this will not adversely affect the operation of the cable and is not grounds for cable renewal.

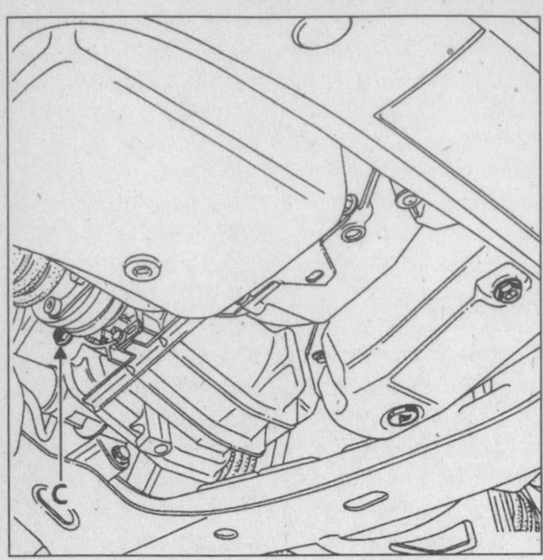

7.11 Final drive filler/level plug (C)

8 Release the selector cable from all relevant retaining clips and withdraw it from under the vehicle.
9 Examine the cable for worn end fittings or a damaged outer casing, and for signs of fraying of the inner wire. The cable inner wire should move smoothly and easily through the outer casing. If the adjuster mechanism is thought to be faulty the cable must be renewed.

Refitting

10 Refitting is a reversal of removal, but adjust the cable as described in Section 4.

7 Speedometer drive – removal and refitting

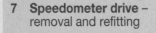

Note: *This procedure applies to the AD4 transmission only.*

Removal

1 The speedometer drivegear can be removed once the final drive cover plate has been unbolted from the rear of the transmission.
2 Firmly apply the handbrake, then jack up the front of the vehicle and support it on axle stands (see *Jacking and vehicle support*). Where fitted, remove the engine compartment undershield.
3 Remove the air cleaner assembly as described in Chapter 4A.
4 Disconnect the wiring and unscrew the vehicle speed sensor from the top of the transmission.
5 Place a suitable container under the final drive housing, to catch the fluid which will be released as the cover plate is removed.
6 Unscrew the securing bolts, and remove the final drive housing cover plate. Recover the gasket.
7 Unscrew the speedometer gear housing from the top of the transmission, then unclip the drivegear and withdraw the gear. Recover the sealing ring.

Refitting

8 Fit a new sealing ring to the speedometer gear housing, and insert the housing into the transmission. Clip the drivegear into the housing and seat the housing in position, making sure the gear is correctly engaged, and tighten securely.
9 Ensure that the cover plate and transmission surfaces are clean and dry, and refit the cover using a new gasket. Fit the cover bolts and tighten them securely.
10 Refit the vehicle speed sensor and reconnect the wiring.
11 It is now necessary to refill the final drive unit. The unit is refilled via the filler/level plug on the right-hand end of the transmission **(see illustration)**. Slacken and remove the filler/level plug, and refill the final drive with the exact amount of the specified type of oil (see the end of *Weekly checks* and Chapter 1A Specifications) until the fluid level is up to the lower edge of the filler/level plug hole. Refit the filler/level plug, tighten it securely and lower the vehicle to the ground.
12 Take the vehicle on a short drive. On your return, park the vehicle on level ground and check the final drive unit oil level as described in Chapter 1A, Section 11.

8 Oil seals – renewal

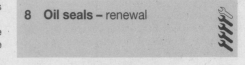

AD4 type transmission

Right-hand differential oil seal

1 Apply the handbrake, then jack up the front of the car and support it on axle stands (see *Jacking and vehicle support*). Remove the right-hand wheel.
2 Referring to Chapter 8, disconnect the complete driveshaft assembly from the transmission noting that where applicable the intermediate shaft bearing must be detached from the rear of the cylinder block. Note that it is not necessary to remove the driveshaft completely, the shaft can be left attached to the hub assembly and freed from the transmission as the hub assembly is pulled outwards. **Note:** *Do not allow it to hang down under its own weight as this could damage the constant velocity joints/gaiters.*
3 Carefully lever off the oil seal protector from the outside of the transmission housing. Note the fitted depth of the old seal, then carefully lever the seal out of position using a flat-bladed screwdriver **(see illustrations)**.
4 Wipe clean the oil seal seating in the casing and apply a smear of oil to the seal lip. Making sure the seal lip is facing inwards, carefully ease the new seal into position over the differential shaft. Press the seal squarely into the transmission until it is positioned at the same depth as the original was prior to removal. If necessary the seal can be tapped into position using a piece of metal tube or a

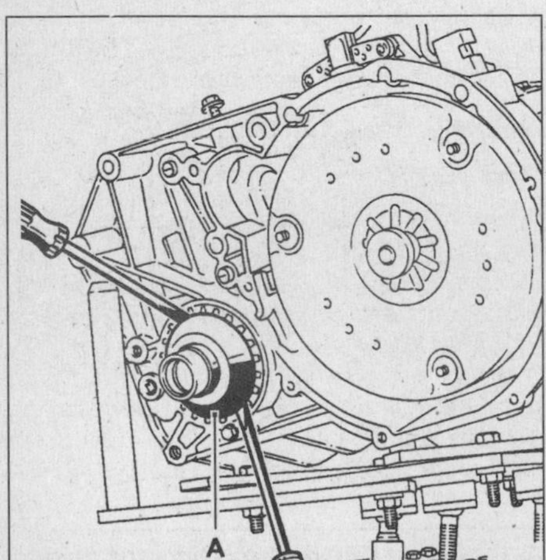

8.3a Using two screwdrivers to prise the oil seal protector (A) from the transmission housing

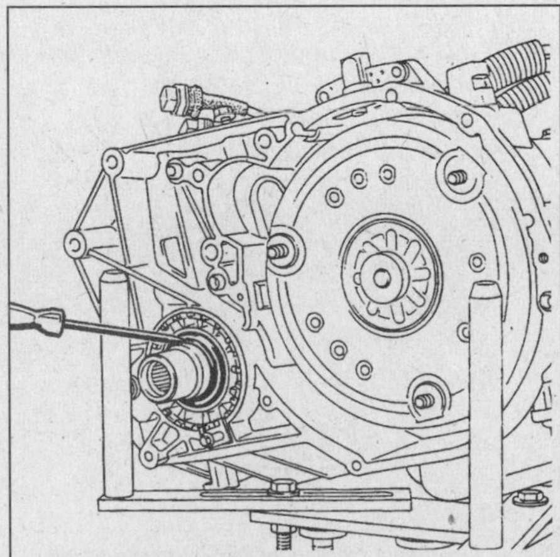
8.3b Levering out the right-hand differential oil seal

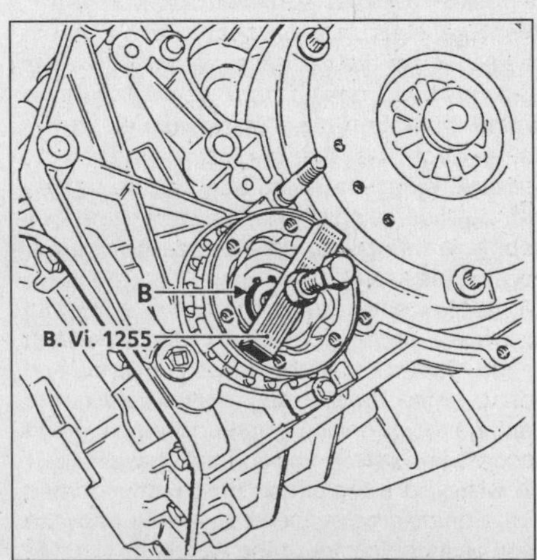

8.9 Renault special tool (B. Vi. 1255) to enable the left-hand drive shaft flange circlip (B) to be removed (AD4 transmission)

socket which bears only on the hard outer edge of the seal.

5 Fit the new seal protector making sure it is pressed securely into position.

6 Carefully refit the driveshaft assembly as described in Chapter 8.

7 Check and, if necessary, top-up the final drive oil level as described in Chapter 1A, Section 11.

8 Refit the roadwheel and lower the car to the ground and tighten the wheelbolts to the specified torque.

Left-hand differential oil seal

Note: *In order to renew the oil seal it will be necessary to obtain a suitable alternative to the Renault service tool (B.Vi.1255)* ***(see illustration)****. This is needed to compress the driveshaft flange spring to allow the retaining circlip to be removed and refitted.*

9 Apply the handbrake, then jack up the front of the car and support it on axle stands (see *Jacking and vehicle support*). Remove the left-hand front roadwheel.

10 Referring to Chapter 8, disconnect the driveshaft from the transmission. Note that it is not necessary to remove the driveshaft completely, the shaft can be left attached to the hub assembly and freed from the flange as the hub assembly is pulled outwards. **Note:** *Do not allow it to hang down under its own weight as this could damage the constant velocity joints/gaiters.*

11 Prise out the cap from the centre of the driveshaft flange to reveal the circlip. Discard the cap, a new one should be used on refitting.

12 Press the driveshaft flange into the transmission (see Note at the start of this sub-Section) and remove the circlip.

13 Carefully release the driveshaft flange until all the spring tension is relieved then remove the driveshaft flange and spring from the transmission.

14 Note the correct fitted position of the original oil seal then carefully lever the seal out of position using a flat-bladed screwdriver.

15 Wipe clean the oil seal seating in the casing. Press the new seal squarely into the transmission, making sure its sealing lip is facing inwards, until it is positioned at the same depth as the original was prior to removal. If necessary the seal can be tapped into position using a piece of metal tube or a socket which bears only on the hard outer edge of the seal.

16 Apply a smear of grease to the sealing lip of the seal and the shoulder of the driveshaft flange. Carefully refit the driveshaft flange and spring to the transmission taking care not to damage the oil seal. Compress the spring and secure the flange in position with the circlip.

17 Make sure the circlip is correctly located in the shaft groove then tap a new cap into position in the centre of the flange.

18 Reconnect the driveshaft to the transmission as described in Chapter 8.

19 Check and, if necessary, top-up the final drive oil level as described in Chapter 1A, Section 11.

20 Refit the roadwheel and lower the car to the ground and tighten the wheelbolts to the specified torque.

Torque converter seal

21 Remove the transmission from the engine as described in Section 11.

22 Remove the retaining strap and carefully slide the torque converter off from the transmission shaft. Be prepared for fluid loss as the converter is removed.

23 Using a flat-bladed screwdriver carefully lever the seal out from the centre of the torque converter, taking great care not to mark the metal bush.

24 Press the new seal squarely into position making sure its sealing lip is facing inwards.

25 Lubricate the lip of the seal with clean transmission fluid and carefully slide the converter onto the transmission shaft.

26 Make sure the torque converter is correctly engaged with the transmission shaft splines then refit the transmission as described in Section 11.

DP0 type transmission

Differential oil seals

27 Disconnect the battery negative terminal (refer to *Disconnecting the battery* in the Reference Section of this manual).

28 Apply the handbrake, then jack up the front of the car and support it on axle stands (see *Jacking and vehicle support*). Remove the relevant roadwheel.

29 Drain the transmission fluid as described in Section 2.

30 Referring to Chapter 8, disconnect the complete driveshaft assembly from the transmission on the side being worked on. Note that it is not necessary to remove the driveshaft completely, the shaft can be left attached to the hub assembly and freed from the transmission as the hub assembly is pulled outwards. **Note:** *Do not allow it to hang down under its own weight as this could damage the constant velocity joints/gaiters.*

31 Note the fitted depth of the old seal, then carefully lever the seal out of position using a flat-bladed screwdriver.

32 Wipe clean the oil seal seating in the casing and apply a smear of oil to the seal lip. Making sure the seal lip is facing inwards, carefully ease the new seal into position over the differential shaft. Press the seal squarely into the transmission until it is positioned at the same depth as the original was prior to removal. If necessary the seal can be tapped into position using a piece of metal tube or a socket which bears only on the hard outer edge of the seal.

33 Carefully refit the driveshaft assembly as described in Chapter 8.

34 Refill the transmission with new fluid as described in Section 2.

35 Refit the roadwheel, lower the car to the ground and tighten the wheelbolts to the specified torque.

Torque converter seal

36 Proceed as described in paragraphs 21 to 26.

9 Fluid cooler – removal and refitting

Removal

1 The fluid cooler is located on top of the AD4 type transmission, or on the rear left-hand side on the DP0 unit **(see illustrations)**. To gain access to the cooler, remove the air cleaner assembly as described in Chapter 4A.

2 To minimise coolant loss, clamp the coolant hoses on either side of the fluid cooler. Alternatively, drain the cooling system as described in Chapter 1A.

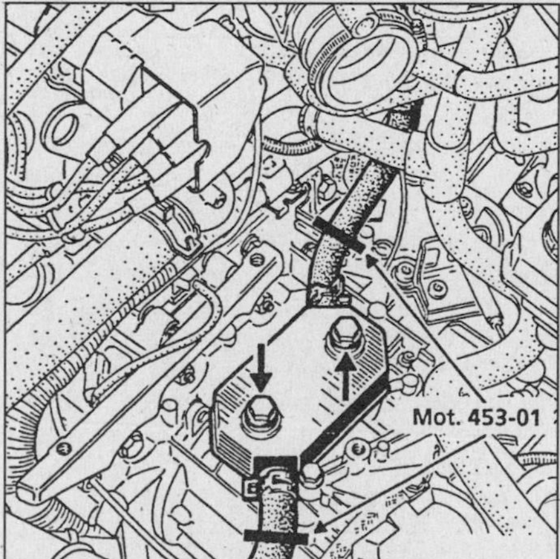

9.1a The fluid cooler is mounted on the top of the AD4 transmission

Arrows show mounting bolts

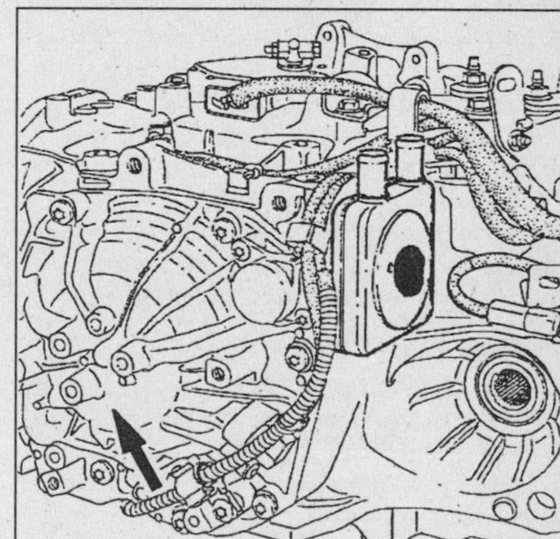

9.1b On the DP0 transmission, the fluid cooler is located on the rear left-hand side

Arrow indicates location of identification engraving

3 Loosen the clips and disconnect the hoses from the fluid cooler – be prepared for some coolant spillage. Wash off any spilt coolant immediately with cold water, and dry the surrounding area before proceeding further.

4 Slacken and remove the mounting bolt(s), and remove the fluid cooler from the transmission. There will be some loss of fluid, so some clean rags should be placed around the cooler to absorb spillage. Make sure that dirt is prevented from entering the hydraulic system.

5 Remove the sealing ring from each mounting bolt, and the sealing rings fitted between the cooler and transmission. Discard all sealing rings; new ones must be used on refitting.

Refitting

6 Lubricate the new seals with clean automatic transmission fluid, then fit the two new seals to the base of the fluid cooler, and a new seal to each mounting bolt.

7 Locate the fluid cooler on the top of the transmission housing, ensuring its lower seals remain in position. Refit the mounting bolt(s) and tighten them to the specified torque setting.

8 Reconnect the coolant hoses to the fluid cooler, and securely tighten their retaining clips. Remove the hose clamps.

9 Refit the air cleaner assembly as described in Chapter 4A.

10 On completion, top-up the cooling system and check the automatic transmission fluid level as described in *Weekly checks* and Chapter 1A.

10 Automatic transmission electronic components – removal and refitting

Note: *Whenever any of the transmission electronic control components are renewed it is necessary to validate the no-load/full-load position of the transmission. To do this, the Renault (XR25) diagnostic equipment is needed. Therefore, it will be necessary to entrust the following work to a Renault dealer if access to the necessary equipment cannot be gained. Failure to validate the no-load/full-load position could lead to incorrect gearchange thresholds, and the instrument panel warning light illuminating randomly.*

Removal

1 Always disconnect the battery negative lead (refer to *Disconnecting the battery* in the Reference Section of this manual) before proceeding as described under the relevant sub-heading.

Multi-function switch (AD4)

2 The multi-function switch informs the electronic control unit of the selector lever position, prevents the starter motor operating when the transmission is in gear, and also controls the reversing lights. The switch is located on the rear of the transmission, above the left-hand driveshaft.

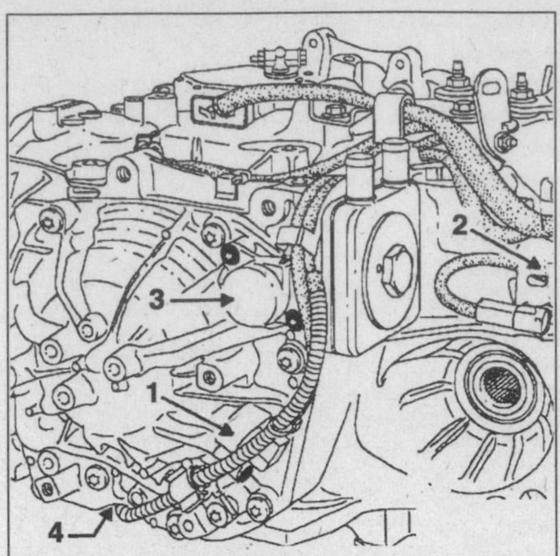

10.13 Sensor locations on the DP0 transmission

1 Input speed sensor
2 Output speed sensor
3 Exchanger flow control solenoid valve
4 Line pressure sensor

3 To remove the switch, trace the wiring back from the switch and disconnect it at the connector.

4 Unscrew the mounting bolt and remove the clamp plate. Unscrew the earth wire bolt, then pull the switch out of the transmission with its sealing ring.

Multi-function switch (DP0)

5 The multi-function switch informs the electronic control unit of the selector lever position, prevents the starter motor operating when the transmission is in gear, and also controls the reversing lights. The switch is located on the top of the transmission.

6 To remove the switch, place the selector lever in position N, then disconnect the end of the inner cable from the balljoint on the switch.

7 Release the outer cable from its support by turning the locking sleeves in opposite directions.

8 Mark the position of the multi-function switch to aid refitting, then unscrew and remove the two mounting bolts.

9 Release the connector slide mechanism and disconnect the modular connector.

10 Unscrew the three mounting bolts of the modular support plate, then unscrew the two mounting bolts of the modular connector plate and disconnect the green connector.

11 Withdraw the multi-function switch from the transmission.

Throttle potentiometer

12 Refer to Chapter 4A, Section 13 or 14.

Speed sensor

13 On the AD4 type, the sensor is mounted onto the top of the transmission, on its front left-hand end. On the DP0 type, the input speed sensor is located on the left-hand end of the transmission, above the wiring support bracket, and the output speed sensor is located just above the left-hand driveshaft **(see illustration)**.

14 If necessary, to improve access, remove the air cleaner assembly and mounting bracket, as described in Chapter 4A.

15 Trace the wiring back from the sensor, and disconnect at the wiring connector.

16 Unscrew the mounting bolt and remove the clamp plate, then pull the sensor out of the transmission with its sealing ring.

Line pressure sensor

17 The sensor is fitted to the base of the transmission, on the front end.

18 To gain access to the sensor, firmly apply the handbrake then jack up the front of the vehicle and support it on axle stands (see *Jacking and vehicle support*). Undo the retaining screws and remove the plastic undercover.

19 Trace the wiring back from the sensor and disconnect it at the wiring connector.

20 Be prepared for some fluid loss as the sensor is removed, then slacken the retaining bolts and remove the sensor retaining plate. Remove the sensor and recover the sealing ring.

Electronic control unit

21 The electronic control unit is located in the left-hand side of the engine compartment, beneath the battery tray.

22 Release the rubber retaining strap, then disconnect the wiring connectors and remove the control unit from the engine compartment.

Refitting

23 Refitting is a reversal of the removal procedure. On completion, reconnect the battery and validate the no-load/full-load position of the transmission.

24 The multi-function switch must be adjusted as follows. Select Neutral, and connect an ohmmeter to the switch terminals. Turn the switch slowly until the internal contacts just close and the meter reads zero resistance. Tighten the switch mounting bolts, then check again that the contacts are closed. Check that all gears can be engaged correctly, and that the starter motor will only operate with P or N selected.

11 Automatic transmission – removal and refitting

Note: *If a new transmission and/or torque converter is being fitted, note that the ECU auto-adaptive values must be reset by a Renault dealer using the XR25 test equipment. The following paragraphs describe the removal and refitting procedure for models fitted with the DP0 transmission, however, the procedure is similar for other models fitted with the AD4 transmission.*

Removal

1 Remove the battery and battery tray as described in Chapter 5A.
2 Apply the handbrake, then jack up the front of the vehicle and support it on axle stands (see *Jacking and vehicle support*). Remove the engine undertray and both front roadwheels.
3 Unclip the wiring loom for the battery and automatic transmission.
4 Remove the air cleaner assembly and the inlet duct as described in Chapter 4A.
5 Disconnect the selector cable end fitting from the multi-function switch on top of the transmission. Release the outer cable from the support bracket by turning the two locking rings in opposite directions. **Do not** move the orange ring as the locking rings are released. However, note that if the orange ring breaks during removal, this will not adversely affect the operation of the cable and is not grounds for cable renewal.
6 Pull out the locking tab and disconnect the transmission wiring harness modular connector. To prevent entry of dust and dirt, wrap a polythene bag over the connector.
7 Unscrew the engine wiring harness support bolts, and remove the support.
8 Unbolt the crankshaft speed/position (TDC) sensor from the top of the transmission and place to one side.
9 Clamp the coolant hoses on either side of the fluid cooler. Alternately, drain the cooling system as described in Chapter 1A. Loosen the clips and disconnect the hoses from the cooler.
10 Unscrew and remove the transmission-to-engine upper mounting bolts.
11 Undo the screws and prise out the fasteners, then remove the front sections of the wheelarch liners on each side.
12 Remove both driveshafts with reference to Chapter 8. Leave their outer ends attached to the hub carriers, and remove both items together.
13 Unbolt the power steering fluid pipe supports from the transmission.
14 Disconnect the wiring for the speed sensors at the connector.
15 Remove the starter motor as described in Chapter 5A.
16 Unbolt the exhaust-to-transmission support stay.
17 Unbolt the rear mounting link from the transmission, then loosen the remaining bolt and swivel the link down.
18 Unscrew the bolts/nuts securing the steering gear to the rear of the subframe. Remove the mounting clamps and carefully prise the steering gear away from the subframe. Tie the track rod ends to the front suspension coils on each side in order to support the steering gear while the subframe is being lowered.
19 Unbolt and remove the horn with reference to Chapter 12.
20 For additional working room, remove the front bumper as described in Chapter 11.
21 Use trolley jacks or axle stands to support the weight of the front subframe, then unscrew and remove the subframe mounting bolts and lower the unit to the floor. Withdraw the subframe from under the vehicle.
22 The left-hand end of the engine must now be supported while the transmission mounting is unbolted from the inner body panel. To do this, use a hoist or engine support bar across the engine compartment. Alternatively, use a trolley jack and block of wood beneath the sump, but in this case take care that the engine is adequately supported. If using a support bar, locate it at the rear left-hand corner and front right-hand corner; first remove the automatic transmission computer, right-hand headlight and inlet ducting. It is also possible to accommodate a support bar by making up a simple bracket bolted to the chassis member on the lower left-hand side of the engine compartment.
23 Release the power steering hydraulic hose from the transmission and tie it to the rear, away from the transmission.
24 Unscrew and remove the bolts securing the transmission mounting bracket to the inner body panel, then carefully lower the transmission until there is sufficient clearance between it and the inner body panel to remove it.
25 The torque converter is attached to the driveplate by three nuts which are accessed through the starter motor aperture. Turn the engine as required to position the nuts in the aperture, then unscrew and remove them. **Note:** *The nuts must be renewed every time they are removed.* Where applicable, unbolt the access plate from the bottom of the transmission.
26 Support the weight of the transmission on a trolley jack, or (preferably) on a transmission cradle.
27 Unbolt and remove the transmission/engine left-hand mounting from the transmission and inner body panel.
28 Lower the transmission and engine as far as possible, but take care not to damage the air conditioning compressor (where fitted).
29 With the jack positioned beneath the transmission taking the weight, slacken and remove the remaining nut/bolts securing the transmission to the engine. Note the correct fitted positions of each nut/bolt, and the necessary brackets, as they are removed, to use as a reference on refitting. Make a final check that all components have been disconnected, and are positioned clear of the transmission so that they will not hinder the removal procedure.
30 With the bolts removed, make sure the torque converter is pushed fully onto the transmission shaft then move the trolley jack and transmission to the left, to free it from its locating dowels.
31 Once the transmission is free, lower the jack and manoeuvre the unit out from under the car. Remove the locating dowels from the transmission or engine if they are loose, and keep them in a safe place. Secure the torque converter in position by bolting a length of metal bar to one of the housing holes, or by tying one of the studs to the crankshaft speed/position (TDC) sensor aperture on the top of the housing **(see illustration)**.

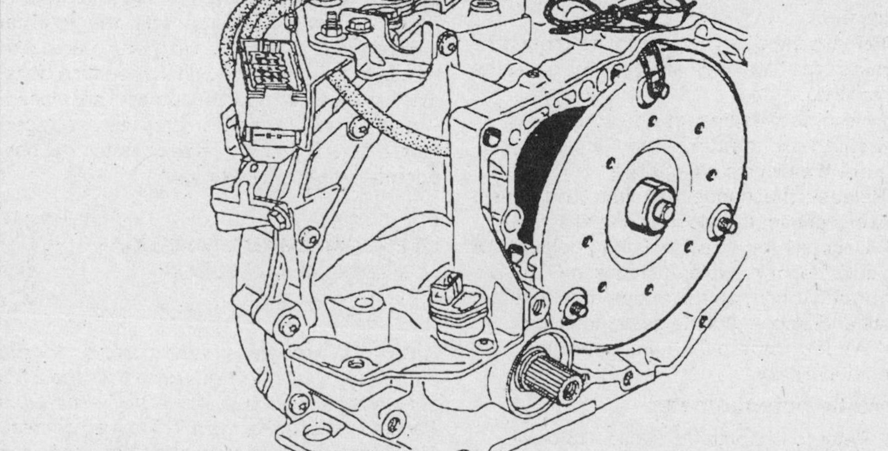

11.31 Torque converter secured in the transmission with string tied through the crankshaft speed/position (TDC) sensor aperture

Refitting

32 The transmission is refitted using a reversal of the removal procedure, bearing in mind the following points.

- *a) Remove the retaining bar and ensure that the torque converter is pushed fully onto the transmission. Apply a smear of high-melting point grease (Renault recommend the use of Molykote BR2) to the converter centre spigot.*
- *b) Ensure the locating dowels are correctly*

positioned prior to installation and clean the torque converter-to-driveplate stud threads.

c) Align the torque converter studs with the driveplate holes as the transmission is refitted. Apply thread locking compound (Renault recommend the use of Loctite Frenbloc) to the ***new*** *retaining nuts and tighten them to the specified torque.*

d) Tighten all nuts and bolts to the specified torque (where given).

e) Refit the driveshafts as described in Chapter 8.

f) Connect the selector cable and adjust as described in Sections 6 and 4.

g) On completion, top-up/refill the transmission with the specified type and quantity of lubricant, as described in Section 2 and/or Chapter 1A.

12 Automatic transmission overhaul – general information

In the event of a fault occurring with the transmission, it is first necessary to determine whether it is of an electrical, mechanical or hydraulic nature, and to do this, special test equipment is required. It is therefore essential to have the work carried out by a Renault dealer if a transmission fault is suspected.

Do not remove the transmission from the car for possible repair before professional fault diagnosis has been carried out, since most tests require the transmission to be in the vehicle.

Chapter 8
Driveshafts

Contents

Degrees of difficulty

Easy, suitable for novice with little experience 	**Fairly easy,** suitable for beginner with some experience 	**Fairly difficult,** suitable for competent DIY mechanic 	**Difficult,** suitable for experienced DIY mechanic 	**Very difficult,** suitable for expert DIY or professional

Specifications

Lubricant

Type/specification	Mobil CVJ 825 or Mobil EXF 57C (special grease is supplied in sachets with gaiter kits – joints are otherwise pre-packed with grease and sealed)
Quantity – manual gearbox models (per joint):	
GE 86 joint (outer joint)	320 g
AC 1700 joint (outer joint)	140 g
RC 462 and RC462 E type joint (inner joints)	180 g

Torque wrench settings	Nm	lbf ft
Driveshaft retaining nut:		
'Nylstop' type with separate washer	250	185
'Enko' type with incorporated washer	280	207
Driveshaft-to-transmission flange bolts:		
Automatic transmission	35	26
Left-hand driveshaft inner gaiter retaining plate bolts:		
Manual gearbox	25	18

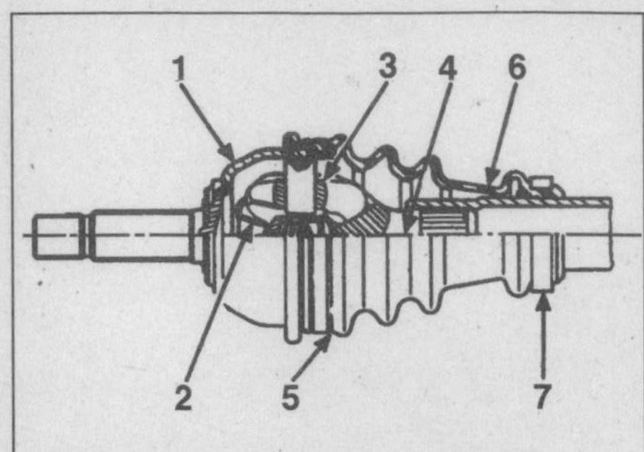

1.2a Sectional view of the spider-and-yoke type outer constant velocity joint

1 *Outer member*
2 *Thrust plunger*
3 *Driveshaft spider*
4 *Driveshaft*
5 *Outer retaining clip*
6 *Gaiter*
7 *Inner retaining clip*

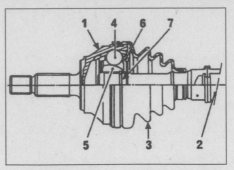

1.2b Sectional view of the ball-and-cage type outer constant velocity joint

1 *Outer member*
2 *Driveshaft*
3 *Gaiter*
4 *Ball bearing*
5 *Inner member*
6 *Ball cage*
7 *Circlip*

1 General information

1 Drive is transmitted from the differential to the front wheels by means of two driveshafts.

2 Both driveshafts are fitted with a constant velocity (CV) joint at their outer ends, which may be of the spider-and-yoke type or of the ball-and-cage type **(see illustrations)**. Each joint has an outer member, which is splined at its outer end to accept the wheel hub and is threaded so that it can be fastened to the hub by a large nut. The joint contains either a spring-loaded plunger or six balls within a cage, which engage with the inner member. The complete assembly is protected by a flexible gaiter secured to the driveshaft and joint outer member.

3 On vehicles with a manual gearbox, a different inner constant velocity joint arrangement is fitted to each driveshaft. On the right-hand side, the driveshaft is splined to engage with a tripod joint, containing needle roller bearings and cups. The tripod joint is free to slide within the yoke of the joint outer member, which is splined and (where applicable) retained by a roll pin to the differential sun wheel stub shaft (on most later models, the roll pin is deleted, and the splined end of the driveshaft joint is sprung to retain it in the differential sun wheel stub shaft). As on the outer joints, a flexible gaiter secured to the driveshaft and outer member protects the complete assembly. On the left-hand side, the driveshaft also engages with a tripod joint, but the yoke in which the tripod joint is free to slide is an integral part of the differential sun wheel. On this side, the gaiter is secured to the transmission casing with a retaining plate, and to a ball-bearing on the driveshaft with a retaining clip. The bearing allows the driveshaft to turn within the gaiter, which does not revolve.

4 On vehicles with automatic transmission, there are two different types of inner joints to the transmission. One type is secured by bolts and the other is a splined-fit in the differential sun wheel stub shaft. As with the outer joints, the complete assembly is protected by a flexible gaiter which is secured to the driveshaft and joint outer member.

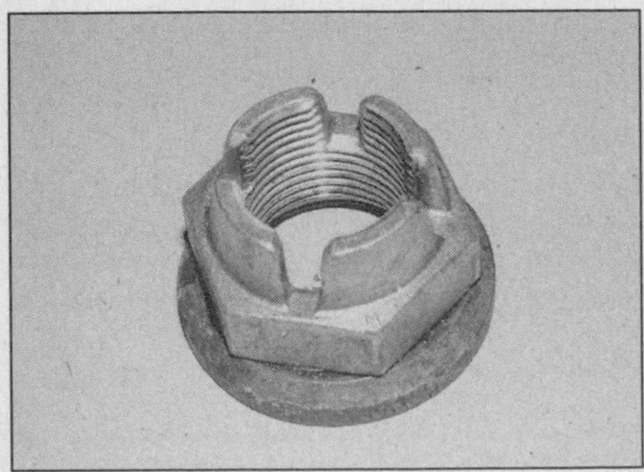

2.1 New Enko type driveshaft securing nut

TOOL TiP

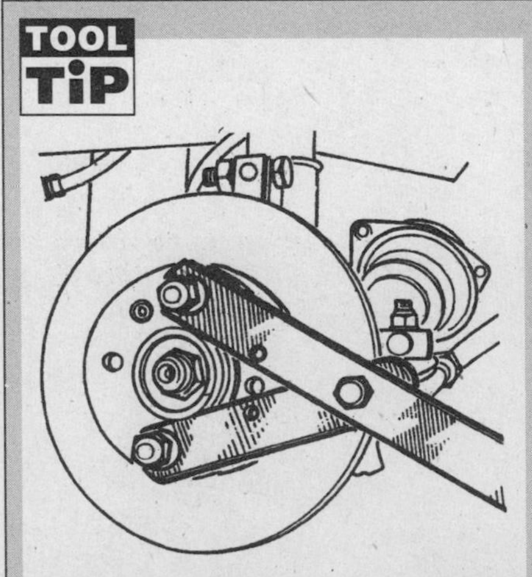

Using a fabricated tool to hold the front hub stationary whilst the driveshaft nut is slackened

2 Driveshaft – removal and refitting

Removal

Note: *When carrying out an operation on this assembly, it is essential to use the new 'Enko' type self-locking nut* ***(see illustration)*** *without applying a coat of locking fluid. This type of nut is gradually being fitted in production across the whole vehicle range. If the vehicle is already fitted with the 'Enko' type nut, it may not be necessary to renew it; it can be re-used four times. The bearing and driveshaft kits are no longer supplied with the 'Nylstop' type nut.*

Note: *On manual transmission models, new driveshaft-to-differential side-gear roll pins (where fitted) will be required on refitting; note that if the original double roll pin is renewed, the new one will be of single coiled type. On later models, instead of a roll pin, there is a spring built into the inner joint to prevent the joint coming of the differential splines.*

Note: *On early models, the driveshaft outer joint splines are coated with locking compound prior to refitting. Therefore it is likely that a puller/extractor will be required to draw the hub assembly off the driveshaft end on removal.*

1 Remove the wheel trim/hub cap (as applicable), then slacken the driveshaft nut with the vehicle resting on its wheels. Also slacken the wheel bolts.

2 Chock the rear wheels of the car, firmly apply the handbrake, then jack up the front of the car and support it on axle stands (see *Jacking and vehicle support*). Remove the appropriate front roadwheel.

3 On models equipped with ABS, remove the wheel sensor as described in Chapter 9.

4 Slacken and remove the driveshaft retaining nut. If the nut was not slackened with the wheels on the ground (see paragraph 1), refit at least two roadwheel bolts to the front hub, tightening them securely, then have an assistant firmly depress the brake pedal to prevent the front hub from rotating, whilst you slacken and remove the driveshaft retaining nut. Alternatively, a tool can be fabricated from two lengths of steel strip (one long, one short) and a nut and bolt; the nut and bolt forming the pivot of a forked tool **(see Tool Tip)**.

5 Unscrew the two bolts securing the brake caliper assembly to the swivel hub, and slide the caliper assembly off the disc. Using a piece of wire or string, tie the caliper to the front suspension coil spring, to avoid placing any strain on the hydraulic brake hose.

6 Slacken and remove the nut securing the steering gear track rod end balljoint to the swivel hub. Release the balljoint tapered

2.6 Using a balljoint separator to release the track rod end balljoint from the swivel hub

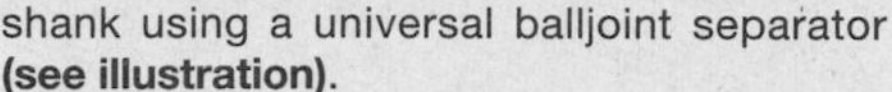

2.7 Withdraw the upper swivel hub-to-strut bolt, noting which way around it is fitted

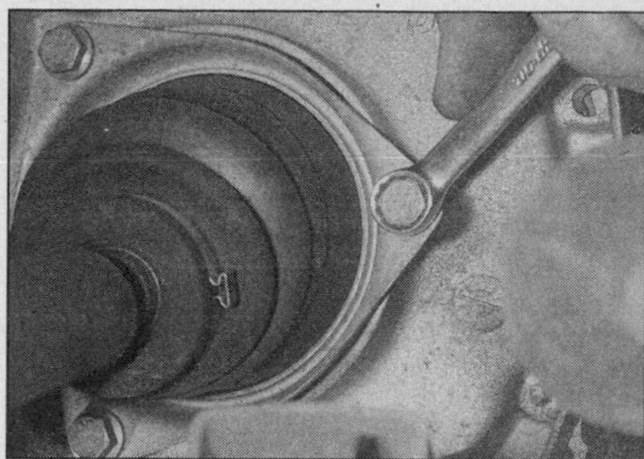

2.9 On the left-hand driveshaft, remove the flexible gaiter retaining plate bolts . . .

shank using a universal balljoint separator **(see illustration)**.

7 Slacken and remove the two nuts and washers from the bolts securing the swivel hub to the suspension strut, noting that the nuts are positioned on the rear side of the strut. Withdraw the upper bolt, but leave the lower bolt in position at this stage **(see illustration)**. Now proceed as described under the relevant sub-heading.

Left-hand driveshaft (manual models)

8 Drain the transmission oil as described in Chapter 7A.

9 Slacken and remove the three bolts securing the flexible gaiter retaining plate to the side of the gearbox/transmission **(see illustration)**.

10 Pull the top of the swivel hub outwards until the driveshaft tripod joint is released from its yoke; be prepared for some oil spillage as the joint is withdrawn **(see illustration)**. Be careful that the rollers on the end of the tripod do not fall off.

11 Remove the lower bolt securing the swivel hub to the suspension strut. Taking care not to damage the driveshaft gaiters, release the outer constant velocity joint from the hub and remove the driveshaft. Note that it is likely the joint will be a tight fit in the hub splines (see Note at the start of this Section). Try tapping the joint out of position using a hammer and a soft metal drift, whilst an assistant supports the hub assembly. If this fails to move the joint, a suitable puller/extractor will be required to draw the hub assembly off the driveshaft end **(see illustration)**. Whilst the driveshaft is removed, support the hub assembly by refitting the bolts to the base of the strut.

Right-hand driveshaft (manual models)

Note: *On later models, the roll pin at the inner end of the driveshaft is deleted, and the splined end of the driveshaft joint is sprung to retain it in the differential sun wheel stub shaft – ignore the references to removing and refitting the roll pins when working on one of these vehicles.*

12 On Scénic models with a two-piece driveshaft, unscrew the two bolts securing the driveshaft inner section retaining plate to engine mounting bracket/bearing carrier **(see illustration)**.

13 Where applicable, rotate the driveshaft until the double roll pin, securing the inner constant velocity joint to the sun wheel shaft, is visible. Using a hammer and a 5 mm diameter pin punch, drive out the double roll pin **(see illustration)**. New roll pins must be used on refitting.

14 Pull the top of the swivel hub outwards until the inner constant velocity joint splines are released from the sun wheel shaft. Remove the sealing ring (where fitted) from the sun wheel shaft splines.

15 Remove the driveshaft as described in paragraph 11.

Both driveshafts (automatic models)

16 On AD4 type transmission, working at the transmission end of the driveshaft, slacken and remove the six bolts and washers securing the driveshaft flange to the transmission flange, rotating the shaft as necessary to gain access to the bolts.

17 Pull the top of the swivel hub outwards, and disengage the inner constant velocity joint from the drive flange/splined shaft. Remove the driveshaft as described in paragraphs 11 and 10.

Refitting

18 All new driveshafts supplied by Renault are equipped with cardboard or plastic protectors, to prevent damage to the gaiters.

2.10 . . . and release the tripod joint from the transmission – manual transmission models

2.11 Using an extractor to press the driveshaft out of the front hub

2.12 Slacken and remove the two retaining bolts (arrowed)

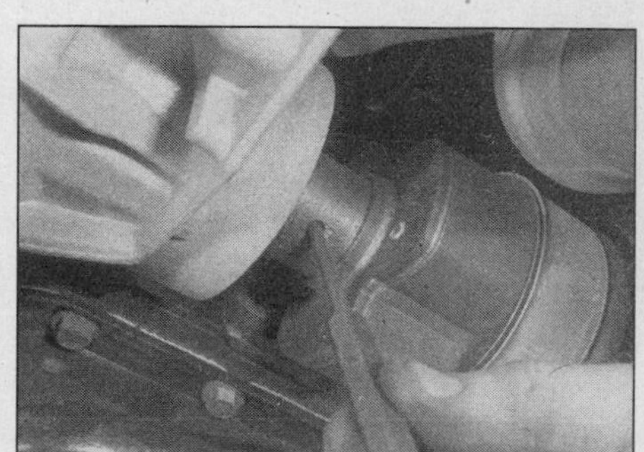

2.13 On the right-hand driveshaft, tap out the roll pins with a suitable pin punch – manual transmission models

Even the slightest knock to the gaiter can puncture it, allowing the entry of water or dirt at a later date, which may lead to the premature failure of the joint. If the original driveshaft is being refitted, it is worthwhile making up some cardboard protectors as a precaution. They can be held in position with elastic bands. The protectors should be left on the driveshafts until the end of the refitting procedure.

Left-hand driveshaft (manual models)

19 Wipe clean the side of the transmission and the outer constant velocity joint splines.

20 Insert the tripod joint into the sun wheel yoke, keeping the driveshaft horizontal as far as possible. Align the gaiter retaining plate with its bolt holes. Refit the retaining bolts, and tighten them to the specified torque. Ensure that the gaiter is not twisted.

21 Ensure both the hub and driveshaft outer constant velocity joint splines are clean and dry, and apply a coat of locking fluid (Renault recommend Loctite Scelbloc – available from your Renault dealer) to the splines of the driveshaft.

22 Move the top of the swivel hub inwards, at the same time engaging the driveshaft with the hub.

23 Slide the hub fully onto the driveshaft splines, then insert the two suspension strut mounting bolts from the front side of the strut. Refit the washers and nuts to the rear of the bolts, and tighten them to the specified torque (see Chapter 10 Specifications).

24 Fit the new driveshaft 'Enko' type retaining nut (see the note at the beginning of this Section), tightening it by hand only at this stage.

25 Reconnect the steering track rod balljoint to the swivel hub, and tighten its retaining nut to the specified torque (see Chapter 10 Specifications).

26 Clean the threads of the caliper bracket mounting bolts, and coat them with thread locking compound (Renault recommend Loctite Frenbloc – available from your Renault dealer). Slide the caliper into position, making sure the pads pass either side of the disc, and tighten the caliper bracket bolts to the specified torque setting (see Chapter 9 Specifications).

27 Using the method employed during removal to prevent the hub from rotating, tighten a new driveshaft retaining nut to the specified torque. Alternatively, lightly tighten the nut at this stage, and tighten it to the specified torque once the vehicle is resting on its wheels again.

28 Check that the hub rotates freely, then remove the protectors (where fitted) from the driveshaft, taking great care not to damage the flexible gaiters.

29 Refit the roadwheel. Lower the car to the ground and tighten the roadwheel bolts to the specified torque. If not already done, also tighten the driveshaft retaining nut to the specified torque.

30 Refill the transmission with the specified type and amount of oil, and check the level using the information given in Chapter 1A or 1B.

Right-hand driveshaft (manual models)

31 Ensure that the inner constant velocity joint and sun wheel shaft splines are clean and dry. Apply a smear of molybdenum disulphide grease to the splines (Renault recommend the use of Molykote BR2 – available from your Renault dealer). Where necessary, fit a new sealing ring over the end of the sun wheel shaft, and slide the O-ring along the shaft until it abuts the transmission oil seal **(see illustration)**.

32 On Scénic models with a two-piece driveshaft, pass the inner end of the shaft through the bearing mounting bracket, then carefully engage with the transmission splines. Secure the shaft by refitting the retaining plate and two securing bolts to the driveshaft inner section engine mounting bracket/bearing carrier.

33 Engage the driveshaft splines with those of the sun wheel splined shaft, and where applicable, make sure that the roll pin holes are in alignment **(see illustration)**. Slide the driveshaft onto the sun wheel splined shaft until the roll pin holes are aligned (where applicable).

34 Where applicable, drive in new roll pins with their slots 180° apart, then seal the ends of the pins with sealing compound (Renault recommend the use of CAF 4/60 THIXO or Rhodoseal 5661 – available from your Renault dealer) **(see illustration)**.

35 Carry out the procedures described in paragraphs 21 to 29.

Both driveshafts (automatic models)

36 On AD4 type transmission, working at the transmission end of the driveshaft, ensure that the inner driveshaft joint flange mating faces are clean and dry. Securely tighten the six bolts and washers securing the driveshaft flange to the transmission flange, rotating the shaft as necessary to gain access to the bolts.

37 On DP0 type transmission, ensure that the inner constant velocity joint and sun wheel shaft splines are clean and dry. Apply a smear of molybdenum disulphide grease to the splines (Renault recommend the use of Molykote BR2 – available from your Renault dealer). Engage the driveshaft inner constant velocity joint with the sun wheel shaft splines.

38 Carry out the procedures described in paragraphs 21 to 29.

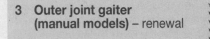

3 Outer joint gaiter (manual models) – renewal

1 Remove the driveshaft (refer to Section 2).

2 Cut through the gaiter retaining clips, and slide the gaiter down the shaft to expose the outer constant velocity joint.

3 Scoop out as much grease as possible from the joint, and determine which type of constant velocity joint is fitted. Proceed as described under the relevant sub-heading.

Ball-and-cage (AC1700) joint

4 Using circlip pliers, expand the joint internal circlip. At the same time, tap the exposed face of the ball hub with a mallet to separate the joint from the driveshaft. Slide off the gaiter and rubber collar.

5 With the constant velocity joint removed from the driveshaft, clean the joint using paraffin, or a suitable solvent, and dry it thoroughly. Carry out a visual inspection of the joint.

6 Move the inner splined driving member from side-to-side, to expose each ball in turn

2.31 Fit the new O-ring (where fitted) onto the sun wheel shaft . . .

2.33 . . . and engage the driveshaft, ensuring that the roll pin holes (arrowed) are correctly aligned

2.34 On the right-hand driveshaft, tap the roll pins securely into position and seal their ends with sealing compound

3.15 Removing the vibration damper from the driveshaft

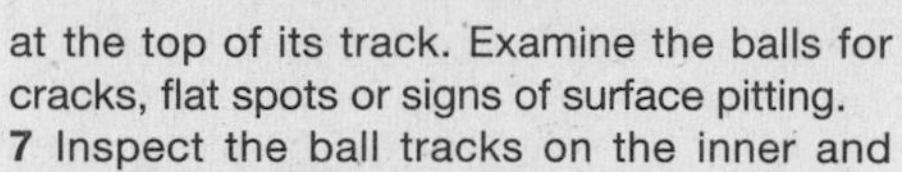

3.19 Renault driveshaft gaiter repair kit

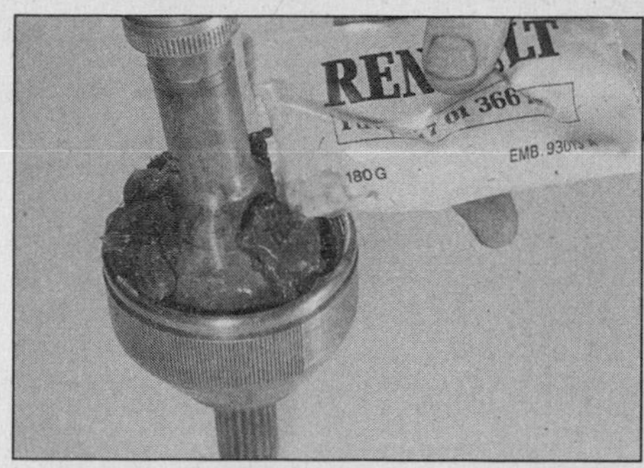

3.21 Pack the joint with the grease supplied in the repair kit . . .

at the top of its track. Examine the balls for cracks, flat spots or signs of surface pitting.

7 Inspect the ball tracks on the inner and outer members. If the tracks have widened, the balls will no longer be a tight fit. At the same time, check the ball cage windows for wear or cracking between the windows.

8 If on inspection any of the constant velocity joint components are found to be worn or damaged, it will be necessary to renew the complete driveshaft assembly, since no components are available separately. If the joint is in satisfactory condition, obtain a repair kit from your Renault dealer consisting of a new gaiter, rubber collar, retaining spring, and the correct type and quantity of grease.

9 Tape over the splines on the end of the driveshaft, then slide the rubber collar and gaiter onto the shaft. Locate the inner end of the gaiter on the driveshaft, and secure it in position with the rubber collar.

10 Remove the tape, then slide the constant velocity joint coupling onto the driveshaft until the internal circlip locates in the driveshaft groove.

11 Check that the circlip holds the joint securely on the driveshaft, then pack the joint with the grease supplied. Work the grease well into the ball tracks, and fill the gaiter with any excess.

12 Locate the outer lip of the gaiter in the groove on the joint outer member. With the coupling aligned with the driveshaft, lift the lip of the gaiter to equalise the air pressure. Fit both the inner and outer retaining clips to the gaiter, and secure each one in position by compressing its raised section. In the absence of the special tool, carefully compress each clip using a pair of side-cutters, taking great care not to cut through the clip

13 Check that the constant velocity joint moves freely in all directions, then refit the driveshaft to the vehicle as described in Section 2.

Spider-and-yoke (GE86) joint

14 Remove the inner constant velocity joint bearing and gaiter (as applicable), as described in Section 4 of this Chapter.

15 Where a vibration damper is fitted, clearly mark the position of the damper on the driveshaft, then use a puller or press to remove it from the inner end of the driveshaft, noting which way around it is fitted **(see illustration)**. Ensure that the legs of the puller or support plate rest only on the damper inner rubber bush, otherwise the damper will distort and break away from the outer metal housing as it is removed.

16 Slide the outer constant velocity joint gaiter off the inner end of the driveshaft.

17 Clean the outer constant velocity joint using paraffin or a suitable solvent, and dry it thoroughly. Carry out a visual inspection of the joint.

18 Check the driveshaft spider and outer member yoke for signs of wear, pitting or scuffing on their bearing surfaces. Also check that the outer member pivots smoothly and easily, with no traces of roughness.

19 If inspection reveals signs of wear or damage, it will be necessary to renew the driveshaft complete, since no components are available separately. If the joint components are in satisfactory condition, obtain a repair kit consisting of a new gaiter, retaining clips, and the correct type and quantity of grease **(see illustration)**.

20 Tape over the splines on the inner end of the driveshaft, then carefully slide the outer gaiter onto the shaft.

21 Pack the joint with the grease supplied in the repair kit **(see illustration)**. Work the grease well into the joint, and fill the gaiter with any excess.

22 Ease the gaiter over the joint, and ensure that the gaiter lips are correctly located in the grooves on the driveshaft and on the joint **(see illustration)**. With the coupling aligned with the driveshaft, lift the lip of the gaiter to equalise the air pressure.

23 Fit the large metal retaining clip to the gaiter. Remove any slack in the gaiter retaining clip by carefully compressing the raised section of the clip. In the absence of the special tool, a pair of side-cutters may be used, so long as great care is taken not to cut the clip **(see illustrations)**. Secure the small retaining clip using the same procedure. Check that the constant velocity joint moves freely in all directions before proceeding further.

24 To refit the vibration damper (when applicable), lubricate the driveshaft with a solution of soapy water. Press or drive the

3.22 . . . then slide the gaiter into position over the joint

3.23a Fit the large gaiter retaining clip . . .

3.23b . . . and secure it in position by carefully compressing the raised section of the clip

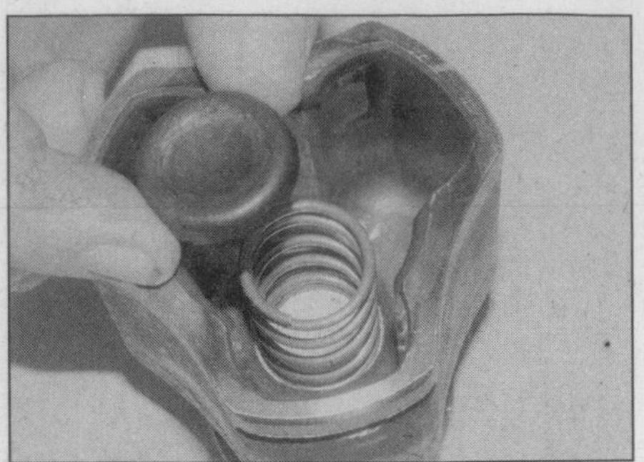
4.4 The joint without a roll pin fitted, has a spring and cup inside

4.5 Remove the circlip . . .

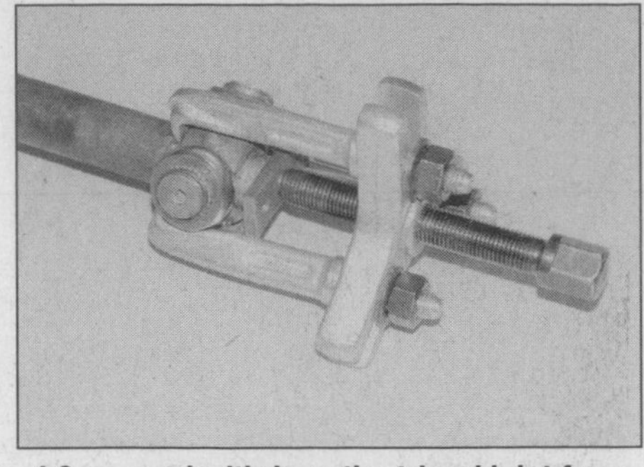
4.6 . . . and withdraw the tripod joint from the driveshaft end, using a puller if required

vibration damper along the shaft, using a tubular spacer which bears only on the damper inner bush, until it is aligned with the mark made prior to removal.

25 Refit the inner constant velocity joint components as described in Section 4, then refit the driveshaft to the vehicle as described in Section 2.

4 Inner joint gaiter (manual models) – renewal

Right-hand driveshaft

Note: *On these type joints, the RC 462 type has a roll pin to hold the driveshaft onto the splines of the differential. The RC462 E type has no roll pin, this is held in position by a spring, fitted internally in the joint. A suitable joint repair kit will be required.*

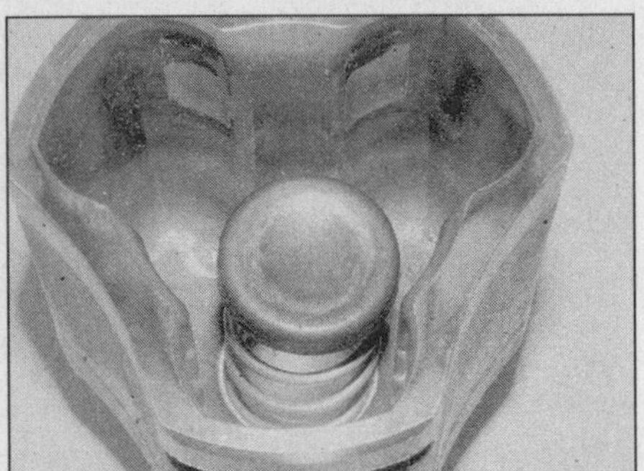
4.13a Refit the spring and cup into the outer part of the joint . . .

1 Remove the driveshaft as described in Section 2.

2 Release the large outer retaining clip and the inner retaining clip, then slide the gaiter down the shaft to expose the joint.

3 Slide the outer member off the tripod joint. Be prepared to hold the rollers in place (where applicable), otherwise they may fall off the tripod ends as the outer member is withdrawn. If necessary, secure the rollers in place using tape after removal of the outer member. The rollers are matched to the tripod joint stems, and it is important that they are not interchanged.

4 On the RC 462 E joint (no roll pin type), remove the spring and cup from inside the outer member of the joint **(see illustration)**.

5 Using circlip pliers, extract the circlip securing the tripod joint to the driveshaft **(see illustration)**. Note that on some models, the joint may be staked in position; if so, relieve the staking using a file. Mark the position of the tripod in relation to the driveshaft, using a dab of paint or a punch.

6 The tripod joint can now be removed **(see illustration)**. If it is tight, draw the joint off the driveshaft end using a puller. Ensure that the legs of the puller are located behind the joint inner member and do not contact the joint rollers. Alternatively, support the inner member of the tripod joint, and press the shaft out using a hydraulic press, again ensuring that no load is applied to the joint rollers.

7 With the tripod joint removed, slide the gaiter and inner retaining collar off the end of the driveshaft.

8 Wipe clean the joint components, taking care not to remove the alignment marks made on dismantling. **Do not** use paraffin or other solvents to clean this type of joint.

9 Examine the tripod joint, rollers and outer member for any signs of scoring or wear. Check that the rollers move smoothly on the tripod stems. If wear is evident, the tripod joint and roller assembly can be renewed, but it is not possible to obtain a replacement outer member. Obtain a new gaiter, retaining clips and a quantity of the special lubricating grease. These parts are available in the form of a repair kit from your Renault dealer.

10 Tape over the splines on the end of the driveshaft, then carefully slide the inner retaining clip and gaiter onto the shaft.

11 Remove the tape, then, aligning the marks made on dismantling, engage the tripod joint with the driveshaft splines. Use a hammer and soft metal drift to tap the joint onto the shaft, taking great care not to damage the driveshaft splines or joint rollers. Alternatively, support the driveshaft, and press the joint into position using a hydraulic press and suitable tubular spacer which bears only on the joint inner member.

12 Secure the tripod joint in position with the circlip, ensuring that it is correctly located in the driveshaft groove. Where no circlip is fitted, secure the joint in position by staking the end of the driveshaft in three places, at intervals of 120°, using a hammer and punch.

13 Where applicable, refit the spring and cup

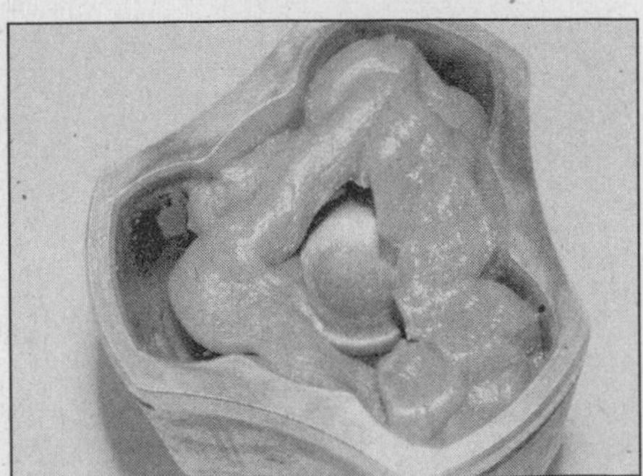
4.13b . . . and pack with the grease supplied in the repair kit

4.14a Pack the gaiter and tripod joint with the remainder of the grease . . .

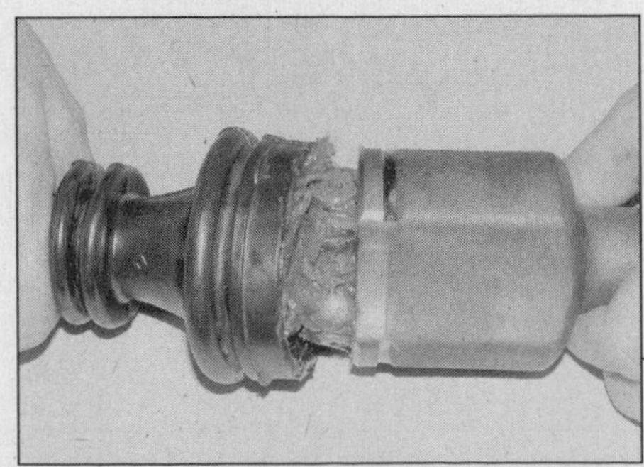
4.14b . . . and slide the halves of the joint together

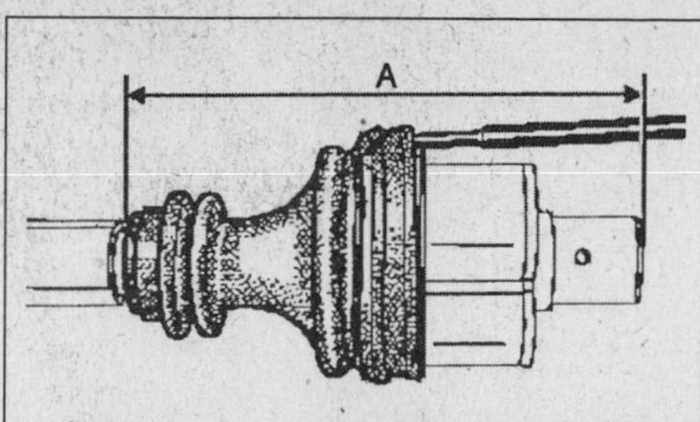

4.17a Fitting dimension for the right-hand driveshaft inner joint gaiter with roll pin – RC462 joint

A = 190 ± 1 mm

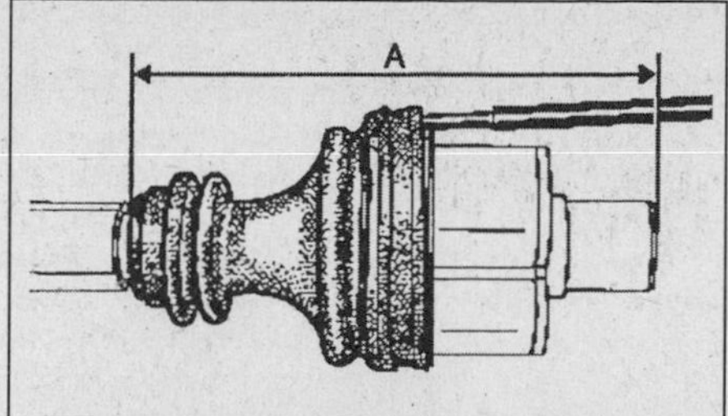

4.17b Fitting dimension for the right-hand driveshaft inner joint gaiter without roll pin – RC462 E joint

A = 203 ± 1 mm

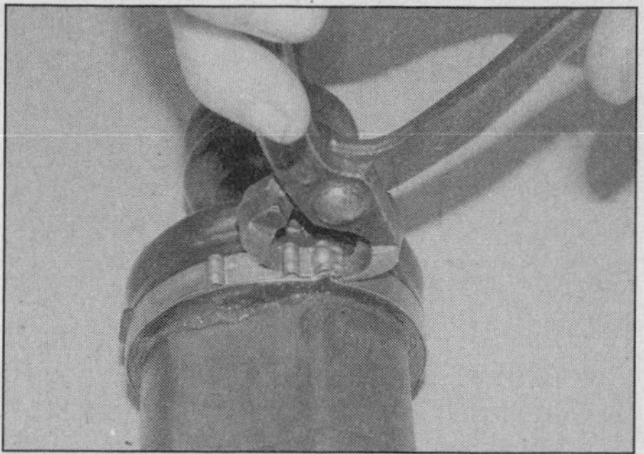

4.18 Using pincers to secure the gaiter retaining clip

in the outer member, then evenly distribute the grease contained in the repair kit around the tripod joint and inside the outer member **(see illustrations)**.

14 Pack the gaiter with the remainder of the grease and slide the two halves of the joint together **(see illustrations)**.

15 Slide the gaiter up the driveshaft. Locate the gaiter in the grooves on the driveshaft and outer member.

16 Fit the inner retaining clip into place over the inner end of the gaiter.

17 Using a blunt rod, carefully lift the outer lip of the gaiter to equalise the air pressure. With the rod in position, compress the joint until the dimension from the inner end of the gaiter to the flat end face of the outer member is as shown **(see illustrations)**. Hold the outer member in this position and withdraw the rod.

18 Slip the new retaining clip into place to secure the outer lip of the gaiter to the outer member. Remove any slack in the gaiter retaining clip by carefully compressing the raised section of the clip. In the absence of the special tool, a pair of pincers may be used **(see illustration)**. Secure the small retaining clip using the same procedure.

19 Check that the constant velocity joint moves freely in all directions, then refit the driveshaft as described in Section 2.

Left-hand driveshaft

20 Remove the driveshaft as described in Section 2.

21 Using circlip pliers, extract the circlip securing the tripod joint to the driveshaft. Note that on some models, the joint may be staked in position; if so, relieve the staking using a file. Using a dab of paint or a hammer and punch, mark the position of the tripod joint in relation to the driveshaft, to use as a guide to refitting.

22 The tripod joint can now be removed. If it is tight, draw the joint off the driveshaft end using a puller. Ensure that the legs of the puller are located behind the joint inner member and do not contact the joint rollers. Alternatively, support the inner member of the tripod joint and press the shaft out of the joint, again ensuring that no load is applied to the joint rollers.

23 The gaiter and bearing assembly is removed in the same way, either by drawing the bearing off the driveshaft, or by pressing the driveshaft out of the bearing. Remove the retaining plate, noting which way round it is fitted.

24 Obtain a new gaiter, which is supplied complete with the small bearing.

25 Owing to the lip-type seal used in the bearing, the bearing and gaiter must be pressed into position. If a hammer and tubular drift are used to drive the assembly onto the driveshaft, there is a risk of distorting the seal.

26 Refit the retaining plate to the driveshaft, ensuring that it is fitted the correct way around.

27 Support the driveshaft, and press the gaiter bearing onto the shaft, using a tubular spacer which bears only on the bearing inner race. Position the bearing so that the distance from the end of the driveshaft to the inner face of the bearing is as shown **(see illustrations)**.

28 Align the marks made on dismantling, and engage the tripod joint with the driveshaft splines. Use a hammer and soft metal drift to tap the joint onto the shaft, taking care not to damage the driveshaft splines or joint rollers. Alternatively, support the driveshaft, and press the joint into position using a tubular spacer which bears only on the joint inner member.

29 Secure the tripod joint in position with the circlip, ensuring that it is correctly located in the driveshaft groove. Where no circlip is fitted, secure the joint in position by staking the end of the driveshaft in three places, at intervals of 120°, using a hammer and punch.

30 Refit the driveshaft to the vehicle as described in Section 2.

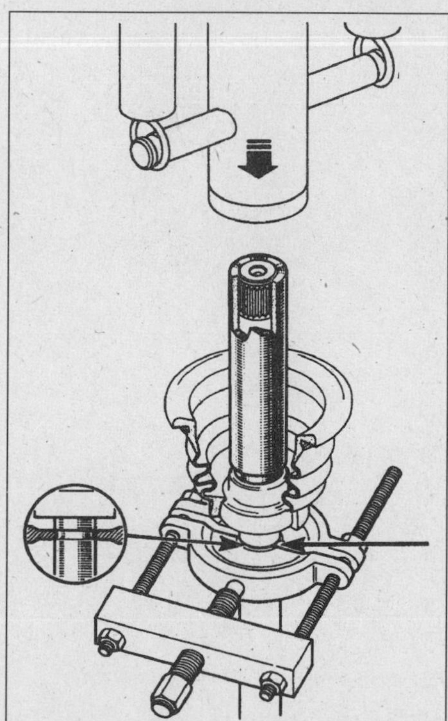

4.27a Pressing the inner bearing/gaiter onto the end of the left-hand driveshaft – manual transmission models

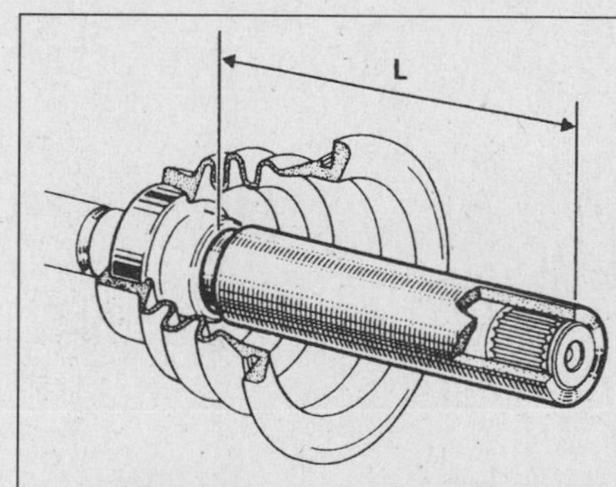

4.27b Fitting dimension for the left-hand driveshaft inner bearing/gaiter – manual transmission models

L = 118 ± 0.2mm (JB1 transmission)
L = 123 ± 0.2mm (JB3 transmission)

5 Gaiter renewal (automatic models) – general information

At the time of writing, no information on driveshaft dismantling was available for these models. The inner joints differ from the manual transmission models, although the driveshafts outer joints are very similar in design to the manual transmission models. If gaiter renewal is necessary, and further information required, then the driveshaft should be removed from the vehicle, as described in Section 2, and taken to a Renault dealer.

6 Driveshaft overhaul – general information

If any of the checks described in Chapter 1A or 1B reveal wear in a driveshaft joint, first remove the roadwheel trim or centre cap (as appropriate) and check that the driveshaft retaining nut is still correctly tightened; if in doubt, use a torque wrench to check it. Refit the centre cap or trim, and repeat the check on the other driveshaft.

Road test the vehicle, and listen for a metallic clicking from the front as the vehicle is driven slowly in a circle on full-lock. If a clicking noise is heard, this indicates wear in the outer constant velocity joint.

If vibration, consistent with road speed, is felt through the vehicle when accelerating, there is a possibility of wear in the inner constant velocity joints.

Constant velocity joints can be dismantled and inspected for wear as described in Sections 3 and 4.

On models with manual gearbox, wear in the outer constant velocity joint can only be rectified by renewing the driveshaft. This is necessary since no outer joint components are available separately. For the inner joint, the tripod joint and roller assembly is available separately, but wear in any of the other components will also necessitate driveshaft renewal.

On models with automatic transmission, wear in either constant velocity joint will necessitate driveshaft renewal; no components for either joint are available separately.

On models with ABS, the reluctor ring is part of the driveshaft and cannot be removed.

7 Intermediate bearing – renewal

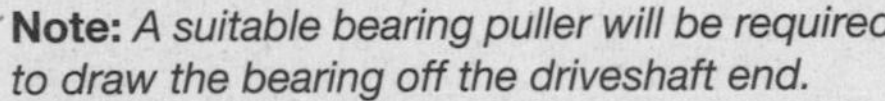

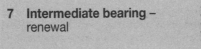

Note: *A suitable bearing puller will be required to draw the bearing off the driveshaft end.*

1 Remove the right-hand driveshaft as described in Section 2.

2 Check that the bearing outer race rotates smoothly and easily, without any signs of roughness or undue free-play between the inner and outer races. If necessary, renew the bearing as follows.

3 Where applicable, remove the bearing retaining circlip **(see illustration)**.

4 Using a long-reach universal bearing puller, carefully draw the bearing off the inner end of the driveshaft.

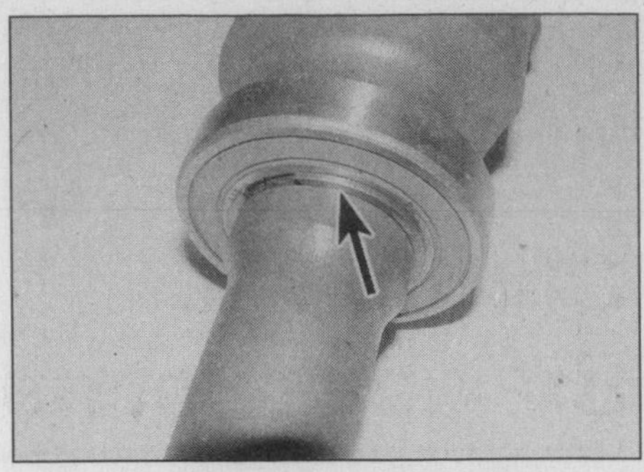

7.3 Remove the bearing retaining circlip (arrowed)

5 Thoroughly clean the contact faces of the driveshaft and the new bearing.

6 Apply a smear of grease to the inner race of the new bearing, then fit the bearing over the end of the driveshaft.

7 Using hammer and a suitable piece of tubing, which bears only on the bearing inner race, tap the new bearing into position on the driveshaft until it contacts the locating shoulder on the shaft.

8 Where applicable, fit the bearing retaining circlip.

9 Check that the bearing rotates freely, then refit the driveshaft as described in Section 2.

Chapter 9
Braking system

Contents

Degrees of difficulty

Easy, suitable for novice with little experience 

Fairly easy, suitable for beginner with some experience 

Fairly difficult, suitable for competent DIY mechanic 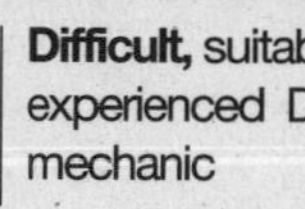

Difficult, suitable for experienced DIY mechanic

Very difficult, suitable for expert DIY or professional

Specifications

ABS sensors

Front sensors:	
Air gap – adjustable	1.0 mm ± 0.6
Resistance	1000 ohms
Rear sensors:	
Air gap – not adjustable	Cannot be checked
Resistance	1000 ohms

Front disc brakes

	New	Minimum
Disc thickness:		
Mégane*:		
A	20.6 mm	17.6 mm
B	22.0 mm	19.8 mm
C	24.0 mm	21.8 mm
Scénic	24.0 mm	21.8 mm
Brake pad thickness (including backing plate)	18.2 mm	6.0 mm
Brake disc diameter:		
1.4 litre and 1.9 litre dTi Mégane	259 mm	
All other models	280mm	
Maximum disc run-out	0.07 mm	

** Depending on model and engine type; consult a Renault dealer.*

Rear disc brakes

	New	Minimum
Disc thickness	11.0 mm	9.5 mm
Brake pad thickness (including backing plate)	11.0 mm	5.0 mm
Brake disc diameter	274 mm	

Rear drum brakes

	New	Maximum
Drum internal diameter*:		
A	203.2 mm	204.4 mm
B	228.5 mm	229.5 mm
Brake shoe thickness (including backing):	New	Minimum
Leading shoe	4.9 mm	2.0 mm
Trailing shoe	3.4 mm	2.0 mm

* Depending on model and engine type; consult a Renault dealer.

Torque wrench settings

Torque wrench settings	Nm	lbf ft
ABS wheel sensor mounting bolts	8	6
Bleed screw	6	4
Front brake caliper:		
Guide pin bolts*	32	24
Mounting bolts	100	74
Front disc-to-hub bolts	14	10
Hydraulic hose union	15	11
Hydraulic pipe union nut	13	10
Master cylinder retaining nuts	23	17
Rear brake caliper:		
Guide pin bolts*	35	26
Mounting bolts	60	44
Rear hub nut*	175	129
Rear stub axle bolts – Scénic	See Chapter 10	
Roadwheel bolts	90	66
Vacuum servo unit mounting nuts	20	15

*Use new fasteners

1 General information

The braking system is of the servo-assisted, dual-circuit hydraulic type. The arrangement of the hydraulic system is such that each circuit operates one front and one rear brake from a tandem master cylinder. Under normal circumstances, both circuits operate in unison. However, in the event of hydraulic failure in one circuit, full braking force will still be available at two wheels.

All models are fitted with front disc brakes, which are actuated by single-piston sliding type calipers, which ensure that equal pressure is applied to each disc pad.

On models with rear drum brakes, the rear drum brakes incorporate leading and trailing shoes, which are actuated by twin-piston wheel cylinders. A self-adjust mechanism is incorporated, to automatically compensate for brake shoe wear. As the brake shoe linings wear, the footbrake operation automatically operates the adjuster mechanism, which effectively lengthens the shoe strut and repositions the brake shoes, to renew the lining-to-drum clearance.

On models with rear disc brakes, the brakes are actuated by single-piston sliding calipers which incorporate mechanical handbrake mechanisms.

On some models, depending on the braking system fitted, a load-sensitive pressure-regulating valve is situated in the hydraulic circuit to each rear brake. The valve is linked to the rear axle and regulates the hydraulic pressure applied to the rear brakes, according to the loading on the axle, and so helps prevent rear wheel lock-up during emergency braking. It does this by varying the hydraulic pressure applied to the rear calipers in proportion to the load being carried by the vehicle.

On all models, the handbrake provides an independent mechanical means of rear brake application.

Warning: When servicing any part of the system, work carefully and methodically; also observe scrupulous cleanliness when overhauling any part of the hydraulic system. Always renew components (in axle sets, where applicable) if in doubt about their condition, and use only genuine Renault replacement parts, or at least those of known good quality. Note the warnings given in 'Safety first!' and at relevant points in this Chapter concerning the dangers of asbestos dust and hydraulic fluid.

2 Hydraulic system – bleeding

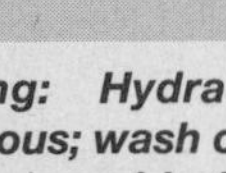

Warning: Hydraulic fluid is poisonous; wash off immediately and thoroughly in the case of skin contact, and seek immediate medical advice if any fluid is swallowed or gets into the eyes. Certain types of hydraulic fluid are inflammable, and may ignite when allowed into contact with hot components; when servicing any hydraulic system, it is safest to assume that the fluid is inflammable, and to take precautions against the risk of fire as though it is petrol that is being handled. Hydraulic fluid is also an effective paint stripper, and will attack plastics; if any is spilt, it should be washed off immediately, using copious quantities of fresh water. Finally, it is hygroscopic (it absorbs moisture from the air) – old fluid may be contaminated and unfit for further use. When topping-up or renewing the fluid, always use the recommended type, and ensure that it comes from a freshly-opened sealed container.

Models not equipped with ABS

General

1 The correct operation of any hydraulic system is only possible after removing all air from the components and circuit; this is achieved by bleeding the system.

2 During the bleeding procedure, add only clean, unused hydraulic fluid of the recommended type; never re-use fluid that has already been bled from the system. Ensure that sufficient fluid is available before starting work.

3 If there is any possibility of incorrect fluid being already in the system, the brake components and circuit must be flushed completely with uncontaminated, correct fluid, and new seals should be fitted to the various components.

4 If hydraulic fluid has been lost from the system, or air has entered because of a leak, ensure that the fault is cured before proceeding further.

5 Park the vehicle on level ground, switch off

the engine and select first or reverse gear then chock the wheels and release the handbrake.

6 Check that all pipes and hoses are secure, unions tight and bleed screws closed. Clean any dirt from around the bleed screws.

7 Unscrew the master cylinder reservoir cap, and top the master cylinder reservoir up to the MAXI level line; refit the cap loosely, and remember to maintain the fluid level at least above the MINI level line throughout the procedure, or there is a risk of further air entering the system.

8 There are a number of one-man, do-it-yourself brake bleeding kits currently available from motor accessory shops. It is recommended that one of these kits is used whenever possible, as they greatly simplify the bleeding operation, and also reduce the risk of expelled air and fluid being drawn back into the system. If such a kit is not available, the basic (two-man) method must be used, which is described in detail below.

9 If a kit is to be used, prepare the vehicle as described previously, and follow the kit manufacturer's instructions, as the procedure may vary slightly according to the type being used; generally, they are as outlined below in the relevant sub-section.

10 Whichever method is used, the same sequence must be followed (paragraphs 11 and 12) to ensure the removal of all air from the system.

Sequence

11 If the system has been only partially disconnected, and suitable precautions were taken to minimise fluid loss, it should be necessary only to bleed that part of the system (ie, the primary or secondary circuit).

12 If the complete system is to be bled, then it should be done working in the following sequence:

a) Right-hand rear brake
b) Left-hand front brake
c) Left-hand rear brake
d) Right-hand front brake

Basic (two-man) method

13 Collect a clean glass jar, a suitable length of plastic or rubber tubing which is a tight fit over the bleed screw, and a ring spanner to fit the screw. The help of an assistant will also be required.

14 Remove the dust cap from the first screw in the sequence. Fit the spanner and tube to the screw, place the other end of the tube in the jar, and pour in sufficient fluid to cover the end of the tube.

15 Ensure that the master cylinder reservoir fluid level is maintained at least above the MINI level line throughout the procedure.

16 Have the assistant fully depress the brake pedal several times to build up pressure, then maintain it on the final downstroke.

17 While pedal pressure is maintained, unscrew the bleed screw (approximately one turn) and allow the compressed fluid and air to flow into the jar. The assistant should maintain pedal pressure, following it down to the floor if necessary, and should not release it until instructed to do so. When the flow stops, tighten the bleed screw again, have the assistant release the pedal slowly, and recheck the reservoir fluid level.

18 Repeat the steps given in paragraphs 16 and 17 until the fluid emerging from the bleed screw is free from air bubbles. If the master cylinder has been drained and refilled, and air is being bled from the first screw in the sequence, allow approximately five seconds between cycles for the master cylinder passages to refill.

19 When no more air bubbles appear, tighten the bleed screw to the specified torque, remove the tube and spanner, and refit the dust cap. Do not overtighten the bleed screw.

20 Repeat the procedure on the remaining screws in the sequence, until all air is removed from the system and the brake pedal feels firm again.

Using a one-way valve kit

21 As their name implies, these kits consist of a length of tubing with a one-way valve fitted, to prevent expelled air and fluid being drawn back into the system; some kits include a translucent container, which can be positioned so that the air bubbles can be more easily seen flowing from the end of the tube.

22 The kit is connected to the bleed screw, which is then opened **(see illustration)**. The user returns to the driver's seat, depresses the brake pedal with a smooth, steady stroke, and slowly releases it; this is repeated until the expelled fluid is clear of air bubbles.

23 Note that these kits simplify work so much that it is easy to forget the master cylinder reservoir fluid level; ensure that this is maintained at least above the MINI level line at all times.

Using a pressure-bleeding kit

24 These kits are usually operated by the reservoir of pressurised air contained in the spare tyre. However, note that it will probably be necessary to reduce the pressure to a lower level than normal; refer to the instructions supplied with the kit.

25 By connecting a pressurised, fluid-filled container to the master cylinder reservoir, bleeding can be carried out simply by opening each screw in turn (in the specified sequence), and allowing the fluid to flow out until no more air bubbles can be seen in the expelled fluid.

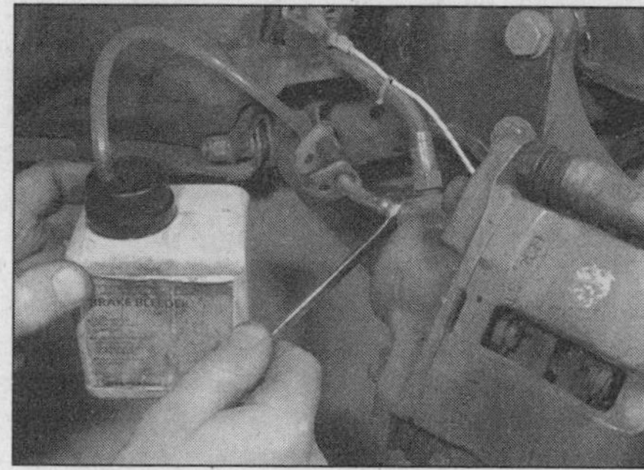

2.22 Bleeding a front brake caliper

26 This method has the advantage that the large reservoir of fluid provides an additional safeguard against air being drawn into the system during bleeding.

27 Pressure-bleeding is particularly effective when bleeding difficult systems, or when bleeding the complete system at the time of routine fluid renewal.

All methods

28 When bleeding is complete, and firm pedal feel is restored, wash off any spilt fluid, tighten the bleed screws to the specified torque, and refit their dust caps.

29 Check the hydraulic fluid level in the master cylinder reservoir, and top-up if necessary (see *Weekly checks*).

30 Discard any hydraulic fluid that has been bled from the system; it will not be fit for re-use.

31 Check the feel of the brake pedal. If it feels at all spongy, air must still be present in the system, and further bleeding is required. Failure to bleed satisfactorily after a reasonable repetition of the bleeding procedure may be due to worn master cylinder seals.

Models equipped with ABS

Caution: On models equipped with ABS, disconnect the battery before disconnecting any braking system hydraulic union and do not reconnect the battery until after the hydraulic system has been bled. Failure to do this could lead to air entering the hydraulic unit. If air enters the hydraulic unit pump, it will prove very difficult (in some cases impossible) to bleed the unit. Refer to Chapter 5A, Section 1 when disconnecting the battery.
Caution: Do not use a pressure-bleeding kit on models equipped with ABS.

32 On models with ABS, due to the complexity of the hydraulic system, special precautions/procedures are necessary to bleed the hydraulic system of air. These procedures differ depending on which part of the system has been disconnected.

33 The basic information given for the conventional system (ignoring the information about pressure-bleeding) also applies to models equipped with ABS. One notable change is the sequence that the complete system is bled in. On models with ABS the order is as follows:

a) Left-hand front brake
b) Right-hand rear brake
c) Right-hand front brake
d) Left-hand rear brake

34 In addition to this, the following bleeding procedures should be used to ensure that all air is removed from the system.

Connecting a caliper/wheel cylinder

Note: *If more than one caliper/wheel cylinder has been removed, carry out this procedure on each brake, working in the order given in paragraph 33.*

35 With the container connected to the bleed screw and the master cylinder topped-up, continue as follows, ensuring that the brake fluid never fails below the MINI level in the reservoir.

36 Open up the bleed screw then have your assistant fully depress the brake pedal and hold it down. Close the bleed screw securely then have your assistant release the brake pedal slowly and wait for approximately 3 seconds. Repeat this procedure at least ten times until the fluid flowing from bleed screw is free of air bubbles.

37 Next build-up pressure in the braking system by having your assistant pump the brake pedal at least 3 times, keep the pedal depressed on the last stroke. Open the bleed screw again and allow the pedal to reach the floor. Securely close the screw then have your assistant release the pedal slowly and wait at least 3 seconds. Repeat this procedure again and check that the fluid flowing from the bleed screw is free of air bubbles.

38 Check the feel of the brake pedal then remove the container and top-up the fluid level (see *Weekly checks*). Ensure that the bleed screw is tightened to the specified torque then refit the dust cap.

Connecting the pressure-regulator

39 Bleed both rear brakes using the information in paragraphs 35 to 38.

Connecting the master cylinder

40 If the master cylinder is disconnected for any reason, to minimise the risk of trapping air in the hydraulic unit it is necessary to bleed the cylinder of air prior to reconnecting the pipes. In order to do this two blanking plugs which screw into the master cylinder ports will be required.

41 With both pipes disconnected, screw the plugs into the master cylinder ports and tighten securely.

42 Fill the master cylinder reservoir then open up the rear port (primary circuit) plug/bleed screw and have an assistant depress and hold the brake pedal. Securely close the plug then have your assistant release the brake pedal slowly and wait for approximately 3 seconds. Repeat this procedure 5 or 6 times.

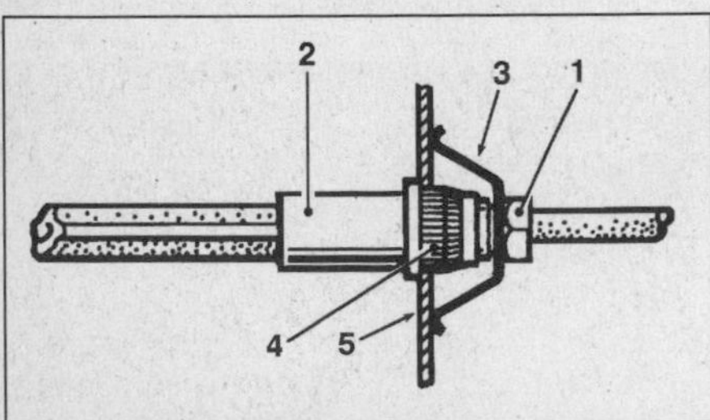

3.2 Typical hydraulic pipe connection to a flexible hose

1 *Union nut*
2 *Flexible hose*
3 *Spring clip*
4 *End fitting*
5 *Bodywork*

43 Repeat the procedure on the master cylinder front port (secondary circuit) to remove all traces of air from the master cylinder.

44 To ensure that the fluid does not escape (allowing air to enter) when the plugs are disconnected, it is necessary to depress the brake pedal slightly (approximately 30 mm) and hold it in position. Special tools are available from accessory shops to hold pedals in position or alternately have an assistant hold the pedal.

45 Remove the plugs from the brake pipes and check that both pipes are full of fluid; if not top them up. With the brake pedal held in position, quickly remove one of the plugs from the master cylinder port and reconnect the brake pipe tightening its union nut to the specified torque. Repeat the operation on the second master cylinder port then wash off any spilt fluid.

46 Following the information given in paragraphs 35 to 38, the complete braking system should then be bled in the specified sequence.

After disconnecting a hydraulic unit

47 Prior to reconnecting the pipes to the hydraulic unit ensure that all pipes and the hydraulic unit ports are full of fluid. This will minimise the amount of air present in the circuit and lessen the risk of getting air trapped in the hydraulic unit. Tighten all union nuts to the specified torque and wash off any spilt fluid.

48 Following the information given in paragraphs 35 to 38, the complete braking system should then be bled in the specified sequence.

3 Hydraulic pipes and hoses – renewal

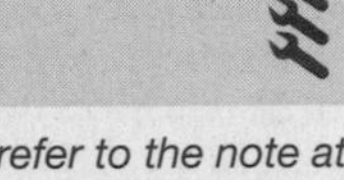

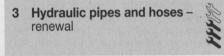

Note: *Before starting work, refer to the note at the beginning of Section 2 concerning the dangers of hydraulic fluid.*

Models not equipped with ABS

1 If any pipe or hose is to be renewed, minimise fluid loss by first removing the master cylinder reservoir cap, then tightening it down onto a piece of polythene to obtain an airtight seal. Alternatively, flexible hoses can be sealed, if required, using a proprietary brake hose clamp; metal brake pipe unions can be plugged (if care is taken not to allow dirt into the system) or capped immediately they are disconnected. Place a wad of rag under any union that is to be disconnected, to catch any spilt fluid.

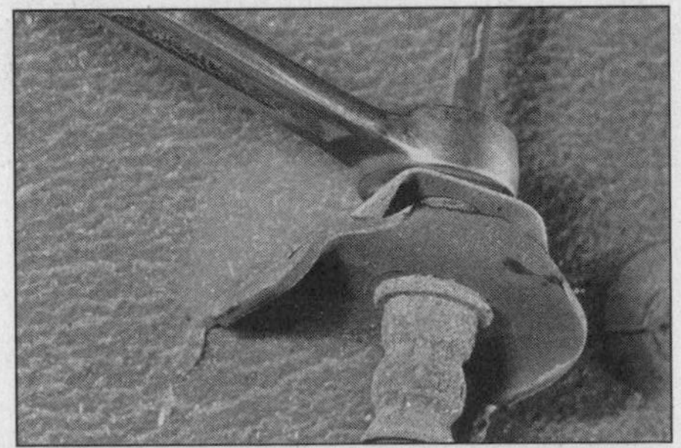

3.3 Using a brake pipe spanner to slacken a hydraulic pipe union nut

2 If a flexible hose is to be disconnected, unscrew the brake pipe union nut before removing the spring clip which secures the hose to its mounting bracket **(see illustration)**.

3 To unscrew the union nuts, it is preferable to obtain a brake pipe spanner of the correct size; these are available from most large motor accessory shops **(see illustration)**. Failing this, a close-fitting open-ended spanner will be required, though if the nuts are tight or corroded, their flats may be rounded-off if the spanner slips. In such a case, a self-locking wrench is often the only way to unscrew a stubborn union, but it follows that the pipe and the damaged nuts must be renewed on reassembly. Always clean a union and surrounding area before disconnecting it. If disconnecting a component with more than one union, make a careful note of the connections before disturbing any of them.

4 If a brake pipe is to be renewed, it can be obtained, cut to length and with the union nuts and end flares in place, from Renault dealers. All that is then necessary is to bend it to shape, following the line of the original, before fitting it to the car. Alternatively, most motor accessory shops can make up brake pipes from kits, but this requires very careful measurement of the original, to ensure that the replacement is of the correct length. The safest answer is usually to take the original to the shop as a pattern.

5 On refitting, do not overtighten the union nuts. It is not necessary to exercise brute force to obtain a sound joint.

6 Ensure that the pipes and hoses are correctly routed, with no kinks, and that they are secured in the clips or brackets provided. After fitting, remove the polythene from the reservoir, and bleed the hydraulic system as described in Section 2. Wash off any spilt fluid, and check carefully for fluid leaks.

Models equipped with ABS

Caution: On models equipped with ABS, disconnect the battery before disconnecting any braking system hydraulic union and do not reconnect the battery until after the hydraulic system has been bled. Failure to do this could lead to air entering the hydraulic unit. If air enters the hydraulic unit pump, it will prove very difficult (in some cases impossible) to bleed the unit. Refer to Chapter 5A, Section 1 when disconnecting the battery.

7 Refer to the information given in paragraphs 1 to 6, noting the following:

a) *If a brake pipe(s) is to be disconnected from the hydraulic unit, it is essential that the unit port(s) are sealed up immediately to prevent fluid loss and allow the entry of air. This will minimise the risk of air getting trapped in the unit (see Caution). Prior to reconnecting the*

4.4 Remove the lower guide pin bolt whilst retaining the guide pin with an open-ended spanner

4.5 Pivot the caliper upwards and away from the disc . . .

4.6 . . . and lift out the pads from the caliper mounting bracket

pipe(s), ensure both the port(s) and pipe(s) are full of fluid (see Section 2).

b) If a brake pipe(s) is disconnected from the master cylinder, it will be necessary to bleed the master cylinder prior to reconnecting the pipe (see Section 2).

4 Front brake pads – renewal

Warning: Renew both sets of front brake pads at the same time – never renew the pads on only one wheel, as uneven braking may result. Note that the dust created by wear of the pads may contain asbestos, which is a health hazard. Never blow it out with compressed air, and don't inhale any of it. An approved filtering mask should be worn when working on the brakes. DO NOT use petrol or petroleum-based solvents to clean brake parts; use brake cleaner or methylated spirit only.

Note: *New caliper guide pin bolts will be required on refitting.*

1 Chock the rear wheels, apply the handbrake, then jack up the front of the vehicle and support it on axle stands. Remove the front roadwheels.

2 Where applicable, trace the brake pad wear sensor wiring back from the pads, and disconnect it from the wiring connector. Note the routing of the wiring, and free it from any relevant retaining clips.

3 Push the piston into its bore by pulling the caliper outwards.

4 Slacken and remove the caliper lower guide pin bolt, using a slim open-ended spanner to prevent the guide pin itself from rotating **(see illustration)**. Discard the guide pin bolt – a new one must be used on refitting.

5 Pivot the caliper away from the brake pads and mounting bracket, and tie it to the suspension strut using a suitable piece of wire **(see illustration)**. If the upper guide pin is also removed, do not allow the caliper to hang down by the hose.

6 Withdraw the two brake pads from the caliper mounting bracket **(see illustration)**.

7 First measure the thickness of each brake pad (friction material and backing plate) **(see illustration)**. If either pad is worn at any point to the specified minimum thickness or less, all four pads must be renewed. The pads should also be renewed if any are fouled with oil or grease; note that there is no satisfactory way of degreasing friction material, once contaminated. If any of the brake pads are worn unevenly, or are fouled with oil or grease, trace and rectify the cause before reassembly.

8 If the brake pads are still serviceable, carefully clean them using a clean, fine wire brush or similar, paying particular attention to the sides and back of the metal backing. Clean out the grooves in the friction material, and pick out any large embedded particles of dirt or debris. Carefully clean the pad locations in the caliper mounting bracket.

9 Prior to fitting the pads, check that the guide pins are free to slide easily in the caliper mounting bracket, and check that the rubber guide pin gaiters are undamaged **(see illustration)**. Brush the dust and dirt from the caliper and piston, but **do not** inhale it, as it is a health hazard. Inspect the dust seal around the piston for damage, and the piston for evidence of fluid leaks, corrosion or damage. If attention to any of these components is necessary, refer to Section 8.

10 If new brake pads are to be fitted, the caliper piston must be pushed back into the cylinder to make room for them. Either use a G clamp or similar tool, or use suitable pieces of wood as levers; take care not to damage the piston seals. Provided that the master cylinder reservoir has not been overfilled with hydraulic fluid, there should be no spillage, but keep a careful watch on the fluid level while retracting the piston. If the fluid level rises above the MAXI level line at any time, the surplus should be syphoned off or ejected via a plastic tube connected to the bleed screw (see Section 2). **Note:** *Do not syphon the fluid by mouth, as it is poisonous; use a syringe or an old antifreeze tester.*

11 Ensuring that the friction material of each pad is against the brake disc, fit the pads to the caliper mounting bracket. Note; Where applicable, the pad with the wear sensor wiring should be fitted as the inner pad.

12 Pivot the caliper down into position over the pads, ensuring that the pad warning sensor wiring is correctly routed. Ensure that the pad anti-rattle springs are correctly positioned against the caliper then press down on the caliper and install the new guide pin bolt **(see illustration)**. Tighten the guide

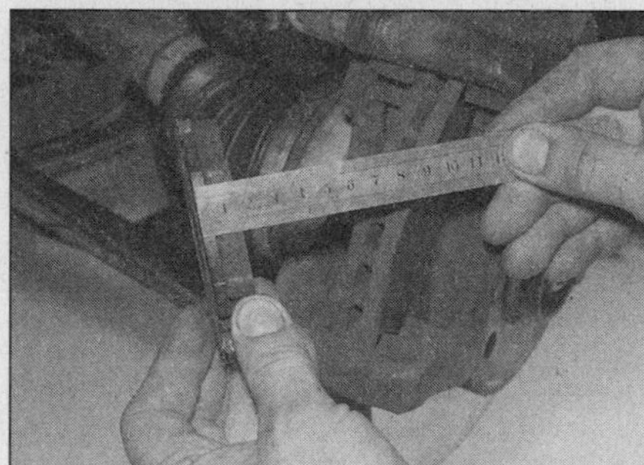

4.7 Measuring brake pad thickness

4.9 Prior to fitting the pads check the guide pin gaiters for signs of wear or damage

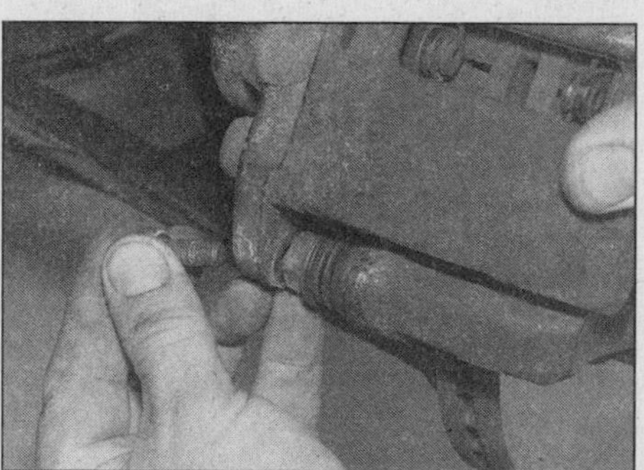

4.12 Pivot the caliper down into position and fit the new guide pin bolt

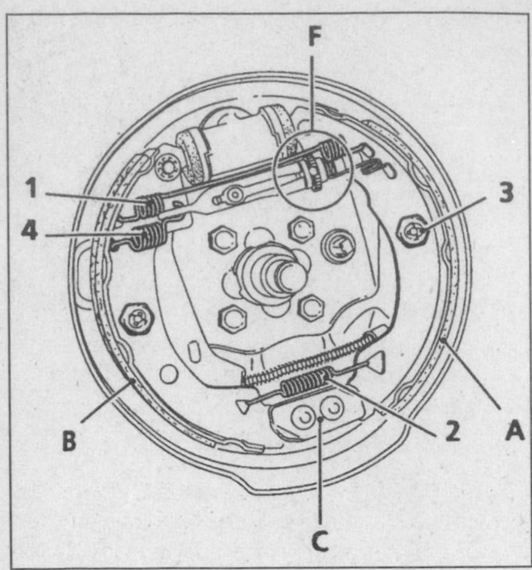

5.6 Rear drum brake assembly

1 *Upper return spring*
2 *Lower return spring*
3 *Retainer spring cup*
4 *Adjuster strut spring*
A *Leading shoe*
B *Trailing shoe*
C *Lower pivot point*
F *Adjuster strut knurled wheel*

pin bolt to the specified torque setting, while retaining the guide pin with an open-ended spanner.

13 Reconnect the brake pad wear sensor wiring connector, ensuring that the wiring is securely clipped in position.

14 Depress the brake pedal repeatedly, until the pads are pressed into firm contact with the brake disc, and normal (non-assisted) pedal pressure is restored.

15 Repeat the above procedure on the remaining front brake caliper.

16 Refit the roadwheels, then lower the vehicle to the ground and tighten the roadwheel bolts to the specified torque setting.

17 Check the hydraulic fluid level as described in *Weekly checks*.

HAYNES HiNT ***New pads will not give full braking efficiency until they have bedded-in. Be prepared for this, and avoid hard braking as far as possible for the first hundred miles or so after pad renewal.***

5 Rear brake shoes – renewal

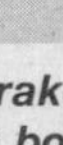

Warning: Brake shoes must be renewed on both rear wheels at the same time – never renew the shoes on only one wheel, as uneven braking may result. Also, the dust created by wear of the shoes may contain asbestos, which is a health hazard. Never blow it out with compressed air, and don't inhale any of it. An approved filtering mask should be worn when working on the brakes. DO NOT use petrol or petroleum-based solvents to clean brake parts; use brake cleaner or methylated spirit only.

1 Remove the brake drum as described in Section 7.

2 Working carefully, and taking the necessary precautions, remove all traces of brake dust from the brake drum, backplate and shoes.

3 Measure the thickness of each brake shoe at several points (friction material and shoe); if either shoe is worn at any point to the specified minimum thickness or less, all four shoes must be renewed as a set. The shoes should also be renewed if any are fouled with oil or grease; there is no satisfactory way of degreasing friction material, once contaminated.

4 If any of the brake shoes are worn unevenly, or fouled with oil or grease, trace and rectify the cause before reassembly.

5 If the all components are in good condition, refit the brake drum as described in Section 7. To renew the brake shoes, proceed as follows.

6 Note the position of each shoe, and the location of each of the springs **(see illustration)**. Also make a note of the self-adjuster component locations, to aid refitting later.

7 Using a pair of pliers, remove the shoe retainer spring cups by depressing and turning them through 90°. With the cups removed, lift off the springs and withdraw the retainer pins **(see illustrations)**.

8 Ease the shoes out one at a time from the lower pivot point, to release the tension of the return spring, then disconnect the lower return spring from both shoes **(see illustration)**.

9 Ease the upper end of both shoes out from their wheel cylinder locations, taking care not to damage the wheel cylinder seals, and disconnect the handbrake cable from the trailing shoe. The brake shoe and adjuster strut assembly can then be manoeuvred out of position and away from the backplate. Do not depress the brake pedal until the brakes are reassembled; wrap a strong elastic band around the wheel cylinder pistons to retain them **(see illustrations)**.

10 With the shoe and adjuster strut assembly on the bench, make a note of the correct fitted

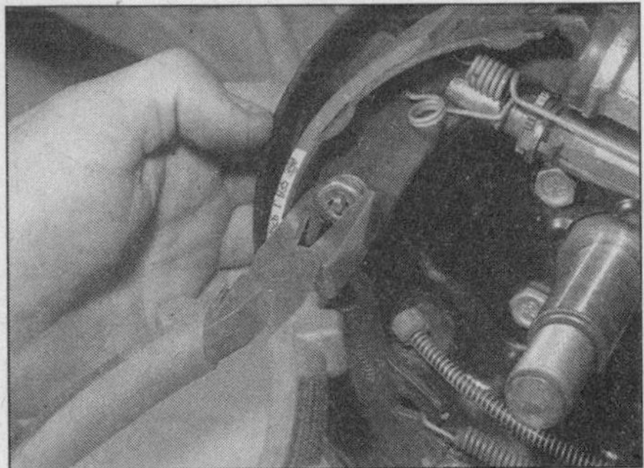

5.7a Using pliers, depress the spring cup and rotate through 90° . . .

5.7b . . . then lift off the spring and remove the retainer pin

5.8 Ease the shoes out from the lower pivot point and remove the lower return spring

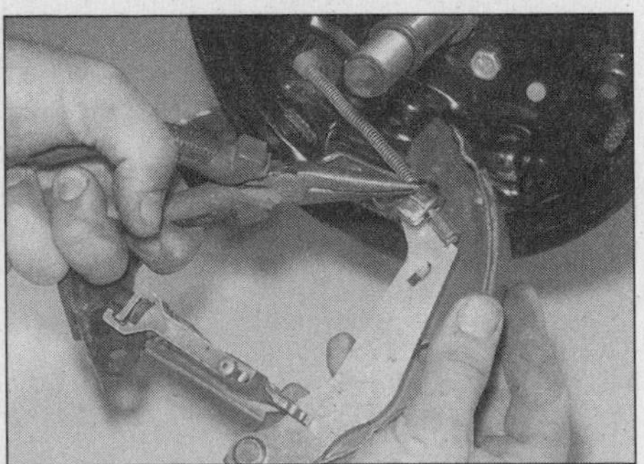

5.9a Remove the shoe assembly from the backplate and detach it from the handbrake cable

5.9b Whilst the shoes are removed wrap a strong elastic band around the wheel cylinder to retain the pistons

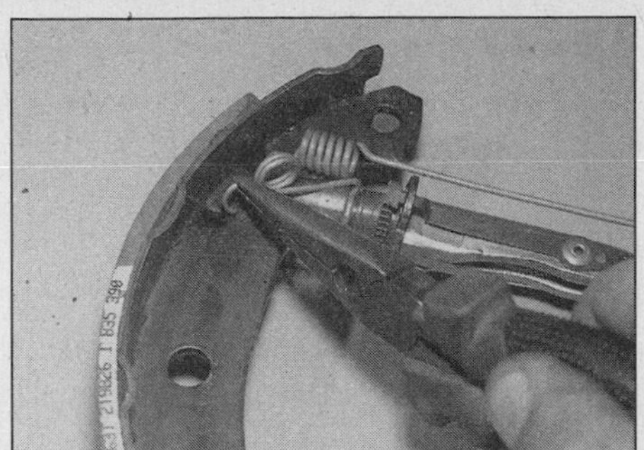

5.10a Unhook the adjuster strut bolt spring from the leading shoe . . .

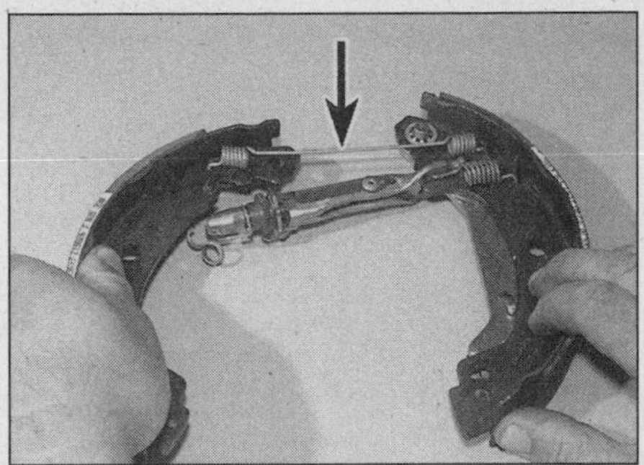

5.10b . . . then separate the shoe from the strut and remove the upper return spring (arrowed)

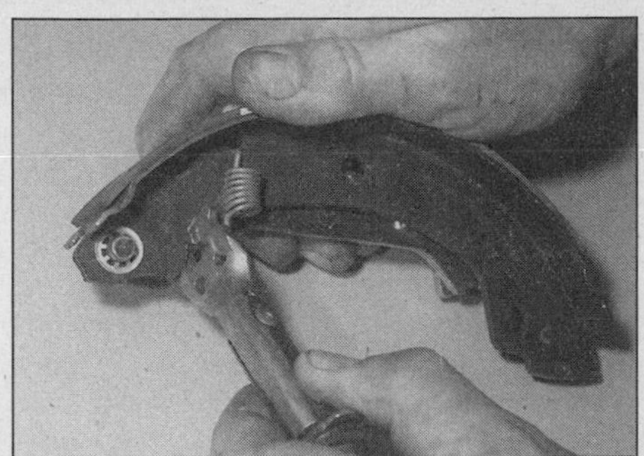

5.10c Unhook the adjuster strut from the trailing shoe . . .

positions of the springs and adjuster strut, to use as a guide on reassembly. Release the handbrake lever stop-peg (if not already done), then detach the adjuster strut bolt retaining spring from the leading shoe. Disconnect the upper return spring, then detach the leading shoe and return spring from the trailing shoe and strut assembly. Unhook the adjuster strut from the trailing shoe, and remove its spring noting which way around it is fitted **(see illustrations)**.

11 Withdraw the adjuster bolt from the strut, and carefully examine the assembly for signs of wear or damage, paying particular attention to the threads of the adjuster bolt and the knurled adjuster wheel, and renew if necessary. Note that left-hand and right-hand struts are not interchangeable; the strut bolts can also be identified by the grooves on the adjuster wheel collars; the left-hand strut bolt has two grooves whereas the right-hand bolt has only a single groove **(see illustration)**.

12 Depending on the type of brake shoes being installed, it may be necessary to remove the handbrake lever from the original trailing shoe, and install it on the new shoe. Secure the lever in position with a new retaining clip. All return springs should be renewed, regardless of their apparent condition; spring kits are available from Renault dealers.

13 Ensure that the components on the end of the strut are correctly positioned, then apply a little high melting-point grease to the threads of the adjuster bolt. Screw the adjuster wheel onto the bolt until only a small gap exists between the wheel and the head of the bolt, then install the bolt in the strut.

14 Fit the adjuster strut retaining spring to the trailing shoe, ensuring that the shorter hook of the spring is engaged with the shoe. Attach the adjuster strut to the spring end, then ease the strut into position in its slot in the trailing shoe.

15 Engage the upper return spring with the trailing shoe. Hook the leading shoe onto the other end of the spring, and lever the leading shoe down until the adjuster bolt head is correctly located in its groove. Once the bolt is correctly located, hook its retaining spring into the slot on the leading shoe **(see illustration)**.

16 Remove the elastic band fitted to the wheel cylinder. Peel back the rubber protective caps, and check the wheel cylinder for fluid leaks or other damage. Also check that both cylinder pistons are free to move easily. Refer to Section 9, if necessary, for information on wheel cylinder renewal.

17 Prior to installation, clean the backplate and apply a thin smear of high-temperature brake grease or anti-seize compound to all those surfaces of the backplate which bear on the shoes, particularly the wheel cylinder pistons and lower pivot point. Do not use too much, and don't allow the lubricant to foul the friction material.

18 Ensure that the handbrake lever stop-peg is correctly located against the edge of the trailing shoe.

19 Manoeuvre the shoe and strut assembly into position on the vehicle and attach the handbrake cable to the trailing shoe lever. Engage the upper ends of both shoes with the wheel cylinder pistons then fit the lower return spring to both shoes, and ease the shoes into position on the lower pivot point.

20 Centralise the shoes relative to the backplate by tapping them. Refit the shoe retainer pins and springs, and secure them in position with the spring cups.

21 Using a screwdriver, turn the strut adjuster wheel until the diameter of the shoes is approx 1.0mm less than the inner diameter of the brake drum. This should allow the brake drum to just pass over the shoes.

22 Slide the drum into position over the linings, but do not refit the hub nut yet.

23 Repeat the above procedure on the remaining rear brake.

24 Once both sets of rear shoes have been renewed, adjust the lining-to-drum clearance by alternately depressing the brake pedal then applying the handbrake. Whilst doing this, have an assistant listen to the rear drums, to check that the adjuster strut is functioning correctly; if this is so, a clicking sound will be emitted by the strut as the pedal/lever is operated.

25 Remove both the rear drums and

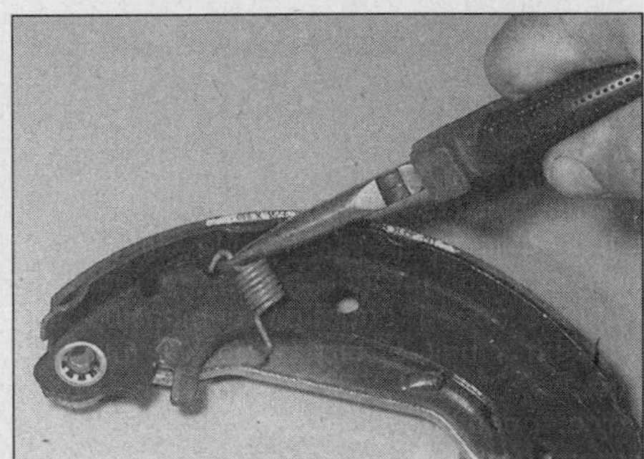

5.10d . . . and remove the spring, noting that it is fitted with its shorter hook engaged with the shoe

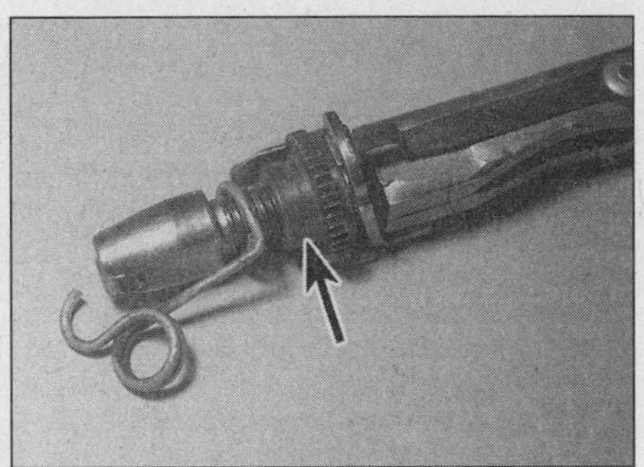

5.11 The adjuster struts can be identified by the grooves (arrowed) on the knurled wheel – left-hand strut assembly shown

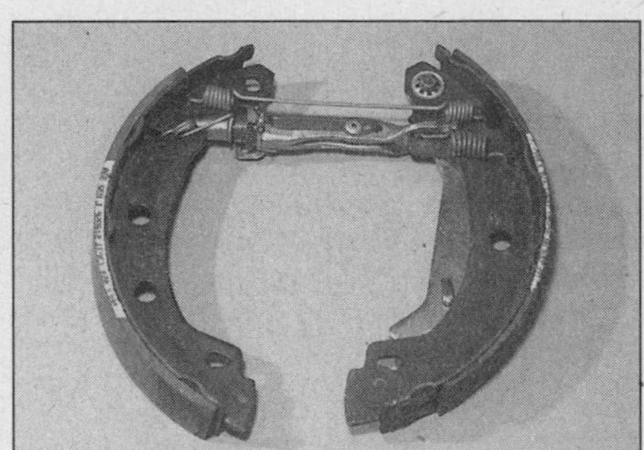

5.15 Ensure that all components are correctly reassembled before refitting

6.3 Using a micrometer to measure brake disc thickness

6.4 Using a dial gauge to measure brake disc run-out

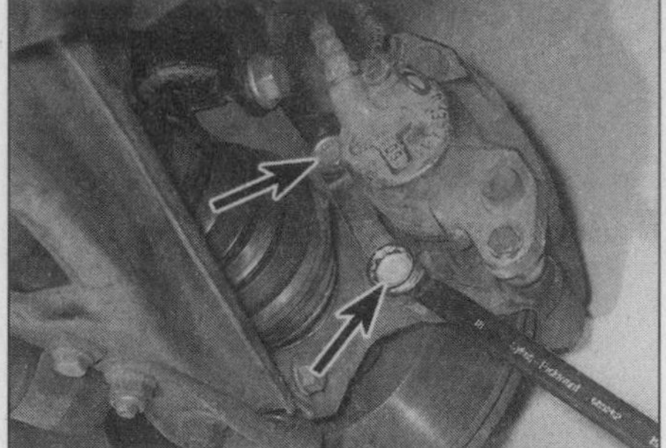

6.6 Remove the mounting bracket bolts (arrowed) and slide the brake caliper off from the disc

adjust the handbrake as described in Section 14.

26 Refit the brake drums as described in Section 7.

27 On completion, check the hydraulic fluid level as described in *Weekly checks*.

New shoes will not give full braking efficiency until they have bedded-in. Be prepared for this, and avoid hard braking as far as possible for the first hundred miles or so after shoe renewal.

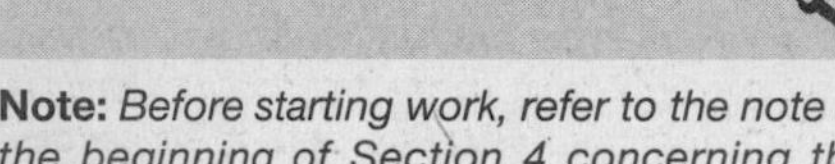

6 Front brake disc – inspection, removal and refitting

Note: *Before starting work, refer to the note at the beginning of Section 4 concerning the dangers of asbestos dust.*

Inspection

Note: *If either disc requires renewal, BOTH should be renewed at the same time, to ensure even and consistent braking. New brake pads should also be fitted.*

1 Apply the handbrake, then jack up the front of the car and support it on axle stands (see *Jacking and vehicle support*). Remove the appropriate front roadwheel.

2 Slowly rotate the brake disc so that the full area of both sides can be checked; remove the brake pads if better access is required to the inboard surface. Light scoring is normal in the area swept by the brake pads, but if heavy scoring or cracks are found, the disc must be renewed.

3 It is normal to find a lip of rust and brake dust around the disc's perimeter; this can be scraped off if required. If, however, a lip has formed due to excessive wear of the brake pad swept area, then the disc's thickness must be measured using a micrometer **(see illustration)**. Take measurements at several places around the disc, at the inside and outside of the pad swept area; if the disc has worn at any point to the specified minimum thickness or less, the disc must be renewed.

4 If the disc is thought to be warped, it can be checked for run-out. Either use a dial gauge mounted on any convenient fixed point, while the disc is slowly rotated, or use feeler blades to measure (at several points all around the disc) the clearance between the disc and a fixed point, such as the caliper mounting bracket **(see illustration)**. If the measurements obtained are at the specified maximum or beyond, the disc is excessively warped, and must be renewed; however, it is worth checking first that the hub bearing is in good condition (Chapters 1A or 1B and/or 10).

5 Check the disc for cracks, especially around the wheel bolt holes, and any other wear or damage, and renew if necessary.

Removal

6 Slacken and remove the two bolts securing the brake caliper mounting bracket to the swivel hub **(see illustration)**. Slide the caliper assembly off the disc and tie the assembly to the front coil spring, using a piece of wire or string, to avoid placing any strain on the hydraulic brake hose.

7 Use chalk or paint to mark the relationship of the disc to the hub, then remove the screws securing the brake disc to the hub, and remove the disc. If it is tight, lightly tap its rear face with a hide or plastic mallet.

Refitting

8 Refitting is the reverse of the removal procedure, noting the following points:

a) Ensure that the mating surfaces of the disc and hub are clean and flat.

b) Align (if applicable) the marks made on removal, and tighten the disc retaining screws to the specified torque setting.

c) If a new disc has been fitted, use a suitable solvent to wipe any preservative coating from the disc, before refitting the caliper.

d) Prior to installation, clean the threads of the caliper bracket mounting bolts and coat them with thread locking compound (Renault recommend Loctite Frenbloc – available from your Renault dealer). Slide the caliper into position, making sure the pads pass either side of the disc, and tighten the caliper bracket bolts to the specified torque setting.

e) Refit the roadwheel, then lower the vehicle to the ground and tighten the wheel bolts to the specified torque. Apply the footbrake several times to force the pads back into contact with the disc before driving the vehicle.

7 Rear brake drum – removal, inspection and refitting

Note: *Before starting work, refer to the note at the beginning of Section 5 concerning the dangers of asbestos dust.*

Removal

Note: *A new hub nut will be required on refitting.*

1 Chock the front wheels, then jack up the rear of the vehicle and support it on axle stands (see *Jacking and vehicle support*). Remove the appropriate rear wheel.

2 Using a hammer and suitable large flat-bladed screwdriver, carefully tap and prise the cap out of the centre of the brake drum **(see illustration)**. If the cap is damaged, it must be renewed.

3 Using a socket and long bar, slacken and remove the rear hub nut and (where fitted) the washer. Discard the hub nut; a new nut must be used on refitting.

4 It should now be possible to withdraw the brake drum and hub bearing assembly from the stub axle by hand. It may be difficult to remove the drum due to the tightness of the

7.2 Levering out the hub cap from the rear brake drum

7.6a If necessary to increase clearance, insert a screwdriver through one of the brake drum holes . . .

7.6b . . . push the handbrake lever inwards so that the stop-peg (arrowed) slips behind the web of the shoe

7.6c Remove the brake drum and slide the spacer off the stub axle

hub bearing on the stub axle, or due to the brake shoes binding on the inner circumference of the drum. If the bearing is tight, tap the periphery of the drum using a hide or plastic mallet, or use a universal puller, secured to the drum with the wheel bolts, to pull it off. If the brake shoes are binding, proceed as follows.

5 First ensure that the handbrake is fully off. From underneath the vehicle, slacken the handbrake cable adjuster locknut, then back off the adjuster nut on the handbrake lever rod. Note that on some models, it will first be necessary to remove the mounting nut(s) and lower the exhaust heat shield to gain access to the adjuster nut.

6 Insert a screwdriver through one of the wheel bolt holes in the brake drum, so that it contacts the handbrake operating lever on the trailing brake shoe. Push the lever until the stop-peg slips behind the brake shoe web, allowing the brake shoes to retract fully. Withdraw the brake drum, and slide the spacer off the stub axle **(see illustrations)**.

Inspection

7 Working carefully, remove all traces of brake dust from the drum, but *avoid inhaling the dust, as it is injurious to health.*

8 Scrub clean the outside of the drum, and check it for obvious signs of wear or damage such as cracks around the roadwheel bolt holes; renew the drum if necessary.

9 Examine carefully the inside of the drum. Light scoring of the friction surface is normal, but if heavy scoring is found, the drum must be renewed. It is usual to find a lip on the drum's inboard edge which consists of a mixture of rust and brake dust; this should be scraped away to leave a smooth surface which can be polished with fine (120 to 150 grade) emery paper. If the lip is due to the friction surface being recessed by wear, then the drum must be refinished (within the specified limits) or renewed.

10 If the drum is thought to be excessively worn or oval, its internal diameter must be measured at several points using an internal micrometer. Take measurements in pairs, the second at right-angles to the first, and compare the two to check for signs of ovality. Minor ovality can be corrected by machining; otherwise, renew the drum.

Refitting

11 If a new brake drum is to be installed, use a suitable solvent to remove any preservative coating that may have been applied to its interior.

12 Ensure that the handbrake lever stop-peg is correctly repositioned against the edge of the brake shoe web. Apply a smear of gear oil to the stub axle, and slide on the spacer and brake drum, being careful not to get oil onto the brake shoes or the friction surface of the drum. Depress the footbrake several times to operate the self-adjusting mechanism until normal, non-assisted pedal action returns.

13 Repeat the above procedure on the remaining rear brake assembly (as necessary).

14 Remove the brake drum(s) and adjust the handbrake as described in Section 14.

7.15a On refitting, fit a new hub nut . . .

7.15b . . . and tighten it to the specified torque setting

15 Once the handbrake is correctly adjusted, refit the drum then fit the washer (where necessary) and a new hub nut. Tighten the nut to the specified torque and tap the hub cap into place in the centre of the brake drum **(see illustrations)**.

16 On completion, refit the roadwheel(s), lower the vehicle to the ground and tighten the wheel bolts to the specified torque.

8 Front brake caliper – removal, overhaul and refitting

Caution: On models equipped with ABS, disconnect the battery before disconnecting any braking system hydraulic union and do not reconnect the battery until after the hydraulic system has been bled. Failure to do this could lead to air entering the hydraulic unit. If air enters the hydraulic unit pump, it will prove very difficult (in some cases impossible) to bleed the unit (see Section 2). Refer to Chapter 5A, Section 1 when disconnecting the battery.

Note: *Before starting work, refer to the note at the beginning of Section 2 concerning the dangers of hydraulic fluid, and to the warning at the beginning of Section 4 concerning the dangers of asbestos dust.*

Removal

Note: *New guide pin bolts will be required on refitting.*

1 Apply the handbrake, then jack up the front of the vehicle and support it on axle stands (see *Jacking and vehicle support*). Remove the appropriate roadwheel.

2 Minimise fluid loss by first removing the master cylinder reservoir cap, and then tightening it down onto a piece of polythene, to obtain an airtight seal. Alternatively, use a brake hose clamp, a G-clamp or a similar tool to clamp the flexible hose.

3 Clean the area around the caliper hose union, then loosen the union. Disconnect the pad wear warning sensor wiring connector (where fitted), and free it from any relevant retaining clips.

4 Slacken and remove the upper and lower caliper guide pin bolts, using a slim open-ended spanner to prevent the guide pin itself from rotating (see Section 4). Discard the bolts, new ones must be used on refitting. Lift the caliper away from the brake disc, then unscrew the caliper from the end of the brake hose; plug the hose end to minimise fluid loss and prevent dirt entry. Note that the brake pads need not be disturbed, and can be left in position in the caliper mounting bracket.

Overhaul

5 With the caliper on the bench, wipe away all traces of dust and dirt, but *avoid inhaling the dust, as it is injurious to health.*

6 Carefully remove the retaining ring from the outside of the caliper dust seal. Withdraw the partially ejected piston from the caliper body, and remove the dust seal. If the piston cannot be withdrawn by hand, it can be pushed out by applying compressed air to the brake hose union hole. Only low pressure should be required, such as is generated by a foot pump.

Caution: As the piston is expelled take great care not to trap your fingers between the piston and caliper.

7 Using a small screwdriver, extract the piston hydraulic seal, taking great care not to damage the caliper bore.

8 Thoroughly clean all components, using only methylated spirit, isopropyl alcohol or clean hydraulic fluid as a cleaning medium. Never use mineral-based solvents such as petrol or paraffin, as they will attack the hydraulic system's rubber components. Dry the components immediately, using compressed air or a clean, lint-free cloth. Use compressed air to blow clear the fluid passages.

9 Check all components, and renew any that are worn or damaged. Check particularly the cylinder bore and piston; these should be renewed (note that this means the renewal of the complete body assembly) if they are scratched, worn or corroded in any way. Similarly check the condition of the guide pins and their gaiters; both pins should be undamaged and (when cleaned) a reasonably tight sliding fit in the caliper bracket. If there is any doubt about the condition of any component, renew it.

10 If the assembly is fit for further use, obtain the appropriate repair kit; the components are available from Renault dealers in various combinations. All rubber seals should be renewed as a matter of course; these should never be re-used.

11 On reassembly, ensure that all components are clean and dry.

12 Soak the piston and the new piston (fluid) seal in clean hydraulic fluid. Smear clean fluid on the cylinder bore surface.

13 Fit the new piston (fluid) seal, using only your fingers (no tools) to manipulate it into the cylinder bore groove.

14 Fit the new dust seal to the piston groove then carefully ease the piston squarely into the cylinder bore using a twisting motion. Press the piston fully into position then seat the outer lip of the dust seal on the caliper body and secure it in position with the retaining ring.

15 If the guide pins are being renewed, lubricate the pin shafts with the special grease supplied in the repair kit and fit the gaiters to the pin grooves. Insert the pins into the caliper bracket and seat the gaiters correctly in the bracket grooves.

Refitting

16 Screw the caliper body fully onto the flexible hose union.

17 Ensure that the brake pads are still correctly fitted in the caliper mounting bracket and refit the caliper, making sure the pad wear sensor wiring is correctly routed.

18 Make sure the pad anti-rattle springs are correctly engaged with the caliper body then press the caliper into position and fit the new guide pin bolts. Tighten both guide pin bolts to the specified torque, starting with the lower bolt, while retaining the guide pins with an open-ended spanner.

19 Tighten the brake hose union nut to the specified torque then remove the brake hose clamp or polythene (where fitted).

20 Bleed the hydraulic system as described in Section 2. Note that, providing the precautions described were taken to minimise brake fluid loss, it should only be necessary to bleed the relevant front brake.

21 Refit the roadwheel, then lower the vehicle to the ground and tighten the roadwheel bolts to the specified torque.

9 Rear wheel cylinder – removal and refitting

Caution: On models equipped with ABS, disconnect the battery before disconnecting any braking system hydraulic union and do not reconnect the battery until after the hydraulic system has been bled. Failure to do this could lead to air entering the hydraulic unit. If air enters the hydraulic unit pump, it will prove very difficult (in some cases impossible) to bleed the unit (see Section 2). Refer to Chapter 5A, Section 1 when disconnecting the battery.

Note: *Before starting work, refer to the note at the beginning of Section 2 concerning the dangers of hydraulic fluid, and to the warning at the beginning of Section 5 concerning the dangers of asbestos dust.*

Removal

1 Remove the brake drum as described in Section 7.

2 Minimise fluid loss by first removing the master cylinder reservoir cap, and then tightening it down onto a piece of polythene, to obtain an airtight seal. Alternatively, use a brake hose clamp, a G-clamp or a similar tool to clamp the flexible hose at the nearest convenient point to the wheel cylinder.

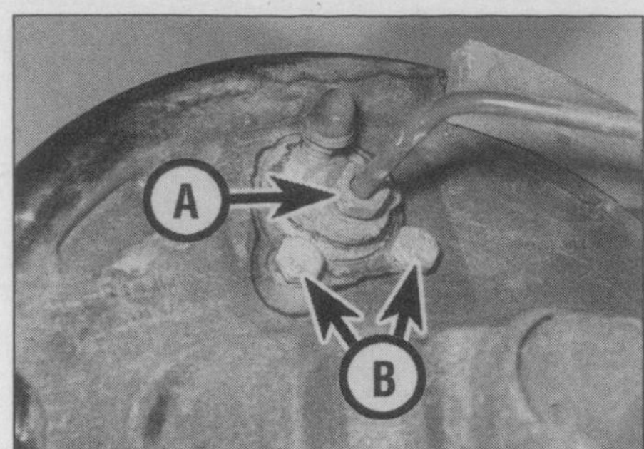

9.4 Rear wheel cylinder brake pipe union nut (A) and retaining bolts (B)

3 Carefully unhook the brake shoe upper return spring, and remove it from both brake shoes. Pull the upper ends of the shoes away from the wheel cylinder to disengage them from the pistons.

4 Wipe away all traces of dirt around the brake pipe union at the rear of the wheel cylinder, and unscrew the union nut **(see illustration)**. Carefully ease the pipe out of the wheel cylinder, and plug or tape over its end to prevent dirt entry. Wipe off any spilt fluid immediately.

5 Unscrew the two wheel cylinder retaining bolts from the rear of the backplate, and remove the cylinder, along with its sealing ring (where fitted), taking great care not to allow surplus hydraulic fluid to contaminate the brake shoe linings.

6 It is not possible to overhaul the cylinder, since no components are available separately. If faulty, the complete wheel cylinder assembly must be renewed.

Refitting

7 Ensure that the backplate and wheel cylinder mating surfaces are clean and dry. On models where a sealing ring is fitted to the cylinder, use a new sealing ring. Where no sealing ring is fitted, apply a smear of sealing compound to the wheel cylinder mating surface.

8 Spread the brake shoes and manoeuvre the wheel cylinder into position. Engage the brake pipe, and screw in the union nut two or three turns to ensure that the thread has started.

9 Insert the two wheel cylinder retaining bolts, tightening them securely, then tighten the brake pipe union nut to the specified torque.

10 Remove the clamp from the flexible brake hose, or the polythene from the master cylinder reservoir (as applicable).

11 Ensure that the brake shoes are correctly located in the cylinder pistons, then carefully refit the brake shoe return spring, ensuring it is correctly located in both shoes.

12 Refit the brake drum as described in Section 7.

13 Bleed the brake hydraulic system as

described in Section 2. Providing suitable precautions were taken to minimise loss of fluid, it should only be necessary to bleed the relevant rear brake.

10 Master cylinder – removal, overhaul and refitting

Caution: On models equipped with ABS, disconnect the battery before disconnecting any braking system hydraulic union and do not reconnect the battery until after the hydraulic system has been bled. Failure to do this could lead to air entering the hydraulic unit. If air enters the hydraulic unit pump, it will prove very difficult (in some cases impossible) to bleed the unit (see Section 2). Refer to Chapter 5A, Section 1 when disconnecting the battery.

Caution: Before starting work, refer to the warning at the beginning of Section 2 concerning the dangers of hydraulic fluid.

Removal

Note: *Depending on the engine type and model range, it may be necessary to remove the inlet/exhaust manifold and heat shield to gain better access to the brake master cylinder assembly (see the relevant Chapters for the removal and refitting procedures).*

1 Pull back or remove any soundproofing that is covering the brake master cylinder assembly **(see illustration)**. Remove the brake fluid reservoir filler cap and fluid level sensor (see *Weekly checks*).

2 Where the reservoir is mounted directly on top of the master cylinder, empty the brake fluid from the reservoir by syphoning it out using a syringe, a pipette or a hydrometer. **Never** syphon the fluid directly by mouth via a tube. If either the master cylinder or the reservoir is to be renewed, the reservoir can now be pulled off the master cylinder – it is a press-fit in the two seals.

3 Where the reservoir is mounted remotely from the master cylinder **(see illustration)**, it can be removed from the bulkhead by unscrewing the nuts securing its mounting bracket then unhook the rubber strap (where applicable) securing the reservoir to the bracket. Invert the reservoir over a suitable container and tip out the brake fluid. The connecting hoses can be disconnected from the reservoir if required and their union can be pulled off the master cylinder – it is a press-fit in the two seals.

4 Wipe clean the area around the brake pipe unions on the side of the master cylinder, and place absorbent rags beneath the pipe unions to catch any surplus fluid. Make a note of the correct fitted positions of the unions, then unscrew the union nuts and carefully withdraw the pipes. Plug or tape over the pipe ends and master cylinder orifices, to minimise the loss of brake fluid, and to prevent the entry of dirt into the system. Wash off any spilt fluid immediately with cold water.

5 Slacken and remove the nuts and washers securing the master cylinder to the vacuum servo unit **(see illustration)**. Remove the master cylinder from the engine compartment along with its sealing ring; discard the sealing ring; a new one must be used on refitting.

6 It is not possible to overhaul the cylinder, since no internal components are available separately. If faulty, the complete master cylinder assembly must be renewed. The only components which can be renewed separately are the reservoir-to-master cylinder seals (which can be pulled out of position) and the master cylinder-to-servo sealing O-ring.

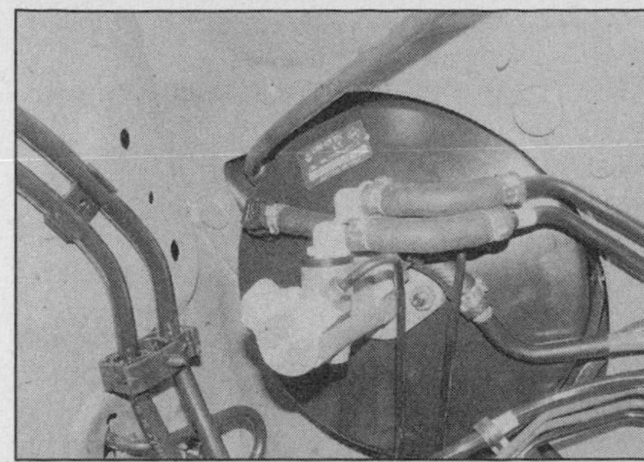

10.1 Location of the brake master cylinder with the soundproofing removed

Refitting

7 Prior to refitting, check that the pushrod end-to-servo unit mating surface distance is correctly set (see Section 12) and adjust as necessary.

8 Ensure that the mating surfaces are clean and dry then fit the new sealing ring to the rear of the master cylinder.

9 Carefully fit the master cylinder to the servo unit, ensuring that the servo unit pushrod enters the master cylinder bore centrally. Fit the retaining nuts and tighten them to the specified torque setting.

10 On models without ABS, wipe clean the brake pipe unions and refit them to the master cylinder ports in the locations noted on removal. Tighten securely the union nuts, taking care not to damage them by overtightening – if the necessary torque wrench and split crowsfoot adapter are available, they can be tightened to the torque wrench setting specified. Refit the master cylinder and fill it with new fluid, then check all disturbed unions for signs of leaks.

11 On models with ABS, refit the master cylinder and fill it with new fluid, then check all disturbed unions for signs of leaks. Bleed all traces of air from the master cylinder as described in Section 2. Wipe clean the brake pipe union and refit them to the master cylinder ports in the locations noted on removal. Tighten securely the union nuts, taking care not to damage them by overtightening – if the necessary torque wrench and split crowsfoot adapter are available, they can be tightened to the torque wrench setting specified.

12 On all models, bleed all traces of air from the complete hydraulic system, as described in Section 2.

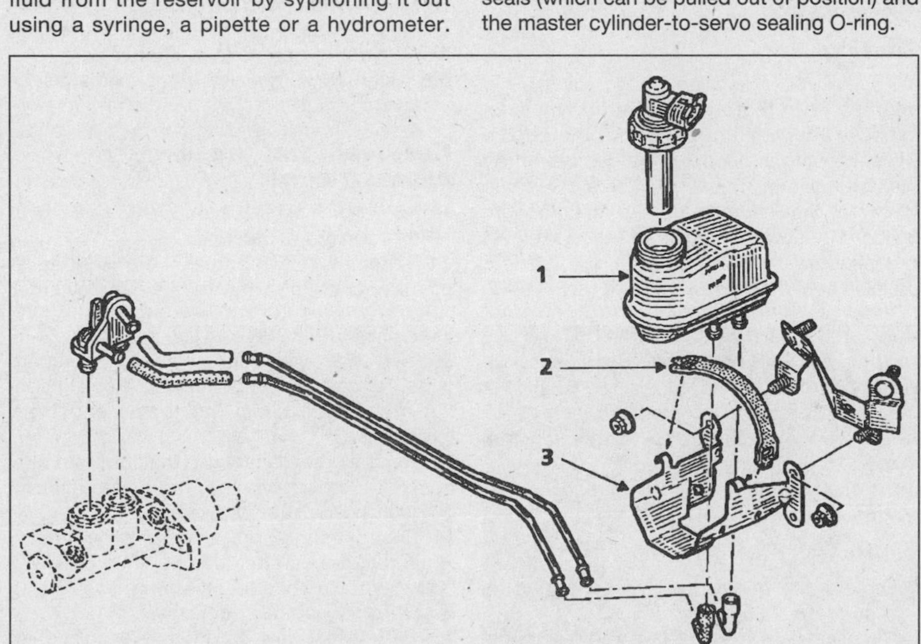

10.3 Models with reservoir mounted on the bulkhead

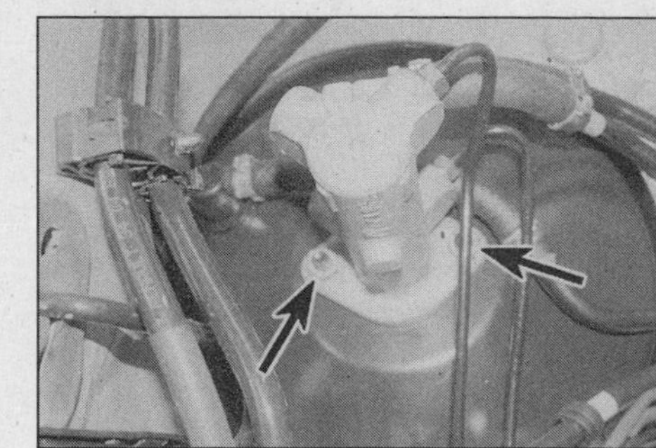

10.5 Master cylinder retaining nuts

9

11 Brake pedal – removal and refitting

Removal

Manual gearbox models

1 Remove the clutch pedal as described in Chapter 6.
2 Slide off the retaining clip and remove the clevis pin securing the vacuum servo unit pushrod to the pedal **(see illustration 12.7)**.
3 Slide the pedal pivot bolt out of position and manoeuvre the brake pedal out from underneath the facia along with its mounting bushes and spacer.
4 Inspect the pedal for signs of wear or damage, paying particular attention to the pivot bushes, and renew worn components as necessary.

Automatic transmission models

5 From inside the vehicle, remove the facia undercover (where fitted) to gain access to the clutch pedal assembly. Slacken and remove the nut from the pedal pivot bolt then remove the pedal as described in paragraphs 2 to 4.

Refitting

Manual gearbox models

6 Apply some multi-purpose grease to the bearing surfaces of the pedal, spacer and bushes. Insert the spacer into the pedal and fit the bushes with their collars outermost. Also apply a smear of grease to the servo unit pushrod clevis and pin.
7 Manoeuvre the pedal assembly into position under the facia, engaging it with the servo unit pushrod, then slide the pivot bolt into position.

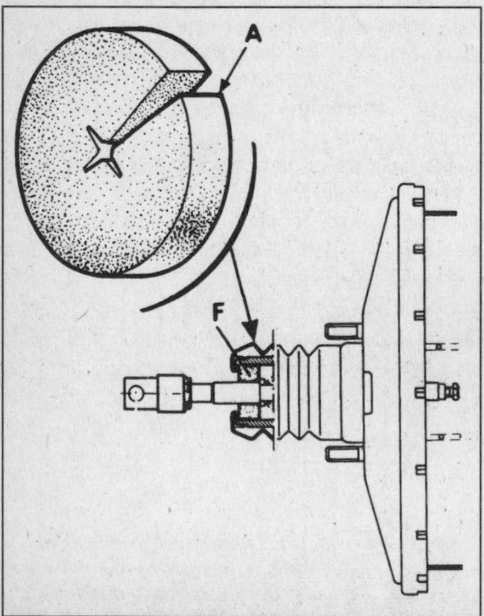

12.7 Vacuum servo unit air filter renewal
A Cut the filter as shown
F Correct position of filter in servo unit

8 Align the pedal with the pushrod and insert the clevis pin. Secure the pin in position with the retaining clip making sure it is securely located in the pin groove.
9 Check the operation of the brake pedal then refit the clutch pedal as described in Chapter 6.

Automatic transmission models

10 Fit the pedal as described above in paragraphs 6 to 8 then securely tighten the pivot bolt nut. Check the operation of the brake pedal before using the vehicle on the road.

12 Vacuum servo unit – general information, testing, removal and refitting

General information

1 Depending on the vehicle model and engine type, the vacuum servo unit can be removed from within the engine compartment or passenger compartment. The both removal procedures are described in this Section.
2 To remove from the engine compartment, the brake master cylinder will have to be removed first as described in Section 10. This procedure will mean that depending on model, it will be necessary to remove the inlet/exhaust manifold(s), heat shields, air filter assembly, and on Scénic models the wiper arms and scuttle panels. The removal and refitting of these components can be found in their relevant Chapters.
3 To remove from inside the passenger compartment the master cylinder retaining nuts will have to be removed from inside the engine compartment. The pedal assembly will also be removed.

Testing

4 To test the operation of the servo unit, depress the footbrake several times to exhaust the vacuum, then start the engine whilst keeping the pedal firmly depressed. As the engine starts, there should be a noticeable 'give' in the brake pedal as the vacuum builds-up. Allow the engine to run for at least two minutes, then switch it off. If the brake pedal is now depressed it should feel normal, but further applications should result in the pedal feeling firmer, with the pedal stroke decreasing with each application.
5 If the servo does not operate as described, first inspect the servo unit check valve as described in Section 13. If the check valve is functioning correctly, renew the servo unit air filter (see paragraph 7).
6 If the servo unit still fails to operate satisfactorily, the fault lies within the unit itself. Repairs to the unit are not possible – if faulty, the servo unit must be renewed.
7 The only item which is available separately is the servo unit air filter. To renew the filter, ease the rubber gaiter off the rear of the servo unit, slide it along the pushrod then carefully hook out the old air filter from the rear of the servo. Make a cut in the new filter as shown **(see illustration)**. Place the filter over the pushrod, slide it securely into position in the servo then refit the rubber gaiter.

12.12 Slide off the retaining clip (arrowed) and withdraw the clevis pin

Removal from engine compartment

Note: *A new master cylinder/servo O-ring seal will be required on refitting.*
8 Disconnect the battery as described in Chapter 5A.
9 Remove the master cylinder as described in Section 10.
10 Disconnect the vacuum hose from the servo unit check valve.
11 From inside the vehicle, remove the retaining clips and remove the undercover (where fitted) from the driver's side of the facia.
12 Slide off the retaining clip and remove the clevis pin securing the vacuum servo unit pushrod to the pedal **(see illustration)**.
13 Slacken and remove the four retaining nuts then return to the engine compartment and manoeuvre the servo unit out of position, along with its gasket **(see illustration)**. The gasket must be renewed if it shows signs of wear or damage.

Removal from passenger compartment

Note: *A new master cylinder/servo o-ring seal will be required on refitting.*
14 Disconnect the battery as described in Chapter 5A. Undo the two master cylinder

12.13 Vacuum servo unit retaining nuts (arrowed)

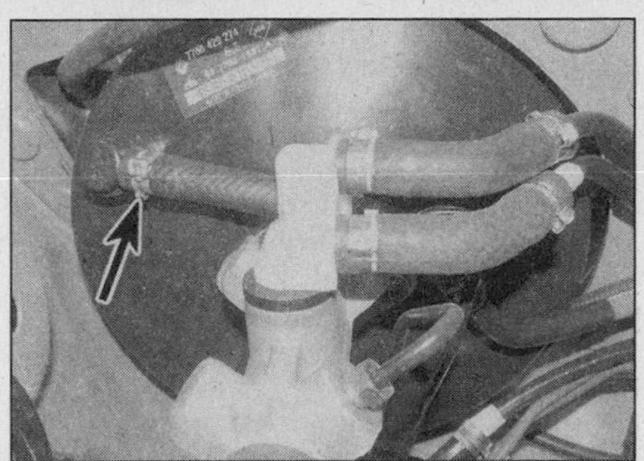

12.15 Remove the vacuum hose (arrowed)

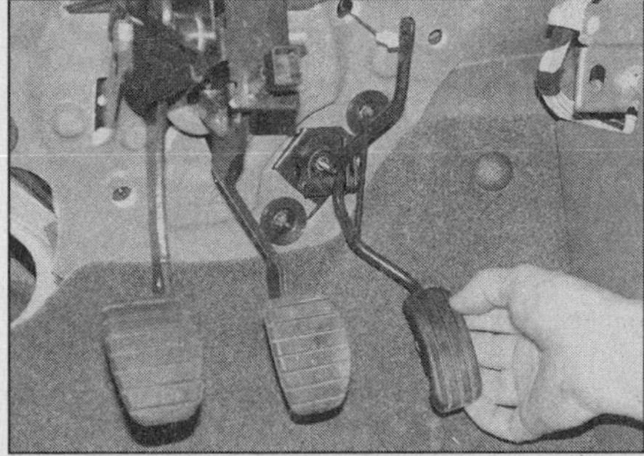

12.16 Removing the accelerator pedal

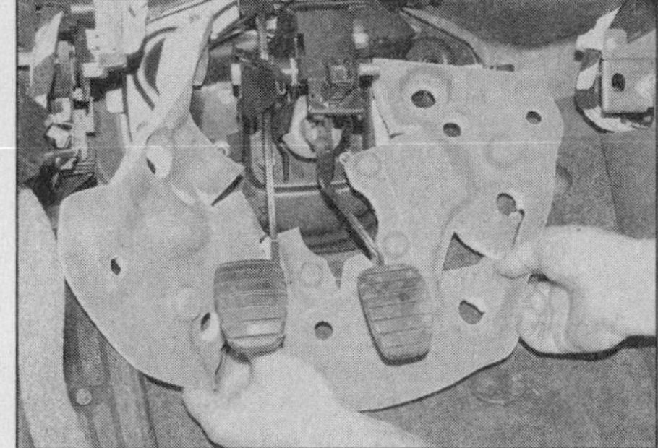

12.19 Removing the soundproofing from around the pedal assembly

securing nuts to disengage it from the servo unit, discard the O-ring seal.

15 Disconnect the vacuum hose from the check valve on the servo unit **(see illustration)**.

16 Working inside the vehicle, disconnect the accelerator cable from the pedal. Undo the accelerator pedal securing nut and remove the pedal **(see illustration)**.

17 Disconnect the brake light switch wiring connector, from above the brake pedal.

18 Remove the clutch pedal travel stop, and disconnect the clutch cable from its linkage on the top of the pedal assembly.

19 Undo the retaining nuts from around the pedal assembly, and remove the soundproofing **(see illustration)**.

20 The pedal assembly, complete with mounting plate and servo can be withdrawn from inside the footwell **(see illustration)**.

21 To remove the servo from the pedal assembly, remove the four nuts securing the servo unit to the pedal assembly mounting plate **(see illustration)**.

22 Extract the spring clip and withdraw the clevis pin securing the servo unit pushrod to the brake pedal. Note the spacer which is located on the inside of the pedal.

Refitting from engine compartment

23 Prior to refitting, check that the servo unit pushrod is correctly adjusted as follows. With the gasket removed, check the dimensions shown **(see illustration)**. If adjustment is necessary, dimension L can be altered by slackening the locknut and repositioning the pushrod clevis, and dimension X can be altered by repositioning the nut (P). After adjustment ensure that the clevis locknut is securely tightened.

24 Inspect the check valve sealing grommet for signs of damage or deterioration, and renew if necessary.

25 Fit a new O-ring seal to the rear of the master cylinder, and reposition the unit in the engine compartment.

26 Ensure that all mating surfaces are clean and dry and fit the gasket to the rear of the servo unit. Manoeuvre the servo unit into position and locate it in the bulkhead.

27 From inside the vehicle, ensure that the servo unit is correctly engaged with the brake pedal then refit the retaining nuts and tighten them to the specified torque setting.

28 Align the pushrod clevis with the brake pedal and slide in the clevis pin. Secure the pin in position with the retaining clip, ensuring it is correctly located in the pin groove. Refit the undercover to the facia.

29 From within the engine compartment, reconnect the vacuum hose to the servo unit.

30 Refit the master cylinder as described in Section 10 and bleed the complete hydraulic system as described in Section 2.

31 Reconnect the battery as described in Chapter 5A.

32 On completion, start the engine and check that there are no air leaks at the servo vacuum hose connection. Check the operation of the servo as described at the beginning of this Section.

Refitting from passenger compartment

33 Prior to refitting, check that the servo unit pushrod is correctly adjusted as follows. With the gasket removed, check the dimensions shown **(see illustration 12.23)**. If adjustment is necessary, dimension L can be altered by slackening the locknut and repositioning the pushrod clevis, and dimension X can be altered by repositioning the nut (P). After adjustment ensure that the clevis locknut is securely tightened.

34 Inspect the check valve sealing grommet for signs of damage or deterioration, and renew if necessary.

35 Fit a new O-ring seal to the rear of the master cylinder, and reposition the unit in the engine compartment.

36 Working inside the vehicle, refit the servo unit to the pedal assembly mounting plate. Ensure that the servo unit pushrod is correctly engaged with the brake pedal and tighten the four mounting nuts securely.

37 Position the spacer on the inside of the brake pedal. Refit the clevis pin, and secure it in position with the spring clip.

38 Offer the assembly into position, aligning the servo with the master cylinder.

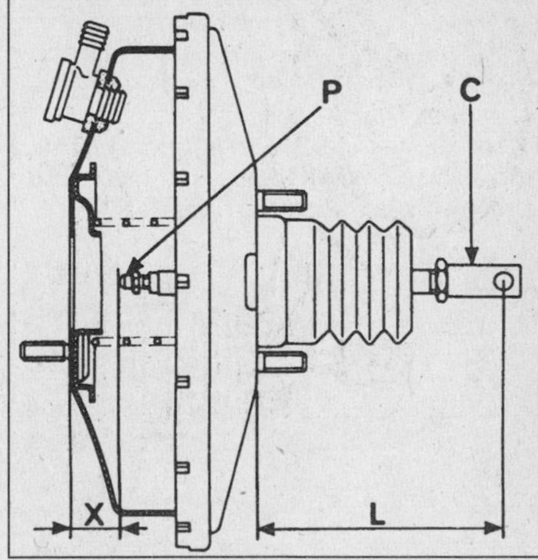

12.23 Vacuum servo unit adjustment dimensions

C Pushrod clevis — *L = 133 mm*
P Pushrod nut — *X = 22.3 mm*

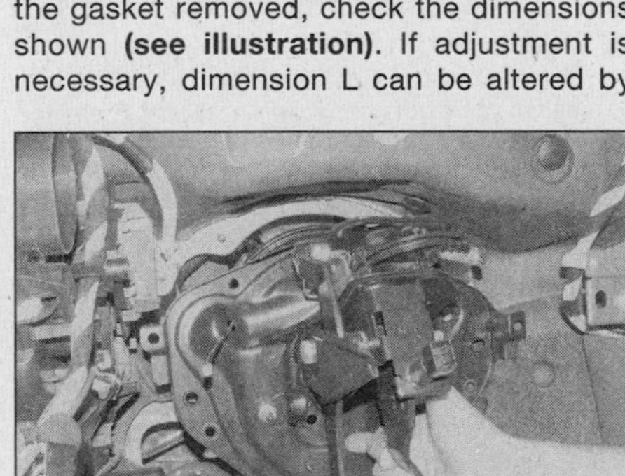

12.20 Withdraw the assembly from the bulkhead – check the master cylinder does not foul the servo

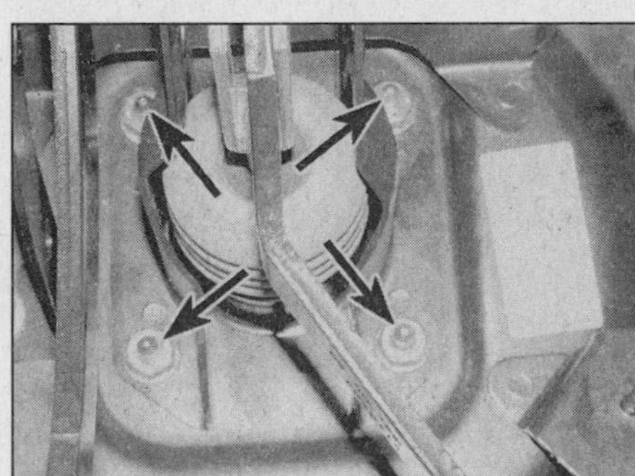

12.21 Remove the four securing nuts (arrowed) to release the servo from the pedal assembly

39 Refit the soundproofing around the pedal assembly, and tighten the mounting plate retaining nuts securely.
40 Reconnect the clutch cable to the pedal linkage, making sure the outer cable is located in the mounting plate correctly. Refit the clutch pedal travel stop.
41 Reconnect the stop-light switch wiring connector, and refit the accelerator pedal and cable.
42 Working inside the engine bay, reconnect the vacuum hose to the servo unit check valve, and refit the master cylinder retaining nuts, tighten them to their specified torque.
43 Reconnect the battery as described in Chapter 5A.
44 On completion, start the engine and check that there are no air leaks at the servo vacuum hose connection. Check the operation of the servo as described at the beginning of this Section.

13 Vacuum servo unit check valve – removal, testing and refitting

Removal

1 Disconnect the hose from the servo unit check valve which is mounted on the front of the servo unit. On right-hand drive models, access to the valve is poor but can only be significantly improved by removing the inlet/exhaust manifold and heat shields (see Chapter 4A or 4B).
2 Withdraw the valve from its rubber sealing grommet, using a pulling and twisting motion. Remove the grommet from the servo.

Testing

3 Examine the check valve for signs of damage, and renew if necessary. The valve may be tested by blowing through it in both directions. Air should flow through the valve in one direction only – when blown through from the servo unit end of the valve. Renew the valve if this is not the case.
4 Examine the rubber sealing grommet and flexible vacuum hose for signs of damage or deterioration, and renew as necessary.

Refitting

5 Fit the sealing grommet into position in the servo unit.
6 Ease the check valve into position, taking care not to displace or damage the grommet, then reconnect the vacuum hose.
7 On completion, start the engine and check that there are no air leaks.

14 Handbrake – adjustment

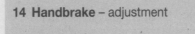

Caution: On drum brake models, if the handbrake is incorrectly adjusted, the rear brake automatic adjustment mechanism will not be able to function correctly. This will lead to the brake shoe-to-drum clearance becoming excessive as the shoe linings wear, resulting in excessive brake pedal travel.
1 The handbrake will normally be kept in adjustment by the action of the rear brake automatic adjusters. Occasionally, the handbrake mechanism may require adjustment to compensate for cable stretch but adjustment should only be needed if the brake shoes, drums, pads, cables or handbrake lever are disturbed.
2 Chock the front wheels, engage reverse gear (or P on automatics) and release the handbrake. Jack up the rear of the vehicle and support it on axle stands (see *Jacking and vehicle support*).
3 Adjust the handbrake cable using the adjuster which is situated on the underside of the handbrake lever. To gain access to the adjuster; it will be necessary to unbolt and remove the exhaust system heat shield which is situated just to the rear of the handbrake lever. Slacken the locknut (where fitted) and back the adjuster nut off until a slight amount of free play is present in the cable **(see illustrations)**.

Drum brake models

4 Remove both rear brake drums as described in Section 7.
5 Check that both the left- and right-hand brake shoe adjuster strut knurled wheels are free to rotate easily then back each wheel off by 5 to 6 teeth.
6 Have an assistant operate the handbrake lever and check that the left- and right-hand brake shoe handbrake levers move smoothly and easily. If not, check the cables/brake shoes for signs of wear or damage before proceeding.
7 With the handbrake lever fully released, check that the stop-pegs on both the left- and right-hand brake shoe handbrake levers are resting against the edge of each rear brake shoe.
8 With the stop-pegs in contact with the shoes, have an assistant slowly operate the handbrake lever whilst you observe the movement of the brake shoe levers. The lever on each rear brake assembly should start to move as the handbrake lever is moved between the first and second notch (click) of its ratchet mechanism, ie, so that the stop-pegs are still in contact with the shoes when the handbrake is on the first notch of the ratchet, but no longer contact the shoes when the handbrake is on the second notch. If adjustment is necessary, slacken the locknut (where fitted) and rotate the adjuster nut.
9 Once the handbrake adjustment is correctly set and both rear brake assembly handbrake levers are operating correctly, where necessary, hold the adjuster nut stationary and securely tighten the locknut. Refit the exhaust system heat shield to the vehicle underbody and securely tighten its retaining bolts/nuts.
10 Refit the brake drums as described in Section 7. Check the operation of the rear brake automatic adjustment mechanism by depressing the brake pedal whilst having an assistant listen to the rear drums. If the adjustment mechanism is functioning correctly, a clicking sound will be emitted by the strut as the pedal is depressed.
11 Once the shoe-to-drum clearance is correctly adjusted, refit the roadwheels then lower the vehicle to the ground and tighten the wheel bolts to the specified torque.

Disc brake models

12 Check that the handbrake cables slide freely by puling on their front ends, and check that the operating levers on the brake calipers move smoothly.
13 Move both of the caliper operating levers as far rearwards as possible, then tighten the

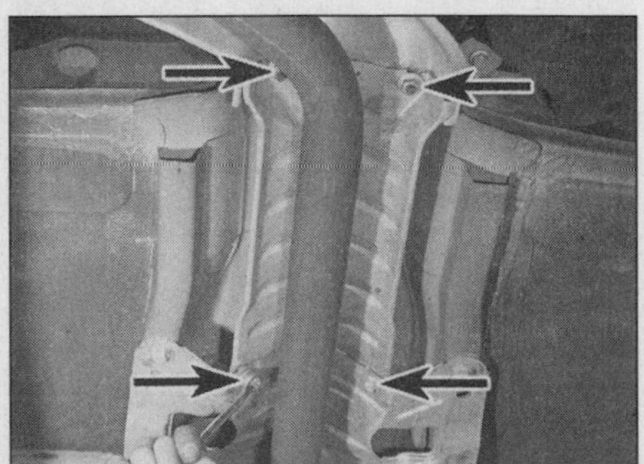

14.3a Undo the retaining nuts and bolts (arrowed) . . .

14.3b . . . and remove the heat shield from underneath the handbrake lever . . .

14.3c . . . to gain access to the handbrake cable adjuster nut

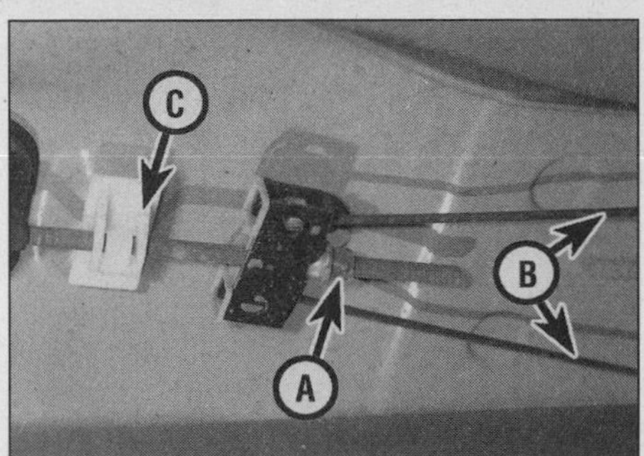

15.4 Slacken the adjuster nut (A) then detach the handbrake cables (B) and unclip the lever rod (C) from its guide

adjuster nut on the handbrake lever operating rod until all free play is removed from both cables. With the aid of an assistant, adjust the nut so that the operating lever on each rear brake caliper starts to move as the handbrake lever is moved between the first and second notch (click) of its ratchet mechanism. Once the handbrake adjustment is correct, hold the adjuster nut and securely tighten the locknut.
14 Refit the heat shield retaining nuts, then lower the vehicle to the ground.

15 Handbrake lever – removal and refitting

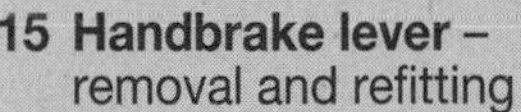

Removal

1 To gain access to the handbrake lever, remove the complete centre console (Scénic models) or the rear section only (all other models) as described in Chapter 11. Disconnect the wiring connector from the handbrake warning light switch and fully release the lever.
2 Chock the front wheels then jack up the rear of the vehicle and support it on axle stands (see *Jacking and vehicle support*).
3 Slacken and remove the retaining nuts/bolts and remove the exhaust system heat shield(s) from underneath the handbrake lever. **Note:** *On some models it may be necessary to separate the exhaust system intermediate pipe front joint to enable the heat shield(s) to be removed (see Chapter 4A or 4B).*

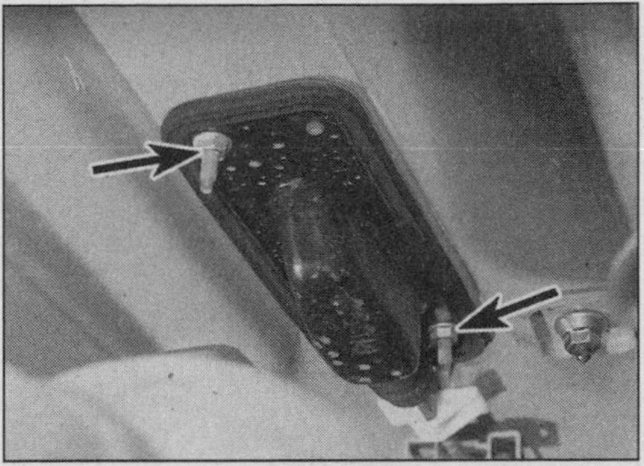

15.6 Undo the retaining nuts (arrowed) and remove the handbrake lever from underneath the vehicle

4 Slacken the locknut (where fitted) then unscrew the adjuster nut to obtain maximum free play in the handbrake cables **(see illustration)**.
5 Unhook the cables from the handbrake lever equaliser plate then unclip the lever rod from its guide.
6 Slacken and remove the lever retaining nuts then manoeuvre the assembly out from underneath the vehicle **(see illustration)**.

Refitting

7 Refitting is a reversal of removal tightening the lever retaining nuts securely. Prior to refitting the heat shield(s), adjust the handbrake cable as described in Section 14.

16 Handbrake cables – removal and refitting

Removal

1 The handbrake cable consists of two sections, a right- and left-hand section, which are linked to the lever assembly by an equaliser plate. Each section can be removed individually as follows.
2 Chock the front wheels, engage reverse gear (or P on automatics) and release the handbrake. Jack up the rear of the vehicle and support it on axle stands (see *Jacking and vehicle support*).
3 Working from underneath the vehicle, undo the nut(s) securing the exhaust system heat shield to the vehicle underbody. Manoeuvre the heat shield out from under the vehicle, to gain access to the handbrake cable adjuster/locking nuts.
4 Slacken the adjuster locknut until there is sufficient slack in the cables to allow it to be disconnected from the equaliser plate.
5 On models with rear drum brakes, remove the rear brake shoes from the appropriate side as described in Section 5. Carefully unclip the outer cable from the brake backplate **(see illustration)**.
6 On models with rear disc brakes, disengage the inner cable from the caliper handbrake lever. Disengage the inner cable, then unclip the outer cable out of its mounting bracket on the caliper **(see illustration)**.
7 Working along the length of the cable, remove any retaining bolts and screws, and free the cable from the retaining clips and ties **(see illustration)**. Remove the cable from under the vehicle.

Refitting

8 Refitting is a reversal of the removal procedure ensuring that the cable is correctly routed and retained by all the relevant clips and ties. Prior to refitting the heat shields, adjust the handbrake as described in Section 14.

17 Rear brake pressure-regulating valve – testing, removal and refitting

Testing

1 On some models, a load-sensitive pressure-regulating valve is fitted into the hydraulic circuit to each rear brake. The valve is mounted onto the underside of the rear of the vehicle and is attached to the rear axle. The valve measures the load on the rear axle, via the movement of the axle, and regulates the hydraulic pressure being applied to the rear brakes to help prevent rear wheels locking-up under hard braking.
2 Specialist equipment is required to check the performance of the valve(s), therefore if

16.5 Unclip the handbrake cable from the backplate

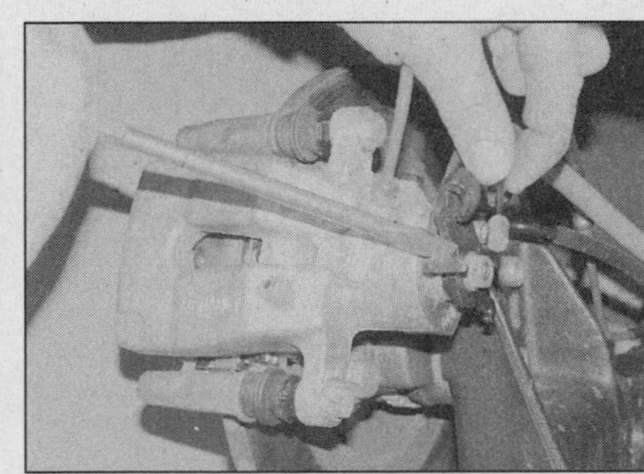

16.6 Disengaging the inner cable from the caliper handbrake lever

16.7 Release the cable from all the relevant retaining clips

9

17.7a Remove the rear brake pressure-regulating valve retaining bolts (arrowed) . . .

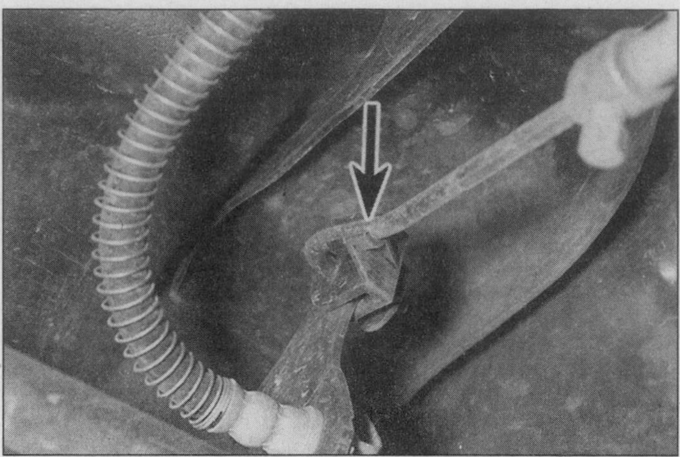
17.7b . . . then unclip the link rod from the axle and remove the assembly from underneath the vehicle

the valve is thought to be faulty the car should be taken to a suitably equipped Renault dealer for testing. Repairs are not possible and, if faulty, the valve must be renewed.

Removal

Note: *Before starting work, refer to the warning at the beginning of Section 2 concerning the dangers of hydraulic fluid.*

3 Minimise fluid loss by first removing the master cylinder reservoir cap, and then tightening it down onto a piece of polythene, to obtain an airtight seal.

4 Chock the front wheels then jack up the rear of the vehicle and support it on axle stands (see *Jacking and vehicle support*).

5 Wipe clean the area around the brake pipe unions on the valve, and place absorbent rags beneath the pipe unions to catch any surplus fluid. To avoid confusion on refitting, make alignment marks between the pipes and valve assembly.

6 Slacken the union nuts and disconnect the brake pipes from the valve. Plug or tape over the pipe ends and valve orifices, to minimise the loss of brake fluid, and to prevent the entry of dirt into the system. Wash off any spilt fluid immediately with cold water.

7 Slacken and remove the retaining bolts then unclip the valve link rod and remove the valve assembly from underneath the vehicle **(see illustrations). Note:** *Do not slacken the link rod clamp bolt. If the bolt is slackened and the link rod length altered the valve will need to be adjusted on refitting.*

Refitting

8 Manoeuvre the valve assembly into position and tighten its retaining bolts securely.

9 Refit the brake pipes to their unions on the valve and tighten the union nuts to the specified torque setting.

10 Clip the valve link rod back into position in its retaining clip and lower the vehicle to the ground.

11 If a new valve assembly is being fitted, it will be noted that a spacer is fitted to the link rod; this is to adjust the link rod length. With the vehicle resting on its wheels, with a full tank of fuel and one person in the driver's seat, slacken the link rod clamp bolt and allow the valve spring to set the link rod length. Securely tighten the clamp bolt and remove the spacer from the link rod. Although not strictly necessary, it is recommended that the valve operation is tested by a Renault dealer.

12 Remove the polythene from the master cylinder reservoir and bleed the complete hydraulic system as described in Section 2.

18 Stop-light switch – removal, refitting and adjustment

Removal

1 The stop-light switch is located on the pedal bracket behind the facia.

2 To remove the switch, reach up behind the facia, disconnect the wiring connector and unscrew the switch from the bracket **(see illustrations)**.

Refitting and adjustment

3 Screw the switch back into position in the mounting bracket.

4 Connect a continuity tester (ohmmeter or

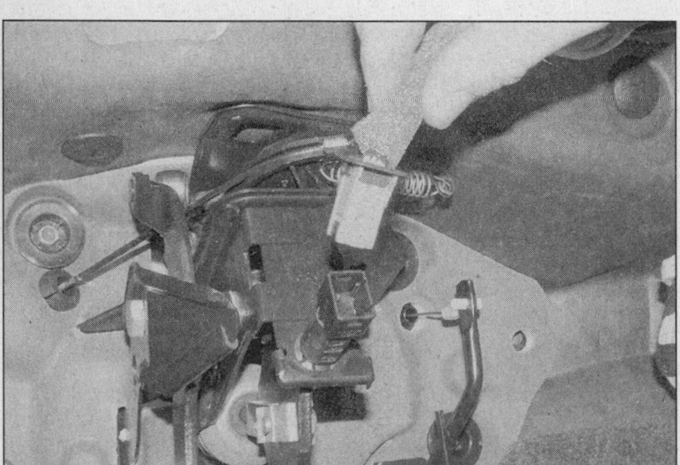
18.2a Disconnect the wiring connector . . .

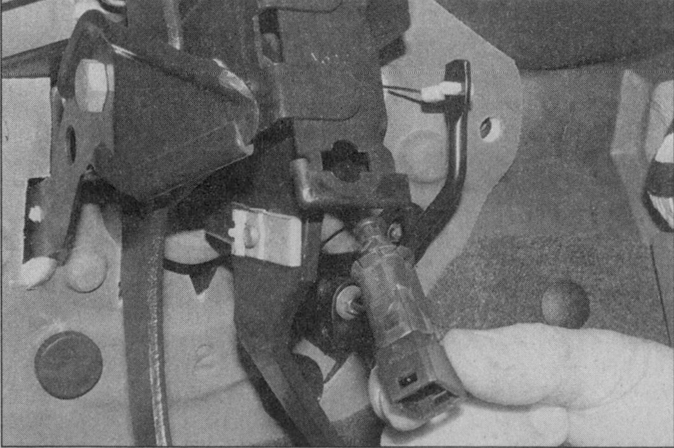
18.2b . . . and unscrew the stop-light switch (facia panel removed for clarity)

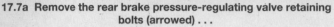

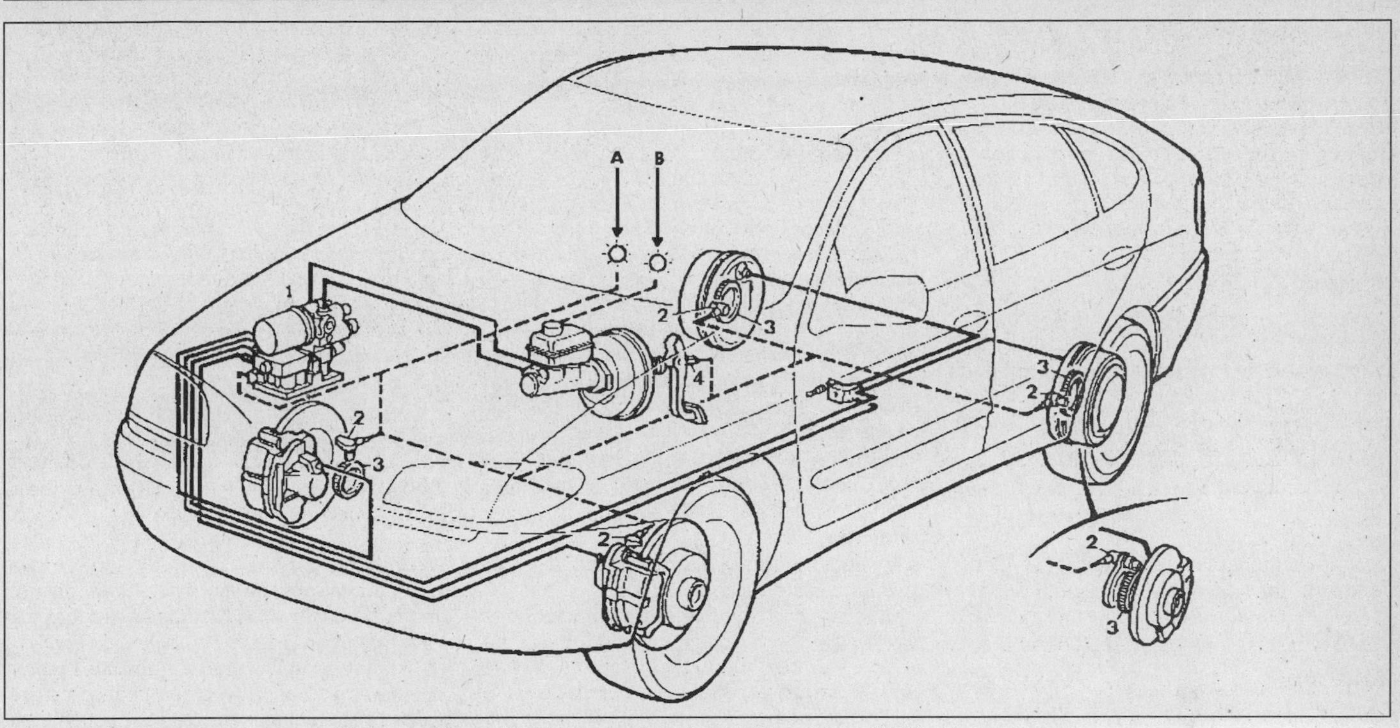

19.1 Location of the Teves anti-lock braking system (ABS) components

A ABS warning light
B Code warning light
1 Hydraulic unit
2 Wheel speed sensor
3 Toothed target ring
4 Stop-light switch

self-powered test light) across the switch terminals. Screw the switch in until an open-circuit is present between the switch terminals (infinite resistance, or light goes out). Gently depress the pedal and check that continuity exists between the switch terminals (zero resistance, or light comes on) after the pedal has travelled approximately 5 mm. If necessary, reposition the switch until it operates as specified.

5 In the absence of a continuity tester, the same adjustment can be made by reconnecting the switch and having an assistant observe the stop-lights (ignition on).

6 Once the stop-light switch is correctly adjusted, remake the original wiring connections, and recheck the operation of the stop-lights.

19 Anti-lock braking system (ABS) – general information

ABS is available on all models. The system comprises of the hydraulic unit and the four roadwheel sensors. The hydraulic unit contains the electronic control unit, the eight hydraulic solenoid valves (two for each brake – one inlet and one outlet) and the electrically-driven pump. The purpose of the system is to prevent the wheel(s) locking during heavy braking. This is achieved by automatic release of the brake on the relevant wheel, followed by re-application of the brake. In the case of the rear wheels both brakes are applied at the same time **(see illustration)**.

The solenoid valves are controlled by the control unit, which itself receives signals from the four wheel sensors (which are fitted to the wheel hubs), which monitor the speed of rotation of each wheel. By comparing these signals, the control unit can determine the speed at which the vehicle is travelling. It can then use this speed to determine when a wheel is decelerating at an abnormal rate, compared to the speed of the vehicle, and therefore predicts when a wheel is about to lock. During normal operation, the system functions in the same way as a non-ABS braking system.

If the control unit senses that a wheel is about to lock, it closes the relevant outlet solenoid valves in the hydraulic unit, which then isolates the relevant brake(s) on the wheel(s) which is/are about to lock from the master cylinder, effectively sealing-in the hydraulic pressure.

If the speed of rotation of the wheel continues to decrease at an abnormal rate, the control unit opens the inlet solenoid valves on the relevant brake(s) and operates the electrically-driven return pump which pumps the hydraulic fluid back into the master cylinder, releasing the brake. Once the speed of rotation of the wheel returns to an acceptable rate, the pump stops; the solenoid valves switch again, allowing the hydraulic master cylinder pressure to return to the caliper/wheel cylinder (as applicable), which then re-applies the brake. This cycle can be carried out many times a second.

The action of the solenoid valves and return pump creates pulses in the hydraulic circuit. When the ABS system is functioning, these pulses can be felt through the brake pedal.

The operation of the ABS system is entirely dependent on electrical signals. To prevent the system responding to any inaccurate signals, a built-in safety circuit monitors all signals received by the control unit. If an inaccurate signal or low battery voltage is detected, the ABS system is automatically shut down, and the warning light on the instrument panel is illuminated, to inform the driver that the ABS system is not operational. Normal braking should still be available, however.

If a fault does develop in the ABS system, the vehicle must be taken to a Renault dealer for fault diagnosis and repair.

20 Anti-lock braking system (ABS) components – removal and refitting

Hydraulic unit

Caution: Disconnect the battery before disconnecting any braking system hydraulic union and do not reconnect the battery until after the hydraulic system has been bled. Failure to do this could lead to air entering the hydraulic unit. If air enters the hydraulic

unit pump, it will prove very difficult (in some cases impossible) to bleed the unit (see Section 2). Refer to Chapter 5A, Section 1 when disconnecting the battery.

Note: *Before starting work, refer to the warning at the beginning of Section 2 concerning the dangers of hydraulic fluid. Blanking plugs will be needed to seal the hydraulic unit unions once the pipes have been disconnected.*

Removal

1 Disconnect the battery negative lead (refer to Chapter 5A).

2 Firmly apply the handbrake then jack up the front of the vehicle and support it on axle stands (see *Jacking and vehicle support*). Remove the right-hand front roadwheel.

3 Unscrew the fasteners and remove the wheelarch liner from underneath the right-hand wing.

4 Release the retaining clip and disconnect the wiring connector from the base of the hydraulic unit.

5 Minimise fluid loss by first removing the master cylinder reservoir cap, and then tightening it down onto a piece of polythene, to obtain an airtight seal.

6 Mark the locations of the hydraulic fluid pipes to ensure correct refitting (the pipes may be colour-coded) **(see illustration)**. Unscrew the union nuts, and disconnect the pipes from the regulator assembly, whilst being prepared for fluid spillage. Seal the hydraulic unit ports with the blanking plugs and plug the pipes to prevent dirt ingress and further fluid loss. **Note:** *If hydraulic unit unions are not securely plugged there is a risk of air entering the hydraulic unit pump (see Caution at the start of this Section).*

7 Slacken and remove the hydraulic unit mounting bolts and remove the assembly from the engine compartment.

Refitting

8 Refitting is the reverse of removal, noting the following points:

a) Prior to reconnection, ensure that the pipes and the hydraulic unit unions are full of fluid (see Section 2). Reconnect the pipes to their original unions and tighten the union nuts to the specified torque.

b) Ensure that the wiring connector is securely held in position with its retaining clip.

c) Bleed the hydraulic system as described in Section 2 then reconnect the battery.

d) On completion, it is recommended that the operation of the ABS system is checked at the earliest opportunity by a Renault dealer using special electronic test equipment.

Electronic control unit

Removal

9 Carry out the operations described in paragraphs 1 to 4.

10 Slacken and remove the hydraulic unit and mounting bracket bolts then carefully manoeuvre the bracket away from the unit. Securely support the hydraulic unit to avoid placing any strain on the hydraulic pipes.

11 Undo the retaining screws then pull the control unit squarely away from the hydraulic unit and remove it from the vehicle.

Refitting

12 Refitting is the reverse of removal, taking great care to ensure that the control unit is correctly engaged with the hydraulic unit connectors.

Wheel sensor

Removal

13 Disconnect the battery negative lead (refer to Chapter 5A).

14 Apply the handbrake, then jack up the front or rear of the vehicle (depending on sensor to be removed) and support securely on axle stands (see *Jacking and vehicle support*). To improve access, remove the roadwheel.

15 Trace the wiring back from the sensor, releasing it from all the relevant clips and ties whilst noting its correct routing, and disconnect the wiring connector **(see illustration)**.

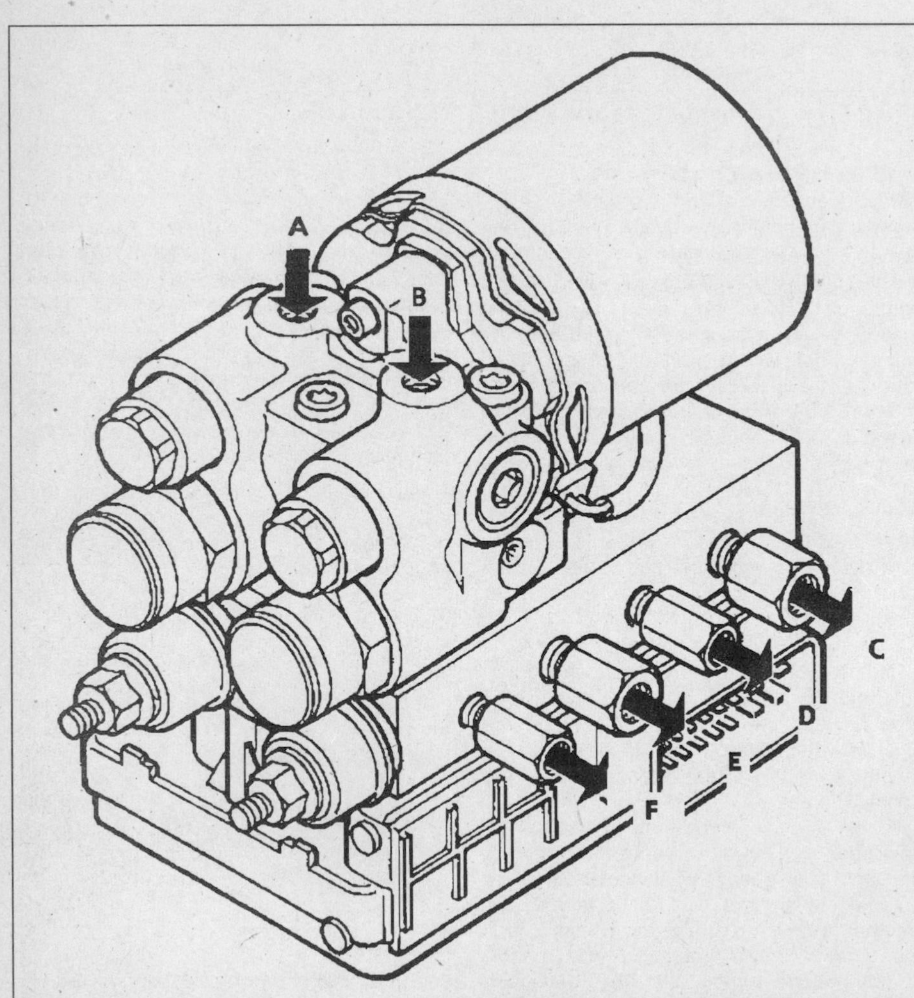

20.6 Hydraulic unit brake pipe union locations

A Inlet from master cylinder (primary)
B Inlet from master cylinder (secondary)
C To front left-hand wheel (yellow)
D To rear right-hand wheel (red)
E To rear left-hand wheel (blue)
F To front right-hand wheel (green)

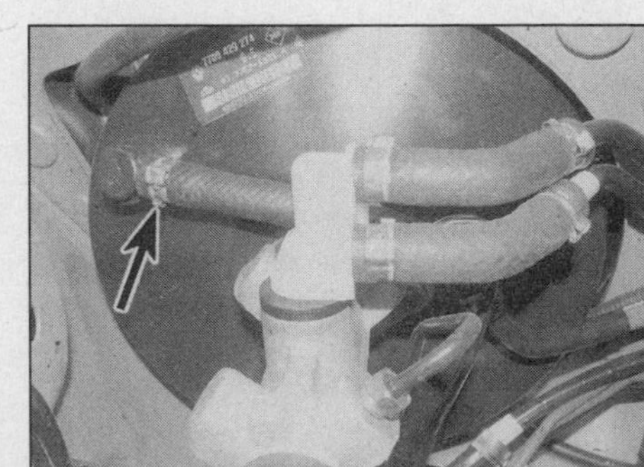

20.15 Disconnect the wheel sensor wiring connectors

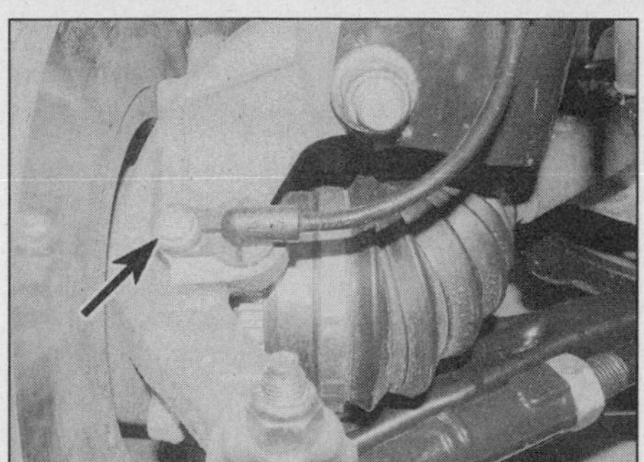
20.16a Front wheel sensor retaining bolt (arrowed)

20.16b Rear wheel sensor retaining bolt (arrowed) – rear disc model

20.16c Rear wheel sensor retaining bolt (arrowed) – rear drum model

16 Slacken and remove the retaining bolt and withdraw the sensor from the hub **(see illustrations)**.

Refitting

17 Ensure that the mating faces of the sensor and the hub are clean, and apply a little multi-purpose grease to the hub bore before refitting.
18 Make sure the sensor tip is clean and ease it into position in the hub. Refit the retaining bolt and tighten it to the specified torque.
19 On the front wheel sensors, check the air gap between the sensor tip and the teeth on the reluctor ring **(see illustration)**. Rotate the hub and repeat the check on several other teeth. If the air gap is not within the range given in the specifications (at the beginning of this Chapter), then the advice of a Renault dealer must be sought to supply shims.
20 Work along the sensor wiring, making sure it is correctly routed, securing it in position with all the relevant clips and ties. Reconnect the wiring connector then lower the vehicle and (where necessary) tighten the wheel bolts to the specified torque.

21 Vacuum pump (diesel engine models) – removal and refitting

Removal

Note: *A new vacuum pump drive dog and gasket will be required before refitting.*
1 If necessary, to improve access to the vacuum pump, remove the air cleaner duct (see Chapter 4B).
2 Release the retaining clip and disconnect the vacuum hose from the pump **(see illustration)**.
3 Slacken and remove the mounting bolts/nuts securing the pump to the left-hand end of the cylinder head, then remove the pump. Recover the pump gasket and discard it; a new one should be used on refitting.

Refitting

4 Ensure that the pump and cylinder head mating surfaces are clean and dry and fit the new gasket to the head.
5 Manoeuvre the pump into position, aligning its drive dog with the camshaft slot, then refit the pump mounting bolts/nuts and tighten them securely.
6 Reconnect the vacuum hose and wiring connector (where applicable) to the pump, making sure the retaining clips are securely located. Where necessary refit the air cleaner duct.

22 Vacuum pump (diesel engine models) – testing and overhaul

1 The operation of the braking system vacuum pump can be checked using a vacuum gauge.
2 Disconnect the vacuum pipe from the pump, and connect the gauge to the pump union using a suitable length of hose.
3 Start the engine and allow it to idle, then measure the vacuum created by the pump. As a guide, after one minute, a minimum of approximately 500 mm Hg should be recorded. If the vacuum registered is significantly less than this, it is likely that the pump is faulty. However, seek the advice of a Renault dealer before condemning the pump.
4 Overhaul of the vacuum pump is not possible, since no components are available separately for it. If faulty, the complete pump assembly must be renewed.

23 Rear brake pads – inspection and renewal

Warning: Renew both sets of rear brake pads at the same time – never renew the pads on only one wheel, as uneven braking may result. Note that the dust created by wear of the pads may contain asbestos, which is a health hazard. Never blow it out with compressed air, and don't inhale any of it. An approved filtering mask should be worn when working on the brakes. DO NOT use petroleum-based solvents to clean brake parts – use brake cleaner or methylated spirit only.

Inspection

1 Chock the front wheels, engage reverse gear (or P) and release the handbrake. Jack up the rear of the vehicle and support it on axle stands (see *Jacking and vehicle support*). Remove the rear wheels.
2 Disconnect the handbrake cable from the caliper operating lever **(see illustration)**.
3 Slacken and remove the caliper guide pin

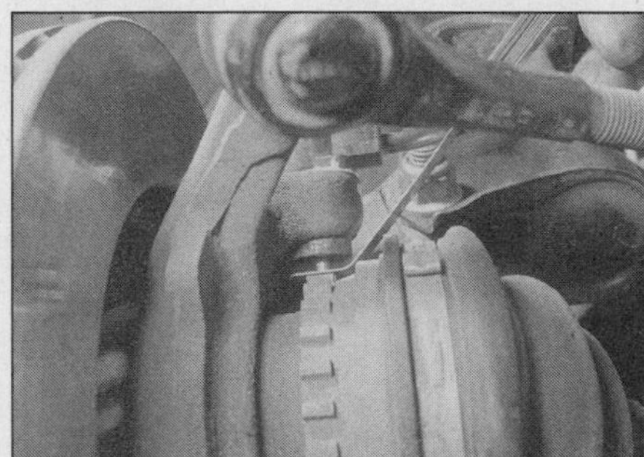
20.19 Checking front wheel sensor-to-reluctor ring clearance

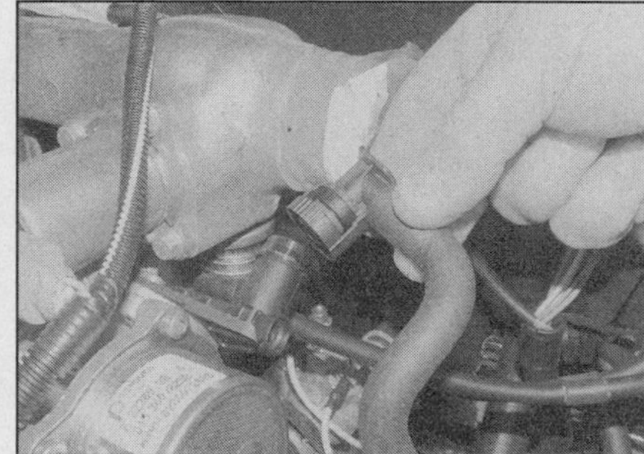
21.2 Disconnecting the hose from the vacuum pump

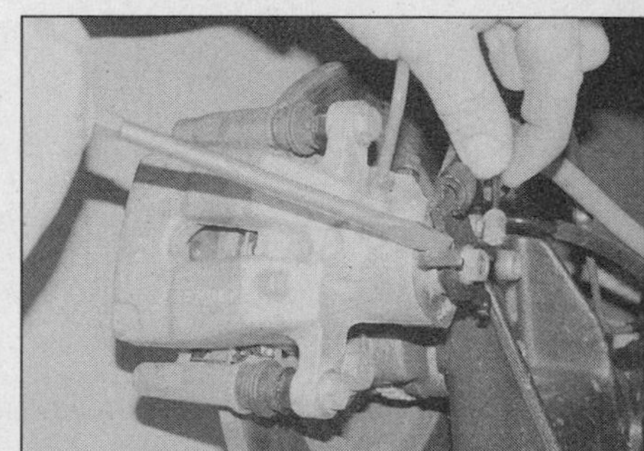
23.2 Releasing the inner cable from the caliper lever

9

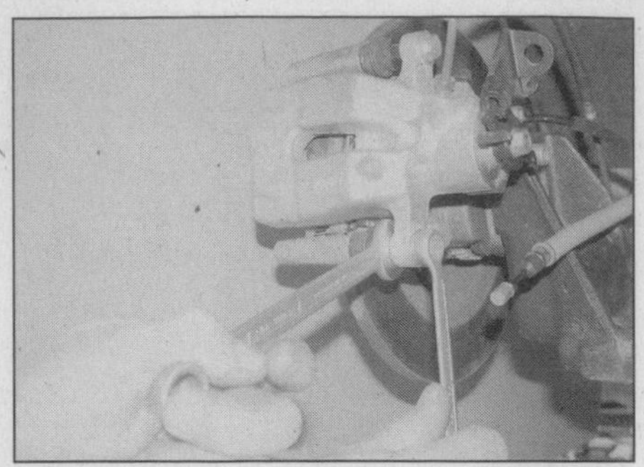
23.3 Slacken the guide pin bolts whilst holding the guide pins with an open-ended spanner

23.5 Withdraw the brake pads

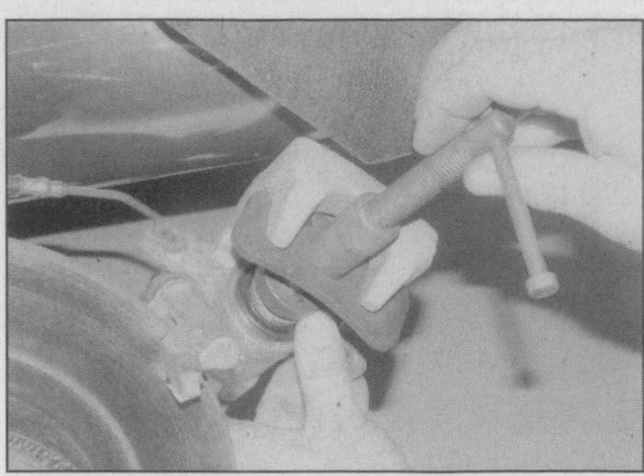
23.9 Using a special tool to retract the piston

bolts, using a slim open-ended spanner to prevent the guide pins themselves from rotating **(see illustration)**.

4 Pivot the caliper away from the brake pads and mounting bracket, and tie it to the underside of the body (eg, exhaust mounting bracket) using a suitable piece of wire. Do not allow the caliper to hang down by the hose, it may damage the brake pipe.

5 Withdraw the two brake pads from the caliper mounting bracket **(see illustration)**

6 First measure the thickness of each brake pad (friction material and backing plate). If either pad is worn at any point to the specified minimum thickness or less, all four pads must be renewed. Also, the pads should be renewed if any are fouled with oil or grease; there is no satisfactory way of degreasing friction material once contaminated. If any of the brake pads are worn unevenly, or fouled with oil or grease, trace and rectify the cause before reassembly. New brake pads are available from Renault dealers.

7 If the brake pads are still serviceable, carefully clean them using a clean, fine wire brush or similar, paying particular attention to the sides and back of the metal backing. Clean out the grooves in the friction material, and pick out any large embedded particles of dirt or debris. Clean the pad locations in the caliper body/mounting bracket.

8 Prior to fitting the pads, check that the guide sleeves are free to slide easily in the caliper body, and that the guide sleeve rubber gaiters are undamaged. Brush the dust and dirt from the caliper and piston, but *do not inhale it, as it is injurious to health.* Inspect the dust seal around the piston for damage, and the piston for evidence of fluid leaks, corrosion or damage. If attention to any of these components is necessary, refer to Section 24.

Renewal

9 If new brake pads are to be fitted, it will be necessary to retract the piston fully into the caliper bore by rotating it in a clockwise direction **(see illustration)**. Provided that the master cylinder reservoir has not been overfilled with hydraulic fluid, there should be no spillage, but keep a careful watch on the fluid level while retracting the piston. If the fluid level rises above the MAXI level, the surplus should be syphoned off (not by mouth – use an old syringe or antifreeze tester), or ejected via a plastic tube connected to the bleed screw (see Section 2).

10 Ensuring that the friction material of each pad is against the brake disc, fit the pads to the caliper mounting bracket.

11 Refit the caliper down into position over the pads, ensuring that the pad anti-rattle springs are correctly positioned against the caliper then press down on the caliper and install the new guide pin bolts. Tighten the guide pin bolts to their specified torque setting, while retaining the guide pin with an open-ended spanner.

12 Depress the brake pedal repeatedly, until the pads are pressed into firm contact with the brake disc, and normal (non-assisted) pedal pressure is restored.

13 Repeat the above procedure on the remaining rear brake caliper.

14 Refit the handbrake cable and check the adjustment as described in Sections 14 and 16. Refit the roadwheels, then lower the vehicle to the ground and tighten the roadwheel bolts to the specified torque setting.

15 Check the hydraulic fluid level as described in *Weekly checks*.

New pads will not give full braking efficiency until they have bedded in. Be prepared for this, and avoid hard braking as far as possible for the first hundred miles or so after pad renewal.

24 Rear brake caliper – removal, overhaul and refitting

Note: *Before starting work, refer to the warnings at the beginning of Section 2 concerning the dangers of hydraulic fluid, and at the beginning of Section 23 concerning the dangers of asbestos dust.*

Removal

1 Chock the front wheels, engage reverse gear (or P) and release the handbrake. Jack up the rear of the vehicle and support it on axle stands (see *Jacking and vehicle support*). Remove the relevant rear wheel.

2 Free the handbrake inner cable from the caliper handbrake operating lever, then tap the outer cable out of its bracket on the caliper body.

3 Minimise fluid loss, either by removing the master cylinder reservoir cap and then tightening it down onto a piece of polythene to obtain an airtight seal (taking care not to damage the sender unit), or by using a brake hose clamp, a G-clamp or a similar tool with protected jaws to clamp the flexible hose at the nearest convenient point to the brake caliper **(see illustration)**.

4 Clean the area around the caliper hose union, and unscrew the union nut **(see illustration)**. Carefully ease the pipe out of

24.3 Brake hose clamp fitted to flexible brake hose

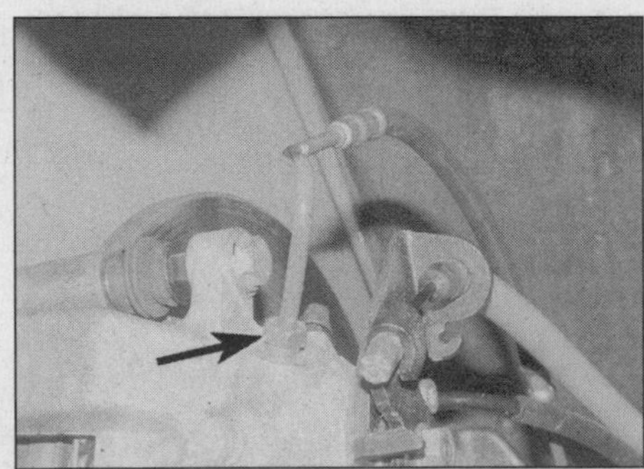
24.4 Remove the brake pipe union (arrowed)

24.11 Using a pair of pliers to refit the handbrake cable

position, and plug or tape over its end to prevent dirt entry. Wipe off any spilt fluid immediately.

5 Slacken and remove the upper and lower caliper guide pin bolts, using a slim open-ended spanner to prevent the guide pin itself from rotating (see Section 23). Discard the bolts, new ones must be used on refitting, then lift the caliper away from the brake disc. Note that the brake pads need not be disturbed, and can be left in position in the caliper mounting bracket.

Overhaul

6 At the time of writing, no further information was available for the overhaul of the rear brake calipers. Consult a Renault dealer regarding the availability of spare parts.

Refitting

7 Ensure that the brake pads are still correctly fitted in the caliper mounting bracket and refit the caliper.

8 Make sure the pad anti-rattle springs are correctly engaged with the caliper body then press the caliper into position and fit the new guide pin bolts. Tighten both guide pin bolts to the specified torque, starting with the lower bolt, while retaining the guide pins with an open-ended spanner.

9 Wipe clean the brake pipe union, and refit the pipe to the caliper. Tighten the brake pipe/hose union nut to the specified torque then remove the brake hose clamp or polythene from the master cylinder reservoir (as applicable).

10 Bleed the hydraulic system as described in Section 2. Note that, providing the precautions described were taken to minimise brake fluid loss, it should only be necessary to bleed the relevant rear brake.

11 Insert the handbrake cable through its bracket on the caliper, and fit the outer cable into position. Reconnect the inner cable to the caliper operating lever **(see illustration)**.

12 Repeatedly apply the brake pedal to bring the pads into contact with the disc. Check and if necessary adjust the handbrake cable as described in Section 14.

13 Refit the roadwheel, lower the vehicle to the ground and tighten the wheel bolts to the specified torque. On completion, check the hydraulic fluid level as described in *Weekly checks*.

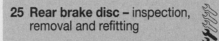

25.4 Remove the caliper mounting frame from the hub assembly

25 Rear brake disc – inspection, removal and refitting

Note: *Before starting work, refer to the warning at the beginning of Section 23 concerning the dangers of asbestos dust. If either disc requires renewal, both should be renewed at the same time, to ensure even and consistent braking (new brake pads should be fitted when fitting new discs). A new rear hub nut will be required on refitting.*

Inspection

1 Chock the front wheels, engage reverse gear (or P on automatics) and release the handbrake. Jack up the rear of the vehicle and support it on axle stands (see *Jacking and vehicle support*). Remove the appropriate rear roadwheel.

2 Inspect the disc as described in Section 6. Note: The disc/hub bearing is supplied from the dealer as a complete assembly.

Removal

3 Remove the brake pads as described in Section 23.

4 Remove the two caliper frame retaining bolts. Remove the frame from the hub assembly **(see illustration)**.

5 Using a hammer and a large flat-bladed tool, carefully tap and prise the cap out of the centre of the brake disc **(see illustration)**.

25.5 Prising out the hub cap from the rear disc

6 Using a socket and long bar, slacken and remove the rear hub nut and withdraw the thrustwasher. Discard the hub nut; a new nut must be used on refitting.

7 It should now be possible to withdraw the brake disc and hub bearing assembly from the stub axle by hand **(see illustration)**. It may be difficult to remove the disc, due to the tightness of the hub bearing on the stub axle. If the bearing is tight, tap the periphery of the disc using a hide or plastic mallet, or use a universal puller, secured to the disc with the wheel bolts, to pull it off.

Refitting

8 Prior to refitting the disc, smear the stub axle shaft with gear oil. Be careful not to contaminate the friction surfaces with oil. If a new disc is to be fitted, use a suitable solvent to wipe any preservative coating from its surface.

9 Slide the disc onto the stub axle, and tap it into position using a soft-faced mallet.

10 Fit the new rear hub nut and washer (where fitted), then tighten it to the specified torque **(see illustration)**. Tap the cap back into position in the centre of the disc.

11 Apply a few drops of locking fluid to the threads of the caliper frame retaining bolts. Offer up the frame and refit the bolts. Tighten both bolts to the specified torque.

12 Refit the brake pads as described in Section 23.

13 Check the handbrake cable adjustment as described in Chapter Section 14.

14 Refit the roadwheels and lower the vehicle to the ground. Tighten the roadwheel bolts to the specified torque.

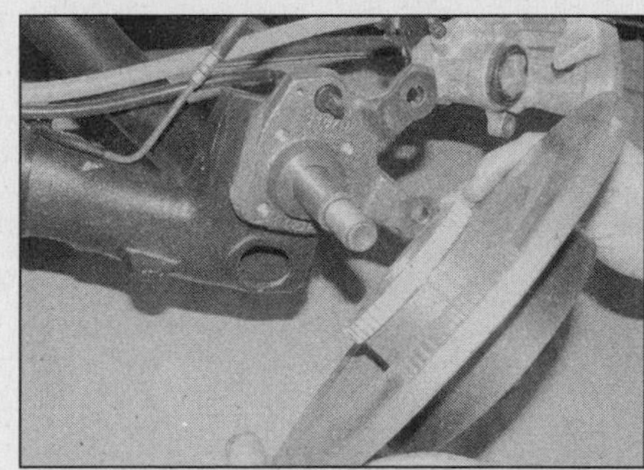

25.7 Slide the rear disc/hub assembly from the stub axle

25.10 Tighten the new rear hub nut to its specified torque

Chapter 10
Suspension and steering

Contents

Degrees of difficulty

Easy, suitable for novice with little experience 	**Fairly easy,** suitable for beginner with some experience 	**Fairly difficult,** suitable for competent DIY mechanic 	**Difficult,** suitable for experienced DIY mechanic 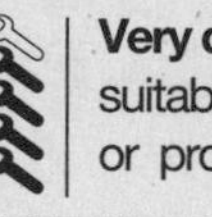	**Very difficult,** suitable for expert DIY or professional

Specifications

Engine designation

Petrol models:	
1.4 litre engine	E7J 764, K4J 750
1.6 litre engine	K4M 700, K4M 701
2.0 litre engine	F4R 740, F4R 741
Diesel models:	
Non-turbo engines – D models	F8Q 620, F8Q 622, F8Q 788
Turbo engines:	
dT models – indirect injection	F8Q 784, F8Q 786
dTi models – direct injection	F9Q 730, F9Q 734
dCi models – direct common-rail injection	F9Q 732

Front suspension

Front hub assembly end play	0 to 0.05 mm

Rear suspension

Rear hub assembly end play	0 to 0.03 mm

Steering

Collapsible safety column intermediate shaft length:	
All models except Scénic:	
Right-hand drive models	373.5 ± 0.5 mm
Left-hand drive models with manual steering	426.6 ± 0.5 mm
Left-hand drive models with power steering	370.4 ± 0.5 mm
Scénic models:	
Right-hand drive models	391.1 ± 0.5 mm
Left-hand drive models with manual steering	426.6 ± 0.5 mm
Left-hand drive models with power steering	378.1 ± 0.5 mm

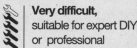

Wheel alignment and steering angles

Front wheel alignment (vehicle unladen)	+0°10' ± 10' (+1 ± 1 mm) toe-out
Rear wheel alignment (vehicle unladen)*:	
Mégane	
All models (except Saloon)	–0° 30' ± 20' (–3.0 ± 2 mm) toe-in
Saloon	–0° 25' ± 20' (–2.5 ± 2 mm) toe-in
Scénic	–0° 25' ± 20' (–2.5 ± 2 mm) toe-in

* **Note:** *The rear wheel alignment is not adjustable*

Torque wrench settings

	Nm	lbf ft
Front suspension		
Anti-roll bar mounting clamp bolts	32	24
Anti-roll bar to lower arms	32	24
Driveshaft retaining nut:		
'Nylstop' type with separate washer	250	185
'Enko' type with incorporated washer	280	207
Lower arm:		
Balljoint clamp bolt	60	44
Balljoint mounting bolt	65	48
Pivot bolt nuts:		
All models except Scénic	90	66
Scénic	100	74
Support arm to inner wing (bolt)	30	22
Support arm to lower arm pivot:		
Bolt	30	22
Nut	90	66
Suspension strut:		
Strut-to-swivel hub bolts	180	133
Strut upper mounting bolts	30	22
Strut upper mounting plate nut	60	44
Subframe-to-underbody bolts:		
Front mounting bolts	60	44
Rear mounting bolts	110	81
Rear suspension		
Axle mounting nuts*	100	74
Rear stub axle to trailing arm mountings	70	52
Shock absorber:		
Lower mounting bolt:		
All models except Scénic	135	100
Scénic	125	92
Upper mounting bolt	100	74
Hub nut*	175	129
Steering		
Hydraulic pipe union nuts:		
Feed pipe (pump to steering rack)	24	18
Return pipe (steering rack to pump):		
Aluminium casting	22	16
Steel casting	28	20
Steering gear pipe (pinion to rack housing)	15	11
Steering column:		
Mounting nuts and bolts	20	15
Universal joint clamp bolt nut	25	18
Steering gear mounting bolts	55	41
Steering wheel retaining bolt*	45	33
Track rod balljoint:		
Clamp bolt	20	15
Retaining nut	35	26
Track rod inner balljoint to steering rack:		
SMI steering gear assembly	50	37
TRW steering gear assembly	80	59

* *Use new fasteners*

1 General information

The independent front suspension is of the MacPherson strut type, incorporating coil springs and integral telescopic shock absorbers. The MacPherson struts are located by transverse lower suspension arms, which utilise rubber inboard mounting bushes and incorporate a balljoint at the outer ends. The front swivel hubs, which carry the wheel bearings, brake calipers and the hub/disc assemblies, are bolted to the MacPherson struts and connected to the lower arms via the balljoints. The anti-roll bar is rubber-mounted onto the subframe, and connects both the lower suspension arms.

The rear suspension is of the open-bar rear axle type, incorporating two torsion bars, two anti-roll bars and an L-section metal crossmember which is connected to both the trailing arms. The two torsion bars and two anti-roll bars are connected at the centre with a shackle/link, and at their outer ends to the trailing arms.

The steering column has a universal joint approximately halfway along its length and a second universal joint at its lower end. The lower universal joint is attached to the steering gear pinion by means of a clamp bolt.

The steering gear is mounted onto the front subframe. It is connected by two track rods and balljoints to steering arms projecting rearwards from the swivel hubs. The track rod ends are threaded to enable wheel alignment adjustment.

Power-assisted steering is available on most models. The hydraulic system is powered a pump, which is driven off the crankshaft pulley via a drivebelt.

Caution: If the vehicle is equipped with a radio/cassette unit with a built-in security code, do not disconnect the battery if you don't know the correct security code.

2 Front swivel hub assembly – removal and refitting

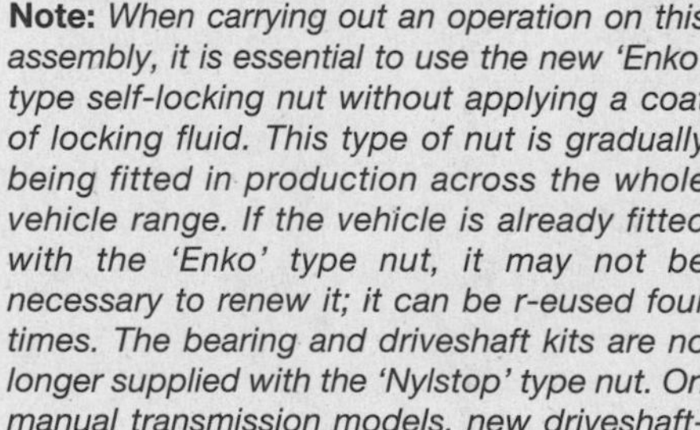

Note: *When carrying out an operation on this assembly, it is essential to use the new 'Enko' type self-locking nut without applying a coat of locking fluid. This type of nut is gradually being fitted in production across the whole vehicle range. If the vehicle is already fitted with the 'Enko' type nut, it may not be necessary to renew it; it can be r-eused four times. The bearing and driveshaft kits are no longer supplied with the 'Nylstop' type nut. On manual transmission models, new driveshaft-to-differential side gear roll pins (where applicable) will be required on refitting.*

Note: *On early models, the driveshaft outer joint splines are coated with locking compound prior to refitting. Therefore it is likely that a puller/extractor will be required to draw the hub assembly off the driveshaft end on removal.*

Removal

1 Remove the wheel trim/hub cap (as applicable) then slacken the driveshaft nut with the vehicle resting on its wheels. Also slacken the wheel bolts.

2 Chock the rear wheels of the car, firmly apply the handbrake, then jack up the front of the car and support it on axle stands (see *Jacking and vehicle support*). Remove the appropriate front roadwheel.

3 On models equipped with ABS, unbolt the wheel sensor and position it clear of the hub assembly (see Chapter 9). Note that there is no need to disconnect the wiring.

4 Slacken and remove the driveshaft retaining nut. If the nut was not slackened with the wheels on the ground (see paragraph 1), refit at least two roadwheel bolts to the front hub, tightening them securely, then have an assistant firmly depress the brake pedal to prevent the front hub from rotating, whilst you slacken and remove the driveshaft retaining nut. Alternatively, a tool can be fabricated to hold the hub stationary (see Chapter 8, Section 2).

5 Slacken and remove the nut securing the steering gear track rod end to the swivel hub then free the balljoint from the hub using a universal balljoint separator.

6 If the hub bearings are to be disturbed, remove the brake disc as described in Chapter 9. If not, unscrew the two bolts securing the brake caliper mounting bracket assembly to the swivel hub, and slide the caliper assembly off the disc **(see illustration)**. Using a piece of wire or string, tie the caliper to the front suspension coil spring, to avoid placing any strain on the hydraulic brake hose. If necessary, unbolt the brake hose/wiring bracket from the strut.

7 Remove the nut and clamp bolt securing the lower suspension arm to the swivel hub. Carefully lever the balljoint out of the swivel hub, taking care not to damage the balljoint or driveshaft gaiters. Note the plastic protector plate which is fitted to the balljoint shank.

8 Remove the two nuts and washers from the bolts securing the swivel hub to the suspension strut, noting that the nuts are positioned on the rear side of the strut **(see illustration)**. Withdraw the bolts and support the swivel hub assembly.

9 Release the driveshaft joint from the hub, and remove the swivel hub assembly from the vehicle. **Note:** *On early models, locking fluid may be applied to the joint splines during assembly, so it is likely that they will be a tight fit in the hub. Use a hammer and soft metal drift to tap the joint out of the hub, or use a puller to draw the swivel hub assembly off the joint splines* **(see illustration)**. Whilst the hub assembly is removed, support the driveshaft to avoid damage to the constant velocity joints/gaiters.

Refitting

10 Ensure that the driveshaft joint and hub splines are clean and dry from any locking fluid.

11 Engage the joint splines with the hub, and slide the hub fully onto the driveshaft. Insert the two swivel hub-to-suspension strut mounting bolts from the front side of the strut, then refit the washers and nuts to the rear of the bolts and tighten them to the specified torque **(see illustration)**.

2.6 Undo the mounting bracket bolts and slide the brake caliper off the disc

2.8 Undo the nuts and remove the suspension strut-to-swivel hub bolts

2.9 Using a puller to draw the hub assembly off the driveshaft joint splines

2.11 Ensure the strut-to-swivel hub bolts are fitted from the front of strut

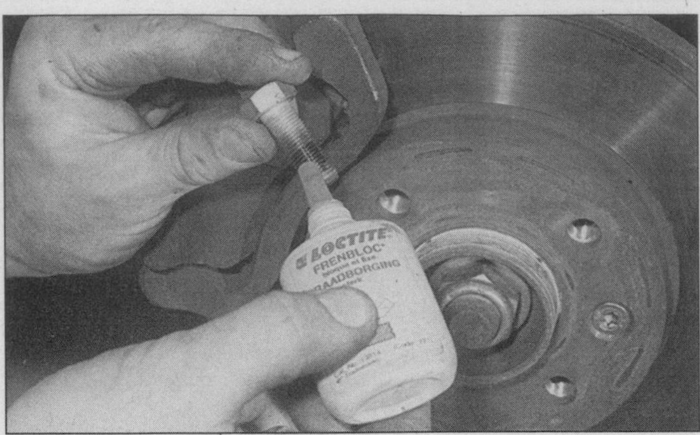

2.16 Apply thread locking compound to the threads of the brake caliper mounting bolts prior to installation

3.4 Circlip fitted to retain the bearing in the hub assembly (arrowed)

12 Slide on the washer and fit the new driveshaft 'Enko' type nut (see note above), tightening it by hand only at this stage.

13 Ensure that the plastic protector is still fitted to the lower arm balljoint, then locate the balljoint shank in the swivel hub. Refit the balljoint clamp bolt, and tighten its retaining nut to the specified torque.

14 Reconnect the track rod end balljoint to the swivel hub, and tighten its retaining nut to the specified torque.

15 On models equipped with ABS, refit the sensor to the hub, and tighten its retaining bolt to the specified torque (see Chapter 9).

16 Refit the brake disc (if removed), aligning the marks made on removal, and tighten its retaining screws to the specified torque. Slide the brake caliper assembly into position over the brake disc. Apply a few drops of locking fluid to the caliper bracket bolt threads (Renault recommend Loctite Frenbloc – available from your Renault dealer) then refit the bolts and tighten them to the specified torque (Chapter 9) **(see illustration)**.

17 Using the method employed during removal to prevent the hub from rotating, tighten a new driveshaft retaining nut to the specified torque. Alternatively, lightly tighten the nut at this stage and tighten it to the specified torque once the vehicle is resting on its wheels again.

18 Check that the hub rotates freely, then refit the roadwheel and lower the vehicle to the ground. Tighten the roadwheel bolts to the specified torque. If not already having done so, also tighten the driveshaft retaining nut to the specified torque.

3 Front hub bearings – checking and renewal

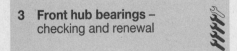

Note: *The bearing is a sealed, pre-adjusted and pre-lubricated, double-row roller type, and is intended to last the car's entire service life without maintenance or attention. Do not attempt to remove the bearing unless absolutely necessary, as it will be damaged during the removal operation. Never overtighten the driveshaft nut in an attempt to 'adjust' the bearing.*

Note: *A press will be required to dismantle and rebuild the assembly; if such a tool is not available, a large bench vice and suitable spacers (such as large sockets) will serve as an adequate substitute. The bearing's inner races are an interference fit on the hub; if the inner race remains on the hub when it is pressed out of the hub carrier, a suitable knife-edged bearing puller will be required to remove it.*

Checking

1 Wear in the front hub bearings can be checked by measuring the amount of side play present. To do this, a dial gauge should be fixed so that its probe is in contact with the disc face of the hub. The play should be as given in the Specifications. If it is greater than this, the bearings are worn excessively, and should be renewed.

Renewal

2 Remove the swivel hub assembly as described in Section 2, then undo the brake disc shield retaining screws and remove the shield from the hub.

3 Support the swivel hub securely on blocks or in a vice. Using a suitable tubular spacer which bears only on the inner end of the hub flange, press the hub flange out of the bearing. If the bearing outboard inner race remains on the hub, remove it using a suitable bearing puller (see note above).

4 Extract the bearing retaining circlip from the inner end of the swivel hub assembly **(see illustration)**.

5 Where necessary, refit the inner race in position over the ball cage, and support the inner face of the swivel hub. Using a suitable tubular spacer which bears only on the inner race, press the complete bearing assembly out of the swivel hub.

6 Thoroughly clean the hub and swivel hub, removing all traces of dirt and grease. Polish away any burrs or raised edges which might hinder reassembly. Check for cracks or any other signs of wear or damage, and renew the components if necessary. As noted above, the bearing and its circlip must be renewed whenever they are disturbed. A replacement bearing kit, which consists of the bearing, circlip, driveshaft nut and washer is available from Renault dealers.

7 On reassembly, check (if possible) that the new bearing is packed with grease. Apply a light film of oil to the bearing outer race and to the hub flange shaft.

8 Before fitting the new bearing, remove the plastic covers protecting the seals at each end, but leave the inner plastic sleeve in position to hold the inner races together.

9 Securely support the swivel hub, and locate the bearing in the hub. Press the bearing into position, ensuring that it enters the hub squarely, using a suitable tubular spacer which bears only on the outer race.

10 Once the bearing is correctly seated, secure it with the new circlip and remove the plastic sleeve. Apply a smear of grease to the oil seal lips.

11 Securely support the outer face of the hub flange then locate the bearing inner race over the end of the hub flange. Press the bearing onto the hub, using a tubular spacer which bears only on the inner race, until it seats against the shoulder **(see illustration)**. Check

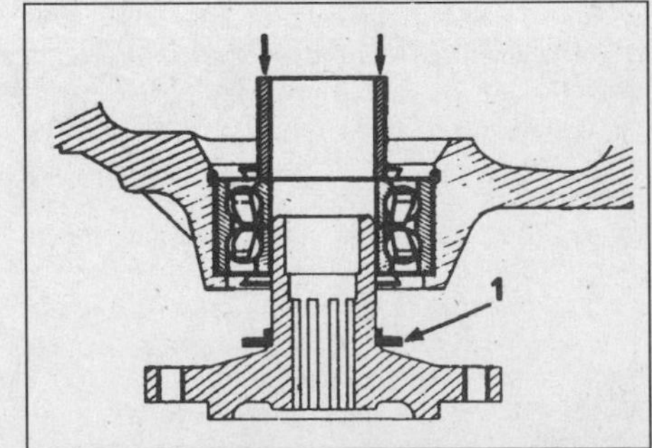

3.11 Pressing the hub assembly onto the hub flange

1 Thrustwasher (where applicable)

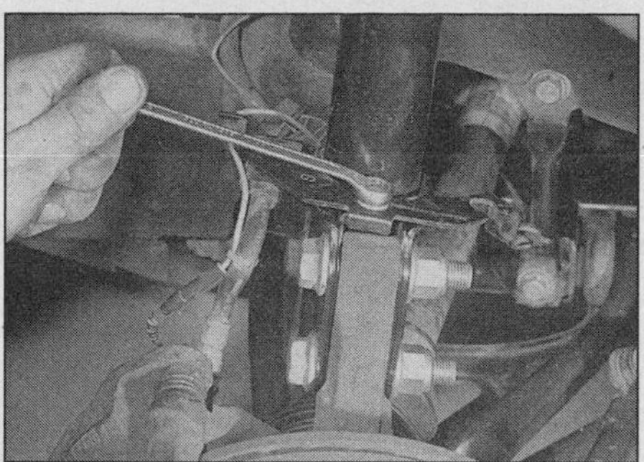
4.2 Undo the retaining bolt and free the hose/wiring bracket from the base of the strut

4.3 Withdraw the bolts securing the strut to the swivel hub, noting which way around they are fitted

4.4 Remove the upper mounting bolts (arrowed) – Mégane

that the hub flange rotates freely. Wipe off any excess oil or grease.

12 Refit the brake disc shield to the swivel hub, and tighten its retaining screws.

13 Refit the swivel hub assembly (Section 2).

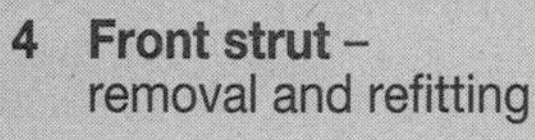

4 Front strut – removal and refitting

Removal

1 Chock the rear wheels, firmly apply the handbrake, then jack up the front of the vehicle and support it on axle stands (see *Jacking and vehicle support*). Remove the appropriate roadwheel.

2 Unscrew the retaining bolt and free the brake hose/wiring bracket from the base of the strut **(see illustration)**.

4.5a On Scénic models, unclip the strut cover . . .

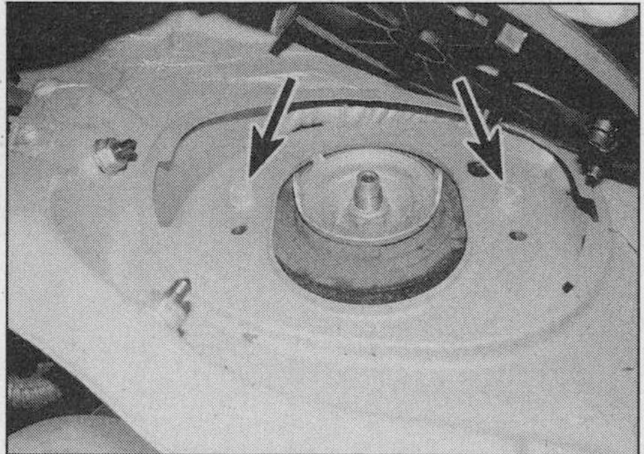
4.5b . . . and remove the upper mounting bolts (arrowed)

3 Remove the two nuts and washers from the bolts securing the swivel hub to the suspension strut, noting that the nuts are positioned on the rear side of the strut. Withdraw the bolts, and support the swivel hub assembly **(see illustration)**.

4 From within the engine compartment, note which bolt holes the strut upper mounting bolts are fitted to, then, whilst an assistant supports the weight of the strut, slacken and remove both bolts **(see illustration)**.

5 On Scénic models the strut mounting bolts are located under the air inlet vent scuttle panels. To gain access, remove both wiper arms (Chapter 12) and the bulkhead sealing strip. Undo the screws and remove the scuttle panels by moving them toward the centre of the windscreen to release the centring pin at each end. Lift off the strut turret sealing covers and remove the bolts as previously described **(see illustrations)**.

6 Release the strut from the swivel hub, and withdraw it from under the wheelarch, taking care to prevent damage to the driveshaft gaiter **(see illustration)**.

Refitting

7 Manoeuvre the strut assembly into position, taking care not damage the driveshaft gaiter. Position the upper mounting plate correctly to align with the relevant set of the mounting bolt holes then refit the mounting bolts and tighten them to the specified torque setting. The rear bolt holes are for use if the vehicle is fitted with power steering and front bolt holes for use when the vehicle is fitted with manual steering; rotate the mounting plate as necessary **(see illustration)**.

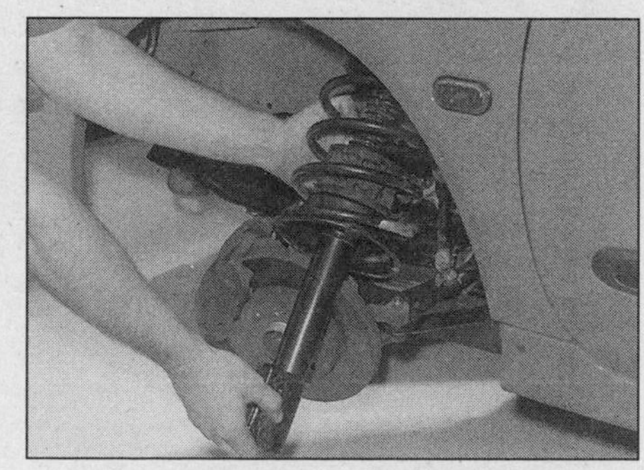
4.6 Manoeuvre the strut out from underneath the wheelarch

8 Insert the two swivel hub-to-suspension strut mounting bolts from the front side of the strut. Refit the washers and nuts to the rear of the bolts, and tighten them to the specified torque.

9 Refit the brake hose/wiring mounting bracket to the strut and securely tighten its retaining bolt.

10 On Scénic models, apply a bead of sealant to the strut turret sealing covers. Refit the air inlet vent scuttle panels, the bulkhead sealing strip and the wiper arms.

5 Front strut – overhaul

Warning: Before attempting to dismantle the front suspension strut, a suitable tool to hold the coil spring in compression must be obtained. Adjustable coil spring compressors are readily available, and are recommended for this operation. Any

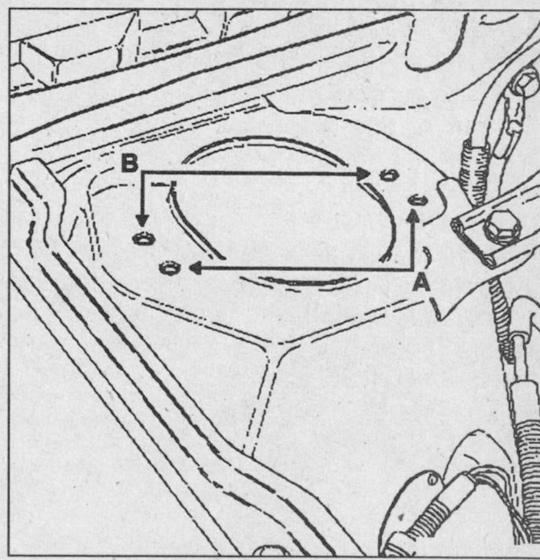

4.7 Ensure the strut mounting is correctly positioned so that the upper mounting bolts are fitted to the correct holes

A Mechanical steering models
B Power steering models

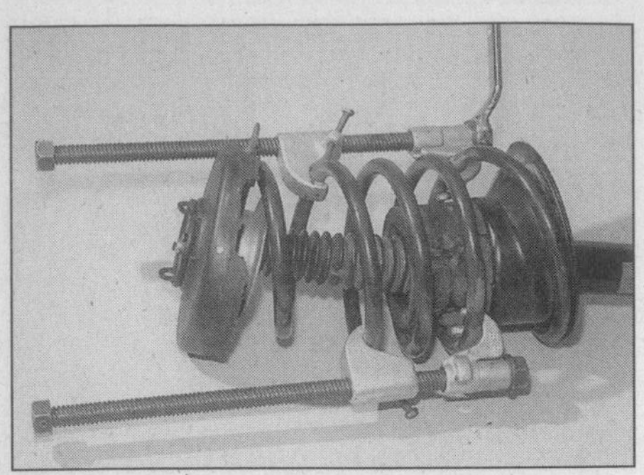

5.1 Using spring compressors, compress the strut coil spring until tension is relieved from the spring seats

5.2 Remove the cover from the upper mounting plate

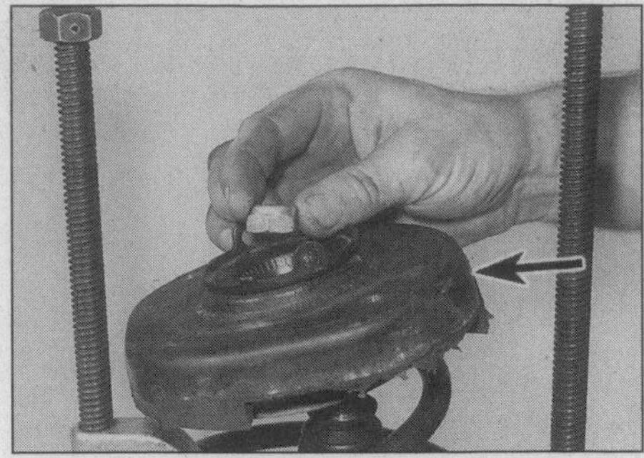

5.3 Remove the nut then lift off the upper mounting plate (arrowed)

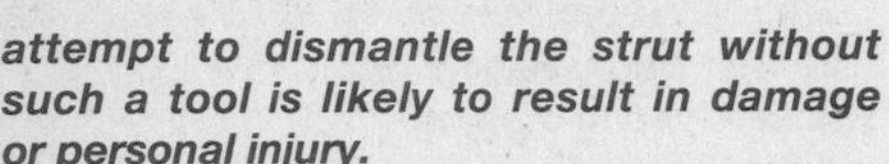

attempt to dismantle the strut without such a tool is likely to result in damage or personal injury.

Note: *A new upper mounting plate nut will be required.*

1 With the strut removed from the car, clean away all external dirt, then mount it upright in a vice. Fit the spring compressor and compress the coil spring until tension is relieved from the spring seats **(see illustration)**.

2 Remove the cover from the upper mounting plate nut then slacken the nut whilst retaining the shock absorber piston with a suitable Allen key **(see illustration)**.

3 Remove the nut and lift off the upper mounting plate **(see illustration)**.

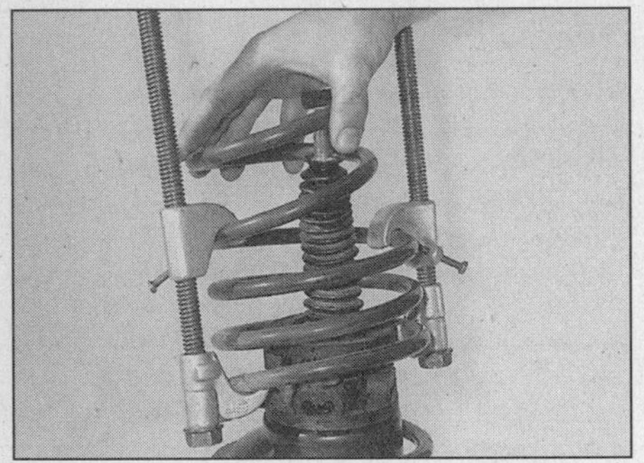

5.4a Lift off the coil spring . . .

4 Lift off the spring, followed by the spring stop/lower seat and the lower seat bearing then slide the dust gaiter off of the piston **(see illustrations)**.

5 Examine the shock absorber for signs of fluid leakage. Check the piston for signs of pitting along its entire length, and check the shock body for signs of damage. While holding it in an upright position, test the operation of the shock absorber by moving the piston through a full stroke, and then through short strokes of 50 to 100 mm. In both cases, the resistance felt should be smooth and continuous. If the resistance is jerky, or uneven, or if there is any visible sign of wear or damage to the shock absorber, renewal is necessary.

6 Inspect all other components for signs of damage or deterioration, paying particular attention to the bearing, and renew any that are suspect.

7 Slide the dust gaiter onto the piston and seat its lower end in the strut.

8 Fit the bearing, ensuring it is the correct way up, followed by the spring stop/lower seat assembly.

9 Refit the coil spring, making sure its lower end is correctly seated against the spring seat stop.

10 Fit the upper mounting plate, aligning its stop with the spring end, then screw on the new nut **(see illustration)**. Retain the shock absorber piston and tighten the mounting plate nut to the specified torque. Refit the cover to the nut.

11 Slowly release the spring compressor, ensuring the spring ends remain correctly seated, and remove it from the strut assembly.

12 Refit the strut to the vehicle as described in Section 4.

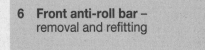

6 Front anti-roll bar – removal and refitting

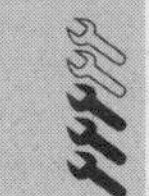

Removal

1 Chock the rear wheels, apply the handbrake, then jack up the front of the vehicle and support it on axle stands (see *Jacking and vehicle support*). Remove both front roadwheels.

2 Remove the engine compartment undershield (where fitted), and the exhaust downpipe as described in Chapter 4A or 4B.

3 On models fitted with a manual gearbox, disconnect the gearchange mechanism from the gearbox as described in Chapter 7A.

4 Slacken and remove the retaining nut and bolt securing each end of the anti-roll bar to

5.4b . . . and the spring stop/lower seat . . .

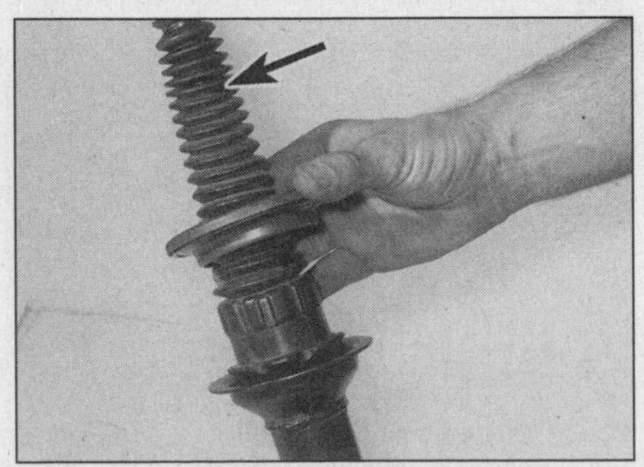

5.4c . . . then remove the lower seat bearing and the dust gaiter (arrowed)

5.10 On refitting ensure the upper mounting plate stop is correctly located against the spring end

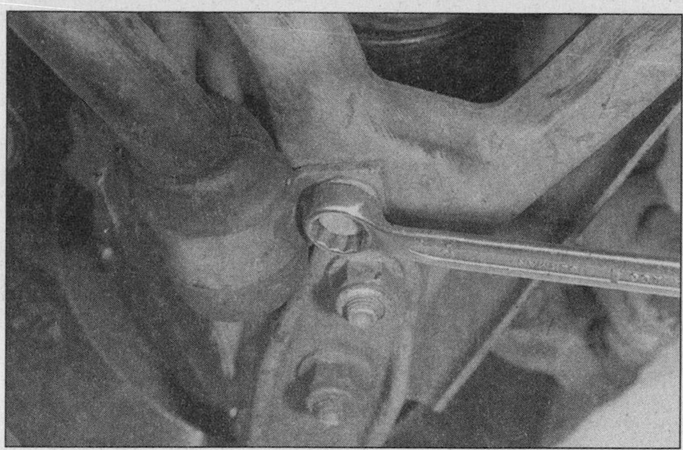

6.4 Removing the mounting clamp nut and bolt from the lower suspension arm

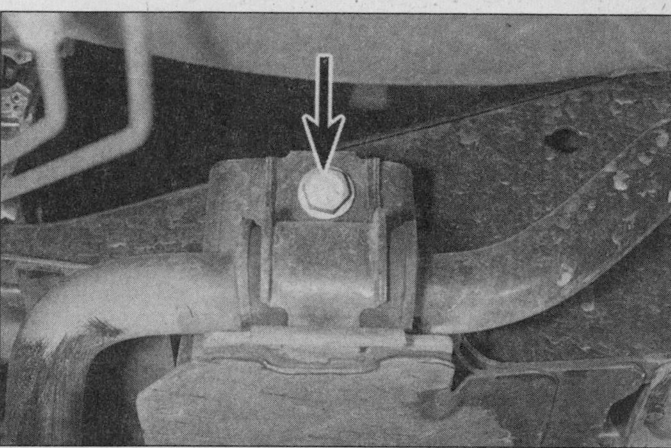

6.5 Remove the retaining bolt (arrowed) and withdraw the anti-roll bar mounting clamps

the lower suspension arms **(see illustration)**. Unhook both clamps and remove them from the undersides of the arms.

5 Slacken and remove the retaining nuts and bolts and remove the anti-roll bar mounting clamps from the subframe **(see illustration)**.

6 Manoeuvre the anti-roll bar out from underneath the vehicle, and remove the rubber mounting bushes.

7 Carefully examine the anti-roll bar components for signs of wear, damage or deterioration, paying particular attention to the mounting bushes. Renew worn components as necessary.

Refitting

8 Fit the mounting bushes onto the anti-roll bar then manoeuvre the anti-roll bar into position underneath the vehicle. Position the bushes so that their splits are against the subframe, then refit the mounting clamps, tightening the bolts lightly only at this stage.

9 Lubricate the bar end mounting rubbers with a smear of multi-purpose grease (Renault recommend the use of Molykote 33 medium grease – available from your Renault dealer). Fit the mounting rubbers to the end of the bar then hook the mounting clamps into position on the lower arms. Refit the mounting clamp bolts and nuts, tightening them lightly only at this stage.

10 On manual gearbox models, reconnect the selector mechanism as described in Chapter 7A.

11 Refit the exhaust downpipe as described in Chapter 4A or 4B, then refit the engine compartment undershield (where applicable).

12 Refit the roadwheels, lower the vehicle to the ground and tighten the wheel bolts to the specified torque.

13 With the vehicle resting on its wheels, rock the vehicle to settle the anti-roll bar in position then tighten the anti-roll bar mounting clamps and the anti-roll bar-to-lower arm mountings to the specified torque.

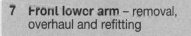

7 Front lower arm – removal, overhaul and refitting

Removal

1 Chock the rear wheels, apply the handbrake, jack up the front of the vehicle and support it on axle stands (see *Jacking and vehicle support*). Remove the appropriate front roadwheel.

2 Working as described in Section 6, disconnect the ends of the anti-roll bar from the lower suspension arms then slacken the mounting clamps and pivot the bar clear of the lower arm.

3 Remove the bolt securing the support bar (where fitted) to the front wing valance, and the nut securing it to the lower arm front pivot. Remove the support bar from the vehicle **(see illustrations)**.

4 Remove the nut and clamp bolt securing the lower suspension arm balljoint to the swivel hub **(see illustration)**. Slacken the lower arm pivot bolts then carefully lever the balljoint out of the swivel hub, taking care not to damage the balljoint or driveshaft gaiters. Remove the plastic protector plate which is fitted to the balljoint shank.

5 Remove the two pivot nuts and bolts, and remove the lower suspension arm from the vehicle.

Overhaul

6 Clean the lower arm and the area around the arm mountings, then check for cracks, distortion or any other signs of damage. On some models, a brake disc cooling shield is clipped to the arm; this should also be removed. Check that the lower arm balljoint moves freely, without any sign of roughness, and that the balljoint gaiter is free from cracks and splits. Examine the shank of the pivot bolts for signs of wear or scoring. Renew worn components as necessary.

7 Inspect the lower arm pivot bushes. If they are worn, cracked, split or perished, they must be renewed. To renew the bushes, support the lower arm, and press the first

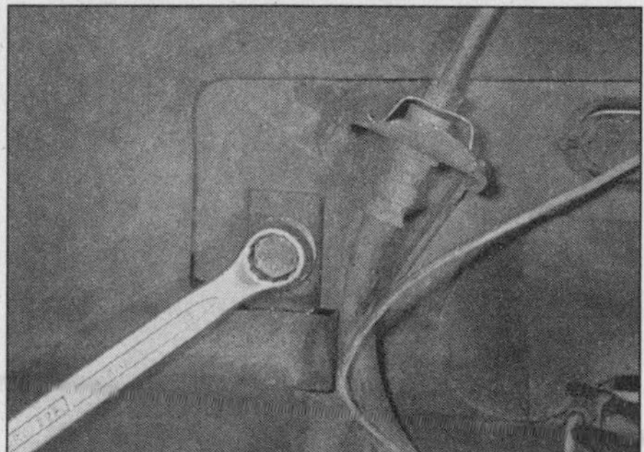

7.3a Undo the upper mounting bolt . . .

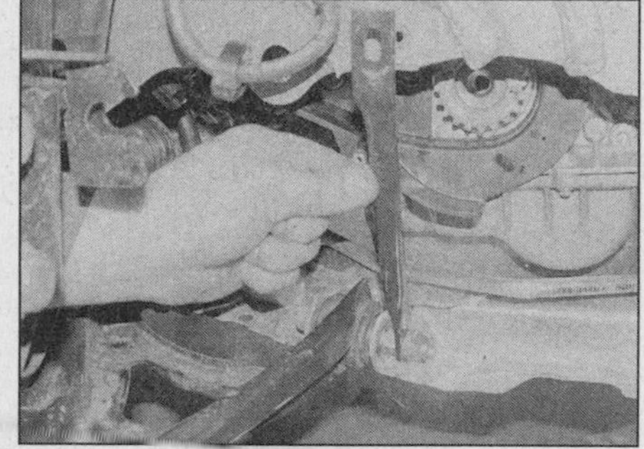

7.3b . . . then unscrew the lower nut from the pivot bolt and remove the support bar

7.4 Remove the clamp bolt and free the lower arm balljoint from the swivel hub

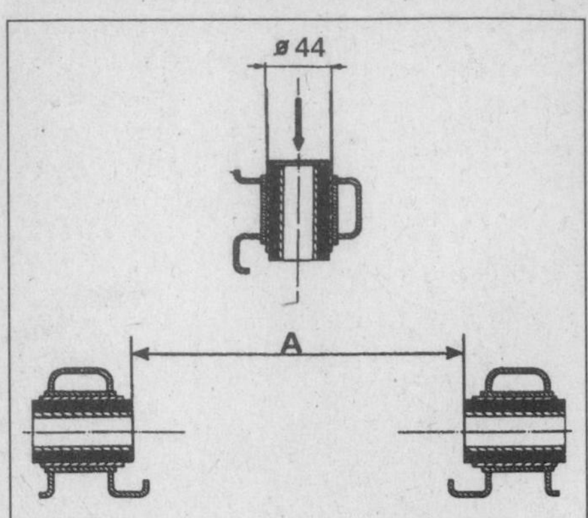

7.7 Front lower arm pivot bush fitting dimension

A = 147 ± 0.5 mm

bush out using a tubular spacer, such as a socket, which bears only on the hard, outer edge of the bush. **Note:** *Remove only one bush at a time from the arm, to ensure that each new bush is correctly positioned on installation.* Thoroughly clean the lower arm bore, removing all traces of dirt and grease, and polish away any burrs or raised edges which might hinder reassembly. Apply a smear of a suitable grease to the outer edge of the new bush. Press the bush into position until the distance A between the inner edges of the lower arm bushes is as shown **(see illustration)**. Wipe away surplus grease and repeat the procedure on the remaining bush.

Refitting

8 Offer up the lower suspension arm, and insert the two pivot bolts from the rear of the suspension arm. Refit the nuts, but tighten them by hand only at this stage.

9 Refit the plastic protector to the lower arm balljoint, then locate the balljoint shank in the swivel hub. Refit the balljoint clamp bolt, and tighten its retaining nut to the specified torque.

10 When applicable, refit the support bar on the front pivot bolt shank. Fit the retaining bolt and nut, tightening both by hand only at this stage.

11 Working as described in Section 6, reconnect the ends of the anti-roll bar to the lower suspension arms, tightening the mounting bolts only lightly at this stage.

12 Refit the roadwheel, lower the vehicle and tighten the roadwheel bolts to the specified torque.

13 With the vehicle standing on its wheels, rock the vehicle to settle the lower arm and anti-roll bar in position. Tighten the lower arm pivot bolts to the specified torque setting then tighten the anti-roll bar mounting clamps to their specified torque settings. Once the pivot bolts and anti-roll bar fixings have been tightened, secure the support bar (where fitted) in position by securely tightening its retaining nut and bolt.

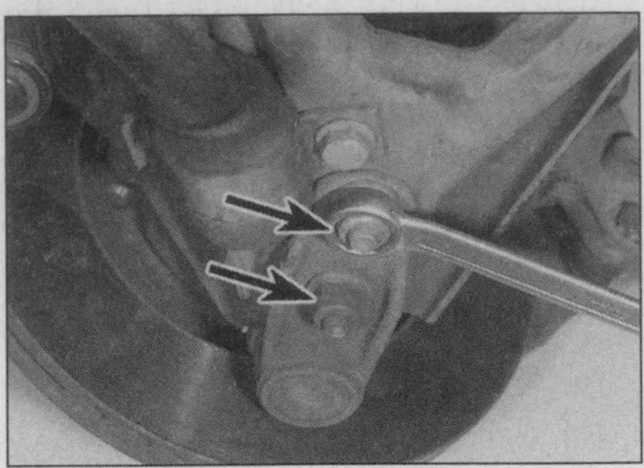

8.2 Remove the nuts and bolts (arrowed) securing the balljoint to the lower arm

8 Front lower arm balljoint – removal and refitting

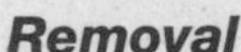

Removal

1 Carry out the operations described in paragraphs 1 to 4 of Section 7.

2 Slacken and remove the nuts and bolts securing the balljoint to the lower arm and remove the balljoint from the vehicle **(see illustration)**.

3 Check that the balljoint moves freely, without any sign of roughness or free play. Examine the balljoint gaiter for signs of damage and deterioration such as cracks or splits. Renew the complete balljoint assembly if damaged; it is not possible to renew the balljoint gaiter separately. The balljoint renewal kit obtainable from Renault dealers contains the balljoint, the plastic protector plate and all fixings.

Refitting

4 Offer up the balljoint then insert the retaining bolts and tighten the retaining nuts to the specified torque.

5 Carry out the operations described in paragraphs 9 to 13 of Section 7.

9 Rear hub bearings – checking and renewal

Note: *The bearing is a sealed, pre-adjusted and pre-lubricated, double-row ball or tapered-roller type, and is intended to last the car's entire service life without maintenance or attention. Check for the availability of parts before proceeding. Never overtighten the hub nut in an attempt to 'adjust' the bearings.*

Checking

1 Chock the front wheels and engage reverse gear (or P). Jack up the rear of the vehicle and support it on axle stands (see *Jacking and vehicle support*). Remove the appropriate rear roadwheel, and fully release the handbrake.

9.4 Rear hub bearing circlip (arrowed) – drum brake

2 Wear in the rear hub bearings can be checked by measuring the amount of side play present. To do this, a dial test indicator should be fixed so that its probe is in contact with the hub outer face. The play should be as given in the Specifications. If it is greater than this, the bearings are worn excessively and should be renewed.

Renewal

Drum brakes

3 Remove the rear brake drum as described in Chapter 9.

4 Using circlip pliers, extract the bearing retaining circlip from the front of the brake drum **(see illustration)**.

5 Securely support the front of the drum hub and press or drive the bearing out of the hub using a tubular drift which bears on the bearing outer race.

6 Thoroughly clean the hub, removing all traces of dirt and grease. Polish away any burrs or raised edges which might hinder reassembly. Check the hub for cracks or any other signs of damage, and renew if necessary. The bearing and its circlip must be renewed whenever they are disturbed. A bearing kit is available from Renault dealers, consisting of the bearing, circlip, spacer, thrustwasher, hub nut and grease cap.

7 On reassembly, check (if possible) that the new bearing is packed with grease. Apply a light film of gear oil to the bearing outer race and stub axle.

8 Securely support the rear of the drum hub then press/tap the bearing into position using a suitable tubular spacer which bears only on the bearing outer race. Ensure that the bearing enters the hub squarely until it is in contact with the hub shoulder.

9 Secure the bearing in position with the new circlip, ensuring the circlip is correctly seated in its groove.

10 Refit the brake drum as described in Chapter 9.

Disc brakes

11 Check the availability of parts. If the bearing is available separately, carry out the procedures as described in paragraphs 4 to 9

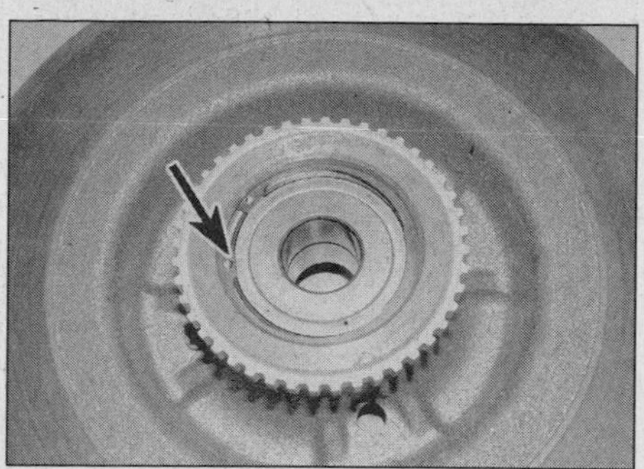

9.11 Rear hub bearing circlip (arrowed) – disc brake

10.2 Remove the lower mounting bolt (arrowed) . . .

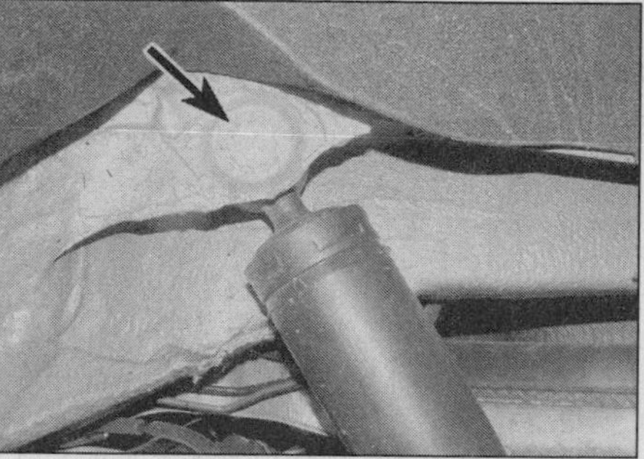

10.3 . . . and the upper mounting bolt (arrowed) then remove the rear shock absorber from the vehicle

to replace the bearing in the disc/hub assembly **(see illustration)**.

12 On most models, the disc/hub and bearing are a sealed assembly and the bearing cannot be removed separately. On these models, renewal of the bearing entails renewing the complete disc/hub assembly as follows.

13 Remove and refit the rear brake disc/hub assembly as described in Chapter 9.

14 Secure the disc/hub assembly with a new hub nut. Tighten the nut to the specified torque and tap the hub cap into place in the centre of the hub.

10 Rear shock absorber – removal, testing and refitting

Removal

1 Chock the front wheels and engage reverse gear (or P). Jack up the rear of the vehicle and support it on axle stands (see *Jacking and vehicle support*). Remove the appropriate rear roadwheel.

2 Using a jack, raise the trailing arm slightly until the shock absorber is slightly compressed. Remove the lower mounting bolt and washer **(see illustration)**.

3 Slacken and remove the upper mounting bolt and remove the shock absorber from the vehicle **(see illustration)**.

Testing

4 Examine the shock absorber for signs of fluid leakage or damage. Test the operation of the shock absorber, while holding it in an upright position, by moving the piston through a full stroke and then through short strokes of 50 to 100 mm. In both cases, the resistance felt should be smooth and continuous. If the resistance is jerky, or uneven, or if there is any visible sign of wear or damage, renewal is necessary. Also check the rubber mountings for damage and deterioration. Renew the shock absorber complete if any damage or wear is evident; the mounting bushes are not available separately. Inspect the mounting bolts for signs of wear or damage, and renew as necessary.

Refitting

5 Prior to refitting the shock absorber, mount it upright in the vice, and operate it fully through several strokes in order to prime it. Apply a smear of multi-purpose grease (Renault recommend the use of Molykote BR2 – available from your Renault dealer) to the shock absorber mounting bolts.

6 Offer up the shock absorber, then install its upper mounting bolt, tightening it by hand only at this stage.

7 Refit the lower shock absorber mounting bolt and washer, again tightening it by hand only. Remove the jack from under the trailing arm.

8 Refit the roadwheel, lower the vehicle to the ground and tighten the roadwheel bolts to the specified torque.

9 Rock the vehicle to settle the shock absorber mounting bushes in position, then tighten both the mounting bolts to the specified torque.

11 Rear anti-roll bar – removal and refitting

The anti-roll bars are integral with the rear axle, see Section 12.

12 Rear axle – removal and refitting

Note: *New axle mounting bolt nuts will be required on refitting.*

Removal

1 Chock the front wheels and engage reverse gear (or P on automatic gearbox). Jack up the rear of the vehicle and support it on axle stands (see *Jacking and vehicle support*). Remove both rear roadwheels.

2 Working as described in Chapter 9, carry out the following:

a) *Detach both handbrake cables from the lever and release the cables from the vehicle underbody so that they are free to be removed with the axle.*
b) *Trace the brake pipes/hoses back from the wheel cylinders/calipers to their unions just in front of the axle* **(see illustration)**. *Disconnect both unions and plug the hose/pipe ends to minimise fluid loss and prevent dirt entry then slide out the retaining clip and free the hose from its mounting bracket. On models with ABS, disconnect the battery before disconnecting the hose unions (see Warnings in Chapter 9).*
c) *Where applicable, unhook the pressure-regulating valve link rod from the rear axle.*
d) *On models with ABS, trace the wiring back from the rear wheel sensors and disconnect the wiring connectors. Free the wiring from all the relevant clips so it is free to be removed with the axle* **(see illustration)**.

12.2a Disconnect the left and right-hand rear brake pipes/hoses at their unions (arrowed) in front of the axle

12.2b Where applicable, disconnect the wiring connector for the ABS

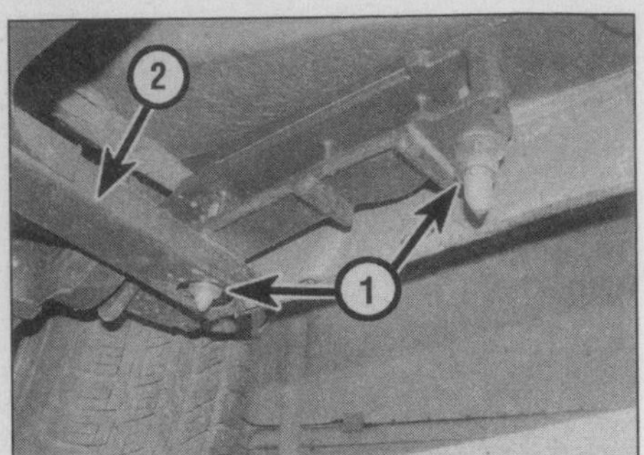

12.5 Remove the axle retaining nuts (1) and remove the bracing bar (2)

3 Support the weight of the rear axle on a trolley jack.
4 Slacken and remove the left- and right-hand shock absorber lower mounting bolts.
5 Slacken and remove the nuts securing the axle in position and remove the bracing bar which is fitted to the axle mounting bolts **(see illustration)**. Discard the nuts, new ones should be used on refitting.
6 Ensure that the axle cables/wiring are freed from all the necessary clips and ties then carefully lower the axle assembly out of position and remove it from underneath the vehicle.
7 To gain access to the axle mounting bolts, remove the rear seat cushion and the sill/side trim panel (see Chapter 11, Sections 25 and 28). Undo the retaining bolt then remove the retaining plate and mounting bolts from the vehicle.

Refitting

8 Where necessary, refit the axle mounting bolts and retaining plate in position, tightening the retaining plate bolt securely.
9 Manoeuvre the axle assembly into position, aligning it with the mounting bolts. Refit the bracing bar to the axle bolts then fit the new mounting nuts and tighten them to the specified torque. Where necessary, refit the trim panel and rear seat cushion.
10 Apply a smear of multi-purpose grease (Renault recommend the use of Molykote BR2 – available from your Renault dealer) to the shock absorber lower mounting bolts. Align the shock absorbers with the trailing arms and refit the mounting bolts, tightening them by hand only at this stage.
11 Working as described in Chapter 9, carry out the following:

a) Reconnect the rear brake lines, tightening the union nuts to the specified torque, and secure them in position with the retaining clips.
b) On models with ABS, reconnect the wheel sensor wiring connectors ensuring the wiring is correctly routed and retained by all the necessary clips.
c) Reconnect and adjust the handbrake cables.
d) Clip the pressure regulating valve link rod back into position.

12 Refit the roadwheels then lower the vehicle to the ground and tighten the wheel bolts to the specified torque.
13 Rock the vehicle to settle the rear axle in position then tighten the shock absorber lower mounting bolts to the specified torque.
14 Bleed the complete braking system as described in Chapter 9.

13 Rear axle overhaul – general information

Note: *Overhaul of the rear axle assembly is a complex task, requiring the use of several special tools. It is also critical that the axle is reassembled correctly, otherwise the vehicle ride height will be incorrect and/or the rear suspension performance will be adversely affected. If in any doubt, it may be best entrusted to a Renault dealer with access to all the necessary equipment.*

1 To remove the two torsion bars or anti-roll bars a suitable slide hammer removal tool will be required (Renault tool Emb. 880).

> **HAYNES HiNT** ***It is possible to improvise a bar removal tool by screwing a long bolt with a flat washer into the bar, and placing the jaws of a spanner against the washer. Striking the spanner sharply with a hammer should free the bar***

2 Mark the torsion bars and anti-roll bars in relation to the trailing arms and centre shackle/link block. Then extract them using the slide hammer.
3 Examine all the components for wear and damage. Check the splines on the torsion bars, anti-roll bars, centre shackle/link block and trailing arms. If a trailing arm or the L-shaped crossmember is damaged, it will be necessary to obtain a new rear axle (supplied with the bearing brackets already fitted, but requiring the original torsion bars and anti-roll bars to be fitted). If the bearing bracket bushes require renewal, proceed as described below, noting that it is not possible to obtain either bush separately. If worn, the complete bearing bracket and bush assembly must be renewed. If it is not wished to renew the bushes, proceed to paragraph 7.
4 Obtain a nut of suitable diameter which just fits inside the bearing bracket pivot shaft, and weld it securely to the shaft inner surface. Support the outer surface of the trailing arm. Press out the bearing bracket shaft, using a spacer which bears on the top of the welded nut.
5 Thoroughly clean the trailing arm bore. Polish away any burrs or raised edges which might hinder reassembly. Apply a smear of multi-purpose grease to the outer diameter of the new bracket pivot shaft, to aid installation.
6 Support the inner edge of the trailing arm. Position the new bearing bracket as shown in relation to the trailing arm. Press the bracket onto the trailing arm shaft until the distance between inner bolt hole centres of the left and right-hand bearing brackets is as shown **(see illustrations)**. Wipe away any excess grease.
7 Commence reassembly of the rear axle by placing it upside-down on blocks of wood positioned under the L-shaped crossmember so that the bearing brackets are free.
8 Use a ruler, and mark each trailing arm on the axis between the centres of the torsion bar and anti-roll bar holes. Clean the anti-roll bar splines, and grease them well with molybdenum disulphide grease. Insert one anti-roll bar so that its drill mark is aligned with the mark made on the trailing arm. Fit the centre shackle/link block to the anti-roll bar so that it is parallel with the upper section of the crossmember. Insert the remaining anti-roll bar from the opposite side, also aligning its circular drill mark with the mark made on the trailing arm.
9 It is now necessary to adjust the shackle/centre link position, in order to avoid any contact with the crossmember during

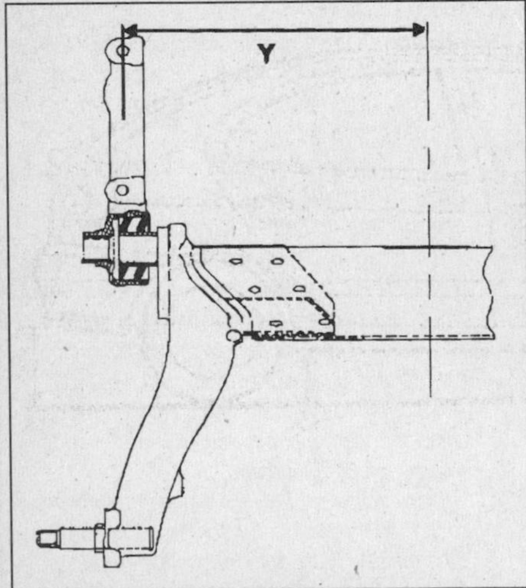

13.6a Measure the centre of the bolt holes from each side suspension arm

Y = 1268 ± 1mm

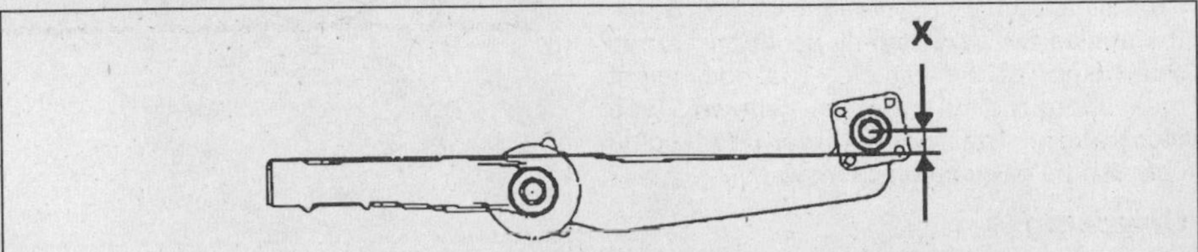

13.6b The centre of the stub axle to the top of the axle assembly

X = 37mm

movement of the rear suspension. First measure the movement possible between the shackle/centre link and the crossmember. Note this measurement, then refer to the table below to obtain the amount of adjustment, in terms of splines, necessary.

Movement (mm)	Number of splines to compensate
2 to 4	1
5 to 6	2
7 to 8	3
9 to 10	4
11 to 12	5
13 to 14	6
15 to 16	7
17 to 18	8
19 to 20	9

10 Withdraw one of the anti-roll bars from the trailing arm. Slide the centre shackle/link off the end of the other anti-roll bar, rotate the shackle/link away from the crossmember by the specified number of splines, then refit it to the anti-roll bar end. Disengage the anti-roll bar and centre shackle/link assembly from the trailing arm splines. Rotate the bar by the specified number of splines, so that the centre shackle/link is parallel to the crossmember again, then relocate the anti-roll bar in the trailing arm splines. Rotate the second anti-roll bar by the same number of splines in the opposite direction, so that its drill mark is at the same position as the one on the opposite bar, then engage its splines with those of the trailing arm and centre link, and slide the bar into position.

11 With the anti-roll bars correctly positioned, use a G-clamp to press the centre shackle/link down until it is parallel with the crossmember. Temporarily refit the torsion bars. Rotate each bar until the position is found where the bar can be freely engaged with the splines on the bearing bracket and bearing, then press the bars fully into position.

12 If a new axle is being fitted, remove the brake pipes from the original and fit them to the new axle. Also transfer the brake caliper mounting brackets, using locking fluid on the threads of the retaining bolts.

14 Vehicle ride height – general information and checking

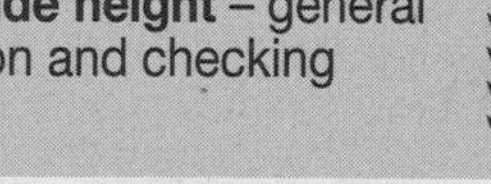

General information

1 The vehicle ride height measurements are used to ensure accuracy when checking the front suspension and steering angles, since the angles will vary slightly according to the ride height of the vehicle. The ride height measuring points are as shown **(see illustration)**. The front and rear ride heights can also be calculated as follows.

Checking

2 To accurately check the ride height, position the unladen vehicle on a level surface, with the tyres correctly inflated and the fuel tank full.

Ride height

3 To check the front ride height, measure and record the dimensions H1 (centre of the wheel axis to the ground) and H2 (subframe to the ground) on both sides of the vehicle. Subtract H2 from H1 to find the underbody height checking dimension.

4 To check the rear ride height, measure and record the dimensions H4 (centre of the wheel axis to the ground) and H5 (centre of the rear trailing arm bush to the ground) on both sides of the vehicle. Subtract H5 from H4 to find the underbody height checking dimension.

5 Note that the difference between the heights on each side must not exceed 5 mm, with the driver's side slightly higher than the passenger side.

6 Check with your local Renault dealer, to check that these dimensions are within the range given for your vehicle. **Note:** *The specification varies according to the model and engine type of the vehicle and were not available to us at the time of writing.*

7 If the ride height differs greatly from that specified, examine the suspension components for signs of wear or damage.

8 If further checks or adjustments are required, take your vehicle to your local Renault dealer who will have the specialised equipment to do this.

15 Steering wheel – removal and refitting

Note: *All models are equipped with a driver's side airbag, and have the word AIRBAG stamped on the steering wheel pad. A new steering wheel retaining bolt will be required on refitting.*

Warning: Refer to the precautions on Airbag Systems in Chapter 12 before proceeding.

Removal

1 Remove the airbag unit (see Chapter 12), and disconnect the horn wiring connector(s)

2 Position the front wheels in the straight-ahead position and engage the steering lock.

3 Slacken and remove the steering wheel retaining bolt then mark the steering wheel and steering column shaft in relation to each other. Discard the bolt; a new one must be used on refitting.

4 Lift the steering wheel off the column splines, taking care not to damage the wiring.

If the wheel is tight, tap it up near the centre, using the palm of your hand, or twist it from side-to-side, whilst pulling upwards to release it from the shaft splines.

Refitting

5 Refitting is a reversal of removal, noting the following points:

a) *Prior to refitting, ensure that the indicator switch stalk is in its central position. Failure to do this could lead to the steering wheel lug breaking the switch tab as the steering wheel is refitted.*
b) *Refit the wheel, aligning the marks made on removal, then fit the new retaining bolt and tighten to the specified torque.*
c) *Ensure the front wheels are still in the straight-ahead position and check that the airbag contact unit is correctly centralised (Chapter 12). On completion, refit the airbag unit as described in Chapter 12.*

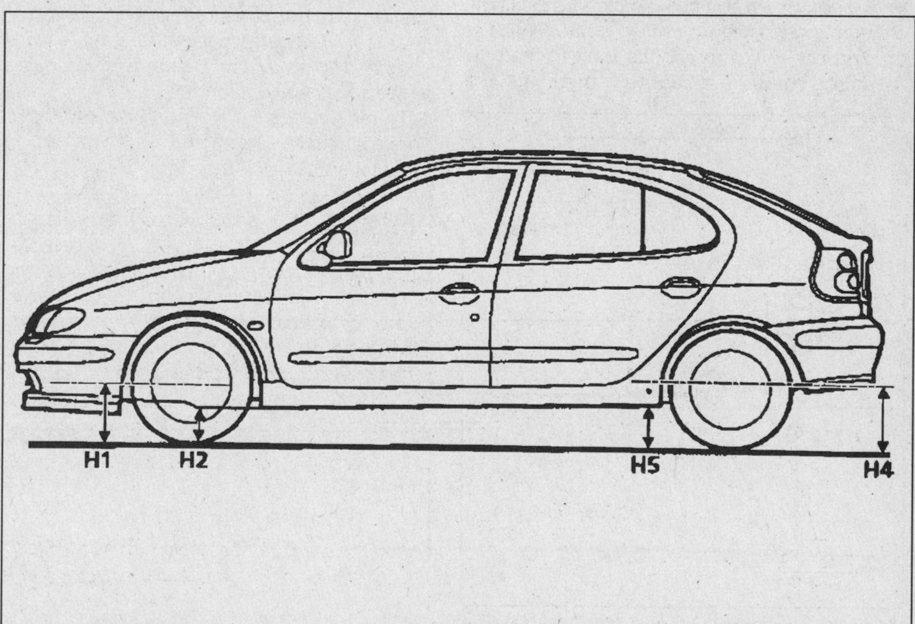

14.1 Underbody height measuring points. Note that H5 is measured from the centre of the trailing arm bush

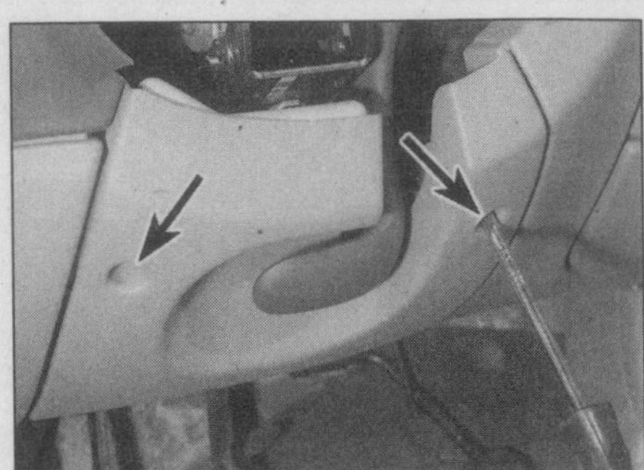
16.4 Undo the retaining screws (arrowed) and remove the steering column trim panel from the facia

16.5 Disconnect the ignition switch wiring and free it from any relevant clips and ties

16.6 Remove the screws (arrowed) securing the facia to the top of the steering column

16 Steering column – removal, inspection and refitting

Warning: All models are equipped with a driver's side airbag, refer to the precautions given in Chapter 12 before proceeding.

Removal

1 Disconnect the battery negative lead (refer to Chapter 5A).

2 Remove the steering wheel as described in Section 15.

3 Remove the complete combination switch assembly as described in Chapter 12, Section 4.

4 Slacken and remove the retaining screws and remove the steering column trim panel from the facia **(see illustration)**.

5 Trace the wiring back from the ignition switch, freeing it from any relevant clips and ties, and disconnect the wiring connectors **(see illustration)**.

6 Undo the two bolts securing the facia to the top of the steering column **(see illustration)**.

7 Apply the handbrake then jack up the front of the vehicle and support it on axle stands (see *Jacking and vehicle support*).

8 Working from underneath the vehicle, release the retaining clip (where fitted) and fold back the protective rubber cover to gain access to the steering column lower universal joint. Using paint or a suitable marker pen, make alignment marks between the steering column universal joint and the steering gear pinion. Slacken and remove the nut and clamp bolt securing the joint to the pinion.

Caution: To prevent damage to the airbag wiring contact unit, before dismantling the steering column, the steering wheel must be locked using a suitable tool with the wheels in the straight-ahead position.

9 From inside the vehicle, slacken and remove the four steering column mounting nuts and bolts **(see illustration)**. Unclip the steering column from the facia then release it from its mountings. On models equipped with power steering, also release the steering column lower gaiter from the bulkhead.

10 Disengage the universal joint from the steering gear pinion, and remove the steering column assembly from the vehicle **(see illustration)**.

16.9 Remove the mounting bolts and nuts . . .

16.10 . . . then free the universal joint and remove the column assembly from the vehicle

Inspection

11 The lower section of the steering column incorporates a telescopic safety feature. In the event of a front-end crash, the intermediate shaft collapses and prevents the steering wheel injuring the driver. Before refitting the steering column, the length of the intermediate shaft must be checked and compared with the figures given in the Specifications **(see illustration)**. If the length is shorter than specified, the complete steering column must be renewed. Damage to the intermediate shaft is also implied if it is found that the clamp bolt at its base cannot be inserted freely when refitting the column.

12 Check the steering shaft for signs of free play in the column bushes, and check the universal joints for signs of damage or roughness in the joint bearings. If damage or wear is found on the steering shaft universal

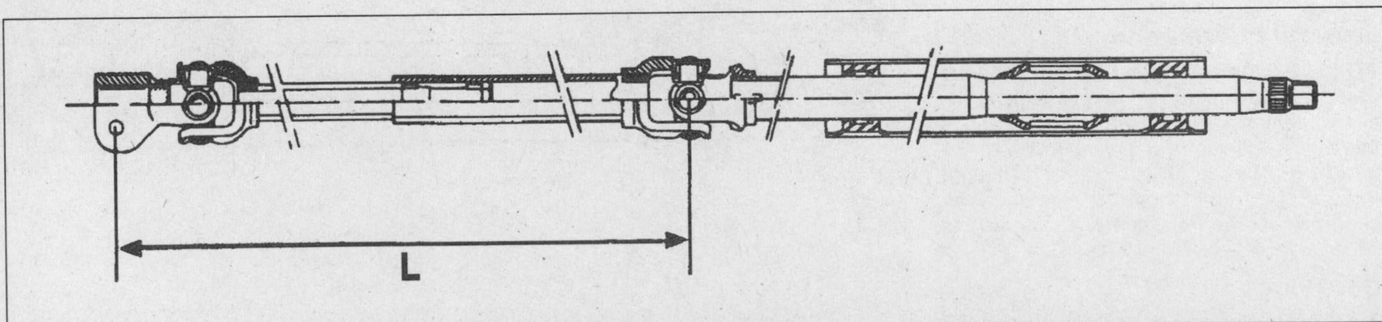

16.11 Steering column intermediate shaft checking dimension
See Specifications for dimension L

joints or shaft bushes, the column must be renewed as an assembly.

13 Inspect the column rubber gaiter/protective cover for signs of damage or deterioration and renew if necessary.

Refitting

14 Manoeuvre the steering column assembly into position. Engage the universal joint with the steering gear pinion, aligning the marks made prior to removal.

15 Refit and tighten the steering column mounting nuts and bolts. On models with power steering, refit the column gaiter to the bulkhead **(see illustration)**.

16 From underneath the vehicle, refit the universal joint clamp bolt and nut, and tighten it to the specified torque. Relocate the protective cover securely in position and (where necessary) secure it in position with a new clip. Lower the vehicle to the ground.

17 Refit the two bolts securing the facia to the top of the steering column, and tighten them securely. Refit the steering column trim panel to the facia.

18 Ensure the ignition switch wiring is correctly routed then reconnect it to the main wiring harness.

19 Refit the combination switch assembly as described in Chapter 12. Refit the airbag contact unit to the steering column.

20 Refit the steering wheel as described in Section 15 and reconnect the battery.

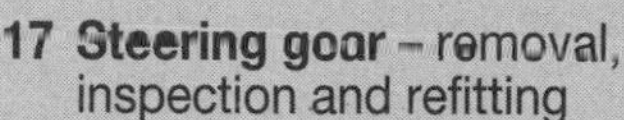

17 Steering gear – removal, inspection and refitting

Note: *New steering gear mounting nuts and bolts will be required on refitting.*

Removal

1 Chock the rear wheels, firmly apply the handbrake then jack up the front of the vehicle and support it on axle stands (see *Jacking and vehicle support*). Remove both front roadwheels and continue as described under the relevant sub-heading.

Manual steering gear

2 Remove the nuts securing the track rod

16.15 Tighten the column mounting nuts and bolts to the specified torque

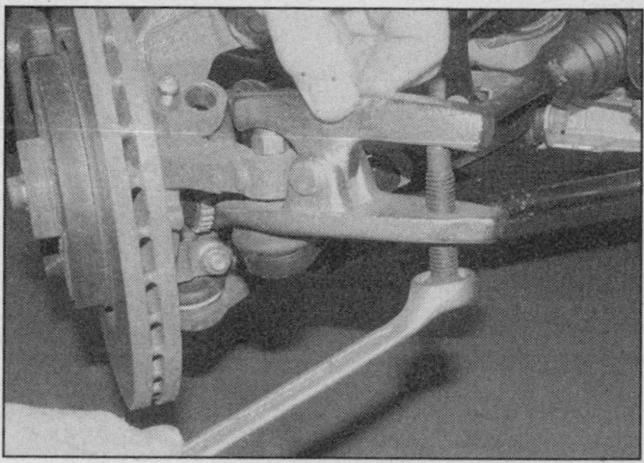

17.2 Using a universal balljoint separator to free the track rod balljoint from the swivel hub

balljoints to the swivel hubs. Release the balljoint tapered shanks using a universal balljoint separator **(see illustration)**.

3 Working from underneath the vehicle, release the retaining clip (where fitted) and fold back the protective rubber cover to gain access to the steering column lower universal joint. Using paint or a suitable marker pen, make alignment marks between the steering column universal joint and the steering gear pinion. Slacken and remove the nut and clamp bolt securing the joint to the pinion.

4 Remove the two nuts and bolts securing the steering gear assembly to the front subframe. Release the steering gear pinion from the universal joint, and manoeuvre the assembly sideways out of position and recover the rubber cover. Discard the mounting nuts and bolts; new ones should be used on refitting.

Power steering gear

5 Remove the exhaust downpipe as described in Chapter 4A or 4B. On left-hand drive models, if necessary, remove the air cleaner housing to improve access to the steering gear assembly.

6 Carry out the operations described in paragraphs 2 and 3.

Caution: To prevent damage to the airbag wiring contact unit, before dismantling the steering column, the steering wheel must be locked using a suitable tool with the wheels in the straight-ahead position.

7 Using brake hose clamps, clamp both the supply and return hoses near the power steering fluid reservoir. This will minimise fluid loss during subsequent operations.

8 Mark the unions to ensure that they are correctly positioned on reassembly, then unscrew the feed and return pipe union nuts from the steering gear assembly; be prepared for fluid spillage, and position a suitable container beneath the pipes whilst unscrewing the union nuts. Disconnect both pipes, and plug the pipe ends and steering gear orifices, to prevent fluid leakage and to keep dirt out of the hydraulic system. Remove the sealing rings from the union nuts and discard them; new ones should be used on refitting.

9 Unscrew the nuts/bolts securing the fluid feed and return pipes to the subframe and position both pipes clear of the steering gear.

10 Slacken and remove the steering gear mounting bolts and nuts then remove the left- and right-hand mounting clamp halves and the mounting rubbers **(see illustrations)**. Discard the mounting nuts and bolts; new ones should be used on refitting.

11 On Scénic models, remove the bolt securing the support bar to the front wing valance on the driver's side, and the nut securing it to the lower arm front pivot bolt and remove the support bar from the vehicle **(see illustration)**.

12 Release the steering gear pinion from the universal joint then manoeuvre the assembly out from the driver's side of the vehicle.

13 It may be necessary to remove the securing bolt from the engine/transmission

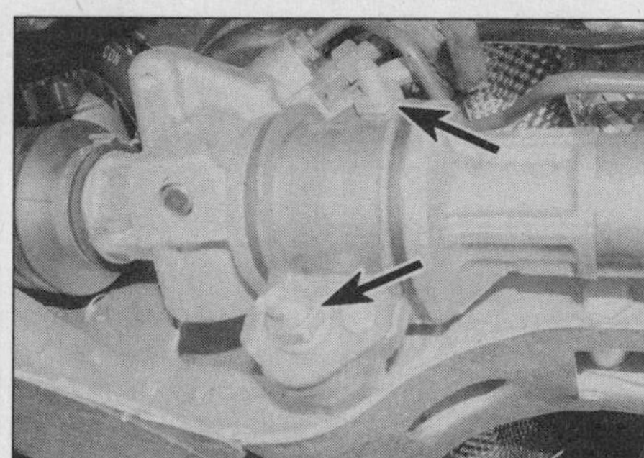

17.10a Undo the steering gear retaining bolt/nut (arrowed) . . .

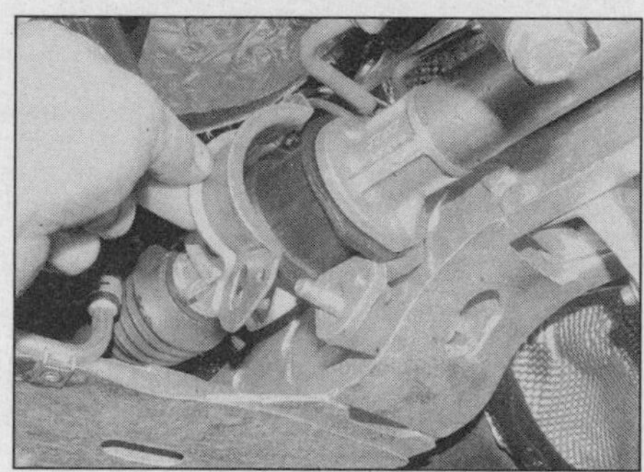

17.10b . . . then remove the mounting clamp

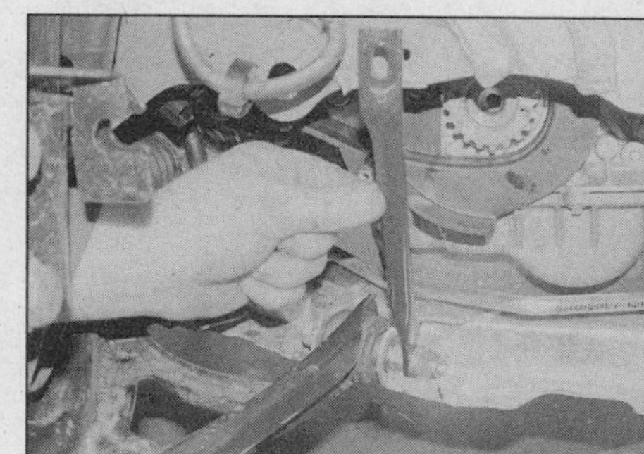

17.11 Removing the support bar

17.13 Where applicable, remove the engine/transmission stabiliser bar

stabiliser bar **(see illustration)** then have an assistant pull the engine/transmission forward as far as possible while the steering gear is manoeuvred from its location.

Inspection

14 Examine the steering gear assembly for signs of wear or damage, and check that the rack moves freely throughout the full length of its travel, with no signs of roughness or excessive free play between the steering gear pinion and rack. On models with power-assisted steering, inspect all the steering gear fluid unions for signs of leakage, and check that all union nuts are securely tightened.

15 Overhaul of the steering gear rack and pinion assembly is not possible. The only components which can be renewed are the steering gear gaiters, the track rod balljoints and the track rods. Track rod balljoint, steering gear gaiter and track rod renewal procedures are covered in other Sections of this Chapter.

Refitting

Manual steering gear

16 Manoeuvre the steering gear assembly and rubber cover into position. Engage the universal joint with the steering gear pinion splines, aligning the marks made prior to removal.

17 Insert the new mounting bolts then fit the nuts and tighten them to the specified torque.

18 Refit the universal joint clamp bolt and nut, and tighten it to the specified torque. Relocate the protective cover and secure it in position with a new cable tie.

19 Reconnect the track rod balljoints to the swivel hubs, and tighten their retaining nuts to the specified torque.

20 Refit the roadwheels, lower the vehicle to the ground and tighten the wheel bolts to the specified torque.

21 On completion check and, if necessary, adjust the front wheel alignment as described in Section 23.

Power steering gear

22 Manoeuvre the steering gear assembly and rubber cover into position from the driver's side of the vehicle. Engage the universal joint with the steering gear pinion splines, aligning the marks made prior to removal.

23 Fit the mounting rubbers to the steering gear and manoeuvre the mounting clamp halves into position. Fit the new mounting bolts and nuts tightening them by hand only at this stage.

24 Fit new sealing rings to the steering pipe unions nuts and reconnect the pipes to the steering gear. Screw each union nut in by a few turns then refit the pipe retaining clip nuts/bolts (as applicable) but do not tighten yet.

25 Tighten the steering gear mounting bolts and nuts to the specified torque setting then tighten the feed and return pipe union nuts to their specified torque settings. The pipe retaining clip nuts/bolts should then be securely tightened.

26 Refit the universal joint clamp bolt and nut, tightening it to the specified torque, then relocate the protective cover securely in position.

27 Reconnect the track rod balljoints to the swivel hubs, and tighten their retaining nuts to the specified torque.

28 Where applicable, refit the support bar to the front wing valance lower arm and the engine/stabiliser securing bolt.

29 Refit the exhaust system downpipe and (where removed) the air cleaner housing as described in Chapter 4A or 4B.

30 Refit the roadwheels, lower the vehicle to the ground and tighten the wheel bolts to the specified torque.

31 Remove the hose clamps and bleed the hydraulic system as described in Section 19.

32 On completion check and, if necessary, adjust the front wheel alignment as described in Section 23.

18.8 Unclip the power steering reservoir from the radiator cowling

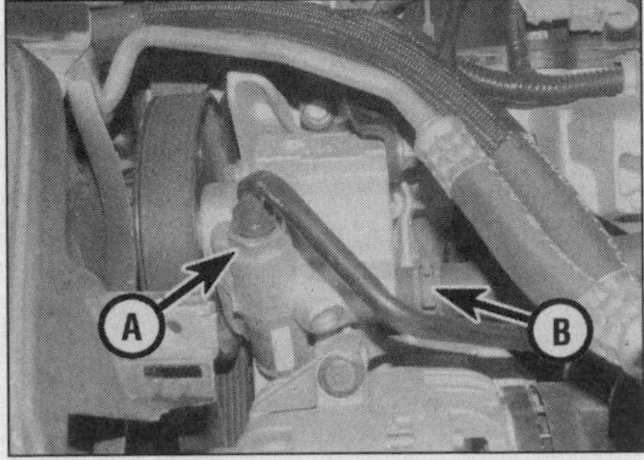

18.12 Power steering pump fluid supply hose (B) and pressure feed pipe union (A) – K4M engine

18 Power steering pump – removal and refitting

Note: *Renault state that a drivebelt must be renewed whenever it is removed.*

Note: *Where an alternator is fitted below the power steering pump, cover it with a plastic sheet or similar to prevent the entry of power steering fluid when the hoses are disconnected.*

Removal

1 Disconnect the battery negative terminal (refer to Chapter 5A).

2 Where fitted, remove the engine undertray and engine top cover.

3 Working as described in Chapter 1A or 1B, release the auxiliary drivebelt tension and disengage the drivebelt from the pump pulley. Note that the power steering pump pulley retaining bolts should be slackened before the belt is removed (except K4J and K4M engines), hold the pulley stationary with a suitable tool while the bolts are slackened.

4 Using brake hose clamps, clamp the pump supply hose. This will minimise fluid loss during subsequent operations.

Engines without air conditioning

5 Remove the three retaining bolts and remove the pulley from the pump, noting which way round it is fitted.

6 Disconnect the fluid supply hose from the pump then slacken the union nut, and disconnect the feed pipe. Be prepared for some fluid spillage as the pipe and hose are disconnected, and plug the hose/pipe end and pump unions, to minimise fluid loss and prevent the entry of dirt into the system. Discard the feed pipe union nut sealing ring, a new one should be used on refitting.

7 Slacken the bolts securing the power steering pump to its mounting bracket and remove the pump from the engine.

Engines with air conditioning

8 Where applicable, detach the power steering fluid reservoir from its mounting and move it to one side without disconnecting the fluid hoses **(see illustration)**.

9 On K4J and K4M engines, undo the nuts securing the fuel injector and fuel rail protective cover at the front of the inlet manifold. Release the wiring harness from the cable clips and remove the cover.

10 Release any fluid hoses/pipes from any clips or brackets to enable the hoses/pipes to be moved to one side, clear of the pump.

11 All models except K4J and K4M engines, remove the retaining bolts and remove the pulley from the pump.

12 Disconnect the fluid supply hose from the pump then slacken the union nut, and disconnect the pressure feed pipe **(see illustration)**. Be prepared for some fluid spillage as the pipe and hose are

18.14 Disconnect the fuel supply hose from the fuel rail for access to the pump rear mounting bolt

disconnected, and plug the hose/pipe end and pump unions, to minimise fluid loss and prevent the entry of dirt into the system. Discard the feed pipe union nut sealing ring, a new one should be used on refitting.

13 On Scénic models, remove the bolt securing the support bar to the inner front wing valance on the driver's side, and the nut securing it to the lower arm front pivot bolt then remove the support bar from the vehicle **(see illustration 17.11)**.

14 On K4J and K4M engines, bearing in mind the information given on depressurising the fuel system in Chapter 4A, and taking suitable safety precautions, disconnect the fuel supply hose from the fuel rail to gain access to the rear mounting bolt **(see illustration)**.

15 Slacken the bolts securing the power steering pump to its mounting bracket and remove the pump from the engine **(see illustrations)**.

16 On K4J and K4M engines, work through the openings in the pump pulley to slacken the bolts securing the front of the pump to the mounting bracket. Undo the rear mounting bolt and withdraw the pump from its mounting bracket **(see illustration)**.

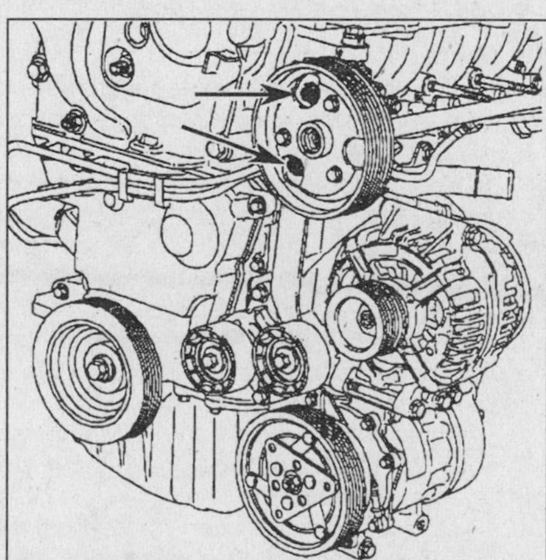

18.16 Slacken and remove the bolts (arrowed) through the openings in the pulley

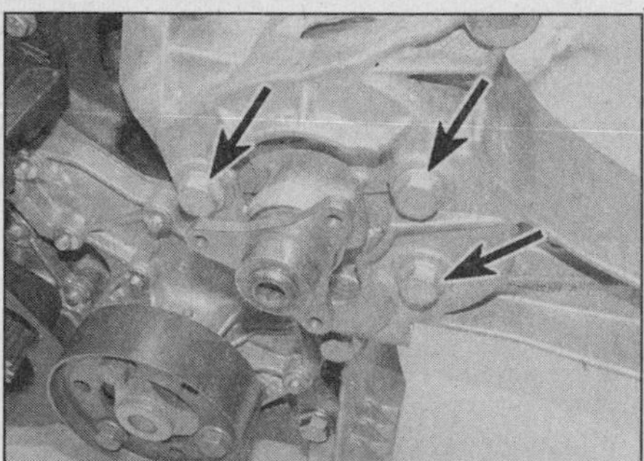

18.15a Slacken and remove the three bolts (arrowed) . . .

17 On models where the steering pump is fitted to the rear of the engine, it may be necessary to remove the securing bolt from the engine/transmission stabiliser bar then have an assistant pull the engine/transmission forward as far as possible while the steering pump is manoeuvred from its location **(see illustration 17.13)**.

Refitting

18 Manoeuvre the pump assembly back into position and securely tighten the mounting bolts.

19 Fit a new sealing ring to the feed pipe union and refit the pipe to the pump, tightening the union nut to the specified torque. Reconnect the supply pipe and securely tighten its retaining clip. Where necessary, refit the feed pipe and wiring mounting clamp bolt and tighten securely.

20 Refit the pulley, ensuring it is the correct way around, and refit the retaining bolts without tightening them at this stage.

21 Fit the drivebelt and tension as described in Chapter 1A or 1B. The pump pulley retaining bolts can then be securely tightened by holding the pulley stationary with a suitable tool.

22 Refit the power steering fluid reservoir and remove the hose clamps from the supply hose.

23 On K4J and K4M engines, refit the fuel rail as described in Chapter 4A.

24 On Scénic models, refit the support bar to the inner front wing valance on the driver's side.

25 Where applicable, refit the stabiliser bar to the engine/transmission and remove any protective covering used to prevent fluid entry into the alternator.

26 On completion, reconnect the battery and bleed the power steering hydraulic system as described in Section 19.

19 Power steering hydraulic system – bleeding

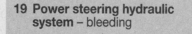

1 This procedure will only be necessary when any part of the hydraulic system has been disconnected, or if air has entered because of leakage.

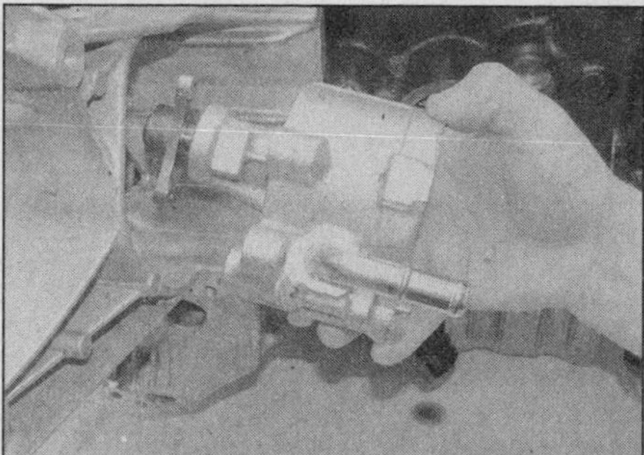

18.15b . . . and remove the power steering pump – F9Q 732 engine

2 Remove the fluid reservoir filler cap, and top-up the fluid level to the maximum mark, using only the specified fluid as described in *Weekly checks*.

3 With the engine stopped, slowly move the steering from lock-to-lock several times to expel trapped air, then top-up the level in the fluid reservoir. Repeat this procedure until the fluid level in the reservoir does not drop any further.

4 Start the engine. Slowly move the steering from lock-to-lock several times to expel any air remaining in the system. Repeat this procedure until bubbles cease to appear in the fluid reservoir.

5 If, when turning the steering, an abnormal noise is heard from the fluid pipes, it indicates that there is still air in the system. Check this by turning the wheels to the straight-ahead position and switching off the engine. If the fluid level in the reservoir rises, air is still present in the system, and further bleeding is necessary.

6 Once all traces of air have been removed, stop the engine and allow the system to cool. Once cool, check that the fluid level is up to the maximum mark on the power steering fluid reservoir; top-up if necessary.

20 Steering gear rubber gaiter – renewal

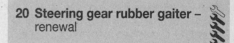

1 Remove the track rod end balljoint as described in Section 21.

2 Mark the correct fitted position of the gaiter on the track rod. Release the retaining clips, and slide the gaiter off the steering gear housing and track rod end.

3 Thoroughly clean the track rod and the steering gear housing, using fine abrasive paper to polish off any corrosion, burrs or sharp edges which might damage the sealing lips of the new gaiter on installation.

4 Recover the grease from inside the old gaiter. If it is uncontaminated with dirt or grit, apply it to the track rod inner balljoint. If the old grease is contaminated, or it is suspected that some has been lost, apply some new molybdenum disulphide grease.

21.3 Track rod end balljoint locking nut (arrowed)

21.4 Using a universal ball joint separator to release the track rod end balljoint from the swivel hub

5 Grease the inside of the new gaiter. Carefully slide the gaiter onto the track rod, and locate it on the steering gear housing. Align the outer edge of the gaiter with the mark made on the track rod prior to removal, then secure it in position with new clips.

6 Refit the track rod balljoint as described in Section 21.

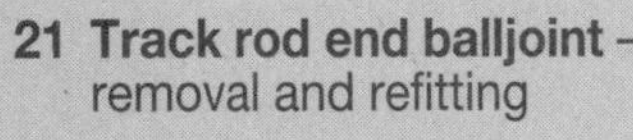

21 Track rod end balljoint – removal and refitting

Removal

1 Apply the handbrake, then jack up the front of the vehicle and support it on axle stands (see *Jacking and vehicle support*). Remove the appropriate front roadwheel.

2 If the balljoint is to be re-used, use a straight-edge and a scriber, or similar, to mark its relationship to the track rod.

3 Holding the balljoint, slacken the locknut by half a turn only, do not move the locknut from this position as it will serve as a reference mark on refitting **(see illustration)**.

4 Remove the nut securing the track rod balljoint to the swivel hub. Release the balljoint tapered shank using a universal balljoint separator **(see illustration)**. If the balljoint is to be re-used, protect the threaded end of the shank by screwing the nut back on a few turns before using the separator.

5 Counting the **exact** number of turns necessary to do so, unscrew the balljoint from the track rod.

6 Carefully clean the balljoint and the threads. Renew the balljoint if its movement is sloppy or if it is too stiff, if it is excessively worn, or if it is damaged in any way. Carefully check the shank taper and threads. If the balljoint gaiter is damaged, the complete balljoint must be renewed; it is not possible to obtain the gaiter separately.

Refitting

7 Screw the balljoint into the track rod by the number of turns noted on removal. This align the marks that were made (if applicable) on removal.

8 Refit the balljoint shank to the swivel hub, and tighten the retaining nut to the specified torque. If difficulty is experienced due to the balljoint shank rotating, jam it by exerting pressure on the underside of the balljoint, using a tyre lever or a jack.

9 Refit the roadwheel, lower the vehicle to the ground and tighten the roadwheel bolts to the specified torque.

10 Check the front wheel toe setting as described in Section 23 then tighten the balljoint clamp bolt to the specified torque.

22 Track rod and inner balljoint – removal and refitting

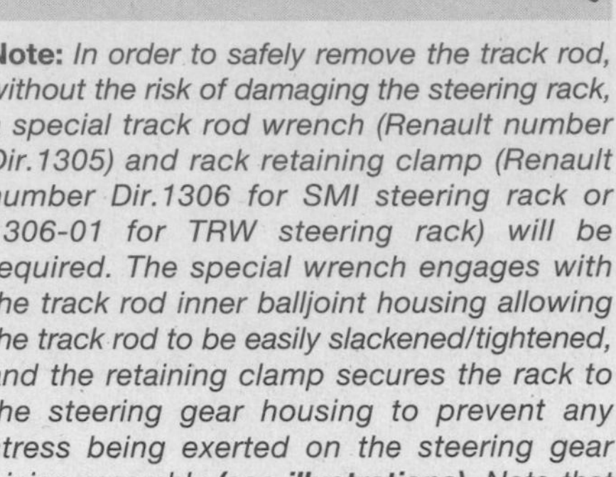

Note: *In order to safely remove the track rod, without the risk of damaging the steering rack, a special track rod wrench (Renault number Dir.1305) and rack retaining clamp (Renault number Dir.1306 for SMI steering rack or 1306-01 for TRW steering rack) will be required. The special wrench engages with the track rod inner balljoint housing allowing the track rod to be easily slackened/tightened, and the retaining clamp secures the rack to the steering gear housing to prevent any stress being exerted on the steering gear pinion assembly* ***(see illustrations)****. Note that without access to the special tools, track rod removal will be difficult, especially without causing damage.*

Note: *There are two different types of steering gear assemblies fitted to these vehicles; the steering racks are manufactured by either SMI or TRW; the type of rack fitted can be identified from the manufacturing markings cast onto the steering gear housing. If work is being carried out on a SMI steering rack note that a new track rod lockwasher assembly must be used on refitting.*

Removal

1 Remove the track rod end balljoint as described in Section 22.

2 Cut the retaining clips, and slide the steering gear gaiter off the track rod. It is recommended that the gaiter is renewed, regardless of its apparent condition.

3 In the absence of the special tools, using a suitable pair of grips, unscrew the track rod inner balljoint from the steering rack end. Prevent the steering rack from turning by holding the balljoint lockwasher/steering rack with a second pair of grips.

Caution: Take care not to mark the surfaces of the rack and balljoint.

4 Remove the track rod assembly from the steering rack. On SMI steering

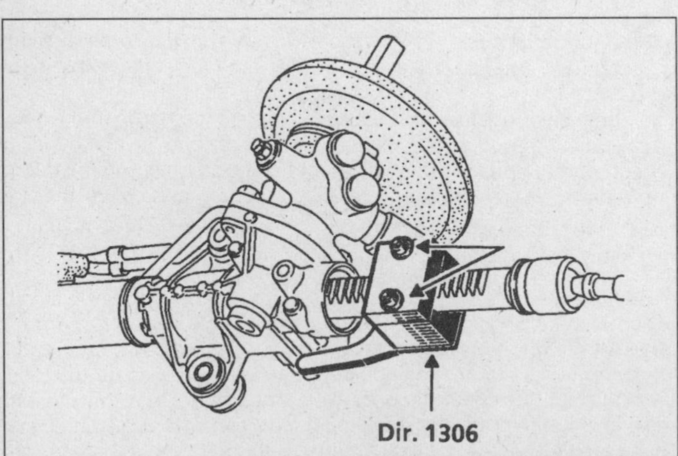

22.0a Steering rack secured with a retaining clamp

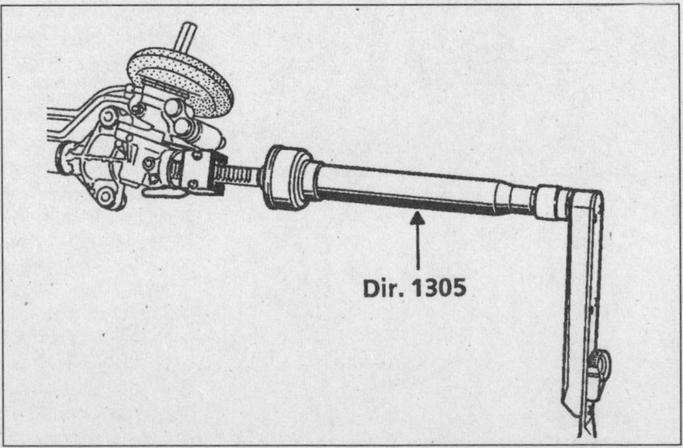

22.0b Track rod balljoints slackened with a special wrench

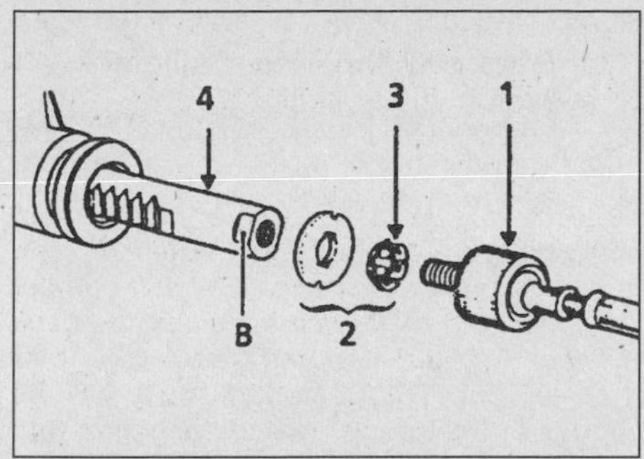

22.7 On models fitted with a SMI steering gear assembly, ensure the new lockwasher and locking ring are correctly assembled and fit them to the end of the track rod

1 Track rod
2 Locking ring
3 Lockwasher
4 Steering gear
B Flats on steering end

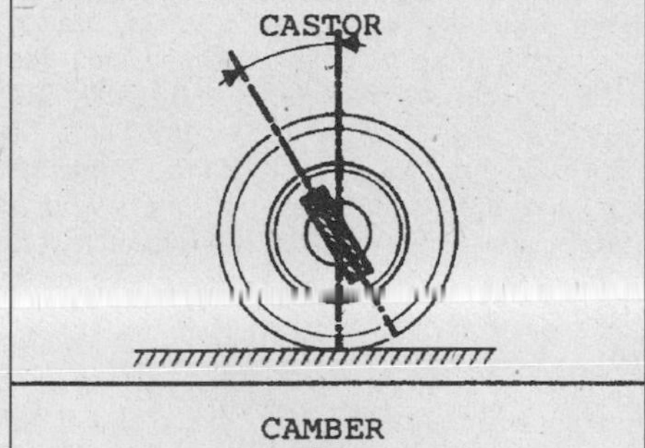

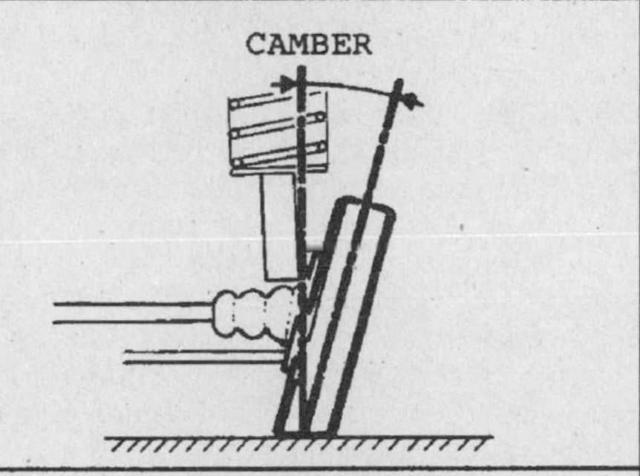

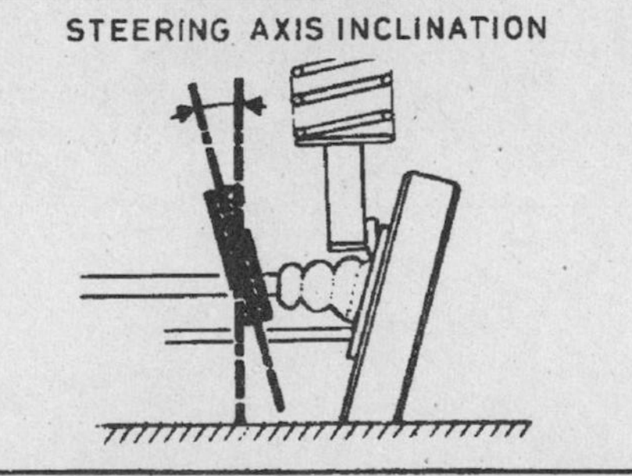

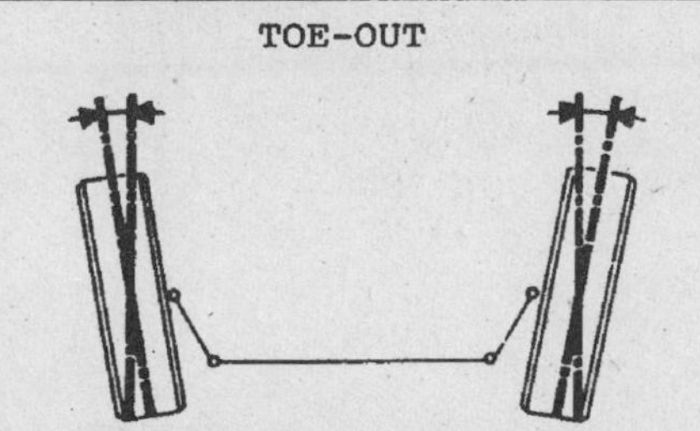

23.1 Wheel alignment and steering angles

gear assemblies, discard the lockwasher assembly; a new one must be used on refitting.

5 Examine the inner balljoint for signs of slackness or tight spots. Check that the track rod itself is straight and free from damage. If necessary, renew the track rod.

Refitting

6 Prior to refitting the track rod remove all traces of locking compound from the rack and track rod threads.

7 On models fitted with a SMI steering gear assembly, ensure the new lockwasher and locking ring are correctly assembled and fit them to the end of the track rod **(see illustration)**.

8 Apply a coat of locking compound (Renault recommend the use of Loctite Frenbloc – available from your Renault dealer) to the threads of the track rod then fit the track rod to the end of the steering rack. Using the method employed on removal, tighten the track rod inner balljoint to the specified torque, taking great care not to marks either the rack or the balljoint. On the SMI steering gear, whilst tightening the track rod ensure the tabs on the lock washer engage with the flats on the steering end.

9 Slide the new gaiter onto the track rod end, and locate it on the steering gear housing. Turn the steering from lock-to-lock to check that the gaiter is correctly positioned, then secure it with new retaining clips.

10 Refit the track rod end balljoint as described in Section 22.

23 Wheel alignment and steering angles – general information

Definitions

1 A car's steering and suspension geometry is defined in four basic settings **(see illustration)** – all angles are expressed in degrees (toe settings are also expressed as a measurement); the steering axis is defined as an imaginary line drawn through the axis of the suspension strut, extended where necessary to contact the ground.

2 Camber is the angle between each roadwheel and a vertical line drawn through its centre and tyre contact patch, when viewed from the front or rear of the car. Positive camber is when the roadwheels are tilted outwards from the vertical at the top; negative camber is when they are tilted inwards. The camber angle is not adjustable

3 Castor is the angle between the steering axis and a vertical line drawn through each roadwheels centre and tyre contact patch, when viewed from the side of the car. Positive castor is when the steering axis is tilted so that it contacts the ground ahead of the vertical; negative castor is when it contacts the ground behind the vertical. The castor angle is not adjustable.

4 Steering axis inclination is the angle between the steering axis and a vertical line drawn through each roadwheels centre and tyre contact patch, when viewed from the front or rear of the car. Steering axis inclination is not adjustable.

5 Toe is the difference, viewed from above, between lines drawn through the roadwheel centres and the car's centre-line. 'Toe-in' is when the roadwheels point inwards, towards each other at the front, while 'toe-out' is when they splay outwards from each other at the front.

6 The front wheel alignment (toe-setting) is adjusted by screwing the track rod in or out of its balljoints, to alter the effective length of the track rod assembly. The rear wheel toe setting is not adjustable.

Checking and adjustment

7 Due to the special measuring equipment necessary to check the wheel alignment and steering angles, and the skill required to use it properly, the checking and adjustment of these settings is best left to a Renault dealer or similar expert. Note that most tyre-fitting shops now possess sophisticated checking equipment. The following is provided as a guide, should the owner decide to carry out a DIY check.

Front wheel alignment (toe-setting)

8 For **accurate** checking, the vehicle **must** be at the kerb weight, ie, unladen and with a full tank of fuel.

9 Before starting work, check first that the tyre sizes and types are as specified, then check the tyre pressures and tread wear, the roadwheel run-out, the condition of the hub bearings, the steering wheel free play, and the condition of the front suspension components (see *Weekly checks* and Chapter 1A or 1B). Correct any faults found.

10 Park the vehicle on level ground, check that the front roadwheels are in the straight-ahead position, then rock the rear and front ends to settle the suspension. Release the handbrake, and roll the vehicle backwards 1 metre, then forwards again, to relieve any stresses in the steering and suspension components.

11 Measure the distance between the front edges of the wheel rims and the rear edges of the rims. Subtract the rear measurement from the front measurement, and check that the result is within the specified range.

12 If adjustment is necessary, apply the handbrake, then jack up the front of the vehicle and support it securely on axle stands (see *Jacking and vehicle support*). Turn the steering wheel onto full-left lock, and record the number of exposed threads on the right-hand track rod end. Now turn the steering onto full-right lock, and record the number of threads on the left-hand side. If there are the same number of threads visible on both sides, then subsequent adjustment should be made equally on both sides. If there are more threads visible on one side than the other, it will be necessary to compensate for this during adjustment. **Note:** *It is most important that after adjustment, the same number of threads are visible on each track rod end.*

13 First clean the track rod threads; if they are corroded, apply penetrating fluid before starting adjustment. Release the rubber gaiter outboard clips, and peel back the gaiters; apply a smear of grease to the inside of the gaiters, so that both are free, and will not be twisted or strained as their respective track rods are rotated.

14 Use a straight-edge and a scriber or similar to mark the relationship of each track rod to its balljoint then slacken the balljoint clamp bolt.

15 Alter the length of the track rods, bearing in mind the note made in paragraph 12. **Note:** *One complete rotation of the track rod equals approximately 30' (3 mm) of adjustment.* Screw them into or out off the balljoints, rotating the track rod using an open-ended spanner fitted to the flats provided on the track rod **(see illustration)**. Shortening the track rods (screwing them into their balljoints) will reduce toe-in/increase toe-out.

16 When the setting is correct, tighten the balljoint clamp bolts. Check that the balljoints are seated correctly in their sockets, and count the exposed threads to check the length of both track rods. If they are not the same, then the adjustment has not been made equally, and problems will be encountered with tyre scrubbing in turns; also, the steering wheel spokes will no longer be horizontal when the wheels are in the straight-ahead position.

17 If the track rod lengths are the same, lower the vehicle to the ground and recheck the toe setting; re-adjust if necessary. When the setting is correct, tighten the track rod balljoint clamp bolts to the specified torque. Ensure that the rubber gaiters are seated correctly, and are not twisted or strained, and secure them in position with new retaining clips.

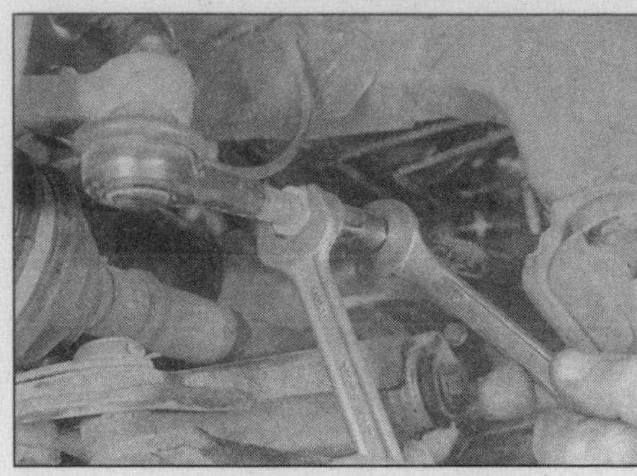

23.15 Adjusting the front wheel alignment (toe setting)

Chapter 11
Bodywork and fittings

Contents

Degrees of difficulty

Easy, suitable for novice with little experience 	**Fairly easy,** suitable for beginner with some experience 	**Fairly difficult,** suitable for competent DIY mechanic 	**Difficult,** suitable for experienced DIY mechanic 	**Very difficult,** suitable for expert DIY or professional

Specifications

Torque wrench setting	**Nm**	**lbf ft**
Seat belt mounting bolts	25	18

1 General information

The bodyshell and floorpan are manufactured from pressed-steel, and form an integral part of the vehicle's structure (monocoque), without the need for a separate chassis. Most components are welded together, but some use is made of structural adhesives.

Various areas of the structure are strengthened to provide for suspension, steering and engine mounting points, and load distribution.

Scénic models are fitted with front wings manufactured from a polymer compound, which can withstand an impact of up to 10 mph (16 km/h) without sustaining permanent damage.

Corrosion protection is applied to all new vehicles. Various anti-corrosion preparations are used, including galvanising, zinc phosphatisation, and PVC underseal. The bonnet, door, and some other vulnerable panels are made of zinc-coated metal, and are further protected by being coated with an anti-chip primer before being sprayed. Protective wax is injected into the box sections and other hollow cavities.

Extensive use is made of plastic for peripheral components, such as the radiator grille, bumpers and wheel trims, and for much of the interior trim. Plastic wheelarch liners are fitted, to protect the metal body panels against corrosion due to a build-up of road dirt.

Interior fittings are to a high standard on all models, and a wide range of optional equipment is available throughout the range.

Caution: If the vehicle is equipped with a radio/cassette unit with a built-in security code, make sure you know the correct security code before you disconnect the battery.

2 Maintenance – bodywork and underframe

The general condition of a vehicle's bodywork is the one thing that significantly affects its value. Maintenance is easy, but needs to be regular. Neglect, particularly after minor damage, can lead quickly to further deterioration and costly repair bills. It is important also to keep watch on those parts of the vehicle not immediately visible, for instance the underside, inside all the wheelarches, and the lower part of the engine compartment.

The basic maintenance routine for the bodywork is washing – preferably with a lot of water, from a hose. This will remove all the loose solids which may have stuck to the vehicle. It is important to flush these off in such a way as to prevent grit from scratching the finish. The wheelarches and underframe need washing in the same way, to remove any accumulated mud which will retain moisture and tend to encourage rust. Paradoxically enough, the best time to clean the underframe and wheelarches is in wet weather, when the mud is thoroughly wet and soft. In very wet weather, the underframe is usually cleaned of large accumulations automatically, and this is a good time for inspection.

Periodically, except on vehicles with a wax-based underbody protective coating, it is a good idea to have the whole of the underframe of the vehicle steam-cleaned, engine compartment included, so that a thorough inspection can be carried out to see what minor repairs and renovations are necessary. Steam cleaning is available at many garages, and is necessary for the removal of the accumulation of oily grime, which sometimes is allowed to become thick in certain areas. If steam-cleaning facilities are not available, there are some excellent grease solvents available which can be brush-applied; the dirt can then be simply hosed off. Note that these methods should not be used on vehicles with wax-based underbody protective coating, or the coating will be removed. Such vehicles should be inspected annually, preferably just before Winter, when the underbody should be washed down, and repair any damage to the wax coating. Ideally, a completely fresh coat should be applied. It would also be worth considering the use of such wax-based protection for injection into door panels, sills, box sections, etc, as an additional safeguard against rust damage, where such protection is not provided by the vehicle manufacturer.

After washing paintwork, wipe off with a chamois leather to give an unspotted clear finish. A coat of clear protective wax polish will give added protection against chemical pollutants in the air. If the paintwork sheen has dulled or oxidised, use a cleaner/polisher combination to restore the brilliance of the shine. This requires a little effort, but such dulling is usually caused because regular washing has been neglected. Care needs to be taken with metallic paintwork, as special non-abrasive cleaner/polisher is required to avoid damage to the finish. Always check that the door and ventilator opening drain holes and pipes are completely clear, so that water can be drained out. Brightwork should be treated in the same way as paintwork. Windscreens and windows can be kept clear of the smeary film which often appears, by proprietary glass cleaner. Never use any form of wax or other body or chromium polish on glass.

3 Maintenance – upholstery and carpets

Mats and carpets should be brushed or vacuum-cleaned regularly, to keep them free of grit. If they are badly stained, remove them from the vehicle for scrubbing or sponging, and make quite sure they are dry before refitting. Seats and interior trim panels can be kept clean by wiping with a damp cloth. If they do become stained (which can be more apparent on light-coloured upholstery), use a little liquid detergent and a soft nail brush to scour the grime out of the grain of the material. Do not forget to keep the headlining clean in the same way as the upholstery. When using liquid cleaners inside the vehicle, do not over-wet the surfaces being cleaned. Excessive damp could get into the seams and padded interior, causing stains, offensive odours or even rot. If the inside of the vehicle gets wet accidentally, it is worthwhile taking some trouble to dry it out properly, particularly where carpets are involved. *Do not leave oil or electric heaters inside the vehicle for this purpose.*

4 Minor body damage – repair

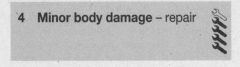

Repairs of minor scratches in bodywork

If the scratch is very superficial, and does not penetrate to the metal of the bodywork, repair is very simple. Lightly rub the area of the scratch with a paintwork renovator or a very fine cutting paste to remove loose paint from the scratch, and to clear the surrounding bodywork of wax polish. Rinse the area with clean water.

Apply touch-up paint to the scratch using a fine paint brush; continue to apply fine layers of paint until the surface of the paint in the scratch is level with the surrounding paintwork. Allow the new paint at least two weeks to harden, then blend it into the surrounding paintwork by rubbing the scratch area with a paintwork renovator or a very fine cutting paste. Finally, apply wax polish.

Where the scratch has penetrated right through to the metal of the bodywork, causing the metal to rust, a different repair technique is required. Remove any loose rust from the bottom of the scratch with a penknife, then apply rust-inhibiting paint to prevent the formation of rust in the future. Using a rubber or nylon applicator, fill the scratch with bodystopper paste. If required, this paste can be mixed with cellulose thinners to provide a very thin paste which is ideal for filling narrow scratches. Before the stopper-paste in the scratch hardens, wrap a piece of smooth cotton rag around the top of a finger. Dip the finger in cellulose thinners, and quickly sweep it across the surface of the stopper-paste in the scratch; this will ensure that the surface of the stopper-paste is slightly hollowed. The scratch can now be painted over as described earlier in this Section.

Repairs of dents in bodywork

When deep denting of the vehicle's bodywork has taken place, the first task is to pull the dent out, until the affected bodywork almost attains its original shape. There is little point in trying to restore the original shape completely, as the metal in the damaged area will have stretched on impact, and cannot be reshaped fully to its original contour. It is better to bring the level of the dent up to a point which is about 3 mm below the level of the surrounding bodywork. In cases where the dent is very shallow anyway, it is not worth trying to pull it out at all. If the underside of the dent is accessible, it can be hammered out gently from behind, using a mallet with a wooden or plastic head. Whilst doing this, hold a suitable block of wood firmly against the outside of the panel, to absorb the impact from the hammer blows and thus prevent a large area of the bodywork from being 'belled-out'.

Should the dent be in a section of the bodywork which has a double skin, or some other factor making it inaccessible from behind, a different technique is called for. Drill several small holes through the metal inside the area – particularly in the deeper section. Then screw long self-tapping screws into the holes, just sufficiently for them to gain a good purchase in the metal. Now the dent can be pulled out by pulling on the protruding heads of the screws with a pair of pliers.

The next stage of the repair is the removal of the paint from the damaged area, and from an inch or so of the surrounding 'sound' bodywork. This is accomplished most easily by using a wire brush or abrasive pad on a power drill, although it can be done just as effectively by hand, using sheets of abrasive paper. To complete the preparation for filling, score the surface of the bare metal with a screwdriver or the tang of a file, or alternatively, drill small holes in the affected area. This will provide a good 'key' for the filler paste.

To complete the repair, see the Section on filling and respraying.

Repairs of rust holes or gashes in bodywork

Remove all paint from the affected area, and from an inch or so of the surrounding 'sound' bodywork, using an abrasive pad or a wire brush on a power drill. If these are not available, a few sheets of abrasive paper will do the job most effectively. With the paint removed, you will be able to judge the severity of the corrosion, and therefore decide whether to renew the whole panel (if this is possible) or to repair the affected area. New body panels are not as expensive as most people think, and it is often quicker and more satisfactory to fit a new panel than to attempt to repair large areas of corrosion.

Remove all fittings from the affected area, except those which will act as a guide to the original shape of the damaged bodywork (eg headlamp shells etc). Then, using tin snips or a hacksaw blade, remove all loose metal and any other metal badly affected by corrosion. Hammer the edges of the hole inwards, to create a slight depression for the filler paste.

Wire-brush the affected area to remove the powdery rust from the surface of the remaining metal. Paint the affected area with rust-inhibiting paint; if the back of the rusted area is accessible, treat this also.

Before filling can take place, it will be necessary to block the hole in some way. This can be achieved with aluminium or plastic mesh, or aluminium tape.

Aluminium or plastic mesh, or glass-fibre matting, is probably the best material to use for a large hole. Cut a piece to the approximate size and shape of the hole to be filled, then position it in the hole so that its edges are below the level of the surrounding bodywork. It can be retained in position by several blobs of filler paste around its periphery.

Aluminium tape should be used for small or very narrow holes. Pull a piece off the roll, trim it to the approximate size and shape required, then pull off the backing paper (if used) and stick the tape over the hole; it can be overlapped if the thickness of one piece is insufficient. Burnish down the edges of the tape with the handle of a screwdriver or similar, to ensure that the tape is securely attached to the metal underneath.

Bodywork repairs – filling and respraying

Before using this Section, see the Sections on dent, deep scratch, rust holes and gash repairs.

Many types of bodyfiller are available, but generally speaking, those proprietary kits which contain a tin of filler paste and a tube of resin hardener are best for this type of repair which can be used directly from the tube. A wide, flexible plastic or nylon applicator will be found invaluable for imparting a smooth and well-contoured finish to the surface of the filler.

Mix up a little filler on a clean piece of card or board – measure the hardener carefully (follow the maker's instructions on the pack), otherwise the filler will set too rapidly or too slowly. Using the applicator, apply the filler paste to the prepared area; draw the applicator across the surface of the filler to achieve the correct contour and to level the surface. When a contour that approximates to the correct one is achieved, stop working the paste – if you carry on too long, the paste will become sticky and begin to 'pick-up' on the applicator. Continue to add thin layers of filler paste at 20-minute intervals, until the level of the filler is just proud of the surrounding bodywork.

Once the filler has hardened, the excess can be removed using a metal plane or file. From then on, progressively-finer grades of abrasive paper should be used, starting with a 40-grade production paper, and finishing with a 400-grade wet-and-dry paper. Always wrap the abrasive paper around a flat rubber, cork, or wooden block – otherwise the surface of the filler will not be completely flat. During the smoothing of the filler surface, the wet-and-dry paper should be periodically rinsed in water. This will ensure that a very smooth finish is imparted to the filler at the final stage.

At this stage, the 'dent' should be surrounded by a ring of bare metal, which in turn should be encircled by the finely 'feathered' edge of the good paintwork. Rinse the repair area with clean water, until all the dust produced by the rubbing-down operation has gone.

Spray the whole area with a light coat of primer – this will show up any imperfections in the surface of the filler. Repair these imperfections with fresh filler paste or bodystopper, and again smooth the surface with abrasive paper. If bodystopper is used, it can be mixed with cellulose thinners, to form a thin paste which is ideal for filling small holes. Repeat this spray-and-repair procedure until you are satisfied that the surface of the filler, and the feathered edge of the paintwork, are perfect. Clean the repair area with clean water, and allow to dry fully.

The repair area is now ready for final spraying. Paint spraying must be carried out in a warm, dry, windless and dust-free atmosphere. This condition can be created artificially if you have access to a large indoor working area, but if you are forced to work in the open, you will have to pick your day very carefully. If you are working indoors, dousing the floor in the work area with water will help to settle the dust which would otherwise be in the atmosphere. If the repair area is confined to one body panel, mask off the surrounding panels; this will help to minimise the effects of a slight mis-match in paint colours. Bodywork fittings (eg chrome strips, door handles etc) will also need to be masked off. Use genuine masking tape, and several thickness of newspaper, for the masking operations.

Before starting to spray, agitate the aerosol can thoroughly, then spray a test area (an old tin, or similar) until the technique is mastered. Cover the repair area with a thick coat of primer; the thickness should be built up using several thin layers of paint, rather than one thick one. Using 400 grade wet-and-dry paper, rub down the surface of the primer until it is smooth. While doing this, the work area should be thoroughly doused with water, and the wet-and-dry paper periodically rinsed in water. Allow to dry before spraying on more paint.

Spray on the top coat, again building up the thickness by using several thin layers of paint. Start spraying at the top of the repair area, and then, using a side-to-side motion, work downwards until the whole repair area and about 2 inches of the surrounding original paintwork is covered. Remove all masking material 10 to 15 minutes after spraying on the final coat of paint.

Allow the new paint at least two weeks to harden, then, using a paintwork renovator or a very fine cutting paste, blend the edges of the paint into the existing paintwork. Finally, apply wax polish.

Plastic components

With the use of more and more plastic body components by the vehicle manufacturers (eg bumpers. spoilers, and in some cases major body panels), rectification of more serious damage to such items has become a matter of either entrusting repair work to a specialist in this field, or renewing complete components. Repair of such damage by the DIY owner is not feasible, owing to the cost of the equipment and materials required for effecting such repairs. The basic technique involves making a groove along the line of the crack in the plastic, using a rotary burr in a power drill. The damaged part is then welded back together, using a hot air gun to heat up and fuse a plastic filler rod into the groove. Any excess plastic is then removed, and the area rubbed down to a smooth finish. It is important that a filler rod of the correct plastic is used, as body components can be made of a variety of different types (eg polycarbonate, ABS, polypropylene).

Damage of a less serious nature (abrasions, minor cracks etc) can be repaired by the DIY owner using a two-part epoxy filler repair material which can be used directly from the tube. Once mixed in equal proportions, this is used in similar fashion to the bodywork filler used on metal panels. The filler is usually cured in twenty to thirty minutes, ready for sanding and painting.

If the owner is renewing a complete component himself, or if he has repaired it with epoxy filler, he will be left with the problem of finding a suitable paint for finishing which is compatible with the type of plastic used. At one time, the use of a universal paint was not possible, owing to the complex range of plastics met with in body component applications. Standard paints, generally speaking, will not bond to plastic or rubber satisfactorily, but professional matched paints, to match any plastic or rubber finish, can be obtained from some dealers. However, it is now possible to obtain a plastic body parts finishing kit which consists of a pre-primer treatment, a primer and coloured top coat. Full instructions are normally supplied with a kit, but basically the method of use is to first apply the pre-primer to the component concerned, and allow it to dry for up to 30 minutes. Then the primer is applied, and left to dry for about an hour before finally applying the special-coloured top coat. The result is a correctly coloured component, where the paint will flex with the plastic or rubber, a property that standard paint does not normally posses.

5 Major body damage – repair

Where serious damage has occurred, or large areas need renewal due to neglect, it means that complete new panels will need welding-in, and this is best left to professionals. If the damage is due to impact, it will also be necessary to check completely the alignment of the bodyshell, and this can only be carried out accurately by a Renault dealer using special jigs. If the body is left misaligned, it is primarily dangerous, as the car will not handle properly, and secondly, uneven stresses will be imposed on the steering, suspension and possibly transmission, causing abnormal wear, or complete failure, particularly to such items as the tyres.

6 Front bumper – removal and refitting

Removal

1 To make access easier, apply the handbrake then jack up the front of the vehicle and support it on axle stands (see *Jacking and vehicle support*).

2 Slacken and remove the screws securing the front wheelarch liners to each end of the bumper **(see illustration)**.

3 On models with front foglights, disconnect the foglight wiring from the back of the light unit.

4 Slacken and remove the bolts securing the left- and right-hand ends of the bumper in position. Where applicable, undo the two bolts securing the rear of the bumper under cover to the subframe **(see illustrations)**.

5 Unscrew the centre retaining bolt from the top of the bumper then, with the aid of an assistant, release the bumper ends and manoeuvre the bumper assembly forwards, away from the vehicle **(see illustrations)**.

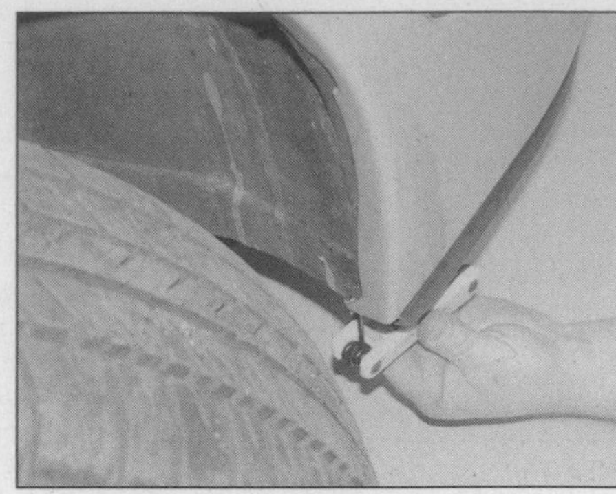

6.2 Undo the lower wheelarch liner retaining screws

6 On models with headlight washers, release the retaining nut(s) and disconnect the washer supply hose(s) as the bumper is withdrawn.

7 Inspect the bumper mountings for signs of damage and renew if necessary.

Refitting

8 Refitting is a reverse of the removal procedure, ensuring that the bumper mounting bolts are securely tightened.

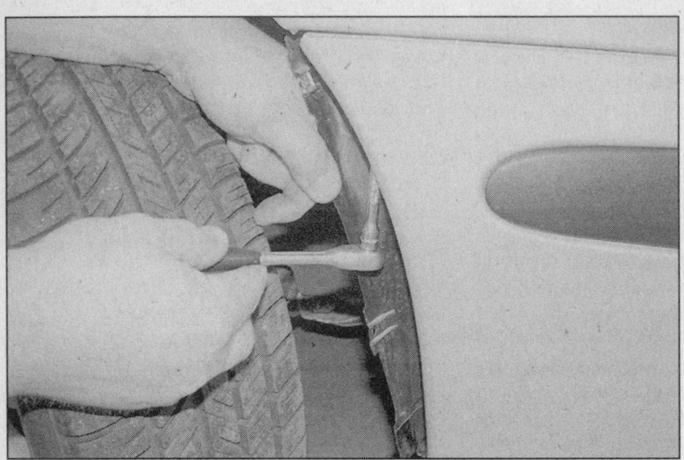

6.4a Remove the bumper end bolts . . .

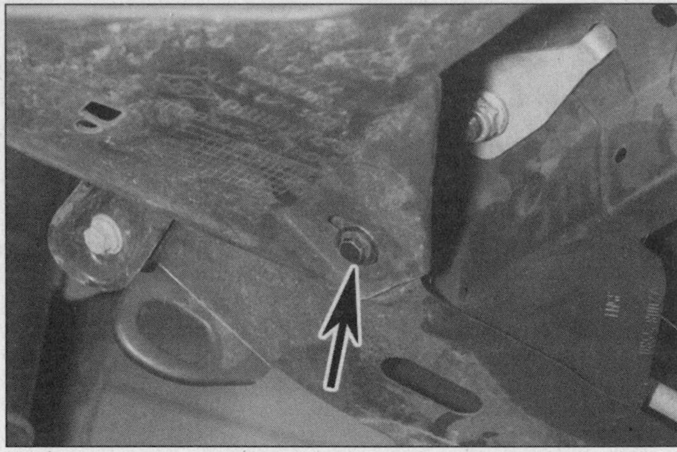

6.4b . . . and the bolts (arrowed) securing the undercover to the subframe

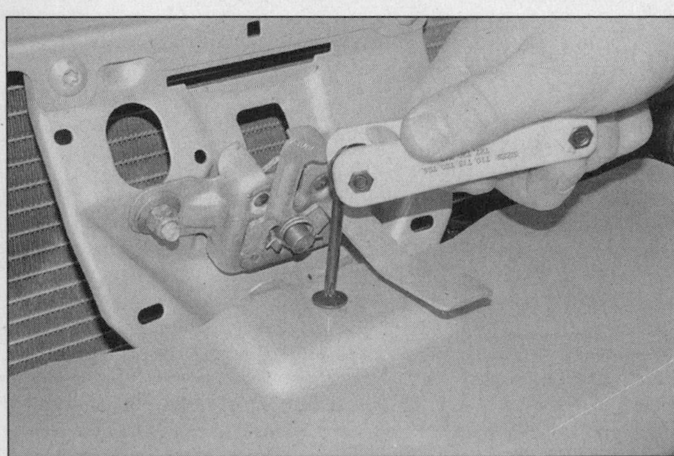

6.5a Undo the retaining bolt from the centre of the bumper . . .

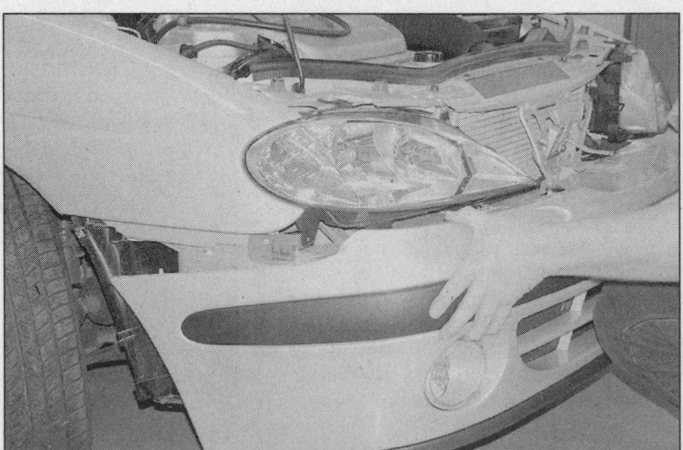

6.5b . . . then release the bumper ends and manoeuvre the bumper forwards and away from the vehicle

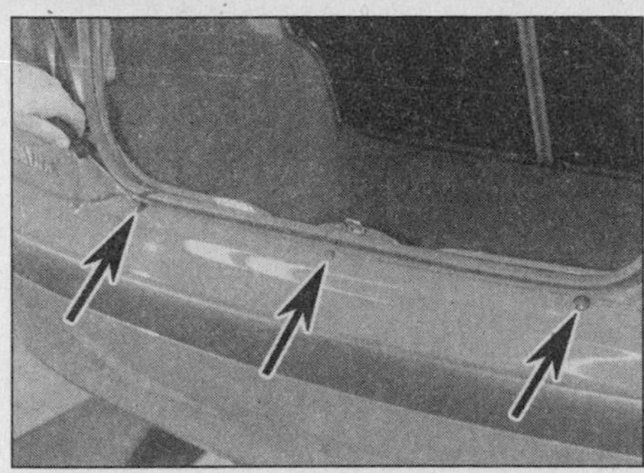
7.1a Remove the three rear bumper upper retaining screws (arrowed)

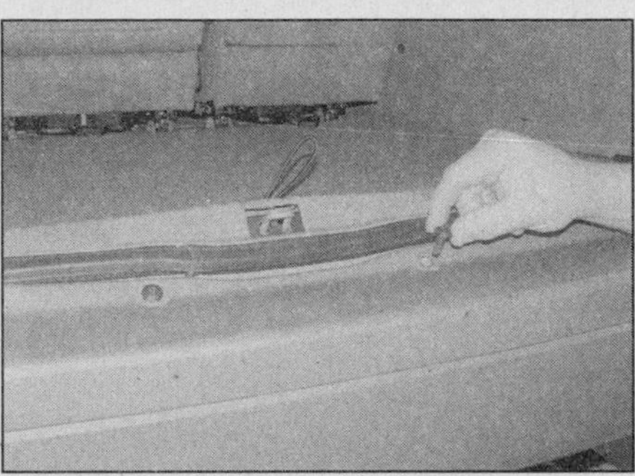
7.1b Remove the inner retaining bolts . . .

7.1c . . . and the four outer . . .

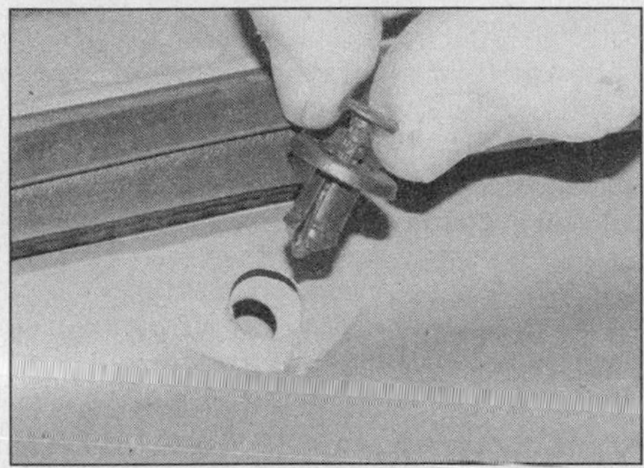
7.1d . . . plastic securing screws/clips – Scénic

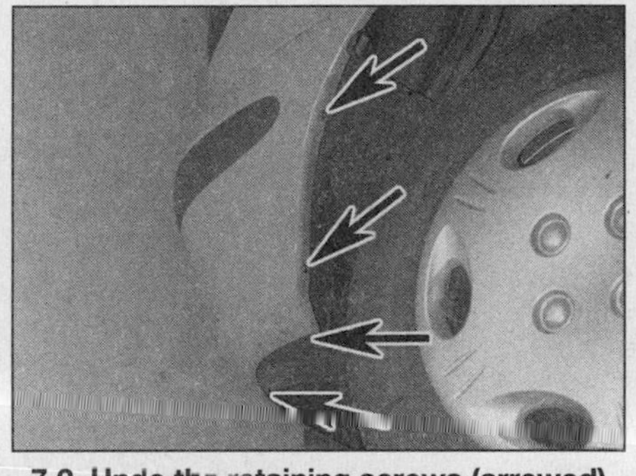
7.2 Undo the retaining screws (arrowed) securing the wheelarch liners to the rear bumper

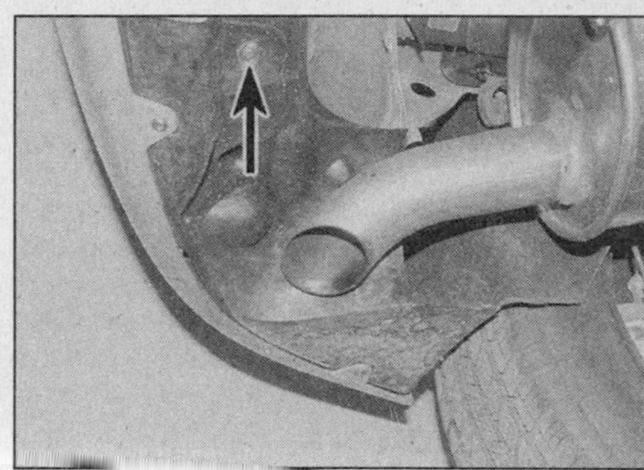
7.3a Remove the retaining screw (arrowed) . . .

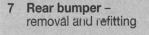

7 Rear bumper – removal and refitting

Removal

1 Open up the tailgate/boot lid then slacken and remove the bumper upper retaining screws. **Note:** *On Scénic models the two outer screws each side are retaining screw/clips. Turn a quarter of a turn and lift out the centre of the plastic screw to remove* ***(see illustrations).***

2 Slacken and remove the screws securing the rear wheelarch liner rear sections to the left- and right-hand ends of the bumper **(see illustration)**.

3 On Scénic models, undo the retaining screw from the plastic trim above the rear exhaust silencer to gain access to the bumper outer retaining bolt **(see illustrations)**.

4 From underneath the vehicle, remove the centre and outer retaining bolts securing the bumper in position **(see illustration)**.

5 Pull back the wheelarch liner, then slacken and remove the bolts securing the left- and right-hand ends of the bumper in position **(see illustration)**.

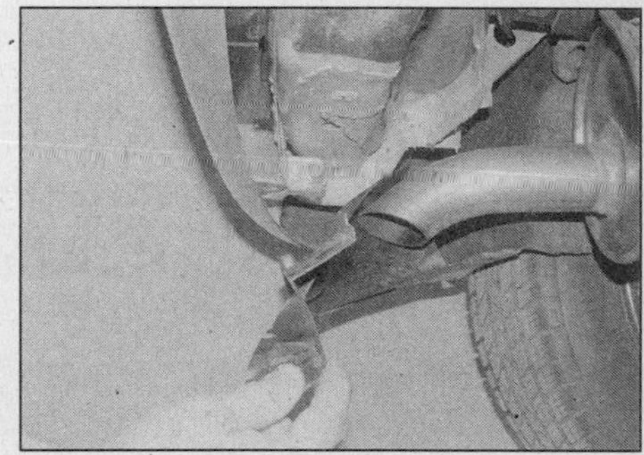
7.3b . . . and withdraw the plastic trim

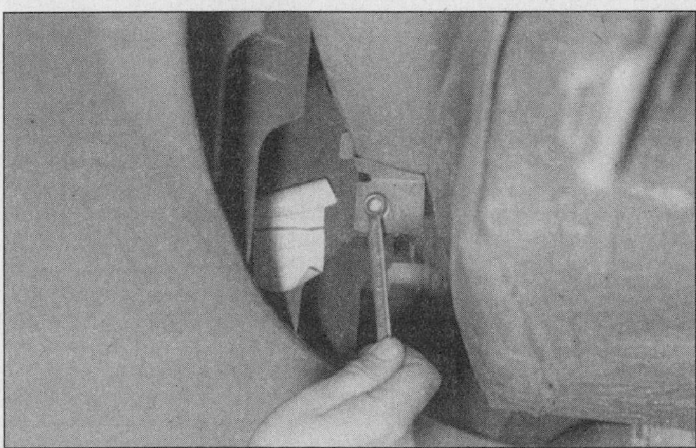
7.4 Removing the centre retaining bolt

7.5 Remove the rear bumper outer end bolts (arrowed)

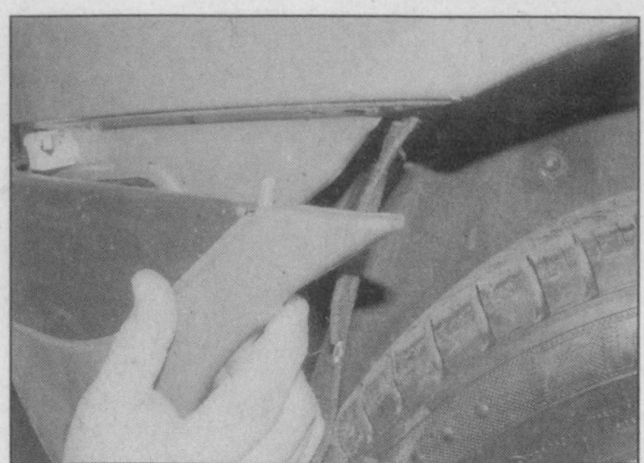

7.6a Release the end locating pegs . . .

7.6b . . . and remove the rear bumper from the vehicle

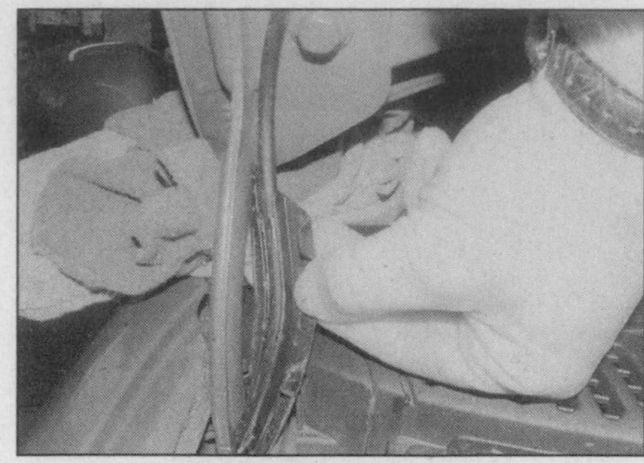

8.2 Unclip the washer hose from the bonnet hinge

6 With the aid of an assistant, carefully release the bumper ends and remove the bumper from the vehicle **(see illustrations)**.

Refitting

7 Refitting is a reverse of the removal procedure, ensuring that the retaining bolts are securely tightened.

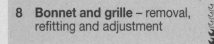

8 Bonnet and grille – removal, refitting and adjustment

Bonnet

Removal

1 Open the bonnet and place a wad of rag underneath each corner of the bonnet to protect against possible damage should the bonnet slip.

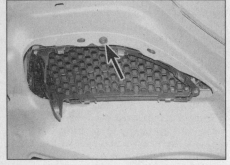

8.8a Undo the retaining screw (arrowed) . . .

2 Remove the sound proofing from under the bonnet (where fitted), then disconnect the washer hose from the right-hand side of the bonnet hinge **(see illustration)**.

3 Using a pencil or felt tip pen, mark the outline of each retaining bolt relative to the bonnet, to use as a guide on refitting.

4 With the aid of an assistant, slacken and remove the left- and right-hand hinge-to-bonnet bolts and carefully remove the bonnet from the vehicle.

5 Inspect the bonnet hinges for signs of wear and free play at the pivots, and if necessary renew; the hinges are secured in position by two nuts and can be removed once the vent panel has been removed from the base of the windscreen.

Refitting and adjustment

6 With the aid of an assistant, engage the bonnet with the hinges. Refit the retaining bolts and tighten them by hand only. Align the bolts with the marks made on removal, then tighten them securely. Where necessary, clip the support struts securely onto the bonnet.

7 Close the bonnet, and check for alignment with the adjacent panels. If necessary, slacken the hinge bolts and re-align the bonnet to suit; the height of the bonnet is altered by moving the rubber stops on the bonnet crossmember. Once the bonnet is correctly aligned, check that the bonnet fastens and releases satisfactorily.

Grille

8 Open the bonnet and remove the retaining screw from the inside of the grille, then unclip the grille from the bonnet **(see illustrations)**. Refitting is a reversal of removal, taking care not to damage the paintwork.

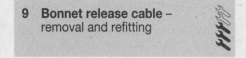

9 Bonnet release cable – removal and refitting

Removal

1 Remove the bonnet lock as described in Section 10.

2 Tie a long piece of string to the end of the release cable and free the cable from all the necessary retaining clips and ties.

3 On all models except Scénic, carefully prise the left- and right-hand front speaker grilles out from the top of the facia panel. Slacken and remove the retaining screws from the left- and right-hand end and unclip the top panel from the main facia and remove it from the vehicle. Unclip the release cable from its bulkhead clips so that it is free to be withdrawn from the vehicle **(see illustration)**.

4 On Scénic models, unclip the release cable from the bulkhead under the facia, around the back of the heater unit **(see illustration)**.

5 On all models, pull the bonnet release handle to remove, then peel back the door sealing strip and carefully unclip the front

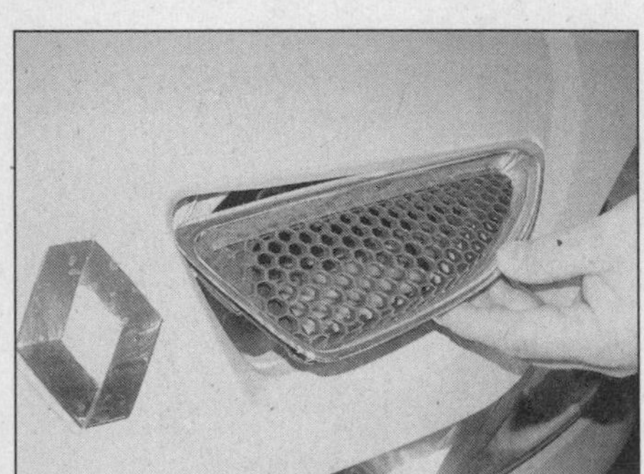

8.8b . . . and unclip the grille from the bonnet

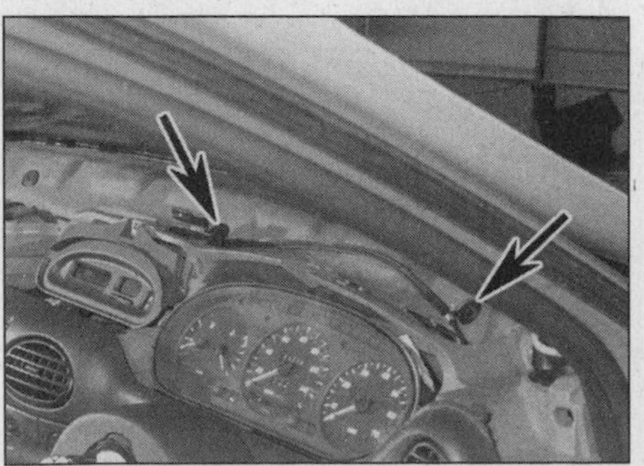

9.3 On right-hand drive models, unclip the bonnet release cable retaining clips situated at the top of the bulkhead

9.4 Bonnet cable (arrowed) is secured behind the heater unit - Scénic

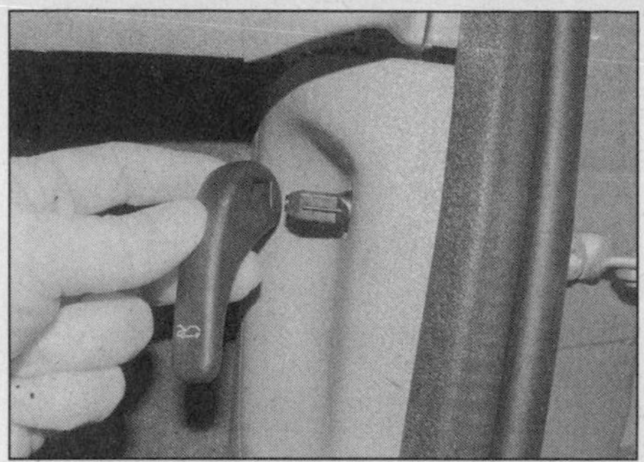

9.5 Pull the bonnet opening lever to release it from the cable assembly

section of the driver's side sill trim panel so that access can be gained to the bonnet release lever retaining screw **(see illustration)**.

6 Slacken and remove the bonnet release lever screw **(see illustration)** then remove the lever from underneath the facia, withdrawing the cable into the passenger compartment. When the end of the string appears from the bulkhead, untie it and leave it in position; the string can then be used on refitting to draw the cable back into position.

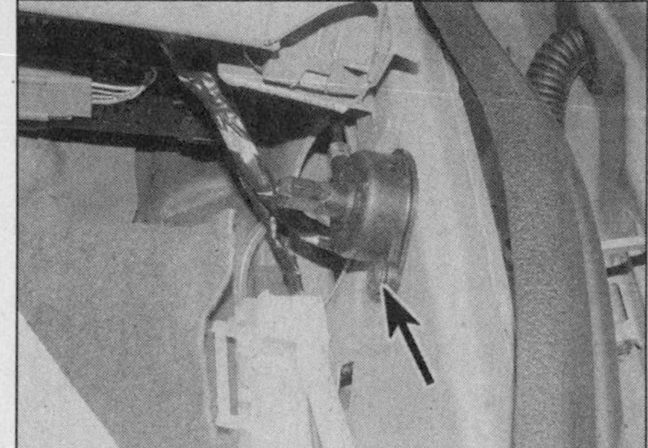

9.6 Undo the retaining screw (arrowed)

Refitting

7 Refitting is the reverse of removal ensuring that the cable is correctly routed, and secured to all the relevant retaining clips. Prior to closing the bonnet, operate the release handle and have an assistant check that the lock hook moves easily and smoothly to its stop.

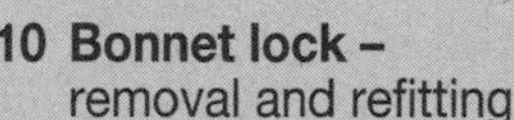

10 Bonnet lock – removal and refitting

Removal

1 Open the bonnet and using a suitable marker pen, make alignment marks between the lock and crossmember.

2 Slacken and remove the retaining nuts and remove the lock mounting plate from the rear of the crossmember, freeing it from the release outer cable.

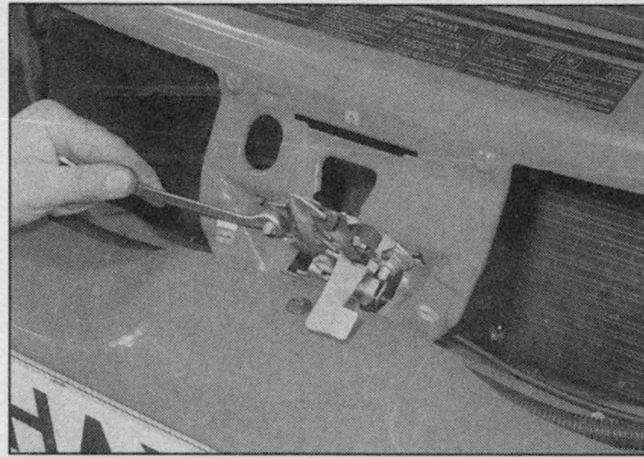

10.3a Remove the retaining nuts . . .

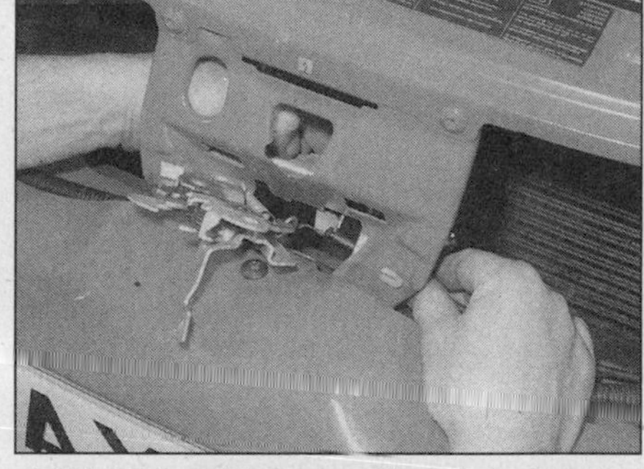

10.3b . . . and the mounting plate, freeing it from the outer cable . . .

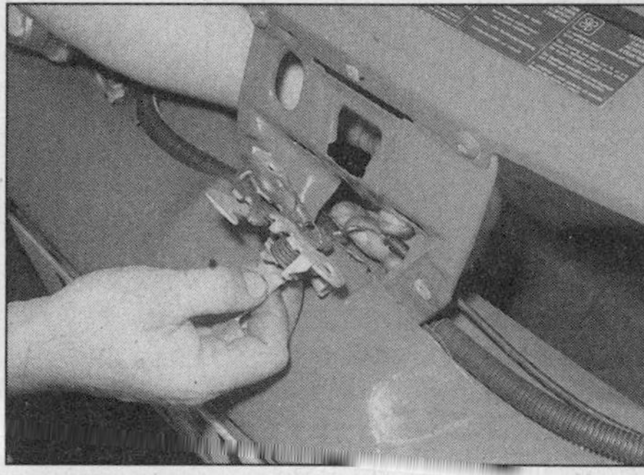

10.3c . . . then detach the lock from the inner cable and remove it from the vehicle

3 Detach the lock assembly from the inner cable and remove it from the vehicle **(see illustrations)**.

Refitting

4 Refitting is the reverse of removal, aligning the lock with the marks made prior to removal. Check the lock operation and lubricate it with multi-purpose grease.

11 Door – removal and refitting

Note: *If the hinge pins are a tight fit, a special tool will be required to pull them out of position. The Renault tool is in the form of a hooked adapter (Car.1055-02) which engages with the head of the pin; a slide hammer is then attached to the adapter and used to force each pin out of position.*

Removal

1 Disconnect the battery negative lead (refer to Chapter 5A).

2 Undo the retaining bolt securing the check link to the pillar **(see illustration)**.

3 Lift up the retaining clip and disconnect the door wiring connector from the pillar **(see illustration)**.

4 Remove the retaining clips from the upper and lower hinge pins **(see illustration)**.

5 Have an assistant support the weight of the door then carefully tap out the upper and lower hinge pins using a hammer and punch; the upper pin is removed in a downwards direction and the lower pin is removed in an

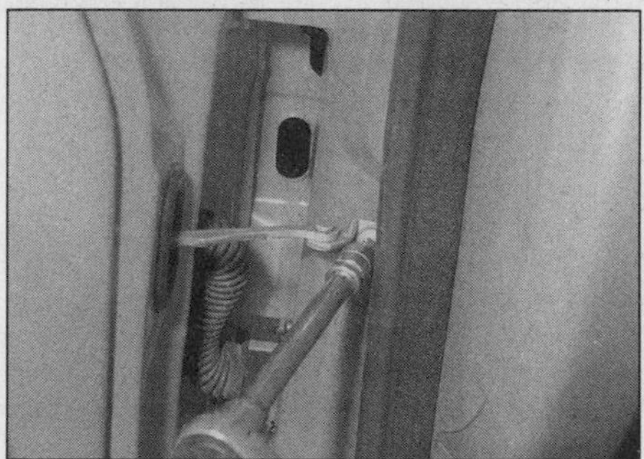

11.2 Slacken the check link retaining bolt

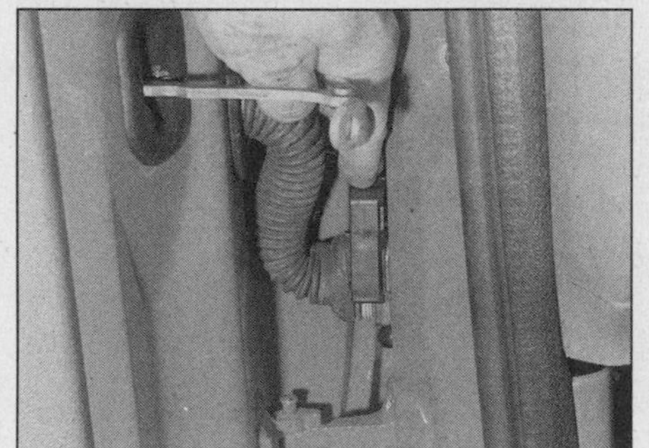

11.3 Lift up the retaining clip and disconnect the door wiring connector

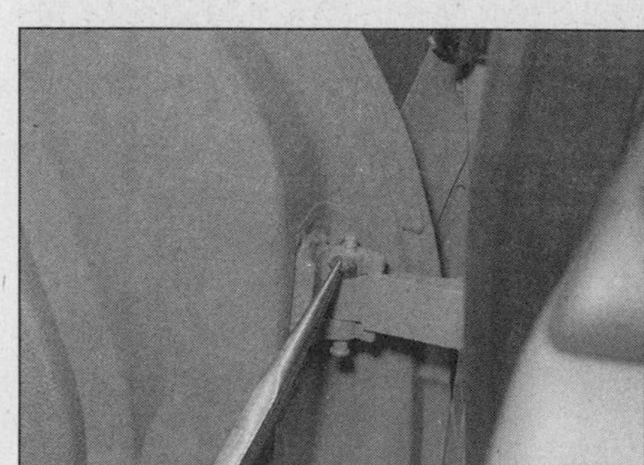

11.4 Remove the retaining clips from the hinge pins

upwards direction **(see illustrations)**. Since it is not possible to hit the pin squarely with a punch, great care must be taken not to bend the pin (see Note at the start of this Section).

6 Once both pins have been removed, move the door away from the vehicle.

7 Examine the hinge pins and bushes for signs of wear or damage and renew if necessary; the bushes are a press-fit in the hinge. It is recommended that the pins are renewed every time they are removed. If the hinges themselves are damaged, it will be necessary to consult a Renault dealer on the best course of action; the hinges are welded in position and cannot be easily renewed.

Refitting

8 Ensure that the bushes are pressed securely into the hinges and lubricate them with a smear of multi-purpose grease.

9 Manoeuvre the door into position and fit the hinge pins; the upper pin is fitted from below and the lower pin from above. Tap the pins fully into position and secure them in position with the retaining clips.

10 Reconnect the wiring connector to the pillar and secure it in position with the retaining clip.

11 Align the check link with the pillar, securely tighten its retaining bolt then reconnect the battery negative lead.

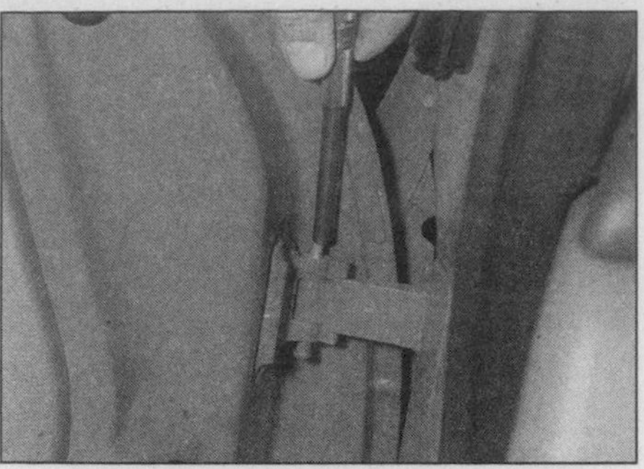

11.5a Tap the hinge pins out of position noting that the upper pin is removed in a downwards direction . . .

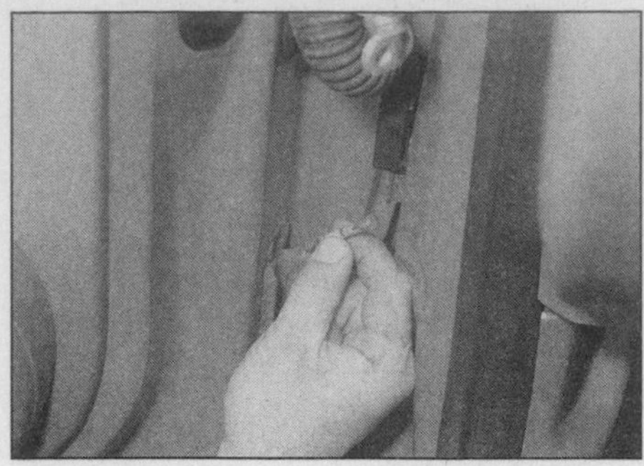

11.5b . . . and the lower pin upwards

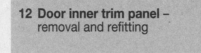

12 Door inner trim panel – removal and refitting

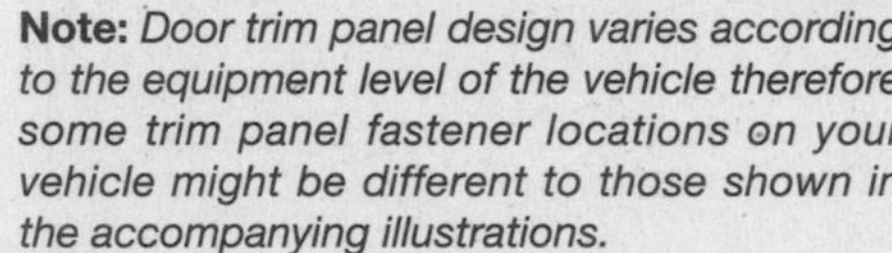

Note: *Door trim panel design varies according to the equipment level of the vehicle therefore some trim panel fastener locations on your vehicle might be different to those shown in the accompanying illustrations.*

Front door trim removal

1 Disconnect the battery negative lead (refer to Chapter 5A) and proceed as described under the relevant sub-heading.

All models except Scénic

2 Unclip the exterior mirror inner trim panel from the front of the door. On Coupé models also unclip the small trim panel from the upper rear corner of the panel **(see illustrations)**.

3 Remove the loudspeaker from the door as described in Chapter 12.

4 Undo the retaining screws securing the storage compartment to the bottom of the trim panel. Move the storage compartment upwards to release it from its retaining clips then remove it from the door. **Note:** *On some models the storage compartment is part of the door trim panel and does not come away separately.* Disconnect the wiring connector(s) (where necessary) as they become accessible **(see illustrations)**.

5 Remove the trim cover from the base of the armrest pocket then slacken and remove the retaining screw and lift the pocket out of position **(see illustrations)**.

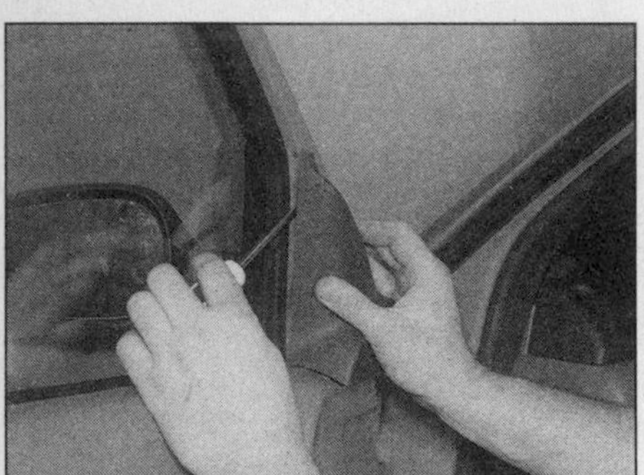

12.2a Unclip the mirror inner trim panel and remove it from the door

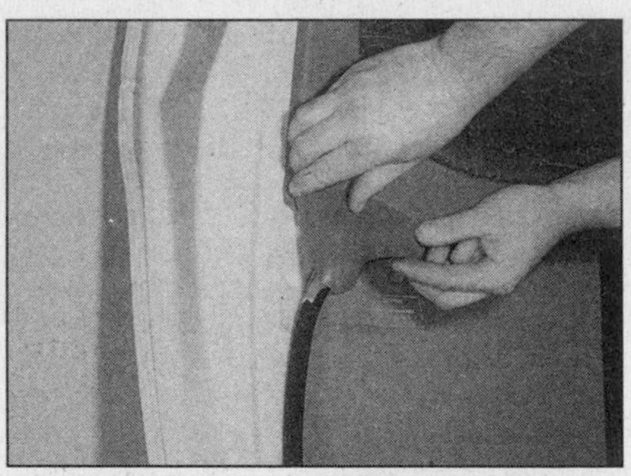

12.2b On Coupé models also unclip the small trim panel from the rear of the door

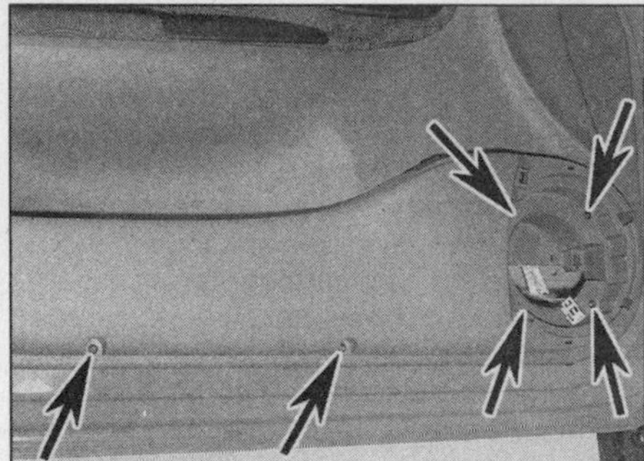

12.4a Undo the retaining screws (arrowed) . . .

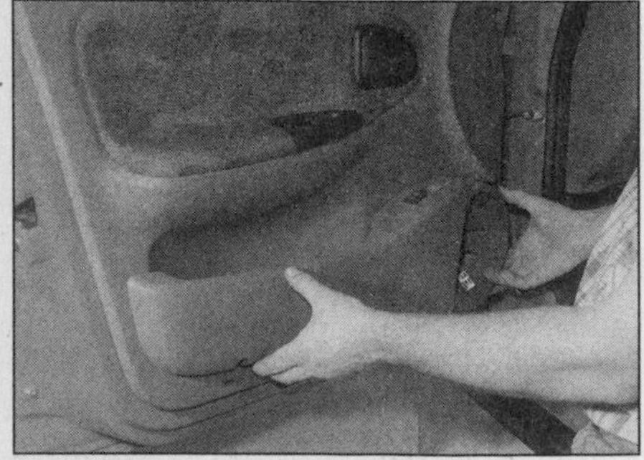

12.4b . . . then unclip the storage compartment and remove it from the door . . .

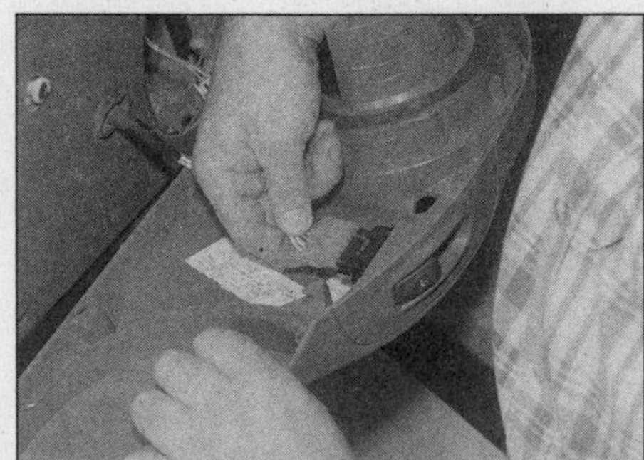

12.4c . . . disconnect the wiring connectors as they become accessible

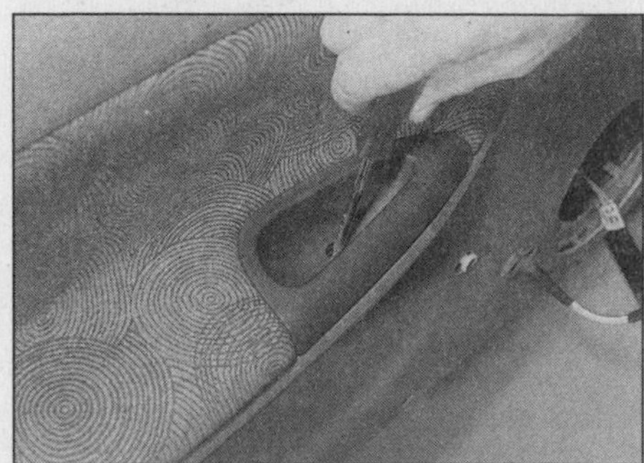

12.5a Undo the retaining screw . . .

12.5b . . . and remove the armrest pocket from the trim panel

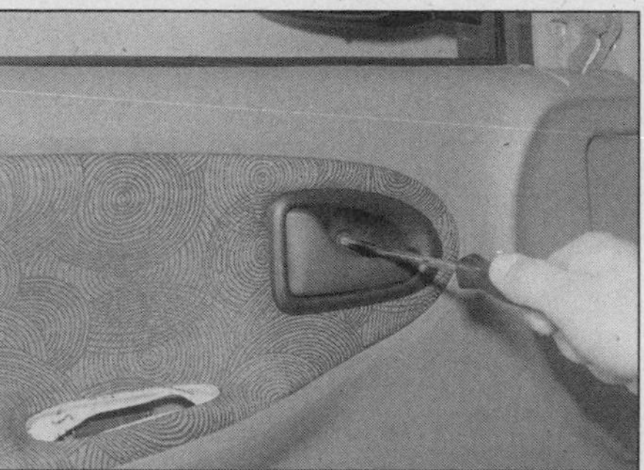
12.6a Undo the retaining screw . . .

12.6b . . . then unhook the lock inner handle from the link rod/cable

6 Undo the retaining screw and remove the lock inner handle, disconnect it from its link rod/cable **(see illustrations)**.

7 On models with manual windows, pull/lever the window regulator handle off its spindle and remove the spacer **(see illustration)**.

8 Make a final check that all the screws have been removed then carefully unclip the base of the trim panel from the door then manoeuvre the panel upwards and out of position **(see illustration)**. **Note:** *The panel is stuck in position with a mastic sealant as well as being clipped in position and some force will be required to unclip it. It is desirable to carefully cut through the sealant with a sharp knife to facilitate removal, but take care to protect the edges of the panel.* As the panel is removed, free the wiring harness noting its correct routing.

Scénic models

9 Unclip the exterior mirror inner trim panel from the front of the door **(see illustration)**.

10 Remove the loudspeaker from the door as described in Chapter 12.

11 Undo the retaining screws at the bottom, and within the speaker aperture, securing the trim panel.

12 Remove the trim cover from the base of the armrest pocket then slacken and remove the retaining screw and lift the pocket out of position **(see illustrations)**. Where applicable, disconnect the wiring from the electric window switches.

13 Undo the retaining screw and remove the lock inner handle, disconnect it from its operating cable **(see illustration)**.

14 On models with manual windows, pull/lever the window regulator handle off its spindle and remove the spacer.

15 Make a final check that all the screws have been removed then carefully unclip the base of the trim panel from the door then manoeuvre the panel upwards and out of position. **Note:** *The panel is stuck in position*

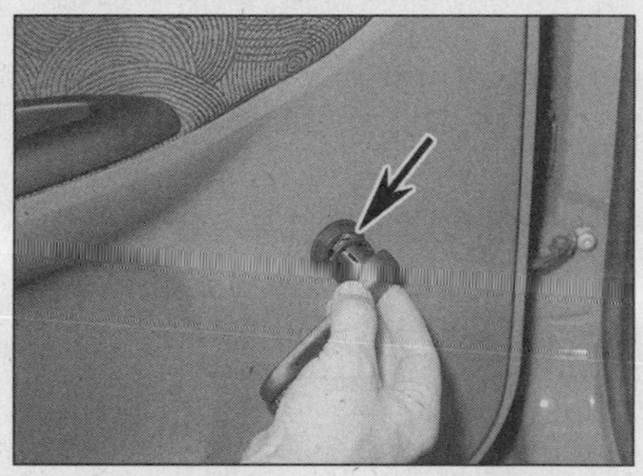
12.7 On models with manual windows, unclip the regulator handle and remove the spacer (arrowed)

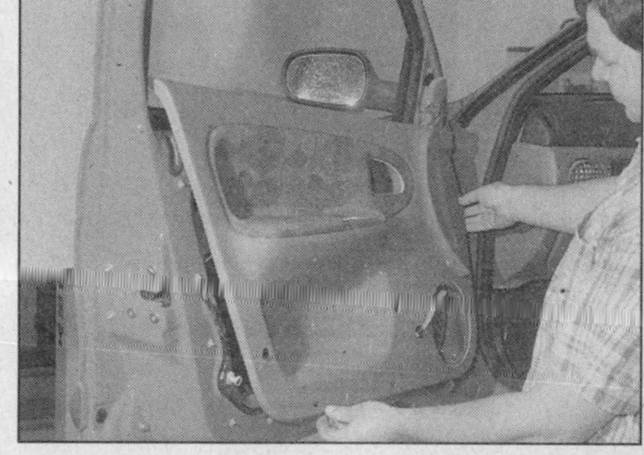
12.8 Unclip the base of the trim panel and remove it from the door

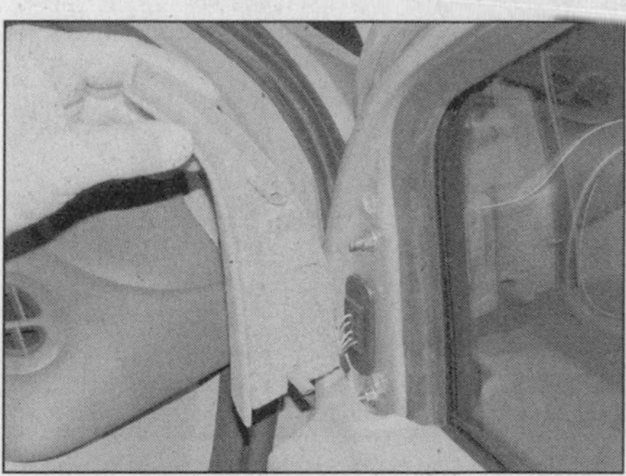
12.9 Unclip the inner door mirror trim panel

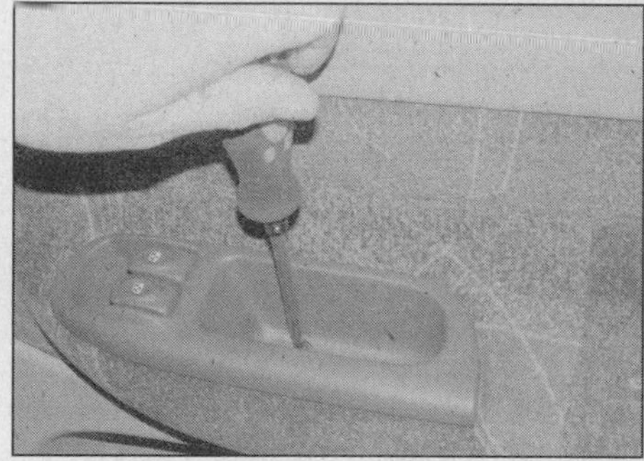
12.12a Undo the retaining screw . . .

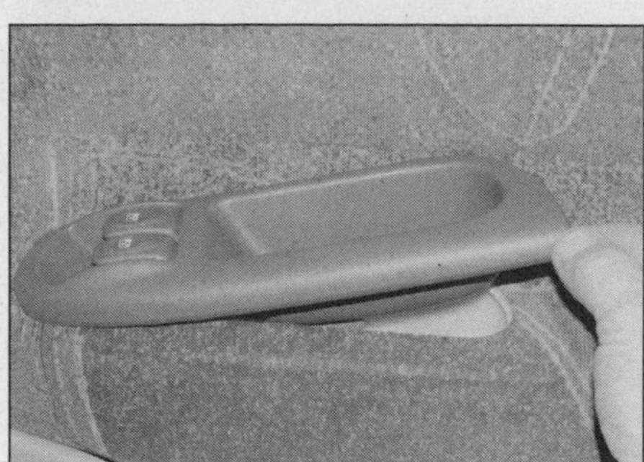
12.12b . . . and release the trim panel

12.13a Undo the retaining screw . . .

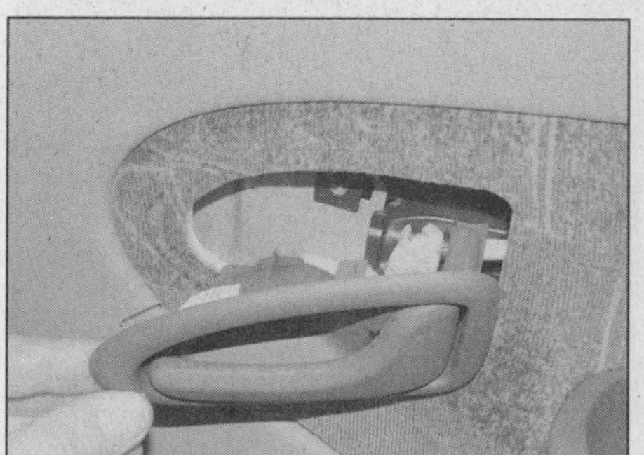
12.13b . . . and release the operating cable

with sealant as well as being clipped in position and some force will be required to unclip it. It is desirable to carefully cut through the sealant with a sharp knife to facilitate removal, but take care to protect the edges of the panel ***(see illustration)***. As the panel is removed, release the blanking plug in the panel to allow the wiring to be pulled through.

16 Disconnect the wiring connector(s) (where necessary) as they become accessible.

Rear door trim removal

17 Disconnect the battery negative lead (refer to Chapter 5A).

18 Undo the trim panel retaining screws from the base of the storage compartment (where fitted) and on Scénic models, also unclip the rear quarter trim panel at the rear of the window.

19 Remove the trim panel as described in paragraphs 5 to 8 (for all models except Scénic) or 11 to 16 (for Scénic models), ignoring the remark about the wiring.

Refitting

20 Refitting of the trim panel is the reverse of removal. Apply a fresh bead of suitable mastic sealant to the panel if the original sealant is unsuitable for further use. Prior to clipping the panel in position, ensure that all the wiring (where applicable) is correctly routed and passed through the relevant apertures.

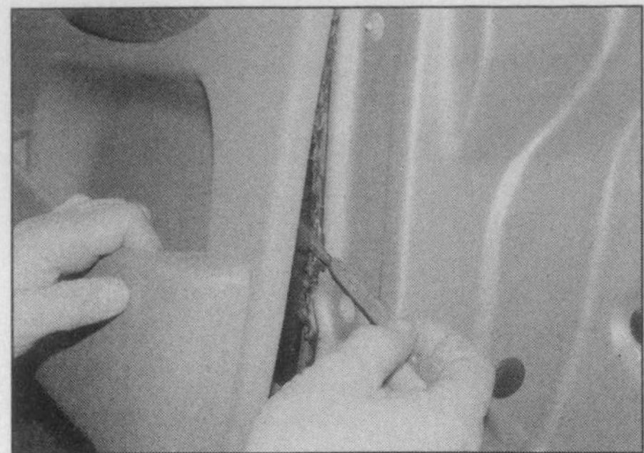

12.15 Cutting the sealant to release the door trim panel

13.1 Removing the lock inner handle

13 Door handle and lock components – removal and refitting

Removal

Inner handle

1 Undo the retaining screw securing the handle to the door, then detach the handle assembly from the link rod/operating cable and remove it from the vehicle **(see illustration)**.

Front exterior handle

2 Remove the door inner trim panel as described in Section 12.

3 Remove the impact absorbing panel from the door. On some models the panel is secured in position with screws whereas on other models it is clipped in position.

4 Detach the link rod/operating cable from the handle then undo the retaining nuts and remove the handle from the door **(see illustrations)**.

Front lock cylinder

5 Remove the door trim panel as described in Section 12.

6 Remove the impact absorbing panel from the door. On some models the panel is secured in position with screws whereas on other models it is clipped in position.

7 Slacken and remove the retaining screws and remove the anti-theft cover/bracket from the lock assembly **(see illustrations)**.

8 Release the retaining clip by rotating it

13.4a Undo the retaining nuts (arrowed) . . .

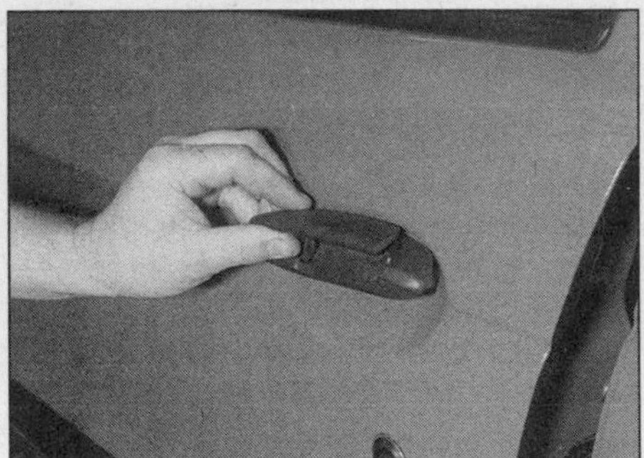

13.4b . . . and remove the exterior handle from the door

13.7a Remove the anti-theft cover from the lock assembly

13.7b Undo the two screws (arrowed) . . .

13.7c . . . and the lower securing bolt . . .

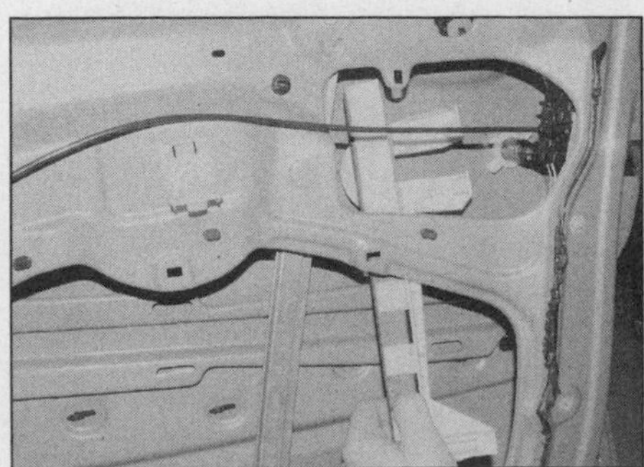

13.7d . . . and remove the anti-theft bracket from the door

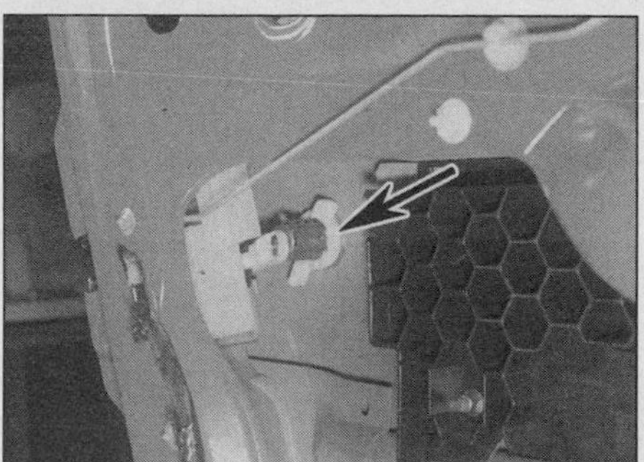
13.8a Rotate the retaining clip (arrowed) through 90° . . .

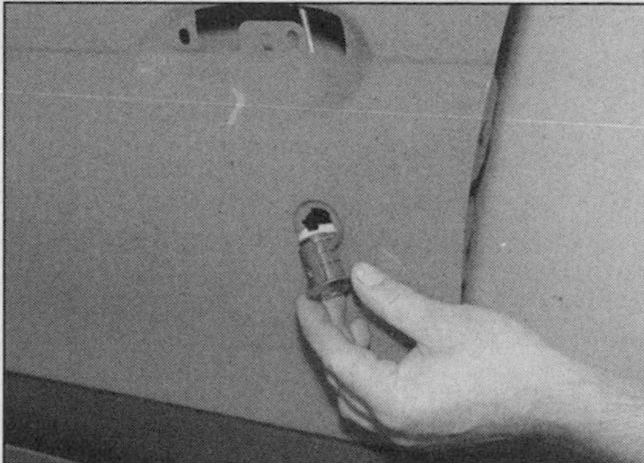
13.8b . . . and remove the lock cylinder from the door

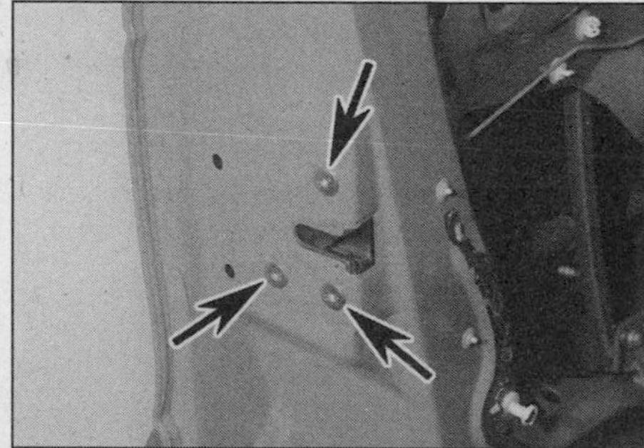
13.11a Undo the retaining screws (arrowed) . . .

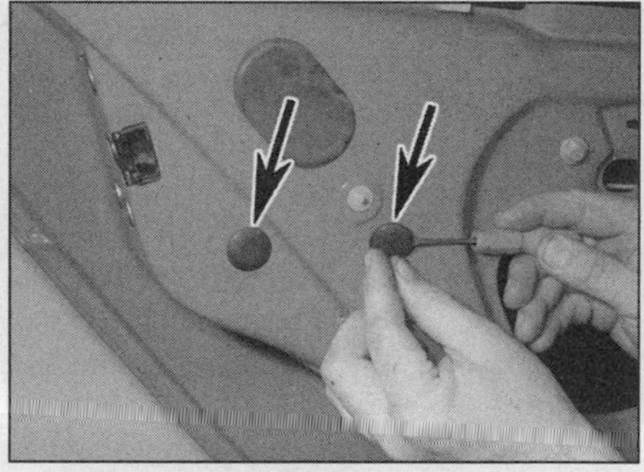
13.13 Prise out the rubber covers (arrowed) to gain access to the rear door exterior handle nuts

13.11b . . . then remove the lock, where necessary release the retaining clip and disconnect the wiring connector (arrowed) from the central locking motor

through 90° then remove the lock cylinder and clip from the door **(see illustrations)**.

Front lock assembly

9 Remove the lock cylinder as described earlier in this Section.

10 Where applicable, detach the lock assembly link rod/operating cable from the exterior handle then release the interior handle link rod from its guide on the door.

11 Slacken and remove the lock retaining screws and remove the lock assembly from the door, disconnecting the wiring connector from the central locking motor (where fitted) **(see illustrations)**.

Rear exterior handle

12 Remove the door inner trim panel as described in Section 12.

13 On Mégane models, prise out the rubber covers from the door to gain access to the handle retaining nuts **(see illustration)**.

14 From inside the door aperture, detach the link rod from the handle then undo the retaining nuts and remove the handle from the door **(see illustration)**.

Rear lock assembly

15 Remove the exterior handle as described in paragraphs 12 to 14.

16 Undo the securing bolts and remove the window glass rear guide as described in Section 14.

17 Release the inner handle operating cable and detach the clips from the door.

18 Undo the retaining screws and remove the lock assembly from the door, complete with link rods and cable, disconnecting the central locking motor wiring connector (where fitted) **(see illustration)**.

Refitting

19 Refitting is the reverse of removal, ensuring that all link rods/cables are clipped securely in position. Prior to refitting the trim panel, reconnect the battery and check the operation of the lock and handles. If all is well, refit the trim panel as described in Section 12.

14 Door window glass and regulator – removal and refitting

Front sliding window

All models except Scénic

1 Position the window glass about 3/4 of the way down then disconnect the battery negative lead.

2 Remove the inner trim panel from the door as described in Section 12.

3 Remove the impact absorbing panel from the door. On some models the panel is secured in position with screws whereas on other models it is clipped in position.

4 On Hatchback and Saloon models, carefully unclip the window inner sealing strip and remove it from the door, noting which way around it is fitted **(see illustration)**. On Coupé models unclip the lower and rear sections of the sealing strip; there is no need to remove the strip completely.

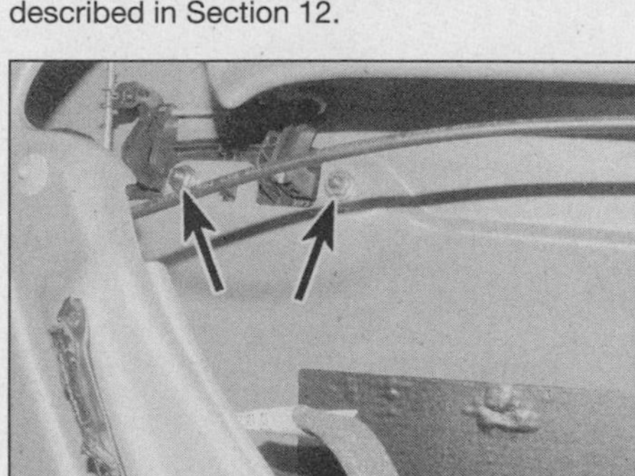
13.14 Undo the two retaining nuts (arrowed) – Scénic

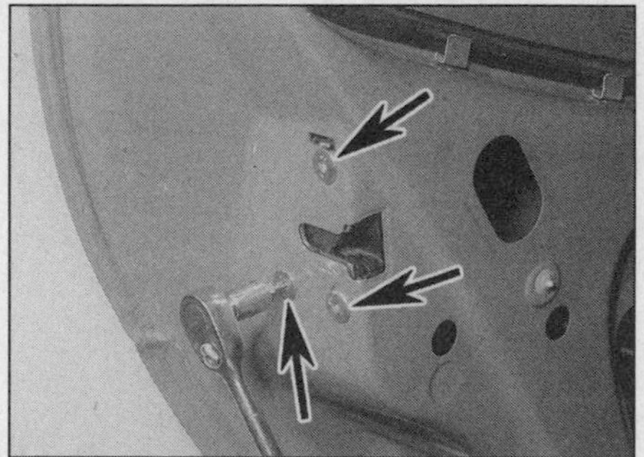
13.18 Undo the retaining screws (arrowed) and manoeuvre the lock assembly out from the rear door

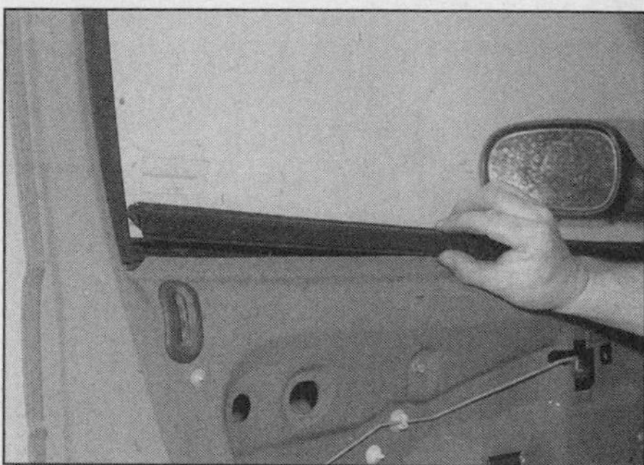
14.4 On Hatchback and Saloon models unclip the window inner sealing strip and remove it from the door

11

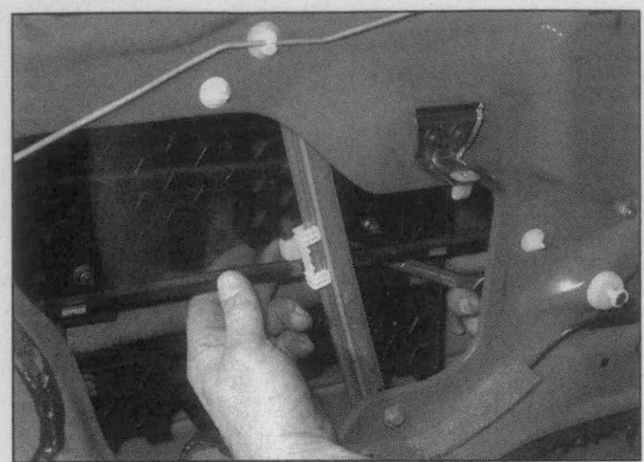

14.5a Using a 13 mm ring spanner, carefully release the retaining clip tangs . . .

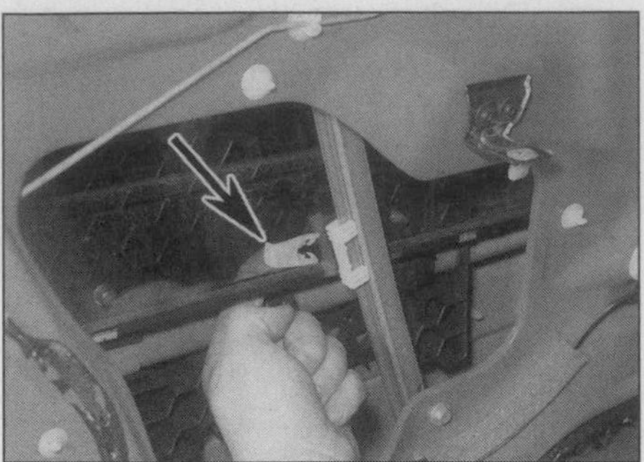

14.5b . . . and pull the retaining clip (arrowed) off from the regulator

14.6a On Hatchback and Saloon models, tilt the glass to free its guide (arrowed) then lift the glass through the top of the door

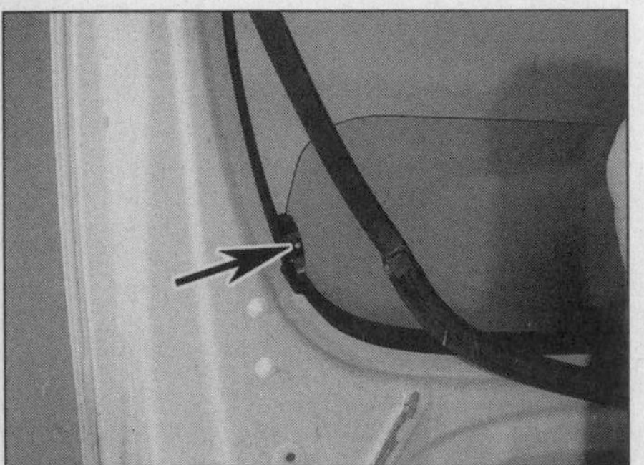

14.6b On Coupé models free the window rear guide (arrowed) . . .

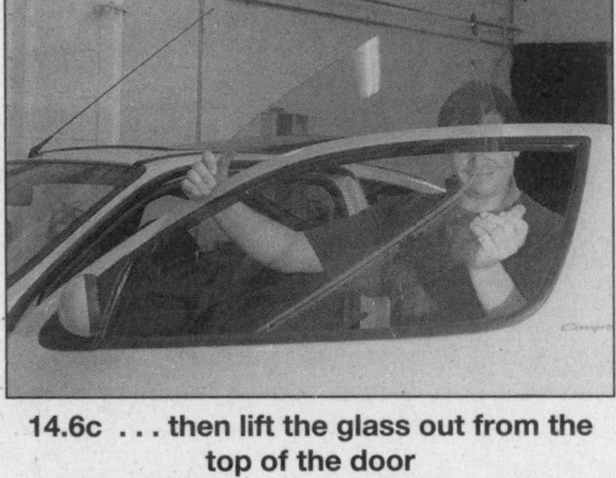

14.6c . . . then lift the glass out from the top of the door

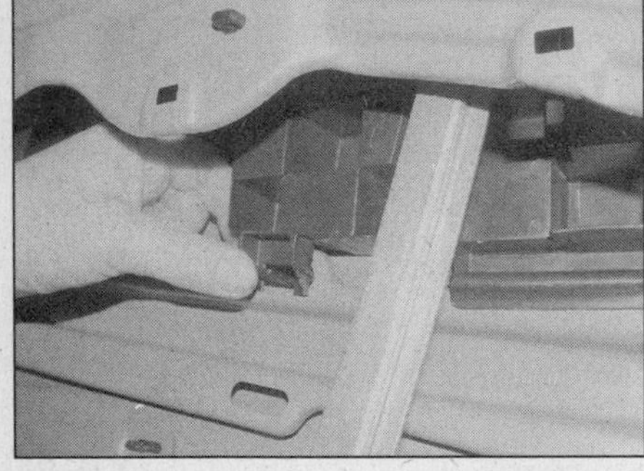

14.9 Unclip the impact absorber and rotate to remove from door panel

14.10 Unclip the window inner seal

5 Remove the window guide retaining clip by sliding it off the regulator; a 13 mm ring spanner is ideal for releasing the retaining clip tangs **(see illustrations)**.

6 Free the window glass from the regulator then lower it slightly. Free the glass rear guide from the sealing strip then tilt the glass and manoeuvre it out of the top of the door **(see illustrations)**.

7 Refitting is the reverse of removal, checking the operation of the window prior to refitting the trim panel.

Scénic models

8 Position the window glass about 3/4 of the way down then disconnect the battery (refer to Chapter 5A). Remove the inner trim panel from the door as described in Section 12.

9 Remove the impact absorbing panel from the door. The panel is clipped in position **(see illustration)**.

10 Carefully unclip the window inner sealing strip and remove it from the door, noting which way around it is fitted **(see illustration)**.

11 Remove the window guide retaining clip by sliding it off the regulator; a 13 mm ring spanner is ideal for releasing the retaining clip tangs **(see illustration)**.

12 Undo the two bolts securing the fixed pillar (between the sliding glass and fixed glass) to the door **(see illustrations)**.

13 Free the window glass from the regulator then lower it to the bottom of the door.

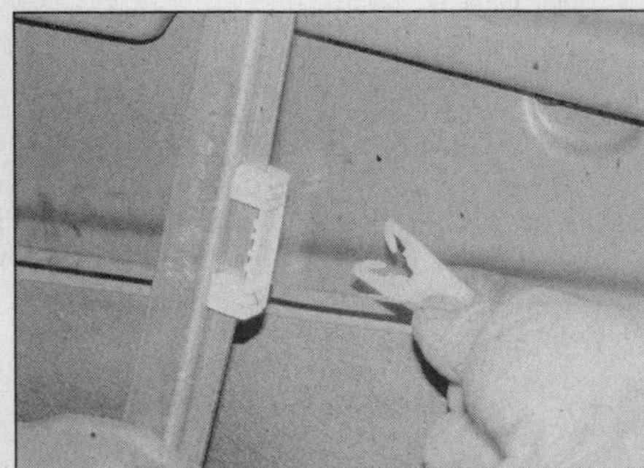

14.11 Release the window guide retaining clip

14.12a Undo the upper securing bolt (arrowed) . . .

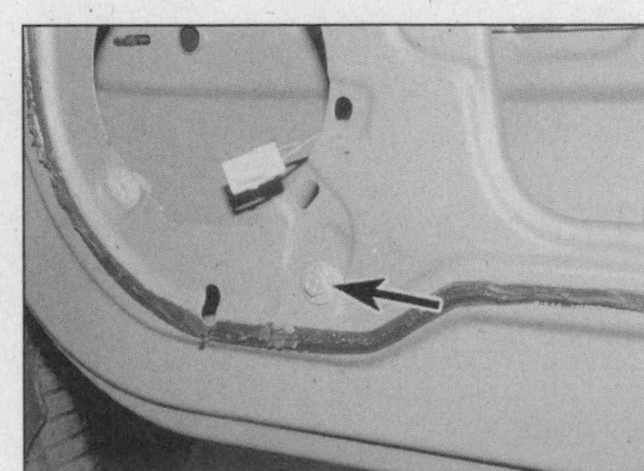

14.12b . . . and the lower securing bolt (arrowed)

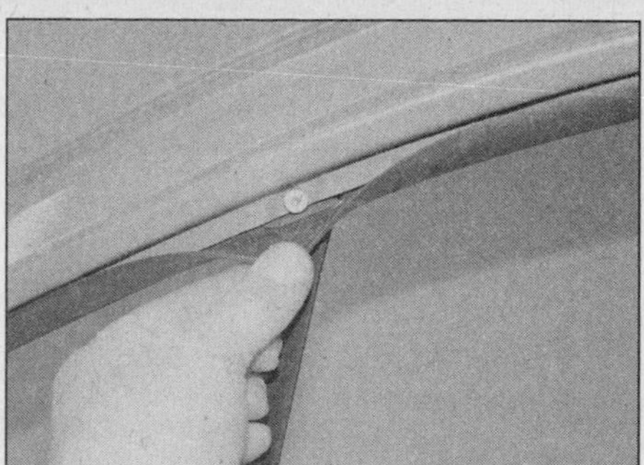
14.14a Undo the upper securing screw . . .

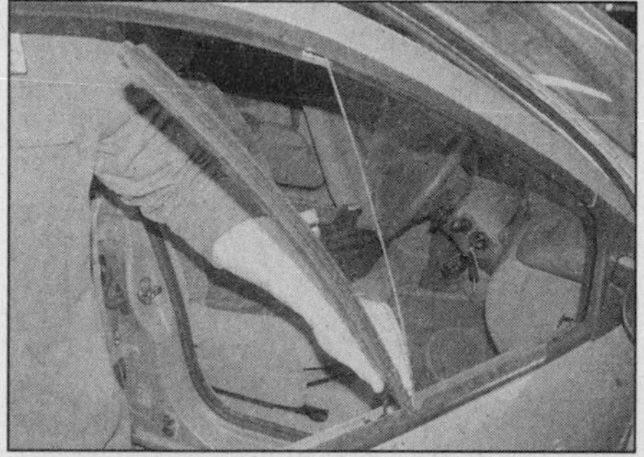
14.14b . . . and twist the guide through 90° to withdraw

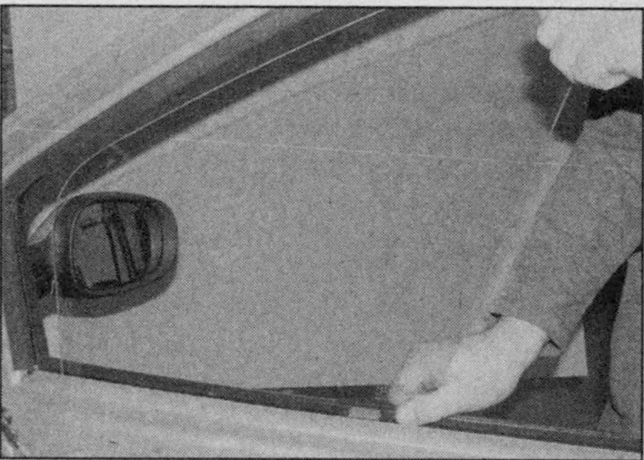
14.17 Slide the glass out from the door frame

14 Remove the trim cap and the fixed pillar upper mounting bolt. Push the pillar down to free the upper location, turn it through 90° and lift it out of the door **(see illustrations)**.

15 Free the glass rear guide from the sealing strip then tilt the glass and manoeuvre it out of the top of the door.

16 Refitting is the reverse of removal, checking the operation of the window prior to refitting the trim panel.

Front fixed window

Scénic models

17 Carry out the operations described in paragraphs 8 to 14. Pull the window rearwards to release it from the door frame at the front, then lift it up and out of the door **(see illustration)**.

18 Refitting is the reverse of removal, checking the operation of the window prior to refitting the trim panel.

Front window regulator

19 Remove the window as described in paragraphs 1 to 6, or 8 to 15, according to model. On models with electric windows disconnect the wiring connector from the window motor.

20 Slacken and remove the regulator and lifting rail mounting nuts and bolts then free the assembly from the door and manoeuvre it out through the door aperture **(see illustration)**.

21 Refitting is the reverse of removal, checking the operation of the window prior to refitting the trim panel.

Rear sliding window

Hatchback and Saloon models

22 Position the window glass about 3/4 of the way down then disconnect the battery negative lead. Remove the inner trim panel from the door as described in Section 12.

23 Carefully unclip the window inner sealing strip and remove it from the door, noting which way around it is fitted.

24 Slacken and remove the bolts securing the window glass to the regulator then free the glass and fully lower the glass in the door **(see illustration)**. If the window is held in place by a retaining clip follow the procedure in paragraph 5.

25 Remove the trim cover to gain access to the window rear guide rail upper retaining screw, then slacken and remove both the upper and lower screws. Free the guide rail from the fixed window then rotate it through 90° and remove it from the door **(see illustrations)**.

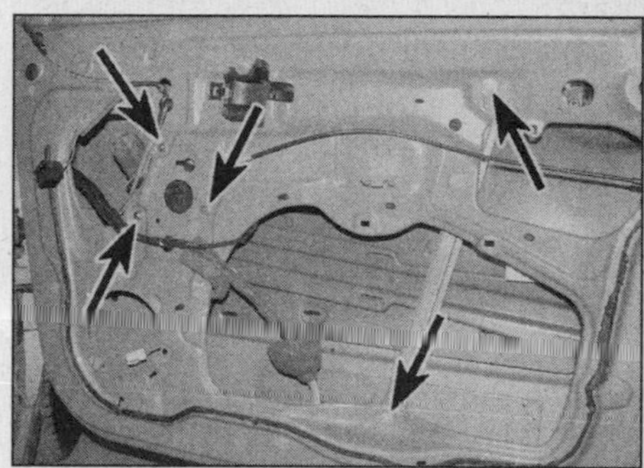
14.20 Undo the retaining nuts and bolts (arrowed) and manoeuvre the regulator assembly out from the door

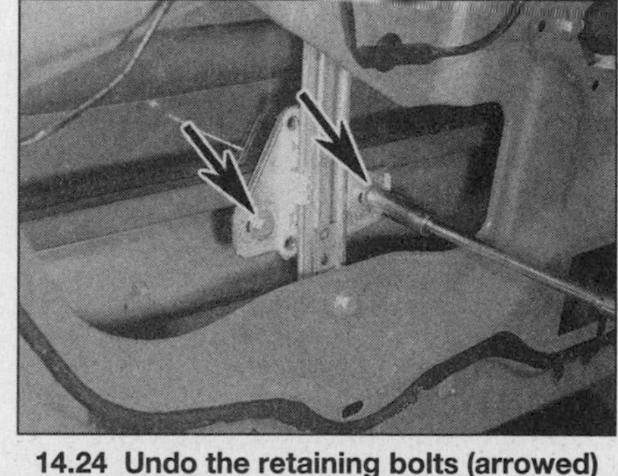
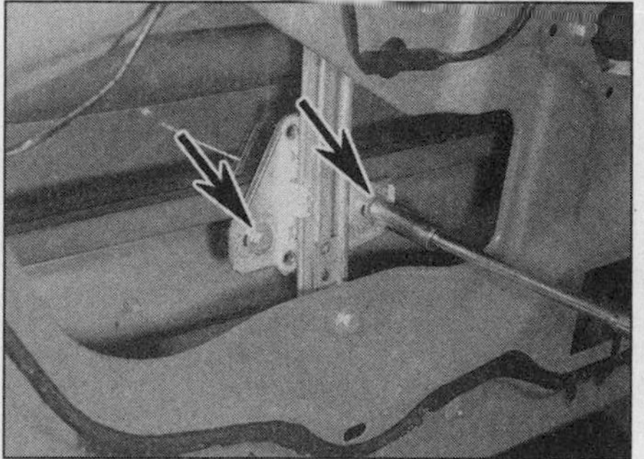
14.24 Undo the retaining bolts (arrowed) and free the glass from the rear door regulator

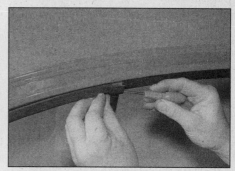

14.25a Prise off the trim cover . . .

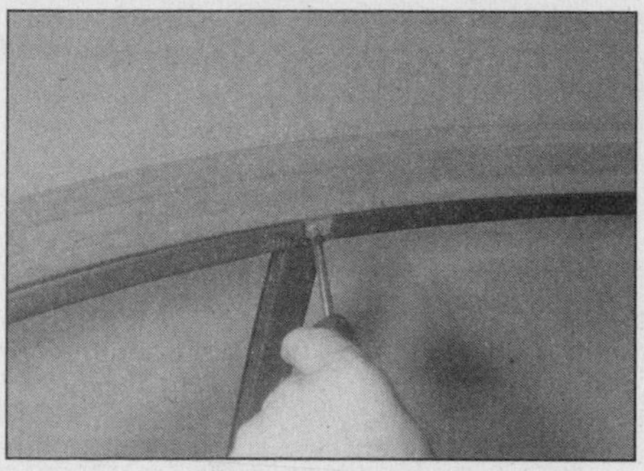
14.25b . . . then slacken and remove the upper retaining screw . . .

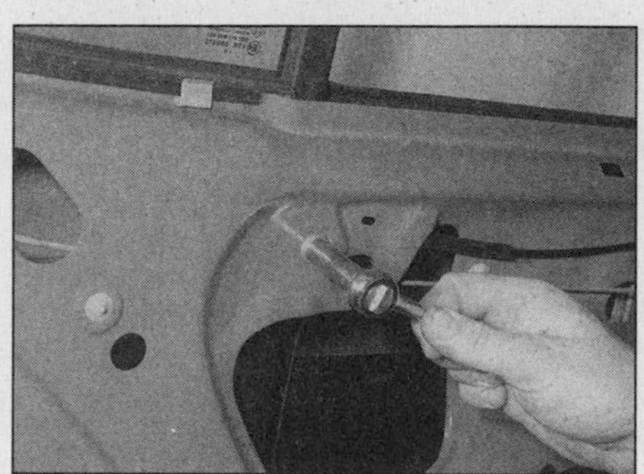
14.25c . . . and the lower screw . . .

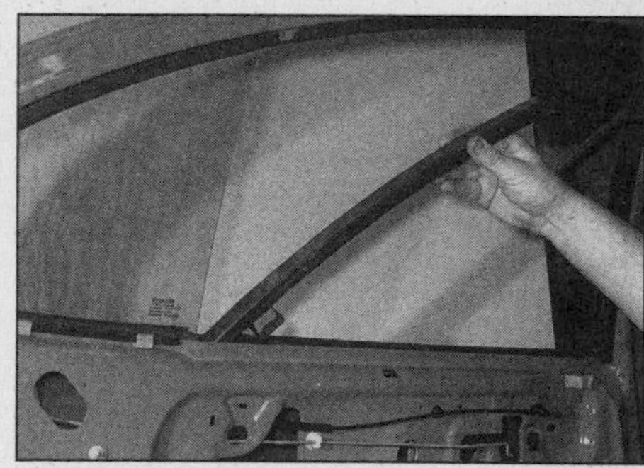
14.25d . . . and manoeuvre the window guide rail out from the top of the door

11

14.26 Removing the rear door window – Hatchback

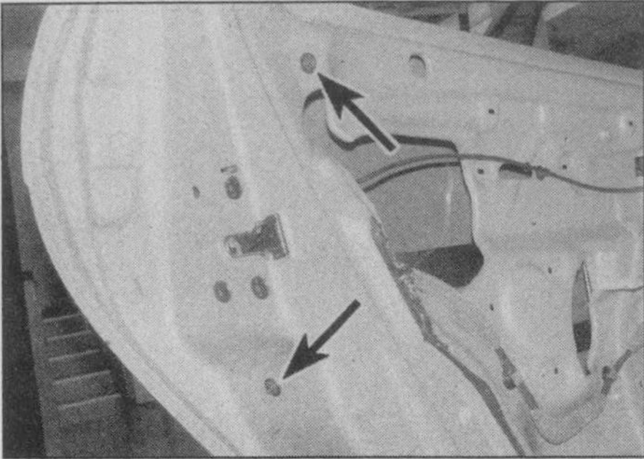

14.29a Undo the two mounting bolts (arrowed) . . .

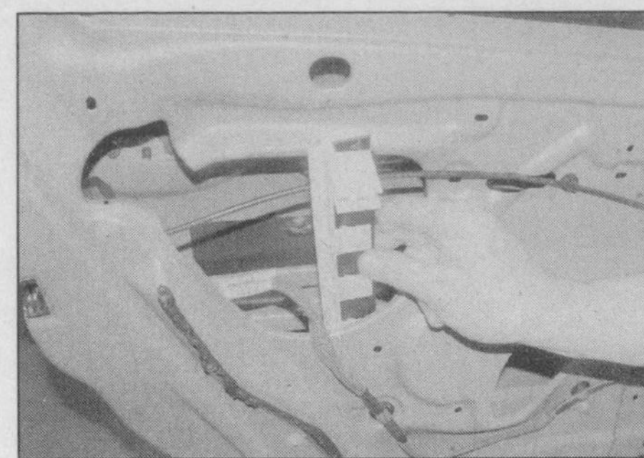

14.29b . . . and remove the rear window guide

26 Carefully lift the window glass out of the top of the door **(see illustration)**.

27 Refitting is the reverse of removal. On models with the window held on the regulator by two retaining bolts, prior to refitting the trim panel, adjust the position of the window glass by slackening the retaining bolts then fully raising the window before securely retightening them; this will ensure that the window is squarely seated in its guides.

Scénic models

28 Position the window glass about 3/4 of the way down then disconnect the battery negative lead (refer to Chapter 5A). Remove the inner trim panel from the door as described in Section 12.

29 Undo the two bolts, one below the lock mechanism on the door rear face, and one on the inner face at the rear, securing the window rear guide to the door **(see illustrations)**.

30 Carefully unclip the window inner sealing strip and remove it from the door, noting which way around it is fitted.

31 Remove the window guide retaining clip by sliding it off the regulator; a 13 mm ring spanner is ideal for releasing the retaining clip tangs **(see illustrations 14.5a and 14.5b)**.

32 Free the window glass from the regulator then lower it to the bottom of the door.

33 Remove the door exterior weatherstrip as follows. Where applicable, remove the emblem on the rear door pillar. Starting at the forward end of the door, ease the weatherstrip up using a flat tool, to free the front locating lug. When the weather strip has been released up to the point where it contacts the rear door pillar, lift it up to free the locating lug, then pull it forwards to release the rear locating pin.

34 Remove the window guide channel front vertical section, pulling it upward to release it from the pad on the upper front edge of the glass.

35 Apply a suitable strip of wide masking tape to the two door frame vertical pillars to protect the pillars as the window is removed.

36 Lift the window upwards, locating it in the recessed slots at the front and rear of the door. Carefully lift the window glass out of the door on the inner side of the frame **(see illustrations)**.

37 Refitting is the reverse of removal, checking the operation of the window prior to refitting the trim panel.

Rear fixed window

Hatchback and Saloon models

38 Remove the sliding window as described in paragraphs 22 to 26. Slide the fixed window glass forwards and remove it from the vehicle.

39 Refitting is the reverse of removal ensuring that the glass is correctly seated in its sealing strip.

Rear side window

Coupé models

40 Open up the window then undo the retaining screw and free the opening mechanism from the motor spindle. Undo the screw securing the opening mechanism to the window and recover the washers, rubbers and end cap from the window, noting the correct fitted location and orientation of each component.

41 Have an assistant support the window then slacken and remove the screws securing the front of the window to its hinges. Recover the spacers, mounting rubbers and the end caps, noting each components correct fitted position and orientation, and remove the window from the vehicle.

42 Refitting is the reverse of removal making sure the window fixing components are correctly positioned. Prior to refitting the window screws, apply a few drops of locking compound to their threads.

Scénic models

43 The rear side windows on Scénic models are bonded in position with a special adhesive. Refer to Section 22 for further information.

Rear window regulator

Hatchback and Saloon models

44 Remove the sliding window as described in paragraphs 22 to 26. On models with electric windows disconnect the wiring connector from the window motor.

45 Slacken and remove the regulator mounting bolts then free the assembly from the door and manoeuvre it out through the door aperture.

46 Refitting is the reverse of removal, checking the operation of the window prior to refitting the trim panel.

Scénic models

47 Position the window glass about 3/4 of the way down then disconnect the battery negative lead (refer to Chapter 5A, Section 1). Remove the inner trim panel from the door as described in Section 12.

48 Carefully unclip the window inner sealing strip and remove it from the door, noting which way around it is fitted.

49 Remove the window guide retaining clip by sliding it off the regulator; a 13 mm ring spanner is ideal for releasing the retaining clip tangs **(see illustrations 14.5a and 14.5b)**.

50 Free the window glass from the regulator and move it to the closed position. Secure the glass to the door frame with masking tape.

51 On models with electric windows

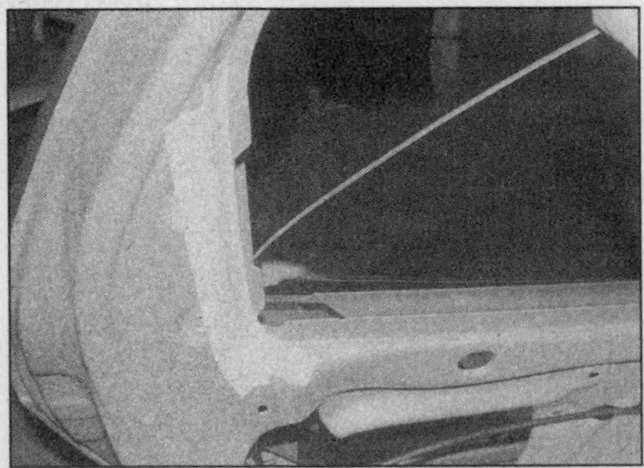

14.36a Lift the glass out through the recessed slots . . .

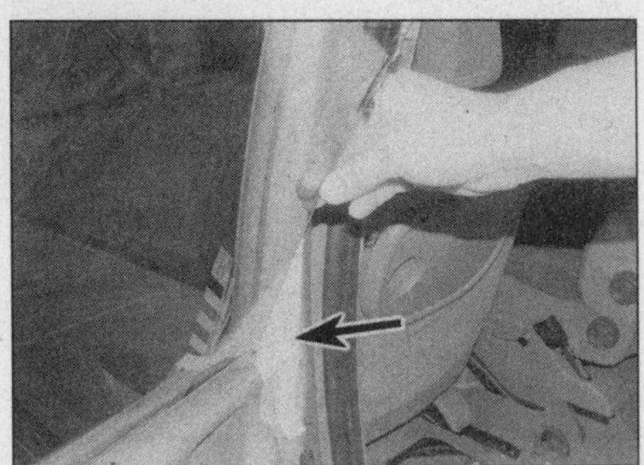

14.36b . . . note the masking tape to prevent scratches to the door frame

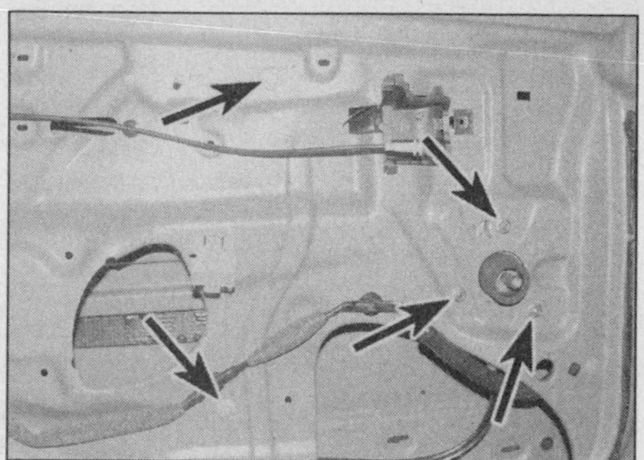

14.52 Rear door window regulator retaining bolts – Scénic

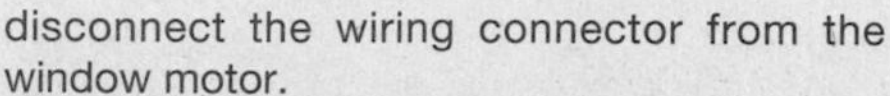

disconnect the wiring connector from the window motor.

52 Slacken and remove the regulator and lifting rail mounting nuts and bolts then free the assembly from the door and manoeuvre it out through the door aperture **(see illustration)**.

60 Refitting is the reverse of removal, checking the operation of the window prior to refitting the trim panel.

15 Boot lid – removal and refitting

Boot lid removal

Coupé models

1 Open up the boot lid and disconnect the battery negative lead.

2 Disconnect the wiring connectors from the boot lid electrical components, noting their correct fitted locations, and tie a piece of string to the end of the wiring. Noting the correct routing of the wiring harness, then release the grommet from the left-hand side of the boot lid and withdraw the wiring **(see illustration)**. When the end of the wiring appears, untie the string and leave it in position in the boot lid; it can then be used on refitting to draw the wiring into position.

3 Draw around the outline of each hinge with a suitable marker pen then unscrew the hinge retaining bolts and remove the boot lid from the vehicle **(see illustration)**.

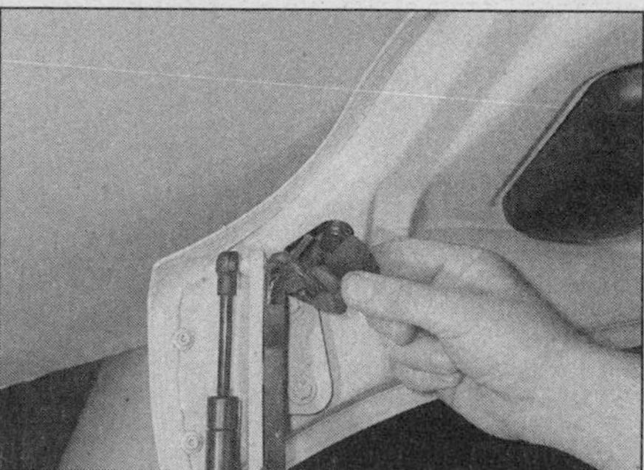

15.2 On Coupé models disconnect the wiring plugs from the boot lid then withdraw the wiring harness from the boot lid

4 Inspect the hinges for signs of wear or damage and renew if necessary; each hinge is secured to the body by two nuts.

Saloon models

5 Lift up the rear seat cushions and fold down the seat backs.

6 Remove the high-level stop-light as described in Chapter 12, Section 7. On models fitted with rear speakers also remove the speaker grilles from the parcel shelf.

7 Carefully prise out the retaining clips securing the front edge of the parcel shelf trim panel in position then slide the trim panel forwards and position it clear of the shelf.

8 Disconnect the boot lid wiring connector, which is clipped to the left-hand side of the shelf, and free the wiring from its retaining clips **(see illustration)**.

9 Open up the boot lid and free the wiring harness grommet from the body. Withdraw the wiring so that it is free to be removed with the boot lid **(see illustration)**.

10 Draw around the outline of each hinge with a suitable marker pen then unscrew the hinge retaining bolts and remove the boot lid from the vehicle.

11 Inspect the hinges for signs of wear or damage and renew if necessary; each hinge is secured to the body by two nuts.

Support strut removal

12 To remove a support strut, using a small flat-bladed screwdriver, carefully lift the retaining clip(s) and unhook the strut from its balljoint(s); on some models one end of the strut may be secured in position with a retaining nut **(see illustration)**.

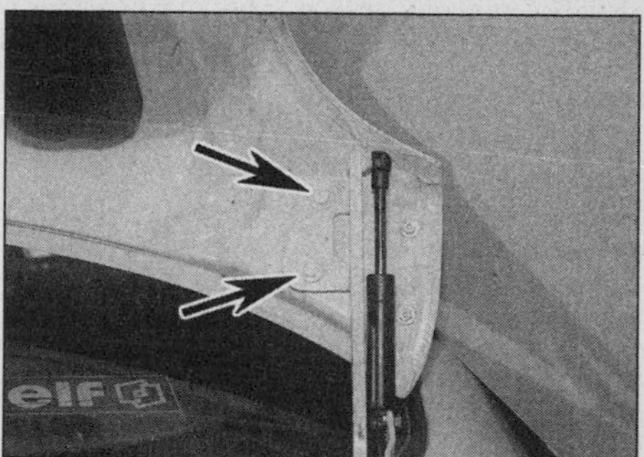

15.3 Undo the retaining bolts (arrowed) and remove the boot lid from the vehicle

Refitting

Boot lid

13 Refitting is the reverse of removal, aligning the hinges with the marks made before removal.

14 On completion, close the boot lid and check its alignment with the surrounding panels. If necessary slight adjustment can be made by slackening the retaining bolts and repositioning the boot lid on its hinges. If the paint work around the hinges has been damaged, paint the affected area with a suitable touch-in brush to prevent corrosion.

Support strut

15 Refitting is the reverse of removal ensuring that the strut is securely clipped in position.

16 Boot lid lock components – removal and refitting

Lock removal

1 Open up the boot lid then disconnect the battery negative lead.

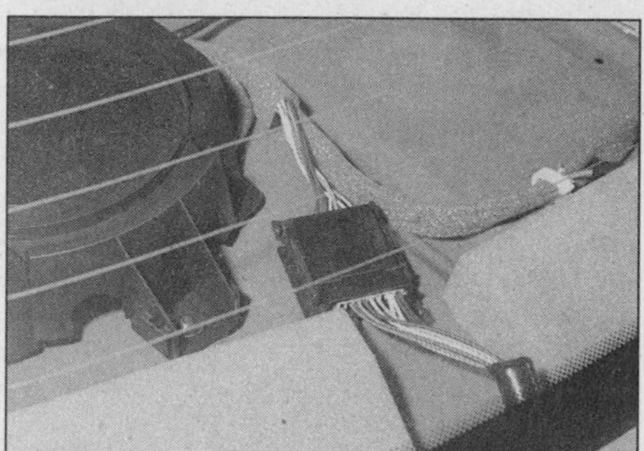

15.8 On Saloon models disconnect the wiring connector located behind the parcel shelf trim . . .

15.9 . . . then release the grommet and withdraw the wiring from the body

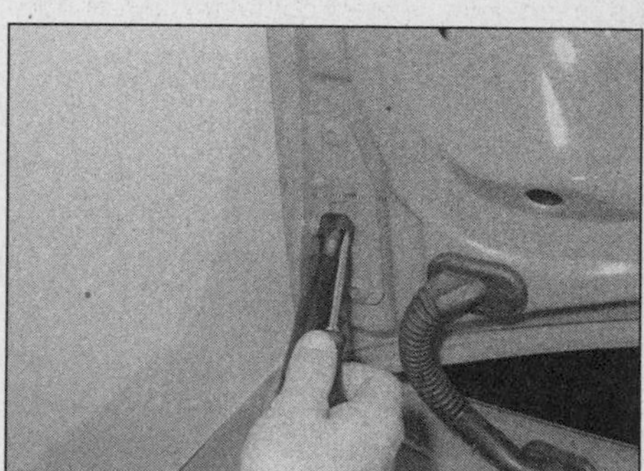

15.12 Release the boot lid support strut from its balljoints by carefully lifting its retaining clips

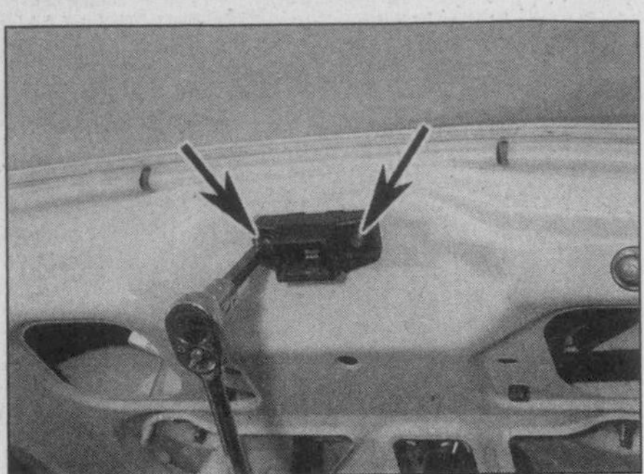

16.2a On Coupé models, undo the two retaining bolts (arrowed) . . .

16.2b . . . then detach the lock from the link rod and remove it from the boot lid

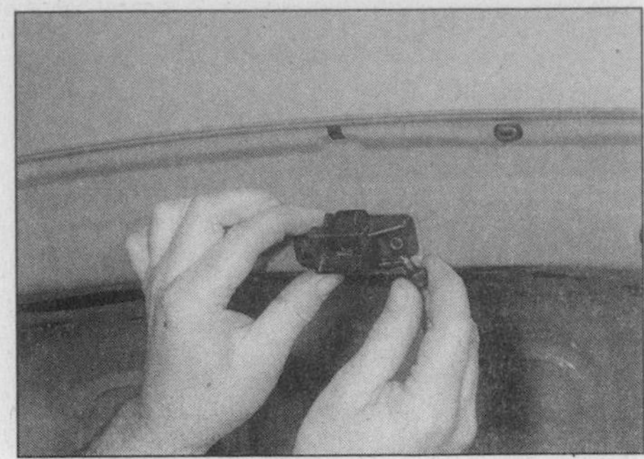

16.3 On Saloon models, undo the retaining bolts and remove the lock from the boot lid

Coupé models

2 Slacken and remove the retaining bolts then remove the lock, unhooking it from the link rod **(see illustrations)**.

Saloon models

3 Undo the retaining bolts and remove the lock from the boot lid, noting which way around it is fitted **(see illustration)**.

Lock button removal

Coupé models

4 Open up the boot lid then disconnect the battery negative lead.

5 Unclip the link rod and detach it from the lock button assembly **(see illustration)**.

6 Disconnect the wiring connector from the

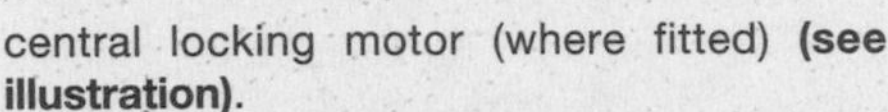

central locking motor (where fitted) **(see illustration)**.

7 Slacken and remove the retaining nuts and manoeuvre the button assembly out of position **(see illustration)**.

Saloon models

8 Unclip the plastic trim cover then release the retaining clip and detach the link rod from the button assembly **(see illustrations)**.

9 Disconnect the drain pipe from the lock then undo the two retaining nuts and manoeuvre the assembly out from the boot lid **(see illustration)**.

Refitting

10 Refitting is the reverse of removal, checking the operation of the lock assembly and (where necessary) the central locking motor.

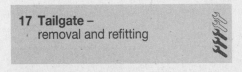

17 Tailgate – removal and refitting

Tailgate removal

All models except Scénic

1 Open up the tailgate then disconnect the battery negative lead.

2 Working as described in paragraphs 25 to 29 of Section 27, remove the upper trim panel from the left-hand rear pillar to gain access to the tailgate wiring connector.

3 Disconnect the tailgate wiring connector then free the wiring grommet and withdraw the wiring harness from the body so that it is

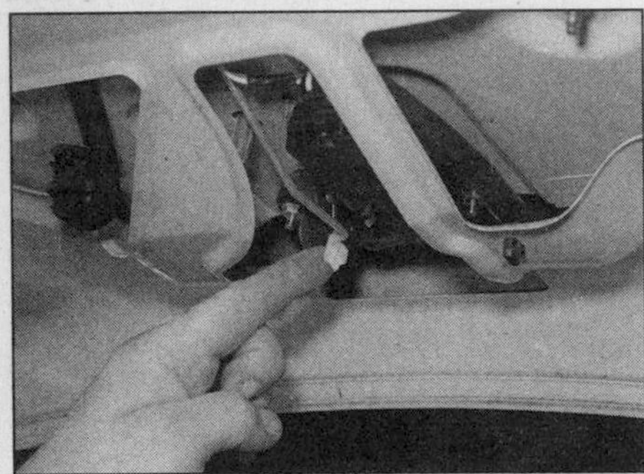

16.5 Unclip the link rod . . .

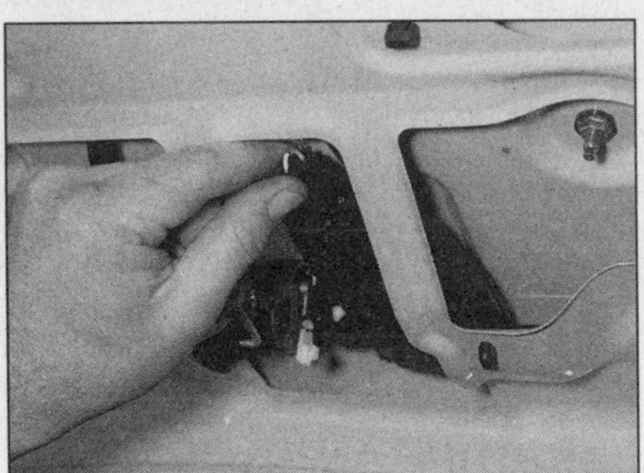

16.6 . . . then disconnect the central locking motor wiring connector

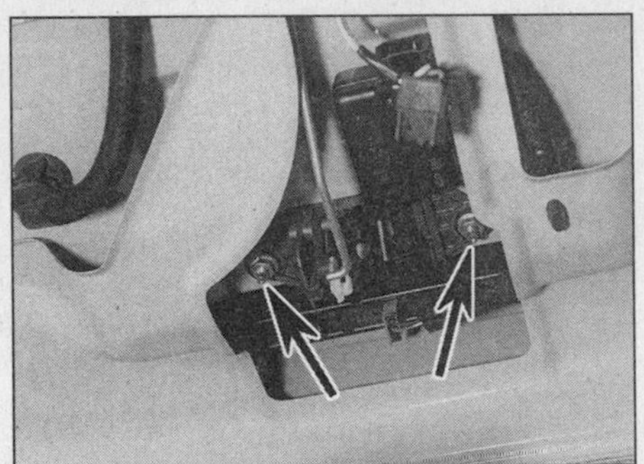

16.7 Undo the retaining nuts (arrowed) and remove the boot lid lock button assembly from the vehicle

16.8a Unclip the plastic trim cover . . .

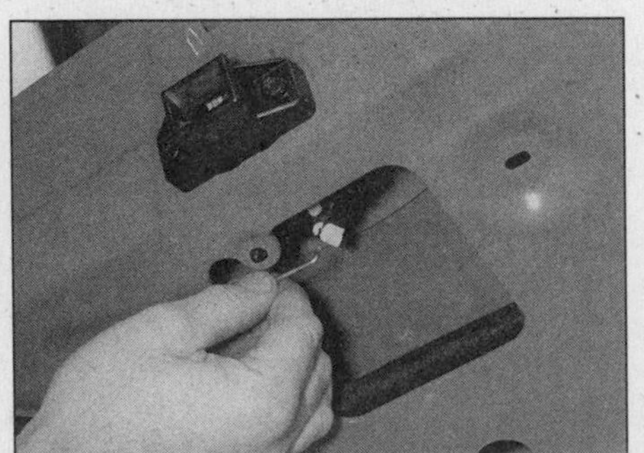

16.8b . . . and detach the link rod from the lock button

16.9 Unscrew the retaining nuts and remove the lock button assembly from the boot lid

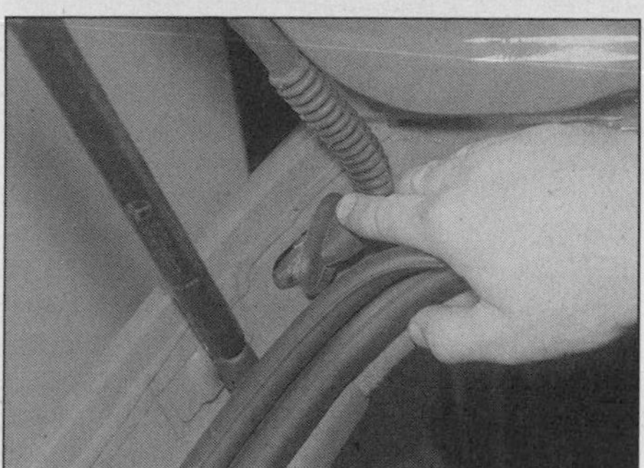

17.3 Disconnect the tailgate wiring connector then withdraw the wiring harness from the body

17.4 Prise out the trim plugs, then undo the hinge retaining nuts and remove the tailgate

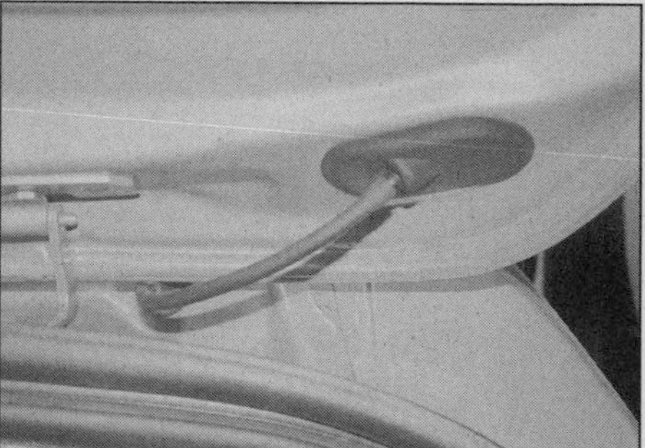

17.11 Disconnect the rear screen washer hose

free to be removed with the tailgate **(see illustration)**.

4 Prise out the trim plugs from the rear of the headlining to gain access to the tailgate hinge retaining nuts **(see illustrations)**.

5 Have an assistant support the tailgate, then carefully lift the retaining clips and detach the support struts.

6 Unscrew the nuts securing the tailgate hinges to the body and remove the tailgate from the vehicle.

Scénic models

7 Open up the tailgate then disconnect the battery negative lead (refer to Chapter 5A).

8 Undo the four tailgate trim panel retaining bolts. Release the retaining clips by carefully pulling on the tailgate closing handles in the trim panel, then withdraw the panel from the tailgate.

9 Noting their locations for refitting, disconnect all the tailgate wiring connectors then release the wiring loom from the retaining clips.

10 Prise out the wiring loom grommet from the side of the tailgate. Disconnect the wiring connector for the high-level stop-light, then withdraw the wiring loom from the tailgate.

11 Disconnect the rear washer fluid hose and withdraw the hose from the tailgate **(see illustration)**.

12 To gain access to the tailgate hinge retaining nuts, remove the trim plugs each side by turning them a quarter turn anticlockwise with a flat-bladed screwdriver **(see illustration)**.

13 Have an assistant support the tailgate, then carefully lift the retaining clips and detach the support struts.

14 Unscrew the nuts securing the tailgate hinges to the body and remove the tailgate from the vehicle.

Support strut removal

15 Have an assistant support the tailgate then, using a small flat-bladed screwdriver, carefully lift the retaining clips and unhook the strut from its balljoints **(see illustration)**.

Refitting

Tailgate

16 Refitting is the reverse of removal. On completion, ensure that the tailgate is correctly aligned with all its surrounding body components (there should be a clearance of up to 4.5 ± 1 mm (except Scénic) or 5.4 ± 1 mm (Scénic)); adjustments can be made by slackening the bolts and repositioning the tailgate adjusters located on either side **(see illustrations)**.

Support strut

17 Refitting is the reverse of removal making sure the strut is clipped securely in position.

18 Tailgate lock components – removal and refitting

Removal

Lock

1 Open up the tailgate then disconnect the battery negative lead (refer to Chapter 5A)

2 Undo the four tailgate trim panel retaining screws/bolts. Release the retaining clips by carefully pulling on the tailgate closing handles in the trim panel, then withdraw the panel from the tailgate.

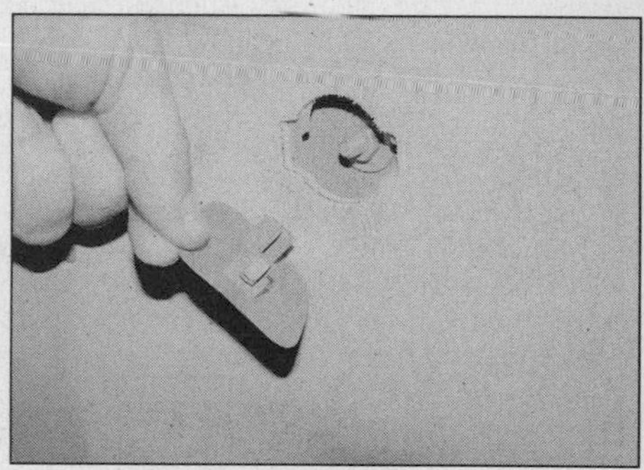

17.12 Prise out the trim plugs for access to the hinge mounting nuts

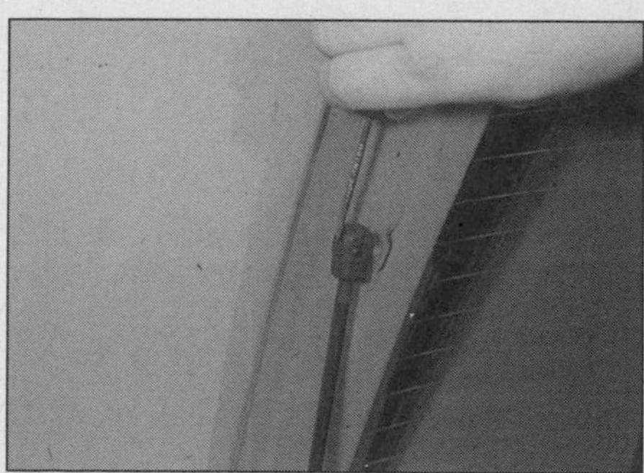

17.15 Release the tailgate support strut from its balljoints by lifting its clips

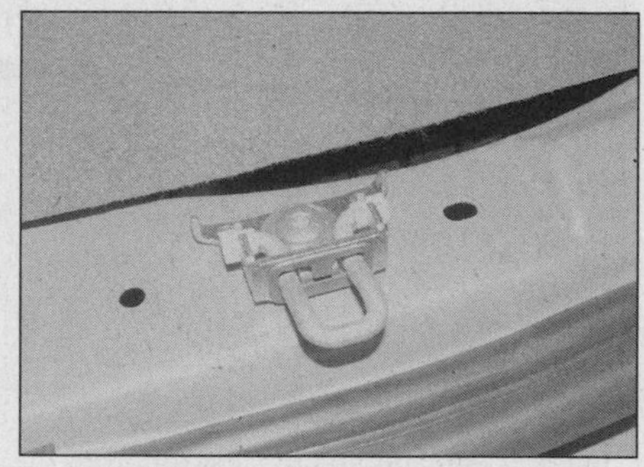

17.16a Slacken the screw to move the adjusting block – Hatchback

17.16b Tailgate adjusting block on Scénic models

18.3 Disconnect the link rod from the lock button . . .

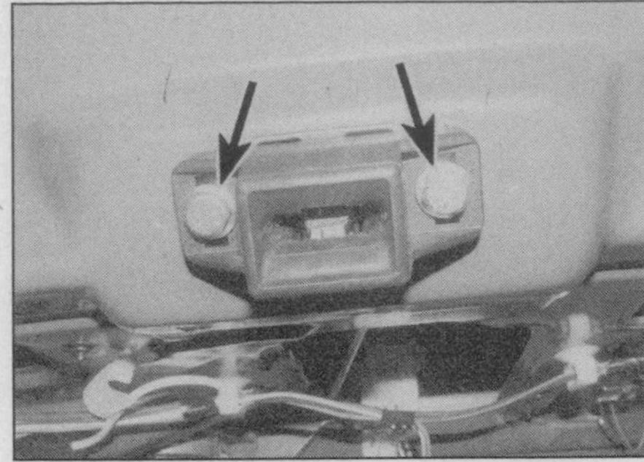
18.4 . . . then undo the retaining bolts and remove the lock from the tailgate

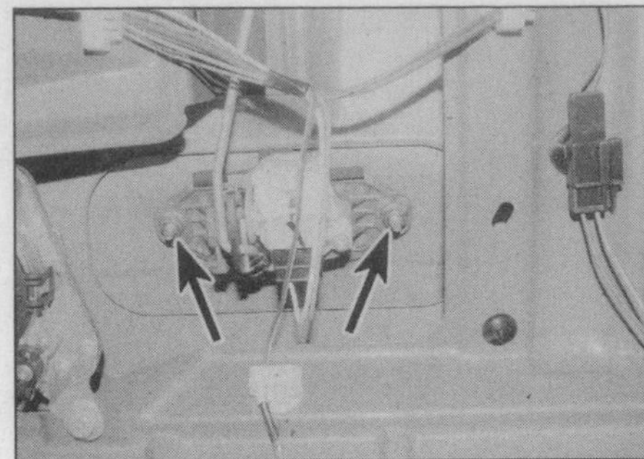
18.6 Undo the retaining nuts and remove the lock button assembly

18.7a Undo the retaining screws . . .

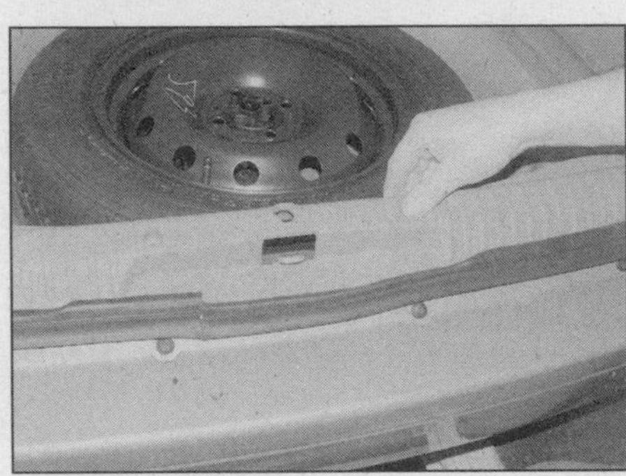
18.7b . . . and release the rear trim panel . . .

3 Detach the link rod from the lock button assembly **(see illustration)**.

4 Slacken and remove the retaining bolts and remove the lock assembly from the tailgate **(see illustration)**.

Lock button

5 Carry out the operations described in paragraphs 1 to 3.

6 Disconnect the wiring connector from the central locking motor (where fitted). Slacken and remove the retaining nuts and clips, then manoeuvre the lock button assembly (and central locking motor – where fitted) out from the tailgate **(see illustration)**.

Lock striker

7 Open up the tailgate and unclip the plastic cover from the lock striker. On Scénic models, unscrew the rear trim from the luggage compartment **(see illustrations)**.

8 Draw around the outline of the striker plate mounting, then undo the bolt(s) and remove the striker from the vehicle.

Refitting

Lock

9 Refitting is the reverse of removal. Check the lock operation before refitting the trim panel.

Lock button

10 Refitting is the reverse of removal, checking the operation of the lock prior to refitting the trim panel.

Lock striker

11 Fit the striker to the vehicle, and refit the bolt(s). Align the mounting plate with the marks made before removal and tighten the bolts securely.

12 Check the operation of the lock, if necessary adjustments can be made by slackening the bolt(s) and repositioning the striker **(see illustration)**, then where applicable, refit the plastic cover.

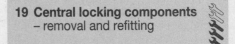

19 Central locking components – removal and refitting

Note: *The following procedures, are for the central locking motors that are separate units and can be renewed without the complete lock assembly. On later models, the central locking motors are part of the lock assembly; if there is a fault with the central locking unit then the complete lock assembly will have to be renewed.*

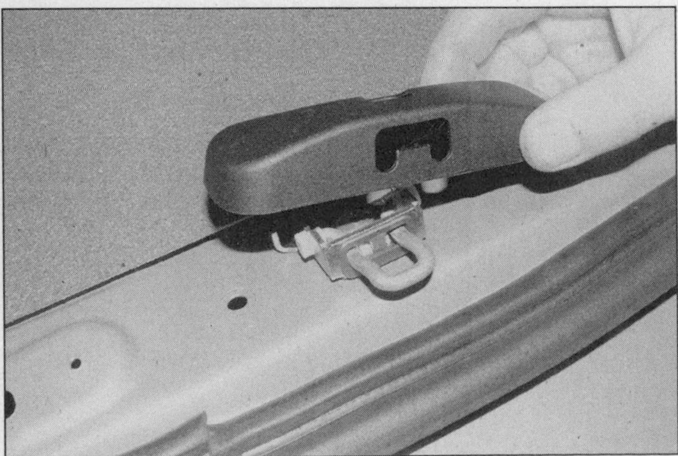
18.7c . . . then unclip the lock striker cover

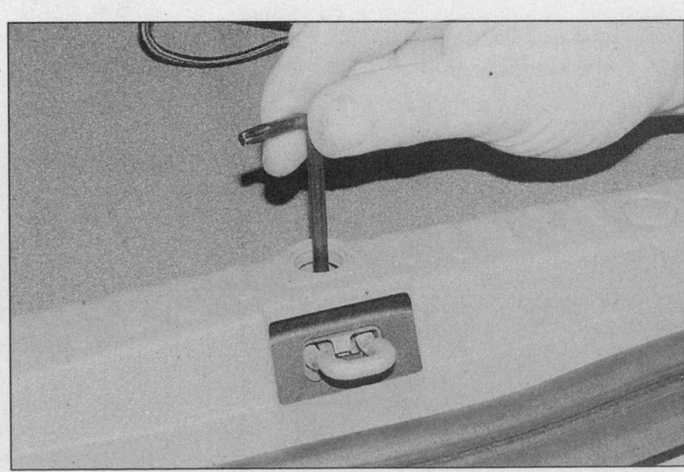
18.12 Adjusting the lock striker through the trim cover – Scénic

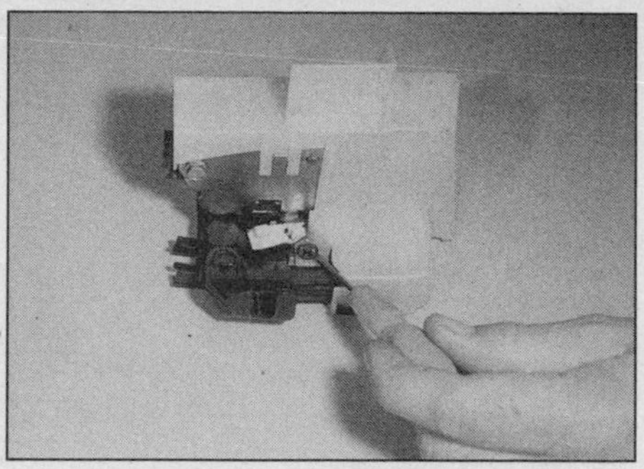

19.2a Prise off the retaining clip . . .

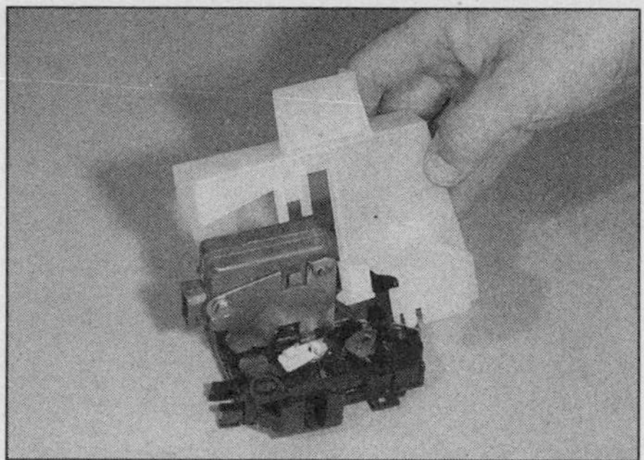

19.2b . . . then unclip the plastic cover and remove it from the door lock

19.3a Undo the retaining screw . . .

Removal

Door lock motor

1 Remove the door lock assembly as described in Section 13.

2 Carefully prise off the retaining clip, taking care not to lose it, then unclip the plastic cover and remove it from the lock **(see illustrations)**.

3 Undo the retaining screw and detach the motor from the lock assembly **(see illustrations)**.

Tailgate lock motor

4 Remove the lock button assembly as described in Section 18.

5 Remove the retaining screw and clip and detach the motor from the mounting bracket.

Boot lid lock motor – Coupé models

6 Remove the lock button assembly as described in Section 16.

7 Remove the retaining screw and clip and detach the motor from the mounting bracket **(see illustration)**.

Boot lid lock motor – Saloon models

8 Open up the boot lid and unclip the lock access cover.

9 Release the retaining clip and detach the link rod from the motor **(see illustration)**.

10 Remove the retaining screw and clip and withdraw the motor from the boot lid, disconnect its wiring connector as it becomes accessible **(see illustrations)**.

Fuel filler flap motor

11 Prise out the retaining clips and peel back the luggage compartment side trim panel to gain access to the motor; on some models it will be necessary to remove the rear light covers to free the panel **(see illustration)**.

12 Disconnect the wiring connector then undo the screw securing the motor mounting bracket to the body **(see illustration)**.

13 Carefully unclip the mounting bracket and

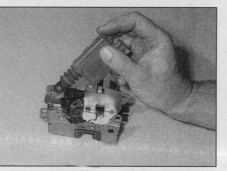

19.3b . . . then pivot the motor away from its mounting bracket and remove it

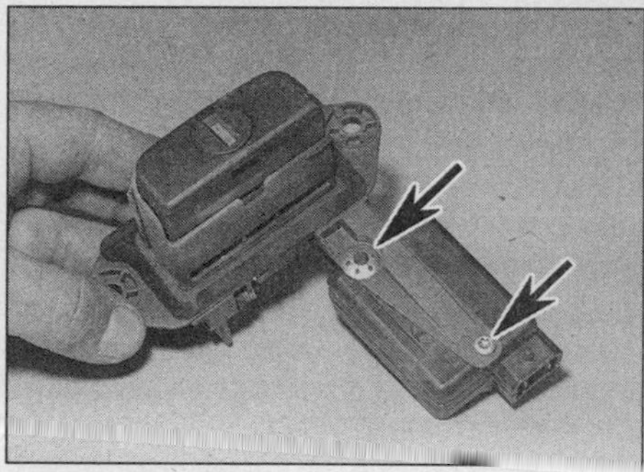

19.7 Boot lid lock motor retaining screw and clip (arrowed) – Coupé models

19.9 On Saloon models remove the access cover and detach the link rod . . .

19.10a . . . then remove the retaining screw and clip (arrowed) . . .

19.10b . . . and remove the central locking motor, disconnecting its wiring connector

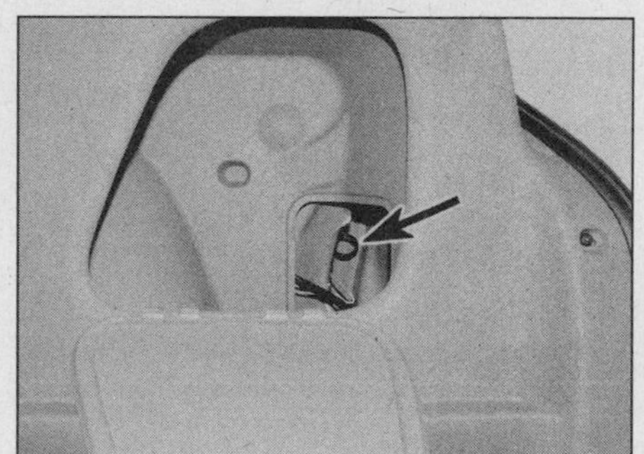

19.11 Pull the ring (arrowed) to release the fuel flap, if motor is not operating – Scénic

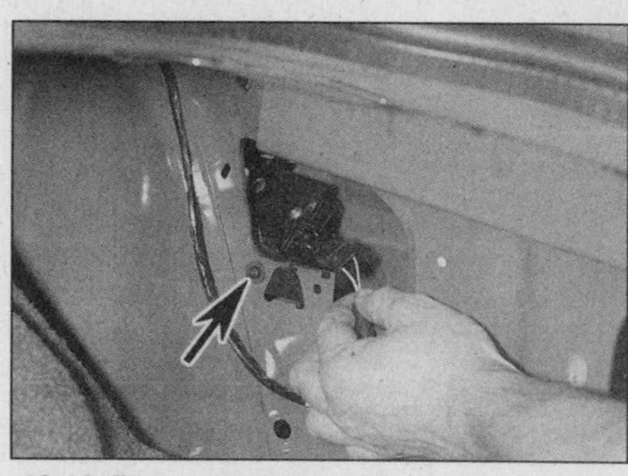

19.12 Disconnect the fuel filler flap wiring plug, then undo the screw (arrowed) . . .

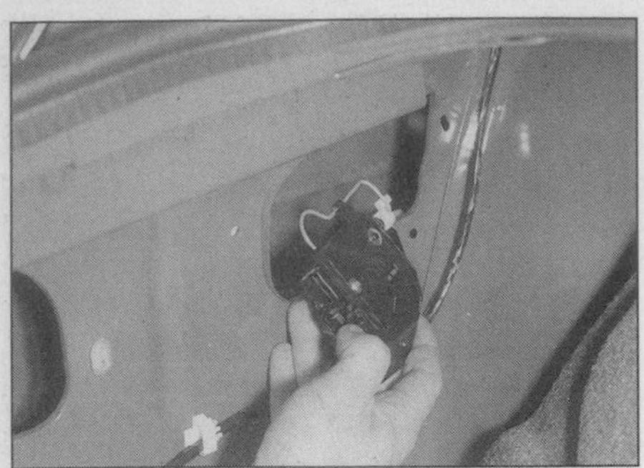
19.13a . . . then unclip and remove the motor and mounting bracket assembly

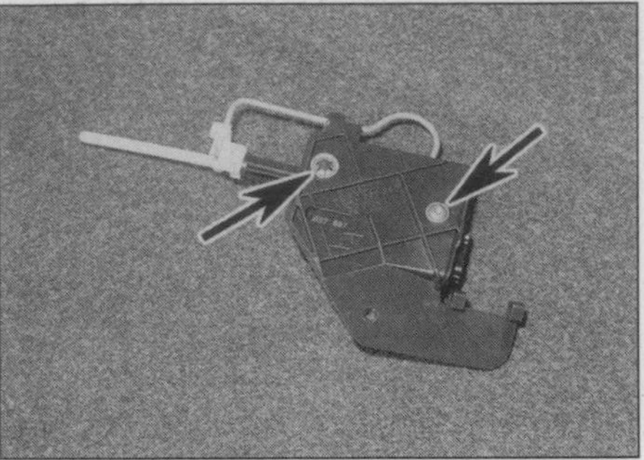
19.13b If necessary, remove the retaining screw and clip and separate the bracket and filler flap motor

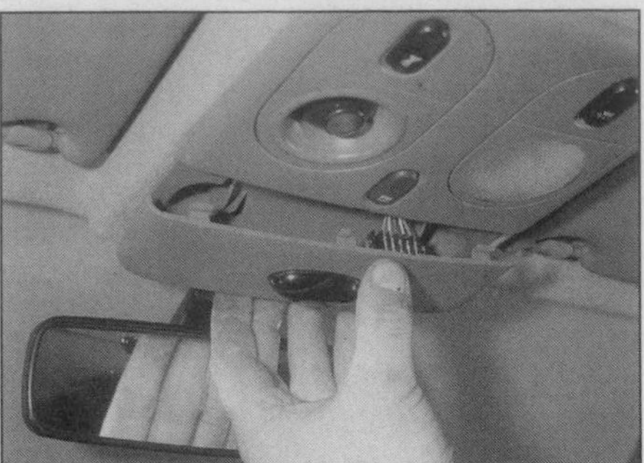
19.14 Carefully unclip the front panel from the roof console and disconnect its wiring connector

remove the motor assembly from the vehicle. The bracket and motor can be separated once the retaining clip and screw have been removed **(see illustrations)**.

Central locking remote receiver

14 Carefully unclip the front panel from the roof console in a forwards direction **(see illustration)**.

15 Disconnect the wiring connector then carefully unclip the central locking printed circuit board and separate it from the panel **(see illustration)**.

Refitting

16 Refitting is the reverse of removal; on refitting the fuel filler flap motor ensure that the flap locking rod is correctly seated in its guide tube. Prior to refitting any trim panels removed for access, thoroughly check the operation of the central locking system.

20 Electric window components – removal and refitting

Note: *If the battery is disconnected with a window open, the window will need reprogramming once the battery is reconnected. To do this, turn on the ignition and fully lower the window to its stop. Hold the switch until the relay clicks then, within two seconds, fully raise the window (it will rise in short steps). Once the window is fully-closed, keep the switch depressed for a few seconds; this initialises the ECU so it learns the fully closed position. Release the switch and check the window operation. Repeat the procedure as necessary.*

Window switches

1 Refer to Chapter 12, Section 4.

Door window winder motors

2 The window winder motors are not available separately, they are part of the window regulator assembly. See Section 14 for the removal of the window regulator assembly. Refer to your Renault dealer for any additional information.

Rear side window opening motor

Coupé models

3 Remove the rear seat side trim panel as described in Section 27, paragraphs 12 to 23.

4 Slacken and remove the motor retaining screws then disconnect the wiring connector and remove the motor from the vehicle **(see illustration)**.

5 Refitting is the reverse of removal.

21 Exterior mirrors and associated components – removal and refitting

Manually-adjusted mirror

All models except Scénic

1 Carefully unclip the top of the mirror inner trim panel from the door then free the trim panel from the adjustment lever and remove it from the door.

2 Remove the seal from the adjustment lever and the insulating foam.

3 Prise out the trim covers and insulation to reveal the mirror retaining nuts then undo the nuts and remove the mirror from the door. Recover the rubber seal which is fitted between the door and the mirror; if the seal is damaged it must be renewed.

4 Refitting is the reverse of removal.

Scénic models

5 Unclip the exterior mirror inner trim panel from the front of the door.

6 Where a mirror with remote adjustment control is fitted, remove the door inner trim panel as described in Section 12, remove the retaining clips securing the mirror adjustment control to the trim panel.

7 Undo the three retaining nuts and remove the mirror from the door. Where fitted, recover the rubber seal which is fitted between the door and the mirror; if the seal is damaged it must be renewed.

8 Refitting is the reverse of removal.

Electrically-operated mirror

All models except Scénic

9 Carefully unclip the top of the mirror inner trim panel and remove the panel from the door.

10 Remove the insulating foam and disconnect the motor wiring connector **(see illustration)**.

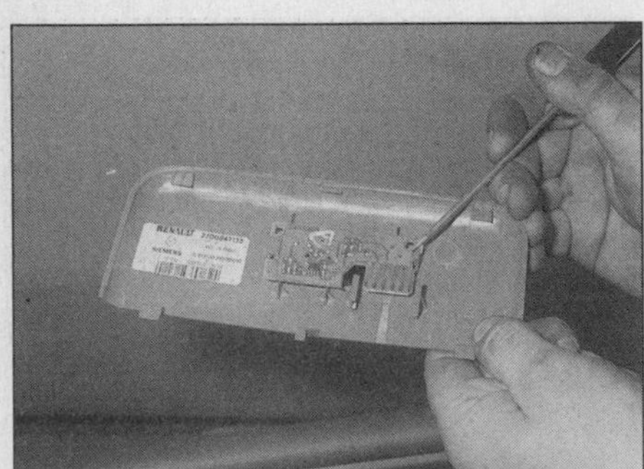
19.15 The central locking remote receiver is clipped into the panel

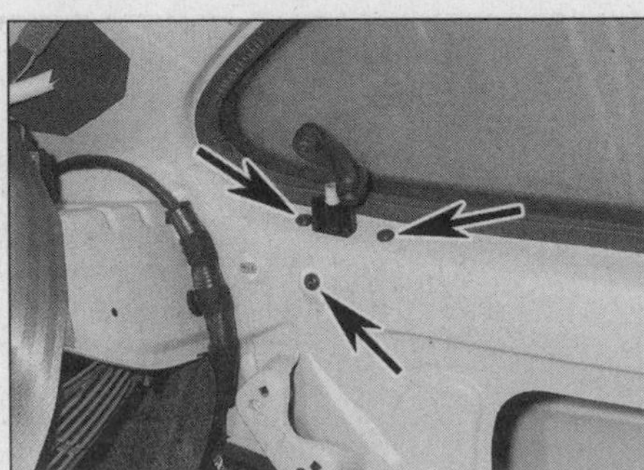
20.4 Rear side window opening motor retaining screws (arrowed) – Coupé

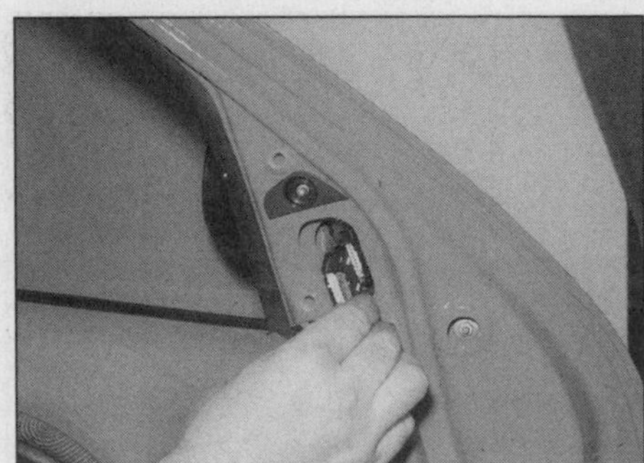
21.10 Disconnect the mirror wiring connector

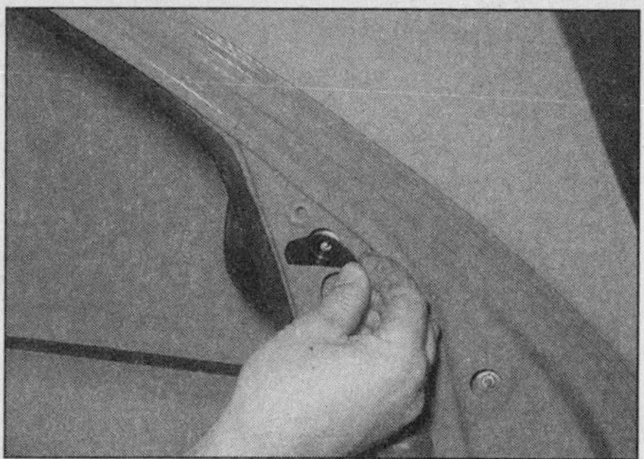
21.11a Remove the covers . . .

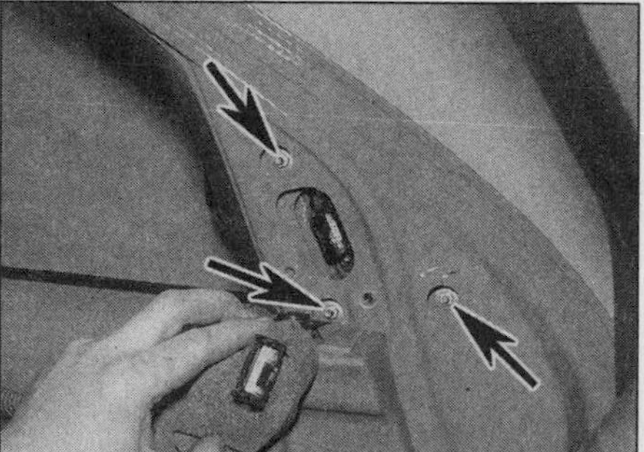
21.11b . . . then slacken the retaining nuts (arrowed) . . .

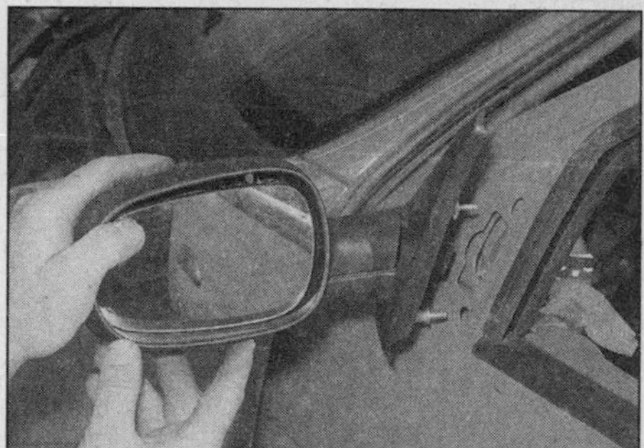
21.11c . . . and remove the mirror

11 Prise out the trim covers to reveal the mirror retaining nuts then undo the nuts and remove the mirror from the door **(see illustrations)**. Recover the rubber seal which is fitted between the door and mirror; if the seal is damaged it must be renewed.

12 Refitting is the reverse of removal.

Scénic models

13 Unclip the exterior mirror inner trim panel from the front of the door **(see illustration)**.

14 Disconnect the wiring block connector from the door mirror assembly **(see illustration)**.

15 Undo the three retaining nuts and remove the mirror from the door **(see illustration)**. Where fitted, recover the rubber seal which is fitted between the door and the mirror; if the seal is damaged it must be renewed.

16 Refitting is the reverse of removal.

Mirror glass

Note: *The mirror glass is clipped into position. Removal of the glass is likely to result in breakage if carried out carelessly.*

17 Tilt the mirror glass fully downwards and insert a wide plastic or wooden wedge in-between the centre of the mirror glass and the mirror housing **(see illustration)**. Carefully prise the glass from the motor/adjuster; take great care when removing the glass; do not use excessive force as the glass is easily broken.

18 Remove the glass from the mirror, where necessary, disconnect the wiring from the mirror heating element **(see illustration)**.

19 On refitting, reconnect the wiring to the glass and clip the glass onto the motor/adjuster, taking great care not to break it. Ensure that the glass is clipped securely into position and adjust as necessary.

Mirror switch

20 Refer to Chapter 12, Section 4.

22 Windscreen, side and rear screen glass – general information

These areas of glass are secured by the tight fit of the weatherstrip in the body aperture, and are bonded in position with a special adhesive. Renewal of such fixed glass is a difficult, messy and time-consuming task, which is beyond the scope of the home mechanic. It is difficult, unless one has plenty of practice, to obtain a secure, waterproof fit. Furthermore, the task carries a high risk of breakage; this applies especially to the laminated glass windscreen. In view of this, owners are strongly advised to have this sort of work carried out by one of the many specialist windscreen fitters.

23 Sunroof – general information

1 Due to the complexity of the sunroof mechanism, considerable expertise is needed to repair, renew or adjust the sunroof components successfully. Removal of the roof first requires the headlining to be removed, which is a complex and tedious operation, and not a task to be undertaken lightly. Therefore, any problems with the sunroof should be referred to a Renault dealer.

2 On models with an electric sunroof, if the

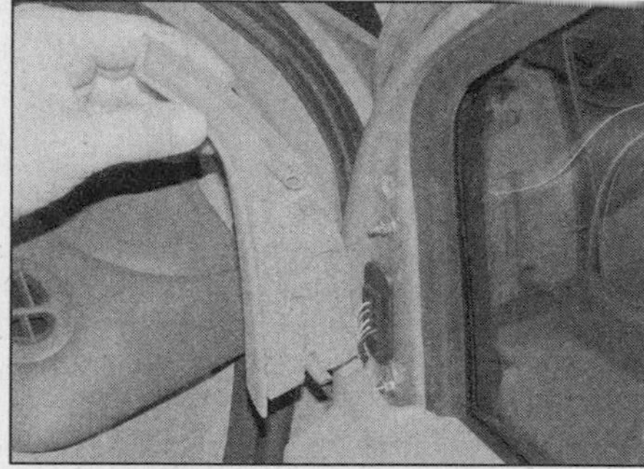
21.13 Unclip the trim cover . . .

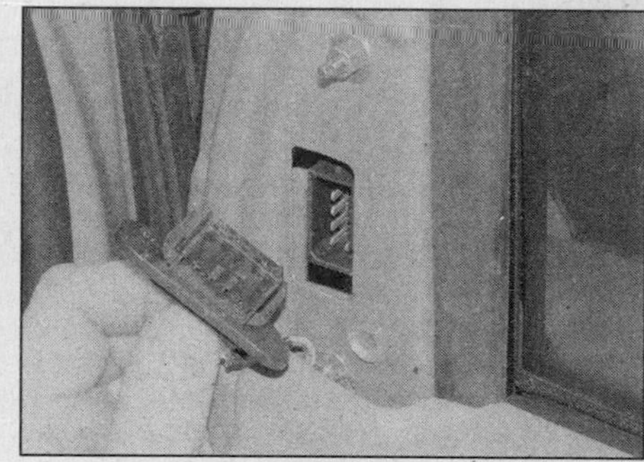
21.14 . . . disconnect the wiring connector . . .

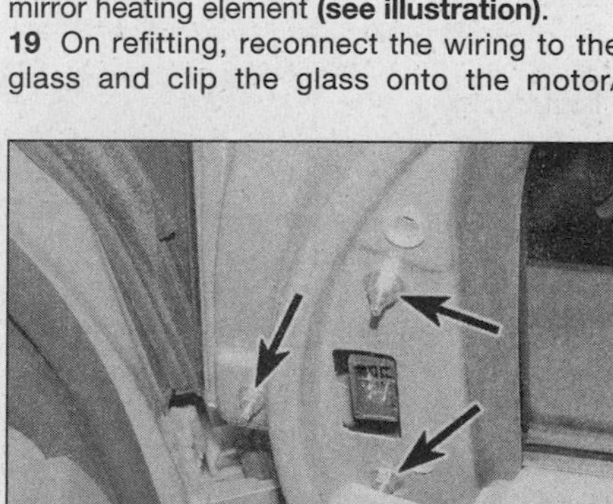
21.15 . . . and undo the three mounting nuts (arrowed)

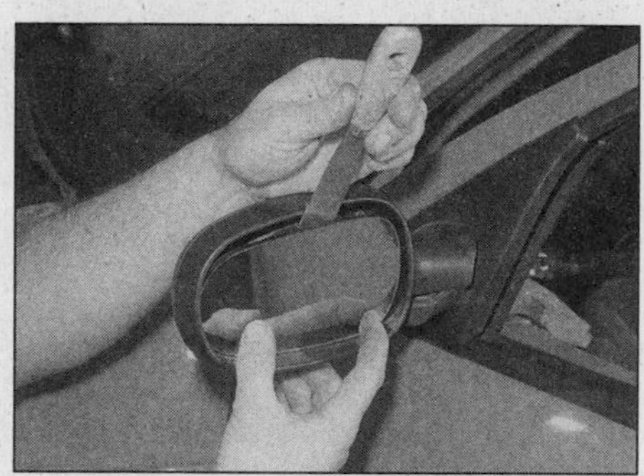
21.17 Carefully prise out the mirror glass . . .

21.18 . . . and disconnect its wiring plugs

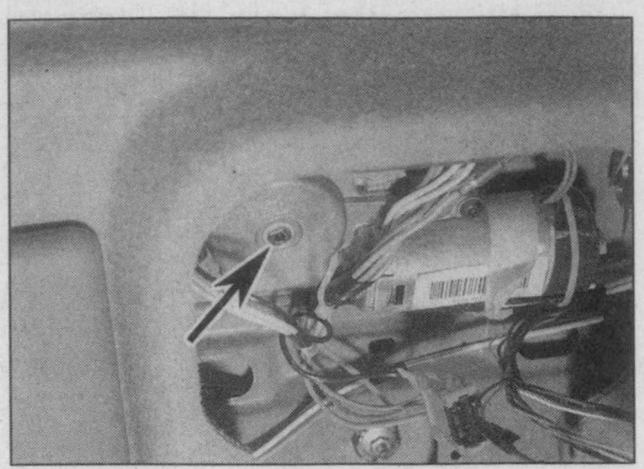

23.2 In an emergency, the electric sunroof can be moved by rotating the motor spindle with a suitable Allen key

sunroof motor fails to operate, first check the relevant fuse. If the fault cannot be traced and rectified, the sunroof can be opened and closed manually using an Allen key to turn the motor spindle **(see illustration)**. To gain access to the motor spindle, it is necessary to remove the complete overhead console from the roof (see Chapter 12, Section 4). Using an Allen key, rotate the motor spindle and move the sunroof to the required position.

24 Body exterior fittings – removal and refitting

Wheelarch liners and body under-panels

1 The various plastic covers fitted to the underside of the vehicle are secured in position by a mixture of screws, nuts and retaining clips and removal will be fairly obvious on inspection. Work methodically around the panel removing its retaining screws and releasing its retaining clips until the panel is free and can be removed from the underside of the vehicle. Most clips used on the vehicle are simply prised out of position. Other clips can be released by unscrewing/prising out the centre pins and then removing the clip.

2 On refitting, renew any retaining clips that may have been broken on removal, and ensure that the panel is securely retained by all the relevant clips and screws.

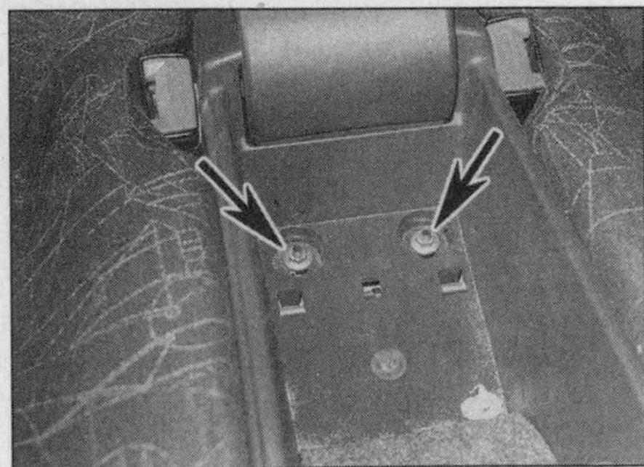

25.10 On Coupé models, undo the retaining nuts (arrowed) situated in the storage compartment . . .

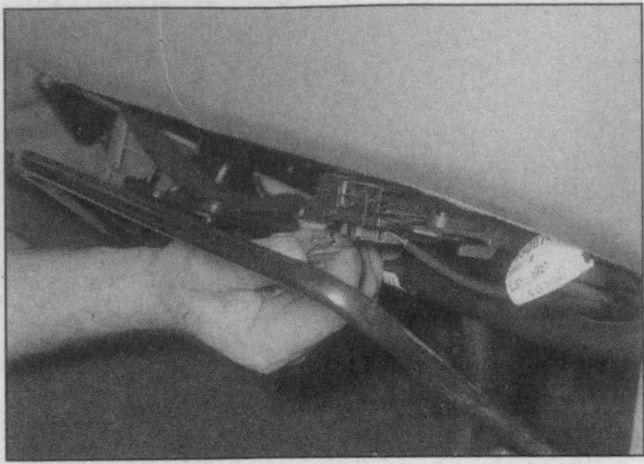

25.3 Disconnect the wiring connectors and remove the front seat from the vehicle

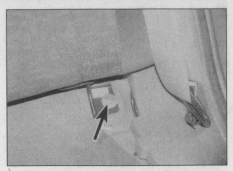

Body trim strips and badges

3 The various body trim strips and badges are held in position with a special adhesive tape. Removal requires the trim/badge to be heated, to soften the adhesive, and then cut away from the surface. Due to the high risk of damage to the vehicle's paintwork during this operation, it is recommended that this task should be entrusted to a Renault dealer.

25 Seats – removal and refitting

Front seat removal

Warning: On models with seat belt tensioners, disable the tensioning mechanism (see Section 26) before removing the seat.

All models except Scénic

1 Firmly apply the handbrake then jack up the front of the vehicle and support it on axle stands (see *Jacking and vehicle support*).

2 From underneath the vehicle, slacken and remove the four seat mounting nuts.

3 From inside the vehicle, lift the front seat out of position, disconnecting its wiring connectors as they become accessible **(see illustration)**.

Scénic models

4 Remove the circular trim cover on the side of the seat, then undo the seat belt retaining bolt working through the trim cover aperture.

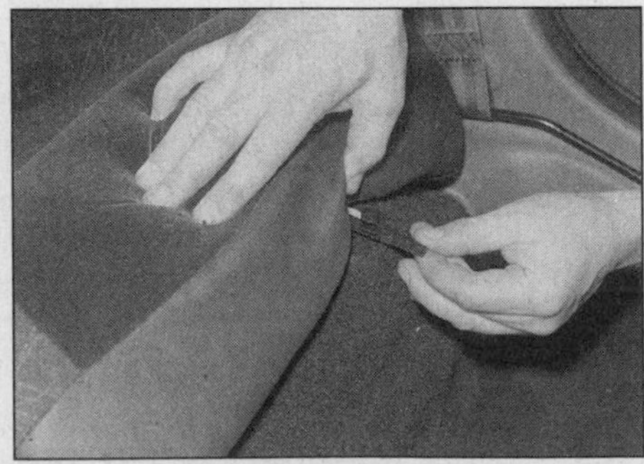

25.11 . . . then slide out the retaining clips to allow the seat cushion to be lifted out of position

25.9 Undo the retaining nut (arrowed)

5 Slide the seat forward and undo the two seat rail rear retaining bolts.

6 Slide the seat rearwards and undo the two seat rail front retaining bolts.

7 Open the covers under the seat and disconnect the seat wiring connectors. Withdraw the seat from the vehicle.

Rear seat removal

Hatchback and Saloon models

8 To remove the rear seat cushions, fold the cushion(s) up and unhook the side front pivots from the floor.

9 To remove the seat back, remove the seat cushion(s) then slacken and remove the retaining nuts from the seat back hinges **(see illustration)**. Release the seat back from its locking pins and remove it from the vehicle.

Coupé models

10 Open up the rear seat storage compartment then peel back the felt cover and unscrew the retaining nuts **(see illustration)**.

11 Using a pair of pliers, pull out the retaining clips from the left- and right-hand side of the seat cushion then lift the cushion out from the vehicle **(see illustration)**.

12 Slacken and remove the seat back retaining nuts and remove the assembly from the vehicle; if the complete seat assembly is to be removed undo the three hinge main securing nuts, if only one side of the seat is to be removed undo the outer hinge nut and smaller nut securing the seat to the centre hinge assembly **(see illustration)**.

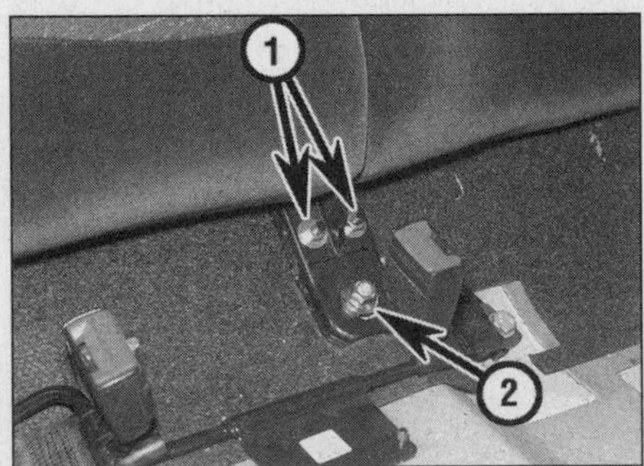

25.12 To remove the complete seat assembly, undo the main centre hinge nut (2); to remove either side of the seat undo the relevant smaller nut (1)

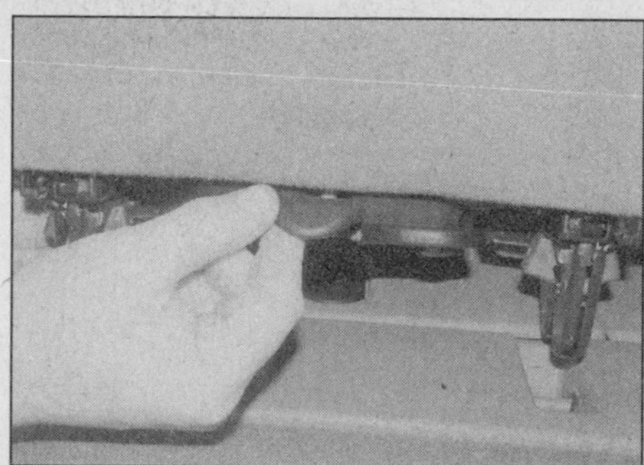

25.14 Pull the lever to release the rear of the seat . . .

Scénic models

13 Lift the release lever on the top (centre seat) or side (side seats) and fold the seat back down until it locks in position.

14 Lift the locking bar at the rear of the seat base and fold the seat assembly forward **(see illustration)**.

15 Lower the two lugs at the seat forward mounting/pivot points and lift the seat out of the vehicle **(see illustration)**.

Refitting

16 Refitting is the reverse of removal ensuring all nuts/bolts are securely tightened. When refitting the rear seats on Scénic models, engage the seat forward mountings/pivots in their locations, lower the seat until it is approximately 100 mm from the floor and release it. The seat will automatically lock into place.

26 Front seat belt tensioning mechanism – general information

Most models covered in this manual are fitted with a front seat belt tensioner system. The system is designed to instantaneously take up any slack in the seat belt in the case of a sudden frontal impact, therefore reducing the possibility of injury to the front seat occupants. Each front seat is fitted with the system, the tensioner being attached directly to the seat belt stalk.

The seat belt tensioner is operated by the same control unit as the airbag (Chapter 12). The tensioner is electrically triggered by a frontal impact above a pre-determined force. Lesser impacts, including impacts from behind, will not trigger the system.

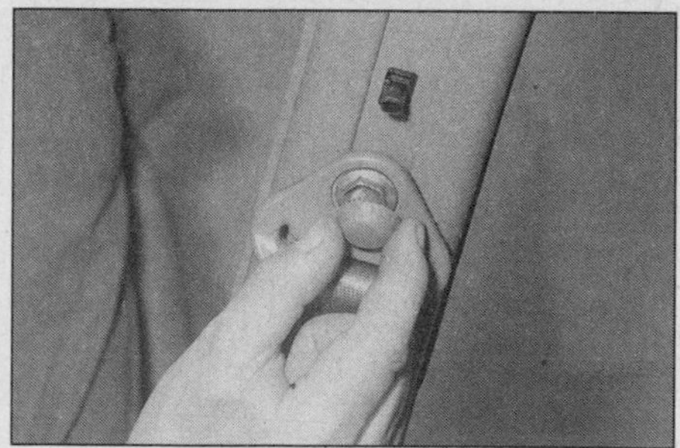

27.4a Remove the trim cover . . .

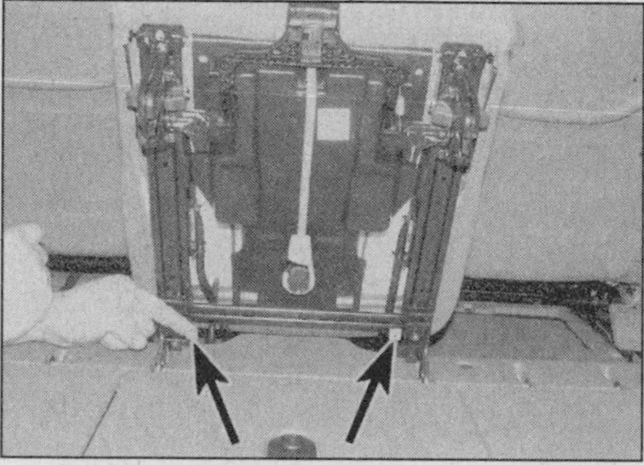

25.15 . . . then release the two front seat catches

When the system is triggered, the gas generator inside the tensioner cylinder ignites. This forces the tensioner piston forwards which then removes all slack from the seat belt by retracting the seat belt stalk. The strength of the explosion in the tensioner cylinder is calibrated to retract the seat belt sufficiently to securely retain the occupant of the seat without forcing them into the seat. Once the tensioner has been triggered, the seat belt will be permanently locked and the assembly must be renewed.

To prevent the risk of injury if the system is triggered inadvertently when working on the vehicle, if any work is to be carried out on the front seats, disconnect the battery and disable the tensioner. To do this, remove the seat belt tensioner/airbag system fuse from the engine compartment fusebox and wait for at least five minutes. This will allow the reserve power capacitors in the control unit to discharge.

Also note the following warnings before contemplating any work on the front seat belts.

Warning: If the seat belt tensioners are activated in an accident, both the tensioners and the control unit must be renewed.

Warning: If the tensioner mechanism is dropped, it must be renewed, even it has suffered no apparent damage.

Warning: Do not allow any solvents to come into contact with the tensioner mechanism.

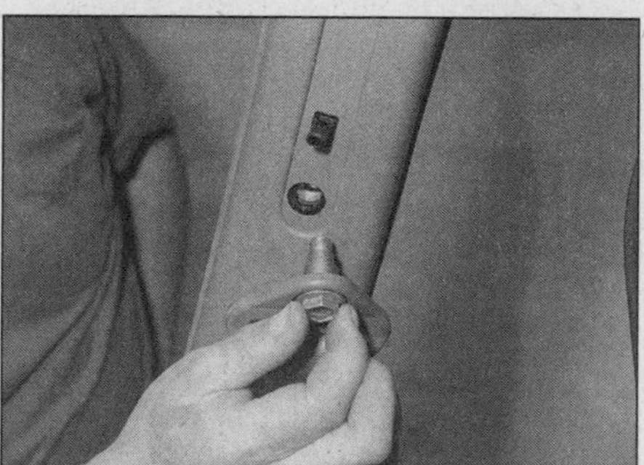

27.4b . . . then unscrew the mounting bolt and detach the seat belt upper mounting from the pillar

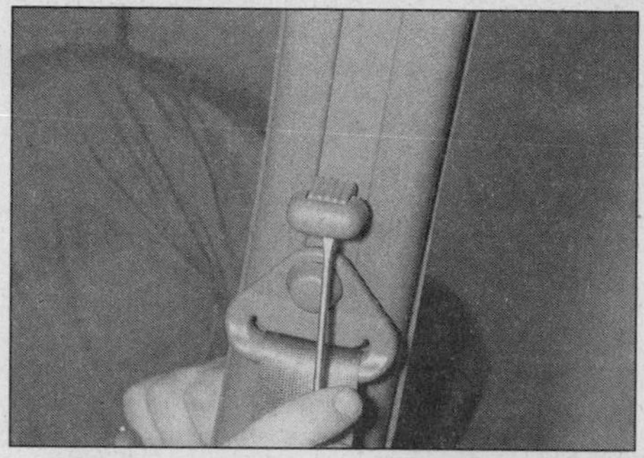

27.3 Lever between the adjustment lever inner and outer sections and remove the lever from the vehicle

Warning: Do not subject the seat to any form of shock as this could accidentally trigger to the seat belt tensioner.

Warning: Do not subject the tensioner assembly to excessive temperatures.

27 Seat belt components – removal and refitting

Warning: On models equipped with front seat belt tensioners refer to Section 26 before proceeding.

Front seat belt removal

Hatchback and Saloon models

1 Disconnect the battery negative lead.

2 To improve access, remove the relevant front seat as described in Section 25.

3 Using a flat-bladed screwdriver, lever between the inner and outer sections of the height adjustment lever button to release the button from its clip **(see illustration)**.

4 Unclip the trim cover then slacken and remove the mounting bolt and free the seat belt from its upper mounting **(see illustrations)**.

5 Peel away the front and rear sealing strips from the door centre pillar.

6 Unclip the centre pillar trim panel (starting at the top and working down) and remove it from the vehicle **(see illustration)**.

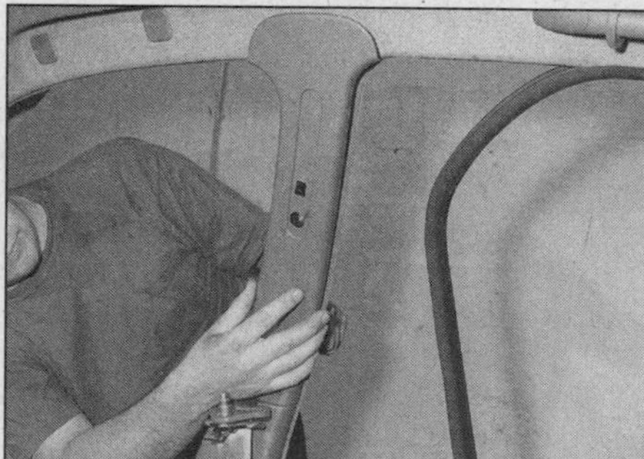

27.6 Peel away the sealing strips then unclip the pillar upper trim panel and remove it from the vehicle

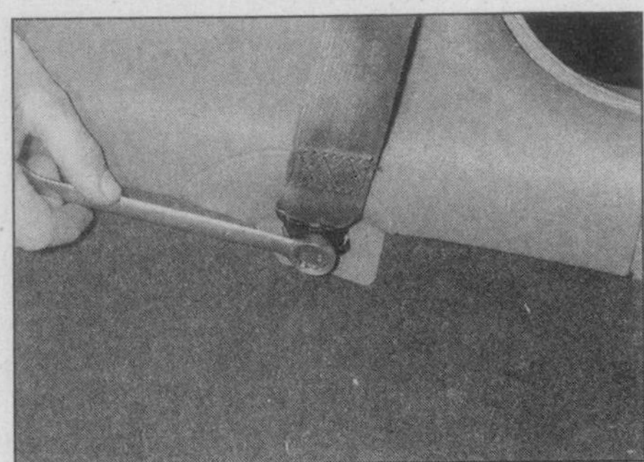
27.7 Unscrew the seat belt lower mounting bolt

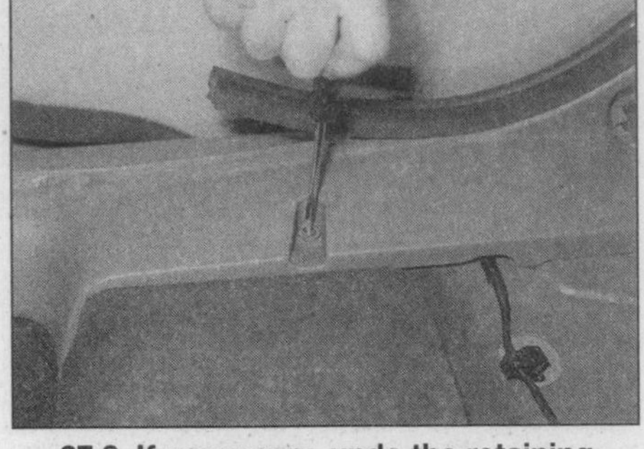
27.8 If necessary, undo the retaining screw to allow the rear door sill trim panel to be unclipped sufficiently to gain access to the front panel rear screw

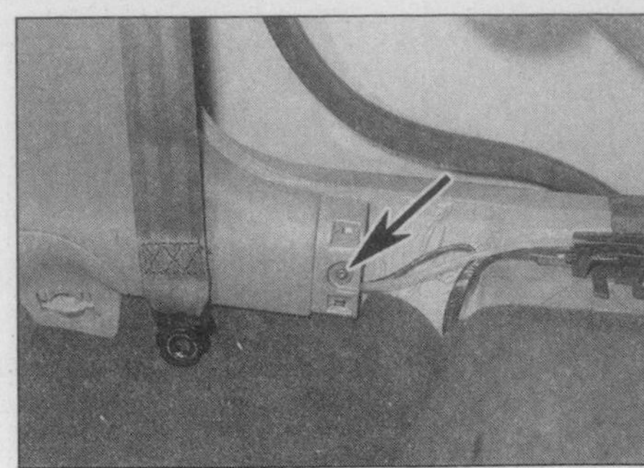
27.9a Slacken the rear screw (arrowed) . . .

7 Remove the trim cover then slacken and remove the seat belt lower mounting bolt **(see illustration)**.

8 Carefully unclip the front of the rear door sill trim panel to reveal the pillar/front sill trim panel rear retaining screw; if necessary, lift up the rear seat cushion and undo the retaining screw to allow the panel to be sufficiently unclipped **(see illustration)**.

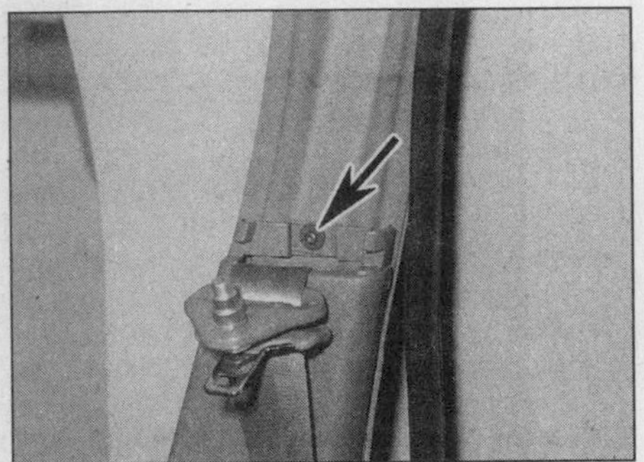
27.9b . . . and the upper screw (arrowed) . . .

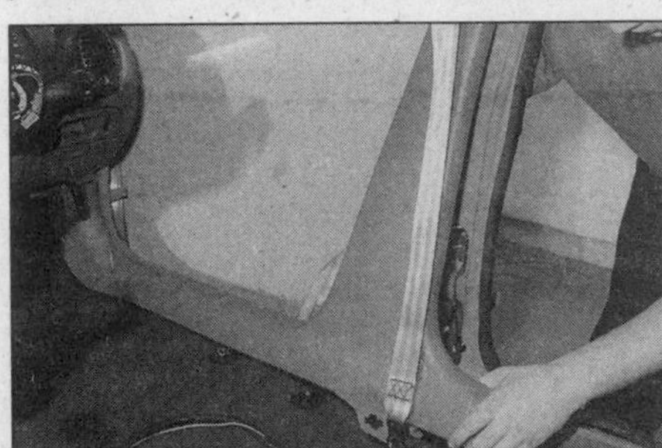
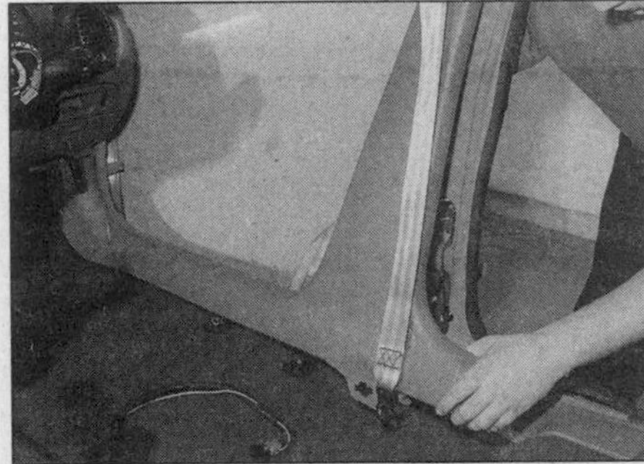
27.9c . . . then unclip the front door pillar/sill trim panel and remove it

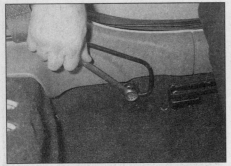

9 Slacken and remove the rear and upper retaining screws then, starting at the rear and working forwards, unclip the trim panel from the door pillar/sill. Free the seat belt from the panel and remove it from the vehicle **(see illustrations)**.

10 Slacken and remove the inertia reel mounting bolt and remove the seat belt assembly from the vehicle.

11 If necessary, the height adjustment mechanism can be removed once its retaining bolts have been undone.

Coupé models

12 Remove the rear seat as described in Section 25 and slide the front seat fully forwards.

13 Remove the trim cap then unscrew the seat belt lower mounting rail retaining bolt. Unhook the rail from the body and free it from the end of the seat belt **(see illustrations)**.

14 Slacken and remove the rear seat belt lower mounting bolt and free the belt from the trim panel **(see illustration)**.

15 Peel the sealing strip from the rear of the door aperture.

16 Undo the retaining screws then unclip the lower section of the rear seat side trim panel and remove it from the vehicle **(see illustrations)**.

17 Using a flat-bladed screwdriver, lever between the inner and outer sections of the

27.13a On Coupé models, unscrew the mounting bolt . . .

27.13b . . . then unhook the lower mounting rail from the body and free it from the end of the seat belt

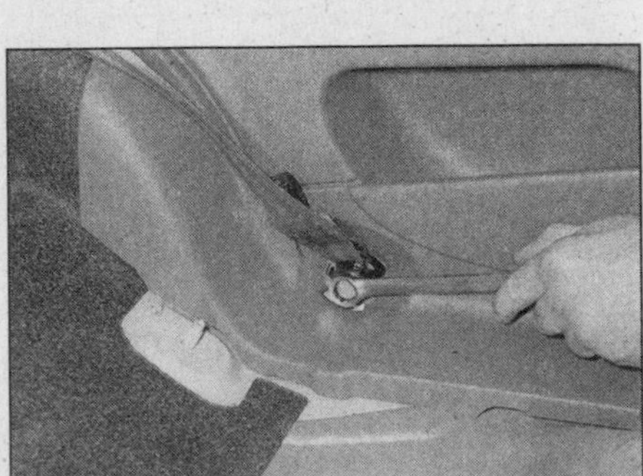
27.14 Unscrew the mounting bolt and free the rear seat belt lower mounting

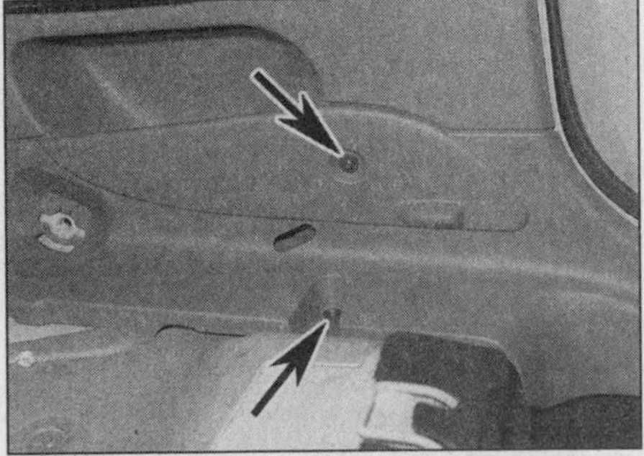
27.16a Undo the retaining screws (arrowed) . . .

27.16b . . . then unclip the lower section of the side trim panel and remove it

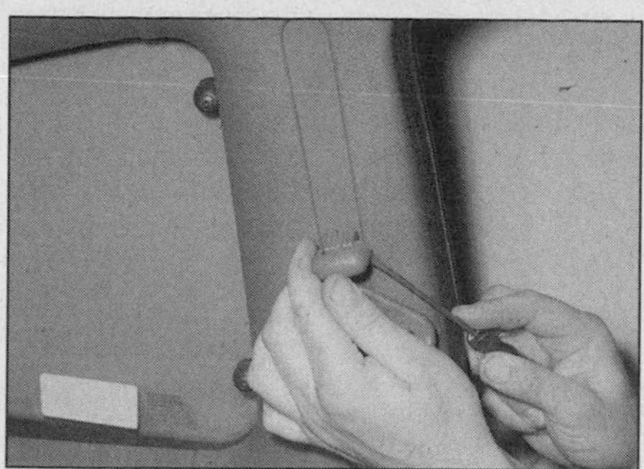
27.17 Remove the height adjustment lever button . . .

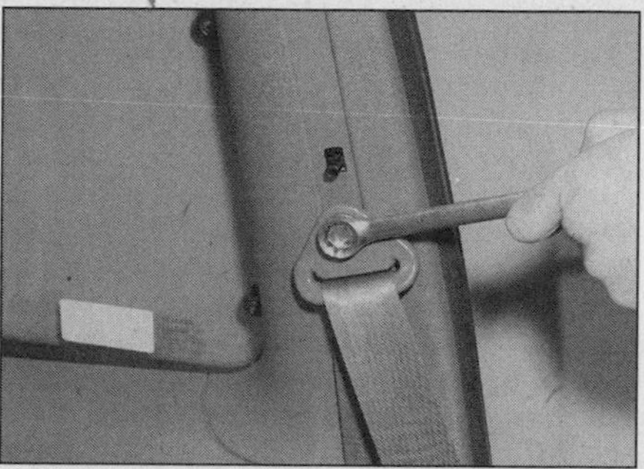
27.18 . . . then remove the trim cover and unscrew the seat belt upper mounting bolt

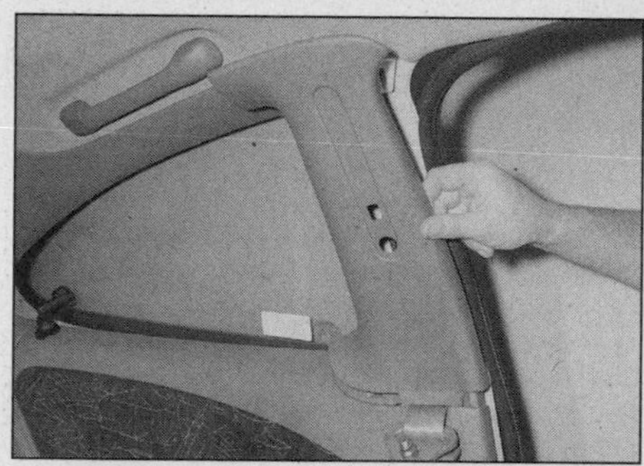
27.19 Unclip the pillar upper trim panel and remove it from the vehicle

height adjustment lever button to release the button from its clip **(see illustration)**.

18 Unclip the trim cover then slacken and remove the mounting bolt and free the seat belt from its upper mounting **(see illustration)**.

19 Unclip the pillar trim panel (starting at the top and working down) and remove it from the vehicle **(see illustration)**.

20 Remove the rear pillar trim panel as described in paragraphs 34 and 35.

21 Slacken and remove the rear seat back locking pin from the side of the vehicle **(see illustration)**.

22 Open up the rear side window then undo the retaining screw securing the opening linkage to the motor spindle **(see illustration)**. Carefully ease the linkage off the spindle.

23 Undo the retaining screws then unclip the side trim panel and remove it from the vehicle, freeing it from the front seat belt **(see illustrations)**.

24 Slacken and remove the inertia reel retaining nuts and remove the front seat belt from the vehicle **(see illustration)**.

Scénic models

25 Disconnect the battery negative lead (refer to Chapter 5A).

26 To improve access, remove the relevant front seat as described in Section 25.

27 Using a flat-bladed screwdriver, lever between the inner and outer sections of the height adjustment lever button to release the button from its clip **(see illustration)**.

28 Unclip the trim cover then slacken and remove the mounting bolt and free the seat belt from its upper mounting **(see illustration)**.

29 Peel away the front and rear sealing strips from the door centre pillar.

30 Unclip the centre pillar lower trim panel (starting at the top and working down), lift it upwards to disengage the three lower locating lugs.

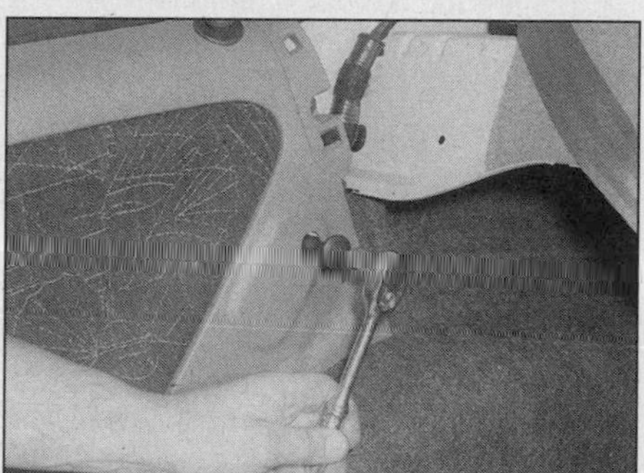
27.21 Unscrew the rear seat back locking pin

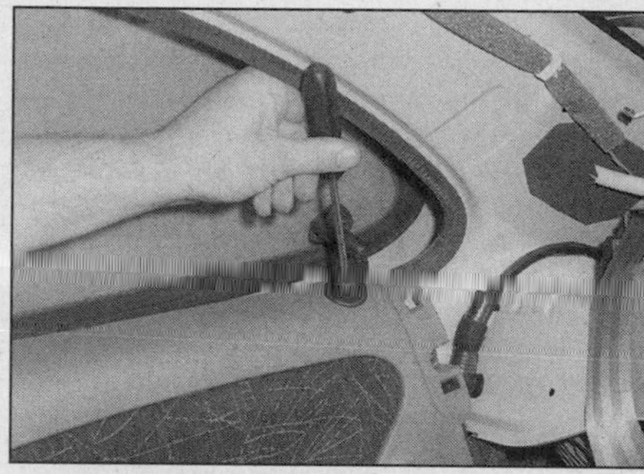
27.22 Undo the retaining screw and free the side window linkage from the spindle

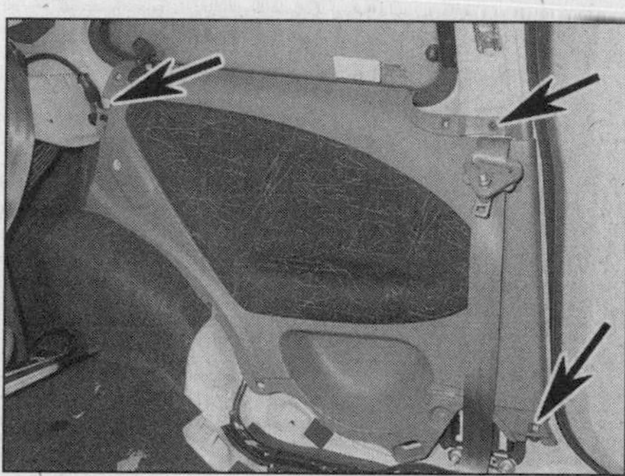
27.23a Undo the retaining screws (arrowed) . . .

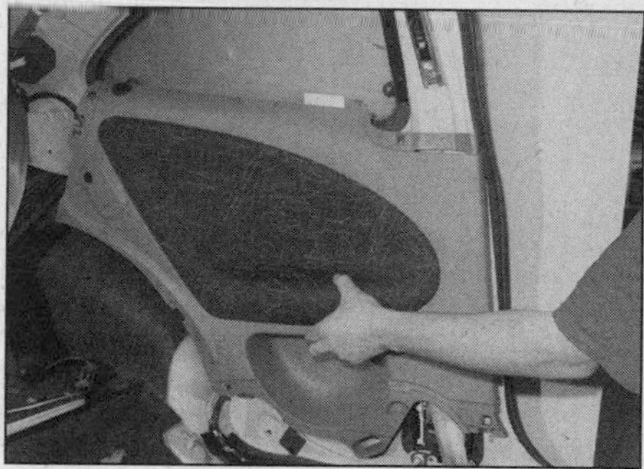
27.23b . . . then unclip the side trim panel and remove it from the vehicle

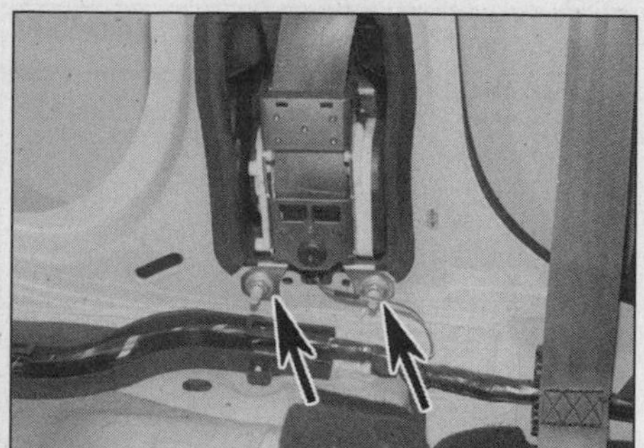
27.24 Front seat belt inertia reel retaining nuts (arrowed) – Coupé

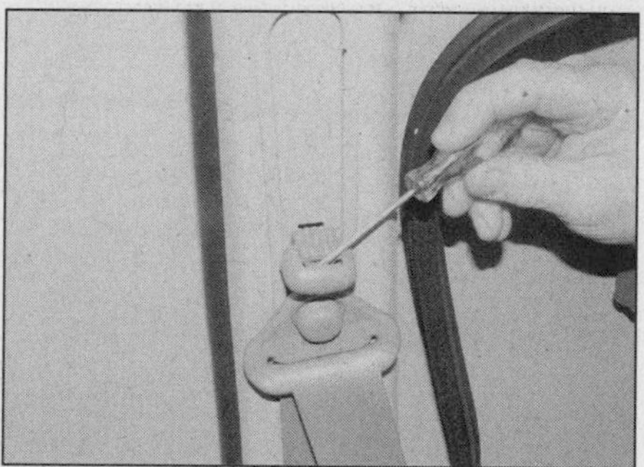
27.27 Unclip the height adjustment button

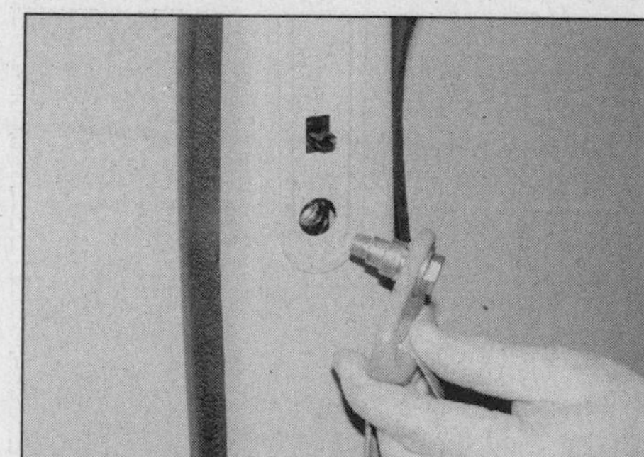
27.28 Slacken and remove the upper seat belt mounting bolt

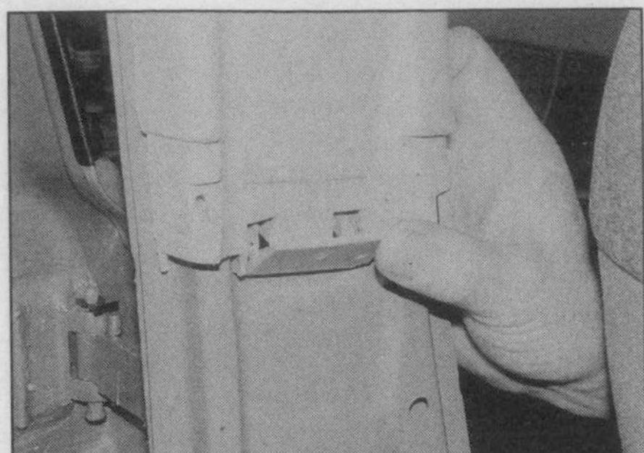

27.31 Release the retaining clip to remove the upper pillar trim panel

31 Unclip the bottom of the upper pillar trim **(see illustration)**, then lift the trim panel upwards and remove it from the vehicle.

32 Fold the rear seats forward for access to the rear inner sill upper trim panel.

33 Using a flat-bladed screwdriver, release the trim panel from the retaining clips around the periphery of the panel **(see illustration).**

34 If working on the right-hand side of the vehicle, open the rear wheelarch cover trim storage compartment door (if fitted), reach through the opening and unclip the luggage compartment light. Withdraw the light and disconnect the wiring connector. If working on the left-hand side, withdraw the alarm system mounting plate and disconnect the wiring at the rear.

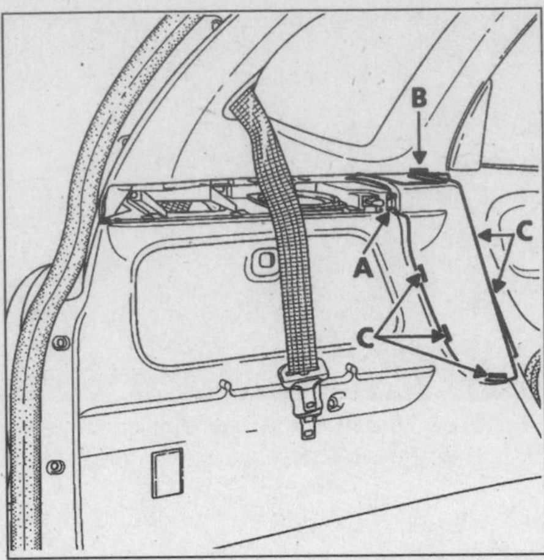

27.33 On Scénic models, release the trim panel from the retaining clips (A, B and C) around the panel periphery

35 Release the speaker grille retaining clips, then lift the grille upwards and pull it towards the centre of the vehicle to remove. Undo the retaining bolts and remove the relevant rear wheelarch cover trim panel by releasing the rear clips then lifting up at the front **(see illustration)**. Where applicable, disconnect the speaker wiring as the panel is removed.

36 Remove the rear inner sill lower trim panel by undoing the four retaining bolts, then releasing the trim panel from the retaining clips along its entire length **(see illustration)**. To gain access to the retaining bolt at the front end of the panel it will be necessary to locally unclip the front inner sill lower trim panel and carefully ease it clear.

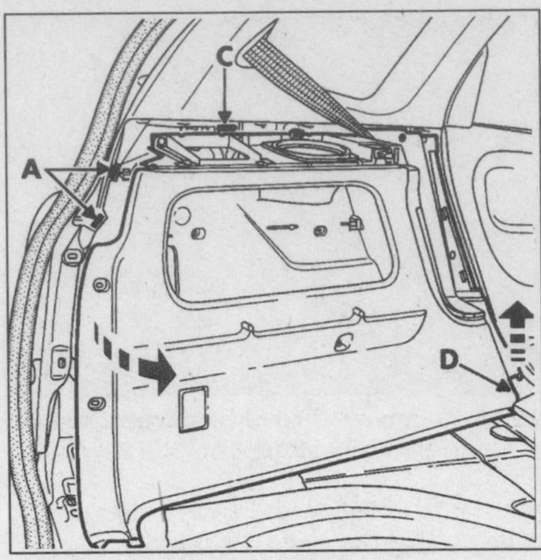

27.35 On Scénic models, remove the relevant rear wheelarch cover trim panel by releasing the clips A, C and D then lift upwards and outwards to remove

37 Release the clip and undo the mounting bolts securing the inertia reel assembly to the body pillar. Remove the front seat belt from the vehicle.

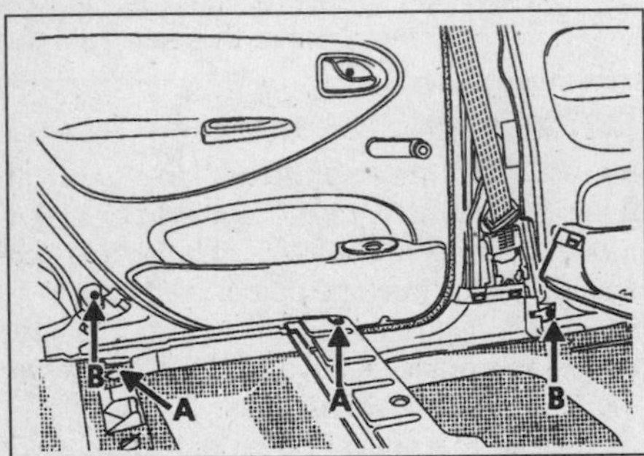

27.36 On Scénic models, remove the rear inner sill lower trim panel by undoing the four retaining bolts A and B, then releasing the panel from the clips along its entire length

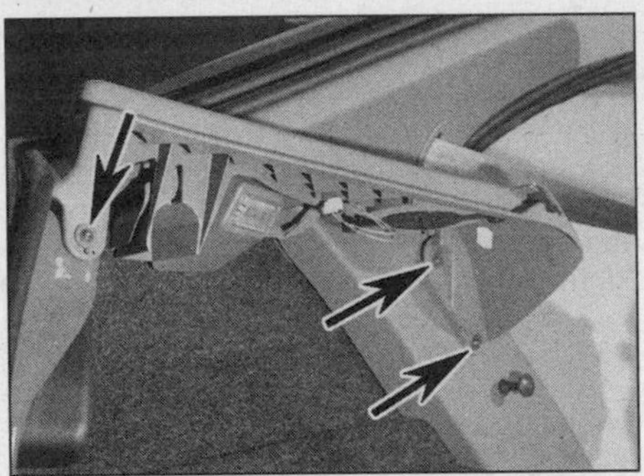

27.39a On Hatchback models undo the retaining screws (arrowed) . . .

Rear seat belt removal

Hatchback models

38 Remove the parcel shelf from the luggage compartment.

39 Fold the rear seats down and disconnect the wiring connectors from the rear loudspeaker on the side that the seat belt is to be removed. Slacken and remove the retaining screws and remove the relevant parcel shelf side mounting panel from the luggage compartment **(see illustrations).**

40 Peel the rear door sealing strip away from the rear seat side trim panel. Slacken and remove the seat locking pin then unclip the trim panel and remove it from the vehicle **(see illustrations).**

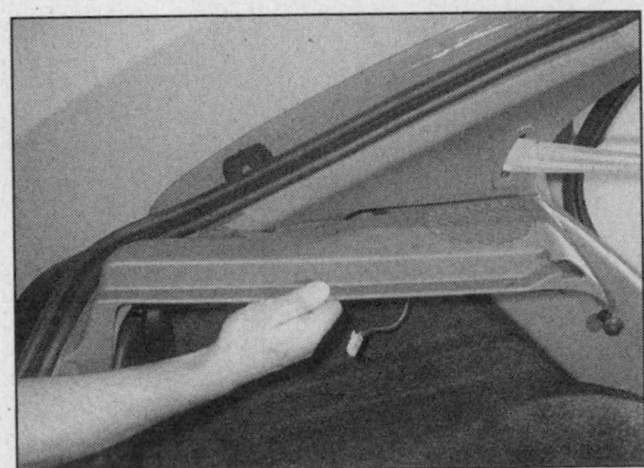

27.39b . . . and remove the parcel shelf side mounting panel

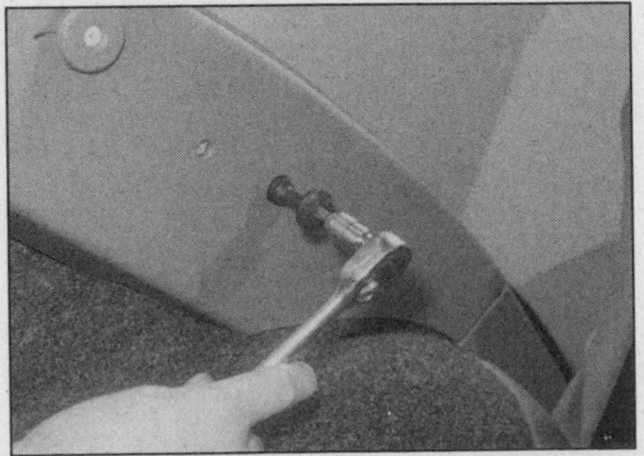

27.40a Unscrew the rear seat back locking pin . . .

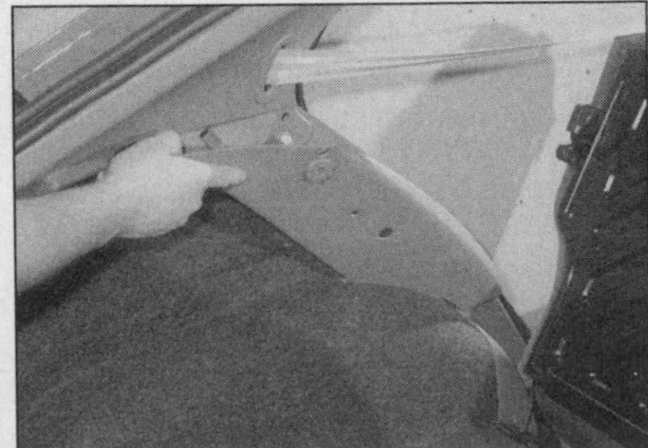

27.40b . . . then unclip the side trim panel and remove it from the vehicle

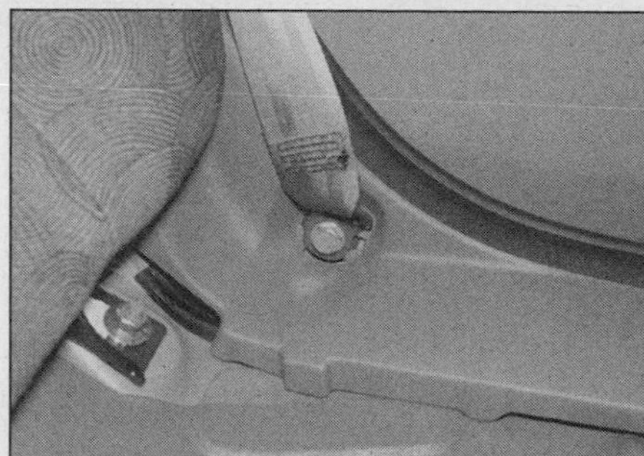
27.41 Unscrew the bolt and free the seat belt lower mounting from the vehicle

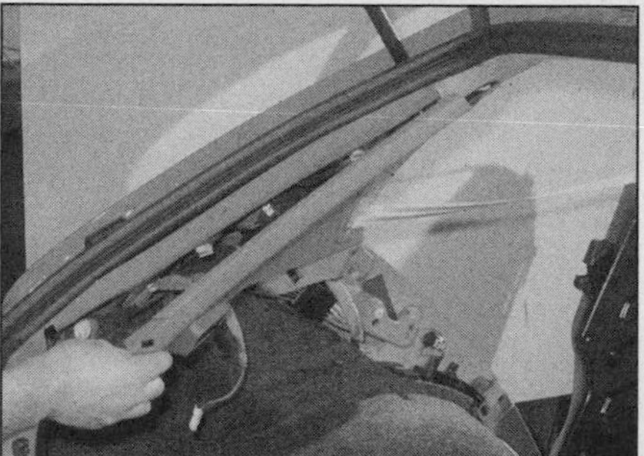
27.42a Unclip the upper trim panel . . .

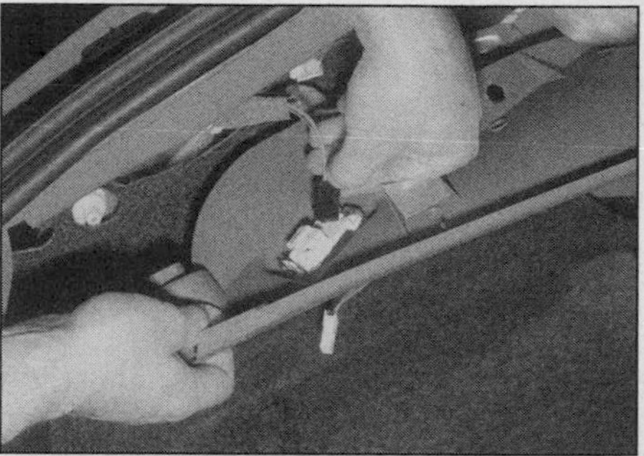
27.42b . . . noting that it will be necessary to disconnect the wiring connector from the light if work is being carried out on the left-hand side

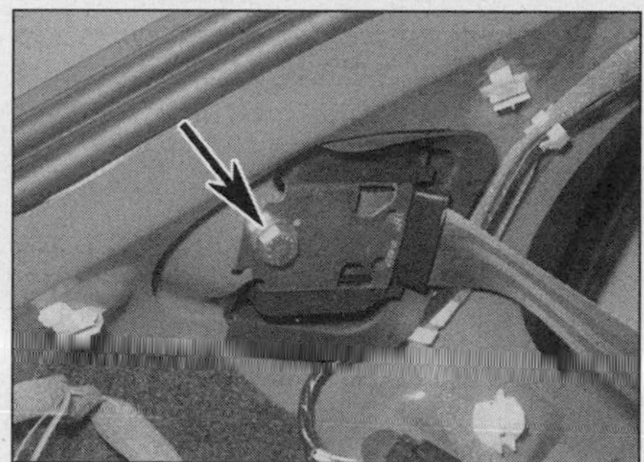
27.43 Rear seat belt inertia reel mounting bolt (arrowed) – Hatchback

27.47 On Coupé models, disconnect the rear window heating element wiring . . .

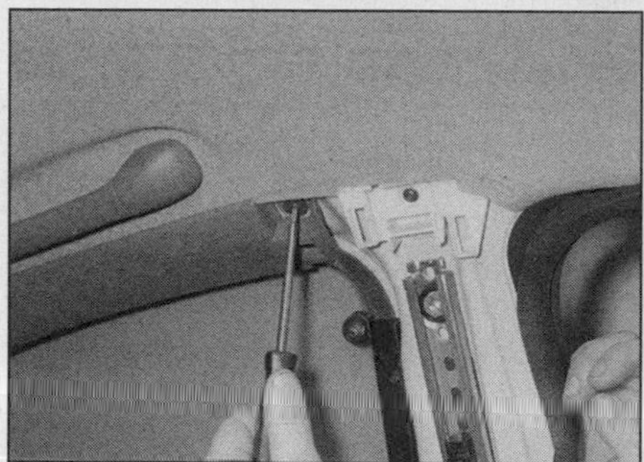
27.48a . . . then undo the retaining screw . . .

41 Slacken and remove the seat belt lower mounting bolt **(see illustration)**.

42 Unclip the upper trim panel from the rear pillar then free the panel from the belt and remove it from the vehicle. If work is being carried out on the left-hand side, it will be necessary to disconnect the luggage compartment light as the panel is removed **(see illustrations)**.

43 Slacken and remove the inertia reel mounting bolt and remove the belt from the vehicle **(see illustration)**.

Coupé models

44 Remove the rear seat cushion as described in Section 25 and fold down the seat back.

45 Slacken and remove the lower mounting bolt and free the belt from the side trim panel.

46 Remove the front pillar upper panel as described in paragraphs 17 to 19, pooling the door sealing strip away from the front edge of the panel.

47 Carefully ease the rear window heated element wiring connector out from the rear pillar trim panel and disconnect the connector **(see illustration)**.

Caution: Take great care not to bend the window wire too much as it is easily broken.

48 Undo the retaining screw then unclip the trim panel from the rear pillar **(see illustrations)**. Free the seat belt from the panel and remove the panel from the vehicle.

49 Slacken and remove the inertia reel mounting bolt and remove the belt from the vehicle.

Saloon models

50 Remove the high-level stop-light as described in Chapter 12, Section 7. On models with rear speakers also remove the speaker grilles from the parcel shelf trim.

51 Unclip and remove the rear seat cushions then slacken and remove the seat belt lower mounting bolt (where necessary).

52 Unclip the relevant seat belt trim cover from the parcel shelf trim **(see illustration)**.

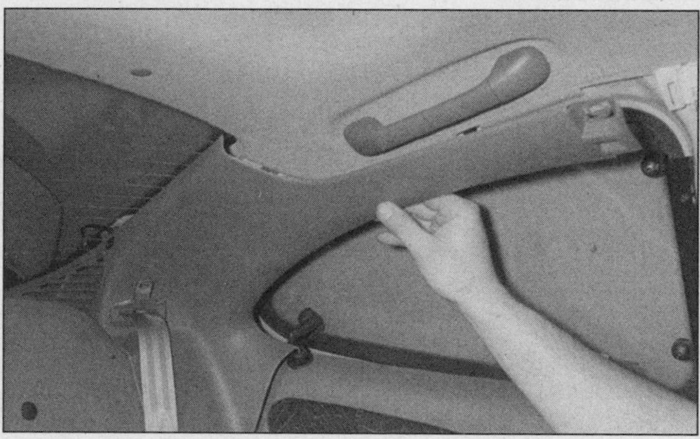
27.48b . . . and unclip the rear pillar trim panel

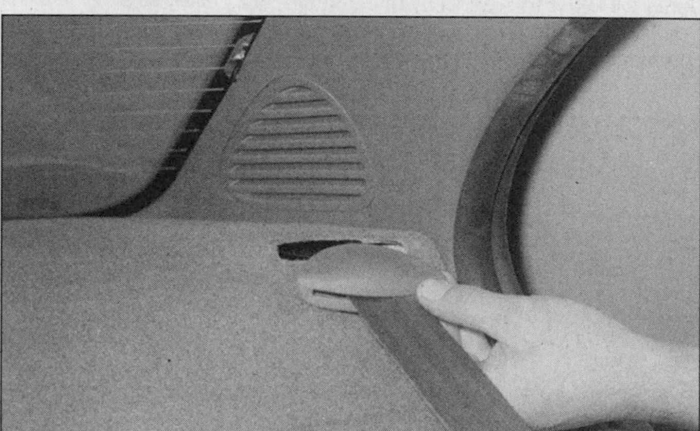
27.52 On Saloon models unclip the relevant seat belt trim cover from the parcel shelf trim

27.53a Prise out the retaining clips (arrowed) . . .

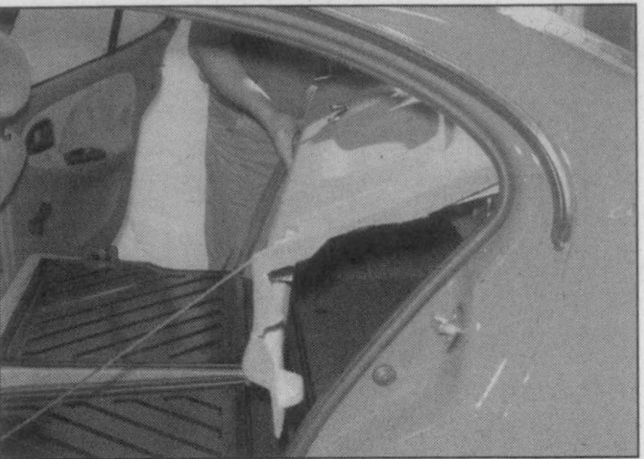
27.53b . . . and release the parcel shelf trim panel in a forwards direction

53 Fold down the rear seat backs then carefully prise out the retaining clips securing the front edge of the parcel shelf trim panel in position. Slide the trim panel forwards and position it clear of the shelf **(see illustrations)**.
54 Undo the inertia reel mounting bolt then remove the belt from the vehicle, freeing it from the parcel shelf trim panel.

Rear side seat belt removal

Scénic models

55 Remove the rear parcel shelf from the luggage compartment.
56 Using a flat-bladed screwdriver, release the three clips on the lower edge of the rear speaker grille, located on the rear wheelarch cover trim panel. Lift the grille upwards and pull it towards the centre of the vehicle to remove.
57 Fold the rear seats forward for access to the rear inner sill upper trim panel.
58 Using a flat-bladed screwdriver, release the trim panel from the retaining clips around the periphery of the panel **(see illustration 27.33)**.
59 Peel away the luggage compartment sealing strip from the base of the tailgate aperture.
60 Lift off the screw caps using a small screwdriver, then undo the luggage compartment sill trim retaining bolts. Remove the trim.
61 If working on the right-hand side of the vehicle, open the rear wheelarch cover trim storage compartment door (if fitted), reach through the opening and unclip the luggage compartment light. Withdraw the light and disconnect the wiring connector. If working on the left-hand side, withdraw the alarm system mounting plate and disconnect the wiring at the rear.
62 Undo the retaining bolts and remove the relevant rear wheelarch cover trim panel by releasing the rear clips then lifting up at the front **(see illustration 27.35)**. Where applicable, disconnect the speaker wiring as the panel is removed.
63 Unclip the cover over the seat belt upper mounting.
64 Undo the two rear quarter trim panel retaining bolts located on the edge of the panel adjacent to the tailgate sealing strip. Release the two centering devices on the lower edge of the panel, then pull the panel away at the area around the tailgate support strut. Free the panel from the support strut mounting through the slot provided.
65 Release the panel from the retaining clips around the window, then pull the panel rearward to release the upper front locating pin. Remove the panel.
66 Undo the seat belt and inertia reel mounting bolts and remove the seat belt assembly.

Rear centre seat belt removal

Scénic models

67 Release the seat belt buckle from its bracket on the headlining, then undo the two trim retaining screws now exposed **(see illustration)**.
68 Remove the inertia reel cover panel, then undo the two inertia reel mounting bolts **(see illustration)**. Remove the seat belt assembly.

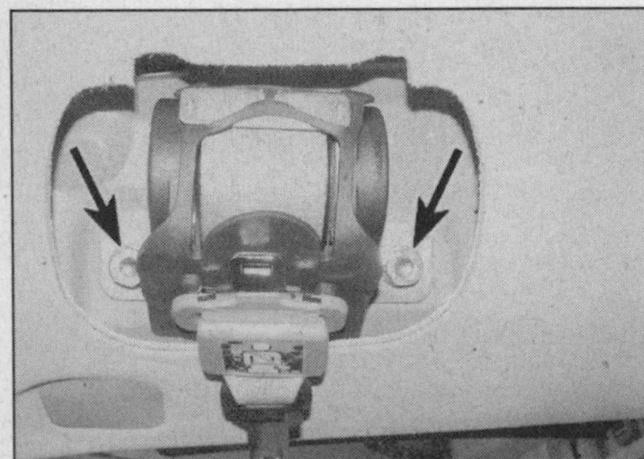
27.68 . . . then undo the two seat belt mounting bolts

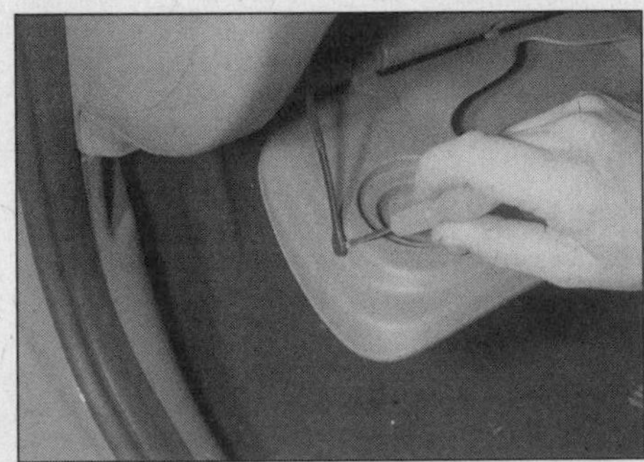
28.6 Carefully unclip the support cables from the sides of the glovebox lid . . .

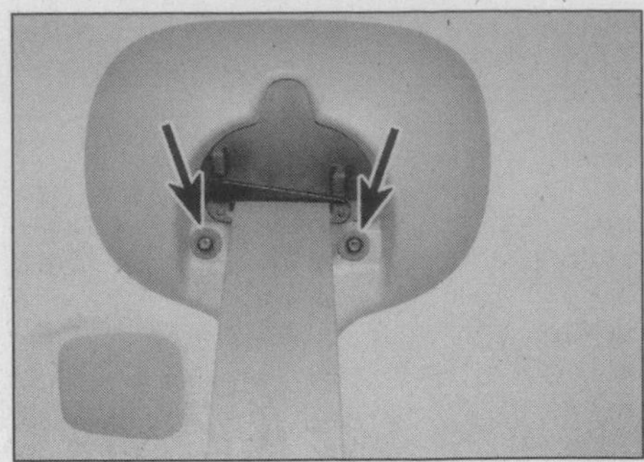
27.67 Undo the two trim retaining screws (arrowed) . . .

Refitting

69 Refitting is the reverse of removal, making sure the inertia reel is correctly engaged with the body and that all mounting bolts are securely tightened. Also ensure that all trim panels removed are correctly clipped into position and retained by all the relevant clips and screws.

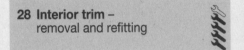

28 Interior trim – removal and refitting

Interior trim panels

1 The interior trim panels are secured using either screws or various types of trim fasteners, usually studs or clips.
2 Check that there are no other panels overlapping the one to be removed; usually there is a sequence that has to be followed that will become obvious on close inspection. Many of the interior trim panels must be removed for access to the seat belt components and details of their removal, together with photographic sequences are given in Section 27.
3 Remove all obvious fasteners, such as screws. If the panel will not come free, it is held by hidden clips or fasteners. These are usually situated around the edge of the panel and can be prised up to release them; note, however that they can break quite easily so replacements should be available. The best way of releasing such clips without the correct type of tool, is to use a large flat-bladed screwdriver. Note in many cases that the adjacent sealing strip must be prised back to release a panel.
4 When removing a panel, **never** use excessive force or the panel may be damaged; always check carefully that all fasteners have been removed or released before attempting to withdraw a panel.
5 Refitting is the reverse of the removal procedure; secure the fasteners by pressing them firmly into place and ensure that all disturbed components are correctly secured to prevent rattles.

Glovebox lid

6 Open up the glovebox lid and unclip the support cables **(see illustration)**.

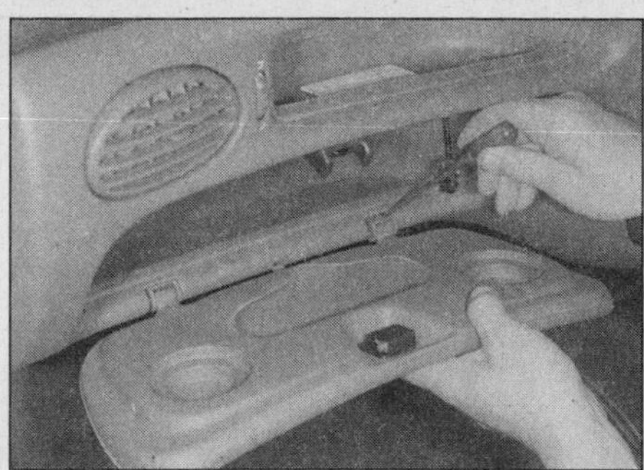

28.7 . . . then carefully unclip the hinges from the facia panel

7 Release the lid by gently pulling it backwards whilst carefully prising its hinge assemblies out from the facia using a screwdriver **(see illustration)**. As the lid is removed, take care not to lose the hinge retaining clips.

8 On refitting ensure that the hinges are securely retained by their clips and the support cables are clipped securely in position.

Carpets

9 The passenger compartment floor carpet is in one piece and is secured at its edges by screws or clips, usually the same fasteners used to secure the various adjoining trim panels.

10 Carpet removal and refitting is reasonably straightforward but very time-consuming because all adjoining trim panels must be removed first, as must components such as the seats, the centre console and seat belt lower anchorages.

Headlining

11 The headlining is clipped to the roof and can be withdrawn only once all fittings such as the grab handles, sun visors, sunroof (if fitted), windscreen and rear quarter windows and related trim panels have been removed and the door, tailgate and sunroof aperture sealing strips have been prised clear **(see illustrations)**.

12 Note that headlining removal requires considerable skill and experience if it is to be carried out without damage and is therefore best entrusted to an expert.

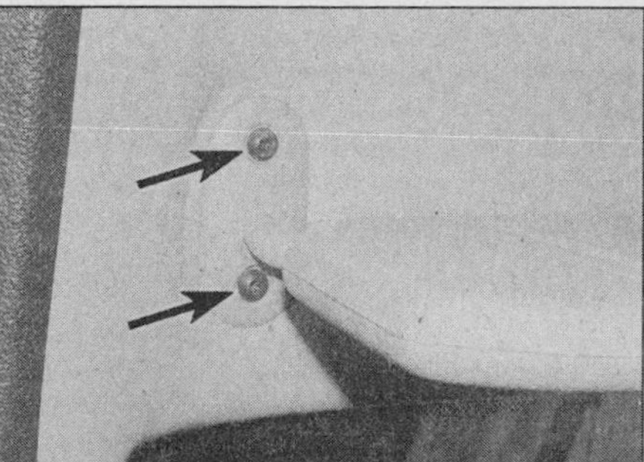

28.11a Undo the two visor mounting screws (arrowed) . . .

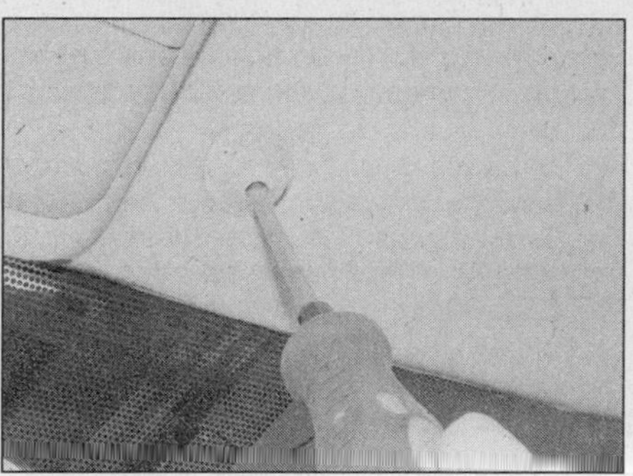

28.11c Slacken the securing screw to release the visor retaining clip

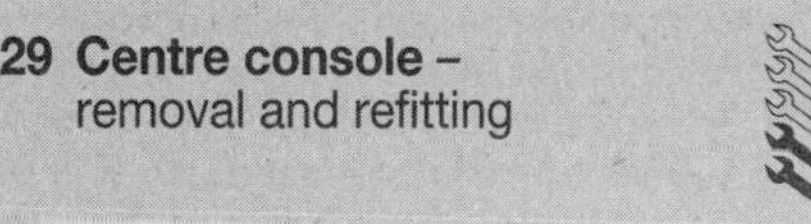

29 Centre console – removal and refitting

Removal

All models except Scénic

1 Disconnect the battery negative lead (refer to Chapter 5A).

2 On models with electric rear windows, remove the window switch panel from the rear of the centre console.

3 On models with manual rear windows, unclip the ashtray and remove it from the rear of the centre console **(see illustration)**.

4 On all models, slacken and remove the rear retaining nut then lift the rear section of the centre console off from the handbrake lever **(see illustrations)**.

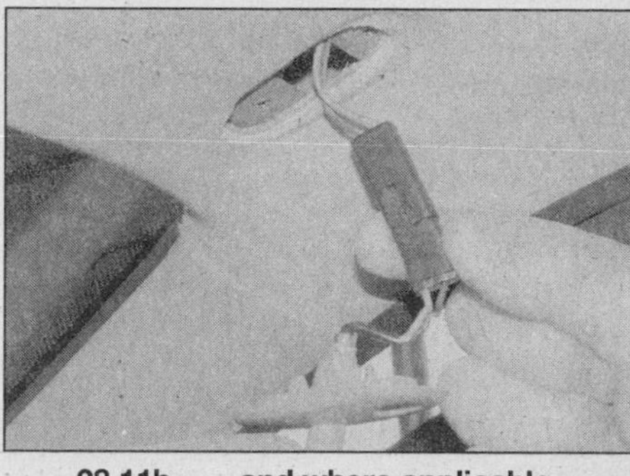

28.11b . . . and where applicable, disconnect the wiring connector

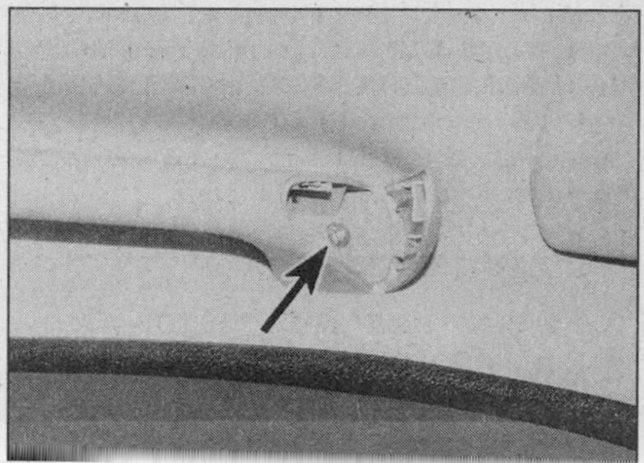

28.11d Unclip the cover, and undo the securing screw to release the grab handle

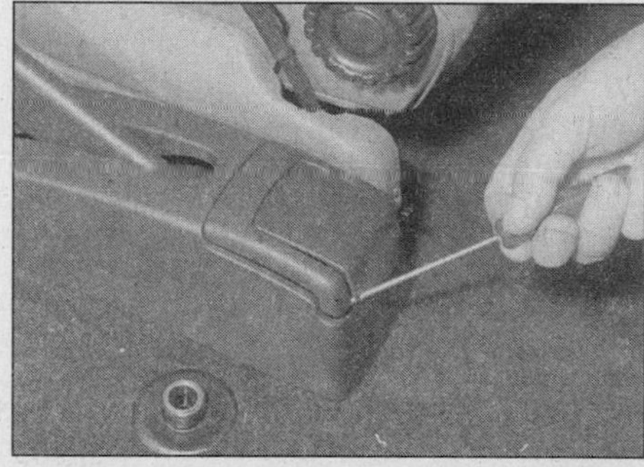

29.3 On models with manual rear windows unclip the ashtray from the centre console rear section

5 On manual transmission models, unclip the gearchange lever gaiter from the console **(see illustration)**.

29.4a Slacken the retaining nut (arrowed) . . .

29.4b . . . then lift the centre console rear section off the handbrake lever

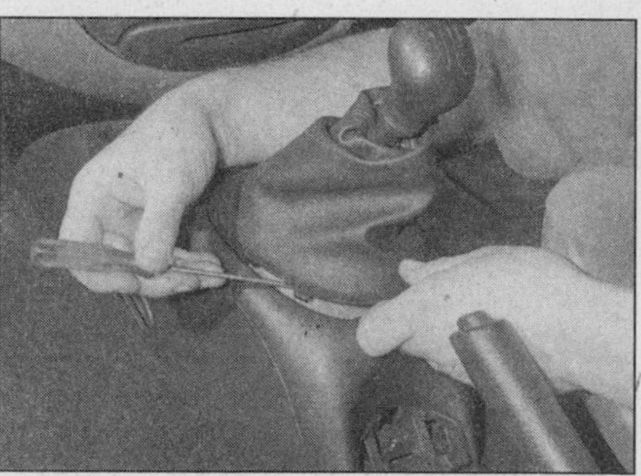

29.5 On manual transmission models unclip the gearchange lever gaiter

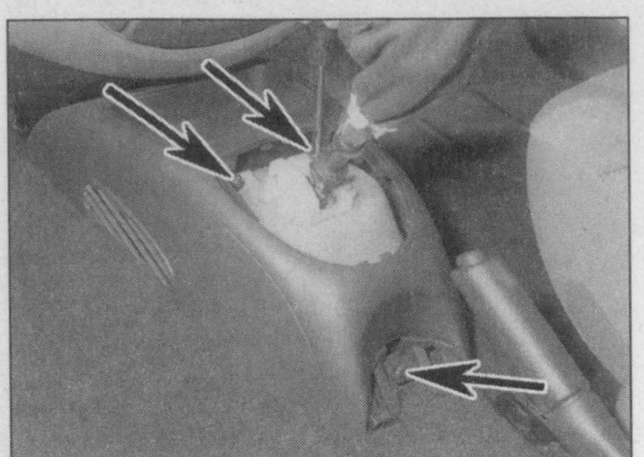

29.7a Slacken the retaining screws (arrowed) . . .

29.7b . . . and remove the front section of the centre console

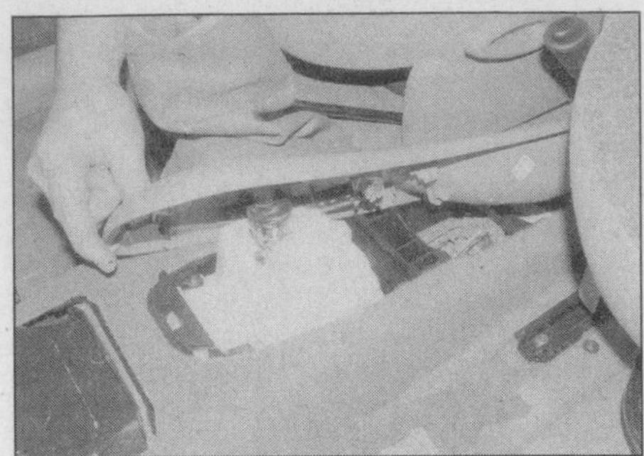

29.9 Release the cover from the centre console

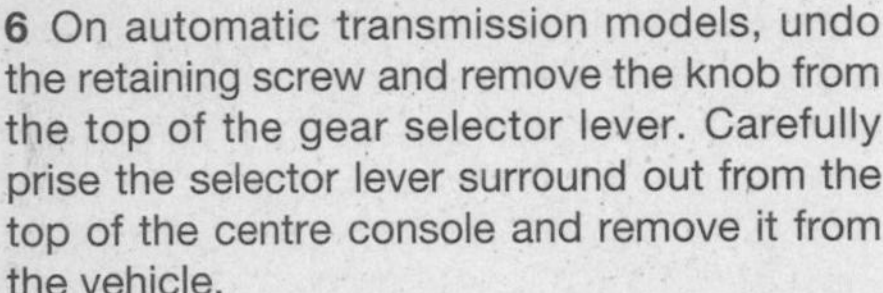

6 On automatic transmission models, undo the retaining screw and remove the knob from the top of the gear selector lever. Carefully prise the selector lever surround out from the top of the centre console and remove it from the vehicle.

7 On all models, slacken and remove the retaining screws then remove the front section of the centre console from the vehicle, disconnecting its wiring connectors (where necessary) as they become accessible **(see illustrations)**.

Scénic models

8 Disconnect the battery negative lead (refer to Chapter 5A).

9 On manual transmission models, unclip the gearchange lever gaiter/cover from the console **(see illustration)**.

10 On automatic transmission models, undo the retaining screw and remove the knob from the top of the gear selector lever. Carefully prise the selector lever surround out from the top of the centre console and remove it from the vehicle.

11 Unclip the centre tray and lift it out over the top of the selector lever.

12 Undo the bolt securing the right-hand centre footwell vent panel under the centre of the facia. Pivot the front of the vent downward to release the locating pin, then move it forward to disengage the rear locating tag. Repeat this procedure to remove the left-hand vent panel **(see illustration)**.

13 Remove the lower centre storage compartment/switch panel by undoing the two screws, one each side. Pivot the compartment/panel upwards to release the clips and centering pins along its top edge, then withdraw the unit. Where applicable, disconnect the wiring connectors and remove the compartment/switch panel **(see illustrations)**.

14 Undo the four bolts, two at the front and two at the rear securing the console to the floor **(see illustrations)**. Pull the handbrake lever up as far as possible then lift the console up at the rear.

15 Move the console rearward, disengage the gear lever/selector and handbrake lever, then remove the console from the vehicle.

Refitting

16 Refitting is the reverse of removal, ensuring all wiring is correctly routed and all fasteners are securely tightened.

30 Facia panel assembly – removal and refitting

Note: *Due to a wide range of models covered in this manual, there may be a slight variation in the procedure of disconnecting the wiring loom from the facia. See Haynes Hint.*

Removal

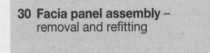

Attach an identification label to each wiring connector as it is disconnected. The labels can then be used on refitting to help ensure that all wiring is correctly routed through the relevant facia apertures.

1 Disconnect the battery negative lead (refer to Chapter 5A). On models with the battery located in the scuttle panel at the rear of the

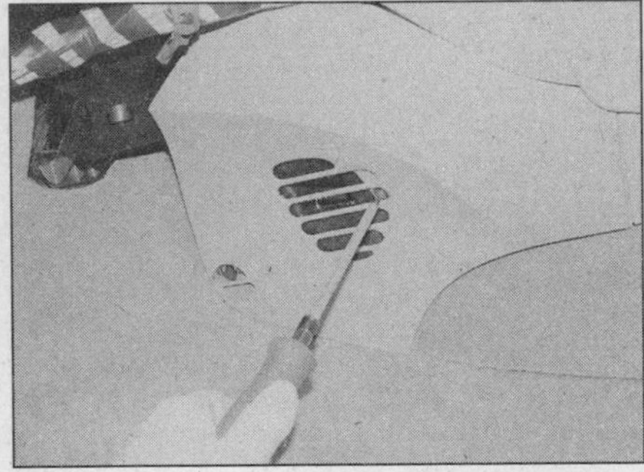

29.12 Slacken the retaining screw and remove the trim panel

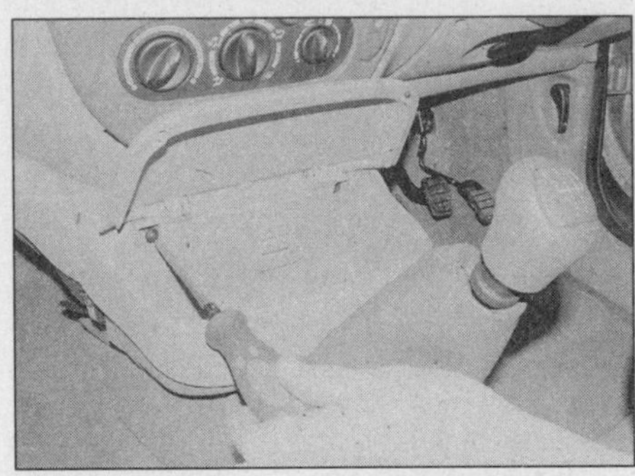

29.13a Undo the two retaining screws . . .

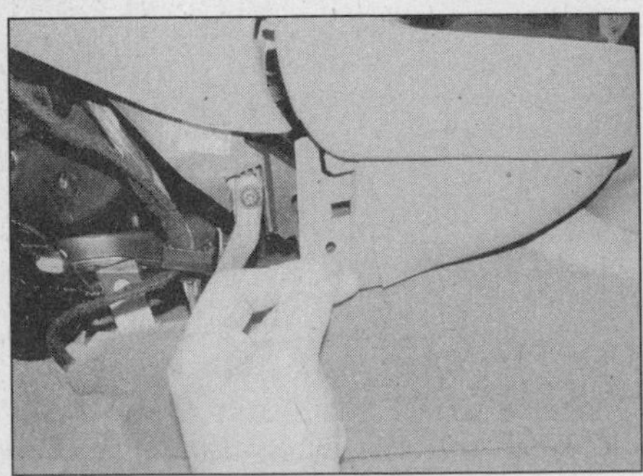

29.13b . . . and unclip each side of the storage compartment

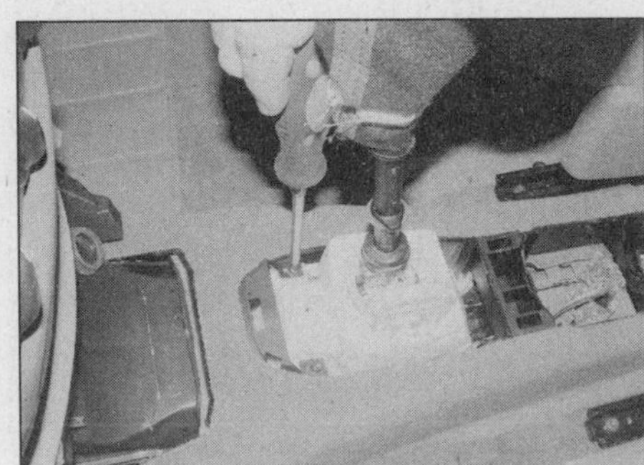

29.14a Slacken and remove the two front retaining screws . . .

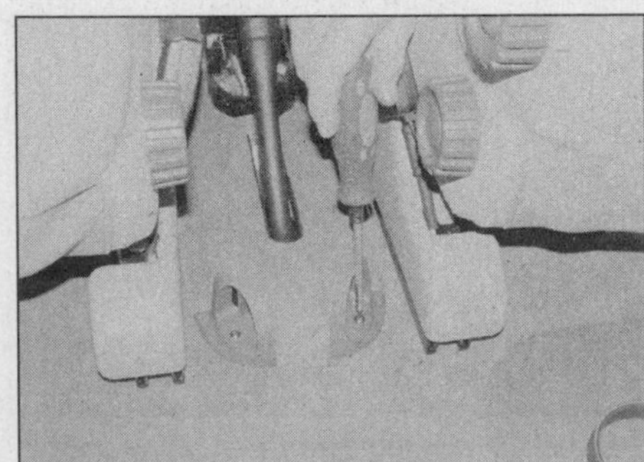

29.14b . . . and the two rear retaining screws – Scénic

30.2 Remove the front seats and lift out the seat spacers – except Scénic

30.7a Remove the lower retaining clips then release the upper clips (arrowed) . . .

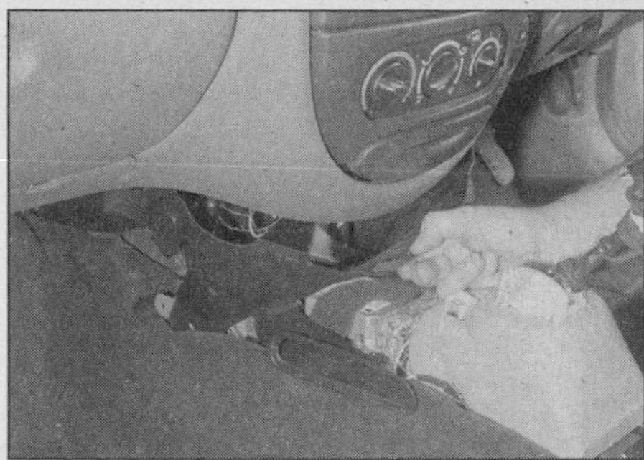

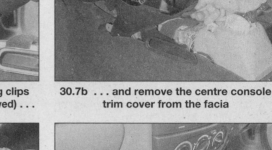

30.7b . . . and remove the centre console trim cover from the facia

engine compartment, remove the battery completely.

2 Remove the front seats as described in Section 25 then, on all models except Scénic, prise out the seat mounting spacers from the floor **(see illustration)**.

3 Remove the steering column as described in Chapter 10.

4 Remove the centre console as described in Section 29.

5 Working as described in Chapter 12, remove the following components.

a) Driver's side switch panel.

b) Instrument panel.

c) Cigarette lighter.

d) Multi-function display.

e) Windscreen wiper arms.

6 Remove the heater control unit as described in Chapter 3.

7 On all models except Scénic, remove the lower retaining clips then release the upper clips and remove the centre console trim cover from the base of the facia panel. Remove the fastener and unclip the heater duct from the base of the facia **(see illustrations)**.

8 Working in the left-hand side of the engine compartment, remove the cover then slide out the front panel from the fuse/relay box. Unclip the fuse/relay panel then release the retaining clips and disconnect the main (engine wiring harness) wiring connectors. Remove the retaining clips and screws and remove the front and rear sections of the left-hand wheelarch liner. Free the bulbholder from the direction indicator side repeater light then release the wiring harness from all the relevant retaining clips so that it is free to be pulled through into the passenger compartment **(see illustrations)**. If necessary to improve access, jack up the front of the vehicle, support it on axle stands (see *Jacking and vehicle support*) and remove the front wheel.

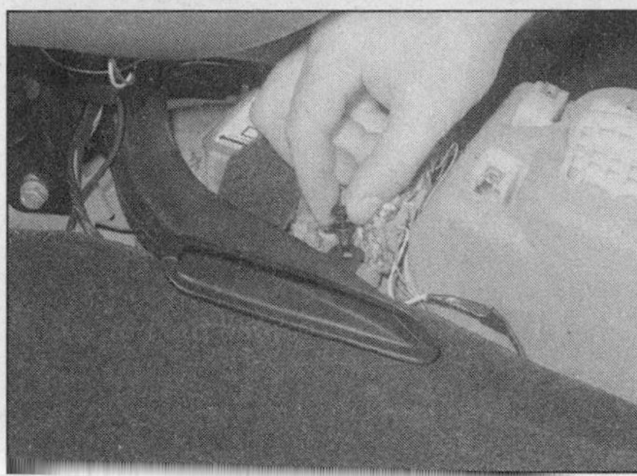

30.7c Remove the fastener . . .

30.7d . . . and unclip the heater duct from the base of the facia

30.8a Remove the fuse/relay box lid then unclip the front panel . . .

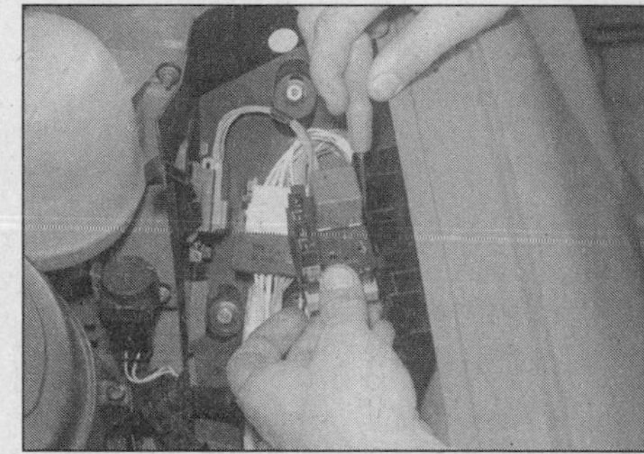

30.8b . . . and release the fuse/relay panel from the box

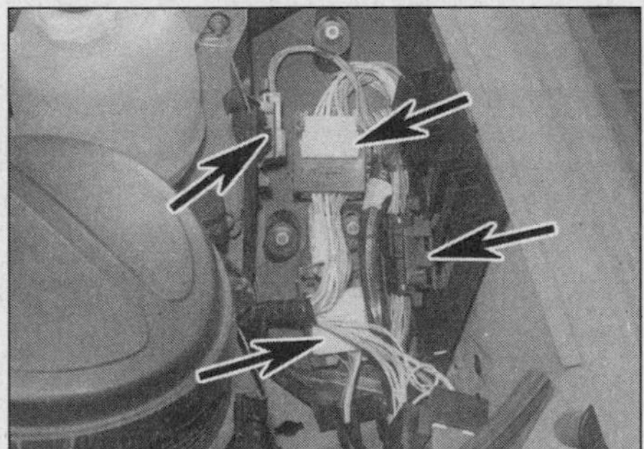

30.8c Disconnect the wiring connectors (arrowed) and free them from their retaining clips

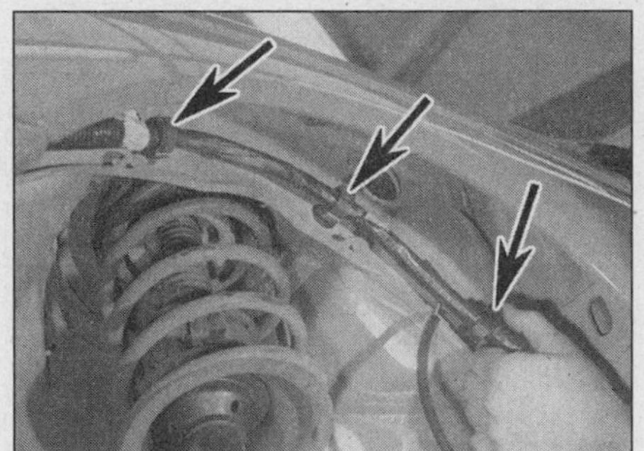

30.8d Free the wiring harness from its retaining clips (arrowed) underneath the wing . . .

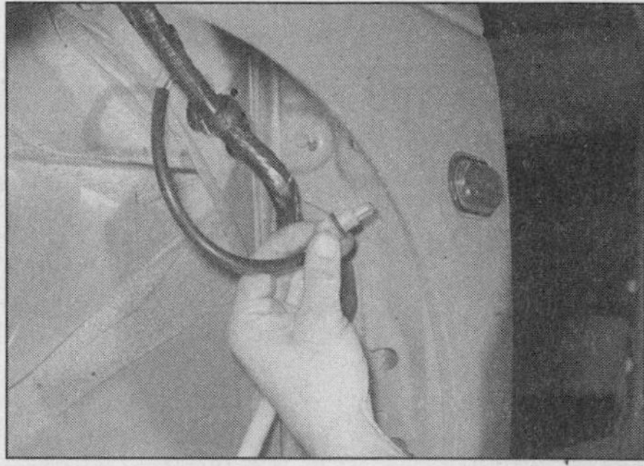

30.8e . . . then detach the bulbholder from the side repeater light . . .

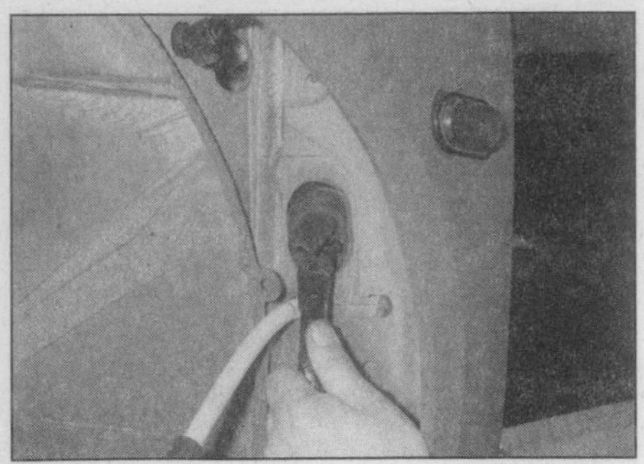
30.8f ... and free the wiring grommet so that the harness is free to be removed with the facia assembly

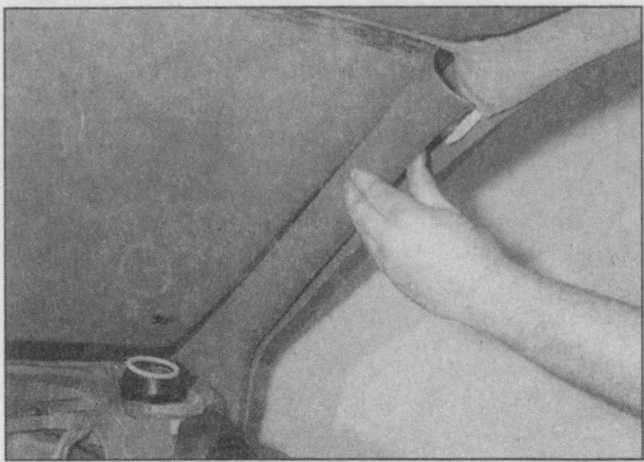
30.12 Unclip the windscreen pillar trim panels and remove them from the vehicle

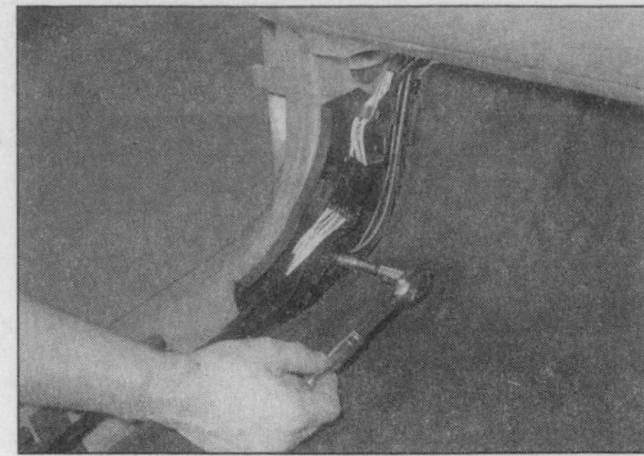
30.14a Unscrew the earth bolts ...

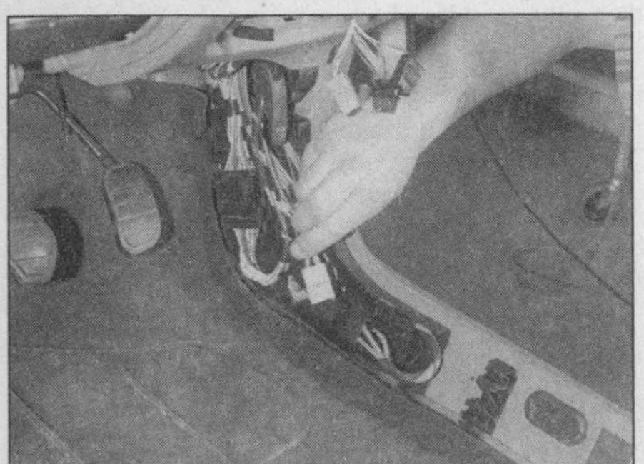
30.14b ... and disconnect the wiring connectors situated behind the left- and right-hand front door pillar/sill trim panels

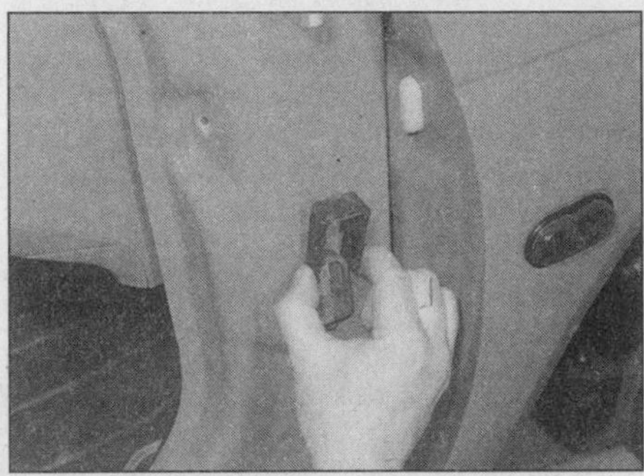
30.15a Slide off the retaining clip ...

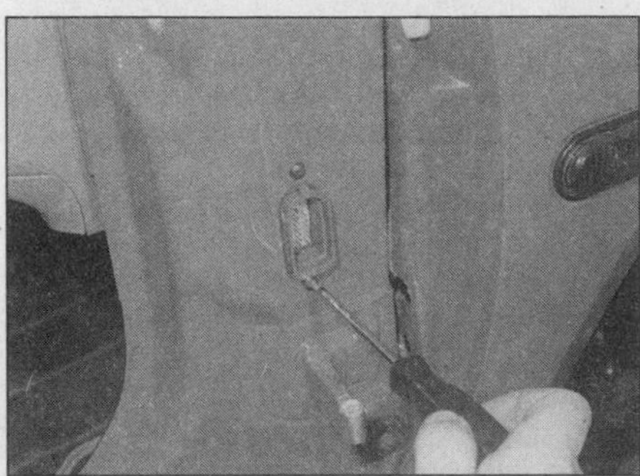
30.15b ... then undo the screws and free the front door wiring connectors from the pillars (shown with doors removed)

9 Peel off the rubber sealing strip from the top of the engine compartment bulkhead.

10 Slacken and remove the retaining screws then carefully unclip the left-hand vent panel from the base of the windscreen and remove it from the vehicle.

11 Working on the right-hand side of the engine compartment, release the large fuses from their retaining clips. Disconnect the wiring connectors from the wiper motor and heater blower motor and release the harness from its retaining clips so that it is free to be pulled through into the passenger compartment. **Note:** *This is not necessary on all models; on some models the wiring harness is not connected to the facia and can be left in position.*

12 Peel the front door sealing strips away from the windscreen pillar trim panels then unclip both panels (starting at the top and working downwards) and remove them from the vehicle **(see illustration)**.

13 On Hatchback models remove the left- and right-hand pillar trim panels as described in the relevant paragraphs of Section 27. On Coupé models remove the rear seat cushion as described in Section 25 then remove the left- and right-hand lower sections of rear seat side trim panels as described in the relevant paragraphs of Section 27.

14 On all models, undo the retaining screws and remove the left- and right-hand door pillar/front sill trim panels (see Sections 27 and 28). Unscrew the retaining screws and free the earth leads from the left- and right-hand sills then disconnect the various facia wiring connectors and free the wiring harness from all its retaining clips so that it is free to be removed with the facia **(see illustrations)**.

15 Release the retaining clips and disconnect the left- and right-hand front door wiring connectors. Slide the retaining clips fully off the connector then undo the screws and free each door wiring connector from the pillar **(see illustrations)**.

16 Refer to the warnings in Section 26, then release the retaining clip and disconnect the wiring connector from the airbag/seat belt tensioning control unit. Remove the fasteners securing the seat wiring loom covers in position then unhook the retaining clips and free both the left- and right-hand front seat wiring from their pivot clips. Lift the carpet and release both left- and right-hand

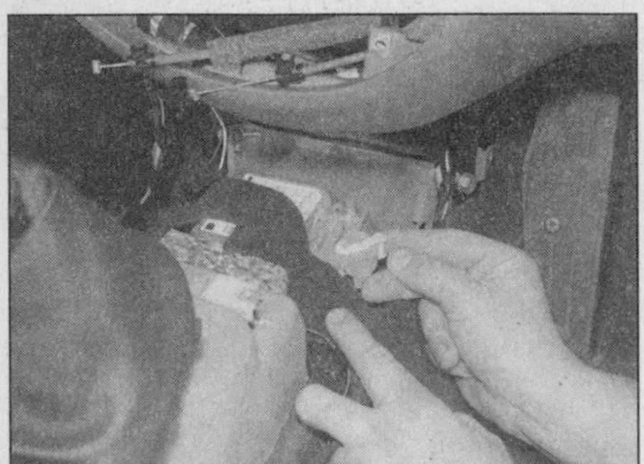
30.16a Disconnect the wiring connector from the airbag/seat belt tensioning control unit ...

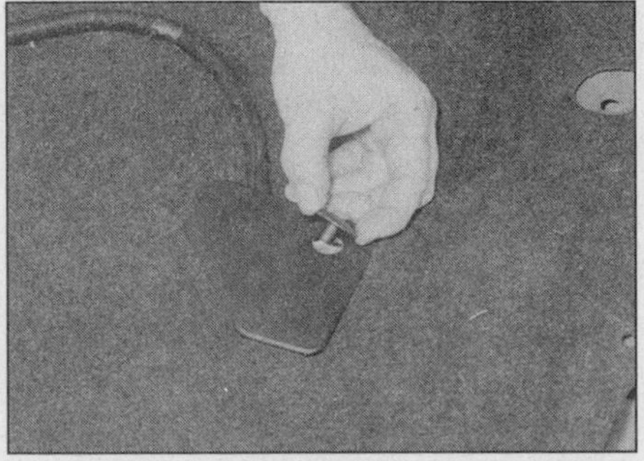
30.16b ... then remove the retaining clip ...

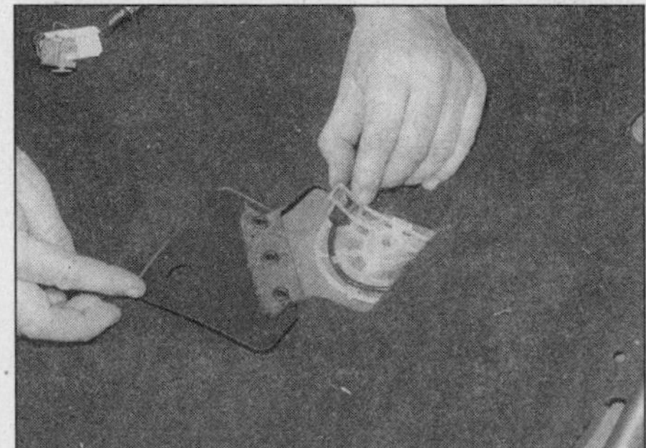
30.16c ... and free the seat wiring from its pivot assembly ...

30.16d . . . so that it is free to be withdrawn from under the carpet and be removed with the facia

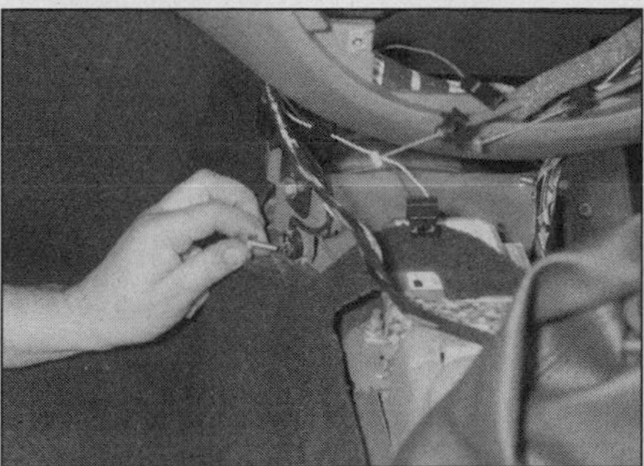
30.17a Undo the earth lead bolt from the left-hand side of the facia . . .

30.17b . . . and disconnect the aerial lead connector

harnesses from their retaining clips so they can be pulled through and are free to be withdrawn with the facia **(see illustrations)**.

17 Slacken and remove the earth bolt from the left-hand side of the centre of the facia and disconnect the aerial lead connector **(see illustrations)**.

18 Slacken and remove the two facia retaining screws which are situated in the heater control panel aperture **(see illustration)**.

19 Carefully prise off the trim covers from the left- and right-hand bottom corners of the facia to gain access to the lower mounting nuts **(see illustrations)**.

20 Slacken and remove the upper and lower mounting nuts from the left- and right-hand ends of the facia **(see illustration)**.

21 With the aid of an assistant, carefully manoeuvre the facia assembly away from the bulkhead **(see illustration)**. As the facia is withdrawn, release the wiring grommets from the bulkhead, noting the correct routing of all the wiring, and release the wiring from all the relevant clips and ties.

Refitting

22 Refitting is a reversal of the removal procedure. Prior to refitting the facia mounting nuts, ensure that all the necessary wiring connectors are fed through the relevant facia apertures and make sure the wiring grommets are correctly seated in the bulkhead. On completion, reconnect the battery and check that all the electrical components and switches function correctly.

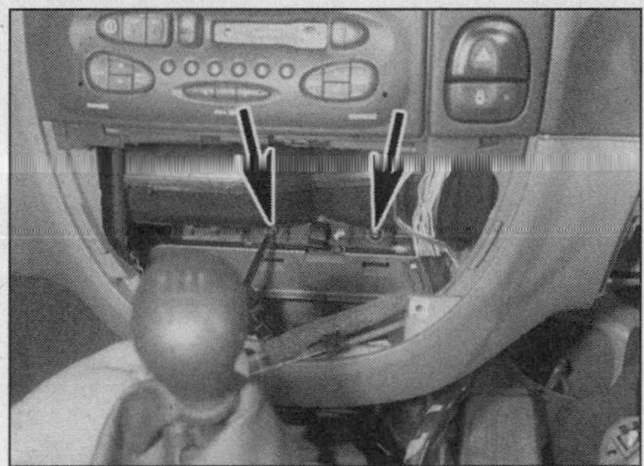
30.18 Remove the retaining screws (arrowed) which are located in the heater control panel aperture

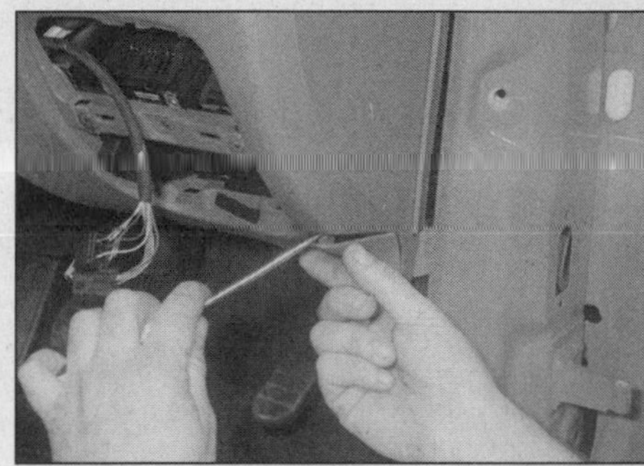
30.19a Unclip the trim covers from the left- and right-hand sides of the facia . . .

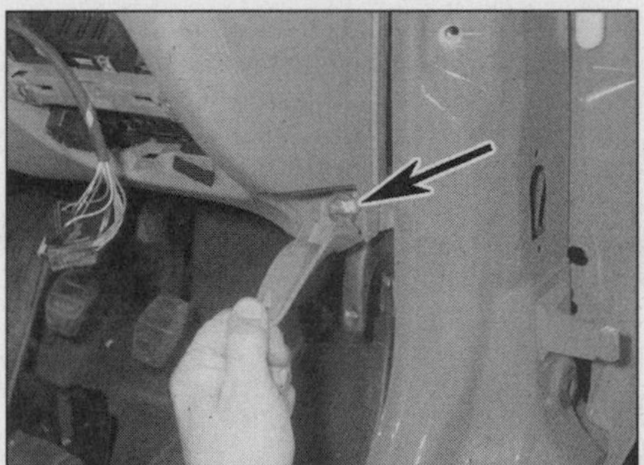
30.19b . . . then slacken and remove the facia lower mounting nuts (arrowed) . . .

30.20 . . . and the upper mounting nuts

30.21 Removing the facia assembly from the vehicle

Chapter 12
Body electrical system

Contents

Degrees of difficulty

Easy, suitable for novice with little experience 	**Fairly easy,** suitable for beginner with some experience 	**Fairly difficult,** suitable for competent DIY mechanic 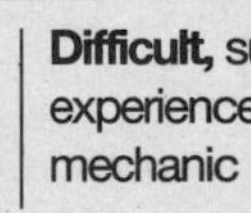	**Difficult,** suitable for experienced DIY mechanic	**Very difficult,** suitable for expert DIY or professional

Specifications

System type	12-volt negative earth
Bulbs	**Wattage**
Direction indicator (orange coloured)	21
Direction indicator side repeater	5
Front courtesy lights	5 or 7
Front foglight	55 (H1 type)
Front sidelight	5
Glovebox illumination light	5
Headlight:	
Single	55/60 (anti-UV. H4 type*)
Dual:	
Main beam	55 (anti-UV. H1 type*)
Dip beam	55 (anti-UV. H7 type*)
High-level stop-light	5
Luggage compartment light	7
Number plate light	5
Rear courtesy lights	5 or 7
Rear foglight	21
Rear sidelight	5
Reversing light	21
Stop/tail	21/5

* **Note***: As the headlights have plastic lenses,* **anti-UV type bulbs** *are used. The headlight may be damaged if any other type of H1, H4, or H7 bulb is used.*

Fuses	See *Wiring diagrams* at the end of this Chapter

Torque wrench setting	**Nm**	**lbf ft**
Driver's airbag unit screws	5	4

1 General information and precautions

Warning: Before carrying out any work on the electrical system, read through the precautions given in 'Safety first!' at the beginning of this manual and in Chapter 5A.

The electrical system is of the 12 volt negative earth type. Power for the lights and all electrical accessories is supplied by a lead-acid type battery which is charged by the alternator.

This Chapter covers repair and service procedures for the various electrical components not associated with the engine. Information on the battery, alternator and starter motor can be found in Chapter 5A.

It should be noted that prior to working on any component in the electrical system, the battery negative terminal should first be disconnected to prevent the possibility of electrical short circuits and/or fires (refer to Chapter 5A).

Caution: Before disconnecting the battery, refer to the information given in 'Disconnecting the battery' in the Reference Section of this manual.

2 Electrical fault finding – general information

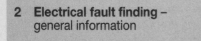

Note: *Refer to the precautions given in 'Safety first!' and in Section 1 of this Chapter before starting work. The following tests relate to testing of the main electrical circuits, and should not be used to test delicate electronic circuits (such as anti-lock braking systems), particularly where an electronic control unit (ECU) is used.*

General

A typical electrical circuit consists of an electrical component, any switches, relays, motors, fuses, fusible links or circuit breakers related to that component, and the wiring and connectors which link the component to both the battery and the chassis. To help to pinpoint a problem in an electrical circuit, wiring diagrams are included at the end of this Chapter.

Before attempting to diagnose an electrical fault, first study the appropriate wiring diagram to obtain a complete understanding of the components included in the particular circuit concerned. The possible sources of a fault can be narrowed down by noting if other components related to the circuit are operating properly. If several components or circuits fail at one time, the problem is likely to be related to a shared fuse or earth connection.

Electrical problems usually stem from simple causes, such as loose or corroded connections, a faulty earth connection, a blown fuse, a melted fusible link, or a faulty relay (refer to Section 3 for details of testing relays). Visually inspect the condition of all fuses, wires and connections in a problem circuit before testing the components. Use the wiring diagrams to determine which terminal connections will need to be checked in order to pinpoint the trouble spot.

The basic tools required for electrical fault-finding include a circuit tester or voltmeter (a 12 volt bulb with a set of test leads can also be used for certain tests); a self-powered test light (sometimes known as a continuity tester); an ohmmeter (to measure resistance); a battery and set of test leads; and a jumper wire, preferably with a circuit breaker or fuse incorporated, which can be used to bypass suspect wires or electrical components. Before attempting to locate a problem with test instruments, use the wiring diagram to determine where to make the connections.

To find the source of an intermittent wiring fault (usually due to a poor or dirty connection, or damaged wiring insulation), a 'wiggle' test can be performed on the wiring. This involves wiggling the wiring by hand to see if the fault occurs as the wiring is moved. It should be possible to narrow down the source of the fault to a particular section of wiring. This method of testing can be used in conjunction with any of the tests described in the following sub-Sections.

Apart from problems due to poor connections, two basic types of fault can occur in an electrical circuit – open circuit, or short circuit.

Open circuit faults are caused by a break somewhere in the circuit, which prevents current from flowing. An open circuit fault will prevent a component from working, but will not cause the relevant circuit fuse to blow.

Short circuit faults are caused by a 'short' somewhere in the circuit, which allows the current flowing in the circuit to 'escape' along an alternative route, usually to earth. Short circuit faults are normally caused by a breakdown in wiring insulation, which allows a feed wire to touch either another wire, or an earthed component such as the bodyshell. A short circuit fault will normally cause the relevant circuit fuse to blow.

Finding an open circuit

To check for an open circuit, connect one lead of a circuit tester or voltmeter to either the negative battery terminal or a known good earth.

Connect the other lead to a connector in the circuit being tested, preferably nearest to the battery or fuse.

Switch on the circuit, bearing in mind that some circuits are live only when the ignition switch is moved to a particular position.

If voltage is present (indicated either by the tester bulb lighting or a voltmeter reading, as applicable), this means that the section of the circuit between the relevant connector and the battery is problem-free.

Continue to check the remainder of the circuit in the same fashion.

When a point is reached at which no voltage is present, the problem must lie between that point and the previous test point with voltage. Most problems can be traced to a broken, corroded or loose connection.

Finding a short circuit

To check for a short circuit, first disconnect the load(s) from the circuit (loads are the components which draw current from a circuit, such as bulbs, motors, heating elements, etc).

Remove the relevant fuse from the circuit, and connect a circuit tester or voltmeter to the fuse connections.

Switch on the circuit, bearing in mind that some circuits are live only when the ignition switch is moved to a particular position.

If voltage is present (indicated either by the tester bulb lighting or a voltmeter reading, as applicable), this means that there is a short circuit.

If no voltage is present, but the fuse still blows with the load(s) connected, this indicates an internal fault in the load(s).

Finding an earth fault

The battery negative terminal is connected to 'earth' – the metal of the engine/transmission and the car body – and most systems are wired so that they only receive a positive feed, the current returning through the metal of the car body. This means that the component mounting and the body form part of that circuit. Loose or corroded mountings can therefore cause a range of electrical faults, ranging from total failure of a circuit, to a puzzling partial fault. In particular, lights may shine dimly (especially when another circuit sharing the same earth point is in operation), motors (eg, wiper motors or the radiator cooling fan motor) may run slowly, and the operation of one circuit may have an apparently unrelated effect on another. Note that on many vehicles, earth straps are used between certain components, such as the engine/transmission and the body, usually where there is no metal-to-metal contact between components due to flexible rubber mountings, etc.

To check whether a component is properly earthed, disconnect the battery and connect one lead of an ohmmeter to a known good earth point. Connect the other lead to the wire or earth connection being tested. The resistance reading should be zero; if not, check the connection as follows.

If an earth connection is thought to be faulty, dismantle the connection and clean back to bare metal both the bodyshell and the wire terminal or the component earth connection mating surface. Be careful to remove all traces of dirt and corrosion, then use a knife to trim away any paint, so that a

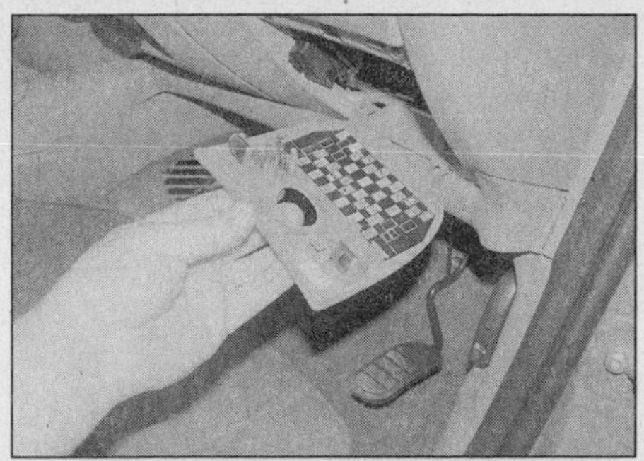

3.1a Most fuses are located behind the cover on the driver's side of the facia . . .

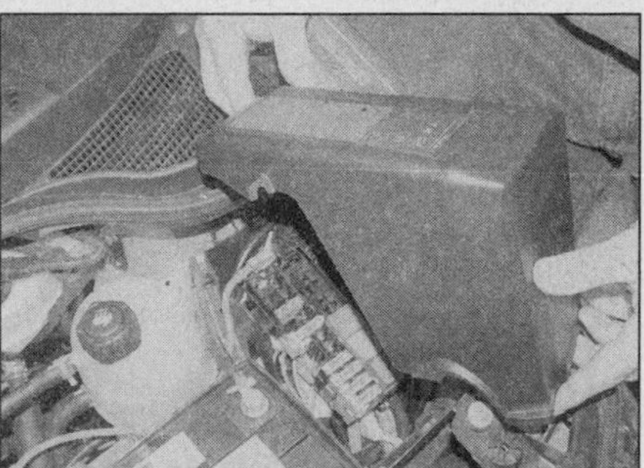

3.1b . . . with the others located in the engine compartment fuse/relay box

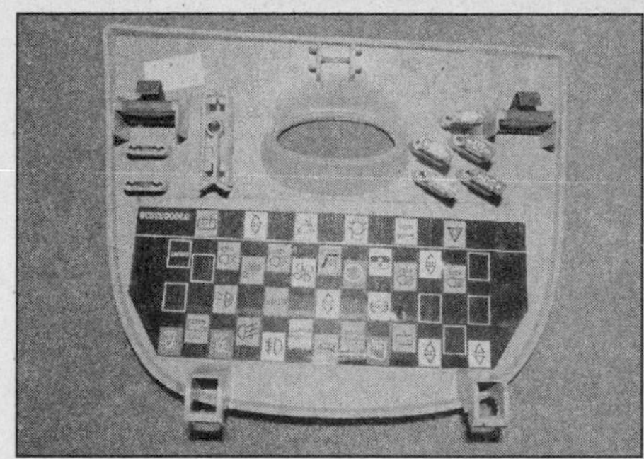

3.3 Pictures of circuits on the inside of the fuse cover

clean metal-to-metal joint is made. On reassembly, tighten the joint fasteners securely; if a wire terminal is being refitted, use serrated washers between the terminal and the bodyshell to ensure a clean and secure connection. When the connection is remade, prevent the onset of corrosion in the future by applying a coat of petroleum jelly or silicone-based grease or by spraying on (at regular intervals) a proprietary ignition sealer or a water dispersant lubricant.

3 Fuses and relays – general information

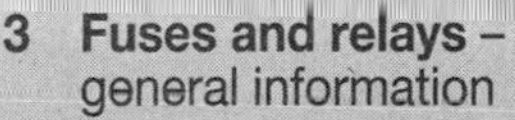

Fuses

1 The majority of fuses are located in the passenger compartment fusebox situated on the driver's side of the facia. Additional fuses and relays, are located in the fuse/relay box on the left-hand side of the engine compartment **(see illustrations)**.

2 To gain access to the main fusebox, open up the cover. To gain access to the fuses in the engine compartment fuse/relay box, simply unclip the cover.

3 A list of the circuits each fuse protects is given on the relevant fusebox cover **(see illustration)**.

4 To remove a fuse, first switch off the circuit concerned (or the ignition), then pull the fuse out of its terminals using the plastic tool provided on the passenger compartment fusebox cover. The wire within the fuse should be visible; if the fuse is blown it will be broken or melted.

5 Always renew a fuse with one of an identical rating; never use a fuse with a different rating from the original or substitute anything else. Never renew a fuse more than once without tracing the source of the trouble. The fuse rating is stamped on top of the fuse; note that the fuses are also colour-coded for easy recognition.

6 If a new fuse blows immediately, find the cause before renewing it again; a short to earth as a result of faulty insulation is most likely. Where a fuse protects more than one circuit, try to isolate the defect by switching on each circuit in turn (if possible) until the fuse blows again. Always carry a supply of spare fuses of each relevant rating on the vehicle, a spare of each rating should be clipped into the base of the fusebox.

Relays

7 The majority of relays are plugged into the relay box which is attached to the passenger compartment fusebox located behind the driver's side of the facia. Other relays can be found in the engine compartment fuse/relay box.

8 To gain access to the relay box behind the facia, remove the driver's side facia switch panel as described in Section 4. Unscrew the fusebox retaining screw then reach up behind the facia and unclip the plastic protector plate from the base of the fusebox. Release the retaining clips and disconnect the four wiring connectors from the base of the fusebox. Release the fusebox from its side retaining clips by pushing it towards the front of the vehicle then carefully manoeuvre the assembly out from underneath the facia. Release the retaining clips and remove the cover to gain access to the various relays **(see illustrations)**. Refitting is the reverse of removal.

9 If a circuit or system controlled by a relay develops a fault and the relay is suspect, operate the system; if the relay is functioning it should be possible to hear it click as it is energised. If this is the case the fault lies with the components or wiring of the system. If the relay is not being energised then either the relay is not receiving a main supply or a switching voltage or the relay itself is faulty. Testing is by the substitution of a known good unit but be careful; some relays are identical

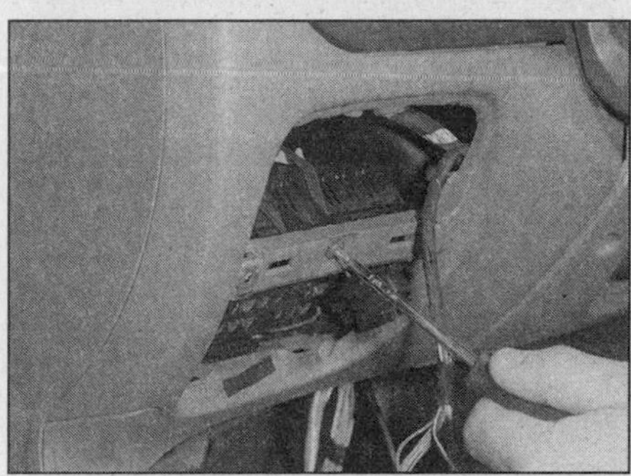

3.8a To gain access to the passenger compartment fusebox relays, undo the retaining screw . . .

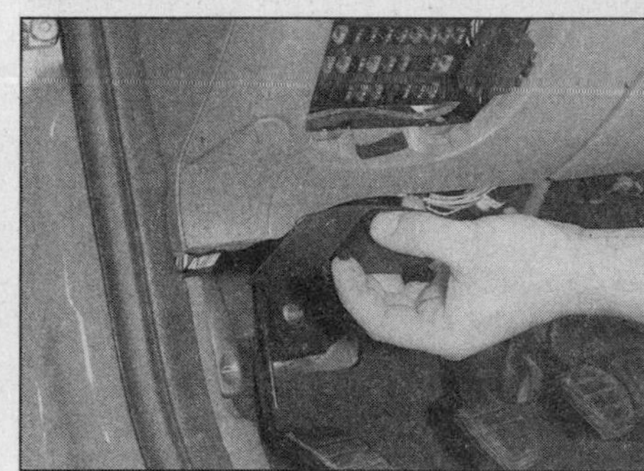

3.8b . . . then unclip the protective cover from the base of the unit

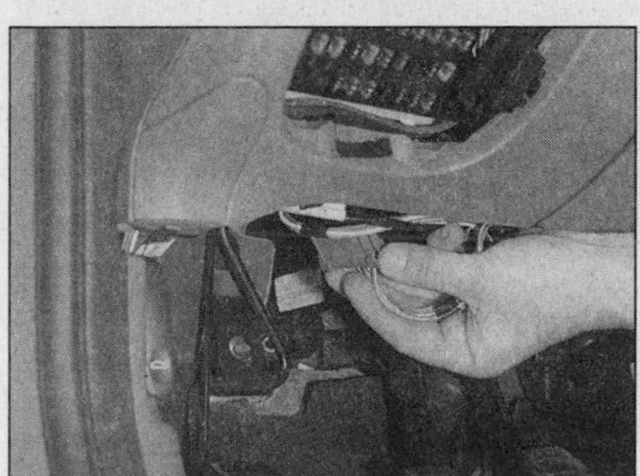

3.8c Disconnect the wiring connectors then unclip the fusebox . . .

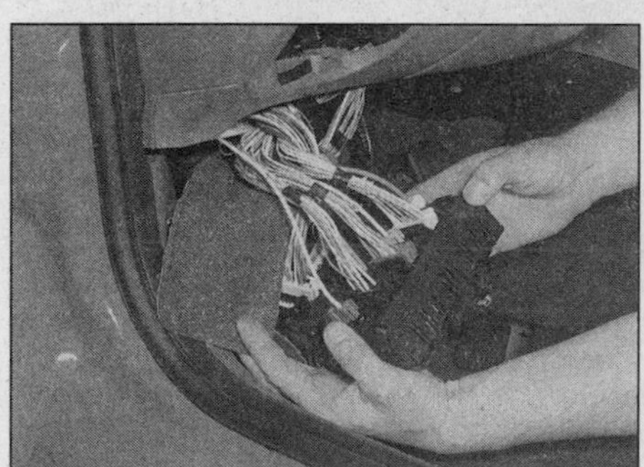

3.8d . . . and remove the cover to gain access to the relays

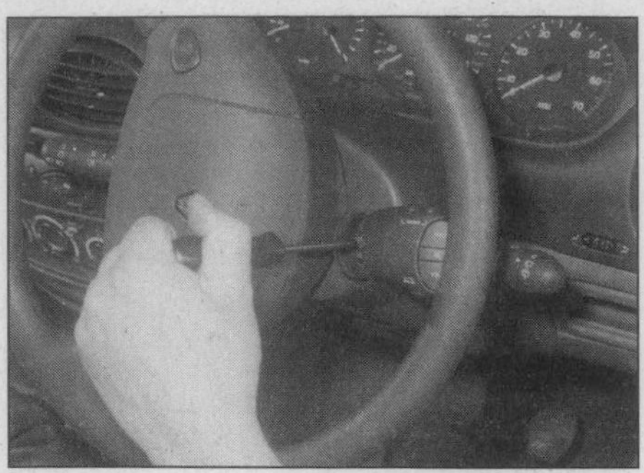
4.2 Unclip the cover and slacken the radio control switch screw a few turns

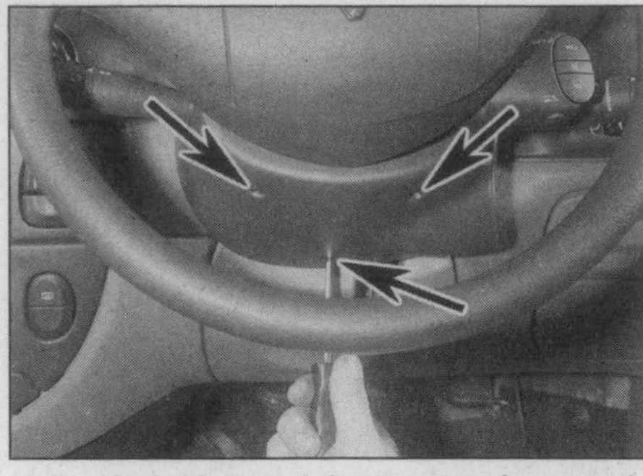
4.3a Undo the retaining screws (arrowed) and remove the steering column lower shroud . . .

4.3b . . . then undo the screws and lift off the upper shroud

in appearance and in operation, others look similar but perform different functions.

10 To renew a relay first ensure that the ignition switch is off. The relay can then simply be pulled out from the socket and the new relay pressed in.

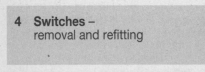

4 Switches – removal and refitting

Note: *Disconnect the battery negative lead (refer to Chapter 5A) before removing any switch, and reconnect the lead after refitting the switch.*

Ignition switch/steering lock

1 Insert the key into the ignition switch so the steering wheel is free to turn.

2 Position the steering wheel so that access can be gained to the radio control switch assembly. Unclip the cover from the inside of the switch and slacken the switch retaining screw by a few turns **(see illustration)**.

3 Slacken and remove the retaining screws and remove the lower half of the steering column shroud. Undo the two retaining screws, positioning the steering wheel as necessary, and remove the upper half of the steering column shroud **(see illustration)**.

4 Undo the retaining screws and remove the steering column lower cover from the facia.

5 Trace the wiring back from the switch and disconnect it from the main harness.

6 Remove the plastic trim cover (where fitted) from around the switch and unscrew the switch retaining screw **(see illustrations)**.

7 Insert the ignition key and turn the key until it aligns with the mark halfway between the A and M (1st and 2nd) switch positions. Hold the key in this position then depress the retaining clip and slide the switch assembly out of position **(see illustrations)**.

8 Refitting is the reverse of removal, making sure the switch is clipped securely into position. Ensure that the wiring is correctly routed and retained by all the necessary clips.

Steering column switches

9 Remove the steering column shrouds as described in paragraphs 1 and 3.

10 To remove an individual switch assembly, disconnect the wiring then remove the retaining screws and slide the switch out of its mounting bracket **(see illustration)**.

11 To remove the complete switch and mounting bracket assembly it will first be necessary to remove the steering wheel (see Chapter 10). Unscrew the radio control switch stalk mounting screw and position the stalk clear. Disconnect the wiring from the switches then slacken the clamp screw a few turns and release the switch clamp by tapping the screw lightly. The complete switch assembly can

4.6a Remove the trim cover from the switch (shown with steering wheel removed for clarity) . . .

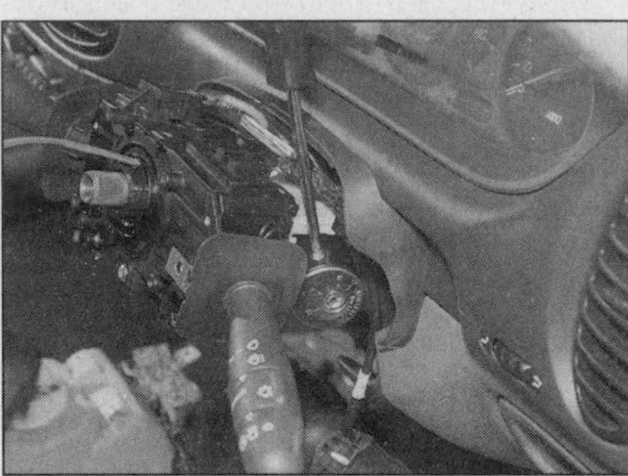
4.6b . . . then remove the switch retaining screw

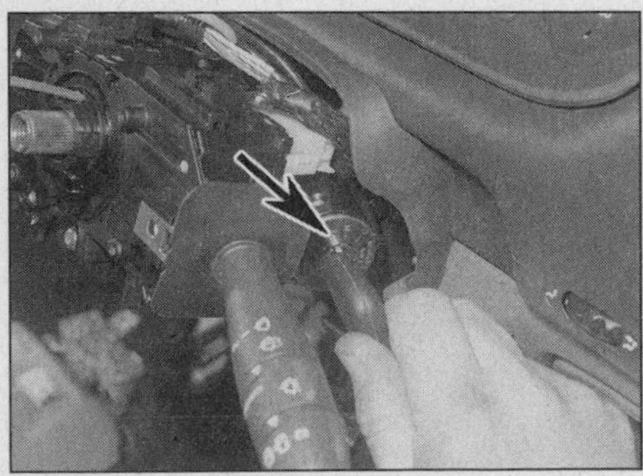
4.7a Insert the key and turn it to align with the mark (arrowed) midway between the A and M marks . . .

4.7b . . . then depress the retaining clip and slide the switch out of position

4.10 Undo the retaining screws and slide the combination switch out of its mounting bracket

4.11 Removing the complete combination switch assembly

4.12 If the complete assembly has been removed, centralise the stalks with the shrouds and tighten the clamp screw

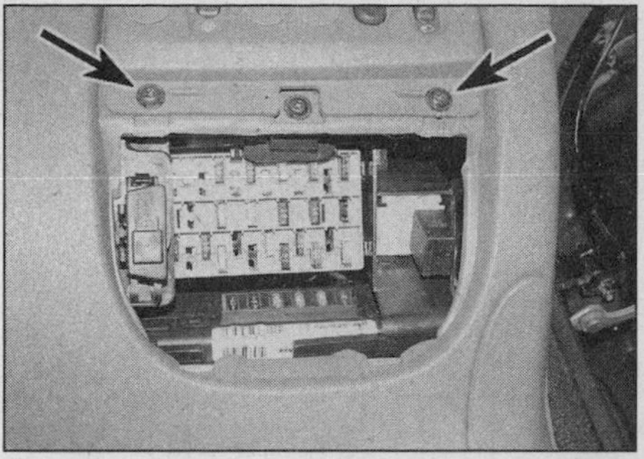
4.13 Remove the fusebox cover then undo the retaining screws (arrowed) . . .

then be lifted off from the top of the steering column **(see illustration)**.

12 Refitting is the reverse of removal ensuring all wiring connectors are securely reconnected. If the complete switch assembly has been removed, prior to refitting the steering wheel, ensure that the switch stalks are correctly positioned in relation to the shrouds; if necessary slacken the mounting clamp screw and reposition the switch correctly before securely retightening the screw **(see illustration)**.

Driver's side facia switches

13 Remove the fusebox cover from the driver's side of the facia then slacken and remove the switch panel retaining screws **(see illustration)**.

14 Remove the switch panel from the facia, disconnecting its wiring connectors as they become accessible. The relevant switch can then be unclipped and removed from the panel **(see illustration)**.

15 Refitting is the reverse of removal.

Centre facia switches

16 Referring to Chapter 3, remove the heater control panel from the facia noting that it is not necessary to remove the panel completely, only to slide it sufficiently out of position so that access can be gained to the relevant switch.

17 Depress the retaining clips then push the relevant switch out of position and disconnect it from the wiring connector **(see illustrations)**.

18 Refitting is the reverse of removal.

Centre console front switches

All models except Scénic

19 Carefully unclip the switch panel and remove it from the front of the centre console disconnecting its wiring connectors as they become accessible.

20 Undo the retaining screws/unclip the switch from the panel.

21 Refitting is the reverse of removal ensuring that the switch panel is clipped securely in position.

Scénic models

22 Undo the bolt securing the right-hand centre footwell vent panel under the centre of the facia. Pivot the front of the vent downward to release the locating pin, then move it forward to disengage the rear locating tag. Repeat this procedure to remove the left-hand vent panel.

23 Remove the centre console switch panel by undoing the two screws, one each side.

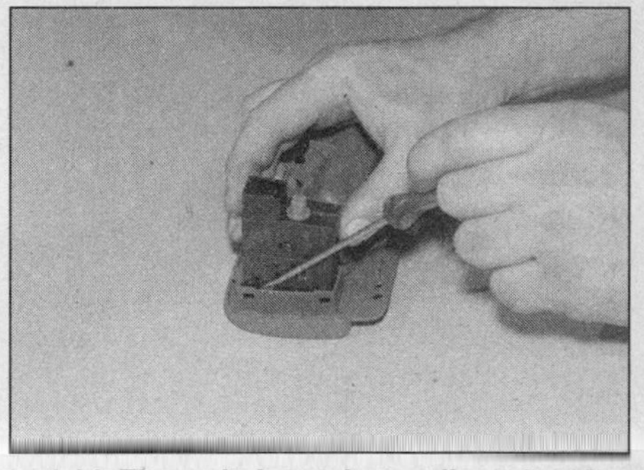
4.14 The switch can be unclipped and removed from the panel

Pivot the panel upwards to release the clips and centring pins along its top edge, then withdraw the unit. Disconnect the wiring connectors and remove the switch panel.

24 To remove the rear window switches, depress the four tabs and push the switch out of the panel. To remove the remaining switches, undo the two mounting bolts.

25 Refitting is the reverse of removal.

Centre console rear switches

26 Carefully unclip the switch panel from the rear section of the centre console and disconnect the wiring connectors. The wiring connector are colour-coded for identification;

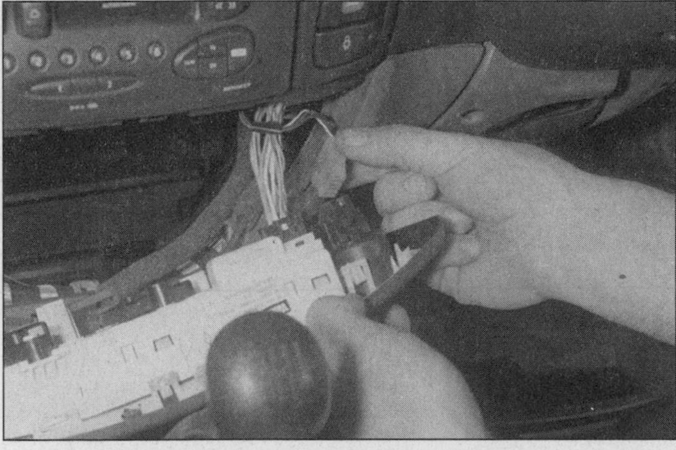
4.17a Withdraw the heater control panel then disconnect the wiring connector . . .

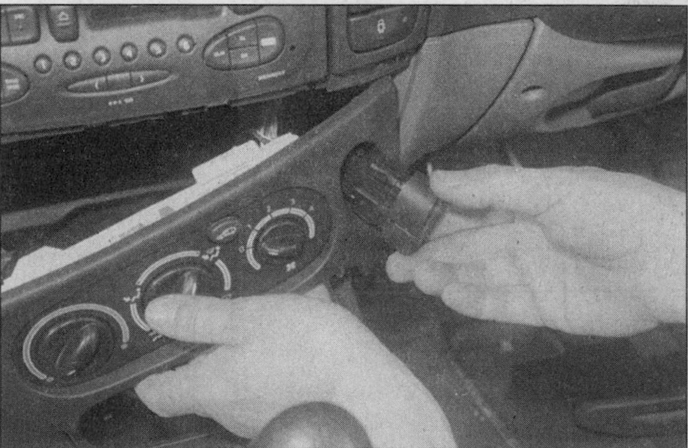
4.17b . . . and unclip the switch assembly

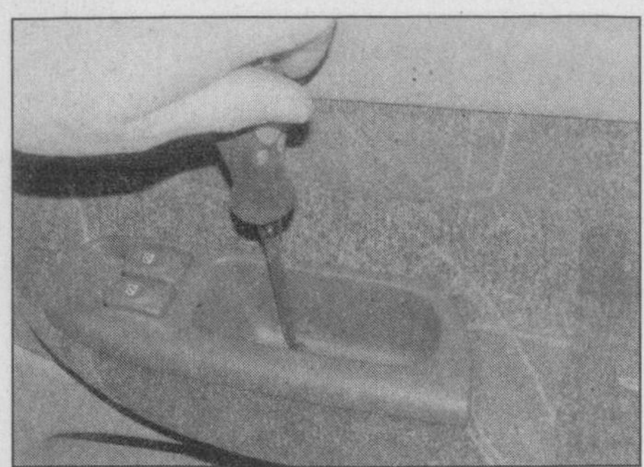
4.30a Undo the retaining screws . . .

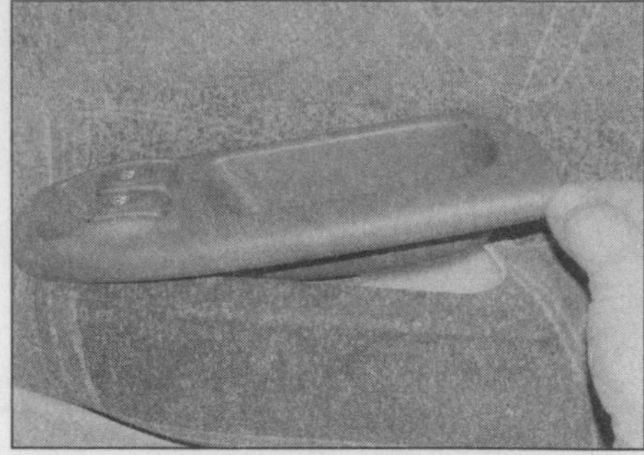
4.30b . . . and unclip the assembly from the door trim panel

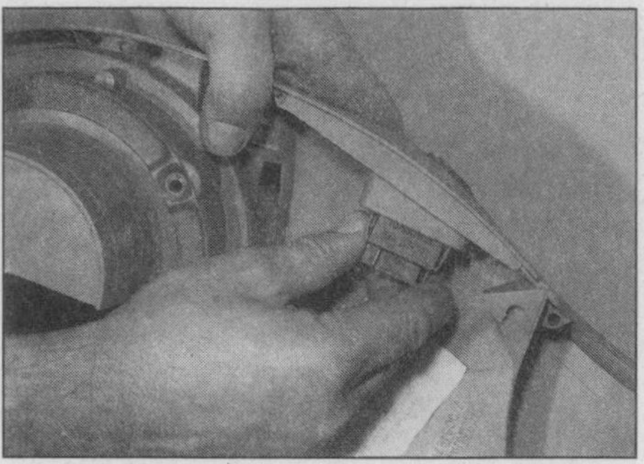
4.31 Depress the retaining clips and slide the window switch out from the storage compartment

the left-hand one is green and the right-hand one grey.

27 Depress the clips and slide the switch(es) out of position noting their correct locations.

28 Refitting is the reverse of removal.

Door-mounted switches

29 On Mégane models, remove the loudspeaker from the door as described in Section 20. Undo the retaining screws and remove the storage compartment from the bottom of the door in an upwards direction, disconnecting the wiring connectors as they become accessible.

30 On Scénic models, undo the retaining screw and unclip the door handle/switch assembly from the door trim panel, disconnecting the wiring connectors as they become accessible **(see illustrations)**.

31 Each switch can then be removed by depressing its retaining clips and sliding it out of position **(see illustration)**.

32 Refitting is the reverse of removal.

Overhead console switches

33 The light switches are integral with the courtesy light units (see Section 6). The sunroof switch can be removed as follows.

34 Slide off the plastic cover from the front of the overhead console, in a forwards direction **(see illustration)**.

35 On Mégane models, slacken and remove the retaining screws then remove the console assembly from the roof, disconnecting its wiring connectors as they become accessible. Slacken and remove the retaining screws to remove the switch from the console **(see illustrations)**.

36 On Scénic models, unclip the light cover from around the switch, then remove the switch assembly **(see illustrations)**.

37 Refitting is the reverse of removal.

4.34 Slide the plastic cover off from the overhead console and disconnect its wiring connector

4.35a Undo the retaining screws (arrowed), then unclip the console and disconnect its wiring connectors

Seat switches

38 Carefully prise the switch panel out from the side of the seat and disconnect it from the wiring connector(s).

39 Reconnect the wiring connector and clip the switch back into position.

Stop-light switch

40 Refer to Chapter 9.

Courtesy light switch

41 Open the door and remove the rubber cover from the switch.

42 Using a small, flat-bladed screwdriver depress the switch retaining clips then carefully ease the switch out from the pillar. Disconnect the wiring connector and tie a piece of string to the wiring to prevent it falling back into the door pillar. If necessary, to avoid damaging the switch/paintwork, remove the pillar trim panel and push the switch out from behind.

43 Refitting is a reverse of the removal procedure. Refit the rubber cover to the

4.35b The sunroof switch is secured to the console by two screws (arrowed)

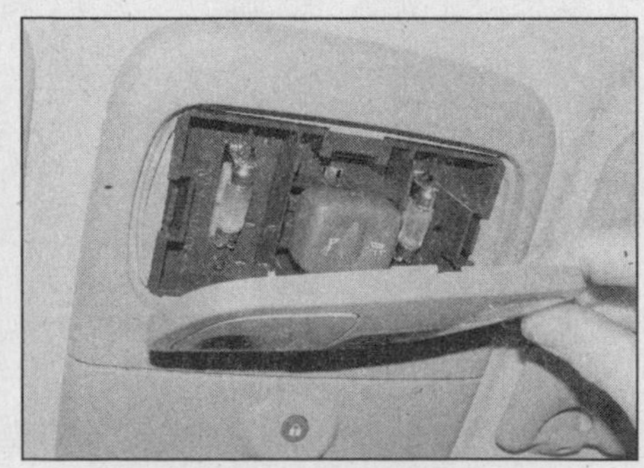
4.36a Unclip the switch cover . . .

4.36b . . . and release the switch assembly

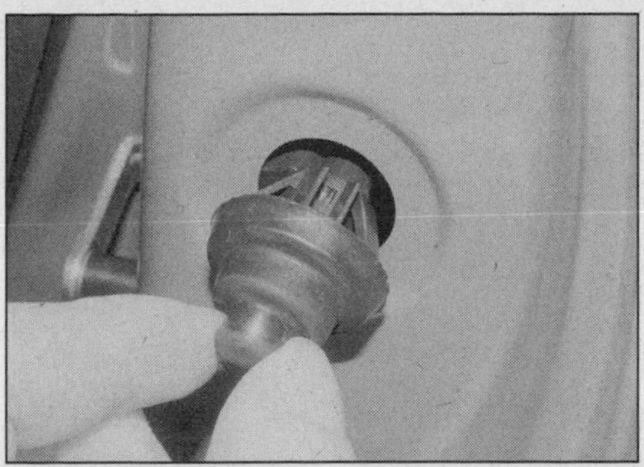

4.43 Refit the rubber cover to the switch before refitting

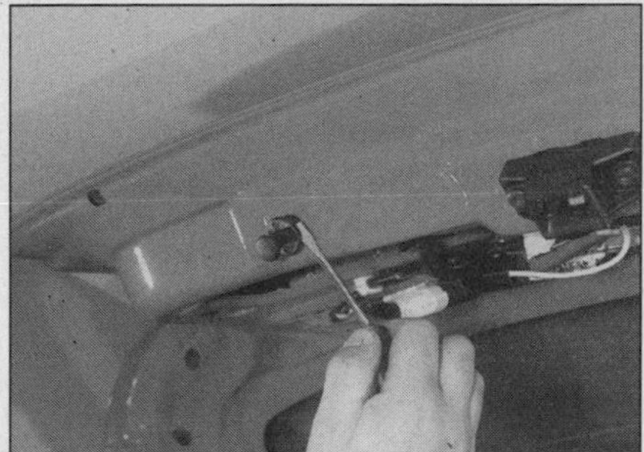

4.44a Prise out the luggage compartment light switch . . .

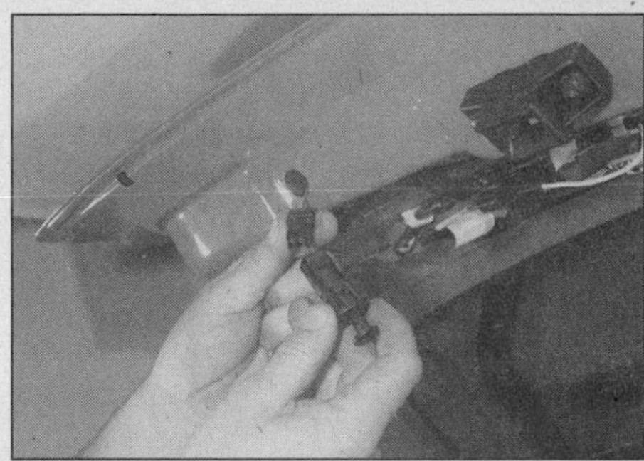

4.44b . . . and disconnect its wiring

switch prior to clipping it into the door pillar **(see illustration)**.

Luggage area light switch

44 Open up the tailgate/boot lid then carefully prise the switch out of position and disconnect its wiring connector. If necessary, to avoid damaging the switch/paintwork, remove the inner trim (where fitted) panel and push the switch out of position **(see illustrations)**.

45 Refitting is the reverse of removal.

Horn switch

Warning: Before carrying out any work on airbags, read through the precautions given in Section 24.

46 Remove the airbag from the centre of the steering wheel as described in Section 25.

47 There are three switches incorporated in the steering wheel **(see illustration)**.

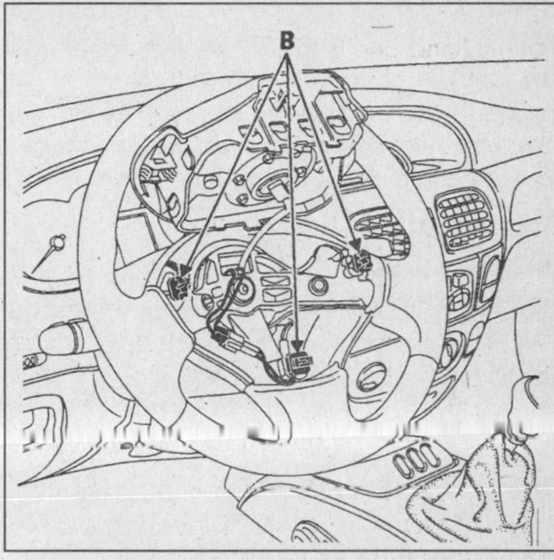

4.47 There are three horn switches (B) incorporated in the steering wheel

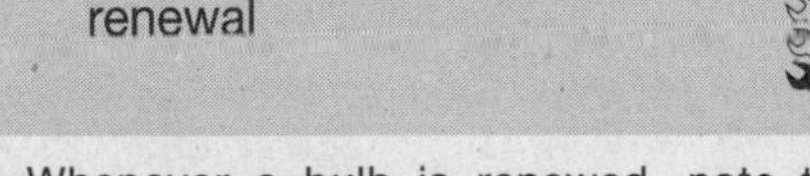

5 Bulbs (exterior lights) – renewal

1 Whenever a bulb is renewed, note the following points.

a) *Disconnect the battery negative lead before starting work (refer to Chapter 5A)*
b) *Remember that if the light has just been in use the bulb may be extremely hot.*
c) *Always check the bulb contacts and holder, ensuring that there is clean metal-to-metal contact between the bulb and its live(s) and earth. Clean off any corrosion or dirt before fitting a new bulb.*
d) *Wherever bayonet-type bulbs are fitted ensure that the live contact(s) bear firmly against the bulb contact.*
e) *Always ensure that the new bulb is of the correct rating and that it is completely clean before fitting it; this applies particularly to headlight/foglight bulbs (see below).* ***Note:*** *As the headlights have plastic lenses,* ***anti-UV type bulbs*** *are used (the headlight may be damaged if any other type of H1, H4, or H7 bulb is used, see specifications).*

Headlight

2 Remove the access cover from the rear of the headlight unit; where a round cover is fitted, twist the cover through 90° to release it, and where a rectangular cover is fitted release the retaining clip **(see illustration)**.

3 Disconnect the wiring connector from the rear of the bulb **(see illustration)**.

4 Unhook and release the ends of the bulb retaining clip and release it from the rear of the light unit. Withdraw the bulb **(see illustrations)**.

5 When handling the new bulb, use a tissue or clean cloth to avoid touching the glass with the fingers; moisture and grease from the skin can cause blackening and rapid failure of this type of bulb.

If the headlight or foglight glass is accidentally touched, wipe it clean using methylated spirit.

5.2 On models with a round access cover, twist the cover through 90° to release it from the headlight

5.3 Disconnect the wiring connector . . .

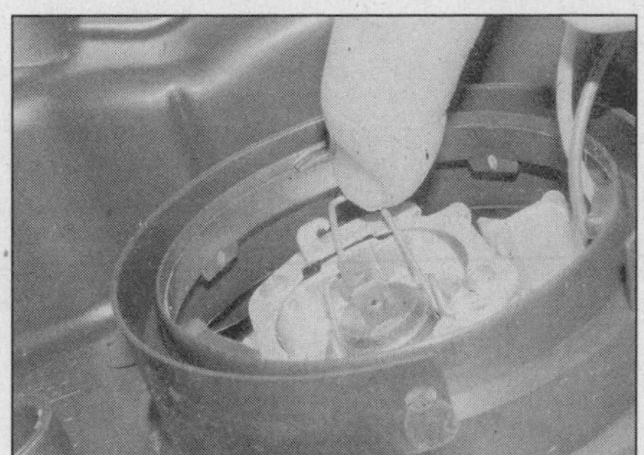

5.4a . . . then release the retaining clip . . .

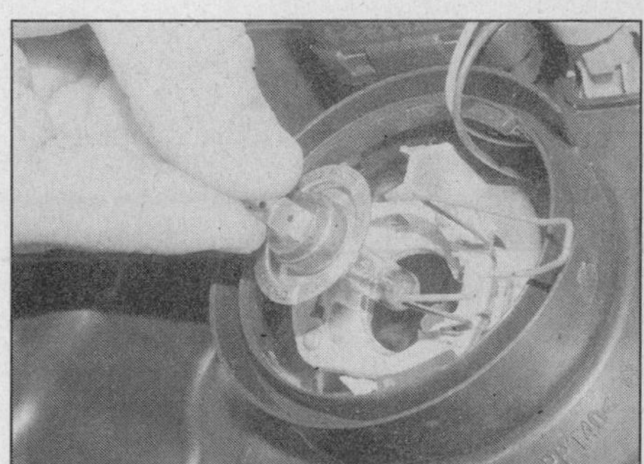

5.4b . . . and withdraw the bulb from the headlight

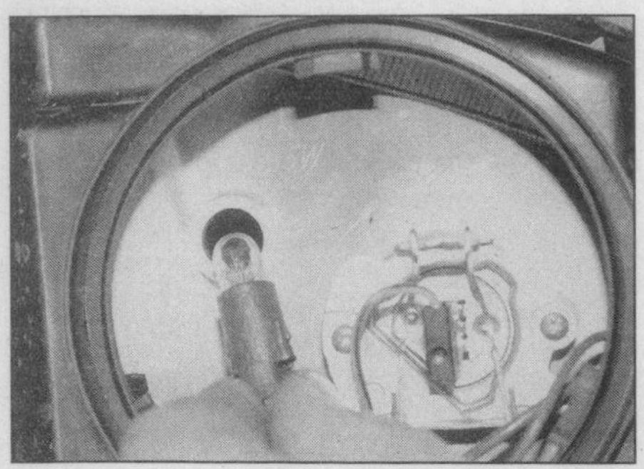
5.9a Free the sidelight bulbholder from the rear of the headlight . . .

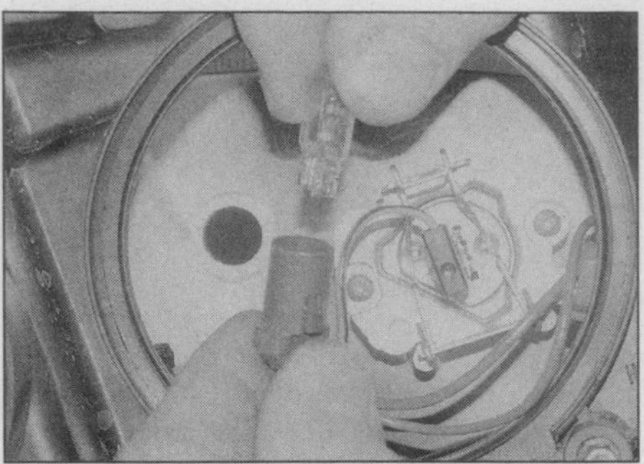
5.9b . . . and pull out the bulb

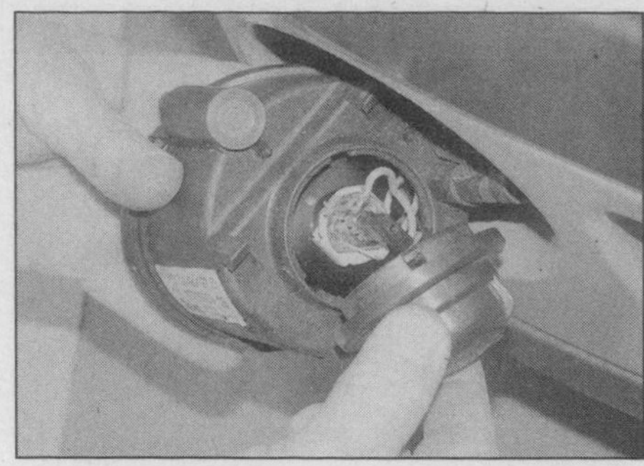
5.12a Twist the rear cover to remove . . .

6 Install the new bulb, ensuring that its locating tabs are correctly located in the light cut-outs, and secure it in position with the retaining clip

7 Reconnect the wiring connector and refit the access cover, making sure it is securely refitted.

Front sidelight

8 Remove the access cover from the rear of the headlight unit (see paragraph 2).

9 Rotate the sidelight bulbholder and release it from the headlight unit. The bulb is of the capless (push-fit) type and can be removed by simply pulling it out of the bulbholder **(see illustrations)**.

10 Refitting is the reverse of the removal procedure making sure the access cover is securely refitted.

Front foglight

11 Remove the foglight as described in Section 7.

12 Rotate the access cover and remove it from the rear of the light unit. Disconnect the wiring connector, then unhook and release the ends of the bulb retaining clip. Withdraw the bulb from the rear of the light unit **(see illustrations)**.

13 When handling the new bulb, use a tissue or clean cloth to avoid touching the glass with the fingers; moisture and grease from the skin can cause blackening and rapid failure of this type of bulb. If the glass is accidentally touched, wipe it clean using methylated spirit.

14 Install the new bulb, ensuring that its locating tabs are correctly located in the light cut-outs, and secure it in position with the retaining clip

15 Reconnect the wiring connector and refit the access cover, making sure it is securely refitted.

16 Refit the foglight as described in Section 7.

Front direction indicator

17 Rotate the bulbholder anti-clockwise and remove it from the rear of the headlight unit. The bulb is a bayonet fit in the holder and can be removed by pressing it and twisting in an anti-clockwise direction **(see illustrations)**.

18 Refitting is a reverse of the removal procedure.

Front indicator side repeater

19 Carefully unclip the light unit and withdraw it from the wing **(see illustration)**.

20 Twist the bulbholder anti-clockwise and remove it from the light. The bulb is of the capless (push-fit) type and can be removed by simply pulling it out of the bulbholder **(see illustrations)**.

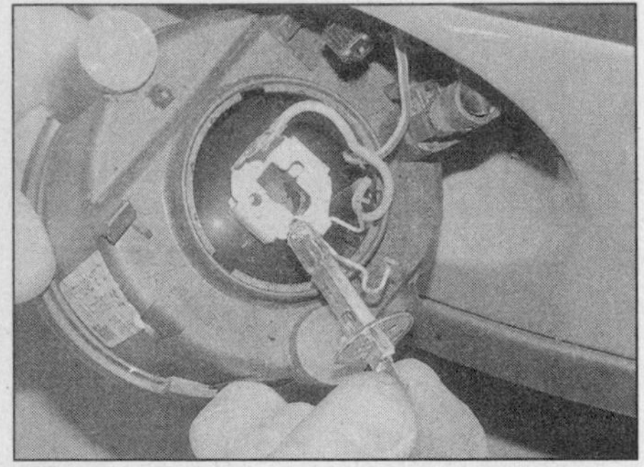
5.12b . . . then release the retaining clip and remove the foglight bulb

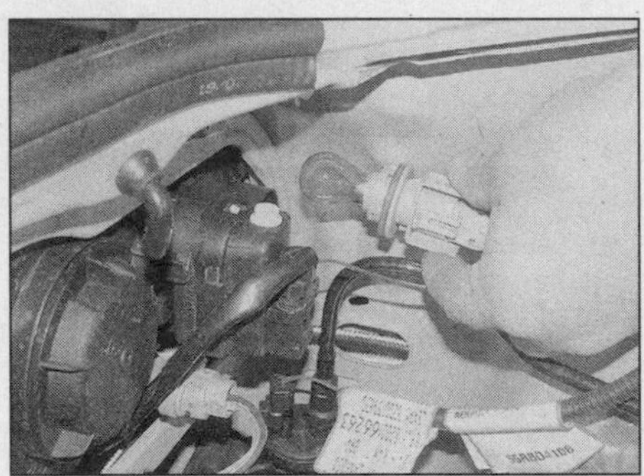
5.17a Rotate the bulbholder anti-clockwise to free it from the direction indicator light . . .

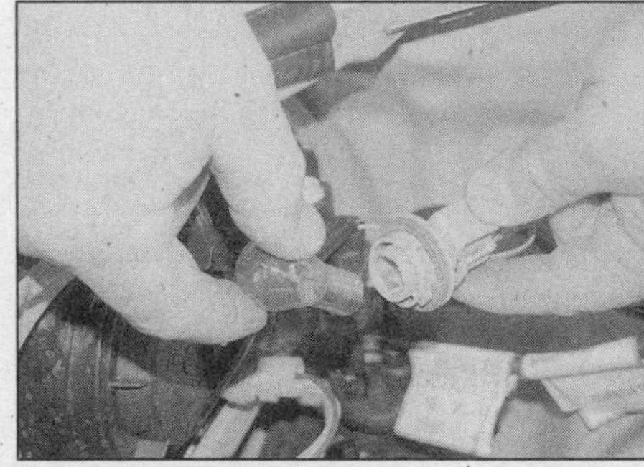
5.17b . . . then push the bulb in and twist it anti-clockwise to free it from the holder

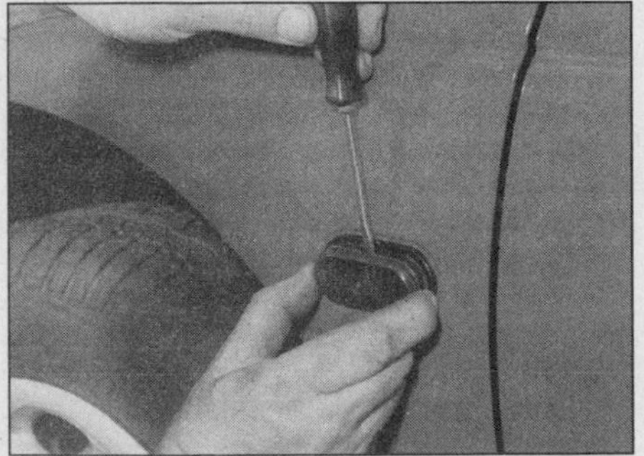
5.19 Carefully prise the side repeater light out from the wing . . .

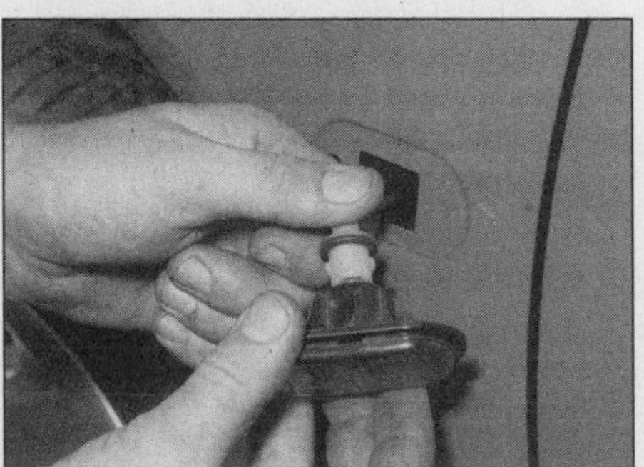
5.20a . . . then rotate the bulbholder to free it from the light . . .

5.20b . . . and pull out the bulb

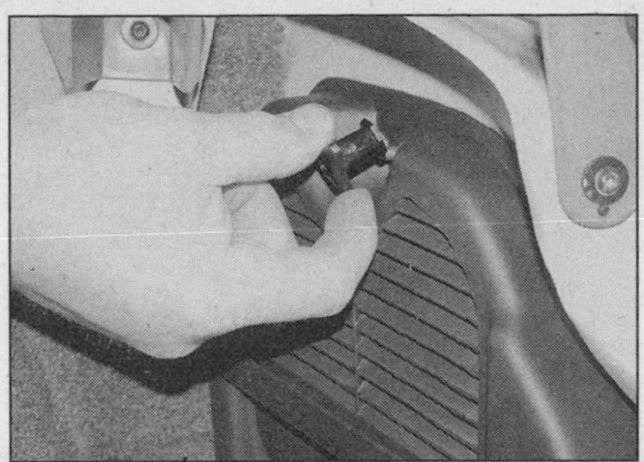

5.22 On Hatchback (shown here) and Coupé models, unscrew the nut and pivot the cover away from the light cluster

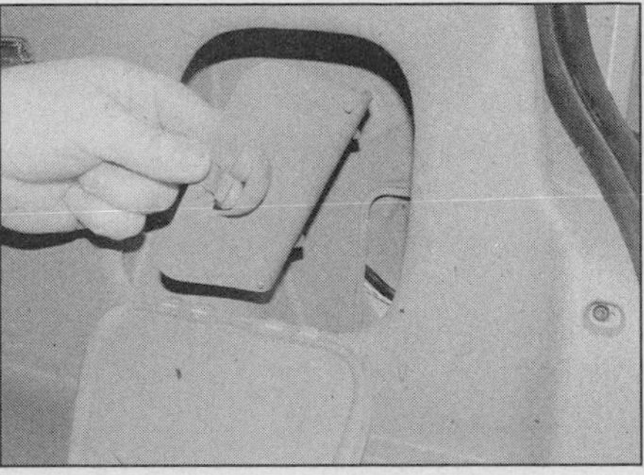

5.23 Unclip the access panel and inner trim cover to reach the back of the rear light cluster

5.24 Depress the retaining clips and remove the bulbholder

21 Refitting is a reverse of the removal procedure.

Rear light cluster

22 On Hatchback and Coupé models, from inside the luggage compartment, unscrew the upper retaining nut and unclip the cover from the rear of the light cluster; on some models it will also be necessary to unhook the cover rubber retaining band **(see illustration)**.

23 On Saloon and Scénic models, unclip the access cover from the rear of the light unit. On Scénic models, the access cover is located inside the wheelarch liner trim panel and it may be necessary to open the flap on the panel to reach inside **(see illustration)**.

24 Release the retaining clips and remove the bulbholder assembly from the rear of the light cluster **(see illustration)**.

25 All bulbs have bayonet fittings. The relevant bulb can be removed by pressing in and rotating anti-clockwise **(see illustration)**. Note that the stop/taillight bulb has offset pins to ensure it is fitted the correct way around.

26 Refitting is the reverse of the removal sequence.

Boot lid-mounted rear lights

Coupé models

27 Open up the boot lid then unclip the cover to access to the rear of the light **(see illustration)**.

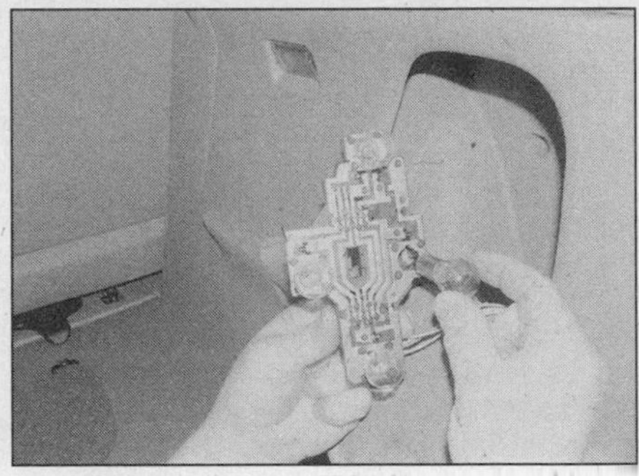

5.25 The bulb can then be removed by pushing it in and turning anti-clockwise

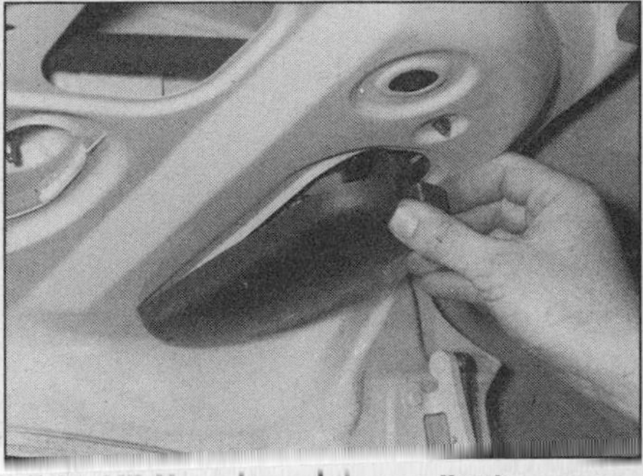

5.27 On Coupé models, unclip the cover then rotate the bulbholder to free it from the light unit

28 Twist the bulbholder and free it from the rear of the light unit then remove the bulb.

29 Refitting is the reverse of the removal sequence.

Saloon models

30 Open up the boot lid then unclip the cover to access to the rear of the light.

31 Release the retaining clips and remove the bulbholder assembly from the rear of the light cluster then remove the bulb.

32 Refitting is the reverse of the removal sequence.

High-level stop-light

33 On Hatchback models, open up the tailgate then depress the retaining clips and slide off the cover from the underside of the light unit **(see illustration)**.

34 On Coupé models, open up the boot lid to gain access to the rear of the light unit.

35 On Saloon models, from inside the vehicle, depress the retaining clips and slide off the cover from the rear of the light unit **(see illustration)**.

36 On Scénic models, open the tailgate and remove the two plugs from the holes behind

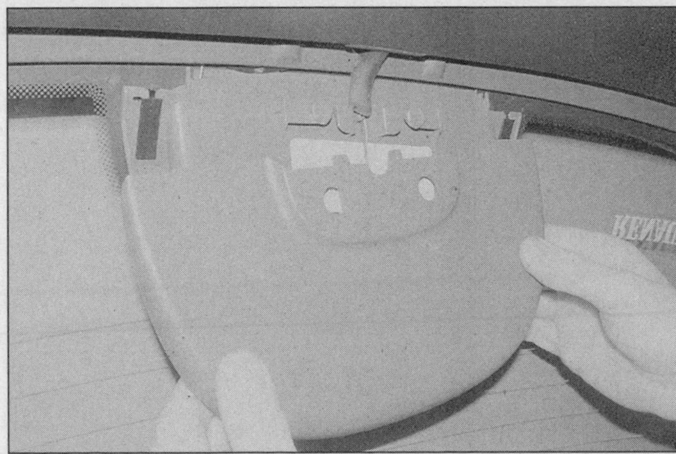

5.33 On Hatchback models, depress the retaining clips and slide the cover off from the high-level stop-light

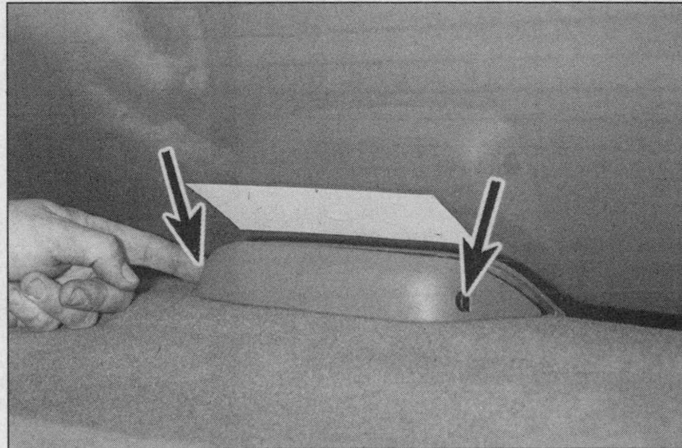

5.35 On Saloon models, depress the retaining clips (arrowed) and slide off the high-level stop-light cover

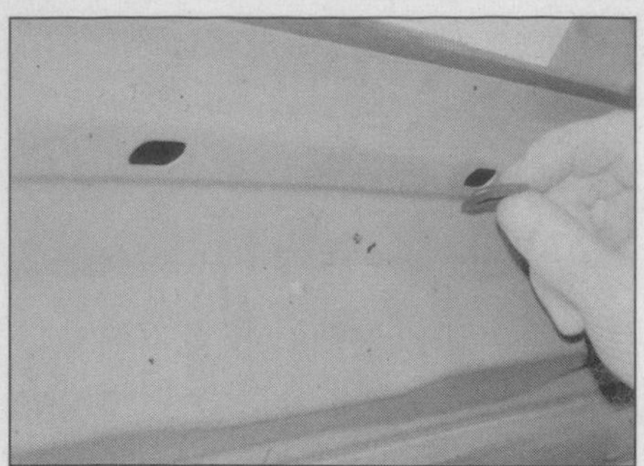
5.36a Remove the plastic plugs in the tailgate . . .

5.36b . . . insert the a screwdriver to release the securing clips . . .

5.36c . . . and withdraw the light unit

the light unit. Insert a screwdriver into each hole in turn and release the light unit from its locating clips. Withdraw the light unit to the outside of the tailgate **(see illustrations)**.

37 On all models, release the retaining clip and pull out the capless (push-fit) type bulb from the bulbholder **(see illustrations)**.

38 Refitting is the reverse of the removal sequence.

Number plate light

39 Carefully prise out the light unit out of position then unclip the cover (where fitted) and remove the bulb from the light unit contacts **(see illustrations)**.

40 Refitting is the reverse of removal ensuring that the bulb and lens are clipped securely in position.

6 Bulbs (interior lights) – renewal

1 Whenever a bulb is renewed, note the following points.

a) Disconnect the battery negative lead before starting work (refer to Chapter 5A).

b) Remember that if the light has just been in use the bulb may be extremely hot.

c) Always check the bulb contacts and holder, ensuring that there is clean metal-to-metal contact between the bulb and its live(s) and earth. Clean off any corrosion or dirt before fitting a new bulb.

d) Wherever bayonet-type bulbs are fitted ensure that the live contact(s) bear firmly against the bulb contact.

e) Always ensure that the new bulb is of the correct rating and that it is completely clean before fitting it).

Front courtesy and reading lights

Combined courtesy/reading light

2 Using a flat-bladed screwdriver, carefully unclip the light unit cover from the overhead console taking care not to damage either the cover or console **(see illustration)**.

3 Each individual bulb can then be removed from the console.

4 Refitting is the reverse of removal.

Separate courtesy and reading lights

5 Using a small, flat-bladed screwdriver, carefully prise the light unit assembly out of position **(see illustration)**.

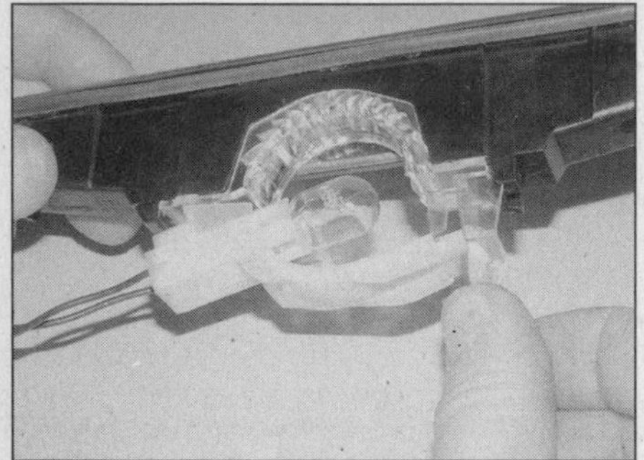
5.37a Unclip the bulbholder from the light unit . . .

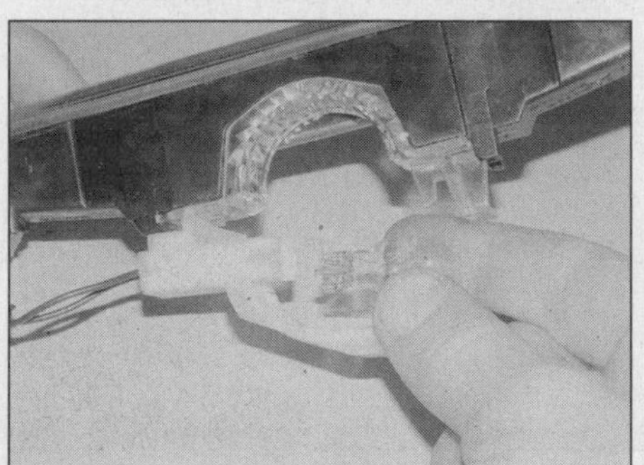
5.37b . . . and pull out the relevant bulb

5.39a Unclip the number plate light . . .

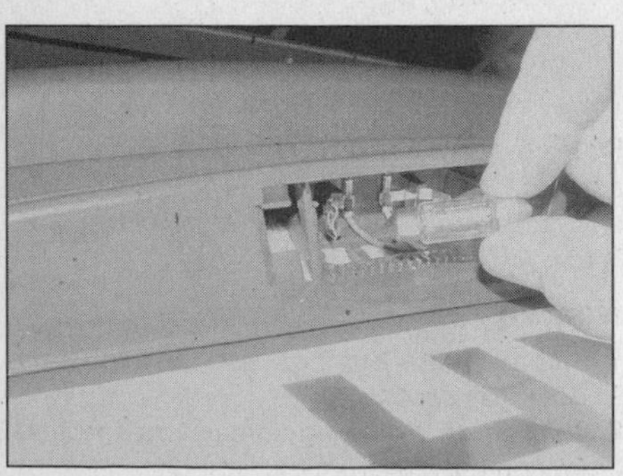
5.39b . . . then unclip the bulb from its contacts

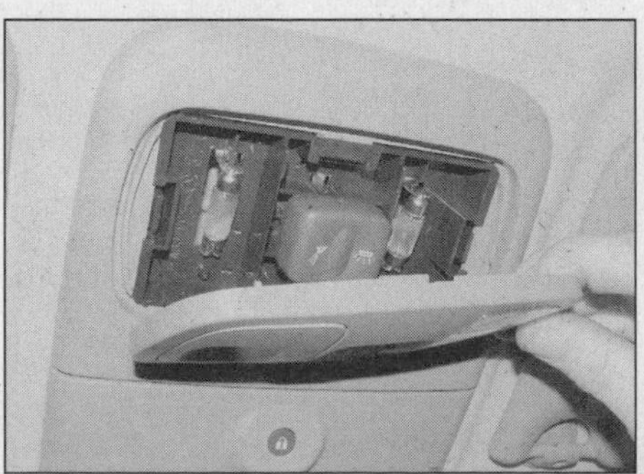
6.2 Unclip the cover to access the bulbs

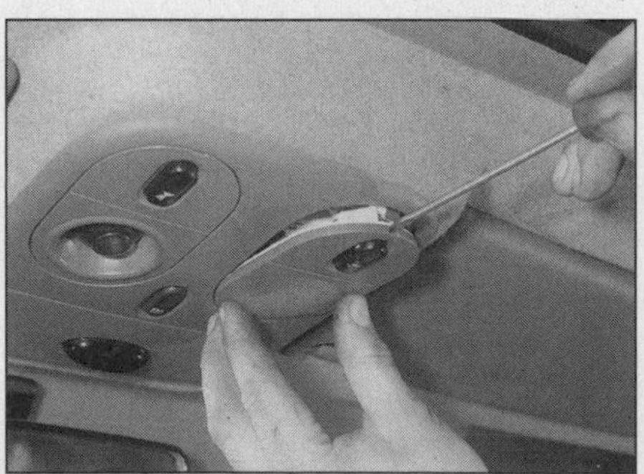
6.5 Carefully prise out the light unit from the overhead console . . .

6.6 . . . then rotate the bulbholder anti-clockwise and pull out the bulb

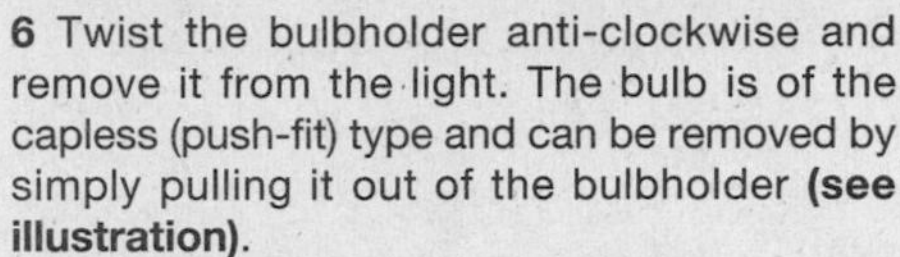

6 Twist the bulbholder anti-clockwise and remove it from the light. The bulb is of the capless (push-fit) type and can be removed by simply pulling it out of the bulbholder **(see illustration)**.

7 Refitting is the reverse of removal.

Rear courtesy light

8 Using a flat-bladed screwdriver, carefully unclip the lens then release the bulb and remove it from the light unit **(see illustration)**.

9 Refitting is the reverse of removal ensuring that the bulb is securely held by the contacts.

Luggage area light

10 Using a flat-bladed screwdriver, carefully unclip the light unit from the trim panel/body and disconnect it from the wiring connector **(see illustration)**.

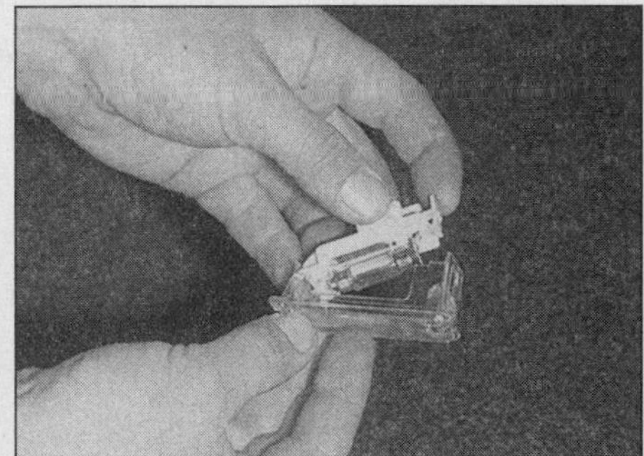

6.11 . . . then unclip the lens from the bulbholder and remove the bulb

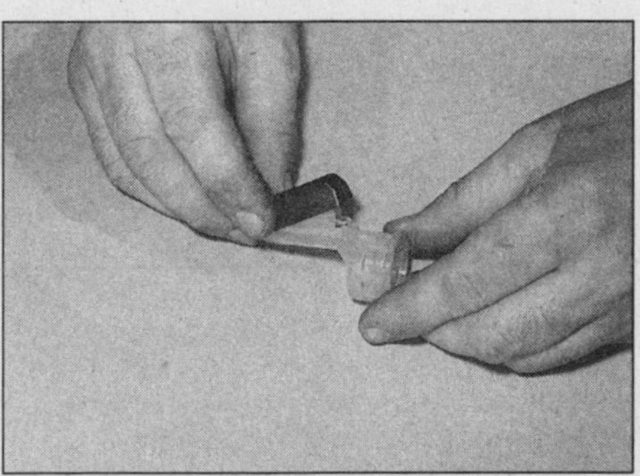

6.19a Unclip the cover from the cigarette lighter surround . . .

6.8 Remove the bulb from its contacts

11 Depress the retaining clip and release the lens from the light unit; the bulb can then be released and removed **(see illustration)**.

12 Refitting is the reverse of removal ensuring that the bulb is securely held by the contacts. **Note:** *On some models, the positive feed (red wire) before ignition for the luggage compartment light is a timer switch. Its feed disappears approximately one hour after switching off the ignition to prevent unwanted discharge from the battery. This modification is gradually being applied to all model ranges.*

Instrument/warning lights

13 The instrument panel is a complete assembly and has no bulbs that can be renewed, the instrument panel is illuminated by soldered LEDs.

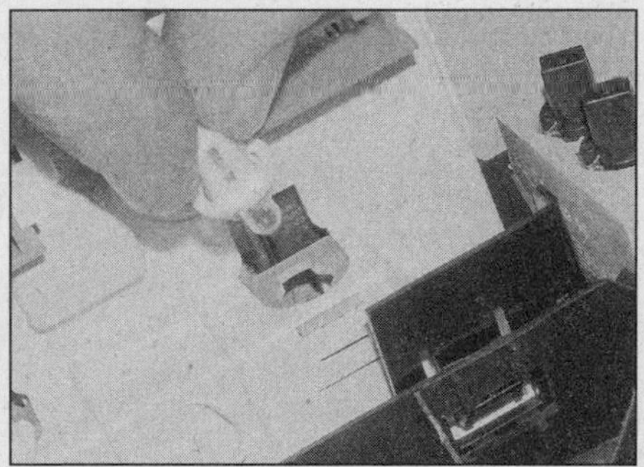

6.16 Removing the clock illumination bulb

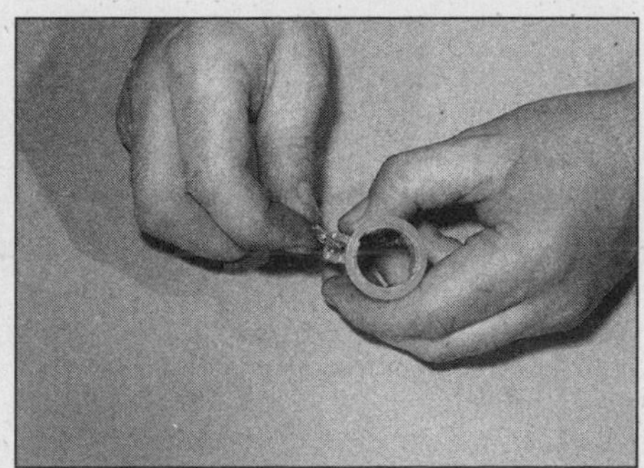

6.19b . . . and pull out the bulb

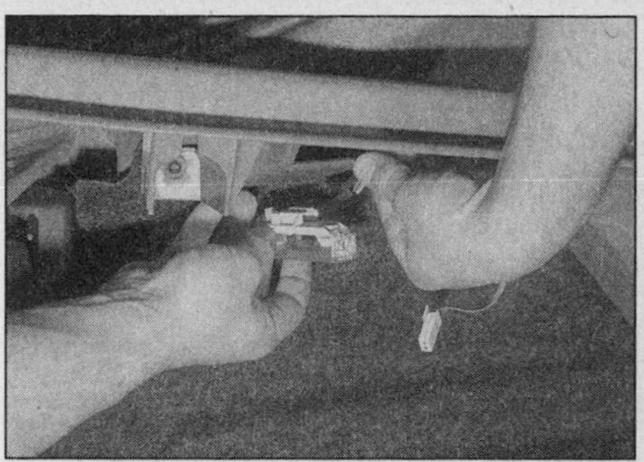

6.10 Prise out the luggage compartment light unit and disconnect its wiring connector (Hatchback) . . .

Glovebox illumination

14 Open up the glovebox and renew the bulb as described in paragraphs 10 to 12.

Multi-function display light

15 Remove the multi-function display as described in Section 11.

16 Twist the bulbholder through 90° and remove it from the display **(see illustration)**.

17 Refitting is the reverse of removal.

Cigarette lighter illumination

18 Remove the cigarette lighter as described in Section 12.

19 Unclip the cover from around the bulb. The bulb is of the capless (push-fit) type and can be removed by simply pulling it out of the bulbholder **(see illustrations)**.

20 Refitting is the reverse of removal.

Switch illumination

21 All of the switches are fitted with illuminating bulbs; some are also fitted with a bulb to show when the circuit concerned is operating. On some switches, these bulbs can be removed by simply twisting the bulbholder through 90° once access has been gained to the rear of the switch. However, on some switches, it will be found that the bulbs are an integral part of the switch assembly and cannot be obtained separately. Bulb replacement will therefore require the renewal of the complete switch assembly.

7 Exterior light units – removal and refitting

Note: *Disconnect the battery negative lead (refer to Chapter 5A) before removing any light unit, and reconnect the lead after refitting the light.*

Headlight

1 Remove the bumper as described in Chapter 11, Section 6.

2 Disconnect the wiring connectors and free the wiring harness from the light unit.

3 On models equipped with a headlight levelling system, disconnect the wiring

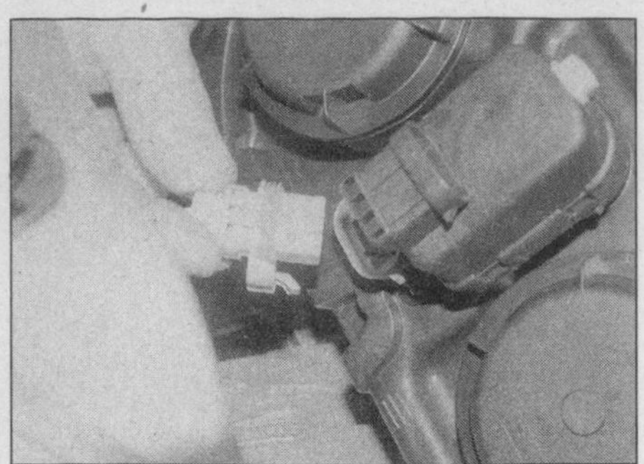

7.3 On models with a headlight levelling system disconnect the wiring connector from the motor

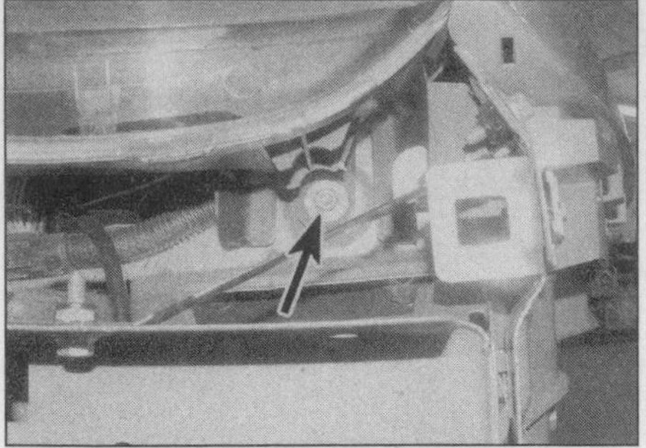

7.4a Slacken and remove the lower mounting bolts (arrowed) . . .

7.4b . . . the inner retaining mounting bolt (arrowed) . . .

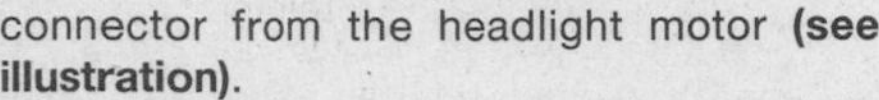

connector from the headlight motor **(see illustration)**.

4 Slacken and remove the bolt securing the headlight unit lower mounting brackets to the body then remove the two upper retaining bolts and manoeuvre the light unit forwards and away from the vehicle **(see illustrations)**.

5 On Scénic models, undo the two retaining bolts and remove the bracket below the headlamp **(see illustration)**.

6 On models equipped with a headlight levelling system, if necessary, remove the motor from the rear of the light unit by rotating it anti-clockwise and carefully unclipping its balljoint from the rear of the reflector assembly **(see illustration)**.

7 Refitting is a direct reversal of the removal procedure. On completion the headlight beam alignment should be checked using the information given in Section 8.

Front foglight

8 Slacken and remove the foglight mounting screw and withdraw the light unit from the bumper, disconnecting its wiring connectors as they become accessible **(see illustrations)**.

9 Refitting is the reverse of removal. If necessary, the foglight aim can be adjusted using the screw on the top of the light unit **(see illustration)**.

Front direction indicator

10 The direction indicator is part of the headlight unit, to remove complete assembly see headlight removal in this Section.

Front indicator side repeater

11 Carefully unclip the light unit and withdraw it from the wing. Free the bulbholder by rotating it anti-clockwise and remove the light unit from the vehicle **(see illustrations 5.19 and 5.20a)**.

12 Refitting is a reverse of the removal procedure.

Rear light cluster

13 On Hatchback and Coupé models, from inside the vehicle luggage compartment, unscrew the upper retaining nut and unclip the cover from the rear of the light cluster; on some models it will also be necessary to unhook the cover rubber retaining band.

14 On Saloon and Scénic models, from inside the luggage compartment, unclip the

7.4c . . . and the upper mounting bolt (arrowed) – Scénic

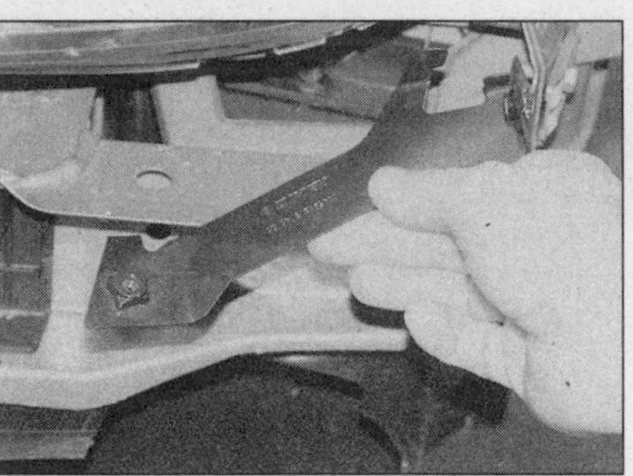

7.5 On Scénic models, remove the support bar from under the light unit

7.6 To remove the headlight levelling motor, rotate it anti-clockwise then carefully unclip its balljoint from the headlight reflector

7.8a Undo the foglight retaining screw . . .

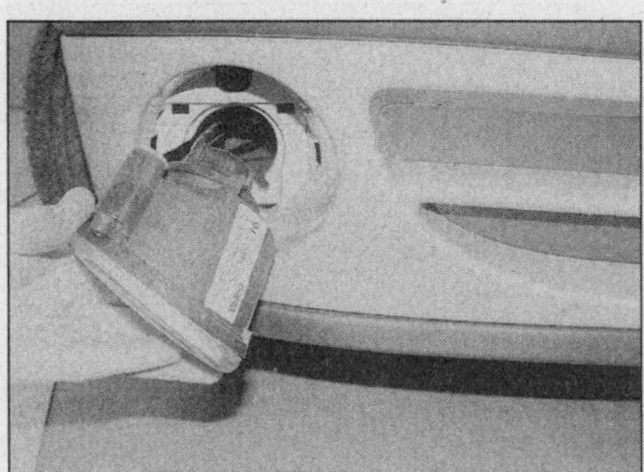

7.8b . . . then withdraw the foglight from the bumper

7.9 Adjusting the front foglight

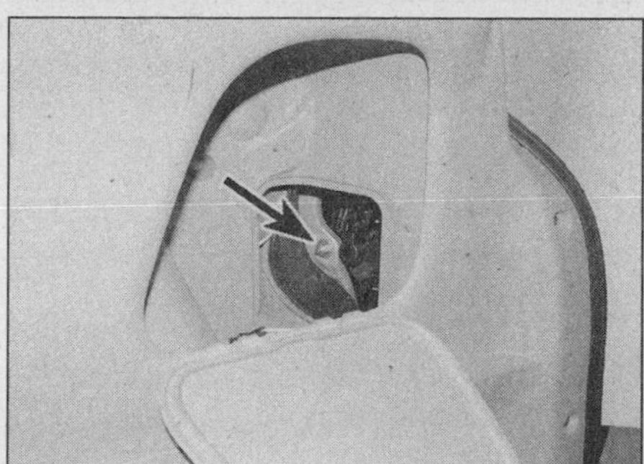

7.14a Undo the two retaining nuts (one arrowed) . . .

access cover from the light unit cover. On Scénic models, the access cover is located inside the wheelarch liner trim panel and it may be necessary to open the open the flap on the panel and reach inside **(see illustrations)**. To further improve access on Saloon models, undo the retaining screws and unclip the light unit cover.

15 Disconnect the wiring connector then undo the retaining nuts and remove the light unit from the rear of the vehicle **(see illustration)**.

16 Refitting is the reverse of removal, ensuring that the retaining nuts are securely tightened.

Boot lid-mounted rear lights

17 Open up the boot lid then unclip the cover to access to the rear of the light.

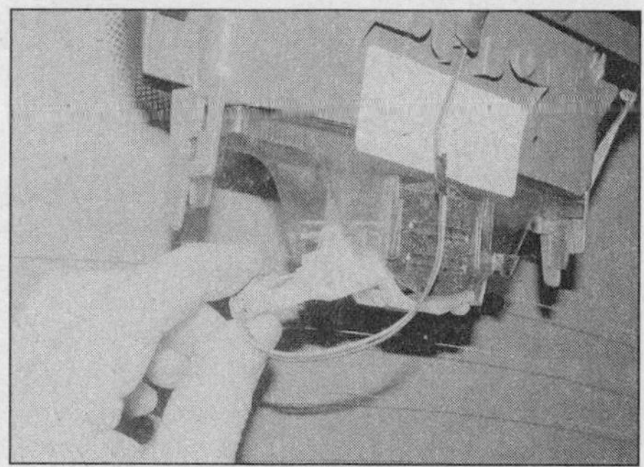

7.21a Disconnect the wiring . . .

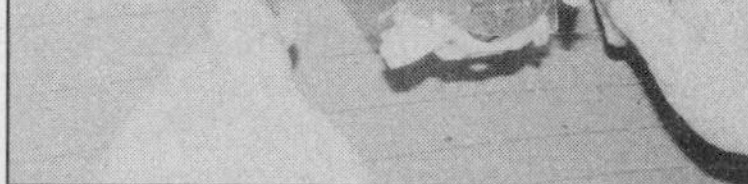

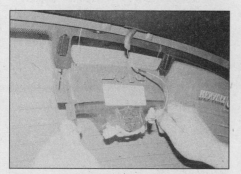

7.21c . . . and slide it of the retaining clips

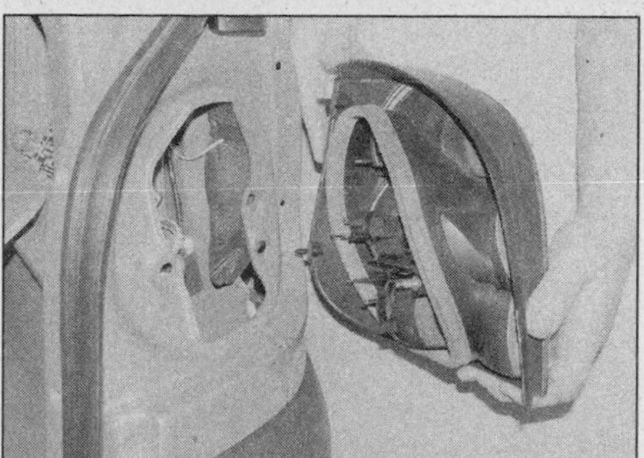

7.14b and withdraw the light unit – Scénic

18 Disconnect the wiring connector then undo the retaining nuts and remove the light unit.

19 Refitting is the reverse of removal.

High-level stop-light

Hatchback models

20 Depress the retaining clips and slide off the cover from the rear of the light unit.

21 Disconnect the wiring connector then release the retaining clip and slide the light assembly off its bracket **(see illustrations)**.

22 Refitting is the reverse of removal ensuring that both the light and cover are clipped securely in position.

Coupé models

23 Open up the boot lid and disconnect the wiring connector from the rear of the light unit.

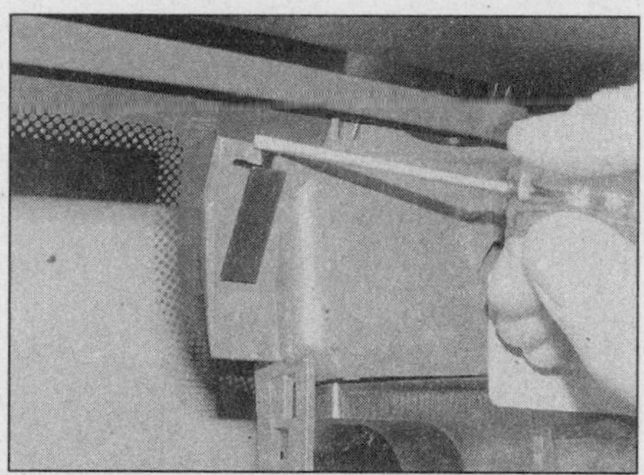

7.21b . . . unclip the light unit . . .

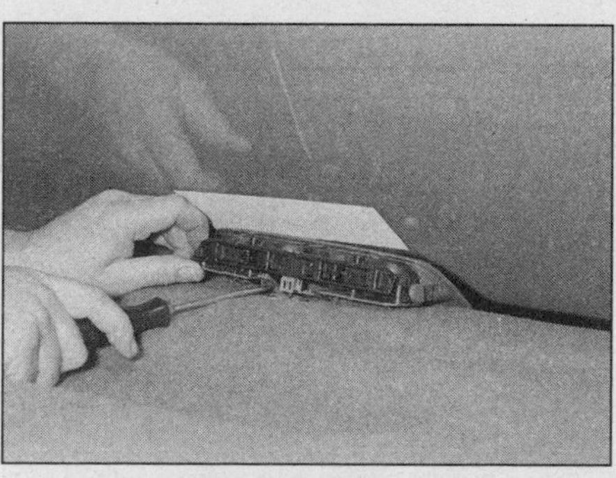

7.27a On Saloon models, release the retaining clips . . .

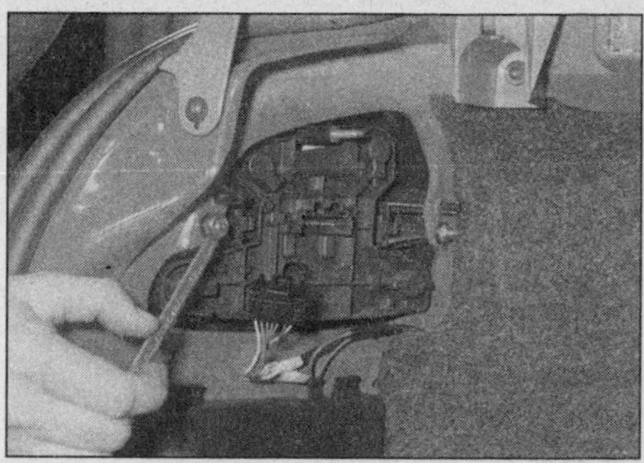

7.15 Undo the retaining nuts and remove the rear light cluster unit – Hatchback

24 Carefully release the retaining clips and push the light unit out from the boot lid.

25 Refitting is the reverse of removal.

Saloon models

26 Depress the retaining clips and slide off the cover from the rear of the light unit.

27 Using a screwdriver, carefully lift the lower retaining clips then slide the light unit forwards and out of position, disconnecting its wiring connector **(see illustrations)**.

28 Refitting is the reverse of removal ensuring that both the light and cover are clipped securely in position.

Scénic models

29 Open the tailgate and remove the two plugs from the holes behind the light unit. Insert a screwdriver into each hole in turn and release the light unit from its locating clips. Withdraw the light unit to the outside of the tailgate **(see illustrations 5.36a, 5.36b and 5.36c)**.

30 Release the retaining clips and remove the bulbholder from the rear of the light unit.

31 Refitting is the reverse of the removal sequence.

Number plate light

32 Carefully prise the light unit out from the tailgate, disconnecting its wiring connector as it becomes accessible.

33 On refitting, reconnect the wiring connector and clip the light unit securely in position.

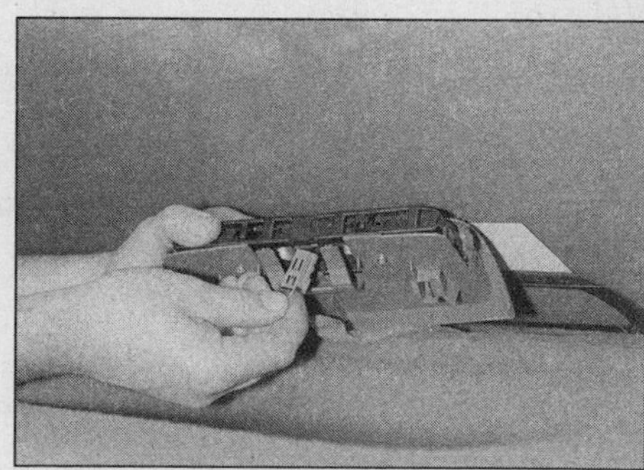

7.27b . . . then slide the high-level stop-light out of position and disconnect its wiring connector

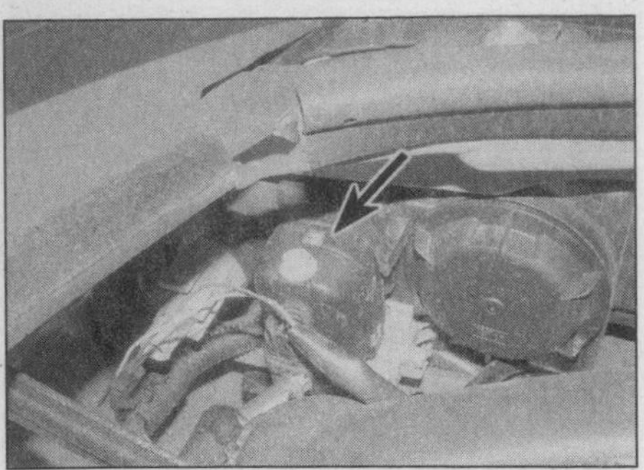

8.2 Headlight levelling motor – adjusting screw arrowed

8 Headlight beam alignment – general information

1 Accurate adjustment of the headlight beam is only possible using optical beam setting equipment and this work should therefore be carried out by a Renault dealer or suitably-equipped workshop.

2 For reference the headlights can be adjusted by rotating the adjuster screws on the rear of the headlight unit. The upper screw adjusts the headlight beam vertical aim and the lower screw the headlight beam horizontal aim; on models equipped with headlight levelling the upper screw is built into the levelling motor **(see illustration)**.

3 On models equipped with a headlight levelling system, ensure that the headlight beam adjuster switch is set to position 0 before the headlights are adjusted. On models not equipped with a headlight levelling system, ensure that the manual adjuster on the rear of each light unit is set to position A before adjustment.

9 Instrument panel – removal and refitting

Removal

1 Disconnect the battery negative lead (refer to Chapter 5A).

2 Carefully prise the left- and right-hand front speaker grilles out from the top of the facia panel to gain access to the facia top panel retaining screws.

3 Slacken and remove the retaining screws from the left- and right-hand end then unclip the top panel from the main facia and remove it from the vehicle **(see illustrations)**.

4 Slacken and remove the retaining screws, then withdraw the instrument panel. Disconnect the wiring connectors as they become accessible **(see illustrations)**.

Refitting

5 Securely reconnect the wiring connectors then clip the instrument panel back into position in the facia. Refit the panel retaining screws and tighten securely.

6 Manoeuvre the facia top panel into position and clip it firmly onto the main facia assembly.

7 Refit the top panel retaining screws, tightening them securely, and refit the loudspeaker grilles.

8 Reconnect the battery and check the operation of the panel warning lights to ensure that they are functioning correctly.

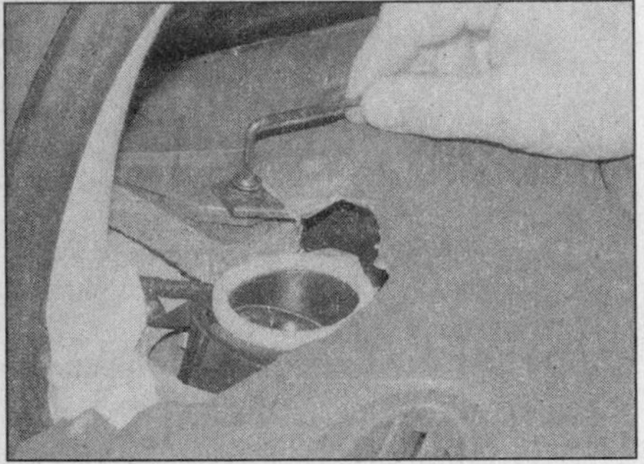

9.3a Slacken and remove the left- and right-hand retaining screws . . .

9.3b . . . then unclip the top panel and remove it from the facia

9.4a Undo the retaining screws (arrowed) . . .

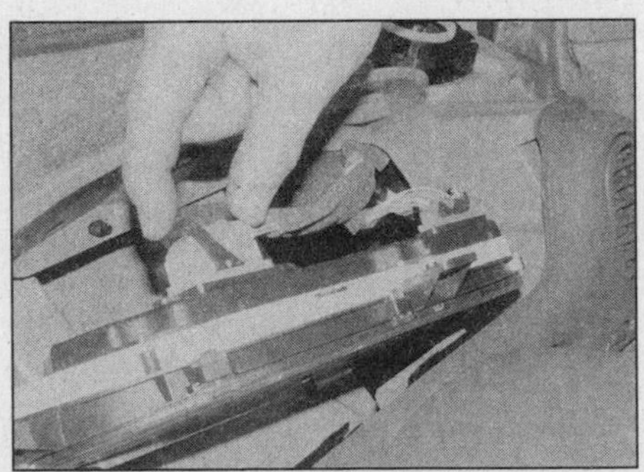

9.4b . . . and remove the instrument panel, disconnecting the wiring connectors as they become accessible

10 Instrument panel components – general information

1 Depending on model specification, the instrument panel has the following functions:

a) Electronic speedometer.
b) Rev counter.
c) Fuel gauge.
d) Engine coolant temperature gauge.
e) Various warning light illuminations.
f) Automatic transmission display.
g) Display for total mileage, trip mileage, oil level and on-board computer (ADAC). Depending on version.
h) Time clock.
i) Trip reset button.

2 The instrument panel is a sealed unit and the only part that can be renewed separately is the instrument glass. If any other components are faulty, the entire instrument panel has to be renewed.

3 The illumination bulbs cannot be replaced on these instrument panels, as they are soldered LEDs.

Self-test

Vehicles without trip computer (ADAC)

4 Press and hold down the trip reset button on the instrument panel and switch the ignition on without starting the engine, release the trip reset button after approx 5 seconds.

The system then checks the following functions simultaneously:

a) The speedometer, by the needle moving at increments of 40 km/h.
b) The rev counter, by the needle moving at increments of 1000 rpm.
c) The fuel gauge, by the needle moving at increments of 1/4 of the scale.
d) The coolant temperature gauge, by the needle moving at increments of 1/4 of the scale.

5 This will carry on checking the instruments until the ignition is switched off.

Vehicles with trip computer (ADAC)

6 Press and hold down the trip computer button on the end of the wiper stalk and switch the ignition on without starting the engine, release the trip computer button after approx 5 seconds.

The system then checks the following functions simultaneously:

a) The speedometer, by the needle moving at increments of 40 km/h.

11.2 Undo the three multi-function display retaining screws

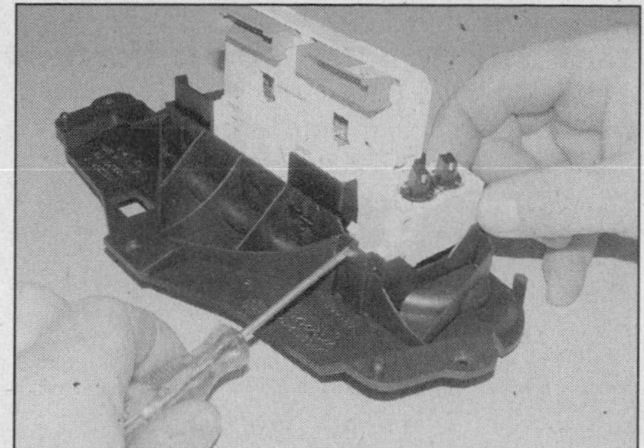
11.3 Unclipping the warning light unit from the display

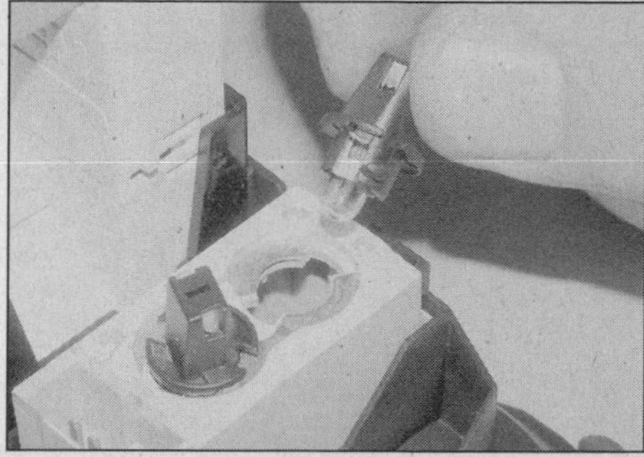
11.4 The bulbs can be removed from the display

b) *The rev counter, by the needle moving at increments of 1000 rpm.*
c) *The fuel gauge, by the needle moving at increments of 1/4 of the scale.*
d) *The coolant temperature gauge, by the needle moving at increments of 1/4 of the scale.*
e) *The trip computer digital display, by making all the segments illuminate at once.*

7 To move to the following tests on the trip computer:

a) *Press the switch on the end of the windscreen wiper stalk; the value displayed should be the amount of fuel remaining in the tank.*
b) *Press the switch on the end of the windscreen wiper stalk again; the value displayed should be the fuel flow in litres/hour (this will only be displayed if the engine is running).*
c) *Press the switch on the end of the windscreen wiper stalk once again; the display should be showing any stored failures, with the letters d, h, J or t.*
- *If d is displayed, there is a failure on the flowmeter information circuit for more than 16 kilometres (10 miles).*
- *If h is displayed, there is a failure on the oil level gauge circuit (disconnected or short circuit).*
- *If J is displayed, there is a failure on the fuel gauge circuit (disconnected for more than 100 seconds).*
- *If t is displayed, there is a failure on the coolant temperature circuit (disconnected).*
- *If there are no letters displayed (only dashes), then this indicates that no failures have been detected.*

8 To exit the self test procedure, press the reset button on the instrument panel. This will erase all the stored failures and reset the trip computer display back to zero. **Note:** *If you wish to keep the stored failure readings, then simply switch the ignition off.*

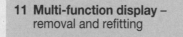

11 Multi-function display – removal and refitting

Note: *On some models, there is a multi-function display panel fitted in the top of the facia panel at the centre. This display is for the radio, temperature and time clock.*

Removal

1 Remove the facia top panel as described in paragraphs 1 to 3 of Section 9.

2 Slacken and remove the retaining screws and remove the multi-function display from the facia, disconnecting its wiring connectors as they become accessible **(see illustration)**.

3 The components from the multi-function display panel can be unclipped from the surround trim panel **(see illustration)** as required.

4 To renew a bulb, twist the appropriate bulbholder anti-clockwise, and withdraw it from the panel **(see illustration)**. The bulb can then be pulled out of the bulbholder.

Refitting

5 Refitting is the reverse of removal.

12 Cigarette lighter – removal and refitting

Removal

1 Disconnect the battery negative lead (refer to Chapter 5A).

2 Remove the ashtray insert then slacken and remove the ashtray mounting bracket retaining screws **(see illustrations)**.

3 Remove the ashtray mounting bracket from

12.2a Remove the ashtray insert . . .

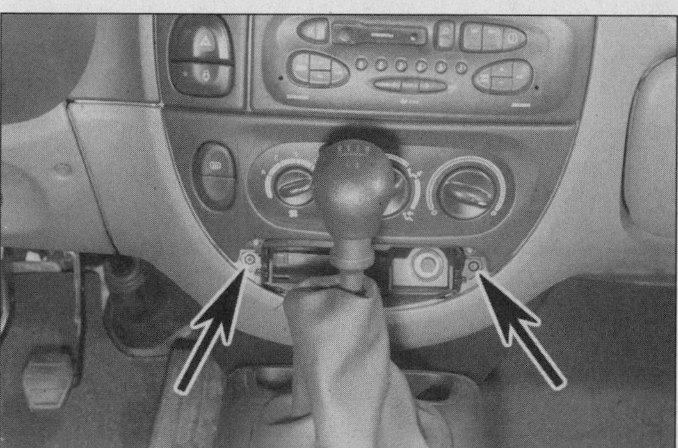
12.2b . . . then slacken and remove the ashtray retaining screws (arrowed)

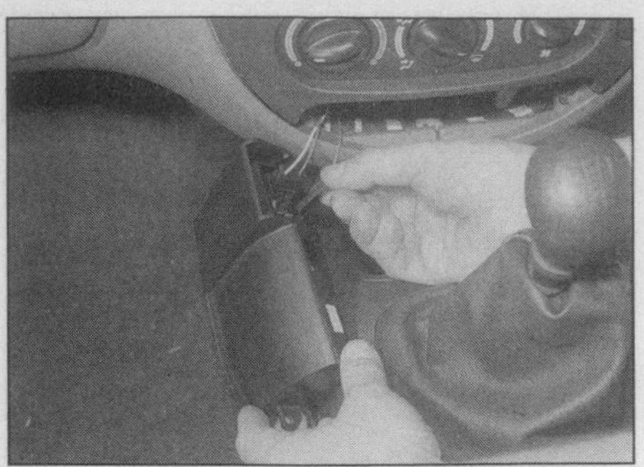

12.3 Withdraw the ashtray from the facia and disconnect its wiring connectors

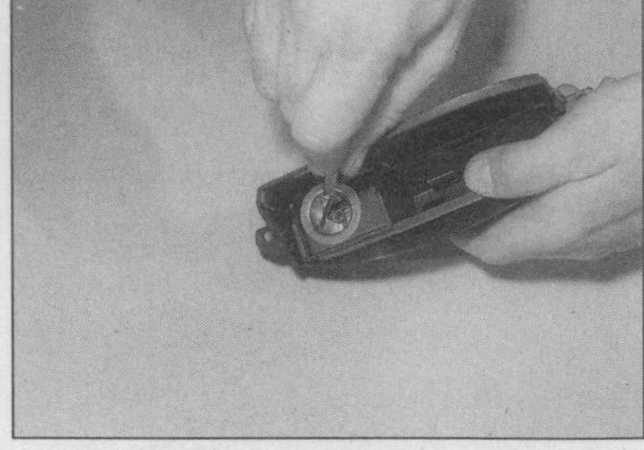

12.4a Release the retaining clips . . .

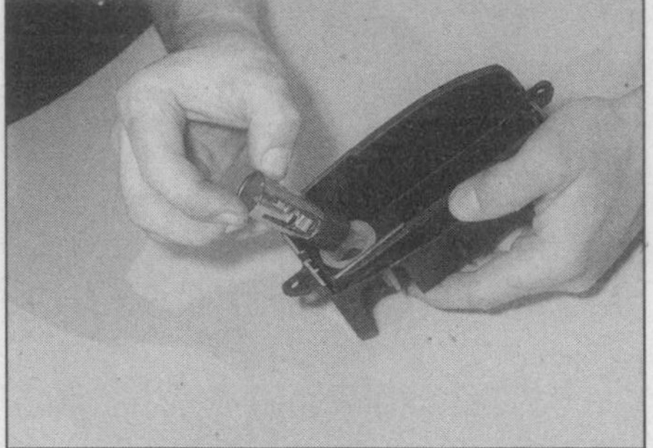

12.4b . . . then slide out the metal insert . . .

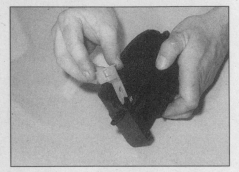

12.4c . . . and remove the plastic surround

the facia and disconnect its wiring connectors **(see illustration)**.

4 Release the retaining clips and slide out the cigarette lighter insert then push the plastic surround out of position **(see illustrations)**.

Refitting

5 Refitting is a reversal of the removal procedure, ensuring that all the wiring connectors are securely reconnected.

13 Clock – removal and refitting

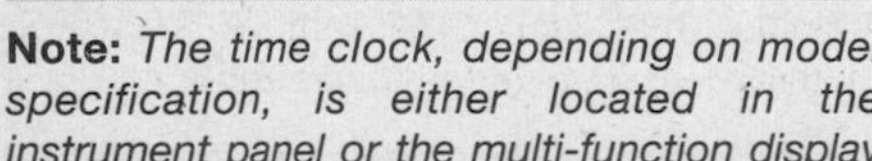

Note: *The time clock, depending on model specification, is either located in the instrument panel or the multi-function display panel. Both are sealed units and if faulty must be renewed as a complete unit.*

Removal

1 If the clock is located in the multi-function display, refer to Section 11.

2 If the clock is located in the instrument panel, refer to Section 9 and 10.

Refitting

3 Refitting is the reverse of removal.

14 Horn(s) – removal and refitting

Removal

Note: *On some models, there may be a second horn fitted on the opposite side.*

1 The horn is located behind the front bumper, on the left-hand side.

2 To gain access to the assembly, firmly apply the handbrake then jack up the front of the vehicle and support it on axle stands (refer to *Jacking and vehicle support*). Where necessary, undo the retaining screws and free the wheelarch liner/cover from the underside of the bumper and wheelarch (as applicable).

3 Disconnect the wiring connector(s) then slacken and remove the mounting bolt(s) and remove the horn(s) from the vehicle.

Refitting

4 Refitting is the reverse of removal.

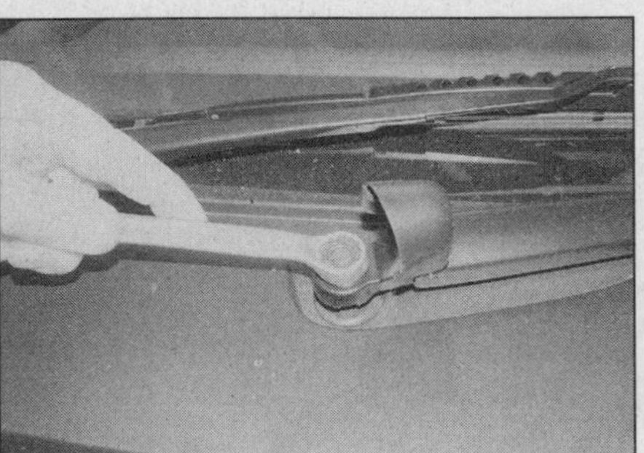

15.2 Lift up the cover then slacken and remove the wiper arm retaining nut

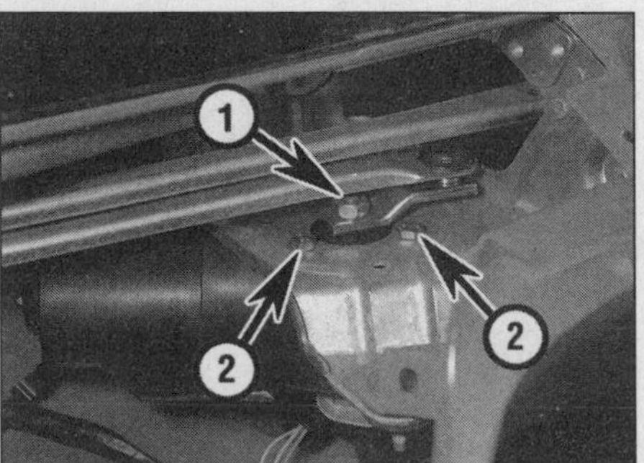

16.4 Remove the spindle nut (1) then unscrew the mounting bolts (2) – one hidden – and remove the wiper motor

15 Wiper arm – removal and refitting

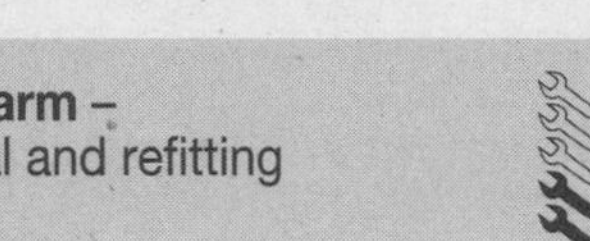

Note: *The wiper arms are a very tight fit on the spindles and it is likely that a puller will be needed to remove them safely, without damage.*

Removal

1 Operate the wiper motor then switch it off so that the wiper arm returns to the at rest position.

2 Lift the wiper arm retaining nut cover then slacken and remove the nut **(see illustration)**.

3 Lift the blade off the glass and pull the wiper arm off the motor and carefully lever the arm off the spindle using a large, flat-bladed screwdriver. If the arm is very tight, free it from the spindle using a suitable puller.

Refitting

4 Ensure that the wiper and spindle are clean and dry then refit the arm. Ensure that the arm is correctly positioned then securely tighten the retaining nut and refit the spindle nut cover.

16 Windscreen wiper motor and linkage – removal and refitting

Wiper motor removal

1 Disconnect the battery lead (refer to Chapter 5A).

All models except Scénic

2 If the battery is located in the rear corner of the scuttle panel, remove the battery as described in Chapter 5A.

3 Working through the aperture, disconnect the wiring connector from the wiper motor.

4 Mark the relative positions of the motor shaft and crank then unscrew the retaining nut and washer and free the wiper linkage from the motor spindle. Unscrew the motor retaining bolts and manoeuvre the motor out of position and remove it from the vehicle **(see illustration)**.

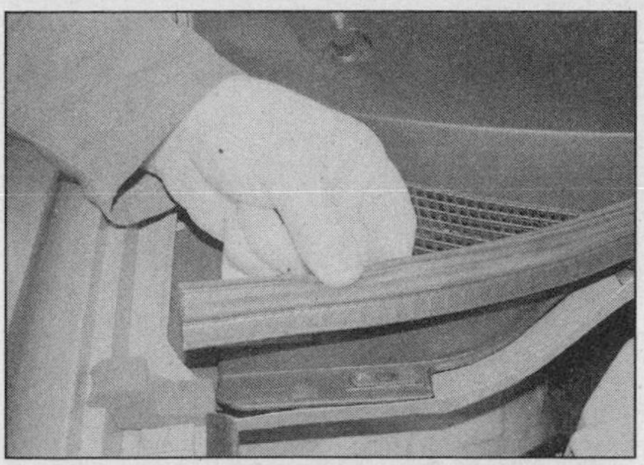
16.5 Peel off the seal from the bulkhead . . .

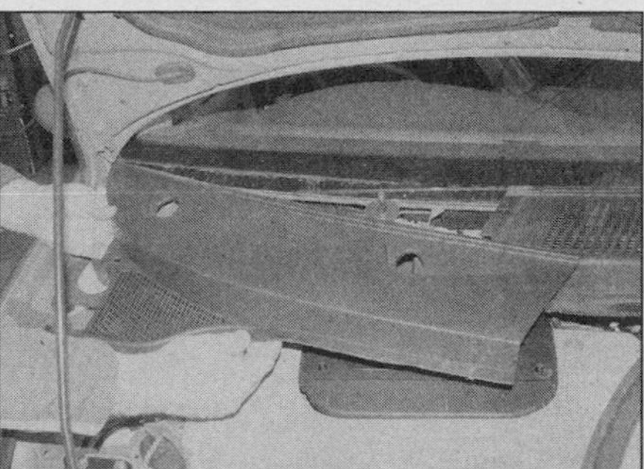
16.6 . . . and remove the air vent panels

16.7 The bulkhead section can be unbolted and removed

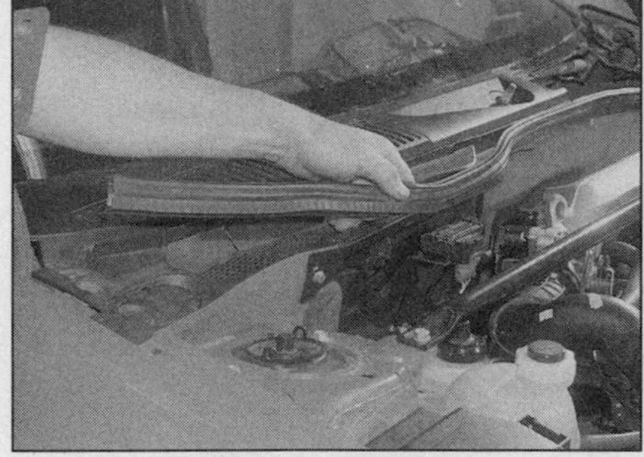
16.15 Peel off the rubber seal from the engine compartment bulkhead

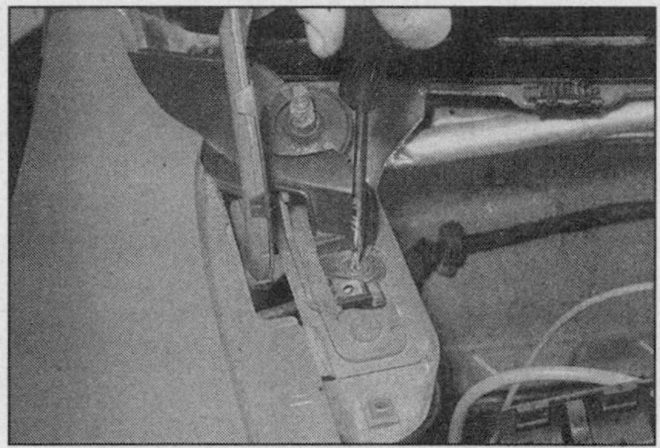
16.16a Undo the retaining screws and small inlet vent panel section from the right-hand side . . .

16.16b . . . and the large vent panel from the left-hand side – Mégane

Scénic models

5 Remove the sealing strip from the top of the engine compartment bulkhead **(see illustration)**.

6 Remove the wiper arms as described in Section 15, then undo the retaining screws and remove both inlet vent panels from beneath the windscreen **(see illustration)**.

7 Undo the retaining bolts and lift out the removable section of the bulkhead scuttle panel in front of the wiper mechanism **(see illustration)**.

8 Disconnect the wiring connector from the wiper motor.

9 Mark the relative positions of the motor shaft and crank then unscrew the retaining nut and washer and free the wiper linkage from the motor spindle. Unscrew the motor retaining bolts and manoeuvre the motor out of position and remove it from the vehicle.

Wiper motor refitting

10 Manoeuvre the motor into position and refit its mounting bolts, tightening them securely.

11 Engage the crank with the motor spindle, aligning the marks made prior to removal, and securely tighten the spindle nut.

12 Reconnect the motor wiring connector then refit/reconnect the battery. On Scénic models, refit the scuttle panel and vent panel components.

Wiper motor and linkage

Right-hand drive models

13 If the battery is located in the rear corner of the scuttle panel, remove the battery as described in Chapter 5A.

14 Remove the wiper arms as described in the previous Section.

15 Open up the bonnet and remove the rubber seal from the top of the engine compartment bulkhead **(see illustration)**.

16 Undo the retaining screws then unclip and remove the remaining inlet vent panel sections from beneath the windscreen **(see illustrations)**. On Scénic models, undo the retaining bolts and lift out the removable section of the bulkhead scuttle panel in front of the wiper mechanism **(see illustration 16.7)**.

17 Remove the covers from the wiper arm spindles then slacken and remove the spindle nuts and washers **(see illustrations)**.

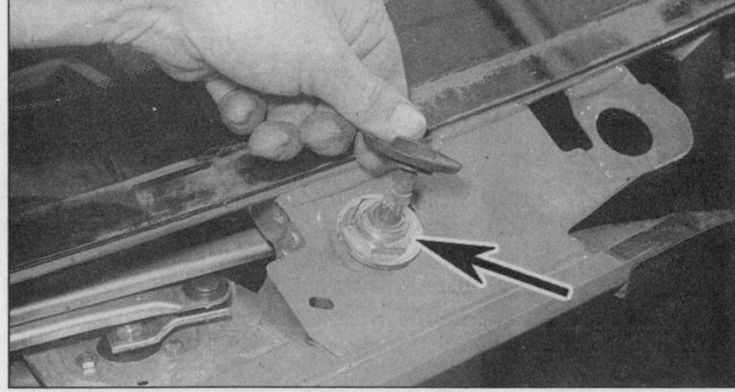
16.17a Remove the rubber covers then slacken and remove the spindle nuts (arrowed) and washers – Mégane

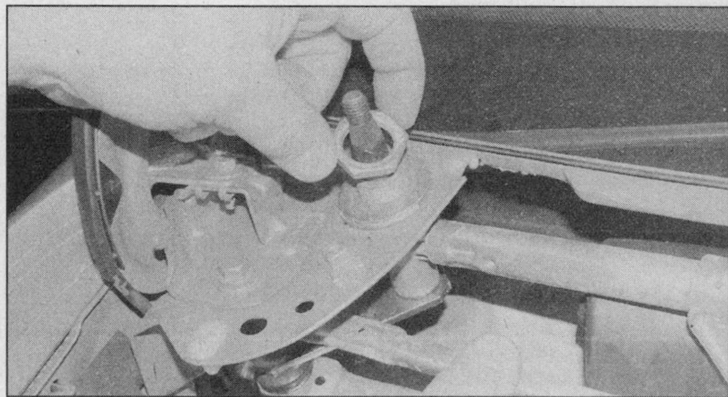
16.17b Remove the rubber covers then slacken and remove the spindle nuts and washers – Scénic

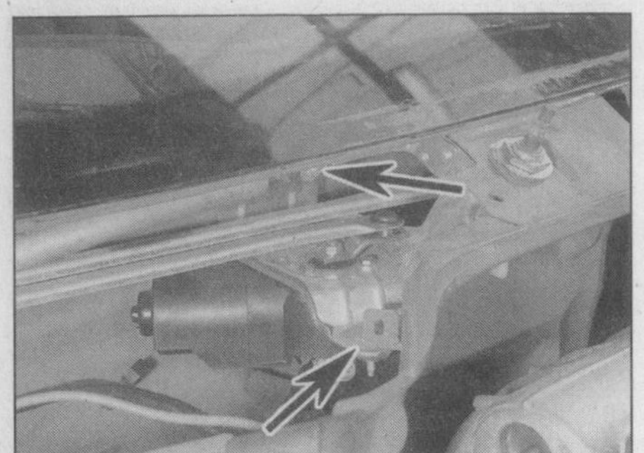
16.18a Undo the mounting bolts (arrowed) . . .

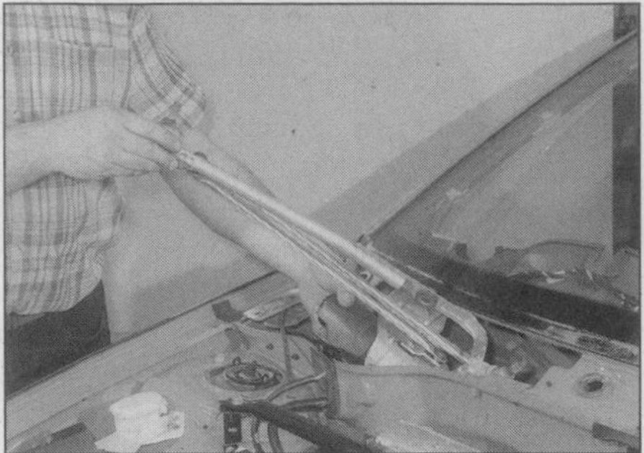
16.18b . . . and manoeuvre the wiper motor and linkage out of position – Mégane

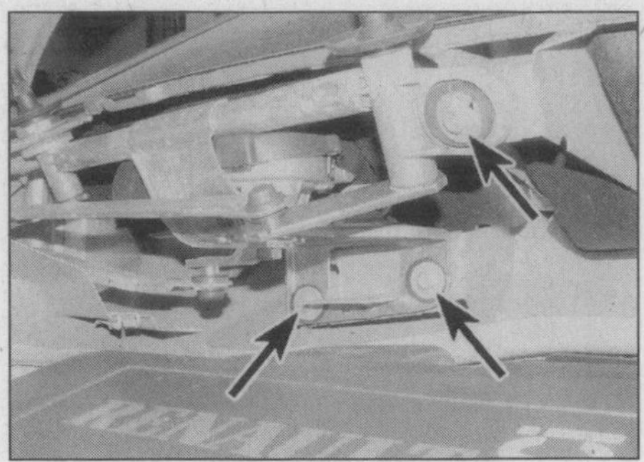
16.18c Undo the mounting bolts (arrowed) . . .

18 Disconnect the wiring connector from the wiper motor then unscrew the mounting bolts and manoeuvre the assembly out of position and away from the car **(see illustrations)**. If necessary the motor and linkage can then be separated as described in paragraph 4.

19 Refitting is a reverse of removal. Prior to refitting ensure that the rubber mounting grommets fitted to the spindle holes are in good condition. Ensure that all fasteners are secure and make sure that the inlet vent panels are correctly clipped in position prior to refitting the wiper arms.

Left-hand drive models without air conditioning

20 Removal and refitting is as described in paragraphs 13 to 19 noting that on all models except Scénic, it will also be necessary to remove the heater blower motor assembly to gain the necessary clearance required to manoeuvre the wiper motor out of position (see Chapter 3).

Left-hand drive models with air conditioning

21 On left-hand drive models with air conditioning, removal of the wiper motor and linkage assembly requires the air conditioning system evaporator to be removed. This means that the refrigerant circuit will have to be discharged/recharged and therefore this task will have to be entrusted to a Renault dealer or other suitably-equipped workshop (see Chapter 3).

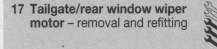

17 Tailgate/rear window wiper motor – removal and refitting

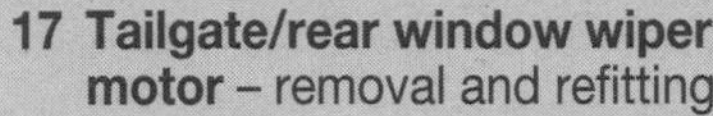

Note: *Where applicable, it may be necessary to remove the rear spoiler to gain access to the rear wiper arm* ***(see illustration)****.*

Removal

1 Disconnect the battery negative lead (refer to Chapter 5A), then remove the wiper arm as described in Section 15.

2 Prise off the spindle cover then unscrew the nut and lift off the spacer from the tailgate wiper motor spindle **(see illustrations)**.

3 On Hatchback models, open up the

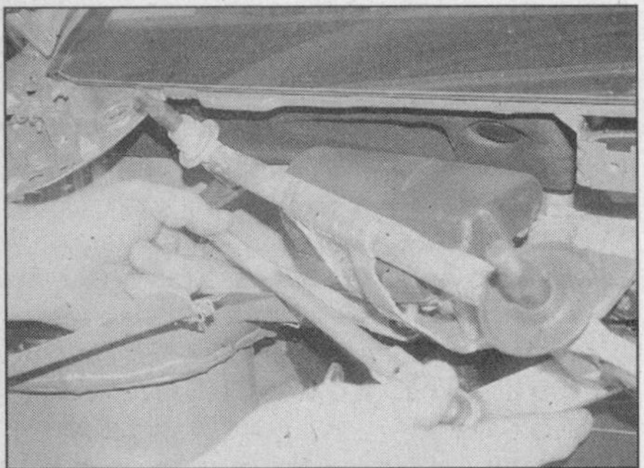
16.18d . . . and manoeuvre the wiper motor and linkage out of position – Scénic

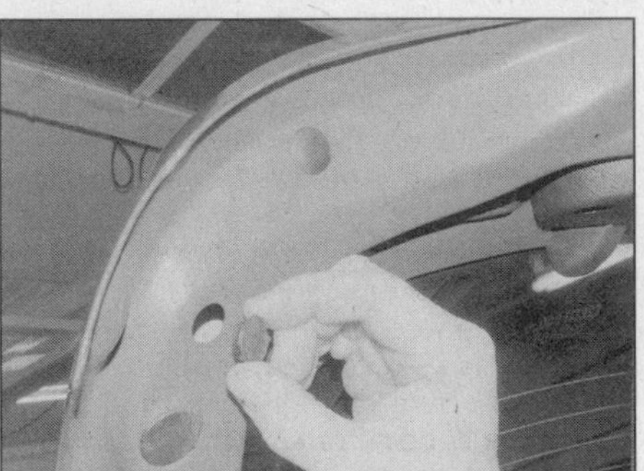
17.0a Remove the rubber grommets from the tailgate . . .

17.0b . . . and undo the retaining bolts to remove the rear spoiler

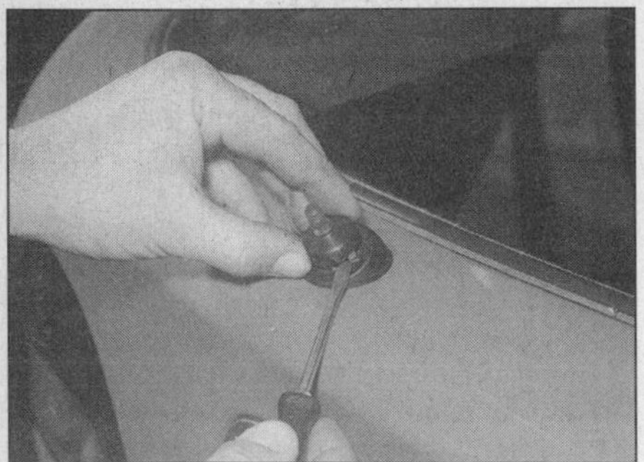
17.2a Prise off the spindle cover . . .

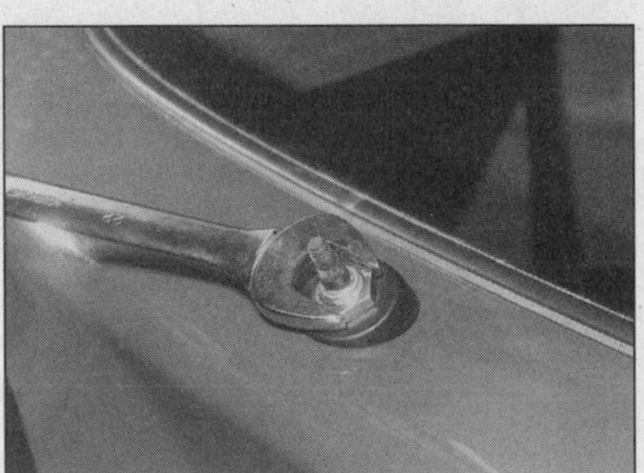
17.2b . . . then unscrew the nut . . .

17.2c . . . and lift off the spacer – Hatchback

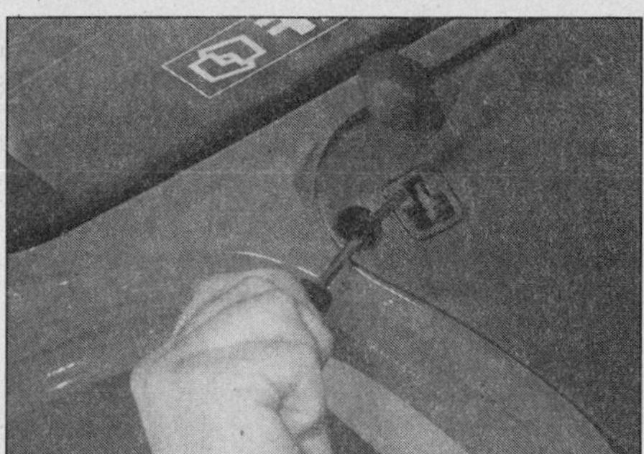

17.3a On Hatchback models, undo the retaining screws and unclip the inner trim panel from the tailgate . . .

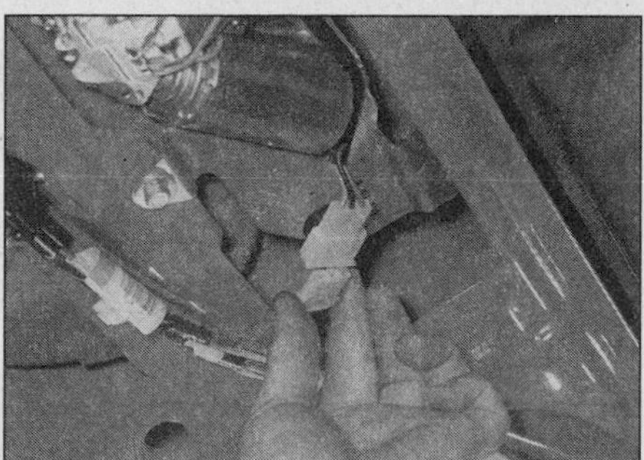

17.3b . . . disconnect the wiring connector . . .

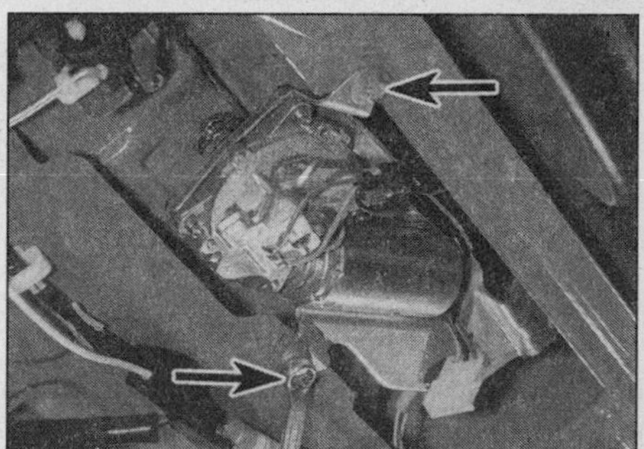

17.3c . . . then undo the retaining bolts (arrowed) and remove the wiper motor from the tailgate

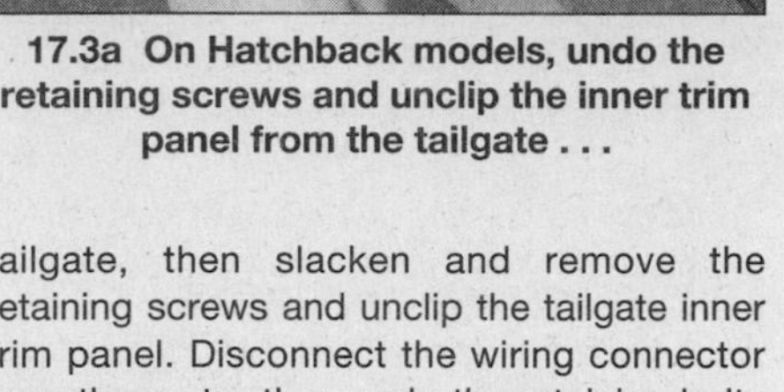

tailgate, then slacken and remove the retaining screws and unclip the tailgate inner trim panel. Disconnect the wiring connector from the motor then undo the retaining bolts and remove the motor from the tailgate. Remove the rubber sealing grommet from the tailgate **(see illustrations)**.

4 On Coupé models, open up the boot lid and disconnect the wiring connector from the motor. Slacken and remove the mounting bolts and remove the wiper motor from the vehicle, taking care not to lose the motor mounting rubbers **(see illustration)**. Remove the rubber sealing grommet from the tailgate.

5 On Scénic models, open up the tailgate and undo the four tailgate trim panel retaining bolts. Release the retaining clips by carefully pulling on the tailgate closing handles in the trim panel, then withdraw the panel from the tailgate. Disconnect the wiring connector from the motor then undo the retaining bolts and remove the motor from the tailgate **(see illustration)**. Remove the rubber sealing grommet from the tailgate.

Refitting

6 Refitting is the reverse of removal. Prior to refitting, inspect the sealing grommet for signs of damage or deterioration and renew if necessary **(see illustration)**.

18 Windscreen/tailgate washer system components – removal and refitting

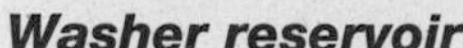

Washer reservoir

1 Working in the engine compartment, undo the retaining nut/screw (as applicable) and remove the washer reservoir filler neck. On Scénic models, remove the wiper arms and air vent panels as described in Section 16.

2 Firmly apply the handbrake then jack up the front of the vehicle and support it on axle stands (see *Jacking and vehicle support*). Remove the right-hand front roadwheel then remove the retaining screws and fasteners and remove the wheelarch liner sections to reveal the reservoir.

3 Release the retaining clip(s) and disconnect the hose(s) from the washer pump union(s) (as applicable). Where there is more than one hose connection, make alignment marks to ensure the hoses are correctly reconnected on refitting.

4 Trace the wiring back from the washer pump to the connector and disconnect it from the main harness; on some models it will also be necessary to release the side repeater bulbholder from the light unit to allow the bulbholder to be removed with the reservoir.

5 Slacken and remove the retaining nut from the front of the reservoir then manoeuvre the reservoir out from underneath the wing.

6 Refitting is the reverse of removal ensuring that the hose(s) are securely reconnected. Refill the reservoir and check for leakage.

Washer pump

7 Remove the reservoir as described earlier in this Section.

8 Carefully ease the pump out from the reservoir and recover its sealing grommet. Wash off any spilt fluid with cold water.

9 Refitting is the reverse of removal, using a new sealing grommet if necessary. Refill the reservoir and check the pump grommet for leaks.

Washer reservoir level switch

10 To gain access to the level switch (where fitted), firmly apply the handbrake then jack up the front of the vehicle and support it on axle stands (see *Jacking and vehicle support*). Remove the front roadwheel then remove the retaining screws and fasteners and remove the rear section of the wheelarch liner.

11 Disconnect the wiring connector from the level switch and carefully ease the switch out from the reservoir and catch the reservoir contents in a suitable container. Recover the sealing grommet and wash off any spilt fluid with cold water.

12 Refitting is the reverse of removal, using a

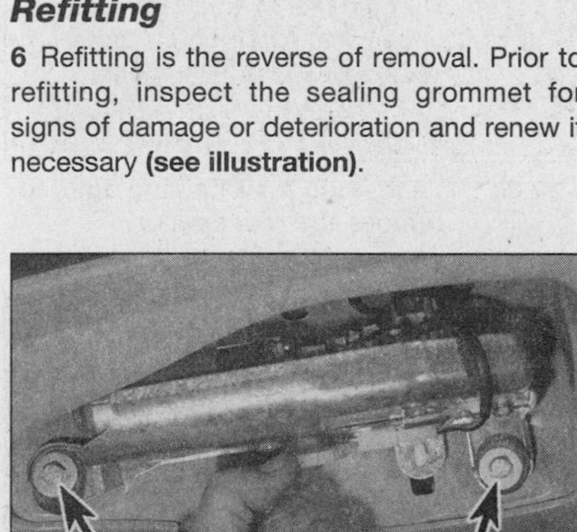

17.4 On Coupé models, disconnect the wiring then undo the mounting bolts (arrowed) and remove the wiper motor

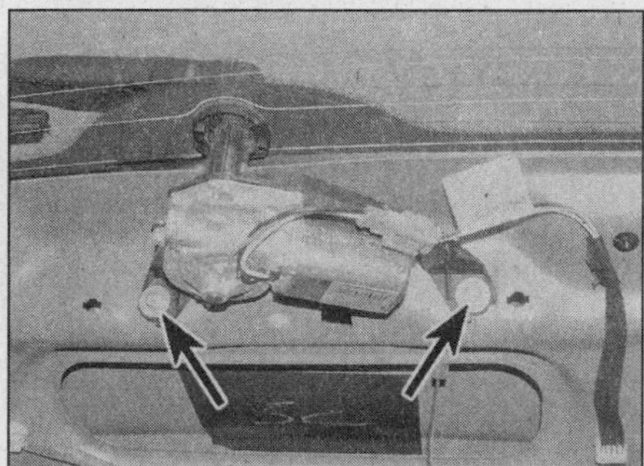

17.5 Undo the two retaining bolts (arrowed) – Scénic

17.6 Prior to refitting ensure that the wiper motor spindle sealing grommet is in good condition

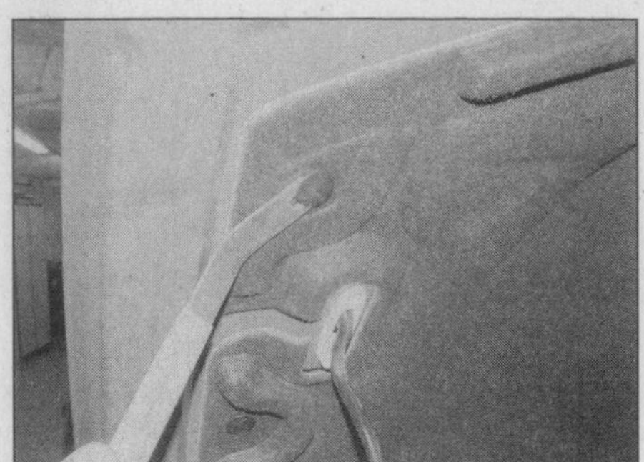

18.13a Unclip the bonnet lining . . .

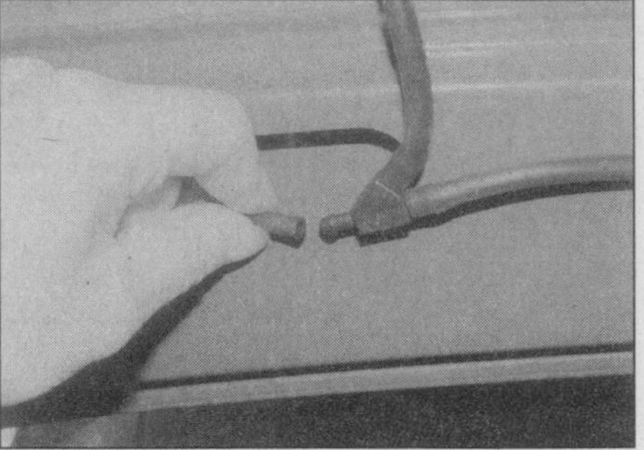

18.13b . . . and disconnect the windscreen washer hose

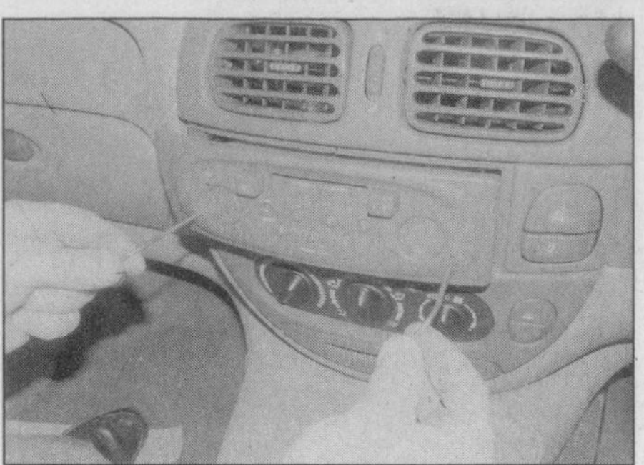

19.3 Release the retaining clips by inserting welding rods into the holes provided

new sealing grommet if the original one shows signs of damage or deterioration.

Windscreen washer jets

13 Open up the bonnet then carefully prise out the retaining clips and peel back the bonnet insulation panel to gain access to the washer jets. Disconnect the washer hoses from the relevant jet then depress the retaining clips and carefully ease the jet away from the bonnet **(see illustrations)**.

14 On refitting, securely connect the jet to the hose and clip it into position in the bonnet. Check the operation of the jet. If necessary adjust the nozzles using a pin, aiming one nozzle to a point slightly above the centre of the swept area and the other to slightly below the centre point to ensure complete coverage.

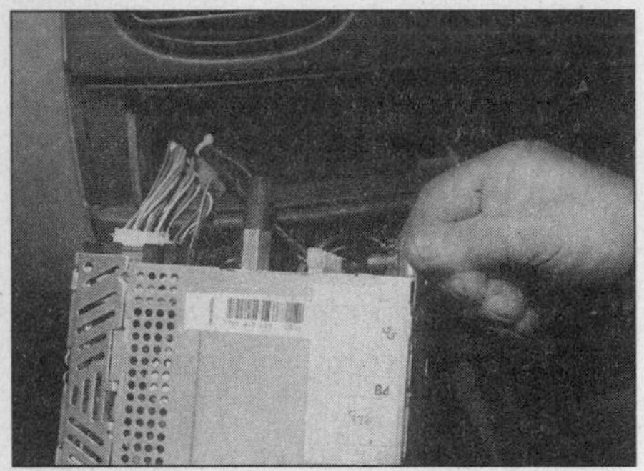

19.4 Slide out the radio/cassette player and disconnect the wiring connectors and aerial lead

Tailgate washer jet

15 Open up the tailgate and peel the sealing strip away from the top of the tailgate aperture so that it is clear of the headlining.

16 Depress the retaining tangs and slide out the retaining clips from the rear of the headlining.

17 Prise out the tailgate hinge access covers from the headlining then carefully peel back the headlining until access can be gained to the washer jet.

18 Unscrew the retaining nut then lift the washer jet and seal away from the roof, disconnecting it from the hose.

19 Refitting is the reverse of removal. If necessary adjust the nozzle using a pin.

19 Radio/cassette player – removal and refitting

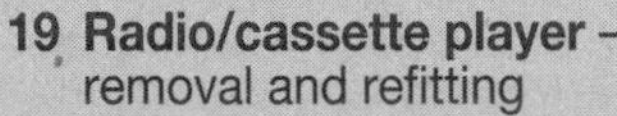

Note: *All the radio/cassette players fitted to the Renault range have DIN standard fixings. A pair of removal clips, obtainable from in-car entertainment specialists, will be required for removal.*

Removal

1 Disconnect the battery negative lead (refer to Chapter 5A)

2 Where applicable, prise the plastic covers from the sides of the radio/cassette player.

3 Insert the removal clips into the holes at the sides of the unit until they snap into place. Pull the clips rearwards (away from the facia) to release the unit. If the removal clips are not available, two lengths of bent welding rod will be required. Insert the rods into the holes in each side of the unit until the retaining clips are felt to release **(see illustration)**.

4 Carefully slide the audio unit out of position whilst ensuring that the wiring does not become trapped or caught. Disconnect the wiring connectors and the aerial lead and remove the unit from the vehicle **(see illustration)**.

Refitting

5 Reconnect the wiring plugs and the aerial cable to the rear of the unit.

6 Push the unit into its housing in the facia until the retaining lugs snap into place.

7 Where applicable, refit the covers to the sides of the unit, then reconnect the battery negative lead.

20 Loudspeakers – removal and refitting

Facia loudspeaker

1 Carefully prise the speaker grille out of position, taking great care not to damage the facia panel or speaker **(see illustration)**.

2 Slacken and remove the retaining screws then manoeuvre the speaker out of position, disconnecting the wiring connector as it becomes accessible **(see illustrations)**.

3 Refitting is the reverse of removal.

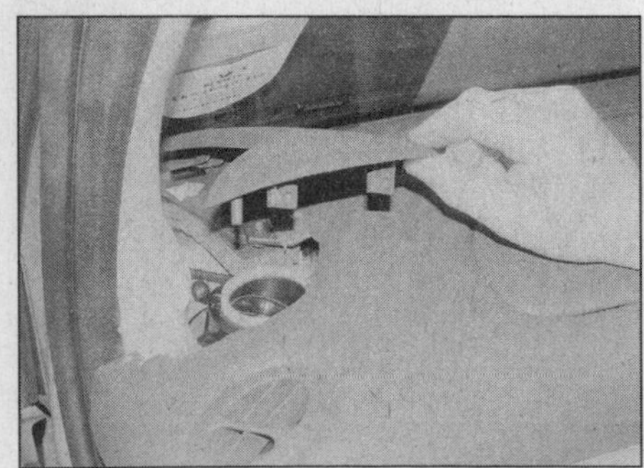

20.1 Carefully prise the speaker grille out from the top of the facia . . .

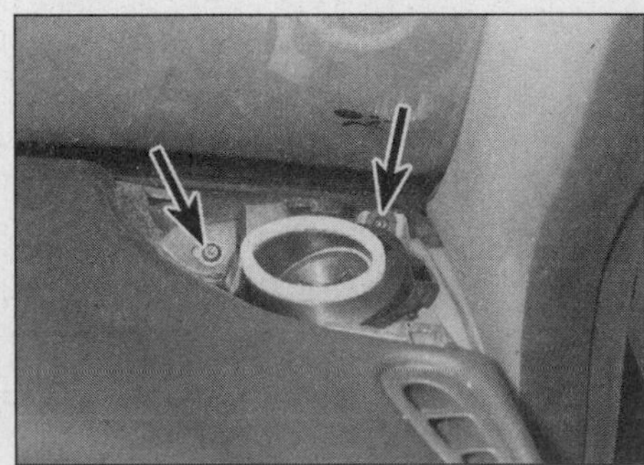

20.2a . . . then undo the retaining screws (arrowed) . . .

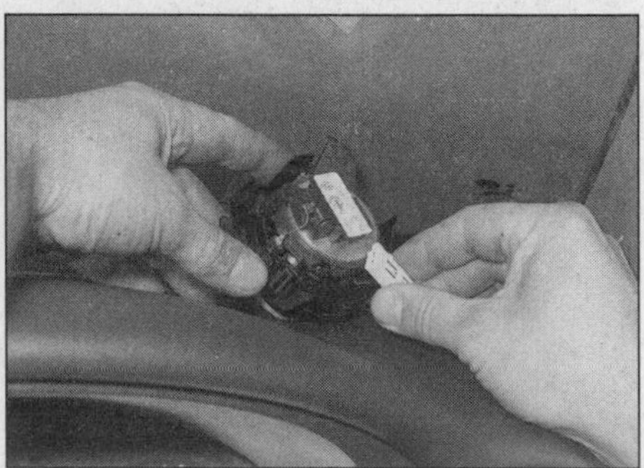

20.2b . . . and lift out the speaker, disconnecting its wiring connector

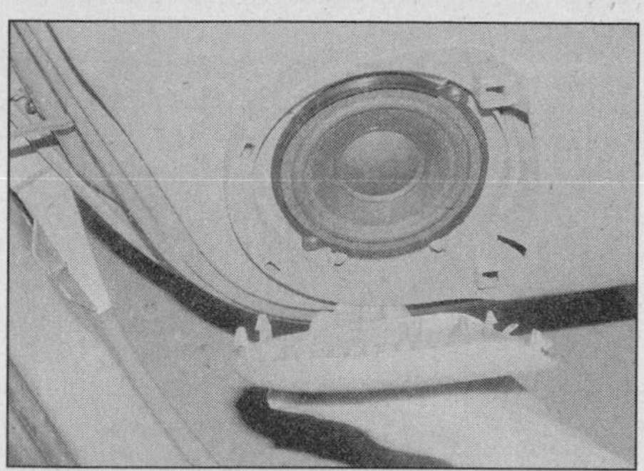
20.4 On models with electric windows, unclip the speaker grille from the door trim panel

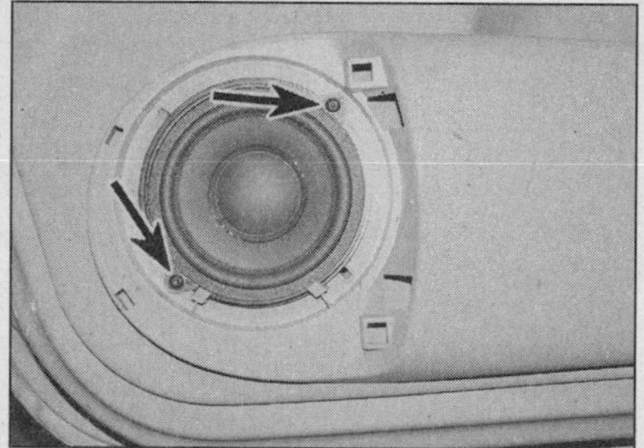
20.5 Slacken and remove the retaining screws (arrowed)

20.7 Speaker is under the rear side shelf – Hatchback

Front door speaker

4 Carefully prise the front of the speaker grille out of position, and remove the grille from the door **(see illustration)**.

5 Slacken and remove the retaining screws then remove the speaker from the door, disconnecting the wiring connector as it becomes accessible **(see illustration)**.

6 Refitting is the reverse of removal.

Rear speaker

Hatchback models

7 From within the luggage compartment, disconnect the wiring connector from the base of the speaker then slacken and remove the retaining screws and remove the speaker from the vehicle **(see illustration)**.

8 Refitting is the reverse of removal.

Coupé and Saloon models

9 Carefully twist and unclip the speaker cover from the rear parcel shelf.

10 Undo the retaining screws and remove the speaker, disconnecting its wiring connectors as they become accessible.

11 Refitting is the reverse of removal.

Scénic models

12 Using a flat-bladed screwdriver, release the three clips on the lower edge of the rear speaker grille, located on the rear wheelarch cover trim panel. Lift the grille upwards and pull it towards the centre of the vehicle to remove **(see illustration)**.

13 Undo the retaining screws and remove the speaker, disconnecting its wiring connectors as they become accessible.

14 Refitting is the reverse of removal.

21 Radio aerial – removal and refitting

Removal

1 The aerial mast is a screw-fit in its base and is easily removed.

2 To remove the complete aerial it is necessary to remove the overhead console. To do this, slide the front cover off the console in a forwards direction and disconnect it from the wiring connector. Slacken and remove the console retaining screws then slide the console assembly towards the front of the vehicle to release it from the roof. Disconnect the wiring connectors and remove the console from the vehicle. Remove the insulating cap (where fitted) then slacken and remove the aerial lead nut **(see illustrations)**. Detach the aerial lead and lift the aerial off from the roof, noting its rubber seal.

Refitting

3 Refitting is the reverse of removal.

22 Anti-theft alarm and engine immobiliser – general information

Note: *This information is applicable only to the anti-theft alarm/engine immobiliser systems fitted by Renault as standard equipment.*

General

1 Most models in the range are fitted with an anti-theft alarm system as standard equipment. The alarm is automatically armed and disarmed using the remote central locking transmitter (where applicable). When the system is activated, the alarm indicator light, located on the roof console, will flash continuously. In addition to the alarm function, the system also incorporates an engine immobiliser.

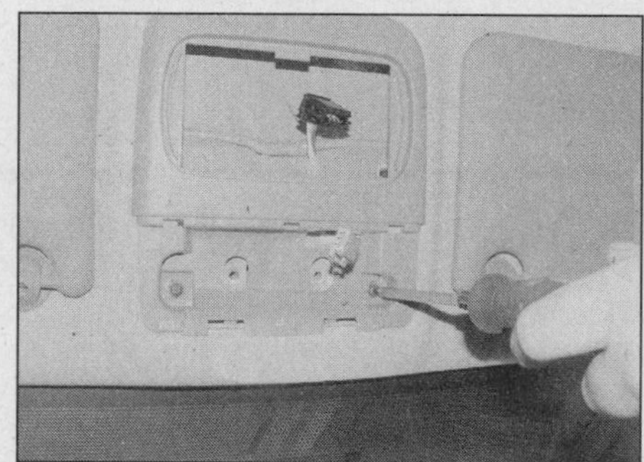
21.2a Remove the retaining screws . . .

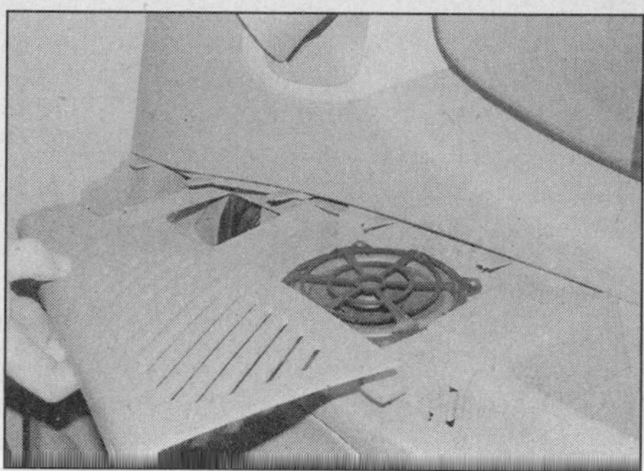
20.12 Unclip the cover to access the rear speaker – Scénic

2 Most models are also fitted with an engine immobiliser device. On models with an anti-theft alarm the immobiliser is also armed and disarmed at the same time as the alarm. On models not equipped with remote central locking, the immobiliser is activated by the coded ignition key. When the immobiliser is armed, the indicator light on the instrument panel will flash continuously.

Anti-theft alarm system

Note: *If the doors are operated using the key, the alarm will not be armed or disarmed (as applicable).*

3 The alarm system has switches on the bonnet, tailgate/boot and each of the doors. It also has ultrasonic sensing, which detects movement inside the vehicle, via sensors mounted on the roof console. If, for some reason the remote central locking transmitter

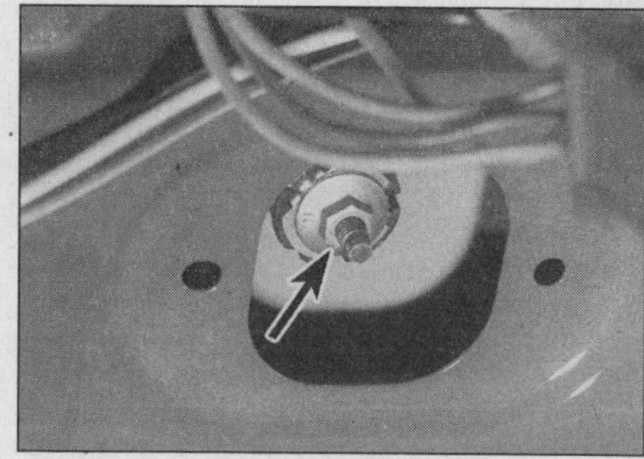
21.2b . . . and undo the aerial retaining nut (arrowed)

fails whilst the alarm is armed, the alarm can be disarmed using the key. To do this, open the door with the key, then enter the vehicle, noting that the alarm will sound as the door is opened. Open up the glovebox and switch the alarm system isolation switch to the OFF position.

4 When the alarm is set using the remote central locking transmitter, the hazard warning light should flash and the alarm siren should 'bleep'. If there is no sound and the hazard warning lights do not flash as the doors are locked, check that the isolation switch is not turned off. If the alarm 'bleeps' but the hazard warning lights do not flash, this indicates that a door or the tailgate/boot/bonnet are not properly shut; as soon as the relevant item is securely closed the hazard warning lights will flash to indicate the alarm system is now active.

5 To de-activate the alarm system, unlock the doors with the remote central locking transmitter then open up the glovebox and, using the ignition key, turn the alarm system isolation switch to the OFF position. To re-activate the system, turn the isolation switch back ON then lock then unlock the vehicle using the remote transmitter; the alarm will be functional again the next time the vehicle is locked with the remote control.

6 Should the alarm system become faulty, the vehicle should be taken to a Renault dealer for examination.

Engine immobiliser

Models with remote central locking

Caution: If the central locking remote transmitter becomes faulty whilst the doors are locked, it will be necessary to use the spare central locking remote transmitter (supplied with the vehicle) to unlock the doors and disarm the immobiliser. If the spare transmitter is not available, then it will be necessary to seek the advice of your Renault dealer; it will not be possible to start the engine without a functioning transmitter.

7 On models with remote central locking, the engine immobiliser is turned on and off using the remote central locking transmitter.

8 When the doors are locked using the transmitter, the immobiliser is switched on and the warning light in the instrument panel flashes continuously. When the doors are unlocked using the transmitter, the warning light will go out. When the ignition switch is turned on, the light should illuminate for a few seconds and then go out; this indicates that the immobiliser has received the correct signal and the engine can be started.

9 If the immobiliser warning light fails to go out when the ignition key is turned or illuminates/flashes whilst the engine is running then the immobiliser system is faulty and the vehicle should be taken to a Renault dealer for testing.

Models without remote central locking

Caution: If ignition key is lost/faulty, it will be necessary to use the spare key (supplied with the vehicle) to unlock the doors and switch on the ignition. If the spare key is not available, then it will be necessary to seek the advice of your Renault dealer; it will not be possible to start the engine without a functioning transmitter.

10 On models not equipped with remote central locking, the engine immobiliser is activated by the coded ignition key.

11 When the ignition switch is turned off and the key is removed, the immobiliser is activated and the warning light in the instrument panel flashes continuously. When the key is inserted and the ignition switch is turned on, the light should illuminate for a few seconds and then go out; this indicates that the immobiliser has received the correct signal from the ignition key and the engine can be started.

12 If the immobiliser warning light illuminates or flashes whilst the engine is running then the immobiliser system is faulty and the vehicle should be taken to a Renault dealer for testing.

Disconnecting the battery

13 Prior to disconnecting the battery, the alarm system must be de-activated by turning the isolation switch in the glovebox off (see paragraph 5). Failure to de-activate the alarm will lead to the siren sounding when the battery is disconnected. Once the battery is reconnected, reactivate the alarm by switching the isolation switch back on again.

23 Electric front seat components – removal and refitting

Renewal of the front seat heater pads and/or electric motors should be entrusted to a Renault dealer. Renewal involves dismantling of the complex seat assembly. Heater pad renewal is especially difficult to achieve successfully. In practice, it will be very difficult for the home mechanic to carry out the job without ruining the upholstery. The only item which is easily removed/refitted is the operating switches (see Section 4).

24 Airbag system – general information and precautions

Both a driver and passenger's airbag are fitted as standard to all the models in the range. The driver's airbag has the word AIRBAG stamped on the airbag unit, which is fitted to the centre of the steering wheel. The passenger airbag also has the word AIRBAG stamped on the passenger airbag unit which is fitted to the passenger side of the facia. The airbag system comprises of the airbag unit(s) (complete with gas generators), the control unit (with an integral impact sensor) and a warning light in the instrument panel.

The airbag system is triggered in the event of a heavy frontal impact above a predetermined force; depending on the point of impact. The airbag is inflated within milliseconds and forms a safety cushion between the driver and steering wheel and (where fitted) the passenger and facia. This prevents contact between the upper body and wheel/facia and therefore greatly reduces the risk of injury. The airbag then deflates almost immediately. The control unit also operates the front seat belt tensioner mechanisms at the same time as the airbag(s) (see Chapter 11).

Every time the ignition is switched on, the airbag control unit performs a self-test. The self-test takes approximately 3 seconds and during this time the airbag warning light in the instrument panel is illuminated. After the self-test has been completed the warning light should go out. If the warning light fails to come on, remains illuminated after the initial period or comes on at any time when the vehicle is being driven, there is a fault in the airbag system. The vehicle should be taken to a Renault dealer for examination at the earliest possible opportunity.

Warning: Before carrying out any operations on the airbag system, to prevent the risk of injury if the system is triggered inadvertently when working on the vehicle, disconnect the battery and disable the system. To do this, remove the seat belt tensioner/airbag system fuse from the engine compartment fusebox and wait for at least five minutes. This will allow the reserve power capacitors in the control unit to discharge. When operations are complete, refit the fuse. Make sure no one is inside the vehicle when the battery is reconnected then, with the driver's door open, switch the ignition on from outside the vehicle.

Warning: Note that the airbag(s) must not be subjected to excess temperatures. When the airbag is removed, ensure that it is stored the correct way up to prevent possible inflation.

Warning: Do not allow any solvents or cleaning agents to contact the airbag assemblies. They must be cleaned using only a damp cloth.

Warning: The airbags and control unit are both sensitive to impact. If either is dropped or damaged they should be renewed.

Warning: Disconnect the airbag control unit wiring plug prior to using arc-welding equipment on the vehicle.

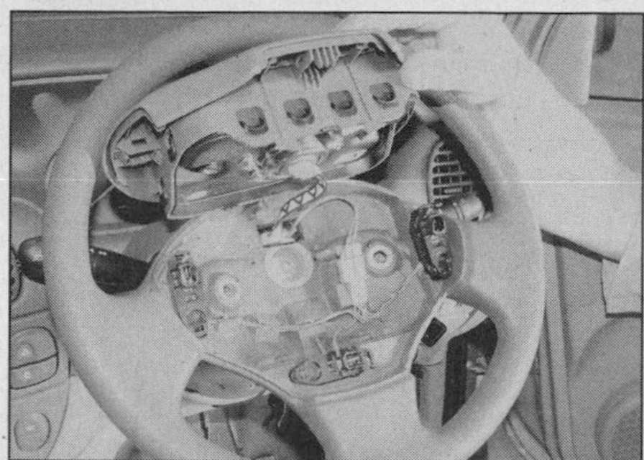

25.3 Lift the driver's airbag away from the steering wheel and disconnect its wiring connector

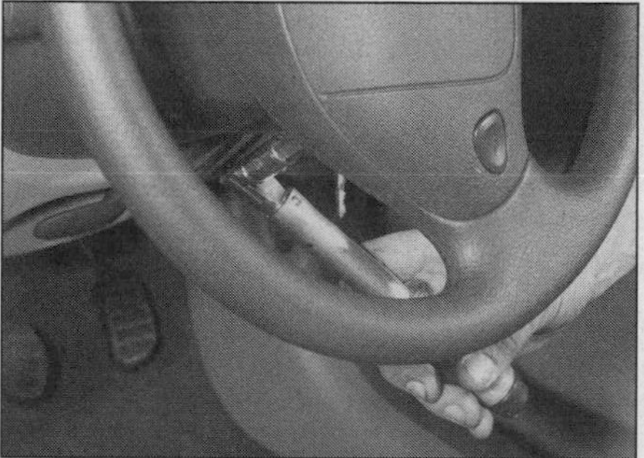

25.4 On refitting, tighten the airbag retaining screws to the specified torque

25.12 Disconnect the wiring connector then undo the retaining nuts (arrowed) and remove the airbag control unit

25 Airbag system components – removal and refitting

Warning: Refer to the warnings in Section 24 before carrying out any of the following operations.

1 Disconnect the battery negative lead (refer to Chapter 5A), remove the seat belt tensioner/airbag system fuse from the engine compartment fusebox and wait for at least five minutes. This will allow the reserve power capacitors in the control unit to discharge and disable the airbag system (see Section 24).

Driver's airbag

Removal

2 Slacken and remove the two airbag retaining screws from the rear of the steering wheel, rotating the wheel as necessary to gain access to the screws.

3 Return the steering wheel to the straight-ahead position then carefully lift the airbag assembly away from the steering wheel and disconnect the wiring connector from the rear of the unit **(see illustration)**. Note that the airbag must not be knocked or dropped and should be stored the correct way up with its padded surface uppermost.

Refitting

4 Ensure that the wiring connectors are securely reconnected and seat the airbag unit centrally in the steering wheel, making sure the wire does not become trapped. Fit the retaining screws and tighten them to the specified torque setting **(see illustration)**.

5 Refit the fuse and, ensuring no one is inside the vehicle, reconnect the battery. With the driver's door open, turn on the ignition switch and check the operation of the airbag warning light.

Passenger airbag

Removal

6 Remove the facia, referring to Chapter 11.

7 Disconnect the wiring connector(s) then slacken and remove the retaining nuts/bolts. Release the airbag unit from its mountings and remove it from the facia.

Refitting

8 Manoeuvre the airbag into position, making sure it is correctly engaged with its mounting tangs, then refit the mounting nuts and tighten them securely. Reconnect the wiring connector(s), ensuring that the wiring is correctly routed and retained by all the necessary clips and ties.

9 Refit the facia as described in Chapter 11.

10 Refit the fuse and, ensuring no one is inside the vehicle, reconnect the battery. With the driver's door open, turn on the ignition switch and check the operation of the airbag warning light.

Airbag control unit

Removal

11 Remove the centre console as described in Chapter 11 to gain access to the control unit which is mounted in front of the gearchange/selector lever.

12 Release the retaining clip and disconnect the wiring connector then unscrew the retaining nuts and remove the control unit from the vehicle **(see illustration)**.

Refitting

13 Refit the control unit, making sure the arrow on the top of the unit is pointing towards the front of the vehicle **(see illustration)**. Refit the mounting nuts and tighten them securely.

14 Reconnect the wiring connector and refit the centre console as described in the relevant Section of Chapter 11.

15 Refit the fuse and, ensuring no one is inside the vehicle, reconnect the battery. With the driver's door open, turn on the ignition switch and check the operation of the airbag warning light.

Airbag wiring contact unit

Note: *The rotary wiring contact unit is part of the combination switch mounting bracket assembly on the steering column and cannot be renewed separately.*

Removal

16 Remove the driver's airbag unit then remove the steering wheel as described in Chapter 10. Ensure that the front wheels are pointing in the straight-ahead position.

17 Unclip the cover from the inner end of the radio control switch assembly and slacken the switch retaining screw by a few turns **(see illustration)**.

18 Undo the retaining screws and remove the lower half of the steering column shroud. Undo the two retaining screws and remove

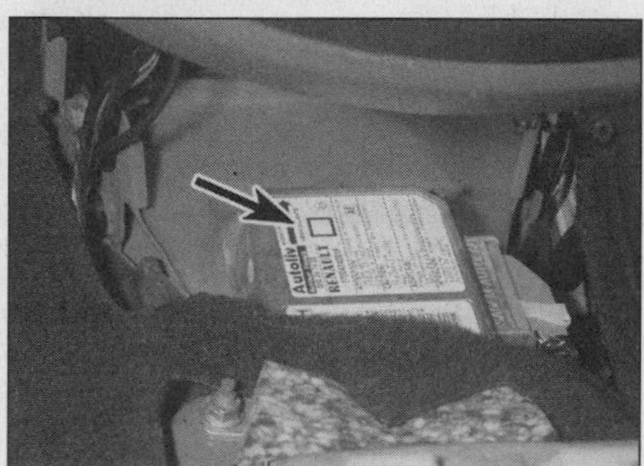

25.13 Ensure that the control unit is fitted with its arrow (arrowed) pointing towards the front of the vehicle

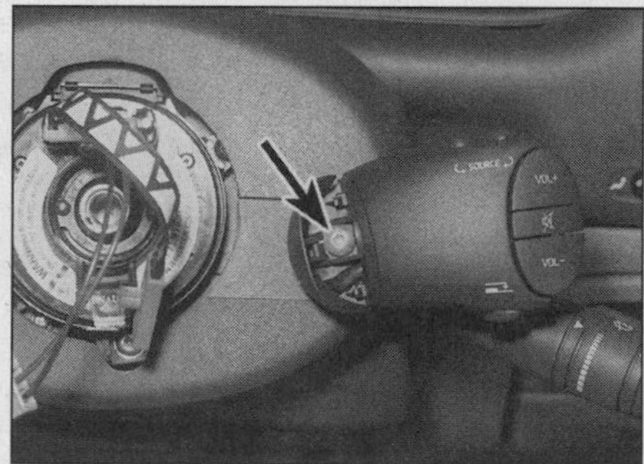

25.17 Undo the retaining screw (arrowed) and free the radio control switch from the steering column

12

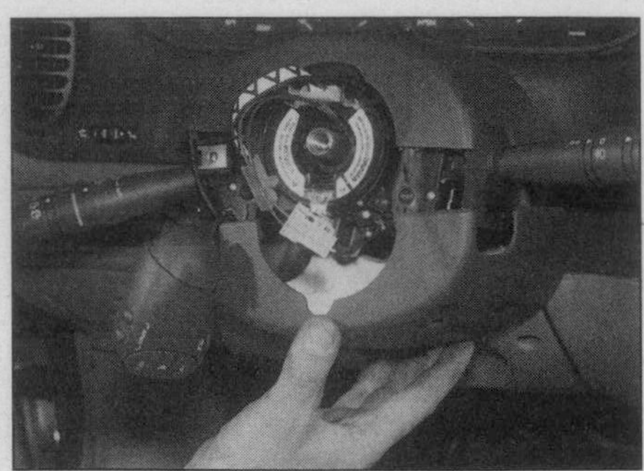

25.18a Undo the retaining screws and remove the lower shroud . . .

the upper half of the steering column shroud **(see illustrations).**

19 Slacken but do not remove the clamp screw, then tap with the screwdriver

25.19 Slacken the screw, then tap gently to release the switch assembly

25.18b . . . then undo the retaining screws (arrowed) and lift off the upper shroud

sharply to release the cone-shaped assembly from the column **(see illustration).** Withdraw the assembly from the steering column.

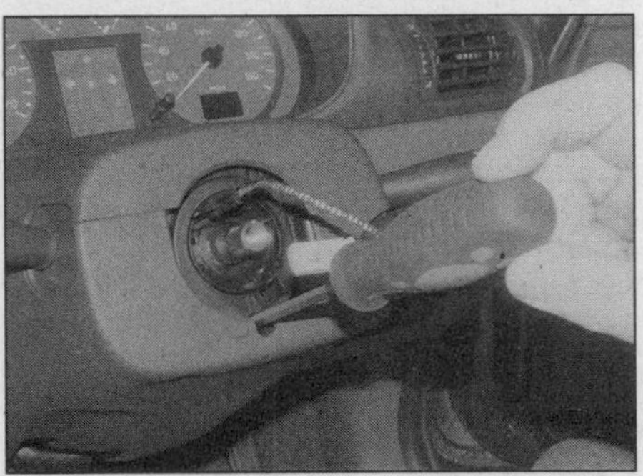

25.21 Tightening the switch clamp screw, after the shrouds have been fitted

Refitting

20 Prior to refitting it is necessary to ensure that the contact unit is correctly centralised, with the wiring connector at the top of the unit, and that the front wheels are pointing in the straight-ahead position. If there is any doubt about the contact unit position, rotate the contact unit insert in an anti- clockwise direction until resistance is felt (do not use force). From this point, rotate the insert clockwise until its wiring connector is positioned at the top of the unit, then rotate it through a further two rotations clockwise. Do not rotate the unit from now on.

21 Slide the switch assembly/contact unit into position, ensure that the switch assembly/contact ring is correctly seated. **Note:** *Do not tighten the switch assembly clamp screw until the shrouds have been fitted* ***(see illustration).***

22 Refit the steering column upper and lower shrouds, tightening the retaining screws securely. Where applicable, retighten the radio switch stalk screw.

23 Refit the steering wheel as described in Chapter 10, then refit the airbag unit as described in paragraphs 4 and 5.

Side airbags

24 The side airbag units are built into the front seats, and their removal requires that the seat fabric be removed. This is not considered to be a DIY operation, and should be referred to a Renault dealer.

Megane/Scenic wiring diagrams

Diagram 1

Key to symbols

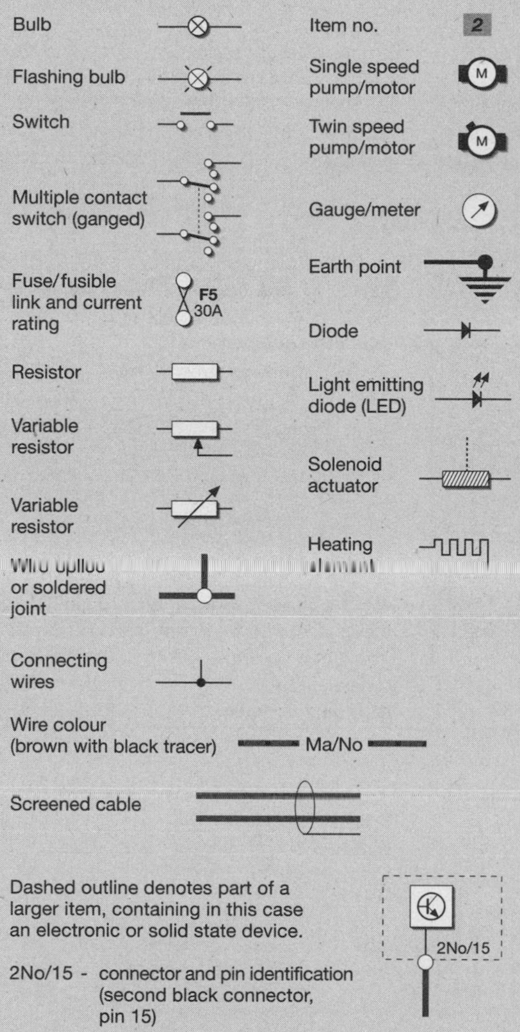

Bulb 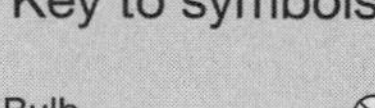

Flashing bulb 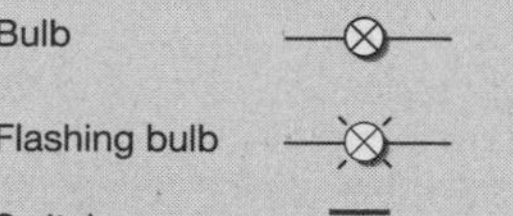

Item no. **2**

Single speed pump/motor 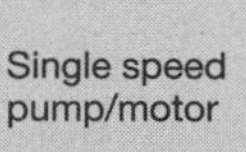

Switch

Twin speed pump/motor 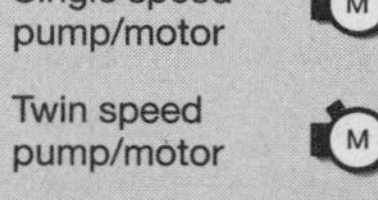

Multiple contact switch (ganged) 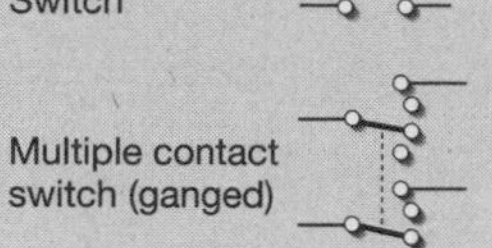

Gauge/meter

Fuse/fusible link and current rating 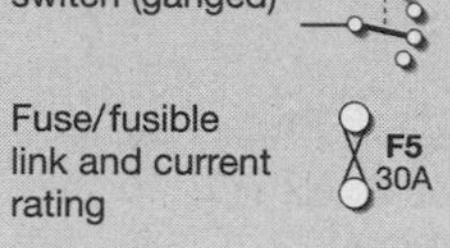

Earth point 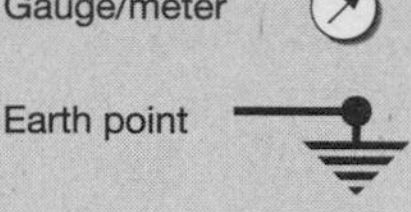

Diode

Resistor

Light emitting diode (LED) 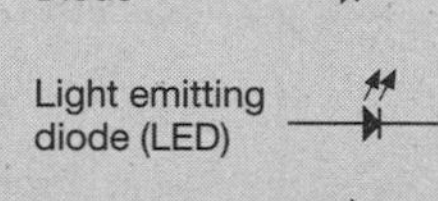

Variable resistor 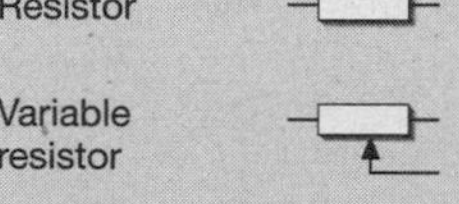

Solenoid actuator

Variable resistor 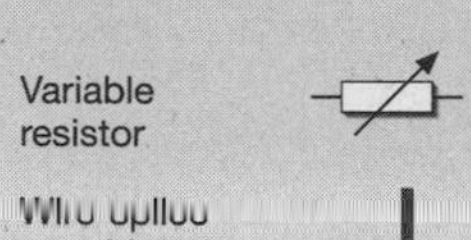

Heating element 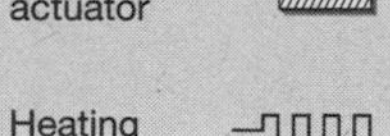 

Wire splice or soldered joint 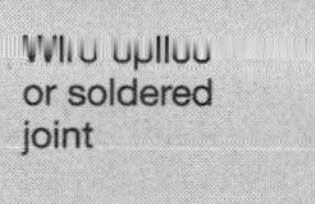

Connecting wires 

Wire colour (brown with black tracer) 

Screened cable 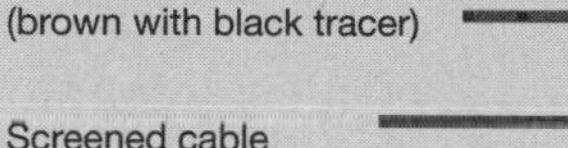

Dashed outline denotes part of a larger item, containing in this case an electronic or solid state device.

2No/15 - connector and pin identification (second black connector, pin 15)

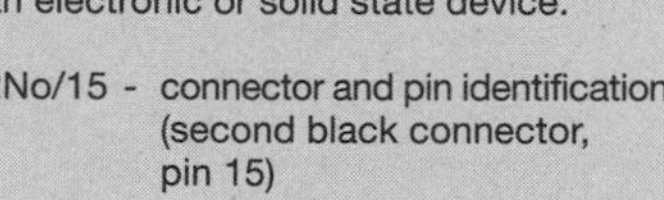

Key to circuits

Diagram 1	Information for wiring diagrams.
Diagram 2	Starting, charging, engine cooling fan, diagnostic socket.
Diagram 3	Safety restraint system, horn, cigar lighter, heater blower, Diesel fuel filter heater.
Diagram 4	Air conditioning, anti-lock brakes.
Diagram 5	Instrument cluster.
Diagram 6	Front & rear foglights, stop & reversing lights, direction indicators & hazard warning lights.
Diagram 7	Side & tail lights, interior lighting, headlights and headlight levelling.
Diagram 8	Clock & external temperature sensor, heated rear screen & mirrors, audio unit.
Diagram 9	Electric mirrors, electric sunroof, front & rear wash/wipe, heated seats.
Diagram 10	Electric front & rear windows, central locking.
Diagram 11	Engine management (petrol models).
Diagram 12	Engine management (Diesel models).

Typical passenger fusebox

Fuse	Rating	Circuit protected
F1	25A	Rear LH electric window
F2	-	Spare
F3	25A	Rear RH electric window
F4	-	Spare
F5	7.5A	Heated mirrors
F6	15A	Circuit breaker - electric mirrors, clock & radio display
F7	15A	Horn
F8	5A	Engine management, engine cooling fan, diagnostic socket, automatic transmission, instrument cluster
F9	5A	Rear foglight
F10	15A	Front foglight
F11	7.5A	LH sidelight
F12	10A	Headlight washers
F13	7.5A	RH sidelight
F14	-	Spare
F15	-	Spare
F16	5A	Anti-lock brakes
F17	25A	Passengers electric window
F18	15A	Stop lights, instrument cluster, heated screen, ABS, rear electric window locking
F19	15A	Reversing lights, rear screen wash/wipe
F20	-	Spare
F21	-	Spare
F22	10A	LH main beam
F23	25A	Driver's electric window (low spec models)
F24	10A	RH main beam
F25	20A	Sunroof
F26	-	Spare
F27	15A	Heated seats
F28	20A	Heating, air conditioning
F29	10A	LH dipped beam
F30	15A	Radio, cigar lighter, instrument illumination, clock
F31	10A	RH dipped beam
F32	-	Spare
F33	-	Dual headlights (shunt)
FA	15A	Hazard warning and direction indicators
FB	5A	Remote control, engine immobiliser
FC	20A	Central locking
FD	20A	Windscreen wiper
FE	25A	Driver's one touch electric window (high spec models)
FF	30A	Heated rear window

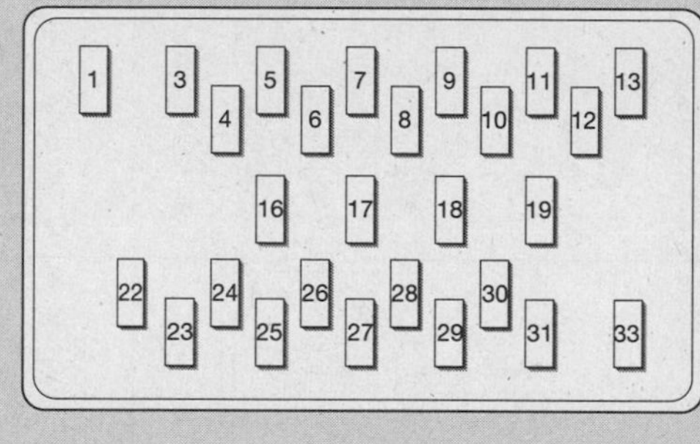

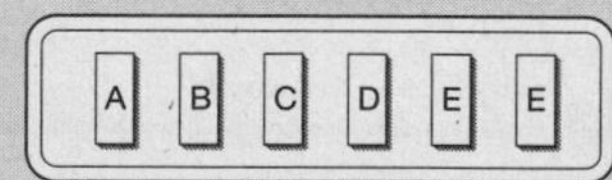

Earth locations

E1	RH inner wing	**E7**	LH front 'A' pilar
E2	On gearbox	**E8**	RH front crossmember
E3	On front of engine	**E9**	Below LH rear light cluster
E4	Base of RH 'A' pilar	**E10**	Below RH rear light cluster
E5	Base of RH 'A' pilar	**E11**	Radio earth
E6	LH front crossmember		

H32357

Diagram 2

Wire colours

Ba	White	**No**	Black
Be	Blue	**Or**	Orange
Bj	Beige	**Rg**	Red
Cy	Clear	**Sa**	Pink
Gr	Grey	**Ve**	Green
Ja	Yellow	**Vi**	Mauve
Ma	Brown		

Key to items

1 Battery
2 Battery +ve protection unit
3 Power feed fusebox
4 Engine relay/fusebox
  a = starter relay
  b = low speed relay
  c = fan relay
  d = injection locking relay
5 Ignition switch
6 Starter motor
7 Alternator
8 Engine cooling fan
9 Engine cooling fan resistor
10 Diagnostic socket
11 Passenger fusebox
12 Multi-timer unit

H32358

Typical starting and charging system (manual transmission)

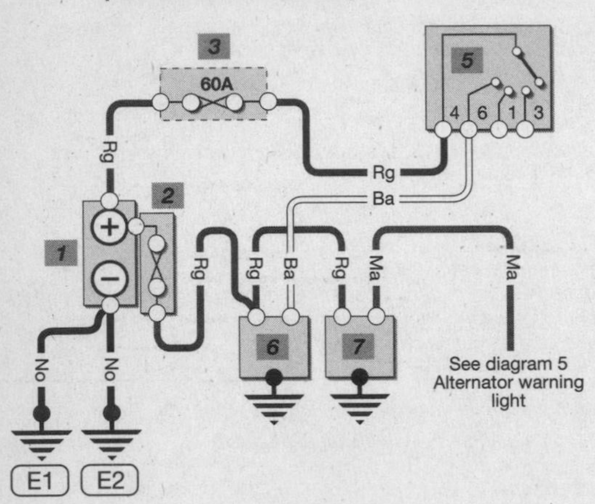

Typical engine cooling fan

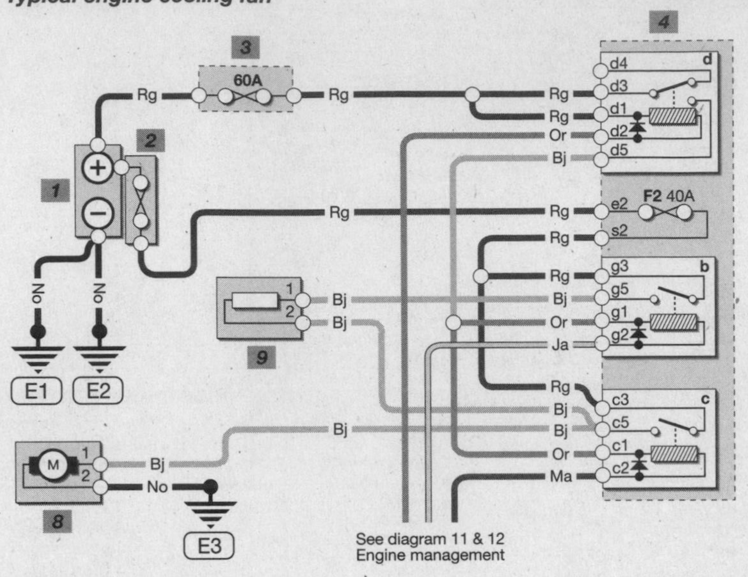

Typical starting and charging system (automatic transmission)

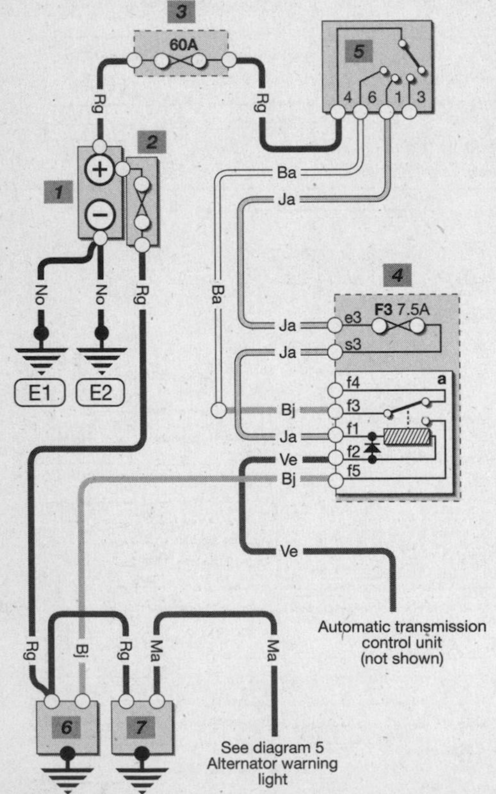

Typical diagnostic socket

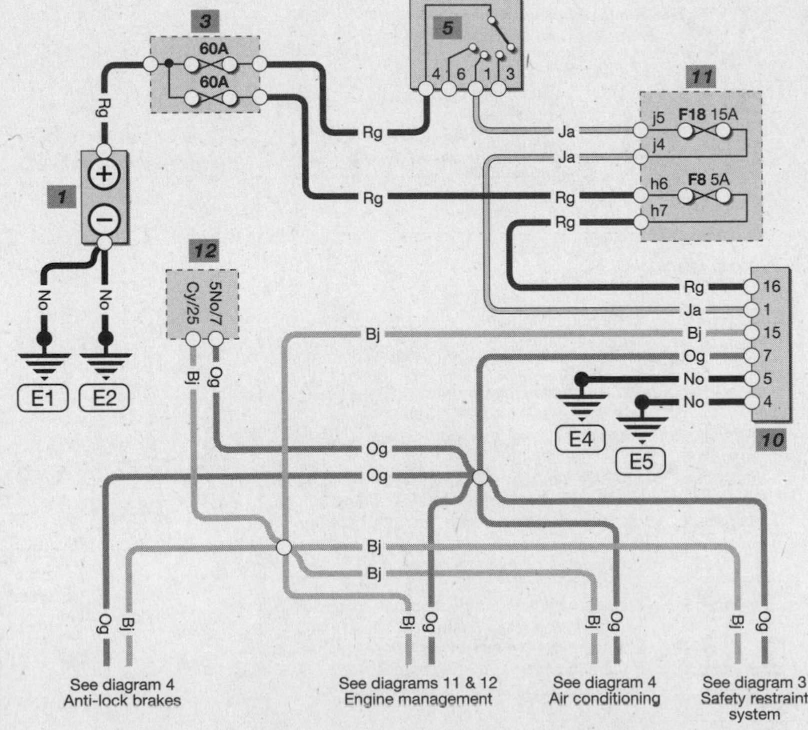

Diagram 3

Wire colours

Ba	White	**No**	Black
Be	Blue	**Or**	Orange
Bj	Beige	**Rg**	Red
Cy	Clear	**Sa**	Pink
Gr	Grey	**Ve**	Green
Ja	Yellow	**Vi**	Mauve
Ma	Brown		

Key to items

1 Battery
2 Battery +ve protection unit
3 Power feed fusebox
4 Engine relay/fusebox
 e = Diesel fuel heater relay
5 Ignition switch
11 Passenger fusebox
15 SRS control unit
16 Driver's seatbelt pretensioner
17 Passenger's seatbelt pretensioner
18 Driver's curtain airbag
19 Passenger's curtain airbag
20 Driver's side airbag
21 Passenger's side airbag
22 Driver's airbag
23 Passenger's airbag
24 Horn/light switch
 a = horn
 b = side/headlight
25 Horn
26 Cigar lighter
27 Diesel fuel filter heater
28 Heater control panel
29 Fan unit
30 Interior lighting rheostat

H32359

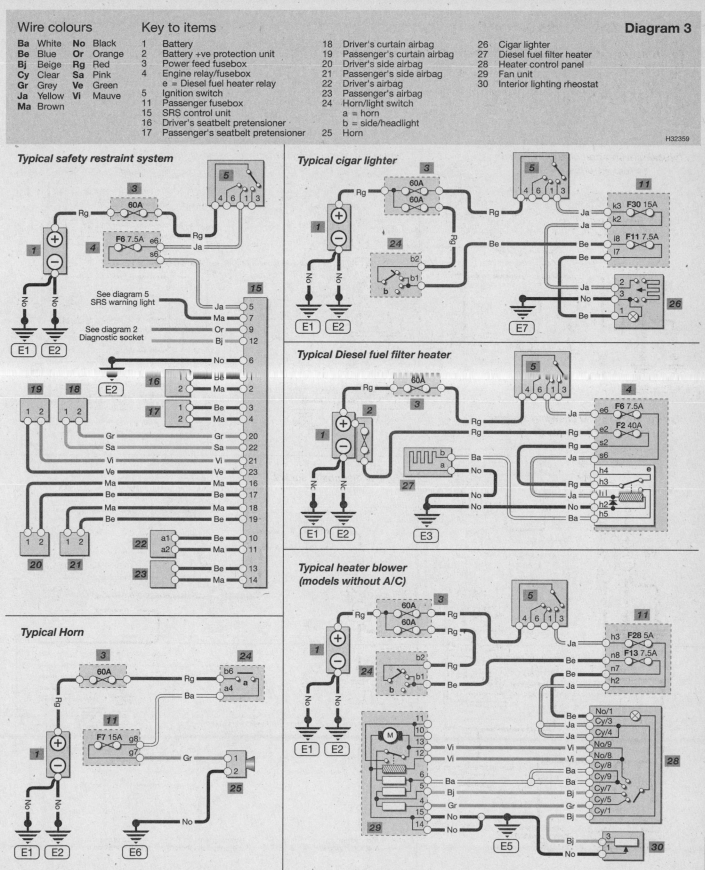

Typical safety restraint system

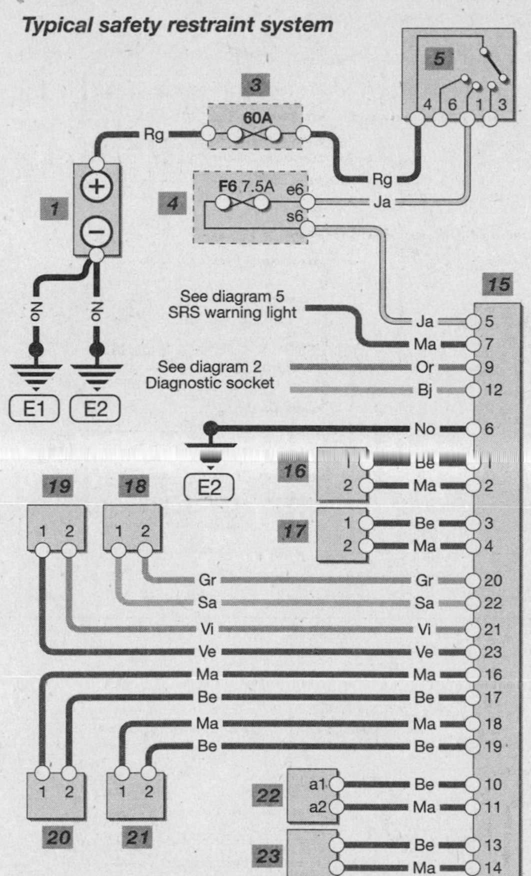

Typical cigar lighter

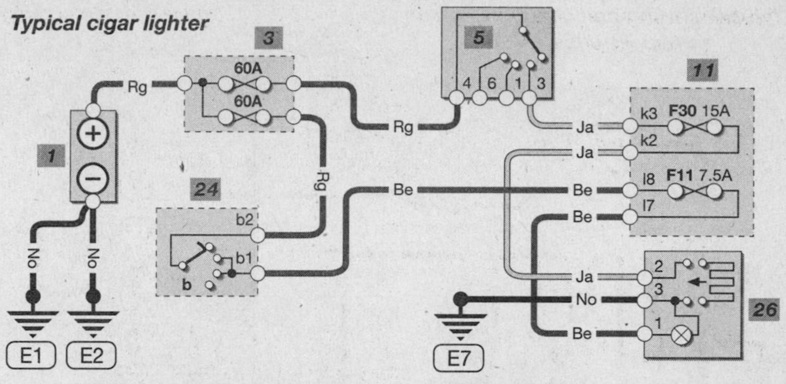

Typical Diesel fuel filter heater

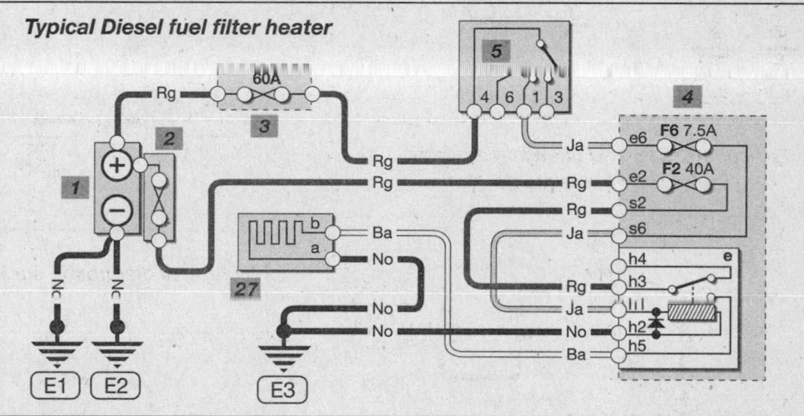

Typical heater blower (models without A/C)

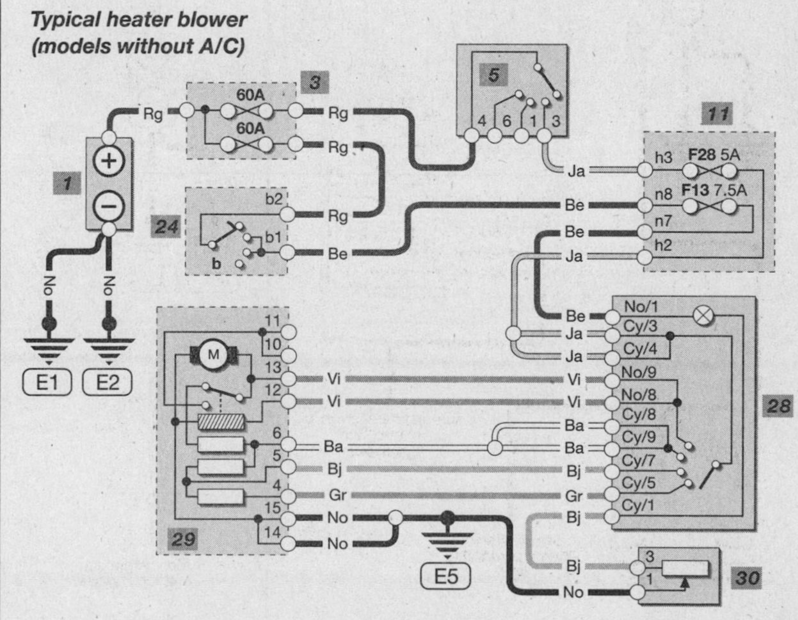

Typical Horn

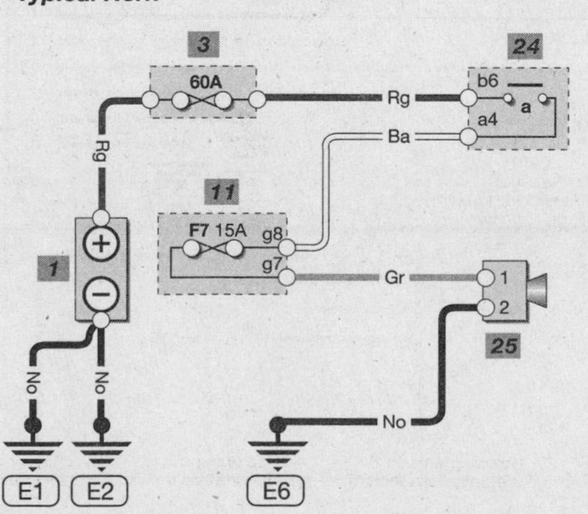

Diagram 4

Wire colours

Ba	White	**No**	Black
Be	Blue	**Or**	Orange
Bj	Beige	**Rg**	Red
Cy	Clear	**Sa**	Pink
Gr	Grey	**Ve**	Green
Ja	Yellow	**Vi**	Mauve
Ma	Brown		

Key to items

1 Battery
3 Power feed fusebox
5 Ignition switch
11 Passenger fusebox
24 Horn/light switch
b = side/headlight
29 Fan unit
30 Interior lighting rheostat
31 A/C control panel
32 A/C monitoring unit
33 A/C pressostat
34 A/C magnetic clutch
35 ABS control unit
36 LH front wheel sensor
37 RH front wheel sensor
38 LH rear wheel sensor
39 RH rear wheel sensor

H32360

Typical air conditioning

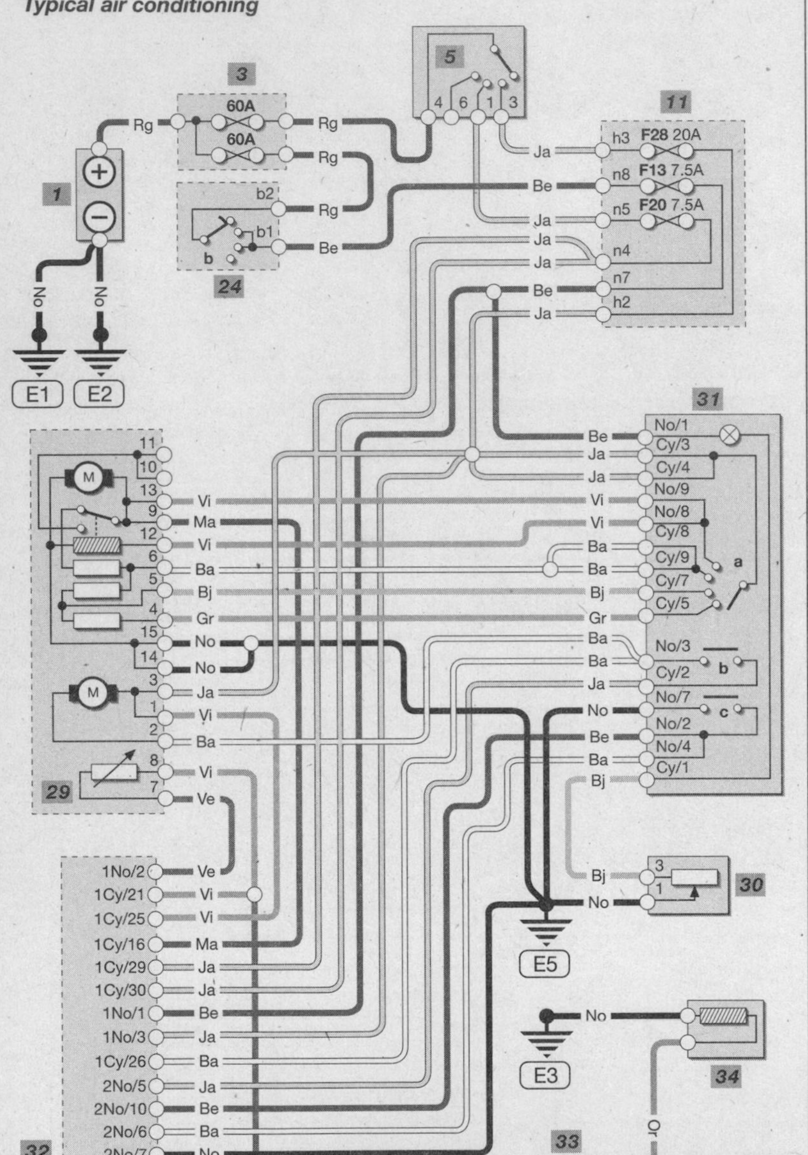

Typical anti-lock brakes

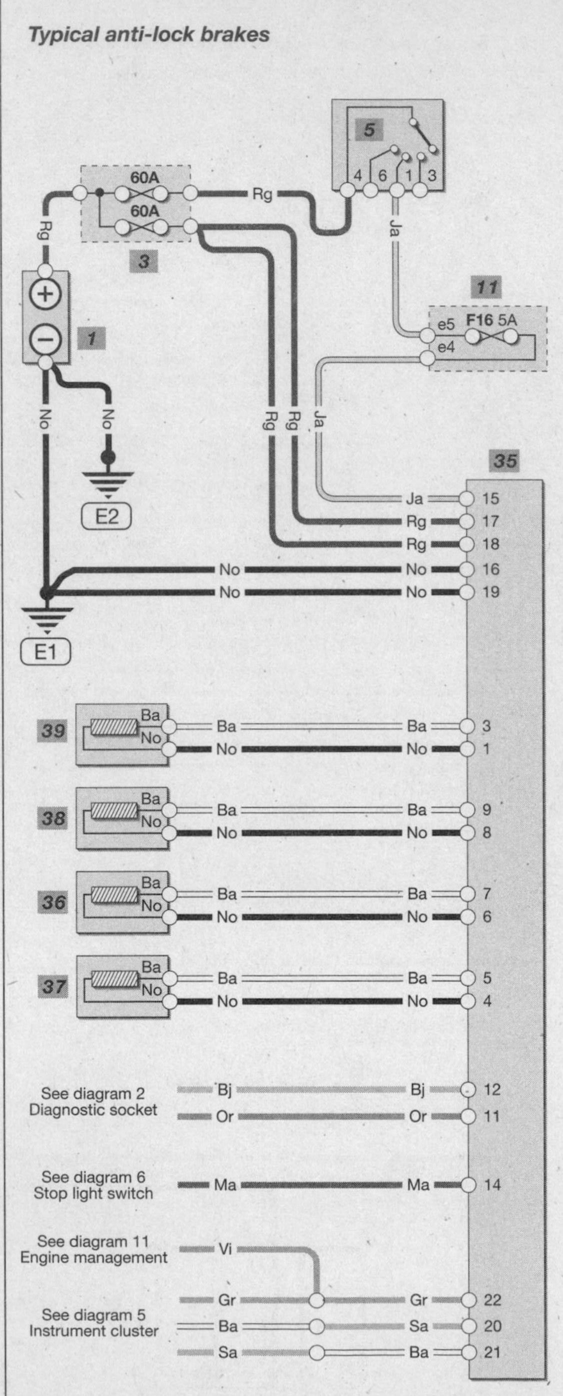

Diagram 5

Wire colours

Ba	White	**No**	Black
Be	Blue	**Or**	Orange
Bj	Beige	**Rg**	Red
Cy	Clear	**Sa**	Pink
Gr	Grey	**Ve**	Green
Ja	Yellow	**Vi**	Mauve
Ma	Brown		

Key to items

1 Battery
3 Power feed fusebox
5 Ignition switch
11 Passenger fusebox
24 Horn/light switch
  b = side/headlight
30 Interior lighting rheostat
45 Coolant temp. sensor/switch
46 Oil level sensor
47 Fuel gauge sender unit/fuel pump
48 Handbrake switch
49 Low brake fluid sensor
50 Low washer fluid switch

51 Instrument cluster
  a = LH indicator warning light
  b = RH indicator wanring light
  c = dipped beam warning light
  d = main beam warning light
  e = front foglight warning light
  f = rear foglight warning light
  g = glow plug warning light
  h = instrument control unit
  i = ABS warning light
  j = brake system warning light
  k = high temperature warning light
  l = low washer fluid warning light

51 Instrument cluster (continued)
  m = SRS warning light
  n = alternator warning light
  o = engine management warning light
  p = oil pressure warning light
  q = heated rear window warning light
52 Wash/wipe switch
  a = trip computer reset button
53 Oil pressure switch

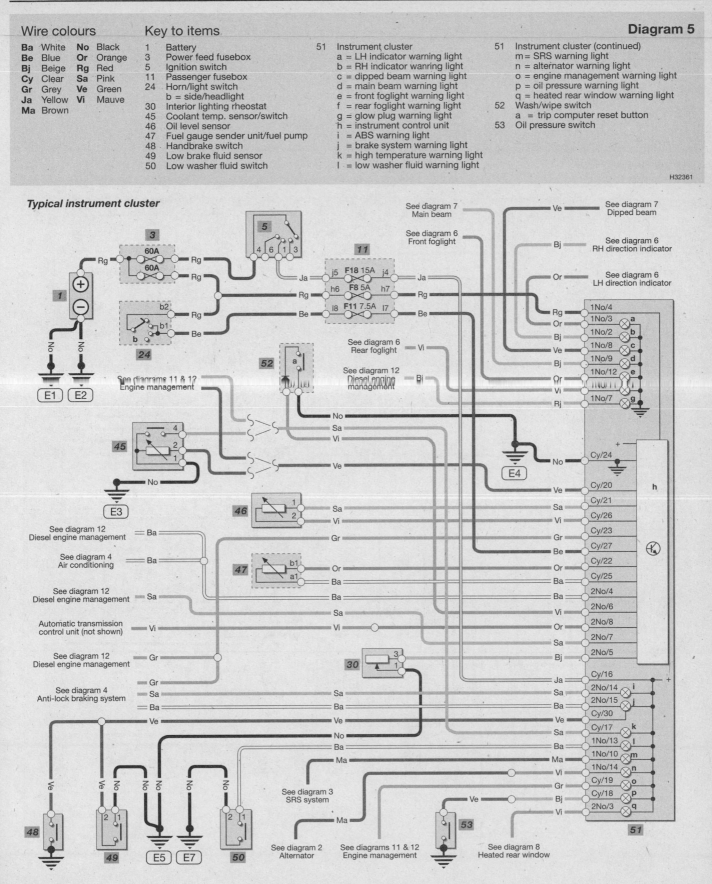

H32361

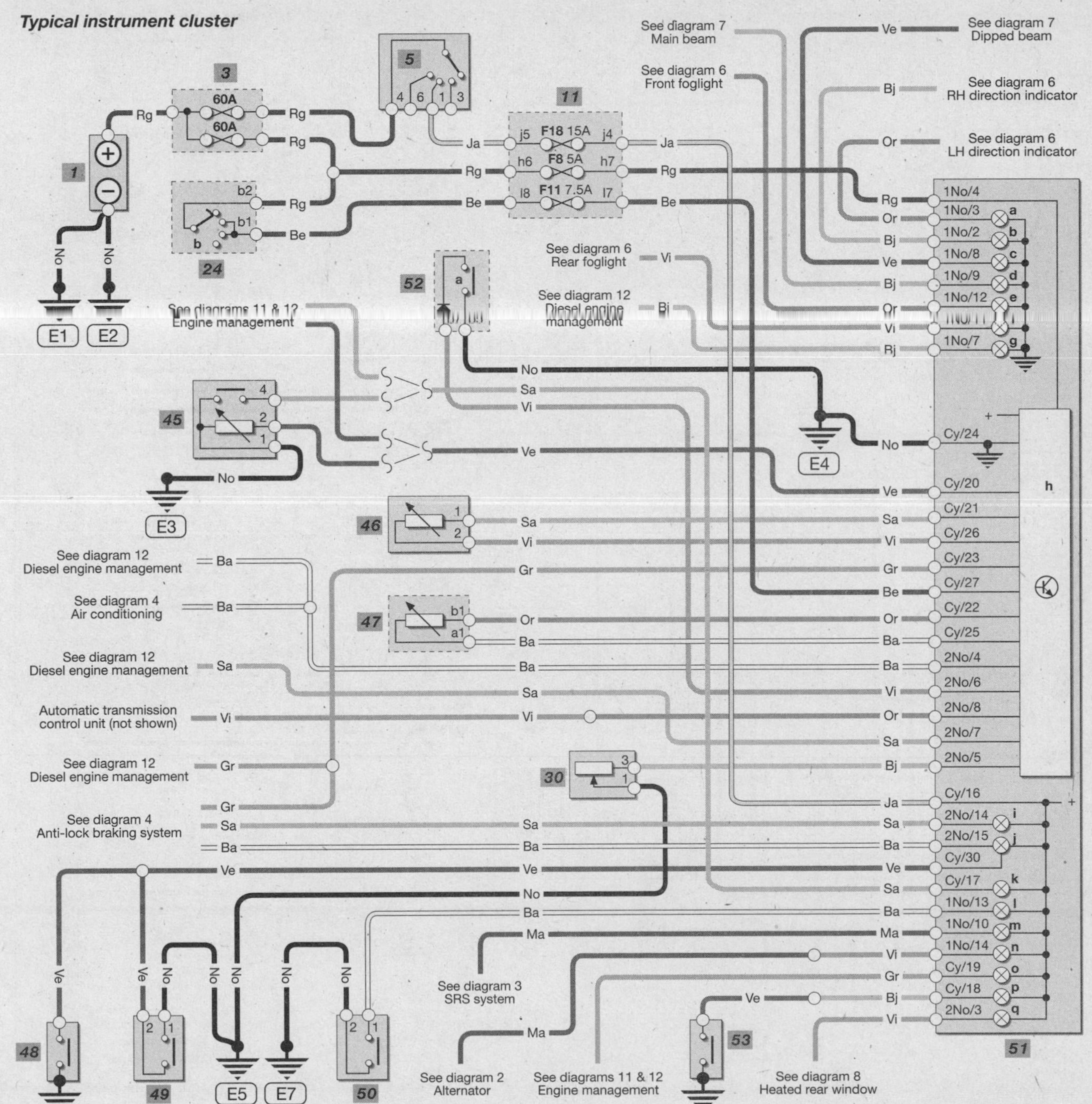

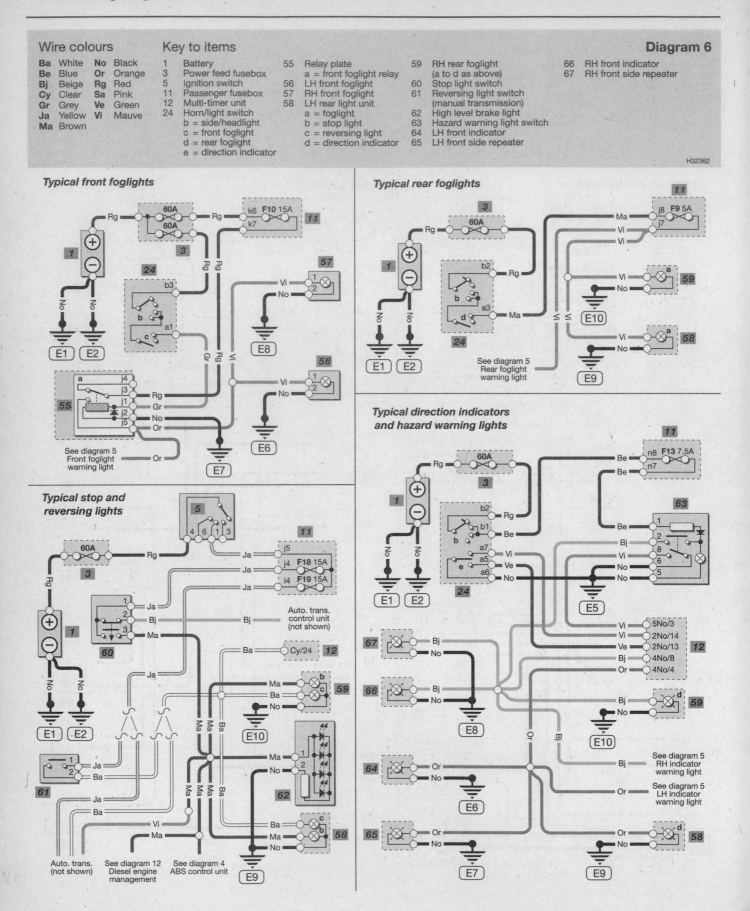

Diagram 6

Wire colours

Ba	White	**No**	Black
Be	Blue	**Or**	Orange
Bj	Beige	**Rg**	Red
Cy	Clear	**Sa**	Pink
Gr	Grey	**Ve**	Green
Ja	Yellow	**Vi**	Mauve
Ma	Brown		

Key to items

1 Battery
3 Power feed fusebox
5 Ignition switch
11 Passenger fusebox
12 Multi-timer unit
24 Horn/light switch
b = side/headlight
c = front foglight
d = rear foglight
e = direction indicator
55 Relay plate
a = front foglight relay
56 LH front foglight
57 RH front foglight
58 LH rear light unit
a = foglight
b = stop light
c = reversing light
d = direction indicator
59 RH rear foglight
(a to d as above)
60 Stop light switch
61 Reversing light switch
(manual transmission)
62 High level brake light
63 Hazard warning light switch
64 LH front indicator
65 LH front side repeater
66 RH front indicator
67 RH front side repeater

H32362

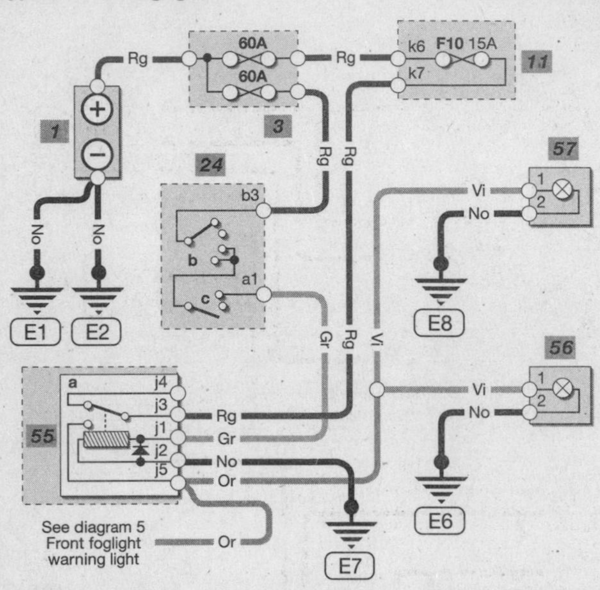

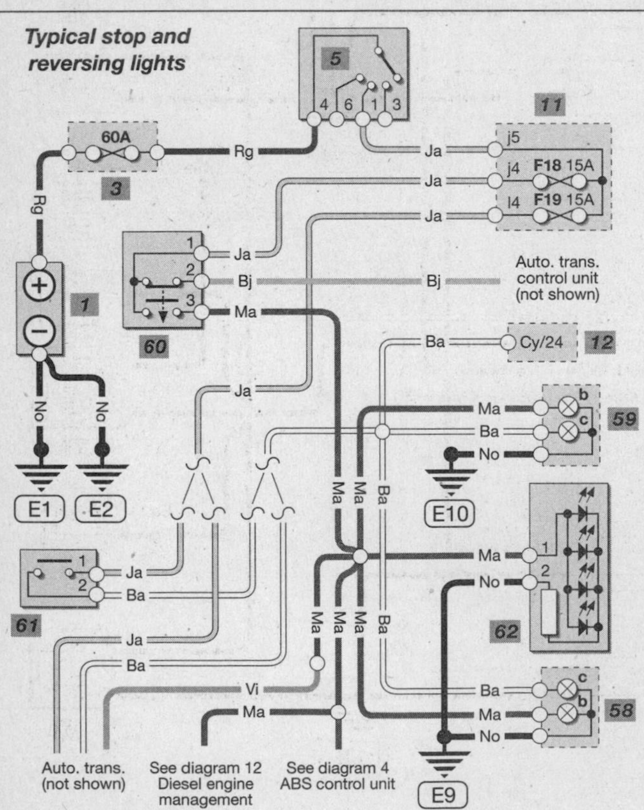

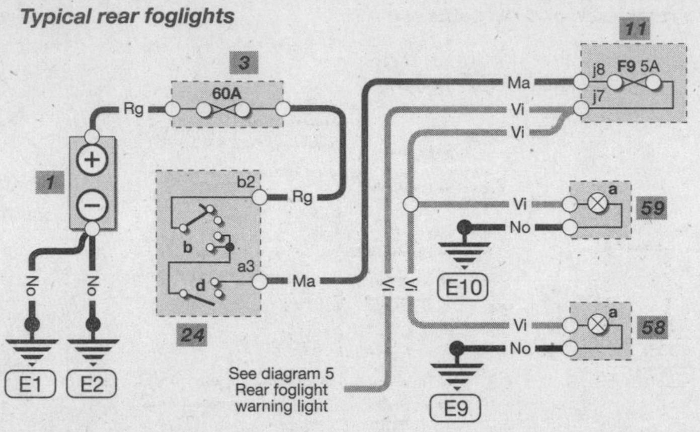

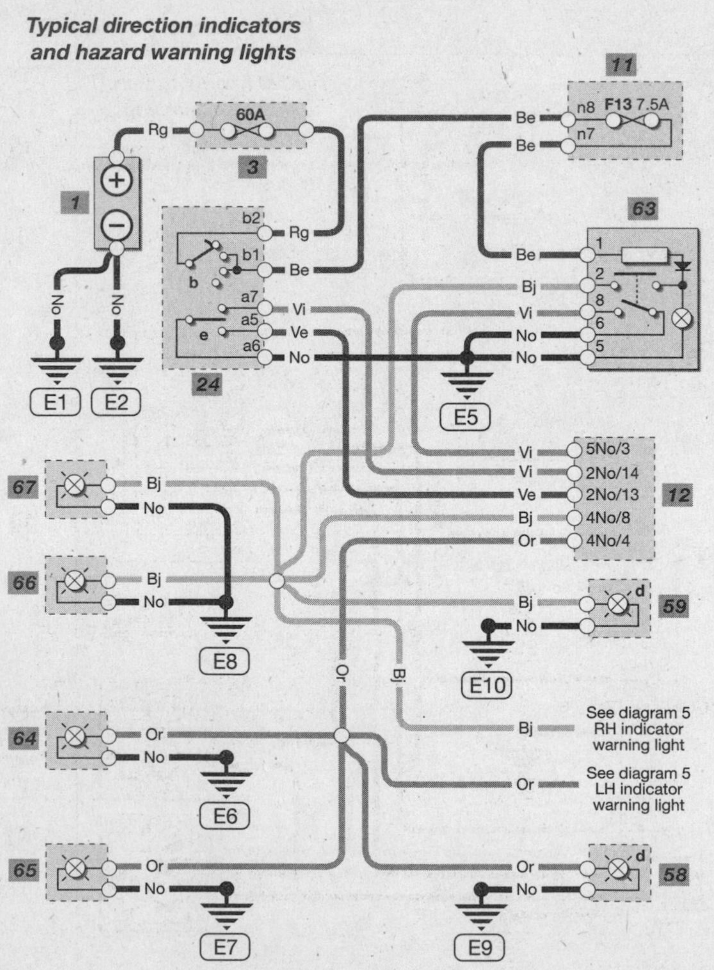

Diagram 7

Wire colours

Ba	White	**No**	Black
Be	Blue	**Or**	Orange
Bj	Beige	**Rg**	Red
Cy	Clear	**Sa**	Pink
Gr	Grey	**Ve**	Green
Ja	Yellow	**Vi**	Mauve
Ma	Brown		

Key to items

1 Battery
3 Power feed fusebox
5 Ignition switch
11 Passenger fusebox
12 Multi-timer unit
24 Horn/light switch
  b = side/headlight
  f = headlight flasher
58 LH rear light unit
  e = tail light
59 RH rear foglight
  e = tail light
70 LH headlight
71 RH headlight
72 Headlight levelling control
73 LH headlight levelling motor
74 RH headlight levelling motor
75 Glove box light/switch
76 Luggage compartment light
77 Luggage compartment light switch
78 Front courtesy light
79 Front map reading light
80 LH rear courtesy light
81 RH rear courtesy light
82 Multi-timer unit
83 Luggage compartment lid switch
84 Driver's door switch
85 Passenger's door switch
86 LH rear door switch
87 RH rear door switch

H32363

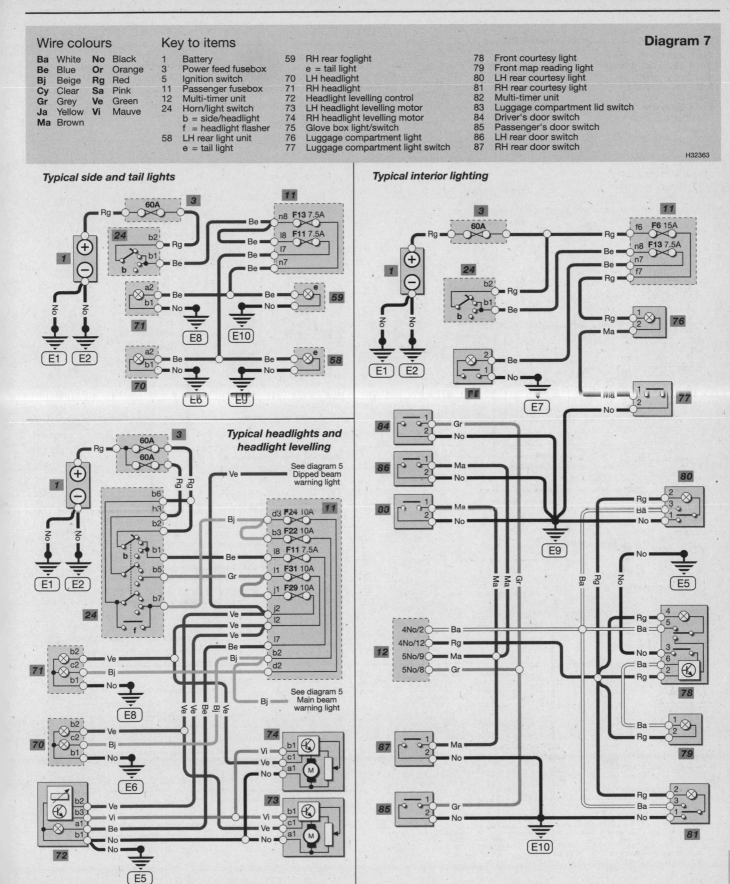

Typical side and tail lights

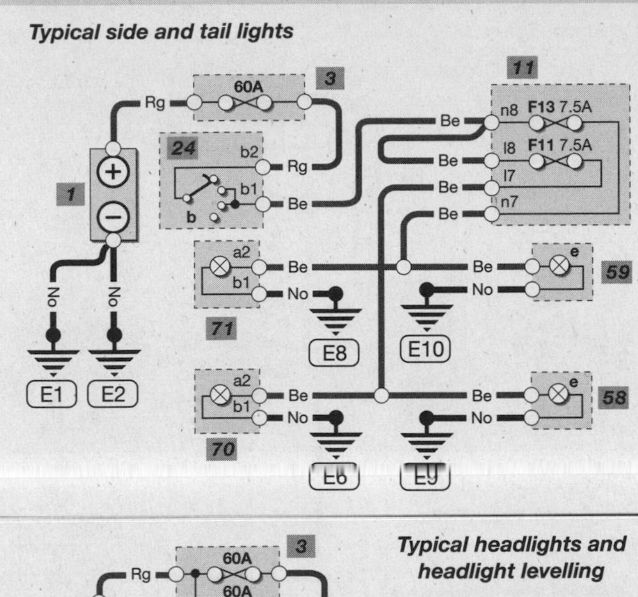

Typical headlights and headlight levelling

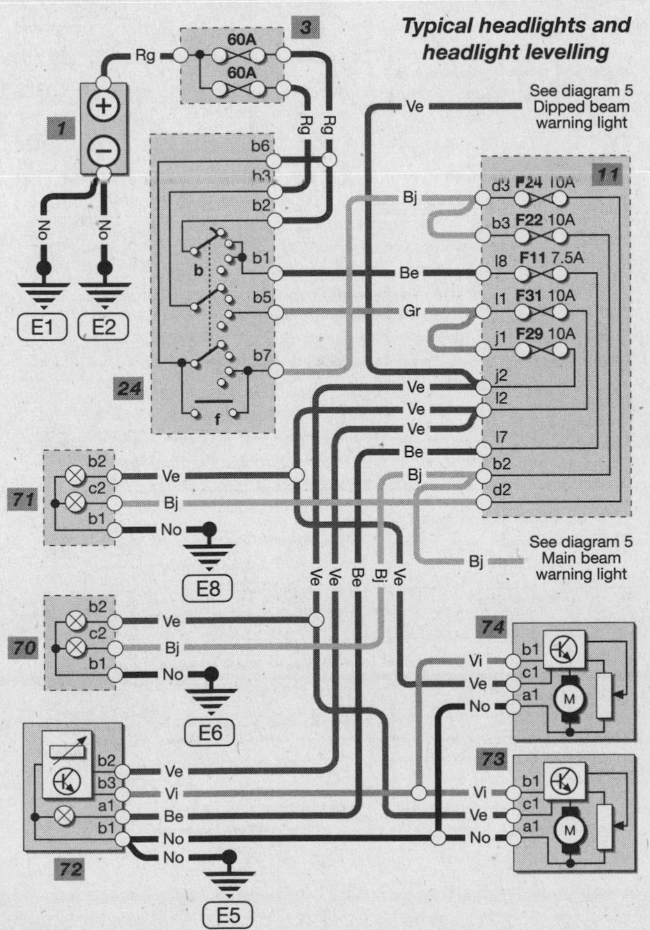

Typical interior lighting

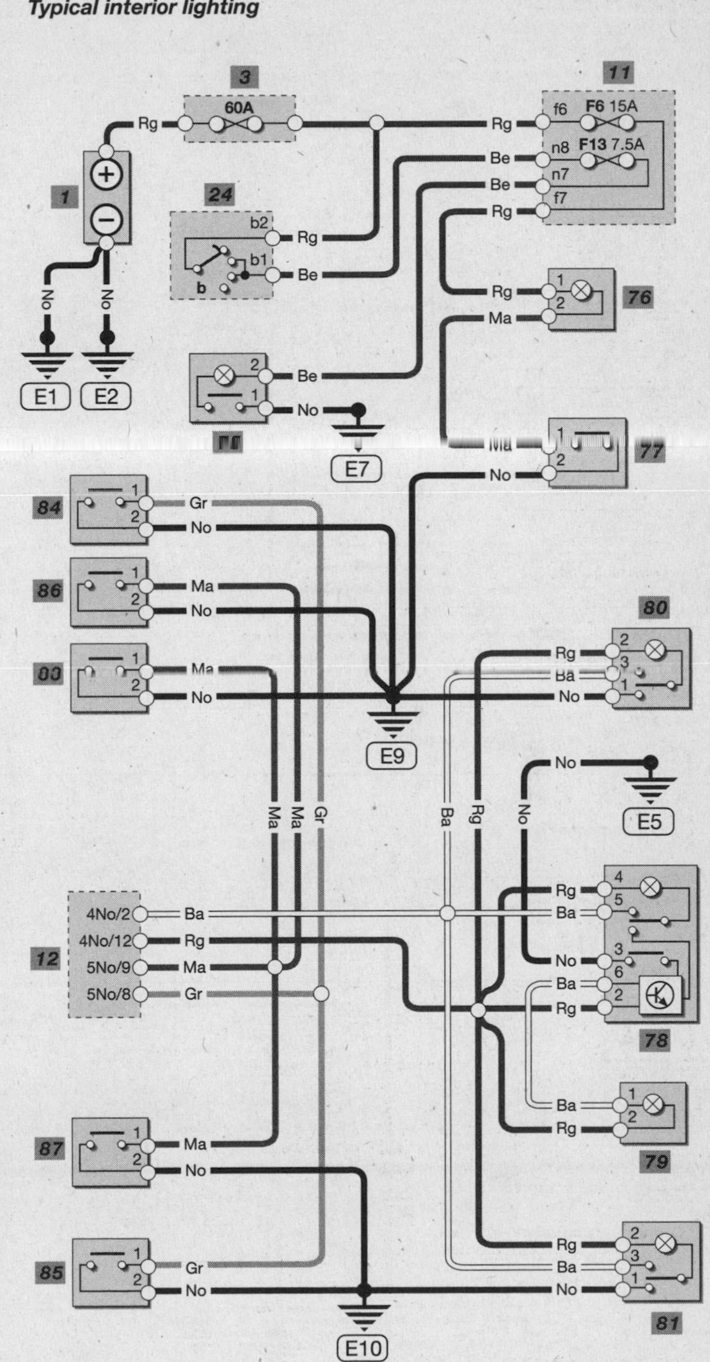

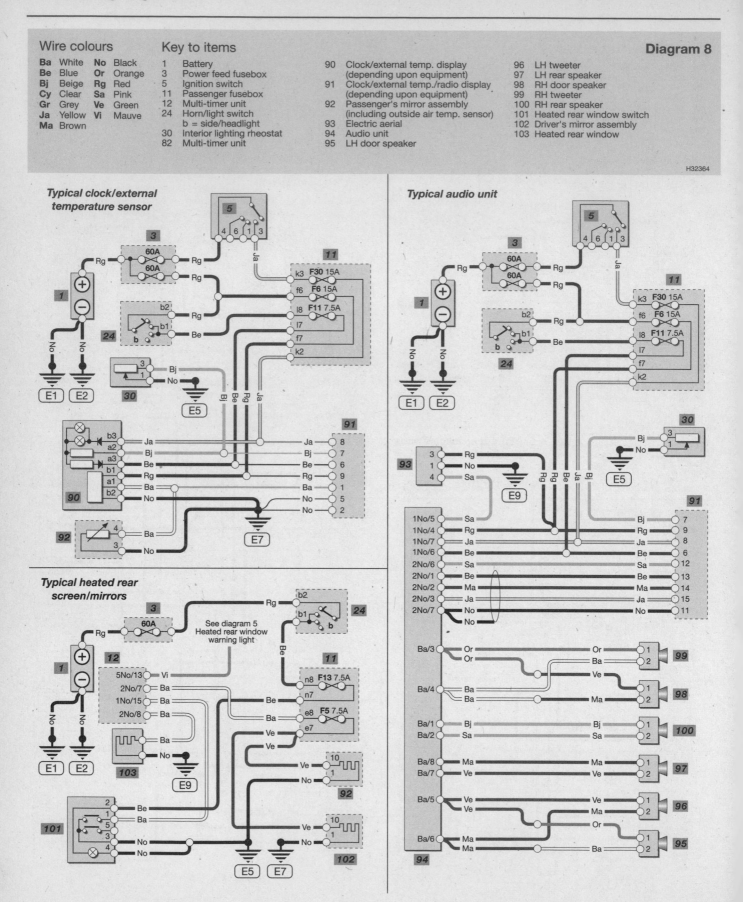

Diagram 8

Wire colours

Ba	White	**No**	Black
Be	Blue	**Or**	Orange
Bj	Beige	**Rg**	Red
Cy	Clear	**Sa**	Pink
Gr	Grey	**Ve**	Green
Ja	Yellow	**Vi**	Mauve
Ma	Brown		

Key to items

1 Battery
3 Power feed fusebox
5 Ignition switch
11 Passenger fusebox
12 Multi-timer unit
24 Horn/light switch
b = side/headlight
30 Interior lighting rheostat
82 Multi-timer unit
90 Clock/external temp. display (depending upon equipment)
91 Clock/external temp./radio display (depending upon equipment)
92 Passenger's mirror assembly (including outside air temp. sensor)
93 Electric aerial
94 Audio unit
95 LH door speaker
96 LH tweeter
97 LH rear speaker
98 RH door speaker
99 RH tweeter
100 RH rear speaker
101 Heated rear window switch
102 Driver's mirror assembly
103 Heated rear window

H32364

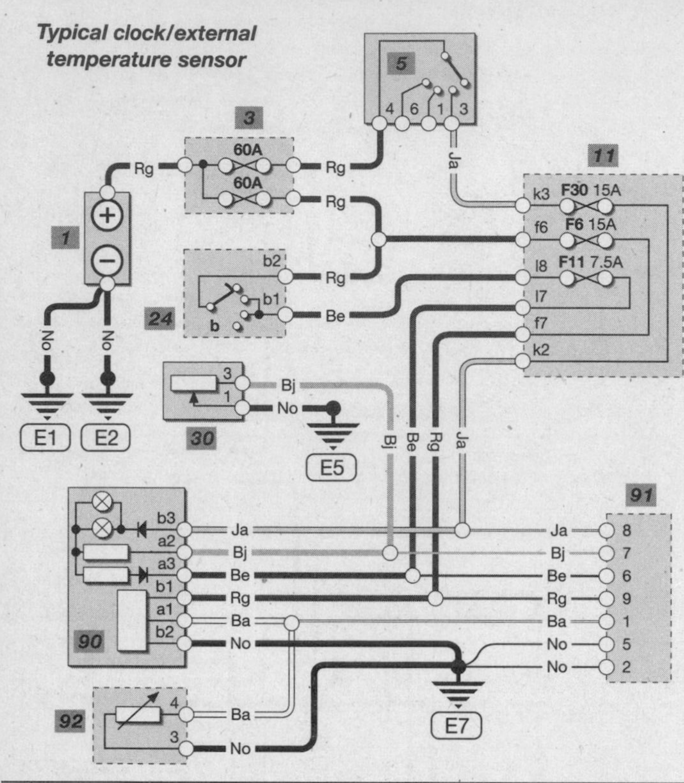

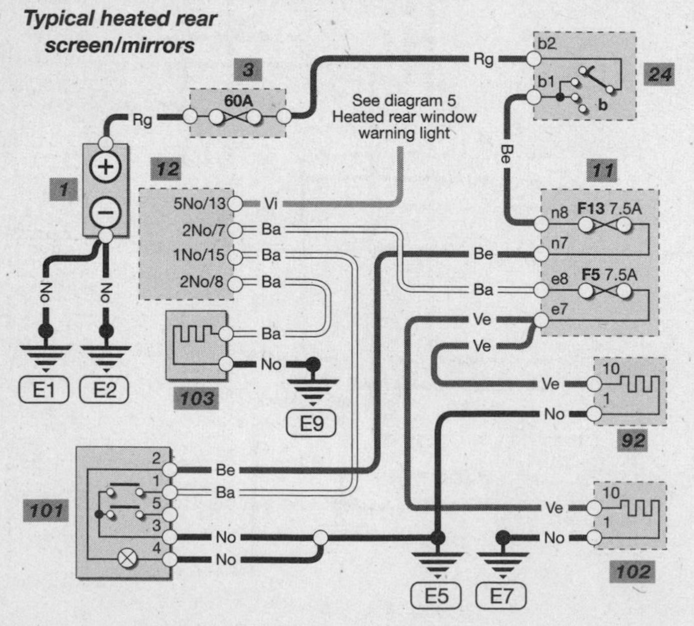

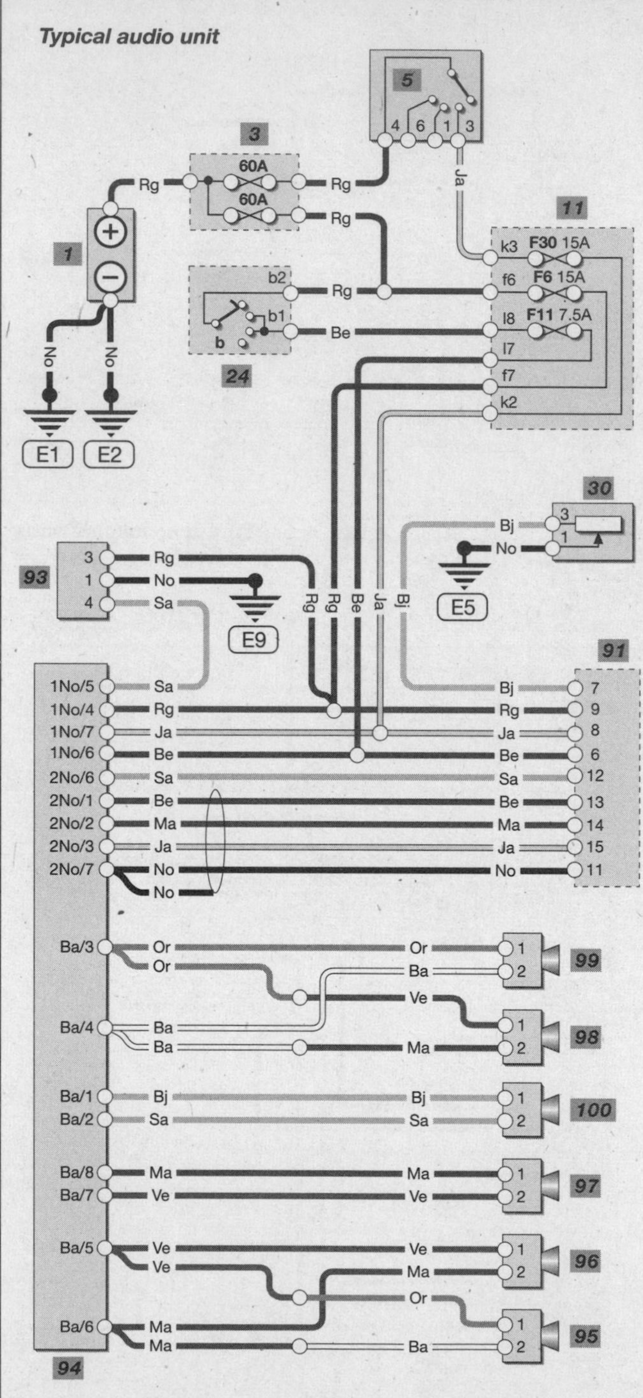

Diagram 9

Wire colours

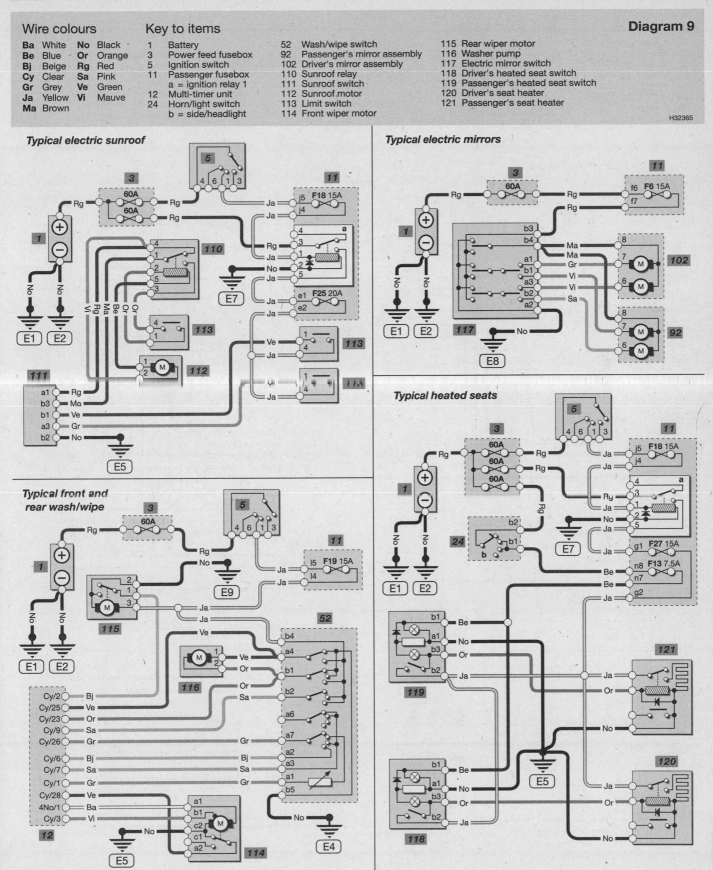

Ba	White	**No**	Black
Be	Blue	**Or**	Orange
Bj	Beige	**Rg**	Red
Cy	Clear	**Sa**	Pink
Gr	Grey	**Ve**	Green
Ja	Yellow	**Vi**	Mauve
Ma	Brown		

Key to items

1 Battery
3 Power feed fusebox
5 Ignition switch
11 Passenger fusebox
a = ignition relay 1
12 Multi-timer unit
24 Horn/light switch
b = side/headlight
52 Wash/wipe switch
92 Passenger's mirror assembly
102 Driver's mirror assembly
110 Sunroof relay
111 Sunroof switch
112 Sunroof motor
113 Limit switch
114 Front wiper motor
115 Rear wiper motor
116 Washer pump
117 Electric mirror switch
118 Driver's heated seat switch
119 Passenger's heated seat switch
120 Driver's seat heater
121 Passenger's seat heater

H32365

Typical electric sunroof

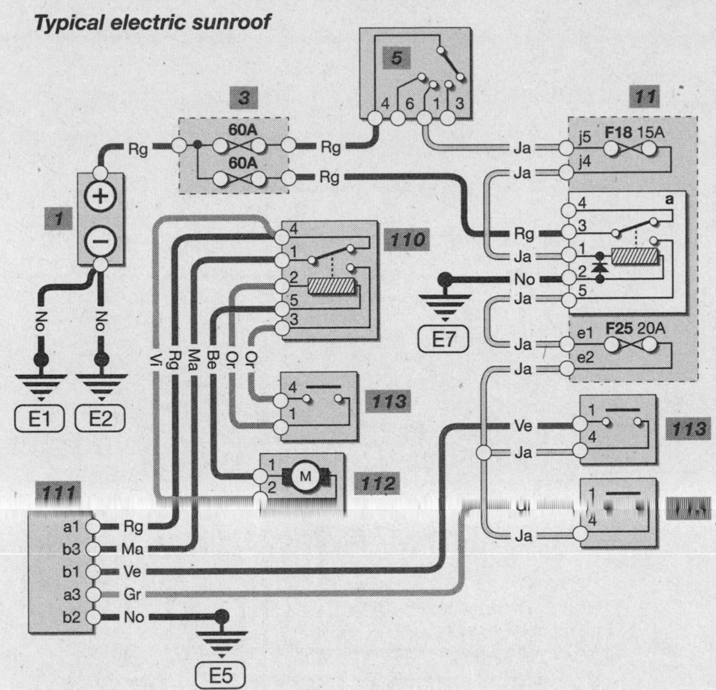

Typical electric mirrors

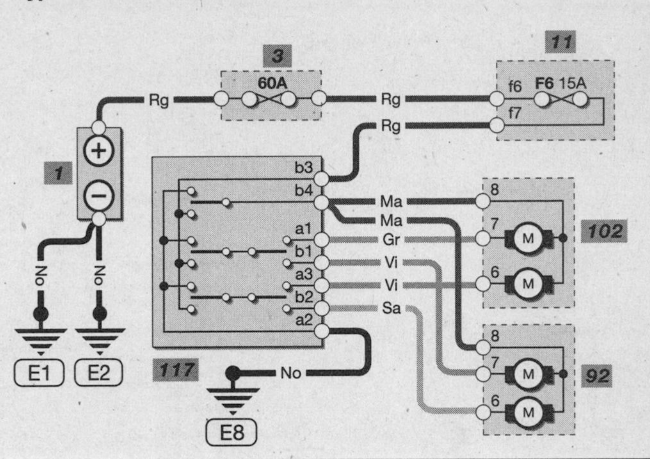

Typical front and rear wash/wipe

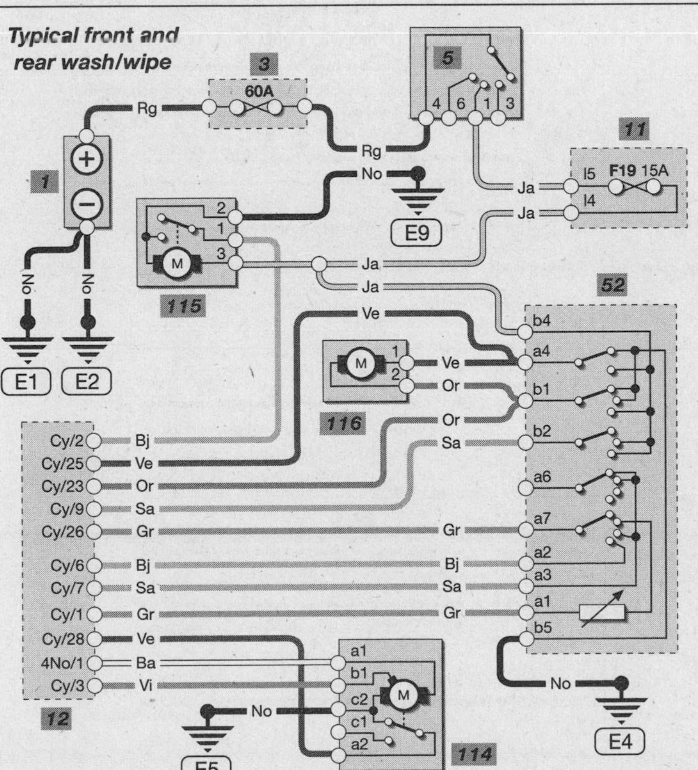

Typical heated seats

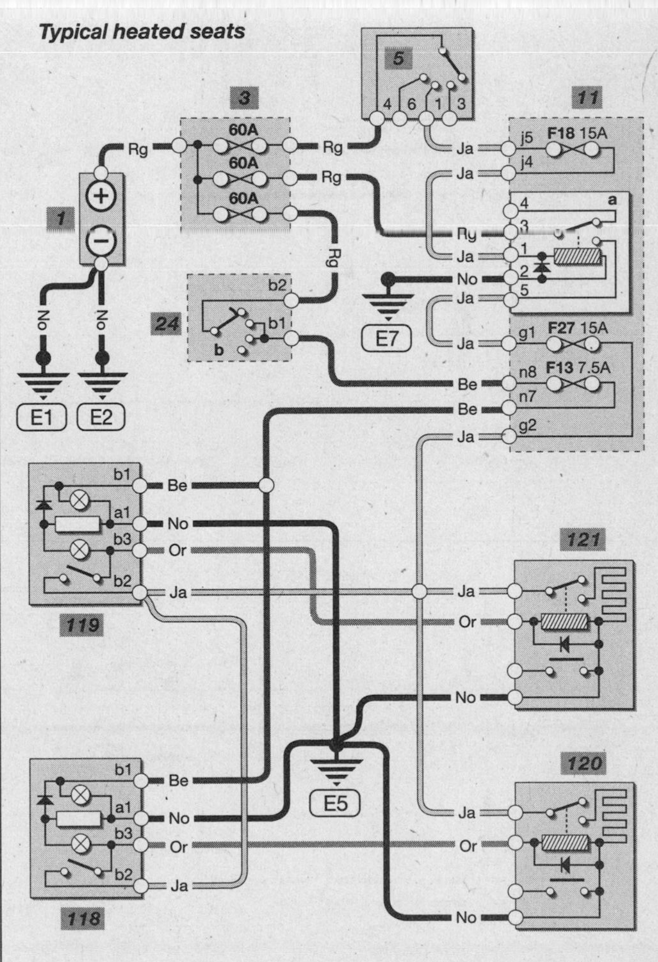

Diagram 10

Wire colours

Ba	White	**No**	Black
Be	Blue	**Or**	Orange
Bj	Beige	**Rg**	Red
Cy	Clear	**Sa**	Pink
Gr	Grey	**Ve**	Green
Ja	Yellow	**Vi**	Mauve
Ma	Brown		

Key to items

1 Battery
3 Power feed fusebox
5 Ignition switch
11 Passenger fusebox
12 Multi-timer unit
24 Horn/light switch
b = side/headlight
125 Driver's switch for front passenger window
126 Driver's switch for front driver's window
127 Passenger's window switch
128 Driver's window motor
129 Passenger's window motor
130 Electric window relay
131 Rear widow locking switch
132 LH rear window switch
133 RH rear window switch
134 LH rear window motor
135 RH rear window motor
136 Central locking interior switch
137 Passenger's door lock motor
138 Driver's door lock motor
139 Fuel filler flap lock motor
140 LH rear door lock motor
141 RH rear door lock motor
142 Boot lid/tailgate lock motor

H32366

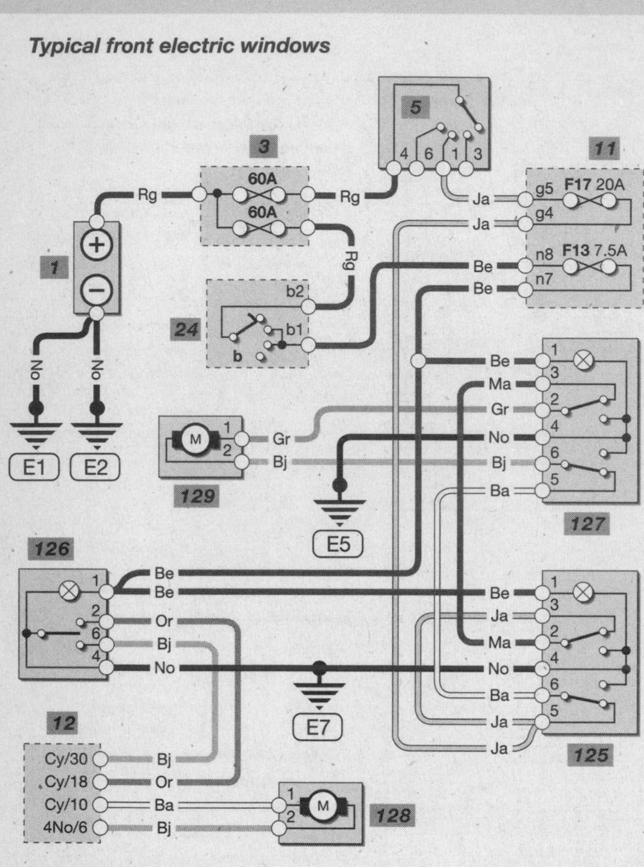

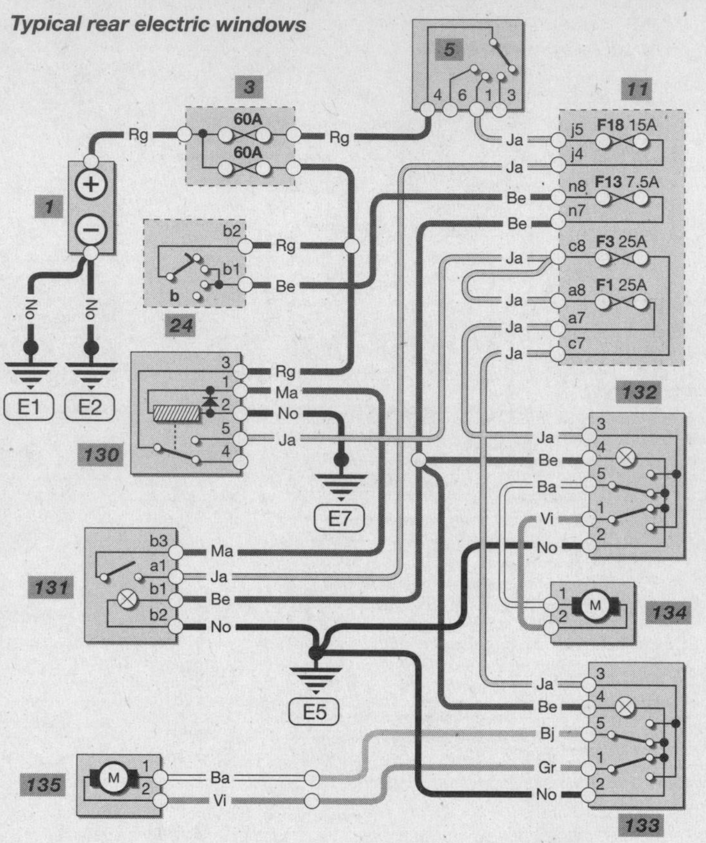

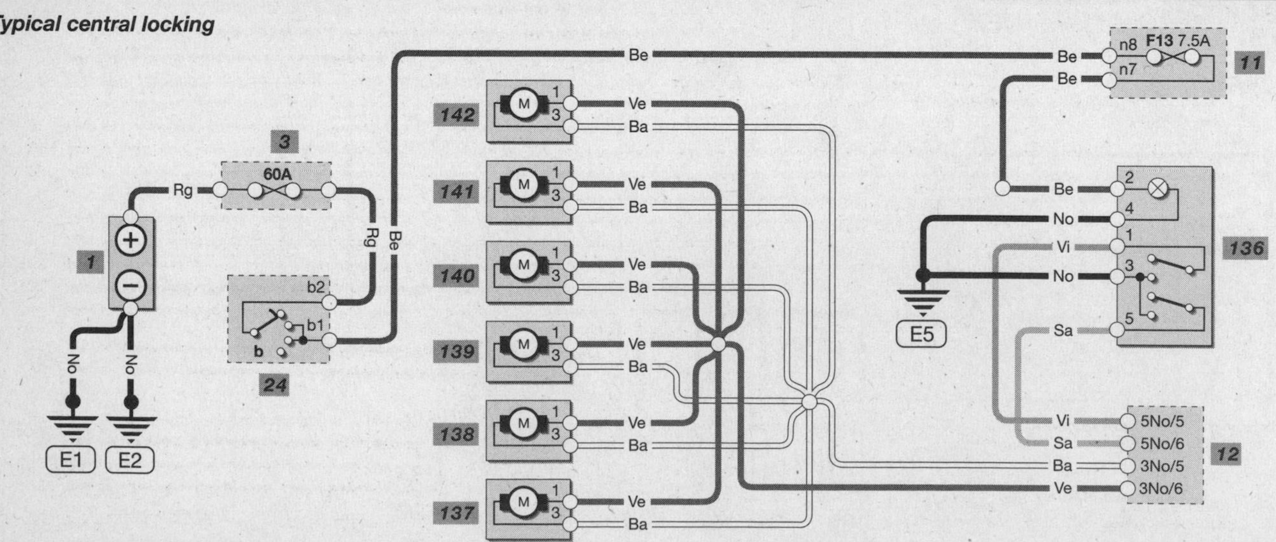

Diagram 11

Wire colours

Ba	White	**No**	Black
Be	Blue	**Or**	Orange
Bj	Beige	**Rg**	Red
Cy	Clear	**Sa**	Pink
Gr	Grey	**Ve**	Green
Ja	Yellow	**Vi**	Mauve
Ma	Brown		

Key to items

1 Battery
3 Power feed fusebox
4 Engine relay/fusebox
  d = injection locking relay
  f = fuel pump relay
5 Ignition switch
11 Passenger fusebox
12 Multi-timer unit
47 Fuel gauge sender unit/fuel pump
145 Inertia switch
146 Fuel injector
147 Throttle potentiometer
148 Inlet air temperature sensor
149 Knock sensor
150 Carbon canister valve
151 Oxygen sensor
152 MAP sensor
153 Idle stepper motor
154 Coolant temperature sensor
155 Engine management control unit
156 TDC sensor
157 Power steering pressure switch
158 Ignition coil

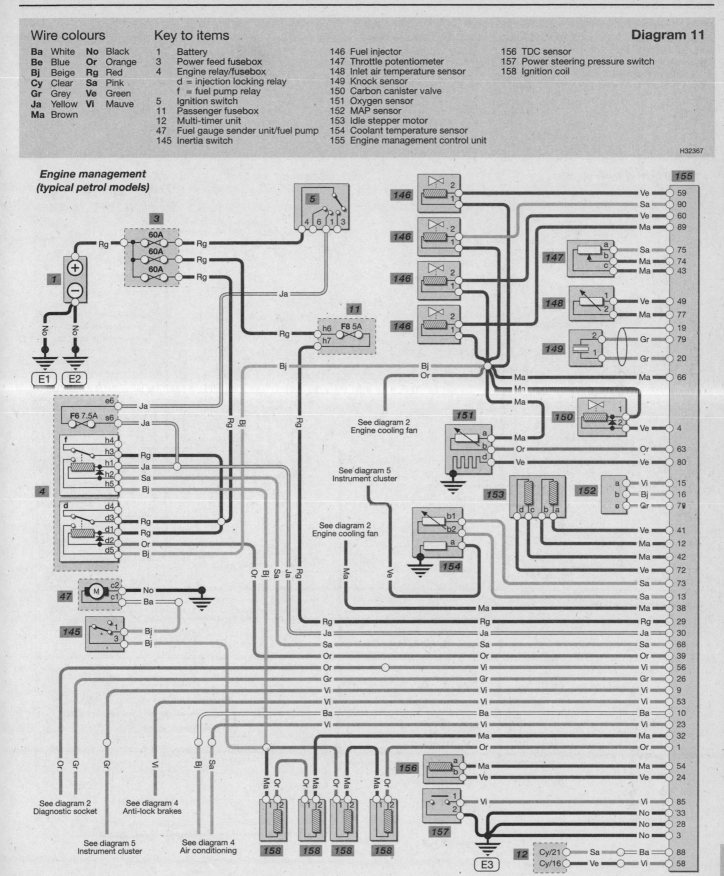

H32367

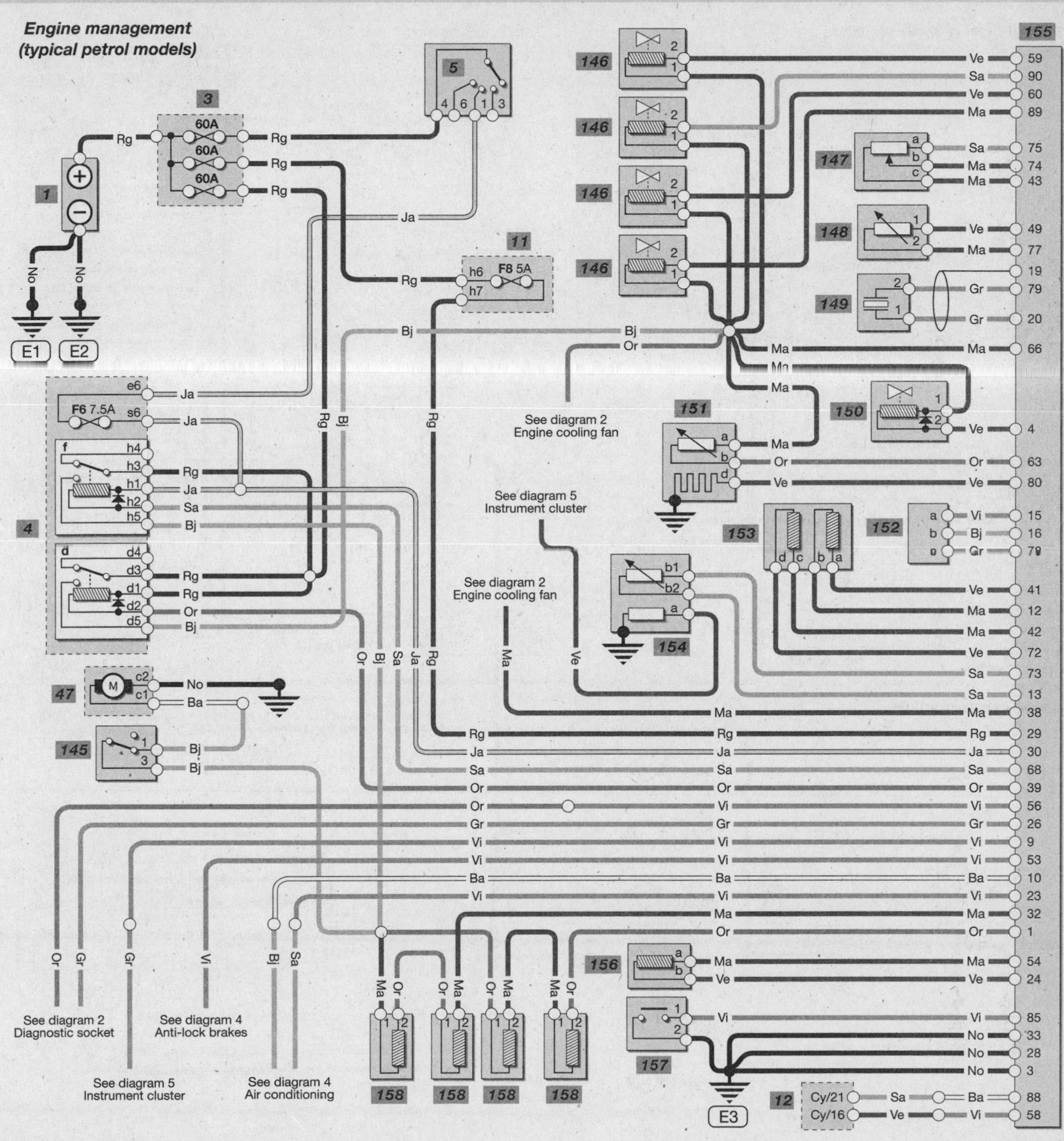

Wire colours

Ba	White	**No**	Black
Be	Blue	**Or**	Orange
Bj	Beige	**Rg**	Red
Cy	Clear	**Sa**	Pink
Gr	Grey	**Ve**	Green
Ja	Yellow	**Vi**	Mauve
Ma	Brown		

Key to items

1 Battery
2 Battery +ve protection unit
3 Power feed fusebox
4 Engine relay/fusebox
d = injection locking relay
5 Ignition switch
12 Multi-timer unit
148 Inlet air temperature sensor
154 Coolant temperature sensor
155 Engine management control unit
156 TDC sensor
157 Preheater unit
158 EGR solenoid valve
159 Diesel pump unit
160 Accelerator potentiometer
161 Glow plug

Diagram 12

H32368

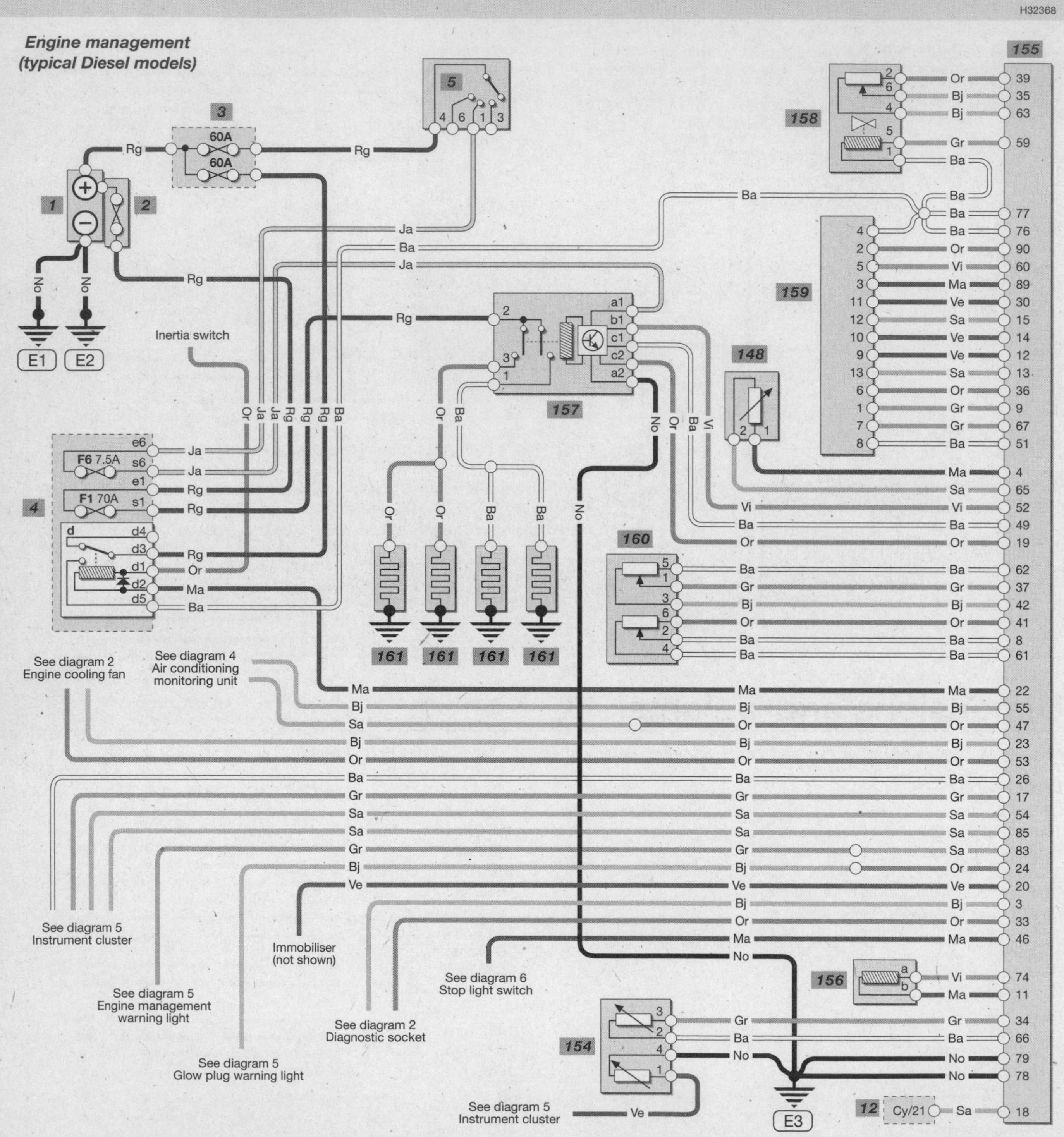

Dimensions and weights

Note: *All figures are typical and vary according to model. Refer to manufacturer's data for exact figures.*

Dimensions

Overall length:	
Hatchback	4164 mm
Saloon (Classic)	4436 mm
Scénic	4169 mm
Overall width (not including door mirrors)	1698 mm
Overall height (unladen):	
Mégane	1420 mm
Scénic	1675 mm
Wheelbase	2580 mm
Front track	1450 mm
Rear track:	
Hatchback	1432 mm
Saloon (Classic)	1422 mm
Scénic	1485 mm
Turning circle:	
Between walls	11.4 metres
Between kerbs	10.7 metres

Dimensions and weights

Weights

Kerb weight:	
Mégane Hatchback:	
1.4 litre 16-valve	1080 kg
1.6 litre manual	1085 kg
1.6 litre automatic	1115 kg
1.9 litre	
dTi	1140 kg
dCi	1145 kg
Mégane Saloon (Classic):	
1.4 litre 16-valve	1090 kg
1.6 litre manual	1090 kg
1.6 litre automatic	1130 kg
1.9 litre:	
dTi	1140 kg
dCi	1150 kg
Scénic:	
1.4 litre 16-valve	1235 kg
1.6 litre manual	1250 kg
1.6 litre automatic	1280 kg
2.0 litre manual	1290 kg
2.0 litre automatic	1320 kg
1.9 litre	1290 kg
Maximum gross vehicle weight:	
Mégane Hatchback:	
1.4 litre 16-valve	1595 kg
1.6 litre manual	1600 kg
1.6 litre automatic	1630 kg
1.9 litre	1650 kg
Mégane Saloon (Classic):	
1.4 litre 16-valve	1610 kg
1.6 litre manual	1620 kg
1.6 litre automatic	1650 kg
1.9 litre:	
dTi	1650 kg
dCi	1675 kg
Scénic:	
1.4 litre 16-valve	1795 kg
1.6 litre manual	1800 kg
1.6 litre automatic	1840 kg
2.0 litre manual	1815 kg
2.0 litre automatic	1845 kg
1.9 litre	1840 kg
Maximum braked towing weight (driver only):	
Mégane Hatchback and Saloon (Classic)	1250 kg
Scénic:	
All models except 1.6 litre automatic and 2.0 litre)	1300 kg
1.6 litre automatic	1250 kg
2.0 litre	1350 kg
Maximum unbraked towing weight (driver only):	
Mégane Hatchback:	
1.4 litre 16-valve	575 kg
1.6 litre manual	580 kg
1.6 litre automatic	595 kg
1.9 litre	605 kg
Mégane Saloon (Classic):	
1.4 litre 16-valve	580 kg
1.6 litre manual	580 kg
1.6 litre automatic	600 kg
1.9 litre:	
dTi	605 kg
dCi	610 kg
Scénic:	
1.4 litre 16-valve	655 kg
1.6 litre manual	660 kg
1.6 litre automatic	675 kg
2.0 litre manual	680 kg
2.0 litre automatic	695 kg
1.9 litre	680 kg

Length (distance)

Inches (in)	x 25.4	= Millimetres (mm)	x 0.0394	= Inches (in)
Feet (ft)	x 0.305	= Metres (m)	x 3.281	= Feet (ft)
Miles	x 1.609	= Kilometres (km)	x 0.621	= Miles

Volume (capacity)

Cubic inches (cu in; in^3)	x 16.387	= Cubic centimetres (cc; cm^3)	x 0.061	= Cubic inches (cu in; in^3)
Imperial pints (Imp pt)	x 0.568	= Litres (l)	x 1.76	= Imperial pints (Imp pt)
Imperial quarts (Imp qt)	x 1.137	= Litres (l)	x 0.88	= Imperial quarts (Imp qt)
Imperial quarts (Imp qt)	x 1.201	= US quarts (US qt)	x 0.833	= Imperial quarts (Imp qt)
US quarts (US qt)	x 0.946	= Litres (l)	x 1.057	= US quarts (US qt)
Imperial gallons (Imp gal)	x 4.546	= Litres (l)	x 0.22	= Imperial gallons (Imp gal)
Imperial gallons (Imp gal)	x 1.201	= US gallons (US gal)	x 0.833	= Imperial gallons (Imp gal)
US gallons (US gal)	x 3.785	= Litres (l)	x 0.264	= US gallons (US gal)

Mass (weight)

Ounces (oz)	x 28.35	= Grams (g)	x 0.035	= Ounces (oz)
Pounds (lb)	x 0.454	= Kilograms (kg)	x 2.205	= Pounds (lb)

Force

Ounces-force (ozf; oz)	x 0.278	= Newtons (N)	x 3.6	= Ounces-force (ozf; oz)
Pounds-force (lbf; lb)	x 4.448	= Newtons (N)	x 0.225	= Pounds-force (lbf; lb)
Newtons (N)	x 0.1	= Kilograms-force (kgf; kg)	x 9.81	= Newtons (N)

Pressure

Pounds-force per square inch (psi; lbf/in^2; lb/in^2)	x 0.070	= Kilograms-force per square centimetre (kgf/cm^2; kg/cm^2)	x 14.223	= Pounds-force per square inch (psi; lbf/in^2; lb/in^2)
Pounds-force per square inch (psi; lbf/in^2; lb/in^2)	x 0.068	= Atmospheres (atm)	x 14.696	= Pounds-force per square inch (psi; lbf/in^2; lb/in^2)
Pounds-force per square inch (psi; lbf/in^2; lb/in^2)	x 0.069	= Bars	x 14.5	= Pounds-force per square inch (psi; lbf/in^2; lb/in^2)
Pounds-force per square inch (psi; lbf/in^2; lb/in^2)	x 6.895	= Kilopascals (kPa)	x 0.145	= Pounds-force per square inch (psi; lbf/in^2; lb/in^2)
Kilopascals (kPa)	x 0.01	= Kilograms-force per square centimetre (kgf/cm^2; kg/cm^2)	x 98.1	= Kilopascals (kPa)
Millibar (mbar)	x 100	= Pascals (Pa)	x 0.01	= Millibar (mbar)
Millibar (mbar)	x 0.0145	= Pounds-force per square inch (psi; lbf/in^2; lb/in^2)	x 68.947	= Millibar (mbar)
Millibar (mbar)	x 0.75	= Millimetres of mercury (mmHg)	x 1.333	= Millibar (mbar)
Millibar (mbar)	x 0.401	= Inches of water (inH$_2$O)	x 2.491	= Millibar (mbar)
Millimetres of mercury (mmHg)	x 0.535	= Inches of water (inH$_2$O)	x 1.868	= Millimetres of mercury (mmHg)
Inches of water (inH$_2$O)	x 0.036	= Pounds-force per square inch (psi; lbf/in^2; lb/in^2)	x 27.68	= Inches of water (inH$_2$O)

Torque (moment of force)

Pounds-force inches (lbf in; lb in)	x 1.152	= Kilograms-force centimetre (kgf cm; kg cm)	x 0.868	= Pounds-force inches (lbf in; lb in)
Pounds-force inches (lbf in; lb in)	x 0.113	= Newton metres (Nm)	x 8.85	= Pounds-force inches (lbf in; lb in)
Pounds-force inches (lbf in; lb in)	x 0.083	= Pounds-force feet (lbf ft; lb ft)	x 12	= Pounds-force inches (lbf in; lb in)
Pounds-force feet (lbf ft; lb ft)	x 0.138	= Kilograms-force metres (kgf m; kg m)	x 7.233	= Pounds-force feet (lbf ft; lb ft)
Pounds-force feet (lbf ft; lb ft)	x 1.356	= Newton metres (Nm)	x 0.738	= Pounds-force feet (lbf ft; lb ft)
Newton metres (Nm)	x 0.102	= Kilograms-force metres (kgf m; kg m)	x 9.804	= Newton metres (Nm)

Power

Horsepower (hp)	x 745.7	= Watts (W)	x 0.0013	= Horsepower (hp)

Velocity (speed)

Miles per hour (miles/hr; mph)	x 1.609	= Kilometres per hour (km/hr; kph)	x 0.621	= Miles per hour (miles/hr; mph)

Fuel consumption*

Miles per gallon, Imperial (mpg)	x 0.354	= Kilometres per litre (km/l)	x 2.825	= Miles per gallon, Imperial (mpg)
Miles per gallon, US (mpg)	x 0.425	= Kilometres per litre (km/l)	x 2.352	= Miles per gallon, US (mpg)

Temperature

Degrees Fahrenheit = (°C x 1.8) + 32

Degrees Celsius (Degrees Centigrade; °C) = (°F - 32) x 0.56

** It is common practice to convert from miles per gallon (mpg) to litres/100 kilometres (l/100km), where mpg x l/100 km = 282*

General repair procedures

Whenever servicing, repair or overhaul work is carried out on the car or its components, observe the following procedures and instructions. This will assist in carrying out the operation efficiently and to a professional standard of workmanship.

Joint mating faces and gaskets

When separating components at their mating faces, never insert screwdrivers or similar implements into the joint between the faces in order to prise them apart. This can cause severe damage which results in oil leaks, coolant leaks, etc upon reassembly. Separation is usually achieved by tapping along the joint with a soft-faced hammer in order to break the seal. However, note that this method may not be suitable where dowels are used for component location.

Where a gasket is used between the mating faces of two components, a new one must be fitted on reassembly; fit it dry unless otherwise stated in the repair procedure. Make sure that the mating faces are clean and dry, with all traces of old gasket removed. When cleaning a joint face, use a tool which is unlikely to score or damage the face, and remove any burrs or nicks with an oilstone or fine file.

Make sure that tapped holes are cleaned with a pipe cleaner, and keep them free of jointing compound, if this is being used, unless specifically instructed otherwise.

Ensure that all orifices, channels or pipes are clear, and blow through them, preferably using compressed air.

Oil seals

Oil seals can be removed by levering them out with a wide flat-bladed screwdriver or similar implement. Alternatively, a number of self-tapping screws may be screwed into the seal, and these used as a purchase for pliers or some similar device in order to pull the seal free.

Whenever an oil seal is removed from its working location, either individually or as part of an assembly, it should be renewed.

The very fine sealing lip of the seal is easily damaged, and will not seal if the surface it contacts is not completely clean and free from scratches, nicks or grooves. If the original sealing surface of the component cannot be restored, and the manufacturer has not made provision for slight relocation of the seal relative to the sealing surface, the component should be renewed.

Protect the lips of the seal from any surface which may damage them in the course of fitting. Use tape or a conical sleeve where possible. Lubricate the seal lips with oil before fitting and, on dual-lipped seals, fill the space between the lips with grease.

Unless otherwise stated, oil seals must be fitted with their sealing lips toward the lubricant to be sealed.

Use a tubular drift or block of wood of the appropriate size to install the seal and, if the seal housing is shouldered, drive the seal down to the shoulder. If the seal housing is unshouldered, the seal should be fitted with its face flush with the housing top face (unless otherwise instructed).

Screw threads and fastenings

Seized nuts, bolts and screws are quite a common occurrence where corrosion has set in, and the use of penetrating oil or releasing fluid will often overcome this problem if the offending item is soaked for a while before attempting to release it. The use of an impact driver may also provide a means of releasing such stubborn fastening devices, when used in conjunction with the appropriate screwdriver bit or socket. If none of these methods works, it may be necessary to resort to the careful application of heat, or the use of a hacksaw or nut splitter device.

Studs are usually removed by locking two nuts together on the threaded part, and then using a spanner on the lower nut to unscrew the stud. Studs or bolts which have broken off below the surface of the component in which they are mounted can sometimes be removed using a stud extractor. Always ensure that a blind tapped hole is completely free from oil, grease, water or other fluid before installing the bolt or stud. Failure to do this could cause the housing to crack due to the hydraulic action of the bolt or stud as it is screwed in.

When tightening a castellated nut to accept a split pin, tighten the nut to the specified torque, where applicable, and then tighten further to the next split pin hole. Never slacken the nut to align the split pin hole, unless stated in the repair procedure.

When checking or retightening a nut or bolt to a specified torque setting, slacken the nut or bolt by a quarter of a turn, and then retighten to the specified setting. However, this should not be attempted where angular tightening has been used.

For some screw fastenings, notably cylinder head bolts or nuts, torque wrench settings are no longer specified for the latter stages of tightening, "angle-tightening" being called up instead. Typically, a fairly low torque wrench setting will be applied to the bolts/nuts in the correct sequence, followed by one or more stages of tightening through specified angles.

Locknuts, locktabs and washers

Any fastening which will rotate against a component or housing during tightening should always have a washer between it and the relevant component or housing.

Spring or split washers should always be renewed when they are used to lock a critical component such as a big-end bearing retaining bolt or nut. Locktabs which are folded over to retain a nut or bolt should always be renewed.

Self-locking nuts can be re-used in non-critical areas, providing resistance can be felt when the locking portion passes over the bolt or stud thread. However, it should be noted that self-locking stiffnuts tend to lose their effectiveness after long periods of use, and should then be renewed as a matter of course.

Split pins must always be replaced with new ones of the correct size for the hole.

When thread-locking compound is found on the threads of a fastener which is to be re-used, it should be cleaned off with a wire brush and solvent, and fresh compound applied on reassembly.

Special tools

Some repair procedures in this manual entail the use of special tools such as a press, two or three-legged pullers, spring compressors, etc. Wherever possible, suitable readily-available alternatives to the manufacturer's special tools are described, and are shown in use. In some instances, where no alternative is possible, it has been necessary to resort to the use of a manufacturer's tool, and this has been done for reasons of safety as well as the efficient completion of the repair operation. Unless you are highly-skilled and have a thorough understanding of the procedures described, never attempt to bypass the use of any special tool when the procedure described specifies its use. Not only is there a very great risk of personal injury, but expensive damage could be caused to the components involved.

Environmental considerations

When disposing of used engine oil, brake fluid, antifreeze, etc, give due consideration to any detrimental environmental effects. Do not, for instance, pour any of the above liquids down drains into the general sewage system, or onto the ground to soak away. Many local council refuse tips provide a facility for waste oil disposal, as do some garages. If none of these facilities are available, consult your local Environmental Health Department, or the National Rivers Authority, for further advice.

With the universal tightening-up of legislation regarding the emission of environmentally-harmful substances from motor vehicles, most vehicles have tamperproof devices fitted to the main adjustment points of the fuel system. These devices are primarily designed to prevent unqualified persons from adjusting the fuel/air mixture, with the chance of a consequent increase in toxic emissions. If such devices are found during servicing or overhaul, they should, wherever possible, be renewed or refitted in accordance with the manufacturer's requirements or current legislation.

OIL CARE
FOLLOW THE CODE
OIL BANK LINE
0800 66 33 66
www.oilbankline.org.uk

Note: It is antisocial and illegal to dump oil down the drain. To find the location of your local oil recycling bank, call this number free.

Spare parts are available from many sources, including maker's appointed garages, accessory shops, and motor factors. To be sure of obtaining the correct parts, it will sometimes be necessary to quote the vehicle identification number. If possible, it can also be useful to take the old parts along for positive identification. Items such as starter motors and alternators may be available under a service exchange scheme – any parts returned should be clean.

Our advice regarding spare parts is as follows.

Officially appointed garages

This is the best source of parts which are peculiar to your car, and which are not otherwise generally available (eg, badges, interior trim, certain body panels, etc). It is also the only place at which you should buy parts if the vehicle is still under warranty.

Accessory shops

These are very good places to buy materials and components needed for the maintenance of your car (oil, air and fuel filters, light bulbs, drivebelts, greases, brake pads, touch-up paint, etc). Components of this nature sold by a reputable shop are usually of the same standard as those used by the car manufacturer.

Besides components, these shops also sell tools and general accessories, usually have convenient opening hours, charge lower prices, and can often be found close to home. Some accessory shops have parts counters where components needed for almost any repair job can be purchased or ordered.

Motor factors

Good factors will stock all the more important components which wear out comparatively quickly, and can sometimes supply individual components needed for the overhaul of a larger assembly (eg, brake seals and hydraulic parts, bearing shells, pistons, valves). They may also handle work such as cylinder block reboring, crankshaft regrinding, etc.

Tyre and exhaust specialists

These outlets may be independent, or members of a local or national chain. They frequently offer competitive prices when compared with a main dealer or local garage, but it will pay to obtain several quotes before making a decision. When researching prices, also ask what 'extras' may be added – for instance fitting a new valve and balancing the wheel are both commonly charged on top of the price of a new tyre.

Other sources

Beware of parts or materials obtained from market stalls, car boot sales or similar outlets. Such items are not invariably sub-standard, but there is little chance of compensation if they do prove unsatisfactory. in the case of safety-critical components such as brake pads, there is the risk not only of financial loss, but also of an accident causing injury or death.

Second-hand components or assemblies obtained from a car breaker can be a good buy in some circumstances, but this sort of purchase is best made by the experienced DIY mechanic.

Jacking and vehicle support

The jack supplied with the car should only be used for changing the roadwheels – see *Wheel changing* at the front of this manual. When carrying out any other kind of work, raise the vehicle using a hydraulic trolley jack, and always supplement the jack with axle stands positioned under the vehicle jacking points.

When using a hydraulic jack or axle stands, always position the jack head or axle stand head under one of the relevant jacking points **(see illustration)**.

Do not jack the vehicle under any other part of the sill, sump, floor pan, or any of the steering or suspension components. With the vehicle raised, the axle stands should be positioned beneath the vehicle jack location points on the sill.

Warning: Never work under, around, or near a raised car, unless it is adequately supported.

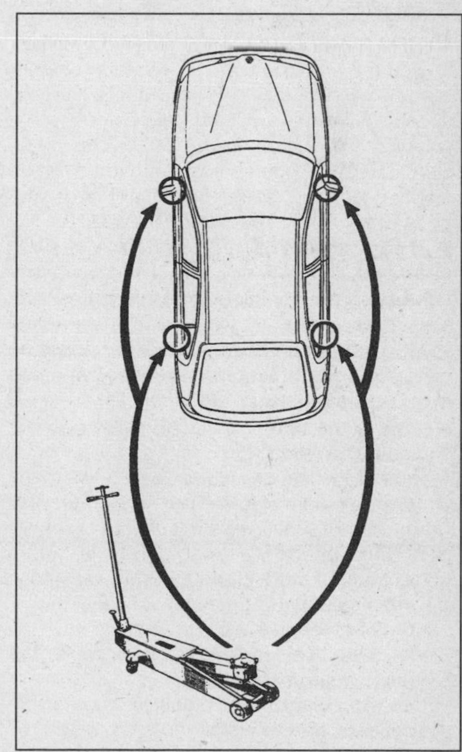

Vehicle jacking points

Vehicle identification numbers

Modifications are a continuing and unpublicised process in vehicle manufacture, quite apart from major model changes. Spare parts manuals and lists are compiled upon a numerical basis, the individual vehicle identification numbers being essential to correct identification of the component concerned.

When ordering spare parts, always give as much information as possible. Quote the car model, year of manufacture, body and engine numbers as appropriate.

The *Vehicle Identification Number (VIN)* plate is located on the door pillar behind the driver's door. The plate carries the VIN number, chassis number, vehicle weight information and various other information, depending on territory **(see illustrations)**.

The *engine number* is located on a meta plate attached to the front of the engine **(se illustration)**.

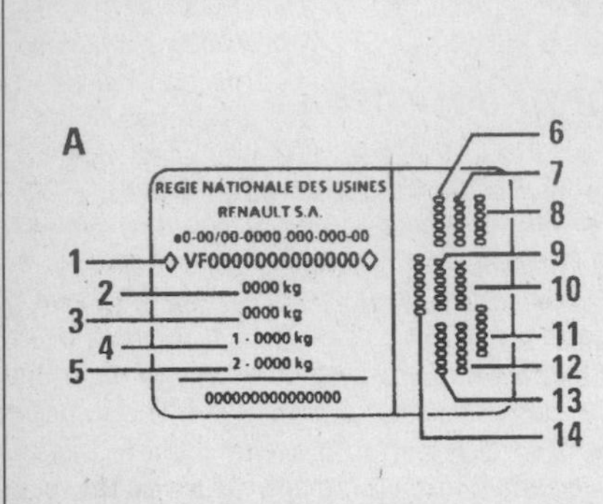

1 Vehicle type and chassis number
2 Maximum permissible all-up weight
3 Maximum permissible total train weight
4 Maximum permissible front axle loading
5 Maximum permissible rear axle loading
6 Technical specifications
7 Paint code
8 Equipment level
9 Vehicle type
10 Trim code
11 Additional equipment code
12 Fabrication number
13 Interior matching trim code

Vehicle identification plate numbers

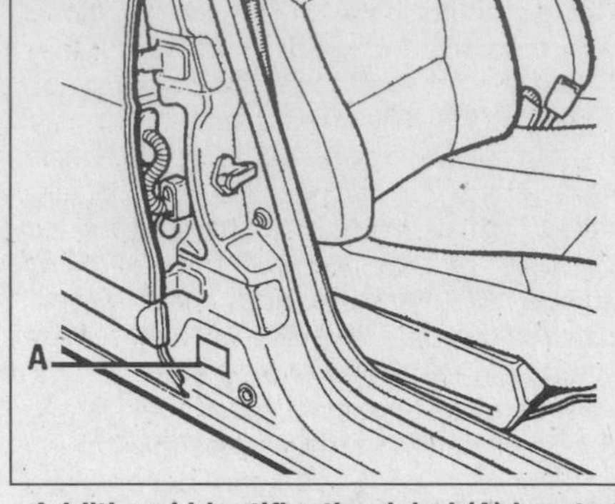

Additional identification label (A) located on the right-hand centre pillar

Engine number location on diesel engines

The chassis number is stamped onto the top of the right-hand front suspension turret (Mégane)

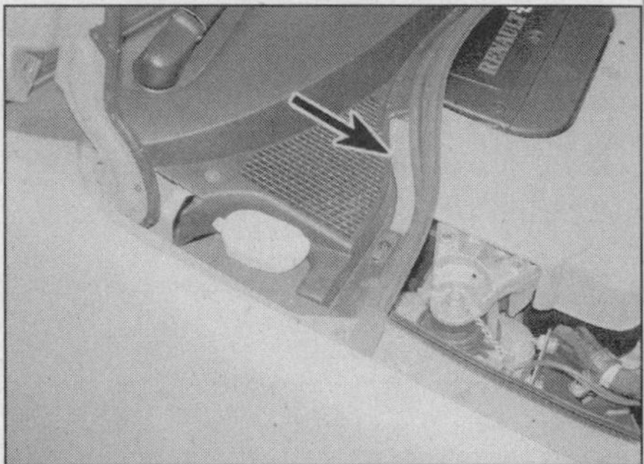

The chassis number is stamped onto the top of the right-hand scuttle panel (Scénic)

Disconnecting the battery

Several systems fitted to the vehicle require battery power to be available at all times, either to ensure their continued operation (such as the clock), or to maintain electronic memory settings which would otherwise be erased. Whenever the battery is to be disconnected, first note the following points, to ensure there are no unforeseen consequences:

a) *First, on any vehicle with central door locking, it is a wise precaution to remove the key from the ignition, and to keep it with you, so that it does not get locked in if the central locking engages when the battery is reconnected.*

b) *If a security-coded audio unit is fitted, and the unit and/or the battery is disconnected, the unit will not function again on reconnection until the correct security code is entered. Details of this procedure, which varies according to the unit fitted and vehicle model, are given in the vehicle owner's handbook. Where necessary, ensure you have the correct code before you disconnect the battery. If you do not have the code or details of the correct procedure, but can supply proof of ownership and a legitimate reason for wanting this information, a Renault dealer may be able to help.*

c) *On vehicles equipped with an original equipment anti-theft alarm system, before disconnecting the battery, de-activate the alarm siren, using the dedicated key. When reconnecting the battery, as soon as the battery is reconnected, the alarm is automatically activated. Use the remote control transmitter to turn off the alarm, then activate the alarm siren using the dedicated key.*

Devices known as 'memory-savers' or 'code-savers' can be used to avoid some of the above problems. Precise details of use vary according to the device used. Typically, it is plugged into the cigar lighter socket, and is connected by its own wiring to a spare battery; the vehicle battery is then disconnected from the electrical system, leaving the memory-saver to pass sufficient current to maintain audio unit security codes and other memory values, and also to run permanently-live circuits such as the clock.

Warning: Some of these devices allow a considerable amount of current to pass, which can mean that many of the vehicle's systems are still operational when the main battery is disconnected. If a 'memory-saver' is used, ensure that the circuit concerned is actually 'dead' before carrying out any work on it!

Introduction

A selection of good tools is a fundamental requirement for anyone contemplating the maintenance and repair of a motor vehicle. For the owner who does not possess any, their purchase will prove a considerable expense, offsetting some of the savings made by doing-it-yourself. However, provided that the tools purchased meet the relevant national safety standards and are of good quality, they will last for many years and prove an extremely worthwhile investment.

To help the average owner to decide which tools are needed to carry out the various tasks detailed in this manual, we have compiled three lists of tools under the following headings: *Maintenance and minor repair*, *Repair and overhaul*, and *Special*. Newcomers to practical mechanics should start off with the *Maintenance and minor repair* tool kit, and confine themselves to the simpler jobs around the vehicle. Then, as confidence and experience grow, more difficult tasks can be undertaken, with extra tools being purchased as, and when, they are needed. In this way, a *Maintenance and minor repair* tool kit can be built up into a *Repair and overhaul* tool kit over a considerable period of time, without any major cash outlays. The experienced do-it-yourselfer will have a tool kit good enough for most repair and overhaul procedures, and will add tools from the *Special* category when it is felt that the expense is justified by the amount of use to which these tools will be put.

Maintenance and minor repair tool kit

The tools given in this list should be considered as a minimum requirement if routine maintenance, servicing and minor repair operations are to be undertaken. We recommend the purchase of combination spanners (ring one end, open-ended the other); although more expensive than open-ended ones, they do give the advantages of both types of spanner.

- ☐ *Combination spanners:*
  Metric - 8 to 19 mm inclusive
- ☐ *Adjustable spanner - 35 mm jaw (approx.)*
- ☐ *Spark plug spanner (with rubber insert) - petrol models*
- ☐ *Spark plug gap adjustment tool - petrol models*
- ☐ *Set of feeler gauges*
- ☐ *Brake bleed nipple spanner*
- ☐ *Screwdrivers:*
  Flat blade - 100 mm long x 6 mm dia
  Cross blade - 100 mm long x 6 mm dia
  Torx - various sizes (not all vehicles)
- ☐ *Combination pliers*
- ☐ *Hacksaw (junior)*
- ☐ *Tyre pump*
- ☐ *Tyre pressure gauge*
- ☐ *Oil can*
- ☐ *Oil filter removal tool*
- ☐ *Fine emery cloth*
- ☐ *Wire brush (small)*
- ☐ *Funnel (medium size)*
- ☐ *Sump drain plug key (not all vehicles)*

Repair and overhaul tool kit

These tools are virtually essential for anyone undertaking any major repairs to a motor vehicle, and are additional to those given in the *Maintenance and minor repair* list. Included in this list is a comprehensive set of sockets. Although these are expensive, they will be found invaluable as they are so versatile - particularly if various drives are included in the set. We recommend the half-inch square-drive type, as this can be used with most proprietary torque wrenches.

The tools in this list will sometimes need to be supplemented by tools from the *Special* list:

- ☐ *Sockets (or box spanners) to cover range in previous list (including Torx sockets)*
- ☐ *Reversible ratchet drive (for use with sockets)*
- ☐ *Extension piece, 250 mm (for use with sockets)*
- ☐ *Universal joint (for use with sockets)*
- ☐ *Flexible handle or sliding T "breaker bar" (for use with sockets)*
- ☐ *Torque wrench (for use with sockets)*
- ☐ *Self-locking grips*
- ☐ *Ball pein hammer*
- ☐ *Soft-faced mallet (plastic or rubber)*
- ☐ *Screwdrivers:*
  Flat blade - long & sturdy, short (chubby), and narrow (electrician's) types
  Cross blade – long & sturdy, and short (chubby) types
- ☐ *Pliers:*
  Long-nosed
  Side cutters (electrician's)
  Circlip (internal and external)
- ☐ *Cold chisel - 25 mm*
- ☐ *Scriber*
- ☐ *Scraper*
- ☐ *Centre-punch*
- ☐ *Pin punch*
- ☐ *Hacksaw*
- ☐ *Brake hose clamp*
- ☐ *Brake/clutch bleeding kit*
- ☐ *Selection of twist drills*
- ☐ *Steel rule/straight-edge*
- ☐ *Allen keys (inc. splined/Torx type)*
- ☐ *Selection of files*
- ☐ *Wire brush*
- ☐ *Axle stands*
- ☐ *Jack (strong trolley or hydraulic type)*
- ☐ *Light with extension lead*
- ☐ *Universal electrical multi-meter*

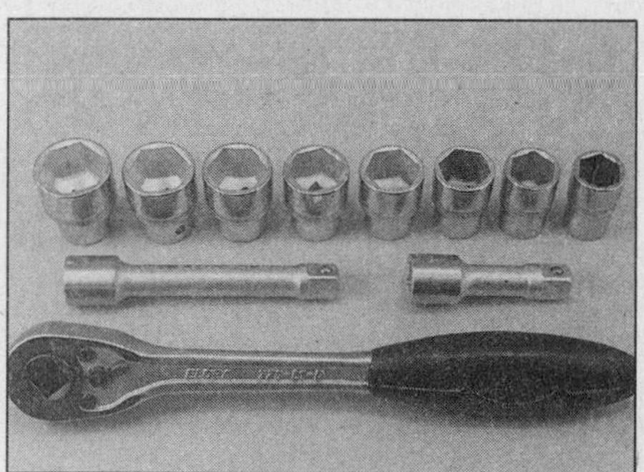
Sockets and reversible ratchet drive

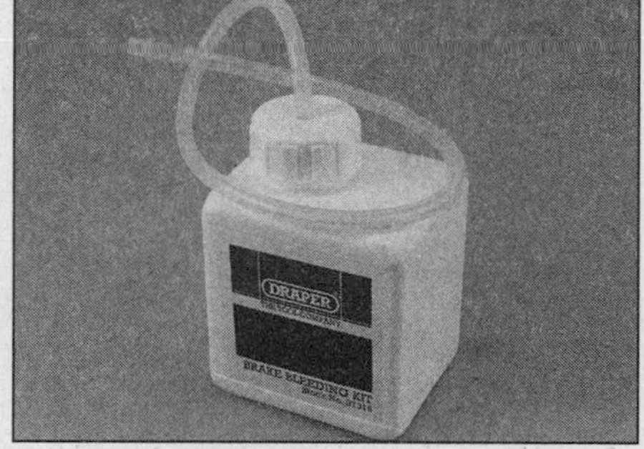
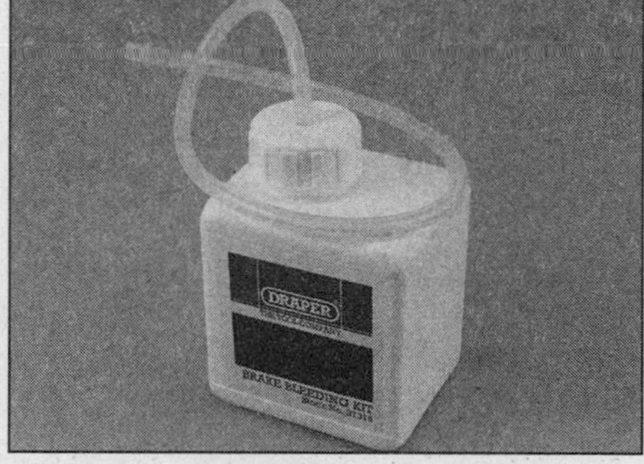

Brake bleeding kit

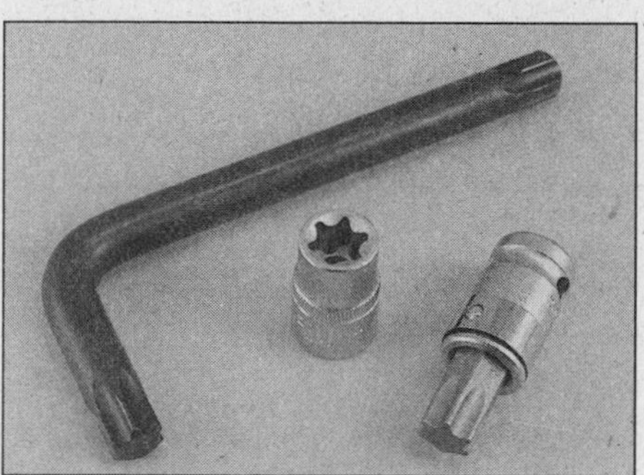
Torx key, socket and bit

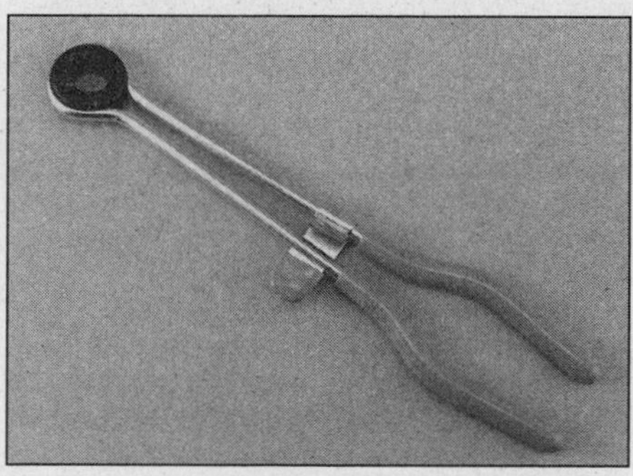
Hose clamp

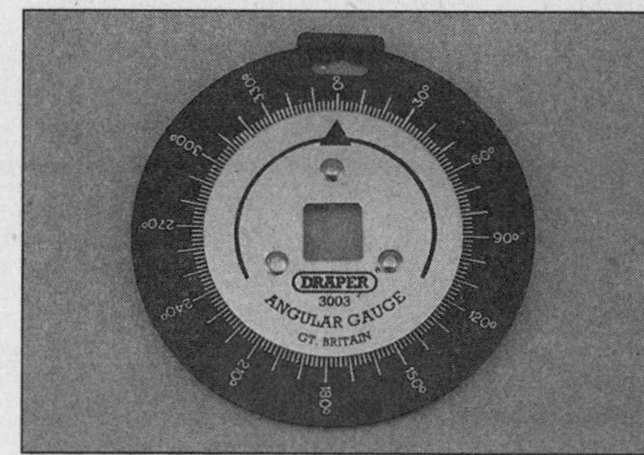

Angular-tightening gauge

Special tools

The tools in this list are those which are not used regularly, are expensive to buy, or which need to be used in accordance with their manufacturers' instructions. Unless relatively difficult mechanical jobs are undertaken frequently, it will not be economic to buy many of these tools. Where this is the case, you could consider clubbing together with friends (or joining a motorists' club) to make a joint purchase, or borrowing the tools against a deposit from a local garage or tool hire specialist. It is worth noting that many of the larger DIY superstores now carry a large range of special tools for hire at modest rates.

The following list contains only those tools and instruments freely available to the public, and not those special tools produced by the vehicle manufacturer specifically for its dealer network. You will find occasional references to these manufacturers' special tools in the text of this manual. Generally, an alternative method of doing the job without the vehicle manufacturers' special tool is given. However, sometimes there is no alternative to using them. Where this is the case and the relevant tool cannot be bought or borrowed, you will have to entrust the work to a dealer.

- ☐ *Angular-tightening gauge*
- ☐ *Valve spring compressor*
- ☐ *Valve grinding tool*
- ☐ *Piston ring compressor*
- ☐ *Piston ring removal/installation tool*
- ☐ *Cylinder bore hone*
- ☐ *Balljoint separator*
- ☐ *Coil spring compressors (where applicable)*
- ☐ *Two/three-legged hub and bearing puller*
- ☐ *Impact screwdriver*
- ☐ *Micrometer and/or vernier calipers*
- ☐ *Dial gauge*
- ☐ *Stroboscopic timing light*
- ☐ *Dwell angle meter/tachometer*
- ☐ *Fault code reader*
- ☐ *Cylinder compression gauge*
- ☐ *Hand-operated vacuum pump and gauge*
- ☐ *Clutch plate alignment set*
- ☐ *Brake shoe steady spring cup removal tool*
- ☐ *Bush and bearing removal/installation set*
- ☐ *Stud extractors*
- ☐ *Tap and die set*
- ☐ *Lifting tackle*
- ☐ *Trolley jack*

Buying tools

Reputable motor accessory shops and superstores often offer excellent quality tools at discount prices, so it pays to shop around.

Remember, you don't have to buy the most expensive items on the shelf, but it is always advisable to steer clear of the very cheap tools. Beware of 'bargains' offered on market stalls or at car boot sales. There are plenty of good tools around at reasonable prices, but always aim to purchase items which meet the relevant national safety standards. If in doubt, ask the proprietor or manager of the shop for advice before making a purchase.

Care and maintenance of tools

Having purchased a reasonable tool kit, it is necessary to keep the tools in a clean and serviceable condition. After use, always wipe off any dirt, grease and metal particles using a clean, dry cloth, before putting the tools away. Never leave them lying around after they have been used. A simple tool rack on the garage or workshop wall for items such as screwdrivers and pliers is a good idea. Store all normal spanners and sockets in a metal box. Any measuring instruments, gauges, meters, etc, must be carefully stored where they cannot be damaged or become rusty.

Take a little care when tools are used. Hammer heads inevitably become marked, and screwdrivers lose the keen edge on their blades from time to time. A little timely attention with emery cloth or a file will soon restore items like this to a good finish.

Working facilities

Not to be forgotten when discussing tools is the workshop itself. If anything more than routine maintenance is to be carried out, a suitable working area becomes essential.

It is appreciated that many an owner-mechanic is forced by circumstances to remove an engine or similar item without the benefit of a garage or workshop. Having done this, any repairs should always be done under the cover of a roof.

Wherever possible, any dismantling should be done on a clean, flat workbench or table at a suitable working height.

Any workbench needs a vice; one with a jaw opening of 100 mm is suitable for most jobs. As mentioned previously, some clean dry storage space is also required for tools, as well as for any lubricants, cleaning fluids, touch-up paints etc, which become necessary.

Another item which may be required, and which has a much more general usage, is an electric drill with a chuck capacity of at least 8 mm. This, together with a good range of twist drills, is virtually essential for fitting accessories.

Last, but not least, always keep a supply of old newspapers and clean, lint-free rags available, and try to keep any working area as clean as possible.

Micrometers

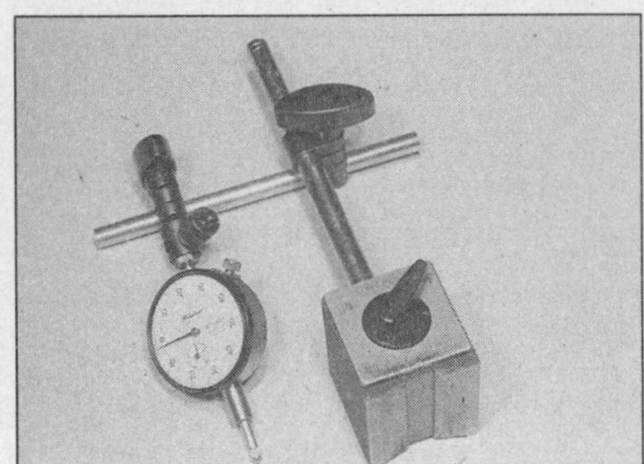

Dial test indicator ("dial gauge")

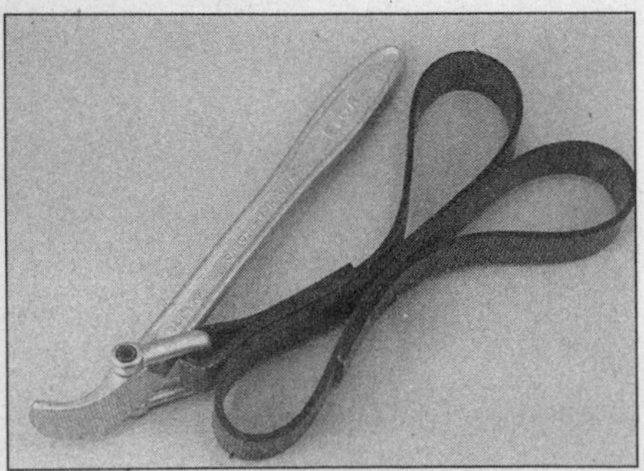

Strap wrench

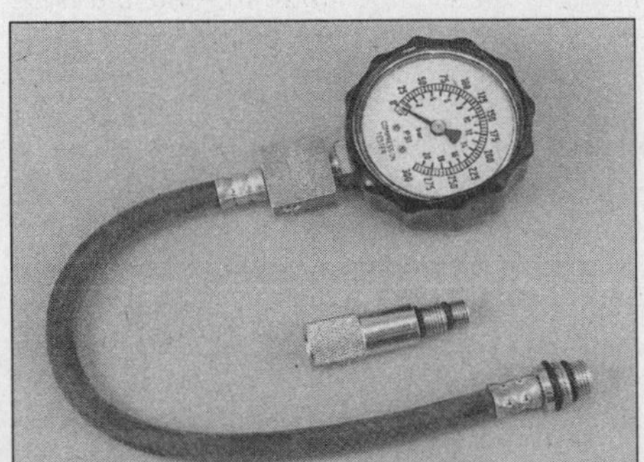

Compression tester

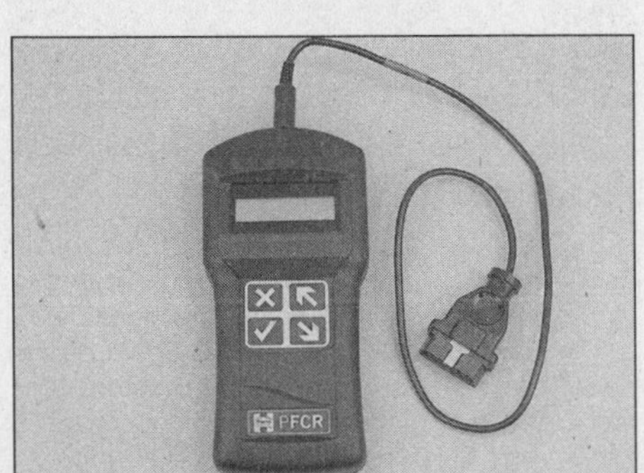

Fault code reader

This is a guide to getting your vehicle through the MOT test. Obviously it will not be possible to examine the vehicle to the same standard as the professional MOT tester. However, working through the following checks will enable you to identify any problem areas before submitting the vehicle for the test.

Where a testable component is in borderline condition, the tester has discretion in deciding whether to pass or fail it. The basis of such discretion is whether the tester would be happy for a close relative or friend to use the vehicle with the component in that condition. If the vehicle presented is clean and evidently well cared for, the tester may be more inclined to pass a borderline component than if the vehicle is scruffy and apparently neglected.

It has only been possible to summarise the test requirements here, based on the regulations in force at the time of printing. Test standards are becoming increasingly stringent, although there are some exemptions for older vehicles.

An assistant will be needed to help carry out some of these checks.

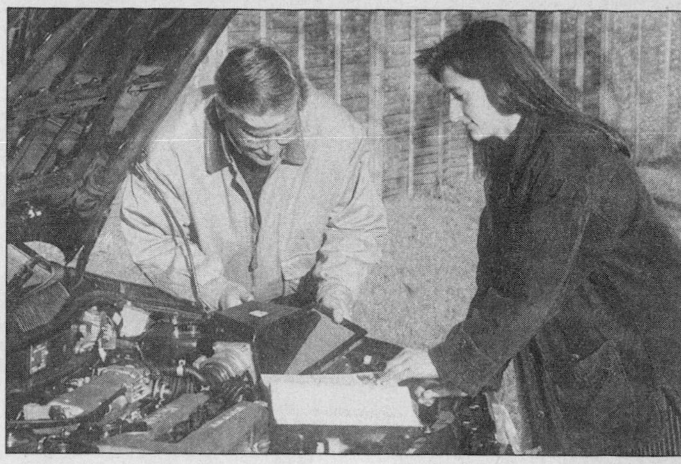

The checks have been sub-divided into four categories, as follows:

1 Checks carried out **FROM THE DRIVER'S SEAT**

2 Checks carried out **WITH THE VEHICLE ON THE GROUND**

3 Checks carried out **WITH THE VEHICLE RAISED AND THE WHEELS FREE TO TURN**

4 Checks carried out on **YOUR VEHICLE'S EXHAUST EMISSION SYSTEM**

1 Checks carried out FROM THE DRIVER'S SEAT

Handbrake

☐ Test the operation of the handbrake. Excessive travel (too many clicks) indicates incorrect brake or cable adjustment.

☐ Check that the handbrake cannot be released by tapping the lever sideways. Check the security of the lever mountings.

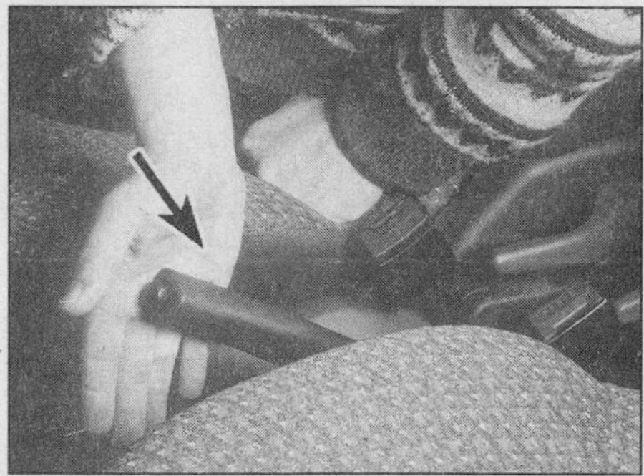

Footbrake

☐ Depress the brake pedal and check that it does not creep down to the floor, indicating a master cylinder fault. Release the pedal, wait a few seconds, then depress it again. If the pedal travels nearly to the floor before firm resistance is felt, brake adjustment or repair is necessary. If the pedal feels spongy, there is air in the hydraulic system which must be removed by bleeding.

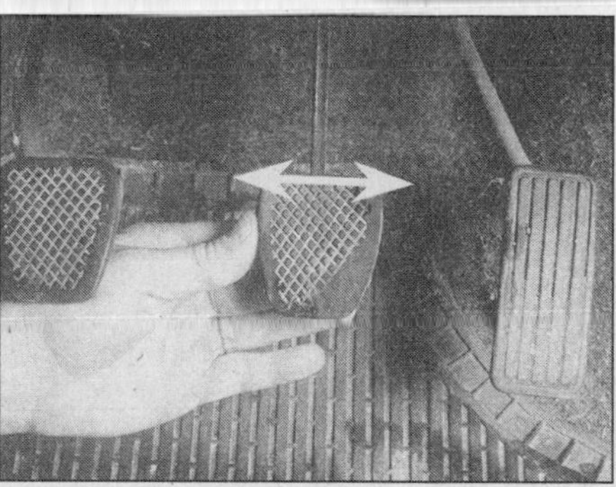

☐ Check that the brake pedal is secure and in good condition. Check also for signs of fluid leaks on the pedal, floor or carpets, which would indicate failed seals in the brake master cylinder.

☐ Check the servo unit (when applicable) by operating the brake pedal several times, then keeping the pedal depressed and starting the engine. As the engine starts, the pedal will move down slightly. If not, the vacuum hose or the servo itself may be faulty.

Steering wheel and column

☐ Examine the steering wheel for fractures or looseness of the hub, spokes or rim.

☐ Move the steering wheel from side to side and then up and down. Check that the steering wheel is not loose on the column, indicating wear or a loose retaining nut. Continue moving the steering wheel as before, but also turn it slightly from left to right.

☐ Check that the steering wheel is not loose on the column, and that there is no abnormal

movement of the steering wheel, indicating wear in the column support bearings or couplings.

Windscreen, mirrors and sunvisor

☐ The windscreen must be free of cracks or other significant damage within the driver's field of view. (Small stone chips are acceptable.) Rear view mirrors must be secure, intact, and capable of being adjusted.

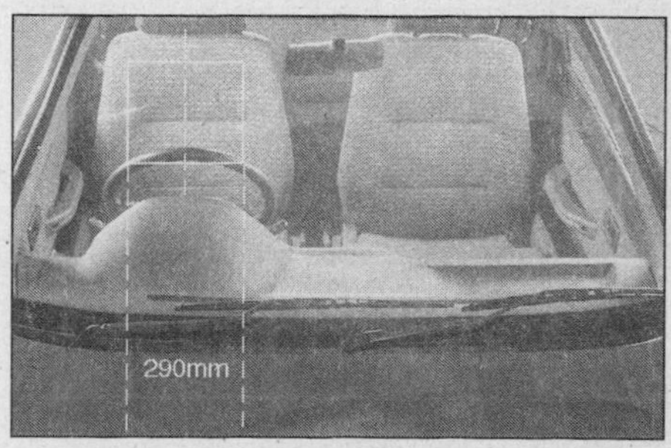

☐ The driver's sunvisor must be capable of being stored in the "up" position.

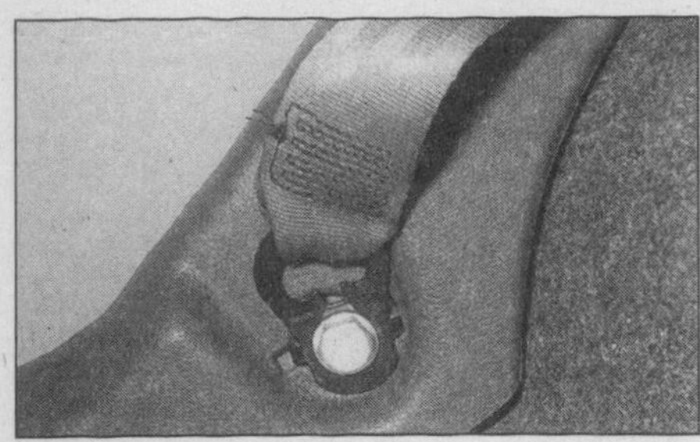

Seat belts and seats

Note: *The following checks are applicable to all seat belts, front and rear.*

☐ Examine the webbing of all the belts (including rear belts if fitted) for cuts, serious fraying or deterioration. Fasten and unfasten each belt to check the buckles. If applicable, check the retracting mechanism. Check the security of all seat belt mountings accessible from inside the vehicle.

☐ Seat belts with pre-tensioners, once activated, have a "flag" or similar showing on the seat belt stalk. This, in itself, is not a reason for test failure.

☐ The front seats themselves must be securely attached and the backrests must lock in the upright position.

Doors

☐ Both front doors must be able to be opened and closed from outside and inside, and must latch securely when closed.

2 Checks carried out WITH THE VEHICLE ON THE GROUND

Vehicle identification

☐ Number plates must be in good condition, secure and legible, with letters and numbers correctly spaced – spacing at (A) should be at least twice that at (B).

☐ The VIN plate and/or homologation plate must be legible.

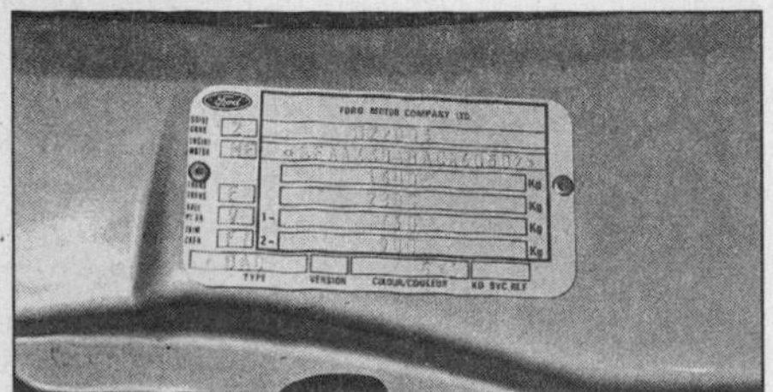

Electrical equipment

☐ Switch on the ignition and check the operation of the horn.

☐ Check the windscreen washers and wipers, examining the wiper blades; renew damaged or perished blades. Also check the operation of the stop-lights.

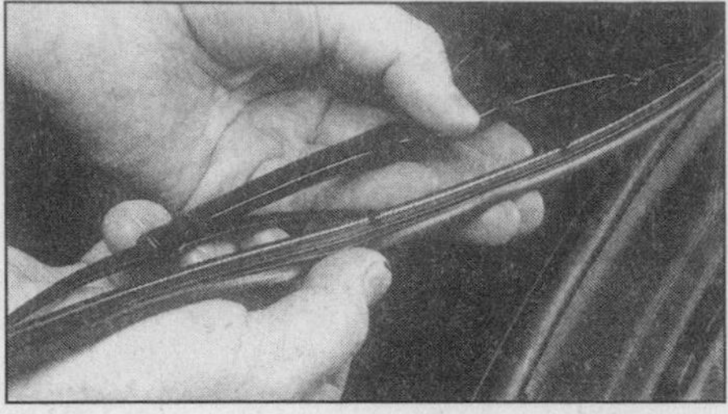

☐ Check the operation of the sidelights and number plate lights. The lenses and reflectors must be secure, clean and undamaged.

☐ Check the operation and alignment of the headlights. The headlight reflectors must not be tarnished and the lenses must be undamaged.

☐ Switch on the ignition and check the operation of the direction indicators (including the instrument panel tell-tale) and the hazard warning lights. Operation of the sidelights and stop-lights must not affect the indicators - if it does, the cause is usually a bad earth at the rear light cluster.

☐ Check the operation of the rear foglight(s), including the warning light on the instrument panel or in the switch.

☐ The ABS warning light must illuminate in accordance with the manufacturers' design. For most vehicles, the ABS warning light should illuminate when the ignition is switched on, and (if the system is operating properly) extinguish after a few seconds. Refer to the owner's handbook.

Footbrake

☐ Examine the master cylinder, brake pipes and servo unit for leaks, loose mountings, corrosion or other damage.

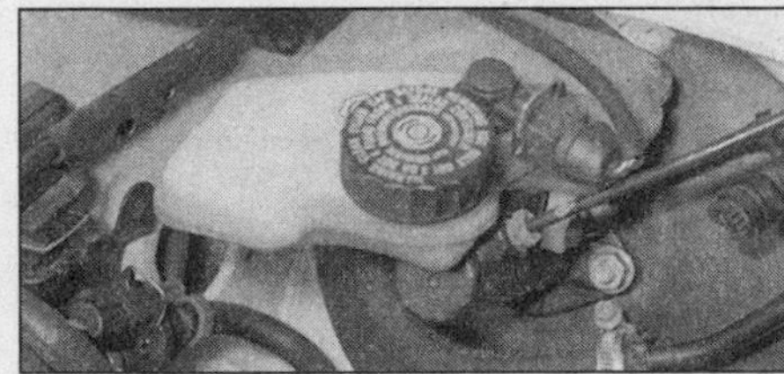

☐ The fluid reservoir must be secure and the fluid level must be between the upper (**A**) and lower (**B**) markings.

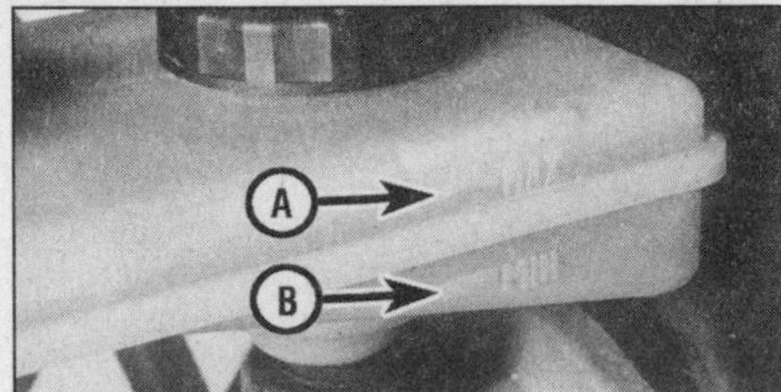

☐ Inspect both front brake flexible hoses for cracks or deterioration of the rubber. Turn the steering from lock to lock, and ensure that the hoses do not contact the wheel, tyre, or any part of the steering or suspension mechanism. With the brake pedal firmly depressed, check the hoses for bulges or leaks under pressure.

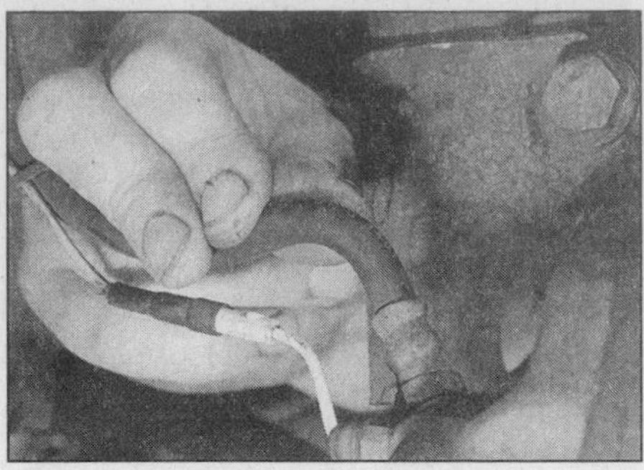

Steering and suspension

☐ Have your assistant turn the steering wheel from side to side slightly, up to the point where the steering gear just begins to transmit this movement to the roadwheels. Check for excessive free play between the steering wheel and the steering gear, indicating wear or insecurity of the steering column joints, the column-to-steering gear coupling, or the steering gear itself.

☐ Have your assistant turn the steering wheel more vigorously in each direction, so that the roadwheels just begin to turn. As this is done, examine all the steering joints, linkages, fittings and attachments. Renew any component that shows signs of wear or damage. On vehicles with power steering, check the security and condition of the steering pump, drivebelt and hoses.

☐ Check that the vehicle is standing level, and at approximately the correct ride height.

Shock absorbers

☐ Depress each corner of the vehicle in turn, then release it. The vehicle should rise and then settle in its normal position. If the vehicle continues to rise and fall, the shock absorber is defective. A shock absorber which has seized will also cause the vehicle to fail.

Exhaust system

☐ Start the engine. With your assistant holding a rag over the tailpipe, check the entire system for leaks. Repair or renew leaking sections.

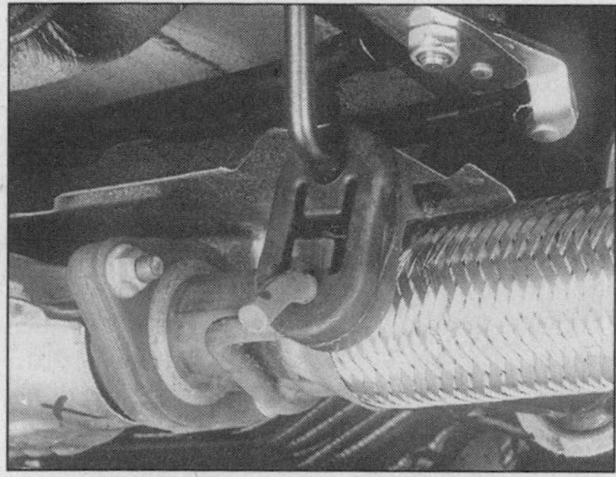

3 Checks carried out WITH THE VEHICLE RAISED AND THE WHEELS FREE TO TURN

Jack up the front and rear of the vehicle, and securely support it on axle stands. Position the stands clear of the suspension assemblies. Ensure that the wheels are clear of the ground and that the steering can be turned from lock to lock.

Steering mechanism

☐ Have your assistant turn the steering from lock to lock. Check that the steering turns smoothly, and that no part of the steering mechanism, including a wheel or tyre, fouls any brake hose or pipe or any part of the body structure.

☐ Examine the steering rack rubber gaiters for damage or insecurity of the retaining clips. If power steering is fitted, check for signs of damage or leakage of the fluid hoses, pipes or connections. Also check for excessive stiffness or binding of the steering, a missing split pin or locking device, or severe corrosion of the body structure within 30 cm of any steering component attachment point.

Front and rear suspension and wheel bearings

☐ Starting at the front right-hand side, grasp the roadwheel at the 3 o'clock and 9 o'clock positions and rock gently but firmly. Check for free play or insecurity at the wheel bearings, suspension balljoints, or suspension mountings, pivots and attachments.

☐ Now grasp the wheel at the 12 o'clock and 6 o'clock positions and repeat the previous inspection. Spin the wheel, and check for roughness or tightness of the front wheel bearing.

☐ If excess free play is suspected at a component pivot point, this can be confirmed by using a large screwdriver or similar tool and levering between the mounting and the component attachment. This will confirm whether the wear is in the pivot bush, its retaining bolt, or in the mounting itself (the bolt holes can often become elongated).

☐ Carry out all the above checks at the other front wheel, and then at both rear wheels.

Springs and shock absorbers

☐ Examine the suspension struts (when applicable) for serious fluid leakage, corrosion, or damage to the casing. Also check the security of the mounting points.

☐ If coil springs are fitted, check that the spring ends locate in their seats, and that the spring is not corroded, cracked or broken.

☐ If leaf springs are fitted, check that all leaves are intact, that the axle is securely attached to each spring, and that there is no deterioration of the spring eye mountings, bushes, and shackles.

☐ The same general checks apply to vehicles fitted with other suspension types, such as torsion bars, hydraulic displacer units, etc. Ensure that all mountings and attachments are secure, that there are no signs of excessive wear, corrosion or damage, and (on hydraulic types) that there are no fluid leaks or damaged pipes.

☐ Inspect the shock absorbers for signs of serious fluid leakage. Check for wear of the mounting bushes or attachments, or damage to the body of the unit.

Driveshafts (fwd vehicles only)

☐ Rotate each front wheel in turn and inspect the constant velocity joint gaiters for splits or damage. Also check that each driveshaft is straight and undamaged.

Braking system

☐ If possible without dismantling, check brake pad wear and disc condition. Ensure that the friction lining material has not worn excessively, (A) and that the discs are not fractured, pitted, scored or badly worn (B).

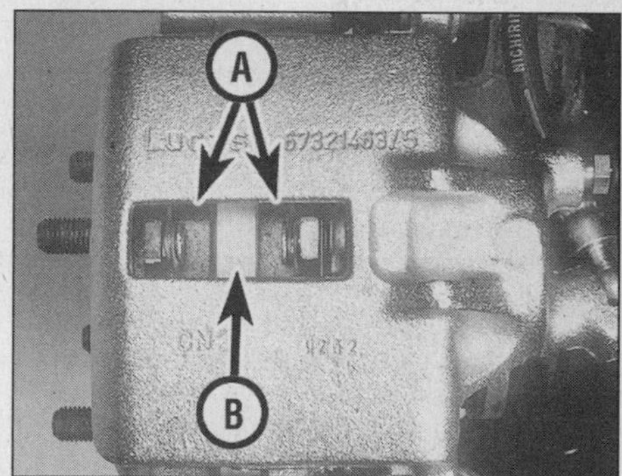

☐ Examine all the rigid brake pipes underneath the vehicle, and the flexible hose(s) at the rear. Look for corrosion, chafing or insecurity of the pipes, and for signs of bulging under pressure, chafing, splits or deterioration of the flexible hoses.

☐ Look for signs of fluid leaks at the brake calipers or on the brake backplates. Repair or renew leaking components.

☐ Slowly spin each wheel, while your assistant depresses and releases the footbrake. Ensure that each brake is operating and does not bind when the pedal is released.

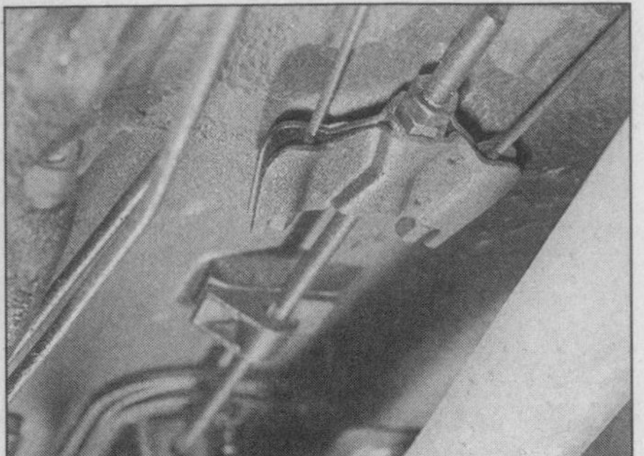

☐ Examine the handbrake mechanism, checking for frayed or broken cables, excessive corrosion, or wear or insecurity of the linkage. Check that the mechanism works on each relevant wheel, and releases fully, without binding.

☐ It is not possible to test brake efficiency without special equipment, but a road test can be carried out later to check that the vehicle pulls up in a straight line.

Fuel and exhaust systems

☐ Inspect the fuel tank (including the filler cap), fuel pipes, hoses and unions. All components must be secure and free from leaks.

☐ Examine the exhaust system over its entire length, checking for any damaged, broken or missing mountings, security of the retaining clamps and rust or corrosion.

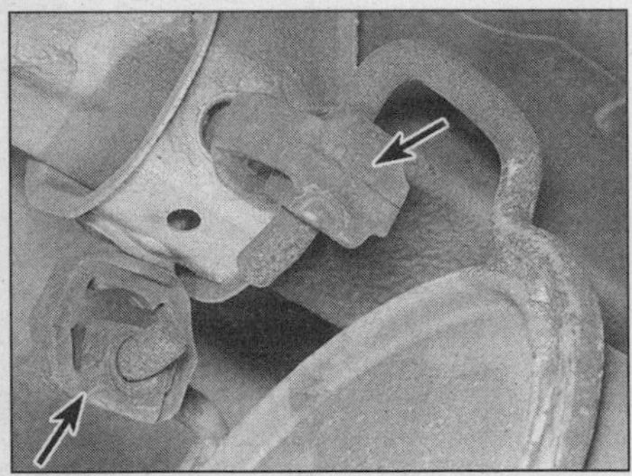

Wheels and tyres

☐ Examine the sidewalls and tread area of each tyre in turn. Check for cuts, tears, lumps, bulges, separation of the tread, and exposure of the ply or cord due to wear or damage. Check that the tyre bead is correctly seated on the wheel rim, that the valve is sound and properly seated, and that the wheel is not distorted or damaged.

☐ Check that the tyres are of the correct size for the vehicle, that they are of the same size and type on each axle, and that the pressures are correct.

☐ Check the tyre tread depth. The legal minimum at the time of writing is 1.6 mm over at least three-quarters of the tread width. Abnormal tread wear may indicate incorrect front wheel alignment.

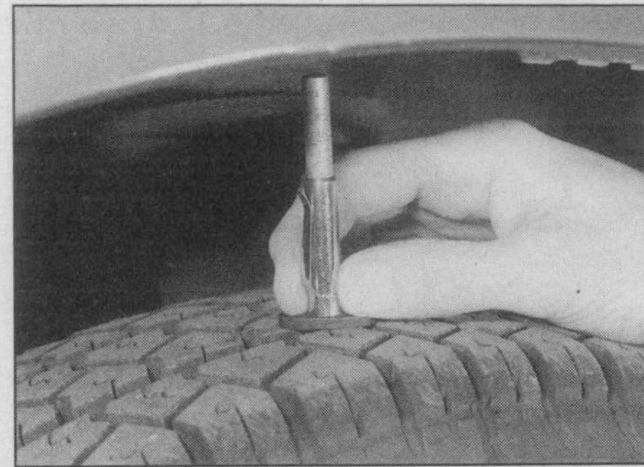

Body corrosion

☐ Check the condition of the entire vehicle structure for signs of corrosion in load-bearing areas. (These include chassis box sections, side sills, cross-members, pillars, and all suspension, steering, braking system and seat belt mountings and anchorages.) Any corrosion which has seriously reduced the thickness of a load-bearing area is likely to cause the vehicle to fail. In this case professional repairs are likely to be needed.

☐ Damage or corrosion which causes sharp or otherwise dangerous edges to be exposed will also cause the vehicle to fail.

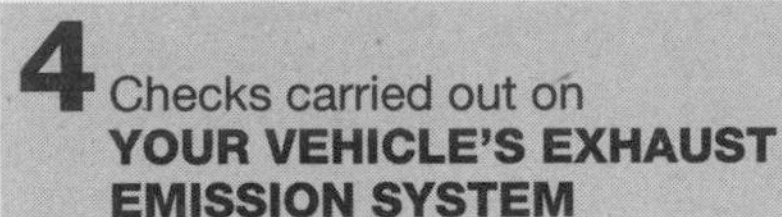

4 Checks carried out on **YOUR VEHICLE'S EXHAUST EMISSION SYSTEM**

Petrol models

☐ Have the engine at normal operating temperature, and make sure that it is in good tune (ignition system in good order, air filter element clean, etc).

☐ Before any measurements are carried out, raise the engine speed to around 2500 rpm, and hold it at this speed for 20 seconds. Allow the engine speed to return to idle, and watch for smoke emissions from the exhaust tailpipe. If the idle speed is obviously much too high, or if dense blue or clearly-visible black smoke comes from the tailpipe for more than 5 seconds, the vehicle will fail. As a rule of thumb, blue smoke signifies oil being burnt (engine wear) while black smoke signifies unburnt fuel (dirty air cleaner element, or other carburettor or fuel system fault).

☐ An exhaust gas analyser capable of measuring carbon monoxide (CO) and hydrocarbons (HC) is now needed. If such an instrument cannot be hired or borrowed, a local garage may agree to perform the check for a small fee.

CO emissions (mixture)

☐ At the time of writing, for vehicles first used between 1st August 1975 and 31st July 1986 (P to C registration), the CO level must not exceed 4.5% by volume. For vehicles first used between 1st August 1986 and 31st July 1992 (D to J registration), the CO level must not exceed 3.5% by volume. Vehicles first used after 1st August 1992 (K registration) must conform to the manufacturer's specification. The MOT tester has access to a DOT database or emissions handbook, which lists the CO and HC limits for each make and model of vehicle. The CO level is measured with the engine at idle speed, and at "fast idle". The following limits are given as a general guide:

At idle speed -
CO level no more than 0.5%
At "fast idle" (2500 to 3000 rpm) -
CO level no more than 0.3%
(Minimum oil temperature 60°C)

☐ If the CO level cannot be reduced far enough to pass the test (and the fuel and ignition systems are otherwise in good condition) then the carburettor is badly worn, or there is some problem in the fuel injection system or catalytic converter (as applicable).

HC emissions

☐ With the CO within limits, HC emissions for vehicles first used between 1st August 1975 and 31st July 1992 (P to J registration) must not exceed 1200 ppm. Vehicles first used after 1st August 1992 (K registration) must conform to the manufacturer's specification. The MOT tester has access to a DOT database or emissions handbook, which lists the CO and HC limits for each make and model of vehicle. The HC level is measured with the engine at "fast idle". The following is given as a general guide:

At "fast idle" (2500 to 3000 rpm) -
HC level no more than 200 ppm
(Minimum oil temperature 60°C)

☐ Excessive HC emissions are caused by incomplete combustion, the causes of which can include oil being burnt, mechanical wear and ignition/fuel system malfunction.

Diesel models

☐ The only emission test applicable to Diesel engines is the measuring of exhaust smoke density. The test involves accelerating the engine several times to its maximum unloaded speed.

Note: *It is of the utmost importance that the engine timing belt is in good condition before the test is carried out.*

☐ The limits for Diesel engine exhaust smoke, introduced in September 1995 are:

Vehicles first used before 1st August 1979:
Exempt from metered smoke testing, but must not emit "dense blue or clearly visible black smoke for a period of more than 5 seconds at idle" or "dense blue or clearly visible black smoke during acceleration which would obscure the view of other road users".

Non-turbocharged vehicles first used after 1st August 1979: 2.5m^{-1}

Turbocharged vehicles first used after 1st August 1979: 3.0m^{-1}

☐ Excessive smoke can be caused by a dirty air cleaner element. Otherwise, professional advice may be needed to find the cause.

Engine

- ☐ Engine fails to rotate when attempting to start
- ☐ Engine rotates, but will not start
- ☐ Engine difficult to start when cold
- ☐ Engine difficult to start when hot
- ☐ Starter motor noisy or rough in engagement
- ☐ Engine starts, but stops immediately
- ☐ Engine idles erratically
- ☐ Engine misfires at idle speed
- ☐ Engine misfires throughout the driving speed range
- ☐ Engine hesitates on acceleration
- ☐ Engine stalls
- ☐ Engine lacks power
- ☐ Engine backfires
- ☐ Oil pressure warning light illuminated with engine running
- ☐ Engine runs-on after switching off
- ☐ Engine noises

Cooling system

- ☐ Overheating
- ☐ Overcooling
- ☐ External coolant leakage
- ☐ Internal coolant leakage
- ☐ Corrosion

Fuel and exhaust systems

- ☐ Excessive fuel consumption
- ☐ Fuel leakage and/or fuel odour
- ☐ Excessive noise or fumes from exhaust system

Clutch

- ☐ Pedal travels to floor – no pressure or very little resistance
- ☐ Clutch fails to disengage (unable to select gears)
- ☐ Clutch slips (engine speed increases, with no increase in vehicle speed)
- ☐ Judder as clutch is engaged
- ☐ Noise when depressing or releasing clutch pedal

Manual transmission

- ☐ Noisy in neutral with engine running
- ☐ Noisy in one particular gear
- ☐ Difficulty engaging gears
- ☐ Jumps out of gear
- ☐ Vibration
- ☐ Lubricant leaks

Automatic transmission

- ☐ Fluid leakage
- ☐ Transmission fluid brown, or has burned smell
- ☐ General gear selection problems
- ☐ Transmission will not downshift (kickdown) with accelerator fully depressed
- ☐ Engine will not start in any gear, or starts in gears other than Park or Neutral
- ☐ Transmission slips, shifts roughly, is noisy, or has no drive in forward or reverse gears

Driveshafts

- ☐ Clicking or knocking noise on turns (at slow speed on full-lock)
- ☐ Vibration when accelerating or decelerating

Braking system

- ☐ Vehicle pulls to one side under braking
- ☐ Noise (grinding or high-pitched squeal) when brakes applied
- ☐ Excessive brake pedal travel
- ☐ Brake pedal feels spongy when depressed
- ☐ Excessive brake pedal effort required to stop vehicle
- ☐ Judder felt through brake pedal or steering wheel when braking
- ☐ Pedal pulsates when braking hard
- ☐ Brakes binding
- ☐ Rear wheels locking under normal braking

Steering and suspension

- ☐ Vehicle pulls to one side
- ☐ Wheel wobble and vibration
- ☐ Excessive pitching and/or rolling around corners, or during braking
- ☐ Wandering or general instability
- ☐ Excessively-stiff steering
- ☐ Excessive play in steering
- ☐ Lack of power assistance
- ☐ Tyre wear excessive

Electrical system

- ☐ Battery will only hold a charge for a few days
- ☐ Ignition/no-charge warning light remains illuminated with engine running
- ☐ Ignition/no-charge warning light fails to come on
- ☐ Lights inoperative
- ☐ Instrument readings inaccurate or erratic
- ☐ Horn inoperative, or unsatisfactory in operation
- ☐ Wipers inoperative, or unsatisfactory in operation
- ☐ Washers inoperative, or unsatisfactory in operation
- ☐ Electric windows inoperative, or unsatisfactory in operation
- ☐ Central locking system inoperative, or unsatisfactory in operation

Introduction

The vehicle owner who does his or her own maintenance according to the recommended service schedules should not have to use this section of the manual very often. Modern component reliability is such that, provided those items subject to wear or deterioration are inspected or renewed at the specified intervals, sudden failure is comparatively rare. Faults do not usually just happen as a result of sudden failure, but develop over a period of time. Major mechanical failures in particular are usually preceded by characteristic symptoms over hundreds or even thousands of miles. Those components which do occasionally fail without warning are often small and easily carried in the vehicle.

With any fault-finding, the first step is to decide where to begin investigations. Sometimes this is obvious, but on other occasions, a little detective work will be necessary. The owner who makes half a dozen haphazard adjustments or replacements may be successful in curing a fault (or its symptoms), but will be none the wiser if the fault recurs, and ultimately may have spent more time and money than was necessary. A calm and logical approach will be found to be more satisfactory in the long run. Always take into account any warning signs or abnormalities that may have been noticed in the period preceding the fault – power loss, high or low gauge readings, unusual smells, etc – and remember that failure of components such as fuses or spark plugs may only be pointers to some underlying fault.

The pages which follow provide an easy-reference guide to the more common problems which may occur during the operation of the vehicle. These problems and their possible causes are grouped under headings denoting various components or systems, such as Engine, Cooling system, etc. The general Chapter which deals with the problem is also shown in brackets; refer to the relevant part of that Chapter for system-specific information. Whatever the fault, certain basic principles apply. These are as follows:

☐ *Verify the fault*. This is simply a matter of being sure that you know what the symptoms are before starting work. This is particularly important if you are investigating a fault for someone else, who may not have described it very accurately.

☐ *Don't overlook the obvious*. For example, if the vehicle won't start, is there fuel in the tank? (Don't take anyone else's word on this particular point, and don't trust the fuel gauge either!) If an electrical fault is indicated, look for loose or broken wires before digging out the test gear.

☐ *Cure the disease, not the symptom*. Substituting a flat battery with a fully-charged one will get you off the hard shoulder, but if the underlying cause is not attended to, the new battery will go the same way. Similarly, changing oil-fouled spark plugs for a new set will get you moving again, but remember that the reason for the fouling (if it wasn't simply an incorrect grade of plug) will have to be established and corrected.

☐ *Don't take anything for granted*. Particularly, don't forget that a 'new' component may itself be defective (especially if it's been rattling around in the boot for months), and don't leave components out of a fault diagnosis sequence just because they are new or recently-fitted. When you do finally diagnose a difficult fault, you'll probably realise that all the evidence was there from the start.

Engine

Engine fails to rotate when attempting to start

☐ Battery terminal connections loose or corroded (*Weekly checks*).
☐ Battery discharged or faulty (Chapter 5A).
☐ Broken, loose or disconnected wiring in the starting circuit (Chapter 5A).
☐ Defective starter solenoid or switch (Chapter 5A).
☐ Defective starter motor (Chapter 5A).
☐ Starter pinion or flywheel ring gear teeth loose or broken (Chapters 2A, 2B, 2C and 5A).
☐ Engine earth strap broken or disconnected (Chapter 5A).

Engine rotates, but will not start

☐ Fuel tank empty.
☐ Battery discharged (engine rotates slowly) (Chapter 5A).
☐ Battery terminal connections loose or corroded (Chapters 1A or 1B).
☐ Ignition components damp or damaged – petrol models (Chapters 1A, 1B and 5B).
☐ Broken, loose or disconnected wiring in the ignition circuit – petrol models (Chapters 1A, 1B and 5B).
☐ Worn, faulty or incorrectly-gapped spark plugs – petrol models (Chapter 1A).
☐ Preheating system faulty – diesel models (Chapter 5C).
☐ Fuel injection system fault – petrol models (Chapter 4A).
☐ Stop solenoid faulty – diesel models (Chapter 4B).
☐ Air in fuel system – diesel models (Chapter 4B).
☐ Major mechanical failure (eg camshaft drive) (Chapter 2A, 2B or 2C).

Engine difficult to start when cold

☐ Battery discharged (Chapter 5A).
☐ Battery terminal connections loose or corroded (Chapter 1A or 1B).
☐ Worn, faulty or incorrectly-gapped spark plugs – petrol models (Chapter 1A).
☐ Preheating system faulty – diesel models (Chapter 5C).
☐ Fuel injection system fault – petrol models (Chapter 4A).
☐ Other ignition system fault – petrol models (Chapters 1A and 5B).
☐ Fast idle valve incorrectly adjusted – diesel models (Chapter 4B).
☐ Low cylinder compressions (Chapter 2A, 2B or 2C).

Engine difficult to start when hot

☐ Air filter element dirty or clogged (Chapter 1A or 1B).
☐ Fuel injection system fault – petrol models (Chapter 4A).
☐ Low cylinder compressions (Chapter 2A, 2B or 2C).

Starter motor noisy or rough in engagement

☐ Starter pinion or flywheel ring gear teeth loose or broken (Chapters 2A, 2B, 2C and 5A).
☐ Starter motor mounting bolts loose or missing (Chapter 5A).
☐ Starter motor internal components worn or damaged (Chapter 5A).

Engine starts, but stops immediately

☐ Loose or faulty electrical connections in the ignition circuit – petrol models (Chapters 1A and 5B).
☐ Vacuum leak at the throttle body or inlet manifold – petrol models (Chapter 4A).
☐ Blocked injector/fuel injection system fault – petrol models (Chapter 4A).

Engine idles erratically

☐ Air filter element clogged (Chapter 1A or 1B).
☐ Vacuum leak at the throttle body, inlet manifold or associated hoses – petrol models (Chapter 4A).
☐ Worn, faulty or incorrectly-gapped spark plugs – petrol models (Chapter 1A).
☐ Uneven or low cylinder compressions (Chapter 2A or 2B).
☐ Camshaft lobes worn (Chapter 2A, 2B or 2C).
☐ Timing belt incorrectly tensioned (Chapter 2A, 2B or 2C).
☐ Blocked injector/fuel injection system fault – petrol models (Chapter 4A).
☐ Faulty injector(s) – diesel models (Chapter 4B).

Engine misfires at idle speed

☐ Worn, faulty or incorrectly-gapped spark plugs – petrol models (Chapter 1A).
☐ Faulty spark plug HT leads – petrol models (Chapter 1A).
☐ Vacuum leak at the throttle body, inlet manifold or associated hoses – petrol models (Chapter 4A).
☐ Blocked injector/fuel injection system fault – petrol models (Chapter 4A).
☐ Faulty injector(s) – diesel models (Chapter 4B).
☐ Ignition fault – petrol models (Chapter 5B).
☐ Uneven or low cylinder compressions (Chapter 2A, 2B or 2C).
☐ Disconnected, leaking, or perished crankcase ventilation hoses (Chapter 4C).

Engine misfires throughout the driving speed range

☐ Fuel filter choked (Chapter 1A or 1B).
☐ Fuel pump faulty, or delivery pressure low – petrol models (Chapter 4A).
☐ Fuel tank vent blocked, or fuel pipes restricted (Chapter 4A or 4B).
☐ Vacuum leak at the throttle body, inlet manifold or associated hoses – petrol models (Chapter 4A).
☐ Worn, faulty or incorrectly-gapped spark plugs – petrol models (Chapter 1A).
☐ Faulty spark plug HT leads – petrol models (Chapter 1A).
☐ Faulty injector(s) – diesel models (Chapter 4B).
☐ Distributor cap cracked or tracking internally – petrol models (where applicable) (Chapter 5B).
☐ Faulty ignition coil – petrol models (Chapter 5B).
☐ Uneven or low cylinder compressions (Chapter 2A, 2B or 2C).
☐ Blocked injector/fuel injection system fault – petrol models (Chapter 4A).

Engine (continued)

Engine hesitates on acceleration

- ☐ Worn, faulty or incorrectly-gapped spark plugs – petrol models (Chapter 1A).
- ☐ Vacuum leak at the throttle body, inlet manifold or associated hoses – petrol models (Chapter 4A).
- ☐ Blocked injector/fuel injection system fault – petrol models (Chapter 4A).
- ☐ Faulty injector(s) – diesel models (Chapter 4B).

Engine stalls

- ☐ Vacuum leak at the throttle body, inlet manifold or associated hoses – petrol models (Chapter 4A).
- ☐ Fuel filter choked (Chapter 1A or 1B).
- ☐ Fuel pump faulty, or delivery pressure low – petrol models (Chapter 4A).
- ☐ Fuel tank vent blocked, or fuel pipes restricted (Chapter 4A or 4B).
- ☐ Blocked injector/fuel injection system fault – petrol models (Chapter 4A).
- ☐ Faulty injector(s) – diesel models (Chapter 4B).

Engine lacks power

- ☐ Timing belt incorrectly fitted or tensioned (Chapter 2A, 2B or 2C).
- ☐ Fuel filter choked (Chapter 1A or 1B).
- ☐ Fuel pump faulty, or delivery pressure low – petrol models (Chapter 4A).
- ☐ Uneven or low cylinder compressions (Chapter 2A, 2B or 2C).
- ☐ Worn, faulty or incorrectly-gapped spark plugs – petrol models (Chapter 1A).
- ☐ Vacuum leak at the throttle body, inlet manifold or associated hoses – petrol models (Chapter 4A).
- ☐ Blocked injector/fuel injection system fault – petrol models (Chapter 4A).
- ☐ Faulty injector(s) – diesel models (Chapter 4B).
- ☐ Injection pump timing incorrect – diesel models (Chapter 4B).
- ☐ Brakes binding (Chapter 9).
- ☐ Clutch slipping (Chapter 6).

Oil pressure warning light illuminated with engine running

- ☐ Low oil level, or incorrect oil grade (*Weekly checks*).
- ☐ Faulty oil pressure sensor (Chapter 5A).
- ☐ Worn engine bearings and/or oil pump (Chapter 2A, 2B or 2C).
- ☐ High engine operating temperature (Chapter 3).
- ☐ Oil pressure relief valve defective (Chapter 2A, 2B or 2C).
- ☐ Oil pick-up strainer clogged (Chapter 2A, 2B or 2C).

Engine backfires

- ☐ Timing belt incorrectly fitted or tensioned (Chapter 2A, 2B or 2C).
- ☐ Vacuum leak at the throttle body, inlet manifold or associated hoses – petrol models (Chapter 4A).
- ☐ Blocked injector/fuel injection system fault – petrol models (Chapter 4A).

Engine runs-on after switching off

- ☐ Excessive carbon build-up in engine (Chapter 2A, 2B or 2C).
- ☐ High engine operating temperature (Chapter 3).
- ☐ Fuel injection system fault – petrol models (Chapter 4A).
- ☐ Faulty stop solenoid – diesel models (Chapter 4B).

Engine noises

Pre-ignition (pinking) or knocking during acceleration or under load

- ☐ Ignition system fault – petrol models (Chapters 1A and 5B).
- ☐ Incorrect grade of spark plug – petrol models (Chapter 1A).
- ☐ Incorrect grade of fuel (Chapters 1A or 1B).
- ☐ Vacuum leak at the throttle body, inlet manifold or associated hoses – petrol models (Chapter 4A).
- ☐ Excessive carbon build-up in engine (Chapter 2A, 2B or 2C).
- ☐ Blocked injector/fuel injection system fault – petrol models (Chapter 4A).

Whistling or wheezing noises

- ☐ Leaking inlet manifold or throttle body gasket – petrol models (Chapter 4A).
- ☐ Leaking exhaust manifold gasket or pipe-to-manifold joint (Chapter 4A or 4B).
- ☐ Leaking vacuum hose (Chapters 4A, 4B or 4C, 5B and 9).
- ☐ Blowing cylinder head gasket (Chapter 2A, 2B or 2C).

Tapping or rattling noises

- ☐ Worn valve gear or camshaft (Chapter 2A, 2B or 2C).
- ☐ Ancillary component fault (water pump, alternator, etc) (Chapters 3, 5A, etc).

Knocking or thumping noises

- ☐ Worn big-end bearings (regular heavy knocking, perhaps less under load) (Chapter 2C).
- ☐ Worn main bearings (rumbling and knocking, perhaps worsening under load) (Chapter 2C).
- ☐ Piston slap (most noticeable when cold) (Chapter 2C).
- ☐ Ancillary component fault (water pump, alternator, etc) (Chapters 3, 5A, etc).

Cooling system

Overheating

- ☐ Insufficient coolant in system (*Weekly Checks*).
- ☐ Thermostat faulty (Chapter 3).
- ☐ Radiator core blocked, or grille restricted (Chapter 3).
- ☐ Electric cooling fan or thermostatic switch faulty (Chapter 3).
- ☐ Inaccurate temperature gauge sender unit (Chapter 3).
- ☐ Airlock in cooling system (Chapter 3).
- ☐ Expansion tank pressure cap faulty (Chapter 3).

Overcooling

- ☐ Thermostat faulty (Chapter 3).
- ☐ Inaccurate temperature gauge sender unit (Chapter 3).

External coolant leakage

- ☐ Deteriorated or damaged hoses or hose clips (Chapters 1A or 1B).
- ☐ Radiator core or heater matrix leaking (Chapter 3).
- ☐ Pressure cap faulty (Chapter 3).
- ☐ Coolant pump internal seal leaking (Chapter 3).
- ☐ Coolant pump-to-block seal leaking (Chapter 3).
- ☐ Boiling due to overheating (Chapter 3).
- ☐ Core plug leaking (Chapter 2A, 2B or 2C).

Internal coolant leakage

- ☐ Leaking cylinder head gasket (Chapter 2A, 2B or 2C).
- ☐ Cracked cylinder head or cylinder block (Chapter 2A, 2B or 2C).

Corrosion

- ☐ Infrequent draining and flushing (Chapters 1A or 1B).
- ☐ Incorrect coolant mixture or inappropriate coolant type (Chapters 1A or 1B).

Fuel and exhaust systems

Excessive fuel consumption

- ☐ Air filter element dirty or clogged (Chapters 1A or 1B).
- ☐ Fuel injection system fault – petrol models (Chapter 4A).
- ☐ Faulty injector(s) – diesel models (Chapter 4B).
- ☐ Ignition system fault – petrol models (Chapters 1A and 5B).
- ☐ Tyres under-inflated (*Weekly checks*).

Fuel leakage and/or fuel odour

- ☐ Damaged or corroded fuel tank, pipes or connections (Chapter 4A or 4B).

Excessive noise or fumes from exhaust system

- ☐ Leaking exhaust system or manifold joints (Chapters 1A, 1B, 4A or 4B).
- ☐ Leaking, corroded or damaged silencers or pipe (Chapters 1A, 1B, 4A or 4B).
- ☐ Broken mountings causing body or suspension contact (Chapters 1A or 1B).

Clutch

Pedal travels to floor – no pressure or very little resistance

- ☐ Badly stretched or broken cable (Chapter 6).
- ☐ Leak or other fault in clutch hydraulic system – where applicable (Chapter 6).
- ☐ Incorrect clutch adjustment (Chapter 6).
- ☐ Broken clutch release bearing or arm (Chapter 6).
- ☐ Broken diaphragm spring in clutch pressure plate (Chapter 6).

Clutch fails to disengage (unable to select gears)

- ☐ Incorrect clutch adjustment (Chapter 6).
- ☐ Clutch friction plate sticking on gearbox input shaft splines (Chapter 6).
- ☐ Clutch friction plate sticking to flywheel or pressure plate (Chapter 6).
- ☐ Faulty pressure plate assembly (Chapter 6).
- ☐ Clutch release mechanism worn or badly assembled (Chapter 6).

Clutch slips (engine speed increases, with no increase in vehicle speed)

- ☐ Clutch friction plate linings excessively worn (Chapter 6).
- ☐ Clutch friction plate linings contaminated with oil or grease (Chapter 6).
- ☐ Faulty pressure plate or weak diaphragm spring (Chapter 6).

Judder as clutch is engaged

- ☐ Clutch friction plate linings contaminated with oil or grease (Chapter 6).
- ☐ Clutch friction plate linings excessively worn (Chapter 6).
- ☐ Faulty or distorted pressure plate or diaphragm spring (Chapter 6).
- ☐ Worn or loose engine or gearbox mountings (Chapter 2A, 2B or 2C).
- ☐ Clutch friction plate hub or gearbox input shaft splines worn (Chapter 6).

Noise when depressing or releasing clutch pedal

- ☐ Worn clutch release bearing (Chapter 6).
- ☐ Worn or dry clutch pedal pivot (Chapter 6).
- ☐ Faulty pressure plate assembly (Chapter 6).
- ☐ Pressure plate diaphragm spring broken (Chapter 6).
- ☐ Broken clutch friction plate cushioning springs (Chapter 6).

Manual transmission

Noisy in neutral with engine running

- ☐ Input shaft bearings worn (noise apparent with clutch pedal released, but not when depressed) (Chapter 7).*
- ☐ Clutch release bearing worn (noise apparent with clutch pedal depressed, possibly less when released) (Chapter 6).

Noisy in one particular gear

- ☐ Worn, damaged or chipped gear teeth (Chapter 7).*

Difficulty engaging gears

- ☐ Clutch fault (Chapter 6).
- ☐ Worn or damaged gear linkage (Chapter 7).
- ☐ Worn synchroniser units (Chapter 7).*

Jumps out of gear

- ☐ Worn or damaged gear linkage (Chapter 7).
- ☐ Worn synchroniser units (Chapter 7).*
- ☐ Worn selector forks (Chapter 7).*

Vibration

- ☐ Lack of oil (Chapters 1A or 1B).
- ☐ Worn bearings (Chapter 7).*

Lubricant leaks

- ☐ Leaking oil seal (Chapter 7).
- ☐ Leaking housing joint (Chapter 7).*

**Although the corrective action necessary to remedy the symptoms described is beyond the scope of the home mechanic, the above information should be helpful in isolating the cause of the condition, so that the owner can communicate clearly with a professional mechanic.*

Automatic transmission

Note: *Due to the complexity of the automatic transmission, it is difficult for the home mechanic to properly diagnose and service this unit. For problems other than the following, the vehicle should be taken to a dealer service department or automatic transmission specialist. Do not be too hasty in removing the transmission if a fault is suspected, as most of the testing is carried out with the unit still fitted.*

Fluid leakage

☐ Automatic transmission fluid is usually dark in colour. Fluid leaks should not be confused with engine oil, which can easily be blown onto the transmission by airflow.

☐ To determine the source of a leak, first remove all built-up dirt and grime from the transmission housing and surrounding areas using a degreasing agent, or by steam-cleaning. Drive the vehicle at low speed, so airflow will not blow the leak far from its source. Raise and support the vehicle, and determine where the leak is coming from. The following are common areas of leakage:

a) Oil pan (Chapter 1A and 7B).
b) Dipstick tube (Chapter 1A and 7B).
c) Transmission-to-fluid cooler pipes/unions (Chapter 7B).

Transmission fluid brown, or has burned smell

☐ Transmission fluid level low, or fluid in need of renewal (Chapter 7B).

General gear selection problems

☐ Chapter 7B deals with checking and adjusting the selector cable on automatic transmissions. The following are common problems which may be caused by a poorly-adjusted cable:

a) Engine starting in gears other than Park or Neutral.
b) Indicator panel indicating a gear other than the one actually being used.
c) Vehicle moves when in Park or Neutral.
d) Poor gear shift quality or erratic gear changes.

☐ Refer to Chapter 7B for the selector cable adjustment procedure.

Transmission will not downshift (kickdown) with accelerator pedal fully depressed

☐ Low transmission fluid level (Chapter 1 and 7B).
☐ Incorrect selector cable adjustment (Chapter 7B).

Engine will not start in any gear, or starts in gears other than Park or Neutral

☐ Incorrect starter/inhibitor switch adjustment (Chapter 7B).
☐ Incorrect selector cable adjustment (Chapter 7B).

Transmission slips, shifts roughly, is noisy, or has no drive in forward or reverse gears

☐ There are many probable causes for the above problems, but the home mechanic should be concerned with only one possibility – fluid level. Before taking the vehicle to a dealer or transmission specialist, check the fluid level and condition of the fluid as described in Chapters 1A, 1B or 7B, as applicable. Correct the fluid level as necessary, or change the fluid and filter if needed. If the problem persists, professional help will be necessary.

Driveshafts

Clicking or knocking noise on turns (at slow speed on full-lock)

☐ Lack of constant velocity joint lubricant, possibly due to damaged gaiter (Chapter 8).
☐ Worn outer constant velocity joint (Chapter 8).

Vibration when accelerating or decelerating

☐ Worn inner constant velocity joint (Chapter 8).
☐ Bent or distorted driveshaft (Chapter 8).
☐ Worn right-hand driveshaft intermediate bearing – where applicable (Chapter 8).

Braking system

Note: *Before assuming that a brake problem exists, make sure that the tyres are in good condition and correctly inflated, that the front wheel alignment is correct, and that the vehicle is not loaded with weight in an unequal manner. Apart from checking the condition of all pipe and hose connections, any faults occurring on the anti-lock braking system should be referred to a Renault dealer for diagnosis.*

Vehicle pulls to one side under braking

- ☐ Worn, defective, damaged or contaminated front or rear brake pads/shoes on one side (Chapters 1A, 1B and 9).
- ☐ Seized or partially-seized front or rear brake caliper/wheel cylinder piston (Chapter 9).
- ☐ A mixture of brake pad/shoe lining materials fitted between sides (Chapter 9).
- ☐ Brake caliper or rear brake backplate bolts loose (Chapter 9).
- ☐ Worn or damaged steering or suspension components (Chapters 1A, 1B and 10).

Noise (grinding or high-pitched squeal) when brakes applied

- ☐ Brake pad or shoe friction lining material worn down to metal backing (Chapters 1A, 1B and 9).
- ☐ Excessive corrosion of brake disc or drum – may be apparent after the vehicle has been standing for some time (Chapters 1A, 1B and 9).

Excessive brake pedal travel

- ☐ Faulty rear drum brake self-adjust mechanism (Chapter 9).
- ☐ Faulty master cylinder (Chapter 9).
- ☐ Air in hydraulic system (Chapter 9).
- ☐ Faulty vacuum servo unit (Chapter 9).
- ☐ Faulty vacuum pump – diesel models (Chapter 9).

Brake pedal feels spongy when depressed

- ☐ Air in hydraulic system (Chapter 9).
- ☐ Deteriorated flexible rubber brake hoses (Chapters 1A, 1B and 9).
- ☐ Master cylinder mountings loose (Chapter 9).
- ☐ Faulty master cylinder (Chapter 9).

Excessive brake pedal effort required to stop vehicle

- ☐ Faulty vacuum servo unit (Chapter 9).
- ☐ Disconnected, damaged or insecure brake servo vacuum hose (Chapters 1A, 1B and 9).
- ☐ Faulty vacuum pump – diesel models (Chapter 9).
- ☐ Primary or secondary hydraulic circuit failure (Chapter 9).
- ☐ Seized brake caliper or wheel cylinder piston(s) (Chapter 9).
- ☐ Brake pads or brake shoes incorrectly fitted (Chapter 9).
- ☐ Incorrect grade of brake pads or brake shoes fitted (Chapter 9).
- ☐ Brake pads or brake shoe linings contaminated (Chapter 9).

Judder felt through brake pedal or steering wheel when braking

- ☐ Excessive run-out or distortion of brake disc(s) or drum(s) (Chapter 9).
- ☐ Brake pad or brake shoe linings worn (Chapters 1A, 1B and 9).
- ☐ Brake caliper or rear brake backplate mounting bolts loose (Chapter 9).
- ☐ Wear in suspension or steering components or mountings (Chapters 1A, 1B and 10).

Pedal pulsates when braking hard

- ☐ Normal feature of ABS – no fault

Brakes binding

- ☐ Seized brake caliper piston(s) or wheel cylinder piston(s) (Chapter 9).
- ☐ Incorrectly-adjusted handbrake mechanism or linkage (Chapter 9).
- ☐ Faulty master cylinder (Chapter 9).

Rear wheels locking under normal braking

- ☐ Seized brake caliper piston(s) or wheel cylinder piston(s) (Chapter 9).
- ☐ Faulty brake pressure regulator (Chapter 9).

Steering and suspension

Note: *Before diagnosing suspension or steering faults, be sure that the trouble is not due to incorrect tyre pressures, mixtures of tyre types, or binding brakes.*

Vehicle pulls to one side

- ☐ Defective tyre (Chapter 1A or 1B).
- ☐ Excessive wear in suspension or steering components (Chapters 1A, 1B and 10).
- ☐ Incorrect front wheel alignment (Chapter 10).
- ☐ Accident damage to steering or suspension components (Chapters 1A, 1B and 10).

Wheel wobble and vibration

- ☐ Front roadwheels out of balance (vibration felt mainly through the steering wheel) (Chapter 10).
- ☐ Rear roadwheels out of balance (vibration felt throughout the vehicle) (Chapter 10).
- ☐ Roadwheels damaged or distorted (Chapter 10).
- ☐ Faulty or damaged tyre (*Weekly Checks*).
- ☐ Worn steering or suspension joints, bushes or components (Chapters 1A, 1B and 10).
- ☐ Wheel bolts loose (Chapter 10).

Excessive pitching and/or rolling around corners, or during braking

- ☐ Defective shock absorbers (Chapters 1A, 1B and 10).
- ☐ Broken or weak coil spring and/or suspension component (Chapters 1A, 1B and 10).
- ☐ Worn or damaged anti-roll bar or mountings (Chapter 10).

Wandering or general instability

- ☐ Incorrect front wheel alignment (Chapter 10).
- ☐ Worn steering or suspension joints, bushes or components (Chapters 1A, 1B and 10).
- ☐ Roadwheels out of balance (Chapter 10).
- ☐ Faulty or damaged tyre (*Weekly Checks*).
- ☐ Wheel bolts loose (Chapter 10).
- ☐ Defective shock absorbers (Chapters 1A, 1B and 10).

Excessively-stiff steering

- ☐ Lack of steering gear lubricant (Chapter 10).
- ☐ Seized track rod end balljoint or suspension balljoint (Chapters 1A, 1B and 10).
- ☐ Broken or incorrectly adjusted auxiliary drivebelt (Chapters 1A or 1B).
- ☐ Incorrect front wheel alignment (Chapter 10).
- ☐ Steering rack or column bent or damaged (Chapter 10).

Excessive play in steering

- ☐ Worn steering column universal joint(s) (Chapter 10).
- ☐ Worn steering track rod end balljoints (Chapters 1A, 1B and 10).
- ☐ Worn rack-and-pinion steering gear (Chapter 10).
- ☐ Worn steering or suspension joints, bushes or components (Chapters 1A, 1B and 10).

Lack of power assistance

- ☐ Broken or incorrectly-adjusted auxiliary drivebelt (Chapters 1A or 1B).
- ☐ Incorrect power steering fluid level (*Weekly Checks*).
- ☐ Restriction in power steering fluid hoses (Chapter 10).
- ☐ Faulty power steering pump (Chapter 10).
- ☐ Faulty rack-and-pinion steering gear (Chapter 10).

Tyre wear excessive

Tyres worn on inside or outside edges

- ☐ Tyres under-inflated (wear on both edges) (*Weekly Checks*).
- ☐ Incorrect camber or castor angles (wear on one edge only) (Chapter 10).
- ☐ Worn steering or suspension joints, bushes or components (Chapters 1A, 1B and 10).
- ☐ Excessively-hard cornering
- ☐ Accident damage.

Tyre treads exhibit feathered edges

- ☐ Incorrect toe setting (Chapter 10).Tyres worn in centre of tread
- ☐ Tyres over-inflated (*Weekly Checks*).

Tyres worn on inside and outside edges

- ☐ Tyres under-inflated (*Weekly Checks*).
- ☐ Worn shock absorbers (Chapters 1A, 1B and 10).

Tyres worn unevenly

- ☐ Tyres out of balance (*Weekly Checks*).
- ☐ Excessive wheel or tyre run-out (Chapters 1A or 1B).
- ☐ Worn shock absorbers (Chapters 1A, 1B and 10).
- ☐ Faulty tyre (*Weekly Checks*).

Electrical system

Note: *For problems associated with the starting system, refer to the faults listed under 'Engine' earlier in this Section.*

Battery will only hold a charge for a few days

- ☐ Battery defective internally (Chapter 5A).
- ☐ Battery electrolyte level low – where applicable (*Weekly Checks*).
- ☐ Battery terminal connections loose or corroded (*Weekly Checks*).
- ☐ Auxiliary drivebelt worn – or incorrectly adjusted, where applicable (Chapters 1A or 1B).
- ☐ Alternator not charging at correct output (Chapter 5A).
- ☐ Alternator or voltage regulator faulty (Chapter 5A).
- ☐ Short-circuit causing continual battery drain (Chapters 5A and 12).

Ignition/no-charge warning light remains illuminated with engine running

- ☐ Auxiliary drivebelt broken, worn, or incorrectly adjusted (Chapters 1A or 1B).
- ☐ Alternator brushes worn, sticking, or dirty (Chapter 5A).
- ☐ Alternator brush springs weak or broken (Chapter 5A).
- ☐ Internal fault in alternator or voltage regulator (Chapter 5A).
- ☐ Broken, disconnected, or loose wiring in charging circuit (Chapter 5A).

Electrical system (continued)

Ignition/no-charge warning light fails to come on

- ☐ Warning light bulb blown (Chapter 12).
- ☐ Broken, disconnected, or loose wiring in warning light circuit (Chapter 12).
- ☐ Alternator faulty (Chapter 5A).

Lights inoperative

- ☐ Bulb blown (Chapter 12).
- ☐ Corrosion of bulb or bulbholder contacts (Chapter 12).
- ☐ Blown fuse (Chapter 12).
- ☐ Faulty relay (Chapter 12).
- ☐ Broken, loose, or disconnected wiring (Chapter 12).
- ☐ Faulty switch (Chapter 12).

Instrument readings inaccurate or erratic

Instrument readings increase with engine speed

- ☐ Faulty voltage regulator (Chapter 12).

Fuel or temperature gauges give no reading

- ☐ Faulty gauge sender unit (Chapters 3, 4A or 4B).
- ☐ Wiring open-circuit (Chapter 12).
- ☐ Faulty gauge (Chapter 12).

Fuel or temperature gauges give continuous maximum reading

- ☐ Faulty gauge sender unit (Chapters 3, 4A or 4B).
- ☐ Wiring short-circuit (Chapter 12).
- ☐ Faulty gauge (Chapter 12).

Horn inoperative, or unsatisfactory in operation

Horn operates all the time

- ☐ Horn contacts permanently bridged or horn push stuck down (Chapter 12).

Horn fails to operate

- ☐ Blown fuse (Chapter 12).
- ☐ Cable or cable connections loose, broken or disconnected (Chapter 12).
- ☐ Faulty horn (Chapter 12).

Horn emits intermittent or unsatisfactory sound

- ☐ Cable connections loose (Chapter 12).
- ☐ Horn mountings loose (Chapter 12).
- ☐ Faulty horn (Chapter 12).

Wipers inoperative, or unsatisfactory in operation

Wipers fail to operate, or operate very slowly

- ☐ Wiper blades stuck to screen, or linkage seized or binding (*Weekly Checks* and Chapter 12).
- ☐ Blown fuse (Chapter 12).
- ☐ Cable or cable connections loose, broken or disconnected (Chapter 12).
- ☐ Faulty relay (Chapter 12).
- ☐ Faulty wiper motor (Chapter 12).

Wiper blades sweep over too large or too small an area of the glass

- ☐ Wiper arms incorrectly positioned on spindles (Chapter 12).
- ☐ Excessive wear of wiper linkage (Chapter 12).
- ☐ Wiper motor or linkage mountings loose or insecure (Chapter 12).

Wiper blades fail to clean the glass effectively

- ☐ Wiper blade rubbers worn or perished (*Weekly Checks*).
- ☐ Wiper arm tension springs broken, or arm pivots seized (Chapter 12).
- ☐ Insufficient windscreen washer additive to adequately remove road film (*Weekly Checks*).

Washers inoperative, or unsatisfactory in operation

One or more washer jets inoperative

- ☐ Blocked washer jet (Chapter 12).
- ☐ Disconnected, kinked or restricted fluid hose (Chapter 12).
- ☐ Insufficient fluid in washer reservoir (*Weekly Checks*).

Washer pump fails to operate

- ☐ Broken or disconnected wiring or connections (Chapter 12).
- ☐ Blown fuse (Chapter 12).
- ☐ Faulty washer switch (Chapter 12).
- ☐ Faulty washer pump (Chapter 12).

Washer pump runs for some time before fluid is emitted from jets

- ☐ Faulty one-way valve in fluid supply hose (Chapter 12).

Electric windows inoperative, or unsatisfactory in operation

Window glass will only move in one direction

- ☐ Faulty switch (Chapter 12).

Window glass slow to move

- ☐ Regulator seized or damaged, or in need of lubrication (Chapter 11).
- ☐ Door internal components or trim fouling regulator (Chapter 11).
- ☐ Faulty motor (Chapter 11).

Window glass fails to move

- ☐ Blown fuse (Chapter 12).
- ☐ Faulty relay (Chapter 12).
- ☐ Broken or disconnected wiring or connections (Chapter 12).
- ☐ Faulty motor (Chapter 12).

Central locking system inoperative, or unsatisfactory in operation

Complete system failure

- ☐ Blown fuse (Chapter 12).
- ☐ Faulty relay (Chapter 12).
- ☐ Broken or disconnected wiring or connections (Chapter 12).

Latch locks but will not unlock, or unlocks but will not lock

- ☐ Faulty switch (Chapter 12).
- ☐ Broken or disconnected latch operating rods or levers (Chapter 11).
- ☐ Faulty relay (Chapter 12).

One motor fails to operate

- ☐ Broken or disconnected wiring or connections (Chapter 12).
- ☐ Faulty motor (Chapter 11).
- ☐ Broken, binding or disconnected lock operating rods or levers (Chapter 11).
- ☐ Fault in door lock (Chapter 11).

A

ABS (Anti-lock brake system) A system, usually electronically controlled, that senses incipient wheel lockup during braking and relieves hydraulic pressure at wheels that are about to skid.

Air bag An inflatable bag hidden in the steering wheel (driver's side) or the dash or glovebox (passenger side). In a head-on collision, the bags inflate, preventing the driver and front passenger from being thrown forward into the steering wheel or windscreen.

Air cleaner A metal or plastic housing, containing a filter element, which removes dust and dirt from the air being drawn into the engine.

Air filter element The actual filter in an air cleaner system, usually manufactured from pleated paper and requiring renewal at regular intervals.

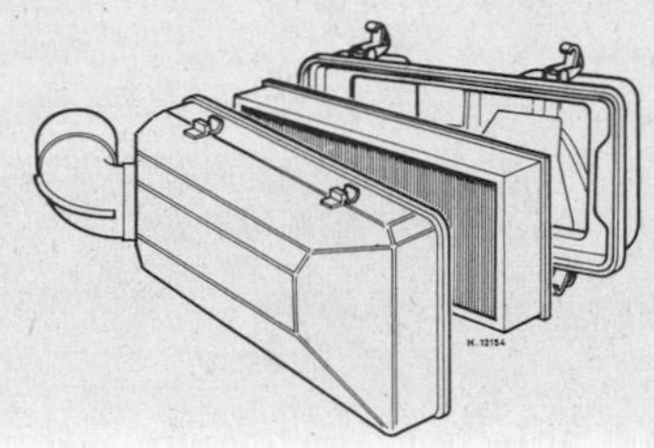

Air filter

Allen key A hexagonal wrench which fits into a recessed hexagonal hole.

Alligator clip A long-nosed spring-loaded metal clip with meshing teeth. Used to make temporary electrical connections.

Alternator A component in the electrical system which converts mechanical energy from a drivebelt into electrical energy to charge the battery and to operate the starting system, ignition system and electrical accessories.

Ampere (amp) A unit of measurement for the flow of electric current. One amp is the amount of current produced by one volt acting through a resistance of one ohm.

Anaerobic sealer A substance used to prevent bolts and screws from loosening. Anaerobic means that it does not require oxygen for activation. The Loctite brand is widely used.

Antifreeze A substance (usually ethylene glycol) mixed with water, and added to a vehicle's cooling system, to prevent freezing of the coolant in winter. Antifreeze also contains chemicals to inhibit corrosion and the formation of rust and other deposits that would tend to clog the radiator and coolant passages and reduce cooling efficiency.

Anti-seize compound A coating that reduces the risk of seizing on fasteners that are subjected to high temperatures, such as exhaust manifold bolts and nuts.

Asbestos A natural fibrous mineral with great heat resistance, commonly used in the composition of brake friction materials. Asbestos is a health hazard and the dust created by brake systems should never be inhaled or ingested.

Axle A shaft on which a wheel revolves, or which revolves with a wheel. Also, a solid beam that connects the two wheels at one end of the vehicle. An axle which also transmits power to the wheels is known as a live axle.

Axleshaft A single rotating shaft, on either side of the differential, which delivers power from the final drive assembly to the drive wheels. Also called a driveshaft or a halfshaft.

B

Ball bearing An anti-friction bearing consisting of a hardened inner and outer race with hardened steel balls between two races.

Bearing The curved surface on a shaft or in a bore, or the part assembled into either, that permits relative motion between them with minimum wear and friction.

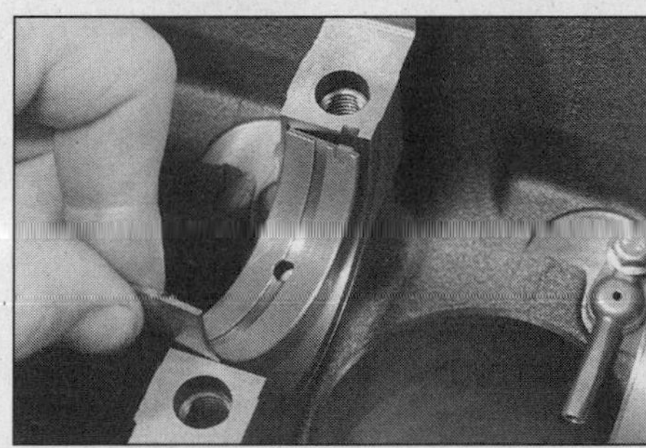

Bearing

Big-end bearing The bearing in the end of the connecting rod that's attached to the crankshaft.

Bleed nipple A valve on a brake wheel cylinder, caliper or other hydraulic component that is opened to purge the hydraulic system of air. Also called a bleed screw.

Brake bleeding Procedure for removing air from lines of a hydraulic brake system.

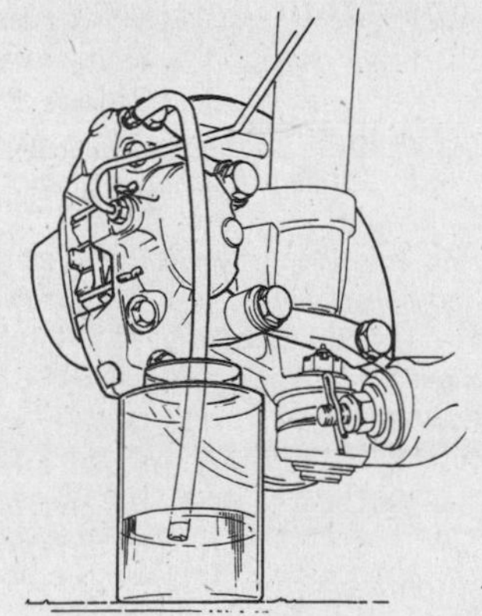

Brake bleeding

Brake disc The component of a disc brake that rotates with the wheels.

Brake drum The component of a drum brake that rotates with the wheels.

Brake linings The friction material which contacts the brake disc or drum to retard the vehicle's speed. The linings are bonded or riveted to the brake pads or shoes.

Brake pads The replaceable friction pads that pinch the brake disc when the brakes are applied. Brake pads consist of a friction material bonded or riveted to a rigid backing plate.

Brake shoe The crescent-shaped carrier to which the brake linings are mounted and which forces the lining against the rotating drum during braking.

Braking systems For more information on braking systems, consult the *Haynes Automotive Brake Manual*.

Breaker bar A long socket wrench handle providing greater leverage.

Bulkhead The insulated partition between the engine and the passenger compartment.

C

Caliper The non-rotating part of a disc-brake assembly that straddles the disc and carries the brake pads. The caliper also contains the hydraulic components that cause the pads to pinch the disc when the brakes are applied. A caliper is also a measuring tool that can be set to measure inside or outside dimensions of an object.

Camshaft A rotating shaft on which a series of cam lobes operate the valve mechanisms. The camshaft may be driven by gears, by sprockets and chain or by sprockets and a belt.

Canister A container in an evaporative emission control system; contains activated charcoal granules to trap vapours from the fuel system.

Canister

Carburettor A device which mixes fuel with air in the proper proportions to provide a desired power output from a spark ignition internal combustion engine.

Castellated Resembling the parapets along the top of a castle wall. For example, a castellated balljoint stud nut.

Castor In wheel alignment, the backward or forward tilt of the steering axis. Castor is positive when the steering axis is inclined rearward at the top.

Catalytic converter A silencer-like device in the exhaust system which converts certain pollutants in the exhaust gases into less harmful substances.

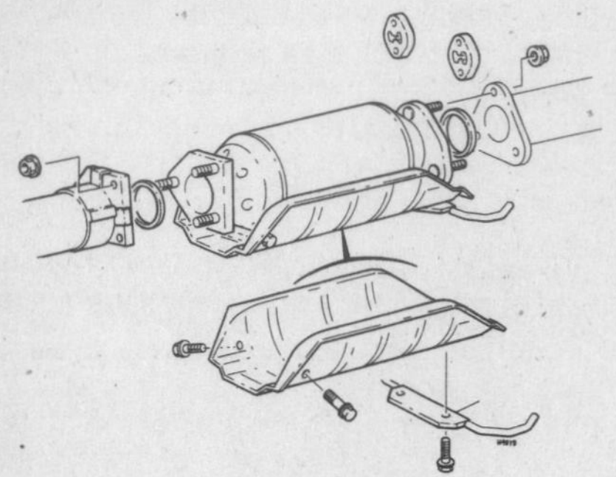

Catalytic converter

Circlip A ring-shaped clip used to prevent endwise movement of cylindrical parts and shafts. An internal circlip is installed in a groove in a housing; an external circlip fits into a groove on the outside of a cylindrical piece such as a shaft.

Clearance The amount of space between two parts. For example, between a piston and a cylinder, between a bearing and a journal, etc.

Coil spring A spiral of elastic steel found in various sizes throughout a vehicle, for example as a springing medium in the suspension and in the valve train.

Compression Reduction in volume, and increase in pressure and temperature, of a gas, caused by squeezing it into a smaller space.

Compression ratio The relationship between cylinder volume when the piston is at top dead centre and cylinder volume when the piston is at bottom dead centre.

Constant velocity (CV) joint A type of universal joint that cancels out vibrations caused by driving power being transmitted through an angle.

Core plug A disc or cup-shaped metal device inserted in a hole in a casting through which core was removed when the casting was formed. Also known as a freeze plug or expansion plug.

Crankcase The lower part of the engine block in which the crankshaft rotates.

Crankshaft The main rotating member, or shaft, running the length of the crankcase, with offset "throws" to which the connecting rods are attached.

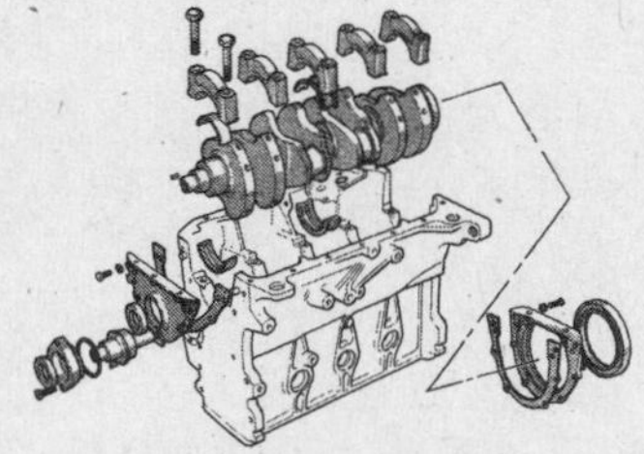

Crankshaft assembly

Crocodile clip See Alligator clip

D

Diagnostic code Code numbers obtained by accessing the diagnostic mode of an engine management computer. This code can be used to determine the area in the system where a malfunction may be located.

Disc brake A brake design incorporating a rotating disc onto which brake pads are squeezed. The resulting friction converts the energy of a moving vehicle into heat.

Double-overhead cam (DOHC) An engine that uses two overhead camshafts, usually one for the intake valves and one for the exhaust valves.

Drivebelt(s) The belt(s) used to drive accessories such as the alternator, water pump, power steering pump, air conditioning compressor, etc. off the crankshaft pulley.

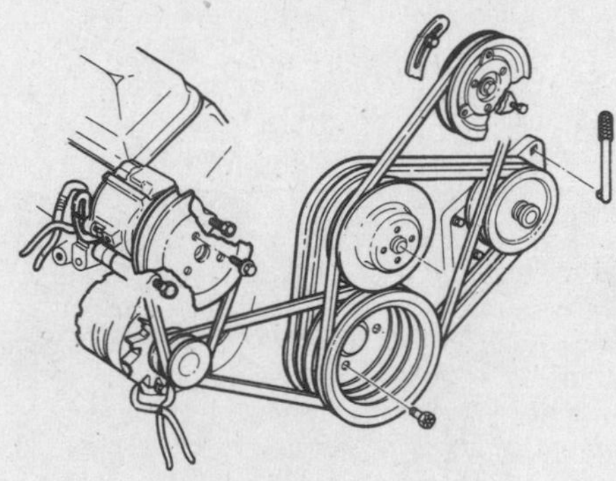

Accessory drivebelts

Driveshaft Any shaft used to transmit motion. Commonly used when referring to the axleshafts on a front wheel drive vehicle.

Drum brake A type of brake using a drum-shaped metal cylinder attached to the inner surface of the wheel. When the brake pedal is pressed, curved brake shoes with friction linings press against the inside of the drum to slow or stop the vehicle.

E

EGR valve A valve used to introduce exhaust gases into the intake air stream.

Electronic control unit (ECU) A computer which controls (for instance) ignition and fuel injection systems, or an anti-lock braking system. For more information refer to the *Haynes Automotive Electrical and Electronic Systems Manual.*

Electronic Fuel Injection (EFI) A computer controlled fuel system that distributes fuel through an injector located in each intake port of the engine.

Emergency brake A braking system, independent of the main hydraulic system, that can be used to slow or stop the vehicle if the primary brakes fail, or to hold the vehicle stationary even though the brake pedal isn't depressed. It usually consists of a hand lever that actuates either front or rear brakes mechanically through a series of cables and linkages. Also known as a handbrake or parking brake.

Endfloat The amount of lengthwise movement between two parts. As applied to a crankshaft, the distance that the crankshaft can move forward and back in the cylinder block.

Engine management system (EMS) A computer controlled system which manages the fuel injection and the ignition systems in an integrated fashion.

Exhaust manifold A part with several passages through which exhaust gases leave the engine combustion chambers and enter the exhaust pipe.

F

Fan clutch A viscous (fluid) drive coupling device which permits variable engine fan speeds in relation to engine speeds.

Feeler blade A thin strip or blade of hardened steel, ground to an exact thickness, used to check or measure clearances between parts.

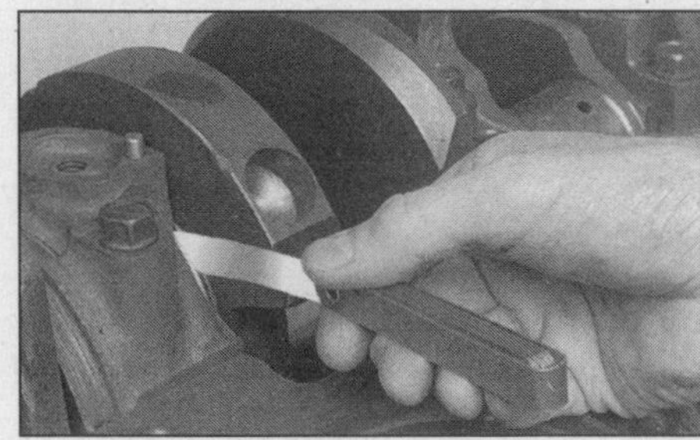

Feeler blade

Firing order The order in which the engine cylinders fire, or deliver their power strokes, beginning with the number one cylinder.

Flywheel A heavy spinning wheel in which energy is absorbed and stored by means of momentum. On cars, the flywheel is attached to the crankshaft to smooth out firing impulses.

Free play The amount of travel before any action takes place. The "looseness" in a linkage, or an assembly of parts, between the initial application of force and actual movement. For example, the distance the brake pedal moves before the pistons in the master cylinder are actuated.

Fuse An electrical device which protects a circuit against accidental overload. The typical fuse contains a soft piece of metal which is calibrated to melt at a predetermined current flow (expressed as amps) and break the circuit.

Fusible link A circuit protection device consisting of a conductor surrounded by heat-resistant insulation. The conductor is smaller than the wire it protects, so it acts as the weakest link in the circuit. Unlike a blown fuse, a failed fusible link must frequently be cut from the wire for replacement.

G

Gap The distance the spark must travel in jumping from the centre electrode to the side electrode in a spark plug. Also refers to the spacing between the points in a contact breaker assembly in a conventional points-type ignition, or to the distance between the reluctor or rotor and the pickup coil in an electronic ignition.

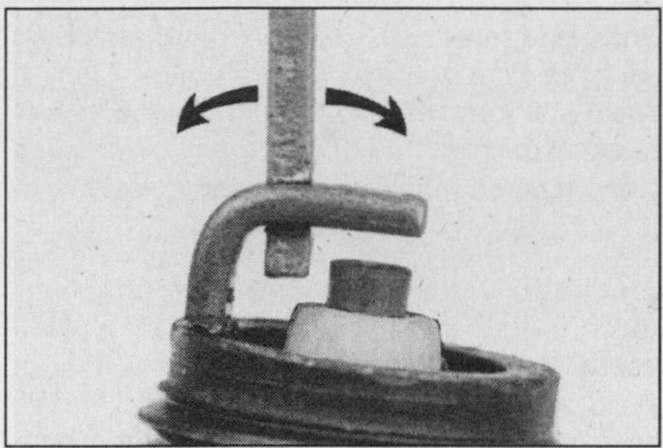

Adjusting spark plug gap

Gasket Any thin, soft material - usually cork, cardboard, asbestos or soft metal - installed between two metal surfaces to ensure a good seal. For instance, the cylinder head gasket seals the joint between the block and the cylinder head.

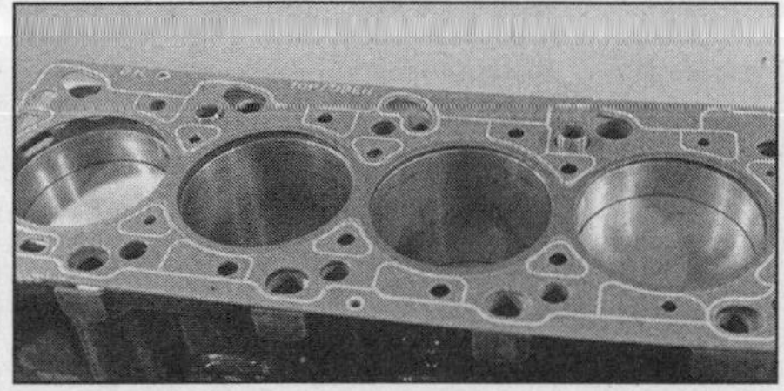

Gasket

Gauge An instrument panel display used to monitor engine conditions. A gauge with a movable pointer on a dial or a fixed scale is an analogue gauge. A gauge with a numerical readout is called a digital gauge.

H

Halfshaft A rotating shaft that transmits power from the final drive unit to a drive wheel, usually when referring to a live rear axle.

Harmonic balancer A device designed to reduce torsion or twisting vibration in the crankshaft. May be incorporated in the crankshaft pulley. Also known as a vibration damper.

Hone An abrasive tool for correcting small irregularities or differences in diameter in an engine cylinder, brake cylinder, etc.

Hydraulic tappet A tappet that utilises hydraulic pressure from the engine's lubrication system to maintain zero clearance (constant contact with both camshaft and valve stem). Automatically adjusts to variation in valve stem length. Hydraulic tappets also reduce valve noise.

I

Ignition timing The moment at which the spark plug fires, usually expressed in the number of crankshaft degrees before the piston reaches the top of its stroke.

Inlet manifold A tube or housing with passages through which flows the air-fuel mixture (carburettor vehicles and vehicles with throttle body injection) or air only (port fuel-injected vehicles) to the port openings in the cylinder head.

J

Jump start Starting the engine of a vehicle with a discharged or weak battery by attaching jump leads from the weak battery to a charged or helper battery.

L

Load Sensing Proportioning Valve (LSPV) A brake hydraulic system control valve that works like a proportioning valve, but also takes into consideration the amount of weight carried by the rear axle.

Locknut A nut used to lock an adjustment nut, or other threaded component, in place. For example, a locknut is employed to keep the adjusting nut on the rocker arm in position.

Lockwasher A form of washer designed to prevent an attaching nut from working loose.

M

MacPherson strut A type of front suspension system devised by Earle MacPherson at Ford of England. In its original form, a simple lateral link with the anti-roll bar creates the lower control arm. A long strut - an integral coil spring and shock absorber - is mounted between the body and the steering knuckle. Many modern so-called MacPherson strut systems use a conventional lower A-arm and don't rely on the anti-roll bar for location.

Multimeter An electrical test instrument with the capability to measure voltage, current and resistance.

N

NOx Oxides of Nitrogen. A common toxic pollutant emitted by petrol and diesel engines at higher temperatures.

O

Ohm The unit of electrical resistance. One volt applied to a resistance of one ohm will produce a current of one amp.

Ohmmeter An instrument for measuring electrical resistance.

O-ring A type of sealing ring made of a special rubber-like material; in use, the O-ring is compressed into a groove to provide the sealing action.

Overhead cam (ohc) engine An engine with the camshaft(s) located on top of the cylinder head(s).

Overhead valve (ohv) engine An engine with the valves located in the cylinder head, but with the camshaft located in the engine block.

Oxygen sensor A device installed in the engine exhaust manifold, which senses the oxygen content in the exhaust and converts this information into an electric current. Also called a Lambda sensor.

P

Phillips screw A type of screw head having a cross instead of a slot for a corresponding type of screwdriver.

Plastigage A thin strip of plastic thread, available in different sizes, used for measuring clearances. For example, a strip of Plastigage is laid across a bearing journal. The parts are assembled and dismantled; the width of the crushed strip indicates the clearance between journal and bearing.

Plastigage

Propeller shaft The long hollow tube with universal joints at both ends that carries power from the transmission to the differential on front-engined rear wheel drive vehicles.

Proportioning valve A hydraulic control valve which limits the amount of pressure to the rear brakes during panic stops to prevent wheel lock-up.

R

Rack-and-pinion steering A steering system with a pinion gear on the end of the steering shaft that mates with a rack (think of a geared wheel opened up and laid flat). When the steering wheel is turned, the pinion turns, moving the rack to the left or right. This movement is transmitted through the track rods to the steering arms at the wheels.

Radiator A liquid-to-air heat transfer device designed to reduce the temperature of the coolant in an internal combustion engine cooling system.

Refrigerant Any substance used as a heat transfer agent in an air-conditioning system. R-12 has been the principle refrigerant for many years; recently, however, manufacturers have begun using R-134a, a non-CFC substance that is considered less harmful to the ozone in the upper atmosphere.

Rocker arm A lever arm that rocks on a shaft or pivots on a stud. In an overhead valve engine, the rocker arm converts the upward movement of the pushrod into a downward movement to open a valve.

Rotor In a distributor, the rotating device inside the cap that connects the centre electrode and the outer terminals as it turns, distributing the high voltage from the coil secondary winding to the proper spark plug. Also, that part of an alternator which rotates inside the stator. Also, the rotating assembly of a turbocharger, including the compressor wheel, shaft and turbine wheel.
Runout The amount of wobble (in-and-out movement) of a gear or wheel as it's rotated. The amount a shaft rotates "out-of-true." The out-of-round condition of a rotating part.

S

Sealant A liquid or paste used to prevent leakage at a joint. Sometimes used in conjunction with a gasket.
Sealed beam lamp An older headlight design which integrates the reflector, lens and filaments into a hermetically-sealed one-piece unit. When a filament burns out or the lens cracks, the entire unit is simply replaced.
Serpentine drivebelt A single, long, wide accessory drivebelt that's used on some newer vehicles to drive all the accessories, instead of a series of smaller, shorter belts. Serpentine drivebelts are usually tensioned by an automatic tensioner.

Serpentine drivebelt

Shim Thin spacer, commonly used to adjust the clearance or relative positions between two parts. For example, shims inserted into or under bucket tappets control valve clearances. Clearance is adjusted by changing the thickness of the shim.
Slide hammer A special puller that screws into or hooks onto a component such as a shaft or bearing; a heavy sliding handle on the shaft bottoms against the end of the shaft to knock the component free.
Sprocket A tooth or projection on the periphery of a wheel, shaped to engage with a chain or drivebelt. Commonly used to refer to the sprocket wheel itself.
Starter inhibitor switch On vehicles with an automatic transmission, a switch that prevents starting if the vehicle is not in Neutral or Park.
Strut See MacPherson strut.

T

Tappet A cylindrical component which transmits motion from the cam to the valve stem, either directly or via a pushrod and rocker arm. Also called a cam follower.
Thermostat A heat-controlled valve that regulates the flow of coolant between the cylinder block and the radiator, so maintaining optimum engine operating temperature. A thermostat is also used in some air cleaners in which the temperature is regulated.
Thrust bearing The bearing in the clutch assembly that is moved in to the release levers by clutch pedal action to disengage the clutch. Also referred to as a release bearing.
Timing belt A toothed belt which drives the camshaft. Serious engine damage may result if it breaks in service.
Timing chain A chain which drives the camshaft.
Toe-in The amount the front wheels are closer together at the front than at the rear. On rear wheel drive vehicles, a slight amount of toe-in is usually specified to keep the front wheels running parallel on the road by offsetting other forces that tend to spread the wheels apart.
Toe-out The amount the front wheels are closer together at the rear than at the front. On front wheel drive vehicles, a slight amount of toe-out is usually specified.
Tools For full information on choosing and using tools, refer to the *Haynes Automotive Tools Manual.*
Tracer A stripe of a second colour applied to a wire insulator to distinguish that wire from another one with the same colour insulator.
Tune-up A process of accurate and careful adjustments and parts replacement to obtain the best possible engine performance.
Turbocharger A centrifugal device, driven by exhaust gases, that pressurises the intake air. Normally used to increase the power output from a given engine displacement, but can also be used primarily to reduce exhaust emissions (as on VW's "Umwelt" Diesel engine).

U

Universal joint or U-joint A double-pivoted connection for transmitting power from a driving to a driven shaft through an angle. A U-joint consists of two Y-shaped yokes and a cross-shaped member called the spider.

V

Valve A device through which the flow of liquid, gas, vacuum, or loose material in bulk may be started, stopped, or regulated by a movable part that opens, shuts, or partially obstructs one or more ports or passageways. A valve is also the movable part of such a device.
Valve clearance The clearance between the valve tip (the end of the valve stem) and the rocker arm or tappet. The valve clearance is measured when the valve is closed.
Vernier caliper A precision measuring instrument that measures inside and outside dimensions. Not quite as accurate as a micrometer, but more convenient.
Viscosity The thickness of a liquid or its resistance to flow.
Volt A unit for expressing electrical "pressure" in a circuit. One volt that will produce a current of one ampere through a resistance of one ohm.

W

Welding Various processes used to join metal items by heating the areas to be joined to a molten state and fusing them together. For more information refer to the *Haynes Automotive Welding Manual.*
Wiring diagram A drawing portraying the components and wires in a vehicle's electrical system, using standardised symbols. For more information refer to the *Haynes Automotive Electrical and Electronic Systems Manual.*

Note: *References throughout this index are in the form "Chapter number"•"page number"*

T

U

V

W

Haynes Manuals – The Complete List

Title	Book No.
ALFA ROMEO	
Alfa Romeo Alfasud/Sprint (74 - 88) up to F	0292
Alfa Romeo Alfetta (73 - 87) up to E	0531
AUDI	
Audi 80 (72 - Feb 79) up to T	0207
Audi 80, 90 (79 - Oct 86) up to D & Coupe (81 - Nov 88) up to F	0605
Audi 80, 90 (Oct 86 - 90) D to H & Coupe (Nov 88 - 90) F to H	1491
Audi 100 (Oct 82 - 90) up to H & 200 (Feb 84 - Oct 89) A to G	0907
Audi 100 & A6 Petrol & Diesel (May 91 - May 97) H to P	3504
Audi A4 (95 - Feb 00) M to V	3575
AUSTIN	
Austin A35 & A40 (56 - 67) *	0118
Austin Allegro 1100, 1300, 1.0, 1.1 & 1.3 (73 - 82)*	0164
Austin Healey 100/6 & 3000 (56 - 68) *	0049
Austin/MG/Rover Maestro 1.3 & 1.6 (83 - May 95) up to M	0922
Austin/MG Metro (80 - May 90) up to G	0718
Austin/Rover Montego 1.3 & 1.6 (84 - 94) A to L	1066
Austin/MG/Rover Montego 2.0 (84 - 95) A to M	1067
Mini (59 - 69) up to H	0527
Mini (69 - Oct 96) up to P	0646
Austin/Rover 2.0 litre Diesel Engine (86 - 93) C to L	1857
BEDFORD	
Bedford CF (69 - 87) up to E	0163
Bedford/Vauxhall Rascal & Suzuki Supercarry (86 - Oct 94) C to M	3015
BMW	
BMW 1500, 1502, 1600, 1602, 2000 & 2002 (59 - 77)*	0240
BMW 316, 320 & 320i (4-cyl) (75 - Feb 83) up to Y	0276
BMW 320, 320i, 323i & 325i (6-cyl) (Oct 77 - Sept 87) up to E	0815
BMW 3-Series (Apr 91 - 96) H to N	3210
BMW 3- & 5-Series (sohc) (81 - 91) up to J	1948
BMW 520i & 525e (Oct 81 - June 88) up to E	1560
BMW 525, 528 & 528i (73 - Sept 81) up to X	0632
CITROËN	
Citroën 2CV, Ami & Dyane (67 - 90) up to H	0196
Citroën AX Petrol & Diesel (87 - 97) D to P	3014
Citroën BX (83 - 94) A to L	0908
Citroën C15 Van Petrol & Diesel (89 - Oct 98) F to S	3509
Citroën CX (75 - 88) up to F	0528
Citroën Saxo Petrol & Diesel (96 - 01) N to X	3506
Citroën Visa (79 - 88) up to F	0620
Citroën Xantia Petrol & Diesel (93 - 98) K to S	3082
Citroën XM Petrol & Diesel (89 - 00) G to X	3451
Citroën Xsara Petrol & Diesel (97 - Sept 00) R to W	3751
Citroën ZX Diesel (91 - 98) J to S	1922
Citroën ZX Petrol (91 - 98) H to S	1881
Citroën 1.7 & 1.9 litre Diesel Engine (84 - 96) A to N	1379
FIAT	
Fiat 126 (73 - 87) *	0305
Fiat 500 (57 - 73) up to M	0090
Fiat Bravo & Brava (95 - 00) N to W	3572
Fiat Cinquecento (93 - 98) K to R	3501
Fiat Panda (81 - 95) up to M	0793
Fiat Punto Petrol & Diesel (94 - Oct 99) L to V	3251
Fiat Regata (84 - 88) A to F	1167
Fiat Tipo (88 - 91) E to J	1625
Fiat Uno (83 - 95) up to M	0923
Fiat X1/9 (74 - 89) up to G	0273
FORD	
Ford Anglia (59 - 68) *	0001
Ford Capri II (& III) 1.6 & 2.0 (74 - 87) up to E	0283
Ford Capri II (& III) 2.8 & 3.0 (74 - 87) up to E	1309
Ford Cortina Mk III 1300 & 1600 (70 - 76) *	0070
Ford Cortina Mk IV (& V) 1.6 & 2.0 (76 - 83) *	0343
Ford Cortina Mk IV (& V) 2.3 V6 (77 - 83) *	0426
Ford Escort Mk I 1100 & 1300 (68 - 74) *	0171
Ford Escort Mk I Mexico, RS 1600 & RS 2000 (70 - 74)*	0139
Ford Escort Mk II Mexico, RS 1800 & RS 2000 (75 - 80)*	0735
Ford Escort (75 - Aug 80) *	0280
Ford Escort (Sept 80 - Sept 90) up to H	0686
Ford Escort & Orion (Sept 90 - 00) H to X	1737
Ford Fiesta (76 - Aug 83) up to Y	0334
Ford Fiesta (Aug 83 - Feb 89) A to F	1030
Ford Fiesta (Feb 89 - Oct 95) F to N	1595
Ford Fiesta (Oct 95 - 01) N-reg. onwards	3397
Ford Focus (98 - 01) S to Y	3759
Ford Granada (Sept 77 - Feb 85) up to B	0481
Ford Granada & Scorpio (Mar 85 - 94) B to M	1245
Ford Ka (96 - 02) P-reg. onwards	3570
Ford Mondeo Petrol (93 - 99) K to T	1923
Ford Mondeo Diesel (93 - 96) L to N	3465
Ford Orion (83 - Sept 90) up to H	1009
Ford Sierra 4 cyl. (82 - 93) up to K	0903
Ford Sierra V6 (82 - 91) up to J	0904
Ford Transit Petrol (Mk 2) (78 - Jan 86) up to C	0719
Ford Transit Petrol (Mk 3) (Feb 86 - 89) C to G	1468
Ford Transit Diesel (Feb 86 - 99) C to T	3019
Ford 1.6 & 1.8 litre Diesel Engine (84 - 96) A to N	1172
Ford 2.1, 2.3 & 2.5 litre Diesel Engine (77 - 90) up to H	1606
FREIGHT ROVER	
Freight Rover Sherpa (74 - 87) up to E	0463
HILLMAN	
Hillman Avenger (70 - 82) up to Y	0037
Hillman Imp (63 - 76) *	0022
HONDA	
Honda Accord (76 - Feb 84) up to A	0351
Honda Civic (Feb 84 - Oct 87) A to E	1226
Honda Civic (Nov 91 - 96) J to N	3199
HYUNDAI	
Hyundai Pony (85 - 94) C to M	3398
JAGUAR	
Jaguar E Type (61 - 72) up to L	0140
Jaguar MkI & II, 240 & 340 (55 - 69) *	0098
Jaguar XJ6, XJ & Sovereign; Daimler Sovereign (68 - Oct 86) up to D	0242
Jaguar XJ6 & Sovereign (Oct 86 - Sept 94) D to M	3261
Jaguar XJ12, XJS & Sovereign; Daimler Double Six (72 - 88) up to F	0478
JEEP	
Jeep Cherokee Petrol (93 - 96) K to N	1943
LADA	
Lada 1200, 1300, 1500 & 1600 (74 - 91) up to J	0413
Lada Samara (87 - 91) D to J	1610
LAND ROVER	
Land Rover 90, 110 & Defender Diesel (83 - 95) up to N	3017
Land Rover Discovery Petrol & Diesel (89 - 98) G to S	3016
Land Rover Series IIA & III Diesel (58 - 85) up to C	0529
Land Rover Series II, IIA & III Petrol (58 - 85) up to C	0314
MAZDA	
Mazda 323 (Mar 81 - Oct 89) up to G	1608
Mazda 323 (Oct 89 - 98) G to R	3455
Mazda 626 (May 83 - Sept 87) up to E	0929
Mazda B-1600, B-1800 & B-2000 Pick-up (72 - 88) up to F	0267
Mazda RX-7 (79 - 85) *	0460
MERCEDES-BENZ	
Mercedes-Benz 190, 190E & 190D Petrol & Diesel (83 - 93) A to L	3450
Mercedes-Benz 200, 240, 300 Diesel (Oct 76 - 85) up to C	1114
Mercedes-Benz 250 & 280 (68 - 72) up to L	0346
Mercedes-Benz 250 & 280 (123 Series) (Oct 76 - 84) up to B	0677
Mercedes-Benz 124 Series (85 - Aug 93) C to K	3253
Mercedes-Benz C-Class Petrol & Diesel (93 - Aug 00) L to W	3511
MG	
MGA (55 - 62) *	0475
MGB (62 - 80) up to W	0111
MG Midget & AH Sprite (58 - 80) up to W	0265
MITSUBISHI	
Mitsubishi Shogun & L200 Pick-Ups (83 - 94) up to M	1944
MORRIS	
Morris Ital 1.3 (80 - 84) up to B	0705
Morris Minor 1000 (56 - 71) up to K	0024
NISSAN	
Nissan Bluebird (May 84 - Mar 86) A to C	1223
Nissan Bluebird (Mar 86 - 90) C to H	1473
Nissan Cherry (Sept 82 - 86) up to D	1031
Nissan Micra (83 - Jan 93) up to K	0931
Nissan Micra (93 - 99) K to T	3254
Nissan Primera (90 - Aug 99) H to T	1851
Nissan Stanza (82 - 86) up to D	0824
Nissan Sunny (May 82 - Oct 86) up to D	0895
Nissan Sunny (Oct 86 - Mar 91) D to H	1378
Nissan Sunny (Apr 91 - 95) H to N	3219
OPEL	
Opel Ascona & Manta (B Series) (Sept 75 - 88) up to F	0316
Opel Ascona (81 - 88) *(Not available in UK see Vauxhall Cavalier 0812)*	3215
Opel Astra (Oct 91 - Feb 98) *(Not available in UK see Vauxhall Astra 1832)*	3156
Opel Astra & Zafira Diesel (Feb 98 - Sept 00) *(See Astra & Zafira Diesel Book No. 3797)*	
Opel Astra & Zafira Petrol (Feb 98 - Sept 00) *(See Vauxhall/Opel Astra & Zafira Petrol Book No. 3758)*	
Opel Calibra (90 - 98) *(See Vauxhall/Opel Calibra Book No. 3502)*	
Opel Corsa (83 - Mar 93) *(Not available in UK see Vauxhall Nova 0909)*	3160
Opel Corsa (Mar 93 - 97) *(Not available in UK see Vauxhall Corsa 1985)*	3159
Opel Frontera Petrol & Diesel (91 - 98) *(See Vauxhall/Opel Frontera Book No. 3454)*	
Opel Kadett (Nov 79 - Oct 84) up to B	0634
Opel Kadett (Oct 84 - Oct 91) *(Not available in UK see Vauxhall Astra & Belmont 1136)*	3196
Opel Omega & Senator (86 - 94) *(Not available in UK see Vauxhall Carlton & Senator 1469)*	3157
Opel Omega (94 - 99) *(See Vauxhall/Opel Omega Book No. 3510)*	
Opel Rekord (Feb 78 - Oct 86) up to D	0543
Opel Vectra (Oct 88 - Oct 95) *(Not available in UK see Vauxhall Cavalier 1570)*	3158
Opel Vectra Petrol & Diesel (95 - 98) *(Not available in UK see Vauxhall Vectra 3396)*	3523
PEUGEOT	
Peugeot 106 Petrol & Diesel (91 - 01) J to X	1882
Peugeot 205 Petrol (83 - 97) A to P	0932
Peugeot 206 Petrol and Diesel (98 - 01) S to X	3757
Peugeot 305 (78 - 89) up to G	0538

* Classic reprint

Title	Book No.
Peugeot 306 Petrol & Diesel (93 - 99) K to T	**3073**
Peugeot 309 (86 - 93) C to K	**1266**
Peugeot 405 Petrol (88 - 97) E to P	**1559**
Peugeot 405 Diesel (88 - 97) E to P	**3198**
Peugeot 406 Petrol & Diesel (96 - 97) N to R	**3394**
Peugeot 505 (79 - 89) up to G	**0762**
Peugeot 1.7/1.8 & 1.9 litre Diesel Engine (82 - 96) up to N	**0950**
Peugeot 2.0, 2.1, 2.3 & 2.5 litre Diesel Engines (74 - 90) up to H	**1607**
PORSCHE	
Porsche 911 (65 - 85) up to C	**0264**
Porsche 924 & 924 Turbo (76 - 85) up to C	**0397**
PROTON	
Proton (89 - 97) F to P	**3255**
RANGE ROVER	
Range Rover V8 (70 - Oct 92) up to K	**0606**
RELIANT	
Reliant Robin & Kitten (73 - 83) up to A	**0436**
RENAULT	
Renault 4 (61 - 86) *	**0072**
Renault 5 (Feb 85 - 96) B to N	**1219**
Renault 9 & 11 (82 - 89) up to F	**0822**
Renault 18 (79 - 86) up to D	**0598**
Renault 19 Petrol (89 - 94) F to M	**1646**
Renault 19 Diesel (89 - 96) F to N	**1946**
Renault 21 (86 - 94) C to M	**1397**
Renault 25 (84 - 92) B to K	**1228**
Renault Clio Petrol (91 - May 98) H to R	**1853**
Renault Clio Diesel (91 - June 96) H to N	**3031**
Renault Clio Petrol & Diesel (May 98 - May 01) R to Y	**3906**
Renault Espace Petrol & Diesel (85 - 96) C to N	**3197**
Renault Fuego (80 - 86) *	**0764**
Renault Laguna Petrol & Diesel (94 - 00) L to W	**3252**
Renault Mégane & Scénic Petrol & Diesel (96 - 98) N to R	**3395**
Renault Mégane & Scénic (Apr 99 - 02) T-reg onwards	**3916**
ROVER	
Rover 213 & 216 (84 - 89) A to G	**1116**
Rover 214 & 414 (89 - 96) G to N	**1689**
Rover 216 & 416 (89 - 96) G to N	**1830**
Rover 211, 214, 216, 218 & 220 Petrol & Diesel (Dec 95 - 98) N to R	**3399**
Rover 414, 416 & 420 Petrol & Diesel (May 95 - 98) M to R	**3453**
Rover 618, 620 & 623 (93 - 97) K to P	**3257**
Rover 820, 825 & 827 (86 - 95) D to N	**1380**
Rover 3500 (76 - 87) up to E	**0365**
Rover Metro, 111 & 114 (May 90 - 98) G to S	**1711**
SAAB	
Saab 90, 99 & 900 (79 - Oct 93) up to L	**0765**
Saab 95 & 96 (66 - 76) *	**0198**
Saab 99 (69 - 79) *	**0247**
Saab 900 (Oct 93 - 98) L to R	**3512**
Saab 9000 (4-cyl) (85 - 98) C to S	**1686**
SEAT	
Seat Ibiza & Cordoba Petrol & Diesel (Oct 93 - Oct 99) L to V	**3571**
Seat Ibiza & Malaga (85 - 92) B to K	**1609**
SKODA	
Skoda Estelle (77 - 89) up to G	**0604**
Skoda Favorit (89 - 96) F to N	**1801**
Skoda Felicia Petrol & Diesel (95 - 01) M to X	**3505**

Title	Book No.
SUBARU	
Subaru 1600 & 1800 (Nov 79 - 90) up to H	**0995**
SUNBEAM	
Sunbeam Alpine, Rapier & H120 (67 - 76) *	**0051**
SUZUKI	
Suzuki SJ Series, Samurai & Vitara (4-cyl) (82 - 97) up to P	**1942**
Suzuki Supercarry & Bedford/Vauxhall Rascal (86 - Oct 94) C to M	**3015**
TALBOT	
Talbot Alpine, Solara, Minx & Rapier (75 - 86) up to D	**0337**
Talbot Horizon (78 - 86) up to D	**0473**
Talbot Samba (82 - 86) up to D	**0823**
TOYOTA	
Toyota Carina E (May 92 - 97) J to P	**3256**
Toyota Corolla (Sept 83 - Sept 87) A to E	**1024**
Toyota Corolla (80 - 85) up to C	**0683**
Toyota Corolla (Sept 87 - Aug 92) E to K	**1683**
Toyota Corolla (Aug 92 - 97) K to P	**3259**
Toyota Hi-Ace & Hi-Lux (69 - Oct 83) up to A	**0304**
TRIUMPH	
Triumph Acclaim (81 - 84) *	**0792**
Triumph GT6 & Vitesse (62 - 74) *	**0112**
Triumph Herald (59 - 71) *	**0010**
Triumph Spitfire (62 - 81) up to X	**0113**
Triumph Stag (70 - 78) up to T	**0441**
Triumph TR2, TR3, TR3A, TR4 & TR4A (52 - 67)*	**0028**
Triumph TR5 & 6 (67 - 75) *	**0031**
Triumph TR7 (75 - 82) *	**0322**
VAUXHALL	
Vauxhall Astra (80 - Oct 84) up to B	**0635**
Vauxhall Astra & Belmont (Oct 84 - Oct 91) B to J	**1136**
Vauxhall Astra (Oct 91 - Feb 98) J to R	**1832**
Vauxhall/Opel Astra & Zafira Diesel (Feb 98 - Sept 00) R to W	**3797**
Vauxhall/Opel Astra & Zafira Petrol (Feb 98 - Sept 00) R to W	**3758**
Vauxhall/Opel Calibra (90 - 98) G to S	**3502**
Vauxhall Carlton (Oct 78 - Oct 86) up to D	**0480**
Vauxhall Carlton & Senator (Nov 86 - 94) D to L	**1469**
Vauxhall Cavalier 1300 (77 - July 81) *	**0461**
Vauxhall Cavalier 1600, 1900 & 2000 (75 - July 81) up to W	**0315**
Vauxhall Cavalier (81 - Oct 88) up to F	**0812**
Vauxhall Cavalier (Oct 88 - 95) F to N	**1570**
Vauxhall Chevette (75 - 84) up to B	**0285**
Vauxhall Corsa (Mar 93 - 97) K to R	**1985**
Vauxhall/Opel Corsa (Apr 97 - Oct 00) P to X	**3921**
Vauxhall/Opel Frontera Petrol & Diesel (91 - Sept 98) J to S	**3454**
Vauxhall Nova (83 - 93) up to K	**0909**
Vauxhall/Opel Omega (94 - 99) L to T	**3510**
Vauxhall Vectra Petrol & Diesel (95 - 98) N to R	**3396**
Vauxhall/Opel 1.5, 1.6 & 1.7 litre Diesel Engine (82 - 96) up to N	**1222**
VOLKSWAGEN	
Volkswagen 411 & 412 (68 - 75) *	**0091**
Volkswagen Beetle 1200 (54 - 77) up to S	**0036**
Volkswagen Beetle 1300 & 1500 (65 - 75) up to P	**0039**
Volkswagen Beetle 1302 & 1302S (70 - 72) up to L	**0110**
Volkswagen Beetle 1303, 1303S & GT (72 - 75) up to P	**0159**
Volkswagen Beetle Petrol & Diesel (Apr 99 - 01) T reg onwards	**3798**
Volkswagen Golf & Bora Petrol & Diesel (April 98 - 00) R to X	**3727**

Title	Book No.
Volkswagen Golf & Jetta Mk 1 1.1 & 1.3 (74 - 84) up to A	**0716**
Volkswagen Golf, Jetta & Scirocco Mk 1 1.5, 1.6 & 1.8 (74 - 84) up to A	**0726**
Volkswagen Golf & Jetta Mk 1 Diesel (78 - 84) up to A	**0451**
Volkswagen Golf & Jetta Mk 2 (Mar 84 - Feb 92) A to J	**1081**
Volkswagen Golf & Vento Petrol & Diesel (Feb 92 - 96) J to N	**3097**
Volkswagen LT vans & light trucks (76 - 87) up to E	**0637**
Volkswagen Passat & Santana (Sept 81 - May 88) up to E	**0814**
Volkswagen Passat Petrol & Diesel (May 88 - 96) E to P	**3498**
Volkswagen Passat 4-cyl Petrol & Diesel (Dec 96 - Nov 00) P to X	**3917**
Volkswagen Polo & Derby (76 - Jan 82) up to X	**0335**
Volkswagen Polo (82 - Oct 90) up to H	**0813**
Volkswagen Polo (Nov 90 - Aug 94) H to L	**3245**
Volkswagen Polo Hatchback Petrol & Diesel (94 - 99) M to S	**3500**
Volkswagen Scirocco (82 - 90) up to H	**1224**
Volkswagen Transporter 1600 (68 - 79) up to V	**0082**
Volkswagen Transporter 1700, 1800 & 2000 (72 - 79) up to V	**0226**
Volkswagen Transporter (air-cooled) (79 - 82) up to Y	**0638**
Volkswagen Transporter (water-cooled) (82 - 90) up to H	**3452**
Volkswagen Type 3 (63 - 73) *	**0084**
VOLVO	
Volvo 120 & 130 Series (& P1800) (61 - 73) *	**0203**
Volvo 142, 144 & 145 (66 - 74) up to N	**0129**
Volvo 240 Series (74 - 93) up to K	**0270**
Volvo 262, 264 & 260/265 (75 - 85) *	**0400**
Volvo 340, 343, 345 & 360 (76 - 91) up to J	**0715**
Volvo 440, 460 & 480 (87 - 97) D to P	**1691**
Volvo 740 & 760 (82 - 91) up to J	**1258**
Volvo 850 (92 - 96) J to P	**3260**
Volvo 940 (90 - 96) H to N	**3249**
Volvo S40 & V40 (96 - 99) N to V	**3569**
Volvo S70, V70 & C70 (96 - 99) P to V	**3573**
AUTOMOTIVE TECHBOOKS	
Automotive Air Conditioning Systems	**3740**
Automotive Brake Manual	**3050**
Automotive Carburettor Manual	**3288**
Automotive Diagnostic Fault Codes Manual	**3472**
Automotive Diesel Engine Service Guide	**3286**
Automotive Electrical and Electronic Systems Manual	**3049**
Automotive Engine Management and Fuel Injection Systems Manual	**3344**
Automotive Gearbox Overhaul Manual	**3473**
Automotive Service Summaries Manual	**3475**
Automotive Timing Belts Manual – Austin/Rover	**3549**
Automotive Timing Belts Manual – Ford	**3474**
Automotive Timing Belts Manual – Peugeot/Citroën	**3568**
Automotive Timing Belts Manual – Vauxhall/Opel	**3577**
Automotive Welding Manual	**3053**
In-Car Entertainment Manual (3rd Edition)	**3363**

* Classic reprint

CL13.4/02

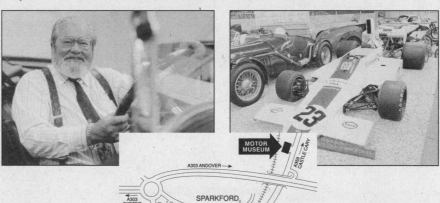